3A210

Teacher's Guide for

THIS IS
AMERICA'S STORY

THIRD EDITION

To the Teacher:

The purpose of the *Teacher's Edition* is to help you use *This Is America's Story* to best advantage in planning and teaching a course in American history. The *Teacher's Edition* differs in two important respects from the textbook for pupils:

1. An opening section, the *Teacher's Guide for This Is America's Story*, explains the organization and features of the book. Part One, The Plan for This Text (pages 1-11), discusses objectives of the course and text, calls attention to the importance of focusing instruction on important concepts and of making history interesting to students, and describes features which make this book teachable. Part Two, How This Text Contributes to the Achievement of Major Objectives (pages 12-30), illustrates ways in which *This Is America's Story* develops the four goals of a junior high school course in American history.

2. Practical suggestions for teaching American history are contained in the annotations found on the regular pages of the text. The annotations in script are related to features found in the book and to uses that can be made of them. Annotations in regular type are concerned with comparisons, interpretation, and analysis. They contain additional information that may prove helpful to you in developing important concepts and ideas.

Your day-by-day work as a teacher will be made easier if you use the *Teacher's Key and Audio-Visual Guide for This Is America's Story*. This separate pamphlet suggests answers to all section and chapter Check Ups, to Unit Review questions, and also to questions raised in map and chart captions. An important part of this publication is the section dealing with audio-visual aids: films, filmstrips, recordings, and tapes. Carefully selected items are listed for each of the ten units of *This Is America's Story*.

You may wish to know also about three supplementary publications for pupils who are using *This Is America's Story*.

1. *Programmed Practice for This Is America's Story* provides self-teaching exercises which are based on the text. The procedure is one that calls for the student to read a block of material in the textbook and then to determine his mastery of it by answering pertinent questions. If necessary the student may again read the material in the text. *Programmed Practice*, therefore, provides for the immediate recall and use of important information read. This procedure reinforces learning and provides the student with the satisfaction of knowing that he understands important points developed by the authors.

2. *Progress Tests for This Is America's Story* is a booklet containing objective-type achievement tests focused on reasoned understanding of information and mastery of essential skills. Tests are provided for each of the units and there are also end-of-year tests.

3. *Practice Exercises and Review Tests* is planned to serve two purposes. Pupils may use the exercises for a self-check and comprehensive review of important information and study skills. By detaching the appropriate pages from the booklet, the teacher may also use the material for a given unit as a classroom test. Material is provided for each of the chapters and units in the text and also for end-of-year review and evaluation.

1966 Teacher's Edition
This Is America's Story
HOUGHTON MIFFLIN COMPANY

PART ONE: *The Plan for This Text*

Objectives of the Course and Text

During the last decade both schools and colleges have been rethinking goals, methods, and subject matter. In consequence a number of "newer" courses have emerged — in science and mathematics, and in English and foreign languages. The forces which had led to a rethinking of courses in the fields mentioned have also affected the social studies. From this ferment, certain points of view with reference to junior high courses in American history are emerging:

1. Understanding the History of Our Country

Although everything that ever happened is history, history becomes meaningful only as information is focused on important concepts or big ideas. Among these are:

How the geographic environment and man's technology affect ways of living.

How this country grew from Thirteen Colonies to a world power.

How the factor of interdependence has been of basic importance in the nation's growth — colonies and mother country, sections of the country with one another, the United States and other countries.

How our government developed; the basic values on which our form of government rests; comparison with totalitarian government.

How our economy developed; the basic values on which the free enterprise system rests; comparison with totalitarian government.

Viewing in historical perspective the role of the United States as a champion of liberty, of democratic institutions, and of the republican form of government.

2. Appreciating Our American Heritage

The American heritage has come down from one generation to the next for centuries. It includes values and ideals, rights and obligations, laws and institutions. It includes also the memory of men and women who made great contributions to our heritage or who sacrificed to keep it from being tarnished and diminished. Teaching in junior high social studies courses should reflect the fact that, during younger adolescence, children reach a peak of idealism and identification with the heroic. These are the years when a reasoned patriotism should be developed.

3. Mastering Basic Study Skills

Students should be taught such basic skills as reading and interpreting the written narrative, maps, charts, graphs, pictures. They should be taught how to organize and make reports and how to develop a time sense.

4. Using the Skills of Analysis and "Critical Thinking"

Students should be taught and encouraged to practice the skills of analysis — identifying issues, using and evaluating primary and secondary sources, identifying various points of view and the assumptions underlying them, reaching conclusions and providing supporting evidence.

This Is America's Story reflects the points of view just listed. For a discussion of how each of them has been developed, the teacher should turn to Part Two, page 12.

1

Focusing Instruction on Important Concepts

It is important to recognize that many students lose interest in history because they fail "to see the forest for the trees." The "trees," in this case, are a mass of facts not clearly related to important ideas, concepts, and issues. A student may find it difficult to get excited once again in Grade 8 over the fact that Columbus discovered America in 1492. But quite possibly he does not know, and would find it interesting to learn, why this voyage became possible in the late 1400's and not a century or two earlier, why Columbus took the route he did, what came of his explorations. There is a thrill for students in reading a narrative that identifies important ideas, concepts, and issues, and provides information to make them meaningful.

This Is America's Story is organized into ten units (see Contents, pages v-ix in the textbook). Each unit deals with a major development in the history of our country. Thus Unit Three, for example, explains how "New Nations Are Born as the New World Shakes Off European Rule." How are the major concepts of this unit identified and developed?

Unit Introduction. (See pages 134-135 in the textbook.) Unit Three begins with a two-page spread that includes a scene which captures the "spirit" of the important events to be described. The scene depicts redcoats and minutemen confronting each other on Lexington Green. The picture of a minuteman is highlighted and this heroic figure becomes a symbol of the unit. At the bottom of page 135 are these words from the Declaration of Independence, "We, therefore, the Representatives of the United States of America . . . declare that these United Colonies are, and of right ought to be free and independent states." The picture and the quotation suggest the "emotional climate" of the period discussed in the unit. So, of course, do the words of the unit introduction. You will also note that the introduction calls attention to the basic questions to be answered in this unit.

Furthermore, the unit story does not end with the independence of the Thirteen Colonies. It includes also the independence movement in Latin America and Britain's granting of responsible government to Canada. The relationship of the latter two move-ments to the struggle of the Thirteen Colonies for liberty is clearly brought out in this text.

Now let us see how part of the unit story is developed in Chapter 9.

Chapter introduction. (See page 165 in the textbook.) The title of Chapter 9 is "The Thirteen English Colonies Win Their Independence." This and other chapters begin with an illustration — in this case, the Liberty Bell. Such a "background picture" suggests the theme of the chapter. The drawings in the foreground of the Liberty Bell introduce people who play important parts in the story — a French soldier, Continental cavalryman and foot soldier, a British grenadier, a Hessian soldier — and these personages are identified in a footnote. The narrative of the chapter introduction clearly states the basic issue which confronted the colonists.

. . . Should the Patriots throw off the British government once and for all? Or should they try to heal the break and continue to live as subjects of King George? These were burning questions in 1775.

In this chapter we shall learn how our forefathers made their decision. We shall study also the war which was fought to win our independence. To aid us in our study, we shall look for answers to the following questions:

1. Why did the Thirteen Colonies decide to declare their independence?
2. What strengths and weaknesses did the Americans have in the Revolution?

3. How did the Thirteen Colonies win their independence?

Note the three *guide questions* at the end of the chapter introduction. These questions call attention to the important issues to be discussed in Chapter 9. This chapter, then, is divided into three sections. The three guide questions are the same as the three section titles on pages 166, 170, and 178.

Section, column, and paragraph headings. A combination of section, column, and paragraph headings carry forward the basic ideas identified in the unit and chapter introductions. These headings make clear exactly what is discussed and provide an effective outline of the chapter (see pages 166-177 in the textbook).

I. Why Did the Thirteen Colonies Decide to Declare Their Independence? (*This is a section heading.*)
 A. Great Britain and the Colonies Drift Farther Apart as Fighting Continues. (*This is a column heading.*)
  1. The colonists fight bravely in the Battle of Bunker Hill. (*This is a paragraph heading as are also #2 and 3 below.*)
  2. Colonial troops force the British to leave Boston.
  3. Blows are struck elsewhere.
 B. The Colonies Declare Themselves Independent.
  1. The attitude of the British government becomes stricter.
  2. Colonial leaders call for independence.
  3. The Second Continental Congress takes a bold step toward independence.
  4. The Declaration of Independence is adopted.
  5. A new nation is born.
II. What Strengths and Weaknesses Did the Americans Have in the Revolution?

 A. What Were the Weaknesses of the United States?
  1. The Patriot forces lacked training and organization.
  2. The Patriots lacked equipment and money.
  3. Loyalists opposed the Patriots.
 B. What Were the Strengths of the United States?
  1. The Patriots fought for a cause they believed in.
  2. The Patriots profited from British blunders.
  3. The Patriots received foreign aid.
  4. General George Washington proves an excellent leader.

If students are encouraged to read unit and chapter introductions carefully, and to note and refer to section, column, and paragraph headings, they will find it much easier to follow the story told in a given chapter.

Section Check Up. A student may wish to read an entire chapter for general impression. But to make sure that important points are not missed, he should stop now and then to recall what has been read and to ask himself what it means. To encourage recall, a Check Up is included at the end of each section. The following Check Up is provided for the first section in Chapter 9, "Why Did the Thirteen Colonies Decide to Declare Their Independence?"

1. (a) How did the Patriots capture Boston? (b) Where else had fighting taken place between the Patriots and the British troops?
2. (a) How did the British king try to stop the rebellion? (b) Why did many colonists begin to favor independence?
3. (a) What steps did the Second Continental Congress take to separate from England? (b) What were the two most important ideas of the Declaration of Independence?

Note that these questions do much more

than turn paragraph headings into question form. Such words as "how," "why," "what steps," "what were the two most important ideas" suggest the type of thoughtful recall which encourages effective learning.

Chapter Check Up. (See pages 188-189 in the textbook.) Each Chapter Check Up includes four kinds of exercises: (1) Words which the student should understand are listed under *Do You Know the Meaning?* (2) Important names, dates, and terms are included under *Can You Identify?* (3) Places which the student should be able to locate on a map are listed under *Can You Locate?* (4) Included in the Chapter Check Up are also questions which encourage the students to use acquired information in thinking about important issues. The following *What Do You Think?* questions are provided for Chapter 9:

1. (a) From 1763 to 1775, did the American colonists enjoy the right to "life, liberty, and the pursuit of happiness" under the government of Great Britain? (b) Did the British government have "the consent of the governed" as far as the colonists were concerned? Give reasons for your answers.
2. Why did it take great courage for the members of the Continental Congress to vote for the Declaration of Independence? . . .
4. American persistence, French aid, and British blundering were important factors in the outcome of the Revolutionary War. Which factor was most important? Why?

Thinking about the unit as a whole. Because each unit deals with a major development in the nation's history, it is important for students to think about the unit as a whole. To encourage this kind of review and re-thinking, for example, is the purpose of *To Clinch Your Understanding of Unit 3.* (See pages 207-209.) Each of the end-of-

unit sections includes (1) a *Summary of Important Ideas,* (2) *Unit Review* questions, (3) a *Gaining Skill* exercise which helps students to use social studies material more effectively, and (4) *Interesting Things To Do,* a list of activities which suggest ways of using information required.

The first two of these contribute substantially to the task of emphasizing important concepts. It was pointed out earlier that an outline of a given chapter could be made from its section, column, and paragraph headings (see page 3). A briefer outline could also be developed from the *Summary of Important Ideas* for Unit Three. Note how point 1, c from the Unit Three outline (pages 207-208) summarizes Chapter 9:

> c. When it became clear that King George III refused to listen to the grievances of the colonists, the Second Continental Congress approved a Declaration of Independence. Many colonists, however, remained loyal to the mother country. The leadership of Washington, the courage of his men, valuable aid from foreign countries, the advantage of fighting on familiar ground, and British blunders helped the Thirteen Colonies win their independence.

The thought-provoking quality of *Unit Review* questions can be illustrated by calling attention to one of those provided for Unit Three. Note also how this question "cuts across" several chapters.

1. (a) How did the English government and the colonists differ in their views on the proper relationship of the mother country and the colonies? (b) Did the same differences exist in the case of Spain and the Spanish colonies? Explain.

A discussion of *Gaining Skill* exercises and examples of *Interesting Things to Do* will be found in Part Two of this Guide.

Making History Interesting

Effective learning cannot take place without the active co-operation of students. It is unfortunate, therefore, that quite a few youngsters "do not like history." Their attitude usually stems from one or more of the following reasons:

1. They may be slow readers who have difficulty getting meaning from the printed page.

2. They may be able youngsters who are not challenged by conventional textbook material and teaching procedures.

3. They may be students whose experience in earlier social studies courses has been unfortunate and not representative of good practice. These students often feel that history is little more than a jumble of names, dates, and events.

In classes in which students are not grouped on the basis of reading comprehension, the teacher may find a range of seven or more years in the ability of youngsters to read. Students in the first of the groups listed need help in becoming better readers and in mastering basic study skills (see pages 23 to 26 of the Guide). They will derive satisfaction and enjoyment from reading exciting historical fiction and biography pitched at 2-3 years below grade level but not labeled as such. (See "For Further Reading," pages A33-A38 in the Reference Section at the end of textbook.) The interest of students in the second group can be aroused by providing more mature reading, and by encouraging them to work on individual or group projects involving the skills of analysis and critical thinking. Students in the third group may also be in one of the other two. Aside from what has already been suggested, the best "cure" for them is exposure to a course in which instruction is focused on important concepts, cause and result relationships are stressed, and sharp and up-to-date interpretations of issues and problems are provided.

Of course motivation is an important consideration in the case of other students who do not fall into one or more of the problem groups already identified. These students, too, will enjoy stimulating supplementary reading, instruction which points up important ideas and issues, and opportunities to develop the skills of analysis and critical thinking. In the rest of this section we shall call attention to ways in which *This Is America's Story* meets the needs of students by presenting history — not as a dull subject requiring rote memory of who, what, when, and where; but as a fascinating study of the why's and wherefore's of man's actions.

History takes on added meaning for students and becomes more interesting to them when they see how events that happened centuries ago have a bearing on the present. The feature, "Linking Past and Present," found at the end of each chapter, carries through this theme of building on the past. (See page 11 of this Guide.) "Links" also appear within chapters where they provide interesting information that gives spice to the narrative by calling attention to how contemporary America has been built on what has gone before. In the section which discusses "a new era in transportation," we find pictures and text that compare toll gates in the early 1800's with toll stations in use on our present-day superhighways:

> Old toll gates, like the one shown above at Milestone Village in Darien, Connecticut, had a bar which could be raised by a wooden wheel. Today, modern toll stations (right) collect the money to pay for many of our superhighways. (page 280)

On page 456 a "Link" compares the shipment of produce from Long Island to market in New York City, 1884, with today's refrigerated "piggy back" cars for long distance shipping. Examples of other "Links" may be found on pages 29, 297, and 632.

Photographs themselves capture a student's interest; hold it when they illustrate a colonial schoolroom (page 108), the old Slater

Mill (page 273), an automobile assembly line about 1914 (page 449), the digging of the Panama Canal (page 587); and then turn the student's interest to the text in search of further information on the "idea" behind the illustration.

Where the stages of an event or the components of an idea need additional emphasis or clarification for students, a cartoon treatment of the subject has been found effective. This type of treatment has been used to explain "Tariff vs. Free Trade" (pages 274-275), "Why Farmers Organized to Protect Their Interests" (pages 490-491), and "How Our Approach to Latin America Has Changed" (pages 670-671). Let us look at "Why Americans Criticized the Confederacy" (pages 214-215) and then refer to the text to see how the cartoon treatment reinforces the discussion of the weaknesses of the government under the Articles of Confederation. Frame 1 in this cartoon (page 214) shows a congressman explaining to angry creditors, "We asked the states for some money months ago, but I don't know if we will ever get it." This frame reinforces the point that Congress was not given the right to tax. Frames 2 and 3 in the cartoon illustrate the difficulties businessmen faced because Congress did not have the power to regulate the trade which was carried on between states. In frame 4 — at the Virginia-Maryland border — a fisherman from Virginia shakes his fist at a resident of Maryland and states: "I claim I've got a right to fish over there but there's no court where I can take you to prove it." This frame gives meaning to the point that still another weakness of the Confederation was that it provided no satisfactory way of settling quarrels between the states.

A "personalized" approach is often used in discussing topics which otherwise might prove difficult. For example, to explain "business cycle," "boom," "depression," and "monopoly" to students and keep their interest throughout, *This Is America's Story* tells about "Mr. Charles Jackson, an American businessman of the 1890's." (See pages 469-

473.) This style of writing is also used to tell what kind of government developed in the English colonies (pages 140-142), to compare an Iowa farm in the 1880's with one in the 1960's (pages 520-521), and to describe the steps by which Canada became an independent nation (pages 651-655). Your students will learn about life in the Spanish colonies from a series of imaginary letters written by "Philip Andrews," a fifteen-year-old boy who visited New Spain in the early 1700's (pages 68-75).

This Is America's Story arouses a student's interest not only through the use of features, illustrations, and imaginative situations, but also by means of vivid narrative. Let us see how this textbook sets the scene for World War I.

> **World War I begins.** On a night early in August, 1914, the citizens of a little Belgian village on the border of Germany awoke with a feeling of fear. Into the village rode the advance guard of the German army. Soon, long columns of gray-clad infantry followed, and there could be heard the rumble and thunder of guns. The citizens knew what all this meant — Germany was at war with France. Belgium was a neutral country, but that fact meant nothing to the German army, which wanted to make a lightning thrust at France. The Belgian villagers had reason to be fearful and sad. As the battle surged around them, their homes went up in flames and many of the people were killed.
>
> At other towns and villages along the border, the news was the same. The million and a half German soldiers invading Belgium and France expected to crush the French army in a few weeks. Gone were the high hopes of leading peaceful lives in a peaceful world. Once more war had come to Europe — the worst war the world had known. . . . (page 600)

The explanation of the growth of a city is an example of the way in which *This Is*

America's Story presents history as "a study of the why's and wherefore's of man's actions." This particular "story" will also help your students to see the broad concept that the geographical environment and man's technology affect ways of living. Students will want to apply what they have learned in this section to their own community. What reasons for its settlement and growth are similar to those given for the city in the textbook? What differences can your students discover? Can they account for them? (See pages 511-512.)

How "The United States Became a Great Industrial Nation" is told in Chapter 22, pages 442 to 466. But the story of the growth of industry can also be told through the lives of the men of that period — Vanderbilt, Hill, Ford, Rockefeller. Note how, in a few paragraphs, *This Is America's Story* presents the rapid growth of the steel industry through the life of Andrew Carnegie (pages 461-462).

Other Features Which Make This Text "Teachable"

We have considered the importance of arousing student interest in history and of focusing instruction on important ideas. Up to this point, however, we have not mentioned certain other features and characteristics which make *This Is America's Story* "teachable." Let us consider first the importance of the prologue and epilogue in a history textbook.

Prologue and epilogue. The first chapter in an American history textbook usually opens with a discussion of events that took place long before the famous voyage of Columbus. The last page of the last chapter perhaps closes with the most recent important development prior to the date the book went to press. Allowing for some slight exaggeration in this statement, it nevertheless helps to explain why prologue and epilogue often serve a useful purpose. The one provides an opportunity to emphasize the basic theme of the book; the latter, to stress the point that what each generation does or does not do vitally affects the welfare of succeeding generations.

The prologue of this book bears the title: *This Is America — Land of Promise; Land of Progress Toward a Better Life*. This prologue stresses in words and illustrations the basic theme in American history: Liberty helped to create freedom of opportunity; freedom of opportunity in turn made possible growth; and growth made possible progress toward a better life.

America Faces the Future, quite appropriately, is the title of our epilogue. Each generation is heir to the heritage of the past; each transmits the heritage, richer or poorer, to the generation which follows. Our generation must cope with many great problems at home — declining natural resources, pollution of air and water, crime and corruption, to list but a few. The greatest challenge to this country, however, is that posed by Communist imperialism — a system based on principles at the polar opposite to those on which our government and way of life are based.

The importance of rich detail. It is not enough to identify a concept and to ask a student to learn it. When this happens the student may memorize the concept and be able to repeat it verbatim. Yet he may be far from understanding it. Depth of understanding is the product of defining terms, providing examples, making comparisons, applying ideas to other situations. In textbook writing, as in teaching, an abstract presentation is a difficult hurdle for the learner to overcome. Let us look at an example of the way a concept can be made meaningful to students. In Chapter 7, "How Were the English Governed?", there is a paragraph about how the spirit of freedom grew in America (see page 139):

The spirit of freedom grows in America. English colonists not only had all the rights of Englishmen, but they enjoyed even greater freedom in the New World than did their countrymen in England. It is not difficult to understand why this was true. For one thing, the settlement of the English colonies, as you know, was carried out chiefly by trading companies or by proprietors. In the early days, the English kings were only mildly interested in what was going on in the New World. They were too busy with affairs in England to worry about the struggling settlements across the sea. This lack of interest on the part of the English government permitted the colonists to enjoy great freedom in managing their own affairs.

We must remember, too, that 3000 miles of ocean lay between the colonies and England. It took weeks or even months to cross the ocean. Naturally the colonies had more freedom to govern themselves than if orders could have been delivered promptly. And the New World itself, with its plentiful land and unlimited opportunities, encouraged this feeling of freedom. Men believed that by overcoming the dangers of the wilderness and building up settlements, they had earned a right to say how they should be governed.

An analysis of these paragraphs reveals the supporting information provided to explain how the spirit of freedom grew in America.

1. The colonies had all the rights of Englishmen.
2. Actually they enjoyed greater freedom than their countrymen in England.
   a. Many colonies were founded by private trading companies and proprietors and therefore were not under the direct control of the English government.
   b. English kings were busy coping with problems in England.
   c. Lack of interest on the part of the English government resulted in considerable freedom for colonists to manage their own affairs.
3. Three thousand miles of ocean separated the colonies from England.
   a. Weeks or even months were needed to cross the ocean.
   b. Orders from England, therefore, could not be delivered promptly.
4. The New World itself encouraged the feeling of freedom.
   a. Land was plentiful; opportunities unlimited.
   b. Colonists believed that by overcoming dangers of the wilderness and building settlements they had earned the right to say how they should be governed.

Correlating narrative and illustrations. Illustrations and other visual aids not only stimulate pupils' interest (page 5), but are an important resource in the development of concepts. Space permits only a few examples of how illustrations can supplement and clarify important points made in the narrative.

The Virginia House of Burgesses has been described as the first representative legislative assembly in America. An illustration on page 142 in the textbook enables the student to see this body in session. This revealing illustration is a photograph of a diorama in the Colonial Historical Park at Jamestown. In studying the photograph the student notes the kind of meeting place used and the number of representatives present. The pictured scene is very different from a present-day meeting of the legislature.

A three-strip cartoon (pages 150-151) makes clear why pioneer farmers, Indians, and fur traders were not agreed on the desirability of having members of the first group settle west of the Appalachians about 1763.

The cartoon is especially useful in explaining why the Proclamation Line of 1763 (discussed on page 152) seemed a good idea to the British government but was unacceptable to frontiersmen in the Thirteen Colonies.

Following the discussion of the Stamp Act Congress (page 153) an old print is included to show colonists protesting against the Act. A man carries a placard portraying a greatly enlarged stamp. Beneath this stamp are skull and cross bones and the inscription, "The Folly of England; The Ruin of America." Other colonists are cheering the man carrying the placard.

The Intolerable Acts are discusssed on page 159 in the text. On the same page is a reproduction of an old English cartoon which represents Boston as a cage suspended from a branch of the Liberty Tree. On the land side of this tree are British soldiers and artillery blocking escape. On the ocean side are British warships. The people in the cage have nothing to eat but raw fish brought them by their fellow Patriots. This cartoon and its caption bring out an English reaction to the Boston Tea Party and the punitive legislation enacted by Parliament.

Frequently a picture provides depth of insight into a problem discussed in general terms. To illustrate, the narrative states that "perhaps as many as a third of the colonists remained loyal to the king." Some Loyalists merely refused to help the Patriot cause; others gave direct aid to the British. In the words of the narrative, ". . . the Patriots naturally regarded them [Loyalists] as traitors . . . attacked their homes and destroyed their property." The picture on page 192 portrays what happened to many Loyalist families. Grandfather leads a horse pulling a cart loaded with the family's possessions. On another horse ride mother and daughter. A son, carrying one bundle on a stick and another in his hand, trudges down the dusty road. To the rear father, rifle in hand, warily looks back to the village they have just left. In the background villagers are shouting, waving sticks, and throwing stones. A dog barks angrily. Where can this uprooted family find refuge?

At several places in the textbook closely related pictures in full color have been grouped with captions to provide a "self-contained" *picture story*. These throw light on certain facets of our heritage. Examples of such pictorial treatment are: Indian America, The Colonial Seaboard, Maritime New England, The Cotton Kingdom, The Old Northwest, The Golden West, The Industrial Age, and The New Pacific World. Each two-page picture story is located in the appropriate chapter, *e.g.* The Cotton Kingdom in Chapter 15, "Cotton Becomes King in the South."

The *picture biography* is another type of "self-contained" pictorial treatment. Artists' drawings, each frame with its own caption, are used to bring out five facets of the lives of important Americans. Note, for example, the presentation of Benjamin Franklin (page 155). Illustrations and captions tell about this man of many interests, who became "spokesman for the colonies."

Other subjects of picture biographies are: Columbus, La Salle, John Smith, Roger Williams, Washington, Jefferson, John Marshall, Eli Whitney, Jackson, Houston, Lincoln, Robert E. Lee, Andrew Carnegie, Thomas A. Edison, Samuel Gompers, Mark Twain, Clara Barton, and Robert Goddard.

Other pictorial features are those dealing with Hamilton, page 237; Clay, Calhoun, and Webster on page 377; our Presidents; and contributions of outstanding Americans of varied backgrounds (pages 528-529).

Correlating narrative and maps. Close integration between narrative and maps is even more important than between narrative and illustrations. Maps should be placed as closely as possible to related narrative, and information in captions should supplement, not duplicate, that in the narrative. The usefulness of maps in explaining a difficult concept can be illustrated in the case of the Navigation Acts (see the narrative and maps, pages 144-145). One of two globes shows colonial exports, which could be sold only to the mother country, being funneled into England. Arrows suggest that some of these would be resold to other countries at a profit. Another globe shows imports which the colonies needed from countries other than England flowing first to the mother country, where they were taxed, and then to the colonies. This map provides an easy-to-understand graphic representation of the financial implications of the Navigation Acts for the mother country and the colonies.

Sometimes a map effectively supplements information provided both in narrative and pictures. The map, "British Driven from Boston," page 167 in the textbook, is an excellent example. This map shows Breed's Hill and the route taken by the British in preparing to attack the Patriots. It brings out the fact that Continental troops ringed the city, and makes clear why the placing of artillery on Dorchester Heights led to the evacuation of Boston. This map also helps students understand why the British were compelled to dislodge the minutemen on Breed's Hill and suggests that this goal could have been achieved more easily had the British seized the neck of the Charlestown Peninsula instead of attempting a direct assault on the hill. In addition, students who study the map will understand why the redcoats left Boston by water rather than by land. Pages 166-167 provide a good illustration of the integration of narrative, picture, and maps in telling a story.

The fact that various projections have been used in drawing the maps included in *This Is America's Story* is important for teaching purposes. Students must be taught to use various projections and to recognize the advantages of each.

An attractive and useful map feature is the special map story following page 432 — *Land of Continuing Growth.* On the maps in this section students can follow step by step (1) the nation's territorial growth and the admission of states and (2) the development of transportation and areas of settlement at various periods. The graphs on these pages show the growth and density of the country's population.

Correlating narrative and charts. The second section of Chapter 7 describes the kind of government that evolved in the Thirteen Colonies (pages 140-143). Two charts (pages 140-141) bring out the fact that power was divided between the mother country and the colonies in the case of both executive and legislative branches of colonial government. In most colonies the governor was appointed by the king. In three colonies this official was appointed by the proprietor and in two he was elected. In either case, however, the king nevertheless had the right to approve or reject. With respect to the legislature, the governor, representing the king and Parliament, appointed members to the upper house. Members sitting in the lower house, however, were elected by the colonists. The two charts bring out these points more clearly than can words. A third chart in this series reveals the basic differences between local government in New England and in the South. In the former, town officials were elected in town meetings. In the South, county officials were appointed by the governor.

Another kind of chart is found on page 175 in the textbook. It illustrates a point already made in the narrative — that the "Continental Congress had little gold or silver . . . [and that] as the war dragged on, Continental paper money bought less and less." The chart pictures Continental silver and paper dollars. Then it shows for each year, 1776-1781, how many of the latter were needed to equal one of the former. The stack of bills needed in 1781, 500 of them, gives meaning to the saying, "not worth a continental."

A graph on page 219 shows the population of each of the United States — more than 700,000 for Virginia and less than 100,000 in the case of Rhode Island, Delaware, and Georgia. This graph is included in the chapter dealing with the Constitutional Convention. On pages 219 and 220 in the textbook the students have read about the Virginia and the New Jersey Plans, and have been told that the former was a "large state" and the latter a "small state" Plan. It seems unlikely that students would know how great was the range in size of population among the Thirteen States. Knowing the great differences in population, students will understand much better the reason for the determined small-state opposition to the Virginia Plan.

"Landmark in the Growth of Human Rights" is the title of a chart (page 230) on the same page as the discussion of our Bill of Rights. This chart uses a winding and broadening path to locate in order great documents from Magna Carta to our Bill of Rights. A brief quotation from each document is included. Since the English landmarks have been mentioned in an earlier chapter (page 138), this chart provides both review and reinforcement of the concept that our present-day freedoms are based on the heritage of the past.

Charts, simple in concept and design, have been used throughout *This Is America's Story* to reinforce and supplement the narrative, to facilitate comparisons and point up relationships, and to measure growth.

Linking Past and Present. Linking the past and the present is a basic purpose of history teaching and of historical writing. At the end of each chapter we have included brief episodes that call attention to ways in which the past lives today. Below are some examples of these "Links" with the central thought of each given in a few words.

Spanish names live on (page 79). Examples are the names of towns and cities, mountains and rivers, and even states.

The message of Valley Forge (page 189). ". . . a reminder of the spirit that rose above hardship and fear of defeat to win . . . independence . . ."

Mayflower II (page 99). This ship, much like the original, is in Plymouth, Massachusetts, harbor for all to see.

French customs live in the land of Louis (page 131). Mardi gras, parishes, the very law itself.

The Cry of Dolores (page 206). The ringing of Mexico's "liberty bell" marks the celebration of Mexican Independence.

Our documents of freedom (page 225). They can be seen today in the National Archives Building.

Our money system (page 242). How it came into being.

Freedom of the press (page 148). The acquittal of John Peter Zenger is a landmark in the establishment of this freedom.

Paul Revere (page 164). His silver work is treasured today; his home still stands in Boston; bells cast by him still ring in New England churches.

The Reference Section. The most important feature of the Reference Section is the treatment provided to help students understand the Constitution of the United States. A total of thirty-two pages are used for this purpose. Headnotes call attention to important provisions in the Constitution and provide the additional information needed to bring out their importance. Difficult words and terms are explained in a column parallel to the text of the Constitution itself.

At the back of the book are also found: (1) *For Further Reading*, a list of books for general reference and suggested readings for each unit, (2) a list of *Important Dates*, (3) information about the *States and Dependencies*, (4) information about *Presidents and Vice-Presidents*, (5) *Sources and Acknowledgments*, (6) an *Index to Names on Maps*, which students will find helpful in locating on maps in the book geographical names appearing in the narrative, and (7) a detailed and carefully worked out *Index*.

PART TWO: How This Text Contributes to the Achievement of Major Objectives

On page 1 we listed four basic goals to be kept in mind in planning a course in American history: understanding the history of our country, appreciating our American heritage, mastering basic study skills, and using the skills of analysis and "critical thinking." In the following pages you will find examples from *This Is America's Story* to illustrate ways in which this book contributes to the achievement of these goals.

Understanding the History of Our Country

Page 1 lists six points of emphasis in developing a basic understanding of our country's history. In pages 12-18 we have called attention (by units) to these and other important concepts developed in *This Is America's Story* and have suggested how such concepts can be made meaningful to students.

UNIT 1. Europe Seeks an Ocean Route to Asia and Discovers a New World in the West

Unit One tells the story of how Western European countries, seeking new routes to the East, found and explored a New World.

1. The demand in Europe for Eastern goods increased after the Crusades. The high prices of these goods and the desire to share in the rich trade caused countries in western Europe to look for new routes. The map on page 26 shows the old trade routes to the East and the routes used by Venice and Genoa in distributing Eastern goods in Europe. See also the paragraph, "Other Europeans are jealous of the Italians."

2. The search for a water route was made easier by important inventions (the compass and astrolabe) and better maps. . . . The map on page 28 shows the route taken by the Portuguese to reach India. On the following page the narrative explains why the Portuguese were able to sell Eastern goods for less than the Venetian merchants. Because Portugal controlled this new route, other European countries looked for different routes to the East.

3. Columbus, believing that Asia was larger and the earth smaller than they actually are, persuaded the rulers of Spain to back an expedition to seek a westward route to the East. . . . The maps on page 31 make clear why Columbus thought he could find a practical route to the East by sailing westward.

In looking for westward routes to the East, the people of western Europe learned more about the New World.

1. Magellan's expedition (1519-22) showed that a new world lay across the westward route to the East. The route followed in the first circumnavigation of the globe is shown on the maps, page 41. Note (page 40) that the spices brought back by the "Victoria" more than paid for the cost of the expedition. Because Magellan's route was too long for trade, France, England, and Holland sent explorers to look for short cuts to Asia. The map on page 43 shows the northwest short cut to Asia sought by England, France, and Holland. The maps on pages 45, 46, and 48 make clear why their efforts were in vain.

2. These explorations opened up the New World. . . .

UNIT 2. European Nations Plant Colonies and Struggle for Control of the New World.

Unit Two tells how European nations settled colonies and developed empires in the

New World. The first of these was Spain.

1. In Mexico and Peru, Cortés and Pizarro conquered Indian empires possessing great wealth; other Spaniards roamed far and wide in search of riches. Priests worked hard to Christianize the Indians. The extract from Balboa's letter to his king (page 60) makes clear what the Spanish hoped to find in the New World. The paragraph (pages 64-65), "Pizarro imprisons the Inca and gains a king's ransom," suggests how great was the wealth of Peru.

2. Within a century Spain acquired Florida and the southwestern part of the present-day United States, Mexico, the West Indies, and all of Central and South America (except Brazil).

3. Spain maintained strict control over her colonies. The methods used by England, Holland, and France in striking at Spain are described on pages 76-77.

England, France, and Holland also established colonies in the New World.

1. The Englishmen who came to America sought freedom to make a better living, to obtain land, to worship as they pleased, and to share in the government. See the cartoon (pages 82-83), "Why Englishmen Went to America." Geographic conditions help to explain why different ways of living developed. These geographic conditions are explained on pages 101-102. Wherever they lived, the English colonists had some things in common — a form of government in which the colonists had a voice, the English language, and the problem of earning a living 3000 miles from the mother country.

2. The French claimed a vast territory, and the small population made a living in the fur trade and by agriculture. The French government strictly regulated life in New France. The French priests were active missionaries among the Indians. The differences between life in New France and in the English colonies are brought out on pages 121-122 and 137-138.

3. Rivalry between France and England led to wars in North America. For the respective advantages of the French and the English colonies in this struggle, see pages 124-125. The English colonists, hemmed in by the French, had reasons of their own for fighting. Defeated in the French and Indian War, France surrendered Canada and the land east of the Mississippi to England and gave French territory west of that river to Spain. . . .

UNIT 3. New Nations Are Born as the New World Shakes Off European Rule.

Unit Three tells about the birth of new nations in the Western Hemisphere. When the English Parliament after 1763 tried to control the American colonies more strictly, the colonists resisted and won their independence (1783).

1. The colonists claimed the rights of Englishmen, and in the New World they enjoyed even greater freedom than their countrymen in England. See paragraph (page 139), "The Spirit of Freedom Grows in America," and pages 140-141 for a discussion of the kind of government which developed in the colonies.

2. . . . After Parliament passed harsh laws to punish Massachusetts for the Boston Tea Party, colonial leaders met in the First Continental Congress. When British soldiers attempted to destroy military supplies stored by the colonists at Concord, fighting began. Note that the mother country felt that the colonies existed for the good of England, pages 143-144. The cartoon (pages 150-151), "Why Britain Tried to Close the Frontier," illustrates one source of disagreement. The chart on page 156 summarizes British and American counter measures during the critical years, 1763-1775. Note also how source extracts, illustrations, and poetry are used (pages 153-163) to bring out the growing tension between mother country and colonies.

3. The Second Continental Congress approved a Declaration of Independence. The narrative (pages 168-170) makes clear how

the colonists finally became convinced that independence was the only solution to their quarrel with England. . . . The factors which made a Patriot victory possible are discussed on pages 176-177.

While Canada remained in the British Empire, the New World colonies of Spain and Portugal . . . became independent.

1. The Loyalists who fled to Canada demanded greater rights to govern themselves. Note that the policies which conciliated the French in 1763 (page 191) later became the source of tension between Canadians and the mother country (pages 195-196). Through the governors and their councils, however, the British Parliament retained its power in Canada until 1846, when responsible government was introduced. . . .

2. Spain's strict control over its colonies, the Creoles' resentment of their lack of opportunities, and the influence of the French and American Revolutions led to unrest and armed revolt in the Spanish colonies. The reasons for the revolt are explained on pages 197-198. Note that these grievances had existed a long time (see pages 68-73). Geographic conditions which made the winning of independence more difficult for the Spanish than for the English colonies are brought out on page 197. Miranda, Bolívar, and San Martín were leaders in the movement for independence from Spain. Brazil also declared its independence from Portugal.

UNIT 4. The United States Is Established on a Firm Basis.

Unit Four tells how our government developed, the forming of the Constitution, and the progress made by the United States in its early years. . . .

1. At the outbreak of the Revolutionary War there was no United States; the Second Continental Congress served as an emergency government. In 1781, the states adopted the Articles of Confederation. . . . The weaknesses of this government led to a demand for a stronger union. The cartoon on pages 214-215 illustrates problems which vexed the colonists.

2. The Constitutional Convention worked out a plan of government which included many important compromises. These are discussed in detail on pages 219-222. . . . Powers not given to the United States by the Constitution were left to the states. Separating powers among the executive, legislative, and judicial branches enabled each branch of the federal government to check the others. The chart on page 229 compares the powers of Congress under the Confederation and under the new Constitution. The illustration on page 232 brings out the relationship of the people to the Constitution and of the latter to our government.

3. With inauguration of Washington as President, the new government began. Alexander Hamilton developed a financial plan to pay the national and state debts, to raise money through tariffs and taxes, and to establish a national bank. His financial policies are discussed on pages 234-236. . . . Differences over how strong the federal government should be led to the formation of political parties.

The United States in time won the respect of other nations.

1. In 1789, a revolution broke out in France. When war against France broke out, the United States, though an ally of France, declared its neutrality. . . . The difficulties encountered by the United States in its effort to remain neutral are brought out on pages 245-246 and 251-252.

2. Influenced in part by the hope of gaining additional territory, the United States went to war with Great Britain in 1812. The maps on page 253 make clear the course of the war on land and sea. This war aroused a new national spirit in the United States and built up American manufacturing. By the purchase of Louisiana the United States had doubled its territory and had gained control of the Mississippi River.

3. By 1825 the Spanish and Portuguese

colonies (from Mexico southward) had achieved independence. The United States sympathized with their struggle for independence; Great Britain, for commercial and other reasons, wanted the new countries to remain independent. To safeguard the Western Hemisphere from European interference, President Monroe announced the Monroe Doctrine. Why both Britain and this country were interested in maintaining the independence of the former Spanish Colonies is discussed on page 257.

UNIT 5. The American Way of Living Changes as the Different Sections Develop.

Unit Five deals with important changes which had taken place in the United States by 1850. Different ways of living developed in various sections of the country. Chapters 14, 15, and 16 discuss how the geographic environment and man's technology affected ways of living in the Northeast, the South, and the West.

1. New England sea captains, barred from English ports after the Revolutionary War, found new markets. American commerce increased greatly after 1815. . . . The map on page 269 shows American trade and trade routes in the early 1800's. Meanwhile, the use of machinery spread from England to America. The rise of manufacturing is discussed on pages 272-274. The picture story (page 291) shows how Eli Whitney developed the principles of interchangeable parts in the manufacture of rifles — a key principle in mass production. . . .

2. By present-day standards, wages, hours, and working conditions were unsatisfactory in the early factories. The growth of industry increased the number and size of cities. Improved transportation and communication (turnpikes, canals, steamboats, railroads, and telegraph) were developed. The important roads are shown on the map, page 279; the important canals on page 281. See also illustrations of early railroad cars on pages 283, 285, and 286, as well as railroad routes on the map, page 284.

3. The invention of the cotton gin increased the planting of cotton. How the cotton gin worked is brought out in the drawing, page 292. The importance of cotton in the economy of the South is suggested by the picture (page 295) and the graph (page 296). Note that the area where most cotton is grown today (page 303) is west of the old cotton kingdom (map, page 293). When land in the Old South "wore out," planters sought new land to the southwest. Though a small part of the population, the plantation owners were the leaders in the South.

4. Differences in ways of living in the North and South led to disagreements. See, for example, the cartoon on pages 274-275 which brings out why North and South differed on the tariff question. The manufacturing North favored protective tariffs, the agricultural South opposed them. The North favored free labor, the plantation South depended on slave labor.

5. The frontier region attracted thousands of pioneer families. The chief routes across the Appalachians are shown on the map, page 309. Illustrations and source extracts provide a vivid story of life on the frontier, pages 312-316. The Ordinance of 1787 provided territorial government for the Northwest Territory and for the admission, in time, of new states. The pattern set by this law was followed in the case of later territories.

The United States became more democratic in the first half of the 1800's.

1. Different ways of living led to rivalry among the three sections. The cartoons on pages 324-325 show what the sections wanted. Andrew Jackson's election as President was hailed as a victory for the West.

2. Jackson refused to recognize the right claimed by South Carolina to nullify a protective tariff law. He also vetoed a bill to renew the charter of the Bank of the United States. When unsound trading in western land caused the government to require that payments be made in gold and silver, a severe panic swept the country.

3. During Andrew Jackson's administration, the right to vote was extended to practically all free men. The graph on page 329 shows how voting restrictions have been removed and how more power has been given voters. National conventions began to nominate the candidates for the presidency. In the 1830's, reformers worked [to improve conditions, and] . . . free public schools were established. . . .

UNIT 6. The United States Expands and Is Torn by War.

Unit Six tells how the United States expanded and how the North and South fought a bitter war. From 1803 to 1853 the United States, through purchase, annexation, treaty, and conquest, expanded until it reached the Pacific. Four of the maps in Chapter 18, pages 349, 351, 362, and 370, show the stages of this territorial expansion. See also the *Map Story* following page 432.

1. Among the reasons for this expansion were (1) a desire to control the inland waterways and to acquire cheap and fertile land, and (2) fear that European countries might become powerful in North America.

2. . . . Pioneers followed the Santa Fe Trail to the Southwest or the Oregon Trail to the west coast. The discovery of gold in California greatly increased the population on the Pacific coast.

A bitter quarrel developed between the North and the South over slavery in the new territories.

1. For a time, compromises like the Missouri Compromise and the Compromise of 1850 checked the quarrel over slavery.

2. Finally, further compromise was rejected. Leaders in the South opposed any limitations on slavery in the territories. . . . The box on page 379 shows clearly how the states lined up in 1848. The maps on the same page also make clear the balance between free and slave states in 1820, 1850, and 1854. The great majority of people in the North opposed the extension of slavery into the territories. How the two sections of the country moved closer to conflict is brought out on pages 383-386 in a series of six dramatic scenes.

3. The victory in 1860 of the Republican Party (which believed that Congress had the power to pass laws prohibiting slavery in the territories) led to the secession of the southern states. The cartoon on page 388 brings out points of view held in the North and in the South.

The Civil War (1861-1865) caused great destruction in the South and led to great changes in both the North and South.

1. The North had a larger population and greater industrial resources; the South had the advantages of fighting in defense of its own soil and of brilliant military leadership.

2. After bitter fighting, the northern plan of blockade and of dividing the South resulted in victory. The maps on page 399 make clear Union strategy on land and sea. Thus, the Union was saved. In the North, the war greatly increased the national debt, but industry also grew stronger. In the South, property damage was great and Confederate money became worthless. . . .

3. Following the assassination of Lincoln, Congress imposed a harsh plan for reconstructing the South, a policy deeply resented by Southerners. . . .

UNIT 7. Modern America Takes Shape.

In Unit Seven you will read how farming and industry developed following the Civil War.

1. The Homestead Act and the transcontinental railroad encouraged settlers to come to the great plains and Rocky Mountain region. Although the Indians fought bitterly against the advancing white man, the region was opened to mining, ranching, and farming. The source extract (pages 428-429) quotes the words of an Indian chief to make clear how Indians felt when their land was taken by white men. The map on page 429 shows where western railroads crossed Indian lands.

2. The growth of industry was made possible by our great natural resources, a large labor supply, foreign investments, inventions, and improved methods for the mass production of goods. . . .

3. The invention and increased use of farm machinery, as well as improved transportation, revolutionized agriculture. The vast improvement in agricultural methods from the early 1800's to today can be seen from the illustrations on pages 485-487.

The growth of industry and increased agricultural production have been accompanied by a number of problems.

1. Business has tended to follow a "boom, panic, and depression" pattern. The "ups and downs" of business have caused suffering to employers and employees and also to the general public. See the story of Mr. Jackson, an American businessman of the 1890's (pages 469-474), and the chart (page 472) which shows why a free flow of money contributes to prosperity.

2. To further their interests, manufacturers have tended to create monopolies. To improve their condition, workers have organized unions. The chart on page 475 illustrates the difference between craft and industrial unions. See also the picture biography of Samuel Gompers, page 477. The government has sought to regulate business, industry, and labor in the public interest.

3. Farming, like manufacturing, has tended to follow a boom and depression pattern. See the explanation of the law of supply and demand, and its application to farm prices (pages 489-490). Among the problems of the farmer are debt, high interest rates, "over-production" and falling prices, and worn-out land. Refer also to the cartoon on pages 490-491 to see what problems confront the farmer. . . .

UNIT 8. New Conditions Bring Changes in American Life.

In Unit Eight you will read how American life has been affected by the Machine Age, by social changes, and by greater opportunities for education and recreation. Since 1820 more than 40 million people have immigrated to the United States. The chart on page 508 shows when the immigrants arrived and where they came from.

1. Among the reasons why immigrants have come to America are the desire for greater freedom and the hope of earning a better living. Immigrants have made great contributions to American life.

2. When the good free land was occupied and the demand for labor had begun to decline, the United States began a policy of restricting immigration.

With the growth of industry in the years after the Civil War, American cities grew rapidly in number and size. Compare our twelve largest cities in 1890 with the twelve largest cities in 1960 (chart, page 512). Note also the three views of Chicago — 1833, 1860's, and 1928 — which show how a city grows. Job opportunities in industry attracted immigrants and reduced the percentage of Americans living in farm areas. . . .

1. Cities began to provide special services (such as pure water supplies) and to build tall buildings and new systems of transportation and lighting.

2. City slums and intemperance were two evils which engaged the attention of Americans.

3. In this period women achieved more rights and became increasingly active outside the home. The picture biography of Clara Barton (page 535) shows how some women put their greater freedom to good use. The illustrations on page 537 show the greater opportunities open to women of today. See also "Women in Politics," pages 550-551.

4. Important population changes included increasing numbers of both babies and older people, the tendency of Americans to be on the move, and the migration of large numbers of Negroes northward.

Industrialization has also affected American farms and small towns. With increased leisure, Americans have more time to become informed and to be entertained. . . .

UNIT 9. The United States Widens Its Horizons.

In this unit you will read about the American Presidents from 1865 to 1920 and how, during their administrations, the United States became more active in foreign affairs. On pages 559-560 you will find short biographical sketches of Presidents Grant through Wilson. The time line on page 592 provides a useful outline of America's involvement in world affairs. Demands for change after the war between the North and the South led, in time, to reforms.

1. Federal legislation established the merit system in civil service, curbed trusts and monopolies, and halted the waste of natural resources. Later, the tariff was cut and the Federal Reserve banking system adopted.

2. An amendment to the Constitution provided for a federal income tax.

3. Some states adopted the initiative, referendum, and recall.

The growth of American farming and industry after 1865 caused the United States to seek new markets. The chart on page 573 shows how the American trade picture has changed since 1865. Commercial expansion led to a more active interest in world affairs.

1. The United States obtained territories outside the country by purchase (Alaska), annexation (Hawaii), and war with Spain (the Philippines, Puerto Rico, and Guam). The maps on page 579 show how the United States expanded across the Pacific. . . .

2. To aid commerce and to protect our possessions, the United States wished for a shorter water route between the east and the west coasts. The desire was fulfilled when the United States leased land from Panama and built the Panama Canal. The map on page 586 will help students understand why the Isthmus of Panama route was chosen for the canal. The map on page 588 is a close-up of the canal.

The basis of American foreign policy was the Monroe Doctrine for the Western Hemisphere and the Open Door for China. . . .

In the early 1900's the United States supported plans for maintaining peace among nations. When World War I broke out in Europe, this country at first sought to remain neutral. Reasons why the United States found it hard not to "take sides" are found on pages 600 and 601.

1. German submarine policy, and the threat to this country implied in a German victory, finally caused the United States to enter the war.

2. President Wilson was able to make the League of Nations a part of the peace settlement. The United States, however, failed to join the League and returned to a policy of isolation after the war.

UNIT 10. The United States Becomes a World Power.

In Unit Ten you will read about our country's part in international affairs from about 1920 to the present and about the Presidents who have guided the country during this period. . . .

1. After World War I, dictatorships gained power in Russia, Italy, and Germany. Because other nations did not want war, the Axis powers were tempted to expand their territories. Refer to the maps on pages 620 and 621 to see the territory occupied by Japan in Asia and by Germany and Italy in Europe.

2. World War II broke out in Europe when Germany invaded Poland in 1939. The United States at first followed a policy of strict neutrality but later gave aid to the victims of aggression. The Japanese attack on Pearl Harbor brought the United States into World War II.

3. The heroic resistance of the British, the unwise German attack on Russia, and the all-out efforts of American industry and manpower contributed to the defeat of the Axis countries in World War II.

World War II was followed by a "cold war" which divided the world into two hostile sides.

1. The nations allied against the Axis powers formed the United Nations to keep peace in the postwar world. Member nations of the UN are shown on the map, page 637. . . .

2. In recent years the United States has continued its efforts for world peace. It also has met Communist aggression by arranging regional defense pacts, working through the UN, helping underdeveloped countries, and building up the defense of the free world.

3. The cold war at times has become a shooting war, as in Korea. Freedom-loving nations must be prepared to resist Communist aggression all over the world. European countries that fell victim to Communist aggression are shown on the map on page 635. See also the map on page 643 which calls attention to trouble spots around the world.

4. The desire of former colonial peoples for freedom, and of underdeveloped peoples to improve their lot quickly, has caused some of them to be impressed with the rapid strides of the Soviet Union toward industrialization.

5. Rapid scientific advances, in fields such as nuclear energy and space exploration, may lead to the use of great sources of power for the good of man rather than his destruction. The picture biography, page 645, tells the story of Robert Goddard, who was a pioneer in modern rocketry.

The relations of the United States with its neighbors to the north and to the south have, in general, become increasingly friendly.

1. Impressed by the growth of the United States, Canada worked toward a union of its provinces. Canada's steady growth and the aid she gave in World War I led England to grant Canada independence within the Commonwealth of Nations. See page 653 for a map of the provinces of Canada, page 654 for the composition of the Commonwealth of Nations, and page 655 for a chart explaining the Canadian form of government.

2. The friendship between the United States and Canada is shown by their long record of settling disputes by peaceful means and the unfortified boundary between the two countries. Canada and the United States depend on each other for commerce and protection.

3. Lack of experience in self-government under Spanish rule and widespread poverty have held back progress in Latin America. Nevertheless, some of these republics are moving ahead rapidly.

4. In the early 1900's the Latin American republics mistrusted the United States. The Good Neighbor Policy and the increasing readiness of this country to help underdeveloped peoples led to improved relations. The chart on page 664 shows the extent to which the countries of Latin America depend on trade with the United States.

5. The Organization of American States provides a means for the United States and Latin American lands to co-operate. "How Our Approach to Latin America Has Changed" is illustrated by a cartoon treatment, pages 670-671.

Since 1920 our country's domestic policies have passed through a series of stages.

1. From 1920 to 1929 the emphasis was on a return to "normalcy," with little government interference in business. This point is developed in Chapter 32, Section 1, "What Goals Did Presidents Harding, Coolidge, and Hoover seek?"

2. During the period of 1930 to 1940 various efforts were made to end the depression and to provide social security.

3. The period of World War II was one of full employment and peak production.

4. Since 1946 the country has generally been prosperous. Rising prices and the failure to achieve full employment, however, have been causes of concern. So also are tensions growing out of efforts to provide equal civil rights for all.

Appreciating Our American Heritage

The pervasive emphasis on "reasoned patriotism" in *This Is America's Story* is suggested in the following quotations dealing with basic American concepts of personal freedom and self-government.

Americans cherish freedom. The rights of Englishmen were the cherished birthright of the colonists. Living 3000 miles from the mother country, they gave new meaning to ancient freedoms. The Declaration of Independence sounded the clarion call that all peoples everywhere have unalienable rights, and among these liberty.

These early Americans had become accustomed to certain rights which their forefathers had won from the kings of England. Building new homes amid the dangers and hardships of an unsettled wilderness strengthened their love of freedom. When stricter regulations by the mother country threatened their rights, the colonists drew up the Declaration of Independence. In this statement, Americans proclaimed that all men were entitled to certain rights. To preserve these rights, our forefathers fought for independence from England. Only after a long and discouraging war did they succeed. Then, to protect their hard-won freedom, they established a government which would be controlled by the people. The voters were to elect representatives to make laws and officials to run the government. (pages 3-4)

I like the organization of the government into [three branches] . . . I approve of the greater House being chosen by the people directly . . . I will now tell you what I do not like. First, [there is no] bill of rights, providing clearly . . . for freedom of religion, freedom of the press, protection against standing armies, . . . and trials by jury . . . a bill of rights is what people are entitled to against every government on earth. . . . (Letter from Jefferson to Madison; page 223)

Freedom has taken on new meaning. The Preamble to the Constitution enumerates the purposes for which the new government was to be established. Through legislation and judicial interpretation such concepts as human rights, freedom, and liberty have taken on new and broader meaning.

We the people of the United States, in order to form a more perfect union, establish justice, insure domestic tranquility, provide for the common defense, promote the general welfare, and secure the blessings of liberty to ourselves and our posterity, do ordain and establish this Constitution for the United States of America. (The Constitution, page 228)

As the United States has grown, so has the American ideal of freedom taken on wider meaning. It includes the right to choose a job, to run a business, to travel and to live where you wish. Our system of free public schools seeks to prepare American boys and girls to live useful and satisfying lives. Americans are free to explore the world of science . . . in search of new knowledge. Yet America will not in truth be the Land of Promise so long as rights and opportunities are denied to any of its citizens. (page 7)

Freedom is ours to defend. There is a reciprocal relationship between rights and responsibilities. This relationship was understood and accepted by the minutemen who fought at Concord. In time of danger millions of Americans have fought to defend their country.

Gentlemen may cry, peace, peace — but there is no peace. The war is actually begun! . . . Our brethren are already in the field! Why stand we here idle? . . . Is life so dear, or peace so sweet, as to be purchased at the price of chains and slavery? . . . I know not what course others may take; but as for me, give me liberty, or give me death! (Patrick Henry spoke thus March 23, 1775; page 161)

. . . As Nathan Hale faced death, his last words were, "I only regret that I have but one life to lose for my country." (page 180)

Ours is a representative form of government. Before coming to America, the English colonists had been represented in Parliament. In the New World they acquired direct representation in the lower houses of the colonial assemblies. After independence had been achieved, legislation was passed, *e.g.* the Northwest Ordinance, to guarantee to people living in the new territories the same rights that were enjoyed by those living in the original states.

The founders of this nation believed the principles of *liberty and self-government* to be all-important. They fought to obtain these rights and, on many occasions, to preserve them . . . because of their efforts, we live today under a government based upon the will of the [people] . . . expressed through elected representatives. (page 705)

The Northwest Ordinance was one of the wisest laws ever passed by any government. This new law gave settlers the rights which mean so much to all Americans. It also set up a form of government which would change as the needs of the settlers changed . . . it promised the people who were willing to brave the dangers of the wilderness that in time they would have a government on equal terms with the older states. (pages 310-311)

Great men have served their country well. It is difficult to appreciate fully the courage displayed by the men who signed the Declaration of Independence. We owe a great

debt to these men and to other great leaders who in time of crisis have accepted heavy responsibilities. Some of them have served in time of war, others in time of peace. Some were in the service of state and nation, others were scientists, inventors businessmen, and philosophers.

And for the support of this Declaration, with a firm reliance on the protection of divine Providence, we mutually pledge to each other our Lives, our Fortunes and our sacred Honor. (Declaration of Independence; page 174)

No American can read the story of our Constitution without realizing what a debt of gratitude we owe to the wise men who wrote it. These men are often called the "Founding Fathers" because in giving the United States its Constitution, they laid the foundation of our nation. This remarkable document has not only given us a strong and stable government but has also protected the liberties which we hold dear. (page 224)

. . . It is rather for us to be here dedicated to the great task remaining before us — . . . that we here highly resolve . . . that this nation, under God, shall have a new birth of freedom; and that government of the people, by the people, for the people, shall not perish from the earth. (The Gettysburg Address; page 405)

Millions of unsung Americans also have helped to build this country. It is possible to identify the great leader by name and to recognize his achievements. Most good citizens, outside of their circle of family and friends, are nameless. Yet they are the men who conquered the wilderness, built the cities, and fought the battles. Their contributions to the building of America are to be seen all around us even if their names are engraved on no great public buildings or huge monuments.

Proud as we are, however, of the famous "names" in our country's story, we must not forget that ordinary Americans have been key figures in building America. Thousands of men and women from our Atlantic seaboard states went west, conquered the wilderness, and established new communities. Wherever they went, they carried with them American ideals. They were joined by groups of "unknown" men from all over the world. And these nameless Americans — from many lands, of all races, of different religions — by their work and their faith in American liberty and democracy have made America what it is today. (page 549)

We recognize that our government is not perfect; our way of life falls short of what we would like it to be. But they can be improved if each individual does his full share. (page 714)

What makes a nation great? Not only wise leaders but a people who have the vision and the will to make a dream come true. The story is no more nor less than the story of the accomplishments of its people. (page 504)

. . . hard work, courage, loyalty, and high ideals . . . built this republic . . . citizens, young and old, must continue to show the same industry, courage, loyalty, and devotion to American ideals if our country is to remain strong and free. . . . (page 8)

Free Americans face the challenge of totalitarianism. Despotic kings and dictators bent on conquest are not new. But none of these pose the threat to the free world that does present-day Communist imperialism. Communism repudiates all religion and democratic ideals, mocks at our government and economic way of life, scorns co-operation with non-Communist nations, seeks to make over the whole world in its image. This is the great challenge which we must meet.

Why is communism a deadly threat? One answer lies in the difference between Communist ideas and the heritage upon which the United States has grown. (1) In the United States the individual is important. Under communism the individual is the servant of the state. (2) Americans cherish personal rights and freedom. Under communism the people have few rights. (3) Our American way of life includes the private ownership of property and the right of the individual to choose his job and to own a business. In Communist countries the government owns the means of production and determines what jobs people will hold. (4) Finally, control of a free government rests in its citizens; the policies of our government are determined by representatives and officials elected by the voters in free elections. In a Communist country, a small group of Communist Party leaders, not the people themselves, determine policies. When elections are held in Communist countries, the people have no opportunity to choose one of several candidates. They are merely allowed to vote "yes" for the candidates selected by the Communist Party. (pages 706-708)

. . . we must preserve those values of liberty and democracy that have made the United States a model for other nations. The world and particularly the new nations of Asia and Africa are watching to see if our free government and way of life can meet the present challenge. The Communists are quick to point out any conditions in the United States which do not square with the principles we proclaim. Our success in making the American way of life work may well sway the world balance in favor of freedom and democracy. (page 712)

. . . I believe . . . that liberty and independence and self-determination, not communism, is the future of man, and that free men have the will and the resources to win the struggle for freedom. (John F.

Kennedy, following the meeting with Premier Khrushchev in early June, 1961; page 694)

. . . when the Constitutional Convention had finished its work, Benjamin Franklin was asked, "What have you given us?" The wise old gentleman replied, "A republic, if you can keep it." Franklin knew that if liberty and self-government were

to endure, citizens must accept responsibilities. This truth applies just as much in the world in which we live today as it did when the United States was created. (page 714)

A nation without a sound heritage rarely reaches greatness. But it is equally true that a nation which does not *guard* its heritage rarely remains great. (page 706)

Mastering Basic Study Skills

Proficiency in history, as in other subjects, depends to a considerable extent on how well students have mastered basic study skills. The various ways in which *This Is America's Story* helps students get the most out of reading a chapter have already been described (see pages 2-4). To help students use the textbook effectively we have also provided a section (see text pages 10-13) which illustrates and explains the purpose of unit and chapter introductions; guide questions, headings, and Check Ups; chapter and unit study equipment; and time lines. In addition to reading narrative for meaning, there are many other basic skills which are important in the study of history: (1) reading maps, (2) reading charts and graphs, (3) obtaining information from pictures, (4) developing a time sense, (5) using the library, and (6) preparing reports. An analysis of each of these skills and suggestions for its development are found in the *Gaining Skill* section at the end of various units.

Reading and interpreting maps. One way of interesting students in reading maps is to call attention to problems which arise when a mapmaker depicts on a flat sheet of paper the land masses and bodies of water that make up the surface of our globe (see pages 54-55 in the textbook).

One way to see the earth as it really is would be from a space capsule orbiting hundreds of miles above the earth's surface. There, before your eyes, would be the vast, round sphere itself! You yourself can get some idea of how the earth looks from space if you bring your eyes close to a globe. On a globe, land and sea areas have the same shape and comparative size as they do on earth. In other words, your globe is a scale *model* of the earth. . . .

Since a globe gives you the most accurate view of the earth, some map makers try to draw pictures of the globe as it looks "in the round." Sometimes they make their maps by copying photographs of a globe. Many of the maps in [Unit One] have been drawn to show parts of the earth more or less as they would appear on a globe seen from different angles. . . .

You probably are acquainted with other kinds of maps, such as those found in an atlas or on your classroom wall. The land areas of the earth may appear different in shape and size on these maps because it is impossible to show accurately the *curved* surface of the globe on a *flat* sheet of paper. The size of the land areas, or their shape, or the distances and directions between them must be changed somewhat. Instead of being exact models or pictures of the globe, such maps are more like useful *diagrams* of the earth's surface. . . .

Map projections are useful for accurate measuring, but all of them distort the appearance of the earth's surface in some way. For example, look at the drawing on page 54 of one of the oldest projections, named after Mercator, the Dutch map maker who invented it. A Mercator map shows accurately the outline of land areas and their direction from one another. But land areas far from the equator appear much larger on this projection than they actually are. Note that there is no North Pole on the Mercator map. Instead of meeting at the North Pole, meridians remain the same distance apart all the way to the top. Note, also, that the parallels are spaced farther apart toward the top of the map. In other words, the top and bottom areas of a Mercator map are in a different scale from the areas near the equator.

A different map projection, named after a German map maker, Mollweide, shows the comparative size of land areas accurately, but distorts their shape (see page 55). As on a Mercator map, the same scale of miles can not be used all over a Mollweide map.

As you refer to maps during your study of American history, you will find it helpful to keep in mind the facts about projections explained above.

Specific suggestions for reading maps are made on page 133 of the textbook:

1. To locate a place.
2. To trace a route.
3. To tell direction.
4. To estimate distance.
5. To compare areas.
6. To see the lay of the land.
7. To understand reasons.
8. To see changes.

Reading and interpreting charts and graphs. *This Is America's Story* contains many charts and graphs. Charts are used to sum up information in a way that makes it easier to understand. Once students have learned how to get the most out of charts, they find them helpful study tools (see pages 552-553 of the textbook).

For example, the chart on page 232 of the textbook pulls together many ideas explained in the text and shows in a "graphic" way the organization of our government. The top chart on page 141 diagrams local government in the Southern and New England Colonies and helps you compare them and note any differences. Throughout the book, you will find charts on political parties which will help you keep all the parties' names straight (pages 240, 338, 415, 568, 686). If you were to put these charts together, you would see the different steps and changes in the growth of political parties throughout our country's history.

Graphs are included in this textbook because statistical information presented in this way is easier to grasp than when only numbers are used. Graphs also facilitate the making of comparisons. The graph on page 175 of the textbook, for example, makes possible comparisons which involve time and amount. Graphs may also be used to show trends. See, for example, the graph on page 296 of the textbook. Trends can be represented in various ways — a rising or falling line, a series of bars, or symbols which represent given quantities. A series of questions on page 553 of the textbook call attention to things which students need to know in reading graphs.

Reading and interpreting illustrations. *This Is America's Story* contains many pictures closely related to the narrative. Students need to be taught to read pictures. Reading a picture, and thinking about what has been discovered, is not the same as taking a casual look at a picture. Specific suggestions for reading pictures are made on pages 420-421 in the textbook.

The pictures in this book can tell you much about America's story if you look at them carefully and think about them.

Sometimes pictures are better than words because they can *show* you how people dressed in past times, what their houses looked like, and the kinds of tools they used. It would take many words to describe the appearance of Americans who lived in the Northeast and the South and on the frontier during the early 1800's. But the drawings on the first pages of Chapters 14, 15, and 16 show you at a glance how typical Americans in the different sections looked at that time (pages 264, 289, 304 of the textbook).

Pictures are especially useful in describing how something works. To see what Eli Whitney's first model of the cotton gin looked like, turn to the picture biography on page 291 and look at the second scene. To understand how the gin actually cleaned cotton, look at the diagram on page 292.

Pictures can also help you understand a story told in words. On page 167 you read how American Patriots at the Battle of Bunker Hill twice drove back the advancing British troops. Now look at the picture on page 168. It shows you how the height of the hill gave the Patriots an advantage over the British who landed at the foot of it and faced a long climb under enemy fire.

In studying pictures you can learn a great deal from details. The illustration on page 105 shows the inside of a colonial ironworks. At the left are the big gear wheels which transmitted power from the outside water wheel. In a modern steel mill such big machinery would be made of steel. Yet in this colonial ironworks the wheels were made of wood. This shows you that in colonial times American industry had barely started to develop. The colonists' use of iron was limited to relatively small parts, like the heads of tools.

Developing a sense of time. The material provided on pages 208-209 in the textbook serves a dual purpose: (1) it explains uses of the time lines included in *This Is America's Story*, and (2) it helps students learn how to use dates in "keeping events straight."

Dates may not seem important by themselves, but they are markers which you can use to tell where you are in your study of history. Dates are needed in history to (1) tell when important events took place, (2) keep events in the right order, and (3) estimate the number of years from the beginning to the end of a historical period.

The time lines which appear at the start of each chapter of the textbook help you to use dates in these three ways. As you read from left to right along the time lines, they *show* the order in which important events took place. By including dates of events already studied, time lines help you to see the relation between important events discussed in different chapters. For example, on the time line for Chapter 10 (page 191) you can see that Canada and Latin America won self-government many years later than the Thirteen Colonies, whose fight for independence was described in Chapter 9.

In some chapters the important events happened many years apart. But in other periods of history, such as the Revolutionary War, described in Chapter 9, many great events were crowded into a few years. Chapter 9, therefore, has a special "close up" time line on page 182 which shows part of the regular chapter time line on a larger scale. On the enlarged part there is room to show the most important dates of the war. . . .

Besides the dates shown on time lines, there are other dates to help you get your bearings in history. For example, dates on a map tell you which of the events shown on the map came first. Look at the map on page 87 which shows the thirteen colonies founded by the English. By reading the date after the name of each settlement, you can tell that Virginia was the first permanent English colony (Jamestown, 1607). You can also tell that Georgia was not founded until 125 years later (Savannah, 1733).

Using the library efficiently. The suggestions found on pages 260-261 of *This Is America's Story* will prove useful in teaching students how to make effective use of local libraries.

Preparing oral and written reports. In history classes students are often asked to make two kinds of reports: (1) book reviews, and (2) reports on subjects of interest to the class. The latter usually involve reading in several books and the organization of the information thus obtained for oral or written presentation. Suggestions on how to prepare reports are found on pages 342-343 of *This Is America's Story*.

Perhaps a student making a report on immigration may wish to include a graph or chart in his report. In preparing a graph or chart he should take into account suggestions of the kind found on pages 552-553 in the textbook.

Let's say you decide to make a chart dealing with immigration to America. Because "Immigration" includes so many things, it will be necessary to limit this topic. Do you see why the topic "Contributions of Immigrants to America, 1850-1920" would be better? The next step is to determine what are the things you should remember about this topic. Ask yourself — which items of information are important? In this way, you will work out the major "categories" of information. Categories might include the names of immigrants, their native countries, and the

fields in which they made contributions. Place each "category" in a separate column: one column for the person's name, another for his accomplishment, and so on.

Providing opportunities for students to practice skills. The old saying, "practice makes perfect," is true for the mastery of study skills. Each teacher has his own views about assignments, evaluation, and remedial teaching designed to make students self-sufficient and effective workers. For each unit we have included under *Interesting Things to Do* a variety of activities, many of which call for using skills such as those described. The following are representative of these activities:

Make a chart of the explorers you read about in Chapter 2, using these headings: Name, Date, Country for Which He Sailed, and Results of Voyage. (page 55)

Prepare a report on Colonial Homes, Colonial Schools, Amusements in Colonial Days. (page 133)

Tell the class about some interesting story you have read describing the conquest of Mexico or Peru, the settling of an English colony, frontier life, the French and Indian Wars. (page 133)

Make a map of the last frontier in the United States showing: the great plains region; Rocky Mountain region; Pacific Northwest and Pacific Southwest; the route of the transcontinental railroad; the cattle country and the long drive; the wheat land; the mining territory. (page 503)

Make a time line showing the important inventions which have made the United States a great manufacturing nation. (page 503)

. . . show on a globe or world map how the Panama Canal . . . shortens the distance between . . . important ports, such as New York to San Francisco, New York to Yokohama. . . . (page 613)

Using the Skills of Analysis and Critical Thinking

Historians and educators agree on the importance of teaching students the skills of analysis and critical thinking. In planning this major revision of *This Is America's Story* we have been mindful of the need to further this objective. Newer interpretations of important events and problems have been included and efforts have been made to state the case for various points of view on important issues.

To acquaint students with primary sources and their uses, such fundamental documents as the Declaration of Independence and the Constitution of the United States are included. The former is found on pages 171-174 in the textbook, with a brief analysis in running text. The Constitution, with headnotes which call attention to important provisions of the Constitution and elaborate on them, and explanations of difficult words and terms, appears on pages A1-A32. References to pertinent parts of the Constitution are frequently made in the running text, as the following excerpts show.

> In the election of 1824 . . . it was found that no candidate had won a majority. In such a case, the Constitution says that the House of Representatives shall choose a President from the three candidates who had won the most votes (page A24). Henry Clay, who had received the fewest votes of the four candidates, asked his supporters to vote for Adams. With this help, Adams was elected by the House. (page 321)

> Another part of Hamilton's program was to set up a *Bank of the United States.* . . . Hamilton believed that Congress could establish the bank under its power to borrow money and regulate currency (page A8). The bank would make the government stronger, so Congress agreed and the bank was established. (page 236)

> For a number of years many people had favored a new form of taxation — a tax on a person's wages or income . . . Congress had tried to levy an income tax before, but the Supreme Court had declared it unconstitutional. In 1913, however, just before Wilson took office, the Sixteenth Amendment was added to the Constitution, permitting Congress to levy such a tax (page A28). At President Wilson's request, an income tax law was passed, and we have had income taxes ever since. (page 568)

Uses of source extracts. A great number of short source extracts have been included in this textbook. The purposes they serve can be illustrated by citing some examples.

A part of a letter from Balboa to King Ferdinand is found on page 60 in the textbook. The explorers had heard rumors of the land we know as Peru and tried to interest the king in financing an expedition to conquer it.

> In the mountains [of Peru] there are certain *caciques* [chiefs] who have great quantities of gold in their houses. It is said . . . that all the rivers of these mountains contain gold; and that they have very large lumps in great abundance . . . and the Indians say that the other sea [Pacific] is at a distance of three days' journey. . . .
>
> They say that the people of the other coast are very good and well-mannered; and I am told that the other sea is very good for canoe navigation, for that it is always smooth and never rough like the sea on this side. . . . They say that there are many large pearls and that the caciques have baskets of them. . . . It is a most astonishing thing and without equal, that our Lord has made you the lord of this land.

The following paragraph suggests the use the authors have made of this source extract.

> What a shrewd letter! Notice that Bal-

boa actually knew very little about this land, since almost every sentence began with "they say" or "it is said." The king apparently noticed this fact, for in spite of the compliment at the end of the letter, he refused aid. If Balboa wished to go to Peru, he had to go "on his own."

The problems confronting the Pilgrims during their first winter in America are suggested in the following paragraph (see page 91 in the textbook) written by Governor Bradford.

> They had now no friends to welcome them nor inns to entertain or refresh their weatherbeaten bodies, no houses or much less towns to repair to, to seek for succor [help]. . . . And for the season, it was winter, and they that know the winters of that country know them to be sharp and violent and subject to cruel and fierce storms, dangerous to travel to known places, much more to search an unknown coast. Besides, what could they see but a hideous and desolate wilderness full of wild beasts and wild men? And what multitudes there might be of them they knew not.

Do these words suggest the horror these men and women must have felt at times? How would this statement be phrased today? The next paragraph on page 91 tells what happened to the Pilgrims during the first winter.

> During the next few months, over half the little band perished of cold, hunger, and disease. When spring came, however, the remaining Pilgrims decided to stay in this new land rather than return to England. In spite of hardships, they had freedom to worship as they chose and to govern themselves.

Were the Pilgrims brave and dedicated people? Had Governor Bradford, in writing about this winter at a later date, overstated the problems facing the settlers?

Thought-provoking questions. One part of the Chapter Check Up is called What Do You Think? Each includes an average of five "thought" questions that cut across the material in the chapter and at times refer to ideas dealt with in earlier chapters. These questions call for comparisons and evaluation. There are no pat answers for them. In discussion of questions of this kind the teacher should make sure that various points of view are identified, that each receives consideration, and that reasons for and against each are clearly stated and evaluated. Doubtless teachers will wish to add other questions of this kind to the list. The following are representative of questions included in What Do You Think? sections:

> What are some advantages that a country has when it is self sufficient? What are some disadvantages? (page 35)

> Why did the early explorers of the interior of North America use water routes rather than land routes? (page 52)

> The French fur trade may have cost France her territory in the New World. Do you agree? Why? (page 130)

> What freedoms do Americans have today that the people in the English colonies did not have? (page 147)

> Washington believed that the United States should not get mixed up in European affairs. So did Monroe. Is it possible to follow the same policy today? Explain why or why not. (page 258)

> Why did the frontier about 1850 jump from the area just west of the Mississippi to the Pacific coast? How could you draw the line of the frontier after that date? (page 372)

> Explain why a high tariff on foreign goods may prevent other countries from buying goods in this country. (page 569)

Why were nations that had suffered staggering losses in World War I ready to spend huge sums for armaments in the 1930's? (page 648)

Why do neighboring countries wish to attract United States investments? Why are these nations nevertheless sometimes uneasy about such investments? (page 675)

Activities which encourage analysis. At the end of each unit is a section headed Interesting Things to Do. It includes activities, many of which call for insight and the ability to analyze. Quite often the student may be asked to "put himself in the shoes" of someone who lived long ago or far away. The following are representative of suggested activities of this kind.

Imagine that you were an Indian boy who saw Columbus land on Guanahani. Write the story as the boy would have told it. . . . (page 55)

Draw a cartoon dealing with one of these subjects: . . . impressment of American seamen . . . feeling of Westerners about New Orleans (prior to 1803); War Hawks and the War of 1812. . . . (page 261)

Write an imaginary conversation between: a Federalist and a Republican; a member of the Constitutional Convention from New Jersey and one from Virginia; a New England merchant and a War Hawk in 1812; . . . a Pennsylvania farmer who joined the Whiskey Rebellion and a government [agent] sent to collect a tax on whiskey. (page 261)

Write a newspaper editorial taking a stand for or against one of these questions of the day: the annexation of Hawaii; war with Spain; . . . the Open Door Policy; the United States and the League of Nations. (page 613)

Three facets of analysis and critical thinking are dealt with in the Gaining Skill section included in the end matter for each unit: "How to Evaluate Information" (pages 612-613), "Developing Opinions and Attitudes" (pages 703-704), and "How to Explore Local History" (pages 502-503).

Evaluating Information. When students read about issues, or take part in discussion of them, they may become aware of lack of agreement as to the facts, the importance to be attached to given facts, and conclusions to be drawn from them. The following general suggestions are made to help students reach sound conclusions:

For several months now, you have been studying the history of the United States. Meanwhile, even as you have been studying American history, more history has been made. Many of the problems you have been reading about in this book are not yet settled. They are going to be worked out in the future, and you are going to have a part in dealing with them. For that reason you will need to keep informed about public affairs through reading, listening to radio and television reports, and taking part in discussions. On many issues you will read conflicting reports and discover differences of opinion. To help you reach sound conclusions, apply these rules to what you read and hear:

(1) Did the reporter himself observe what he describes?

(2) Is the reporter qualified to make an accurate report?

(3) Is the reporter trustworthy?

(4) Is there a special reason why a reporter who usually is trustworthy may not be in a particular case?

(5) Is the report a statement of fact or of opinion?

Incidentally, you should listen to both sides of a question. It is important for you to know what people whose opinions differ from yours think about various issues. (pages 612-613)

Developing opinions and attitudes. The discussion of this subject brings out how *tastes* and *standards* help to shape opinions and the way people behave. The point is then made that behavior which reflects unlawful opinions and attitudes is bound to be unlawful. The following suggestions call attention to basic principles that should be reflected in views and opinions expressed in a free America:

One way is to read in order to be *informed* and to discuss the issue with others who are informed. Another is to seek the views of *experts* on the issue in question. A third is to check each position on the issue to see if it is in conflict with the *basic social beliefs* of Americans. Some of these basic beliefs are:

All persons should be judged on their merits.

All persons should possess equal rights and liberties.

The rights of no person should be exercised so as to interfere with the rights of others.

The actions of no person should threaten the welfare of the people or the security of the nation. (page 704)

Exploring local history. Reconstructing the history of a community is a useful approach to helping students develop skill in analysis. The following list includes topics and sources of information that should receive consideration in planning this type of a project. Students will enjoy the challenge of trying to piece together "evidence" that will help them understand what life was like in their community long ago.

Some American communities were first settled in the early 1600's; others have been started much more recently. But any community, old or young, contains interesting records and remains which you may use to get a better understanding of the past.

Just as this book has presented the story of the nation's early beginnings, so you can prepare an account of your own community's beginnings and growth. Your class could write a play, an article for the local newspaper, or even a book of stories about your community's "yesterdays."

The topics of local history you may wish to learn about are the same as those we have followed in this book in describing early life in the various sections of the country: when and where settlements were made, early settlers, and how people lived long ago.

Here are some of the sources you may investigate to gather this information:

1. Written sources . . .
2. Oral sources . . .
3. Remains . . .
4. Pictorial sources . . .

Of course, this list is quite incomplete. Not all these materials may be available in your community. Even if they were, you could not be expected to use them all. But by setting up committees, a great many sources can be investigated and a surprising amount of information collected. (pages 502-503)

In these pages we have tried to do two things:

1. To focus attention on widely accepted goals for the teaching of history and to suggest procedures appropriate to these ends.

2. To demonstrate that *This Is America's Story* has been written with these goals in mind and to suggest ways of using this textbook to the best advantage.

We wish you all success in the important task of teaching the nation's history to young Americans.

HOUGHTON
★ MIFFLIN ★
SOCIAL STUDIES
★ ★ PROGRAM ★ ★

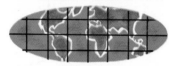

HISTORY
★ ★ ★

THIS IS
AMERICA'S STORY

THIRD EDITION

HOWARD B. WILDER

ROBERT P. LUDLUM

HARRIETT McCUNE BROWN

WITH THE EDITORIAL ASSISTANCE OF

HOWARD R. ANDERSON

HOUGHTON MIFFLIN COMPANY · BOSTON

NEW YORK · ATLANTA · GENEVA, ILL. · DALLAS · PALO ALTO

The statue of "Liberty Enlightens the World" has been seen by millions of Americans returning to their native land as well as by millions of immigrants coming to begin new lives in America. To all people who see it this statue represents the freedom for which our country stands.

This team of authors, editor, and consultants combine experience in Teaching and writing history with experience in curriculum development.

ABOUT THE AUTHORS AND EDITOR

The authors and editor of *This Is America's Story* combine a rich and varied experience in the teaching and writing of history:

HOWARD B. WILDER served for many years as teacher of history and as Head of the Social Studies Department at Melrose High School, Melrose, Massachusetts. He is co-author of the senior high school text *The Making of Modern America*.

ROBERT P. LUDLUM, President of Blackburn College, Carlinville, Illinois, formerly taught history at Texas A. & M. University and at Hofstra University in New York. He is co-author of *American Government*.

HARRIETT McCUNE BROWN has had wide experience in the teaching of history in the junior high school grades in Los Angeles, California. She is co-author of *America Is My Country* and *Our Latin American Neighbors*.

HOWARD R. ANDERSON, a specialist in the teaching of history, has served as Director of Social Studies in the Ithaca, New York, schools, as President of the National Council for the Social Studies, and as Social Science specialist in the United States Office of Education. He is co-author of *The History of Our World*.

Consultants

For valuable suggestions in the Third Edition of *This Is America's Story*, authors and publisher are indebted to **JOHN D. HICKS**, who has been Professor of American History at the Universities of Nebraska, Wisconsin, and California, and to **RAYFORD W. LOGAN**, Professor of History at Howard University. Professor Hicks has contributed to many historical publications and is the author of *The Populist Revolt* and co-author of *The Federal Union* and *The American Nation*. Professor Logan also has contributed to many historical publications and is the author of *The African Mandates in World Politics* and *The Negro in American Life and Thought: The Nadir, 1877–1901*.

This Is America's Story is told in 32 chapters grouped in 10 units which follow a chronological sequence. The title of each chapter and unit makes clear what is the "big idea" developed in each.

CONTENTS

OUR HISTORICAL HERITAGE

On the following pages and elsewhere in this book, color photographs show famous buildings, monuments, paintings, and other handiwork from America's past which can still be seen today at museums and historic sites. By studying them, we can better understand how people lived during the different periods of our history. For example, thousands of people have sensed the brave spirit of America's beginnings while visiting *Mayflower II* (right), a reconstruction of the little ship which brought the Pilgrims to Plymouth.

The history of this country is closely related to the history of Canada and of Latin America. See also Chapters 3, 6, and 31.

A famous statue (left) on Lexington Green recalls the determination with which the minutemen defended their rights in 1775 and launched a new nation. Below, the original "Star-Spangled Banner" which floated over Fort McHenry hangs in the Smithsonian Institution in Washington.

Note the emphasis in Unit Five on how people lived and how technological change affected ways of living. Ways of living are also brought out in Units Two and Eight. This text stresses comparisons.

Unit Five • THE AMERICAN WAY OF LIVING CHANGES

Unit Six • THE UNITED STATES EXPANDS AND IS

One of the last of the old paddle-wheel steamers still cruises on the Ohio River. Now called the *Belle of Louisville*, its annual races against the *Delta Queen* create great excitement.

At Fort Dix, N.J., history-conscious soldiers fire the kind of cannon used in the Civil War.

A steam engine (above) made in Bristol, R.I. helped to power our growing industry in the 1880's.

Antique cars from the dawn of the Automobile Age wait at a crossing near Hill City, South Dakota, while railroad fans enjoy a ride behind an old steam locomotive.

The threat of Communist imperialism and this country's role as the leading power in the Free World are brought out in Unit Ten.

Unit Ten • THE UNITED STATES BECOMES A WORLD LEADER   614

Useful reference material and interesting supplementary readings are cited.

Reference Section

A veteran of World War II, the retired battleship *North Carolina* is shown here being towed upriver to Wilmington, N.C., where it is now a state war memorial open to visitors.

New York City helicopter passengers see the American landmark known the world over as a symbol of liberty.

Places mentioned in the text can be found on one of the maps.

LIST OF MAPS

HISTORICAL MAPS

Columbus' pilot drew a map of the Caribbean Sea (below) on an ox-hide, placing "west" at the top and showing the newly discovered islands. John White mapped the islands off the Carolina coast (right) where he helped found the "lost colony" of Roanoke in 1585.

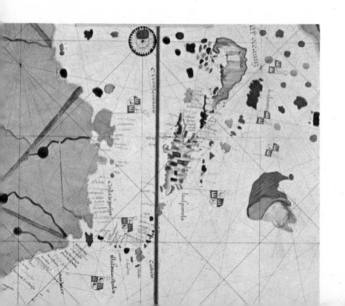

x

This feature combines pictures and narrative to give students some appreciation for each section.

xi

OUR HISTORICAL HERITAGE

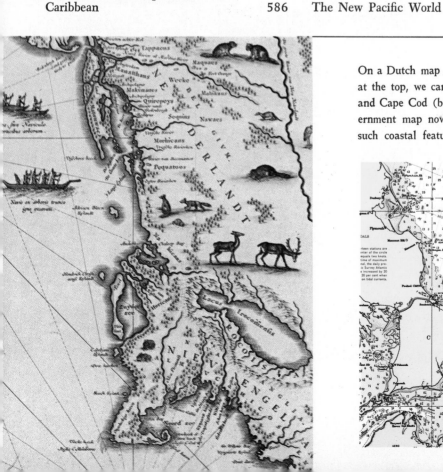

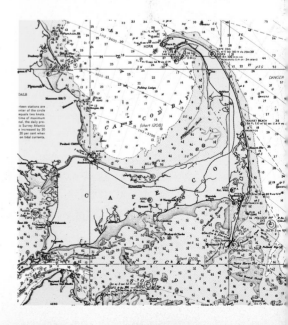

On a Dutch map (left) dated 1635, with "west" at the top, we can recognize Long Island (top) and Cape Cod (bottom). Below, a modern government map now gives us accurate details of such coastal features as Cape Cod.

This Is America

Alaska · Arizona

Florida · Georgia

Kansas · Kentucky

SUPPOSE YOU WERE ASKED to describe America. Here are a few of the answers you might give:

- a nation of about 200 million people whose ancestors came from countries all over the world.

- a vast country of three and a half million square miles, extending from the Atlantic to the Pacific, with two of its fifty states far to the north and west. (To the right you see the fifty state flags.)

- a land blessed with an abundance of natural resources — fertile soil, forests, and minerals.

- a leader in trade and industry, whose farms and factories not only supply the needs of its own people but also send goods to the peoples of other lands.

- a republic, governed under the oldest written constitution in the world.

- a country in which important officers of the national, state, and local governments are chosen by, and are responsible to, its citizens.

- a world power which seeks peace and stands ready to defend liberty.

Minnesota · Mississippi

New Jersey · New Mexico

Oregon · Pennsylvania

Utah · Vermont

Land of Promise

Alabama

Arkansas

California

Colorado

Connecticut

Delaware

Hawaii

Idaho

Illinois

Indiana

Iowa

Louisiana

Maine

Maryland

Massachusetts

Michigan

Missouri

Montana

Nebraska

Nevada

New Hampshire

New York

North Carolina

North Dakota

Ohio

Oklahoma

Rhode Island

South Carolina

South Dakota

Tennessee

Texas

Virginia

Washington

West Virginia

Wisconsin

Wyoming

The early settlers, shown above landing in New Jersey, were followed by millions of people from many lands. Americans still share the traditions of these other lands. Here Scottish pipers from Ohio perform on a peak in North Carolina (right).

These statements give us a picture of America today. But they do not explain why and how the United States has grown to its present position of power and leadership. Compared to the countries of Europe and many of those in Asia, the United States is a young nation. Two hundred years ago there was no nation named the "United States." There were only thirteen small English colonies huddled along our Atlantic coast. And 200 years earlier even those colonies did not exist; only Indian hunters inhabited this land. How has it been possible for America as we know it today to develop out of an untamed continent of dense forests and rolling prairies?

"The driving force behind our progress," President Truman once said, "is our faith in our democratic institutions. That faith is embodied in the promise of equal rights and equal opportunities which the founders of our Republic proclaimed to their countrymen and to the whole world." It was the search for equal rights and opportunities that led small groups of people to leave England in the 1600's and

The colonists had certain rights, granted in royal charters (above). Because they defended their rights and fought for more freedom, we enjoy today the right of choosing our own leaders by such means as political conventions (left).

brave the dangers of the Atlantic to settle in the American wilderness. These settlers had their individual reasons for going to America. Some wanted to escape persecution by their rulers; others wished to worship in their own way; still others were moved by the spirit of adventure. But all of them had one thing in common — they had a dream, a dream of a new and freer life.

These early Americans had become accustomed to certain rights which their forefathers had won from the kings of England. Building new homes amid the dangers and hardships of an unsettled wilderness strengthened their love of freedom. When stricter regulations by the mother country threatened their rights, the colonists drew up the Declaration of Independence. In this statement, Americans proclaimed that all men were entitled to certain rights. To preserve these rights, our forefathers fought for independence from England. Only after a long and discouraging war did they succeed. Then, to protect their hard-won freedom, they established a government which would be

Liberty, freedom under law, representative and republican government are major themes developed in this textbook.

3

controlled by the people. The voters were to elect representatives to make laws and officials to run the government.

The promise of equal rights and opportunities played an important part in the filling in of the vast unsettled continent which lay west of the thirteen original states. More and more people came to America to seek their fortune or simply to find land which they could call their own. Sometimes an unusual event, such as the discovery of gold in California in 1849, caused the stream of immigration to become a flood. But year after year, restless Americans moved westward in search of fresh opportunities, while newcomers left Europe to start a new life in America. In a series of giant strides the United States acquired new territories which stretched to the Pacific. As pioneers settled in these new territories, states were carved out which possessed the same rights of self-government as did the older states in the East.

The thrilling story of westward expansion is told in Chapters 5, 16, 18, and 21.

The first arrivals at Jamestown (left) had to clear a place for themselves in the wilderness. By hard work, Americans have created a rich and fruitful homeland, like the rolling countryside of Virginia (below).

4

Land of Progress
Toward a Better Life

The filling in of the continent brought about changes in the American way of life. Canals and railroads were built to carry the growing numbers of people and the goods they needed. Factories with new machines produced an increasing variety of goods. People moved from farms to towns where factories were located. The towns grew into cities, and around the larger cities there developed clusters of suburbs where people who worked in the cities lived. To run machines, to work in mines, to farm the soil, and to carry farm produce and other goods to market required more workers. New jobs meant new opportunities for a better life for many people living in other lands.

As soon as they arrived, industrious Americans began making things for themselves. Among them was paper (above). Now huge machines mass-produce not only paper but such new materials as cellophane (right).

These two pictures tell better than words the great change brought about by the machine age.

5

Early American scientists like John Bartram (above) began studying the world about them. Giant radar receivers in California (right) have extended our search for knowledge to the galaxies of outer space.

They came to our shores by the millions in the late 1800's and early 1900's. The skill and enterprise of our growing population, America's wealth of natural resources, and modern inventions and scientific discoveries have enabled Americans to develop the highest standard of living in the world.

The task of fulfilling the promise of equal rights and opportunities is never-ending. To make sure that the liberties of all Americans would not be forgotten, ten amendments were added to the United States Constitution soon after it was established as the basis of our government. These amendments, called the Bill of Rights, guarantee to individuals the right to speak and write freely and to worship as they wish. Americans are also protected in their right to have fair trials and to own property.

Free enterprise, under which producers **6** are free to make consumer goods that they believe can be sold, is also a factor. In the Soviet Union production is chiefly for heavy industry and military purposes.

The educating of Americans to be intelligent, productive citizens began in simple colonial schools (above). It continues on a vast scale and today places importance on science, as in this high-school physics laboratory (left).

As the United States has grown, so has the American ideal of freedom taken on wider meaning. It includes the right to choose a job, to run a business, to travel and to live where you wish. Our system of public schools seeks to prepare American boys and girls to live useful and satisfying lives. Americans are free to explore the world of science on their own in search of new knowledge. Yet America will not in truth be the Land of Promise so long as rights and opportunities are denied to any of its citizens.

Such liberties and opportunities do not exist in all countries. In Communist Russia and Red China and the nations they control, all power rests in the hands of a few leaders. Factories and all means of production belong to the state. Citizens have no real voice in their government, nor are they free to choose their jobs or to live where

7

At Plymouth the Pilgrims built a meeting house where they could express their deep religious beliefs. A modern chapel (right) stands as a landmark at the Air Force Academy in Colorado, where Americans today train to defend their country.

they wish. They cannot speak freely or even know the full truth about events going on in the world, since newspapers, books, and radio are under the government's control.

In this book you will read America's story. You will learn how our country was discovered and how it grew to be a great nation. In it you will study the lives of famous men and women. But remember that it was the hard work, courage, loyalty, and high ideals of all Americans which built this republic. And citizens today, young and old, must continue to show the same industry, courage, loyalty, and devotion to American ideals if our country is to remain strong and free in the challenging years ahead. To defend these ideals, we must understand them. As in the past, Americans today can find inspira-

Stress that the welfare of our country depends on "the hard work, courage, loyalty, and high ideals of all Americans."

8

tion and new understanding in the words of American leaders who have tried to express what freedom meant to them:

- *They that can give up essential liberty to obtain a little temporary safety deserve neither liberty nor safety.*
  — BENJAMIN FRANKLIN

- *Those who deny freedom to others deserve it not for themselves. . . .* — ABRAHAM LINCOLN

- *Where the press is free, and every man able to read, all is safe.*
  — THOMAS JEFFERSON

- *Next in importance to freedom and justice is popular education, without which neither freedom nor justice can be permanently maintained.* — JAMES A. GARFIELD

- *Our country — this great republic — means nothing unless it means the triumph of a real democracy, the triumph of popular government, and . . . an economic system under which each man shall be guaranteed the opportunity to show the best that there is in him.* — THEODORE ROOSEVELT

- *We shall not . . . finally achieve the ideals for which this nation was founded so long as any American suffers discrimination as a result of his race, or religion, or color, or the land of origin of his forefathers.* — HARRY S. TRUMAN

- *A democracy smugly disdainful of new ideas would be a sick democracy. A democracy chronically fearful of new ideas would be a dying democracy.* — DWIGHT D. EISENHOWER

- *Let every nation know, whether it wishes us well or ill, that we shall pay any price, bear any burden, meet any hardship, support any friend, oppose any foe to assure the survival and the success of liberty.* — JOHN F. KENNEDY

This book has been written to help you understand America's history. One way to tell this story would be to mention all the events which took place year by year from 1492 to the present. You would find it very difficult, however, to study American history in this fashion. Instead of one book you would have to study many books. Even more important, you would not be able to tell what the really important events were or how certain events were related to others.

To help you follow America's story. In order to make our country's history meaningful, *This Is America's Story* is organized by units and chapters. There are ten *units* in all. Look back to the Table of Contents (pages v–xi). You will see that the title of each of these units deals with a major de-

velopment in America's story. For example, Unit One tells about the discovery of America (*Europe Seeks an Ocean Route to Asia and Discovers a New World in the West*).

Every unit begins with a two-page *introduction* like the one, reduced in size, shown below. It pictures a scene which captures the "spirit" of the events to be described in that particular unit. Within this scene, something which you can remember as an emblem or a symbol of the unit — in Unit One, for example, a ship — is "highlighted" in white. Underneath the picture in each unit introduction, there is a brief preview which tells you in a general way the events you will study in that particular unit.

You will also find in the Table of Contents that each unit contains two or more

Unit and chapter introductions effectively combine pictures and text. Encourage students to study both.

UNIT INTRODUCTION

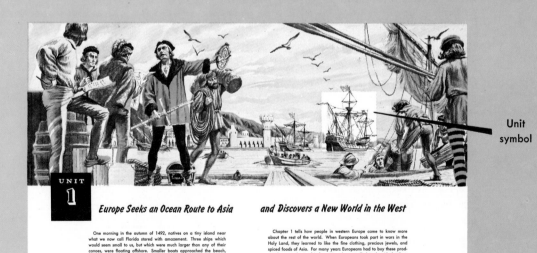

Unit symbol

UNIT 1

Europe Seeks an Ocean Route to Asia and *Discovers a New World in the West*

One morning in the autumn of 1492, natives on a tiny island near what we now call Florida stared with amazement. Three ships which would seem small to us, but which were much larger than any of their canoes, were floating offshore. Smaller boats approached the beach, and men leaped ashore — men unlike any of the people on the island had ever seen before. The natives stared at the strangers — at their white skin, their beards, and their clothes. Although neither the island people nor their white visitors realized it, this was a fateful event in the history of the world. It was the day when the story of America began.

As you probably have guessed, the man leading the white strangers was Christopher Columbus. The scene above shows Columbus and his ships about to leave the little Spanish port of Palos. But why was Columbus intent on undertaking a dangerous journey on unknown seas? And why did Columbus' ship (highlighted in the drawing) become a symbol of exciting possibilities to Europeans? To answer these questions, we need to understand what had been happening in Europe.

Chapter 1 tells how people in western Europe came to know more about the rest of the world. When Europeans took part in wars in the Holy Land, they learned to like the fine clothing, precious jewels, and spiced foods of Asia. For many years Europeans had to buy these products from merchants of Italian cities who controlled trade with the East. But kings of European countries wanted to find their own routes to Asia and the Far East. That is why the king and queen of Spain gave Columbus money to see if he could reach Asia by sailing westward around the globe. Instead, Columbus discovered a New World.

In Chapter 2 you will learn that Europeans were disappointed because the new lands found by Columbus were not a part of Asia. You will also learn how they kept trying to find a short cut through or around the New World to the Far East. In so doing they learned more about the New World and gradually became interested in it for its own sake.

We ever held it certain that in going toward the sunset we would find what we desired.
— CABEZA DE VACA

14

chapters. The chapters within each unit take up some portion of the unit's story. Thus in Unit One, Chapter 1 tells about the discovery of America, while Chapter 2 describes how explorers increased their knowledge of the New World. Chapters also begin with an illustration, as shown below. The background picture in color might be called a "setting" for the chapter, since it shows a scene or suggests an idea which you can connect in your minds with this part of America's story. The drawings in the foreground introduce you to the kinds of people who played important parts in the events of the chapter. Here you can see what the "cast of characters" looked like, how they dressed, and the kinds of tools or weapons they used.

To help you get the most out of reading a chapter. Each chapter begins with an introductory section called *What this chapter is about.* Each chapter introduction ends with *guide questions* which list important ideas to be discussed in that chapter (see below).

To help you locate quickly the answers to the guide questions, the chapter is divided into two or more sections. The titles of these sections correspond exactly to the guide questions (see example below). Within each major section of a chapter, two other types of headings have been used which also are shown below: *column headings,* to indicate general topics, and *paragraph headings.* If you read carefully the unit and chapter introductions and make use of the different kinds of headings, you will find it much easier to follow America's story.

To help you understand and remember. *This Is America's Story* includes *study helps* which appear regularly, so that you will not miss important points in our story. To understand better what you are reading, you must stop now and then to recall what you have read and to ask yourself what it means. As you finish reading each section of a chapter, use the questions under *Check Up* to test your grasp of what you have just read. Then when

Section, column, and paragraph headings provide an effective outline for each chapter.

CHAPTER INTRODUCTION

Guide questions

A PAGE OF TEXT

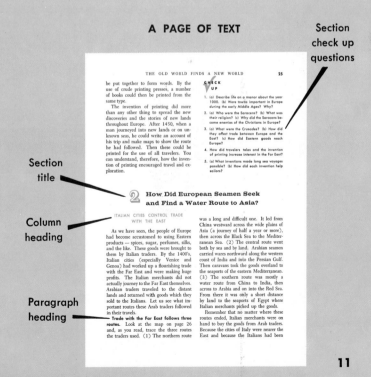

Section check up questions

Section title

Column heading

Paragraph heading

you have read the entire chapter, use the various exercises under the *Chapter Check Up:* (1) *Do You Know the Meaning?* calls attention to important words you should know. (2) *Can You Identify?* lists some names, dates, and terms which are important. (3) *Can You Locate?* gives a list of locations you should be able to find on a map. (4) *What Do You Think?* includes questions that help you think about and apply what you have read. Below you will find a sample of these review items.

Following the Chapter Check Up, you will find a special feature called *Linking Past and Present.* These links are interesting examples of the many ways in which the past affects our lives today. Sometimes a link will be shown in pictures (see pages 29 and 142).

To help you think about the unit as a whole. Each unit is provided with a special section of study aids (see below, for example, *To Clinch Your Understanding of Unit 1*).

Each end-of-unit section includes four types of exercises: (1) The *Summary of Important Ideas* brings together the important ideas stressed in the whole unit. (2) The *Unit Review* provides questions which will help you to think through these ideas. (3) The *Gaining Skill* section will help you to develop skills that will enable you to use social studies materials more effectively. (4) The list of *Interesting Things to Do* suggests ways of using what you have learned, thus adding to your knowledge of the unit.

To find out when and where. Every event takes place at some place and time. Only by knowing the *when* and *where* of different happenings will you know the full story. To help you keep straight the time order of various events, you will find a time line near the beginning of each chapter. Below there is a sample time line and an explanation of how to use it. On pages 208–209, under the heading — *How to Build a Time Sense* — you will find other helpful hints. Also, in

The Chapter Check Up not only calls attention to important information but includes questions which encourage the student to use information learned.

END OF CHAPTER AND UNIT

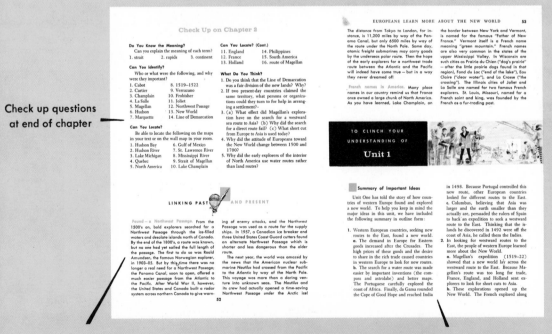

Check up questions at end of chapter

Linking Past and Present

Study aids at end of unit

the reference section at the end of the book there is a list of *Important Dates.*

Throughout your book you will find clear and attractive maps on which you can locate places, boundaries, routes, rivers, and mountains named in the text. All maps are listed in the Table of Contents on pages x–xi.

Source materials. The past comes alive when we follow history to its sources, the actual words of famous persons who lived in the past. These may be in the form of speeches, documents, or eyewitness accounts of important events. Throughout *This Is America's Story* you will find quotations from source materials. You will also find such famous documents as the Declaration of Independence and the Constitution. Helpful notes and explanations appear with the Constitution on pages A1–A32.

To help you to locate information. To locate information on a particular subject quickly, learn to use the *General Index* at the end of this book. At the beginning of the General Index, you will find suggestions on how to use an index. Preceding the General Index is an *Index to Names on Maps.* Refer to this when you want to find on a map a city, river, mountain, or other location.

For easy reference. The reference section in the back of the book contains other helpful information. The section called *For Further Reading* (starting on page A33) includes (1) a list of reference books which will be useful throughout your study of *This Is America's Story* and (2) lists of interesting books for each of the ten units. As you begin the study of each unit, plan to read at least one book from the list for that unit. Two charts — one listing the *States and Dependencies of the United States* and the other listing the *Presidents and Vice-Presidents of the United States* — contain much information in a form easy to read.

To get the most out of your reading of *This Is America's Story,* use all the various aids described above.

Call attention to the fact that the scale for all time lines is not the same.

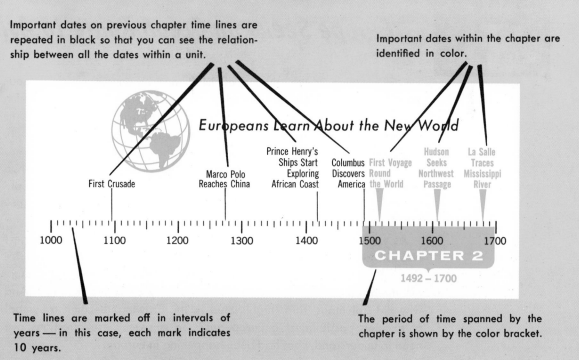

CHAPTER TIME LINE

Important dates on previous chapter time lines are repeated in black so that you can see the relationship between all the dates within a unit.

Important dates within the chapter are identified in color.

Europeans Learn About the New World

First Crusade

Marco Polo Reaches China

Prince Henry's Ships Start Exploring African Coast

Columbus Discovers America

First Voyage Round the World

Hudson Seeks Northwest Passage

La Salle Traces Mississippi River

1000   1100   1200   1300   1400   1500   1600   1700

CHAPTER 2

1492–1700

Time lines are marked off in intervals of years — in this case, each mark indicates 10 years.

The period of time spanned by the chapter is shown by the color bracket.

UNIT 1

Europe Seeks an Ocean Route to Asia

One morning in the autumn of 1492, natives on a tiny island near what we now call Florida stared with amazement. Three ships which would seem small to us, but which were much larger than any of their canoes, were floating offshore. Smaller boats approached the beach, and men leaped ashore — men unlike any the people on the island had ever seen before. The natives stared at the strangers — at their white skin, their beards, and their clothes. Although neither the island people nor their white visitors realized it, this was a fateful event in the history of the world. It was the day when the story of America began.

As you probably have guessed, the man leading the white strangers was Christopher Columbus. The scene above shows Columbus and his ships about to leave the little Spanish port of Palos. But why was Columbus intent on undertaking a dangerous journey on unknown seas? And why did Columbus' ship (highlighted in the drawing) become a symbol of exciting possibilities to Europeans? To answer these questions, we need to understand what had been happening in Europe.

and Discovers a New World in the West

Unit introductions such as this one focus attention on causes and results.

Chapter 1 tells how people in western Europe came to know more about the rest of the world. When Europeans took part in wars in the Holy Land, they learned to like the fine clothing, precious jewels, and spiced foods of Asia. For many years Europeans had to buy these products from merchants of Italian cities who controlled trade with the East. But kings of European countries wanted to find their own routes to Asia and the Far East. That is why the king and queen of Spain gave Columbus money to see if he could reach Asia by sailing westward around the globe. Instead, Columbus discovered a New World.

In Chapter 2 you will learn that Europeans were disappointed because the new lands found by Columbus were not a part of Asia. You will also learn how they kept trying to find a short cut through or around the New World to the Far East. In so doing they learned more about the New World and gradually became interested in it for its own sake.

> *We ever held it certain that in going toward the sunset we would find what we desired.*
>
> — CABEZA DE VACA

At the beginning of each chapter are five features designed to arouse interest and prepare pupils for studying the chapter: (1) a preview suggesting the theme to be developed, (2) a picture illustrating an aspect of this theme, (3) questions which

The Old World Finds a New World

Beyond Its Horizon

serve as headings for the main sections of the chapter, (4) the "cast of characters" for the chapter, (5) a time line.

What this chapter is about —

The history of our country might be compared to the steps in a long, long walk — a long march from the past to the present. Many people have taken part in this march of history, and we ourselves are taking the step which marks the present. What the future steps may be, we do not know. But, looking back at the steps taken in the past and at the people who took them, we may learn how to direct our own steps better in the present and the future.

The march of American history did not begin in this country, but in Europe. In our first chapter, therefore, we shall turn back to Europe. We shall turn back to a time when castles along the European coast looked out upon the unknown sea (see picture above). You will learn how Europeans took the first step in the long march — how they ventured out onto the sea and discovered a new world. In this chapter you will find answers to the following questions:

▶ 1. How did changes in Europe lead to important geographical discoveries?

▶ 2. How did European seamen seek and find a water route to Asia?

▶ 3. Why did Columbus sail westward, and what did he accomplish?

At the beginning of each chapter you will find pictures of a "cast of characters" — the kinds of people who play important parts in the chapter. The Chapter 1 "cast," shown above, includes (from left to right) a serf, Crusader, Arab trader, king and queen, and geographer.

16

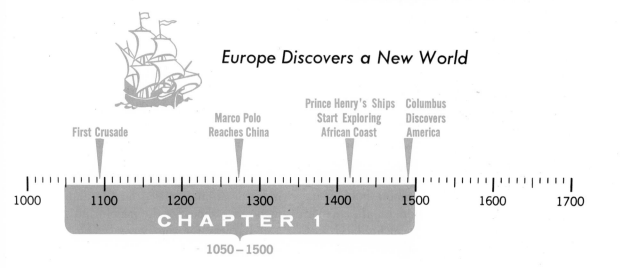

Europe Discovers a New World

First Crusade

Marco Polo
Reaches China

Prince Henry's Ships
Start Exploring
African Coast

Columbus
Discovers
America

1000   1100   1200   1300   1400   1500   1600   1700

CHAPTER 1

1050–1500

How Did Changes in Europe Lead to Important Geographical Discoveries?

HOW PEOPLE LIVED IN WESTERN EUROPE ABOUT THE YEAR 1000

In western Europe about the year 1000, during a period called the Middle Ages (about 500–1400 A.D.), each little neighborhood lived by itself. It was almost as if the villages were separate islands. The people of one village hardly knew what happened in villages only a few miles away. To understand the life of most of the people, suppose that you were living in Europe about that time. What would your life be like?

Your home and its furniture are very simple. You and your father and mother and brothers and sisters live in a cottage built of wood. It has no windows. The roof of the cottage is of thatch, that is, a thick covering of straw or reeds or leaves. The hard-packed earth is the only floor. There are just two openings in the cottage. One is the door, and one is a hole in the roof to let out the smoke from the fire. Unfortunately, the hole also lets in the rain. There is no chimney, and your mother has no oven in which to do her baking. In summer she cooks out-of-doors over an open fire.

There is little furniture in your cottage, and what there is, is rough. A box with a straw mattress on it is the bed. The table is made of boards laid on trestles. (A trestle is a support similar to a sawhorse.) There are some three-legged stools and a chest. Your food is cooked in an iron pot and eaten from dishes made of baked and hardened clay. You have no lamps or even candles. This doesn't matter, however, because nobody in the family can read and everyone goes to bed at sundown and gets up at sunrise.

Your food and clothing are uninteresting. Your mother has spun the yarn, woven the cloth, and made the clothing that you and other members of your family wear. Most of it is of wool or coarse linen.

Your meals are simple and consist of the same things over and over again — mostly bread and a little meat. You eat few vegetables and fruits. There is no tea or coffee and very little milk. You have salt, but no pepper or any other spices. You use no sugar, and if your food is sweetened at all, it is with honey or occasionally with fruit juices.

Each chapter time line (1) shows in **17** *color the years discussed in the chapter, and (2) the sequence of important events.*

Paragraph headings are complete sentences. Bring out that the headings on pages 17 and 18 are the main points in the sub-section, "How people lived in Western Europe about the year 1000."

18 EUROPE DISCOVERS A NEW WORLD IN THE WEST

You live on a manor. Your cottage is one of a dozen or more which stand together by the side of a winding, unpaved road. The cottages form a village belonging to a noble, or a knight, whose large house is nearby. The village and the farms around it are called a *manor,* and the noble who owns it is called the *lord* of the manor. The noble holds your father and the other men on the manor as *serfs.* They have to farm his land part of the time, help build and repair his roads and bridges, and serve him in other ways.

Your father and the other serfs, in fact, are not much better off than slaves. They may not be sold, as slaves can be, but they have to remain on the manor — they are "bound to the soil," as the saying is. If a new lord takes over the land, they must serve him. Serfs cannot own their land outright, nor are they allowed to go elsewhere to find land of their own or to find other jobs. They may not even leave the manor without the lord's permission.

The manor is nearly self-sufficient. We have seen how you and your family and your neighbors live on the manor. But is there any connection between your manor and others? The truth is that your manor has very little to do with others. It is almost *self-sufficient.* By self-sufficient we mean it can get along by itself, without receiving many products from the outside world and without making many things to sell or trade. The food eaten on the manor is grown on it. The manor has its own blacksmith shop and its own mill where all the grain is ground. From the hides of animals raised on the manor the men make shoes for the people and saddles and harness for the horses. The women dye wool from the manor's own sheep and make it into cloth. The blacksmith and the wheelwright (wheel maker) make the wagons and farm tools and keep them in repair. Only a few products, such as salt, iron, and millstones, need to be brought into the manor from outside.

"But aren't there any towns?" you ask. Yes, there are towns, but most of them are small and unimportant. Towns are for trade. (Farm families even today go to town to buy the things they do not grow or make at home.) As we have seen, however, the manors are almost self-sufficient. Most people in the Middle Ages have little need for towns.

•

You have just learned what life was like in western Europe about the year 1000. Gradually this life began to change.

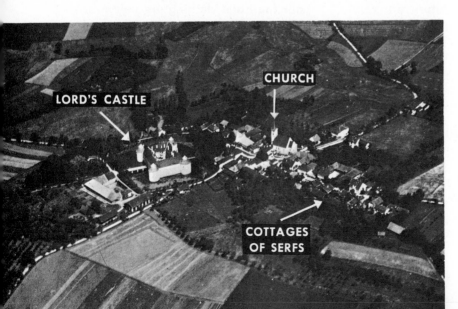

LORD'S CASTLE

CHURCH

COTTAGES OF SERFS

AN AIRPLANE VIEW of this present-day Austrian village gives an idea of what a manor might have looked like in the Middle Ages. Note how the buildings are huddled together, surrounded by fields.

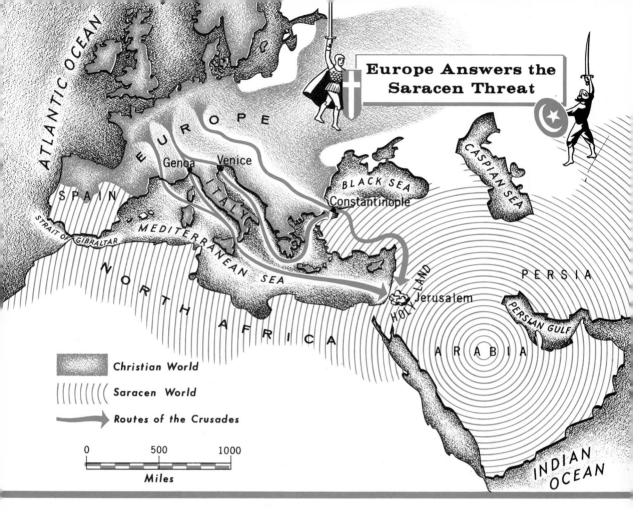

Europe Answers the Saracen Threat

ATLANTIC OCEAN

EUROPE

SPAIN

Genoa   Venice

ITALY

STRAIT OF GIBRALTAR

MEDITERRANEAN SEA

NORTH AFRICA

BLACK SEA
Constantinople

CASPIAN SEA

PERSIA

HOLY LAND   Jerusalem

PERSIAN GULF

ARABIA

INDIAN OCEAN

Christian World

Saracen World

Routes of the Crusades

0   500   1000
Miles

MAP STUDY   The circled lines on this map show you how the Saracens expanded their power into Africa and even into Europe. (1) Where was the homeland of Mohammed's followers? Trace the routes followed by the Crusaders to the Holy Land. Most members of the First Crusade traveled to the Holy Land by way of Constantinople. Later Crusaders followed the sea routes. (2) Name two Italian ports from which sea routes started.

WHY LIFE IN WESTERN EUROPE BEGAN TO CHANGE

In the early Middle Ages, western Europe had little to do with other parts of the world. Indeed, as we have seen, each manor to a large extent lived by itself. To be sure, lords of different manors sometimes fought each other or banded together under some more powerful lord to make war on his enemies. Such wars gave Europeans some knowledge of what was going on outside their tiny villages. Later, Europeans began to take a greater interest in more distant parts of the world. This came about because of wars between Europeans and people called *Saracens*, who lived in countries to the south and southeast of Europe. As a result of these wars, life in Europe began to change. Let us see how this happened.

The Saracens threaten to overrun Europe. About the year 600 a new religion, called *Islam* (or Mohammedanism), grew up in Arabia. (Find Arabia on the map on this page.) Just as Christianity is based upon the teachings of Christ, so Islam is

References are made to maps in the text. Encourage pupils to use the maps.

20 EUROPE DISCOVERS A NEW WORLD IN THE WEST

based upon the teachings of a great religious leader named Mohammed. The Saracens in Arabia believed that the religion taught by Mohammed was the only true religion. They sent armies to conquer other people and force them to accept the religion of Mohammed. Soon they conquered all of North Africa and crossed the Strait of Gibraltar into Spain. For centuries the Saracens pushed hard against the Christians in Europe, threatening always to gain more territory. The map on page 19 shows how much land the Saracens conquered. Thinking of all these conquests, the people of Europe wondered, "What is to become of us if the Saracens force their way even farther into Europe?"

Christians are aroused against the Saracens. Europeans naturally did not want to be conquered by anybody. Least of all did they want to be conquered by the Saracens who sought to spread the religion of Islam, for almost all Europeans were Christians. Today we have many Christian churches (Catholic, Episcopal, Presbyterian, Methodist, Lutheran, Baptist, and others). But in the Middle Ages there was only one great Christian Church in western Europe, the Roman Catholic Church. Christians were willing to serve and fight for their Church. Their loyalty to the Church helped to unite the people in an age when western Europe was split up into small, weak kingdoms and when rich nobles who held many manors were as powerful as kings.

Christians disliked the Saracens for another reason. The Saracens had captured Palestine, at the eastern end of the Mediterranean Sea. Because Christ had lived in Palestine, Christians called it the Holy Land. They liked to make long trips there to worship and to visit the scenes of Christ's life. The Saracens interfered with such visits and sometimes stopped them altogether. Surely, the Christians thought, the blessing of God would be given to the people who helped recapture the Holy Land!

Christians make war against the Saracens. In 1095 the Pope, head of the Roman Catholic Church, held a great meeting. He urged the Christians to war upon the Saracens and to recover the Holy Land. Filled with enthusiasm by the Pope's words, knights by the thousands put on their armor and seized swords, battle-axes, lances, and shields. Eager for battle, the knights mounted their war horses and rode off to capture the Holy Land. This expedition was called a *Crusade,* meaning "for the cross," and the knights who took part in it were called Crusaders. On his garments each man had sewed a large cross, the symbol of the Christian religion. Look at the picture on page 16 to see how a Crusader looked.

Knights from all over Europe gathered at the city of Constantinople and formed a great army for the First Crusade. (See map on page 19 for the routes of the Crusades.) They fought their way to the Holy City of Jerusalem and captured it in 1099. The Christians, however, were unable to keep their hold on the Holy Land. Other Crusades followed, and warfare between the Christians and Saracens continued during the next 200 years. In the end the Crusaders failed and the Holy Land remained in the hands of the Saracens. But during these 200 years Europe itself changed greatly. How did this happen?

The Crusades help to increase trade. During the Crusades thousands and thousands of people went from Europe to the lands at the eastern end of the Mediterranean. There they became familiar with many useful articles and luxuries they had not known at home. They found that

Although the Crusades were a failure, the results of the Crusades were very important.

such spices as pepper, nutmeg, cloves, cinnamon, and ginger made their food taste better. They learned to sweeten their food with sugar. They learned to use soap and to take baths more often! They admired the precious stones — diamonds, rubies, emeralds, pearls, and sapphires — that they saw there. In the East also they found drugs to heal the sick, dyes (like indigo) to color cloth, and fragrant perfumes. They discovered many things — lovely glass and china, beautiful swords and armor and other metal products, gorgeous silks and other costly fabrics, colorful rugs — that were better made in the East than in Europe.

All these articles helped to make life more pleasant and more comfortable. When the Crusaders returned home, they told their neighbors and families about these luxuries. Naturally Europeans wanted these good things for themselves.

They soon learned they could buy these luxuries from Italian merchants.

Italian merchants carry Eastern goods to Europe. Even before the Crusades, certain Italian cities, like Venice and Genoa, had been carrying on some trade with the Eastern lands touching the Mediterranean Sea. During and after the Crusades, when Europeans began to demand more goods from the East, the Italian merchants were glad to supply them. Their trade increased rapidly. Their ships, called galleys, began to go more and more often to the ports of the eastern Mediterranean. There they exchanged such goods as woolen cloth, leather, and tin for the spices, fine silks, and jewels wanted by Europeans.

The galleys of the Italian merchants not only sailed the Mediterranean but went into the Atlantic and carried goods to seaports along the west coast of Europe.

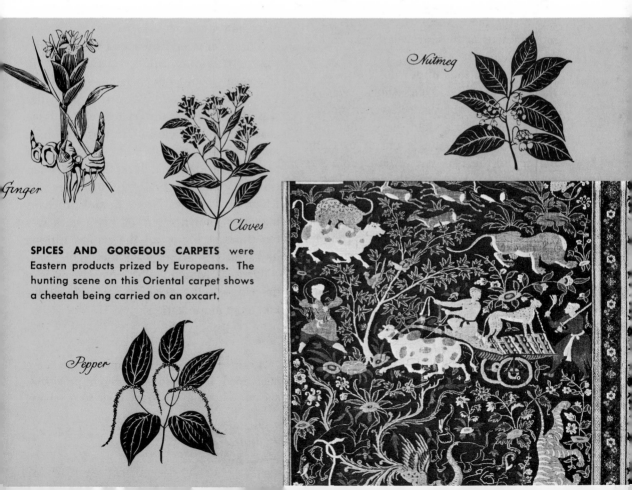

Ginger

Cloves

Nutmeg

Pepper

SPICES AND GORGEOUS CARPETS were Eastern products prized by Europeans. The hunting scene on this Oriental carpet shows a cheetah being carried on an oxcart.

Other merchants then carried these goods by river and by land far into the interior. It therefore became necessary to improve the roads, which up to this time had been little used. Also, wherever the merchants went, they needed market places in which to trade their goods. Around these market places towns grew up. As time passed and trade increased, the towns grew into cities. Life in western Europe had indeed begun to change.

TRAVELERS' TALES AROUSE EUROPEAN INTEREST IN THE FAR EAST

While these changes were taking place, travelers began to go from Europe to visit the strange new lands of the East: Persia, India, China, and the Spice Islands.[1] (Find these lands on the map on page 26.) The travelers came back with exciting stories which made Europeans eager to know still more about these lands. The most famous of these travelers was named Marco Polo.

Marco Polo tells about the wonders of the East. Marco Polo's home was in Italy, in the city of Venice. When he was only seventeen years old, he set out with his father and his uncle on an overland journey to the Far East. Marco Polo was gone for 24 years, from the year 1271 to 1295. During that time he traveled over a great part of Asia, even seeing the Pacific Ocean. So unusual were his travels that he visited some places not seen again by Europeans for 600 years.

What wonders Marco Polo saw and heard others describe! He reported that once he saw a city so large that to go all around it a man would have to walk a hundred miles. Later he saw one even larger. (Travelers of all times have sometimes exaggerated what they saw to make a better story. Marco Polo exaggerated here and there, but his story still had much truth in it.) Marco Polo marveled at seeing the Chinese people burning coal. He didn't know what it was, so he described it as "a kind of black stone, which is dug out of the mountains and burns like wood."

Marco Polo found that the people of the East had the finest carpets in the world. They had splendid silk cloth. They had spices of all kinds, ebony and other fine woods, gold and silver, pearls and precious stones, fine harness for horses, and excellent weapons for soldiers. The women wore costly bracelets on their arms and legs, and the men sometimes wore even costlier ones. Their cities were so rich and had so much trade that a single one of them was visited by thousands of boats each year.

The ruler over China and much of the rest of Asia was called the *Great Khan*. Europeans could not imagine, said Marco Polo, how rich and powerful this ruler was. One of his many palaces was so large that the wall enclosing it was one mile long on each side. In the palace itself there was a dining hall where 6000 men could eat at one time. In his wars the Khan used armies larger than Europeans had ever known. One of his armies was ten times as big as all the armies Europe had sent on the First Crusade!

Here in Marco Polo's own words is a description of the Khan's marvelous system of communication:

[1] Today Persia is known as Iran. The Spice Islands are part of the East Indies and belong to Indonesia.

＊ From the city of Kanbalu there are many roads leading to the different provinces, and . . . upon every great high road, at the

The books listed for this unit (see "For Further Reading"—Books for Unit One) relate the experiences of many explorers who "had a story to tell."

distance of twenty-five or thirty miles, . . . there are stations, with houses of accommodation for travelers. . . . These are large and handsome buildings, having several well-furnished apartments, hung with silk, and provided with everything suitable to persons of rank. . . . At each station four hundred good horses are kept in constant readiness, in order that all messengers going and coming upon the business of the grand khan, and all ambassadors, may have relays, and, leaving their jaded [exhausted] horses, be supplied with fresh ones . . . . In consequence, . . . ambassadors to the court, and the royal messengers, go and return through every province . . . of the empire with the greatest convenience and facility; in all which the grand khan exhibits a superiority over every other emperor, king, or human being.

In the intermediate space between the post-houses, there are small villages settled at the distance of every three miles. . . . In these are stationed the foot messengers, likewise employed in the service of his majesty. They wear girdles round their waists, to which several small bells are attached, in order that their coming may be perceived at a distance; and as they run only three miles, that is, from one of these foot-stations to another . . . , the noise serves to give notice of their approach, and preparation is accordingly made by a fresh courier to proceed with the packet instantly upon the arrival of the former. . . . At each of these three-mile stations there is a clerk, whose business it is to note the day and hour at which the one courier arrives and the other departs; which is likewise done at all the post-houses.

Marco Polo's stories make people want to visit the Far East. The wonders which have just been described are only a few of those Marco Polo heard of and saw. After he returned to Europe, a book was written about his adventures. Those who could read spread the news. Throughout Europe people talked about the stories the book contained. When they learned that

SUN OR STAR

HORIZON

ASTROLABE

Eastern goods cost only a fraction of what the Italian merchants charged for them, they began to ask, "Why can't other Europeans go to the East, as Marco Polo has done, and find out more about it? Why can't we find a way there, perhaps by sea, and get some of the riches of the East by exchanging our goods for theirs?"

INVENTIONS AND IMPROVEMENTS MAKE LONG OCEAN VOYAGES POSSIBLE

About the time that Europeans were talking about finding a way to the Far East, changes were taking place in Europe itself which were to make that very thing possible. As you know, people in western Europe did little traveling or trading before the Crusades. They also did very little reading or writing. Interest in learning was centered chiefly among priests and leaders of the Church. They conducted schools and preserved what few books there were. These books were written in Latin, which few people could read, and contained only knowledge of past centuries. Very little new knowledge was added. But as Europe began to take an

CROSS-STAFF

tell, by looking at certain stars, how far north or south of the equator he was. In this manner he was able to figure out his *latitude*. Then clocks came into use, and careful tables of times and distances were made. By looking at certain stars again, and by using these tables and his clock, a captain could tell how far east or west he was. Thus he knew his *longitude*. To know the latitude and longitude of a place locates it exactly. Of course, sailing still depended largely on the captain's skill. But these instruments, as you can see, made sailing much safer than it had been and made long ocean voyages possible.

The maps and charts which travelers and other sailors began to make also were a help to sailors. A ship's captain with new and better maps could find his way more easily.

A new method of printing is invented. For hundreds of years only one copy of a book could be made at a time. It had to be copied slowly by hand, letter by letter. About the middle of the 1400's a new method of printing was invented. The new method used what we call movable type. For each letter of the alphabet there were sets of tiny separate letters which could

interest in trade and travel, more people began to read and write and study. Men became interested in the learning of the ancient Greeks and Romans, which had been forgotten for hundreds of years. They also made progress in science. They heard about or developed certain inventions which made it easier to sail ships out of sight of land.

New instruments aid sailors. For one thing, people in Europe learned about the compass. To us a compass is a common article, but it was new to the Europeans of that time. First they learned to magnetize an iron needle so that it always pointed north. Next they learned to put the needle in a little box above a card on which north and the other directions were marked. Then they had a compass similar to the ones we have today.

A captain who has a compass can tell in which direction his boat is sailing. But a captain needs to know not only in what direction he is going but where he is. For this purpose, instruments called the cross-staff and the astrolabe (*ass'troh-layb*) were used. With their aid a captain could

EARLY PRINTING PRESS

be put together to form words. By the use of crude printing presses, a number of books could then be printed from the same type.

The invention of printing did more than any other thing to spread the new discoveries and the stories of new lands throughout Europe. After 1450, when a man journeyed into new lands or on unknown seas, he could write an account of his trip and make maps to show the route he had followed. Then these could be printed for the use of all travelers. You can understand, therefore, how the invention of printing encouraged travel and exploration.

CHECK UP

1. (a) Describe life on a manor about the year 1000. (b) Were towns important in Europe during the early Middle Ages? Why?

2. (a) Who were the Saracens? (b) What was their religion? (c) Why did the Saracens become enemies of the Christians in Europe?

3. (a) What were the Crusades? (b) How did they affect trade between Europe and the East? (c) How did Eastern goods reach Europe?

4. How did travelers' tales and the invention of printing increase interest in the Far East?

5. (a) What inventions made long sea voyages possible? (b) How did each invention help sailors?

Check Ups at the end of each section help pupils to evaluate their mastery of important facts and concepts.

 How Did European Seamen Seek and Find a Water Route to Asia?

ITALIAN CITIES CONTROL TRADE WITH THE EAST

As we have seen, the people of Europe had become accustomed to using Eastern products — spices, sugar, perfumes, silks, and the like. These goods were brought to them by Italian traders. By the 1400's, Italian cities (especially Venice and Genoa) had worked up a flourishing trade with the Far East and were making huge profits. The Italian merchants did not actually journey to the Far East themselves. Arabian traders traveled to the distant lands and returned with goods which they sold to the Italians. Let us see what important routes these Arab traders followed in their travels.

Trade with the Far East follows three routes. Look at the map on page 26 and, as you read, trace the three routes the traders used. (1) The northern route

was a long and difficult one. It led from China westward across the wide plains of Asia (a journey of half a year or more), then across the Black Sea to the Mediterranean Sea. (2) The central route went both by sea and by land. Arabian seamen carried wares northward along the western coast of India and into the Persian Gulf. Then caravans took the goods overland to the seaports of the eastern Mediterranean. (3) The southern route was mostly a water route from China to India, then across to Arabia and on into the Red Sea. From there it was only a short distance by land to the seaports of Egypt where Italian merchants picked up the goods.

Remember that no matter where these routes ended, Italian merchants were on hand to buy the goods from Arab traders. Because the cities of Italy were nearer the East and because the Italians had been

Encourage pupils to refer to the maps, which are closely linked to the text.

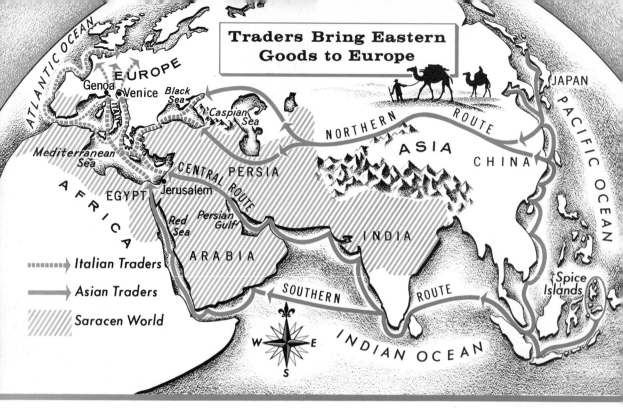

Traders Bring Eastern Goods to Europe

MAP STUDY Marco Polo followed the trade routes on his journeys to and from Asia. Note that the Saracen world lay across the routes, between Europe and Asia. Why were Asian goods called "Eastern"? To answer, look at the compass "star" on the map.

given special privileges by the Saracens, the merchants from other countries of Europe did not have a chance to share in this profitable trade. In other words, the Italian cities had what we call a *monopoly* of the Eastern trade.

Other Europeans are jealous of the Italians. You can imagine how jealous of the Italian cities the other seafaring countries of Europe were. They looked at the trade routes controlled by the Italians. They saw Italian purses growing fat while their own grew thin. Europeans had some goods which they traded to the Italians in exchange for the luxuries of the East. But their goods were not as valuable as the Eastern goods, so they had to make up the difference by paying gold and silver to the Italian merchants. Countries cannot keep on buying more than they sell, any more than a person can keep on spending more than he earns.

There was another reason, too, why the countries of Europe resented the Italian monopoly of trade. You remember that during the early Middle Ages the nobles were almost as powerful as the kings and that people had no feeling of loyalty to their country. This condition had gradually changed. Kings had slowly overcome the lords and were becoming the heads of strong, united countries. For the first time the people of France and England, Portugal and Spain, knew what it meant to feel proud of their countries. They wanted their countries to become wealthy and powerful, and they knew that trade with the East would help to make them so. The kings too were eager to become rich. They stood ready to furnish ships and money, and to send daring sailors to find the way to distant lands.

Europeans seek new routes to the East. It is small wonder, then, that sailors of these new nations began to dream of other routes to India and the Far East. They said, "Venice and Genoa control the well-known routes to Asia. Why not look for a new way by water so that we can have our share of the riches of the East?" Indeed, what could stop them? They now had instruments to make sailing safer. They had maps and charts to guide them. And what is more, they had dreams of adventure and fame and wealth. Such dreams keep men pressing onward in spite of failures and hardships.

PORTUGUESE SAILORS REACH INDIA BY WATER

Prince Henry of Portugal encourages exploration. The little country of Portugal was the first to find a water route to the East. Much of the credit for this discovery belongs to a member of the Portuguese royal family, Prince Henry. Prince Henry's great interest was the sea. By exploring the west coast of Africa, he hoped to make the natives Christians and to build up a profitable trade for his country in gold and ivory. But perhaps Prince Henry also had hopes that by venturing farther and farther into the unknown sea along the African coast, the Portuguese might find an all-water route to the East.

To help carry out these ambitions, Prince Henry built a school for sailors at the southwestern tip of Europe. Here he gathered ship captains, students of navigation (the science of sailing ships), makers of maps and instruments, travelers, and shipbuilders. Soon the sailors and ships of Portugal became the finest of those times. Prince Henry himself became known as "Prince Henry the Navigator."

Portuguese sailors explore the western coast of Africa. Prince Henry began to send ships down the west coast of Africa

PORTUGAL has honored Prince Henry the Navigator with this monument in Lisbon. Prince Henry stands at the head of a line of Portuguese explorers and missionaries who followed the routes he opened up.

to explore and to trade. He commanded each captain to build a six-foot stone tower on the coast marking the farthest point he had reached. No one at that time, of course, realized how huge the continent of Africa is. It took great courage, therefore, to sail ships ever southward along what seemed a never-ending coast. Many sailors believed the terrible tales they had heard about the unknown seas — that there were whirlpools waiting to suck ships into the depths of the ocean, that evil monsters were lurking below the surface to destroy them, that the Devil himself lay in wait for those who dared sail the unknown waters! Because of these stories sailors would often turn back from the "Great Sea of Darkness," as they called it. But Prince Henry commanded the captains to keep on, and stone towers were built farther and

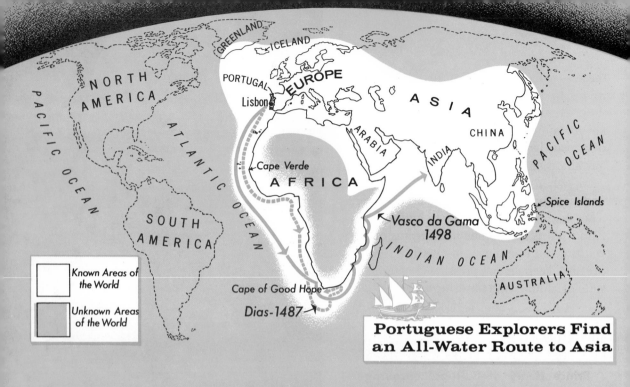

Portuguese Explorers Find an All-Water Route to Asia

MAP STUDY The white areas in this map show what parts of the Old World were known to Europeans in the 1400's. Notice how Portuguese explorers like Dias and da Gama "lighted up" the formerly unknown coast of Africa. What continents did Europeans still know nothing about at this time?

farther south on the coast of western Africa.

In time, the Portuguese found natives who were glad to exchange slaves and gold dust for horses. It was not long before Portugal built up a rich trade along the African coast. But Prince Henry was not satisfied. Ever southward he urged his ship captains. At the time of his death in 1460, his ships had rounded Cape Verde. (Look at the map on this page to see how far that was.)

India is reached at last. After Prince Henry's death, Portuguese captains continued to explore the coast of Africa. At last, late in 1487, Bartholomew Dias (*dee'*ahs) sailed around the southern tip. When he was quite sure that the way was now clear to sail on to India, he hastened back with the news. The king of Portugal joyfully named the southern end of Africa the Cape of Good Hope. Several years later, in 1498, another Portuguese explorer proved that Dias was right. Vasco da Gama (duh *gam'*uh) sailed around the Cape of Good Hope and up the eastern coast of Africa. Then, pointing the prow of his ship eastward, he crossed the Indian Ocean to India! There he set up a stone tower to mark the end of the search for a water route to the East. Then he sailed for home with a shipload of spices, silks, and jewels as proof that he had indeed reached India.

Portuguese explorers make the known world larger. Before Prince Henry's ships began their voyages of exploration, people knew little about the world. (Look again at the map above.) But the Portuguese explorers added a great deal to the knowledge of geography. As the cap-

Phonetic spelling is used to help students pronounce difficult names and words.

28

Note that we can learn history from remains as well as from written records. Perhaps some of your students have found Indian arrowheads, or fragments of pottery, or seen them in a museum.

THE OLD WORLD FINDS A NEW WORLD 29

tains returned from their trips, the map makers would add a new part of the coast to the maps. These maps gave the people of Europe a much better idea of what their world was like.

PORTUGAL CONTROLS THE ALL-WATER ROUTE TO INDIA

Portugal grows rich from her Eastern trade. Portugal understood at once the value of the all-water route to the East which da Gama found. He had brought back a cargo worth 60 times what his voyage had cost! If you could buy for a penny something which you could sell for 60 cents, you would be pleased. The king of Portugal, the ship captains, and the merchants felt just that way about it. They increased the number of ships sailing to the East. Also, they set up trading posts in India and sent soldiers to guard the posts. Portugal was now the sole master of the new all-water route to India!

The Italian cities lose their trade to Portugal. In the early 1500's, Lisbon, capital of Portugal, became the most important port in Europe. Sailors thronged her streets and taverns, while ship captains and merchants sat in quiet rooms and made plans for future voyages. Heavily laden vessels from India sailed into her harbor. They carried valuable Eastern goods — precious stones, spices, cloth. The ships of other nations were waiting in Lisbon to transport these goods to other ports of Europe. As you know, the Italian cities of Venice and Genoa had long been Europe's leading ports. Because water transportation was cheaper, Portuguese merchants were now able to sell Eastern goods at lower prices than the Italian merchants. That is why Lisbon became the leader in the rich Eastern trade which had once been the monopoly of the Italian cities.

This feature is frequently used to make the past seem less remote from the students' own experience.

LINKING PAST AND PRESENT

The Vikings came to America almost 1000 years ago, but we can see today what their ships looked like. The ship's hull shown above was buried with a Viking chief and preserved for centuries in the clay soil of Norway. Dug up in recent times, it now is in a Norwegian museum. By studying its lines, craftsmen were able to build a full-size model of a Viking ship (right). Note the shields and the dragon's head on the bow.

1. By what routes did early traders bring goods from the East?

2. (a) What European cities controlled trade with the East? (b) Why were other European countries jealous of these cities?

3. Why were the people of western Europe interested in finding new routes to the Far East?

4. (a) Who was Prince Henry the Navigator? (b) How did Portugal find an all-water route to the East? (c) What were the results of this discovery?

3 Why Did Columbus Sail Westward, and What Did He Accomplish?

Even before da Gama reached India, the voyages of earlier Portuguese ship captains had led Europeans to wonder about other routes to the Far East. After all, a water route controlled by the Portuguese would be no better for the other nations of Europe than the old routes controlled by the Italian cities. Some people had a daring new idea: Why not try to find a water route to the Far East and its riches by sailing *westward?* Today we know that about the year 1000, Viking warriors from Scandinavia had sailed westward and found land across the Atlantic Ocean. But the Vikings lost interest in the new lands, and very few Europeans in the late 1400's even knew about their voyages.

Columbus plans to sail westward to Asia. One man was sure that he could reach Asia by sailing west instead of east. Christopher Columbus was a dreamer, but he had the courage to try to make his dreams come true. Columbus loved the sea and had become a sailor when he was fourteen years old. When he was not actually on shipboard, he made maps and charts for a living. He studied the charts of others, read the reports of new voyages, and talked with other seamen. Slowly his great dream about sailing westward to Asia changed from a dream into a definite plan.

Columbus thought his plan would be easier to carry out than it really was. Because he planned to sail into unknown seas, he had to guess what he would find, and he guessed wrong. He believed that the earth was round, but he thought it was much *smaller* than it is. Also, he thought that Asia was much *larger* than it is. Naturally, therefore, he thought that the distance he would have to sail westward from Europe to reach Asia was much *shorter* than it is. As the first globe on the next page shows, Columbus knew nothing of the two great continents that would block his way to Asia.

Columbus prepares for his voyage. Columbus was sure that it would be easier and cheaper to reach Asia by sailing westward than by sailing all the way around Africa as the Portuguese were trying to do. But Columbus was not a rich man. He could not buy ships, pay for supplies for a long voyage, or hire crews to sail the ships. He needed help to carry out his bold plan.

As we have learned, the kings of Europe were eager for greater wealth, and had already helped some ship captains to make important voyages. So Columbus turned to the monarchs of Spain and Portugal for help. But for years no one

Pupils will find it easier to understand this paragraph if they study the globes on page 31.

Columbus Discovers the New World

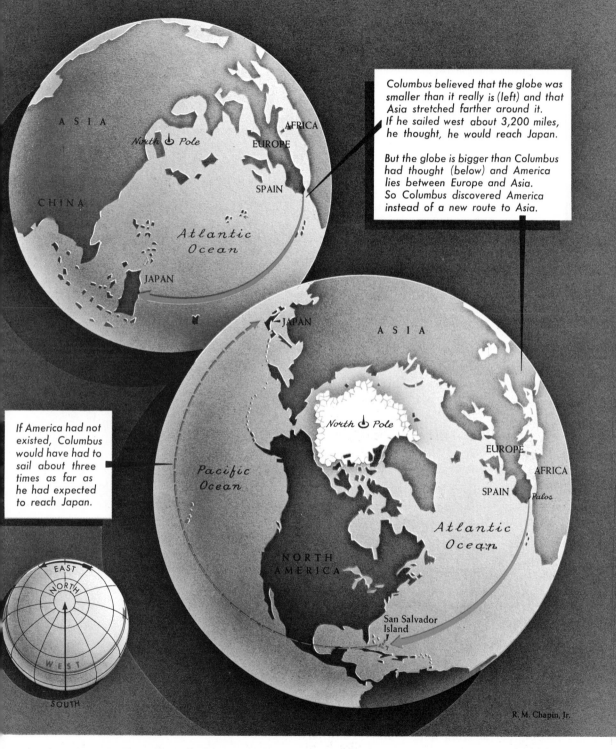

Columbus believed that the globe was smaller than it really is (left) and that Asia stretched farther around it. If he sailed west about 3,200 miles, he thought, he would reach Japan.

But the globe is bigger than Columbus had thought (below) and America lies between Europe and Asia. So Columbus discovered America instead of a new route to Asia.

If America had not existed, Columbus would have had to sail about three times as far as he had expected to reach Japan.

R. M. Chapin, Jr.

MAP STUDY The two globes on this page are slightly tipped towards you. Note the location of the North Pole in each. The globe at the top shows how Columbus thought he could sail across the Atlantic from Europe to Asia. The globe below shows how America actually blocked his way.

Note that the Vikings in reaching North America **31** via Iceland and Greenland crossed shorter stretches of open sea than did Columbus.

The Journal of Christopher Columbus is another primary source. Why did Columbus record the distance sailed as less than it really was?

32   EUROPE DISCOVERS A NEW WORLD IN THE WEST

would listen to his story, and Columbus became worn out and discouraged. He almost gave up hope of ever being able to try out his plan. Finally he persuaded King Ferdinand and Queen Isabella of Spain to give him ships and money to prepare for the westward voyage to Asia.

At last everything was ready and the time to set sail arrived. It was quite early in the morning of Friday, August 3, 1492. In the harbor of the Spanish village of Palos, Columbus stood on the deck of a small ship, the *Santa Maria,* giving orders to the crew of 40 men. The *Santa Maria* sailed slowly from the harbor and put out to sea. Two other ships, the *Niña (nee'-nyah)* and *Pinta,* each with some 25 men on board, also sailed under Columbus' command. For years Columbus had dreamed of this day and planned for it. Now he and his companions were going to try to reach Asia by sailing westward into unknown seas.

Columbus discovers a new world. What a voyage it was! The tiny ships were mere specks upon the endless waves. The men grew fearful as day after day the ships slid westward through unknown waters. This was the dreadful Great Sea of Darkness, where the Devil and his monsters lay in wait! Columbus restlessly walked the deck, keeping watch on everything — the wind, the sails, the weather, the men. He kept a record of each day's progress. Soon he had to keep two records. One, which he kept for himself, gave the true distance they had come from Spain. The other, which he let the crew see, showed the distances covered each day as much less than they really were. He did this so that the men would not worry at being so far from home. But at last, ten weeks after the little port of Palos had dropped from sight behind them, they saw sure signs of land. We can imagine how

triumphant Columbus must have felt! We can do even more; we can read his own story of his triumph. Here is part of it, as it appears in *The Journal of Christopher Columbus:*

✳ WEDNESDAY, 10TH OF OCTOBER. — The course was W.S.W. [West of Southwest], and they went at the rate of 10 miles an hour, occasionally 12 miles, and sometimes 7. During the day and night they made 59 leagues,[1] counted [for the sailors' sake] as no more than 44. Here the people could endure no longer. They complained of the length of the voyage. But the Admiral [as Columbus referred to himself] cheered them up in the best way he could, giving them good hopes of the advantages they might gain from it. . . .

THURSDAY, 11TH OF OCTOBER. — The course was W.S.W., and there was [a rougher] sea than there had been during the whole of the voyage. They saw sandpipers, and a green reed near the ship. Those on the *Pinta* saw a cane and a pole, and they took up [from the sea] another small pole which appeared to have been worked with iron; also another cane, a sand-plant, and a small board. The crew of the caravel *Niña* also saw signs of land, and a small branch covered with berries. Everyone breathed afresh and rejoiced at these signs. . . .

After sunset the Admiral returned to his original west course, and they went along at the rate of 12 miles an hour. . . . As the caravel *Pinta* was a better sailor, and went ahead of the Admiral, she found the land, and made the signals ordered by the Admiral. The land was first seen by a sailor named Rodrigo de Triana. But the Admiral, at ten in the previous night . . . , saw a light, though it was so uncertain that he could not affirm it was land. . . . It seemed to few to be an indication of land; but the Admiral made certain that land was close. . . . The Admiral asked . . . the men to keep a good look-out on the forecastle, and to watch well for land; and

[1] A league was about 4 miles.

who discovered a New World, grew up in the busy Old World seaport of Genoa on the Italian coast.

SHIPWRECK gave young Columbus his first taste of the Atlantic Ocean. Like most Genoese boys, Columbus had gone to sea, following the old Mediterranean trade route to the East. Then, on a voyage to bring Asian goods from Genoa to the Netherlands, Columbus' ship was sunk by pirates. He clung to an oar and swam six miles to the shore of Portugal.

A REUNION with his brother, who was a mapmaker in Portugal, gave Columbus a fresh start. He learned about Portuguese explorations in the Atlantic and began to dream of finding a new way to Asia.

A WESTWARD ROUTE to Asia was the daring plan Columbus proposed to King Ferdinand and Queen Isabella of Spain. For years Columbus sought their help. Finally, they gave him three ships, and he set out.

"ASIA, AT LAST!" was Columbus' first thought when he sighted land after more than two months of sailing westward through unknown seas. His plan had worked! He hastened ashore to look for the gold and spices of the East. But Columbus had found something even more important than a new route to Asia. He had discovered America.

to him who should first cry out that he saw land, he would give a silk doublet [jacket], besides the other rewards promised by the Sovereigns [Ferdinand and Isabella] which was 10,000 [gold coins] to him who should first see it. At two hours after midnight the land was sighted at a distance of two leagues. . . .

FRIDAY, 12TH OF OCTOBER. — The vessels were hove to [stopped], waiting for daylight; and on Friday they arrived at a small island . . . called, in the language of the Indians, Guanahani (gwah-nah-*hah'*nee). Presently they saw naked people. The Admiral went on shore in the armed boat, and Martin Alonzo Pinzon, and Vicente Yanez, his brother, who was captain of the *Niña*. The Admiral took the royal standard, and the captains went with two banners of the green cross, . . . with an F and a Y [for Ferdinand and Ysabel] and a crown over each letter, one on one side of the cross and the other on the other. Having landed, they saw trees very green, and much water, and fruits of diverse kinds. The Admiral called to the two captains, and to the others who leaped on shore . . . and said that they should bear faithful testimony that he . . . had taken . . . possession of the said island for the King and for the Queen. . . .

Why was Columbus' voyage important? On October 12, 1492, Columbus had landed on the island which he named San Salvador (called Guanahani by the Indians). This island lies in the Bahama Islands about 400 miles southeast of Florida. Still seeking the mainland of Asia, Columbus sailed along the coasts of two other islands, Cuba and Hispaniola (his-pahn-*yoh'*lah), before returning to Spain. Because he thought these islands were part of the East Indies off the eastern coast of Asia, he called them "the Indies." Today, as a result of Columbus' mistake, this group of islands is called the West Indies.

By using section, sub-section, and **34** paragraph headings the class can prepare an outline of the chapter.

What had Columbus accomplished? He
had not reached Asia; he had not discovered a route between Europe and the East.
But what he had found was even more
important. Although he did not know it
at the time, Columbus had discovered
America.

CHECK UP

1. Why were some European countries interested in a westward route to the East?

2. (a) Why did Columbus think he could reach
the East by sailing westward? (b) Why did
he fail?

3. Why was Columbus' voyage important?

Pupils can test their knowledge of Chapter 1 by using the study helps on this page.

Check Up on Chapter 1

Do You Know the Meaning?

The following words are important in
understanding Chapter 1. Knowing their
meaning will also help you to increase your
vocabulary. Can you explain the meaning of
each word?

1. serf
2. manor
3. monopoly
4. self-sufficient
5. compass
6. navigation
7. astrolabe
8. latitude
9. longitude
10. trade route
11. printing press
12. spices

Can You Identify?

When you identify a name, a term, a date,
or a place in history, you point out its meaning and its importance. Can you tell who or
what the following were, and why they were
important?

1. Middle Ages
2. Crusades
3. Saracens
4. Islam
5. 1498
6. Far East
7. Columbus
8. San Salvador
9. Prince Henry
10. October 12, 1492
11. Dias
12. da Gama
13. Ferdinand and Isabella
14. Marco Polo
15. Pope
16. Holy Land

Can You Locate?

Geography has been called the key to history. If you know the location of the places
mentioned in each chapter, the story will have
more meaning for you. Be able to locate the
following places on maps in your text or on
the wall map in your classroom.

Can You Locate? (Cont.)

1. Africa
2. Asia
3. Europe
4. China
5. Pacific Ocean
6. India
7. Genoa
8. Lisbon
9. Portugal
10. Venice
11. Spain
12. Cape of Good Hope
13. Spice Islands
14. Cape Verde
15. Indian Ocean
16. Black Sea
17. route of da Gama
18. Red Sea
19. Persian Gulf
20. Atlantic Ocean
21. Mediterranean Sea

What Do You Think?

The study of history should teach us to
understand and apply what we have learned.
Can you use the knowledge gained in this
chapter to answer the following questions?
Be sure to give reasons for your answers.

1. (a) What are some advantages that a
country has when it is self-sufficient?
(b) What are some disadvantages?

2. What connection did the Crusades have
with the discovery of America?

3. Was Marco Polo an explorer? Why has he
not received more recognition for his long
travels?

4. (a) Would you give Prince Henry or da
Gama the credit for discovering a new
route to the East? (b) Do Venice and
Genoa deserve any credit for this discovery?

5. Columbus called the people he found in
1492 "Indians." (a) Why did he give
them this name? (b) Why are they still
called Indians?

The questions listed under "What Do You Think?" call for comparisons, evaluation, and the ability to draw conclusions.

LINKING PAST AND PRESENT

One reason for studying history is that it helps us to understand the world in which we live today. For the past is not dead; it is linked to the present in many ways. This feature of your textbook, "Linking Past and Present," appears at the ends of chapters. In it you will find interesting bits of information which show that events and people of times past have left their mark on the present day.

Why America, not Columbia? How does it happen that the two great continents of the New World are not named for the man who discovered them? The reason lies in the past. One of the many explorers who followed Columbus to the New World was an Italian called Amerigo Vespucci (in Latin, *Americus Vespucius*). Vespucci's account of his voyages to the New World greatly impressed a famous German map maker. This map maker began to put the name *Terra America* ("land of Americus") on his maps. Because many seamen and explorers used these maps, "America" soon became an accepted name.

In the 1700's and 1800's, however, poets and other writers often referred to our nation as "Columbia," after Columbus, of course. Columbia became a poetic or literary name for America. For example, you may be familiar with the old patriotic song, "Columbia, the Gem of the Ocean."

Columbus is not forgotten. Although the Americas were not named for Columbus, the New World has used his name in other ways. Most of our 50 states have a city, town, or county named after Columbus — such as Columbus, Ohio, and Columbia, South Carolina. Columbia University in New York City bears his name, and the great river of our Northwest is called the Columbia. One of the republics of South America is named Colombia. And two cities in Panama are Cristóbal and Colón — Spanish for "Christopher" and "Columbus."

Prince Henry the Navigator. The Portuguese seamen and navigators who sailed on voyages of discovery and opened the age of exploration studied at Prince Henry's school of navigation on Cape Saint Vincent. In 1960, on the 500th anniversary of Prince Henry's death, sea captains again gathered at Cape Saint Vincent to honor the great patron of navigation and exploration. But this time they came from many parts of the world. Several nations sent ships to take part in a great naval review off the cliffs of southwestern Portugal. To watch the parade of the international fleet, scientists, historians, and statesmen from many nations met at the site of Prince Henry's school. The school itself no longer exists, but a lighthouse now stands on the site of its ruins.

The first Americans. When Europeans reached the New World, they found black-haired, copper-skinned people already living there. Columbus called these natives "Indians," because he thought he had reached the East Indies. As a result of his mistake, these first Americans have been called Indians ever since.

At that time, it has been estimated, there were about 10,000,000 Indians in what we now call Latin America, and perhaps 900,000 in North America north of Mexico. Who were these first Americans and where did they come from? They were Asian people, who had migrated from the Old World to the New, long before the Europeans. These people had crossed from Siberia to Alaska and then spread southward through North America and South America. These migrations, of course, took place over thousands of years. In the United States today, there are over 500,000 Indians — direct descendants of the first Americans.

Although the interior of North America was unknown, the map maker had a fair knowledge of the Atlantic coast and an excellent knowledge of the lands bordering the Caribbean. Can your students explain why this was so?

Europeans Learn More About the New World

What this chapter is about —

Across empty spaces on old maps like the one shown above, the words *Terra Incognita* often appear. These Latin words mean "unknown land," or "unexplored country." The map makers wrote *Terra Incognita* on the maps to show that they did not know what the unexplored parts of the world were like and therefore could not draw those areas accurately.

Before Christopher Columbus began the voyage described at the end of the last chapter, the map makers might have written *Terra Incognita* over a large portion of the world. They knew little about the Atlantic Ocean except the waters near Europe. And although the voyage of Columbus added to the knowledge of map makers, it also left many questions unanswered. Columbus had crossed the Atlantic Ocean and had touched land. But nobody, including Columbus, knew for certain what land it was. If it was Asia, then what part of Asia? If it was not Asia, what was it?

In this chapter you will learn how Europeans found out more about this new land. As you read, you will find answers to the following questions:

▶ 1. How did explorers find a New World blocking the westward route to Asia?
▶ 2. What explorers sought short cuts to Asia through the New World?
▶ 3. How did the search for short cuts to Asia open up the New World?

People in our story for this chapter — seaman, ship captain, map maker, and inland explorer.

1 How Did Explorers Find a New World Blocking the Westward Route to Asia?

Many people had looked upon Columbus as a foolish adventurer when he set sail from Palos, Spain in 1492. But when he returned the next year saying that he had reached the Indies, he was hailed as a hero. Europeans thought he had found a direct water route to Asia. Ferdinand and Isabella gave him the grand title of "Admiral of the Ocean Sea"! The story of his discovery was printed and read in many countries. Columbus himself, however, was not content with discovering islands. He wished to find the mainland of Asia and claim its rich trade for Spain.

Columbus fails to find Asia. Late in 1493 Columbus sailed westward again. This time he commanded seventeen vessels, instead of the small expedition of three ships that he had on his first voyage. Twice more, in later years, Columbus paced the deck as his ships plowed across the Atlantic. In these various journeys he touched at Puerto Rico, Hispaniola, Jamaica, Cuba, and other islands of the Caribbean Sea. (Look at the map on page 39.) Although Columbus never saw the mainland of North America, he sailed along the coasts of South America and of Central America. Never did he find what he was seeking — the riches of India. Yet he would not admit that the land he saw was not part of Asia. In his heart, however, he must have suspected the truth, because on his second voyage he made his men swear that they were sure they had reached Asia. If Columbus himself had felt no doubts, would he have thought it necessary to demand such an oath? The discoverer of the New World died in 1506 without knowing why his name would become famous.

Cabot also fails to find Asia. The success of Columbus' first voyage led other explorers to sail westward. In 1497, a captain named John Cabot set out from an English port in a small ship with a crew of only eighteen men. Cabot was an Italian navigator who had lived many years in London and now sailed under the English flag. Like Columbus, Cabot had an idea that he could reach the East by sailing west. He had received permission from the king of England to make the attempt. In fact, if the king had given him help when he first asked for it, Cabot might have been first to find the New World!

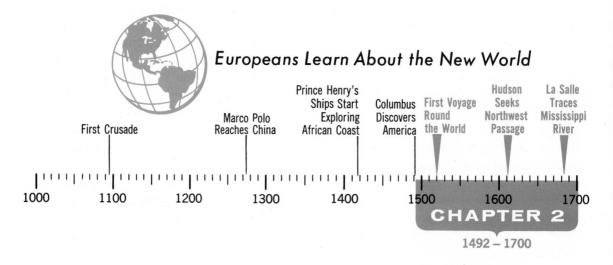

Europeans Learn About the New World

First Crusade

Marco Polo Reaches China

Prince Henry's Ships Start Exploring African Coast

Columbus Discovers America

First Voyage Round the World

Hudson Seeks Northwest Passage

La Salle Traces Mississippi River

1000   1100   1200   1300   1400   1500   1600   1700

CHAPTER 2

1492 – 1700

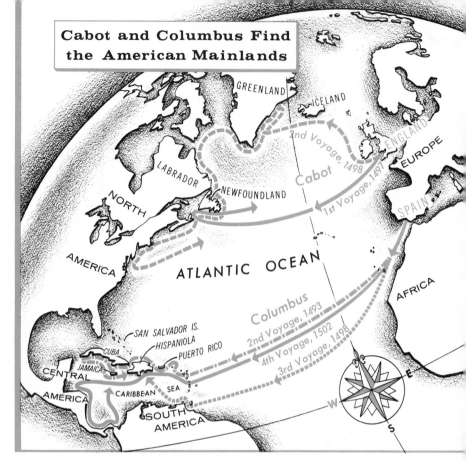

Cabot and Columbus Find the American Mainlands

MAP STUDY

Columbus continued his search for Asia in later voyages to the Caribbean area. Exploring its islands and shores, he established a base for later Spanish exploration. Other sea captains, such as John Cabot, explored the American coastline farther north.

Sailing farther north than Columbus had done, Cabot crossed the Atlantic in two months. He came to the northern coast of what we know as North America. Cruising along this coast, Cabot felt sure that he had reached Asia, but he did not find the rich cities he expected. Soon his supplies ran low, and he had to return to England. Cabot tried again the next year to reach Asia. Not only did he fail to find it, but we are not sure that he himself ever returned from the trip. Although Cabot had actually discovered the mainland of North America, this discovery meant little at the time, for he had not found the wealth of Asia.

Europeans become familiar with the notion of a New World. If Columbus and Cabot did not realize the truth about the new lands, others soon did. Daring ship captains sailing under the flag of Spain were busy exploring the coasts of South America, Central America, and Florida. You will read later, in Chapter 3, that one adventurous Spaniard, Balboa, even crossed the Isthmus of Panama and found an endless stretch of ocean on the other side. Before long, explorers had seen a good deal of these lands without finding any proof that they were part of Asia. They knew that Cabot had failed to find Asia farther north. They began to realize that these new lands were not part of the old world they had known, but were instead a great new world.

At first Europeans were not interested in the New World for its own sake. This may seem strange to you unless you remember that they were eager to find a westward route to Asia. To them the new land was only a barrier blocking the path to the East. For many years men tried to find a passageway through or around the American continents.

Be sure that students trace Magellan's voyage on the maps, page 41.

40 EUROPE DISCOVERS A NEW WORLD IN THE WEST

Magellan finds a way around the world. Ferdinand Magellan, a fearless Portuguese captain, was one of these men. He undertook a voyage which was to prove that Columbus' idea had been right — that Asia could be reached by sailing westward. Because he was not popular in his own country of Portugal, Magellan went to Spain with a plan for reaching India by finding a passage through the land Columbus had discovered. The king of Spain gave him permission to try.

In the fall of 1519, Magellan sailed from Spain with five ships and some 240 men. The ships plowed across the rough Atlantic and then turned south along the coast of South America. As they sailed ever southward, the weather grew steadily colder and more bitter. Then for six weeks the ships fought through the narrow, bleak, and stormy strait near the tip of the continent. (Today this strait is called the Strait of Magellan. Follow Magellan's travels on the map (on the facing page).) At last Magellan and his men came out into a wide sea so calm and quiet that they named it Pacific, which means "peaceful."

For four and a half dreary months they sailed across the Pacific. Hunger, thirst, and disease tortured the men until finally they reached the Philippine Islands. From there Magellan's men cruised south to the Spice Islands, where they picked up a load of cloves. Then, in a long sweep, they sailed around southern Africa and back to Spain. Every kind of disaster happened to the expedition — storms, hunger, sickness, death, mutiny, desertion. But at last, in 1522, the men who remained alive anchored once more in a Spanish harbor. Their shipload of valuable spices more than paid for the cost of the expedition!

Only eighteen men, aboard one ship, had come home to Spain. Magellan himself was not among them; he had been killed fighting natives in the Philippine Islands. These eighteen men, however, had performed a marvelous feat — they had sailed completely around the world. Since Magellan was not alive to receive the honors, the king of Spain presented to the

Page references to maps help students to relate geography and history.

COMPARE Magellan's tiny ship with the "Triton," a nuclear-powered submarine that retraced Magellan's route round the world in 1960. Magellan's voyage took three years. The "Triton" covered almost 42,000 miles *under water* in 84 days.

ROUND THE WORLD IN 1522 — AND TODAY

Magellan's "Victoria" was the first ship to sail round the world

U. S. Navy's "Triton" made the first underwater voyage round the world

SIZE OF MAN

586

0   100   200   300   400

LENGTH IN FEET

Voyage of Magellan and His Crew

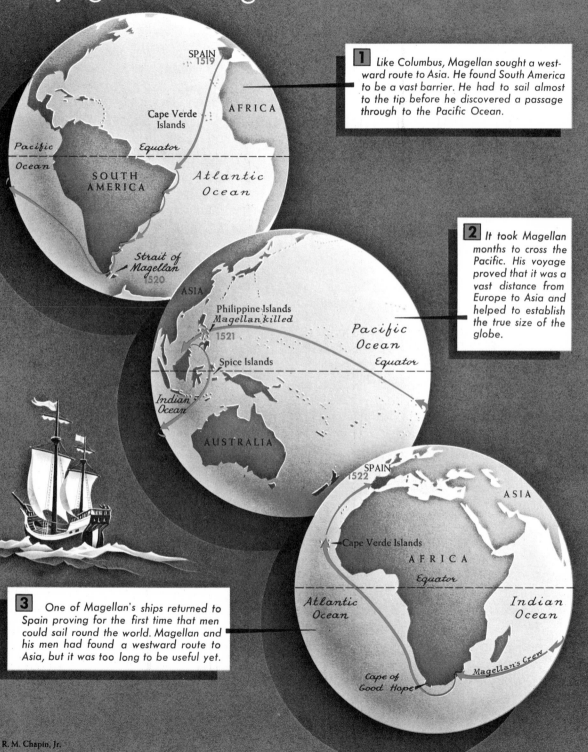

1 Like Columbus, Magellan sought a westward route to Asia. He found South America to be a vast barrier. He had to sail almost to the tip before he discovered a passage through to the Pacific Ocean.

SPAIN
1519

Cape Verde
Islands

AFRICA

Pacific
Ocean

Equator

SOUTH
AMERICA

Atlantic
Ocean

Strait of
Magellan
1520

2 It took Magellan months to cross the Pacific. His voyage proved that it was a vast distance from Europe to Asia and helped to establish the true size of the globe.

ASIA

Philippine Islands
Magellan killed
1521

Spice Islands

Pacific
Ocean
Equator

Indian
Ocean

AUSTRALIA

SPAIN
1522

ASIA

Cape Verde Islands

AFRICA
Equator

Atlantic
Ocean

Indian
Ocean

3 One of Magellan's ships returned to Spain proving for the first time that men could sail round the world. Magellan and his men had found a westward route to Asia, but it was too long to be useful yet.

Cape of
Good Hope

Magellan's Crew

R. M. Chapin, Jr.

MAP STUDY Above you see three different views of the globe as if it were turning from west to east (that is, toward the right-hand side of the page). Start at Spain in the top globe and trace Magellan's route around the world and back to Spain again. How many times did his expedition cross the equator?

Line of Demarcation→

Spain and Portugal Divide the World

North Pole

ASIA

EUROPE

SPAIN
PORTUGAL

AFRICA

INDIAN OCEAN

NORTH AMERICA

West   East →

Lands Open to Portugal

Lands Open to Spain

SOUTH AMERICA

BRAZIL

PACIFIC OCEAN

ATLANTIC OCEAN

MAP STUDY The Line of Demarcation marked off the areas to be claimed by Spain and those to be claimed by Portugal. Note that the Line reserved almost all of the New World for Spain. What small part of the New World could Portugal claim?

men was extremely important to the people of Europe. In the first place, it furnished absolute proof that the world was round. Magellan's crew had sailed west from Europe and, without retracing their course, had come back to their starting point. What was even more important, the voyage showed that Asia was an enormous distance west of Europe, and that a great land stretched fully across the path from Europe to the Far East. Magellan had indeed found a westward route to the Far East, but it was too long and dangerous for merchant ships to follow. Yet Europeans were not discouraged. Magellan's discovery led them to search for a short cut through the New World to Asia.

CHECK UP

1. Why did Columbus make more than one voyage westward across the Atlantic?

2. (a) What led Cabot to sail westward? (b) How successful was his expedition?

3. (a) What was Magellan's purpose in sailing westward? (b) What two things did Magellan's voyage prove?

captain of the surviving ship a coat-of-arms with a globe bearing these words: "You first sailed around me."

Magellan's voyage reveals the size of the world. The voyage of Magellan and his

Not until 1580 was the second voyage around the world completed by Francis Drake, an Englishman. This suggests how large loomed the dangers encountered by Magellan.

What Explorers Sought Short Cuts to Asia Through the New World?

Spain and Portugal divide the world. By the early 1500's only two countries had profited from the search for water routes to the Far East. These countries were Spain and Portugal. As you know, Portugal was growing rich from her trade with India and the Far East, but she would not allow any other countries to share that trade. She also claimed for herself the land her explorers had discovered in

Africa. Spain had found and claimed territory in the New World which might some day prove to be valuable.

As soon as Columbus had claimed for Spain what he thought to be Asia, it looked as though Spain and Portugal might be rivals for the same lands in the East. So these countries had asked the Pope to decide which new lands should belong to each of them. In 1493 the Pope drew an imaginary line west of the Cape Verde Islands and extending around the world from pole to pole. Portugal was to have the lands east of this line; Spain the lands that lay west of it. This *Line of Demarcation,* as it came to be called, was shifted farther west by a treaty between Spain and Portugal the next year. As the map on page 42 shows, Spain claimed most of the New World, while Portugal claimed Africa, India, and large areas in the Far East.

England, France, and Holland seek a share in the trade with the Far East. What about the other countries of Europe, such as England, France, and Holland? They had no share in the new lands and the profitable trade. These other countries, watching Portugal grow rich from her trade with the East, wanted to get a share of that trade for themselves. They asked, "Can't we find another route to the East and thus get ahead of Portugal as Portugal has gotten ahead of the Italian cities?"

One question led to another. Magellan's route to the East around the New World was, as we have seen, too long and too difficult to be valuable for trade. So, many Europeans asked: "Can't we find a better, shorter path? Perhaps there is a *northwest* passage which would give us a good, direct route to the East." Knowing little of what we now call North America, they believed they might find a waterway *through* it. For over a hundred years, daring men sent out by France, Holland, and England sailed up and down the Atlantic coast seeking a Northwest Passage, which they never found. Let us follow some of these bold sailors on their explorations.

Verrazano searches the coast. Among the first to seek a route through the New World was Verrazano (vehr-rah-*tsah*'noh). Although he was an Italian by birth, his most important voyage was made under

the flag of France. This voyage took place in 1524, just two years after Magellan's men completed their famous voyage around the world. Verrazano sailed westward to look for a passage to Asia. As the map on page 45 shows, he followed the coast of North America from what is now North Carolina as far north as Newfoundland. But he found no passage through the land, and returned disappointed to France.

Cartier explores the St. Lawrence River. Some ten years later another explorer for France, Jacques Cartier (*zhahk* car-*tyay*'), followed Verrazano to America. Cartier discovered and explored the mighty St. Lawrence River. Three or four times he crossed from France to the St. Lawrence, seeking a passage to the East. He sailed up and down the river and spent winters in camps upon its banks. He found an Indian village far inland where the city of Montreal now stands. There he came

MAP STUDY This map shows why Europeans searched hard for a Northwest Passage to Asia. The broad line shows an imaginary Northwest Passage. Note how much shorter than Magellan's actual route a northwest route would have been.

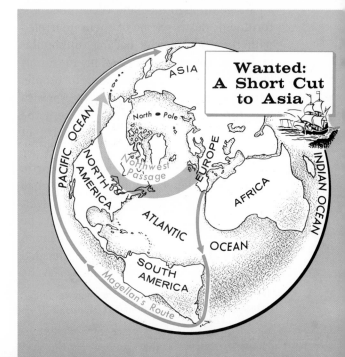

CARTIER questions Indians on the shores of the St. Lawrence about a Northwest Passage to the Pacific. Note the basket of American vegetables — corn and squash.

upon rapids which prevented his ships from going farther up the river. To his great disappointment, Cartier realized that the St. Lawrence was not a passage to the Far East, but only a river (map, next page).

Many explorers or captains who sought a passage through the New World met misfortune or death. Some of them quarreled with their men, some became unpopular at home, some died at sea or in far-off lands. But Cartier was more fortunate. After all his adventures in North America he returned safe and sound and spent the rest of his life quietly in the ports of France.

Frobisher seeks a passage farther north. Although Cartier had failed to reach Asia by sailing up the St. Lawrence River, Europeans still thought there must be a passage somewhere. An Englishman named Captain Martin Frobisher decided to search farther north. In June, 1576, he

set sail from England with three small vessels. Hardly had they left the English coast when one of the three ships was lost in a storm. The crew of the second ship grew fainthearted and soon deserted to return home. But Captain Frobisher kept on his course. Far to the north he went, touching Greenland and rounding its southern tip. At last he came to the stretch of water we now call Frobisher Bay. Unable to make his way against the ice, he was forced to turn back (map, page 46).

Though Captain Frobisher made two more voyages to the same region, he failed in his search for a Northwest Passage. He continued as a captain for many years after his third voyage, sailing the seas and fighting the Spaniards and the French.

Champlain explores the Great Lakes region. Although captain after captain returned to Europe without having found a short cut to Asia, new explorers always were ready to take the place of the old. Each hoped he would succeed where others had failed. One of these explorers was a Frenchman named Samuel de Champlain (sham-*plain'*). Champlain came to America for the first time in 1603. For years he roamed the coasts and the forests, the rivers and the lakes of America.

Champlain explored the Atlantic coast all the way from the mouth of the St. Lawrence River to the southern part of what is now Massachusetts. He sailed up the St. Lawrence and founded the town of Quebec, the first permanent French settlement in America. Continuing up the river to what is now Montreal, he turned south and pushed on to the southern end of a beautiful lake which has been named Lake Champlain in his honor. On a later trip Champlain traveled still farther inland, moving north and west from the St. Lawrence. He made his way along other rivers into the northern part of Lake

The explorations of Champlain provided valuable **44** information about the unknown interior of North America. Compare the maps on pages 37 and 45.

Huron. From there he swung down to Lake Ontario and then back to Quebec. To follow his explorations, look at the map on this page. It took a bold and energetic man to travel such distances in an unknown wilderness.

Champlain learned, and taught to others, much about the geography of North America. When he died in 1635, map makers could draw plainly and exactly many thousands of square miles of North America that had been unknown before Champlain's lifetime. But still he had found no short cut to Asia.

Henry Hudson finds a river. Another mariner who tried to find a passage to Asia was an Englishman named Henry Hudson. Hudson was employed by Dutch merchants to try to find a route to China. In the year 1609 he set out in a small ship named the *Half Moon*. At first he attempted to reach Asia by sailing north of Europe, but his little ship ran into dangerous ice and snow. Hudson then turned and set his course westward across the Atlantic toward the New World. He reached North America and traveled down the coast as far as Chesapeake Bay. But Hudson soon found he could not reach China by way of this bay. Sailing northward again, he came upon the broad river which now bears his name. He passed through the large bays at the mouth of the river. How his hopes must have risen as he sailed between the beautiful wooded banks! Perhaps this was the long-looked-for passage! But the river grew narrow, the water ceased to be salt, and Hudson finally realized that this was not a strait through America but only a river. Failure again!

MAP STUDY   The routes of three explorers for France are shown below. (1) Which of the three came to America first? (See the small map set in the upper left-hand corner.) (2) How far up the St. Lawrence did Cartier travel? (3) What lakes did Champlain explore?

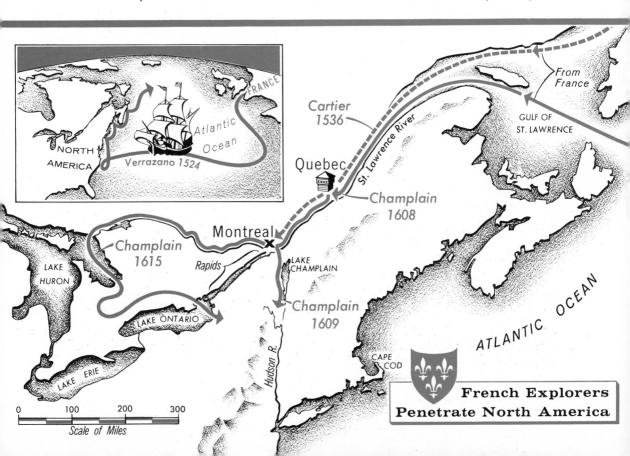

French Explorers Penetrate North America

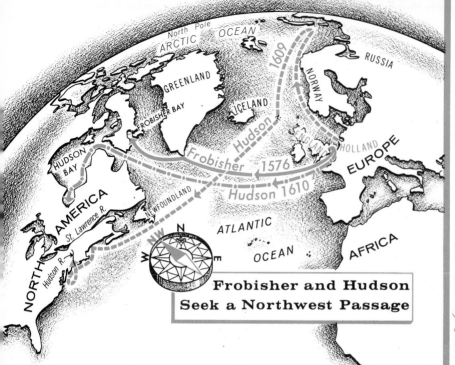

MAP STUDY

On his first voyage Henry Hudson sought a northeast route to Asia around Europe. Discouraged by ice, he turned west to the New World. Note that he sailed from Holland on his first trip. From what country did he sail in 1610?

The maps in this chapter illustrate different projections. Do your students understand the advantages and limitations of each?

Frobisher and Hudson Seek a Northwest Passage

Henry Hudson discovers a great bay. Hudson's next voyage brought not only failure but death. In 1610 he hoisted sail again, this time under the banner of his mother country, England. In the small ship *Discovery,* he headed once more into the setting sun on a voyage from which he was never to return. This time, like Frobisher, he turned far north. He and his crew fought their way through an ice-blocked strait and there, before their eyes, a great body of clear water stretched to the south and west.

All summer long, Hudson and his men sailed the waters of this huge bay, seeking a passage to Asia. When winter came, the little company had to camp on the frozen shores of the bay. By spring they had only a small quantity of cheese and biscuit left. The crew had suffered so many hardships that they could stand no more. They forced Hudson, with his young son and a few loyal men, into a boat and set them adrift. Henry Hudson was never heard of again. Only four members of the crew managed to make their way back to England. Today the name Hudson Bay reminds us of the brave explorer who perished in its icy waters without finding the passageway he sought. (The map on this page shows Hudson's explorations.)

Marquette and Joliet explore the Mississippi. Daring captains, like Verrazano and Frobisher, as you have read, touched only the edges of North America. Other explorers, such as Cartier and Champlain, made their way up rivers which were natural pathways, pushing deeper and ever deeper into this New World. In time, still other adventurous explorers spread in many directions through the wilderness of the interior, hoping to find an easy way through the New World.

Following Champlain's death, certain Frenchmen pushed hundreds of miles beyond the town of Quebec to Lake Superior. There they established a church, where a French priest preached to the Indians. This priest was Father Jacques Marquette (mar-*ket'*). From the Indians he heard tales of a "great water" which emptied into an even greater one. This, he thought,

In our day both ice breakers and submarines have gone by water from the Atlantic to the Pacific north of North America (see page 52).

The fur trade became so important to New France that it discouraged farming and other settled living. In the long run this hurt New France.

EUROPEANS LEARN MORE ABOUT THE NEW WORLD   47

must be the short cut to Asia which so many had been seeking.

In 1673, with an explorer named Louis Joliet (*joh'lih-et'*), Father Marquette set out to find this short cut. Marquette and Joliet and five companions left Lake Michigan in two bark canoes. (Look at the map on page 48 to trace their route.) They paddled up the Fox River, carried their canoes

BUILDING A BIRCH-BARK CANOE

across to the Wisconsin River, and floated down to the Mississippi. Here at last, they believed, was the great passage to Asia. But after they had paddled hundreds of miles down the Mississippi to the mouth of the Arkansas River, they knew they had not found the long-sought passage. The Mississippi, they realized, flowed southward and emptied into the Gulf of Mexico. It would not lead them to Asia. Sadly they

turned back and returned to Lake Michigan, this time by way of the Illinois River.

La Salle reaches the mouth of the Mississippi. When Joliet was returning to Quebec to report on his journey, he met an expedition headed by another Frenchman. This man was Robert Cavelier, Sieur de La Salle (luh *sal'*). He was well educated, the son of a proud old French family. But he had given up the easy living of a noble to risk his life exploring the wilds of North America. You can imagine that he listened eagerly to the story of how Joliet and Marquette had found the "great water." La Salle's ambition was to obtain for France the rich fur trade of the Great Lakes and the upper Mississippi. In the years that followed, he dreamed of an even greater plan. Why not find the mouth of the Mississippi and claim for France the vast interior of North America?

It was several years before La Salle was ready to set out on his search for the mouth of the Mississippi. His first attempt was not successful. After terrible sufferings he had to return to the fort which he had built on Lake Ontario. But La Salle refused to give up. He and his men set out again, even though it was winter. This time everything went well. They traveled by canoe across Lake Erie, Lake

HENRY HUDSON and his crew watch from the deck of the "Half Moon" as they sail up the Hudson River, hoping to find a passage through the continent. (This picture is from a "diorama," a model of a scene. Watch for later dioramas in the book.)

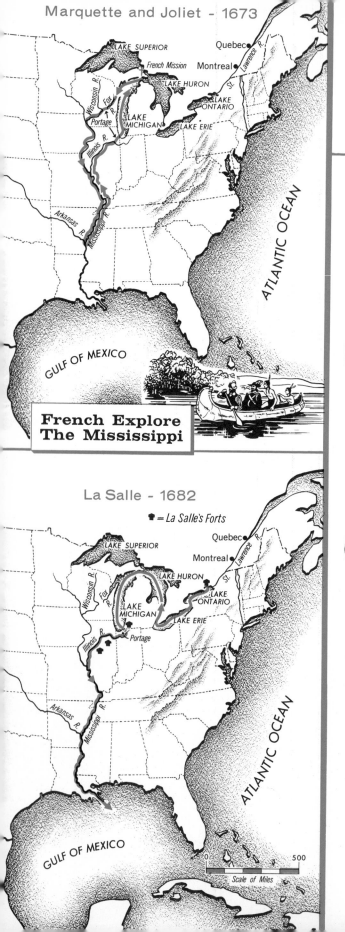

Marquette and Joliet - 1673

French Explore The Mississippi

La Salle - 1682

⚑ = La Salle's Forts

↑**MAP STUDY**

On these maps you see the routes of Frenchmen who explored the Mississippi River and thus opened up a water route into the interior of North America. The dotted lines show the boundaries of our present-day states. Can you name some of the states through which La Salle or Marquette and Joliet passed?

Huron, and Lake Michigan. At the lower end of Lake Michigan they set out on foot for the Illinois River, dragging their canoes on sleds which they had built. In canoes again, they paddled down the Illinois. Ice floated in the Mississippi when they reached it, but the weather grew warmer as they went south. At last, in April, 1682, they reached the Gulf of Mexico. (Trace La Salle's journey on the map on this page.) La Salle claimed for the French king the huge river valley from the Great Lakes to the Gulf of Mexico.

La Salle met an untimely death. In a later expedition he was murdered by his own men because of the hardships they had been forced to endure. But La Salle's travels had important results. Now the French had found a route, mostly by water, which cut North America in two. They also could claim as their territory the enormous stretches of land covered by their explorers.

CHECK UP

1. (a) How did Spain and Portugal come to claim all the newly discovered lands? (b) How did England, France, and Holland feel about this arrangement? Why?

2. How did the following explorers find that these rivers were not short cuts to Asia: (a) Cartier (St. Lawrence), (b) Hudson (Hudson), (c) Marquette and Joliet (Mississippi)?

3. (a) Why did La Salle want to explore the Mississippi Valley? (b) What route did he follow?

LA SALLE
a young French nobleman, sailed up the St. Lawrence River to seek his fortune in America.

This portage (frame 3) is a reason French explorers used canoes.

AS AN INTERPRETER, La Salle went west with the French governor of Canada to establish trade with the Indians for furs. La Salle soon realized that North America was not just a barrier to trade with Asia, but was itself a rich land.

A WATER ROUTE to the interior of North America was planned by La Salle. He built the "Griffin," first sailing ship on the Great Lakes, in order to bring supplies west and carry furs back to Canada. The "Griffin" sank on its first voyage, but La Salle continued to search for river routes leading inland.

WINTER ICE did not stop La Salle from starting his quest for the Mississippi. Heading southwest, he and his men pulled their canoes on sleds until they found open water in which to launch them.

JOURNEY'S END came after months of paddling when La Salle saw the wide horizon of the Gulf of Mexico. He had followed the Mississippi to its mouth. His own plans for trading posts and settlements failed, but La Salle had helped to open up the vast interior of North America for his fellow Frenchmen and others who came after him.

3 How Did the Search for Short Cuts to Asia Open Up the New World?

Geographic knowledge of America grows. Europeans wished at first that America did not exist. Because they wanted to reach the Far East, they searched for a short and easy route through or around the New World to Asia. We have seen that they did not succeed. But their explorations resulted in a great deal of new and accurate geographical information. Each explorer drew maps and wrote reports of what he had seen.

La Salle reached the mouth of the Mississippi just 190 years after Columbus reached San Salvador. During that time, knowledge of geography had been increased tremendously. To see how much knowledge had been gained, you can look at just two maps. The first one, on page 28, shows how little Europeans knew about the world before their explorations began. The other is the map on page 51, showing what was known about North and Central America in 1700. Comparing these maps, you can see how much was learned in the search for a short cut to Asia.

The land belongs to the discoverer. Besides their desire to find a short cut to Asia, explorers had another reason for braving hardships and dangers. They wanted to make their countries more powerful by claiming land in the New World. It became the rule of exploration that new land belonged to the European country whose explorers were the first to see it. For example, when Cartier discovered the St. Lawrence River, he took possession of all the nearby country in the name of his king, Francis I of France. He put up a marker to warn all comers that the land was French. Explorers sent out by other countries claimed land in the same way.

This rule of "finders, keepers" was used by European nations to decide what territory in the New World belonged to them. Let us see how this rule worked out.

What belonged to whom? Among the explorers you have studied, Columbus and Magellan sailed, of course, for Spain. John Cabot and Martin Frobisher were explorers for England. Verrazano, Cartier, Champlain, Marquette, Joliet, and La Salle served France. And Hudson explored for both Holland and England. If North America were to be divided according to the explorations and claims of these men, what would each country own about the year 1700?

France would hold a huge territory. She would claim the northern Atlantic coast, the land from the mouth of the St. Lawrence to the Great Lakes, and the great stretch southward along the Mississippi. England's territory would be a narrow strip along the Atlantic coast from the present state of Maine to Florida. (By 1700, as you will learn in Chapter 4, England had taken over the Dutch claims along the Hudson River.) England would also claim a large area around Hudson Bay. To Spain, whose further explorations you will read about in the next chapter, would belong the whole southern part of North America. (Spain also claimed most of South America as well.) The map on the next page shows that the division of North America worked out about that way.

The bold explorers who searched this land did not find the waterway to the East which they were seeking, but they accomplished something even more important. They turned the attention of Europe away from Asia to the New World

A good opportunity to use maps in Teaching.

50

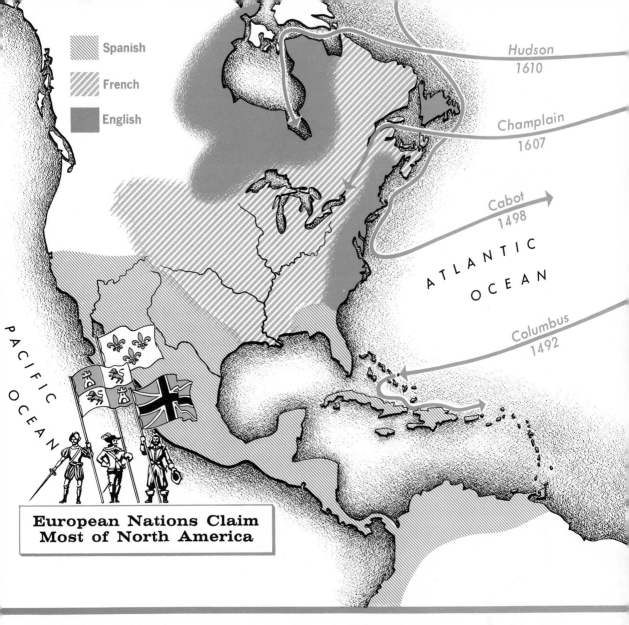

Spanish

French

English

Hudson
1610

Champlain
1607

Cabot
1498

ATLANTIC
OCEAN

PACIFIC
OCEAN

Columbus
1492

**European Nations Claim
Most of North America**

MAP STUDY   Use the key on this map to tell what parts of North America were claimed by England, Spain, and France. (Remember, though, that the boundaries between these areas were vague, and claims often overlapped.) The routes shown here are those of the chief explorers whose travels gave the different European nations their claims. For which country did each of these explorers sail?

Explanatory statements are included with maps, graphs, and pictures to make their meaning clear.

itself. They opened up a huge continent for the countries of Europe to settle. Europeans no longer looked upon America as a barrier blocking their way to the East; they became interested in it for its own sake. In the next unit you will see how these countries became rivals for land and wealth in the New World.

**CHECK
UP**

1. (a) Why did European nations send explorers to America? (b) How was it decided what land belonged to each country?

2. (a) What regions in North America were claimed by France, England, and Spain about 1700? (b) What region had Holland lost, and to whom?

51

Check Up on Chapter 2

Do You Know the Meaning?

Can you explain the meaning of each term?

1. strait　　　2. rapids　　　3. continent

Can You Identify?

Who or what were the following, and why were they important?

1. Cabot
2. Cartier
3. Champlain
4. La Salle
5. Magellan
6. Hudson
7. Marquette
8. 1519–1522
9. Verrazano
10. Frobisher
11. Joliet
12. Northwest Passage
13. New World
14. Line of Demarcation

Can You Locate?

Be able to locate the following on the maps in your text or on the wall map in your room.

1. Hudson Bay
2. Hudson River
3. Lake Michigan
4. Quebec
5. North America
6. Gulf of Mexico
7. St. Lawrence River
8. Mississippi River
9. Strait of Magellan
10. Lake Champlain

Can You Locate? (Cont.)

11. England
12. France
13. Holland
14. Philippines
15. South America
16. route of Magellan

What Do You Think?

1. Do you think that the Line of Demarcation was a fair division of the new lands? Why?
2. If two present-day countries claimed the same territory, what persons or organizations could they turn to for help in arranging a settlement?
3. (a) What effect did Magellan's exploration have on the search for a westward sea route to Asia? (b) Why did the search for a direct route fail? (c) What short cut from Europe to Asia is used today?
4. Why did the attitude of Europeans toward the New World change between 1500 and 1700?
5. Why did the early explorers of the interior of North America use water routes rather than land routes?

LINKING PAST AND PRESENT

Found — a Northwest Passage. From the 1500's on, bold explorers searched for a Northwest Passage through the ice-filled waters and desolate islands north of Canada. By the end of the 1800's, a route was known, but no one had yet sailed the full length of the passage. The first to do so was Roald Amundsen, the famous Norwegian explorer, in 1903–05. But by this time there was no longer a real need for a Northwest Passage; the Panama Canal, soon to open, offered a much easier passage from the Atlantic to the Pacific. After World War II, however, the United States and Canada built a radar system across northern Canada to give warn-

ing of enemy attacks, and the Northwest Passage was used as a route for the supply ships. In 1957, a Canadian ice breaker and three United States Coast Guard cutters found an alternate Northwest Passage which is shorter and less dangerous than the older route.

The next year, the world was amazed by the news that the American nuclear submarine *Nautilus* had crossed from the Pacific to the Atlantic by way of the North Pole. This voyage was more than a daring venture into unknown seas. The *Nautilus* and its crew had actually opened a time-saving Northwest Passage *under* the Arctic ice!

The distance from Tokyo to London, for instance, is 11,200 miles by way of the Panama Canal, but only 6500 miles by way of the route under the North Pole. Some day, atomic freight submarines may carry goods by the underseas polar route. Then the hope of the early explorers for a northwest trade route between the Atlantic and the Pacific will indeed have come true — but in a way they never dreamed of!

French names in America. Many place names in our country remind us that France once owned a large chunk of North America. As you have learned, Lake Champlain, on the border between New York and Vermont, is named for the famous "Father of New France." Vermont itself is a French name meaning "green mountain." French names are also very common in the states of the upper Mississippi Valley. In Wisconsin are such cities as Prairie du Chien ("dog's prairie" — after the little prairie dogs found in that region), Fond du Lac ("end of the lake"), Eau Claire ("clear water"), and La Crosse ("the crossing"). The Illinois cities of Joliet and La Salle are named for two famous French explorers. St. Louis, Missouri, named for a French saint and king, was founded by the French as a fur-trading post.

The summaries bring out important concepts developed in the unit. Ask pupils to provide evidence supporting the major points made.

TO CLINCH YOUR
UNDERSTANDING OF
Unit 1

Summary of Important Ideas

Unit One has told the story of how countries of western Europe found and explored a new world. To help you keep in mind the major ideas in this unit, we have included the following summary in outline form:

1. Western European countries, seeking new routes to the East, found a new world.
   a. The demand in Europe for Eastern goods increased after the Crusades. The high prices of these goods and the desire to share in the rich trade caused countries in western Europe to look for new routes.
   b. The search for a water route was made easier by important inventions (the compass and astrolabe) and better maps. The Portuguese carefully explored the coast of Africa. Finally, da Gama rounded the Cape of Good Hope and reached India in 1498. Because Portugal controlled this new route, other European countries looked for different routes to the East.
   c. Columbus, believing that Asia was larger and the earth smaller than they actually are, persuaded the rulers of Spain to back an expedition to seek a westward route to the East. Thinking that the islands he discovered in 1492 were off the coast of Asia, he called them the Indies.

2. In looking for westward routes to the East, the people of western Europe learned more about the New World.
   a. Magellan's expedition (1519–22) showed that a new world lay across the westward route to the East. Because Magellan's route was too long for trade, France, England, and Holland sent explorers to look for short cuts to Asia.
   b. These explorations opened up the New World. The French explored along

the St. Lawrence, the Great Lakes, and the Mississippi. The English explored to the north of present-day Canada, and the Dutch along the Hudson River.

c. European explorers greatly increased man's knowledge of the New World. Spain, France, and England — each claiming the lands they explored — divided North America among themselves.

Unit Review

1. (a) Why did people living in Europe in the year 1000 take little interest in the outside world? (b) Why did the demand for Eastern goods in western Europe increase after the Crusades?
2. (a) Why were Spain and Portugal interested in a new route to the East? (b) Why did the great geographic discoveries take place when they did?
3. (a) Why did the search for new routes to the East continue after Portugal's discovery of an all-water route to India? (b) What countries took a leading part in this search? (c) In what directions was the search made? (d) With what success?
4. (a) Why did Portugal and Spain ask the Pope to help settle their claims to newly discovered lands? (b) How might such a question be settled today?
5. (a) What became the basis for claims to lands in the New World? (b) What areas were claimed by Spain, England, France, and Holland?

Gaining Skill

How Maps Represent the Earth

One way to see the earth as it really is would be from a space capsule orbiting hundreds of miles above the earth's surface. There, before your eyes, would be the vast, round sphere itself! You yourself can get some idea of how the earth looks from space if you bring your eyes close to a globe. On a globe, land and sea areas have the same shape and comparative size as they do on the earth

Take time to discuss this material with your students. It will help them to use maps with understanding.

itself, seen from space. In other words, your globe is a scale *model* of the earth.

On most globes you can see a pattern of intersecting lines. Long ago map makers drew these imaginary lines to help them locate places exactly on the globe and on maps projected from it. Lines drawn from the North Pole to the South Pole are called *meridians* or *longitude* lines. Lines drawn east to west and parallel to the equator are called *parallels* or *latitude* lines (see diagram below). Both sets of lines are numbered.

Since a globe gives you the most accurate view of the earth, some map makers try to draw pictures of the globe as it looks "in the round." Sometimes they make their maps by copying photographs of a globe. Many of the maps in this unit have been drawn to show parts of the earth more or less as they would appear on a globe seen from different angles. For example, the map on page 31 of Columbus' route shows the globe as it would look from a point in space above North America, with the North Pole tipped toward you. On page 46 the map of Hudson's explorations shows only a portion of the globe as it might appear from a point above the Atlantic Ocean, with the North Pole almost on the "horizon."

You probably are acquainted with other kinds of maps, such as those found in an atlas or on your classroom wall. The land areas of the earth may appear different in shape and size on these maps because it is impossible to show accurately the *curved* surface of the globe on a *flat* sheet of paper. The size of the land areas, or their shape, or the distances and directions between them must be changed somewhat. Instead of being exact models or pictures of the globe, such maps are more like

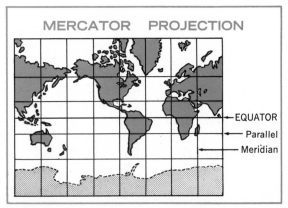

MERCATOR PROJECTION

EQUATOR

Parallel

Meridian

useful *diagrams* of the earth's surface.

In order to draw their diagrams, map makers often *project* the outlines of land areas from a globe onto the paper, much as we use a slide-projector to cast an image on a screen. Maps made in this way are called *projections*.

Map projections are useful for accurate measuring, but all of them distort the appearance of the earth's surface in some way. For example, look at the drawing on page 54 of one of the oldest projections, named after Mercator, the Dutch map maker who invented it. A Mercator map shows accurately the outline of land areas and their direction from one another. But land areas far from the equator appear much larger on this projection than they actually are. Note that there is no North Pole on the Mercator map. Instead of meeting at the North Pole, meridians remain the same distance apart all the way to the top. Note, also, that the parallels are spaced farther apart toward the top of the map. In other words, the top and bottom areas of a Mercator map are in a different scale from the areas near the equator.

A different map projection, named after a German map maker, Mollweide, shows the comparative size of land areas accurately, but distorts their shape (see drawing below). As on a Mercator map, the same scale of miles can not be used all over a Mollweide map.

Other map makers have succeeded in working out projections which distort land areas and shapes less than do the maps shown here. As you refer to maps during your study of American history, you will find it helpful to keep in mind the facts about projections explained above.

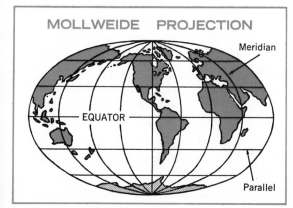

MOLLWEIDE PROJECTION

Meridian

EQUATOR

Parallel

Interesting Things to Do

The activities suggested below may be fun and will help you remember what you have already learned. Those marked with an asterisk (*) are suggested for the whole class. There are others for people who like to write, for instance, or to speak, draw, or read.

*1. Start a game to help you learn the dates, events, and men mentioned under "Can You Identify?" in the Chapter Check Ups. On large cards print the name or date in large letters on one side; on the other side print a brief identification. Example: *da Gama* (on one side); *Portuguese explorer who sailed east to India* (on the other side). Choose teams and see which team can identify most.

*2. Make a chart of the explorers you read about in Chapter 2, using these headings: Name, Date, Country for Which He Sailed, and Results of Voyage.

3. Make a picture map showing the voyages of Dias and da Gama. Draw in the monsters and whirlpools in the Great Sea of Darkness, Prince Henry's school, the stone towers on the African coast, and so on.

4. Look up Joaquin Miller's poem *Columbus*. Read it to the class.

5. Imagine that you were an Indian boy who saw Columbus land on Guanahani. Write the story as the boy would have told it. Or write a newspaper account of one of these events: (a) da Gama reaches India; (b) Columbus tells the Spanish rulers about his discovery; (c) Magellan's crew returns to Spain; (d) La Salle reaches the Gulf of Mexico.

6. On a map of the United States see how many cities, rivers, and lakes you can find that are named after explorers.

7. Report to the class on the life of one of these explorers: Marquette, Joliet, La Salle, Cartier, Champlain, Magellan, Cabot.

8. Have you read a story or seen a motion picture about the Crusades, early trade with Asia, or explorations in America? Tell the class about the story.

This type of writing encourages pupils to try to put themselves in the shoes of others.

European Nations Plant Colonies an

The first paragraph recalls the old world described in Unit One.

Not often does an old world find a new one. For hundreds of years Europeans had seen little of the world. Throughout their lives many never traveled more than a few miles from their place of birth. Even the Crusaders, who had journeyed long distances, knew only about Europe and the nearby areas of Africa and Asia. But early in the 1500's daring explorers found a whole new world in the Western Hemisphere.

These are three basic questions to be answered in Unit Two.

What was this New World like? What riches might be found there? What countries would claim the New World and become wealthy and powerful? At first, Europeans had very little information with which to answer these questions. But their imaginations were stirred by the tales told by returning explorers, just as we are excited today when space pilots venture into the unknown regions beyond our planet.

Unit One told the story of bold captains and explorers who found out more and more about the New World, especially North America. In Unit Two we shall learn how ever-increasing numbers of Europeans came to the Americas. Chapter 3, for example, describes how Spaniards

Struggle for Control of the New World

came to gain wealth and power. As a result, Spain founded a mighty empire chiefly in Mexico and South America. Within this empire there developed a way of life which combined Spanish customs with those of the Indians conquered by the Spaniards.

In Chapter 4 we shall study the beginnings and growth of English colonies in the New World. Unlike the Spaniards, most English settlers came to the New World in search of new homes where they could enjoy a freer way of life. That is why, in the scene above of the founding of Jamestown, Virginia, one of the first houses is highlighted. Chapter 5 describes ways of living in the Thirteen English Colonies in North America.

Finally, in Chapter 6 we shall learn what regions in North America were settled by the French. This chapter also tells how conflicts arose between the French and English colonies and what the outcome was.

Quotations from sources help to make the past live. Do your pupils think Raleigh "promised" too much? Can they suggest why he did?

I never saw a more beautiful country, all fair green grass . . . the deer crossing in every path . . . the air fresh . . . and every stone that we stooped to take up promised either silver or gold by [its] complexion.

— SIR WALTER RALEIGH

The chapter preview recalls the wealth that flowed from the New World to Spain. Today divers are recovering gold and jewels from sunken galleons off Florida and Bermuda.

Spain Establishes a Great Empire

What this chapter is about —

A gallant ship bearing the white-and-gold banner of Spain is heading eastward across the Atlantic. Its fore and aft decks are high above the water, and its sails are gaily decorated with paintings. High up in the crow's-nest a sailor looks anxiously in all directions for swift-sailing pirate ships. For this is a treasure galleon of the Spanish fleet, carrying riches to Spain. Piled in the hold is treasure to stagger the imagination — heavy bars of gold and silver, boxes of pearls and emeralds. What a prize for a bold pirate!

Are these the riches of Asia? Have the Spaniards at last found a passage to the Far East? No, this ship with its precious load has come from Spain's colonies in the New World. And it is carrying only a frac-

tion of the wealth that is transported every year to the mother country from her American colonies.

In this chapter you will learn how Spain established a great empire in the New World and how she grew rich and became the envy of other European nations. You will find out what life in Spanish America was like — why, for example, the Spanish built many mission churches like the one shown above. As you read, look for answers to these questions:

▶ 1. How did Spain explore and conquer much of the New World?

▶ 2. What was life like in Spanish America?

▶ 3. How did England and other nations threaten Spain's power?

Compare the cast of characters for Chapters 3, 4 and 6.

People in our story — Spanish adventurer, Aztec warrior, Spanish missionary, Indian man and woman, and Mexican rancher.

Refer pupils to the map on page 63, and point out how near Cuba and Hispaniola were to the mainland.

1 How Did Spain Explore and Conquer Much of the New World?

Spain gets a head start in the New World. Columbus, you remember, discovered several islands in the Caribbean Sea — Cuba, Hispaniola, Puerto Rico, and others. Although he found little gold, he was so sure he had discovered islands off the coast of Asia that Spain sent over ships with men and supplies to found settlements. Soon more and more settlers came to take up land and develop large farms called plantations. Bold adventurers and penniless soldiers also flocked to Cuba and Hispaniola in the hope of making their fortunes. But little gold was ever found in the islands. The only way to become wealthy was to farm the rich soil or to raise cattle, and this was too slow for men who dreamed of great riches. So from these settlements adventurous men set out to explore the New World. Thus the islands of the Caribbean became stepping-stones to the nearby mainland.

The New World attracts many Spaniards. Many Spaniards were eager to come to the New World. In those days, young men of the upper class in Spain, as well as many others, chose soldiering as a career. In the early 1500's, however, Spain's armies were not always at war, and many soldiers wanted adventure and riches. The New World, unknown and unexplored, beckoned to them. What brave *caballero* (cah-bah-*yay*′roh), or gentleman of Spain, wouldn't risk his life for fame and fortune?

We must also remember that the Spanish people were deeply religious, and believed it their duty to convert heathen people to Christianity. Thus, you see, the New World offered a chance not only to gain riches but also to save souls. So from Spain to the New World came dashing caballeros, stouthearted soldiers, and courageous priests — in search of converts for their Church, gold for their king, or wealth for themselves.

Tales could be told about many of these Spanish explorers, sometimes called *conquistadors,* or conquerors. But we shall describe in detail the adventures of only three. You will probably recognize their names: Balboa, Cortés, and Pizarro.

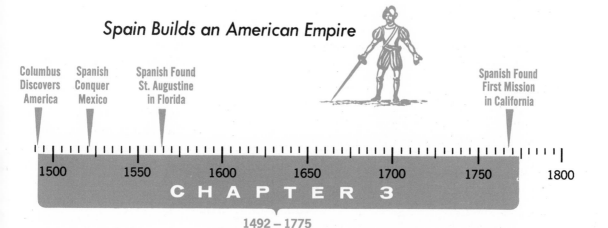

Spain Builds an American Empire

| Columbus Discovers America | Spanish Conquer Mexico | Spanish Found St. Augustine in Florida | | | Spanish Found First Mission in California |

1500 1550 1600 1650 1700 1750 1800

C H A P T E R 3

1492 – 1775

BALBOA, standing on a peak on the Isthmus of Panama, discovers the shining Pacific Ocean.

BALBOA DISCOVERS THE PACIFIC

The first of these Spanish explorers was Vasco Nuñez de Balboa (Balboa for short), a tall and haughty man and an excellent swordsman. He owned a plantation in Hispaniola but was restless and unhappy there, for the love of adventure was in his blood. Balboa heard tales from the Indians about a land rich in gold. This land (which we now know was Peru) could be reached by sea from the other side of the Isthmus of Panama. Balboa seized upon this chance to make a name for himself. He wrote a letter to King Ferdinand of Spain, describing the land and asking for help. Here is part of his letter:

✻ In the mountains [of Peru] there are certain *caciques* [chiefs] who have great quantities of gold in their houses. It is said . . . that all the rivers of these mountains contain gold; and that they have very large lumps in great abundance . . . and the Indians say that the other sea [Pacific] is at a distance of three days' journey. . . . They say that the people of the other coast are very good and well-mannered; and I am told that the other sea is very good for canoe navigation, for that it is always smooth and never rough like the sea·on this side. . . .

They say that there are many large pearls and that the caciques have baskets of them. . . . It is a most astonishing thing and without equal, that our Lord has made you the lord of this land.

What a shrewd letter! Notice that Balboa actually knew very little about this land, since almost every sentence began with "they say" or "it is said." The king apparently noticed this fact, for in spite of the compliment at the end of the letter, he refused aid. If Balboa wished to go to Peru, he had to go "on his own."

Balboa crosses the Isthmus of Panama. On a September day in 1513 Balboa, with about 200 Spaniards, set out from a small settlement on the Caribbean side of the Isthmus. The Spaniards were armed with crossbows, swords, and firearms. Hundreds of Indian slaves accompanied them. You can see on the map, page 63, that the distance to be covered was not great. But there were many hardships to be overcome. The jungle was alive with stinging insects and poisonous snakes. Hostile natives threatened the Spaniards' lives. And the tangled vines and swamps of the tropical jungle slowed their march to a mile or two a day.

The reliability of a source is influenced by his information and what purpose he has in mind.

60

(among other things) where the author got

Call attention to cross references. Students sometimes ignore them.

SPAIN ESTABLISHES A GREAT EMPIRE 61

At length Balboa and his men came to high mountains which their Indian guides told them looked upon the "other sea" to the south. As they neared the summit of the mountains, Balboa ordered his men to wait. He climbed the last steep distance alone. There before him, as far as his eye could see, stretched a vast, shimmering sea! Eagerly he beckoned to his men to join him so that they could see the great water. They were the first white men to look upon the Pacific Ocean from the shores of the New World.

Balboa claims the Pacific Ocean for Spain. Four days later they reached the waters of the Pacific. With the banner of Spain fluttering in the breeze and his drawn sword in his hand, Balboa stepped into the waves and claimed the sea and all the lands that bordered it for his royal master. Balboa named his discovery the South Sea because it lay directly south of the place where he had started his march (map, page 63). It was not until after Magellan's voyage that the sea was called Pacific, the name we use today.

Balboa returned with news of his discovery. He made plans to set sail on the South Sea to search for gold. But a new governor had been appointed in Panama. The governor and other Spaniards were jealous of Balboa and prevented him from carrying out his plan to find the land of gold which he had described to the king. The unfortunate Balboa was finally accused of treason and was killed.

HERNANDO CORTÉS CONQUERS MEXICO

Balboa was not the only Spaniard to listen to tales of rich lands. Sailors who had touched the coast of the mainland opposite Cuba brought back stories of a great land to the north and west (Mexico) where much treasure was to be found.

This land, they said, was ruled by a tribe of civilized Indians called *Aztecs*. All the neighboring tribes paid tribute to the Aztec emperor. The governor of Cuba decided to check up on these stories. He planned to send an expedition to explore the land, convert the Indians, and perhaps discover the treasure.

Cortés sets out for Mexico. As leader of the expedition, the governor chose an ambitious soldier by the name of Hernando Cortés. Cortés was then about 33 years old, with flashing dark eyes and a jovial manner. The son of a poor Spanish nobleman, he had left home at nineteen and sailed to the New World to make his fortune. He had helped Spanish forces subdue the Indians in Cuba and later became a well-to-do plantation owner. Like Balboa, he was eager for adventure. He gladly agreed to become leader of the expedition.

Cortés left Cuba early in 1519 with eleven ships, 600 men, several priests, a few horses and cannon, and many Indian slaves or workers. (Turn to page 63 and follow his course on the map as you read.) The Spanish fleet landed in Mexico where the city of Veracruz now stands, and Cortés took possession of the land for Spain. From the natives of that region he heard more about the Aztecs and their emperor, who was called Moctezuma (mahk-teh-*zoo′* muh).[1]

Cortés meets with Aztec messengers and "burns his bridges" behind him. In the meantime, swift runners carried to Moctezuma news of white-skinned, bearded strangers who rode on great beasts and had weapons which made sounds like thunder. The Aztecs had a legend about a

---

[1] Though this ruler is often called "Montezuma," the spelling "Moctezuma" is more accurate.

Note preferred spelling and pronunciation.

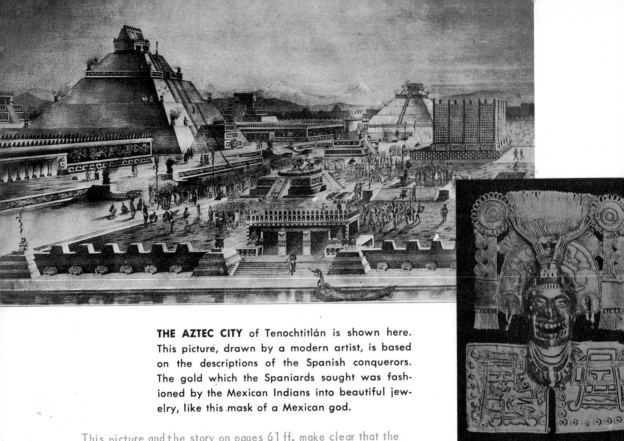

THE AZTEC CITY of Tenochtitlán is shown here. This picture, drawn by a modern artist, is based on the descriptions of the Spanish conquerors. The gold which the Spaniards sought was fashioned by the Mexican Indians into beautiful jewelry, like this mask of a Mexican god.

This picture and the story on pages 61 ff. make clear that the Aztecs were more numerous and civilized than tribes found farther north.

"fair god" who once ruled their land. Hundreds of years before, he had departed in a great canoe, promising that he would one day return to them. Was it possible, wondered Moctezuma, that the leader of these strange beings was their ancient god? Moctezuma dared take no chances, so he sent messengers with words of greeting and dazzling gifts. Among the gifts were two plates as large as wagon wheels, one of gold and one of silver!

Cortés was more anxious than ever to meet a king who owned such treasure. He made a bold decision. He would overpower this king and win his wealth and lands for Spain, and also, of course, for Cortés and his men. He would no longer take orders from the governor of Cuba, but instead would make his own decisions. Cortés wisely sent a letter to the Spanish king, telling him what he planned to do.

Then he announced his decision to his men and told them that he was founding a new colony.

Cortés was a leader who inspired others to follow him, and his men gladly agreed to his daring plan. To make sure that no men turned fainthearted, Cortés burned all his ships! He learned that the Indian tribes along the coast, who hated the Aztec rule, would be glad to join him in fighting against Moctezuma. In August, 1519, the little band of white men and their Indian allies set out for Tenochtitlán (tay-nohch-tee-*tlahn'*), the capital city of the Aztecs, which was located in the mountains of central Mexico.

Cortés arrives at Tenochtitlán. Two months later the weary Spaniards stood looking in amazement upon the Aztec capital. The city was built on islands in a large but shallow lake, and was con-

Bring out why the Indians along the coast   **62**   sided with the Spaniards.

Perhaps a pupil may wish to report on Aztec, Mayan, or Inca ruins, and what they tell us about how these Indians lived.

SPAIN ESTABLISHES A GREAT EMPIRE

63

nected with the mainland by three raised roads, or causeways. Crisscrossing the city were many canals which served as streets, and gaily colored canoes darted back and forth. Alongside these canals were footpaths. Most of the buildings were dazzling white in the bright sunshine. Great temples to Aztec gods towered above the city.

The Spaniards were met by Moctezuma, ruler of the Aztecs. A tall and dignified man, dressed in blue and gold, he was carried on a couch borne by his subjects. When he alighted, a carpet was put down to protect his golden sandals from the earth. On all sides important Aztec officials stood without daring to raise their eyes in the presence of their ruler. Moctezuma and Cortés gravely exchanged gifts, and the Spaniards slowly entered the city.

Although he feared the strangers, Moctezuma treated them as honored guests. They lived for some months in the city, storing up gold and treasure by trade with the Indians. The natives did not appear to be hostile, but Cortés realized that his small band was greatly outnumbered by the Aztecs.

The Spaniards fight their way out of Tenochtitlán. Then Cortés received news that the governor of Cuba had sent an expedition to Mexico to take him prisoner. With some of his followers, Cortés left the city and returned to the coast. There he captured the leader of the expedition. By describing the treasure that would be theirs when the Aztecs were conquered, Cortés persuaded the others to join him. Returning to Tenochtitlán with his recruits, Cortés discovered that in his absence fighting had broken out between the Spaniards and the Aztecs. When they found that Spaniards could be killed, the Aztecs realized that the white strangers were not gods and had turned on them in fury.

After several days of bitter street fighting, Cortés decided that he and his men must get out of the city. Even their cannon and arms were no match for thousands of Aztec warriors. Loaded down with gold and jewels, the Spaniards tried to steal away in the darkness of night, but their

MAP STUDY

The locations of the chief Indian peoples found by the Spanish in America are shown here in color. Besides the Aztecs and Incas, the Spanish also conquered the Mayas, whose civilization had been one of the oldest and most advanced in the New World. Notice that the Spanish explorers set out from island bases discovered by Columbus.

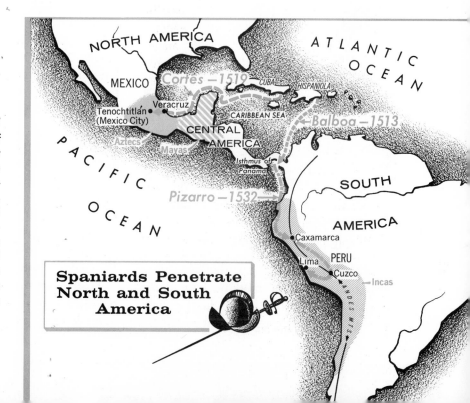

Spaniards Penetrate North and South America

flight was discovered. A fierce battle followed. Many Spaniards plunged into the lake and drowned; hundreds of others were killed by Aztec knives and arrows. Cortés and those of his men who escaped had suffered a terrible defeat. It is said that Cortés sat under a tree outside the city and wept over the loss of 450 of his valiant men.

Tenochtitlán finally surrenders to Cortés. Cortés knew that he must continue his attempt to conquer Tenochtitlán and the Aztec warriors. He must succeed or he could never return to Cuba — unless he wished to be hanged for treason. But it was not until 1521 that the city finally surrendered. Cortés then tore down the capital of the Aztecs and built in its place a Spanish city which he called Mexico City. Christian churches soon replaced the temples of the Aztecs.

Cortés continues his conquests. Cortés did not stop with the conquest of the Aztecs. As commander of the Spanish forces in Mexico, he sent expeditions throughout the Aztec empire and into Central America. Some of these expeditions he himself led. Cortés seized the gold and silver mines and other wealth that he found and forced the Indians to work for the Spaniards. When he died at the age of 62, Spanish rule had spread from northern Central America through Mexico and into what is now the southwestern United States. Although we may not approve of his methods, we must admire the courage and persistence of this conqueror of Mexico.

PIZARRO CONQUERS PERU

After Balboa's death, Spaniards began to hear more about the land he had hoped to conquer (page 60). This land, which we now call Peru, was the home of highly civilized Indians. They were ruled by a tribe whose leaders were called Incas, meaning "children of the sun." These Indians were clever farmers who knew how to irrigate lands which were too dry for crops. They also wove fine cloth and made beautiful articles of pottery and metal. What was more important to the gold-hungry Spaniards, the Incas were said to wear golden shoes and to eat from golden dishes. Here, indeed, was a land worth finding!

Pizarro reaches Inca Land. The man who determined to conquer Peru was Francisco Pizarro (pih-*zahr'* oh). He had crossed the Isthmus with Balboa and was an old hand at exploration. Pizarro was not a nobleman like Cortés and Balboa; his family was a humble one, and he had never learned to read or write. He was a harsh man, but he made a good explorer because he could endure hardships and disappointments without becoming discouraged.

Pizarro knew that he and his men would have great difficulty in conquering the Inca ruler, who lived high in the Andes Mountains. So Pizarro spent several years getting ready for his great venture. He landed safely on the coast of Peru, where he remained for some time "sizing up" the situation. At last, in the autumn of 1532, Pizarro set out for the Inca cities with a band of only about 180 Spaniards. Pizarro, however, was counting on firearms and horses to overcome the much greater numbers of the Supreme Inca. He and his men struggled up the steep mountainsides, leading their horses after them, and came at last to the city of Caxamarca (kah-hah-*mahr'* kah), where the haughty Inca ruler awaited them.

Pizarro imprisons the Inca and gains a king's ransom. The ruler, Atahualpa (ah-tah-*wahl'* pah), with thousands of his

A PERUVIAN INDIAN, dressed in the costume of an Inca warrior, poses by a ruined Inca fortress. The Peruvian Indians made fine utensils in graceful and amusing shapes, like this little vase in the shape of a crab.

subjects gathered about him, sat on a throne of gold in the great square. We may well imagine that he did not fear this small band of white men with their weapons, for he had never before seen a gun. The Spaniards decided to give Atahualpa a chance to become a Christian and a subject of the king of Spain. A priest talked to him through an interpreter, telling him about the Christian religion and urging him to accept the Christian God. Atahualpa listened, but was not impressed. He pointed to the sun and said, "My god still lives in the heavens and looks down upon his children." Then he dashed to the ground the Bible which the priest had offered him. This was too much for the religious Spaniards and Pizarro gave the signal to fire. While the Inca looked on in horror from his golden throne, the Spaniards massacred thousands of his subjects. Pizarro took Atahualpa prisoner.

When the royal prisoner saw how eager the Spaniards were for gold, he made a bargain with Pizarro for his freedom. Touching the wall of a small room as high above his head as he could reach, Atahualpa promised to fill the room with gold if his captors would release him. Pizarro agreed, and during the days which followed, a steady stream of Indians entered the room with gold objects from palaces and temples. At last the room was filled. This was indeed a king's ransom! The room contained treasure worth about fifteen million dollars in gold. Atahualpa had carried out his side of the bargain, but Pizarro had no intention of keeping his promise. For him the bargain was simply an easy way to get the Inca gold. Later on, he found an excuse to kill Atahualpa, who was strangled to death by the Spaniards.

Pizarro meets a violent death. It was not long before Pizarro conquered other cities, and soon he controlled the whole Inca empire (see map, page 63). He

Here is another instance of Spanish zeal to exploit them.

Christianize the Indians as well as to

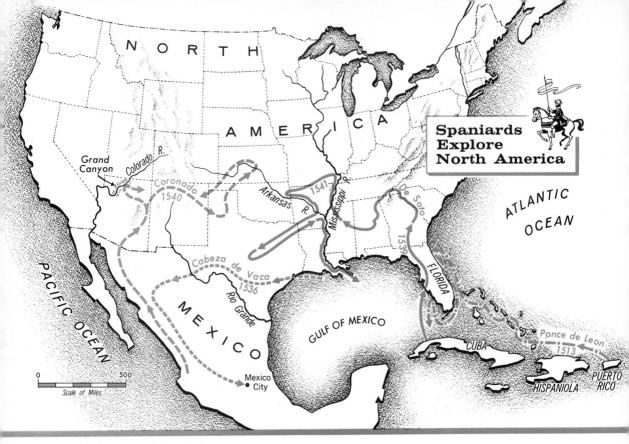

Spaniards
Explore
North America

MAP STUDY The faint lines in the background of this map show the boundaries of our present-day states. They help you to see what parts of North America the Spaniards explored. (1) Across what present-day states did each of the explorers shown here travel? (2) Which explorers set out from the islands claimed for Spain by Columbus?

founded the Spanish city of Lima (*lee'-muh*), which grew to be one of the important cities of the New World. Pizarro, however, did not have a chance to enjoy the wealth and fame for which he had worked so hard. His harsh treatment of the Indians led to many revolts and endless fighting. There also was much jealousy and plotting among the Spaniards themselves. Pizarro died as violently as he had lived, for he was finally assassinated by his own countrymen.

SPAIN GAINS WEALTH AND POWER
FROM HER NEW WORLD EMPIRE

Other explorers extend Spain's claims in the New World. So far you have learned about Balboa, Cortés, and Pizarro.

There were, of course, many other famous explorers who claimed for Spain the regions they explored while searching for fame and treasure. You probably know about some of them.

(1) Ponce de Leon (*pohn' say day lay-ohn'*) discovered Florida while searching for a "fountain of youth." Though nothing came of Ponce de Leon's expedition, other Spaniards founded a settlement at St. Augustine, Florida, in 1565. It is the oldest city in the United States.

(2) Another Spaniard, Cabeza de Vaca (*kah-bay' sah day vah' kah*), wandered for nine years through Mexico and what is now the state of Texas.

(3) Francisco Coronado (*kor-uh-nah'-doh*) marched hundreds of weary miles through a large part of what is our South-

Bring out that rumors or legends encouraged explorations, even as they had Balboa, Cortés, and Pizarro. Would the success of the last two cause rumors to be believed more readily?

Ponce de Leon and Coronado to make

west, seeking cities of gold that the Indians told about. Coronado reported that he reached a region which "is the best I have ever seen for producing all the products of Spain, for besides the land itself being very fat and black and being very well watered by rivulets and springs and rivers, I found prunes like those of Spain and nuts and very good sweet grapes and mulberries." But Coronado found no gold, and his Indian guides confessed that the stories they had told were false, "believing that as the way was through such uninhabited deserts, and from the lack of water, they would get us [the Spaniards] where we and our horses would die."

(4) Hernando de Soto was the first white man to discover the Mississippi River, reaching it about 140 years before La Salle (page 47). The Spaniards, however, did nothing to colonize the area at the time, so La Salle claimed it for France later on. (Locate the routes of these various explorers on the map on page 66.)

Spain's new empire stretches far. Priests, officers of the government, traders, and settlers followed the Spanish conquistadors. During the hundred years after Columbus first set foot upon the New World, Spain carved out a great empire in America. It included all of South America (except Brazil, which Portugal claimed), all Central America, and Mexico. It also included Florida, the coast around the Gulf of Mexico, the southwestern part of what is now the United States, and all the islands of the West Indies. (The map on page 71 shows the mighty empire of Spain.)

This enormous area was divided into two parts: (1) As shown on the map, the part called New Spain included Mexico and the West Indies. (2) The name Peru was given to Spanish possessions in South America except for Venezuela.

Make sure that pupils refer to the map on page 71 as they read this section.

Spain becomes the richest and most powerful nation in Europe. The Spaniards stripped the Aztec and the Inca kingdoms of stored-up wealth. Then they forced the Indians to dig still more gold and silver from the mines of Mexico and Peru. Treasure ships kept moving across the Atlantic, and during the 1500's the riches of her New World empire helped to make Spain the wealthiest country in Europe.

Wealth means power. Spain's newfound wealth made her, for a time, Europe's most powerful nation. She was able to build strong colonies in America and to send soldiers to protect them. A huge navy guarded her great fleet of merchant ships against attack.

Spain's power reached its height in the latter half of the 1500's. Philip II, an earnest Catholic, ruled over a vast empire in Europe and the New World. His power was still further increased because the Pope at Rome looked to him to convert heathen in his great realm and to defend the cause of the Catholic Church everywhere. When people thought of all Philip's land, his wealth, his power, they said, "When Spain moves, the whole world trembles."

CHECK UP

1. For what reasons did Spaniards come to the New World?

2. (a) How did Balboa add to Spain's claims in the New World? (b) What peoples and lands did Cortés and Pizarro conquer for Spain? (c) What were the results of these conquests?

3. What other explorers extended Spain's claims in the New World? Tell where in each case.

4. What effect did its empire in the New World have on Spain?

2 What Was Life Like in Spanish America?

Exciting as are the stories of Spanish explorers and conquistadors, they do not tell us all we want to know about the Spanish empire in the New World. What about the people who lived in the Spanish colonies? How were they governed? What kind of homes did they live in and what kind of work did they do? How did the Spaniards get along with the Indians they had conquered?

Instead of studying life in Spanish America in the usual way, we shall read about it in imaginary letters written by a fifteen-year-old boy whom we shall call Philip Andrews. Let us suppose that Philip, son of an English father and a Spanish mother, went to New Spain in the early 1700's to visit his uncle. Although there was no real Philip Andrews, these letters give a true picture of life in the Spanish colonies. Imagine that the letters were found long after Philip wrote them, and that the finder put in the headings and the pronunciations. Remember, too, that a boy in the 1700's wrote more formal letters, even to his parents, than would boys and girls today.

THE SPANISH GOVERNMENT CONTROLS THE SPANISH COLONISTS

ON SHIPBOARD, BOUND
FOR NEW SPAIN

Dear Father and Mother,

What good luck I have had — and at the very beginning of my trip, too! One of my fellow passengers on the ship is a Spanish official. In talking with him I have learned a great deal about the Spanish colonies even before reaching them. So in this first letter I can give you a general idea of New Spain and its government, even though I have not yet arrived there.

The government controls almost everything. The most striking thing about the Spanish colonies is how carefully everything is controlled by the government. For example, the number of people who come to the Spanish colonies is limited. No one but Catholics born in Spain itself may settle there, and everyone who enters New Spain must have a permit to do so.

Another thing the government manages with great care is the trade with her colonies. Only Spanish merchants, using Spanish vessels, can trade with New Spain. Every spring a great fleet of heavily guarded merchant ships sails to Veracruz from Spain. The ships are loaded with manufactured goods, such as fine cloth, shoes, and tools. These Spanish goods are traded for corn, cattle, hides, and other products of New Spain.

The people in the colonies do not like the way trade is regulated by the mother country. They have to buy what they need from the merchants at Veracruz. The colonists must also sell what they make or grow to the same merchants. The colonists have nothing to say about the prices of the goods they buy or the goods they sell. And they are not allowed to grow anything produced in Spain because, if they did, Spanish merchants would not be able to sell their own products in the colonies. What the colonists want is to be free to trade with other countries.

Another example of control is the way New Spain is governed. The king of Spain appoints a colonial governor, called a *viceroy*. This official has great power, while the people have no real share in the

68

(Continued on page 71)

INDIAN AMERICA

Long before Europeans came to America, the Indians had developed their own customs and skills. This valuable heritage is kept alive by Indians today. In the Southwest, dolls (above) are still costumed like the dancers who impersonate the *kachinas*, or spirits. At left, an Indian is shown making a picture of the moon spirit by the ancient art of letting grains of colored sand trickle through his fingers. At Taos, New Mexico, stands the great Pueblo (below), an adobe apartment house in which Indians have lived for over 200 years. (The domes in the foreground are outdoor ovens.) Early pueblos were described as "cities of gold," a legend which lured the first Spaniards into the Southwest.

"Old Broken Nose" (right) is one of the traditional masks worn by the False Face Society, a men's club of the Iroquois Indians in New York.

The colorful costume of the plains Indians included the well-known warbonnet (right) and leather vests decorated with beadwork (above). It was natural for the Cheyenne Indians to choose a design of horsemen for this vest since their way of life depended on swift horses. Two braves are shown below escaping on horseback from a prairie fire in a painting by a modern Indian artist, Blackbear Bosin, of the Kiowa and Comanche tribes.

government. The viceroy and his assistants control the lives of the people, issuing all sorts of regulations. As you can see, the people of New Spain are far from free to do as they like.

Your affectionate son,
PHILIP

THE SPANIARDS AND THE INDIANS

ON SHIPBOARD

Dear Mother and Father,

I have been talking again with my friend, the Spanish official. One question I asked him was how the Spaniards get along with the Indians. He says that when the Spanish conquerors first reached the New World, they cared nothing for the Indians. They killed the Indians and drove them away from their homes. The Spanish government, however, did not approve of mistreating the Indians. In order to protect them and to help civilize them, the government established a new system back in the 1500's.

The Indians work for the Spaniards. When a Spanish captain had conquered a region, the land and the Indians on it were divided among him and his followers. The Spaniards were supposed to see that the Indians were treated kindly, converted to Christianity, and allowed plots of land to farm for themselves. In return, the Indians were supposed to work on the estates or in the mines of the owners for a small sum. When I asked my friend how this plan worked out, he shook his head and said that the Spanish landowners paid little attention to laws issued in far-off Spain. As far as I can tell, the Indians were no better off than serfs living in Europe in the Middle Ages. They were not allowed to leave the land and were forced to work the fields for the owners for no pay at all.

Spain's Empire in the New World

MAP STUDY New Spain and Peru were the two large divisions of the Spanish empire in America. What areas were included in New Spain? Note that the division called Peru was much larger than the present-day country of that name.

They were often shamefully overworked and sometimes almost starved. My friend says that Spanish priests tried to make the lot of the Indians easier, but found it difficult to help them. He claims, however, that even under this system the Indians were probably no worse off than they had been under the rule of the Aztecs.

The Indians become Christians. A priest who is returning to New Spain tells me that the Spaniards have tried all along to make Christians of the Indians. Spanish priests have always preached to the Indians, and they have founded churches throughout New Spain. In distant territories they have also made settlements called "missions." In these missions the priests care for the Indians and educate them as well as teach them the Catholic religion. When I reach New Spain, I shall try to visit one of these missions.

We are not far from New Spain now, and in my next letter I should be able to tell you some things I have learned first-hand. We expect to land at Veracruz and go from there to Mexico City. I am looking forward to seeing many new and interesting things when we finally arrive there.

Your affectionate son,
PHILIP

LIFE IN MEXICO CITY

In Mexico City

Dear Mother and Father,

Since I last wrote you I have reached New Spain! In this letter I shall tell you what Mexico City is like.

Mexico City is the largest and richest city in New Spain, and it is also one of the most beautiful. Part of it is surrounded by a shallow lake, so that goods for the great market place in the center of the city may travel by water as well as by land. The city is built around a large central plaza or public square where the Cathedral and viceroy's palace stand. There are also wide, well-paved roads running through the city at right angles. Where necessary, earth and stones have been thrown into the lake, and the roads have been built on top of this filled-in land. Most of the houses here are two stories high with iron balconies across the front. Each house is built around an open-air courtyard where the members of the family can sit without being seen by their neighbors or passers-by in the street.

Mexico City is the capital of New Spain. This city is different from the others in New Spain, for it is the capital. The highest officer, the viceroy, lives here. As the representative of the king of Spain he is head of the government and has many duties and responsibilities. The viceroy appoints other government officers who also live in the city. Actually, Mexico City is like the capital of Spain itself but on a smaller scale, and the viceroy and his attendants are similar to the king and his court.

Another sign that Mexico City is the capital is the great Cathedral. This beautiful church is said to be the largest in the New World. The Cathedral is the church of the archbishop of New Spain, who is the highest Catholic official in the province. The presence of the archbishop draws many officers of the Church to Mexico City,

TAXCO, an important silver-mining center, shows the kind of town built by the Spanish in the New World. Looming over the narrow streets and jumbled roofs are the twin towers of the church.

Compare the "Spanish" city of Taxco with the Aztec capital (page 62).

MONK'S CHAIR

CANDLE HOLDER

METAL CHEST

CANDLE STICK

SETTEE

SPANISH COLONIAL FURNITURE

just as the viceroy attracts government officers. In addition to the Cathedral, there is also the University of Mexico. This university and the one at Lima, Peru, were both founded in 1551. They are the two oldest universities in the New World. There are many other less important churches and schools, too.

Mexico City is known for its splendor and ceremony. Great parades are held in honor of important events, such as the arrival of a new viceroy or the departure of an old one. Frequently there are solemn religious processions. At other times gay parties are given by the rich at their expensive homes in or near the city. These men and women dress in elegant silks and wear costly jewels. But thousands and thousands of poor people do not share in this wealth and luxury. They do all the hard work and live in miserable one-room huts on the edge of the city.

There are four classes of people in New Spain. I think you would be interested in the classes of people who live in New Spain: (1) The Spaniards born in Spain are at the very top and hold the important positions in the Church and the government. (2) The Spaniards look down on the *Creoles* (pronounced *cree'*ohls in English, cray-*oh'*lace in Spanish), who are of Spanish blood but born in New Spain. Many of the landowners, merchants, and

businessmen are Creoles. (3) Then there is a large class of *mestizos* (mes-*tee'*-sohz), who are part Spanish and part Indian. They work as laborers and skilled craftsmen in the cities, and many of them are miserably poor. (4) The lowest class in Mexico is made up of the unfortunate Indians who work in the fields and the mines, as I have told you before.

In a short time I expect to take a trip into other parts of New Spain to see what life is like away from the capital. During my journey I plan to visit Uncle Pedro.

Your affectionate son,
PHILIP

THE HACIENDAS AND THE MISSIONS

IN NORTHERN NEW SPAIN

Dear Mother and Father,

I left Mexico City some time ago and began a trip on horseback through the country. I have seen how people live in many parts of New Spain. I want to tell you especially about two important ways of living in order to give you a clearer idea of the Spanish colonies.

A visit to a hacienda. First of all, I'll tell you about what are called the *haciendas* (hah-sih-*en'*duhz). These are large estates or ranches owned by rich people. They are to be found throughout

How would each of these classes be likely to **73** feel about the way Spain controlled the colony (see page 68)?

CATTLE first came to the New World in Spanish ships. This painting shows how they were unloaded. The Spaniards also introduced horses to the New World. Many of them ran wild or were captured by Indians.

the country, and I have stopped at many of them. If I describe the one owned by Uncle Pedro, you will get a good picture of them all.

Uncle Pedro's house is built around a courtyard, as are those in Mexico City. The family stays out-of-doors most of the time and therefore pays little attention to the furnishings inside the house. Near the house itself is a church where the family and the Indians worship. There are stables for horses, and not far away are many huts occupied by the Indian *peons* (*pee'*unz), or peasants, who do all the hard tasks on the hacienda. At the house they cook and clean and serve. They also take care of the crops and of the huge herds of cattle which are the chief part of their master's wealth.

Uncle Pedro, like the masters of all the haciendas, is a splendid horseman and spends many hours every day in the saddle. He rides for pleasure, and also to keep an eye upon the work being done on the hacienda. The life of the family is comfortable but not exciting. Their time is spent in entertaining visitors (like me!)

Note similarities between life on the hacienda

and in visiting their friends. Everybody who passes by is welcome at the hacienda for as long as he wants to stay. The family amuses the guests with dances, riding, and occasionally a bullfight. In these fights a wild bull is let into an enclosure where a man is waiting. The bull attacks the man, who tries to kill it with a sword.

A visit to a mission. I stayed at many haciendas besides Uncle Pedro's as I traveled northward from Mexico City. Life on the haciendas is peaceful and easy-going. It is even more peaceful in the missions, which I visited next. These missions belong to the Catholic Church. They were founded among uncivilized Indians far beyond the Spanish settlements. The courageous priests who started the missions devoted their lives to teaching the Christian faith to these Indians. They often endured severe hardships and great suffering for the sake of their religion. The priests have made Christians of the Indians nearby, and hold church services for them in the missions. Hundreds of Christian Indians live around a mission. They take care of the crops and tend the cattle

and the feudal manor (see page 18).

and do the other necessary work. At most of the missions, under the direction of the priests, the Indians have spent years and years in building churches of great beauty. These churches have heavy walls and high towers, and inside they are gorgeously decorated. The woodwork is delicately carved, and many of the churches have religious scenes painted on the walls.

Close by the churches are schools and workshops for the Indians. The Indians pass slowly back and forth — to work, to worship, and to learn. Over all gleams the brilliant sunshine; now and then the bell tolls in the tower of the church. You cannot imagine a scene more peaceful and orderly than this one.

I am soon to return home, and how glad I shall be to see you! I hope that my letters have reached you safely, and that they have given you a good idea of what I have seen of the life of the people in New Spain.

Your affectionate son,
PHILIP

The missions brought a practical kind of education as well as religion to the Indians.

This ends Philip's letters. They tell about the life in New Spain and, in fact, throughout the Spanish colonies in the New World. If Philip had visited Peru, he would have discovered some differences in the way the people lived there, but his letters in general would have been much the same.

CHECK UP

1. (a) In what ways did Spain regulate life in her New World colonies? (b) What groups of people especially profited from these regulations?

2. (a) How did Spain try to help the Indians? (b) Why were these plans not always successful?

3. (a) Describe Mexico City in the days of Spanish control. (b) What classes of people lived in New Spain?

4. (a) Describe life on the haciendas. (b) What was the purpose of the missions? (c) Describe the life of the Indians who lived around the missions.

3 How Did England and Other Nations Threaten Spain's Power?

You have learned how Spain built up a huge empire in the New World and became the leading power in Europe. How do you suppose other European powers felt about Spain's important position in the world? As you may guess, they resented the power of Spain. As smaller children may fear a bigger boy who is a bully, so the countries of Europe feared Spain. They were also jealous of her huge possessions in the New World. They believed that Spain had no more right to the riches of the new lands than they themselves had. In fact, when he heard of the Line of Demarcation dividing the newly found lands between Spain and Portugal (page 43), the king of France scornfully asked, "Who can show me the will of Father Adam leaving all the world to Spain and Portugal?" Naturally England, France, and Holland were eager to lessen the power of Spain.

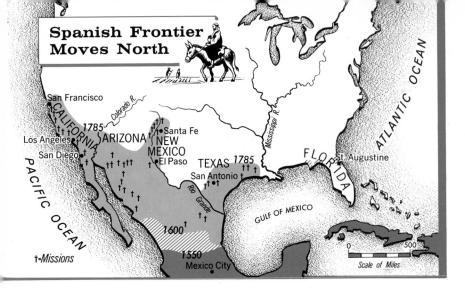

San Francisco

Colorado R.

1785

Los Angeles
San Diego

CALIFORNIA

ARIZONA

Santa Fe
†† ††
NEW
MEXICO
El Paso

TEXAS 1785

San Antonio

Rio Grande

Mississippi R.

FLORIDA

St. Augustine

ATLANTIC OCEAN

PACIFIC OCEAN

GULF OF MEXICO

1600

1550
Mexico City

†=Missions

0   500
Scale of Miles

MAP STUDY

Spanish settlers gradually followed the missions northward into what is now the United States. This map shows you how far the Spanish frontier of settlement had reached by 1550, by 1600, and by 1785.

EUROPEAN NATIONS DEFY SPAIN IN THE NEW WORLD

Spain loses trade and treasure. One way for other nations to strike at Spain was to carry on a secret trade with her colonies. Even though Spanish regulations forbade such trade, non-Spanish traders would make agreements to deliver goods in the seaport towns. They would anchor off the coast and land their merchandise at night in small boats. One English captain boldly sailed his armed ship into a port and landed 200 Negro slaves which he sold under the very eyes of the Spanish officials! This illegal trade took much wealth from the pockets of Spanish merchants.

Another way to strike at Spain was by actually attacking her merchant and treasure ships. In the 1500's, armed ships from France, Holland, and England roamed the seas. They captured Spanish ships and plundered rich towns along the coasts of Spanish America. Spain was like a dog with a piece of meat, being attacked by other dogs. The treasure and other booty snatched by these raiders cannot be valued exactly but must have been worth millions of dollars. Later on, raiding sea rovers even helped themselves to Spanish

territory. French pirates took over the western end of Hispaniola and attacked Spanish trade in the Caribbean. English pirates established themselves on the coast of Central America. Dutch pirates took over an island off the coast of what is now Venezuela.

The sea dogs of England nip at Spain. The English were the most successful in striking at Spain. When Columbus discovered the New World, England was not a powerful country. Wars between rival noble families had left her weak. Under the capable rule of Queen Elizabeth I (1558–1603), however, England rapidly grew stronger. Because England was an island, Englishmen had learned to be good sailors and skillful shipbuilders. This fact made it easier for them to prey on Spanish shipping. The captains of the English vessels which swooped down upon the ships of Spain came to be known as "sea dogs."

Francis Drake "singes the beard" of the king of Spain. The most famous of all the sea dogs was Francis Drake. Brought up in a little English coast town, he had learned the ways of the sea before he was ten years old. Drake felt a bitter hatred for the Spaniards. For many years he

England, France, and Holland, teeling threatened in the colonies and on the seas.

by Spanish might in Europe, struck at Spain

Bring out the Spanish and English viewpoints regarding Drake. This is an example of why it is difficult to write history which will not be regarded as biased by some group.

SPAIN ESTABLISHES A GREAT EMPIRE   77

proved his boldness and skill by capturing Spanish vessels and attacking Spanish towns. Once he and his men landed on the Isthmus of Panama and coolly seized a Spanish mule-train bearing costly treasure! After this the Spaniards called him "Drake the Dragon," and the king of Spain offered a sum equal to $200,000 to anyone who could kill him.

In 1577 Drake left England in his ship, the *Golden Hind,* on a dangerous expedition. The Spaniards had never been attacked in their "Spanish lake," as they boastingly called the South Sea (Pacific Ocean). Why not follow Magellan's route to the Pacific and surprise the Spaniards? Drake crossed the Atlantic, and after sixteen days of difficult sailing, succeeded in passing through the Strait of Magellan. Up the western coast of South America he sped, capturing many an unsuspecting ship and frightening the people in the coast towns. His greatest prize was the Spanish treasure ship known as the "Glory of the South Sea." Taking the ship completely by surprise, Drake seized precious stones, chests full of gold pieces, and tons of pure silver. At last the *Golden Hind* was loaded with priceless treasure.

How to return home? With all of Spanish America aroused against him, Drake decided that the longest way round was indeed the shortest way home! He continued up the coast of California, crossed the Pacific, and sailed around Africa to England (map, page 71). His expedition was the second to sail around the world. Drake's voyage was also important for other reasons. Not only had he brought home treasure that was worth millions, but he had proved that the South Sea was no more a Spanish lake than it was an English one. When he arrived home, he was given a great welcome. Queen Elizabeth, standing on the deck of the *Golden Hind,* rewarded him by making him a knight — Sir Francis Drake.

SPAIN STRIKES BACK BUT IS DEFEATED

Philip of Spain prepares to attack England. King Philip of Spain was furious at the attacks of the sea dogs on his ships and his people. Drake's latest success was too much for a king of Spain to endure. He notified the queen of England that Drake was nothing but a pirate and ought to be hanged. But Philip of Spain had a deeper reason for being angered at England. Several European countries, of which England was one of the most important, had broken away from the Roman Catholic Church earlier in the 1500's. As

SIR FRANCIS DRAKE has captured a Spanish galleon and is towing it in this picture of the battle with the Armada. Note that a sail has fallen across the bow of the Spanish ship.

Spain's trade and commercial policies, involvement in a series of wars, and failure to develop a sound economy were other reasons.

78   EUROPEAN NATIONS COLONIZE THE NEW WORLD

the most powerful Catholic ruler in Europe, Philip decided that the time had come to crush England. He gathered a fleet of 130 war vessels, put on board 19,000 soldiers and 8000 sailors, and sent them to attack England. This great expedition was called the *Invincible Armada,* which means "unconquerable fleet."

The Spanish Armada is defeated. When the Armada reached the English Channel, it was met by about 150 English vessels. Among the commanders of the English fleet were Sir Francis Drake and Captain Martin Frobisher, the explorer. The English ships could move about faster and shoot better than those of the Spaniards. They darted back and forth around the ships of the Armada, firing quickly and sailing away before the heavy enemy ships could return their fire. The English also launched fire ships and let them drift among the Spanish vessels.

For days the battle raged, but finally the Spaniards fled up the English Channel with the English in pursuit. Then nature came to England's aid. A fierce gale blew

up, and many of the enemy ships which had survived the battle were driven ashore or swamped. The rest of the Armada was hopelessly scattered. Proud Spain had suffered a terrible defeat. She lost a third of her ships and thousands of men.

After the defeat of the Armada in 1588 Spain's power began to decline. For almost a century Spain had been the strongest nation in Europe, but England had proved to the world that Spain could be beaten. Other countries could now make settlements in parts of the New World not controlled by Spain, without fear of interference. In the next chapter, for example, we shall learn how the English founded colonies in North America.

CHECK UP

1. (a) Why were other nations jealous of Spain? (b) How did they strike at Spain's power?

2. How did England win a great naval victory over Spain?

"What Do You Think?" encourages the student to use concepts developed in the chapter in new contexts. Many of these questions require the use of such skills as the ability to outline, to draw conclusions, and to compare and contrast.

Check Up on Chapter 3

Do You Know the Meaning?

1. mission	4. hacienda	7. peon
2. Creole	5. sea dog	8. conquistador
3. caballero	6. mestizo	9. viceroy

Can You Identify?

1. Balboa
2. Ponce de Leon
3. South Sea
4. Cortés
5. Pizarro
6. Coronado
7. de Soto
8. Incas
9. Aztecs
10. Spanish Armada
11. Drake
12. Philip II
13. New Spain
14. Moctezuma
15. Atahualpa
16. Queen Elizabeth I

Can You Locate?

1. Mexico	6. Veracruz
2. Andes	7. Hispaniola
3. Peru	8. Caribbean Sea
4. Lima	9. West Indies
5. Mexico City	10. Cuba
11. Isthmus of Panama	

What Do You Think?

1. Moctezuma considered the Spaniards bloodthirsty because they killed for gold and power. The Spaniards considered the Aztecs bloodthirsty because the Indians sacrificed human beings to their gods. Do you

What Do You Think? (Cont.)

think one practice worse than the other? Why?

2. Why was the defeat of the Spanish Armada important?

3. How were Cortés and Pizarro, with only small forces of men, able to conquer Mexico and Peru?

4. What religion would you expect to find in Mexico, Central America, and South America today? Why?

5. Some historians have argued that Spain's New World empire actually came to be a handicap to the mother country, in spite of the wealth it produced. Why do they think this? What is your opinion?

Some points to consider: inflow of precious metals caused inflation, keeping open sea-lanes to the New World was a drain on resources, "easy wealth" from the New World made Spain less interested in developing industry.

LINKING PAST AND PRESENT

Our oldest city. The oldest city in the United States was founded not by Englishmen but by Spaniards. St. Augustine, Florida, was more than forty years old when the first English settlers came to Jamestown, Virginia. Founded in 1565 to protect the land Ponce de Leon had discovered, St. Augustine was laid out like a city of Spain with a plaza or square in the center. A Spanish fort begun in the 1630's is still standing today. Other Spanish landmarks also remain — the cathedral, the ancient schoolhouse, and the oldest house of any kind in the United States. St. Augustine today is a resort town and a shipping center.

Spanish names live on. The Spaniards who came to the New World left lasting evidence of their explorations in Florida and the Southwest. We find towns and cities, mountains and rivers, and even states with Spanish names. Florida, for instance, was named by the Spanish explorer Ponce de Leon. Because it was Easter time when he reached the new land, he named it "Florida" after the Spanish name for Easter — *Pascua florida.*

As for the name "California," the story goes that in the 1500's people in Europe were reading a book about an imaginary island rich in gold and jewels and called California. When ship captains returned to Mexico from exploring our southwest coast, they described the land in glowing terms to Cortés. He remarked, "Yes, this must truly be the island of California." And so, in spite of the geographical error, the land was named. The states of Colorado, Nevada, and Montana also have Spanish names.

Many towns and cities in our Southwest date back to Spanish days. In 1609 a group of young Spanish caballeros founded the city of Santa Fe ("Holy Faith") in New Mexico. Their descendants still live there, proud of their ancestry and of their old adobe houses built over 300 years ago. In Texas, such cities as San Antonio ("Saint Anthony") and El Paso ("the pass") were founded by the Spaniards. Most of the 21 missions founded in California have become towns and cities and still keep their Spanish names — San Diego, San Francisco, Santa Barbara, and so on. In 1781 the Spaniards founded a town which they called *Nuestra Señora la Reina de Los Angeles* ("Our Lady the Queen of the Angels"). That tiny Spanish town has become the third largest city in the United States. Its long Spanish name has been shortened to Los Angeles.

Many geographical names in the Southwest are also Spanish: Sierra Nevada ("snowy mountain ridge"); Colorado ("red") River; Rio Grande ("great river"). Spanish words, too, have made their way into the English language. In our Southwest and other parts of the country, you often hear such words as plaza, corral, rodeo, patio, siesta, adobe, avocado.

Englishmen Establish Vigorous
Colonies in North America

Ask your pupils to "translate" the words of the
poem into their own "language."

What this chapter is about —

. . . The heavy night hung dark
The hills and waters o'er,
When a band of exiles moored their bark
On the wild New England shore.

Not as the conqueror comes,
They, the true-hearted, came;
Not with the roll of the stirring drums,
And the trumpet that sings of fame. . . .

What sought they thus afar?
Bright jewels of the mine?
The wealth of seas, the spoils of war?
They sought a faith's pure shrine!

Most of you are familiar with these verses from the poem about the Pilgrims and their landing on the shores of New England. Unlike the dashing Spanish conquerors, these simple English folk sought homes in a New World. Their interest was not in treasure — the "bright jewels of the mine" — but in beginning a new life, a life in which they would be free to worship as they chose.

Even before the Pilgrims landed at Plymouth, another settlement had been made far to the south in what is now Virginia. In the years that followed, still other groups landed along the coast of North America. These settlers came to the New

People in our story — colonial proprietor, Virginia settler, Puritan settler and wife, and Quaker.

World for many different reasons. Most of them were English men and women, though there were also people from many European countries. Out of the various settlements founded by these people grew the English colonies, which, in turn, developed into the United States of America. In this chapter you will read about the early beginnings of our country. As you read, keep in mind these questions:

▶ 1. Why and how did Englishmen go to the New World?
▶ 2. How did the first successful English colony get its start?
▶ 3. How were the New England Colonies founded?
▶ 4. What Southern Colonies were founded?
▶ 5. How were the Middle Colonies founded?

Why and How Did Englishmen Go to the New World?

You remember that while Spain was building her huge empire in the New World, England was still a small and weak country. England's growing strength, however, was shown when she defeated the Spanish Armada. By the early 1600's, Englishmen began to take an interest in founding colonies of their own in North America.

At that time, the only way to cross the ocean was in small sailing ships. These were usually crowded and uncomfortable, and they were at the mercy of the wind and weather. It might take months to make the crossing, or the ships might be lost in the Atlantic gales and never reach their destination. The northern part of the New World was little known and unsettled. Why, then, were English men and women willing to undergo the hardships that lay ahead of them if they became colonists?

Of course, some of them went to the New World in a spirit of adventure just

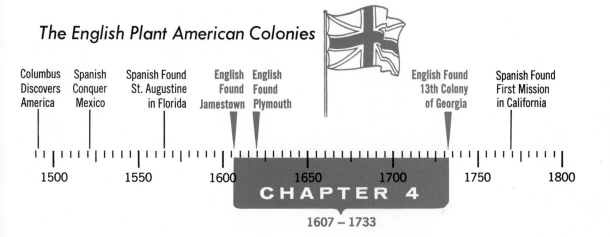

The English Plant American Colonies

| Columbus Discovers America | Spanish Conquer Mexico | Spanish Found St. Augustine in Florida | English Found Jamestown | English Found Plymouth | | English Found 13th Colony of Georgia | Spanish Found First Mission in California |

1500   1550   1600   1650   1700   1750   1800

CHAPTER 4

1607 – 1733

Why Englishmen Went to America

"You can't farm my land any longer. I can make more money raising sheep."

"You go to the same church the King goes to, or you'll go to jail!"

as the Spaniards did, hoping to find gold. But most of the English colonists had other reasons. Let us see what they were.

THE SETTLERS SOUGHT FREEDOM

America meant freedom to earn a better living. There were several reasons why English men and women were ready to leave England for the New World. For one thing, most of the English people had once been farmers. They had rented land from wealthy landowners and raised crops. But there came a time when the landowners could make more money by raising sheep and selling the wool to be made into clothing. So the landowners fenced off much of the farm land and made it into pastures for the sheep. Only a few men were needed to tend the large flocks which grazed on the land where formerly many people had lived.

For this reason large numbers of unfortunate people were not only homeless but jobless as well. They wandered about looking for work. Many were forced to

beg or steal food. The government in England treated such wanderers very harshly. But the New World offered these people a chance to make a better living.

America meant greater freedom to own land. In England in the early 1600's, there were many people who could never hope to own land. Land belonged chiefly to the upper classes and was handed down to the oldest son, so that younger sons had no land of their own. But in the New World there was plenty of land for everyone. Even poor people could become landowners in America.

America meant freedom of religion. There was still another reason why men left England. In Europe in the 1600's the ruler of a country usually controlled the religion of his subjects. People were not free to worship as they wished. In England, for example, the people were supposed to accept the king as the head of the Church of England.[1] They were ex-

[1] The Episcopal Church in America today has a form of worship similar to that of the Church of England.

The four frames in the cartoon are discussed in this **82** order in the narrative: 1, 4, 2, 3. Mark Twain's story, The Prince and the Pauper, describes the inequalities which existed in England at a somewhat earlier period.

"The King will do all the governing from now on. He doesn't want any complaints from you!"

"In America there are acres of land, just for the taking — gold, too, and furs! No King's officers to bother you! Just sign here for your passage!"

pected to attend the services of this church, agree to its teachings, and give money for its support.

Many Englishmen did not like these religious restrictions. Devout Catholics could not accept the teachings of the Church of England which differed from those of the Catholic Church. They also believed it wrong to accept anyone but the Pope in Rome as the rightful head of the Church. On the other hand, there were people who felt that the Church of England was too much like the Catholic Church. These people wanted either to make more changes in the Church of England or to separate from it entirely and set up their own church organizations. But all who did not obey the religious laws of England, no matter what the reason, were likely to be severely punished. Many Englishmen wished to go far away, to America, and there be free to worship as they pleased.

America meant freedom to share in government. Although the people in England during the 1600's had more rights

than those in many lands, they were not satisfied with their government. King James I (who followed Queen Elizabeth) and his son Charles I believed that God had given to kings the right to govern their kingdoms. James and Charles thought that their subjects should accept without question whatever the king felt was good for them. Many Englishmen believed they were losing their rights under such a government. If they went to colonies in America, might they not regain the right to share in their government? They were willing to trade the comforts of their old homes for freedom in a new land.

HOW COLONIES WERE STARTED

Suppose you were an Englishman of the 1600's and you wanted to settle in America for one of the reasons just described. What would you do? You couldn't start across the Atlantic Ocean in the first rowboat you found! You would have to get in touch with men who were interested in founding colonies.

It is important to note that the English were less **83** oppressed than most European peoples. This fact helps to explain why they wished still greater freedom.

It has been said that "The upper classes sent their purses and not their persons." Note that the British government did not control the colonization movement in the same way as had the Spanish government.

84   EUROPEAN NATIONS COLONIZE THE NEW WORLD

Trading companies finance colonies.
No matter what your personal reason for going to the New World might be, most of the men who wanted to establish colonies were interested in making money. You remember how rich the Portuguese merchants had grown from their trade with India. English merchants and businessmen wanted colonies in the New World for the same reason — they hoped to grow rich by founding colonies and trading with them. But not many individual merchants had enough money to fit out ships and to stand the losses if these were sunk. So groups of merchants formed trading companies. Each merchant paid in a share of the money needed, and each expected to receive a share of the profits.

A charter must be obtained. Besides money for ships and supplies, two other things were necessary before a colony could be started. These were (1) per-mission to settle in a certain region; and (2) the right to set up a government there. Permission to settle and to establish a government was granted by the king in a document, or paper, called a *charter*. Usually charters were given to trading companies. Sometimes, however, they were given to rich nobles who were friends of the king. Nobles who founded colonies were called *proprietors*. Both proprietors and trading companies needed men and women willing to make the long, dangerous voyage to colonies in America. So, if you wanted to settle in America, you would find it necessary to seek out a proprietor or a trading company and make the necessary arrangements.

Poor people can go to the New World.
If you had some money, as many colonists did, you would be expected to pay for your passage and for your supplies. But if you had no money, you could still get

THESE THREE SHIPS are models of the tiny vessels that brought the first English settlers to Jamestown. Here they are shown anchored in the James River for the celebration of the 350th anniversary (1957) of the founding of Jamestown.

Be sure that your pupils understand that indentured servants were neither slaves nor serfs.

ENGLISHMEN ESTABLISH VIGOROUS COLONIES

85

to the colonies, provided you were willing to give up your freedom for a few years. You could make a bargain with the ship's captain for your passage. He would transport you without cost and would collect the price of your passage from someone in the colony who wanted to buy your services. You would then have to repay this person by working for him during a certain period of time — from four to seven years. You would be called an *indentured servant.* When you had served out your time, you could then take up land of your own. Such an arrangement may seem to us like a hard bargain, but thousands of people seized the opportunity to come to the English colonies as indentured servants.

We know now why Englishmen were willing to become colonists and what arrangements had to be made to get colonies started. In the rest of this chapter we shall learn how the Thirteen English Colonies were actually founded.

CHECK UP

1. For what reasons did Englishmen settle in the New World?

2. (a) What was a trading company? (b) What things were needed in order to start a colony?

Summarizing paragraphs often provide a transition to the next section of the chapter.

2 How Did the First Successful English Colony Get Its Start?

Starting a settlement in a new and distant land, as you can well imagine, was far from easy. Indeed, the first attempts of Englishmen to found a colony in the New World met with failure.

Sir Walter Raleigh's attempt to start a colony fails. In the latter part of the 1500's, at a time when the English sea dogs were swooping down on Spanish treasure ships, there lived an adventurous Englishman named Sir Walter Raleigh. Raleigh persuaded Queen Elizabeth to let him try to establish a colony in the New World. He sent out an expedition which explored the coast of what is now North Carolina and found good soil and favorable climate. To this general region the name of Virginia was given.

Although Raleigh spent a large sum of money, his efforts to plant a colony in the New World ended in failure. A group of colonists sent out to the island of Roanoke, off the Carolina coast, mysteriously disappeared. When a ship from England visited Roanoke some years later, it found no sign of the colony; the fort was deserted and the people had vanished. To this day no one knows exactly what happened to the lost colony of Roanoke. After this failure, 20 years passed before another attempt was made to found an English colony.

Jamestown is founded. On a day late in April, 1607, three little ships sailed into the mouth of Chesapeake Bay. The men aboard them had spent many long and dreary days crossing the Atlantic. But relief filled their hearts as they drew near the shores which were clad in the soft green of spring. Near the southern end of the bay they found the mouth of a wide river. Guiding their vessels slowly up this river, they finally chose a pleasant spot to go ashore. There they set to work to build a village.

These men who arrived in America in 1607 were colonists sent out by the *London Company*. The London Company had been formed to develop trade in North America. It had a charter from King James I to make settlements along the coast of what are now the states of Virginia and North Carolina. In honor of James I, the colonists named the river the *James* and their village *Jamestown*. (See map on page 87.)

Life is difficult in Jamestown. Brave people these were, to leave their homeland and cross 3000 miles of ocean to set up new homes in an unknown wilderness! And they needed to be brave, for many hardships and dangers awaited them. They fell sick from drinking the river water and from the dread fever carried by mosquitoes from nearby swamps. Hostile Indians lurked in the surrounding forests, ready to attack the settlers at every opportunity.

Food was scarce in those early days. Yet quite a few of the colonists foolishly spent their time digging for gold instead of planting crops. Many of the men were unused to hard work, and considered themselves too good to labor with their hands. For food, therefore, the colonists depended upon wild fowl and animals, the scanty supplies which might come from England, and what corn they could obtain from the Indians. By autumn of the first year barely one third of the men who had first set foot at Jamestown were still alive.

John Smith becomes the leader. Very likely the little settlement would have perished completely in those early years but for the efforts of one man, Captain John Smith. It was Captain Smith who saw to it that defenses were built against the Indians. He was firm in his dealings with the Indians and forced them to show respect for the new colony. Smith also insisted that the men work, that they plant corn for food and not spend their time digging for gold. He established the policy of "no work, no food." Even a lazy man will work rather than starve! In September, 1609, however, Captain Smith was badly burned by an explosion of gunpowder. He went back to England to receive treatment for his burns and to escape some violent quarrels with other colonists. He never returned to Virginia.

Jamestown is saved. Dark days fell upon Jamestown after the departure of Captain John Smith. Food was so scarce in the winter of 1609–10 that it was known as the "starving time." When spring came, the 60 men who remained alive were ready to give up and go back to England. But just as they reached the mouth of the river, they met several ships bringing supplies and more colonists. Greatly encouraged, they returned to the settlement. Jamestown was saved from failure.

The colony grows stronger. Fortunately, the bitter struggle of these early years at Jamestown was not repeated. The little settlement grew steadily stronger. More settlers came from England, among them men who were skilled in carpentry or some other useful trade. The early settlers at Jamestown had been men and boys, but in 1619 a shipload of women settlers came over from England. Now the men were able to marry and establish homes.

MAP STUDY

The Thirteen English Colonies and their earliest settlements stretched along the Atlantic coast. (1) Which were the New England Colonies? (2) The Middle Colonies? (3) The Southern Colonies? Notice that people from Massachusetts helped to settle the other New England Colonies (see close-up at lower right).

References to particular maps reflect the maps. Point out to students how following up such references will help them understand what they read in the Text.

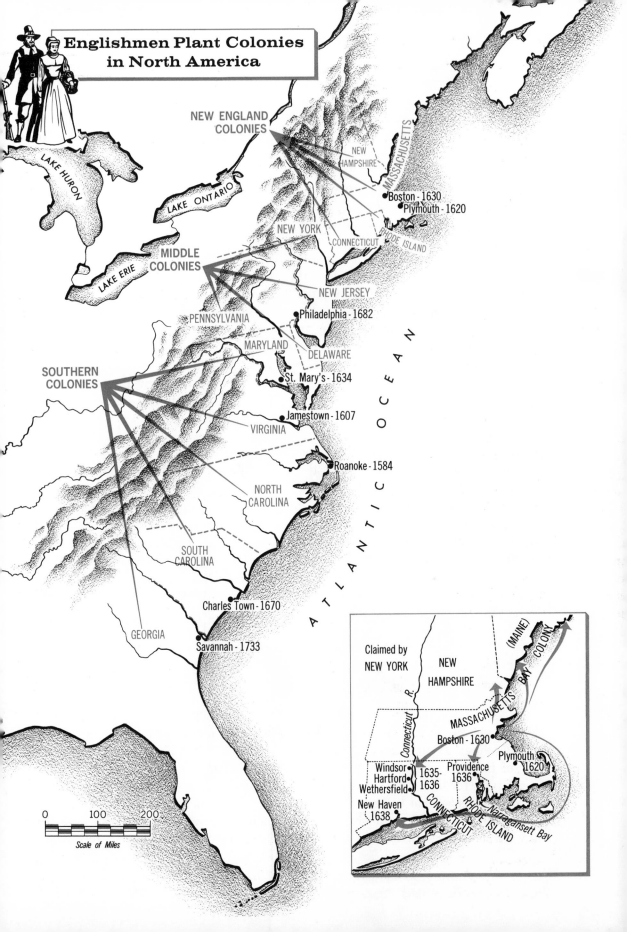

Englishmen Plant Colonies in North America

LAKE HURON

LAKE ONTARIO

LAKE ERIE

NEW ENGLAND COLONIES

NEW HAMPSHIRE

MASSACHUSETTS

Boston - 1630
Plymouth - 1620

NEW YORK

CONNECTICUT

RHODE ISLAND

MIDDLE COLONIES

NEW JERSEY

PENNSYLVANIA

Philadelphia - 1682

MARYLAND

DELAWARE

St. Mary's - 1634

SOUTHERN COLONIES

Jamestown - 1607

VIRGINIA

Roanoke - 1584

NORTH CAROLINA

SOUTH CAROLINA

Charles Town - 1670

GEORGIA

Savannah - 1733

ATLANTIC OCEAN

0   100   200
Scale of Miles

Claimed by NEW YORK

NEW HAMPSHIRE

(MAINE)

MASSACHUSETTS BAY COLONY

Connecticut R.

Boston - 1630

Windsor
Hartford   1635-
Wethersfield 1636

Providence
1636

Plymouth
1620

New Haven
1638

CONNECTICUT

RHODE ISLAND

Narragansett Bay

One of the early settlers, named John Rolfe, learned from the Indians how to produce fine tobacco. This plant was unknown to Europeans until they learned about it from the American Indians. Smoking soon became popular in England, so the Jamestown colonists found it easy to sell all the tobacco they could grow. The colony at last began to prosper. Workers were needed to grow tobacco, and many indentured servants were imported. About this time, also, a Dutch vessel brought a shipload of Negro indentured servants from Africa to Jamestown. The Negroes proved very useful as workers in the tobacco fields. Small farms gave way to larger plantations. The colony now spread far beyond the limits of Jamestown and became known as Virginia.

The settlers are given a voice in their government. Jamestown began as a colony of the London Company, and for some time it was ruled by men selected by the Company. In 1619, however, when the colony of Virginia was twelve years old, the settlers were allowed to choose representatives from their own number to help make laws for the colony. This group of representatives was called the *House of Burgesses.* The colonists now had a part in their government.

People who choose the men and women to make their laws are said to have *representative government.* The establishment of the House of Burgesses in 1619 is important because it helped plant the idea of representative government, or self-government, in the colonies of England.

•

Jamestown was the first successful English settlement in what is now the United States. During the next hundred years or so, twelve other English colonies were established on the Atlantic coast. So that the story of their founding will be clearer, we shall divide these colonies into three groups: (1) the New England Colonies; (2) the Southern Colonies; (3) the Middle Colonies.

CHECK UP

1. (a) Why was life hard for the early settlers of Jamestown? (b) How did conditions improve?

2. How did the Jamestown colonists obtain a share in their government?

In theory all Englishmen were represented in Parliament. The English colonists felt they were represented in their colonial assemblies but found it hard to believe they were represented in a Parliament 3000 miles away.

3 How Were the New England Colonies Founded?

SETTLEMENTS ARE MADE IN MASSACHUSETTS

At the same time that the first settlers were landing at Jamestown, another group of English people moved to the city of Leyden in Holland. These were humble men and women who at home had wished to separate from the Church of England and worship as they saw fit. For this rea-son, they were called *Separatists.* Because they had been persecuted in England, they fled to Holland. But they were not happy there. The language, customs, and people of Holland seemed strange to them. These English wanderers, or *Pilgrims,* as they later came to be called, did not want their children to forget English ways. Also, the Separatists were farmer folk who did

JOHN SMITH

went looking for adventure as a soldier in Europe before turning west to help colonize America.

A HARD FIGHTER against the Turks in eastern Europe, Smith finally was wounded and captured in battle. Sold as a slave in Turkey, he finally escaped and made his way back to England. There he soon decided that the New World might be a better place for an active young man and joined a party of colonists which arrived in Virginia in 1607.

BREAD-WINNER for the starving colonists of Jamestown, Smith bartered with suspicious Indians for corn. He kept the colony alive for two years until an injury forced him to return to England.

AS AN EXPLORER, Smith came back to America after he recovered from his wounds. He cruised up and down the New England coast looking for good places to plant new colonies. When he returned to England, he made a careful map of his discoveries and wrote a book praising the New World as a rich land.

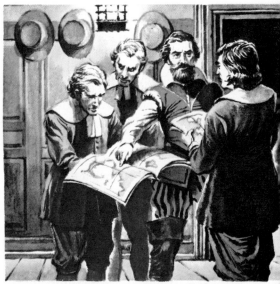

A GOOD SALESMAN for the New World, Smith tirelessly showed his book and map to would-be colonists, including the Pilgrims who later settled Plymouth. Although he never returned to America, he encouraged many Englishmen to go there.

THE INDIAN SAMOSET startled the Pilgrims by greeting them in English. He had learned a few words from fishermen who had touched the New England shore. Samoset and the Pilgrims became good friends.

not like working in a city. They decided to seek new homes in America.

The Pilgrims go to America. Some of the Pilgrims returned to England to make plans for their new venture. They were joined by other Separatists who wished to leave England. Because they were poor people, they had to get help. One of the trading companies agreed to furnish a ship and supplies. In return, the Pilgrims agreed to work for seven years as servants of the company. Everything they produced was to go to the company except supplies which they needed for their own use.

In September, 1620, the Pilgrims set sail from Plymouth, England, in a tiny vessel called the *Mayflower*. There were 102 persons on board. Fierce Atlantic storms drove the *Mayflower* far north of her destination. In November, 1620, she finally came to anchor in a harbor in what is now Massachusetts. The charter of the Pilgrims gave them permission to settle on land owned by the London Company in Virginia. But the land they had reached was outside of the region owned by the Company. What were they to do?

The Pilgrims plan a government. Before they went ashore from the *Mayflower*, some of the men gathered in the little cabin to discuss their problem. Because their charter did not hold good in their new location, they decided they would make their own plans for managing their affairs. After thinking about the kind of life they wanted to lead, they drew up an agreement in which they said:

✳ In the name of God, Amen. We whose names are underwritten, . . . having undertaken . . . a voyage to plant the first colony in the northern parts of Virginia, do . . . solemnly [agree] to enact . . . such just and equal laws . . . from time to time, as shall be thought [best] for the general good of the Colony, unto which we promise all . . . obedience.

This important agreement is known as the *Mayflower Compact*. Later on, a governor was chosen and laws were made. When the settlement grew larger, the people elected representatives to an assembly. Here, as in Jamestown, the beginnings of self-government appeared early in the life of an English colony.

The Pilgrims settle in Plymouth. The Pilgrims landed on the bleak shore and gave the name of Plymouth to their settlement. The dangers and discomforts they faced were described by one of their leaders in these words:

★They had now no friends to welcome them, nor inns to entertain or refresh their weatherbeaten bodies, no houses or much less towns to repair to, to seek for succor [help]. . . . And for the season, it was winter, and they that know the winters of that country know them to be sharp and violent and subject to cruel and fierce storms, dangerous to travel to known places, much more to search an unknown coast. Besides, what could they see but a hideous and desolate wilderness full of wild beasts and wild men? And what multitudes there might be of them they knew not.

During the next few months, over half the little band perished of cold, hunger, and disease. When spring came, however, the remaining Pilgrims decided to stay in this new land rather than return to England. In spite of hardships, they had freedom to worship as they chose and to govern themselves.

Life in Plymouth became more bearable as time went on. Friendly Indians taught the Pilgrims how to hunt, to fish, and to plant corn. Under Governor William Bradford they finally settled their debts with the London merchants and obtained the rights to the land they lived on. As time passed, the Plymouth Colony grew stronger, though it never became very large.

The Puritans establish Massachusetts Bay Colony. Plymouth Colony soon had a neighbor. This was the Massachusetts Bay Colony, which was founded by English people known as *Puritans*. The Puritans did not wish to separate from the Church of England, as the Separatists did, but wanted to change or "purify" the Church. But like the Separatists, they

were persecuted by the English government for their religious beliefs. Most of the Puritans were well-to-do, middle-class Englishmen. Some already belonged to a trading company called the Massachusetts Bay Company, which had been granted land and a charter by the king. They said, "If the Separatists can make a success of a colony in the New World, so can we. Why not buy out those company members who do not wish to go to America, and move our whole Massachusetts Bay Company and its charter across the Atlantic Ocean to Massachusetts?" And this is just what they did.

JOHN WINTHROP, the Puritan leader, scans the Massachusetts shore before leaving ship to take charge of the new colony.

Note that the settlers of Massachusetts Bay brought their charter to America. Why was this important?

WATER POWER was important to settlers in all the colonies. This colonial mill in Virginia was powered by the tides of Chesapeake Bay. The tide coming in from the Bay (at right) turned the mill wheel as the pond (left) filled with water.

The Puritans arrive in Boston. In the spring of 1630, eleven vessels filled with colonists left old England for New England. An important Puritan named John Winthrop was the governor of the colony. There was no trouble getting colonists, for at that time the Puritans were being persecuted more severely than ever in England. Before the summer was over, 2000 men, women, and children had settled in Boston or nearby.

Although many more colonists arrived in the next ten years, the Puritans had a constant struggle to make a living on the rocky soil of New England. The winters were cruelly cold, and large numbers died of disease. But the Puritans were sturdy, courageous people, and their leaders were able men. It was not long before mills were built to grind grain and saw lumber, and a few shops started to make much-needed household articles. The colonists began to carry on a lively trade with England, exchanging furs, fish, and lumber for goods they needed.

Massachusetts Bay and Plymouth unite. Massachusetts Bay Colony, which began with a larger number of people than had founded Plymouth, grew more rapidly than its neighbor. In 1691 the two col-

onies were united, and from that time on they were called Massachusetts. Plymouth itself was never considered one of the Thirteen Colonies.

The Puritans refuse religious freedom to others. Strange though it may seem to us, the Puritans who had come to Massachusetts to worship in their own way were not willing to allow others to do the same. Persons who were not members of the Puritan Church might live in the Bay Colony if they obeyed the strict Puritan rules, but they could have no share in the government. They had to pay taxes to support the Church, but they were not permitted to criticize it. As you can see, there was no real religious freedom among the Puritans. The idea of respecting the religion of others, or religious *tolerance,* was unheard of in early Boston.

OTHER COLONIES ARE SETTLED IN NEW ENGLAND

Rhode Island is founded. The strict Puritan rule in Massachusetts Bay led some settlers to leave that colony and start other colonies in New England. Soon after the Bay Colony was founded, for example, a young minister named Roger

It was commonplace in Europe at this time to deny the full rights of citizenship to people who did not belong to the state church.

Williams began to preach ideas that displeased the Puritan leaders. He said that the white men had no right to the lands they had cleared and settled unless they bought them from the Indians. He also insisted that every man had the right to worship God as he saw fit.

The Puritan leaders were so angered by these ideas that they decided to send Roger Williams back to England. Learning of their plans, Williams fled from Massachusetts Bay Colony in the winter of 1636. He was aided by the Indians, who looked upon him as their friend. He moved southward from one Indian village to another until he reached the shores of Narragansett Bay. There he settled, with five friends, at the place where the city of Providence now stands. Other settlers also made their homes nearby, and in time the colony became known as Rhode Island. (See page 107 for a picture biography of Roger Williams.)

The Rhode Islanders did not agree among themselves on many questions, but they did hold fast to one idea — that each person had the right to worship God in his own way. For the first time, religious freedom was permitted by the people of an American colony. Gradually, the idea of freedom of religion, like the idea of self-government, came to be accepted in the remaining English colonies.

Colonists from Massachusetts settle Connecticut and New Hampshire. The Rhode Islanders were not the only people who left Massachusetts Bay Colony to start settlements where they could live according to the ideas they thought best. A pastor of the Bay Colony, Thomas Hooker, had a number of followers who wanted to worship in their own way. They also thought they could find better land for farming. In the same year that Roger Williams began his settlement at Providence (1636), Hooker and his followers left Massachusetts. Taking their cattle and whatever belongings they could carry, they pushed westward through the wilderness until they reached the broad Connecticut River. Hooker's group and other colonists from Massachusetts built villages at Hartford, Windsor, and Wethersfield. Still another group, seeking to follow its own ideas of worship, started a trading center at New Haven. After a good many years the different settlements in this region were united into a single colony known as Connecticut.

Meanwhile, small settlements had been made north of the Bay Colony by men from England. Adventurous settlers from Massachusetts Bay joined with these groups from England to make the beginnings of the colony of New Hampshire. (Find Connecticut, Rhode Island, and New Hampshire on the map, page 87.)

CHECK UP

1. (a) Why did the Pilgrims decide to go to America? (b) What help did they get? (c) What steps did the Pilgrims take to form a government for their colony?

2. (a) How was Massachusetts Bay Colony founded? (b) Why did it grow rapidly?

3. (a) What other colonies were founded by people from Massachusetts? (b) Why were these colonies established?

COLONIAL HOUSES

EARLY BARK WIGWAM   LOG HOUSE   SALT-BOX HOUSE   DUTCH HOUSE

4 What Southern Colonies Were Founded?

The settlement of one southern colony, Virginia, was described earlier in this chapter. Other southern colonies soon followed.

As we have learned, the kings of England sometimes granted large tracts of land to nobles, who became known as owners or proprietors of this land. The proprietors rarely came to America themselves, but they held control of the land granted to them. They in turn could establish colonies and parcel out sections of land to settlers. Colonies established in this way on land owned by proprietors were known as *proprietary colonies*. The earliest of these proprietary colonies to be settled was Maryland.

Maryland offers religious toleration. Two shiploads of colonists landed in 1634 near the mouth of the Potomac River. Here they founded a settlement called St. Mary's. These people had been sent out from England to establish a colony on land given by the king to Lord Baltimore. Baltimore was a devout Catholic. He hoped not only to gain some profit from the colony but also to provide a refuge where Catholics might worship as they wished. This did not mean, however, that only Catholics could make their homes in the colony.

Many settlers soon flocked to Maryland, as Lord Baltimore's colony came to be called. Other towns were founded, including a settlement called Baltimore. For the most part, Maryland was a colony of farmers. Wealthier folk and those who would bring other settlers to Maryland obtained large estates. Less fortunate people were able to purchase small farms. In addition to paying for their land, all paid a small tax to the proprietor.

In time, the Catholics in the colony were outnumbered by the people of other religious beliefs. In 1649, at the urging of the proprietor, a law called the *Toleration Act* was passed. This act said that no man who was a Christian should be persecuted because of his beliefs. Under the Toleration Act both Catholics and Protestants were free to worship in their own ways. The Toleration Act of Maryland was another important step toward religious freedom in the colonies.

Stamp collectors can bring in many more stamps which tell about this country's early history.

AMERICAN POSTAGE STAMPS honor the founding of colonies as refuges for people not welcome in Europe. From left, the stamps show (1) two ships bringing the first Catholics to Maryland. (2) People of other religions also came to Maryland, like the Puritans shown arriving from Virginia in a small boat. (3) William Penn founded Pennsylvania for Quakers, and (4) James Oglethorpe brought debtors to Georgia.

Proprietors settle the Carolinas. South of Maryland was Virginia, and south of Virginia lay a vast stretch of land which Charles II, king of England, had given to a group of noblemen. They called the region Carolina after the Latin name for Charles, *Carolus*. In 1670, a group sent out by these proprietors founded a settlement which they called Charles Town (later Charleston), also after the king. Even before this date, people from Virginia had made their way into the northern part of Carolina.

In time, the colony broke up into two parts. North Carolina included the settlements founded by Virginians. South Carolina included Charles Town and other nearby settlements. (Look at the map on page 87.) South Carolina, especially, grew rapidly. The fertile soil and warm climate encouraged tobacco raising. Later on, rice also became an important crop. Large plantations, worked by indentured servants and by many Negro slaves, grew up. The fine harbor of Charles Town made it easy to trade with England.

Georgia is founded by James Oglethorpe. Between South Carolina and Spanish Florida lay a large tract of land which was not colonized for a long time. Finally, a man named James Oglethorpe made a settlement on this land. There were two main reasons for founding a colony here: (1) The English were anxious to prevent Spain from extending its settlements north from Florida. The planting of an English colony south of the Carolinas would help to keep the Spaniards out. (2) Oglethorpe was much interested in the unfortunate people who were sent to English prisons simply because they could not pay their debts, or because they had committed some trifling crime. Oglethorpe hoped to give these prisoners, who were cruelly treated, a new start in life. He and a number of other men obtained permission from the king to make settlements in this region.

It was not until 1733 that Oglethorpe brought about a hundred settlers from England. They founded a village which was called Savannah. The colony itself was named Georgia after George II, who was then king of England. Many people from the British Isles settled in Georgia, but it grew slowly. Like the Carolinas, it became chiefly a colony of large farms or plantations.

CHECK UP

1. (a) Why was Maryland founded? (b) How was religious freedom established there?

2. How were the Carolinas settled and developed?

3. For what two main reasons was Georgia founded?

The fact that Georgia at first excluded Catholics and Negro slaves and restricted the size of land holdings were factors.

5 How Were the Middle Colonies Founded?

Between New England and the Southern Colonies there grew up another group of settlements known as the Middle Colonies. Not all of these started as English settlements. If you look at the map on page 97, you will see that New York and the Hudson River region were originally settled by the Dutch. Perhaps you remember that Henry Hudson discovered this river while he was sailing for the Dutch and that he claimed that region for Holland (page 45).

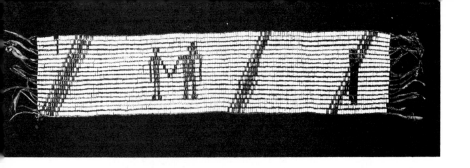

The Dutch found New Netherland. In the early 1620's, the Dutch founded a settlement, called New Amsterdam, on the island of Manhattan. They traded about $24 worth of goods to the Indians for the island. The Dutch also occupied the entire Hudson River valley, and their settlements extended from New Amsterdam to Fort Orange, where Albany, New York, is today. Large estates along the Hudson were given by the Dutch to all landlords or *patroons* who brought 50 settlers with them to work the land. Smaller plots of land were given free to others who wished to do their own farming. The whole colony was called New Netherland. In time the Dutch spread their control south to the Delaware River. There they took over some settlements that had been made earlier by Sweden. Fur trading with the Indians was the most important business of the Dutch, and New Netherland soon became a prosperous colony.

New York and New Jersey take the place of New Netherland. The founding of New Netherland by the Dutch greatly troubled the English. By looking at the map on page 87 you can see how completely New Netherland (New York) separated the New England colonies from the English settlements to the south. So long as New Netherland belonged to the Dutch, the English colonies could not be joined together. Then too, the English cast envious eyes on the splendid harbor at New Amsterdam, with its thriving trade. Bitter feeling between England and Holland in Europe gave the English an excuse to attack New Netherland.

In 1664, an English fleet appeared in the harbor of New Amsterdam. The Dutch colony was governed at that time by Peter Stuyvesant, a peppery old man with a wooden leg. Stuyvesant was eager to offer battle, but the people of New Amsterdam refused to back him up. So, in spite of

The Dutch also established themselves firmly in the East Indies.

NEW YORK by 1680 had become a prosperous village because of the fur trade. This old drawing shows the fort at the tip of Manhattan Island (left). The neat rows of houses built in the Dutch style have long since given way to towering skyscrapers.

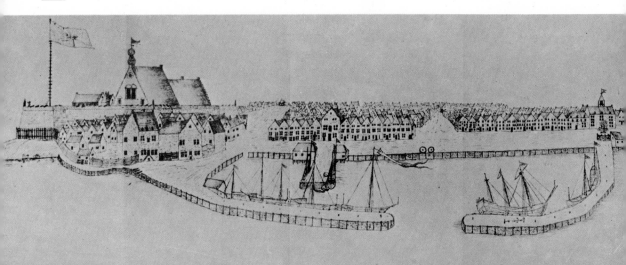

his fussing and fuming, the settlement surrendered without striking a blow, and New Netherland became an English possession. The Duke of York, the brother of the king of England, was made proprietor of the former Dutch territory, and the colony was renamed New York in his honor. The town of New Amsterdam became New York also. The land east of the Delaware River was granted by the duke to two English nobles, who gave their colony the name of New Jersey.

Pennsylvania is settled by Quakers. One of the most famous of the proprietors was William Penn. His father was an admiral in the British navy and an important man in England. Through his father young William became acquainted with the nobles who were making settlements in America.

As a young man, William Penn joined one of the most persecuted religious groups in England, the *Quakers*. The Quakers believed that they should do what their consciences told them was right. They not only refused to follow the Church of England but in many ways disobeyed the government. For example, they believed that war was wrong, and refused to take part in it. Like many other Quakers, Penn was thrown into prison for teaching what he believed to be the truth. After he was released, he was anxious to found a colony where Quakers would not be persecuted.

It happened that the king owed Penn's father a large sum of money. When his father died, Penn told the king he was willing to take a grant of land in America in payment of the debt. The king agreed to Penn's suggestion. No doubt he was very pleased to pay his debt in land and at the same time get many Quakers to leave England. The king gave the name of Pennsylvania (or "Penn's woodlands") to the region west of the Delaware River between

Dutch and Swedes Claim River Valleys

Fort Orange - 1614 (Albany)

NEW NETHERLAND 1609 - 1664

New Amsterdam - 1626 (New York)

NEW SWEDEN 1638 - 1655

Fort Christina - 1638 (Wilmington)

ENGLISH (1664)

DUTCH (1655)

ATLANTIC OCEAN

Connecticut R.

Hudson R.

Delaware R.

0   50   100
Scale of Miles

MAP STUDY The Dutch and Swedes made the first settlements in what later became the English colonies of New York, New Jersey, and Delaware. The Dutch took over the Swedish colonies in 1655, but the English seized all the Dutch lands in 1664.

the present states of New York and Maryland.

Penn's colony becomes prosperous. William Penn arrived in Pennsylvania with a group of settlers in 1682. They laid out the capital city according to Penn's plans and named it Philadelphia, which means "City of Brotherly Love." Penn believed in religious freedom and welcomed people of all faiths to his colony. Large numbers of Quakers and Englishmen of other religions flocked to Pennsylvania. People from other lands also settled in the colony. Among them were thrifty and hard-working Germans who had been treated harshly in their own country. These Germans came to be known as Pennsylvania Dutch.[1]

[1] In the German language, the word for "German" is *Deutsch (doytch),* which the English settlers mispronounced as "Dutch."

This type of problem has been solved by permitting conscientious objectors to render noncombatant service.

Penn was a wise and kind proprietor who treated his colonists fairly and expected honest work from them. The colonists found that land in Pennsylvania was cheap and easy to get. They had little fear of Indian attacks because Penn made friends with the neighboring Indians and treated them honestly. For these reasons, Pennsylvania grew rapidly and became a successful colony. By the late 1700's, Philadelphia had become the largest and busiest city in the Thirteen Colonies.

Delaware becomes a separate colony. Unfortunately, Penn's first grant of land did not include any coastline. Penn was able to obtain from the Duke of York the land now known as Delaware. This land, which had first been controlled by the Swedes, then by the Dutch, and finally by the Duke of York, became a part of Pennsylvania. A number of years later it was made into a separate colony under the name of Delaware.

•

Thus ends the story of how the Thirteen English Colonies were founded. Our next chapter will show how people lived in these English colonies.

CHECK UP

1. (a) Where did the Dutch settle in the New World? (b) Why did the English object? (c) What happened to the Dutch colony?

2. (a) Who founded and settled Pennsylvania? (b) Why did it become a successful colony? (c) How were New Jersey and Delaware settled and how did they become English colonies?

Check Up on Chapter 4

Do You Know the Meaning?

1. proprietor
2. charter
3. patroon
4. tolerance
5. representative government
6. indentured servant
7. religious freedom
8. trading company

Can You Identify?

1. Pilgrims
2. John Smith
3. 1607
4. 1619
5. 1620
6. 1630
7. Puritans
8. Roger Williams
9. Lord Baltimore
10. William Penn
11. James Oglethorpe
12. London Company
13. House of Burgesses
14. Massachusetts Bay Company
15. Toleration Act
16. Peter Stuyvesant
17. Mayflower Compact
18. Quakers
19. William Bradford
20. New Netherland

Can You Locate?

1. Boston
2. Providence
3. New Haven
4. Savannah

Can You Locate? (Cont.)

5. Charleston
6. New York (city)
7. Jamestown
8. Plymouth
9. Philadelphia
10. Delaware River
11. Connecticut River
12. Hartford

What Do You Think?

1. (a) Why were the first settlements in the New World made near mouths of rivers or bays? (b) Why did people who left the earlier settlements often settle near rivers?

2. What three colonies led the way in promoting religious tolerance? Explain why.

3. What freedoms which we cherish today had their beginnings in England and the English colonies?

4. From what you have read about the Spanish and the English colonies, which would you expect to attract more settlers? Why?

5. Some historians have said that the growing of tobacco insured the success of the Virginia colony. Explain why.

Questions 1, 2, 4 and 5 call for the ability to use information in thinking about questions that have not been answered in so many words.

Jamestown comes to life again. In 1957, Americans celebrated the 350th anniversary of Jamestown, the first English town in America. Visitors to Jamestown found themselves stepping back into the 1600's. Riding at anchor in the James River were full-sized models of the three tiny ships which brought the English settlers to Virginia. The old village with its wooden palisades had been rebuilt, and ladies and gentlemen in the dress of the 1600's strolled through the streets.

Visitors could step into thatch-roofed houses like those in early Jamestown and see in the museum the tools, weapons, and dishes used by the settlers. They could look at the old church tower, the foundation of the first government building, and the gravestones in the old graveyard.

Jamestown did not have a long life. After Williamsburg became the capital of Virginia in 1699, the little town was gradually abandoned. As years went by, the marshy peninsula became an island in the James River, and the town fell into ruins. But this old and valuable part of our American heritage has now been brought to life again and is being preserved for us and for future Americans.

Mayflower II. In the spring of 1957, the *Mayflower* sailed into Plymouth Harbor once more! *Mayflower II* was sent to America as a gift from the British people. Made of sturdy oak, the new *Mayflower* had been carefully built as much like the old Pilgrim ship as possible. The captain and the crew of about 30 were experienced in handling sailing ships; all were eager for the adventure. Except for a radio and navigation instruments which were required by law, the ship was fitted out like the original. Quarters were small; there was no refrigeration.

The food put aboard for the crew was similar to what the Pilgrims ate — dried and salted meat, ship's biscuit, and cheese — although some canned goods were added.

On April 20, *Mayflower II* set sail from Plymouth, England, for Plymouth, Massachusetts. People on both sides of the Atlantic waited eagerly for news of the gallant little ship and its crew. When the *Mayflower* finally appeared near Cape Cod, she was greeted by ships and aircraft of all kinds. Fifty-four days after setting sail, the *Mayflower* dropped her anchor in Plymouth Harbor. Captain and crew, dressed like the Pilgrims, were rowed ashore. A great crowd cheered as they watched this "landing of the Pilgrims." *Mayflower II* will remain in a permanent berth at Plymouth, a symbol of the courage and endurance of these early settlers of America.

The Dutch left their mark. Even though Holland held territory in North America for only a short time, we have many reminders today of the early Dutch settlers. Santa Claus, for instance, was introduced into this country by the Dutch colonists. They also introduced the game of bowling. The Dutch Reformed Church, now called the Reformed Church in America, has thousands of members today. In many parts of America you can see modern Dutch colonial houses, patterned after the old Dutch homes. They have sloping roofs with dormer windows, as shown on page 93, and often a "Dutch door" — that is, a door with separate upper and lower halves. They may also have a "stoop," or porch, with two seats cozily facing each other. In many villages along the Hudson River, old stone houses built by the Dutch over 300 years ago are still standing.

Perhaps some of your pupils have visited Jamestown and Plymouth and would be willing to tell what they saw.

How Did People Live in the

English Colonies?

Discuss with class the meaning of each rhyme. How does this material differ from that in a present-day primer.
What this chapter is about —

In Adam's fall
We sinned all.

Thy life to mend,
This Book attend.

The Cat doth play,
And after slay.

A Dog will bite
A Thief at night.

An Eagle's flight
Is out of sight.

The idle Fool
Is whipt at School.

This is a quotation from the *New England Primer*. If you had lived in New England in the 1700's, you would probably have learned to read and spell from this primer. As you can see, schoolbooks of colonial days were not much like ours today. In fact, in many ways life in the colonies was different from life today.

In order to understand what life was like in the English colonies, what do we need to know? Certainly we ought to know what kinds of houses the colonists lived in, how they earned their living, what clothes they wore, and what food they ate. (The picture above shows the kind of fireplace the colonists used to cook food.) We should also know about their schools, their religion, and their amusements. This

People in our story — colonial farmer and family, plantation owner, frontiersman, craftsman.

100

chapter will tell you about such things, and it will also point out how ways of living differed throughout the colonies. As you read, keep in mind these questions:

▶ 1. How did the colonists live in New England?

▶ 2. What was life like in the Southern Colonies?

▶ 3. What was life like in the Middle Colonies?

▶ 4. How did people live in the frontier region?

Do pupils know what geographical conditions caused the first settlers in your state to settle where they did? Do the same factors still influence ways of living?

How Did the Colonists Live in New England?

In different parts of the world today, ways of living are affected by *geographical conditions*. By geographical conditions we mean such things as temperature, rainfall, soil, the land surface, and so on. For example, we should not expect the Eskimos of the cold Arctic to live as the tribesmen of hot central Africa do. In somewhat the same way, people's ways of living differed in the Thirteen Colonies. Of course, geographical conditions in the English colonies did not differ as much as do conditions in the Arctic and central Africa. But they varied enough to influence the lives of the colonists.

Geographical conditions in New England and the South are different. If you will look at the map on page 115, you will see that back of the Atlantic coast

a line of hills and mountains extends from the northeast to the southwest. You will also notice that these hills and mountains are much closer to the coast in the North than in the South. This means that the Southern Colonies had much more level land for farming than did the colonies in the North. In the North the soil is full of stones, and farmers must work harder to grow crops. Then, too, the winters in the North are longer and colder than they are in the South. Farming at first was very important in all the colonies. Because of the different geographical conditions, however, farming remained important much longer in the Southern Colonies than in the Northern Colonies.

Now look again at the map. See how many rivers lead back from the coast, like

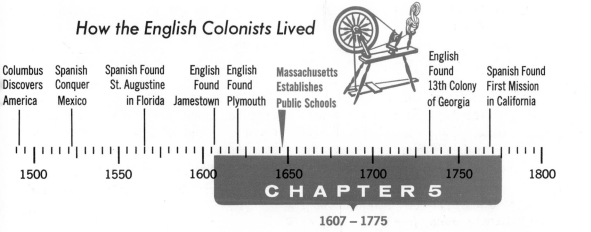

How the English Colonists Lived

| Columbus Discovers America | Spanish Conquer Mexico | Spanish Found St. Augustine in Florida | English Found Jamestown | English Found Plymouth | Massachusetts Establishes Public Schools | English Found 13th Colony of Georgia | Spanish Found First Mission in California |

1500   1550   1600   1650   1700   1750   1800

CHAPTER 5

1607 – 1775

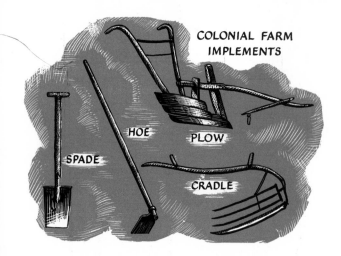

COLONIAL FARM IMPLEMENTS

SPADE

HOE

PLOW

CRADLE

threads worked into a piece of cloth. These rivers were the highways of the colonies, because no good roads existed. At the mouths of many of the rivers, especially in the North, were good harbors. Because of these good harbors, trade and shipping became important in the North.

Keeping these geographical conditions in mind, let us examine the life of the English colonies. The easiest way to do this will be to study closely one of the sections — New England — and then to compare the others with it.

New Englanders make their living in various ways. In spite of poor soil and long, hard winters, many New Englanders were farmers. (You must remember that in colonial days it was difficult to transport food long distances, so each section of the colonies had to grow its own.) Some men, however, became fishermen. In the ocean off the New England coast they caught so many fish that they could not sell them all at home. Therefore, they built ships large enough to carry the fish to sell in the other colonies, in Europe, and in the West Indies. These ships brought back goods received in exchange for the fish. All this trade called for men to build ships and to make their fittings (such as sails, rope, and anchors), and for merchants to sell the goods the ships brought home. Other men began to make articles needed

on land. In this way New England became a region of fishermen, sailors, merchants, and skilled workmen as well as farmers.

Many men in New England learned their trades by serving as *apprentices.* An apprentice was a boy who was learning a trade from a master — a sailmaker, a carpenter, a blacksmith. The boy worked for his master for several years and lived with his master's family. He received low wages while he was an apprentice, and a small sum of money and some clothes when he finished his apprenticeship. By that time he had learned his trade and could work for himself.

What was the colonial New England home like? New Englanders lived in the seaports and in small villages surrounded by farms. Their houses were plain and strongly built. If you had entered one of these houses, you would have found yourself in a small hall. To one side would be the kitchen, which also served as a dining room and living room. On the other side of the hall would be a bedroom, and there would be another bedroom upstairs. The immense fireplace in the kitchen could hold logs so big that two men were needed to put them in place. Here the mother did all the cooking in kettles hung over the fire or placed on the coals. (Look back at the picture on page 100.) The furniture was simple and homemade, and there were not many dishes or eating utensils.

Food in New England was good, and there was plenty of it. Families obtained their meat from cattle, pigs, and fowl raised at home, and the supply was increased by wild game which the men and boys shot in the forest. Almost every family had a garden and grew many of the same vegetables we eat today. Of course there were no refrigerators, and foods could

(Continued on page 105)

Make a "cause and effect" analysis of material in this paragraph.

102

The
Colonial Seaboard

When he saw the above sign in Old Saybrook, Connecticut, a weary colonial traveler knew from the picture on it that he was approaching the Black Horse Tavern.

An architect was brought over from England to design a palace (above) in New Bern, North Carolina, for William Tryon, the royal governor of the colony. Although the palace later was burned, it has now been reconstructed from the architect's plans. During the Revolution, the Tryon Palace became North Carolina's State Capitol. The stately brick building shown at right was built in Pennsylvania in 1735 to house another important branch of colonial government, the Assembly. It, too, became a patriot headquarters and gained its famous name of "Independence Hall" when the Declaration of Independence was signed within its walls in 1776.

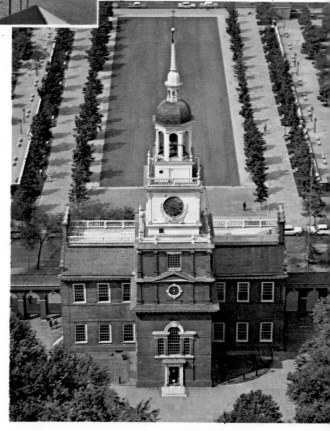

John Singleton Copley painted this portrait (left) of colonial Boston's most famous silversmith, Paul Revere. Revere-made silver, such as the punchbowl shown below, proved that the colonies need not depend on England for master craftsmanship.

Pewter dishes, the pride of the colonial housewife, are displayed in the kitchen (right) of the Thompson House in Setauket, Long Island. Game provided the colonists with part of their food. Note the wild ducks hanging near the window.

Since "do-it-yourself" was the usual rule in colonial times, women became expert at needlework. The design of the chair seat shown at left includes deer and an oak tree in the center with acorns on its branches and butterflies above it.

In Massachusetts Bay colony church and state were not separate.

HOW DID THE ENGLISH COLONISTS LIVE? **105**

not be canned as they are now. The colonists pickled and dried vegetables and kept fruits in covered stone jars for use in winter.

The family's clothes were made at home. Wool from their own sheep was spun into thread and woven into cloth by the women. Skins were tanned for shoes and for harness and for men's clothing. In winter the men wore leather breeches and heavy coats. Those who could afford it had Sunday clothes of fine cloth from England, but there were few ribbons, ruffles, or bright colors.

In the seaports one might see larger houses belonging to rich merchants and shipowners. These houses had beautiful, expensive furniture made by skilled cabinetmakers. The kitchens were used chiefly for cooking, and the family lived in large comfortable living rooms. But we must remember that all colonial houses lacked the comforts we take for granted today. They had no gas, no electricity, no central heating, no bathrooms, no running water, no telephones, no window screens, and few rugs.

Religion is important in colonial New England. In the heart of every New England village stood its church, for the New Englanders were deeply religious. Many of them were Puritans. They were conscientious people who believed that they must lead lives of righteousness. God was just, they believed, but He would surely punish evildoers. To the Puritans many things were evil and life was serious. They disapproved of light-hearted amusements such as dancing, card playing, and boisterous sports. The church was the center of their social life, and before or after services on Sunday everyone met his friends and heard the news. The Puritan ministers were stern, God-fearing men. They had great influence among the people and were consulted on every question.

You would not have enjoyed Sundays in the days of the Puritans. The churches were unheated, and the hard benches were uncomfortable. The men sat in one part of the church, and the women and girls in another. The boys usually sat together in the balcony, and if there was any noise, the offenders were punished in front of the whole congregation! Everybody was required by law to attend church services. The people listened to long sermons both morning and afternoon. Prayers alone often lasted three quarters of an hour.

Can your students figure out step by step how this work was done?

IRONWORKING was practiced by the colonists as early as the 1600's. This painting shows a scene at the Saugus ironworks in Massachusetts. Heavy rollers, powered by water wheels, flattened the hot iron into plates.

During the rest of the day, no one could work or travel or amuse himself in any way. Instead, people were expected to read the Bible and think about religion. Although we might not wish to live as the Puritans did, we cannot help admiring them. They lived in the way they thought was right, no matter how difficult that way was.

Not all New Englanders were Puritans, of course. In Chapter 4 you read how Roger Williams founded the colony of Rhode Island, which was open to settlers of different beliefs. The rules for behavior on Sunday were less strict in Rhode Island than in Puritan Massachusetts.

Punishments are severe in colonial New England. The Puritans tried to make the colonists lead righteous lives by passing many strict laws. They expected these laws to be obeyed. If the laws were broken, people were punished in ways that we would consider very cruel today. There were fifteen crimes which carried the punishment of death. There were also severe punishments for less serious crimes. For swearing, a man might have a hot iron thrust through his tongue. For getting drunk, he might have to wear a large red letter "D" around his neck for all to see.

Certain kinds of punishment were widely used in colonial days. A man who lied might have to sit with his hands and legs fastened in a board called the *stocks.* Or he might have to stand on a platform with his head and hands locked in a wooden board called a *pillory.* There was a *whipping post,* also, where a man was given a certain number of lashes with a whip on his bare back. A man or woman sentenced to the *ducking stool* was tied to a chair at the end of a long pole and ducked into a pool of water! The stocks, the pillory, and the whipping post often stood in front of the church where passers-by could jeer or even throw things at the unfortunate lawbreakers.

Of course, we must remember that these punishments were also common in England in those days. And it is not surprising that the stern Puritans believed strict punishment was the only way to keep people from breaking the laws.

New Englanders believe in education. Because it was very important for every Puritan to be able to read the Bible, more children in New England were sent to school than in any other section. In fact, as early as 1647, Massachusetts passed a law requiring all villages with a certain

THE DUCKING STOOL was ordered for this Puritan woman. She may have been guilty of gossiping or nagging at her husband. The jeers of her neighbors probably hurt more than the ducking.

ROGER WILLIAMS

left England with his young wife to seek freedom for his beliefs in the American wilderness.

Lone Journey (Unit 2 bibliography) tells the story of Roger Williams.

ACCUSED in Massachusetts of having "wrong ideas," the young minister defended himself before an assembly of Puritan leaders. Williams would not give up his demands for religious freedom and justice for the Indians, so the Puritans banished him.

A REFUGEE in the wintery woods, Williams was given shelter by the Indians he had tried to befriend. He bought a piece of land from the Indians in what is now the state of Rhode Island. There Williams established a little settlement which he named Providence.

"WELCOME!" was the greeting Williams gave to others who came to Providence to escape the harsh laws in Massachusetts and elsewhere. Williams believed that each person had a right to his own beliefs. Within the Providence colony, everyone was free to worship God in whatever way his own faith and conscience told him was right.

THE FATHER OF HIS COLONY, Williams came back from a trip to England with a charter from the king, granting his settlement independence of Massachusetts and the right to manage its own affairs.

number of families to provide schools. Reading and writing and arithmetic were about the only subjects taught. Children did not learn much more than you learn in the first few grades of school, but what they learned they learned thoroughly. *Hornbooks* taught them the ABC's. A hornbook was a wooden frame holding a piece of paper protected by a transparent covering. Textbooks were difficult and rather dull. Books like the primer mentioned on page 100 taught religion and correct conduct along with reading. Teachers were strict. A boy who misbehaved in school would be promptly switched.

In larger communities, there were a few more advanced schools called Latin grammar schools. And in 1636, only six years after the colony itself was established, Massachusetts had a college. A minister named John Harvard gave all of his books

A HORNBOOK

and half of his money to start it. Other people contributed what they could. Today Harvard College is the oldest institution of higher learning in the United States. In the early days, however, it was not much like our idea of a college, for its chief purpose was to prepare young men to be ministers.

Reading matter increases as New England grows. Everybody has to work hard just to make a living in a newly settled country. There is little spare time for reading. It is not surprising, therefore, that for many years the colonists had few books, newspapers, or magazines. But after 1700 the greatest hardships were over and more reading matter appeared. Because New Englanders were so interested in religion, some of the first books were books of sermons and books on religious subjects. Almanacs were an especially popular form of reading material. In them people could read useful information about crops, the weather, health, and so on. Almanacs were often the only reading matter in country districts. As the colonies grew older, people liked to read about their early history. And as the colonies grew larger, people read newspapers to find out what was happening

COLONIAL SCHOOLROOMS looked like this one built in 1763. Notice the British flag and the bell on the teacher's desk. What did the pupils use to write with?

108

outside their own settlement. But colonial newspapers were very different from those of today. They came out only once a week and were quite short. The news they contained was days and even weeks old.

•

Ways of living in New England differed from those in the other colonies. Now that we know what New England was like, we can compare the other sections with it.

CHECK
UP

1. Explain how the geography of a region can affect the life of the people.

2. In what ways did New Englanders make their living?

3. Describe a colonial New England home.

4. (a) In what ways did religion affect life in New England? (b) How was education provided for?

2 What Was Life Like in the Southern Colonies?

Southern climate and soil encourage the growth of plantations. The life of the South was very different from that of New England. The South even looked different. The wide plains along the southern coast were not dotted with small farms and farm villages as was the rolling New England countryside. The fertile plains were covered, instead, with large farms called plantations. In fact, the Southern Colonies are often called the "plantation colonies."

The people who settled in the South did not find a harsh climate or unfriendly soil to discourage them from farming, as did New Englanders. Instead, southern farmers found rich soil which easily produced valuable crops. Tobacco was the first and most important product. Later, rice and indigo (used in making dyes) were grown in the southernmost colonies. Such crops brought high prices, and every farmer wanted to raise as much as he could. Because these crops wore out the soil, farmers wanted to let some land lie idle each year to recover its fertility. For these reasons, successful men bought more and

more land. In this way large plantations were established.

Plantations require many workers. No plantation owner could farm his land all by himself, because the plantations often covered several hundred and sometimes even several thousand acres. The owners, therefore, needed laborers to help them. One way to obtain laborers was to hire indentured servants (including, at first, Negroes). These servants were poor people who would work for a master in America if he would pay the cost of their passage across the Atlantic. The other way in which plantation owners secured laborers was to buy Negro slaves. The master owned the slave for life and had complete control of him. The master usually preferred slaves to indentured servants, because the servants were entitled to their freedom after only a few years of work. Slavery, therefore, became widespread in the South, especially after 1700.

To supply the needs of the many workers on a large plantation was a task in itself. Many specially trained workers were needed, as you will see in the following

Worn out land was sometimes abandoned. In the late 1700's a few farmers experimented with crop rotation, but this practice did not appeal to those largely interested in a single crop.

description, written by the daughter of a plantation owner:

* My father had among his slaves carpenters, coopers, sawyers, blacksmiths, tanners, curriers, shoemakers, spinners, weavers and knitters. . . . His carpenters and sawyers built and kept in repair all the dwelling houses, barns, stables, plows, harrows, gates, etc., on the plantations. . . . His coopers made the hogsheads the tobacco was prized [packed] in. . . . The tanners and curriers . . . tanned and dressed the skins . . . to the full amount of the consumption of the estate, and the shoemakers made them into shoes for the Negroes. . . . The blacksmith did all the iron work required by the establishment, as making and repairing plows, harrows, teeth chains, bolts, etc., etc. The spinners, weavers, and knitters made all the coarse cloths and stockings used by the Negroes, and some of finer texture worn by the white family. . . .

My father kept no steward or clerk about him. He kept his own books and superintended, with the assistance of a trusty slave or two, and occasionally of some of his sons, all the operations at or about the house. . . .

Of course, not all plantations were as large as this one, nor were all Negroes taught trades. Most of the slaves were field hands, often brutally treated by white overseers. Slavery itself was debasing for both slaves and master.

Commerce grows in the South. Southern planters found it profitable to raise huge crops of tobacco and other products, which they sold to England. With the profits from these crops, they bought in England many things for their personal use, such as fine furniture and clothing. In this way a thriving trade grew up between the plantation owners and the merchants of England. Such seaports as Charleston, South Carolina, and Savannah, Georgia, became the centers of this trade.

Life on the southern plantation is different from life in New England. Instead of dwelling close together in villages as did the New Englanders, the wealthy southern colonists lived far apart on their big plantations. The best location for a plantation was on a river so that the tobacco or other crops could be loaded onto a ship from the planter's own wharf. Near the river stood the owner's house, which was often large and expensive. The kitchen usually was in a separate building so that heat from the fires would not add to the discomfort of the owner's family during the warm summers. The cabins of the servants or the slaves stood a little distance away. From the big house on the river the owner rode out to direct the work on the plantation.

The planter and his family lived a pleasant and unhurried life. Their spare time was spent in visiting or in entertaining, and in hunting, horse-racing, and other sports. The house was often gay with the laughter of friends or relatives. At parties men wore velvet coats, knee-length satin or velvet breeches, long silk stockings, and shoes with large silver buckles. The women were even more elegant, with full-skirted dresses of flowered silk and high-heeled satin shoes. The Southerners' comfortable manner of living and their stylish clothes were a contrast indeed to the stern life and somber dress of the Puritans in New England.

The South and New England also differ in matters of education and religion. In regions where ways of living were so very different, you might also expect to find differences in education and religion. Each snug New England village could have its own school, but the southern plantations were so widely scattered that the children had to be taught at home. Or, in some cases, teachers from England

Negroes did skilled work not only on the large plantations but also in the cities. Some, having gained freedom, worked for themselves.

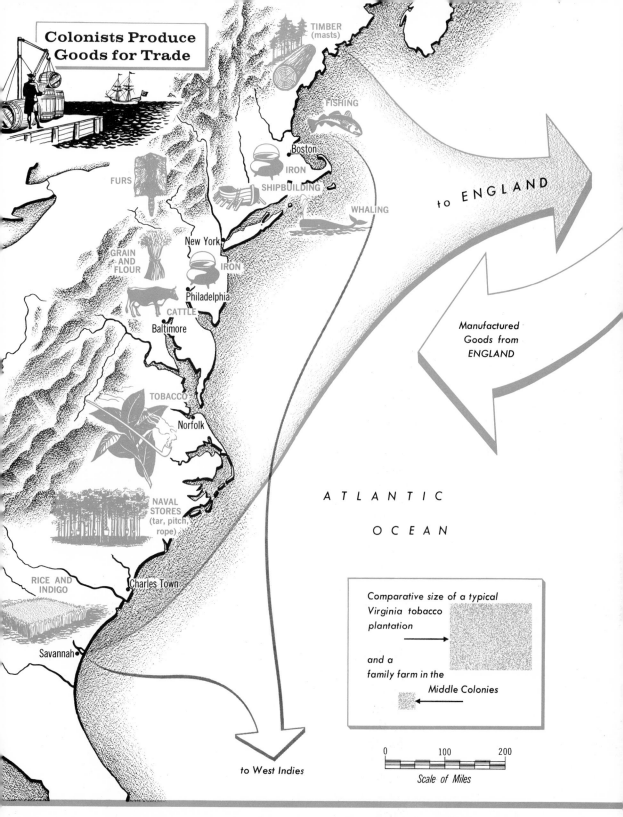

Colonists Produce
Goods for Trade

TIMBER
(masts)

FISHING

FURS

Boston

IRON

SHIPBUILDING

WHALING

to ENGLAND

Manufactured
Goods from
ENGLAND

GRAIN
AND
FLOUR

New York

IRON

Philadelphia

CATTLE

Baltimore

TOBACCO

Norfolk

NAVAL
STORES
(tar, pitch,
rope)

ATLANTIC

OCEAN

RICE AND
INDIGO

Charles Town

Savannah

Comparative size of a typical
Virginia tobacco
plantation

and a
family farm in the
Middle Colonies

to West Indies

0   100   200

Scale of Miles

MAP STUDY The chief goods produced for trade by the different colonies are named on this map. (1) What were the chief products of the New England Colonies? (2) Of the Middle Colonies? (3) Of the Southern Colonies? (Remember that farming was the most important way of earning a living in all the colonies.

This point should be stressed.

Historic Williamsburg, Virginia, has been restored and rebuilt so that it looks today as it did in colonial times.

VISITORS on the campus of the College of William and Mary meet by the statue of one of the royal governors of Virginia. This college, founded in 1693, is the second oldest in our country.

taught the children from several plantations. The sons of rich planters were often sent to college in England. Others, however, went to the College of William and Mary in Virginia. This was the second college founded in the English colonies. Because of their gay life, there was less interest in reading among the southern planters than in New England. As for the children of Negro slaves and indentured servants, little effort was made to educate them.

As education differed in the two sections, so did religion. Most of the Southerners belonged to the Church of England rather than to a strict Puritan church, like the one in Massachusetts. Although the Southerners went to church on Sunday, religion did not influence their lives as much as it did the lives of people in New England. Nor were ministers as powerful in the South as they were in New England. Punishments were severe but people were not punished for small misdeeds.

CHECK UP

1. (a) Why did large plantations develop in the South? (b) What kinds of workers were used on the plantations?

2. (a) How did the South differ from New England in home life? (b) In commerce? (c) In education? (d) In religion?

3 What Was Life Like in the Middle Colonies?

Between New England and the South lay the Middle Colonies. This section was not exactly like either of the others. Not only was it located between them on the map, but its way of life was midway between the other two.

The soil and climate of the Middle Colonies, for example, were better for

Make sure that pupils can name and locate the Middle Colonies (use map, page 87).
HOW DID THE ENGLISH COLONISTS LIVE?   113
Refer also to the map, page 111.

crops than those of New England but not quite so good as those of the South. In manufacturing and commerce, the Middle Colonies ranked next to New England. Their trade was carried on in two big seaports: New York at the mouth of the Hudson River, and Philadelphia near the mouth of the Delaware River.

The Middle Colonies were a mixture in other ways. There were not only big estates like the southern plantations but also many small farms and farm villages like those in New England. Instead of one religion, like that of the Puritans in Massachusetts, the Middle Colonies had Quakers, Catholics, and people of other religions. In fact, as you have learned, the idea of religious freedom was established from the beginning in Pennsylvania, where all Christians were free to settle. There were more schools in the Middle Colonies than in the South, but not so many as in New England. Even the people were more of a mixture than in either of the other two sections. Colonists from many European countries settled in the Middle Colonies. There were thousands of Germans and Scotch-Irish (Scottish people who had lived for a time in Ireland). There were also French, Irish, Scots, Swedes, and, of course, the Dutch. The Middle Colonies, as you can see, were indeed well named.

CHECK UP

1. In what ways was life in the Middle Colonies a mixture of both northern and southern ways of living?

2. What kinds of people settled in the Middle Colonies?

COLONIAL BOATMEN pole their barge-like riverboats, loaded with products, along the Delaware River. Roads were so bad that colonial farmers and craftsmen had to rely on boats to carry their products to market. This kind of boat (called the Durham boat) was used to ferry George Washington's army across the Delaware River on the eve of the Battle of Trenton during the Revolutionary War.

4 How Did People Live in the Frontier Region?

So far, we have been reading about colonial life in the older and more settled parts which lay along the Atlantic seaboard. To the west, back of these settlements, was another region, called the *frontier*. If we are to get a true picture of life in the English colonies in the 1700's, we should know something about this western region.

Why did people move to the frontier? The frontier was the farthest edge of settled country, where only a handful of white men lived. Death lurked in the western forests; back-breaking labor was necessary to provide food and shelter. Why, then, did men and women leave safe and settled communities to live in the wilderness?

Here are some of the reasons: (1) As we know, there are always men who love adventure. The frontier attracted such men, even though they faced dangers and hardships. (2) There were others who disliked settled communities where they were told what to do and what not to do. These men longed to live alone in the wilderness, trusting to their wits and snapping their fingers at laws and governments. They went west to be free to live in their own way. (3) In the streams and forests of the West were animals whose furs could be sold for a good price in the East. Some men, therefore, went to the frontier region to be trappers and fur traders. (4) Still others moved west because land was cheap there. Cheap land attracted people who did not have enough money to buy land near their old homes along the coast. Indentured servants, for example, often moved to the frontier to begin new lives for themselves after they had served their time and become free. (5) Lastly, many people who found life unpleasant in Europe journeyed directly to the frontier where they could live and worship as they pleased without interference. The Scotch-Irish, in particular, passed through the Middle Colonies and settled in large numbers on the frontier.

How did the pioneers move westward? When pioneers went west, they followed the easiest routes inland. They tried to find routes which had no steep ups and downs. (The old rule of the woods is, "Never go over anything you can go around; never step on anything you can step over.") Best of all routes were the rivers. On rivers the pioneers could travel by canoe or raft or boat rather than having to cut a path through the forest. Next best were the valleys and the gaps in the hills. The map on the next page shows the main routes that the settlers followed.

Some of the pioneers made their way up the Connecticut River. Others went up the Hudson to the Mohawk River and west on that stream. Others followed the Susquehanna River. Still others went up the Potomac, and thence up the Shenandoah River. Then they pushed into the

COLONIAL LIGHTING

114

This point is illustrated on the map, page 115. Refer to it as you read the next two paragraphs.

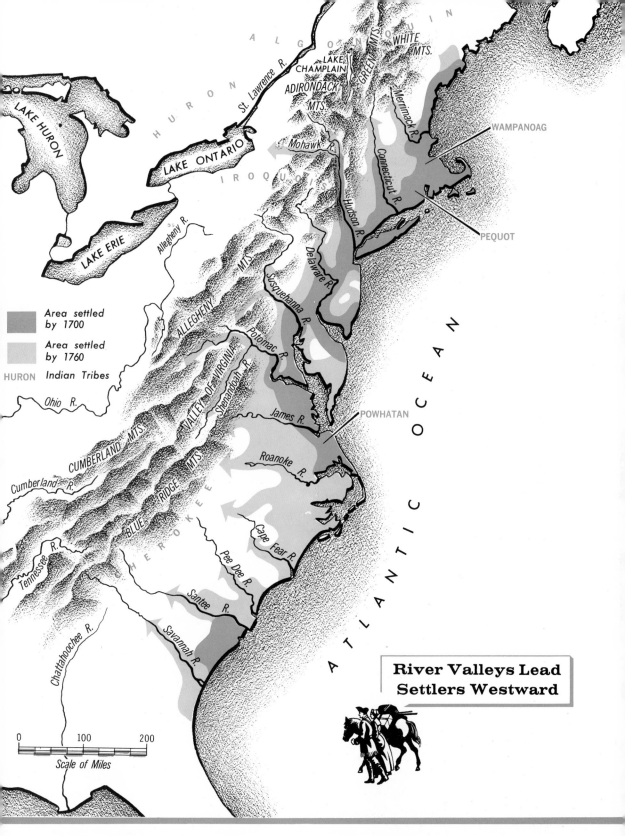

LAKE HURON

LAKE ONTARIO

LAKE ERIE

St. Lawrence R.

HURON

A L G O N Q U I N

LAKE
CHAMPLAIN

ADIRONDACK
MTS.

GREEN MTS.

WHITE
MTS.

Merrimack R.

WAMPANOAG

I R O Q U O I S

Mohawk R.

Hudson R.

Connecticut R.

PEQUOT

Allegheny R.

Delaware R.

ALLEGHENY MTS.

Susquehanna R.

■ Area settled
by 1700

▨ Area settled
by 1760

HURON Indian Tribes

Ohio R.

ALLEGHENY

Potomac R.

VALLEY OF VIRGINIA

Shenandoah R.

James R.

POWHATAN

CUMBERLAND MTS.

Roanoke R.

Cumberland R.

BLUE RIDGE MTS.

C H E R O K E E

A T L A N T I C   O C E A N

Tennessee R.

Pee Dee R.

Cape Fear R.

Santee R.

Savannah R.

Chattahoochee R.

**River Valleys Lead
Settlers Westward**

0   100   200

Scale of Miles

MAP STUDY Early settlers followed the river valleys inland from the Atlantic coast. What chief
rivers did the settlers follow westward? The colored areas on this map show you what
regions they had settled by 1700 and by 1760. As the settlers moved inland, they
came in contact with Indian tribes whose names appear in color.

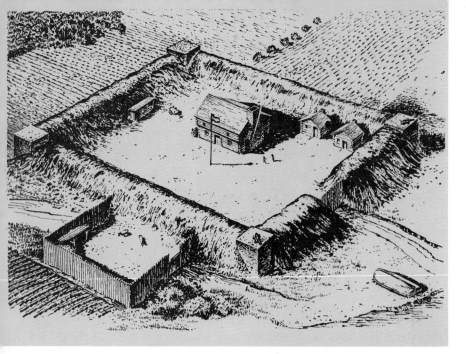

THE DUTCH built this early frontier fort near what is now Hartford, Connecticut. In this fort the walls were huge mounds of earth, but log stockades (lower left) protected the settlers' animals. Notice the small cannon mounted at two of the corners.

great Valley of Virginia between the Blue Ridge Mountains on the east and the Allegheny Mountains on the west. The land along these routes was quite well occupied by 1760, as the map on page 115 shows.

Just before the American Revolution broke out in 1775, pioneers began to pass through the gaps in the Allegheny Mountains to the land sloping slowly down to the Mississippi River. They traveled in groups, some by water, some by land. They went on foot and on horseback, their household goods strapped to the backs of pack horses. When they reached a spot where they wished to settle, they stopped. As pioneers moved steadily westward, the frontier — the farthest edge of settlement — moved westward also.

Frontier life is dangerous. Pioneers faced many dangers. For one thing, they were nearest to the French possessions in Canada and the Ohio Valley. If a war broke out, they would be the first to be attacked. Another danger was the Indians. The Indians hated the white men who kept cutting down their forests and killing their game. At any time they might pounce upon the lonely settlements, so the settlers always had to keep a keen watch for savages on the warpath.

To protect themselves against these ever-present dangers, the pioneers usually fortified their settlements. They drove pointed logs into the ground to make a high fence called a *stockade.* At the corners of the stockade they built two-story cabins, called *blockhouses,* from which to keep watch in time of peace and to shoot in time of war. They kept food and water and ammunition inside the stockade for use during Indian attacks. Bold pioneers who built their cabins and cleared their farms outside of the stockade took refuge inside when warlike Indians came near.

When the Indians were peaceful, the settlement served as a trading post where the white men bargained with the Indians for furs. Some white men, however, preferred to trap the wild animals themselves instead of getting the furs from the Indians. These men were absent from the settlement most of the time and used it

Paul Wellman describes the struggles 116 *between white men and Indians in Indian Wars and Warriors (East).*

This is a useful interpretive summary of the chapter.

only as headquarters — a place to buy what they needed and to sell the skins of the animals they caught.

What kinds of houses and furniture were used on the frontier? The pioneers lived in the wilderness, far from the older settlements. They had to make or grow whatever they needed. A pioneer's cabin was likely to be small, perhaps twelve feet wide and fourteen feet long. It was built of logs a foot or more in diameter, fitted together at the corners. The spaces between the logs were plastered with sticky clay. The roof was made of long shingles. The door consisted of heavy logs split in two, called *puncheons.* The curved sides of the puncheons formed the outer part of the door; on the inside the flat sides were crisscrossed by strong timbers. The window was made by cutting out a section of one or two logs. A huge fireplace occupied nearly all of one end of the cabin. Across the inside of the chimney was fastened a pole, called a *lug pole,* from which hung a chain to support the kettle.

Most of the furniture was homemade, for furniture was too heavy to carry any distance. Beds were made of dogwood poles with woven elm bark or hickory slats. Stools were built by fitting three legs into the curved portion of a puncheon. The legs might be cut to slightly different lengths so that the stool would stand firmly on the uneven floor. Several puncheons laid flat side up on a rough frame formed a table. To build a cupboard, the pioneer laid boards across wooden pegs that had been driven into the log walls of the cabin.

Frontier food and clothes are simple. In the wilderness there were plenty of wild animals which the pioneer could shoot or trap for food. There were birds also, and the streams were full of fish and turtles. The pioneer could grow corn and wheat after fields were cleared in the forest. Then, too, he might have a cow or two and some pigs. In the 1700's, some frontier farmers began to raise a few head of cattle.

The clothes of the pioneers, like their furniture, were homemade. The hides of animals were often used for this purpose. The deerskin shirt and the coonskin cap were two sure marks of the frontiersman. Sometimes he wore homespun shirts, and his wife was usually dressed in homespun.

•

This description has shown you that ways of living differed in the various sections of the colonies. These differences were strengthened by the fact that people in one section had little to do with people in other sections. Indeed, travel was so difficult that many a colonist was born and lived and died without going outside his own colony. The colonists thought of themselves as Virginians, Pennsylvanians, or New Yorkers, rather than as Americans.

Yet we must remember that in spite of differences all the sections were alike in certain ways. All the colonies — New England, Middle, and Southern — were colonies of England. All had governments that were much alike. Most of the colonists spoke English, and this common language helped to bind them together. But

FRONTIER FURNITURE

Compare houses and furniture on the frontier and in the older settlements (see pages 102, 105, 110).

what drew the English colonies most closely together were their common problems — the need to make a living 3000 miles from Europe, to cut down the forests and make farms, and to deal with the Indians. It was because of their likenesses and common problems that the Thirteen Colonies were able at a later time to unite into one country.

CHECK UP

1. For what reasons did people move to the frontier?

2. (a) By what kinds of routes did the pioneers move westward? (b) How did the pioneers protect themselves from dangers?

3. What were houses, furniture, food, and clothing like on the frontier?

Check Up on Chapter 5

Do You Know the Meaning?

1. frontier
2. pioneer
3. apprentice
4. stockade
5. blockhouse
6. plantation
7. stocks
8. pillory
9. puncheon
10. lug pole
11. indigo
12. ducking stool
13. homespun
14. almanac
15. geographical conditions

Can You Identify?

1. Harvard College
2. Scotch-Irish

Can You Locate?

1. Potomac River
2. Shenandoah River
3. Mohawk River
4. Allegheny Mts.
5. Blue Ridge Mts.
6. Susquehanna River

What Do You Think?

1. Would you say that life in a New England village or on a southern plantation more nearly resembled life on a European manor in the Middle Ages? Explain.

2. How did a school in colonial days differ from your school today?

3. What qualities would you expect to find in a typical frontiersman? Why?

4. Do geographical conditions have much effect on ways of living in your community? Explain.

5. Are people today more or less dependent on geographical conditions than people were 300 years ago? Why? In answering, consider transportation, houses, farming, sources of power, etc.

This question calls attention to the fact that an advanced technology makes it easier for man to live well, whatever the geographic environment.

LINKING PAST AND PRESENT

Colonial Williamsburg. To see how people lived in the English colonies before the Revolutionary War, try sometime to visit Williamsburg, Virginia. This famous city was the capital of Virginia from 1699 to 1779. After the capital was moved to Richmond, Williamsburg declined in importance and became a quiet little town. Then in the 1930's, John D. Rockefeller, Jr., arranged to have it

rebuilt as it was in the 1700's.

Today the main streets look much as they did 200 years ago. The houses have been furnished as they were in colonial days; even the gardens are planted with the favorite shrubs and flowers of the colonists. You see the stately Capitol, flying the British flag as of old; the beautiful palace, once home of the royal governors; and even the jail, where the jailer waits to show you around. Shops of colonial times display their wares — you see the wig-maker's shop, the bake shop, the blacksmith shop. To carry out the spirit of colonial days, the guides who take you around wear clothes in the style of the 1700's.

The Indians today. Although the early settlers took over lands belonging to the Indians and developed their own ways of living in America, the "first Americans" still live among us. During the years that the white men were seizing their lands, the Indian people died in great numbers because of war, starvation, and white men's diseases, such as smallpox and measles. But today the Indian population is again increasing and there are over 500,000 in the United States alone. About half of them live on the reservations set aside by the United States government.

While most of the Indians live in western states, over 100,000 still live on land east of the Mississippi River. The states of New York, Wisconsin, North Carolina, Michigan, and Mississippi have reservations where Indian people live and work. Though they work at all types of jobs, they also make baskets, do beadwork, and carry on other fine handicrafts. Some of the eastern Indians continue to hold a colorful council meeting, with dances and feasts, every year. (See Chapter 21 for the western Indians.)

The men who settled America owed a great deal to the Indians. Without their help the white men would have had a harder time making homes in the wilderness. From the Indians white men learned how to stalk game in the forest, to catch fish in the streams, to use canoes, and to find their way through the endless forests over old Indian trails. Few explorers and trappers dared to set out without an Indian guide. From the Indians the white men learned to plant corn, beans, tomatoes, pumpkins, and tobacco.

Today we have many reminders of the Indians who once inhabited this land. From east to west, from north to south are rivers, lakes, and cities with Indian names — Lake Huron, Lake Winnipesaukee in New Hampshire, the Mississippi River, the cities of Chippewa Falls, Wisconsin, and Walla Walla, Washington. You can probably name many others.

John Smith named New England. Most people know that John Smith was a leader of the Jamestown colony, but few realize that this remarkable Englishman explored the north Atlantic coast and gave New England its name. In 1614, after he had returned to Europe from Virginia, Smith set out with two ships on a trading expedition to America. Reaching the coast of what is now Maine, Smith explored the shore as far south as Cape Cod. He made an excellent map of that region which he called "New England," giving names to many rivers and bays. The Charles River, flowing into Massachusetts Bay, was named after Prince Charles, who later became king of England. Farther down the coast, Smith found an excellent harbor which he called "Plimouth." It was here that the Pilgrims landed six years later.

After Smith returned to England with a cargo of fish and furs, he wrote a book called "A Description of New England," which included his map. This and other of Smith's books on New England and Virginia gave valuable information about America. The Pilgrims, the Puritans, and later colonists used Smith's books and maps. The name given by John Smith — New England — has lasted to this day, along with other names such as Plymouth, Charles River, and Cape Ann.

The World of Captain John Smith links world events with periods in John Smith's life.

France Gains, Then Loses,
a Huge Empire in North America

The fur trade was the backbone of the French economy; fearless French priests sought to Christianize and educate the Indians.

What this chapter is about —

In the dead of winter in the year 1704, a band of Indians from the French territory of Quebec traveled southward to the Massachusetts border. Quietly one night they approached the frontier settlement of Deerfield. Without warning the Indians swooped down upon the village and attacked the sleeping settlers. Burning houses lit the dreadful scene. Next day the wintry sun looked down upon smoking ruins. Many men, women, and children had been slain and others had been carried into captivity by the Indians.

Why did Indians from French territory attack an English settlement? You will learn the answer in this chapter. You will also read how France in the end lost her New World empire, leaving England supreme in North America. But first you will get acquainted with New France itself. Many Frenchmen in the New World were trappers who hunted in the wilderness and brought their furs to trading posts on the frontier (see picture above).

To help you understand the chapter, we shall answer the following questions:

▶ 1. What was New France like in the 1700's?

▶ 2. Why did the French and the British come to blows in North America?

▶ 3. What were the results of the French and Indian wars?

People in our story — fur trapper, French missionary, Indian braves, French Canadian and British soldiers.

1   What Was New France Like in the 1700's?

We have read how Spain and England founded settlements in the New World and how these settlements grew into prosperous colonies. Now we are ready to learn the story of French settlement in the New World. France, you remember, claimed an immense territory in North America. This was called New France. It sprawled across much of what is now Canada and stretched far down the Mississippi to the Gulf of Mexico. (The map on page 51 shows the size of New France. Notice how large it was, compared with the territory of the English colonies along the Atlantic coast.)

The population and settlements of New France are small. While Englishmen were busy making settlements along the Atlantic coast of North America, Frenchmen were still exploring the interior. As a result, although the French territory in North America was huge, only a few settlements had been made. Indeed, the little settlements along the St. Lawrence seemed lost amid the vast forests which covered the land. By 1750 there were only about 80,000 Frenchmen in all of New France, while in the English colonies there were over 1,500,000 people.

Quebec and Montreal were the only towns of any size. Quebec, built upon rocky bluffs high above the St. Lawrence River, was the first French town in New France. Founded about the same time as Jamestown, Quebec had only a hundred colonists at the end of its first 20 years. Even after that, it grew very slowly. Montreal had its beginning as a fur-trading post in an Indian town. The other French settlements were mostly tiny forts along the St. Lawrence, the Great Lakes, and the Mississippi River. These were held by a few soldiers and were used as fur-trading posts. Thus, while the English colonists had been busy building towns and clearing farms, the French had spent much more of their time and energy in exploring and fur trading.

The people and government of New France differ from the English colonies. In several ways the people in the settlements of New France were not like the

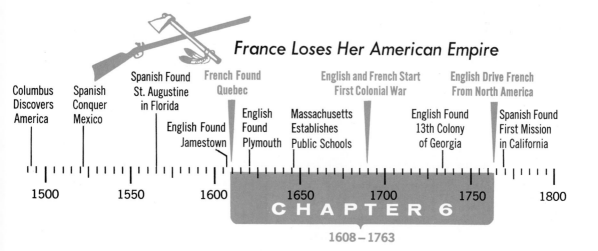

France Loses Her American Empire

Columbus Discovers America	Spanish Conquer Mexico	Spanish Found St. Augustine in Florida	French Found Quebec	English and French Start First Colonial War		English Drive French From North America	
		English Found Jamestown	English Found Plymouth	Massachusetts Establishes Public Schools	English Found 13th Colony of Georgia	Spanish Found First Mission in California	

1500   1550   1600   1650   1700   1750   1800

CHAPTER 6

1608–1763

English colonists. As we know, Englishmen came to the New World to seek a better life for themselves and their families. Most of them were energetic and self-reliant people who wanted to succeed in their new homes. Many of the French, on the other hand, were officials and soldiers who came to America because their government wanted to build up the colony of New France. These Frenchmen were not especially interested in settling permanently in the New World.

The French colonists did not take part in the government, as the English colonists did. There was, in fact, no self-government in the French settlements. New France was ruled by a governor appointed by the king of France. The colonists had nothing to say about making the laws or spending the money for the colony. As for religion, since France was a Catholic country, all the settlers were members of the Catholic Church.

Fur trading is important in New France. Most of the people of New France did not live in the towns. Many of them were fur traders who paddled their canoes up the waterways of the interior to collect furs trapped by the Indians. These furs were carried back to Quebec or Montreal and shipped to Europe where they brought high prices. Although the trade in furs brought large profits, it kept the young men of New France from building settlements and developing the country as the English colonists did.

There were farmers in New France, too. But much of the farm land along the St. Lawrence and along the coast was granted by the king to important Frenchmen, in the form of huge estates. The farmers living on the land had to work for the owners most of the time, much as the serfs of the Middle Ages worked for the lord of the manor (page 18). This was not like the system in the English colonies, where every man could own his own land if he had the price. It is no wonder that many French colonists preferred the free and profitable life of the fur trader to the life of the farmer.

French missionaries work among the Indians. The French were interested in winning the Indians to Christianity. Like the Spaniards, they sent out priests to convert the natives. Father Marquette, who helped Joliet explore the Mississippi (page 47), was a French missionary. The missionaries endured severe hardships, traveling endless miles in canoes and on foot to reach the Indians. Even while the black-robed priests lived among the In-

Governors in the English colonies also were appointed by the kings. But the English colonists were represented in the legislature; the French were not.

EUROPEANS first heard about Niagara Falls from the French missionary priest shown in this painting. Father Hennepin, who explored with La Salle, described the falls in a book he wrote about his travels.

Father Hennepin explored westward as far as present-day Minneapolis.

dians, their life was full of danger. During the long winters they not only faced starvation but almost froze to death in their crude huts. Many priests were tortured, and some were even killed by the Indians. In spite of their hardships, the courageous missionaries labored unceasingly among the Indians and gained for the French the friendship of several of the Indian tribes.

The influence of New France remains to this day. Although France later lost her territory in North America, French customs and language and religion have lasted to this day. In the Canadian province of Quebec, French is spoken much more than English. Public notices are printed in both languages. For instance, a common sign is: "No Smoking. *Défense de Fumer.*" The bus drivers say to the passengers getting on and off: *"Prenez garde! Be careful!"* The spires of French Roman Catholic churches still rise above the villages of the province, and along the roads the traveler sees many religious shrines. The descendants of the French settlers are numerous in Quebec, and they have kept so many of their French customs that a visitor might think he was still in French territory.

CHECK UP

1. How did New France differ from the English colonies in (a) population, (b) size, and (c) government?

2. In what ways did the people in New France earn a living?

3. What reminders of France can be found in present-day Quebec?

The rivalry for beaver fur is described in Trappers and Mountain Men. An exciting story, Captured by the Mohawks, deals with the adventures of Radisson, the French fur trader and one of the founders of the Hudson's Bay Company.

2 Why Did the French and the British Come to Blows in North America?

Have you ever thrown a rock into a quiet pool and watched the ripples spread out in ever-widening circles? In much the same way, an event in history may have effects which are felt in some far-distant spot. In the 1600's and the 1700's, for

BLOCKHOUSES, like this one in Maine, protected English settlements from Indian raids. From its eight sides lookouts could keep watch in every direction.

example, wars broke out in Europe between France and England, and the ripples caused by these wars spread across the Atlantic to their colonies in the New World. Let us see how this came about.

France and England become rivals. From 1643 to 1715, France was ruled by King Louis XIV. Because he was only five years old when he became king, the affairs of state were carried on by the chief government official. After 1661, however, Louis XIV was absolute master of France. He was an ambitious king, and under his leadership France became powerful. He even had plans to bring other parts of Europe under his control. Louis was also interested in strengthening the colony of New France in order to increase the power and prosperity of France. Such ambitions worried the English. "If Louis extends his power," they thought, "he will endanger our trade and our colonies, and perhaps threaten the British Isles themselves." Fear of French power during Louis XIV's

reign and afterward caused England to fight a series of four wars with France. The wars began in 1689 and ended in 1763. Of course, the two countries were not actually at war during all these years, but they were watching each other closely even when they were not fighting.

When the mother countries were at war, it was only natural that the French and English colonists in America should go to war, too. The colonists, as well as the mother countries, were determined not only to protect the land they already had won in America but to gain more territory. The English colonists, in particular, wanted more room to the west for their settlements to grow. Thus the stage was set for war between New France and the colonies of England. Just as we often try to pick the winner before a football game by comparing the two teams, let us consider the strong points of each side in the struggle between the colonies.

What advantages did France have over the English in America? France had several advantages over the English: (1) France, as you already know, controlled more land in North America than did England.

(2) This vast area was ruled by a single powerful government, while each of the thirteen English colonies had a separate government. The French governor did not have to ask thirteen separate colonial legislatures for money and other aid. He was in a position where he could issue orders to the people of New France, who had to obey them. During a war, therefore, New France was organized in such a way that the French could act quickly.

(3) The French government in Europe did not depend on the colonists in New France to do much fighting. The government sent soldiers and ships to protect them. This meant that the French were well prepared when the wars began.

(4) Finally, the French had strong allies among such Indian tribes as the Hurons and the Algonquins (al-*gong'*-kwinz). From the days of the early explorers the French had kept on friendly terms with these Indians and had traded freely with them. French missionaries had lived among them. When war came, the French could count on aid from these tribes.

What advantages did the English colonies have? The English colonies had their strong points, too: (1) There were many more settlers in the English colonies who could help fight than there were in New France.

(2) The English colonists were not scattered over a wide area, but occupied a smaller and more thickly settled region. For this reason the English colonies could be defended more easily than could the French.

(3) Most of the English settlers had come to America to establish homes. Because they had families and land to defend, they had more reason to fight than did many of the wandering French fur traders.

(4) Finally, the English colonies also had Indian allies — the Iroquois (*ear'* oh-kwoy), whose tribes were the most warlike in the eastern part of North America. The Iroquois and the French had been enemies since the days when Champlain (page 44) and his companions went with some friendly Indians to the shores of the lake which bears his name. There they met a party of Iroquois braves who were old enemies of the Indians in Champlain's party. Fighting broke out. The guns which the white men fired terrified the Iroquois and killed a number of them. At a later time the French and the Iroquois also came to blows over the fur trade in the Great Lakes region. When the French and the English were at war, therefore, the Iroquois aided the English.

**C H E C K
U P**

1. Why did France and England fight in North America?

2. (a) What advantages did France have in the wars with England in North America? (b) What advantages did England have?

AN ENLARGED SECTION of this chapter's time line shows when England and France were actually at war between 1689 and 1763, as well as the major events crowded into this period.

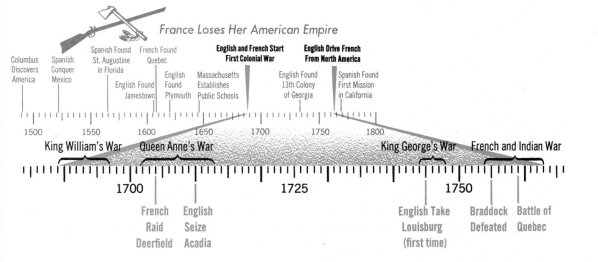

What Were the Results of the French and Indian Wars?

As we have said, whenever England and France went to war in Europe, their colonists went to war in America. In America the first three wars were named for the king or queen who happened to be ruling England at the time. They were King William's War, Queen Anne's War, and King George's War. (See the special time line for these wars on page 125.)

Neither side wins in the first three wars. These first three wars between the

THE GOVERNOR of Massachusetts, wearing fine clothes and a wig, watches colonial volunteers prepare to sail from Boston to attack the French fort of Louisburg. Notice the smartly uniformed drummer boy at right.

colonists accomplished very little. The French, with their warlike Indian allies, made frequent raids on unprotected English settlements. Many a frontier settlement like Deerfield, Massachusetts, heard with terror the bloodcurdling war whoops of the Indians as they burst suddenly from the forest. Many a family grieved because a father or mother, sister or brother, fell victim to the cruel tomahawk or was carried into captivity. The English struck back by attacking the chief forts of the French in America — Quebec on the St. Lawrence River, and the great fortress of Louisburg on Cape Breton Island. (Find these forts on the map on the next page.) They failed to capture Quebec, and although they succeeded in capturing Louisburg, they had to surrender it when peace was made. France did recognize England's claims to Acadia (Nova Scotia) and Newfoundland. But these three wars made no important change in the English and French possessions in America, and neither side won a clear-cut victory. Though hard-fought, the wars in America were overshadowed by the bigger wars in Europe.

Both England and France claim the Ohio Valley. The fourth war, called the French and Indian War, started in North America. It began because both the French and the English wished to control the rich lands along the Ohio River. The French wanted to build a line of forts and trading posts that would connect their settlements on the lower Mississippi River with the rest of New France. Such a plan would not only strengthen their empire but would also keep the English from settling in the Ohio River Valley.

The English, however, were unwilling

This paragraph makes **126** clear the importance of the Ohio Valley.

to let France have this land without a struggle. They did not wish to be limited to a narrow strip of land along the Atlantic seaboard. More English settlers were arriving each year. Many of the better lands along the coast were already cleared and occupied, and more and more settlers were anxious to push westward. About this time a group of Virginia colonists formed a company to settle the lands in the Ohio River Valley. The king of England granted 200,000 acres of land to the Ohio Land Company, as it was called.

The French begin to fortify the disputed territory. When the governor of New France learned of this grant in 1749, he sent an expedition to the Ohio country. As the expedition traveled down the Allegheny River and part of the Ohio River, it left lead plates as land markers to claim the region for France. The French also warned the Indians to have nothing to do with the English. Shortly afterwards, the French began to build forts on Lake Erie and at points southward toward the Ohio River. (The map on this page shows the location of some of the forts.)

The English try to drive the French out of the Ohio Valley. England, in turn, became alarmed at the French advance into the Ohio region. In the autumn of 1753 a messenger was sent through the wilderness to the forts which the French had built in the disputed region. The messenger was George Washington, who at that time was just 21 years old. He carried a letter from the governor of Virginia to the French commander of the forts. This letter warned the French to leave the territory because it belonged to England. Over difficult trails, through snow and rain, young Washington made his way to deliver his message. But the French commander refused to heed the warning, and Washington started back. On his return trip he

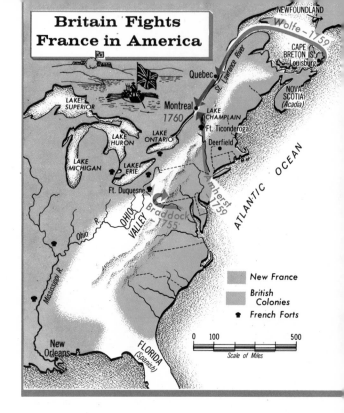

MAP STUDY The British attacked French territory in America along the routes marked by arrows on this map. The Ohio Valley territory was a "no man's land" claimed by both the French and English.

narrowly escaped death when he slipped off a raft and nearly drowned.

The next year Washington returned to the Ohio country, this time with a small group of soldiers. They had been sent out to seize Fort Duquesne (doo-*cane'*), a French fort at the fork where two streams join to form the Ohio River (see the map above). But Washington and his men were outnumbered. They not only failed to capture Fort Duquesne but were forced to surrender and return to Virginia. With this clash the French and Indian War began. To carry on the war, both England and France sent soldiers to America.

General Braddock is defeated by the French. In 1755 the British decided to attack several of the most important French forts. General Edward Braddock,

Virginia's charter gave that colony land from sea to sea. In the Revolutionary War Virginia backed George Rogers Clark's expedition which ousted the British from the Northwest Territory. See page 184.

SHELTERED BY TREES, Indians and French forest fighters ambush General Braddock's army near Fort Duquesne. In this painting the artist has shown the English general falling from his horse as he tries to rally his confused men.

Generals whose experience had been gained on the battlefields of Europe did not understand ambush and surprise attack.

the British commander-in-chief in America, set out to capture Fort Duquesne. Braddock's force of English regulars and Virginians, accompanied by George Washington, moved westward toward Fort Duquesne. As they went, they had to build a road through the wilderness.

Braddock paid little heed to the advice on Indian fighting given him by colonial soldiers. Said he, "These savages may, indeed, be a formidable [threatening] enemy to your raw American militia, but upon the King's regular and disciplined troops . . . it is impossible they should make any impression." But Braddock's overconfidence had tragic results. As the English troops advanced through the wilderness in long columns, a force of French and Indians took them by surprise. The red coats of the English soldiers made fine targets for the hidden enemy. Braddock's brave troops were badly defeated and had to retreat. But the road which they had built

became a main route for pioneers who later pushed their way into the Ohio Valley.

French successes continue. Following Braddock's defeat, French good fortune continued. The British failed to send enough troops to America, and their commanders (like General Braddock) were not used to fighting in the wilderness. The American colonies themselves were slow to work together and to furnish the money and the soldiers needed for victory. As a result, the French won most of the battles during the next two years, capturing several important British forts.

William Pitt takes a hand. The fortunes of war began to change in 1758. The man most responsible for this change was not a soldier but a leader of the English government. His name was William Pitt. Pitt persuaded the colonies to furnish more troops and money. He inspired the British to fight harder. Pitt also sent younger and more vigorous commanders to America. Now it was England's turn to win victory after victory. The great French fort at Louisburg was again attacked by a large British army and forced to surrender. The English were also able to capture several forts along the western frontier. Among them was Fort Duquesne, which the English renamed Fort Pitt in honor of William Pitt. From that small fort has grown the modern city of Pittsburgh, a great center of industry.

Two gallant generals face each other at Quebec.   The battle which was to decide the outcome of the war took place at Quebec, four years after Braddock's defeat. The British forces were under the command of General James Wolfe. Wolfe was an able leader who had taken part in the capture of Louisburg. In the early summer of 1759, a British fleet, carrying thousands of soldiers under Wolfe's command, sailed up the broad St. Lawrence and anchored below the city of Quebec.

It was impossible, however, to attack this French stronghold directly. Located on a high cliff, Quebec was protected by strong walls and many cannon.

General Louis Montcalm, the French leader, had vowed to defend Quebec or die. He knew what Wolfe did not suspect — that it would be difficult for the French to defend Quebec for any length of time. Although Montcalm had more soldiers than Wolfe, many of them were untrained. The city was short of food, and no help could be expected from France while the English navy controlled the St. Lawrence. Montcalm's only hope was to hold Quebec until winter, when ice on the river would force the English fleet to withdraw.

The Battle of Quebec decides the fate of New France.   Meanwhile, from across the river, Wolfe's cannon were bombarding the city but doing little damage. Because winter was approaching, Wolfe decided on a daring move. One night a thin line of British soldiers toiled up the cliffs

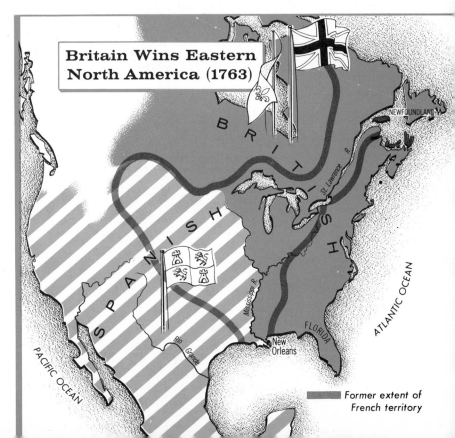

MAP STUDY
Britain defeated France and won control over all eastern North America. Britain also acquired Florida from Spain. What land did Spain receive from France?

Britain Wins Eastern North America (1763)

NEWFOUNDLAND

B R I T I S H

St. Lawrence R.

S P A N I S H

Mississippi R.

Rio Grande

New Orleans

FLORIDA

ATLANTIC OCEAN

PACIFIC OCEAN

Former extent of French territory

at a point left undefended by the French. The next morning the French were amazed to see the British forces forming their lines on a broad plain outside the city walls. Montcalm ordered his troops to attack the enemy. Although the French fought bravely, they were no match for the well-trained English regulars. General Montcalm was fatally wounded. As he lay dying, he said, "I am glad that I need not live to see the surrender of Quebec." General Wolfe also received a fatal wound. When he learned that the enemy was retreating, his last words were: "Now I can die in peace."

British troops entered Quebec, pulled down the French flag, and hoisted the British flag. The Battle of Quebec has been called one of the great battles in the world's history. It is important because it decided whether North America would be chiefly French or British. The British easily captured Montreal, and there was little more fighting in North America. Although the war continued in other parts of the world, the British won victory after victory. In 1763 the conflict was finally ended by a treaty called the Peace of Paris.

France gives up all claims in North America. The peace treaty of 1763 was a humiliating blow to the proud French nation. Great Britain took from France all of her territory east of the Mississippi River except New Orleans. <u>As the map (page 129)</u> shows you, this vast territory included the settlements in what we now call Canada as well as the region south of the Great Lakes. Spain, which had sided with France in the war, had to give Florida to England. To make up for this loss, France gave to Spain New Orleans and the French claims west of the Mississippi River. Except for two small islands off the coast of Newfoundland and some islands in the West Indies, France lost all her possessions in the New World.

CHECK UP

1. (a) What were the names of the first three wars between the French and English in North America? (b) What was the outcome of these three wars?

2. (a) What dispute led to the outbreak of the French and Indian War? (b) Why did France win most of the battles in the early years?

3. (a) Why did England begin to win? (b) What battle decided the outcome of the war?

4. What were the terms of the peace treaty?

Pupils should compare maps on pages 127 and 129 to understand the vast changes in the New World landholdings which resulted from the 1763 peace settlement.

Check Up on Chapter 6

Do You Know the Meaning?

1. province   2. missionary

Can You Identify?

1. Algonquins   7. Battle of Quebec
2. Iroquois   8. Peace of Paris
3. Braddock   9. William Pitt
4. Wolfe   10. 1763
5. Montcalm   11. George Washington
6. Fort Duquesne   12. New France
       13. Ohio Land Company

Can You Locate?

1. Louisburg   4. New Orleans
2. Quebec (city)   5. Ohio River
3. Montreal   6. St. Lawrence River

What Do You Think?

1. The French fur trade may have cost France her territory in the New World. Do you agree? Why?

2. The wars between France and England in Europe from 1689 to 1763 affected their

What Do You Think? (Cont.)

colonies in the New World as well. Give an example to show that today, also, events in one area may have effects in other parts of the world.

3. Why were the French so successful in gaining Indian allies?

4. England and her colonists in America did not agree on how much each had contributed to winning the war against the French. Can you see why? Explain.

5. (a) Why was the outcome of the French and Indian War important to England? (b) To France? (c) To us today?

LINKING PAST AND PRESENT

French customs in the land of Louis. French influence remains strong in Louisiana, which was named for King Louis XIV of France. French people settled the region, and their descendants still carry on many colorful customs of their ancestors. Perhaps some of you have attended the famous *Mardi gras* (*mar'-dih grah'*) in Louisiana's largest city, New Orleans. The Mardi gras is a French carnival which takes place the last few days before Lent. The city is thronged with merry-makers in every kind of costume, dancing

and parading in the streets and watching the spectacular floats. Then, at midnight before the first day of Lent, the Mardi gras ends.

Because of its past, Louisiana is the only state where laws are patterned after French rather than English law. It is also the only state which is divided into parishes instead of counties. The parishes were originally districts of the Catholic Church. When Louisiana became a state, these districts took the place of counties, but continued to be called parishes.

TO CLINCH YOUR

UNDERSTANDING OF

Unit 2

Encourage pupils to read this summary carefully. A point by point discussion will provide an excellent review.

Summary of Important Ideas

Unit Two has told how European nations settled colonies and developed empires in the New World.

1. Spain established a great empire in the New World.

a. In Mexico and Peru, Cortés and Pi-

zarro conquered Indian empires possessing great wealth; other Spaniards roamed far and wide in search of riches. Priests worked hard to Christianize the Indians.

b. Within a century Spain acquired Florida and the southwestern part of the present-day United States, Mexico, the West Indies, and all of Central and South America (except Brazil).

c. Spain permitted only Spanish Catholics to settle in her colonies, regulated colonial trade for her own benefit, and denied the colonists a share in the government. The Spaniards held the high positions in the Church and the government and looked down on the Creoles and mestizos. Large churches and universities were built in Spanish America before the English settled successful colonies in the New World.

d. Wealth from the New World helped make Spain powerful and aroused the fear and envy of England, France, and Holland. Eager to share her wealth and reduce her power, they struck at Spain.

2. England, France, and Holland also established colonies in the New World.

a. The Englishmen who came to America sought freedom to make a better living, to obtain land, to worship as they pleased, and to share in the government. Geographic conditions help to explain why different ways of living developed. Some of the English colonies offered less freedom than others, but colonists often left older settlements to found new settlements where they could live as they wished. Wherever they lived, the English colonists had some things in common — a form of government in which the colonists had a voice, the English language, and the problem of earning a living 3000 miles from the mother country. The Dutch colony of New Netherland was annexed by the English in 1664.

b. The French claimed a vast territory which included most of present-day Canada and the land drained by the Mississippi. The small population made a living in the fur trade and by agriculture. The French government strictly regulated life in New France. The French priests were active missionaries among the Indians.

c. Rivalry between France and England in Europe led to wars which extended to North America. The English colonists, feeling themselves hemmed in by the French, had reasons of their own for fighting. Defeated in the French and Indian War, France surrendered Canada and the land east of the Mississippi to England and gave French territory west of that river to Spain. Nevertheless, the French language and French ways of living have survived to this day in parts of the New World.

Unit Review

1. (a) What kinds of people helped to establish Spain's empire in the New World? (b) Why was each group interested in coming to the New World?
2. How did the discovery of great riches in Mexico and Peru affect (a) the Indians, (b) the spread of Spanish exploration and colonization, and (c) Spain's position as a world power? Explain in each case.
3. (a) Why did Englishmen come to America? (b) How did English efforts at colonization differ from those of Spain and France?
4. (a) To what extent were geographic conditions responsible for differences in ways of living in New England, the Middle Colonies, and the South? (b) Why was life on the frontier different from life along the seaboard?
5. Compare Spanish, English, and French colonies in the New World about 1750. Take into account (a) size, (b) government, (c) chief ways of making a living, and (d) relations with Indians.
6. (a) Why did colonial wars break out between the French and the English in North America? (b) What advantages did each side possess? (c) Why did the English win? (d) How did the English victory affect the future of North America?

Gaining Skill

How to Read Maps

Not only printed words but many maps have been used in this book to tell our nation's story accurately and clearly. You will find it helpful to "read" these maps as carefully as you read the printed words. Here are some ways in which you can use the maps:

1. *To locate a place.* On page 61 you are told that Cortés sailed from Cuba and landed on the Mexican coast near the present-day city of Veracruz. On the map, page 63, locate the place from which Cortés started and the place where he landed.

2. *To trace a route.* On pages 66–67 you learned that Coronado was the first explorer to see the land which is now divided into several of our western states. Trace the route of Coronado's expedition on the map, page 66.

3. *To tell direction.* On pages 43–45 you are told that European explorers, such as Hudson and Frobisher, sought a *northwest* passage through America to Asia. Trace their routes on the map on page 46, and use your ruler to check whether or not they followed the *general* direction shown by the compass needle.

4. *To estimate distance.* You have read on page 67 that the Spanish de Soto was the first explorer to view the Mississippi River. Look at the map on page 66. Use the scale of miles to estimate the distance de Soto traveled west across what is now the southern United States to make his great discovery. You can mark the distance on a piece of paper and compare it with the scale.

5. *To compare areas.* On page 121 you read about the size of New France. On the map on page 51 you can see the French and English possessions in North America. Note that the territory claimed by France is much larger than the English territory along the eastern coast of North America. Try to estimate the difference in size.

6. *To see the lay of the land.* On page 114 you are told that the pioneers used river valleys and gaps in the mountains in going inland. Study the map on page 115, and locate routes taken by the pioneers. Note that the river valleys in the Southern and Middle Colonies run westward, but that the river valleys in New England run north and led settlers in that direction.

7. *To understand reasons.* On page 96 you read about the colony the Dutch founded along the Hudson River. Look at the maps on pages 87 and 97. Why do you suppose the English wanted to conquer this colony? Note that the Dutch controlled important river valleys and separated the English colonies north and south of them.

8. *To see changes.* On page 113 you read that the English settlers moved steadily inland. Look at the map on page 115 again and the key at the left. Note the lands along the coast which the English had settled by 1700. Now compare this area with the area which had been settled by 1760.

Interesting Things to Do

Projects marked with an asterisk (*) are for the whole class.

*1. Make a chart showing the Thirteen English Colonies. Arrange them under the section (New England, Middle Colonies, Southern Colonies) to which they belong. Use these headings for your chart: Name of Colony, Date, Who Founded It, Reasons for Founding.

*2. Make more cards for your game, "Can You Identify?" (page 55), using the names, terms, and dates given at the ends of Chapters 3, 4, 5, and 6.

3. Write entries in an imaginary diary kept by a boy or girl who went with (a) Jamestown settlers in 1607, (b) Pilgrims in 1620, (c) Puritans in 1630.

4. Find pictures showing costumes worn by French, English, Spanish, and Dutch colonists. Show the pictures to the class.

5. Prepare a report on a topic from this unit. Possible subjects are: Colonial Homes, Colonial Schools, Amusements in Colonial Days, Ponce de Leon, Roger Williams, General Montcalm.

6. Tell the class about some interesting story you have read describing (a) the conquest of Mexico or Peru, (b) the settling of an English colony, (c) frontier life, (d) the French and Indian Wars. Visit the library or see the reading list at the end of this book for suggestions.

New Nations Are Born as the

It would be helpful to review the ties that bound America to Europe.
What ties exist today?

Unit Three tells the story of how the New World cut many of the ties that bound it to the Old World. It is a thrilling story of battles and heroic struggles for freedom. Brave men fought against great odds for what they believed to be right. Old empires died and new nations were born as the spirit of freedom swept through the New World.

About 1763, England was the proud mistress of territory that stretched from the Atlantic Ocean to the Mississippi River, and from the Gulf of Mexico to Hudson Bay. All the people living within this territory were English subjects and owed allegiance to the king of England. How, then, did it happen that only twelve years later, the king's troops and American minutemen stood face to face, with guns in their hands, as shown above? And by 1783 Great Britain, apparently so powerful and secure in America, had lost a large share of her American colonies. For even a longer time, about 300 years, Spain had ruled an empire which stretched from California to the southern tip of South America. Yet in the early 1800's Spain lost control of its New World empire. Again, how did this happen?

The colonists were English subjects 134 (citizens) and hence ruled by the King of England. The English felt that Parliament had the same right to make laws for the colonists as for people in England.

ew World Shakes Off European Rule

These paragraphs outline the material in Unit Three.

The first three chapters of this unit tell what happened to the Thirteen English Colonies. Chapter 7 describes the kind of government that developed in the English colonies and the relations between the colonies and the mother country. Chapter 8 tells how stricter regulations by the British government caused growing resistance among the colonists. Words gave way to blows when colonial minutemen met British regulars at Lexington and Concord. Chapter 9 relates the story of the war in which the Thirteen Colonies won their independence.

The final chapter of Unit Three tells what happened somewhat later in other parts of the New World. We shall find out how the Spanish colonies, led by a handful of devoted leaders, gained their independence. And we shall read how Canada gained control of its own affairs, even though it remained a part of the British Empire.

Inclusion of independence movements in Latin America and the development of self-government in Canada in this unit brings out the common experience shared by New World nations.

We, therefore, the Representatives of the united States of America . . . declare that these United Colonies are, and of Right ought to be Free and Independent States. . . . — DECLARATION OF INDEPENDENCE

How Were the English

Colonists Governed?

This approach brings the content of the chapter closer to the lives of the students.

What this chapter is about —

Have you ever stopped to think what *rights* you have because you are an American? Imagine, for example, that you and your family are starting off for church. There is no law in the United States that says what church you must attend; you have the right to decide how and where you worship. In other words, freedom of religion is one of your rights as an American. Or suppose that your father does not like a law that has been proposed by Congress. If he wishes, he may criticize the action of Congress to his friends. He may write a letter to a newspaper telling what he thinks. Or he may even hire a hall and make a public protest if he wants to! This is an example of freedom of speech, which is a right very precious to Americans. Perhaps you can think of other rights which we enjoy.

How did we get these rights? Some of them developed in America. Others, as we shall discover in this chapter, were brought to the colonies by English settlers who cherished them dearly. We shall learn about the governments under which the colonists lived. We shall find that in each colony laws were made by colonial assemblies. (The picture above shows the building where the lawmakers met in Virginia.) We shall also learn how England regulated the trade of the colonies, and how the mother country and the colonies disagreed about colonial government and trade regu-

The chart on page 230 suggests the roots of American liberties.

People in our story — royal governor, colonial lawmakers, colonial sea captain, English naval officer.

136

lations. As you read, keep in mind these questions:

▶ 1. What rights did the English colonists bring to the New World?

▶ 2. What kind of government grew up in the English colonies?

▶ 3. Why did England and her colonies disagree over colonial affairs?

This section calls attention to basic differences among Spanish, French, and English colonies. Note how these differences affected the lives of typical colonists.

1 What Rights Did the English Colonists Bring to the New World?

Colonists of Spain, France, and England lead different lives. Let us pay a visit to three men living about the year 1750 in three widely scattered places in the New World. The first man is Fernando, a Spanish colonist. Fernando lives in Mexico City, where he is a merchant. As we learned in Chapter 3, Fernando has little freedom. Although he is a loyal Spaniard and a good Catholic, he has no part in the government of New Spain or of Mexico City. That is all controlled by the viceroy. Fernando is not free to criticize the government or the king. Even his business is very strictly controlled by the government.

We turn now to a cabin on a large estate in the St. Lawrence Valley. This is the home of Pierre in New France. Pierre's life, also, is not very free. Like Fernando in New Spain, Pierre is loyal to the Catholic Church and to his king, but he has no share in the government. The king's representatives have almost complete power over the inhabitants of New France. Pierre has no land of his own. He lives on the estate of a powerful landowner. He is allowed to keep a share of the crops he raises, but he must perform many duties for the landowner. He must even accept the owner's advice on such matters as getting married!

The last stop in our journey is at the little home of Jonathan Blake in the colony of Massachusetts. Jonathan was a free man when he came from England to make a better living, and his life in America is much freer than that of Fernando or Pierre. He owns his house and his farm, which he is free to manage as he wishes. Moreover, he has a right to share in the government of the colony. He may vote for

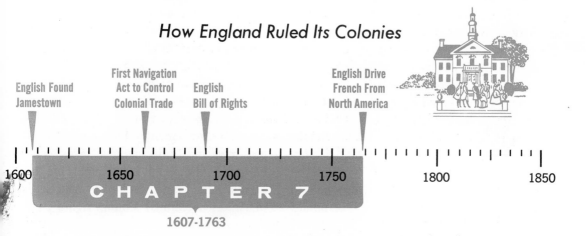

How England Ruled Its Colonies

English Found Jamestown

First Navigation Act to Control Colonial Trade

English Bill of Rights

English Drive French From North America

1600   1650   1700   1750   1800   1850

CHAPTER 7

1607-1763

representatives to serve in the assembly for the whole colony. This assembly decides many important questions, including the taxes which each colonist must pay. Jonathan also has certain other rights. For example, he cannot be punished for a crime unless he has been found guilty by a group of his fellow men called a *jury*.

Jonathan does not possess greater freedom than Fernando or Pierre because of what he himself has done. He owes much to his English ancestors, who loved freedom and insisted upon having certain rights. Let us see how this came about.

Englishmen limit the king's power. At the time the New World was being settled, England, France, and Spain all had kings. But, while the monarchs of France and Spain had become all-powerful in their countries, the people of England had from time to time limited the power of their kings. In fact, whenever a king tried to interfere with certain rights which Englishmen considered their own, the people protested. Three of these protests play a part in our story. They were important steps in the struggle to limit the power of English kings and to increase the rights of the English people.

(1) The first of these steps was taken long ago, in 1215. At that time England was ruled by a worthless tyrant named King John, who wished to govern just as he pleased. But a group of nobles forced him to set his seal to a document, or official paper, called *Magna Carta*, a Latin term which means "Great Charter." In Magna Carta, King John had to accept certain limits upon his power. He agreed that nobles and "freemen" (landholders) should not be punished at the whim of the king, but must be judged by a jury under the laws of the land. The king also had to agree to consult a Great Council of nobles

and church officers on many matters. To be sure, the nobles were looking after themselves when they forced King John to accept this document. In time, however, the rights promised in Magna Carta came to apply to all men in England.

(2) Another ruler who was forced to heed the people's wishes was Charles I. King Charles, who was king when the Puritans left England (page 91), was determined to rule as he saw fit. He paid little attention to *Parliament,* the body of English lawmakers made up of nobles and representatives of the people. He also collected taxes without Parliament's consent. So loud became the protests against these high-handed acts that Charles was obliged to agree to a statement called the *Petition of Right.* This stated that Englishmen should not be taxed without the consent of Parliament. When Charles failed to keep his written promise, an uprising in England cost him his throne and his life.

(3) Still another English king, James II, trampled on the rights of the Parliament and the people. In 1689, after James II had been forced to flee from England, a document called the *Bill of Rights* was drawn up. No English king since then has seriously interfered with the rights of Englishmen listed in the Bill of Rights.

English rights are transplanted to America. By accepting these important papers — Magna Carta, the Petition of Right, and the Bill of Rights — English kings admitted that their people possessed important rights. Englishmen, for example, had the right to a fair trial by a jury and to lay complaints before the king. They also had a right to elect representatives to Parliament. Parliament was to pass laws and to decide what taxes were to be paid. These rights are important to us because the English colonists who settled in America claimed similar rights in the

If the date 1215 were to be included on the time line on page 137, that line would have to be extended to the left nine inches!

KING JOHN faces the English nobles who demand that he place his seal on Magna Carta.

The first charter granted to the London and Plymouth Companies in 1606 gave "Americans" a basis for claiming the rights of Englishmen.

New World. In the early charters giving permission to start colonies in North America, the king declared that the settlers were to have the same "liberties . . . as if they had been abiding and born within this our realm of England." That is why Jonathan Blake enjoyed more freedom than Pierre or Fernando. We shall see in the next chapter that these rights meant so much to the English colonists that they were willing to fight to protect them.

The spirit of freedom grows in America. English colonists not only had all the rights of Englishmen, but they enjoyed even greater freedom in the New World than did their countrymen in England. It is not difficult to understand why this was true. For one thing, the settlement of the English colonies, as you know, was carried out chiefly by trading companies or by proprietors. In the early days, the English kings were only mildly interested in what was going on in the New World. They were too busy with affairs in England to worry much about the struggling settlements across the sea. This lack of interest on the part of the English government permitted the colonists to enjoy great freedom in managing their own affairs.

We must remember, too, that 3000 miles of ocean lay between the colonies and England. It took weeks or even months to cross the ocean. Naturally the colonies had more freedom to govern themselves than if orders could have been delivered promptly. And the New World itself, with its plentiful land and unlimited opportunities, encouraged this feeling of freedom. Men believed that by overcoming the dangers of the wilderness and building up settlements, they had earned a right to say how they should be governed.

It would be wrong, however, to think that the English colonists were entirely their own masters. They lacked certain rights which Americans today take for granted. It was still dangerous, for example, for a man to criticize the king or his officers too loudly. Furthermore, there were many colonists, such as Negro slaves and indentured servants, who were not free. And in some colonies, settlers had less freedom than in others. Nevertheless, by 1750 government throughout the English colonies allowed greater freedom than could be found elsewhere in the New World or in most parts of Europe. Let us see what this government was like.

CHECK UP

1. What rights did the English colonists bring to the New World?

2. Why did the English colonists have greater freedom than people in England?

One reason was because India and "sugar colonies" such as Jamaica and Barbados brought more wealth to the mother country.

139

2. What Kind of Government Grew Up in the English Colonies?

The three charts summarize and diagram information presented on pages 140-141. Make sure your students can "read" them.

Imagine that we have come from the Old World to visit the Massachusetts colony about the year 1750. Suppose, too, that we have a letter of introduction to Jonathan Blake from his brother in England. When we knock at the door of his humble dwelling and show him our letter, he greets us courteously. He asks us to sit down on stools and benches before the dancing flames in his huge fireplace. When we question him about the government of the English colonies, he replies in words like these:

Colonial governments are much alike. "The government of one colony may differ slightly from the government of another, but in all colonies conditions are much the same. A colonial government is really like the government in England, only on a smaller scale. In each colony there is a governor in charge, just as the king is the head of the government in England. Each colony also has a body of lawmakers,

called a *legislature*. The legislature is like the Parliament in England. In addition, there are courts to try cases in each colony, just as there are courts in England. But these colonial governments do not have the last word in their affairs. They have to take orders from England. For example, Parliament may pass laws which the colonies in America have to obey. Then too, laws passed by the legislature of a colony may be set aside by England. This is not often done, however. Our colonial governments really have a good deal of power in carrying on the affairs of the colonies."

Colonial governors are chosen in various ways. "The governors of the different colonies do not inherit their positions as the king of England does. Nor are they all chosen in the same way. In Rhode Island and Connecticut, the governors are elected by the voters. This gives the people of these colonies a good deal more power than the citizens of other colonies enjoy. In three other colonies — Maryland, Pennsylvania, and Delaware — the governor is chosen by the proprietor of the colony. In these cases, however, the governor selected by the proprietor must be approved by the king.

"You may be wondering about the eight remaining colonies: Massachusetts, New Hampshire, New York, New Jersey, Virginia, North and South Carolina, and Georgia. Most of these colonies were founded by trading companies or proprietors, who at the start had the power to appoint governors. But for one reason or another, the king has taken over the government of all these colonies. Their governors are now appointed by the king and are responsible to him. So, you see, the

EACH COLONY HAD A GOVERNOR

1 In most colonies — The King APPOINTED — The Governor

2 In Maryland, Delaware and Pennsylvania — The Proprietor APPOINTED — KING MUST APPROVE CHOICE — The Governor

3 In Rhode Island and Connecticut — The Governor was ELECTED

The COLONISTS

colonists do not have a great deal to say about choosing their governors."

The voters choose the lawmakers. "Our governors are very important and powerful people," Jonathan goes on, "but they share the work of government with the legislatures. Most legislatures have two branches or houses — an upper house and a lower house which is often called an *assembly*. The upper house is small. Its members are appointed by the governor rather than elected, and it is not as important as the lower house. The lower house is made up of representatives elected by the voters. Each town or county in the colony is allowed to send one or more representatives to this lower branch. So the people, through their representatives, do have a voice in the passing of laws and the voting of taxes.

"Not everybody, of course, has the right to vote for these representatives to the legislature. Women cannot vote. Nor are all the men who have reached the age of 21 allowed to vote, either. Usually only those who are free men and who own a certain amount of land or other property are given this right. In some places,

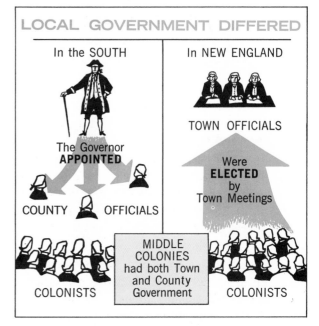

LOCAL GOVERNMENT DIFFERED

In the SOUTH — The Governor APPOINTED — COUNTY OFFICIALS — COLONISTS

In NEW ENGLAND — TOWN OFFICIALS — Were ELECTED by Town Meetings — COLONISTS

MIDDLE COLONIES had both Town and County Government

property owners must also belong to a certain church in order to vote. Here in Massachusetts Bay Colony, in earlier times, only members of the Puritan Church were allowed to vote."

The colonists manage their local governments. "I hope," says Jonathan, "that I have given you a clear picture of the government of our colonies. But no doubt you also want to know how each neighborhood or locality is governed. Well, here in New England each town takes care of its own affairs. Town meetings are held from time to time. In these meetings all the voters of the village or town can take part because the town is small. The voters can voice their opinions, vote for local officers, and decide what to do about local affairs. As you can see, the town meeting allows a great deal of self-government.

"Of course I have never traveled very far from home, but I am told that in the Southern Colonies they do not have town meetings. Because of the large plantations, the population is scattered thinly over the countryside and there are fewer settlements. So their local government is carried on by counties, each county

POWER WAS DIVIDED

ENGLAND

The GOVERNOR represented King and Parliament

AMERICA

e appointed PPER HOUSE f Legislature

he LOWER HOUSE f the Legislature epresented the Colonists ho ELECTED them

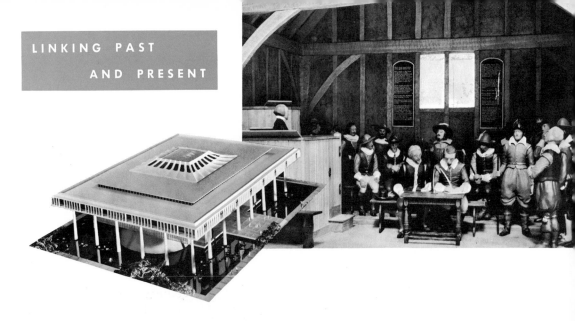

An architect's model (above) shows a design proposed for a new Capitol to house the legislature of our newest state, Hawaii. The 50 state legislatures which today represent the people of our 50 states are all "descendants" of the Virginia House of Burgesses, the fir[st] legislative assembly in America. The fir[st] meeting of the Virginia assembly in 1619 [is] shown above by a diorama in the Coloni[al] Historical Park at Jamestown.

This "power of the purse" was important then and is in our day.

covering a large area. The business of the county is in the hands of a sheriff, an officer of the militia, and several justices of the peace. These officials are appointed by the governor, not elected by the voters. In the Middle Colonies, I believe, there is a mixture of town and county government. I myself am glad I live in New England where we have town meetings."

Conflicts often arise in colonial government. "Of course," Jonathan continues, "although we get along pretty well, we do have disputes and quarrels. Sometimes a governor wishes to have his own way regardless of the wishes of the people. But the legislature of each colony has the right to vote on all bills for taxes, and in most colonies it votes the governor's salary. So the governor cannot afford to be too highhanded.

"Then, too, the people do not always agree among themselves. There may be disagreements between the people who live in large towns and those who live on farms. Or arguments may arise between people who live in the settled regions along the seacoast and those who live on the frontier. Disputes also develop between those who are well-to-do and those who are not. Not everybody can have his own way. But, on the whole, our form of government works very well. I think we are fortunate to have as great a part in ruling ourselves as we have."

•

Jonathan's story makes it plain that by 1750 the English colonists had come a long way on the road to self-government. The colonists were used to certain rights and to having a share in their own government. These are precious things, and men who possess them do not willingly give them up. As we shall see, the colonists guarded these rights, fought and bled for them, and handed them down to their children and their grandchildren. In this way we, today, have received a priceless heritage which we must never take for granted.

These sentences bring out the importance **142** *of helping pupils to develop positive attitudes toward American traditions, institutions, and way of life.*

1. In what ways were the governments of the English colonies alike?

2. In what ways did the government in England have control over the colonial governments?

3. (a) How were the governors of the various colonies selected? (b) How were the members of the legislatures chosen? (c) Who had the right to vote in the colonies?

This sub-section presents the English point of view; the American (colonial) viewpoint is given on pages 144ff. Help pupils see the "arguments" supporting each side.

3 Why Did England and Her Colonies Disagree Over Colonial Affairs?

See if pupils sense which would cost more. What is likely to happen to a country which exports raw materials and buys manufactured goods?

Although English colonists had rights and some voice in their government, they were subject to control by the mother country. In fact, England had some very definite ideas about colonies and how they should be run. What were these ideas and how did the colonists feel about them?

ENGLAND SAYS THAT COLONIES EXIST FOR THE GOOD OF ENGLAND

Englishmen believed that the colonies existed for the benefit of the mother country. After all, they reasoned, the colonies had been started by England. The colonists enjoyed certain rights, including some self-government, only because England allowed it. And England provided armies and ships to help protect the colonies from the Indians and the French. The feeling in England, therefore, was that the colonies owed much to the mother country and should be willing to obey laws and regulations which would benefit England.

Trade means wealth for England. What did England want of her colonies? She expected them to add to her wealth. To be sure, no gold or silver mines, such as those which enriched Spain, had been discovered. There was another way, however, by which the colonies could bring riches to the mother country. This was through trade. For example, the colonies produced plentiful supplies of certain goods which Great Britain desired. Among them were tobacco, indigo, rice, and the materials used in building ships. On the other hand, the colonists needed many articles manufactured in England — clothes, hats, kettles, weapons, and tools.

For a number of reasons, England wanted its American colonies to sell most of their raw materials to the mother country and in turn buy from England most of the manufactured products the colonists needed. Manufacturing articles for the colonies would bring employment to many people in England as well as profits to manufacturers. There would also be good profits for shipbuilders, shipowners, and

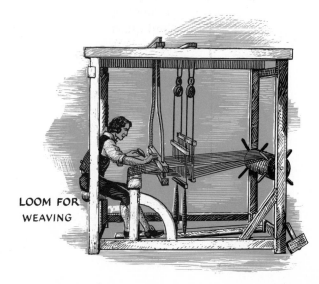

LOOM FOR WEAVING

merchants if goods passing to and from the colonies were carried in English vessels or in vessels built in the English colonies. But how, thought Englishmen, can we keep so profitable a trade for ourselves alone?

England passes laws to control colonial trade.   In order to protect England's trade with her colonies, Parliament had from time to time passed laws known as *Navigation Acts.* Two of the most important of these were passed by Parliament in the 1660's. The Navigation Acts included the following regulations:

(1) The colonists were required to export certain of their products only to Britain or to other British colonies. At first, only a few products — such as sugar, tobacco, and indigo — had to be sold to England. As time went on, however, more articles produced by the colonists were added to the list.

(2) All goods coming to the colonies from other countries must first pass through England. For example, if a cargo of tea were sent from China to Philadelphia, it must be taken to England first. There it could be taxed by the government and then shipped on to Philadelphia.

(3) All goods going to or coming from the colonies were to be carried by ships built in England or in the colonies, Three fourths of the crews of these vessels, said the Navigation Acts, must be Englishmen or colonists.

England controls colonial manufacturing.   In early days the settlers had little time or opportunity to manufacture goods. As the colonies became larger and more settled, some manufacturing began. Goods were not made in factories, as they would be today, but by people in their homes. In time, colonial manufacturing grew until it threatened to hurt the sale of goods made in England. So Parliament

passed other acts to make sure that articles made in the colonies would not interfere with the sale of English goods. Colonists might make their own clothes or hats, for example, but they could not manufacture clothes or hats to sell in other colonies or in other countries. Colonists might also manufacture iron, but were not allowed to make it into finished articles.

The colonists did not suffer as much from these laws controlling trade and manufacturing as you might expect. Because certain articles had to be sold to England the colonists were sure of a good market for these goods. Colonial shipbuilding and shipping increased because goods were supposed to be carried in English or colonial vessels. It is true, too, that England's colonial regulations were far less strict than those of Spain. Nevertheless, England felt free to regulate colonial trade and manufacturing with little thought for the wishes of the colonists.

THE COLONISTS SAY THAT THE COLONIES EXIST FOR THEIR OWN BENEFIT

The settlers in America did not agree that the purpose of the colonies was to make England wealthy. In fact, they did not believe they owed the mother country anything. The colonists remembered that in crossing the ocean to settle in the New World, they had faced countless hardships and dangers. They had worked hard to build new homes in the wilderness and had fought off hostile savages. Even though England had furnished help in the wars against France, they themselves had also contributed money and troops. Indeed, the colonists felt they had done most of the work of building the new empire in America. For this reason they believed their trade should not be regulated.

Make sure that pupils see that the Acts helped the colonists in some ways.

How the Navigation Acts
Regulated Trade

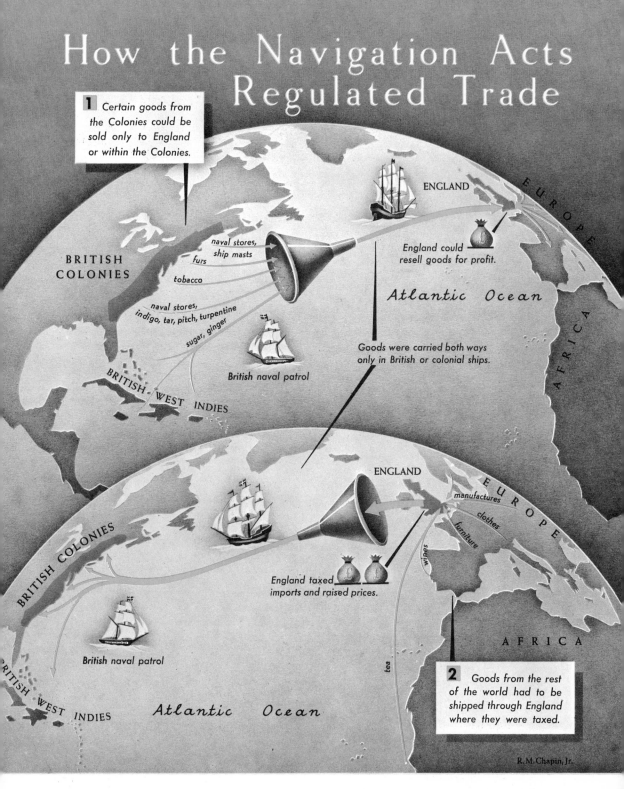

1 Certain goods from the Colonies could be sold only to England or within the Colonies.

ENGLAND

England could resell goods for profit.

BRITISH COLONIES

Atlantic Ocean

naval stores, ship masts

furs

tobacco

naval stores, indigo, tar, pitch, turpentine

sugar, ginger

British naval patrol

BRITISH WEST INDIES

EUROPE

AFRICA

Goods were carried both ways only in British or colonial ships.

ENGLAND

manufactures

clothes

furniture

wines

BRITISH COLONIES

England taxed imports and raised prices.

British naval patrol

BRITISH WEST INDIES

Atlantic Ocean

EUROPE

AFRICA

tea

2 Goods from the rest of the world had to be shipped through England where they were taxed.

R. M. Chapin, Jr.

MAP STUDY These maps show how Britain tried to limit the amount of trade which her colonies could carry on directly with the rest of the world. (1) How did Britain control the export of colonial goods to foreign countries? (2) How did Britain regulate colonial imports of goods from other countries?

Use this map to review and explain points made on pages 143-144.

TRADE FLOURISHED in the colonial port of Charles Town (now Charleston), South Carolina, shown in this old engraving. The description below the picture reports that in the 1700's "between 200 and 300" ships entered the port every year.

The colonists ignore many of the trade laws. For many years no serious trouble developed over British laws regulating colonial trade. England was too busy with affairs at home and with her efforts to defeat France to bother very much about enforcing these laws. Although some officers were appointed to enforce the Navigation Acts, many of them never crossed the Atlantic to carry out their duties in the colonies. The officers who were stationed at the colonial seaports did not try hard to keep the settlers from trading with other countries. So *smuggling* (shipping goods secretly and against the law) was common and very profitable. For instance, colonial merchants smuggled tea from Holland instead of buying it from English merchants whose prices were higher. When colonial merchants and planters gathered in taverns or talked by their firesides, they often grumbled about the British regulations. But they did not go beyond the point of grumbling.

The colonists disagree with England about colonial government. England and her American colonies had some differences of opinion, also, about how the colonies should be governed. Although the colonists were loyal to the king, they believed it was only right that they should be allowed to manage their own affairs. The spirit of freedom was strong in America; and England, after all, was far away. The colonists felt that Englishmen, including the king and his advisers, knew little about conditions in America. The king and Parliament, on the other hand, thought otherwise. They believed that England possessed wide powers of government over her settlements in America. One government officer spoke of the colonies as "these American children, planted by our care, nourished up by our indulgence [kindness] to a degree of strength . . . , and protected by our arms."

Before 1763, however, Great Britain did not often insist upon using her powers of government. To be sure, from time to time a charter was taken away from a colony or proprietor. And the British government continued to claim the right to tax the colonists and to set aside laws passed in the colonies. But these powers were not often used.

•

To sum up, the colonists did not entirely agree with England over the mother country's right to control their government and their trade, but there had been no actual conflict. It is easy to see, however, that any move by England to enforce the trade laws or govern more strictly in the colonies was likely to lead to trouble.

CHECK UP

1. (a) Why did Englishmen believe that the colonies existed for the benefit of England? (b) Why did the English colonists feel that they owed England nothing?

2. (a) What were the provisions of the Navigation Acts? (b) What was the attitude of the colonists toward the laws regulating colonial trade?

3. How did the colonists and the English leaders disagree on the way the colonies should be governed?

Check Up on Chapter 7

Do You Know the Meaning?

1. smuggle
2. county
3. legislature
4. jury
5. trial
6. town meeting
7. representative
8. petition
9. regulate
10. justice of the peace

Can You Identify?

1. Magna Carta
2. Parliament
3. 1215
4. Petition of Right
5. English Bill of Rights
6. Navigation Acts

What Do You Think?

1. Why are the great documents of *English* freedom (page 138) mentioned in an *American* history textbook?

What Do You Think? (Cont.)

2. (a) What kinds of questions were settled at a town meeting in the New England colonies? (b) Was the town meeting an example of representative government? Why?

3. What freedoms do Americans have today that the people in the English colonies did not have?

4. Why did the English colonies escape the strict regulation imposed on the Spanish and French colonies?

5. Why did the English colonists actually suffer little from England's regulation of their trade and manufacturing before 1763?

Questions 1, 3, and 4 get at points which students should be able to "figure out."

LINKING PAST AND PRESENT

The town meeting. Many New England towns still hold town meetings, just as they did in colonial days. At appointed times, all the voters gather to discuss and then to vote directly on any problems that have to do with running the town's affairs. This is democracy in its simplest form, for every voter

has a direct voice in how things are run. He hears how the town's money is being spent, and if anything is going on that he doesn't like, he is free to stand up and say so.

Of course, this kind of government is possible only in communities of the right size. The town meeting system never got started in the southern colonies or in the frontier region because people in those areas lived too far apart to get together for meetings. Also, in most cities there are too many voters for town meetings to be practical. Instead, citizens elect some city officials, and others are appointed.

Freedom of the press. Freedom of the press (the right to print one's opinions without restriction) has always been important to Americans. In the 1730's, an immigrant from Germany named John Peter Zenger published the New York *Weekly Journal.* Zenger printed a series of articles criticizing the policies and actions of the royal governor of New York. For one thing, the governor had interfered in the election of a representative to the colonial assembly. Although the governor's candidate had lost anyway, Zenger's paper did not hesitate to expose the governor's unfair action. In further issues, the

paper told about other ways in which the governor had abused his power, and called upon the people of the colony to defend their liberties. Finally, Zenger was arrested, and four issues of his newspaper were burned in front of the City Hall.

At his trial, Zenger was defended by Andrew Hamilton, a well-known lawyer from the neighboring colony of Pennsylvania. Hamilton argued that the publisher had printed the truth about the governor's administration and that it was every man's right to criticize an unjust government. Although the judge made known his feeling that Zenger was guilty, the twelve jurymen took only a few minutes to return a verdict of "not guilty." The courageous publisher was set free. Zenger returned to his printing shop and continued to attack the governor in his newspaper! His trial was an important landmark in establishing the freedom of the press in America.

Peter Zenger, Fighter for Freedom tells the interesting story of this valiant publisher.

The American Colonists

Resist Strict Control by England

How would this bulletin have been written if it had been released in England?

What this chapter is about —

If radio or television had existed in the year 1775, these two news announcements might have come suddenly over the air:

(March 23) We interrupt this program to bring you a special news bulletin. A Virginia leader today advised Americans to prepare for war! In a speech before the Virginia Convention, Patrick Henry, well-known statesman, said that there was no longer any hope for peace. Declaring that Americans must fight if they wish to be free, Henry ended his fiery speech with these defiant words: "I know not what course others may take; but as for me, give me liberty or give me death!"

(April 19) The top news story of the moment comes from Boston. Fighting broke out today between American colonists and soldiers of the British army! A column of his Majesty's soldiers, marching to Concord, Massachusetts, to destroy war supplies, clashed with colonists assembled on the Common at Lexington. Shots were fired and several colonists were killed. Heavy fighting later took place at Concord Bridge.

Fighting between Great Britain and her American colonists! Only twelve years before, at the end of the French and Indian War in 1763, no one would have guessed that this would happen. Something must have gone seriously wrong to provoke such

People in our story — colonial printer, Son of Liberty,
colonial woman, British officer, American minuteman.

"Why, there's plenty of land here for us! The Indians don't farm it."

"The settlers are spoiling our hunting grounds. Let's drive out all the white men!"

defiant words and violent acts. In this chapter we shall learn about events between 1763 and 1775 which led to fighting between the mother country and her American colonies. To help us understand the course of events, we shall seek answers to these questions:

▶ 1. How did England try to tighten her control over the Thirteen Colonies?

▶ 2. How did the American colonists react to stricter control by England?

▶ 3. What happened when England punished the colonists for their resistance?

Can your pupils explain how each of the characters pictured felt about the fur trade, and why?

1 How Did England Try to Tighten Her Control Over the Thirteen Colonies?

England considers new plans for its colonies. If we had been present at a meeting of the king's ministers [1] in London at the close of the French and Indian War in 1763, we might have heard George Grenville, the chief or *Prime Minister,* address his companions in words like these:

"Gentlemen, a great war has just ended. After long and hard fighting we have defeated our powerful enemy, France. Victory has brought us a vast territory in

[1] In England the members of the king's cabinet are called ministers.

America. Today England is the proud ruler of the greatest empire in the world.

"All this is very gratifying. But our victory has also brought problems. Now that we have gained additional territories in America, we must decide how they shall be governed. We shall need to send an army to keep order in these new lands of ours.

"Governing our American colonies and keeping an army there is going to be very expensive. In the war just ended, we already have spent a great deal. We have had to borrow money, and the only way we can repay this debt is by increasing

This is a useful approach for presenting **150** *the English point of view.*

"If we had only kept those settlers out in the first place, we wouldn't be in this mess!"

view Grenville's reasoning was sound. He and the other members of the British government were convinced that the colonies should be governed more efficiently and contribute more money to pay expenses. And while Grenville was working out a plan to strengthen British power in America, news arrived which made him more certain than ever that he was right.

Pontiac's War convinces Grenville he is right. You remember that pioneers had been settling in the Ohio region beyond the Allegheny Mountains. This fact angered the Indians in the territory because they considered it their land. In the spring of 1763, they united in a plan to get rid of the white men once and for all.

The leader of the Indians was a great warrior and chief named Pontiac. He persuaded the various western tribes to attack all the British forts and settlements in the Ohio region, so as to drive out the English at one blow. At first the attacks were successful. Most of the forts were captured and many settlers were killed and their homes burned. Later, however, more British forces were sent to help the frontiersmen, and Pontiac was defeated.

Pontiac's War showed, said Grenville, that it was necessary to have an army in America to keep control over the Indians. He also decided there would be less trouble

taxes. But the many landowners here in England are even now groaning about the heavy taxes they are required to pay. I do not want to tax the people of England any more than is necessary. I am convinced, moreover, that the colonies can contribute some of the money we need. And there is good reason why they should. If we have to keep an army in America, won't the colonists benefit more by it than the taxpayers of England?"

Grenville didn't actually say these words, but we may be sure that they tell what he was thinking. From his point of

Note that only 12 years separate the end of the war with the French and the outbreak of fighting in the Revolution.

American Colonists Resist England

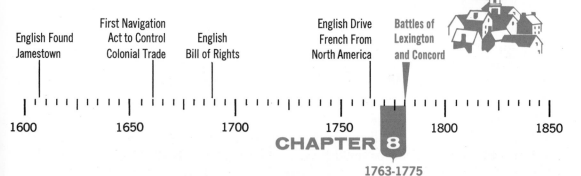

CHAPTER 8
1763-1775

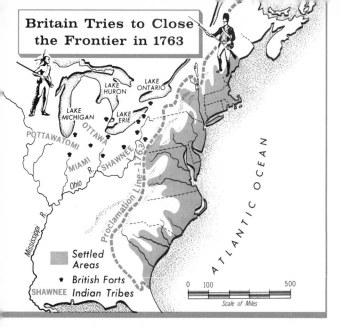

LAKE HURON
LAKE ONTARIO
LAKE MICHIGAN
LAKE ERIE
OTTAWA
POTTAWATOMI
MIAMI
SHAWNEE
Ohio R.
Proclamation Line—1763
Mississippi R.
ATLANTIC OCEAN

Settled Areas
British Forts
SHAWNEE Indian Tribes

0   100   500
Scale of Miles

MAP STUDY   In 1763 the British forbade colonial settlers to go west of the line shown above. The names in color are those of Indian tribes that lived in the Ohio region.

if the white settlers and the Indians were kept apart and settlement of the Ohio region was delayed.

Grenville puts into effect a new program for the colonies.   Grenville and the British government took steps to tighten their control over the American colonies:

(1) *The Proclamation of 1763.* In 1763 Grenville issued a proclamation stating that no settlements were to be made west of the Allegheny Mountains except by special permission. If any settlements were there already, the settlers were "forthwith to remove themselves." All trade with the Indians would be closely controlled by the British government. To guard the fron-

Call attention to the chart on page 156. The fact that the western land for administrative purposes was united with the Province of Quebec angered the Americans.

tier, Grenville proposed to send 10,000 British soldiers to the American colonies.

(2) *Strict enforcement of the Navigation Acts.* Grenville also called for strict enforcement of the Navigation Acts. He realized that if smuggling could be stopped, greater profits would flow into the pockets of English merchants and manufacturers. More taxes on goods would also be collected. To carry out Grenville's idea, new officers were sent to America with strict orders to search for smugglers and to punish lawbreakers.

(3) *The Stamp Act.* Finally, to raise more money in the colonies, Parliament, at Grenville's suggestion, passed the *Stamp Act* in 1765. This law required that stamps sold by the British government must be placed on a great many articles, such as legal papers, newspapers, almanacs, calendars, and playing cards. Some of the stamps cost only a few cents, but others were quite expensive.

The British government felt that the Stamp Act and other laws were fair. They little dreamed what a storm would be aroused in the colonies.

CHECK UP

1. (a) Why did Grenville think the American colonies should contribute more money for defense and other government expenses? (b) How did Pontiac's War convince Grenville that he was right?

2. What were the three parts of Grenville's program?

2   How Did the American Colonists React to Stricter Control by England?

Grenville's program angers the colonists.   Each part of Grenville's program was disliked by one group or another in

the colonies. The settlers in the Ohio region, for example, were angry over the Proclamation of 1763. After the defeat of the French in the French and Indian War, they had expected to be free to settle this region. They wanted no meddling by a faraway government in what they considered their own affairs. So they defied the Proclamation of 1763, and continued to settle wherever they pleased. As for the colonial merchants and shipowners, they did not want to have the Navigation Acts enforced, because smuggling had brought them large profits.

THE COLONISTS TAKE ACTION AGAINST THE STAMP ACT

No "taxation without representation." The greatest excitement in the colonies was caused by the Stamp Act. In England most people agreed with Grenville that the colonies should be taxed to help pay for the army in America and for other colonial expenses. The stamp tax seemed to Englishmen a fair way to do this. The colonists, however, took a very different point of view. Americans believed that taxes should be voted by colonial legislatures whose members were chosen by the colonists themselves. They opposed taxation by Parliament because the colonists were not represented in that body. If Parliament could vote a stamp tax without their consent, what other articles might be taxed in the future? "Why not our lands?" questioned Samuel Adams, a Boston man. "Why not the produce of our lands, and everything we possess or make use of? . . . If taxes are laid upon us in any shape without our having a legal representative where they are laid, are we not reduced from . . . free subjects to the miserable state of . . . slaves?"

Many other colonists protested loudly against the Stamp Act and against "taxation without representation." In the Virginia House of Burgesses, young Patrick Henry, a member from the frontier region,

rose to speak against the act. Though not yet 30 years old, Patrick Henry spoke with great force and power. He declared that it was the right of the colonists to vote their own taxes. Aroused by Henry's speech, the House of Burgesses condemned the Stamp Act. News of this bold action spread to other colonies and caused heated discussion.

The Stamp Act Congress protests. Later in the year (1765), a *Stamp Act Congress* met in New York. Delegates came from nine of the colonies. A formal protest was drawn up and sent to England. In this protest the delegates expressed their loyalty to the mother country. They declared, however, that the right to tax the colonists belonged not to Parliament but to the assemblies of the people in the colonies.

The Sons of Liberty are organized. Nor was this all. In various colonies men

THE STAMP ACT angered people throughout the colonies. In this old print a New Yorker carries a poster attacking the British government's policy. Other colonists cheer him on.

banded together in groups called "Sons of Liberty" to protect their rights. Feeling ran high against officials who had been appointed to distribute the hated stamps. In Boston a mob strung up a dummy of Andrew Oliver, who had been appointed to sell the stamps there. Crowds also destroyed Oliver's office and wrecked the home of a prominent British official. Stamp sellers in other colonies were also threatened, and many of them resigned their positions. Steps were taken to destroy the stamps and to prevent their being landed in America.

A colonial "boycott" brings repeal of the hated Stamp Act. The colonists protested against the Stamp Act in still another way. Many colonists refused to buy goods from England. It was this *boycott,* or refusal to buy British goods, which had the greatest effect in England. The king's ministers were not much troubled by the Sons of Liberty or the protests of the Stamp Act Congress. But when trade with the American colonies dropped off sharply, British merchants and manufacturers began to complain.

In 1766, Parliament repealed (removed) the Stamp Act. At the same time, however, Parliament declared that it "had, hath, and of a right ought to have full power" to pass laws for governing the colonies "in all cases whatsoever." In other words, Parliament still insisted on its right to tax the colonies if it pleased, even though the colonies did not send representatives to Parliament. But the people in America paid little attention to this declaration. All that mattered to them was that the hated Stamp Act had been repealed. Throughout the colonies there was great rejoicing. Bells rang, crowds shouted, and people throughout the colonies proclaimed their loyalty to the mother country.

NEW LAWS AROUSE NEW PROTESTS IN THE COLONIES

The British government should have learned a lesson from its experience with the Stamp Act. The American colonists had made it clear that they would resist any interference with what they considered their rights. But King George III and his ministers did not take kindly to having their plans blocked by a group of colonists across the Atlantic Ocean. In addition, the British government still felt it was necessary to raise money in America to help pay the cost of governing and protecting the colonies.

The Townshend Acts anger the colonists. Within a year after the repeal of the Stamp Act, Parliament passed new laws to regulate the colonies. These laws became known as the *Townshend Acts* because they were proposed by Charles Townshend (*town'*zend), a minister of the king. He was unfriendly to the colonists, and his attitude was, "Let these Americans dare disobey these acts, and we shall see who is master."

Every one of the Townshend Acts angered the colonists. What were these acts, and why did the colonists object to them?

(1) Once again the Navigation Acts were to be strictly enforced. So that the British might look for smuggled goods, officers were to use general search warrants called *writs of assistance.* These writs (legal papers) would allow them to enter and search any house or building. The colonists were distressed to learn that their homes could be searched by any officer who had a writ of assistance.

(2) The Townshend Acts placed duties, or taxes, on a number of goods imported into the colonies. The list included such articles as lead, paper, paint, glass, and tea. The purpose of these duties was to raise money. The colonists were angry

Bring out that the writs of assistance would not be legal today. Search warrants specify the place to be searched and what is sought.

BENJAMIN FRANKLIN
began his lifelong search for new ideas when he was a printer's helper in colonial Philadelphia.

Bring out that the great men of this period, Franklin, Washington (page 179), Jefferson (page 249), had wide interests and talents along many lines.

A CIRCULATING LIBRARY, the first in America, was founded by young Franklin and his friends so they could share their books with each other. Franklin became a successful printer and publisher. He believed not only in spreading knowledge as widely as possible but in putting good ideas to work.

A GOOD CITIZEN, Franklin busied himself with public improvements, such as paving Philadelphia's muddy streets. Always eager to improve anything, he invented a new kind of street lamp, a stove, bifocal eyeglasses, and the lightning rod.

SCIENCE interested Franklin so much that he installed a special lightning rod in his home so that he could study sparks of electricity from the atmosphere. His experiments made him famous in Europe as well as America.

SPOKESMAN for the colonies was a natural role for Franklin because of his bold mind and his reputation abroad. Franklin presented American protests against the Stamp Act to the English Parliament (above). He spent the rest of his life representing Americans abroad and persuading them to work together at home.

BRITAIN vs. THE COLONISTS

Year	British actions	American actions
1763	Frontier closed by proclamation	Settlers ignore proclamation
1764	Navigation Acts enforced strictly	
1765	Stamp Act passed	Stamp Act Congress protests, British goods boycotted
1766	Stamp Act repealed	
1767	Townshend Acts passed	British goods boycotted
1768		
1769		
1770	Townshend Acts repealed, except for tea tax	—Boston Massacre—
1771		
1772		
1773	Cheap tea shipped to colonies	Boston Tea Party
1774	Intolerable Acts passed	First Continental Congress protests, British goods boycotted
1775	Troops raid Lexington and Concord	Minutemen resist

BRITISH ATTEMPTS to control the colonists and the colonists' protests against these attempts resulted in a widening split between Britain and the Americans.

because this law seemed to tax them without their consent.

(3) The money raised from the duties was to be used to pay British officers in America, including the governors of royal colonies. The colonists objected strongly to this plan, because it took away the right of their assemblies to control the salaries of colonial officials.

(4) Still another law forbade the New York Assembly to meet. This law was intended to punish the Assembly for not voting money to support British soldiers stationed in the colony. If such a thing could happen in New York, thought the colonists, might not all the colonies soon lose their assemblies?

The colonists resist the Townshend Acts. A new storm of protests broke out

in the colonies. Little groups of men gathered in the streets or sat in the taverns and argued angrily against the Townshend Acts. Led by Samuel Adams, the Massachusetts legislature sent to the other colonies a letter urging all to work together against these latest acts of Parliament. As in the case of the Stamp Act, however, Americans were not content with words alone. They started boycotting British goods on a large scale. Merchants agreed among themselves not to import goods from England, nor to buy and sell goods brought from England by others. As a result, trade between England and the colonies again dropped off sharply.

The Boston Massacre strengthens opposition. In Boston, Massachusetts, feeling ran especially high. Soldiers who had been sent there to maintain order only made matters worse. The British wore bright scarlet uniforms, and the Bostonians taunted them by calling them "redcoats" and "lobster-backs." On a snowy night in March, 1770, when a fire alarm had brought many people into the streets, a crowd of boys began throwing snowballs at a sentry. Other soldiers hurried to the sentry's aid. Soon a threatening crowd gathered. Some of the soldiers fired into the crowd, killing several citizens, among them Crispus Attucks, a Negro. This incident became known as the *Boston Massacre*. The wrath of the people of Boston was so great that the British troops had to withdraw to a fort in the harbor.

News of the Boston Massacre swept like wildfire through the colonies. There is no telling what might have happened if Parliament had not decided, at that very time, to repeal the Townshend duties. The duties were taken off, not so much because the colonists had protested as because the boycott was hurting English merchants and manufacturers. But in repealing the Townshend Acts, Parliament retained the threepenny tax on tea to show that it had the right to tax the colonists.

Tea causes more trouble. For a time after the repeal of the Townshend Acts in 1770, there was fairly good feeling between the colonists and the mother country. But suddenly, in 1773, the government of Great Britain took an unwise step that led once more to trouble. It allowed the British East India Company (a company which carried on trade with the Far East) to send tea directly to America. In other words, its ships did not have to stop first in England and pay the usual heavy tax. This arrangement made it possible for the East India Company to sell its tea in America at a very low price. But the colonists still had to pay the threepenny tax.

Although the colonists would be getting tea at a bargain price, they were not pleased. They asked suspiciously, "Is this a trick to make us forget that we must pay a tax on tea?" American merchants also became alarmed. Those who had been selling tea smuggled from Holland could not meet the low price of the East India Company. They feared that their business would be ruined.

Boston holds a tea party. Merchants and patriotic colonists made up their minds that the British East India Company should not be allowed to sell tea in the colonies. In some places, when ships carrying the tea reached America, the tea was landed and locked up in storehouses. In other ports the ships were turned back to England. At Boston, where feeling was especially strong, trouble broke out. One night in 1773, a party of men dressed up as Indians boarded the tea ships in Boston Harbor. Let us hear the story of the Boston Tea Party as told by a man who was there:

＊ It was now evening, and I immediately dressed myself in the costume of an Indian, equipped with a small hatchet, . . . with which, and a club, after having painted my face and hands with coal dust in the shop of a blacksmith, I repaired to Griffins Wharf, where the ships lay that contained the tea. When I first appeared in the street, after being thus disguised, I fell in with many who were dressed, equipped, and painted as I was, and who fell in with me, and marched in order to the place of our destination. . . . The commander of the division to which I belonged, as soon as we were on board the ship . . . ordered me to go to the captain and demand of him the keys to the hatches and a dozen candles. I made the demand accordingly, and the captain promptly replied, and delivered the articles; but requested me at the same time to do no damage to the ship or rigging. We then were ordered by our commander to open the hatches, and take out all

Bring out that this tax was retained as proof of right to tax, not because it would bring in much money.

THE BOSTON TEA PARTY was staged by the colonists as a protest against "taxation without representation." When this modern-day painting was first printed, the caption with it read, "They brewed independence in the world's largest teapot."

the chests of tea and throw them overboard, and we immediately proceeded to execute his orders; first cutting and splitting the chests with our tomahawks, so as thoroughly to expose them to the effects of the water. In about three hours from the time we went on board, we had thus broken and thrown overboard every tea chest to be found in the ship, while those in the other ships were disposing of the tea in the same way, at the same time. We were surrounded by British armed ships, but no attempt was made to resist us. We then quietly returned to our several [homes], without having any conversation with each other, or taking any measures to discover who were our associates. . . .

As news of the Boston Tea Party spread through the colonies, there was much excitement. Many colonists rejoiced at the bold action of the citizens of Boston. They agreed with the following jingle by an American poet:

When a certain great king, whose initial is G,
Shall force stamps upon paper, and folks to drink tea;
When these folks burn his tea and stamp paper, like stubble,
You may guess that this king is then coming to trouble.

But other colonists were upset. They felt that the colonists had a right to protest against unjust laws but not to take the law into their own hands. They did not believe it was right to destroy property.

The colonists originally had claimed that the colonial legislatures should levy internal taxes but had conceded Parliament's right to regulate trade. In time they also challenged Parliament's right to do the latter.

1. What did the colonists mean by "no taxation without representation"?

2. (a) In what ways did the colonists protest against the Stamp Act? (b) What was the result?

3. (a) What were the Townshend Acts? (b) How did the colonists resist them?

4. Why did colonists in Boston decide to hold a "Tea Party"?

In answering this question students should bring out that the colonial position grew increasingly firm.

3 What Happened When England Punished the Colonists for Their Resistance?

Laws planned to punish Massachusetts arouse the colonists. When news of the Boston Tea Party reached faraway Britain, most Englishmen agreed that the colonists had gone too far. George III and his ministers were angry, and felt that the unruly colonists must be taught a lesson. For this reason several laws were passed in 1774 to punish Massachusetts. One of these laws closed the port of Boston, so that its people could not trade with the outside world until the owners of the tea had been paid for their loss. Another law took away from Massachusetts many rights of self-government. More troops were sent to Boston, and their commander, General Thomas Gage, was appointed governor of Massachusetts.

To the colonists these laws seemed so harsh that they called them the *Intolerable Acts* (intolerable means unbearable). When news of the Intolerable Acts spread to other colonies, people felt sorry for Massachusetts and angry at the British government. Food and supplies poured into Boston from other colonies. The Virginia House of Burgesses proclaimed a day of prayer and fasting as a protest against the Intolerable Acts.

Patriots throughout the colonies work together. You may wonder how it was that the other colonies heard about Massachusetts' punishment and responded so quickly. The colonists who resisted strict control by the British came to be known as *Patriots*. Even before the Intolerable Acts, Patriots in all the colonies had found a way to work together. Samuel Adams had suggested that a committee be

THIS ENGLISH CARTOON made fun of the Boston Patriots, showing them as "caged" by the Intolerable Acts with nothing to eat but fish.

Can pupils point out things in this cartoon which reflect an anti-colonial bias?

COLONEL JOHN STARK of New Hampshire was among the Patriots who left their farms and trades to answer the call to defend the colonies. Colonel Stark fought at Bunker Hill and later battles of the Revolution.

formed in Boston to write letters to, or "correspond" with, citizens of other towns. They would tell what was happening or what they believed should be done to protect their rights. Similar committees were soon formed by Patriots in many Massachusetts towns. These groups became known as *Committees of Correspondence.* The committees in the various colonies began to correspond with each other. By the time the Intolerable Acts were passed, there were Committees of Correspondence throughout the colonies.

The First Continental Congress meets. Because of what was happening to Massa-

chusetts, the colonists decided to hold a meeting to discuss how they could (1) protect their rights and (2) settle their differences with the mother country. In September, 1774, over 50 men, representing twelve of the colonies, assembled in Carpenters' Hall, Philadelphia. This meeting has become known as the *First Continental Congress.* (People in the English colonies on the continent of North America were commonly called Continentals by the British.)

The delegates to the First Continental Congress thought of themselves as Englishmen, and they wanted to defend their rights as English subjects. They all felt that such laws as the Stamp Act, the Townshend Acts, and the Intolerable Acts were unfair to the colonies. But they were not agreed on what action to take. Some of the bolder men, including Patrick Henry and Samuel Adams, thought that firm steps should be taken. They believed that George III and Parliament should be shown that the colonists' rights must be respected! Other delegates advised the colonists to move carefully. They did not wish to anger the mother country any further or to endanger American trade with her. Hardly any of the delegates even thought of separating from Great Britain.

Before returning to their homes, the delegates to the First Continental Congress agreed that Massachusetts should not obey the Intolerable Acts and if necessary should resist them with force. The Congress drew up a paper addressed to the king which protested that the Intolerable Acts were "unjust" and "cruel." The Congress also protested against being taxed without representation. In addition, the Congress proposed a plan to boycott English goods throughout the colonies. Each town was urged to form a committee to publish the

The colonists thought of themselves as Englishmen doing their utmost to preserve the "rights of Englishmen."

THE COLONISTS RESIST ENGLISH CONTROL   161

names of those who failed to co-operate in this plan. Finally, the delegates arranged for another Continental Congress to meet in May, 1775, if relations between the colonists and the mother country were no better by that time.

The colonies prepare to fight. In the past, the protests of the colonies and their boycotts of British goods had brought results. The Stamp Act had been repealed; the Townshend Acts had been abandoned. This time, however, the British government stood firm. Either the colonies must give in or they must fight. Which should it be? As the year 1774 drew to a close and 1775 began, more and more colonists came to believe that they must fight. Groups of men all over the colonies began to meet for military drill. Massachusetts defied its governor, General Gage, and started to organize an army.

Most of the colonists still did not expect to break away from Great Britain. They thought that firm resistance to the laws they disliked, and perhaps a little fighting, would bring the British government to its senses. Then the hated laws would be changed, and the Americans would go on as before — as loyal colonists of Great Britain. Yet could they? Rising before a body of fellow-Virginians on March 23, 1775, the fiery Patrick Henry cried:

⋇ Gentlemen may cry, peace, peace — but there is no peace. The war is actually begun! The next gale that sweeps from the north will bring to our ears the clash of resounding arms! Our brethren are already in the field! Why stand we here idle? What is it that gentlemen wish? What would they have? Is life so dear, or peace so sweet, as to be purchased at the price of chains and slavery? Forbid it, Almighty God! I know not what course others may take; but as for me, give me liberty, or give me death!

The British act. The British could not remain idle while the men of Massachu-

Did Patrick Henry's views square with Those of most Americans?

"THE BRITISH ARE COMING!" Hearing a galloping horse, a farmer leans out his window to hear Paul Revere shout the famous warning. Soon many farmers like this one in his nightshirt were dressed, armed, and ready to meet the British soldiers.

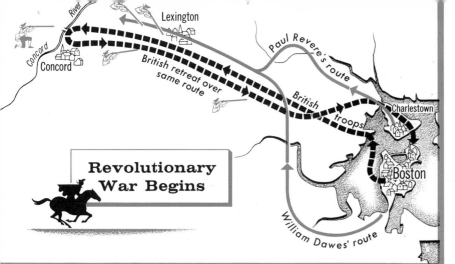

MAP STUDY

Warned by Revere and Dawes, colonial minutemen gathered to meet the British troops. (1) Where were the first shots fired? (2) Where did the British turn back? Fighting continued along the route of the British retreat.

Concord is located 19 miles west and a little to the north of Boston.

setts defied the government by gathering arms and ammunition. In April, General Gage planned to send a force of soldiers to the town of Concord, some eighteen miles from Boston, to destroy war supplies which the Patriots had collected there. He hoped also to capture the Patriot leaders, Samuel Adams and John Hancock, who were staying in the town of Lexington between Boston and Concord. On the night of April 18, Gage ordered his men to set out from Boston for Lexington and Concord.

Paul Revere warns the Patriots. The Patriots, however, were on the watch. Their soldiers were called *minutemen* because they could assemble quickly from their homes. Ready to ride into the country and rouse the minutemen were Paul Revere, a silversmith of Boston, and a companion named William Dawes. As the poet Longfellow wrote of Paul Revere:

He said to his friend, "If the British march
By land or sea from the town tonight,
Hang a lantern aloft in the belfry arch
Of the North Church tower as a signal light,
One, if by land, and two, if by sea;
And I on the opposite shore will be,
Ready to ride and spread the alarm
Through every Middlesex village and farm,
For the country folk to be up and to arm."

The friend kept watch in Boston, and learned that the redcoats were preparing to march. The poet goes on:

Meanwhile, impatient to mount and ride,
Booted and spurred, with a heavy stride
On the opposite shore walked Paul Revere. . . .

And lo! as he looks, on the belfry's height
A glimmer, and then a gleam of light!
He springs to the saddle, the bridle he turns,
But lingers and gazes, till full on his sight
A second lamp in the belfry burns! . . .

So through the night rode Paul Revere;
And so through the night went his cry of
    alarm
To every Middlesex village and farm.

The poet does not tell us so, but Paul Revere was captured by the British after he had reached Lexington and had warned Adams and Hancock. Neither Revere nor Dawes reached Concord, but a third messenger succeeded. He roused the farmers along the way to Concord and gave the alarm in the town. (See map above.)

A shot is "heard round the world." When the British soldiers reached Lexington in the early morning of April 19, 1775, they found a band of determined minutemen barring their way. Shots were fired. Eight of the Patriots were killed and ten

162

more were wounded. Then the British marched on to Concord six miles away. There they burned the courthouse and destroyed military supplies collected by the colonists. At a bridge on the edge of town, the British met another group of determined minutemen, and several volleys were fired by each side. But the fighting was not over. As the British soldiers marched back to Boston, other Patriots seized guns and took their positions along the road. From behind stone walls and trees the Americans poured a withering fire upon the British. Before the redcoats reached Boston, nearly 300 were killed, wounded, or missing.

What would happen next? Blood had been shed on both sides. Possibly the colonists still could have gone back to resisting the laws they disliked with written pro-

This fighting might have been more disastrous for the British had not fresh troops met the retreating column.

tests and fiery speeches. But the colonists did not put down their arms. Instead, they went on to defend their rights and create a new nation. For this reason another poet (Ralph Waldo Emerson) said of the fighting at Concord:

By the rude bridge that arched the flood,
Their flag to April's breeze unfurled,
Here once the embattled farmers stood,
And fired the shot heard round the world.

CHECK UP

1. (a) What were the Intolerable Acts? (b) Why were they passed?

2. (a) Why did the First Continental Congress meet? (b) What actions did the delegates take?

3. (a) What led to fighting at Lexington and Concord? (b) What were the results?

Check Up on Chapter 8

This question reinforces the idea that there were two points of view, each

Do You Know the Meaning?

1. boycott
2. patriot
3. prime minister
4. delegate
5. repeal
6. proclamation
7. intolerable
8. writ of assistance

Can You Identify?

1. Grenville
2. Townshend
3. Stamp Act
4. Patrick Henry
5. Paul Revere
6. George III
7. 1765
8. minutemen
9. redcoats
10. Continental
11. Sons of Liberty
12. Boston Tea Party
13. Boston Massacre
14. Pontiac
15. Samuel Adams
16. Crispus Attucks
17. April 19, 1775
18. Proclamation of 1763
19. First Continental Congress
20. Committees of Correspondence

Can You Locate?

1. Concord
2. Lexington
3. Boston

What Do You Think?

1. (a) Why did Englishmen fail to understand the American colonists? (b) Why were the colonists unable to see England's side of the quarrel?

2. Do you think that if England had treated the colonists more wisely, they would have been content to remain under British control? Give reasons for your answer.

3. Did the repeal of the Stamp Act mean that Parliament had changed its attitude on the question of taxing the American colonists? Explain.

4. Tell in your own words what Patrick Henry said in the Virginia House of Burgesses (page 161). Do you agree with what he said? Why?

5. American people today have to pay a "stamp" tax to the government on such articles as playing cards. Why do we not object?

reasonable to those who held it. But those on neither side seemed able to "put themselves in the shoes" of the other side.

Reminders of the minutemen. On the village green at Lexington, Massachusetts, a great boulder marks the spot where the minutemen assembled against the British regulars on April 19, 1775. On the boulder are engraved these words, believed to have been spoken by the minuteman leader, Captain John Parker:

> Stand your ground.
> Don't fire unless fired upon.
> But if they mean to have a war
> Let it begin here.

Beyond Lexington, in the town of Concord, is the spot where the minutemen "fired the shot heard round the world." Here, a large bronze figure of a minuteman, rifle in hand, stands beside his plow. The old wooden bridge "that arched the flood" is long since gone; but a concrete copy of it now crosses the Concord River. Our country has honored these early Patriots with the Minuteman National Historic Site, which includes many historic spots on the Lexington-Concord road.

It is interesting to know that two British redcoats killed in the clash at Concord were buried nearby. A stone marks their resting place, and each year a group of their countrymen decorates the grave.

"Yankee Doodle, keep it up!" Americans were being called Yankees as far back as the 1760's, when the Americans and the British fought together in the French and Indian War. The redcoats in their fine uniforms used to poke fun at the untrained co-lonial soldiers, calling them "Yankee Doodles." (A "doodle" was a silly fellow.) One Englishman wrote some new verses to an old tune, ridiculing the Yankee Doodles. But the joke backfired. The Americans liked the catchy tune and, in spite of the redcoats' laughter, were soon singing "Yankee Doodle" as a marching song. "Yankee Doodle" continued to be popular in America long after the Revolution, and as you know, it is still one of our national songs.

The nickname Yankee has lasted also. In the war between the North and South, Northerners were called Yankees. During the two World Wars, American troops — northern or southern — were called Yanks by the Europeans. And today in Mexico and other parts of Latin America, we are referred to as "Yanquis." So a name given in fun 200 years ago has become a common word today.

Paul Revere. In a busy downtown part of Boston stands a house that was already old when Paul Revere bought it in 1770. He lived in it for 30 years. It is the only house built in the 1600's that still stands in a large American city. The windows are of small panes in diamond shape, joined by lead frames, and the second floor juts out over the first. Paul Revere was a skilled metal worker, who could make anything from beautiful silver bowls and tea sets to large bronze church bells. Pieces of his silverwork are treasured today; and his bells are still rung in the steeples of many New England churches.

Longfellow's poem insures that students will remember Revere as the man who warned the minutemen. The story in the poem can be compared with Revere's own account (see Rebels and Redcoats).

The story of the Liberty Bell is told on page 189.

9

The Thirteen English Colonies
Win Their Independence

Perhaps your pupils can divide themselves into Patriots and Loyalists to debate this issue.

What this chapter is about —

Serious and honest men do not overthrow one government and set up another unless they believe their rights and liberties can be maintained in no other way. For this reason many of our forefathers hesitated to cast off the rule of Great Britain. One of them, Thomas Jefferson, said: "Prudence, indeed, will dictate that Governments long established should not be changed for light and transient [quickly passing] causes."

Yet British soldiers and American Patriots had died in the fighting at Lexington and Concord on April 19, 1775. An open break between the colonies and the mother country had taken place. Should the Patriots throw off the British government once and for all? Or should they try to heal the break and continue to live as subjects of King George? These were burning questions in 1775.

In this chapter we shall learn how our forefathers made their decision. We shall study also the war which was fought to win our independence. To aid us in our study, we shall look for answers to the following questions:

▶ 1. Why did the Thirteen Colonies decide to declare their independence?

▶ 2. What strengths and weaknesses did the Americans have in the Revolution?

▶ 3. How did the Thirteen Colonies win their independence?

People in our story — French soldier, Continental cavalryman and foot soldier, British grenadier, Hessian soldier.

1 Why Did the Thirteen Colonies Decide to Declare Their Independence?

Encourage pupils to read clarifying information in footnotes.

GREAT BRITAIN AND THE COLONIES
DRIFT FARTHER APART AS
FIGHTING CONTINUES

News of the fighting at Lexington and Concord spread quickly through the colonies. Meanwhile the British troops of General Gage remained in Boston while Patriot recruits gathered in the towns surrounding the city. These men had guns but no uniforms. They had little training, but they did have the courage to face the king's soldiers.

The colonists fight bravely in the Battle of Bunker Hill. During the night of June 16, 1775, a force of 1200 Americans stealthily climbed Bunker Hill and Breed's Hill overlooking the city of Boston. (Look at the map on page 167.) If they could hold these hills, the Patriots might force the English troops to leave Boston. When the morning light came, the startled British found that the Americans had taken up their position on Breed's Hill.[1]

General Gage sent a body of redcoats to drive off or capture the bold Americans. While the citizens of Boston watched intently from their housetops, the lines of British soldiers advanced in perfect order toward the summit of the hill. Twice they nearly reached the top, only to be driven back by the sharpshooting Americans. Dead and dying covered the hillside. But the Patriots were running short of powder. When the redcoats attacked a third time, the Americans were forced to withdraw from the hill. The British were fond of boasting that their regular troops were the finest in the world. Yet in the Battle of Bunker Hill, Patriot farmer lads stood up to the regulars and caused more than twice as many losses as they suffered themselves.

Colonial troops force the British to leave Boston. During the months following the Battle of Bunker Hill, the Pa-

[1] The Patriots received orders to seize Bunker Hill, but instead they fortified themselves on Breed's Hill nearby. Although the battle was fought on Breed's Hill, it has always been called the Battle of Bunker Hill.

If the Patriots could hold these hills and bring up artillery, the British would have to leave Boston. Artillery put into position on Dorchester Heights (see map, page 167) later drove out the British.

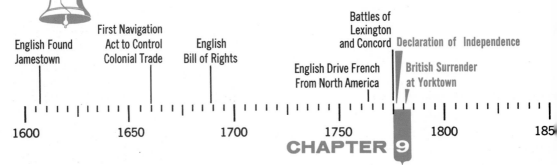

American Colonies Win Independence

English Found Jamestown

First Navigation Act to Control Colonial Trade

English Bill of Rights

English Drive French From North America

Battles of Lexington and Concord

Declaration of Independence

British Surrender at Yorktown

| 1600 | 1650 | 1700 | 1750 | 1800 | 185 |

CHAPTER 9

1775-1783

THE BATTLE OF BUNKER HILL is dramatized in this diorama. The Patriots are armed and ready for the uphill attack of the British troops at left. In the background, across Boston Harbor, are the homes and shipyards of Boston.

The Patriots, armed with rifles, fought from behind an embankment. The British made direct attacks and neglected to cut off the escape route.

triot forces surrounded Boston, but were unable to drive the British out of the city. Then, early in 1776, cannon which had been dragged hundreds of miles overland from Fort Ticonderoga in northeastern New York reached the Patriots outside Boston. The Patriots planned to place these cannon on Dorchester Heights, another hill overlooking the city and harbor. On a night early in March, 1776, the Patriots succeeded in occupying Dorchester Heights. General Howe, the new British commander, decided that he could no longer hold Boston. On March 17, 1776, the British troops embarked on ships in the harbor and sailed away to Halifax, Nova Scotia. The Patriots entered Boston and held it from then on. There were no more major battles in New England during the Revolutionary War.

Blows are struck elsewhere. In the months between the fighting at Lexington (April, 1775) and the capture of Boston (March, 1776), the colonists struck other blows. A group of Patriots led by Ethan Allen seized Fort Ticonderoga (from which the cannon were later taken to Boston) and the British fort at Crown Point, also in northeastern New York. Encouraged by these victories, two Amer-

ican expeditions invaded Canada. The Americans seized Montreal, but they failed to take Quebec. In the end, both expeditions withdrew. Far to the south, in the Carolinas, more fighting took place. At Moore's Creek, North Carolina, Patriots defeated a group of colonists who took the side of the British. Also, a British attack on Charleston, South Carolina, was successfully turned back. The map on page 168 shows where these battles took place.

MAP STUDY British troops drove the Patriots from heights in Charlestown, near Boston. How did the Americans later force the British to leave Boston?

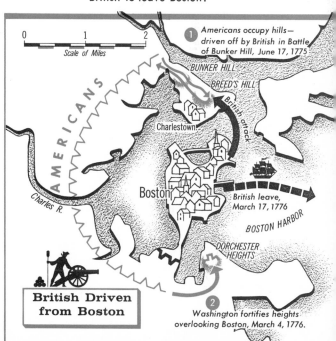

① Americans occupy hills— driven off by British in Battle of Bunker Hill, June 17, 1775

BUNKER HILL
BREED'S HILL
British attack
Charlestown

British leave, March 17, 1776

BOSTON HARBOR

Boston

AMERICANS

Charles R.

DORCHESTER HEIGHTS

British Driven from Boston

② Washington fortifies heights overlooking Boston, March 4, 1776.

0   1   2
Scale of Miles

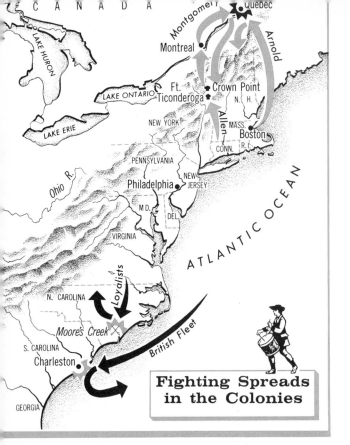

Hessians are pictured on page 165. The hiring of soldiers was a common practice in Europe.

Fighting Spreads in the Colonies

MAP STUDY   After seizing Fort Ticonderoga, Americans (colored arrows) invaded Canada but were turned back. At what points did the Patriots defeat early British efforts to win control of the South?

THE COLONIES DECLARE THEMSELVES INDEPENDENT

The attitude of the British government becomes stricter. Between the spring of 1775 and the spring of 1776, as we have seen, the colonists had taken up arms. Even so, most of them still hoped to remain British subjects. They believed that their willingness to shed blood would show King George III and his ministers how bitterly they opposed strict control by the mother country. As a result, the colonists (and many people in England, too) hoped that the British government would change its attitude. But, instead of adopting a milder attitude toward America, the king decided to be even more firm. He agreed with the British general at Boston, who wrote that the colonists "will be lions whilst we are lambs, but if we take the resolute part [firm stand] they will undoubtedly prove very meek."

Stricter laws were adopted, which greatly hurt the trade and industry of the colonies. The king refused to listen to the grievances of his American subjects, and proclaimed them to be rebels. What is more, he hired German soldiers, called Hessians, to serve in his armies in America. This act greatly angered the colonists. It was bad enough to have British redcoats swaggering up and down their streets. It was still worse for the country to be occupied by hired soldiers speaking a strange language. Many Americans were forced to admit that there was little hope for fair treatment from the mother country.

Colonial leaders call for independence. Must the colonies, then, throw off the government of Great Britain and become independent? A few leaders thought so and said so. One of these was Samuel Adams. For years he had been protesting against such measures as the Stamp Act, the Townshend Acts, and the Intolerable Acts. He was convinced that the colonies must break away from England. Such views made Samuel Adams unpopular with many of his countrymen and caused the British to regard him as a dangerous person. But he continued to urge bold action. He was not disturbed when he learned that the British were on their way to Lexington to capture him. Instead he exclaimed: "What a glorious morning this is!" Even after the fighting at Lexington and Concord some Americans still sought some way to patch up their differences with the mother country, but Adams came out more strongly than ever in favor of independence.

Pupils should turn to page 175 to learn how public opinion was divided on the subject of breaking with England.

The most stirring arguments in favor of independence came from the pen of Thomas Paine. Tom Paine, who had recently come to America from England, wrote a pamphlet called *Common Sense*. In it he called upon Americans to break away from Great Britain. This, wrote Paine, was the common-sense thing to do. Why should a huge continent be tied to a little island thousands of miles away? Why should the colonists submit to laws which hurt their trade and industry? Why should American colonists go on swearing loyalty to a king who cared nothing for them, and who had sent armies to oppress them? "Everything that is right or reasonable," declared Paine, "pleads for separation." And, he wrote:

✳ The Sun never shined on a cause of greater worth. 'Tis not the affair of a City, a County, a Province, or a Kingdom; but of a Continent — of at least one eighth part of the [inhabited world]. 'Tis not the concern of a day, a year, or an age; [but of forever] even to the end of time. . . .

Paine's pamphlet, which appeared early in 1776, sold like wildfire. By their firesides and in taverns, men throughout the colonies talked about the ideas so forcefully expressed by Paine. Many who had been opposed to independence, or who had been uncertain, now felt they wanted the colonies to become independent.

The Second Continental Congress takes a bold step toward independence. As we learned in Chapter 8, the First Continental Congress had arranged for the meeting of another Congress if ill feeling between Great Britain and the colonies should continue. In 1775, shortly after the battles at Lexington and Concord, the Second Continental Congress began its sessions in Philadelphia. Among its members were most of the important colonial leaders.

At first, the majority of the delegates in Congress hoped to come to terms with King George and his government. As the months passed, however, the chances of a peaceful settlement grew dimmer. To more and more Americans, independence seemed the only answer. At length, the Congress yielded to this growing demand for independence. Early in June, 1776, Richard Henry Lee of Virginia rose to his feet. He said he had been directed by his colony to present a motion. As the delegates listened, he read it: "Resolved, that these United Colonies are, and of right ought to be, free and independent states."

You can imagine the excitement in Congress in the days that followed. Delegates gathered in little groups to discuss independence and the all-important motion of Richard Henry Lee. Meanwhile, a committee was appointed to draw up a Declaration of Independence. The member of the committee who did most of the writing of the Declaration was Thomas Jefferson. This tall, thirty-three-year-old Virginian had a rare gift for expressing his thoughts in clear, inspiring words. Soon he had prepared a Declaration for the Congress to consider.

The Declaration of Independence is adopted. Jefferson's Declaration did two important things:

(1) It expressed a bold new idea of the rights of the people. Before this time most men had believed that whatever rights they had were granted to them by the government under which they lived. But Jefferson believed that all men are born with certain rights which cannot be taken from them by any government. In the Declaration he expressed this belief in these ringing words:

✳ We hold these truths to be self-evident, that all men are created equal, that *they are*

The entire continent (and South America, too) did in time separate from Europe. But the Thirteen Colonies at this time had a population of less than four million.

endowed by their Creator with certain unalienable Rights, that among these are Life, Liberty and the pursuit of Happiness.

Jefferson went on to say that the purpose of a government is "to secure these rights," and governments must have "the consent of the governed." Whenever a government does not protect these rights or have the consent of the governed, "it is the Right of the People to alter or to abolish it." Then the people should set up a new government, in such a form as to bring about "their Safety and Happiness."

(2) In the second place, the Declaration of Independence broke all ties with England. The colonies had suffered patiently, wrote Jefferson, under the harsh laws of Great Britain. Now "it is their right, it is their duty, to throw off such Government. . . . We, therefore, the Representatives of the united States of America, in General Congress, Assembled, . . . do . . . solemnly . . . declare, That these United Colonies are, and of Right ought to be Free and Independent States." Jefferson ended the Declaration with these solemn words:

✳ And for the support of this Declaration, with a firm reliance on the protection of divine Providence, we . . . pledge to each other our Lives, our Fortunes and our sacred Honor.

The Declaration of Independence is reproduced in full on the next four pages. This famous document should be read by every American.

A new nation is born. After a few days of discussion, Congress adopted the Declaration of Independence on July 4, 1776. After long months of uncertainty the fateful step had been taken! No longer were our forefathers fighting as British subjects for their rights in the British Empire. Now they were founders of a new nation. No longer would they refer to the "United Colonies." Now they spoke proudly of the *United States of America!* July 4, 1776, is one of the most significant days in American history.

**C H E C K
U P**

1. (a) How did the Patriots capture Boston? (b) Where else had fighting taken place between the Patriots and the British troops?

2. (a) How did the British king try to stop the rebellion? (b) Why did many colonists begin to favor independence?

3. (a) What steps did the Second Continental Congress take to separate from England? (b) What were the two most important ideas of the Declaration of Independence?

People were given these rights "by their Creator" (not by a king), and these rights could not be taken away. Jefferson was speaking for all mankind. That is why the Declaration of Independence has had so great an influence on other peoples.

2 What Strengths and Weaknesses Did the Americans Have in the Revolution?

As news of the Declaration of Independence spread through the states, people received it with mixed feelings. Despite their happiness they wondered: What will happen now? How can the United States succeed against the might of Great Britain? It was one thing for the Congress to declare the United States free and independent; it was another thing to win this independence. What chance had thirteen small states against the army and navy of the strongest nation in the world?

(Continued on page 175)

THE DECLARATION OF INDEPENDENCE

Help students understand the conditions under which people have the right to institute a new government.

When in the Course of human events, it becomes necessary for one people to dissolve the political bands which have connected them with another, and to assume among the powers of the earth, the separate and equal station to which the Laws of Nature and of Nature's God entitle them, a decent respect to the opinions of mankind requires that they should declare the causes which impel them to the separation. [1]

(*The Right of the People to Control Their Government*)

We hold these truths to be self-evident, that all men are created equal, that they are endowed by their Creator with certain unalienable Rights, that among these are Life, Liberty and the pursuit of Happiness. That to secure these rights, Governments are instituted among Men, deriving their just powers from the consent of the governed, That whenever any Form of Government becomes destructive of these ends, it is the Right of the People to alter or to abolish it, and to institute new Government, laying its foundation on such principles and organizing its powers in such form, as to them shall seem most likely to effect their Safety and Happiness. Prudence, indeed, will dictate that Governments long established should not be changed for light and transient causes; and accordingly all experience hath shown, that mankind are more disposed to suffer, while evils are sufferable, than to right themselves by abolishing the forms to which they are accustomed. But when a long train of abuses and usurpations, pursuing invariably the same Object evinces a design to reduce them under absolute Despotism, it is their right, it is their duty, to throw off such Government, and to provide new Guards for their future security. Such has been the patient sufferance of these Colonies; and such is now the necessity which constrains them to alter their former Systems of Government. The history of the present King of Great Britain is a history of repeated injuries and usurpations, all having in

[1] In punctuation and capitalization the text of the Declaration follows accepted sources.

direct object the establishment of an absolute Tyranny over these States. To prove this, let Facts be submitted to a candid world.

(*Tyrannical Acts of the British King*)

He has refused his Assent to Laws, the most wholesome and necessary for the public good.

He has forbidden his Governors to pass Laws of immediate and pressing importance, unless suspended in their operation till his Assent should be obtained; and when so suspended, he has utterly neglected to attend to them.

He has refused to pass other Laws for the accommodation of large districts of people, unless those people would relinquish the right of Representation in the Legislature, a right inestimable to them and formidable to tyrants only.

He has called together legislative bodies at places unusual, uncomfortable, and distant from the depository of their Public Records, for the sole purpose of fatiguing them into compliance with his measures.

He has dissolved Representative Houses repeatedly, for opposing with manly firmness his invasions on the rights of the people.

He has refused for a long time, after such dissolutions, to cause others to be elected; whereby the Legislative powers, incapable of Annihilation, have returned to the People at large for their exercise; the State remaining in the mean time exposed to all the dangers of invasion from without, and convulsions within.

He has endeavoured to prevent the population of these States; for that purpose obstructing the Laws for Naturalization of Foreigners; refusing to pass others to encourage their migrations hither, and raising the conditions of new Appropriations of Lands.

He has obstructed the Administration of Justice, by refusing his Assent to Laws for establishing Judiciary powers.

He has made Judges dependent on his Will alone, for the tenure of their offices, and the amount and payment of their salaries.

He has erected a multitude of New Offices, and sent hither swarms of Officers to harass our People, and eat out their substance.

He has kept among us, in times of peace, Standing Armies without the Consent of our legislatures.

He has affected to render the military independent of and superior to the Civil power.

He has combined with others to subject us to a jurisdiction foreign to our constitution, and unacknowledged by our laws; giving his Assent to their Acts of pretended Legislation:

For quartering large bodies of armed troops among us:

For protecting them, by a mock Trial, from Punishment for any Murders which they should commit on the Inhabitants of these States:

For cutting off our Trade with all parts of the world:

These acts were cited to justify the Declaration of Independence.

For imposing Taxes on us without our Consent:

For depriving us in many cases, of the benefits of Trial by Jury:

For transporting us beyond Seas to be tried for pretended offences:

For abolishing the free System of English Laws in a neighbouring Province, establishing therein an Arbitrary government, and enlarging its Boundaries so as to render it at once an example and fit instrument for introducing the same absolute rule into these Colonies:

For taking away our Charters, abolishing our most valuable Laws, and altering fundamentally the Forms of our Governments:

For suspending our own Legislatures, and declaring themselves invested with power to legislate for us in all cases whatsoever.

He has abdicated Government here, by declaring us out of his Protection and waging War against us.

He has plundered our seas, ravaged our Coasts, burnt our towns, and destroyed the lives of our people.

He is at this time transporting large Armies of foreign Mercenaries to compleat the works of death, desolation and tyranny, already begun with circumstances of Cruelty & perfidy scarcely paralleled in the most barbarous ages, and totally unworthy the Head of a civilized nation.

He has constrained our fellow Citizens taken Captive on the high Seas to bear Arms against their Country, to become the executioners of their friends and Brethren, or to fall themselves by their Hands.

He has excited domestic insurrections amongst us, and has endeavoured to bring on the inhabitants of our frontiers, the merciless Indian Savages, whose known rule of warfare, is an undistinguished destruction of all ages, sexes and conditions.

(*Efforts of the Colonies to Avoid Separation*)

In every stage of these Oppressions We have Petitioned for Redress in the most humble terms: Our repeated Petitions have been answered only by repeated injury. A Prince, whose character is thus marked by every act which may define a Tyrant, is unfit to be the ruler of a free people.

Nor have We been wanting in attentions to our British brethren. We have warned them from time to time of attempts by their legislature to extend an unwarrantable jurisdiction over us. We have reminded them of the circumstances of our emigration and settlement here. We have appealed to their native justice and magnanimity, and we have conjured them by the ties of our common kindred to disavow these usurpations, which, would inevitably interrupt our connections and correspondence. They too have been deaf to the voice of justice and of consanguinity. We must, therefore, acquiesce in the necessity, which denounces our Separation, and hold them, as we hold the rest of mankind, Enemies in War, in Peace Friends.

The Declaration points out that the colonies did not separate from England until they had made every effort to find a peaceful solution to their differences.

Note how the word "united" is used in this section; also the words "state" and "states."

174   THE DECLARATION OF INDEPENDENCE

(*The Colonies Are Declared Free and Independent*)

We, therefore, the Representatives of the united States of America, in General Congress, Assembled, appealing to the Supreme Judge of the world for the rectitude of our intentions, do, in the Name, and by Authority of the good People of these Colonies, solemnly publish and declare, That these United Colonies are, and of Right ought to be Free and Independent States; that they are Absolved from all Allegiance to the British Crown, and that all political connection between them and the State of Great Britain, is and ought to be totally dissolved; and that as Free and Independent States, they have full Power to Levy War, conclude Peace, contract Alliances, establish Commerce, and to do all other Acts and Things which Independent States may of right do. And for the support of this Declaration, with a firm reliance on the protection of divine Providence, we mutually pledge to each other our Lives, our Fortunes and our sacred Honor.

THE DECLARATION OF INDEPENDENCE was signed in bold handwriting by John Hancock, President of the Congress, so that, as he said, "George the Third might read it without his spectacles." Later, the other delegates added their signatures.

WHAT WERE THE WEAKNESSES OF THE UNITED STATES?

✳ **The Patriot forces lacked training and organization.** Against Britain's armies of well-trained regulars, the Patriots seemed ill-matched. For one thing, the men in the Continental Army had little experience in military tactics and fighting in open battle. Their training had been limited largely to frontier warfare against the Indians and the French. Their officers, too, had little experience compared to British officers. What is more, the Continental Army was loosely organized. Its men had joined up, not because they had been ordered to do so, but of their own free will. Such volunteers felt free to return to their homes whenever their short terms of service were finished. As a result, the leaders of the army could hardly tell from day to day how many men were under their command. Also, the colonies had no real navy. Against the strongest navy in the world the Americans could send not one first-class man-of-war!

✳ **The Patriots lacked equipment and money.** In order to carry on a war, the Patriots needed equipment and supplies — muskets and cannon, bullets and powder, uniforms and food. Unfortunately, the Second Continental Congress had little money to buy these things. Nor did Congress have the power to tax the people. It could only ask the states to give money, and the sums received were disappointingly small. Congress also tried to buy supplies with paper money which it printed in large quantities. But people did not like to accept this money in payment for goods. Paper money is not worth much unless it can be exchanged for gold and silver, or unless the government which issues it is strong. The Continental Congress had little gold or silver, and it was a new and weak government. As the war dragged on, Continental paper money

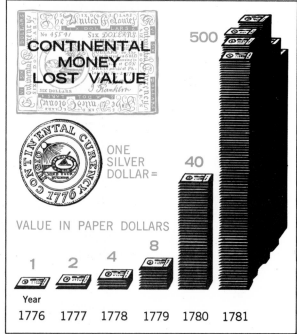

A SILVER DOLLAR was designed, but Congress lacked silver to make coins. The graph shows how the Continental paper money lost value. How many paper dollars equaled a silver dollar by 1781?

bought less and less. "Not worth a continental" became a way of saying that something was worthless.

✳ **Loyalists opposed the Patriots.** Our forefathers of the Revolution not only had to fight the forces of the king; they also had to face foes within their own villages and towns. Even after the Declaration of Independence had been signed, a large number of people, perhaps as many as a third of the colonists, remained loyal to the king. These people were known as *Loyalists* or *Tories*. Some Loyalists merely refused to aid the Patriot cause. Others furnished food and shelter for the king's armies or actually joined the British forces. Although the Loyalists thought they were doing right, the Patriots naturally regarded them as traitors. Sometimes Loyalists were "tarred and feathered" or run out of town on a rail. Patriots attacked their homes and destroyed or seized their property.

175

By using the heavy-type paragraph headings, pages 176-177, and including the main points under each, an outline can be developed on "What Were This Country's Sources of Strength in the Revolutionary War?"

WHAT WERE THE STRENGTHS OF THE UNITED STATES?

In spite of all their handicaps, the Patriots managed to fight on year after year and finally to defeat the British. How did they do it?

The Patriots fought for a cause they believed in. The Continental soldiers, among whom were 5000 Negro troops, lacked training and supplies, but at least they were fighting in their own country. Hardy men, accustomed to outdoor life, they knew how to use firearms and how to make the most of their scanty supplies. The officers and men who had fought against the French and Indians had learned the value of alertness and self-reliance. And they were fighting for a noble cause — freedom and the safety of their homes and families. The British armies, on the other hand, were filled with soldiers who had been forced into service. Far from their homelands across the ocean, the British and Hessian soldiers naturally did not fight with the same spirit as the Americans.

The Patriots profited from British blunders. The mistakes which the British generals made also aided the Patriots' cause. Many of these generals had been appointed because they had wealthy and powerful friends in the home government. They looked with contempt upon the poorly trained colonial troops and doubted they would fight very hard or very long. Like the members of an overconfident athletic team, the British commanders grew careless. Instead of striking swift, hard blows at the Continental Army, they pursued it in a leisurely way. The British officers made serious blunders and allowed almost certain victory to slip through their fingers.

The Patriots received foreign aid. The Patriots were aided by liberty-loving men from Europe who hastened to this country to serve in the Continental Army. Among these volunteers was the Marquis de Lafayette. This dashing young French nobleman defied the orders of the king of France in order to come to America to fight for freedom. With Lafayette came the Baron de Kalb, who gave his life for American independence. Other famous foreign soldiers joined our forces. They included the Baron von Steuben (who had fought under the great military leader, King Frederick of Prussia) and two Polish officers and lovers of liberty, Pulaski (poo-*lah'*ski) and Kosciusko (kos-ee-*us'*koh) (see illustration, next page). Americans were grateful for the help of these Europeans who loved freedom.

Even more important was the assistance given the United States by foreign governments. At the start of the fighting, American representatives were sent to France in the hope of getting help. Because France was an old enemy of Great Britain, Congress reasoned that the French government

Many Negro slaves who served in the Continental Army received their freedom after the war.

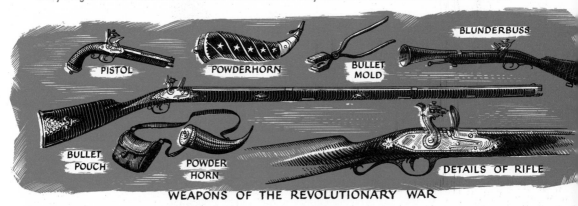

WEAPONS OF THE REVOLUTIONARY WAR

might seize the chance to strike at the British by aiding America. Benjamin Franklin, America's wise and able statesman, worked long and hard to gain the help of France. When it appeared that the Americans had some chance of defeating the British, the French king agreed to help the Patriots. A treaty was signed by which France and the United States became military allies. France was to send money, supplies, soldiers, and ships to aid the Americans in their fight for independence.

When France became our ally, Great Britain declared war on France. Then, other European nations were drawn into the struggle. France persuaded its ally, Spain, to enter the war against Great Britain. During the later years of the war, Spanish as well as French ships kept the British navy busy. Because Dutch bankers lent large sums of money to the American states, Great Britain also declared war on Holland.

General George Washington proves an excellent leader. An important reason for our country's victory was the leadership of George Washington. In the spring of 1775, the Second Continental Congress appointed Washington Commander-in-Chief of the Continental Army. Congress could hardly have made a better choice. Born in Virginia on February 22, 1732, the son of a well-to-do planter, Washington had had a good deal of military experience. As we learned in Chapter 6, Washington had led forces against the French and Indians. He also had experience in government affairs, and had served as a member of the First Continental Congress.

Tall, broad-shouldered, and dignified, Washington was a splendid leader. His bravery and calm manner inspired officers and men alike. He refused to give up in the face of shrinking armies, lack of

TWO POLISH OFFICERS who fought for American independence — Kosciusko and Pulaski — were honored on this stamp issued by Poland in 1932, on the 200th anniversary of George Washington's birth.

money and supplies, and unfair criticism. Through the darkest days of the Revolutionary War, Washington fought on without wavering. Many fainthearted Patriots were encouraged by the steady strength of their commander.

The courage of the Continental soldiers, Washington's leadership, and help from foreign countries — all these made possible America's victory in the Revolutionary War. But the struggle was not easy, nor was success certain at any time. Month after month the Patriots were called upon to meet disappointment, to endure hardship, and to fight desperately. These were, as Tom Paine wrote, "the times that try men's souls." But even when the future seemed blackest, our forefathers refused to admit defeat.

CHECK UP

1. (a) What were the weaknesses of the Patriots in the War for Independence? (b) What were their strengths?

2. (a) What were the British weaknesses during the American War for Independence? (b) What were their strengths?

Washington and the Revolution (see Books for Unit Three) is the story of an army that would not stay beaten.

3 How Did the Thirteen Colonies Win Their Independence?

As you read about the Revolutionary War, remember that the men who fought and died on the battlefields were ordinary men who had left their work and shouldered their rifles to face the trained British armies. Back in their homes— in towns, on farms and plantations, and in log cabins along the frontier — families eagerly waited for news of what was happening. In those days there was no radio or television to give up-to-the-minute reports. Days, sometimes weeks, passed before word of battles reached people at home. For reports of the war, they had to depend on soldiers passing by, a peddler on the road, a letter, or an old newspaper. Eagerly these scraps of information were shared with neighbors. What sorrows must have followed the dark days of the war when all seemed lost! What joy must have greeted the final victory!

THE MIDDLE STATES BECOME A BATTLEGROUND

The early fighting, as we have seen, broke out around Boston (page 162). Later, New York became the center of the fighting. There were two chief reasons why this was so: (1) The city of New York had the finest harbor along the coast. The British needed to control it if they were to keep their army supplied. (2) By holding the line of the Hudson River and Lake Champlain to the north, the British could keep New England cut off from the rest of the colonies. With the colonies divided, the British would find it easier to conquer first one section and then another.

The British take New York City. Hoping to prevent the British from seizing New York, Washington moved his forces from Boston to Long Island. (See map on this page.) There they were attacked late in the summer of 1776 by the British forces from Halifax under General Howe. The Americans were badly defeated. Under cover of darkness and fog, however, the American army managed to escape to the north of New York City. The British took possession of the city, where they were given a royal welcome by wealthy Loyalists. They remained in control of New York until the end of the war.

MAP STUDY   Sea power enabled the British to take New York, then Philadelphia. But Washington kept up the fight until the British held only New York City in the Middle States. What major battles (marked by crossed swords) are shown here?

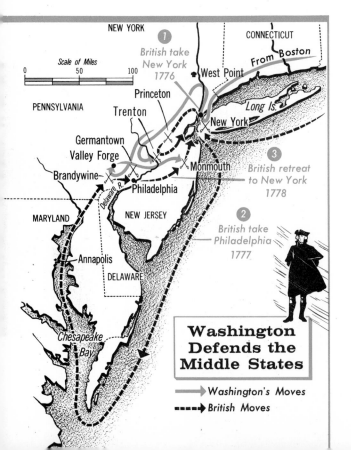

Washington Defends the Middle States

→ Washington's Moves
----► British Moves

178

GEORGE WASHINGTON

loved the outdoors as a youth and helped survey new land in his native Virginia.

DEFENSE of the Virginia frontier was entrusted to the hardy young Washington during the French and Indian War. His small force was surrounded at Fort Necessity (above), and he suffered defeat again with Braddock. Having learned military leadership the hard way, Washington returned after the war to his home at Mount Vernon.

MOUNT VERNON was a big plantation, and experimenting to improve fruit trees was one of Washington's many tasks. He worked hard until called to lead the army in the Revolution.

AS COMMANDER-IN-CHIEF, Washington rallied the hardpressed American troops through the early years of the war, including the grim winter at Valley Forge. With spring, however, news came of the French alliance, and Washington and his men celebrated this fresh hope of victory (above).

THE TRUST which Americans had in their wartime leader was shown when they elected him as our first President. Like a good soldier, Washington took the oath of office to lead his countrymen through more difficult years.

This helps to explain why French regulars were a welcome addition during the last couple years of fighting.

180   NEW NATIONS ARE BORN IN THE NEW WORLD

Nathan Hale gives his life for his country. Wishing to learn of the plans of the British, General Washington called for volunteers to go into New York City. One of the volunteers was twenty-one-year-old Captain Nathan Hale. Before the war this brave young man had been a schoolteacher in Connecticut. Washington chose Nathan Hale for the dangerous task of finding out about the British plans. In disguise Hale made his way into New York City, but was captured by the British and hanged as a spy. As Nathan Hale faced death, his last words were: "I only regret that I have but one life to lose for my country."

Washington retreats into New Jersey. More bad fortune followed the loss of New York. Washington lost 2600 of his best men and large supplies of ammunition and guns when the British captured two American forts on the Hudson River. Perhaps the British forces could have ended the Revolution by immediately attacking Washington's discouraged men. But it is said that General Howe did not wish to destroy the Patriot army because he hoped to win the Americans back to loyalty to Britain. Now that the Patriots had tasted defeat, he hoped they might give in. This, as General Howe was to learn to his sorrow, was a bad mistake.

In the autumn of 1776, General Washington was forced to retreat southward across New Jersey. Howe and the British troops pursued him slowly. Toward the end of the year, the Continental forces crossed the Delaware River into Pennsylvania. (See Washington's route on the map on page 178.) These were discouraging days for the American commander-in-chief. Many of his soldiers had lost hope and had returned to their farms and their jobs. He had expected to find additional troops in New Jersey, but not even a hundred men appeared! At the same time that Washington moved into Pennsylvania, approaching British troops caused Congress to flee from its meeting place in Philadelphia. The American cause seemed hopeless. It is said that some of the British generals were so sure the war was about over

THE "TURTLE," an early submarine, raised Patriot hopes of fighting the powerful British navy. A one-man crew had to steer and propel the little vessel by hand. The Patriot plan was to drill holes in British ships with the long screw (left of the open hatch) and attach explosives. But the submarine's attack on a British warship in New York harbor failed.

that they sent their belongings to their ships to be ready to sail for home.

Victories at Trenton and Princeton cheer the Patriots. Washington, however, refused to give up hope. He decided on a bold move. In the bitter cold of Christmas night, 1776, he and his men turned and recrossed the Delaware River. They fell upon 1400 Hessian soldiers stationed at Trenton, New Jersey, who had been celebrating the holiday. Washington's men took them by surprise and captured a thousand prisoners. Then Washington moved back a few miles. Lord Cornwallis, sent in a hurry to capture Washington, thought he had "the old fox" in a tight place. Once again, however, the American leader showed his skill and daring. Leaving his campfires burning brightly to deceive the British, Washington and his men stole away in the darkness. The next morning Cornwallis was awakened by the dull boom of distant cannon. It was Washington's army attacking three regiments of British soldiers at nearby Princeton! Washington soundly defeated these enemies, too.

The daring victories at Trenton and Princeton gave new courage to the Patriots. Although their cause was far from won, Americans could face the future with more hope.

The British plan to crush the Americans. In 1777 the English commanders made plans to cut off New England by seizing control of the Hudson Valley. An army from Canada, under General John Burgoyne (Gentleman Johnny, as the English called him), was to march south by way of Lake Champlain to Albany. There it was to be met by General Howe's forces from New York City. A third army was to march from Fort Oswego on Lake Ontario eastward across New York State to join the other two armies in Albany.

The plan was a good one, but it did not work. The third force never reached Albany. It was met on the way by American troops at Oriskany (or-*iss*'kuh-nih) in one of the bloodiest battles of the war. After the fighting at Oriskany, the third British force retreated to Oswego. As for General Howe, instead of sending troops to aid Burgoyne, he ordered the army in New York City to board a fleet bound for Chesapeake Bay. After landing, Howe and the army marched north toward Philadelphia.

Saratoga is a turning point in the war. Burgoyne, left on his own, marched south as far as Fort Ticonderoga. But the farther the British advanced, the greater their troubles became. Angry New Yorkers and New Englanders cut down trees to block their way. They also burned crops and drove off cattle, leaving the countryside bare of supplies. In the face of such obstacles Burgoyne and his men advanced slowly. When the General sent 700 Hessians eastward to get supplies, Patriots surrounded and defeated them near Bennington, in the present state of Vermont. At length Burgoyne joined battle with American forces near Saratoga, New York (map, page 183). The British were defeated. Greatly outnumbered, and with no chance of receiving help, General Burgoyne surrendered his whole army on October 17, 1777.

Burgoyne's surrender was a turning point in the war. It was the American victory at the Battle of Saratoga and the capture of Burgoyne and his men that persuaded the French king to give aid to the American cause (page 177). Without this aid the Patriots might have had too little money and too few supplies to keep their armies in the field.

Washington winters at Valley Forge. Now let us return to General Howe, who, with his army, had turned toward Philadelphia. Washington tried to stop him at

French aid proved decisive in the Yorktown campaign which ended the war (see page 187).

Brandywine and Germantown but was defeated in both battles. Howe succeeded in capturing Philadelphia (map, page 178).

General Howe and his men spent the winter of 1777–78 in Philadelphia. For them it was a gay and comfortable time. They had warm homes to shelter them and plenty to eat. There was a constant round of dances and parties. But this winter, so pleasant for Howe's men, proved a nightmare for the Continental Army.

Washington and his troops set up camp nearby at Valley Forge. Food was scarce. Rough, hastily built log huts were all the shelter the soldiers had against the wintry winds and drifting snow. Their ragged clothing gave them little protection against the bitter cold. Many a poor soldier lacked shoes, and few had enough bedding to keep them warm during the long winter nights. The Continental money was worth so little that the farmers would not take it in exchange for food. They preferred to sell their pigs and cattle to the British for gold or silver. Under such conditions some of the Continental soldiers became discouraged and returned home; many others fell sick. But Washington knew the value of the victory at Saratoga, and moved calmly and encouragingly among his cold and hungry men. The German Baron von

Steuben drilled the Patriot troops all winter to get them ready for more fighting in the spring.

Fighting ends in the middle states. In mid-June, 1778, the British abandoned Philadelphia and began a march across New Jersey toward New York City. Washington pursued the British troops and would almost certainly have defeated them at Monmouth, New Jersey, except for the cowardly action of an American officer, General Charles Lee. Instead of following Washington's orders to attack, Lee ordered his men to retreat! The British reached New York, where Washington kept them bottled up until the end of the war. No other important battles took place in the middle states.

A traitor plans to betray his country. One event occurred, however, which was a serious blow to the American cause. Among the Patriot leaders who had fought brilliantly early in the war was Benedict Arnold. He had attacked Quebec at the start of the war and had taken a leading part in the famous Battle of Saratoga which led to Burgoyne's surrender. Arnold was an ambitious man who felt that he deserved more credit than he had received for his services to the Patriot cause. Instead, he was criticized and court-mar-

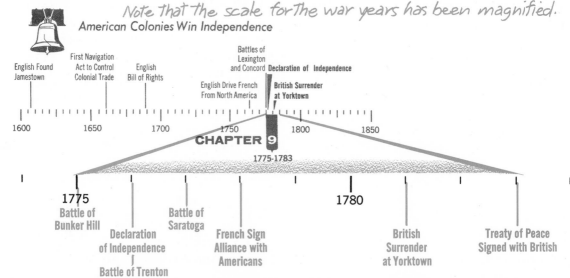

Note that the scale for the war years has been magnified.

American Colonies Win Independence

English Found Jamestown

First Navigation Act to Control Colonial Trade

English Bill of Rights

English Drive French From North America

Battles of Lexington and Concord

Declaration of Independence

British Surrender at Yorktown

1600 1650 1700 1750 1800 1850

CHAPTER 9

1775-1783

1775 1780

Battle of Bunker Hill

Declaration of Independence

Battle of Trenton

Battle of Saratoga

French Sign Alliance with Americans

British Surrender at Yorktown

Treaty of Peace Signed with British

American Victories Win the Revolutionary War

→ British **→** Americans

CANADA

Quebec

Montreal

1 Burgoyne is trapped 1777

LAKE CHAMPLAIN

Burgoyne

Oriskany

Saratoga

Bennington

LAKE HURON

LAKE MICHIGAN

LAKE ONTARIO

Ft. Oswego

Hudson R.

New York

British Fleet

Ft. Detroit

LAKE ERIE

Hamilton

Wabash R.

Illinois R.

Ft. Pitt

Lafayette

Washington

Ft. Vincennes

Ohio R.

Ft. Cahokia

Clark

ATLANTIC OCEAN

Yorktown

3 Cornwallis is trapped 1781

Cornwallis

Kaskaskia

Mississippi R.

2 Clark wins the West 1778-9

King's Mt.

Cornwallis

Greene

Cowpens

Marion

Wilmington

French Fleet

0   100   200   300
Scale of Miles

Cornwallis

Charleston

1778

MAP STUDY Three significant American victories brought about the final defeat of the British. Where were these victories and in what order did they take place? Note how the French fleet aided the land troops in the trapping of Cornwallis at Yorktown.

tialed for misusing his powers as military governor of Philadelphia. Moreover, Arnold had fallen deeply in debt. His need for money and his wounded pride tempted him to enter the pay of the British. He not only furnished the British with military secrets but influenced Washington to place him in command of the fort at West Point, New York. Arnold planned to turn the fort over to the British.

The plot to surrender West Point was discovered in 1780 by the capture of Major André (*ahn'*dray), the English officer with whom Arnold was dealing. André was executed as a spy, but Arnold managed to reach the British lines in safety. During the remainder of the war he fought under the British flag. Years later he died in England, an unhappy man. His name came to mean "traitor" in his

André was executed for spying as Nathan Hale **183** had been by the British (see page 180).

Seldom have so many owed so much to so few (200 men)! Clark's victorious campaign gave this country a claim to the entire Northwest Territory (see map, page 183).

184   NEW NATIONS ARE BORN IN THE NEW WORLD

native land, and he was looked upon with contempt even in Great Britain.

WAR IS WAGED ON THE FRONTIER AND AT SEA

George Rogers Clark strikes blows for freedom in the West. At the same time that the war was being carried on in the middle states, fighting had also been taking place in the frontier region to the west. (See the map on page 183.) It was a different sort of fighting, however, from that waged by Washington and his men. For the most part it consisted of Indian raids upon helpless frontier settlements. To the savages the Loyalists and British whispered this warning, "If the Patriots win the war, they will push their settlements farther and farther into the West. Soon the Indians' hunting grounds will become white men's farms." Backed by the British, the Indians carried on terrifying raids not only west of the Appalachian Mountains but in New York and Pennsylvania. Colonel Henry Hamilton, the English commander at Detroit, was even reported to have given gifts to the Indian braves who brought him human scalps.

A bold young frontiersman named George Rogers Clark decided to put an end to the Indian attacks in the West. He obtained permission from the governor of Virginia to lead an expedition into the West. In 1778, he led a force of two hundred men down the Ohio River. Clark surprised and captured the British frontier forts in the present state of Illinois. Vincennes (vin-*senz'*), in what is now Indiana, also came under his control.

Clark gains control in the West. Colonel Hamilton was alarmed by the young frontiersman's success. With his British soldiers and Indian allies, Hamilton recaptured the fort at Vincennes from the handful of Americans Clark had left there. Although the British commander expected Clark to attack him, he thought nothing would happen until the spring of 1779. Instead, the daring American led a little band of men against Vincennes in midwinter. Wading across swamps and flooded lands in icy water that reached to their waists, the frontiersmen surprised Hamilton and captured Vincennes again. Clark's victories gave the Americans a hold on the vast area between the Great Lakes, the Ohio River, and the Mississippi. After Clark's campaign the Indians were less of a menace to the frontier.

American privateers prey on enemy shipping. Meanwhile, Americans were waging war on sea as well as on land. From the harbors of New England, fishing vessels and merchant ships which had been fitted out with guns and crews sailed forth to seize enemy shipping. These *privateers,* as they were called, captured many a British merchant vessel and brought it to

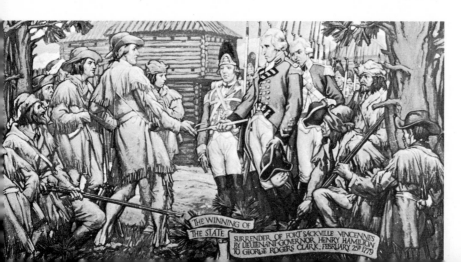

THE WINNING OF THE STATE SURRENDER OF FORT SACKVILLE VINCENNES BY LIEUTENANT-GOVERNOR HENRY HAMILTON TO GEORGE ROGERS CLARK, FEBRUARY 25TH 1779

GEORGE ROGERS CLARK receives the sword of the British officer who surrendered Vincennes (Fort Sackville), in this scene from a mural painting.

port. The cargo of the captured ship was then sold and the money divided among the crew of the privateer. Later in the war, as British men-of-war kept a close watch along the coast for privateers, fewer American ships dared to venture out.

The Americans build a navy. When they were colonists of Britain, the Americans, of course, had no navy; they had always depended for protection on the British fleet. Now this powerful fleet was fighting against the Americans, not for them. Early in the war Congress had begun to build a navy. John Paul Jones, a Scottish seaman who had settled in Virginia a few years before the war, advised Congress to build small, speedy ships. During the whole Revolutionary War, however, there were only about 40 ships in the United States Navy. Before the end of the war all but six of these were either captured or sunk by their crews to prevent the enemy from taking them.

John Paul Jones wins respect for the American navy. Our navy, although small, gave a good account of itself. The most famous sea fight of the Revolution took place between a British man-of-war and a ship built in France and commanded by John Paul Jones. Jones had been cruising along the British coast with his vessel, the *Bonhomme Richard* (buh-*nawm'* ree-*shahr'*), and three other ships. Coming upon a fleet of merchant ships guarded by two British warships, he attacked the larger enemy warship, called the *Serapis* (seh-*ray'*pis).

During the bloody three-hour battle, the *Bonhomme Richard* suffered great damage and was leaking badly. Jones ran his ship so close to the *Serapis* that their cannon almost touched. The British commander called out, "Have you lowered your flag?" In words that have become famous, Jones replied, "I have not yet begun to fight," and went on shooting. Soon the decks of the

JOHN PAUL JONES and his victory over the "Serapis" are shown on the two faces of this medal issued by the Continental Congress in honor of the naval hero.

Bonhomme Richard were littered with dead and wounded men. But the *Serapis* also had been badly damaged. When its mainmast fell, the British commander surrendered to Jones.

John Paul Jones had shown that Americans could fight on sea as well as on land. Although he spent most of his later life in Europe, his body was brought back to the United States after his death. He now lies in an honored grave at the Naval Academy in Annapolis.

THE WAR IN THE SOUTH BRINGS VICTORY TO THE AMERICANS

The British change their plans. After three years of fighting, the British faced a difficult problem. Several campaigns in the middle states had brought them no

GEORGE WASHINGTON fired the first cannon shot at Yorktown, as shown in this diorama. Tradition says that Washington's shot hit a house where British officers were at dinner.

nearer to defeating the Patriots than they had been in 1775. When France entered the war in 1778, the British had to face the power of that country as well. Expecting to gain the aid of large numbers of Loyalists, they shifted the war to the southern states. From the close of 1778 to the end of the war, nearly all the fighting took place in the South.

British and American forces battle in the South. At first it seemed that the British had made a wise decision. They won victories which gave them control of Georgia and most of South Carolina. Only a few roving bands of Patriots courageously kept up the fight. Led by daring leaders such as Francis Marion (nicknamed "the Swamp Fox"), these bands hid in swamps, but stole forth from time to time to pounce on small British forces.

At last, the Americans were able to check the British in the South. Late in 1780 the English leader, General Cornwallis, set out to conquer North Carolina. Part of his army, however, was defeated by frontiersmen at King's Mountain on the border of North and South Carolina. Then, Washington sent one of his ablest generals, Nathanael Greene, to lead the Patriot troops in the South. The Americans won an important victory at Cowpens in South Carolina but were pursued far into North Carolina by the main British army. Because supplies were hard to obtain, Cornwallis was forced to give up his hold on North Carolina and withdrew his army to the coast. (See the map on page 183 for the war in the South.)

The Patriots' cause looks hopeless. Even though Cornwallis had been prevented from taking North Carolina, the Americans were becoming discouraged over the course of the war. Washington, as you know, had been using most of his troops to keep the British bottled up in New York. It was now the spring of 1781. The Patriots had been fighting for six long years and victory still seemed far away. Men were restless at being kept in the army, and food and supplies were always scarce. Even Washington was becoming discouraged and feared the end was near. But then Cornwallis made a move which gave Washington his chance to strike a crushing blow at the British.

Cornwallis is caught in a trap. Lord Cornwallis had marched his men northward into Virginia, which was defended only by a small American force under Lafayette. "That boy cannot escape me," Cornwallis boasted scornfully. But "that boy," Lafayette, whose forces were not

Maurois has written an interesting book about this able Frenchman:
Lafayette in America.

The map on page 183 shows what happened. Victory or defeat hinged on the outcome of this naval battle won by Admiral DeGrasse. The French fleet maintained an effective blockade.

strong enough to meet the British, managed to slip away. Cornwallis then began to fortify Yorktown, which was located on a peninsula extending into Chesapeake Bay. At this base he expected supplies and more troops to come by sea from New York. This was a fatal mistake. A large French fleet from the West Indies closed the entrance to Chesapeake Bay, and a British fleet sent to relieve Cornwallis was driven off.

Washington, meanwhile, had made a bold move. Leaving New York, he joined his army with several thousand French soldiers and raced to Virginia. A force of about 16,000 American and French troops closed in on Cornwallis at Yorktown.

Cornwallis surrenders. Although the British fought desperately, they knew their cause was hopeless. Surrounded on all sides, Cornwallis and his entire army finally surrendered on October 19, 1781.

✳ At about twelve o'clock [according to an eyewitness], the combined army [Americans and French] was arranged and drawn up in two lines, extending more than a mile in length. The Americans were drawn up in a line on the right side of the road, and the French occupied the left. At the head of the former the great American commander . . . took his station, attended by his aides. At the head of the latter was posted the excellent Count Rochambeau and his [staff]. The French troops, in complete uniform, displayed a martial and noble appearance; their band of music . . . produced while marching . . . a most enchanting effect. The Americans, though not all in uniform, nor their dress so neat, yet exhibited an erect soldierly air, and every countenance [face] beamed with satisfaction and joy.

Between the two armies of victorious men the British troops marched out to surrender, their bands playing "The World Turned Upside Down." The victory at Yorktown meant the end of the war.

You can well imagine the rejoicing that followed the surrender of Cornwallis. Bonfires sent their flames high into the

MAP STUDY

The peace treaty of 1783 left the boundaries of the United States uncertain in three places. (1) Where were these places? (2) What natural waterways did the boundary follow? (3) To what other country besides the United States did Britain cede territory? (To answer, compare this map with the map on page 129.)

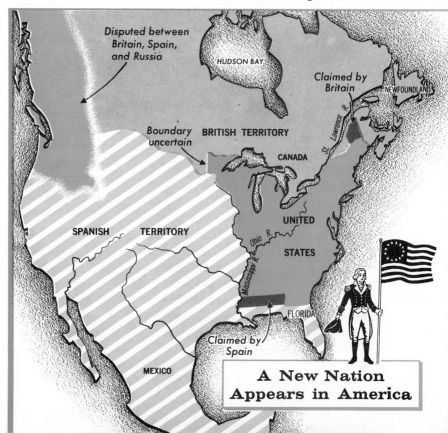

A New Nation Appears in America

sky, bells rang, and prayers were said in thanksgiving. Independence won at last!

American independence is recognized. Although the actual fighting in America was over in 1781, the treaty of peace was not signed until 1783. By this treaty Great Britain recognized the United States as an independent nation. The new nation's territory was to stretch from Canada to Florida, and from the Atlantic Ocean to the Mississippi River. The river itself, however, was to be open to the trade of both Great Britain and the United States. American fishermen were to be permitted to fish off Newfoundland and the mouth of the St. Lawrence River. In a separate treaty Great Britain returned Florida to Spain. To see how North America looked in 1783, look at the map on page 187.

King George III said sourly that considering the "knavery" of the Americans, perhaps it might "not in the end be an evil" that they had left the British Empire. As for the Americans, the opinions of George III were no longer important to them. They had won their freedom and founded a new nation.

CHECK UP

1. (a) Why were the early days of fighting discouraging to the Patriots? (b) How did Washington keep the Patriot cause alive?

2. (a) How did the British plan to end the war in 1777? (b) Why did the plan fail? (c) Why was the Battle of Saratoga important?

3. (a) How did George Rogers Clark win control of the West for the Americans? (b) How successful were the Americans in fighting at sea?

4. (a) Why did the British shift the war to the South? (b) Where did battles take place there? (c) How was Cornwallis trapped at Yorktown?

5. What were the terms of the peace treaty ending the war?

The Check Up questions provide an excellent basis for reviewing the Revolutionary War.

Check Up on Chapter 9

Do You Know the Meaning?

1. privateer	6. abolish
2. statesman	7. recruit
3. rebel	8. man-of-war
4. revolution	9. unalienable
5. endow	10. alter
	11. declaration

Can You Identify?

1. Thomas Paine	12. 1781
2. Nathan Hale	13. 1783
3. Benedict Arnold	14. Burgoyne
4. John Paul Jones	15. Nathanael Greene
5. Cornwallis	16. Richard H. Lee
6. Howe	17. Thomas Jefferson
7. Hessian	18. George Washington
8. Valley Forge	19. Benjamin Franklin
9. Lafayette	20. George Rogers Clark
10. Loyalist	21. Declaration of Independence
11. 1777	

Can You Identify? (Cont.)

22. Bunker Hill	24. Second Continental Congress
23. July 4, 1776	

Can You Locate?

1. Oriskany	8. Princeton
2. Saratoga	9. Ticonderoga
3. Trenton	10. Delaware River
4. Hudson River	11. New York City
5. Yorktown	12. Philadelphia
6. Vincennes	13. King's Mountain
7. Cowpens	14. Chesapeake Bay

What Do You Think?

1. (a) From 1763 to 1775, did the American colonists enjoy the right to "life, liberty, and the pursuit of happiness" under the government of Great Britain? (b) Did the British government have "the consent of the governed" as far as the colonists were concerned? Give reasons for your answers.

2. Why did it take great courage for the members of the Continental Congress to vote for the Declaration of Independence?
3. (a) What do Nathan Hale's words and actions tell us about his character? (b) How was it possible for Benedict Arnold, who had served his country well, to turn traitor?
4. American persistence, French aid, and British blundering were important factors in the outcome of the Revolutionary War. Which factor was most important? Why?

Encourage pupils to list examples and explain what is meant by each. There may be no agreement on which was most important.

LINKING PAST AND PRESENT

The Liberty Bell. The chief attraction in Independence Hall in Philadelphia is the grand old Liberty Bell. Although the Bell is chipped and cracked, you can see on it the date when it was cast (1753) and the names of its makers. Around the base you can still read this inscription from the Bible: "Proclaim liberty throughout all the land unto all the inhabitants thereof." The Liberty Bell pealed out the birth of our nation in 1776 and later our victory in the Revolutionary War. Through the years it tolled in solemn tones to announce the deaths of beloved American patriots. In 1835 the Bell rang for the last time — it had cracked badly. On June 6, 1944, however, Americans heard its voice again, this time over a nation-wide radio broadcast. The Bell was struck with a rubber mallet to celebrate the landing of Allied troops on the coast of France during World War II.

The message of Valley Forge. Every year thousands of Americans visit places made famous during the Revolutionary War, places which remind us that our freedom was dearly bought. One spot a visitor never forgets is Valley Forge, Pennsylvania, where the Continental Army spent the winter of 1777–1778. The old camp grounds have been restored and look much as they did almost 200 years ago. You see the crude log huts that gave poor shelter to Washington's ragged, hungry soldiers. Beyond are the grounds where, in spite of cold and snow, Baron von Steuben drilled the troops in preparation for the spring campaign. You see the houses where Washington, Lafayette, and other officers were quartered. As you remember that desperate winter when the American cause seemed lost, you realize that Valley Forge is more than an old camp ground. It is a reminder of the spirit that rose above hardship and fear of defeat to win the independence we enjoy today.

The Stars and Stripes. Our flag is almost as old as the nation itself. For close to 190 years, it has flown over the land of the free. The design for our nation's first flag was voted upon by the Continental Congress on June 14, 1777. (We now celebrate that day each year as Flag Day.) It was agreed that this flag should have thirteen stripes — one for each state — alternating red and white, and thirteen white stars on a blue field.

For a while, a new stripe and a new star were added whenever a state joined the Union. But it soon became clear that this would spoil the beauty of the flag. So in 1818 the number of stripes was reduced to thirteen, but a star continued to be added for each new state. Our flag grew with our nation until in 1912 it had 48 stars. The number of stars remained the same until 1959, when Alaska and Hawaii were admitted to the Union. Today the flag proudly displays 50 stars on its field of blue.

Perhaps pupils who have visited Philadelphia can tell interesting facts about the Liberty Bell or Valley Forge, or describe their visit to the Betsy Ross House.

Can students identify the various Latin American flags?

The Spirit of Independence
Affects Canada and Latin America

What this chapter is about —

"I swear before . . . the God of my fathers, I swear by my honor and by my native land, that I will give no rest to my arm or repose to my soul until I have broken the chains that oppress us. . . ."

The man who spoke these solemn words was not an English colonist pledging himself to support the American Revolution, but a patriot from Spanish Venezuela in South America. As we shall see in this chapter, the revolution of the Thirteen British Colonies was only one of several explosions that shook the New World loose from the Old. As a result of these explosions, other new nations grew up in the Western Hemisphere. (See in the background picture above the flags adopted by some of these nations.) By 1825, Spain's colonies had cut with a bloody sword the ties that bound them to their mother country. Brazil was no longer a colony of Portugal but an independent nation. Of all the European countries that had carved out empires in America, only Great Britain still held an important colony — Canada. Yet even Canada, which took no part in the wars for independence, followed a path which led her finally to self-government.

It is important for us as Americans to know something about the neighbors who share the Western Hemisphere with us. This chapter will tell what happened in Canada and in Latin America after the

People in our story — Nova Scotia settler and wife, French Canadian farmer, Latin American cavalryman and patriot officer.

American Revolution. It will tell how Canada carried on a "peaceful" revolution, and how the Spanish and Portuguese colonies gained their independence. To follow the important points in the story, look for answers to the following questions as you read:

1. How was Canada affected by the American Revolution?
2. How did Canada win self-government by a "peaceful" revolution?
3. How did the Spanish colonies gain their independence?
4. How did Brazil become independent?

Before introducing the Time line, ask pupils to read the Gaining Skill material on page 208.

1 How Was Canada Affected by the American Revolution?

Before we can understand how Canada was affected by the American Revolution, we must first turn back to the year 1763. This was the year, you remember, when Great Britain gained the territory of New France from her defeated rival.

The British government tries to gain the loyalty of New France. "What is to become of us now?" This was the question that the French people in North America were asking in 1763. "Will our new rulers force us to stop speaking our own language and prevent us from going to our own church?" Although the terms of surrender gave the French settlers the right to keep their native speech and religion, there were many fears that this agreement would not be carried out. The French colonists also wondered: "Will the

lands on which we have built our homes be taken from us and given to Englishmen?"

The French colonists learned to their relief that the British government had no thought of forcing them to adopt English customs and speech. As we know, the Thirteen British Colonies at this time were beginning to talk of liberty and of defending their rights. Great Britain realized that if the French settlers felt wronged, they might listen gladly to this dangerous talk among the British colonists to the south. So Great Britain continued much the same kind of government as the French colonists were accustomed to. They were also promised the right to worship in the Roman Catholic Church and to keep their lands. By fair treatment England hoped

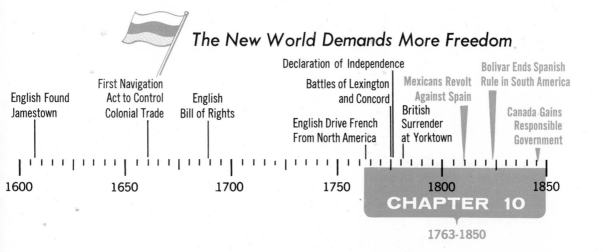

The New World Demands More Freedom

English Found Jamestown

First Navigation Act to Control Colonial Trade

English Bill of Rights

Declaration of Independence

Battles of Lexington and Concord

English Drive French From North America

Mexicans Revolt Against Spain

British Surrender at Yorktown

Bolivar Ends Spanish Rule in South America

Canada Gains Responsible Government

1600   1650   1700   1750   1800   1850

CHAPTER 10

1763-1850

LOYALISTS left their old homes in the Thirteen Colonies rather than stay where they were not wanted. This painting shows a Loyalist family in flight, hoping to find a refuge in British Canada.

to win the trust and loyalty of the French Canadians.

The American invasion of Canada fails. Great Britain was quite right in thinking that the trouble in the Thirteen Colonies might have an effect upon Canada.[1] Soon after fighting had broken out between the American colonies and the mother country, Ethan Allen and a force known as the Green Mountain Boys made a surprise attack. As you have already learned (page 167), they captured the British forts of

[1] Because you are familiar with the name "Canada," we are using that term instead of the more correct term "British North America." Actually, the entire region was not called "Canada" until 1867.

Crown Point and Ticonderoga on Lake Champlain. Ethan Allen's bold capture of these two forts opened the way to Canada. Knowing that Great Britain would use Canada as a base from which to attack the colonies, the Continental Congress decided to act quickly. American forces were sent to invade Canada. They seized and held Montreal for several months, but were unable to take the capital at Quebec. When British reinforcements came up the St. Lawrence, the American troops were forced to retreat from Canada.

The American colonies fail to get aid from the French in Canada. The American Patriots knew that the French Canadians had no great love for the British. So the Continental Congress sent a committee to Montreal to try to secure help for the American colonies from the French Canadians. The committee included Benjamin Franklin, famous for his powers of persuasion. But the citizens of Montreal had no great love for the Americans, either. They did not like the rough American soldiers who occupied their city. They were angered when the soldiers tried to make them accept worthless paper money in return for food and supplies. In fact, the more the people of Montreal saw of the American colonists, the less eager they were to join in the movement for independence. The committee failed in its mission, and all hope of getting aid from Canada faded.

From this time on, the two large British possessions in North America went separate ways — the Thirteen Colonies won their independence, while Canada continued a possession of Great Britain.

Many American Loyalists sail to Nova Scotia. Although Canada did not unite with the American colonies, it was greatly affected by the American Revolution. You have already learned that not everyone

Britain's conciliatory policy after 1763 **192** (see page 191) reassured the French Canadians, just as it angered the Americans (see page 152).

QUEBEC, one of the New World's oldest settlements and now a modern city, stands high above the St. Lawrence River. Here you can see the rugged cliffs that helped protect the fort (the walled open area in the lower part of the picture) from attack.

in the Thirteen Colonies was in favor of independence from the mother country. Probably one third of the colonists were Loyalists, who sided with Great Britain. After the war the bitter feeling against the Loyalists still remained. Some of them returned to England, but many wished to stay in North America. Why not go to the British possessions to the north? The British government in Canada was ready to welcome the Loyalists and to make arrangements for transporting them. They were promised free land, tools, and supplies so that they could start a new life.

After the treaty of peace was signed in 1783, a flood of Loyalists boarded ships in New York City, eager to go to their new homes. There were well-dressed aristocrats who took with them their Negro slaves and such possessions as they had managed to save. There were also merchants, doctors, lawyers, soldiers, workmen, and farmers. Some of the wealthiest and best-educated people of the old colonies were lost to the United States by this Loyalist migration.

Thirty thousand strong, these homeless refugees set sail for Nova Scotia. The ships anchored at Halifax, the capital city of Nova Scotia. You can imagine how crowded the city must have been with thousands of people needing food and shelter and land on which to settle. Before long, land was given to the Loyalists and they spread out to build settlements and to clear fertile farm lands in Nova Scotia.

The migration of Loyalists helps to explain the **193** close ties between Canada and the mother country. It also brought to Canada a group that would not be satisfied with the government established in 1763.

Some went to New Brunswick, directly north of what is now Maine, and to nearby Prince Edward Island. Soon Nova Scotia and the surrounding territory became a strong British colony. (See the map on the next page.)

Other Loyalists reach Canada by land. During the Revolution, many Loyalists had moved into Canada from the western sections of the colonies. After the war, as many as ten thousand crossed the border from New York State into Canada. Most of these people settled north of Lake Ontario and along the upper St. Lawrence, west of Montreal. This territory was part of what had been the old French province of Quebec. The new settlers were given land and tools by the government, and soon log cabins and little villages sprang up in the wilderness.

English-speaking people form the beginnings of British Canada. New France, you will remember, had never been thickly populated. At the time it passed into the hands of the British, its population numbered only about 80,000. You can easily see that the thousands of Loyalists who moved from the United States brought about a great change in the population. The French were no longer in a majority except in the eastern part of old Quebec. Moreover, English-speaking people continued to arrive in Canada in large numbers. Many Americans along the frontier pushed into the Great Lakes region in the early 1800's. Immigrants came in large numbers from the British Isles, too. We may say, therefore, that the American Revolution affected Canadian history because it led to the beginning of the British Canada that we know today.

English-speaking Canadians demand and receive more rights. The Revolution had another effect upon our neighbor to the north. The British people in the prov-ince of Quebec were not satisfied to live under the laws made to govern the French Canadians. They wanted a government in which they would be represented as they had been in the American colonies. The French Canadians, on the other hand, who lived in the older (eastern) part of Quebec, wished to remain French and keep their French customs. They had little desire to take part in government. How was Great Britain to please both the British and French Canadians?

In 1791 it was decided to divide old Quebec into the two provinces of Upper and Lower Canada. (Look again at the facing map.) Upper Canada was the western part of old Quebec where many Loyalists had settled. Lower Canada was the eastern part of Quebec where the French were in the majority. Each province was to have its own government, headed by a governor appointed by Great Britain. Each governor, in turn, was to choose leading citizens to serve on his *council*. There was also to be an assembly elected by the voters in each province. Of course, the British people in Upper Canada were pleased with this arrangement. At the same time, Great Britain hoped that the French people of Lower Canada would gradually learn British ways by taking part in the government.

CHECK UP

1. (a) What did the British do to gain the loyalty of the French in Canada after 1763? (b) Why did the American Patriots fail to win the French Canadians to the cause of independence?

2. In what parts of Canada did Loyalists from the Thirteen Colonies settle?

3. (a) Why were the British people in Canada dissatisfied? (b) Why was Quebec divided into two provinces? (c) How were the two provinces to be governed?

Similar governments had been founded in the Thirteen Colonies. See charts, pages 140-141.

2 How Did Canada Win Self-Government by a "Peaceful" Revolution?

It was not long before Canadians began to find fault with their new government, and a quarrel with Great Britain followed. In fact, during the 1800's this quarrel led to a revolutionary change in the government. <u>Revolutions need not be bloody wars; they may be brought about peacefully.</u> In this section we shall see how a peaceful revolution brought self-government to the Canadians.

The British plan of government keeps a tight rein on Canada. The governments set up in Upper and Lower Canada did not give people the same rights of self-government that had existed in the Thirteen Colonies. Those in authority in Great Britain realized that costly mistakes had led to the loss of the Thirteen Colonies. They were determined that the same thing should not happen in Canada. They agreed that Parliament should not tax a British colony.

But these leaders also thought, "We lost the Thirteen Colonies not only because we taxed them but also because we gave them too great freedom in handling their own affairs. We must 'tighten the reins' on our remaining colony in America so that there will be no chance for another revolt. We shall allow the people to elect assemblies and give them power to raise their own taxes to run the government. But the assemblies will not have full power to make laws. A governor sent from England, and his council, will really control the government of each province. In this way the Canadian people will not get ideas about liberty and self-government."

Canadians demand reforms in their government. The Canadians of each province soon realized that the governor and his council held the real power over the government. These men paid little attention to the wishes of the assembly. They ran the government for their own good and the good of the mother country, rather than for the good of Canada. In other words, the government of the provinces was not *responsible* to the people of Canada. More and more people began to demand what they called *responsible government*. They wanted their elected

A useful clarification of the term "revolution".

Canada Is Divided

HUDSON BAY

Chief settled areas
English-speaking majority
French-speaking majority

TERRITORY OF THE HUDSON'S BAY COMPANY

St. Lawrence R.

LOWER CANADA

Ottawa R.

UPPER CANADA

Montreal

Quebec

NEW BRUNSWICK

NOVA SCOTIA

Halifax

NEWFOUNDLAND

Prince Edward Is.
CAPE BRETON IS.

Boston

New York

Loyalists

ATLANTIC OCEAN

SPANISH TERRITORY

UNITED STATES

MAP STUDY
In 1791 two new provinces of Upper and Lower Canada were formed out of the old province of Quebec. Note that New Brunswick, Nova Scotia, Newfoundland, and Prince Edward Island were separate British colonies.

assemblies to have the real power to govern the provinces. They also wanted more freedom from Britain in managing their affairs.

In Lower Canada, where the British and the French lived side by side, the feeling against the governor and his council was especially bitter. The French people feared that the British government was trying to make them accept the English language and customs. This they would never do. They were French and intended to remain so. Because the French had a majority in the assembly, they even refused to vote taxes to run the government if they disliked the governor's plans. Some fiery leaders urged revolt.

In Upper Canada the quarrel was not between the two nationalities. Instead, it was between those who wanted responsible government and the wealthy people who controlled the government and meant to keep on doing so. As the quarrel grew more bitter, reform leaders urged the people to rebel if their demands were not granted. There was much talk of independence. In 1837 things came to a head. Riots and fighting broke out, but were soon stopped by government troops.

Lord Durham recommends changes in the Canadian government. The British government was shocked by the riots and the bitter feeling that caused them. Wise people in England said, "Our present policy in Canada has failed. We must do something different or we may lose the Canadian provinces as we did the Thirteen Colonies." Accordingly, England sent Lord Durham, a wise and able statesman, to study conditions in Canada and recommend what should be done.

Lord Durham's report proved a turning point in Britain's attitude, not only toward Canada but also toward her colonies all over the world. He warned Great Britain to give up the idea that colonies existed for the good of the mother country. He said that the elected representatives of the people (the assembly) must be given more power. The only way to keep the Canadian provinces in the British Empire, Lord Durham believed, was to give their people the same rights that Englishmen enjoyed — in other words, responsible government. He also suggested that the two Canadas be united again under one government.

Canada receives responsible government. Soon after Lord Durham made his report, Upper and Lower Canada were once more joined in a single province under one governor. But it was several years before England was ready to give Canada responsible government. Finally, in 1846, responsible government was introduced in Canada. The governor appointed to the council representatives from the party that controlled the elected assembly. This council now determined the policies of the government. Thus the Canadians gained control of their affairs except for such matters as defense, trade with other nations, and the making of treaties. Over these matters the British Parliament still had control.

Responsible government in Canada had been brought about without a war. As soon as the Canadians had won their demands, all talk of independence died down. Great Britain had shown her faith in the ability of the Canadian provinces to govern themselves. They, in turn, felt new loyalty and affection for the mother country.

C H E C K
U P

1. (a) Why did the assemblies elected by the people of Upper and Lower Canada have little power? (b) Why did Canadians want responsible government?

2. (a) What changes in the Canadian government did Lord Durham recommend? (b) How was the plan for responsible government carried out?

Stress this point and bring out changes that followed from it.

3 How Did the Spanish Colonies Gain Their Independence?

In the early part of the 1800's, even before Canada obtained responsible government, stirring events were taking place in the Spanish colonies in Mexico, Central America, and South America. Uprisings against Spanish rule broke out in one colony after another. The revolt of the Spanish colonies reminds us in some ways of the revolt of the English colonies. Both had grievances against the mother country because of taxes and trade regulations. Both fought bloody battles to win independence.

Several differences, however, made the winning of independence much more difficult for the Spanish colonies than for the English colonies. (1) The Thirteen English Colonies occupied a narrow strip of land along the seacoast. But the territory of the Spanish colonies stretched across most of South America, Central America, Mexico, and a part of the present United States. (2) In many places, great mountain ranges and dense jungles separated the settlements in Spanish America. You can imagine how difficult it was to send messages and to move armies from one place to another. (3) Another difference was in government. The English colonists cherished certain rights and had a good deal of self-government. But in the Spanish colonies, the people were under the iron rule of the Spanish king and had no chance to try self-government. When we consider that they won their independence in spite of these difficulties, we realize what a remarkable achievement it was.

THE COLONIES OF SPAIN HAVE REASON FOR REVOLT

What grievances did the Spanish colonists have? In Chapter 3 we have already learned how strictly Spain controlled the trade of her colonies. As time went on, those who wanted to make money through trade grew more and more bitter about these regulations. But probably the most serious complaint of the colonists arose among the Creoles (people of Spanish blood born in the New World). The Creoles held few if any of the important public offices in their own colonies. Instead, positions in the Church and government were nearly always given to Spaniards (people born in Spain). The Spaniards looked down upon the Creoles as inferiors. It is easy to understand why proud Creoles of fine family and excellent education resented the attitude of the Spaniards.

There were other grievances also. Many of the colonists believed that the time had come for the people to have something to say about how they were governed. To Spain such ideas seemed dangerous, and she tried hard to prevent them from spreading in her colonies. Colonists were not allowed to buy books or papers unless they had been approved by the Spanish authorities. No printed information about the American Revolution could be circulated in the Spanish colonies. In fact, no Spanish colonist was allowed to visit the United States without special permission, for fear he would bring back ideas of independence.

The American and French Revolutions influence the Spanish colonies. In spite of these strict rules, news trickled in from other parts of the world. The people in the Spanish colonies learned that the English colonies had actually won their independence. They also heard exciting stories of a great revolution which had swept

It is impossible to "quarantine" ideas, today more so than ever. Consider the movement toward independence of former colonial peoples in this century.

TOUSSAINT L'OUVERTURE, born a plantation slave in Haiti, led that colony's struggle for independence from France. He declared the slaves free and drew up a constitution providing for self-government. In 1804 the Negro republic of Haiti became the first Latin American colony to win independence (page 661).

France, beginning in 1789. During the French Revolution, the French people threw off the rule of the king and the nobles and set up a republic. Such news was passed from one person to another in the Spanish colonies and was eagerly discussed. If other people could break the chains that bound them, why could not the Spanish colonists do the same? Young Creoles who returned from study in Europe began to work enthusiastically for independence. In many parts of the colonies secret societies were organized to plan a revolution against Spain. Fortunately for the colonies, in the early

1800's Spain became entangled in European wars. She was too busy to pay much attention to her colonies in America, and they chose this time to revolt.

MEXICO ESTABLISHES HER INDEPENDENCE

The long struggle for Mexican independence is begun by Father Hidalgo. *"Viva la Independencia!* Long live Independence!" These stirring words were uttered in 1810 by Father Miguel Hidalgo (hih-*dal'*goh), a parish priest in the small Mexican village of Dolores. Hidalgo had devoted his life to helping and teaching the downtrodden Indians of Mexico, whose life under Spanish rule was full of hardships. He had made secret plans for a revolt against the Spaniards who ruled Mexico. Independence, Father Hidalgo hoped, would bring about better conditions for the Indians.

The "Cry of Dolores," as Hidalgo's slogan is called, started his Indian followers on the path of revolution. Although at first they captured several towns, the poorly trained Indians were no match for the Spanish troops who were sent against them. Hidalgo was defeated, taken prisoner, and executed. His head was carried through the streets in an iron cage as a warning of what would happen to those who dared to revolt against Spain.

The revolution did not end with Hidalgo's death. Thousands of his followers fled to the mountains, where they continued to fight under new leaders. Many mestizos (people who were part Indian and part Spanish) joined the revolt. Through long, discouraging years they carried on their fight, making surprise attacks on different towns and then retreating into the hills.

MEXICO CITY'S GREAT CATHEDRAL, begun by the Spanish in 1573, glows under artificial lighting at night. The streaks of light were traced by headlights of automobiles passing by while this time-exposure photograph was being shot.

The Creoles take over the movement for independence and succeed. By themselves the Indians and mestizos of Mexico probably would never have won the fight for independence. But the Creoles, who had been watching the unequal struggle between the rebels and Spaniards, saw a chance to use the revolution to gain control of Mexico. They schemed to join the rebels, and when independence was won, take over the government for themselves.

An ambitious young Creole officer named Agustín de Iturbide (ee-toor-*bee'*day) was the leader in this plan. He tricked the Indian leaders into accepting his aid. Together the Creole and Indian forces captured Mexico City and forced the Spaniards to leave. After Iturbide and his soldiers declared Mexico's independence in 1821, they had no further use for the Indians who had fought for so long.

Mexico and Central America win independence. Iturbide was not interested in democratic ideas; he wanted control of Mexico for himself and other Creoles. So the revolution, which was begun to help the Indians, ended with Iturbide being crowned emperor of Mexico! However, many Creoles did not like the idea of an emperor, and after a year Iturbide was exiled. The Republic of Mexico was at last established in 1824, after fourteen years of fighting. About the same time the Spanish provinces in what is now Central America also announced their independence.

BOLIVAR AND SAN MARTIN FREE SOUTH AMERICA

While Mexico was carrying on her revolution against Spain, much had been happening in South America. The story of its

In the case of the Spanish colonies (as in the **199** Thirteen Colonies) independence did not mean repudiation of the cultural heritage from the mother country.

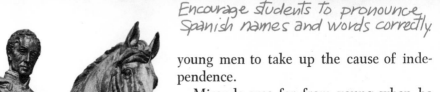

A STATUE of Simón Bolívar stands in Bogotá, Colombia, capital city of one of the countries he freed from Spain.

independence is the story of three great leaders — Miranda, Bolívar, and San Martín. As you read about what they did, you will want to refer to the map on page 201.

Miranda is the father of the revolution in Venezuela. Francisco Miranda (mee-*rahn*'duh), who was born in Venezuela, spent most of his life working for the cause of freedom in South America. For a time he lived in Europe. There he went from one European government to another, trying to interest them in helping the Spanish colonies win their independence. After the United States gained her freedom, he also appealed to our government for help. Miranda founded patriotic societies for young Creoles who had gone to Europe to be educated. His fiery speeches led many

young men to take up the cause of independence.

Miranda was far from young when he returned to Venezuela in 1810 to lead a revolution against Spain. As the white-haired old man rode through the streets of Caracas (kuh-*rah*'kus), capital of Venezuela, the people cheered wildly. But a year later, a frightful earthquake destroyed Caracas and ended the revolution for the time. Miranda was captured by the Spanish and put in prison, where he died.

Bolívar becomes leader of the Venezuelan revolution. There now appears in our story one of the most interesting men in the pages of history. Young Simón Bolívar (boh-*lee*' vahr) will live forever in the memory and in the hearts of South Americans. He has become a symbol of liberty to the people of South America, and means as much to them as George Washington does to us.

Bolívar was the son of one of the wealthy and powerful Creole families of Caracas. He was a handsome and dashing young man, with a slim figure and flashing black eyes. Like many young Creoles, Bolívar was trained as a soldier. He married a beautiful young Spanish girl, but their happiness was cut short by her tragic death not long afterward. Feeling that he had little left to live for, Bolívar went to Europe. There he met Miranda, and was inspired by the old patriot's enthusiasm. Bolívar decided to devote the rest of his life to freeing his beloved land. It was Bolívar who made the oath mentioned at the beginning of this chapter. He was the man who became the leader of the revolutionists in Venezuela after Miranda's death.

Bolívar wins independence for northern South America. Bolívar had little trouble in gathering together a revolutionary army to fight the Spaniards. He was

Patriots Liberate Latin America

PACIFIC OCEAN

UNITED STATES

MEXICO

Rio Grande

1810
Dolores

Mexico City

1791
HAITI

COLOMBIA

1810
Caracas

VENEZUELA

GUIANA

1819

Bolívar

Amazon River

PERU

Lima

1824
Ayacucho

BRAZIL
(Portuguese)

San Martín

CHILE

ANDES MTS.

Rio de Janeiro

1822

ARGENTINA

Paraná R.

1818

Buenos Aires

1810

ATLANTIC OCEAN

Spanish empire

Revolution breaks out

Battles

New Nations Appeared in Latin America by 1826

ATLANTIC OCEAN

MEXICO

Colonies

HAITI

CENTRAL AMERICA

GREAT COLOMBIA

PACIFIC OCEAN

PERU

EMPIRE OF BRAZIL

BOLIVIA

PARAGUAY

CHILE

ARGENTINE CONFEDERATION

MAP STUDY Revolutions against colonial rule broke out in widely separated parts of Latin America at different times. How can you tell on this map where the important outbreaks took place? Only after years of fighting did the campaigns of leaders such as Bolívar and San Martín (colored arrows) win final independence from Spain. (Haiti won independence from France and Brazil from Portugal.) The inset map shows the new nations that had shaken off colonial rule by 1826.

Use the maps on page 201 in reading about campaigns of Bolívar and San Martín.

202   NEW NATIONS ARE BORN IN THE NEW WORLD

the kind of person who naturally attracts men and makes them eager to follow his leadership. Bolívar collected an army of 2100 men, many of them tough cowboys of the Venezuelan plains. When he found the Spanish troops in Venezuela too strong for him, Bolívar decided on a daring move. He led his soldiers on a difficult march over the towering Andes Mountains into neighboring Colombia. He surprised the Spanish forces there and defeated them.

Bolívar now felt strong enough to return and strike at the Spanish troops in Venezuela. In 1821, he put them to flight in an important battle in the western part of that country. Soon all of northern South America was freed from Spain's control. Wherever Bolívar went, he was greeted with wild enthusiasm. The title of Liber-

ator was given to him by the grateful people. But Bolívar knew that his work was not yet finished. Other colonies were still fighting for their freedom. No part of South America could actually be independent, Bolívar realized, until every Spanish fort was taken and every Spanish soldier driven out. His next step was to conquer the strong Spanish forces in Peru.

San Martín becomes a leader in the south. In this new undertaking Simón Bolívar had the help of another great leader, José de San Martín (sahn mahr-*teen'*). San Martín was born in Argentina. Although he had spent 20 years in the army of Spain, he still loved his native land. Soon after a revolt in Argentina drove out the Spanish government (1810), San Martín sailed home to join the rebel forces. Although his own country had freed itself, San Martín, like Bolívar, realized that the Spanish forces must be defeated throughout South America.

San Martín frees Chile. Chile and Peru were still under Spain's control. So San Martín asked himself this question: Why not cross the Andes to Chile, free that country, and then go by sea to attack Peru? San Martín set about drilling an army and collecting supplies for this difficult campaign. He was joined by Chilean patriots who had fled from home after a bad defeat by the Spaniards. At last, after three years of preparations, the Army of the Andes began its bold march. With cannon and equipment, the soldiers toiled over snowy heights. They took sleds to pull their cannon through the snow, movable bridges to cross mountain streams, and extra shoes for the mules. Up, up they climbed, and then down into Chile. This march is said to be one of the greatest military feats in history.

San Martín's surprise attack was successful, and a year later all Chile was freed from Spanish control.

SAN MARTÍN of Argentina, a brilliant military leader, freed Chile after crossing the Andes Mountains.

PIONEERS who settled the inland regions of Uruguay have been honored with this unusual monument in Montevideo. Women and children and the family's few possessions traveled in oxcarts like this one while the men rode horseback.

San Martín enters Peru. After defeating the Spanish troops in Chile, San Martín undertook the second part of his plan. In 1821, he and his army landed on the coast north of the city of Lima, capital of Peru. While the Spanish forces moved farther inland, San Martín entered Lima. The people of the city greeted him with great joy. Shortly afterward, the independence of Peru was proclaimed. But San Martín knew that the strong Spanish forces remaining in Peru must be defeated if freedom was really to be won. He also knew that he did not have enough men to defeat the Spaniards.

San Martín resigns in favor of Bolívar. Meanwhile, Bolívar was advancing southward with his army. When San Martín heard this, he made arrangements to meet Bolívar to discuss plans for the final defeat of the Spanish forces. No one knows exactly what happened at this meeting. Both men wanted independence for all of South America. But Bolívar was an ambitious man who craved fame and glory. San Martín, on the other hand, had no ambition to become famous. Bolívar must have persuaded San Martín to leave his army in Peru and allow Bolívar to complete the conquest. At any rate, on the eve of victory San Martín, who had accomplished so much for the cause of independence, left Peru. He later went to Europe where he spent the rest of his life.

Spanish control in South America comes to an end. With the two armies united under his command, Bolívar swept on to victory. In 1824, he defeated the last strong Spanish forces in the Battle of Ayacucho (ah-yah-*koo'* choh). This victory not only freed Peru but won independence for all of Spanish South America. At last the dreams of Miranda, Bolívar, San Martín, and all the thousands of other patriots had come true.

After winning independence, the former Spanish colonies became free republics with governments patterned after that of the United States. The people of each republic were to elect a president and a legislature. These new republics, however, faced many difficulties. The men who fought for liberty had no experience in governing themselves, as had the people of the Thirteen English Colonies. For the next hundred years and more, the people of the Latin American republics were to suffer wars and revolutions and the harsh rule of dictators before they began to learn the ways of self-government.

CHECK UP

1. (a) What complaints did the Spanish colonies have against Spain? (b) How did the revolutions in the Thirteen Colonies and in France affect the Spanish colonists?

2. How did Mexico win its independence?

3. (a) What parts of South America were freed by Bolívar? (b) By San Martín? (c) How was a final defeat of the Spanish forces in South America brought about?

Self-government evolved over centuries in Western Europe. When self-government is "imposed" on people lacking experience with free institutions, it works less well.

See page 198 for the effect of these wars on Spain and her colonies.

 # How Did Brazil Become Independent?

We have yet to tell the story of Brazil, the largest of the Latin American countries. Unlike the rest of South America, Brazil was discovered and settled by the Portuguese. Even today Brazilians speak Portuguese instead of Spanish. Let us consider briefly how this happened.

The Portuguese claim and colonize Brazil. A Portuguese sea captain named Pedro Cabral (kuh-*brahl'*) set out from Portugal in 1500 to follow da Gama's route to India. The story goes that a storm blew his little fleet so far to the west that he reached the bulge of South America nearest to Africa. Since the land lay east of the Line of Demarcation (see map, page 42), he claimed it for Portugal. Portugal was much more interested at the time in her rich trade with India, but a few settlements were made in Brazil.

The Portuguese soon discovered that the fertile soil of Brazil would grow sugar cane. This news brought many settlers, and it was not long before great plantations were producing sugar for most of Europe. Brazil did not have a huge Indian population like Mexico or Peru. So large numbers of Negroes were brought over to Brazil to work on the plantations. Brazil was governed by a royal governor and was divided into several districts, each one headed by a Portuguese nobleman.

In the early 1800's there were about three million people in Brazil. The capital city, Rio de Janeiro (*ree'* oh duh zhuh-*nair'*oh), had about 100,000 inhabitants, and there were several towns along the coast. Both gold and diamonds were mined in Brazil. But for the most part the life of the people centered about the plantations, with their miles of sugar cane, their sugar mills and workers' huts.

Brazil becomes the home of the king of Portugal. The story of how Brazil became independent is not one of long and bloody struggle like that of the Spanish colonies. In 1808, the people of Brazil learned that the royal family of Portugal was coming to live in their capital city because of wars which were then raging in Europe. These wars forced John, the Portuguese ruler, and hundreds of Portuguese nobles to seek refuge across the sea.

At first, the colonists of Brazil were pleased and honored to have the royal family and the nobles in their midst. It was not long, however, before ill feeling broke out between the Portuguese and the Brazilians. The Portuguese, used to the splendor of a European court, looked with scorn upon the upper classes of Brazil. The native Brazilians, in turn, resented the fact that King John gave important positions in the government to his Portuguese subjects. Soon, in spite of the many good things King John had done for Brazil, Brazilians began to talk about independence from Portugal.

Dom Pedro refuses to leave Brazil. When the wars in Europe were over and conditions again became normal, the king returned to Portugal with his court. He left his young son, Pedro, to rule Brazil in his place. Dom Pedro was a handsome and headstrong prince, much loved by the Brazilians because of his interest in the welfare of their country. When he was ordered by the government of Portugal to return to that country, he angrily refused. Portuguese troops tried to force his return, but instead he obliged them to take ship for Europe.

Brazil becomes independent of Portugal. The Portuguese government refused

The Brazilians felt much as did reasons (see page 197). *the Creoles and for similar*

PICTURESQUE CHURCHES and cobblestone streets are typical features of Ouro Preto, a colonial city which has been called the "Williamsburg" of Brazil. The Brazilian government has preserved the city to look as it did in 1750.

to accept Dom Pedro's decision to remain in Brazil. When this news reached Dom Pedro, he tore the Portuguese colors from his uniform and cried: "It is time! Independence or death!" The people of Brazil were wild with delight at this defiance of Portugal. In 1822, Pedro was crowned Pedro I, Emperor of Brazil. By the end of the next year all Portuguese troops had been driven out, and Portugal was forced to agree to the independence of Brazil.

Pedro I was followed by his son Pedro II, a man respected and admired by everyone. During the fifty years he reigned as emperor he accomplished many things for his people. Brazil then became a republic, but Brazilians still remember Pedro II with gratitude.

He ended the African slave trade, emancipated the slaves, and encouraged immigration.

Thus ends our story of how the spirit of freedom which began in the Thirteen English Colonies affected Canada and Latin America, our neighbors to the north and the south. In later chapters we shall follow the more recent story of Latin America and Canada. And we shall discover how the United States and her neighbors have gotten along together.

CHECK UP

1. How did Brazil become a Portuguese colony?

2. What ways of living developed in Brazil?

3. How did Brazil win independence?

Check Up on Chapter 10

Do You Know the Meaning?

1. Creoles
2. exile
3. dictator
4. liberator
5. refugee
6. council
7. responsible government

Can You Identify?

1. Hidalgo
2. 1810
3. 1821
4. 1824
5. 1846
6. Durham
7. San Martín
8. Pedro I
9. Upper Canada
10. Lower Canada
11. Cabral
12. Iturbide
13. Miranda
14. Bolívar
15. Battle of Ayacucho

Can You Locate?

1. Nova Scotia
2. New Brunswick
3. Rio de Janeiro
4. Venezuela
5. Colombia
6. Chile
7. Peru
8. Andes
9. Mexico
10. Brazil
11. Central America
12. Halifax

Can You Locate? (Cont.)

13. Argentina
14. Caracas
15. Prince Edward Island

What Do You Think?

1. Why did Canada's peaceful revolution take so much longer to achieve than the American Revolution?
2. Spain tried to keep ideas of revolution and democracy out of her colonies. Is it possible for a government to do this for any length of time? Why?
3. There is said to be a bond of friendship between Chile and Argentina which dates back to the early 1800's. Explain why.
4. Compare the difficulties faced by Bolívar and San Martín in winning South American independence with those faced by Washington in the fight for independence in the Thirteen Colonies.
5. Why were the Creoles more active and successful in the Latin American independence movement than the Indians?

Questions 1 and 4 are useful in encouraging pupils to compare the independence movement in the United States with those in Canada and Latin America.

LINKING PAST AND PRESENT

Canada's Acadians today. Large numbers of the early French settlers in Nova Scotia, called the Acadians, settled in Louisiana after the British forced them to leave their homes. But many Acadians stayed in Nova Scotia. Their descendants live there today, speaking the French language and carrying on customs brought to America centuries ago from northern France. Visitors from all over the world go to the tiny village of Grand Pré to see Evangeline Park, where the original Acadian village once stood. The old well and the willow trees that Longfellow wrote about in his poem "Evangeline" are still there.

The Cry of Dolores. The countries of Latin America celebrate their independence days much as we do. If you are ever in Mexico City in the middle of September, you can join the Mexican people in their independence celebration. On the night of September 15, in the great plaza before the National Palace, thousands of people gather in a gay, noisy fiesta. Then, just at midnight, the President of Mexico steps out onto a balcony of the palace. The noise dies down; a bell over the main entrance of the palace begins to ring. It is Mexico's "liberty bell," brought here from Father Hidalgo's church in Dolores. Now the President steps forward and gives

Hidalgo's cry: "Viva la Independencia!" The crowd roars back, "Viva!" Skyrockets burst overhead, fireworks explode, and Mexico begins its celebration of independence, which lasts all through the next day. (See picture, page 660.)

To develop skill in outlining, students might be asked to develop an outline of Chapter 10, based initially on section and heavy type paragraph headings. Then they can compare their outlines with 2a and b of the Summary.

TO CLINCH YOUR
UNDERSTANDING OF
Unit 3

▪ Summary of Important Ideas

In Unit Three you have read about the birth of new nations in the Western Hemisphere.

1. When the English Parliament after 1763 tried to control the American colonies more strictly, the colonists resisted and won their independence (1783).
 a. The colonists claimed the rights of Englishmen, and in the New World they enjoyed even greater freedom than their countrymen in England.
 b. The British Parliament felt justified in taxing the colonists. The colonists objected to "taxation without representation" and to stricter government control (use of writs of assistance, for example). They boycotted British goods in order to secure repeal of the hated laws. Because Parliament passed harsh laws to punish Massachusetts for the Boston Tea Party, leaders from the various colonies met in the First Continental Congress. When British soldiers attempted to destroy military supplies stored by the colonists at Concord, Massachusetts, fighting began.
 c. When it became clear that King George III refused to listen to the grievances of the colonists, the Second Continental Congress approved a Declaration of Independence. Many colonists, however, remained loyal to the mother country. The leadership of Washington, the courage of his men, valuable aid from foreign countries, the advantage of fighting on familiar ground, and British blunders helped the Thirteen Colonies win their independence.

2. While Canada remained in the British Empire, the New World colonies of Spain and Portugal followed the example of the United States and became independent.
 a. The Loyalists who fled to Canada from the Thirteen Colonies demanded greater rights to govern themselves. Through the governors and their councils, however, the British Parliament retained its power in Canada until 1846, when responsible government was introduced. A council appointed from the elected assembly now controlled the government. So, although Canada did not break away from the British Empire, the Canadians obtained a form of government that was responsible to them.
 b. Spain's strict control over its colonies, the Creoles' resentment of their lack of opportunities, and the influence of the French and American Revolutions led to unrest and finally to armed revolt in the Spanish colonies. Miranda, Bolívar, and San Martín were leaders in the movement

for independence from Spain. In addition, Brazil declared its independence from Portugal. By 1825, the former Spanish and Portuguese colonies in Central and South America had become independent states.

Unit Review

1. (a) How did the English government and the colonists differ in their views on the proper relationship of the mother country and the colonies? (b) Did the same differences exist in the case of Spain and the Spanish colonies? Explain.

2. (a) Why did the colonists object to the Stamp Act and the use of writs of assistance? (b) Why did Parliament pass these acts? (c) How did the colonists go about persuading Parliament to repeal laws they did not like?

3. What were the advantages (a) of the Thirteen Colonies and (b) of England in the Revolutionary War? (c) Why did the colonists win the war?

4. (a) What were the chief points in the Declaration of Independence? (b) Why is it one of the world's great documents?

5. (a) What stand did Canada take during the American Revolution? Why? (b) What does the term "responsible government" mean? (c) How did Canada achieve responsible government?

6. (a) Why did the Spanish colonies revolt when they did? (b) Who were the great leaders in this revolt? (c) How did Brazil break away from Portugal?

Gaining Skill

How to Build a Time Sense

Dates may not seem important by themselves, but they are markers which you can use to tell where you are in your study of history. Dates are needed in history to (1) tell when important events took place, (2) keep events in the right order, and (3) estimate the number of years from the beginning to the end of a historical period.

The time lines which appear at the start of each chapter help you to use dates in these three ways. As you read from left to right along the time lines, they *show* the order in which important events took place. By including dates of events already studied, time lines help you see the relation between important events discussed in different chapters. For example, on the time line for Chapter 10 (page 191) you can see that Canada and Latin America won self-government many years later than the Thirteen Colonies, whose fight for independence was described in Chapter 9.

On the time lines you will also recognize the dates of certain events which you have studied in earlier units. The story of France's North American empire, told in Chapter 6, ended in 1763 when the British took over French Canada. In Chapter 10 this same date, 1763, is used to begin the story of how the Canadians gradually won self-government within the British Empire.

In some chapters the important events happened many years apart. But in other periods of history, such as the Revolutionary War, described in Chapter 9, many great events were crowded into a few years. Chapter 9, therefore, has a special "close-up" time line on page 182 which shows part of the regular chapter time line on a larger scale. On the enlarged part there is room to show the most important dates of the war in the right order.

Besides the dates shown on time lines, there are other dates to help you get your bearings in history. For example, dates on a map tell you which of the events shown on the map came first. Look at the map on page 87 which shows the thirteen colonies founded by the English. By reading the date after the name of each settlement, you can tell that Virginia was the first permanent English colony (Jamestown, 1607). You can also tell that Georgia was not founded until 125 years later (Savannah, 1733).

In the same way, the dates mentioned in the text can help you keep events straight. To illustrate the value of dates, let's see if

Questions 1, 4, 5, and 6 are especially useful in encouraging students to think about the independence movements.

you can figure out the answers to some questions based on the following summary:

In 1215 King John of England granted certain rights to his subjects in the Magna Carta. When the English colonists started coming to the New World in 1607, they claimed the rights of Englishmen. After the close of the French and Indian War in 1763, the English government tried to tighten its control over the colonies. Within two years Parliament had passed the Stamp Act, only to repeal it one year later after the colonists protested. In 1767 Parliament put a tax on tea which the colonists thought was against their rights. The Boston Tea Party took place in 1773 when colonists dumped English tea into the harbor. The Revolutionary War broke out a year and a half later and did not end until 1783 when the colonists won their independence.

1. When did King John grant Magna Carta?
2. When did Englishmen start coming to America?
3. For how many years had Englishmen claimed the rights granted by Magna Carta when English colonists first came to America?
4. When did the French and Indian War end?
5. When the war ended, for how many years had Englishmen claimed the rights of Magna Carta?
6. When was the Stamp Act passed? When was it repealed?
7. How many years after the tea tax was passed did the Boston Tea Party take place?
8. When did the Revolutionary War begin?
9. How many years did the Revolutionary War last?
10. What is the correct order of these events: the end of the Revolutionary War, the Stamp Act, the end of the French and Indian War, the Boston Tea Party?

Interesting Things to Do

The projects marked with an asterisk (*) are for the whole class to do.

*1. Add to your card game the names, terms, and dates under "Can You Identify?" for Chapters 7, 8, 9, and 10. You now have enough cards for the class to hold a lively drill.
*2. Make a chart in the form of a ladder called "Steps That Led to the Revolution." Starting with the bottom rung of the ladder, place in their correct order the chief events from 1763 to 1776 that led to the Revolution. You should have eight or ten events.
*3. Learn the Declaration of Independence (page 171) from the beginning to the sentence ending "to effect their safety and happiness."
4. Draw a cartoon illustrating the feeling of the colonists about the Stamp Act, the Proclamation of 1763, or the Intolerable Acts.
5. Select eight or ten important leaders in Revolutionary days and prepare a "clues" program for the class. Give one clue at a time to see how soon your classmates can identify the person being described.
6. Imagine that you had fought on the Patriot side in one of the famous battles of the Revolution. Using books in the library, write an account of what happened. Be sure to check the Unit Three book list at the end of this book for titles that will be helpful.
7. Find out what historical programs are given regularly on television or radio. Report to the class, giving name, channel or station, and time.
8. Form a committee to find out more about how the principal Latin American countries won their independence. Each member of the committee might choose one of the Latin American countries and use the library to find out how that country achieved independence. Report your findings to the class.

Independent workers should be encouraged to do the reading and organization of ideas necessary for good reports.

The United States Is Established

A new nation must make a place for itself among nations just as a young man must make his way in the world. The average young man wants to be successful in his job, popular among his friends, happy in his family life. When he first goes to work, he has had little experience and is untested. What he does will help to determine whether he travels the path to success and happiness, or another road that leads to disappointment and failure.

The men who helped the United States win its independence had high hopes for the nation's future. They wanted it to be strong and prosperous and respected, and they wanted its citizens to be happy under the new government. For the nation to become independent, therefore, was not enough. It had to establish a strong government for its people and win the respect of other nations. Much depended on the leaders it chose, such as John Adams, our second President, who is shown above on his first visit to the new capital city at Washington. Like the boy waving the flag in the picture, the young United States was unknown

on a Firm Basis

For an overview of the entire unit, students might read the summary on pages 259-260.

and untried. Only the test of time would determine whether the hopes of the founders were to be fulfilled.

In Unit Three we learned how our country became free and independent. In this unit we shall find out how it overcame the difficult problems which faced the young nation. Chapter 11 tells of the troubled times that followed the American Revolution and how our Constitution drew the thirteen states together in a firm union. Chapter 12 explains how the government of our new republic got off to a firm start. Two important steps it took were to put the United States on a sound financial basis and to build a permanent capital. (Note in the picture above that only one end of the Capitol Building had been completed when John Adams became President.) In Chapter 13 we shall find out how our country doubled in size and won a place for itself among the nations of the world.

> *A just and solid republican government maintained here will be a standing monument and example for the aim and imitation of the people of other countries. . . .* — THOMAS JEFFERSON

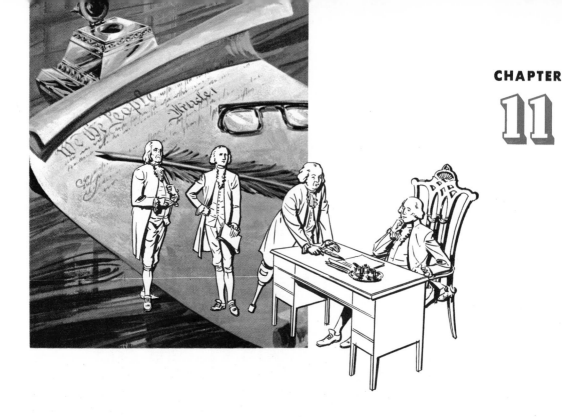

The Thirteen States Create a Firm
Union Under the Constitution

*Students may wish to read more about these men and report to the class.
See, for example, Our Independence and the Constitution.*

What this chapter is about —

All our lives we act according to rules. We obey family rules at home, school rules in school, traffic rules when we walk or ride on the street. When we play football or basketball or baseball, we are expected to follow the rules of the game. If it were not for rules, groups of people could not live or work or play together.

A nation, too, must have rules or agreements for running its affairs. These rules are part of its system of government. When the United States declared its independence, however, there were no rules for running its government; in fact, there was no government for the thirteen states as a whole. But during the Revolutionary

War, the thirteen states worked together to win independence.

After the Revolutionary War a group of outstanding Americans met to undertake the difficult task of planning a new government for the whole nation. These men succeeded in drawing up a remarkable plan which has lasted, with few changes, to the present day. This plan is called the Constitution. In this chapter we shall learn how the Constitution was drawn up. We shall answer these questions:

▶ 1. How was the United States governed after the Revolutionary War?

▶ 2. How did the Constitution become the foundation of our government?

People in our story — Benjamin Franklin, James Madison, Gouverneur Morris, George Washington.

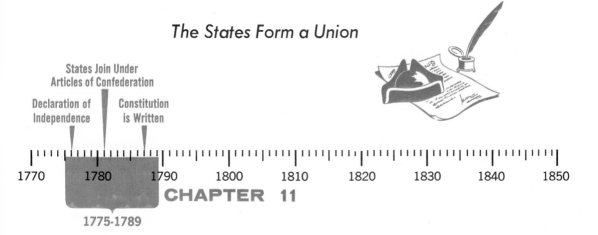

The States Form a Union

States Join Under
Articles of Confederation

Declaration of   Constitution
Independence   is Written

1770   1780   1790   1800   1810   1820   1830   1840   1850

CHAPTER 11

1775-1789

How Was the United States Governed After the Revolutionary War?

We are so used to thinking of the "United States government" that we often forget that it has not always existed. Our strong government under the Constitution did not start until 1789, several years after the United States was born. In the first years of our nation's life, the states were not firmly united as they are now. They had to learn by experience that a strong union was necessary if the United States was to become a successful nation. In order to understand how our Constitution came to be written, we need to know what kind of government the United States had in the years just after it won independence. This story takes us back to the days before the Revolutionary War.

The Thirteen Colonies had little success in working together. In the mid-1700's, although all of the Thirteen British Colonies were subject to the mother country, each had its own separate government. The colonists did not think of themselves as united. They did not even think of themselves as Americans, but as Virginians, Rhode Islanders, and so on.

The colonists, to be sure, had some things in common. They all belonged to the same mother country, and most of them spoke the same language. In times of danger it was natural for them to draw closer together. Yet even common dangers failed to bring about any real union among the colonies.

When the French and Indian War broke out, for instance, they talked about uniting to defend themselves against the French and Indians. In 1754, representatives from most of the colonies met in Albany, New York, to consider a plan for common defense. A council was to be elected which would have power to make treaties with the Indians, build forts, and raise armies to protect all the colonies. Although the *Albany Plan of Union,* as it was called, offered advantages, the colonies failed to adopt it. Each colony wanted such complete control of its own affairs that it refused to allow the representatives of any other colony to have a voice in them. The colonies were not willing to work together in a common cause.

The struggle for independence brings a kind of union. Only when England tightened its control of the colonies (Chapter 8) did the colonists begin to work together to protect their rights. As you know, they sent representatives to the First and

Bring out why the colonies were **213** *more willing to unite in opposing Britain than in fighting the French and Indians.*

Why Americans Criticized the Confederation

"We asked the states for some money months ago, but I don't know if we will ever get it."

"It's not fair! He got his boxes from another state where the tax on foreign goods is lower than ours."

Second Continental Congresses. The Second Continental Congress met for the first time in May, 1775, and continued to hold meetings until March, 1781. It was this Congress which declared independence and managed the affairs of the United States during the Revolutionary War. The Continental Congress directed the war, raised what money it could, and made the alliance with France. But no real powers were definitely given to it by the people or the states. It was an emergency government, held together by the common desire to win the war.

The Articles of Confederation are adopted after a long delay. Meanwhile, the states realized that a regular government was needed for the nation, and the members of Congress worked out a definite plan for such a government. The states were to be joined in a union known as the *Confederation*. The plan for this union was called the *Articles of Confederation*.

When the new plan was sent to the states for approval, it ran into trouble. At that time, about half the states had claims to large areas of land west of the Appalachian Mountains. (The map on page 216 shows the land claimed by the states.) Naturally these states wanted to keep their western lands, but the states that had no western claims did not agree. They were afraid of remaining forever small and weak in comparison with their large, strong neighbors. They believed that the western lands should be turned over to the United States, and refused to accept the Articles of Confederation until this was done. Finally the states claiming western lands agreed to give up their claims, and the Articles were approved. Because of this delay, the new government was not established until 1781, when the war was almost over.

What was the new government like? The government of the Confederation was not like our national government today. There was no President with power to carry out the laws and no Supreme Court to settle important disputes. To run the nation's business there was a Congress made up of representatives from each

This map makes clear why claims **214** *overlapped. Note the land claimed by Virginia, for example.*

"If I have to pay a tax on every load of vegetables I bring across the state line, I'll go out of business!"

"I claim I've got a right to fish over there but there's no court where I can take you to prove it."

state. Whether large or small, each state was to have only one vote. And in most matters nine states had to agree before the Confederation could act.

The new government under the Articles of Confederation could (1) wage war and make peace, and organize an army and navy when needed; (2) control the relations of the United States with other nations; (3) regulate trade with the Indians and other Indian affairs; (4) arrange for carrying the mail; (5) borrow money to pay necessary expenses; and (6) ask each of the states to contribute money to pay the expenses of the Confederation.

The Confederation proves to be a weak government. When the new government came into power, it did not work well. For one thing, the country was upset after long years of war. Farming and business had been neglected. Prices were high, and food and goods were scarce. These conditions would have added to the problems of any government. But the main trouble was that the Articles of Confederation did not give the central government enough power. Americans had just fought a war because the British Parliament had insisted on its right to tax the colonists and to regulate their trade. For this reason the states were afraid to turn over these dearly won rights even to a central government of their own.

Among the many weaknesses of the Articles of Confederation, these were some of the most important:

(1) Congress was not given the right to tax. It could not force the citizens to pay taxes, but had to ask the state governments for money. Usually the states did not pay as much as they were asked to pay. The result was that Congress never had enough money, and the government was always in debt.

(2) Another difficulty was that Congress did not have the power to regulate the trade which was carried on between states. The businessmen in each state, of course, wanted to make as much profit as they could. They persuaded their state governments to keep out the products of other states by taxing such products heavily. For

A summary of five important powers **215** *given the central government under the Articles. The sixth did not provide adequately for raising revenue. See *1 in next column. See also The chart on page 229.*

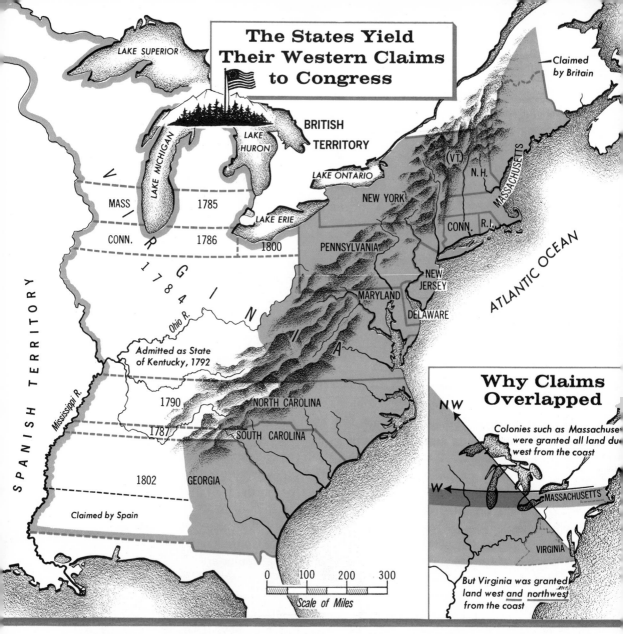

The States Yield Their Western Claims to Congress

LAKE SUPERIOR

BRITISH TERRITORY

Claimed by Britain

LAKE MICHIGAN

LAKE HURON

LAKE ONTARIO

LAKE ERIE

VERMONT (VT.)

N.H.

NEW YORK

MASSACHUSETTS

MASS 1785

CONN. 1786

1800

PENNSYLVANIA

CONN. R.I.

ATLANTIC OCEAN

NEW JERSEY

V I R G I N I A 1784

Ohio R.

MARYLAND

DELAWARE

Admitted as State of Kentucky, 1792

SPANISH TERRITORY

Mississippi R.

1790

NORTH CAROLINA

1787

SOUTH CAROLINA

1802

GEORGIA

Claimed by Spain

0   100   200   300
Scale of Miles

Why Claims Overlapped

NW

Colonies such as Massachusetts were granted all land due west from the coast

W

MASSACHUSETTS

VIRGINIA

But Virginia was granted land west and northwest from the coast

MAP STUDY The dates here tell when eastern states gave up their claims to western lands (shown by broken lines). Why had the claims of some states overlapped? (See inset.)

example, New Jersey farmers who took their vegetables to New York City had to pay a tax not only on the vegetables but also on the boats that carried them. If this sort of thing continued, trade between the states would be sharply cut down. Yet Congress lacked the power to deal with such matters.

(3) Still another weakness of the Confederation was that it provided no satisfac-

tory way of settling quarrels among the states. For example, Pennsylvania and Connecticut almost came to blows over a piece of territory claimed by both states. Yet Congress had no power to set up United States courts to settle disputes between states.

The states see a need for changing the government. Considering the weaknesses of the Articles of Confederation and the

216

Use of color improves geographic the attractiveness of the book.   *presentation and also adds to*

confusion which naturally follows a war, it is not surprising that many Americans were dissatisfied. People tended to blame the government if they were out of work or had to pay high taxes. Indeed, by 1785 the affairs of the United States were in such a state that thoughtful men realized something must be done. Unless a stronger union were established, they feared that there would soon be no union at all.

At this very time Virginia and Maryland were having a dispute about navigation on the Potomac River and Chesapeake Bay. In 1785, representatives from Maryland and Virginia met and agreed on regulations for boats sailing these waters. This success led them to think that it would be a good idea if other states could join them and agree upon a plan for regulating trade.

A meeting is called to improve the government. Maryland and Virginia asked the other states to send representatives to discuss this problem at a meeting to be held at Annapolis, Maryland, a year later. Only five of the thirteen states sent representatives. These men talked of how unsuccessful the Confederation had been. They decided to see if the government could be improved. For this purpose they invited all of the states to send representatives to still another meeting, or convention, to be held in Philadelphia. This time twelve of the thirteen states accepted. Only Rhode Island refused to send delegates.

CH**E**CK
U P

1. What attempts at union had been made before the Articles of Confederation were adopted?

2. What powers did the central government have under the Articles of Confederation?

3. What were the chief weaknesses of this government?

How Did the Constitution Become the Foundation of Our Government?

THE CONSTITUTIONAL CONVENTION MEETS IN PHILADELPHIA

George Washington is elected chairman. Early in June, 1787, about 30 men sat in a small room on the first floor of the State House in Philadelphia where the Declaration of Independence had been signed. In spite of the summer heat, the doors and windows were closed because the men wished to keep their meetings secret. Loose dirt had been shoveled onto the street outside so that they would not be disturbed by the clatter of the wheels of passing carriages and wagons. All the men were dressed in the style of the times: knee breeches with silver buckles just below the knee, silk stockings, low shoes, long waistcoats, and open coats extending almost to their knees.

Near one end of the room was a raised platform upon which stood a large chair with a gilded half-sun carved on its high back. In this chair sat a man well over six feet tall and weighing more than 210 pounds. This man was George Washington, who had been the choice of all for chairman of the meeting. Fifty-five years old at the time of this meeting, George Washington was dignified, serious, and thoughtful. As commander of the army

This account contains detailed information to help pupils visualize the place of meeting and leading participants.

THE MARYLAND STATE CAPITOL, in Annapolis, is the oldest state capitol building still in use. It witnessed many important events while serving as our country's national capitol in 1783–1784.

which had won our independence, he was respected by everybody in the United States. His election as chairman was both natural and wise. Although he did not take much part in the discussions that followed, the members paid close attention to the advice he did give them.

Able men attend the Convention. All together, 55 men attended the Philadelphia Convention. These men were well known in their states. In a day when there were few colleges, many of the men nevertheless had attended college. Most of them had been leaders in the Revolution, and most of them lived in the older villages and cities near the coast.

As Washington glanced about the room, he recognized the faces of many friends and acquaintances. One of these people was a fellow Virginian, much younger than himself, upon whom Washington depended a great deal. This was *James*

Madison, a short, slender man, 35 years of age. He spoke quietly and modestly, but the members listened carefully to his words, because Madison knew a great deal about governments. For one thing, he had studied the governments of many countries. He had also served as a member of the governments of Virginia and of the United States, both during and after the Revolution. The careful notes taken by Madison give us a great deal of information about what went on in the meetings of the Convention.

Benjamin Franklin, wise, humorous, and at 81 the oldest member present at the meeting, also played a useful part. Franklin had first entered Philadelphia one cold Sunday morning years before, when he was seventeen years old. He was a poor apprentice then, and had just run away from his master in Boston. His clothes were dirty and mussed from traveling, and his pockets were "stuffed out with shirts and stockings." He had walked the streets of Philadelphia munching a "great puffy roll" he had bought, and carrying two others under his arms.

Much had happened to the runaway apprentice since that day long ago. He had tried many things and had succeeded at all of them. To name but a few of his activities, he had been a writer, a publisher of a newspaper, and an inventor. He had also served as an official of the United States at home and as her representative abroad. In 1787, he was president, or governor as we should say now, of Pennsylvania. During the meetings he moved about slowly, giving good advice, soothing members when they disagreed, and cheering everybody with a wise comment or a funny remark.

Gouverneur Morris, born in New York, attended the meeting as a representative of Pennsylvania. His body was crippled

During the period covered by this unit the nation's capital was located in four different cities.

(for he had a wooden leg and could not use one arm), but his mind was keen and alert. He was an effective writer. His sentences were clear, direct, and graceful. He is responsible for most of the actual language used in the document describing the new plan of government agreed upon by the Convention.

PLANS FOR A NEW GOVERNMENT ARE WORKED OUT

The men who gathered at Philadelphia included many of the wisest men in the United States. As we shall see, they would need all their experience and wisdom to solve the difficult problems that lay ahead.

The Articles of Confederation are discarded. The states had been invited to send delegates to Philadelphia for one purpose — to improve the Articles of Confederation. Yet the meeting had hardly begun when the men agreed on a bold step. They decided to discard the unsatisfactory Articles of Confederation and draw up an entirely *new* plan of government. A written plan of government is called a *constitution*. Because this meeting voted to write a constitution, it has been called the *Constitutional Convention*.

"But," asked the members of the Constitutional Convention, "if we are to have an entirely new government instead of patching up the old one, what kind of Constitution shall we write?" Gouverneur Morris supplied the answer to this question. He said that the Constitutional Convention must plan a national government strong enough to work successfully, yet not strong enough to break down the authority of the states. Such a plan would not be easy to work out. If the states turned over too much power to the central government, they might be seriously weak-

ened. On the other hand, if the states did not give up enough power to make the United States strong, the central government would not work much better than it had under the Confederation.

Virginia proposes a plan for a strong government. Soon after the meetings began, some of the members placed a plan before the Convention. It was called the *Virginia Plan* because it had the support of the Virginia representatives. According to this plan, the government of the United States was to be made up of three parts: (1) a Congress to make the laws; (2) a separate branch of the government, headed by a President, to enforce these laws; and (3) United States courts to see that justice was done under the laws. Under the Virginia Plan, Congress was to be divided into two houses. The members of the first house were to be elected by

WHICH OF THE THIRTEEN STATES had the most people? Which had the fewest?

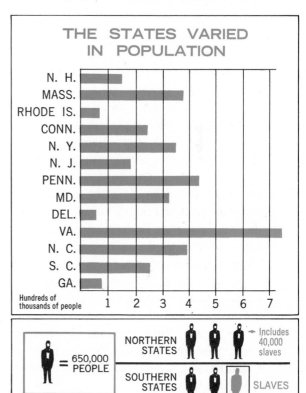

THE STATES VARIED IN POPULATION

Encourage pupils to refer to the Constitution. Difficult terms are explained and interpretative notes provided.

220   THE UNITED STATES IS ESTABLISHED

the people directly. States with small populations, like Delaware, might have only one representative. States with large populations, like Virginia, would have perhaps ten or more. The members of the second house were to be elected by the first house.

Here was a plan which would set up a central government based upon the people. It would make the government of the United States much stronger and the state governments weaker.

New Jersey offers a plan for a weaker government. A number of the members of the Constitutional Convention objected to the Virginia Plan. Some said, "We cannot be sure that the voters will elect capable representatives to Congress. The state governments, not the people, should choose the representatives." Others said, "The Virginia Plan will take too much power from the states. They will be too weak and the national government too strong." The members from the smaller states added still another objection: "The large states with greater populations will have so many representatives in Congress that the small states will have little to say about the passing of laws."

A delegate from the small state of New Jersey offered another plan to the Convention. In the *New Jersey Plan,* each state (regardless of its size) would send an equal number of representatives to Congress. This plan would make certain that the states would remain strong, and that the small states would have the same number of votes as the large ones. But a number of delegates objected to the New Jersey Plan because (1) the representatives would be chosen by the state governments, not the people; and (2) the people in the large states would not be represented fairly. In other words, the large states would have no more votes in Congress than the small states.

An agreement is reached at last. For many days the Convention discussed these two plans carefully. The large states naturally wanted the Virginia Plan; the small states favored the New Jersey Plan. This was the most important disagreement that the Convention had to deal with. If the Constitutional Convention was to succeed, an agreement somehow had to be reached between the members who wanted the Virginia Plan and those who wanted the New Jersey Plan. If an agreement is to be made among men who disagree, each side must give way a little. This is called a *compromise.* The delegates at the Convention were determined to work out a compromise. One man told the Convention he would rather "bury his bones" in Philadelphia than go home without making a strong union.

Finally, each side gave way a little, and a compromise was reached. It was agreed that Congress should have two houses: the *House of Representatives* and the *Senate.* In the House, a state would be represented according to the number of people living in the state. Of course this would give the large states more representatives than the small states. But in the Senate the states would be equal, each having two senators and two votes. Equal representation in the Senate would protect the small states, since every law had to be approved by both houses. And the arrangements for the House and the Senate meant that both the people and the states would be represented. (See Article I, Sections 2c and 3a of the Constitution on page A3.[1])

Once this plan, called the Great Compromise, was agreed upon, both the small states and the large ones were willing to

---

[1] Pages A1, A2, etc., are in the appendix (reference section) at the end of this book.

GEORGE WASHINGTON presides as delegates sign the Constitution. James Madison is second from the right. Who is standing in the middle of the group at the left?

work together to finish writing the Constitution.

Many other compromises appear in the Constitution. All summer long the members of the Convention labored over the new plan of government. As other difficult problems arose, they, too, were settled by compromises. Here are a few of them:

(1) As we have just learned, the number of representatives that each state might have in the House was to depend upon the number of people living in the state. But many more Negro slaves lived in the South than in the North. How should they be counted? If each slave was counted separately, the number of southern votes in the House would be greatly increased. In another compromise it was agreed to count five slaves as three instead of five persons (page A3).

(2) The members disagreed on another important question: Should Congress have the power to control commerce with foreign countries? The northern states, where many people made a living by shipping, wanted Congress, not the states, to regulate foreign trade. But the southern states bought many articles from Europe. They were afraid that Congress might tax these goods, which would add to their cost. The South also feared the slave trade might be stopped by Congress. So another compromise was made. Congress was given the power to regulate commerce with foreign countries and between the states, but it could not stop the slave trade for the next 20 years.

(3) Still another serious question was raised: how should the President be elected? The Constitution made the President a very important official. If Congress were to elect him, he might be afraid to do anything Congress did not like for fear it might not elect him again. On the other hand, there were members of the Convention who did not trust the judgment of the people in selecting a President. So another compromise was made. The President and Vice-President were to be chosen by a group of men called *electors*. Each state would select as many electors as it had senators and representatives. If no candidate for President had the votes of more than half the electors, the House

Nor could exports be taxed, another point in **221** which the South was interested.

These powers were essential to an effective central government.
Government under the Articles lacked These powers. (See page 215.)

222 THE UNITED STATES IS ESTABLISHED

of Representatives would decide between the candidates (pages A11–A12).

The Constitution contained other compromises, too, for the members of the Convention were determined to form a better, stronger union than the Confederation. The Convention discussed each problem until the members felt they had solved it. As tempers rose during the discussion, Franklin would tell a story. He told one about "a certain French lady, who, in a dispute with her sister, said, 'I don't know how it happens, Sister, but I meet with nobody but myself that's always in the right!'" In good humor once more, the members would return to their work.

The Convention's work is completed. At last the Constitution was completed, and its members were ready to return home. Although nobody was completely satisfied, the members believed that they had written the best Constitution possible. The new central government would be stronger than the old, because it had been given important powers which the Confederation government did not have. These powers included the right to tax and to control trade among the states. At the same time the states still possessed enough powers to control their own local affairs. But would the new government be strong enough to be successful? Or would it be too strong? Only time would tell.

Before the meeting broke up, Franklin rose and pointed to the half-sun on Washington's chair. "I have often and often in the course of this session," he said, "looked at that [half-sun] without being able to tell whether it was rising or setting. But now at length I have the happiness to know that it is a rising and not a setting sun." With their work completed, on September 17, 1787, the members said good-bye to each other and left Philadelphia for their homes.

SHALL THE CONSTITUTION BE ACCEPTED?

Let the people choose. The members of the Constitutional Convention had worked long and hard to write what they believed to be a good plan of government. But the only way they could find out how their countrymen felt was to send the Constitution to the states for approval. In each state the voters elected representatives to decide whether or not to accept the new form of government. Meanwhile, throughout the country — in homes, in taverns, and in the streets — the Constitution was the chief topic of conversation. Some Americans strongly favored the new government; many others opposed it.

Some Americans feared the strong government provided by the Constitution. Those Americans who opposed the Constitution feared that it would set up too strong a central government. They could not forget that, only a few short years before, they had fought a long war to protect their precious liberties against the tyranny of a strong central government in England. Now they saw that the government planned in the Constitution would be able to tax the people, to make laws, and to compel the people to obey them. Those who disliked the Constitution asked: "What is to prevent this new strong government from taking away our rights as did the British government before the Revolution?"

Jefferson suggests a Bill of Rights. These fears were well expressed by Thomas Jefferson, who himself had written the Declaration of Independence. Jefferson had not attended the Constitutional Convention because he had been sent to represent the United States in France. When he received a copy of the Constitution, he found much in it to approve, but he also found important weaknesses. He wrote to James Madison:

* I like the organization of the government into legislative, judiciary and executive [branches]. I like the power given the [Congress] to levy taxes, and . . . I approve of the greater House being chosen by the people directly. . . . I will now tell you what I do not like. First, [there is no] bill of rights, providing clearly . . . for freedom of religion, freedom of the press, protection against standing armies, . . . and trials by jury in all matters [that may be tried] by the laws of the land. . . . Let me add that a bill of rights is what the people are entitled to against every government on earth. . . .

Friends of the Constitution campaign for its adoption. In answer to objections like Jefferson's, the friends of the Constitution said that the rights of the people would be perfectly safe. They also pointed out that no laws could be passed by Congress without the consent of the people's representatives in the House. They explained the ways in which the new union would be better than the Confederation.

To win over their countrymen, those who favored the Constitution spoke at meetings in the various states. They also explained the new union in articles printed in the newspapers or in small pamphlets. The most famous of these articles was a series called *The Federalist*, written by James Madison, Alexander Hamilton, and John Jay. These articles gave a clear explanation of the Constitution and presented strong arguments for accepting it.

The Constitution is accepted. Slowly those who approved the Constitution gained support. Delaware accepted the Constitution first, then Pennsylvania. So did New Jersey, Georgia, Connecticut, Massachusetts, Maryland, South Carolina,

AMERICANS throughout the country read the new Constitution to see what the new government would be like. Here nine-year-old Daniel Webster, who later became a famous senator, reads the Constitution in a New Hampshire store.

and New Hampshire. This made <u>nine states</u>, and it had been agreed that if nine states accepted the Constitution, it should become the new government.

In some of these states, however, the Constitution had won by only a small number of votes. Its friends had been compelled to promise that they would work for the addition of a bill of rights to

Pledge of Allegiance

I pledge allegiance to the Flag of the United States of America and to the republic for which it stands; one nation under God, indivisible, with liberty and justice for all.

Most young people have repeated this Pledge many times in school. When they say the Pledge, they are promising to be loyal to the American Flag and to the United States. In addition, they are saying what our country means to its citizens: a united nation in which every American is entitled to liberty and justice.

The Pledge of Allegiance was written in 1892 by a man named Francis Bellamy. It made its first public appearance in a magazine for which Bellamy worked, *The Youth's Companion*. Many Americans, reading the Pledge, felt that it expressed in a few words the deep feeling of loyalty which they felt toward their country. Today the Pledge has become a traditional part of American school life.

---

protect the liberties of the people. Two important states, Virginia and New York, still had not accepted the Constitution. In Virginia, Patrick Henry, the fiery speaker of Revolutionary days, worked against accepting the Constitution. He feared the great power given the central government. Yet without Virginia the new government would lack the support of the largest state. And without New York the new government would be separated into two parts.

At last the people's representatives in Virginia accepted the Constitution by the close vote of 89 to 79. In New York the Constitution won by the votes of only three representatives. (The remaining two states, North Carolina and Rhode Island, did not accept the Constitution until nearly two years after the other states had agreed to establish the new government.)

The Congress of the Confederation arranged that the new government should begin in the spring of 1789. The states were asked to hold elections for the new President and congressmen. A new and stronger union was to be tried at last.

No American can read the story of our Constitution without realizing what a debt of gratitude we owe to the wise men who wrote it. These men are often called the "Founding Fathers" because in giving the United States its Constitution, they laid the foundation of our nation. This remarkable document has not only given us a strong and stable government but has also protected the liberties which we hold dear. (On pages A1–A32 at the end of this book, you will find the complete Constitution, as well as notes to help you read it with greater understanding.)

CHECK UP

1. Who were some of the outstanding men present at the Constitutional Convention?

2. (a) What was the Virginia Plan? (b) The New Jersey Plan? (c) How was the disagreement between large and small states settled?

3. What other important compromises were adopted by the Convention?

4. (a) Why did some men oppose the Constitution? (b) What did Jefferson think should be added to it? Why?

Samuel Adams opposed the Constitution **224** *It is difficult today to understand how men could believe that the states could survive without a stronger central government.*

Do You Know the Meaning?

1. elector
2. tyranny
3. compromise
4. confederation
5. constitution
6. convention
7. central government

Can You Identify?

1. Great Compromise
2. 1787
3. 1789
4. James Madison
5. *The Federalist*
6. Congress
7. President
8. Senate
9. Gouverneur Morris
10. George Washington
11. Benjamin Franklin
12. House of Representatives
13. Virginia Plan
14. New Jersey Plan
15. Albany Plan of Union
16. Articles of Confederation

What Do You Think?

1. Should the Articles of Confederation be blamed for all the troubled conditions in the United States following the Revolution? Why?

On page 215 other reasons are mentioned.

What Do You Think? (Cont.)

2. The Constitution has been called a "bundle of compromises." What does this statement mean?
3. Some people, arguing against the strong government outlined in the Constitution, pointed out that Americans had just fought a war to win freedom from another strong government. How would you have answered their arguments?
4. When the United Nations organization was being planned, a dispute arose between large and small nations similar to that between large and small states at the Constitutional Convention. Do you think that small nations should have equal rights with large ones in the United Nations? Should each nation, regardless of size, have the same vote in determining what action should be taken by the UN? Why?
5. Which man do you think contributed most to the success of the Constitutional Convention? Why?

LINKING PAST AND PRESENT

Our documents of freedom. One thing no visitor to Washington, D.C., should miss is a trip to the National Archives Building. For it is here that you can see the original documents on which our freedom is based — the Declaration of Independence and the Constitution of the United States. You can step up close and look at these important old documents in their cases. They are written by hand on parchment that is now yellowed and cracked with age. Although the ink has faded, you can still read much of the writing. Our government in recent years has done everything possible to preserve these priceless documents. They have been sealed in glass cases filled with helium gas. The tinted glass of the cases protects the documents from bright light, and the helium keeps moisture constant. At night the cases are lowered on an electric elevator into a strong safe on the floor below. Each morning they are raised again to the main floor. Every year thousands of visitors go to see the documents which are a precious heritage from the past.

Savings bonds. Have you ever lent money to the United States government? To pay for the costs of the War for Independence, the young United States issued bonds — that is, it borrowed money on its promise to repay the money with interest. In the same way, our government has borrowed money from you if you have ever bought a savings bond. The $18.75 which you give for a $25 savings bond is a loan to the United States government. These bonds promise to repay $25 after a period of several years. The difference between $18.75 and $25 represents the interest that has collected over this period of time.

Names of the states.   When our Constitution was adopted, there were only thirteen states in the Union. Now, only about 175 years later, there are fifty. Have you ever wondered where some of the states got their names?

Many of the states are named after Indian tribes or have names taken from Indian languages. "Alibama" was the name of an Indian tribe living in what is now Alabama. Missouri was the name given to the river by the Indians. It meant "muddy water." In the language of the Sioux Indians, Dakota meant "alliance of friends." Kentucky is taken from an Indian name meaning "tomorrow" or "Land of Tomorrow," and Idaho comes from the Indian words "Edah hoe" which meant "Light of the Mountains." Ohio was an Iroquois name which meant "great." In another Indian tongue, "michi" meant "great" and "gama" meant "water." Thus we have Michigan, the name first given to the lake and then to the state. Connecticut comes from the Indian word "quonecktacut," meaning "long river" or "river of pines."

There are other Indian names. Arkansas was the Algonquin name for the Quapaw Indians. Illinois is an Indian word believed to mean "river of men." Iowa means "sleepy ones," a word applied to a Sioux tribe by other Indians. Kansas, meaning "people of the South Wind," was the name of another Sioux tribe. Massachusetts was an Algon-

quin name for "the place near the big little hills." Minnesota, in Sioux language, meant "sky-colored water." Nebraska signified "flat river." Mexico was the name of an Aztec war god whose name is carried on in our state of New Mexico. Oklahoma takes its name from a Choctaw word for "red people." Tennessee was the Indian name for the chief town of the Cherokees, on what is now the Little Tennessee River. Texas is believed to have meant "friends." Utah comes directly from the name of the Ute Indians. Wisconsin, spelled in different ways, meant "meeting of the rivers," while Wyoming meant "mountains and valleys."

Some of our states, as you have read (pages 79 and 131), were named by Spanish or French explorers — states like Florida, California, and Louisiana. Montana is a Spanish word that means "mountainous" while Nevada means "snow-clad."

Several states were named by the early settlers or proprietors in memory of places in Europe or in honor of kings or queens or nobles. Maryland was named in honor of Queen Henrietta Maria, wife of King Charles I of England. New Jersey took its name from the island of Jersey off the coast of England, and New Hampshire was named by its settlers in memory of the English county of Hampshire. Delaware gets its name from Lord De La Warr, an English governor of Virginia who came to America in 1610.

Two men in our own history are also honored. The state of Washington was named in memory of George Washington, and the District of Columbia recalls Christopher Columbus. The smallest state once had the largest name! It was called "The State of Rhode Island and Providence Plantations." Because it was so awkward, the name was shortened to "Rhode Island," for the island of Rhodes in the Mediterranean.

As for the two newest states, Alaska is an Eskimo word meaning "great land," and Hawaii probably comes from a native word meaning "homeland."

Can pupils explain the origin of place names near their community?

The New Government
Is Successfully Launched

What this chapter is about —

It was noon on Thursday, April 30, 1789. A large crowd had gathered in Wall Street in New York City. Onto the balcony of Federal Hall stepped George Washington. He wore a dark brown suit with knee breeches, white silk stockings, and shoes with silver buckles. A sword hung at his side. His hair was carefully powdered and drawn into a short queue at the back of his head.

Catching sight of the tall, dignified figure on the balcony, the people below applauded loudly. George Washington placed his hand upon a large Bible and slowly spoke the following words: "I do solemnly swear that I will faithfully execute the office of President of the United States

and will, to the best of my ability, preserve, protect, and defend the Constitution of the United States." As he finished, the crowd broke into shouts of "God bless our Washington! Long live our beloved President!" Washington turned and went inside to address the members of the new Congress.

Thus did our country begin to govern itself under the new Constitution. The Articles of Confederation had been tried and found unsatisfactory; now the new Constitution was to be tried. We Americans today know that the Constitution is strong and lasting, but the people who lived in 1789 did not know how it would work out. Would the new government un-

People in our story — the first President and his Cabinet: Knox, Randolph, Jefferson, Hamilton; and Washington.

der the Constitution be any better than the Confederation? Would it last longer? Everywhere thoughtful Americans were wondering what the future of the new government would be.

In this chapter we shall find out more about the new government under the Constitution. We shall answer the following questions:

▶ 1. What kind of government did the Constitution establish?

▶ 2. How did the new government settle certain important problems?

▶ 3. How did political parties get started?

The heavy-type paragraph headings and the CheckUp questions on page 233 suggest important points included.

1 What Kind of Government Did the Constitution Establish?

✳ We the people of the United States, in order to form a more perfect union, establish justice, insure domestic tranquillity, provide for the common defense, promote the general welfare, and secure the blessings of liberty to ourselves and our posterity, do ordain and establish this Constitution for the United States of America.

These now famous words, which every American should know, form the introduction or *preamble* to the Constitution of the United States of America. "We the people . . . establish this Constitution. . . ." What a long way Americans had traveled along the road of self-government! In a day when almost every country in the world accepted the rule of kings, the makers of our Constitution had created a government based on the right of the people to rule. At a time when laws in other countries were issued in the name of the king, Americans had accepted as their highest law a constitution issued in the name of the people!

Our central government has important powers. Those who planned the new government hoped that it would bring a "more perfect union" and "insure domestic tranquillity" (maintain order). In Chapter 11 we learned that the Confederation had done neither of these because it was weak. But the makers of the Constitution gave the new central government important powers which the Confederation

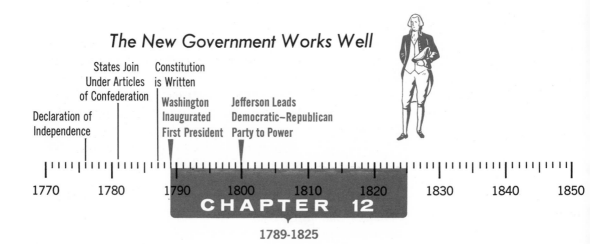

The New Government Works Well

Declaration of Independence

States Join Under Articles of Confederation

Constitution is Written

Washington Inaugurated First President

Jefferson Leads Democratic–Republican Party to Power

1770   1780   1790   1800   1810   1820   1830   1840   1850

CHAPTER 12

1789-1825

lacked. (For some of the most important powers, see the chart on this page.)

Certain powers are left to the states. If the Constitution created a strong central government, what powers, then, were left to the states? The members of the Constitutional Convention were careful to divide the powers so that the states would not be swallowed up by the United States government. They gave the United States control over all matters that concerned the Union or *all* the states. (Turn to pages A8–A9 to read the list of powers granted to the national government.) On the other hand, each of the states was left free to control affairs that did not affect the other states. As a matter of fact, the Constitution leaves to each state all powers not definitely given to the United States.

Let us see how this division of powers worked out. Because war concerns all the states, the United States government was given the power to declare war. This was clearly stated in the Constitution. But each state has the power to make its own laws for punishing crimes like murder or theft, because these laws affect only the people within the state where the crime takes place. You will not find this power of the states mentioned in the Constitution, but it belongs to the states since it is not definitely given to the central government.

Americans want the rights of the people protected. The new government was strong. But was it too strong? Americans love freedom and even today do not want government to put too many limits upon their liberties. So Americans look closely at the power of their government. Of freedom and government, one wise American said:

Who are a free people? Not those whose government is reasonable and just, but those whose government is so checked and

---

WHAT CONGRESS COULD DO

 Powers under the **Confederation**
Powers added by the **Constitution**

1. Declare war and make peace, and organize an army and navy. Call on the militia (soldiers trained by each state).

2. Control the relations of the United States with other nations and Indian tribes.

3. Regulate trade with the Indians. Regulate trade passing from one state into another (interstate commerce) and trade with foreign nations.

4. Borrow money to pay expenses.

5. ~~Ask each state to raise money~~ to pay expenses of the central government.
   --Impose direct taxes--

6. Coin all money and regulate its value.

7. Organize courts to decide all disputes about the United States Constitution and laws, disputes between state governments, and between citizens of different states.

8. Govern the capital city of the United States and territory not yet made into states.

9. Make rules for naturalization of new citizens. Issue patents to inventors.

10. Do anything else, not definitely stated, which is necessary to carry out any powers which are mentioned.

---

controlled that it cannot be anything but reasonable and just.[1]

The original Constitution did contain a few statements guaranteeing some rights to the people. Even so, you remember, Thomas Jefferson and other Americans feared that the new government might interfere with the rights of the people. They thought the Constitution should be changed (*amended* is the legal word) to

[1] Paraphrased from *Letters from a Pennsylvania Farmer* by John Dickinson.

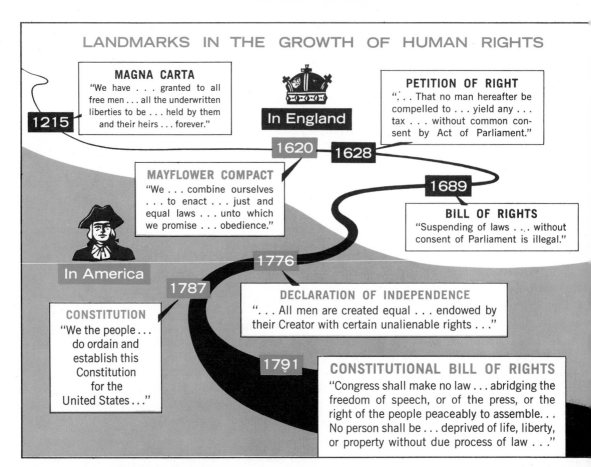

LANDMARKS IN THE GROWTH OF HUMAN RIGHTS

In England

1215

MAGNA CARTA
"We have . . . granted to all free men . . . all the underwritten liberties to be . . . held by them and their heirs . . . forever."

1620

1628

PETITION OF RIGHT
"'. . . That no man hereafter be compelled to . . . yield any . . . tax . . . without common consent by Act of Parliament."

MAYFLOWER COMPACT
"We . . . combine ourselves . . . to enact . . . just and equal laws . . . unto which we promise . . . obedience."

1689

BILL OF RIGHTS
"Suspending of laws . . . without consent of Parliament is illegal."

In America

1776

1787

DECLARATION OF INDEPENDENCE
". . . All men are created equal . . . endowed by their Creator with certain unalienable rights . . ."

CONSTITUTION
"We the people . . . do ordain and establish this Constitution for the United States . . ."

1791

CONSTITUTIONAL BILL OF RIGHTS
"Congress shall make no law . . . abridging the freedom of speech, or of the press, or the right of the people peaceably to assemble. . . No person shall be . . . deprived of life, liberty, or property without due process of law . . ."

THE DOCUMENTS from which brief quotations appear above marked significant steps by which the human rights of all people came to be recognized. (1) Which of the documents were English? (2) Which were American?

This listing is helpful but students should read the Bill of Rights itself.

prevent the government from ever interfering with the rights they held dear.

The Bill of Rights guards our liberties. In 1791, ten amendments were added to the Constitution. These amendments are called the *Bill of Rights* because they state the rights of the American people under their government. The words are somewhat difficult for anyone but a lawyer to understand fully, but they mean a great deal. Because there is a Bill of Rights in our Constitution, you are not in danger of losing your freedom as are the boys and girls and men and women who live under a dictator.

Here are a few of the rights people in America enjoy: (1) An American may hold any religious beliefs he pleases, and

may worship as he sees fit. (2) Americans may meet together in peaceful groups if they wish, and they may freely ask the government to change laws which they believe are wrong. (3) An American may speak or write his opinions freely, even though he criticizes the government. (4) An American charged with a serious crime may claim the right to be tried by a jury in a court of law. (5) Private houses may not be entered and searched by officers of the law except for good reason.

Turn to pages A20–A23 to read the entire Bill of Rights. We Americans must never forget how many of our personal liberties we owe to the Bill of Rights and the rights which are guaranteed in other parts of the Constitution.

Make sure that students can define the italicized words. Italics are used to identify important terms.

THE NEW GOVERNMENT IS SUCCESSFULLY LAUNCHED   **231**

The Constitution can be amended.
One section of the Constitution (Article V) explains how it can be changed or amended. There is more than one method. But the most common way has been for an amendment to be proposed by Congress and approved by the legislatures in three fourths of the states. So wisely planned was our Constitution that only 24 amendments have been added since it was adopted almost two centuries ago!

The new government has three branches. So far we have been speaking of the government in general terms. "The government," we have said, "can do this. It cannot do that." Actually, the United States government is organized into three separate parts, or branches (chart, page 232). Each branch has its own special duties. One branch makes the laws. This is the *legislative* branch, or Congress, and consists of the House of Representatives and the Senate. The second branch puts the laws into effect and sees that they are obeyed. This is the *executive* branch and is headed by the President. The third branch decides cases growing out of the breaking of laws, and also decides whether the laws themselves violate the Constitution. This is the *judicial* branch. It consists of the Supreme Court and the less important federal courts. To divide the government in this way into separate branches, each with its own powers, is called *separation of powers.*

Why are powers separated? Why did the members of the Constitutional Convention divide the government so carefully into three separate branches? The reason is that they wanted to prevent tyranny, that is, cruel or unjust use of power. They believed that if wide powers are given to a single man or a few men, they are likely to be misused. For example, a policeman might easily become a tyrant if he could make the rules and then arrest and punish anybody whom he accused of breaking the rules. But if one man

---

Our Government Grows by Interpretation and Custom

Our national government has grown much larger and more powerful than the makers of the Constitution ever dreamed it would be. Only 24 amendments have been added to the Constitution, but the government has grown in other ways too:

(1) In settling cases, the Supreme Court sometimes must decide just what the words in the Constitution mean. For instance, the Constitution states that Congress may make any laws "which shall be necessary and proper" for carrying out its specific powers (page A9). The Supreme Court has interpreted this to mean that Congress may use added powers if they are necessary to carry out powers stated in the Constitution. By giving this phrase a broad meaning, the Court has enabled the national government to grow more powerful.

(2) Certain customs or ways of doing things have grown up over the years. Although these customs are not provided for in the Constitution, they are just as closely followed as if they were. Our two-party political system is an example of such a custom. Another one is the President's Cabinet. The Constitution provides for the appointment of heads of departments under the President. But it says nothing about their acting together as a group to advise the President, nor does it use the word "Cabinet." Yet, even though the Constitution is silent on political parties and the Cabinet, each has become an important part of our government.

The flexibility of the Constitution permits adaptation and change without formal amendment.

OUR GOVERNMENT HAS THREE BRANCHES

Senate

House of Representatives

100 members

435 members

The President

Supreme Court

EXECUTIVE **LEGISLATIVE** **JUDICIAL**

Circuit Courts of Appeal

The Cabinet

Other Agencies

Agriculture

District Courts

Commerce

State

Interior

Treasury

Housing & Urban
Development

Defense

Labor

**The
Government**

Post Office

Health, Education & Welfare

Attorney General (Justice)

The Constitution

"We the People . . ."

makes the rules, if a second man arrests the people who he believes have broken the rules, and if still a third man decides whether the arrested people really have broken the rules, there is less chance for mistakes or tyranny.

Each branch has power to check the others. Even though they had divided the government into three branches, the members of the Constitutional Convention were not sure they had gone far enough. One branch of the government still might do the wrong thing. To prevent this, the Constitution provides that one branch may check another. For example, if Congress passes an unwise law, the President may disapprove or *veto* it. This prevents Congress from becoming too strong. Or if Congress dislikes a man chosen by the

President to help him enforce the laws, the Senate may refuse to approve his appointment. The President will then have to select someone else. Also, the Supreme Court may check Congress and the President by deciding the meaning of a law in case of a dispute. It can even declare a law *unconstitutional* (contrary to the Constitution) so that it is no longer a law. There are other ways in which one branch of the government may check the others. This way of limiting power is called a *system of checks and balances*. The Constitutional Convention believed that this system would make it difficult for any one branch to become too powerful.

Section 1 has given only a general idea of what our government under the Constitution is like. What is most important to realize is that our Constitution is a *living* document, capable of being changed to meet new conditions. In the 175 years since it was put into operation our country has grown tremendously in size, population, and power. To keep pace with these changes our government has expanded enormously. In fact, if the members of the Constitutional Convention could visit the many government buildings in our capital city today, they would be completely bewildered to see the many activities of our government. Yet the Constitution was so skillfully drawn up that the plan of government it provides serves us as well in this age of jet airplanes and space satellites as it did the people of George Washington's day.

CHECK UP

1. (a) What important powers does the national government have under the Constitution which it did not have under the Articles of Confederation? (b) How did the Constitution divide government powers between the states and the national government?

2. (a) What part of the Constitution protects the rights of the people? (b) What are some of these rights?

3. (a) How can the Constitution be changed? (b) How many amendments have been added to it?

4. (a) What are the three branches of the national government? (b) What are the duties of each branch?

5. (a) How may the President check the actions of Congress? (b) How may Congress check the President? (c) How may the Supreme Court check the President or Congress?

Latter-day Presidents also have to cope with some of these problems. But they can profit from the experience of predecessors.

How Did the New Government Settle Certain Important Problems?

The day set for the new government to take over was March 4, 1789. On that day, however, only a few of the newly elected members of Congress had arrived in New York, the temporary capital. At that time travel (by horse, stagecoach, or ship) was slow. Congress met at last in the early part of April.

As you know, George Washington, the most famous and best-loved man in the United States, had been elected President. John Adams of Massachusetts, a prominent leader in the Revolution, became Vice-President. Washington was notified by Congress of his election and journeyed to New York City from his home at Mount Vernon in Virginia. It was not until April 30 that he was inaugurated

(sworn in) as President of the United States in the ceremony described at the beginning of this chapter.

The new government is set in motion. Although the Constitution outlined the general plan and the powers of each branch, all the details of government had to be worked out by the new Congress and the President. For instance, how was the government to raise money for its expenses? The Constitution called for a Supreme Court and other courts. How many should there be? How many judges should be chosen for the Supreme Court? Who would be the best men for these important positions? The President could not handle all the executive affairs of the government alone. What departments

---

The President's Cabinet

The Cabinet today includes other department heads besides the four original posts. The following members have been added through the years: Postmaster General and Secretaries of Navy, Interior, Agriculture, Commerce, and Labor. In 1947, the War and Navy Departments were combined into one department, headed by the Secretary of Defense. (The Secretaries of the Army, the Navy, and the Air Force now serve under the Secretary of Defense and are not members of the Cabinet.) In 1953, the Department of Health, Education, and Welfare was created, and its Secretary became a Cabinet member. In 1965, the Department of Housing and Urban Development was also established.

When the President calls a meeting of his Cabinet, other government officers may attend. The Ambassador to the United Nations and the Vice-President are often present.

---

should be created to help him? These were only a few of the problems facing the new government.

A great deal was accomplished in the first few years. In 1789, Congress passed a law establishing the Supreme Court and other lower federal courts. The Supreme Court was to have a Chief Justice and five Associate Justices,[1] to be chosen by the President and approved by the Senate. John Jay, a well-known statesman and lawyer from New York, was made Chief Justice. Congress also created several departments to help manage government affairs.

Washington chooses a Cabinet. One of the departments created by Congress

was the *Department of State.* This department was to have charge of our relations with foreign countries. At the head of this department, as *Secretary of State,* Washington placed the brilliant Thomas Jefferson. A trusted old soldier of the Revolution named Henry Knox was placed at the head of the *War Department.* It was his job as *Secretary of War* to manage the army and handle all military affairs. Alexander Hamilton was appointed to the difficult position of *Secretary of the Treasury.* He was head of the *Treasury Department* and was responsible for raising money and handling the finances of the government. In addition, Washington appointed Edmund Randolph as *Attorney General.* His job was to advise the government on legal matters. Washington not only depended on these four men to run their departments but also turned to them for advice and aid in solving the problems of his government. In time they became known as the President's *Cabinet.* Through the years new departments have been created, so today the Cabinet is much larger.

The new government faces difficult financial problems. The first serious problem the new government faced had to do with money matters. The United States owed a great deal of money. During the Revolutionary War the Continental Congress, having little money, had been forced to borrow to meet its expenses. The government of the Confederation, as we have learned, did not have much money either. By 1789, the sums that had been borrowed had not been repaid.

A government, like a person, cannot succeed if it fails to pay its bills. It loses the faith and respect of its citizens and of other nations. If the new government was to be a success, then, it would have to find ways to pay the money it owed.

---

[1] The number of judges on the Supreme Court has changed several times. At present there are nine, including the Chief Justice.

Hamilton was well suited for the job of putting government finances in order. The man who would have charge of raising money and paying the government debts was Alexander Hamilton, Secretary of the Treasury. This young man was born in the West Indies, but he moved to New York City when he was fifteen years old. He attended college there, but left to become an officer in the American armies during the Revolution. He was so capable that George Washington appointed him a member of his military staff. After the war he became a lawyer. He was a member of the Constitutional Convention and believed firmly in a strong central government. As a matter of fact, by writing most of the essays in *The Federalist,* he helped bring about the adoption of the Constitution. Hamilton was only 32 years old when he became Secretary of the Treasury, but he was well fitted for the task. He was hard-working, intelligent, and shrewd about money matters.

Hamilton tackles the problem of the nation's debts. Hamilton found that he had to deal with not one but many debts. The United States had borrowed money both in Europe and from its own citizens. The separate states had borrowed, too. When a government borrows, it gives the lender a promise to repay the loan at a certain time. This promise is called a *bond.* To persuade people to lend the money, the government offers to pay something extra — three or four cents each year for the loan of each dollar. This extra payment is called *interest.*

In the uncertain years after the Revolution many people had serious doubts that the United States would pay its debts. For this reason the bonds which had been issued had fallen sharply in value. Hamilton wanted to combine the national and state debts into one large debt and to

This policy would also further unite the country.

issue new bonds for the full value of all the money that was owed. These bonds could then be paid off in an orderly manner and the honor of the United States upheld. Congress voted to accept this excellent plan.

Hamilton makes a bargain. There were some congressmen, however, who did not want to include the debts of the different states in this plan. "What has the United States to do with paying what the *separate states* have borrowed?" they asked. Hamilton replied that the reason the states had borrowed was to help win independence for the country as a whole. Therefore, he felt, the national government should pay these debts. But some states, like Virginia, had already paid off their debts. These states, mostly in the South, objected to this part of Hamilton's plan.

It happened that at this same time Congress was debating where to establish the nation's permanent capital. The southern states were very anxious to have the capital in the South, so Hamilton made a bargain. He suggested that if the southern congressmen would vote for taking over the state debts, he would use his influence

EARS OF CORN (left) or tobacco leaves (right) were carved on the columns of the new capitol building in Washington, D.C. The architect chose native American plants for his design.

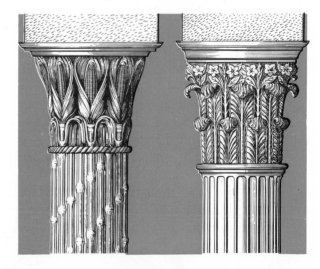

to get the capital located in the South. His offer was accepted. Congress voted to take over the state debts, and it was agreed to locate the new capital on the banks of the Potomac River between Maryland and Virginia. This is how Washington, in the District of Columbia, became the capital of the United States. For ten years, however, until the new city could be built, Philadelphia was our country's capital.

Hamilton proposes the United States Bank. Another part of Hamilton's program was to set up a *Bank of the United States.* The government would help manage the bank and keep its money there. The bank would lend money to the government and issue paper money. Hamilton believed that Congress could establish the bank under its power to borrow money and regulate currency (page A8). The bank would make the government stronger, so Congress agreed and the bank was established.

Hamilton suggests a new tax. Where was the government to get the money it needed to pay its bills? Soon after Congress was established, it had passed a law placing a tax on goods brought or *imported* into the United States from other countries. This kind of tax is called a *tariff.* For example, nails brought into the country were taxed one cent a pound; molasses from the West Indies, 2½ cents a gallon. There were also taxes on imported tea, coffee, sugar, paper, shoes, and so on.

Because the tariff failed to raise enough money, Hamilton recommended another tax called an *excise.* This is a tax on goods manufactured and sold *within* the country. At Hamilton's suggestion, Congress placed an excise on all whiskey made and sold in the United States.

A rebellion against the whiskey tax fails. The farmers who lived far back from the coast strongly objected to Hamilton's plan for a tax on whiskey, because it hit them directly. These farmers raised

corn. There were no railroads or highways in those days, and corn was too bulky to ship to distant markets. Therefore, the farmers made their corn into whiskey. The whiskey occupied less space and was much easier to take to market. Of course, the farmers did not like to be taxed for making their whiskey. In western Pennsylvania in 1794, they angrily refused to pay the tax, and carried on what is called the *Whiskey Rebellion.* But President Washington knew that no government is worthy of the name unless its laws are obeyed. The whiskey tax was a law, and the Pennsylvania farmers were disobeying it. President Washington raised an army of 15,000 soldiers supplied by the states and forced the Pennsylvanians to pay the tax.

The government is well established. In 1795, Hamilton left his place as Secretary of the Treasury and became a lawyer again. He could be proud of what he had accomplished. His plans had solved the money problems of the new government. Americans had begun to trust the government, and this, in turn, helped to make it successful. The new government had earned respect by arranging to pay back the money it owed. And by putting down the Whiskey Rebellion, it had shown that its laws must be obeyed. In brief, the new government was firmly established.

CHECK UP

1. (a) What is the President's Cabinet? (b) What are the duties of Cabinet members?

2. (a) What serious financial problems did the new government face? (b) How did Hamilton plan to put the government's financial affairs in order? (c) Why was the Bank of the United States established?

3. (a) What two kinds of taxes did the government use to raise money? (b) What was the Whiskey Rebellion?

How a tariff works is explained on page 275.

THE BANK of the United States at Philadelphia (left) was founded by Hamilton as Secretary of the Treasury. He enabled the government to issue sound money, such as this $10 goldpiece.

Alexander Hamilton

INCOME from tariff duties was needed, so Hamilton ordered the first Coast Guard cutter (far left) to enforce laws against smuggling. To encourage trade, he built the first federal lighthouse at Cape Henry, Virginia (left).

★ ★

The real issue was how strong the central government should be.

3 How Did Political Parties Get Started?

Hamilton's plans lead to political parties. As we have seen, Hamilton's plans were accepted by Congress and put into effect. Not all the people of the United States, however, believed the plans were wise. An American who disliked the plans might have expressed himself in words like these: "What good to me is Hamilton's new system of repaying the debts of the United States? Of course, it is fine for those who own the bonds. But only wealthy people own them. My neighbors and I own none. I have nothing to do, either, with Hamilton's bank. As for his

taxes, the tax on whiskey hurts a poor farmer like me. Worst of all, Hamilton's plans may make the government too strong. What will prevent it from being tyrannical just as the British government was before the Revolution?"

Many people held much the same views. Some were poor farmers and workingmen in cities. Others, who were well-to-do, were not troubled by the paying of debts and taxes but feared that the United States government might become too powerful. They wished the states to be stronger and the power of the United

States to be limited. One of those who shared these feelings was Thomas Jefferson. In fact, Jefferson became the leader of the men who opposed Hamilton's program.

When people who hold the same idea unite to influence the government, we say that they have formed a *political party*. Thomas Jefferson's followers came to be known as the *Republican Party*.[1] Those who supported Hamilton's ideas formed what was called the *Federalist Party*. When a President or members of Congress were to be chosen, each party tried to get its own men elected.

Political parties develop during Washington's administration. The Federalist and Republican Parties began during Washington's first term as President. George Washington himself did not join either party, although his sympathies lay with the Federalists. He was so respected by the American people, however, that both Jefferson and Hamilton asked him to serve a second term. Washington was elected a second time in 1792. During his second term the Federalist Party became powerful.

When the election of 1796 drew near, Washington felt that two terms as President were enough for one man and announced that he did not wish a third term. He started the custom, which continued until the day of President Franklin D. Roosevelt, that no man should serve more than two terms as President. This custom has now been made law by the Twenty-Second Amendment to the Constitution (page A31). When Washington left the presidency, he went back to Virginia to live on his beloved plantation,

[1] The full name of Jefferson's party was *Democratic-Republican,* but this soon became shortened to *Republican.* It should not be confused with the Republican Party of today. It really was the ancestor of the present Democratic Party.

Mount Vernon. There he died some two years later at the age of 67.

John Adams, Federalist, is elected President. As Washington's second term as President drew to a close, bitter rivalry arose between the Federalists and the Republicans over the presidential election. By a narrow margin the Federalists elected John Adams of Massachusetts as the second President of the United States. Adams had had much experience in the service of his country and had served as Vice-President during both of Washington's terms as President. He was a man of ability and absolute honesty, never swerving from what he believed to be right.

Honest and capable as he was, John Adams was not a popular President. People found him cold, even rude at times, and in general hard to get along with. What is more, during the excitement of a quarrel with France, the Federalists in Congress adopted some very harsh laws. One of these, called the *Sedition Act,* limited the right of the people to criticize the President and Congress. The Republicans attacked this law because it interfered with the right of free speech. As a result, both John Adams and the Federalist Party became unpopular, and Adams was defeated in the election of 1800. Thomas Jefferson, leader of the Republicans, was elected President in his place.

Thomas Jefferson, Republican, becomes President. Born in Virginia on April 13, 1743, Thomas Jefferson was a graduate of the College of William and Mary. He had one of the most active minds in the United States, and he read widely throughout his life. Almost every subject — architecture, art, science, religion, government — interested him. He was an inventor, an architect, a musician, and a writer. Six feet two and one-half inches tall, with sandy hair, he was a commanding figure in any group.

Refer to the chart on page 240. Similar charts for later periods in history are found on pages 338, 415, 568, and 686.

JOHN MARSHALL

America's greatest judge first served his country as a young minuteman in Virginia.

A HARD FIGHTER, Marshall won officer's rank in the Continental Army and led his men at the Battle of Germantown. After serving on Washington's staff at Valley Forge, he returned to Virginia where he became a lawyer.

VIRGINIA FEDERALISTS found a vigorous spokesman in Marshall at the state convention called to vote on the new federal Constitution. Marshall's arguments for a stronger union helped persuade the delegates to ratify. Now a prominent Federalist, Marshall was sent abroad to settle America's troubles with France.

AMERICA'S RIGHTS would be defended, not bought, was Marshall's proud answer to the French leader who demanded a bribe before negotiating. Later, as Secretary of State, Marshall made peace with France on honorable terms, avoiding full-scale war. This service, together with his reputation as a lawyer, gained Marshall an appointment to the Supreme Court.

AS CHIEF JUSTICE for 34 years, Marshall had to decide difficult questions arising for the first time under the Constitution. His firm rulings strengthened the idea of government by law.

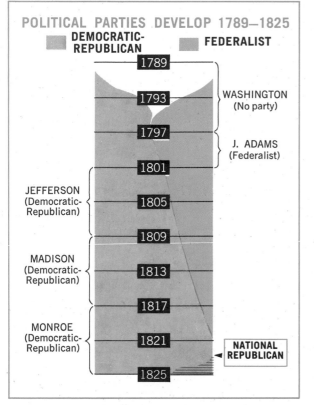

POLITICAL PARTIES DEVELOP 1789–1825

■ DEMOCRATIC-REPUBLICAN   ■ FEDERALIST

1789
1793 } WASHINGTON (No party)
1797
1801 } J. ADAMS (Federalist)

JEFFERSON (Democratic-Republican) { 1801 1805

MADISON (Democratic-Republican) { 1809 1813

MONROE (Democratic-Republican) { 1817 1821 1825

NATIONAL REPUBLICAN

FORMATION of the first political parties is shown by widening bands of blue and gray during Washington's presidency. Narrowing of the blue band shows a decline in Federalist strength until the party was replaced by a new political group during Monroe's second term.

Although Thomas Jefferson was a wealthy man who had enjoyed every advantage, he dressed plainly and disliked ceremony or show. Instead of riding in a fine carriage to his inauguration, he walked! Jefferson believed that the future of the country rested on its development as a nation of small farmers. He placed great trust in the sound judgment of the people as a whole and believed that education was important for every citizen in a democracy. It was he who wrote in the Declaration of Independence that "all men are created equal" and that they are all entitled to "life, liberty, and the pursuit of happiness."

When he became President, Jefferson, like Washington and John Adams before

him, had had much experience. He had been a member of the legislature of Virginia, a member of the Second Continental Congress, and governor of Virginia. He had represented the United States in Europe. Jefferson had also been Secretary of State under Washington and Vice-President under Adams. As President he served two terms, from 1801 to 1809.

The Federalist Party disappears. During Jefferson's administrations the Republican Party grew stronger. The Republicans elected the next two Presidents — James Madison, who served from 1809 to 1817, and James Monroe, who was President from 1817 to 1825. During these years, on the other hand, the Federalist Party became weaker and weaker. Finally, in Monroe's first term, it disappeared, and Monroe was re-elected without opposition. Because there was only one political party, the years of Monroe's presidency are called the *Era of Good Feeling.*

The Era of Good Feeling, however, did not last long. As new problems arose, new political parties and new leaders appeared. Political parties have continued to play an important part in our government.

•

In telling about political parties, we have got a little ahead of our story. As we have seen, the new government had made an excellent start. It had dealt wisely with its problems and had won the respect of its citizens. In Chapter 13 we shall see how the new government also won the respect of foreign nations.

CHECK UP

1. (a) How did political parties develop during Washington's presidency? (b) What were these parties called, and what did each party stand for?

2. (a) Who were the first five Presidents? (b) To what party, if any, did each belong?

This is a good place to review the contributions **240** of the Federalists to the establishment of the new nation.

The Presidents of Our Country

GEORGE WASHINGTON 1789–1797

From Virginia. Commander of the Continental Army during the Revolutionary War and chairman of the Constitutional Convention, Washington was a natural choice for first President. "The Father of His Country" served two terms in New York City, the nation's temporary capital. Climaxing a lifetime of public service, Washington devoted all his strength and wisdom to launching the new government successfully.

JOHN ADAMS 1797–1801

Federalist from Massachusetts. Short and plump, and fearlessly honest, our second President was the first to live in the White House in the new capital at Washington. Adams, who had been Washington's Vice-President, was the only President whose son also became Chief Executive. He and Thomas Jefferson both died on July 4, 1826, the fiftieth anniversary of the Declaration of Independence, which Adams had helped Jefferson to write.

THOMAS JEFFERSON 1801–1809

Democratic-Republican from Virginia. Chief author of the Declaration of Independence, this tall, sandy-haired man was our most versatile Chief Executive — musician, architect, inventor, and educator, as well as statesman. He doubled the size of the country with the Louisiana Purchase in 1803, the greatest peacetime acquisition of land in the history of our nation. One of Jefferson's proudest accomplishments was having founded the University of Virginia.

JAMES MADISON 1809–1817

Democratic-Republican from Virginia. The "Father of the Constitution" — also drafter of the first ten Amendments — was our smallest President. Though frail and soft-spoken, he faced enemy gunfire while in office when the British attacked Washington during the War of 1812. He was the first President whose inaugural costume was completely American-made. Madison's wife, Dolly, became famous as a gracious White House hostess.

JAMES MONROE 1817–1825

Democratic-Republican from Virginia. Soldier, lawyer, member of the Continental Congress, and Secretary of State under Madison. Monroe's presidency was called "the Era of Good Feeling," and he was elected to a second term almost without opposition. He proclaimed that European interference would not be welcome in the Western Hemisphere, a statement which became known as the Monroe Doctrine.

Check Up on Chapter 12

Be sure that students can use and define these terms.

Do You Know the Meaning?

1. preamble	9. tariff
2. finances	10. excise
3. amendment	11. veto
4. legislative	12. political
5. executive	13. capital
6. judicial	14. federal
7. inaugurate	15. unconstitutional
8. administration	16. separation of powers
17. checks and balances	

Can You Identify?

1. Bill of Rights	10. Republican Party
2. Cabinet	11. Federalist Party
3. Supreme Court	12. Sedition Act
4. Congress	13. Alexander Hamilton
5. President	14. Thomas Jefferson
6. John Adams	15. 1789
7. James Monroe	16. Whiskey Rebellion
8. James Madison	17. Henry Knox
9. John Jay	18. Edmund Randolph
19. Era of Good Feeling	

What Do You Think?

1. Why do you suppose the Supreme Court today has nine rather than eight or ten judges?
2. If you had lived in the days of Thomas Jefferson and Alexander Hamilton, to which political party would you have belonged? Why?
3. The Bill of Rights lists the rights of citizens. Explain why citizens also have certain responsibilities that go along with these rights.
4. Why is it that a Constitution drawn up 175 years ago meets so well the needs of our great country today?
5. Although the parties themselves have changed, our country has always had two major political parties since the early 1800's. (a) What are the advantages of a two-party system of government? (b) Why have new political parties developed throughout our country's history?

These questions demand more than recall of information read.

LINKING PAST  **AND PRESENT**

Our money system. The next time you do any figuring with money, give thanks to Thomas Jefferson for our simple decimal system. During and after the Revolution, people had money troubles because there was no uniform money system. Thirteen states as well as Congress issued money. Also, people used Spanish dollars, pistoles, and pieces of eight; French francs; and British sovereigns, pounds, and shillings.

In 1789, the only coins being made in the United States were large copper pennies, called Franklin pennies. When Alexander Hamilton became Secretary of the Treasury, he urged Congress to establish a mint for making coins. Thomas Jefferson recom-

mended that the new money be based on the decimal system, or a system of tens. Ten cents were to make one dime, ten dimes one dollar. The dollar was to be the unit of currency, so that money would be figured in dollars or decimal fractions of dollars. By using the decimal point, cents could be written as hundredths of a dollar, as $4.25 or $.09. Such numbers are easy to add, subtract, multiply, or divide.

Congress accepted the recommendations of Hamilton and Jefferson, and in 1792 the first coins were minted. Later, the government also issued nickels, quarters (of a dollar), and half dollars. Today, most countries use a decimal money system.

Information about Fort McHenry can be found in American Heritage Book of Great Historic Places.

The United States Gains the
Respect of Other Nations

A weak country is unable "to compel" respect; a strong one may not earn it.

What this chapter is about —

Nations do not live by themselves alone any more than people do. The border of one nation is also its neighbor's border. Nations trade with one another. The citizens of one country travel in many other countries. In a hundred ways the affairs of one nation are linked with those of the other countries of the world. Just as people must learn to live with others, so nations must manage wisely their relations with other countries. Each country wishes to be strong enough to be respected by other countries.

We have learned in Chapters 11 and 12 how the United States managed its affairs at home during its first years of independence. In this chapter we shall study how the United States found a place for itself among the nations of the world. We shall also find that, despite its efforts to remain at peace, the United States was drawn into a second war with Great Britain. As you read, look for answers to these questions:

▶ 1. What problems did the United States have with Great Britain and France?

▶ 2. How did our country gain a vast territory beyond the Mississippi?

▶ 3. Why did the United States go to war with Great Britain a second time?

▶ 4. How did President Monroe warn Europe against interfering in the Americas?

People in our story — French general, western militiaman, American naval officer and seaman, British admiral.

1 What Problems Did the United States Have with Great Britain and France?

The United States in 1789 was a weak nation. Although we think of our country as strong and powerful, we need to remember that in 1789 this was not true. At that time the United States covered a large amount of land, but in other ways it was small and weak. The nation contained fewer than four million people. The regular American army consisted of only 672 officers and men. There was no navy. Also, the United States was just beginning a new kind of government, and no one knew how it would work out. In 1789, few countries allowed their people as much voice in the government as the people of the United States had under the Constitution.

In addition, our young republic was hemmed in on three sides by territory belonging to powerful European countries. As the map on page 187 shows, the territory of Great Britain stretched like a fence all along our northern boundary. To the west and south we were hemmed in by Spanish territory. The United States and Great Britain were not good friends. This was natural, because the American Revolution had left bitter feelings on both sides. The United States and Spain were not friendly either. In fact, the best friend the United States had at that time was France. As you remember, France and the United States became allies during the American Revolution, and the French gave valuable help to the Patriots. The friendship of the two nations continued after the Revolutionary War had ended.

The French Revolution leads to war in Europe. Americans would have been pleased if they had been left alone, in a peaceful world, to try out their new gov-

ernment and to build their nation. But this was not to be. Once more, as in the French and Indian wars (page 126), events in Europe changed the course of America's history. Less than three months after George Washington became the nation's first President, the great revolution which we mentioned in Chapter 10 began in France. For hundreds of years the French people had had little liberty. Their kings had ruled them with a strong hand and had given them little voice in their government. The nobles, who possessed many privileges, had oppressed them, too. Now the people of France were determined to make a change. In 1789 they began a revolution which lasted for many years. The revolutionists drew up a constitution for a new government and later executed the French king.

The French Revolution was different from the American Revolution in a very important way. The purpose of the American Revolution had been to win freedom from another country. The French Revolution was a revolt by the people of France against the government of France. This revolution greatly alarmed the ruling classes of other countries in Europe. What was to prevent this uprising from spreading to these countries? If this should happen, their governments might be overthrown as France's had been. Such fears soon led two European countries — Austria and Prussia — to go to war with France. This was the beginning of a series of wars which in time involved most of the countries in Europe. These wars lasted, almost without a pause, until 1815.

The United States remains neutral. What was the United States to do about

The United States Wins Respect Abroad

States Join
Under Articles
of Confederation

Constitution
is Written

Jefferson Leads
Democratic–Republican
Party to Power

Washington
Inaugurated
First President

Declaration of
Independence

Louisiana
Purchase

War of 1812

Monroe
Doctrine
Proclaimed

1770   1780   1790   1800   1810   1820   1830   1840   1850

CHAPTER 13

1789-1823

her treaty of alliance with France? Many Americans, among them Thomas Jefferson, were glad to see the French people get rid of their king and govern themselves. These Americans were grateful for the help France had given in the American Revolution. They felt that the United States owed help to France in return. On the other hand, could the United States afford to be drawn into a war among European nations? Great Britain had joined in the wars against France. If we helped France, the United States might have to fight Great Britain again.

George Washington felt very strongly that Europe's quarrels were not our concern. We were far from Europe, he said, and should be putting our efforts into organizing our government and building a strong and prosperous nation. Matters were made worse by "Citizen" Edmond Genêt, the ambassador sent by the new French republic to the United States. In his efforts to gain aid for France, Genêt set out to arouse the sympathy of the American people for France.

Worried and uncertain what to do about France, President Washington asked the advice of Hamilton, Jefferson, and the rest of his Cabinet. Hamilton and Jefferson clashed over this matter as they did on

so many subjects. But, in spite of our friendship with France, both these men agreed that the United States should stay out of the European war. Even Jefferson realized that the United States was too weak to wage war out of friendship for France. So President Washington signed an official paper declaring that the United States would be "friendly and impartial" to both sides in the war. In other words, the United States would remain *neutral*.

It was all very well for the United States to declare that it would be neutral in the European war. But it is difficult for a nation to be neutral. Countries at war object if they feel that any act of a neutral nation harms them or helps their enemies. When the United States declared that as a neutral nation it had the right to trade with the warring nations, trouble began.

THE UNITED STATES HAS TROUBLE
WITH GREAT BRITAIN

The British seize American ships and seamen. The chief threat to America's neutrality came from Great Britain, owner of the world's most powerful navy. She did not intend to permit the United States to aid the French by shipping them the goods they needed. Britain, therefore, set out to stop such trade. The following

In England press gangs "persuaded" Englishmen to join the Navy. Was a person born in the Thirteen Colonies before July 4, 1776, a British citizen by birth?

246   THE UNITED STATES IS ESTABLISHED

description tells what happened time and again a little distance off the eastern coast of the United States:

"The sails of an American schooner flash in the sun as she skims south before a fair wind. Her hold is filled with a cargo to be traded in the French islands of the West Indies. Suddenly the lookout spies a British frigate upon the horizon. Quickly the British ship overtakes the schooner and forces it to stop. A boat is lowered from the British warship and a scarlet-coated officer is rowed to the schooner. He clambers aboard, followed by some of his men. He demands the right to inspect the cargo and to see the crew. After a glance at the cargo he declares that the schooner is breaking Britain's rules of the sea, and seizes the schooner in the name of Great Britain. He also claims that some members of the crew are Englishmen who are needed as sailors in the

A BRITISH OFFICER impresses an American seaman into the British navy. Such actions angered citizens of the young republic.

British navy. He then leaves some of his men on board to help sail the schooner to the nearest British port, and takes back to his ship the sailors he said were Englishmen. They will be *impressed* into (forced to serve in) the Royal Navy."

The practice of seizing Englishmen for the Royal Navy wherever they were found was common in those days. Sailors were badly needed to man British warships, and the British were not too much concerned if the men they seized were actually Americans. They insisted that anyone who was born an Englishman always remained an Englishman, and took the attitude, "What are you going to do about it?"

The British still hold forts on the American border. The actions of the British made Americans furious. They insisted their ships had the right to sail the seas without interference. As if this were not enough, the United States had another complaint against Great Britain. British soldiers still occupied forts along the northwestern boundary of the United States. The map on page 187 shows where this boundary was. The British kept soldiers in these forts because, for one thing, Americans had not paid certain debts they had owed to Englishmen since before the Revolutionary War. The British also held the forts because they wanted to profit from the fur trade on American soil.

John Jay makes a treaty and prevents a war. In spite of these difficulties with the British, President Washington worked to maintain peace. He did not want the weak young nation to fight a dangerous war. So in 1794 he sent John Jay (who was Chief Justice of the Supreme Court) to England to seek an agreement with the British government. Washington hoped such an agreement would put an end to the trouble between the two countries.

AMERICANS began to build a navy when war with France seemed likely. In this picture drawn in 1800 we see how ships of that time were built. Workmen carried lumber up the scaffolding as they constructed the hull of the frigate "Philadelphia."

Jay did obtain an agreement, which is called Jay's Treaty. Among other things, the treaty stated that the British should turn over the forts along the Great Lakes to the United States. But the British did not promise to stop searching American ships and impressing American sailors.

Many Americans disliked Jay's Treaty because the British did not promise to stop interfering with American ships. President Washington, however, was certain that the treaty would prevent war between Great Britain and the United States. The treaty was approved in 1795, and Washington's judgment proved correct. The danger of war between the two countries was removed for the time being.

TROUBLE BREWS WITH FRANCE

Soon after Jay's Treaty with Great Britain had been signed, serious trouble began between the United States and France. Jay's Treaty itself was partly to blame. The treaty, many Frenchmen believed, showed that the United States was becoming more friendly with Great Britain and less friendly with France. The French decided that American ships should not be allowed to carry goods which might reach the enemies of France. Following the example set by Great Britain, French ships began to capture American ships. In a short time more than 300 American vessels had been seized by the French.

The XYZ Affair angers Americans. War with Great Britain had been avoided by sending John Jay to arrange a treaty. So John Adams, who was now President, took a similar step to avoid war with France. He sent three men to France to try to make a treaty. At the beginning of their talks, the French representatives demanded the payment of a large amount of money before they would even talk about a treaty. The Americans proudly refused to pay what they felt was a bribe. They wrote to the President to tell him what had happened. In their letters, however, they did not use the real names of the three French representatives. They called them simply X, Y, and Z. Hence this event is known as the XYZ *Affair*.

The United States fights an undeclared war with France. The people of the United States were upset when they heard about the XYZ Affair. "Millions for defense," they cried, "but not one cent for

Jay's Treaty also gave American ships certain **247** trading privileges in the British East and West Indies.

tribute!" So angry did Americans become that they came to blows with France. The few naval vessels which the government built attacked French vessels, and armed American ships of all kinds captured French ships whenever they could. Our government also began to recruit an army. Despite the fighting, however, the United States and France were not officially at war, since Congress never did declare that a state of war existed.

France and the United States reach an agreement. While the feeling against France was at its height, President Adams learned that the French government wanted to end the conflict. At once he sent representatives to France, and in 1800 an agreement was signed. This agreement ended the treaty of alliance we had had with France since 1778 (page 177). It also cleared the way for the ships of both nations to sail the ocean in peace. Thus ended the unofficial war with France.

Our disputes with Great Britain and France showed that it was not easy for the United States to make a place for itself among the nations of the world. To end the dispute with Great Britain, the United States had been obliged to make a bargain. But in the dispute with France, Americans showed that, if necessary, they would fight for their rights.

C H E C K
U P

1. Why did the United States want to remain neutral in the wars between France and England?

2. (a) What rights did this country want as a neutral nation? (b) How did England interfere with these rights?

3. (a) In what ways did Jay's Treaty provide a satisfactory settlement of the dispute with Britain? (b) How was it unsatisfactory?

4. (a) What events led to our undeclared war with France? (b) How was the dispute ended?

The map on page 251 shows the importance of the port of New Orleans to Americans. See also source extract, page 250.

2 How Did Our Country Gain a Vast Territory Beyond the Mississippi?

One piece of good fortune stands out in the early relations of our country with European nations. The story has to do with the pioneers who had moved into the territory west of the Appalachian Mountains. As we know, western settlers for the most part earned their living by trapping and farming. But it is not enough to trap animals or to grow a crop of corn. In order to earn a good living, a man must *sell* his furs or his produce in a market where people need them and will pay well for them. The settlers of the West had no roads over which to haul

their produce to market. The easiest way to move their goods was to load them onto flatboats or rafts. These could be floated down streams to the Ohio River, and from the Ohio down the Mississippi to New Orleans. There the goods could be shipped to Europe or to an east coast port.

The Mississippi River and New Orleans are important to the West. Because it was a water highway, the Mississippi River was important to the United States. But the United States did not control the Mississippi. The river was the boundary between the United States and the vast

THOMAS JEFFERSON

As a student, he began clearing a site for his future home in the land he would help to free.

The many talents of Jefferson are made clear in a well-illustrated book, *Thomas Jefferson and His World*.

WORDS became splendid weapons in the American Revolution when Jefferson wrote them down in the Declaration of Independence. Stating his own deep belief in human liberty, the young Virginian set up ideals for all of the American Patriots.

SPACE in which a free nation could grow to greatness was gained by Jefferson as President when he bought the vast Louisiana Territory from France. Interested in everything American — plants, minerals, wildlife — Jefferson here questions visiting Indian chiefs about the lands west of the Mississippi.

A BETTER WAY to do anything always fascinated Jefferson, who himself designed an improved plow to break and turn the soil. On his estate at Monticello, Jefferson not only tried out his own inventions but experimented with new plants and ideas from Europe. Like Franklin, he believed that knowledge is power.

A GREAT FUTURE for America could be assured, Jefferson believed, if Americans were educated to make the most of their freedom. He founded the University of Virginia and, in his 80's, saw the buildings he had designed nearing completion.

Spanish territory to the west. (See map, page 187.) Nor did we own New Orleans, which also belonged to Spain. Americans were allowed to reload their goods on ocean-going boats in New Orleans, but they were never sure when such permission might be withdrawn. If it were, the western settlers would have no way of getting their goods to market.

New Orleans becomes French. In 1802, the Westerners saw their worst fears realized. Permission to use the port of New Orleans was withdrawn. Even before this happened, President Jefferson had learned, to his surprise, that New Orleans no longer belonged to Spain! By a secret treaty, France had obtained from Spain not only New Orleans but also the vast territory of Louisiana, which lay west of the Mississippi River.

France at this time was governed by Napoleon, a great soldier who seemed likely to conquer all of Europe. Napoleon also had plans to establish a French empire in America. Suppose he were to undertake wars of conquest in North America as he had in Europe? Jefferson clearly saw the danger. He wrote to the American representative in France:

✶The [transfer] of Louisiana . . . by Spain to France, works most sorely on the United States. . . . There is on the globe one single spot, the possessor of which is our natural and habitual enemy. It is New Orleans, through which the produce of three-eighths of our territory must pass to market, and [this western territory] . . . will ere long yield more than half of our whole produce, and contain more than half of our inhabitants. . . . The day that France takes possession of New Orleans . . . we must marry ourselves to the British fleet and nation.

In this statement Jefferson pointed out that we might have to join forces with the British and fight Napoleon to keep the French out of New Orleans. But Jefferson did not wish to "marry" the British. Nor did he want to fight if he could help it. If only — thought Jefferson — if only I could *buy* New Orleans, then I could satisfy the Westerners and also avoid the danger of war with France. Accordingly, Jefferson suggested to France that the United States wanted to buy New Orleans.

Jefferson acquires all of Louisiana. Jefferson's suggestion was made just when Napoleon was about to plunge into another war. Napoleon wanted to be free to fight in Europe without worrying about territory in America, and he needed money to meet the costs of war. Also, his plans for a colonial empire were not going well. So he offered to sell not only the city of New Orleans but the whole of Louisiana! Quickly the price was set at $15,000,000,

French sea-power had helped win the Revolutionary War; lack of it caused Napoleon to abandon plans for colonial empire.

FLATBOATS carried animals, produce, and passengers down the western rivers. River travel, the only cheap means of transportation, was vitally important to Westerners.

MAP STUDY

(1) What countries owned territory north and south of the United States? (2) What countries claimed the area to the northwest of the Louisiana Purchase?

The United States Purchases Louisiana

and in 1803 the United States took possession of Louisiana.

The map on this page gives a clear idea of the importance of the *Louisiana Purchase*. Not only had it brought full control of the Mississippi River, but it also had doubled the size of the United States. Jefferson called the purchase of Louisiana "a great achievement," and so it was. In the Louisiana Territory there would be space for thousands, indeed for millions, of Americans. By this single peaceful act the way was paved for the United States to grow into a larger and more powerful nation.

CHECK UP

1. Why were the Mississippi River and New Orleans important to the United States?

2. How was Jefferson able to buy all of Louisiana?

Two great wars in this century (1914-1918; 1939-1945) have been called World Wars I and II. The Seven Years War (1756-1763) and the Wars of the French Revolution and Napoleon (1792-1815), in both of which this country was involved, were also "world wars."

3 Why Did the United States Go to War with Great Britain a Second Time?

THE UNITED STATES COMES TO BLOWS WITH GREAT BRITAIN

In 1803 a new war broke out between Napoleon and Great Britain. Once more each side tried to injure the other by preventing American ships from carrying supplies to the enemy. Once more the British navy stopped American vessels and impressed men from their crews. France also captured American vessels when she could, although she did not impress sea-men. Once again Americans wondered, "What should the United States do?"

Jefferson tries to avoid war. This time it was Thomas Jefferson who, as President, was expected to answer the question. Jefferson hated war because of the fearful loss of human life and the destruction of property. But was it possible to force Britain and France to respect the rights of American ships at sea without fighting? Jefferson believed there was a way. "The

251

The embargo was similar in intent to colonial boycotts; its outcome was different. American (not British) merchants were hurt most by the embargo. Make sure pupils understand why.

252 THE UNITED STATES IS ESTABLISHED

European nations," he thought, "badly need the goods sold by this country. They also need to make profits by selling some of their goods in the United States. If we threaten to stop trading with Great Britain and France, these countries will agree to let our ships and men alone."

To carry out his idea, Jefferson planned (1) to refuse to buy European goods and (2) to place an *embargo* on American shipping. The Embargo Act, passed in 1807, forbade American vessels to leave for any foreign ports.

Jefferson's plan was tried in several forms, both by him and by James Madison, who became President in 1809. Though intended to hurt France and Great Britain, Jefferson's plan in fact nearly ruined American merchants and shipowners. When the embargo made it unlawful for their vessels to sail the seas, some of the merchants defied the law and sailed anyway. So, in spite of the Embargo Act, France and Great Britain continued to seize American ships.

The United States moves closer to war with Great Britain. So far as interference with our shipping was concerned, we had almost as much reason to go to war with France as with Great Britain. But an important reason why feeling ran stronger against Great Britain was to be found in our own country. The people of the West and South believed that the British encouraged the Indians to make war against the settlers on the frontier. In 1811 an Indian chief named Tecumseh led the Indians north of the Ohio in a bloody war against the frontiersmen. There were rumors that the British in Canada had furnished Tecumseh and his braves with supplies and guns. As a result, bitter feeling against the British spread among the frontiersmen.

Many settlers in the West and South also wanted the United States to add to her territory. They looked northward to Canada, which was British, and southward to Florida, which belonged to Spain. At this time Spain and Great Britain were allies If the United States should fight Britain, both Canada and Florida might be conquered.

In Congress there was a group of young men who were keenly interested in developing the West. Among these young men were Henry Clay of Kentucky and John C. Calhoun of South Carolina. So constantly did they talk of war that they earned the nickname of "War Hawks." When these War Hawks told why they wanted war, they spoke not only of British violations of American rights on the seas but also of capturing Canada and Florida. One member of Congress exclaimed that when he heard the War Hawks speak he heard but "one word — like the [cry of the] whip-poor-will . . . one eternal monotonous tone — Canada, Canada, Canada!"

The United States, though unprepared, goes to war with Great Britain. Pushed on by the War Hawks, Congress declared war on England in June, 1812, while Madison was President. The United States was not prepared for war. Its army and navy were pitifully small. There were fewer than 7000 men in the regular United States Army, and few good leaders. To the regular army might be added the soldiers supplied by the states, called *militia*. There were not enough militia, however, and they were usually poorly trained. The United States had only sixteen seagoing vessels in its navy when the war began. Although Congress declared war, it did not provide funds for enlarging this navy. Congress did not vote enough money, either, for carrying on the war.

The war is unpopular in New England. Not only was the United States poorly prepared, but many Americans opposed

The War of 1812

THE WAR AT SEA

1. British fleet blockades the American coast.

2. American frigates and privateers slip out to raid British shipping.

3. American ships win control of lakes on Canadian border.

ENGLAND

• Ghent

Atlantic Ocean

CANADA

EUROPE

British Trade Routes

UNITED STATES

L. Erie

L. Ontario

L. Champlain

British Blockade

THE WAR ON LAND

1. Americans invade Canada but fail to conquer it.

2. British invade America but are beaten back.

CANADA

St. Lawrence R.

L. Champlain

York (Toronto)

L. Ontario

UNITED STATES

L. Erie

Baltimore

Washington

Chesapeake Bay

Mississippi R.

British Blockade

New Orleans

SPANISH FLORIDA

MAP STUDY

Overwhelming seapower enabled the British to put pressure on America by a blockade and to attack at widely separated points. (1) On what lake did American naval power help turn back a British land attack? (2) Why did the war end in a draw?

R. M. Chapin, Jr.

It is important for pupils to understand how our actions may seem to other peoples.
See Building the Canadian Nation.

254 THE UNITED STATES IS ESTABLISHED

the war. The war was especially unpopular in New England. The people of this section wanted to send their merchant ships to sea in spite of the danger of capture by the British. Even if only a few of the ships escaped capture, the goods they carried sold at such high prices that the voyages made large profits. The New Englanders had disliked Jefferson's embargo plan because it had interfered with their trade. When war came, the British fleet blockaded the Atlantic coast and interfered even more with New England shipping.

As the war continued, New Englanders became more and more dissatisfied. Finally, late in 1814, a meeting was held at Hartford, Connecticut. This meeting is called the Hartford Convention. The Convention protested the government's war policy and declared that if Congress violated the Constitution, the states could take steps to protect their rights. The war closed, however, before the Hartford Convention put its words into action.

THE WAR OF 1812 HAS NO WINNER

As you have just read, the United States entered the war without a big army or navy, without enough money, and without the wholehearted support of all the people. How did the United States fare under so many handicaps?

Neither side makes much headway in the war on land. Because one of the purposes of the war had been to seize Canada, an attack was launched at once against that country. But the fighting along the Canadian border was unsuccessful. Although the Americans attempted several invasions between 1812 and 1814, they could not capture Canada. On the other hand, the British could not successfully invade the northern United States.

In 1814, the British did raid our Atlantic coast and burn some American towns. In August of that year, they even sailed up Chesapeake Bay, seized the city of Washington, and burned the Capitol. The story goes that British troops ate a dinner which had been cooked for the President of the United States and then burned the White House.[1]

Americans felt better, however, when a British attack on Baltimore failed. During the battle, the sight of the American flag still flying over Fort McHenry after a heavy bombardment led Francis Scott Key to write the "Star-Spangled Banner." (See the picture of Fort McHenry on page 243.) Americans were also proud when in January, 1815, General Andrew Jackson defeated a British army attempting to capture

[1] In 1813, American soldiers invading Upper Canada had set on fire the government buildings in the capital city, now called Toronto. The British burned our Capitol and the White House in revenge.

AMERICAN SAILORS row Commodore Oliver Hazard Perry to a new ship after escaping from a sinking vessel during the Battle of Lake Erie in 1813.

AMERICAN TROOPS advanced steadily through heavy gunfire to defeat the British at the Battle of Chippewa on Canadian soil. The Americans had been drilled hard all winter and surprised the British by their coolness under fire.

New Orleans. In this battle more than 2000 British soldiers were killed and wounded, while only a very few Americans were lost. Actually, a peace treaty had been signed in Europe before the battle of New Orleans took place. But the slow sailing vessels of that time had not brought the news of peace soon enough to prevent the battle.

Americans win some victories at sea. United States warships gave a good account of themselves. Although our army officers lacked training, American seamen and naval officers knew their jobs. For years they had sailed the seas and defended their rights. American fleets, hastily built on inland waters, defeated the British on Lake Erie and Lake Champlain. Commodore Oliver Hazard Perry reported a victory against the British on Lake Erie in a message that has never been forgotten. "We have met the enemy," he wrote, "and they are ours."

American sailors won glory on the high seas as well as on the lakes. In the first year of the war, individual American ships fought desperate but victorious duels with British vessels. The fighting spirit of the Americans is shown by the words of Captain James Lawrence. Although his vessel was badly battered and he himself was dying of a wound, Captain Lawrence nevertheless ordered his crew, "Don't give up the ship!" American vessels were often better built and armed than the British ships they fought against. The British were amazed at our victories because for centuries Britain had "ruled the waves" and her navy had usually won against all enemies.

As the war continued, however, the larger British fleet drove most of the American vessels into port and kept them there. It is true that armed American merchant vessels, or privateers, captured large numbers of English trading ships. But though American sailors fought hard, sea victories alone could not have won the war.

Both sides gladly end the war. In 1814, the great wars which had raged in

A British victory, making possible British would have posed a problem nevertheless.

control of the mouth of the Mississippi,

Europe for more than 20 years were coming to an end. Great Britain was tired of fighting and wanted peace in America as well as Europe. Because the United States had failed to capture Canada and wanted to resume normal trade, Americans also were glad to make peace. So a treaty ending the war was signed at the city of Ghent, in Belgium, on Christmas Eve, 1814. By the Treaty of Ghent everything was restored to what it had been before the war. Nothing was said about the impressment of sailors or the seizure of ships, which had been reasons for declaring war. But with the European wars over, the need for these impressments ended. An American statesman commented, "We have obtained nothing but peace."

Allow Time for a thorough discussion of these outcomes.

THE WAR OF 1812 HAS IMPORTANT EFFECTS

The war brings about a united and stronger nation. At first glance you might suppose that the war had no important results in the United States, but that is not so. Although the treaty changed nothing, the war itself did have important results:

(1) The war helped to create what may be called a national spirit. This means a pride and confidence in the strength and power of the nation. In the years immediately after the War of 1812, the people of New England, the South, and the West forgot many of their differences in their pride in being Americans. They turned their backs on Europe and devoted themselves to building a greater and more powerful United States.

(2) The war helped to build up manufacturing in this country. Before the war, most manufactured articles used by Americans were imported from other countries. Trade in these articles almost ceased because of Jefferson's plan for avoiding war

by stopping trade and because of the dangers of wartime shipping. Unable to obtain manufactured goods from abroad, people in the United States began to manufacture many of the articles they needed.

(3) In addition, the War of 1812 produced new leaders. Two outstanding generals in the war — Andrew Jackson and William Henry Harrison — later became Presidents of the United States. Other men who played important parts in the war continued to be leaders for many years to come.

The war affects the attitude of other nations toward the United States. The War of 1812 also had effects outside our boundaries:

(1) The people of Canada had taken no part in the troubles between the United States and Great Britain which led to war. You can imagine how the Canadians felt when they learned that their neighbor to the south wished to seize their territory. A feeling of bitterness against the Americans developed in Canada. This feeling lasted for many years.

(2) As a result of the war, European nations developed greater respect for the United States. The United States had shown, for a second time, that it was willing to fight if necessary. In the future, Europe would be more ready to let the United States control its own affairs.

CHECK UP

1. (a) How did Jefferson try to keep the United States out of the European war? (b) Why did his plans fail?

2. (a) What sections of the country favored war with Great Britain in 1812? Why? (b) Which section opposed it? Why?

3. (a) What were some important results of the war? (b) In what way was the war a failure?

4   How Did President Monroe Warn Europe Against Interfering in the Americas?

The United States faces European threats to the Americas. Several years after the War of 1812, our country took a bold step which showed that she was becoming a strong nation. By the early 1820's, as you have read in Chapter 10, the New World colonies of Spain and Portugal had won their freedom. It was well known that the king of Spain wanted to regain his colonies and was trying to get the help of other European powers. Great Britain was opposed to such a plan. She wanted the new nations of Latin America to remain independent so that they could carry on trade with anyone they wished, including Britain. The United States, naturally, was sympathetic toward the new countries which, like herself, had won independence. In addition, the United States did not want to see Spain or any other European nation seize territory in the Western Hemisphere. This could happen not only in Latin America but in other parts of the Americas. At this time, for example, Russia owned Alaska and claimed land even farther south on the Pacific coast.

The Monroe Doctrine is proclaimed. The United States government decided to make its position perfectly clear. In a message to Congress in 1823, President Monroe declared that (1) the United States would consider it an unfriendly act if European nations interfered with any of the new governments in the Americas;

(2) the United States would oppose the establishment of any new colonies in this hemisphere; (3) the United States on its part would not meddle in European affairs.

In other words, Monroe warned Europe, "The New World is not your concern. Keep out of it and we will keep out of Europe's business." The United States was able to take this firm stand because it knew that Great Britain, with its strong navy, also wished European nations to keep their hands off America. Monroe's official statement, which is known as the *Monroe Doctrine*, was one of the most important steps ever taken by our government. For years the Monroe Doctrine was the foundation of our relations with European countries.

•

This chapter has told the story of how our young nation took its place among other nations. The United States had protected itself — sometimes by treaty, and once or twice by war. It had doubled its territory. It had even felt able to warn all of Europe: "Keep out!" The United States was no longer the weak and small nation it had been in 1789.

CHECK UP

1. (a) Why did President Monroe issue the Monroe Doctrine? (b) What important statements did it contain?

2. What was Great Britain's attitude toward the Latin American republics? Why?

The British had expressed a willingness to issue a joint declaration opposing European intervention in the Americas.

Check Up on Chapter 13

Do You Know the Meaning?

1. neutral	3. militia	5. impress
2. embargo	4. doctrine	6. oppress

Can You Identify?

1. XYZ Affair	3. Fort McHenry
2. Jay's Treaty	4. Monroe Doctrine

Can You Identify? (Cont.)

5. War Hawks	11. Embargo Act
6. 1803	12. Napoleon
7. 1812–1814	13. Tecumseh
8. 1823	14. Treaty of Ghent
9. Henry Clay	15. Oliver Hazard Perry
10. John C. Calhoun	16. Andrew Jackson
17. Hartford Convention	

Can You Locate?

1. New Orleans	3. Washington, D. C.
2. Florida	4. Louisiana Purchase

What Do You Think?

1. Do you think the United States should have declared war on England in 1812? Give reasons for your answer.

What Do You Think? (Cont.)

2. Washington believed that the United States should not get mixed up in European affairs. So did Monroe. Is it possible for us today to follow the same policy? Explain why or why not.

3. Many Englishmen believed that the United States, in declaring war on England, was helping Napoleon. Why?

4. The United States tried to remain neutral in the European wars of the early 1800's. In much the same way, our country tried to remain neutral early in World War I and in World War II. Why is it difficult to stay neutral during a general war?

5. Some have said that Napoleon made the United States a great power. Can you explain why they think so?

This question gets at an important point that needs to be understood.

LINKING PAST AND PRESENT

The Star-Spangled Banner. All Americans know the stirring music of our national anthem. The story of how it came to be written goes back to the War of 1812. In September, 1814, a British fleet in Chesapeake Bay was trying to capture Baltimore, Maryland. The British planned to bombard Fort McHenry, which guarded the city. About this time, a young American lawyer named Francis Scott Key boarded a British ship to ask for the release of a friend who was being held prisoner. The release was granted, but the two men were forced to remain aboard because the bombardment of Fort McHenry was about to begin.

As the shells began to pour into the fort, Key anxiously watched the Stars and Stripes over the fort. The flag was still there "at the twilight's last gleaming," but would it survive the "perilous fight"? Next morning, in the "dawn's early light," Key saw with joy that "our flag was still there." The British had failed to take Fort McHenry! Key wrote the first verse of his song on the ship, and then completed it after he was released. The words were set to music, and the inspiring song soon became popular. But it wasn't until over a hundred years later, on March 3, 1931, that Congress made "The Star-Spangled Banner" the official national anthem of the United States.

Today, the American flag flies day and night over the grave of Francis Scott Key in Baltimore, Maryland, as well as over Fort McHenry, which is now a national shrine. The original flag which inspired the national anthem survived the British bombardment. Tattered and stained, with one of its stars shot out, it can be seen in the Smithsonian Institution at Washington.

Summary of Important Ideas

Unit Four has told about the forming of the Constitution and the progress made by the United States in its early years.

1. Our country lacked an effective government until the Constitution was adopted.
a. At the outbreak of the Revolutionary War there was no United States but only thirteen American colonies. The Second Continental Congress served as an emergency government. In 1781, the states adopted the Articles of Confederation. Under the Articles, the central government had the power to wage war and make peace, to control relations with foreign countries, and to borrow money. But Congress did not have the right to levy taxes or control commerce among the states. The weaknesses of this government led to a demand for a stronger union.
b. The Constitutional Convention met in Philadelphia in 1787. The delegates worked out a plan of government which included many important compromises. The new government went into effect when nine states approved the new Constitution. The contest was close in most states because many Americans feared a strong government. Under the Constitution, Congress could levy taxes and regulate commerce between the states. Federal courts were provided. Powers not given to the United States by the Constitution were left to the states. Separating powers among the executive, legislative, and judicial branches enabled each branch of the federal government to check the others.

c. In 1789, with the inauguration of Washington as President, the new government began. Alexander Hamilton developed a financial plan to pay the national and state debts, to raise money through tariffs and taxes, and to establish a national bank. The government gained respect for its laws by putting down the Whiskey Rebellion. Differences over how strong the federal government should be led to the formation of political parties.

2. The United States in time won the respect of other nations.
a. In 1789, a revolution broke out in France. When other European countries went to war against France, the United States, though an ally of France, declared its neutrality. During wars which lasted until 1815, both France and Great Britain seized American shipping and in other ways interfered with American rights. The United States protested to both countries, boycotted European goods, and placed embargoes on American shipping.
b. Influenced in part by the hope of gaining additional territory, the United States went to war with Great Britain in 1812. This war aroused a new national spirit in the United States and built up American manufacturing. Earlier (1803), the United States had bought Louisiana from Napoleon. Thus, the national territory was doubled, and the country gained control of the Mississippi.
c. During the early 1800's, the Spanish and Portuguese colonies (from Mexico southward) declared their independence. By 1825 all had ceased to be colonies. The United States sympathized with these

This summary combines ideas from three chapters under two major headings. Can your students suggest a way of using three headings? If so, what would they be?

countries in their struggle for independence; and Great Britain, for commercial and other reasons, wanted the new countries to remain independent. To safeguard the Western Hemisphere from European interference, President Monroe announced the Monroe Doctrine.

Unit Review

1. (a) How was our country governed during the early years of the Revolutionary War? (b) Under the Articles of Confederation? (c) What were the weaknesses of these governments? (d) Why was a convention called in Philadelphia in 1787? (e) What were the chief compromises in the Constitution drawn up by this convention?

2. (a) What powers were written into the Constitution to strengthen the new government? (b) Why were these ideas included in the Constitution: (1) division of powers between the state and national governments; (2) separation of powers between branches of the central government? (c) What is the Bill of Rights?

3. (a) What was Hamilton's financial plan? (b) How did it cause political parties to be formed? (c) How did his plan add to the nation's strength?

4. (a) Why did the United States remain neutral when France went to war with England and other European countries? (b) Why did France and England fail to respect the rights of the United States as a neutral? (c) How did Jefferson try to compel other countries to respect our rights? (d) How successful was he? Why?

5. (a) Why did the United States go to war with England in 1812? (b) What were the results?

6. (a) How was the United States able to purchase all of Louisiana in 1803? (b) Why was this purchase important?

7. (a) Why were both the United States and Great Britain opposed to the restoring of Spanish rule in the colonies which had revolted from Spain? (b) What were the provisions of the Monroe Doctrine?

The first parts of these four questions deal with important aspects of United States foreign policy.

Gaining Skill

How to Use the Library

In studying history you will often want to find information in other books, as well as in magazines and newspapers. To find these materials, you will need to know how to use the library. Ask your teacher or the librarian to explain how books are classified and numbered on the shelves of your library.

Usually reference books (encyclopedias, atlases, the *World Almanac,* dictionaries) are kept separately. Fiction and biography are usually arranged alphabetically on separate shelves. Look for a book of fiction under the author's name, and for biography under the name of the person who is the subject of the book. Other books are classified by subject and are assigned numbers indicating the subject. If the Dewey Decimal System is used, history books will be found in the 900's.

In using reference books, the first step is to select the proper type of book. In doing the projects suggested in *Interesting Things to Do* for Unit Four, for example, what type of reference book would you use in the case of numbers 3, 6, and 7 — an encyclopedia, atlas, the *World Almanac,* or some other reference book? Explain why in each case.

After selecting the proper book, the next step is to use the index. In using the index to locate information, it is important to look under all the *key words.* For example, you may want to learn more about the Louisiana Purchase before writing the article suggested in number 7. The obvious key words are "Louisiana" and "Purchase." If you were to look in the index which appears in the front of the *World Almanac,* you would find no entry under "Purchase." Under "Louisiana," you would find a number of subheadings, including: "Area, capital, rank; Descriptive; Population." You might find another subheading, "Purchase," or a separate entry, "Louisiana Purchase," below. Other entries in the *World Almanac* also might give information about the Louisiana Purchase. For example, look up this entry: "United States: Territorial Expansion."

Most libraries have a card-index file which lists books by author, title, and subject. If you know the name of the author who wrote a book you want to find, you can look under his name. But if you want to locate books dealing with the Constitutional Convention or the life of George Washington, you must look for cards on those subjects. In each case, what are the key words to look for? When you find a card for a book that you want to use, make a note of the *call number* found in the upper left-hand corner of the card, and ask the librarian where you can find the book.

In considering question number 4 on page 225, you may want to learn something about the planning of the United Nations organization at the San Francisco Conference. This information can be found in books and in magazine articles. Magazine articles are listed in the *Readers' Guide to Periodical Literature*. Each volume of this guide covers about a two-year period. You will want to look particularly in the volume including 1945, the year in which the UN was formed. The articles are classified according to subject matter, and the subject headings are listed alphabetically. In looking up information about the San Francisco Conference and the UN, what are the key words? When you find a key word, be sure to note all *cross-references* (references to other headings). Ask your teacher how to locate a cross-reference. For information on more recent events you will, of course, want to look at more recent volumes of the *Readers' Guide*. If, for example, you want to keep up to date on the exploration of space, you should look up articles listed in the latest volume.

Interesting Things to Do

Items marked with an asterisk (*) are for the whole class.

*1. Make cards for the new names, words, and dates given in Unit Four. Hold a "spell down" with the cards to see who can identify the greatest number.

*2. Learn the Preamble to the Constitution given on page A2. Look up the meaning of any words you do not know.

*3. On an outline map show how the territory of the United States had expanded by 1803. Use one color for the territory granted to the United States in the Treaty of 1783; use a different color for the Louisiana Territory.

4. Draw a cartoon dealing with one of these subjects: (a) weakness of the Confederation; (b) impressment of American seamen; (c) XYZ Affair; (d) feeling of the Westerners about New Orleans; (e) War Hawks and the War of 1812; (f) New England's opposition to the War of 1812; (g) growth of national pride after the War of 1812; (h) Monroe Doctrine.

5. Write an imaginary conversation between: (a) a Federalist and a Republican; (b) a member of the Constitutional Convention from New Jersey and one from Virginia; (c) a New England merchant and a War Hawk in 1812; (d) George Washington and a Frenchman seeking aid from the United States in the early 1790's; (e) a Pennsylvania farmer who joined the Whiskey Rebellion and a government officer sent to collect the tax on whiskey.

6. Choose a committee to give a program on "The American Navy in the War of 1812." Your committee will want to consult books in your school or public libraries for details. Prepare talks on the following battles: (a) Captain Perry and the battle of Lake Erie; (b) the battle of Lake Champlain; (c) the battle between the *Constitution* and the *Guerrière* (gair-ee-*air'*); (d) Captain Lawrence and the battle between the *Chesapeake* and the *Shannon;* (e) the battle between the *Constitution* and the *Java;* (f) the British attack on Baltimore (Fort McHenry).

7. Write a newspaper article, such as might have appeared at the time, on one of the following subjects: adoption of the Constitution; inauguration of Washington; Purchase of Louisiana; war is declared in 1812; Monroe presents the Monroe Doctrine to Congress.

Projects such as these are a test of whether or not students have grasped basic ideas developed in the text.

Relate this unit to the discussion of life in various parts of colonial America (see Chapter 5).

UNIT
5

The American Way of Living Change.

If George Washington could have visited the United States in the 1840's, he would have been amazed at the changes which had taken place since his death in 1799. His thoughts might have run something like this:

"I find it hard to realize that over 20 million people now live in the United States, and that towns like St. Louis (shown above) have grown up on the banks of the Mississippi. In my day there were only 4 million Americans, and most of them lived along the Atlantic coast. . . . Here is a boat run by steam which moves ahead fast against the current of a river! In my time we depended on the wind to drive our boats. . . . What is this engine belching smoke and sparks which carries people across the countryside? When I traveled from Mount Vernon to New York in 1789, I depended on horses. . . . I see large buildings where machines spin thread to weave it into cloth. Who ever heard in my day of a machine that could spin eighty threads at one time? . . . I can hardly believe that this country could change so greatly in only 50 years!"

262

s the Different Sections Develop

In this unit we shall read about the important changes which took place in our country during the half century after Washington became our first President. Also, we shall see how the different parts of the country developed their own characteristic ways of life. Chapter 14, for example, tells how the Northeast became the shipping and manufacturing center of the nation. Inventions like the steamboat pictured above played an important part in this kind of growth as well as in the development of the South and West. Chapter 15 shows how the South became a great cotton-producing section and how slavery became firmly established there. Chapter 16 tells how Americans settled in the land beyond the Appalachians and developed the West into the most democratic section of the country. In Chapter 17 we shall read how Americans gained a greater voice in their government and came to enjoy more advantages.

How many different means of transportation can your students identify in this picture?

Where . . . wigwams stood . . . we behold the foundations of cities laid, that, in all probability, will rival the glory of the greatest upon earth. . . .
— DANIEL BOONE

The Northeast Becomes the Center
of Trade and Manufacturing

What this chapter is about —

If we should glance at a newspaper printed ten years ago, we would find that some of the events reported in bold headlines on the front page have little importance today. On the other hand, an invention, a scientific discovery, or the starting of a new kind of business, which received little attention in the newspapers, may turn out to have far-reaching effects on the life of the nation.

In the early 1800's, certain changes were taking place in the Northeast. Although people did not realize it at the time, these changes would greatly affect life in this country. One was a tremendous increase in shipping and trade. The swift clipper ships, their sails spread to catch the wind (see picture above), carried American trade all over the world. Another change was the introduction of new inventions in the United States. In this chapter you will learn how, by the 1850's, these changes had helped to make the Northeast the center of trade and manufacturing. You will also learn how inventions changed travel and communication. In this chapter we shall try to answer the following questions:

▶ 1. How did the Northeast become the center of trade and manufacturing?

▶ 2. How did machines change ways of living in America?

▶ 3. What changes were made in travel and communication?

People in our story — New England harpooner and sea captain, factory worker, factory owner, and inventor.

Maritime New England

On a ship's bow, the gilded figurehead above represented "Asia," source of spices, silk, and other luxuries prized by Americans in the early 1800's. The figurehead at left portrays one of the Yankee captains who brought back Asian cargoes to the busy port of Boston (painting, below).

Salem merchants paid tariff on their imports at the Custom House (left) where the author Nathaniel Hawthorne once worked. Note the gold American eagle on the roof and the cupola, built to provide a good view of incoming vessels.

The wooden figure of a sperm whale shown at right served as a weather vane. It was carved by a Rhode Island craftsman at a time when many New England seamen ranged the seas to bring back the whale oil needed to fuel American lamps.

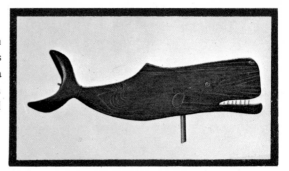

An old print (above) shows the dangers of whaling. In small boats, whale hunters close in for the kill while trying to avoid the huge creature's flailing tail. Many copies of prints like this were published by the firm of Currier & Ives and hung on the walls of American homes. Note the icebergs. Whales were hunted in both Arctic and Antarctic seas, and a voyage might last as long as three years. Whaling called for sturdy, efficient ships like the *Charles W. Morgan* (right), now moored at Mystic Seaport in Connecticut.

1 How Did the Northeast Become the Center of Trade and Manufacturing?

Note that all of the former Middle Colonies (see map, page 87) are not included in the term Northeast.

COMMERCE FLOURISHES IN THE NORTHEAST[1]

Imagine that you could turn the clock back and visit Boston harbor in the 1840's. All along the waterfront many kinds of ships are tied up. Though some of these vessels carry foreign flags, most of them fly the Stars and Stripes of the United States. Here is a fleet of fishing vessels unloading cargoes of cod which have been caught off the Grand Banks of Newfoundland. Yonder is a *packet ship* engaged in carrying goods and passengers to Europe. Beyond her is a *freighter,* built to carry bulky cargoes such as grain or lumber. Nearby, with towering masts and the sharp, slender lines which suggest great speed, is a *clipper ship,* pride of the merchant fleet. Next to her is a *whaler,* just returned from an exciting voyage to the Pacific. The scene is one of bustling activity. Shouting fills the air as sweating

[1] We are using the term *Northeast* rather than New England because the Middle Atlantic states of New York, Pennsylvania, and New Jersey were also affected by the growth of commerce.

workers load and unload cargoes. And as American sailors work at "trimming ship," they talk of strange ports and strange people at the far ends of the earth.

Other harbors of the Northeast, such as New York or Salem, Massachusetts, were also humming with activity in the 1840's. The Atlantic ports, however, had not always been so busy. What had been happening to American shipping and trade since colonial times?

American shipping suffers after the Revolution. As you learned in Chapter 5, New Englanders had begun in colonial days to build and sail ships and to engage in trade. In fact, one of the reasons for the Revolution was that England had tightened her control over American trade (pages 152, 154). During the Revolutionary War, however, many Yankee ships had been captured or sunk by the British navy. Many hardy seamen had been killed, and others had given up a life of seafaring to join the pioneers going west.

In addition to losing ships and sailors, Americans lost most of their markets.

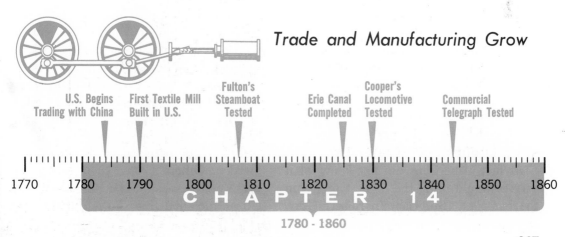

Trade and Manufacturing Grow

| | U.S. Begins Trading with China | First Textile Mill Built in U.S. | Fulton's Steamboat Tested | | Erie Canal Completed | Cooper's Locomotive Tested | | Commercial Telegraph Tested |

1770 1780 1790 1800 1810 1820 1830 1840 1850 1860

C H A P T E R   1 4

1780 - 1860

CAPTAIN ROBERT GRAY buys furs from the Oregon Indians on the Pacific coast. Captain Gray became famous not only for his China trade but also for his discovery of the Columbia River, which he named after his ship. This voyage gave the United States a claim to the Oregon country.

After the United States broke away from England, many of the ports of the British Empire were closed to Yankee ships. Especially serious to Yankee merchants was the loss of trade with the West Indies. Americans had made large profits in this trade before the Revolution. For these reasons American trade and shipping declined in the years after the Revolutionary War.

Americans open trade with China. But energetic American merchants and sea captains refused to be defeated. "If we can't trade in British ports," they said, "we will find new places to trade. Why not send ships across the Pacific to China and other parts of the Far East?" In 1784 the *Empress of China* set sail from New York, bound for China. A year later, she returned laden with silks and tea from the Chinese city of Canton. About the same time, the *Grand Turk* left Salem, Massachusetts, bound for the Orient.

At first, Americans did not know what cargoes would bring the highest profits in the Far East. But Captain Robert Gray, skipper of the *Columbia* out of Boston,

spent a winter off the coast of Oregon. From there he sailed westward to China. In China he found he could get a good price for the furs which he had purchased from the Oregon Indians. Captain Gray then returned from China to the east coast of the United States by sailing west around Africa and across the Atlantic. He was the first American to sail around the world! (The map on the next page shows his route.) After Gray's return, more and more ships that were engaged in the Far Eastern trade stopped along the west coast of North America. There they traded with the Indians, exchanging cheap trinkets for valuable furs. And the furs in turn were bartered in the Far East for the luxuries and other goods of the Orient.

Merchants find new markets in Europe for American goods. Soon American merchants opened up trade with other countries. Some sailed into the Baltic Sea, bent on trade with Russia, Denmark, and Sweden. Others steered their vessels into the Mediterranean Sea to trade with the cities which dotted its shores. The Mediterranean trade, however, turned out to be

American Ships Trade with the World

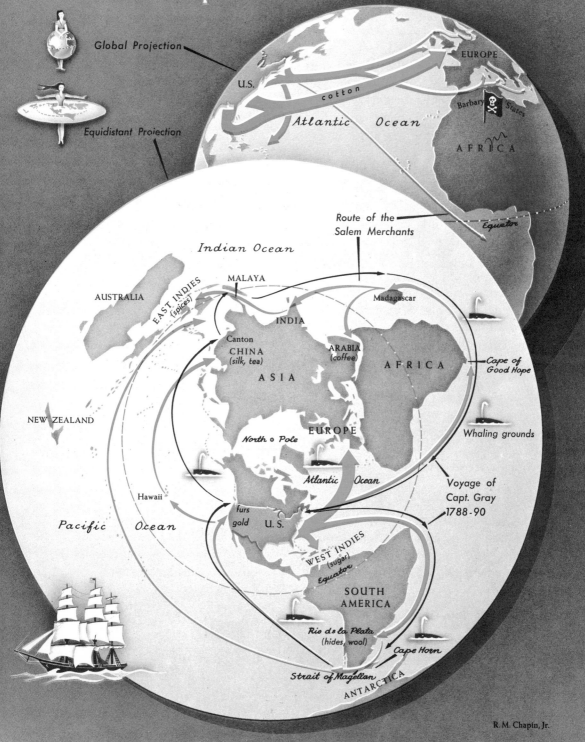

Global Projection

Equidistant Projection

EUROPE

U.S.

cotton

Atlantic Ocean

Barbary States

AFRICA

Equator

Route of the Salem Merchants

Indian Ocean

AUSTRALIA

MALAYA

EAST INDIES (spices)

INDIA

Madagascar

Canton
CHINA (silk, tea)

ARABIA (coffee)

AFRICA

ASIA

Cape of Good Hope

NEW ZEALAND

EUROPE

North o Pole

Whaling grounds

Atlantic Ocean

Voyage of Capt. Gray 1788-90

Hawaii

furs gold

U.S.

Pacific Ocean

WEST INDIES (sugar)

Equator

SOUTH AMERICA

Rio de la Plata (hides, wool)

Strait of Magellan

Cape Horn

ANTARCTICA

R. M. Chapin, Jr.

MAP STUDY (1) Compare the width of the trade lanes shown on the maps. Which would you say was larger, American trade with Europe or with Asia? (2) Where did American ships have trouble with pirates? (3) What was the chief product which American traders sought in the West Indies? (4) In the East Indies?

This map shows how far-flung United States commercial ventures were in the early 1800's.

dangerous. The rulers of several countries on the northern coast of Africa (called the Barbary states) seized whatever merchant ships they could lay their hands on. Sailors who were captured were thrown into prison or sold into slavery. For years the American government, like the governments of European countries, attempted to bribe the pirates into letting their ships alone, but with little success. Finally, President Jefferson, though a man of peace, decided to teach the Barbary pirates a lesson. In 1801, the United States sent a naval squadron to make war on the Barbary pirates. Although the American fleet fought valiantly, it was many years before our trading ships could sail the Mediterranean Sea in complete safety.

Whaling and fishing increase. At the same time that more and more American merchant ships were setting sail for trade with Europe and the Orient, larger fleets of fishing vessels and whaling ships put to sea. Whale oil was in demand for lamps, and whalebone had many uses. Whaling was hard and dangerous, and the voyages were very long. Often two or three years passed before the weary sailors caught sight of the familiar landmarks of their home ports.

American sailors on the seven seas bring wealth to the Northeast. The far-flung voyages of American merchantmen,

THIS SAILOR-FIGURE was carved in 1851 as a ship's compass-holder. After only one voyage, the figure was removed because sailors said its eyes moved at night and kept them from watching the compass!

fishing vessels, and whalers made shipping in the Northeast even more important than it had been before the Revolution. Shipping centers such as New York, Boston, and Salem once more hummed with activity. As one writer has said, "In the spicy warehouses that overlooked Salem Harbor there came to be stored hemp from Luzon, gum copal from Zanzibar, palm oil from Africa, coffee from Arabia, tallow from Madagascar, whale oil from the Antarctic, hides and wool from the Rio de la Plata, nutmeg and cloves from Malaysia." Young men, scarcely old enough to vote, became captains of merchantmen, made great fortunes, and retired before middle age.

PREPARING OIL ABOARD WHALING SHIP

Kerosene came to be **270** used in the 1860's.

THE "FLYING CLOUD," a model of which appears below, was designed by the master-builder of clipper ships, Donald McKay (right). This model shows the "Flying Cloud" with extra sails set on the spars of her foremast (left) to catch every last breath of wind. Note the graceful lines of her hull, shaped to cut swiftly through the water.

American shipping is hurt by the War of 1812. As we learned in Chapter 13, President Jefferson's embargo interfered with American shipping. The War of 1812 also kept American merchant vessels off the high seas. As trade dwindled, warehouses overflowed with goods, sailors lost their jobs, and ships rotted from disuse. A traveler reported that the streets along the New York waterfront were deserted and that grass had begun to grow upon the wharves!

Once the War of 1812 was over, however, men of the Northeast turned again to the sea to seek their fortunes. Shrewd Yankee skippers soon were to be found on all the seas and in many a distant port. Packet ships (that is, ships with fixed sailing dates) made regular trips with passengers and freight between English and American ports.

The swift clipper becomes queen of the seas. In the 1840's, New England shipbuilders brought out a new kind of ship particularly designed for speed. Known as clipper ships, these slender vessels were especially useful in the China trade. They carried a tremendous spread of sail and ate up distance at unheard-of speed. The clipper ships became the pride of American sailors and the envy of the rest of the world. The most famous clippers were designed by Donald McKay of Boston. His *Flying Cloud* made the trip from New York around the "Horn" (Cape Horn) to San Francisco in 89 days. Sailing before a strong wind, she could cover as much as 375 miles in a day. McKay's clippers, says one writer, "were as truly the creations of imagination, faith, and vision as are any other American dreams, which now take the shape of towering buildings, or lofty bridges spanning our rivers, or the long highways uniting our towns and cities, our plains and mountains and deserts into one great land."

In the era of clipper ships (the 1840's and '50's) American shipping reached a high peak. American vessels and traders were everywhere. But the days of the clipper ships were numbered. Already ocean-going steamboats had appeared. The English perfected these boats and began to make them of iron. American sailors, however, still clung to their speedy wooden clippers and looked down in scorn upon the steamboats with their squat, ugly lines and belching smoke. But the day was not far distant when wooden vessels driven by wind would have to give way to the new rulers of the sea.

INVENTIONS HELP MAKE THE NORTHEAST THE MANUFACTURING CENTER OF THE NATION

Along with its flourishing shipping and trade, the Northeast became the manufacturing center of the United States. This would hardly have been possible if an important step in the history of mankind had not taken place in England in the late 1700's. *Men began to use machines on a large scale to do the work formerly done by human hands.* So rapid and so far-reaching was this change in the methods of producing goods that it became known as the *Industrial Revolution.* The Industrial Revolution has had a greater and longer-lasting effect on people's lives than all the wars ever fought.

English inventors pave the way for the Industrial Revolution. The Industrial Revolution began when men invented new machines for spinning thread and weaving cloth. Before the middle of the 1700's, almost every home had its spinning wheel (for making thread) and its hand loom (for weaving cloth). But the spinning wheel was slow; it took many hours to make enough thread to weave a garment. In the 1760's, an Englishman named James Hargreaves built a machine called a *spinning jenny* (possibly named after his wife, Jenny) to take the place of the spinning wheel. This machine could spin eight threads instead of one. Later improvements made it possible to spin 80 threads at one time.

In a few years another Englishman, Edmund Cartwright, invented a loom which could be run by water power. With this loom a weaver could work much faster, and could make wider cloth, than with the old hand loom. Constant improvements were made in spinning machines and power looms. Later, steam as well as water power was used to drive the machines.

The first factories are started. Before these machines were invented, as you have just read, all the spinning and weaving had been done in the homes. But the new machines were expensive, and families could not afford to own them. Also, it was necessary for the machines to be located near streams so that they could be driven by a water wheel. Richard Arkwright is often given the credit for establishing the first *factory.* He put spinning jennies and looms into one building and employed workers to run them. Soon other factories were built, and it was not many years before England was turning out large quantities of cloth. Because these factories manufactured woven fab-

Note that the word revolution is here used to describe a fundamental change in manufacturing.

THE OLD SLATER MILL (the white building behind the train) used machines powered by Pawtucket Falls, which you see at the right of the picture. What different kinds of early transportation do you find in this picture?

See also the "Link" on page 288.

rics, or *textiles,* they were known as textile factories.

Samuel Slater introduces the new machines in America. England jealously guarded the secrets of her new textile machines so that no other country would benefit by them. A law was passed that no one could take a machine, or even the plans of one, out of the country. But no law can control what a man may carry in his head! In 1789, there appeared in the United States an Englishman named Samuel Slater, who settled in Pawtucket, Rhode Island. Slater had worked in English factories, and he was sure he remembered the textile machines well enough to build them in this country. He was right. Within a year he had built from memory a spinning machine which would spin 72 threads at the same time. Slater then established mills in Rhode Island and Massachusetts with textile machines like those found in Great Britain. After Slater had shown the way, a number of other cotton mills were started in New England.

Manufacturing increases rapidly during the War of 1812. At first, the Industrial Revolution was slow in getting started in the United States. The chief reason was that Americans were used to getting manufactured goods from England and other countries of Europe, in exchange for food and raw materials. As we know, however, President Jefferson's embargo, and later the War of 1812, interfered with American trade. During the war Americans were cut off almost entirely from British goods. But the Americans were self-reliant people, and they said, "If we can't get manufactured goods from England, why not start factories and make the articles we need ourselves?" This is just what they did. New factories sprang up in many places. In 1814, Francis Lowell opened a textile factory in Waltham, Massachusetts. It was the first factory in which all the steps needed to make raw cotton into finished cloth took place under one roof. Factories began to produce not only cotton, woolen, and linen fabrics but also a great variety of articles made out of leather, iron, and felt. This method of bringing workers together to produce goods by machinery in factories is called the *factory system.*

New England and the middle states lead in manufacturing. Most of the early American factories, especially the textile mills, were located in New England. There were several reasons for this. (1) New

There had been manufacturing in New England in colonial days.

Why Southerners Liked Free Trade

Southerner: "This is a nice deal for us. The English buy our cotton and we can get anything we want from the English factories — cheap!"

Northerner: "Those English manufacturers have a head start. Their goods are so cheap that they'll put us out of business before we can get going!"

The bibliography lists books about invention and industrial development: Men of Science and Invention and Miracle in Motion: The Story of America's Industry.

England had swift-rushing streams which supplied the needed water power. (2) Because the hillsides of New England were stony and hard to farm, many people were willing to leave their farms and work in the new factories. (3) New England had plenty of ships to carry the products of the factories to other sections of the United States and to other countries.

The factories established in the middle states (New York, Pennsylvania, and New Jersey) manufactured many articles made of iron. In Pennsylvania there were deposits of iron ore which had been used in the production of iron even in colonial times. In the 1800's, the variety of iron goods made in this country began to increase — iron rims for wooden wagon wheels, guns, stoves, axes, and other tools. The South and the West were much slower in starting manufacturing. In the early 1800's, those regions had few factories.

Howe invents the sewing machine. Americans did not merely copy machines from England. They also invented new ones. The textile industry, for example, badly needed a machine which would sew cloth. Several inventors had tried to make such a machine, but Elias Howe was the first to succeed. Howe had been born on a New England farm. Like all farmers of that time, he had learned to repair and even to make many kinds of tools. He had also worked in a factory where he became familiar with machinery. Howe knew that the man who invented a workable sewing machine would make his fortune. He worked hard and suffered many disappointments as one attempt after another ended in failure.

At last, in 1845, Howe perfected a sewing machine which was run by a hand-turned wheel. People were slow to buy his invention, however, and although he finally became rich, he and his family almost starved before money started coming in. Howe's machine not only lightened the work of the housewife but was widely used in clothing factories. Garments made on the sewing machine could be produced and sold much more cheaply than hand-sewn clothing.

Several factors were related: population, availability of capital.

resources, access to markets,

Southerner: "We don't manufacture much in the South. Now everything we need costs more. And if we don't buy from the English, maybe they won't buy our cotton."

Northerner: "Now we can compete with the English! The tariff gives us a chance to show what we can do and build up America!"

Note that not all people in a country benefit from a protective tariff. The reaction of Southern planters is given on page 376.

THE GOVERNMENT ENCOURAGES AMERICAN MANUFACTURERS

Cheap English goods threaten American manufacturers. As we have seen, manufacturing increased rapidly during the War of 1812. But American factory owners found themselves in difficulty in the years that followed the war. When trade was once more possible, English merchants shipped large quantities of goods to their former customers in America. The British goods were cheap in price (1) because the English factories were larger and more efficient than American factories, and (2) because English manufacturers wanted to dispose of large quantities of goods which had piled up during the war. As a result, the United States was flooded with English-made goods which sold at lower prices than American-made goods. Of course, many people bought the cheaper British goods.

Factory owners in the United States were alarmed. Orders were falling off, factories were shutting down, and ruin seemed certain for the new industries. The factory owners sought help from the government. They asked for a *tariff*, that is, a tax on imported goods. Why did the factory owners believe that a tariff would protect them from the less expensive goods imported from England?

How does a protective tariff work? Suppose Mr. Jones in your town owns a shoe factory. Of course, he wants to make a profit. To do this he must sell his shoes for a price higher than the cost of the materials and labor used in making them. In other words, if it costs Mr. Jones $6 to make a pair of shoes, he would expect to sell them for, let us say, $7 a pair. But in a nearby town lives Mr. Smith, who also manufactures shoes. Perhaps his factory is more efficient or he can hire workers for lower wages. At any rate, Mr. Smith is able to make shoes of the very same style and quality for $5 a pair. So Mr. Smith can afford to sell his shoes for $6 a pair and still make the same profit as Mr. Jones. Naturally people will buy the less expensive shoes. Mr. Jones's business will fall off. But, if $1 could somehow

The cartoon plus the example of Mr. **275** *Jones help students understand an abstract idea.*

be added to the price of Mr. Smith's shoes, he and Mr. Jones would compete on even terms.

By substituting "the United States" for Mr. Jones and "Great Britain" for Mr. Smith, we can understand the situation after the War of 1812. If a protective tariff were placed on goods brought into this country, English-made products would cost the buyer as much as the same articles made in the United States. To sell their goods on even terms with the British, American manufacturers therefore wanted a tariff on foreign goods.

Tariffs are established on foreign goods. The American manufacturers appealed to Congress for help. In 1816, a tariff law was passed which placed taxes, or *duties,* on many imported articles. This tariff was of great help to many American factory owners. But there was another side to the tariff question. Many Americans disliked it. They knew that if England could not sell manufactured goods in the United States, she was not so likely to buy American food and raw materials. This meant that our trade with England would decline. Thus, the tariff of 1816 was a blow to the shipowners, who clamored loudly against it. So also did the Southerners who had

tobacco and cotton to sell. Many buyers also protested, since every person who bought manufactured articles would have to pay the higher prices of American goods.

As the years passed, manufacturing increased rapidly in New England and the middle states. So also did the demand for higher tariff duties and for tariff protection on more kinds of goods. In 1824 and again in 1828, Congress passed new and higher tariff laws.

CHECK UP

1. (a) What happened to American shipping during and just after the Revolution? (b) Explain how and where American merchants and sea captains found new markets.

2. (a) How did the War of 1812 hurt shipping? (b) Why were the clipper ships important?

3. (a) Explain the term "Industrial Revolution." (b) What inventions in England paved the way for the Industrial Revolution? (c) How were the new machines introduced into the United States?

4. (a) How did the War of 1812 affect manufacturing in the United States? (b) Why were so many of the early factories located in New England?

5. (a) Why did factory owners demand a tariff on imported manufactured goods? (b) How would a tariff help them?

 ## How Did Machines Change Ways of Living in America?

Working conditions in the early factories are poor. We should remember that early factories were nothing like our modern factories with hundreds of complicated machines, thousands of workers, and long assembly lines. The early factories were usually large wooden buildings, without good lighting or ventilation.

They were cold in the winter and hot in the summer. They had none of the comforts and conveniences found in most factories today. There were no restrooms or cafeterias; there were no doctors or nurses to take care of sick and injured employees.

Large numbers of women and children, as well as men, worked in these factories.

See the picture of a factory (mill) on page 273.

NEW YORK IN 1800 was a busy commercial city of about 60,000 people. At the left is a famous old coffeehouse where merchants and traders met to carry on business with each other. Compare this view of the city with the picture on page 96.

The fact that children were permitted to work in factories was one reason why wages were low.

Children as young as seven or eight worked for long hours. The eight-hour day was unheard of at that time. Employees were on the job from sunrise to sunset, working from twelve to fifteen hours a day! In spite of the long hours, workers earned very little. The men made perhaps five dollars a week, the women about two dollars, and the children often only a dollar a week.

The workers, however, were not always as dissatisfied with these conditions as we might expect. Most of them came from nearby farms where they had been used to hard work and long hours. Although their wages were low, the prices of the things they needed to buy were low also. Nor did the workers have to remain in the factories to make a living. In fact, the young women workers often expected to marry and live on farms, and the men felt they could always strike out for the West where there were plenty of opportunities to make a new start. The only trouble was that the West got farther and farther away, and it took more and more money to start a new life there.

The factory system brings important changes in the worker's life. As time went on, it became clear that the factory system was making great changes in American life. In earlier days, when goods had been made in the homes, the worker had been his own master. He had owned his tools and could work whatever hours he wished. Furthermore, the worker took pride in what he produced with his own hands and brain. With the coming of factories, however, workers lost much of their freedom as well as the pleasure they had had in their work. The machines and the tools they used were no longer theirs. The articles they made did not belong to them but to their employer. If they wished to keep their jobs, they had to work the number of hours set by the employer and to accept the wages he offered to pay them. Often the factory owner knew and cared little about the conditions under which his employees worked.

Early labor unions try to improve conditions. Although it is true that American workers were better off than those in other lands, their lot was far from easy. More and more immigrants were coming to America, which meant that factory owners had no trouble in getting workers. Wages were kept low because if one man

 Labor unions are discussed in Chapter 23.

THE STAGECOACH "SEVENTY-SIX," drawn by ten white horses, carried passengers in New York about 1850. Here a new load of passengers are about to go bumping, tossing, shaking on their way as friends and families see them off.

quit his job, there were plenty of others to take his place.

In order to improve working conditions, a few groups of workers banded together to form labor unions. Most of the members were in the larger cities. The unions were made up of craftsmen or skilled workers engaged in the same work. The chief object of these unions was to win shorter hours and better wages. Workers also demanded greater opportunities for free education for their children. A number of unions flourished during the 1830's but soon declined. It was not until several years after the Civil War that labor unions became numerous and strong.

The factory system leads to the growth of cities. Another change brought about by the use of machines was the growth of cities. As more factories were established, more and more people left the farms and moved near the factories. After 1820 large numbers of the workers who came from Europe settled in the factory towns. Wherever towns were conveniently located, they became centers for transporting goods. Within the towns

stores and shops began to increase, and banks and warehouses were established. Before too long, many small factory towns became busy industrial cities.

During the Revolutionary War there had been only five towns of over 8000 people in the United States. In 1840, there were 44 towns of over 8000; by 1860, there were 141! These figures show that cities grew rapidly in size and number. But we should remember that the majority of Americans still continued to live on farms or in small villages.

City dwellers enjoy new comforts. The growth of industry brought new conveniences to Americans, especially to those living in cities. Candles gave way to oil-burning lamps. Stoves took the place of fireplaces for cooking and heating. The floors of many rooms were covered with carpets. In the kitchen tinware was now being used in place of heavy iron and copper utensils. More and more, comfortable furniture was to be found in most homes. The larger cities used gas for lighting their streets and built water systems to take the place of wells and springs.

Call attention to Daniel Boone's prophecy on page 263. The 1960 census listed 130 cities with a population of over 100,000.

CHECK UP

1. (a) Describe working conditions in early factories. (b) What changes did the factory

system bring about in workers' lives? (c) How did labor unions try to improve conditions?

2. How did the factory system affect the growth of cities?

What Changes Were Made in Travel and Communication?

While the Northeast was developing into a manufacturing and trading section, other important changes were taking place throughout the nation. One change was in the means of transportation. Roads and canals were built which connected the eastern part of the country with the western section. Amazing new inventions made it easier for farmers to get their goods to market and for manufacturers to sell their products where they were needed. Let us see how this came about.

ROADS AND CANALS INCREASE TRADE AND TRAVEL

Do you remember that the first Congress under the Constitution, which was supposed to meet on March 4, 1789, did not open until a month later (page 233)? Poor roads throughout the country helped to cause this delay. Roads were unpaved, and often were just a succession of deep holes, choking dust, or oozing mud. Carriages jounced and swayed over these rough roads, and it was often impossible to travel from one town to the next by carriage. Many people went on horseback. Whenever possible, boats were used to transport passengers and heavy freight.

The Cumberland Road connects the East and the West. As time went on and larger numbers of people moved westward, better and faster transportation was needed. A great forward step was taken in 1811. The United States government began building the *Cumberland* or *National Road*. The surface of the National

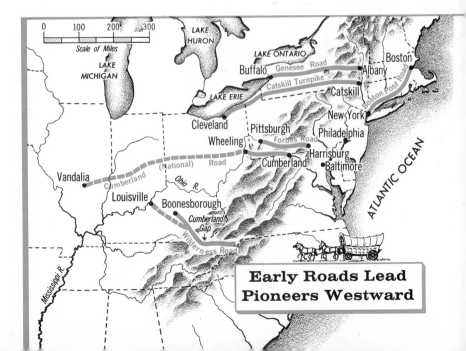

Note that most of the roads ran east and west. Why was that?

MAP STUDY

Broken lines show the extension of the Cumberland Road and the Louisville branch of the Wilderness Road (page 307). Why didn't the Wilderness Road run in a straight line from Virginia to Kentucky?

Early Roads Lead Pioneers Westward

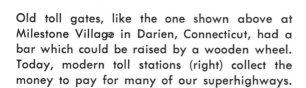

Old toll gates, like the one shown above at Milestone Village in Darien, Connecticut, had a bar which could be raised by a wooden wheel. Today, modern toll stations (right) collect the money to pay for many of our superhighways.

Road, which cost as much as $13,000 a mile, was made of crushed rock. At first, the road ran from Cumberland, Maryland, to Wheeling on the Ohio River. (See map, page 279.) Later, other stretches were added to the National Road. In time it reached Vandalia, Illinois, not far from the Mississippi River. The National Road became the main overland route to the West. Over it streamed a continuous procession of wagons, coaches, riders on horseback, cattle, pack horses, and people on foot. The merchants of Pennsylvania and Maryland made good profits by selling food and other necessities to travelers using the National Road.

Turnpikes are built. Many people, especially Westerners, thought the states should build other new roads. But the state governments had little money, so private companies began to build them. The new roads were much better surfaced than colonial roads. Over them rolled stagecoaches and canvas-covered *Conestoga* wagons. These wagons were used to carry freight or to transport families with their household belongings to new homes in the West. Often the procession of coaches and wagons would be interrupted by large herds of sheep or cattle on their way to market. At certain points along the roads travelers were halted at toll gates, where they had to pay a toll or tax. These toll charges helped to pay the companies for the cost of building and keeping up the roads. At first the toll gate was only a pole, or pike, set across the road and raised or turned aside to let travelers pass. The roads came to be called *turnpikes*.

Canals furnish cheap water routes. Travel by water was also becoming more important. Lakes and rivers had been used for transportation since the days the Indian braves had glided over the water in their canoes. Unfortunately, however, long distances often separated rivers and lakes from one another. Rapids or waterfalls also hindered water travel. To overcome these difficulties, canals were dug around rapids or to connect bodies of

It is difficult to exaggerate the importance of the Erie Canal in the days before the railroad. The route of the New York Central later ran parallel to the canal.

THE NORTHEAST BECOMES THE CENTER OF TRADE   **281**

water. By using the canals people could travel many miles by water. (The map on this page shows where some important canals were located.) Travel by canal, although slow, was much cheaper than over roads. Canal boats were usually towed by horses or mules driven along the bank of the canal. So many canals were built that the period from 1825 to 1850 has been called the *Canal Era*.

The Erie Canal was the most important of the early canals. Governor DeWitt Clinton of New York realized what canal trade would mean to New York City. It was largely because of his dreams and determination that the Erie Canal was built. Completed in 1825 after eight years of hard work, the canal was 40 feet wide and 363 miles long. It ran through the Mohawk River valley in upstate New York, connecting Albany with Lake Erie. The Erie Canal made possible an all-water route from the harbor of New York City to the Great Lakes. Boats could go northward up the Hudson River to Albany and then westward on the canal to Buffalo on Lake Erie. At the opening of the canal, Clinton traveled on a canal boat from Buffalo to New York City, a ten-day trip. He poured water carried from Lake Erie into the Atlantic Ocean to celebrate the joining of these waters by the canal.

The Erie Canal rapidly became the busiest and most important route between the West and the Atlantic seaboard. Before the canal was built, the cost of moving goods between Buffalo and New York City was about $100 a ton. The canal immediately reduced the cost to about $10 a ton. In addition, goods could be transported in little more than one third of the time which had been required before. New York City, already the largest city in the United States, grew even more rapidly because of the canal trade. Products from the Great Lakes region could be shipped by water all the way to New York and from there to other ports along the Atlantic coast or to Europe. In turn, manufactured goods from the eastern states and Europe were shipped to the West by means of the canal.

THE STEAM ENGINE MARKS A NEW ERA IN TRANSPORTATION

In the early 1800's a new kind of power caused a revolution in transportation and

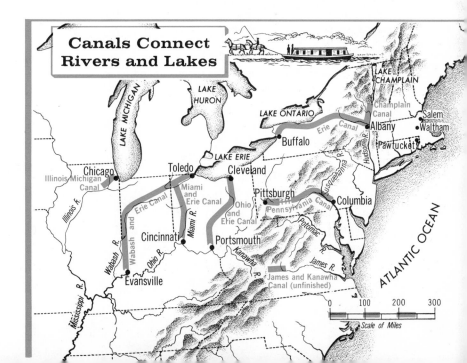

MAP STUDY

Boats were pulled on rails over hills between the two sections of the Pennsylvania Canal. (1) Which of the canals linked inland waterways and the Atlantic Ocean? (2) Which linked the Great Lakes with the Ohio River?

Canals Connect Rivers and Lakes

The steam engine revolutionized not only manufacturing but also transportation by land and water.

282   WAYS OF LIVING CHANGE AS THE NATION DEVELOPS

greatly changed ways of living in the United States. This power was steam. Man had known for some time that steam could be put to work. A Scotsman named James Watt had invented the first practical steam engine in the last half of the 1700's. Factory owners in England and in America began to use the steam engine to run machines. It was not only more efficient than water power, but steam-driven machinery could be set up anywhere. There was plenty of coal and wood in the United States to use as fuel for the steam engine. It was only natural for men to ask the question, "Why cannot steam be used to move boats or wagons as well as to run machines in factories?"

John Fitch fails to develop a successful steamboat. One of the first men to seek an answer to this question was John Fitch, a Connecticut clockmaker who had moved to Philadelphia. In 1787, he launched on the Delaware River a crude vessel driven by steam. Later, Fitch built another steamboat which made trips between Philadelphia and Trenton. But John Fitch lacked the skill and the money needed to develop a fully successful steamboat. He died a penniless and brokenhearted man.

Robert Fulton builds the first successful steamboat. Another American, named Robert Fulton, receives the credit for making the steamboat a success. Born into a humble family in Pennsylvania, Fulton had little education. He became an artist and earned his living by selling his pictures. At the age of 21, he went to Europe, where he soon became more interested in machines and inventions than in art. He began to experiment with the idea of putting a steam engine in a boat. If successful, such a boat would not have to depend upon the winds or the currents of rivers. It might even move faster than many a sailing ship.

After patient planning and much hard work, Fulton at last launched a steamboat in 1803. The vessel sank immediately! Undiscouraged, Fulton built another. Although this one floated and could move under its own power, it was very slow. Fulton returned to the United States and started work on still another steamboat.

Early in 1807, Fulton's new steamboat was nearly completed in a shipyard on the East River in New York City. Those who had watched it being built had laughed at the inventor and had called his boat "Fulton's Folly." But Fulton kept on with his work. On a day in August, the *Clermont,* as the boat was called, was ready for a trial trip up the Hudson.

A CANAL BOAT drawn by a single horse glides along a canal in the Ohio countryside as a steamboat speeds ahead on a nearby river. In the background is the tree-shaded home of William Henry Harrison, who became President in 1841.

HORSE-DRAWN "TRAINS" carried passengers on the Baltimore and Ohio Railroad for a few years before steam-driven trains came into common use.

What a queer sight she was to the people who lined the river banks! Smoke and sparks poured from her smokestack, her engines clattered noisily, paddle wheels splashed at her sides. But she moved steadily up the river and made the trip to Albany and back — a distance of about 300 miles — in 62 hours. Robert Fulton wrote after this journey had been completed:

✳ The power of propelling boats by steam is now fully proved. The morning I left New York there were not perhaps 30 persons in the city who believed that the boat would ever move one mile per hour or be of the least [use]; and, while we were putting off from the wharf, which was crowded with spectators, I heard a number of sarcastic remarks. This is the way ignorant men compliment [inventors].

The steamboat proves valuable. No longer was the steamboat called "Fulton's Folly." New and improved steamboats were quickly built. In fact, in a few years steamboats loaded with goods and passengers were puffing up and down the principal rivers. Steamboat travel in these early days, however, had many dangers. Hidden rocks, floating logs, swift currents, and exploding boilers often caused accidents. Sometimes the boats caught fire from sparks out of their own smokestacks. Then

passengers and crew worked together to put out the blaze. And there was danger of collision when rival steamboats took part in reckless races.

In spite of these dangers, steamboat travel steadily increased. Steamboats on the Great Lakes brought many settlers to the West and carried goods to and from that region. By the late 1830's, the steamboat also had been tried successfully on the ocean. But, as we learned earlier in this chapter, Americans clung to their swift sailing vessels and allowed the English to get ahead of them in this new form of ocean transportation.

Steam railroads are begun. While the steamboat was being developed, other inventors were trying to use the steam engine to improve travel on land. One of the earliest was Oliver Evans, an American inventor. Evans was so certain that railroads could be built that he made the following prophecy in 1812:

✳ The time will come when people will travel in stages moved by steam engines from one city to another as fast as birds fly — fifteen to twenty miles an hour. . . . A carriage will set out from Washington in the morning, and the passengers will breakfast at Baltimore, dine in Philadelphia, and sup at New York the same day.

To accomplish this, two sets of railways will be laid . . . nearly level . . . made of wood

Recall that clipper ships sailed as much as 375 miles in 24 hours. ← **283**

or iron, on smooth paths of broken stone or gravel, with a rail to guide the carriages so that they may pass each other in different directions and travel by night as well as by day; and the passengers will sleep in these stages as comfortably as they do now in steam stage-boats.

Although Evans's ideas seem very sensible to us today, most people of his time scoffed at them. But rails (wooden at first and later covered with strips of iron) had already been laid for short distances. Over these rails carriages were drawn by horses.

An Englishman named George Stephenson invented the first successful steam-driven locomotive. Then in 1830, the *Tom Thumb,* a locomotive built by Peter Cooper, made a successful trial run out of Baltimore, Maryland. This run was made on the Baltimore and Ohio road, a "railroad" on which coaches had been pulled by horses. On one occasion the *Tom Thumb* raced a horse-drawn coach. The locomotive passed the horse and was on the way to victory when it broke down. The horse won!

What were the early trains like? The early railroad trains seem like quaint toys when compared with the streamlined trains of today. The engines were crude open wagons and burned wood instead

The map shows that most railroads ran east and west. Note how lines radiate from key cities: Boston, New York, Philadelphia, Chattanooga, St. Louis, Chicago.
MAP STUDY (1) Why did more railroads run east and west than north and south? (2) At what cities did several important railroads meet?

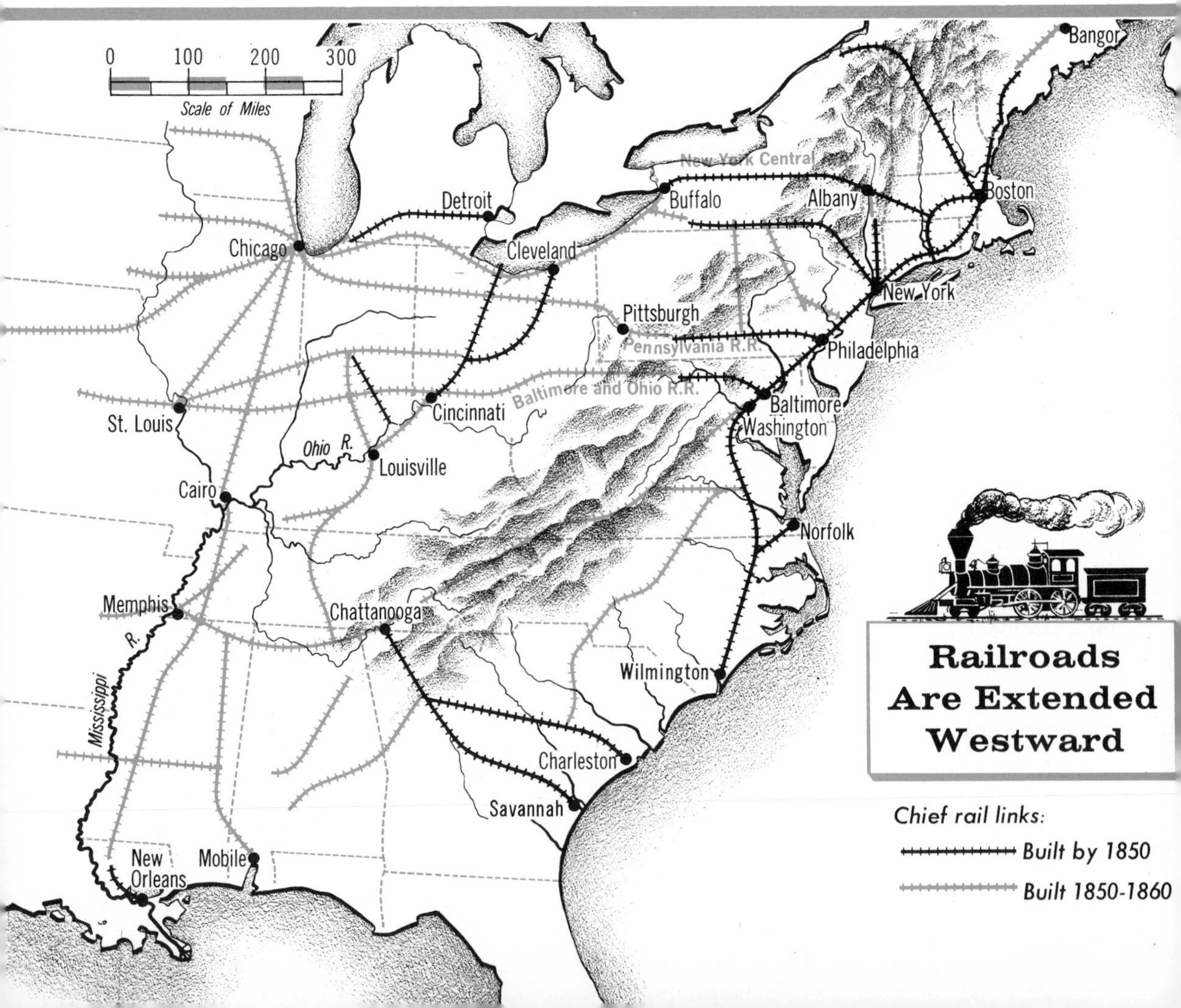

Railroads
Are Extended
Westward

Chief rail links:
+++++++++ Built by 1850
+++++++++ Built 1850-1860

THE "WEST POINT," one of the country's earliest locomotives, made its first trip in South Carolina in 1831. To celebrate the occasion, the train carried a band!

of coal. They were capable of so little speed that races between steam-driven and horse-drawn trains were fairly close. Many people refused to trust these new inventions. They not only considered them dangerous but claimed that God had not intended human beings to be carried so swiftly by mechanical means. Those who were bold enough to try the new railroads found them thoroughly uncomfortable. The earliest cars were little more than stagecoaches on rails. Poor springs and uneven roadbeds gave the riders a bad jolting. Smoke and soot blew in the faces of the passengers, and sparks burned holes in their clothing. Farmers complained that the terrific noise of the locomotives caused their hens to stop laying eggs and the cows to lose their milk!

Charles Dickens, the famous English writer, had this to say about a train ride during his visit to the United States in 1842:

✶ The train calls at stations in the woods, where the wild impossibility of anybody having the smallest reason to get out, is only to be equaled by the apparently desperate hopelessness of there being anybody to get in. It rushes across the turnpike road, where there is no gate, no policeman, no signal: nothing but a rough wooden arch, on which is painted "WHEN THE BELL RINGS, LOOK OUT FOR THE LOCOMOTIVE." On it whirls headlong, dives through the woods again, emerges in the light, clatters over frail arches, rumbles upon the heavy ground, shoots beneath a wooden bridge which intercepts the light for a second like a wink, suddenly awakens all the slumbering echoes in the main street of a large town, and dashes on haphazard, pell-mell, neck-or-nothing, down the middle of the road. There — with mechanics working at their trades, and people leaning from their doors and windows, and boys flying kites and playing marbles, and men smoking, and women talking, and children crawling, and pigs burrowing, and unaccustomed horses plunging and rearing, close to the very rails — there — on, on, on — tears the mad dragon of an engine with its train of cars; scattering in all directions a shower of burning sparks from its wood fire; screeching, hissing, yelling, panting; until at last the thirsty monster stops beneath a covered way to drink [to take on water, that is], the people cluster round, and you have time to breathe again.

Railroads in the United States grow rapidly. The early locomotives and coaches were constantly improved, and railroads spread rapidly. In 1830, there were about 30 miles of railroad track in the United States. Ten years later, there were 2800 miles; in 1850, about 9000 miles. The early railroads ran short distances, usually connecting two important cities. But three great roads, the Baltimore and Ohio, the Pennsylvania, and the New York Central, were begun in this early period. The map on page 284 shows where the railroad lines

A TYPICAL RAILROAD STATION in the mid-1800's was a center of bustling activity whenever a train steamed in to unload or take on passengers.

were built. At that time most of the lines ran east and west. For many years, there were few railroads connecting the North and the South.

Why were railroads important? Of all the new methods of transportation which developed in the United States in the early 1800's, the railroads proved to be the most important. The factories in the Northeast wanted markets for their manufactured goods. The railways made it easy for the factories to ship goods to the western farmers who needed them. In turn, the railroads carried the products of the West to the eastern markets. All this could be done more swiftly than by road or canal. The railroads also provided transportation between points where water travel was impossible.

By making it easier for people to travel and for products to be shipped back and forth, the railroads helped to bind the West and the Northeast more closely together.

These were the two great advantages of the railroad.

A NEW INVENTION REVOLUTIONIZES COMMUNICATION

A means of rapid communication is needed. Although methods of transportation had improved greatly in the early 1800's, people still had no way of send-

ing messages swiftly. To communicate with someone at a distance, it was necessary to travel to see the person or to send him a letter. As settlers moved farther westward, it became even more important to be able to communicate easily and quickly with people at great distances. Then, too, the railroads needed some way of sending messages rapidly. Early railroads had only a single track. It was very difficult to control train traffic when messages could not be sent ahead of the trains from station to station.

Morse invents the telegraph. Samuel F. B. Morse discovered a way to fill this need. Like Robert Fulton, Morse was a successful artist who also had a keen interest in science. He was particularly interested in electricity. Morse believed that he could send messages through a wire by the power of electricity. He began a series of experiments to prove his idea.

By 1837 Morse was greatly encouraged. He had succeeded in inventing the instrument which is called the *telegraph*. This instrument could send sounds through 1700 feet of copper wire. To make use of the sounds, Morse invented the *Morse Code,* a system of dots and dashes representing the letters of the alphabet. But in order to prove that his invention was really useful, he had to raise money enough to

286

The invention by Morse was the first of those that have made communication nearly instantaneous.

build a longer telegraph line. Morse and his friends tried vainly for years to interest members of Congress in the plan. Often he was so poor that he had hardly enough money to support his family; often he went hungry himself. At length, when Morse was almost heartbroken with disappointment, Congress voted money for his project. A telegraph line was built from Washington to Baltimore, a distance of about 40 miles.

MORSE'S FIRST TELEGRAPH

The telegraph is successful. In May, 1844, Morse in Washington prepared to send a message over the telegraph to friends in Baltimore. "What hath God wrought!" he tapped out on the telegraph key. The message was received clearly at the other end of the line and sent back to him correctly. The telegraph was a success.

The need for the telegraph had been so great that lines were rapidly built. They soon connected all the larger cities along the east coast. The telegraph made it possible to put out newspapers containing the day's news from all over the nation. Private and business messages could be

sent speedily; railroads were greatly aided in dispatching their trains. Morse's telegraph had done much to bring people closer together.

CHECK UP

1. (a) What was the National Road? (b) Why was it important? (c) What were turnpikes?

2. (a) Why were many canals built? (b) Why was the Erie Canal important?

3. (a) How was the first successful steamboat developed? (b) Why were steamboats important? (c) What were early trains like? (d) Why were railroads important?

4. (a) How was the telegraph developed? (b) Why was it important?

For more information on how the telegraph affected newspapers, see page 336.

Check Up on Chapter 14

Do You Know the Meaning?

1. factory	8. spinning jenny
2. textile	9. power loom
3. toll	10. telegraph
4. communication	11. labor union
5. tariff	12. packet ship
6. invention	13. clipper ship
7. manufacture	14. turnpike

Can You Identify?

1. Erie Canal	4. Cumberland Road
2. 1807	5. Edmund Cartwright
3. 1816	6. Richard Arkwright

Can You Identify? (Cont.)

7. 1825	14. James Hargreaves
8. 1830	15. Donald McKay
9. 1844	16. Samuel Slater
10. Robert Gray	17. Francis Lowell
11. Northeast	18. Robert Fulton
12. Morse Code	19. Samuel F. B. Morse
13. Elias Howe	20. Industrial Revolution

Can You Locate?

1. Vandalia	3. Cumberland, Md.
2. Albany	4. Baltimore

Can You Locate? (Cont.)

5. Buffalo   7. New York City
6. Lake Erie   8. Hudson River

What Do You Think?

1. How have working conditions improved since the days of the early factories?
2. (a) Skilled workmen often opposed the use of new machines to produce goods. Why? (b) How do you feel about this problem?

What Do You Think? (Cont.)

3. How did the Erie Canal make New York City the greatest port on the Atlantic seaboard?
4. What effect do you think the building of the early railroads had on New Orleans? Why?
5. The wars between Britain and France speeded the industrial development of both Britain and the United States. Why?

LINKING PAST AND PRESENT

Carrying the mail. Today it costs only a few cents to mail a one-ounce letter which will be delivered in a short time anywhere in the United States. For a few cents more the letter will go even faster by air mail or special delivery. In colonial days, mail service was much more uncertain. Important letters were sent by post-riders on horseback, who had a regular route from one city to another. For ordinary mail, people would ask someone going in the right direction to carry a letter. It would be passed along in this way until it reached the person to whom it was addressed. During the Revolution, the Continental Congress established a post office department, and Benjamin Franklin was appointed its head. Later, under the Constitution, Congress made use of its power "to establish post offices and post roads" (page A8) and set up the Post Office Department, which has continued ever since.

The postal service grew slowly. In the early 1800's, each adult sent an average of only one letter a year. You can understand why when you realize that it cost 25 cents for each quarter-ounce to send a letter from Maine to Georgia, and it took 20 days to

The first United States postage stamps were issued in 1847.

get there! As railroads spread across the country, mail service improved. The first regular air mail service began in 1918 when United States Army pilots began to fly mail between New York, Philadelphia, and Washington, D.C. Today the mail is carried by rapid trains and by planes which cross the country in a few hours.

Slater's Mill. Samuel Slater's first textile mill was destroyed by a flood in 1807, but his second mill, built in 1793, can still be seen in Pawtucket, Rhode Island. A museum has been set up in the old mill as a memorial to Slater. Some original pieces of the machinery that he built from memory are on display, and you can see exhibits that tell Slater's story and show how cloth was made in the past. For example, a woman in the costume of the 1700's shows how spinning and weaving were done by hand before power-driven machines were invented. You can also watch flax plants being broken down into long fibers and spun into linen yarn. The sights at the old Slater Mill remind us how the American textile industry has developed from the machines of the past.

Recall what was said in Chapter 5 about differences in geographical conditions.

Cotton Becomes King

in the South

What this chapter is about —

Many of you who read this book live in large cities. That fact has much to do with the way you live. It affects the type of house you live in, the kind of school you attend, and the way in which you spend your free time. Others of you live in farm communities. Your way of life will differ somewhat from that of city dwellers. Some of you have lived in more than one community or section of the country. You know that ways of living are not the same all over the United States.

In the mid-1800's, differences in ways of living in different sections of the country were much more marked than they are today. The Northeast, as we saw in Chapter 14, had become a manufacturing, ship-

ping, and trading center. The South continued, as it had in colonial times, to be a great farming region. By 1860, however, cotton had outdistanced all other farm products and become the South's chief crop.

This chapter tells how "cotton became king." We shall learn how cotton growing changed ways of living in the South and made slavery seem so important. We shall answer the following questions:

▶ 1. How did the cotton gin make cotton the leading crop in the South?

▶ 2. How did the people of the South live in the years before 1860?

▶ 3. How did differing ways of living tend to divide the North and South?

People in our story — slaves, plantation owner and wife, small farmer and wife.

Compare dress and occupations in the South, the Northeast (page 264), and on the frontier (page 304).

1 How Did the Cotton Gin Make Cotton the Leading Crop in the South?

From the days of the first settlers, the South had been a farming region. By the year 1790, it had changed very little since colonial times. Slaves still did the work on the large plantations and in the homes. Large crops of indigo, tobacco, and rice were still being grown and exported. Although some cotton was grown, it was not as profitable as the other crops. The cotton bolls (pods) contained seeds and fibers which were hard to separate. Until the seeds were taken out, the cotton fiber could not be used for making cloth. The seeds had to be picked out by hand; it took a man a whole day to clean enough cotton fiber to weigh a pound.

Eli Whitney invents the cotton gin. Plantation owners had long wanted a machine to clean cotton faster and more easily than it could be done by hand. A man named Eli Whitney invented a machine to do this job. Even as a lad, Whitney had had a keen interest in mechanical things. He is said to have taken his father's watch apart and put it together again so cleverly that he was not discovered. After being graduated from Yale College, young Whitney decided to become a teacher. He soon received an offer to teach

in a Carolina school. What happened thereafter is best told by Whitney himself in a letter to his father:

✳ I went from New York with the family of the late Major General Greene to Georgia. I went immediately with the family to their Plantation about twelve miles from Savannah with an expectation of spending four or five days and then proceeding into Carolina to take the school as I have mentioned in former letters. During this time I heard much said of the extreme difficulty of ginning Cotton, that is, separating it from its seeds. There were a number of very respectable gentlemen at Mrs. Greene's who all agreed that if a machine could be invented which would clean cotton [rapidly], it would be a great thing both to the country and to the inventor. I . . . happened to be thinking on the subject and struck out a plan of a Machine in my mind. . . . In about ten days I made a little model, for which I was offered, if I would give up all right and title to it, a hundred guineas [about $500]. I concluded to [give up] my school and turn my attention to perfecting the Machine. I made one before I came away which required the labor of one man to turn it and with which one man will clean ten times as much cotton as he can in any other way before known and

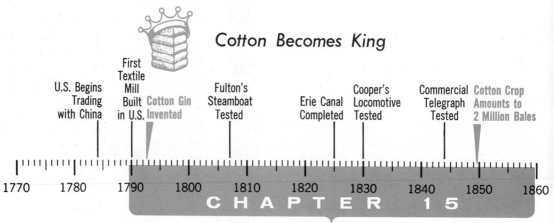

Cotton Becomes King

| U.S. Begins Trading with China | First Textile Mill Built in U.S. | Cotton Gin Invented | Fulton's Steamboat Tested | Erie Canal Completed | Cooper's Locomotive Tested | Commercial Telegraph Tested | Cotton Crop Amounts to 2 Million Bales |

1770　1780　1790　1800　1810　1820　1830　1840　1850　1860

C H A P T E R　1 5

1790 - 1860

ELI WHITNEY

A poor farm boy in New England, he set up his own forge and sold homemade nails to neighbors.

Oral reports will bring out Whitney's contributions to Southern agriculture and Northern industry. See suggestions for preparing reports, page 342.

COLLEGE became Whitney's goal. It took him five years to earn enough money to enter Yale, where he was fascinated by the scientific instruments in the college museum. After graduation, he found a new field for his mechanical skill while visiting a Georgia plantation.

A MACHINE to clean cotton was greatly needed, according to his southern friends. Whitney set to work and soon could show them a successful model. To meet the demand for his cotton gin, Whitney went into the manufacturing business.

A CONTRACT to make 10,000 muskets for the army was a challenge to Whitney. He discarded the old, slow method in which each gun was handmade with no two alike. Instead, he set up a factory where each worker turned out standardized parts which followed a single design.

MASS PRODUCTION was proved a success when Whitney showed President Jefferson that he could quickly assemble a gun by using interchangeable parts at random.

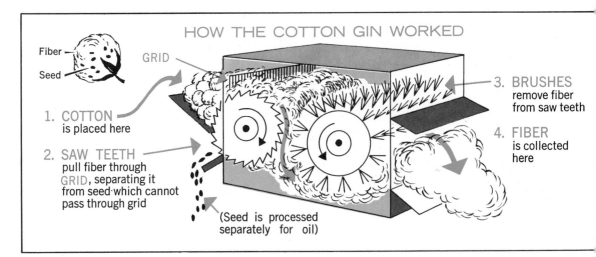

HOW THE COTTON GIN WORKED

Fiber
Seed

GRID

1. COTTON
is placed here

2. SAW TEETH
pull fiber through
GRID, separating it
from seed which cannot
pass through grid

(Seed is processed
separately for oil)

3. BRUSHES
remove fiber
from saw teeth

4. FIBER
is collected
here

also cleanse it much better than in the usual mode. This machine may be turned by water or with a horse, with the greatest of ease, and one man and a horse will do more than fifty men with the old machines. It makes the labor fifty times less, without throwing any class of People out of business.

Whitney made his first *cotton gin* in 1793. His invention, however, brought him little money and a great deal of trouble. In order to have the sole right to build and sell his invention, an inventor must obtain a *patent* from the government. Whitney took out a patent on his cotton gin, but because the idea of the invention was simple, others copied it and built cotton gins from which he received no profit. It took Whitney several years to prove that he alone had the right to build and sell cotton gins.

The South grows more cotton. Although Whitney himself gained little profit from the cotton gin, his invention was a history-making event in the South. As we have learned in Chapter 14, new machines for spinning thread and weaving cloth were being used in the Northeast and in England. More and more cotton was needed to keep these machines busy. With the cotton gin to clean cotton, the South could grow and sell much more cotton than ever before.

Southerners quickly realized that Eli Whitney's invention gave them a chance to become wealthy. Farmers and plantation owners turned from the crops they had been producing and planted cotton instead. They also enlarged their farms and plantations so as to raise more cotton. But the soil in parts of the Old South [1] (particularly in Maryland, Virginia, and North Carolina) proved rather unsatisfactory for cotton growing. The best soil for cotton was in South Carolina and Georgia. Even the good cotton lands were often spoiled because the planter was too eager to make quick profits. Growing cotton on the same land year after year wears out the soil. Instead of trying to keep the soil in good condition by changing crops or using fertilizer, however, many cotton growers preferred to raise as much cotton as possible and then move on to new lands.

Southerners seek better land for cotton. To the southwest of the older settled South lay vast stretches of unsettled, fertile lands covered with dense forests. The many rivers which flowed through this fertile region could be used to float cargoes of cotton to the towns on the Gulf of Mexico.

[1] By the *Old South* we mean the original southern colonies which were among the first thirteen states: Maryland, Virginia, North and South Carolina, and Georgia.

See the Constitution, Article I, Section 8.

From these towns the cotton could be shipped to Europe.

During the fifty years following the invention of the cotton gin, great numbers of people pushed south and west into these unsettled lands. Some of the men who moved into the wilderness were planters from Virginia and the Carolinas, who took their families and their slaves with them. Others came from the foothills and backwoods. The latter were people who owned no slaves and had little wealth but hoped by hard work to become owners of rich plantations.

The newcomers drove away the Indians and staked out farms. They cleared the dense underbrush and timber from the land. Often settlers were so eager to start planting cotton that they did not cut down the taller trees. Instead, the planters left these trees standing but killed them by "girdling" them, that is, by removing a ring of bark near the ground. To fill the need for workers, hundreds of slaves were sold to these new cotton planters of the "lower South" by the plantation owners in Virginia and the Carolinas.[1] In time, stately homes and broad fields of growing cotton appeared where earlier there had been only endless stretches of dark and silent forest. Some of the more adventurous people even took up lands in the region of Texas far beyond the Mississippi.

Cotton is King. By the 1840's, a wide belt of land extending southwest from the Carolinas had been settled. Its most important product, in fact the leading product of the entire South, was cotton. To be

[1] Congress had passed a law in 1808 that no more slaves could be brought into the United States. But by that time the births among slaves kept the number increasing. There was no law to forbid buying and selling slaves within the United States, although all the northern states had abolished slavery within their borders.

Though the slave trade was outlawed, African Negroes were "smuggled in."

sure, large quantities of tobacco were still grown in the older states of Virginia and the Carolinas. Sizable crops of rice were also raised in South Carolina and Georgia, and sugar cane grew in abundance in Louisiana. But cotton outranked all other southern products. In 1790, just before Whitney's invention of the cotton gin, the United States had produced about 4000 bales of cotton, each bale weighing 500 pounds. By 1850, the output of cotton had climbed to over two million bales! Most of it was grown in the newly settled lands of the South, which became known as the *Cotton Kingdom*.

Slowly but surely the lower South grew in importance. Its population increased faster than that of the older southern states. Louisiana (1812), Mississippi (1817), and Alabama (1819) became states of the Union. Mobile and New Orleans, ports of the lower South, became more important centers of trade than Charleston and Savannah. Because there were few factories or mines or centers of industry in the South, most Southerners thought their prosperity depended on the raising of cotton. That is why they used to say, "Cotton is King."

MAP STUDY (1) What states formed the Old South? (2) The Cotton Kingdom?

CHECK UP

1. (a) Why did the South grow much more cotton after the invention of the cotton gin? (b) What changes in ways of living came about as a result?

2. (a) Why did the cotton planters need more land? (b) Where did they find it? (c) What three cotton states had been added to the Union by 1819?

3. What was meant by the expression "Cotton is King"?

These statistics should help to destroy the stereotype that all of the antebellum South was plantation country and that all Southerners owned slaves.

How Did the People of the South Live in the Years Before 1860?

Plantation owners were the leaders of the South. As the South devoted itself more and more to the raising of cotton, a small group of planters became very rich and powerful. Cotton could be grown most profitably on large plantations worked by slaves. (This system of growing one crop on large tracts of land with slave labor is called the *plantation system.*) But slaves cost money. In the 1850's a good field hand — a slave who worked in the fields — was worth as much as $1200 to $2000. By 1860, only about one white family out of four in the South owned slaves. In fact, out of a white population of 5,500,000, fewer than 10,000 men owned 50 or more slaves. These owners of many slaves and large plantations made the greatest profits and controlled most of the wealth of the South. The plantation families were the leaders of their neighborhoods and of the South as a whole. Plantation owners also became important spokesmen for the South in the halls of Congress.

How were the plantations managed? All cotton plantations were managed in much the same way. At the end of the short southern winter the land was plowed. Soon the cotton was planted. Through the long summer the plants had to be carefully tended day by day, to keep out weeds and to prevent damage by insects. In early autumn the cotton was ready to pick. Then into the fields would go the pickers, each with a long bag slung over his shoulder. Bending low in back-breaking labor, the men, women, and children would pluck the cotton from the plants and push it into the bags. Prizes were often given to the fastest pickers.

A typical plantation covered hundreds of acres and required the work of fifty to a hundred slaves. Each morning the field hands gathered at a central place. The master directed them where to go and what to do that day. Often the master hired a man called an *overseer* to take charge of this work on the plantation for him. When the orders were given, the slaves scattered to their places of work. All day long, through the seasons of plowing and planting and harvest, the slaves labored in the fields under the eye of the master or the overseer.

When at last the cotton was picked, it

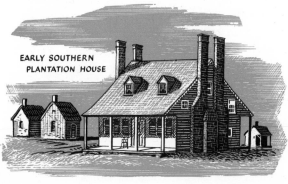

EARLY SOUTHERN PLANTATION HOUSE

The "spokesmen" for any section are likely to be representative of the most important group in the section at that time—merchants, or industrialists, or ranchers, or mine owners.

NEW ORLEANS became a leading port for the Cotton Kingdom. Here river steamers unload cotton bales to be reshipped to textile mills in New England and Great Britain.

was taken to the cotton gin. The larger plantations had their own cotton gins, worked in the early days by horses or water power, and later by steam. The gins removed the seeds from the tough fiber. The clean cotton then was packed into big bales, almost as tall as a man and two or three feet wide. If the plantation was located on a river, the bales were piled on a wharf ready to be loaded on steamboats. From other plantations the bales were hauled in wagons to the river bank.

The bales were shipped down the rivers to the ports, such as Mobile in Alabama and New Orleans in Louisiana. From there they were shipped to the factories of the Northeast or of England. The machines in these factories, as we have learned, made the cotton into yarn and the yarn into cloth.

What was the life of the plantation family? The plantation owner and his family usually lived in a large, comfortable house surrounded by spreading trees and graveled walks. Many of these houses had tall porches with roofs supported by huge white pillars. The porches not only shaded the houses from the intense summer sun but also gave them a grand appearance. Inside the houses were spacious halls and large rooms with high ceilings and tall windows. On the walls one usually could see oil portraits of the family's ancestors. (See the picture on page 299 of a plantation house dating from this period.)

The owner or master supervised the affairs of the plantation. He taught and directed his slaves in their work and gave instructions to his overseer if he employed one. The master's wife not only directed the house servants and managed the affairs of the home but looked after the health and welfare of the slaves. Sons of the owner took little part in running the plantation until they had finished college. Daughters learned from their mothers how to supervise the work of the house-

See *In Calico and Crinoline: Women, 1608-1865.*

295

True Stories of American

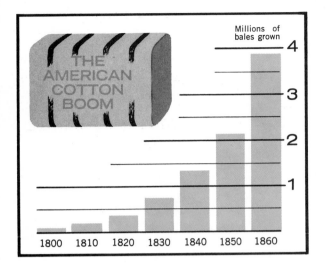

THE AMERICAN COTTON BOOM

Millions of bales grown

1800 1810 1820 1830 1840 1850 1860

hold. Much of the young people's time, however, was spent at neighborhood parties and in riding, hunting, and visiting.

How did the slaves live? All the hard work on the plantation was done by the slaves. The field hands worked from early in the morning until nightfall. The more fortunate of the slaves were house servants. On a large plantation each member of the family had his own slave as a personal servant. A few slaves worked as carpenters and blacksmiths or took care of the horses. The great majority of the Negro men, women, and children, however, were field hands. The slaves naturally were not willing workers, and they showed this in various ways. Most slaves simply did not work any harder than they

had to. Many slaves tried to escape. Occasionally slaves would rise in rebellion and use violence against their masters.

The slave quarters were located not far from the master's house. They usually consisted of a group of crude log cabins, chinked with mud. Many cabins contained only a single room, often without windows. At one end was a big fireplace which furnished heat in cold or rainy weather, and over which the family's food was cooked. The furniture was rough and there was little of it. The slave's food was simple. It consisted largely of pork, corn meal, and molasses, provided each week by the master, and perhaps some vegetables grown by the slave in his own garden plot. A few pieces of cheap clothing made on the plantation were expected to last the slaves a whole year.

Slaves were owned by their master, of course, and were completely under his control. Yet life in the slave quarters on many a plantation was not always unhappy. During the day the small children played merrily, often with the younger white children from the "great house." On special occasions the slaves were allowed to attend picnics or to hunt 'coon and 'possum. Of course there were some harsh masters who treated slaves cruelly, whipping them if they misbehaved or ran away.

SLAVE DWELLINGS

The first steam vessel to cross the Atlantic Ocean was the "Savannah" (above), which made the voyage from Savannah, Georgia, to England in 1819. America's first nuclear-powered merchant ship (above right), which was tested at sea in 1962, was also given the name of "Savannah" after the pioneer steamship. The first "Savannah" was a 98-foot wooden ship whose steam engine drove it at a top speed of about six miles an hour. Its nuclear namesake, almost 600 feet long, can travel at about thirty miles an hour.

In general, however, slaves were too valuable to be mistreated. The greatest fear of the slave was that he and his family would be sold. When this happened, the members of the family often were separated and might never see each other again.

The small farmers are the largest group in the South. Since only a small number of southern families lived on plantations, you are probably wondering how the rest made their living. In the cities and towns there were doctors, lawyers, tradesmen, and skilled workers. The great majority of southern whites, however, owned and worked small farms. These farms were located in the less fertile areas of the South, often on land which was being cleared or which had been abandoned by the big planters. Even so, about half the cotton crop was grown by farmers with little land.

In contrast to the plantation owners, the small farmers had to work with their own hands for a living. Their homes were humble. Some of them owned a slave or two, but on most small farms the work was done by the members of the family. Besides cotton, they raised food crops, especially corn. The year's crop of cotton on each farm amounted to only a few bales. But if the small farmers worked hard and were fortunate enough to have good crops for a season or two, they might make enough money to buy more land. They hoped that someday they too might own broad cotton fields and numerous slaves.

The mountain whites live like frontiersmen. One group of southern whites who lived apart from the rest of the people were the mountain whites. They were descendants of sturdy pioneers who had pushed their way through the wilderness to the slopes of the Appalachian Mountains. Like their fathers and grandfathers, they continued to live the simple life of the frontiersman. Much of their time was spent in fishing in the mountain streams or hunting for wild game.

All members of a slave family were the property **297** of the master. He had the same legal right to sell a slave as a horse.

Though they were poor and though many of them could not read or write, the mountain whites were a proud and independent people. They wished to be left alone to live as their fathers had. They seldom saw other people except on occasional trips to the lowlands, where they sold whiskey made from corn grown in their small garden patches. Otherwise, the mountain whites were out of touch with the outside world. For this reason, they had little interest in slavery or in the aims of the great planters.

CHECK UP

1. (a) What was the plantation system? (b) Why were the plantation owners the leaders in the South? (c) How did the plantation slaves live?

2. (a) How did the small farmers of the South live? (b) The mountain whites?

In the Northeastern states at the time of the Revolutionary War, many household servants and other workers were slaves.

3 How Did Differing Ways of Living Tend to Divide the North and South?

When the United States became independent near the end of the 1700's, there were some differences between the North and the South. These differences, however, were not very great. In both the North and South most people made their living by farming. There were few cities, and almost as many of these were to be found in the South as in the North. Not much manufacturing was carried on in either North or South.

Different ways of living and thinking develop in the North and the South. As the years rolled by, the differences between the North and the South became steadily greater. In the North, as we have learned, more and more attention was paid to manufacturing, to trade, and to business. More cities grew up in the North. Most of the nation's railroads were built there, too. But the South, as we have just seen, continued to be a land of farms and plantations. Cotton became King, and the growing and selling of cotton was the most important way of making a living in the South.

People whose lives are quite different are apt to think differently — to see things in different ways. If a tariff law was to be passed, for instance, a Northerner might say: "This tariff will keep out foreign goods and help me sell mine at a higher price." But a Southerner might say: "This tariff won't help me get better prices for my cotton and other crops I sell. It will, however, raise the price of tools, clothes, and other things I buy from England."

The northern states free their slaves. Another difference between the North and the South was their thinking about slavery. When slaves were first brought to the colonies, they had been used in the North as well as in the South. As time went on, it was found that slaves were more useful in farm work than in factories. But most farms in the North, unlike the plantations of the South, were too small to make good use of large groups of slaves.

Because slavery was not suited to the North, it was easy to give it up. One by one, in the years after the Revolutionary War, the northern states freed their slaves.

(Continued on page 301)

THE *Cotton Kingdom*

In the 1820's the painter and naturalist John James Audubon traveled down the Mississippi River, sketching the birds found along its banks. Audubon settled in New Orleans to complete his great series of illustrations, *The Birds of America* (see his water color of a falcon, left). Meanwhile, more and more of the wilderness which Audubon studied was being cleared for rice, sugar, and cotton plantations. Their owners built splendid houses, such as Oaklawn Manor (below) at Franklin, Louisiana. Its white columns gave the house the stately look of a Greek temple and also provided shady porches which were popular in the warm South. Plantation life became famous for its lawn parties and dances where the ladies appeared in the latest imported fashions (above).

A painting (left) done in 1847 shows the landing at Wetumpka, Alabama, one of the many upriver towns where cotton was loaded onto steamboats.

Gulf seaports like Mobile and New Orleans thrived on the cotton trade. At home, the well-to-do merchants of New Orleans looked down on the busy streets from their second-story balconies (right), sheltered by ornamental ironwork. Seen from the balcony at left is the Cabildo (the government headquarters under Spanish rule) and next to it, the Cathedral of St. Louis. To provide the fastest service to New Orleans, riverboats took short cuts through the Mississippi bayous (below), lighting their way at night with iron baskets of blazing pinewood on either side of the bow.

These Negroes were known as *freedmen.* By the early part of the 1800's, slavery had disappeared from all the states north of Maryland. (In colonial times the boundary between Pennsylvania and Maryland had been surveyed by two men named Mason and Dixon. This line, called *Mason and Dixon's Line,* came to be the boundary between slave and free states.)

In the 1700's some Southerners question slavery. In colonial times and for some time after, many Southerners did not favor slavery, even though they used slave labor. Slaves were expensive to own. They had to be taken care of, even in years when crops were small or sold for low prices. Some Southerners also questioned whether it was right to own slaves. George Washington hoped the day would come when slavery would cease. He made arrangements to have his own slaves freed at his death. Men like Patrick Henry and Thomas Jefferson had doubts about slavery because it did not agree with the ideas of freedom expressed in the Declaration of Independence. Jefferson, in fact, proposed a scheme for freeing Negroes and sending them back to Africa.

If slavery was wrong or not always profitable, why was it not given up in the South? For one thing, freeing slaves would have been very costly to their owners. Not only had large sums been paid out for slaves but a great deal had been spent in caring for them year after year. To set the slaves free, their owners thought, would be giving up property that was very valuable. And what would happen to the Negroes once they were freed? All their lives they had been fed and clothed. They had little education or training to help them earn a living. Freedom would raise many problems for them as well as for the white people.

The cotton gin establishes slavery firmly in the South. Eli Whitney's invention of the cotton gin in 1793 did much to discourage the thought of ending slavery in the South. Cotton raising became profitable, and most Southerners believed that large quantities of cotton could not be grown without the work of Negro slaves. As more and more land was given over to cotton, the demand for slaves increased. By 1840, there were many more slaves in the South than before the invention of the cotton gin. Yet the price of the average slave had more than doubled. In short, the more important the cotton crops and plantations became to Southerners, the more important slavery became to them also. No longer did Southerners talk about slavery as an evil which in time might disappear.

Southerners defend slavery. Many people in the South were upset by the words and acts of certain Northerners who criticized slavery. These Northerners believed it was wrong for any person to own another human being. The most outspoken of them wanted slavery *abolished,* or ended, at once. In later chapters we shall learn more about these people, who were called *abolitionists.*

The more slavery was attacked by the abolitionists, the more vigorously Southerners defended it. Southerners especially resented criticisms from people of a different part of the country. It was one thing for a Southerner to express doubts about slavery; it was quite another thing to have someone else say that slavery was wrong.

Leading men of the South wrote books and made speeches claiming that slavery was a good thing. They declared that the Bible mentioned slavery and that it was perfectly natural for one man to own another. John C. Calhoun, one of the greatest statesmen of the South, announced that "there has never yet existed a wealthy and civilized society in which one portion of the community did not in

These paragraphs point out that in the 1700's the South had reasons for wishing to abolish slavery, but reasons also for not acting vigorously to achieve emancipation.

fact live on the labor of the other." Southern churches had once doubted whether slavery ought to continue. As cotton became even more important, however, and as abolitionists criticized the South, southern churches began to defend slavery. Some church organizations which had members both in the North and the South broke into separate branches.

Some Southerners argued that slavery was a benefit to the Negro. Was he not better off on a well-run plantation than as a savage in the jungles of Africa? And was he not happier than many of the white workers in the northern factories? When there was no work, the northern factories closed down. Workers were out of a job and had no wages to support their families. "At least," said the Southerner, "the average slave is fed and clothed. Some attention is given to his health. And he has no worries about losing his job."

How far apart would the North and South grow? The North and South, then, developed different ways of living. In the North there were more and more factories, trade increased, cities grew in number and in size. Men and women who came from Europe to make new homes in America preferred to settle in the North where they did not have to compete with slave labor. In the South, Cotton was King. Southerners and their slaves were too busy raising their crops to build and work in factories. Southern planters used their money to buy tools and more land and more slaves. Cotton became the chief export of the United States.

It was not that one section was better than the other; the point was that they were different. Honest and intelligent men in the North might prefer business to farming and believe slavery to be wrong. Equally honest and intelligent men in the South might prefer managing cotton plantations to managing factories and believe that the slave system was right. They argued that slaves were better off than northern factory workers who had to work under unhealthy conditions and for very low wages. But Northerners could answer that factory workers were free to leave their jobs if they so chose.

As time went on, however, the differences between the two sections became greater and greater. And as the North and South grew farther apart, the argument over slavery became steadily more dangerous and threatening. One Southerner burst out that "rather than yield our dearest rights and privileges" — meaning slavery — "we should see the Union scattered to the winds." Would it come to this? Would the cotton-growing South and the bustling industrialized North become so different that they could no longer remain parts of the same country?

CHECK UP

1. Why did slavery disappear in the North?

2. (a) How did Southerners feel about slavery before 1793? Why? (b) After 1793? Why?

3. (a) On what grounds did abolitionists object to slavery? (b) How did Southerners defend slavery?

Check Up on Chapter 15

Do You Know the Meaning?

1. field hands
2. overseer
3. plantation system
4. cotton gin

Do You Know the Meaning? (Cont.)

5. patent
6. freedman
7. abolitionist
8. mountain whites

The fact that the South did not get its share of these immigrants helps to explain why the economy of the South developed more slowly and became less diversified than that of the North.

Can You Identify?

1. Eli Whitney 3. lower South
2. 1793 4. Mason and Dixon's Line

Can You Locate?

1. Louisiana 3. Alabama
2. Mobile 4. Mississippi

What Do You Think?

1. Why was slavery not especially profitable before the invention of the cotton gin?
2. Why did the plantation owners buy more slaves instead of hiring free workers?
3. If slavery had been profitable in the North, do you think it would have been continued? Explain your answer.
4. Some historians have argued that dependence on cotton planting and on slave labor hurt the South and slowed its development. What do you think?
5. Between 1789 and 1850 the North and South grew farther and farther apart. Why? Give as many reasons as you can.

These questions should be discussed thoroughly.

LINKING PAST AND PRESENT

Cotton today. Cotton growing is no longer the chief occupation in the South, although it is still an important crop. Besides cotton, rice, sugar, and tobacco, which have long been grown in the South, farmers now also grow a large variety of fruits and vegetables and raise cattle as well. Industries such as mining, lumbering, textile manufacturing, and steelmaking have made the South an important industrial region. For many years, cotton growing has been moving westward into Arkansas, Texas, Arizona, and California. Texas alone produced over four million bales of cotton in a recent year — the largest crop of any state, while Mississippi was the only one of the old cotton-growing states to produce a million bales.

Mountain people today. The people who moved into the valleys and slopes of Kentucky and Tennessee were, as we know, a proud and independent people. And so are their descendants today. Although some of these mountain people are beginning to move into towns and cities, many of them still prefer to live simple, rugged lives in the hills, far from the centers of population. The ancestors of many of the mountain people came to America from England and Scotland soon after the time of Queen Elizabeth I and of Shakespeare, the great English poet and writer of plays. Because they have lived apart, their speech today has some resemblance to that spoken in England when Elizabeth was queen. And their favorite songs, handed down from one generation to another, were sung by the people of Shakespeare's England. No other group in our country is so closely linked to England's past as the mountain people of Kentucky and Tennessee.

A mechanical cotton picker. As you have read, the invention of the cotton gin in 1793 had important results in the development of the South. The cotton gin, by greatly speeding up the process of separating the seed from the fiber, brought about a tremendous increase in cotton growing. In more recent years, another new machine has speeded cotton harvesting. This is the mechanical cotton picker. Picking cotton by hand is a slow, exhausting, back-straining job. A person who can pick a bale of cotton in a week is rated as a "good picker," but mechanical pickers can now pick 20 or more bales in a day, thus reducing both hard labor and expenses.

Democracy Marches Westward

with the Frontier

Find out what your students know about each of the persons pictured in the cast of characters, and sources of their information.

What this chapter is about —

Come my tan-faced children,
Follow well in order, get your weapons
  ready,
Have you your pistols? have you your
  sharp-edged axes?
Pioneers! O pioneers!

All the past we leave behind, . . .
Fresh and strong the world we seize, world
  of labor and the march,
Pioneers! O pioneers!

We detachments steady throwing,
Down the edges, through the passes, up
  the mountains steep,

Conquering, holding, daring, venturing
  as we go the unknown ways,
Pioneers! O pioneers!

These verses by an American poet, Walt Whitman, pay tribute to the men and women who braved hardship and danger to plant homes deep in the western wilderness. The westward march of American pioneers is one of the most stirring chapters in the history of our country. Many Americans set out from safe and settled communities in covered wagons (see picture above) to start a new life in the West. These people left us a

People in our story — backwoodsman, Indian scout, surveyor, land company agent, pioneer family.

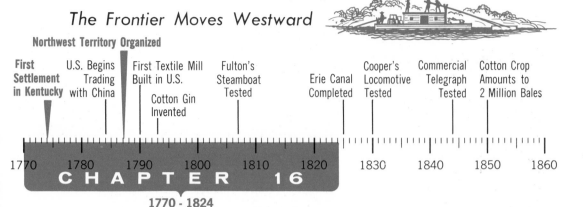

The Frontier Moves Westward

Northwest Territory Organized

First Settlement in Kentucky | U.S. Begins Trading with China | First Textile Mill Built in U.S. | Cotton Gin Invented | Fulton's Steamboat Tested | Erie Canal Completed | Cooper's Locomotive Tested | Commercial Telegraph Tested | Cotton Crop Amounts to 2 Million Bales

1770   1780   1790   1800   1810   1820   1830   1840   1850   1860

CHAPTER 16

1770 - 1824

valuable heritage. By their courage and labor they changed vast stretches of unbroken wilderness into fruitful farm lands and thriving communities. In so doing, they also added to the nation's wealth and power. Furthermore, in the new frontier settlements that grew up, Americans developed a more democratic way of living than existed in other parts of the country at that time.

We learned in Chapter 5 about the early pioneers and their life in the new settlements west of the Atlantic seaboard.

In this chapter we shall see how pioneers pushed still farther westward and filled in the regions beyond the Appalachian Mountains. Let us keep in mind the following questions:

▶ 1. How did the westward march of pioneers begin?

▶ 2. What plan was worked out for governing new territories?

▶ 3. How did the West grow in the first half century of the new republic?

▶ 4. How did conditions in the West encourage a democratic way of life?

Bring out means of transportation available to people moving westward before about 1820 and afterwards.

1 How Did the Westward March of Pioneers Begin?

What was the West? Before beginning our story of the westward movement, we need to understand clearly what is meant by "the West." Today, as you know, Americans use different terms to describe the West. For example, we speak of the Far West (the Rocky Mountain region and the Pacific coast), the Southwest (Arizona, New Mexico, and Texas), or the Middle West. In 1800, however, people referred only to "the West." They

used this term to describe any frontier region or territory that lay between the well-established settlements and the untamed wilderness. As Americans moved steadily westward, the frontier moved westward also.

Different groups of pioneers push back the frontier. First to feel the call of the West was the Indian trader or "long hunter." He usually traveled alone into the wilderness, armed with his hunting

305

knife and long rifle (from which probably came the term *long hunter*). He lived in the open and killed game for food. The long hunter was as skilled as the Indians in the ways of the woods. He hunted for furs and traded trinkets with the Indians for more furs. In the spring he returned to a settlement with his pack of furs. The most famous of these men was Daniel Boone, who spent many exciting years pushing his way into wilderness regions little known to white men.

After the long hunter came the *backwoodsman*. The backwoodsman built a shelter or a rough log cabin in the wilderness. He began to cut down trees and to plant crops between the tree stumps. But he was only half a farmer. For the rest, he was a hunter, an Indian trader, and, if need be, an Indian fighter.

Sometimes this backwoodsman sold his land and moved even farther west to begin all over again. Sometimes he stayed and slowly changed his way of living. Either way, the *pioneer farmer* replaced the backwoodsman. This farmer cut down more trees. He put up fences and built a better house and a barn. He plowed more and more land and planted more crops. As his neighbors did the same thing, the wild animals began to disappear, and trapping and hunting died out. The farmer and his neighbors built a school and a church. A sawmill was set up to cut boards from logs; a gristmill was built to grind the farmers' grain. Soon a storekeeper started a shop nearby. Before long, a village had grown up. In a few years the region was well settled. It was no longer the true West. That term now applied to unsettled places still farther west.

The West moves with the frontier. This same process was repeated over and

over again as our country expanded. In the early 1600's, any place a few miles back from the Atlantic coast was frontier and would have been called the West. As pioneers moved inland along the rivers, the West moved also. On the eve of the Revolution, pioneers had begun to make their way through the gaps in the Appalachian Mountains. In the late 1700's, the Ohio River Valley was the West. In the early 1800's, the Mississippi River Valley became the West. Still later the West was the Pacific coast. So, you see, the term "the West" was applied to different areas at different periods of our nation's history. In this chapter you will learn how the region between the Appalachian Mountains and the Mississippi River was settled and how it grew.

Americans early begin the settlement of the Old Southwest. Even before the Revolutionary War, restless pioneers had begun to push through the Appalachian Mountains to the rich lands beyond. Most of these pioneers came from Virginia and North Carolina. They settled in what became known as the *Old Southwest*. This was the region south of the Ohio River, between the Appalachian Mountains and the Mississippi River. Look at the map on page 309. You will see that rivers like the Cumberland and the Tennessee rise in the Appalachian Mountains and flow westward and northward into the Ohio. It was chiefly along these rivers that pioneers first made their way into the fertile valleys west of the Appalachian Mountains.

Settlements are made in Tennessee and Kentucky. The earliest settlement in the Old Southwest was made in what is now eastern Tennessee. Several years before the Revolution (1769), a group of hardy pioneers crossed the mountains from

Use the map on page 309 to help students understand why the pioneers followed the routes they did in settling the Old Southwest.

DANIEL BOONE and his band of pioneers cleared the Wilderness Road. Note the buckskin clothing and the long guns of the frontiersmen in this diorama.

Bring out that the Wilderness Road was by no means an improved road.

North Carolina. They settled on the Watauga (wah-*taw'*gah) River, which flows into the Tennessee River. Soon they were joined by a young Scotch-Irishman named James Robertson, who became a leader of the Watauga settlement. In a few years there were other settlements on nearby rivers. In 1779, James Robertson led a few pioneers far into the wilds of middle Tennessee. They started a town on the Cumberland River which was called Nashville.

The first settlement to be made in what is now Kentucky was the town of Harrodsburg. In 1774, a group of settlers led by James Harrod founded this town in the Kentucky wilderness. But Daniel Boone, the famous hunter and scout, was chiefly responsible for opening the way into the bluegrass country of Kentucky. He blazed a trail through the mountains by way of

Cumberland Gap and along the Kentucky River. In 1775, he led a band of pioneers over his Wilderness Road to a site on the Kentucky River, which they named Boonesborough. A third town, founded as the Revolutionary War began, was named Lexington, in honor of the first battle of the war. By the end of the Revolution, the settlements of Harrodsburg, Boonesborough, and Lexington had all become important towns in Kentucky.

CHECK
UP

1. What three kinds of pioneers were important in settling the West?

2. (a) Where was "the West" in the early 1600's? (b) In the late 1700's? (c) In the early 1800's?

3. Where and how were early settlements made in Tennessee and Kentucky?

Make sure that students understand how the frontier changed to a settled area, and why this was a continuing process.

2 What Plan Was Worked Out for Governing New Territories?

The early westward trickle of brave pioneers grew into a steady flow after the Revolutionary War. Times were hard in the East, and adventurous Americans were attracted to the fertile lands beyond the Appalachians.

The spread of western settlements brings new problems. As the frontier settlements grew, governing them became a difficult matter. The problem first arose in the Old Southwest, much of which was claimed by Virginia and North Carolina. Long distances and poor traveling conditions made it hard for these two states to govern the regions beyond the mountain barrier. Besides, the frontier settlers showed a spirit of independence. They were not content to remain forever under the control of older eastern states but wanted to set up governments of their own.

As we learned in Chapter 11, the Articles of Confederation were not adopted until the states with western lands agreed to give up their land claims to the central government. The first land to be turned over to the national government lay north of the Ohio River, a rich region known as the Old Northwest. Thousands of people in the East wanted to settle in the Old Northwest. But they were unwilling to go until they knew how much, if anything, they would have to pay for land. Also, they wanted to know what kind of government they might have there. Congress answered these questions by passing two important laws regulating affairs in the Old Northwest.

Congress arranges for surveying lands in the Northwest. To start with, the lands of the Northwest needed to be surveyed. New settlers naturally would want to know the exact boundaries of their land, and records of the boundaries would have to be kept by the government. The system set up by Congress in the *Ordinance of 1785* is probably familiar to those of you who live in states carved out of the Old Northwest or in states west of the Mississippi. The land was divided into squares six miles across, called *townships*. Each township was divided into 36 *sections* one square mile in area. Each section contained 640 acres, which could be divided into quarter sections of 160 acres each or into even smaller plots. Section Number Sixteen of each township was to be given to the people to rent or sell to help pay for public schools. (See the diagram on page 310.) This arrangement of townships gave maps of the Old Northwest a square and regular appearance not found in maps of the East. In the older states there was no such regular pattern.

The Ordinance of 1785 also provides for the sale of land. Laying out townships was only part of the land problem in the Northwest. Should the land be sold or given free to the men who settled it? Congress needed money badly. Under the Ordinance of 1785, Congress decided that the land should be sold at auction *by sections* to the highest bidder. (A section, you remember, contained 640 acres.) The least that could be paid for the land was one dollar an acre.

Although this price seems very low today, dollars were hard to earn in those days. Few men could get together enough money to buy a section of land at $640. The result was that land companies were formed by businessmen in the East. They bought up the land in the Northwest and

Settlers Cross the Appalachians

MAP STUDY The arrows in this map show you the general routes followed by the pioneers who crossed the Appalachians to settle the West. (1) What was the dividing line between the Old Northwest and the Old Southwest? (2) What settlements shown here were in the Old Northwest? (3) In the Old Southwest?

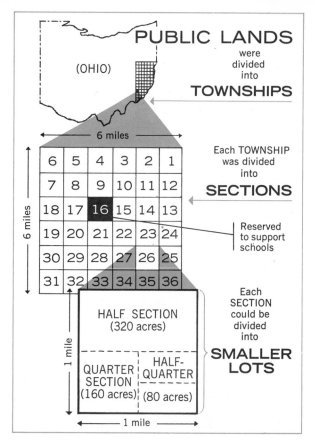

PUBLIC LANDS were divided into TOWNSHIPS

(OHIO)

6 miles

Each TOWNSHIP was divided into SECTIONS

6	5	4	3	2	1
7	8	9	10	11	12
18	17	16	15	14	13
19	20	21	22	23	24
30	29	28	27	26	25
31	32	33	34	35	36

6 miles

Reserved to support schools

Each SECTION could be divided into SMALLER LOTS

HALF SECTION (320 acres)

QUARTER SECTION (160 acres)

HALF-QUARTER (80 acres)

1 mile

1 mile

WESTERN LAND was divided in three stages as shown by this chart. At first, townships were sold a whole section at a time. The buyers resold the land in smaller plots. After 1820, a settler could buy an eighth of a section directly from the government.

offered free transportation to pioneers who would settle there. The land companies planned to divide the land into smaller lots, which could then be sold to settlers at a good profit.

The Northwest Territory is organized. An even more important step was taken by the Congress of the Confederation in 1787. In this year Congress passed a famous law called the *Northwest Ordinance*. This law set up a plan of government for the *Northwest Territory,* the new name given to the Old Northwest. (The word *territory,* as used here, means land belonging to the United States which has not yet been made into states.)

The Northwest Ordinance provided for three steps which had to be taken before the people of the territory could have complete self-government:

(1) As long as the number of settlers in the Northwest remained small, its affairs were to be managed by a governor and three judges chosen by Congress.

(2) When the number of adult free men in the territory reached 5000, they could elect an assembly. This assembly, together with an upper house or council, would make laws for the territory. The territory could also have a delegate in Congress who might suggest laws and make speeches, but who could not vote.

(3) Whenever 60,000 free inhabitants had settled in a given district, that district could take steps to become a state. The people of the district had to prepare a constitution and then request permission of Congress to enter the Union as a state. If Congress approved, the district would enter the Union as a full-fledged state "on equal footing with the original states in all respects whatsoever." It was expected that from three to five states would be carved out of the huge Northwest.

In addition, the Northwest Ordinance listed a number of rights which all people in the Northwest Territory should have. They were to have freedom of worship, freedom of speech, the right to trial by jury, and protection from unreasonable punishments. Public education for all was to be encouraged. The Northwest Ordinance also forbade slavery forever in the Northwest Territory.

The Northwest Ordinance becomes the pattern for United States territories. The Northwest Ordinance was one of the wisest laws ever passed by any government. This new law gave settlers the rights which mean so much to all Americans. It also set up a form of government which would change as the needs of the settlers changed. The law arranged a simple government for a small group of struggling pioneer settlements. Yet it promised the people who were willing to brave the dangers of the wilderness that in time they would have a government on equal terms with the older states.

The Northwest Ordinance became a model of government for other territories of the United States. As pioneers opened up new land farther west or southwest, territorial governments of the same kind were set up by Congress. The Northwest Ordinance did much to encourage the American dream of liberty and self-government.

CHECK UP

1. (a) How did the Ordinance of 1785 provide for the division of the lands of the Old Northwest? (b) How was the land to be sold? (c) Why were land companies organized?

2. (a) What three steps in the government of the Northwest Territory were provided by the Northwest Ordinance? (b) What rights were guaranteed the people living there?

3. Why was the Northwest Ordinance important?

Locate on the map, page 309, the settlements mentioned on pages 311-312. Why were they located along bodies of water?

 ## How Did the West Grow in the First Half Century of the New Republic?

Settlers throng into the Northwest Territory. After the Ordinance of 1787 had been adopted, pioneers flocked by the hundreds into the Northwest Territory, hungry for the new lands. Many of them took the old road that Braddock had cut through western Pennsylvania (page 128). They traveled by horseback or in slow wagon trains to Pittsburgh. There they built big flatboats. Whole families, with their household goods and even cattle aboard, floated down the Ohio. When they came to the place where they wanted to stop, they ran their clumsy rafts ashore.

Towns grow up in the Northwest Territory. In April, 1788, forty-seven settlers floated down the Ohio in a flatboat which they had named the *Mayflower*. They stopped where the Muskingum River joins the Ohio and founded Marietta, the first town in the Northwest Territory. (See the map on page 309.) These men had been sent out by the Ohio Land Company. One of the first things they did was to build a stockade to protect themselves from the Indians. Other settlers followed, and it was not long before a group of log cabins clustered about the stockade. Within two years Marietta was a thriving village with churches and schools and a population of a thousand.

This story was repeated in other parts of the Northwest Territory. A few months after Marietta was settled, Cincinnati was founded farther down the Ohio. By 1790, the town boasted 1300 inhabitants. Six

FRONTIER STOCKADE

FRONTIER SETTLERS had to be constantly alert for Indian raids. Here Indians attack the frontier outpost which in later years became the city of St. Louis. A few settlers (notice the plowman) have been caught outside the stockade.

years later, Moses Cleaveland started the city on Lake Erie which bears his name.[1] In 1803, United States troops built Fort Dearborn on Lake Michigan where the great city of Chicago now stands. A pioneer settlement grew up around the fort.

Indian troubles develop in the Northwest. Life was a struggle for the pioneers of the Northwest. In addition to such hardships as back-breaking labor, freezing winters, and lack of ordinary comforts, the pioneers lived in constant danger of Indian attacks. The Indians had signed treaties surrendering much of the land north of the Ohio to the white men. But the Indians did not live up to their promises, partly because they did not understand the meaning of the treaties they had signed. Furthermore, those who had not

actually signed the treaties did not feel bound to keep them. The Indians deeply resented the presence of the white men, who drove away the wild animals on which the Indians depended for food. The settlers in turn resented and feared the Indians.

Washington settles the Indian problem in the Northwest. When George Washington became President, he had to decide what to do about the Indians of the Northwest. The pioneers of the Northwest were loyal Americans, and they of course looked to the national government to help them. Washington realized that the Indians must be defeated if he wished to keep the loyalty of the Westerners. Furthermore, the Indians were defying the authority of the United States, and this could not be allowed.

The first two expeditions Washington sent against the Indians were ambushed and defeated. Finally, Washington sent General Anthony Wayne, a hero of the Revolutionary War, to subdue the un-

[1] The name of the city is now spelled Cleveland. Nobody knows for certain just how or why the first "a" was dropped out. One story is that a newspaper owner left it out to shorten the name and make it look better at the top of his paper.

This explains the origin of the term "Indian why the Indians were "Indian Givers."

Giver." Be sure, however, to bring out

defeated Indians. With well-trained troops and Indian guides, Wayne marched slowly westward into the Indian country. He met and crushed the Indian braves in northwestern Ohio. Completely beaten, the Indians agreed to leave the settlers alone. They also signed new treaties giving up more land north of the Ohio River. Wayne's expedition settled the Indian problem in the Northwest for some years to come. The white settlers no longer had to live in fear of deadly attacks.

New states add stars to the flag of the United States. Soon after George Washington had become President, new states began to come into the Union. The fourteenth state to add its star to the flag was Vermont. Although we do not usually think of Vermont as "western," at the time of the Revolution it was part of the frontier. Vermont had set up its own state government at the beginning of the Revolution but was not officially recognized by Congress until 1791.

Parts of the Old Southwest petitioned for statehood soon afterward. Kentucky became a state in 1792, and Tennessee followed in 1796. The rest of the Old Southwest was later organized into the Mississippi Territory. This was the region settled by the southern cotton planters (page 293). It was only a few years before there were enough people living in the Mississippi Territory to form two states, Mississippi (1817) and Alabama (1819).

In the Northwest, after the Indian troubles were settled, the population of the Ohio region grew so rapidly that in 1803 Ohio became a state. Indiana and Illinois followed in 1816 and 1818. Michigan entered the Union in 1837. When Wisconsin became a state in 1848, five states filled the Northwest Territory. As we shall see in later chapters, several other states (Louisiana, Maine, Missouri, Arkansas, Florida, Texas, Iowa, and California) joined the Union in the first half of the 1800's. In little more than half a century the young nation had grown to include 31 states.

CHECK UP

1. What towns grew up in the Northwest Territory?

2. How was the Indian problem settled in the Northwest?

3. (a) What states were made from the Old Southwest? (b) From the Old Northwest?

A report on the early history of Vermont, the rival claims of New Hampshire and New York to the area, and how Vermont "became independent," should prove interesting.

How Did Conditions in the West Encourage a Democratic Way of Life?

Today the life of a boy on a Kansas farm is very different from that of a boy in a large city like Chicago or New York. So also in frontier days, life in the West was very different from life in the older settlements of the East and South. But the differences in those days were even greater.

The Westerner is a new type of American. If we could have known some of the men and women who went west, we would understand clearly why Westerners were different from Southerners or Easterners. Let us visit a typical cluster of frontier cabins somewhere along the lower Ohio River soon after 1800. In these cabins live three men whom we shall call Robert Adams, John Lyon, and Thomas MacKenzie.

Before these three men moved west, their ways of living were very different. Back home, Robert Adams belonged to a wealthy and respected New England family, which from colonial days had been engaged in shipbuilding and trade. John Lyon was the son of a recent immigrant, and had known little but poverty and hard knocks all his life. Thomas MacKenzie was of Scotch-Irish descent. He came from a tiny farm in the back country of Virginia, where he had made a scanty living only by thrift and very hard work.

If Adams, Lyon, and MacKenzie had met in the East, there is little chance that they would have become friends. But here in the new lands beyond the mountains all three faced the same problems and dangers. After staking out their farms, they cleared the land of trees and built homes for their families. They planted and harvested their crops. Because they had been able to bring along only a few household articles by flatboat or wagon, these pioneers depended on their own skill to make most of the things they needed in the home or on the farm. When tasks required the labor of more than one man, neighbor helped neighbor. In addition, all the settlers joined, when necessary, in protecting their little settlement from hostile Indians.

It is not surprising that in the new West men like Adams, Lyon, and MacKenzie became close friends. Along the frontier, nobody asked his neighbor, "Who are your parents?" or "How much money have you?" What counted in the new settlements was a man's strength and bravery, his ability to stand hardship, and his willingness to help his neighbors.

A pioneer describes life on the frontier. The best way for us to gain a true understanding of the qualities of the frontiersmen is to read what they themselves said about their life. The description which follows was written at a later time by an actual pioneer in Ohio. This is what he said:

★ I can hardly realize how greatly things have changed since that period, and what a primitive and simple kind of life prevailed. . . . Houses and barns were built of logs, and were raised by the collection of many neighbors together on one day, whose united strength was necessary to the handling of the logs. . . .

The best axmen were given charge of the placing of the logs on the wall, and some one of experience took the general direction. . . . The first two side logs were put in place . . . ; then the end logs were notched down in their places; then two more side logs would be rolled up on skids, and notched

This source extract makes clear how a log cabin was built. Encourage

PIONEER NEIGHBORS BUILDING LOG HOUSE

students to contrast methods used then with those used today in building a frame house.

A FRONTIER POST OFFICE drew settlers from miles around whenever there was a mail delivery. Here, frontiersmen get together at the Tranquility, Tennessee, post office.

in their places. At the corners the top of the log, as soon as it was put in place, would be dressed up [trimmed] by the cornerman; and when the next logs were rolled up they would be notched, which notch would be turned downwards upon the saddle made to receive it. . . . This kept the logs in their places like a dovetail and brought them together so as to form a closer wall. The ends of the skids would be raised on each new log as it was laid down to make a way for the next. The logs on these skids would be rolled as long as the men could handle them from the ground, but when the wall got too high, then they would use forks, made by cutting a young notched tree, with which the logs would be pushed up. By using a fork at each end of the log, it could be pushed up with ease and safety. The men understood handling timber, and accidents seldom happened, unless the logs were icy or wet. . . .

I was often at these raisings, because we had raisings of the kind to do, and it was the custom always to send one from a family to help, so that you could claim like assistance in return. At the raisings I would take the position of cornerman, if the building was

not too heavy, as it was a post of honor, and my head was steady when high up from the ground. In chopping on the corners we always stood up straight, and it required a good balance.

This kind of mutual help of the neighbors was extended to many kinds of work, such as rolling up the logs in a clearing, grubbing out the underbrush, splitting rails, cutting logs for a house, and the like. When a gathering of men for such a purpose took place, there was commonly some sort of mutual job laid out for the women, such as quilting, sewing, or spinning up a lot of thread for some poor neighbor. This would bring together a mixed party, and it was usually arranged that after supper there should be a dance or at least plays which would occupy a good part of the night and wind up with the young fellows seeing the girls home in the short hours or, if they went home early, sitting with them by the fire in that kind of interesting chat known as sparking.

The flax crops required a good deal of handling, in weeding, pulling, and dressing, and each of these processes was made the

315 Note that the "get-togethers" also included women.

occasion of a joint gathering of boys and girls and a good time. As I look back now upon those times, I am puzzled to think how they managed to make such small and crowded houses serve for large parties, and how they found room to dance in an apartment of perhaps eighteen feet square, in which there would be two large beds and a trundle bed (which was low enough to be pushed under a higher bed and so put out of the way in the daytime), besides the furniture, which, though of no great quantity, took some room. And then, if these were small houses, they often contained large families. I have often seen three or four little heads peeping out from that part of a trundle bed that was not pushed entirely under the big bed, to get their share of the fun going on among the older ones, while the big beds were used to receive the hats and bonnets and perhaps a baby or two, stowed away until the mothers were ready to go home.

The Westerner is intensely democratic. The simple and rugged life of the pioneer helped him to develop ideas different from those found in older and more settled parts of the country. First of all, deep in the hearts of all frontiersmen was a strong feeling of equality. On the frontier every man was as good as the next man and had as good a chance to succeed. Each person had the same kind of house, ate the same kind of food, wore the same kind of clothes, did the same kind of work, and faced the same dangers. It has been said that democracy means, not "I am as good as you are," but "You are as good as I am." That is the way the Westerners felt.

The feeling of equality bred by the hardships of frontier living caused Westerners to have a firm faith in democratic government. They believed that all men should share the right to vote and the right

to hold government office, an idea that disturbed many Easterners. As we shall see, this belief began to spread to other parts of the country.

The Westerner develops other qualities. In addition to their strong democratic feeling, frontiersmen were usually optimistic; that is to say, they looked on the bright side of things. Everywhere they saw signs of the great progress they and their friends had made in settling the wilderness. They saw that unlimited opportunities lay ahead for those who were willing to work. This made them hopeful, energetic, and cheerful. On the other hand, they were inclined to be loud and boastful about themselves and the West. To the Easterner, the man from the West seemed rough and ignorant, lacking in manners and education.

The West works for its own interests in Congress. As new states were organized beyond the Appalachian Mountains, the West was able to send its own representatives to Congress in Washington. These representatives asked Congress to help meet the needs of the West. First, they wanted cheaper land. As you know, western settlers had to pay the government or the land companies for the land they settled on. In 1820, a land law was passed by Congress which partly satisfied the western demand for cheap land. Under the new law a man could now buy 80 acres (or one eighth of a section) at $1.25 an acre, or $100 in all. Formerly, you remember, a man had to buy a whole section, which cost at least $640. After 1820, any man who could get together $100 could own a good-sized farm.

Secondly, western congressmen asked for better transportation. Good transportation was very important to Westerners because they had to get their products to

Note what is said about the size of (and furniture in) a pioneer home.

market in order to make a living. But canals and roads were expensive. The western states believed that the national government should share the cost with them. Time and again they asked for aid. So, the national government began the Cumberland Road, which ran from Maryland westward (page 279), and helped pay for it. After the success of the Erie Canal, several western states also received help in building canals to connect important rivers with the Mississippi and with the Great Lakes.

During the early 1800's, the representatives of the frontier states boldly voiced their demands in Congress. As a result, Congressmen from the East and the South realized that the West had become a new and important section of the United States with interests of its own.

CHECK UP

1. (a) What problems and dangers did Westerners face? (b) What characteristics did frontier life develop in Westerners?

2. (a) What two things did western representatives in Congress ask the government to do for the West? (b) How successful were they?

Today the national government pays most of the cost of toll-free, limited-access superhighways.

Check Up on Chapter 16

Do You Know the Meaning?

1. ordinance
2. democratic
3. optimistic
4. township
5. section
6. long hunter
7. backwoodsman
8. blaze (a trail)
9. territory (U.S.)

Can You Identify?

1. Old Northwest
2. Old Southwest
3. 1787
4. Daniel Boone
5. Anthony Wayne
6. James Robertson
7. Ordinance of 1785
8. Northwest Ordinance

Can You Locate?

1. Cleveland
2. Chicago
3. Pittsburgh
4. Ohio River
5. Marietta
6. Cincinnati
7. Tennessee
8. Kentucky
9. Nashville
10. Tennessee River
11. Cumberland River
12. Muskingum River
13. Watauga River
14. Kentucky River
15. Lexington, Ky.
16. Cumberland Gap
17. Harrodsburg
18. Boonesborough

Can You Locate? (Cont.)

19. Mississippi Territory
20. Northwest Territory

What Do You Think?

1. Do "frontier" conditions exist anywhere in the United States today? Explain.
2. Why was slavery prohibited in the Northwest Territory but not in the land south of the Ohio?
3. (a) What is the American "West" today? (b) Why has this term not always meant the same thing or applied to the same region?
4. Alaska and Hawaii became states in 1959. They had been territories for many years but their admission to the Union had been delayed. (a) Had they failed to meet the requirements outlined in the Northwest Ordinance? (b) Why had their statehood been delayed?
5. Does the United States today have any possessions that might become states? Explain.

Boone country. Kentucky has many reminders of Daniel Boone — famous frontiersman, Indian fighter, explorer, and long hunter. The old Wilderness Road, over which he led settlers into Kentucky, still bears the same name but is now a paved modern road, part of U.S. Highway 25. All that remains of the settlement at Boonesborough is an old graveyard; but the spot where the fort used to stand is now marked by a monument. Boone Creek, Boone Hill, and Boone County in northern Kentucky remind us that this region was Daniel Boone's "stamping ground." An early settlement at Harrodsburg, which Boone helped to found, has been rebuilt and shows what a pioneer settlement was like. And in Frankfort, Kentucky, the graves of Daniel Boone and his wife, Rebecca, are marked by a tall stone monument.

Conestoga wagons and prairie schooners. A familiar scene in a western movie or television program is the pioneer train of covered wagons lumbering westward across prairie or desert. One of the earliest types of covered wagon, the Conestoga (kon'ess-toh'guh), took its name from a valley in southeastern Pennsylvania, not far from Philadelphia. This fertile valley was settled in colonial times by German farmers. To haul their crops to market, they built a special type of wagon with broad, heavy wheels, well-suited for travel over rough and hilly country. The wagon box was curved up at each end to keep the heavy loads from shifting on the hills. The wagon was covered with a large hood of tough homespun cloth to protect passengers and goods from sun, rain, and heat. Conestogas proved so practical that they came to be widely used in the days before the railroads. Thousands of pioneers moving westward carried their goods and families in Conestoga wagons.

The heavy Conestoga wagons used on eastern roads were not practical for travel west of the Mississippi River. The pioneers who crossed the western prairies and mountains learned to build lighter wagons which could be drawn by two or four horses or oxen. When these canvas-covered wagons rolled across the wide prairies, they reminded people of schooners on the ocean. For this reason they came to be called prairie schooners. A few of the prairie schooners have been preserved in western museums — reminders of the pioneer days of the West.

Western Reserve. Anyone living in northeastern Ohio knows that this section is often called the Western Reserve. The story of that name takes us far back in American history. When Connecticut gave up its western lands to Congress in 1786, the state kept back a large piece of land on the shore of Lake Erie. Part of this Western Reserve, as it was called, was given to citizens of Connecticut who had lost property in the Revolution. Part was sold to a land company. In 1800 the Western Reserve was added to the Northwest Territory, and in 1803 it became part of the new state of Ohio. Although the region was then divided into several counties, the old name held on. Today that part of Ohio is still often called the Western Reserve. Located in it are the important cities of Cleveland, Akron, Sandusky, Ashtabula, and Youngstown. Western Reserve University in Cleveland also carries on the old name.

Why "buck"? You have all heard the word "buck" used to mean dollar. But did you know that the word goes back to the days of the long hunters in the early West? When a hunter returned home with his pack of skins, he would sell them to get the supplies he needed. The skin of the buck deer was worth the most, so the frontiersman would figure the cost of an article as so many bucks (buckskins). Gradually this word came into general use as slang for a dollar and is still used today.

What counties, towns, or places near your community bear the names of pioneer settlers? What can your students find out about these men?

The Nation as a Whole Becomes
More Democratic

Note the relationship of this chapter to the last three.

What this chapter is about —

In the last three chapters you have learned about important changes in the Northeast, the South, and the new West. But what was taking place in the nation *as a whole,* from the time George Washington first became President until the 1850's?

You already know that in its first years the young nation was placed on a firm foundation and won the respect of other countries. In this chapter you will find that during the first half of the 1800's more Americans had greater opportunities for "life, liberty, and the pursuit of hap-

piness." Democratic ideas spread throughout the country. As the number of voters increased, more Americans took an interest in election campaigns. Americans also became more concerned with people who were less fortunate than themselves. The average American found better opportunities to get an education and to improve his life. Many of these changes began or gathered strength during the 1830's. As a result, they have become linked with the name of Andrew Jackson, who was President at that time. In this chapter we shall find answers to these questions:

People in our story — political speaker,
reformers, schoolteacher and pupils.

319

▶ 1. Why did Americans celebrate Andrew Jackson's election as President?

▶ 2. What important steps did Jackson take as President?

▶ 3. How did more Americans win a larger share in the government?

▶ 4. How was the life of the American people improved?

▶ 5. How did political parties struggle to control the government?

1 Why Did Americans Celebrate Andrew Jackson's Election as President?

As pioneers pushed back the frontier and more western states joined the Union, the democratic ideas of the Westerners influenced the other parts of the country. The man who best represented the new, rough-and-ready democracy of the frontier was Andrew Jackson of Tennessee. Jackson was the first man from a western state to be elected President of the United States. Let us see how this came about.

The North, South, and West become rivals. We have learned in this unit that the three sections of our country were developing in very different ways. The North was interested in manufacturing and shipping. The South specialized in growing certain crops, particularly cotton, for export. The rapidly growing West wanted cheap land for its settlers and good transportation for its products. The special interests of the North, South, and West were often in conflict, and for this reason the three sections became rivals. The members of Congress were frequently more concerned with the welfare of their own sections than with the welfare of the nation as a whole.

President John Quincy Adams spends four unhappy years in the White House. In the election of 1824, each section of the country was determined to place in the White House a man who would advance its own interests. New England supported John Quincy Adams, son of President John Adams and Secretary of State under President Monroe. The South supported William Crawford of Georgia. Out of the West came two "favorite sons," Henry Clay of Kentucky and Andrew Jackson of Tennessee. When the votes were counted, it

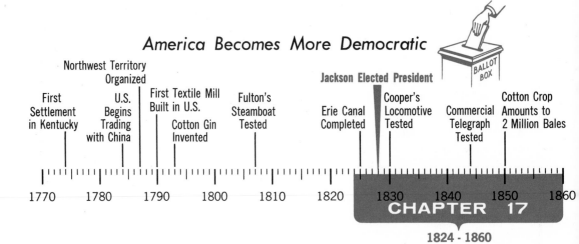

America Becomes More Democratic

Northwest Territory Organized

First Settlement in Kentucky

U.S. Begins Trading with China

First Textile Mill Built in U.S.

Cotton Gin Invented

Fulton's Steamboat Tested

Erie Canal Completed

Jackson Elected President

Cooper's Locomotive Tested

Commercial Telegraph Tested

Cotton Crop Amounts to 2 Million Bales

1770   1780   1790   1800   1810   1820   1830   1840   1850   1860

CHAPTER 17

1824 - 1860

Read the language of the Constitution to the class.

was found that no candidate had won a majority.

In such a case, the Constitution says that the House of Representatives shall choose a President from the three candidates who had won the most votes (page A24). Henry Clay, who had received the fewest votes of the four candidates, asked his supporters to vote for Adams. With this help, Adams was elected by the House.

John Quincy Adams is the only President in the history of our country whose father had been President before him. He was extremely capable, with a long record of government service. As Secretary of State under President Monroe, he had made important decisions which greatly affected our country's future. But Adams was a stern man who would not sacrifice his principles, even if it made him unpopular. Congress quarreled with him and repeatedly opposed him. His years as President were filled with trouble and disappointment.

Andrew Jackson becomes President amid great excitement. When the House of Representatives chose Adams as President, Jackson and his friends were furious. Because Jackson had received more popular votes than Adams in the regular election, they claimed that Jackson had been robbed of the presidency and that the will of the people had not been carried out. They set to work at once to make sure that Jackson should be elected in 1828. So well did they work, and so unpopular was President Adams, that Jackson won an easy victory over his rival in 1828. Adams retired from the White House a bitter and disappointed man. But he soon entered Congress as a Representative from Massachusetts and served with distinction for many years.

On March 4, 1829, the city of Washington was filled with excitement. That was

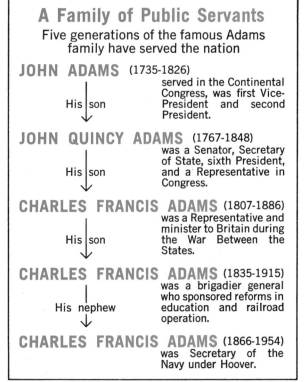

A Family of Public Servants

Five generations of the famous Adams family have served the nation

JOHN ADAMS (1735-1826)

served in the Continental Congress, was first Vice-President and second President.

His son ↓

JOHN QUINCY ADAMS (1767-1848)

was a Senator, Secretary of State, sixth President, and a Representative in Congress.

His son ↓

CHARLES FRANCIS ADAMS (1807-1886)

was a Representative and minister to Britain during the War Between the States.

His son ↓

CHARLES FRANCIS ADAMS (1835-1915)

was a brigadier general who sponsored reforms in education and railroad operation.

His nephew ↓

CHARLES FRANCIS ADAMS (1866-1954)

was Secretary of the Navy under Hoover.

the day when Andrew Jackson was to take office. "A monstrous crowd is in the city," commented Daniel Webster. "I never saw anything like it before. Persons have come five hundred miles to see General Jackson, and they really seem to think that the country is rescued from some dreadful danger." A vast sea of people watched Jackson take the oath of office on the steps of the Capitol. Afterwards, a surging throng pressed close to shake the hand of the new President. At a reception in the White House even wilder scenes took place. Aristocrats and frontiersmen, "statesmen and stable-boys, fine ladies and washerwomen, white people and black" thronged the house and grounds. So great was the crush of people that glasses were broken, furniture upset, and carpets and chairs streaked with mud.

Jackson is the people's idol. What was the reason for all this excitement? Andrew Jackson was a popular hero. His election was a triumph for his supporters, and they wished to celebrate it with him. Some people, however, were shocked at the behavior of the crowd at the inauguration and wondered what would happen to the United States with a "crude" Westerner as President.

It is easy to understand why Jackson was the idol of the people, not only in the West but in other parts of the country too. Like many of them, he had a humble background. Like them he had faced danger, hardship, and poverty. He was born of Scotch-Irish parents on the Carolina frontier. When scarcely fourteen years old, he was taken by the British during the Revolution. To his dying day he bore the scar of a saber cut received when he refused to shine the boots of an English officer.

When he was a young man, Jackson moved to Tennessee. Although he had little schooling, he practiced law and became a judge in the frontier communities. After Tennessee became a state, he was sent to Washington as its representative in Congress. As General Jackson, he became known to the whole nation when he won a victory over the British at New Orleans in the War of 1812. At the time Jackson became President, he was 62 years old.

Jackson appealed to many people not only because of what he had done but also because of the kind of man he was. Bold and courageous, he seemed to love a fight. As a boy he never would admit he was beaten; as a young man he had fought several duels. He never hesitated to stand up for what he thought was right. Jackson was a man of action and of violent feelings. He had a fiery temper, which was easily aroused against those he thought were his enemies. His quick temper and lack of schooling sometimes led him to make mistakes. But he was honest and hard-working. He was as loyal to his friends as he was bitter toward his enemies. And Jackson, as all Americans knew, believed sincerely in democracy.

C H E C K

U P

1. (a) How did the North, South, and West become rivals? (b) What part did this rivalry play in the election of 1824?

2. For what reasons did Andrew Jackson become a popular hero?

These paragraphs explain why Jackson was a popular hero. As President he became less popular in certain sections of the country and with certain groups.

What Important Steps Did Jackson Take as President?

Jackson has definite ideas about a President's authority. Andrew Jackson was a new kind of President. He was a born leader who felt it his duty to carry out the will of the people who had elected him. Jackson, therefore, was not slow to tell Congress and the Supreme Court that he, the President, knew what was best for the country. Some of his actions caused bitter feelings, as we shall see, but on the whole he served the nation well.

Jackson extends the spoils system. Soon after Jackson became President, he dismissed a large number of government officials, mostly postmasters. Many of these officials had held their positions for years and expected to hold them for the rest of their lives. But Jackson wanted to appoint

Other strong Presidents have also strengthened the office of President at the expense of the legislative branch.

ANDREW JACKSON

In the wilderness beyond the mountains, he started a career which led to the White House.

Can your students suggest another "highlight" in Jackson's career?

AN EARLY SETTLER in Tennessee, Jackson became a popular lawyer and commander of the frontier militia. When the British threatened New Orleans in the War of 1812, he marched south to defend the city.

OUTSIDE NEW ORLEANS, he and his men spent the night hurriedly digging in to meet the British attack. Old Hickory's victory the next morning made him a national hero and later helped win him nomination for the presidency.

"THE PEOPLE'S CHOICE," Jackson was swept into the White House by wildly enthusiastic supporters. But when some of them claimed that states had the right to override federal laws or even to secede from the Union, Jackson proved himself a forceful as well as popular President.

"OUR FEDERAL UNION — it must be preserved!" was Jackson's toast at a banquet. With this dramatic answer to his followers, Jackson showed his determination to keep the growing nation united at all costs.

Westerner: "Fine! That makes land easier to buy, but we need money to develop the West and the eastern bankers are sitting on it. The federal government should help us build roads and bridges."

Northerner: "Well, we don't want all our money used to build up the West. By the way, there'll be no slavery in the West, will there? We want no more slave states."

people of his own party to take the places of the officials he had dismissed. Many of these people had worked hard to get Jackson elected. When a man who is elected to office rewards his supporters in this way, he is using what is called the *spoils system.* This name comes from the old saying, "To the victor belong the spoils." (When used in this way, the word *spoils* means "rewards.")

Before Jackson's election, the spoils system had been used to fill positions in the state governments more freely than in the national government. Some earlier Presidents had filled vacant government jobs with their supporters, but Jackson was the first President to use the spoils system widely. This was not a good practice. Officials chosen chiefly as a reward for their support of a person or a party, rather than for ability, often do poor work.

South Carolina protests against the high tariff. Soon after Jackson became President, a quarrel arose over the tariff.

We learned in Chapter 14 that the manufacturers of the Northeast kept demanding higher tariffs in order to get better prices for their manufactured products. But the people of the South manufactured very little themselves. They were farmers and had to buy many manufactured products. So Southerners naturally opposed tariff laws which raised the prices of these products. Nevertheless, tariff laws were passed in 1816, 1824, and 1828.

The tariff of 1828 was a poorly planned law. When the people of South Carolina learned about it, their state legislature drew up a statement protesting against the action of Congress in passing the law. This statement was largely the work of John C. Calhoun. Calhoun was a famous South Carolinian who at that time was Vice-President of the United States. In his protest Calhoun declared that, under the Constitution, Congress had no power to pass tariff laws which favored one section or group over another. When Congress

Civil service (the merit system) has done away with the spoils system.

Southerner: "Wait a minute! You can open up the West if we can move there with our slaves. But build the roads yourself. We don't want the federal government to get too strong!"

went beyond its specific powers to pass a law, said Calhoun, it was the right of any state to *nullify* that law (to declare that the law was not in force). The idea that a state could set aside a law of Congress was called *nullification.*

South Carolina threatens nullification. Calhoun's protest showed how deeply South Carolina felt about the tariff. South Carolina did nothing more, however, until a new protective tariff law was proposed in 1832. Southern members of Congress fought this measure but failed to defeat it. South Carolina now decided to act. A special meeting of delegates, called by the South Carolina legislature, nullified the tariff laws of 1828 and 1832. The delegates also said that if any steps were taken to force the state to accept the hated tariff laws, it would *secede* (withdraw) from the United States.

Andrew Jackson's hot temper boiled over when he learned what South Carolina had done. Above everything else he loved the United States. He had fought under its flag; he had sworn to enforce its laws. "If one drop of blood be shed [in South Carolina] in defiance of the laws of the United States," he said, "I will hang the first man of them I can get my hands on to the first tree I can find." A senator from South Carolina told a friend that he questioned whether Jackson meant what he had said. "I tell you," replied the friend, "when Jackson begins to talk about hanging, they can begin to look for the ropes."

A compromise tariff ends nullification. In a proclamation President Jackson used milder language, but he was no less firm. "To say that any state may at pleasure secede from the Union," he wrote, "is to say that the United States is not a nation." He stated that he would enforce the tariff laws, and he called upon the people of South Carolina to aid him. Meanwhile, he prepared to send an army to South Carolina to enforce the law. Maybe the old General would lead the army himself!

Fortunately, Henry Clay of Kentucky suggested a compromise tariff. Clay's bill provided that the tariff would be lowered gradually over a period of ten years. Congress passed the bill in 1833, and South Carolina withdrew its nullification. Both sides felt they had won a victory: South Carolina, because the tariff had been lowered; and President Jackson, because he had put an end to the threat of secession. The affair, however, showed that the South would fight to protect its interests. And although Jackson had won his point, the question of whether a state could secede from the Union had not been definitely settled. This question was to come up again, as we shall see, in a more serious quarrel between the North and the South.

Jackson puts an end to the second United States Bank. Meanwhile, President Jackson began an attack upon the

POLITICAL SPEAKERS drew interested crowds from all over the countryside in the 1800's as more people gained the right to vote in elections.

Bank of the United States. The first Bank of the United States had been founded as part of the plans of Alexander Hamilton (Chapter 12). It had been followed by the second Bank of the United States in 1816. By the time Jackson entered the White House, this bank had become wealthy and powerful. For this very reason Jackson distrusted it. He believed that the officers of such a powerful bank could influence government officials to pass laws friendly to it. He felt it was undemocratic to put such power in the hands of a few wealthy persons and so decided to put an end to the bank.

The second bank had been given a charter to run until 1836. At that time, if the bank were prevented from getting a new charter, it could be put out of business. But in 1832 — four years before the old charter was up — the friends of the bank persuaded Congress to pass a bill giving the bank a new charter. They thought that President Jackson would not dare to take action just before an election. This trick failed. Jackson sent the bill back to Congress with a stinging veto. When he was

triumphantly re-elected in 1832, Jackson felt that the people approved his attack upon the bank. He was more determined than ever to destroy it. Under Jackson's orders, the Secretary of the Treasury withdrew all the government money deposited in the bank and placed it in certain state banks, nicknamed "pet banks." When its charter expired in 1836, the second Bank of the United States went out of existence. Thus Andrew Jackson was successful in his fight against the bank, as he had been successful in the quarrel over nullification.

 CHECK
UP

1. (a) What was the spoils system? (b) Why did President Jackson make use of it?

2. (a) Why did the North favor a high tariff? (b) Why did the South oppose it?

3. (a) What were Calhoun's ideas about nullification? (b) What did South Carolina do in protest against the tariff law of 1832? (c) How was the tariff quarrel settled?

4. (a) Why did Jackson oppose the United States Bank? (b) How did he put an end to it?

The Check Up questions will help 326 the student discover how well he understands important ideas developed in Section 2.

3 How Did More Americans Win a Larger Share in the Government?

By the middle of the 1800's the people of the United States had gained a larger share in the government than they had ever had before. How did this come about?

Requirements for voting become more democratic. First of all, an important change took place in the laws which stated who should have the right to vote. Not every citizen was allowed to vote when our government was established. In the thirteen original states a man had to be a property owner before he could vote.[1] In the frontier communities, however, there grew up a strong spirit of equality and democracy. So when the first three new states were created — Vermont, Kentucky, and Tennessee — their voting requirements were more democratic. Vermont and Kentucky did not require a man to own property in order to vote. They gave the right to vote to all free white men over 21 years of age. Although Tennessee did not go so far, it allowed more freedom in voting than did the older states of the East.

Later, as other states were formed in the West, they followed the example of Vermont and Kentucky and let all free men vote. Gradually the older states dropped their property requirements for voting. By 1860, all free white men could vote in all the states.

Elections become more democratic. In other ways, also, the people won more control of the government. For example, the laws were changed so that certain government officials, formerly appointed, now were elected directly by the voters. Then, too, the method of choosing a President be-

came more democratic. In early days the members of Congress belonging to each political party nominated the various candidates for President. By 1840, however, presidential candidates were selected by party *conventions*, as they are today. The conventions were made up of delegates chosen by the people. Thus the people had a greater share in deciding which men should run for President. The voters also were allowed to elect the presidential electors, who, according to the Constitution, choose the President (page A11).

Although changes such as these began soon after the nation was founded, they

---

Republic and Democracy

Perhaps you have heard our government sometimes called a *republic*, sometimes a *democracy*. Neither name appears in the Constitution, but today the United States is both. In a republic supreme power rests in the people who may vote. These voters control the government through the representatives and officials they elect. A democracy is a government in which the great majority of the people can vote for candidates of their choice.

Today a number of countries that are ruled by Communists *call* themselves republics or democracies but actually are not. Whether these governments are headed by a single dictator or a small group of powerful men, they and not the people make decisions. To call these countries "republics" or "democracies" is to ignore the true meaning of these words.

The United States is a true republic because it is governed by elected officials; it is also a true democracy because the great majority of adult citizens have the right to vote.

---

[1] We should remember that because land was cheap and easily obtained in our country's early days, this voting requirement was not too difficult to meet.

This footnote makes an important point.

were hastened by the election of Andrew Jackson as President. Throughout his period in office, Jackson worked hard to give all citizens a greater share in the government. The West had reason to be proud of him, for he was easily the most outstanding American of his time.

CHECK UP

1. How had voting requirements changed by 1860?

2. How did the methods of choosing presidential candidates and electing the President become more democratic?

Bring out some present-day reform movements.

4 How Was the Life of the American People Improved?

REFORMERS SEEK TO IMPROVE CONDITIONS

It is important in a democracy like ours that the people shall have the right to vote and hold public office. But many Americans, during and after Jackson's administration, believed that this was not enough. They thought that people should also have the chance to live useful, happy lives. At this time, more Americans had the opportunity to read, and there were more books, magazines, and newspapers to make them think. They read and thought about many things, but in particular they thought about the statement in the Declaration of Independence that all men are endowed with the rights of "life, liberty, and the pursuit of happiness." Looking about them, they saw their rich, young country with unlimited opportunities for all. Yet, wherever they looked, they also saw many unfortunate people whose lives were full of hardship and unhappiness. These people, often through no fault of their own, were not enjoying full, free, and happy lives.

Reformers work to change conditions. Many men and women throughout the country decided that something should be done to improve conditions. Such people were called *reformers*. When reformers found conditions that they thought were evil or undemocratic, they tried to change or *reform* them. They wrote books and articles telling what they thought was wrong, and what they thought should be done to correct it. They held meetings, and people flocked to hear what they had to say. They wrote new laws that were supposed to improve conditions and tried to get the laws passed. What were some of the conditions that reformers wanted to improve?

Reformers in the North fight to abolish slavery. A group of reformers in the North, believing it wrong for one person to own another, insisted that slavery be abolished. As we learned in Chapter 15, these people were called *abolitionists*.

One of the leading abolitionists was a young New Englander named William Lloyd Garrison. He went to Baltimore, Maryland, to help manage an abolitionist newspaper. There he worked hard trying to convince people that slavery was wrong. The newspaper failed, but in the last issue Garrison wrote, "My pen cannot remain idle, nor my voice be suppressed, nor my heart cease to bleed, while two million of my fellow-beings wear the shackles of slavery. . . ."

THE GROWTH OF DEMOCRACY IN AMERICA

EARLY 1800'S

The President

ELECTORS — Elect →

U. S. Senators

Candidates nominated by party groups in Congress

E L E C T

State Legislatures — U. S. House of Representatives

E L E C T

VOTERS

TODAY

By 1840   By 1860   By 1913

Convention Delegates — nominate Candidates →

(17th Amendment)

The President

U. S. House of Representatives

ELECTORS pledged to a candidate

U. S. Senators

State Legislatures

E L E C T

VOTERS

VOTING RESTRICTIONS

VOTER

Only CHURCH members	Only PROPERTY owners	Only FREEMEN —no slaves	Only MEN— No women	
Removed after the Revolution	Removed by 1860	Removed by 13th and 15th Amendments, 1865-70	Removed by 19th Amendment, 1920	Ballot Box

---

Garrison returned to Massachusetts, and on January 1, 1831, he published a new newspaper, *The Liberator.* In it he thundered: "I am in earnest — I will not equivocate — I will not excuse — I will not retreat a single inch — *and I will be heard.*" Garrison's fiery words against slavery aroused bitter feeling in the North as well as the South, and he was mobbed on the streets of Boston. Nevertheless, he continued to fight slavery in every way he could think of — through his paper, through his friends, and through hundreds of speeches and meetings.

Another abolitionist leader was Theodore D. Weld, a serious-minded young man who early decided to become a minister. Weld and some of his friends went from village to village in Ohio preaching abolition. At first, mobs tried to break up these meetings. But Weld and his friends were no more discouraged than Garrison was.

Negroes themselves were among the most effective abolitionists. Frederick Douglass, who had escaped from slavery in Maryland, published his own newspaper and described the horrors of slavery. In a few years, as a result of the work of Garrison, Weld, Douglass, and others, a strong antislavery group was at work in the North.

The movement against slavery began simply as one of many reforms. But before long it aroused stronger feeling than any other reform movement. And, as we shall see in Chapter 19, it helped to bring about a war between the North and the South.

Reformers become interested in criminals and the insane. In the early 1800's, people who had committed even minor crimes were sent to prison, where they were cruelly treated. Little effort was made to help them become better citizens and lead useful lives when their prison terms were over. Conditions in the prisons themselves were often very bad. Jails were dirty, and the prisoners did not receive proper food, medical care, or exercise. Prisoners had nothing to do to keep them busy. Young people who had made only a single mistake were housed with experienced criminals. Many people came out of prison worse men and women than they had been before they went in.

Insane persons also were harshly treated. Today we believe that insanity is sickness of the mind. We think that the insane person is no more to be blamed than

someone who is physically ill. But in earlier times insanity was looked upon as a disgrace. Insane people were kept in miserable quarters; sometimes they were chained to walls. They were dirty, ragged, and ill-fed. Their keepers jeered at them and treated them cruelly.

A number of kindhearted people became interested in the suffering of prisoners and the insane. Chief among them was a Massachusetts woman named Dorothea Dix. Miss Dix spoke and wrote unceasingly about the bad conditions under which the criminals and the insane lived. As a result of her efforts, associations were formed to study better methods of treating these people. Punishment of prisoners became less brutal. New asylums were built for the insane. The work begun by Miss Dix has been carried on from that day to this.

Aid is given to the blind. Samuel G. Howe was another person who became interested in helping less fortunate people. His heart was stirred by the problems of the blind. He wished them to be educated and trained, so that they could earn a living and lead useful lives. In the 1830's, Howe raised money to begin this work. He started the Perkins Institute for the Blind in Boston, where thousands of blind people have been cared for and taught useful trades. Since that time other organizations have also aided the blind.

Temperance leaders fight the liquor evil. A good deal of attention was also given to the evils of alcoholic drinks. Those who became the victims of liquor frequently lost their jobs and sometimes committed crimes. They brought disgrace and suffering to their families. To overcome this evil, *temperance* societies were formed. These societies tried to teach people the bad effects of alcohol and to persuade them to stop drinking. Some

This Institute still serves its original purpose.

FREDERICK DOUGLASS, an escaped slave, became an abolitionist leader. During the Civil War he helped raise Negro regiments for the Union army.

A COUNTRY SCHOOL-TEACHER hears lessons from half his class as the other half studies or fidgets or draws pictures. Boys and girls of all ages attended class together in this log schoolhouse of over a century ago.

temperance leaders went further and tried to get state legislatures to pass laws forbidding the sale of liquor. Maine passed such a law in 1846, and several other states followed her example.

Women ask for their rights as citizens. Among those who took part in the temperance movement and other reforms were many women. But they found it hard to get people to listen to them. Although more and more girls and women were taking jobs in factories, most people thought that a woman's place was in the home. Women did not have the same rights and opportunities as men. They could not get as good an education, and most kinds of jobs were closed to them. Women could not vote. When a woman married, her husband was allowed to manage any property she owned. People frowned on women who took an active part in public meetings and expressed their ideas.

As women reformers worked for one reform or another, they became interested in winning more freedom for themselves and for other women. In 1848, a convention for women's rights was held at Seneca Falls, New York. The delegates drew up a declaration of rights asking for all the

privileges belonging to them as citizens of the United States. Many years were to pass, however, before women were to win equal rights and opportunities with men.

EDUCATION MOVES AHEAD

We have seen that during and after the time when Andrew Jackson was President, thoughtful people found many conditions that needed to be improved. One of the things they were most concerned about was education. Education is very important in a democracy. Since all citizens have the opportunity to vote and take part in the government, all citizens should be able to read and write and keep themselves well-informed.

Public education starts slowly. In the early 1800's there were few opportunities for education as we know it today. It is true, of course, that American leaders had been thinking about education for a long time and had been trying to do something about it. You will remember that the early colonists set up schools of various kinds. Later, when the Northwest Ordinance was adopted, it stated that knowledge was necessary for good government

Students might read again the material on   **331**   education in colonial America (Chapter 5).
Then they can see more clearly the changes which took place in the 1800's.

WESLEYAN COLLEGE, in Macon, Georgia, the first college for women, opened in 1836. A few years earlier, in 1833, Oberlin College in Ohio had accepted women students.

and for the happiness of mankind. It declared that in the Northwest Territory "schools and the means of education shall forever be encouraged." In Virginia, Thomas Jefferson tried to start a system of schools that would help to educate even poor children. Jefferson was far ahead of his times in his thoughts about education.

For many reasons, however, none of these plans to provide education for all of the people was succeeding very well. In the West, many families were struggling so hard to get started in their new homes that they had little time to think about schooling. In the South, only the children of wealthy planters received much education. As you know, public schools had

been established in the North and especially in New England. But these schools suffered during the Revolutionary War and the unsettled years which followed. Parents who could afford it usually sent their children to private schools. In many states the practice in the public schools was to have parents pay a share of the cost of their children's education. Poor children could attend these schools only if their parents were willing to take a "pauper's" oath. By this oath they declared that they were too poor to pay any part of the cost of educating their children. It is not surprising that most poor people kept their children out of school rather than take the oath.

During the 1830's, people began to demand that schools be paid for by taxation. Workers felt that their sons and daughters should have a chance to get an education. They believed that schooling, like voting, should be shared by all.

Free public schools are established. The foremost leader in the fight for better education was Horace Mann. As secretary of the Massachusetts Board of Education, Mann insisted that free public schools should be open to the children of all the people, rich and poor alike. Not everyone agreed with Mann. At first many wealthy people said, "Why should we be taxed to pay for the education of the poor?" But gradually the idea of schools supported entirely by public taxation was accepted. Horace Mann also started *normal schools* for training teachers. Leaders in other states likewise worked hard to bring about free public education. School terms were made longer, more subjects were taught, and textbooks were improved. By 1850, elementary schools supported by taxes were common in the northern states.

The fight for free schools was aimed chiefly at the elementary school. During

The "pauper's" oath brings out clearly how the attitude toward tax-supported schools has changed.

(*Continued on page 335*)

The Old Northwest

The little figures above were carved by a Wisconsin lumberjack and remind us that settling the Northwest Territory was hard work. As the trees were felled for firewood or lumber, prosperous farms appeared on the cleared land (left). Painted by an amateur artist in the 1840's, this farm in Illinois was owned by Swedish immigrants. Farm products were shipped east on new railroads such as the Erie and the Baltimore & Ohio (below). Thomas Rossiter's painting *Opening the Wilderness* shows puffing locomotives at a terminal in the woods.

Before photography was invented, people ordered family portraits from traveling painters when they came to town. A "baby picture" of the early 1800's appears at right.

A typical frontier cabin when Lincoln was a youth is shown at left. Iron pots were used to cook food in the fireplace, and yarn for clothing was homespun on the wheels.

When Lincoln became a successful lawyer, his home in Springfield, Illinois, had a separate kitchen (right) with plastered walls and a cast-iron cooking stove. The rug on the floor was braided from old rags.

these same years, however, young people were also given more opportunities to continue their schooling. Boston had established the first high school in 1821, and other northern cities soon followed her example. More colleges were founded. Instead of preparing students to be ministers only, the colleges began to add such subjects as history and law. In addition, young women began to find it easier to carry on their schooling. Formerly, education beyond the elementary grades was considered unnecessary for women. *Seminaries* or private schools were now opened for them, and a few colleges accepted women students.

Very few Negroes have an opportunity to go to school. Although two Negroes were graduated from New England colleges before the Civil War — John B. Russworm from Bowdoin in 1826 and Jonathan Gibbs from Dartmouth in 1853 — most had no opportunity to gain a formal education. Negroes and friendly whites established elementary schools for free Negroes in northern cities and in Washington, D.C. But neither Negroes nor poor whites went to school in the slave states. A small number of plantation owners, however, provided teachers for their slaves even though such instruction was forbidden by state laws. A few American Negroes went abroad to Europe for their college and professional education.

OPPORTUNITIES FOR READING INCREASE

At the same time that American children were finding more chances to get an education, the grown-ups found greater opportunities for reading. Larger numbers of people in the settled North and South did not have to work so long and had more time for reading. Better means of lighting also made reading easier in the evening hours. Most important of all was the fact that there was much more being written in America for people to read.

American authors produce an American literature. American authors began to write about our nation's history and about American life. Because Americans were proud of their country, these books were eagerly read. Some of the earliest were written by Washington Irving and James Fenimore Cooper, both New Yorkers. Irving's *Legend of Sleepy Hollow* and *Rip Van Winkle* not only were interesting stories but showed what life was like in the Hudson Valley. Cooper wrote exciting tales of Indians and frontiersmen. To this day American boys read *The Last of the Mohicans* and *The Deerslayer*. A southern writer, William Gilmore Simms of South Carolina, wrote many novels, describing the way people lived on the southern frontier.

Edgar Allan Poe, who grew up in Virginia, wrote poems which were both beautiful and sad. People still read *The Raven* and *Annabel Lee*. Poe is also famous for his weird short stories, like *The Tell-Tale Heart,* and the first American detective stories, such as *The Gold Bug.*

It happened that many of the best-known writers lived near Boston. One of these was Henry Wadsworth Longfellow. His poems, such as *Hiawatha, Evangeline, Paul Revere's Ride* (of which a little is quoted in Chapter 8), and *The Courtship of Miles Standish,* delighted the people. John Greenleaf Whittier not only composed poems, such as *Snow-Bound,* about the beauties of nature, but also tried to rouse people against slavery and war. A friend and colleague of William Lloyd Garrison, he has been called "the abolitionist poet." Nathaniel Hawthorne wrote about New England life in short stories like *The Great Stone Face* and novels like *The House of the Seven Gables.*

Masters feared that if slaves could read, they would be stirred to revolt by abolitionist publications smuggled into the South.

"VAINLY EVANGELINE STROVE . . . to cheer him." Longfellow's famous poem told how the Acadians were driven from their homes in Nova Scotia.

Oliver Wendell Holmes was noted for humorous writings in which he poked fun at people and events of his day. Perhaps the most famous of the New England writers was Ralph Waldo Emerson. Emerson did not write stories, but was a serious thinker who pointed out the good and bad things in American life. He believed that every man had the ability to live a worthwhile life. He had great faith, also, in America.

Inexpensive newspapers are printed. Beginning in the 1830's, Americans were able to keep better informed about what was going on in the world. Earlier newspapers had been expensive and had not sold in large quantities. In 1833, the New York *Sun* started publishing a daily paper which sold on the street corners for a penny. This paper was so successful that other newspapers also put out penny dailies. When the telegraph came into use, the news could be sent much more quickly from a distance. Better printing presses were also invented. Because of these changes, the average person was able to buy each day, for a small cost, more news

than kings of former days had been able to command.

•

These improvements and reforms showed that the character of the United States was beginning to change. Although Americans were still busy earning a living, they began to have time for other things. They had time to read newspapers and books and to provide schools for their children. Americans began to feel responsible for unjust treatment of unfortunate people, and wanted to help the slaves, the handicapped, and the insane.

CHECK UP

1. (a) What is a reformer? (b) What were some of the conditions that reformers sought to change?

2. (a) Why did people come to believe in free public education? (b) How were opportunities for education improved?

3. (a) Who were some of the outstanding American authors in the first half of the 1800's? (b) How were Americans able to become better informed about what was going on in the world?

Today newspapers cost more than a penny. But **336** radio and television also help to keep people abreast of recent happenings.

In England, during the 1600's and 1700's, the Whig Party wished to limit the king's power. The Whig Party, therefore, was a good name for these opposed to ''King Andrew I'' and his beliefs.

5 How Did Political Parties Struggle to Control the Government?

Two new political parties develop. At the same time that the changes just described were taking place in American life, there was also a change in political parties. The Federalist Party died out soon after Monroe became President (page 240). For a few years there was only one political party, the Republican or Democratic-Republican. After Monroe left the presidency, however, the Democratic-Republican Party split into two parts. The friends and supporters of Andrew Jackson became known in the 1830's as the *Democratic Party.* Many of the same kinds of men who had supported Thomas Jefferson were members of the Democratic Party. It came to stand for low tariffs and states' rights (page 376), and opposed a strong federal government. Many Southerners and Westerners were Democrats.

Those who disliked "King Andrew I," as they called Andrew Jackson, formed a political party to oppose him and his beliefs. This party was called at first the National Republican Party but later became known as the *Whig Party.* It stood chiefly for high tariffs and a strong federal government. It included many men who had belonged to the Federalist Party in earlier years or who held the same beliefs. The Whig Party was strong in the East.

Martin Van Buren follows Jackson as President. As Jackson's second term drew to a close, he made clear to the Democrats that he wanted his Vice-President, Martin Van Buren of New York, to follow him as President. The Democrats easily elected Van Buren in 1836. Although Van Buren was a skillful politician, his years as President were unhappy ones. Scarcely had he been inaugurated when the country was hit by a severe financial *panic.* Fear and hard times swept the nation.

The United States was prosperous in the early 1830's. The panic followed a period of great prosperity in the United States. In the West there had been an enormous increase in the buying of government land. Many of the buyers did not intend to farm the land; they planned to sell it later and make a profit. Such people are known as *speculators.* To pay for the land, they borrowed paper money issued by the western banks. But many of these banks, called *wildcat banks,* put out paper money without enough gold or silver to back it up. For a time things went well; as prices of western land rose, big profits were made.

In the South, people planted more and more cotton, and thus were able to sell more and more to English factories. This meant greater prosperity for the South. Western farmers sold large amounts of foodstuffs to the South and became more prosperous. With money to spend, the Southerners and Westerners bought manufactured goods from the East. Factories multiplied, people had jobs, businesses of all kinds increased. For a time the whole country prospered. Even England was affected, for Americans were buying great quantities of luxuries and other goods from English traders.

Prosperity ends in the Panic of 1837. Suddenly the period of prosperity ended and a financial panic followed. One of the reasons for the panic was a step taken by President Jackson shortly before he left office. Jackson announced that all sales of government land in the West must be paid for in gold or silver (hard cash), not in paper money.

When the land speculators asked the wildcat banks for hard cash, they were unable to get it. So the speculators began to sell their land holdings, and land

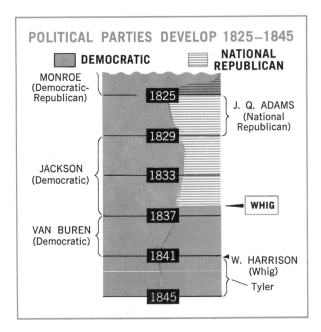

POLITICAL PARTIES DEVELOP 1825–1845

■ DEMOCRATIC　**≡ NATIONAL REPUBLICAN**

MONROE (Democratic-Republican)

1825

J. Q. ADAMS (National Republican)

1829

JACKSON (Democratic)

1833

◀ WHIG

1837

VAN BUREN (Democratic)

1841

◀ W. HARRISON (Whig)
　Tyler

1845

LED BY JACKSON, Democratic-Republicans became known as the Democratic Party. The National Republican Party disappeared, and Jackson's opponents drew together in the new Whig Party.

prices dropped sharply. At the same time, people became fearful when they realized that the government did not have much faith in the paper money issued by the western banks. They rushed to the banks to exchange their paper money for gold and silver. The fear soon spread to the East. Everywhere people demanded hard cash. Because the banks couldn't pay it, they had to close their doors.

Hard times become widespread. English manufacturers and traders failed because they could not collect money owed them by American businessmen. American manufacturers went out of business because people could no longer buy their articles. Factories closed; people lost their jobs. Cotton planters also suffered because English manufacturers could no longer buy their cotton. Western farmers grew poor because the South no longer bought their products.

The Whigs elect Harrison and Tyler. Many people blamed the unlucky Martin

Van Buren for the Panic of 1837. The Whigs made the most of this. As their candidate for President in 1840, they chose William Henry Harrison of Ohio. For Vice-President they selected John Tyler of Virginia. Harrison, who was 67 years old at this time, had won fame as a general in the army. In 1811 he had defeated the Indians at Tippecanoe, a small river in Indiana. He also fought bravely and well in the War of 1812. The Whigs emphasized Harrison's military record and his nickname of "Old Tippecanoe." They conducted a noisy campaign, with many parades and enthusiastic speeches. "Tippecanoe and Tyler too!" they shouted, and soon their shouts were loud with triumph as they won the election.

William Henry Harrison was the first President elected by the Whig Party. He was also the first President of the United States to die in office. Tired out by the campaign, he died only one month after taking the oath of office. The Vice-President, John Tyler, took his place. But Tyler was not a strong believer in Whig ideas. He had been nominated for Vice-President chiefly to win the votes of Southerners who otherwise might not have voted for Harrison. He had many bitter conflicts with Whig leaders and with Congress.

Quarrels within the Whig Party helped to cause its defeat in 1844. Four years later another Whig President was elected, but in the 1850's the party disappeared. The Democratic Party, however, has continued to exist up to the present day.

CHECK UP

1. (a) What two new political parties developed while Jackson was President? (b) What did each stand for?

2. (a) Why was there great prosperity in the United States during the early 1830's? (b) What caused the Panic of 1837?

JOHN QUINCY ADAMS 1825–1829

National-Republican from Massachusetts. Lawyer, Harvard professor, and an able Secretary of State under Monroe, John Quincy Adams was a short, sharp-witted man like his father, the second President. During his administration as President, Adams tried, unsuccessfully, to have Congress approve government promotion of scientific research and education. Defeated for re-election, he served in the House of Representatives until his death in 1848.

ANDREW JACKSON 1829–1837

Democrat from Tennessee. First President to be born in a log cabin, Jackson grew up on the Carolina frontier. He tried teaching school and then became a lawyer, judge, and general. During the War of 1812 he showed such toughness that his troops came to call him "Old Hickory." A strong-willed President, Jackson was given another nickname — "King Andrew I" — by his opponents. He was the first President to ride on a railroad train.

MARTIN VAN BUREN 1837–1841

Democrat from New York. The first President born an American citizen rather than a British subject, Van Buren was called the "Little Magician" because of his skill in politics. He had been Jackson's Vice-President and ally in New York politics before being elected to the presidency. Defeated for re-election, because many people blamed him for the Panic of 1837, he later ran for President unsuccessfully as the candidate of the Free Soil Party.

⇁ WILLIAM HENRY HARRISON 1841

Whig from Ohio. An Indian fighter and frontier governor, Harrison became famous as the general who defeated the Indians in the Battle of Tippecanoe. Later, he served in Congress and as minister to Colombia. Harrison had retired to his farm in Ohio when he was nominated by the Whigs. At 68, "Old Tippecanoe" was the oldest man ever to be inaugurated President, and he became the first to die in that office.

JOHN TYLER 1841–1845

From Virginia. Tyler had been a Democrat before the Whigs nominated him as Harrison's running mate. First Vice-President to become President through the death of his predecessor, Tyler insisted that he was not just an acting President but should have the full title and powers of the presidency. Later in life Tyler tried in vain to reconcile the North and South. He was serving in the Confederate Congress at the time of his death.

Check Up on Chapter 17

Question #1, especially the last part of it, deserves attention.

Do You Know the Meaning?

1. nullify
2. secede
3. panic
4. reformer
5. temperance
6. seminary
7. antislavery
8. wildcat bank
9. spoils system

Can You Identify?

1. Henry Clay
2. Andrew Jackson
3. John C. Calhoun
4. Edgar Allan Poe
5. Dorothea Dix
6. Horace Mann
7. 1832
8. 1837
9. Samuel G. Howe
10. Democratic Party
11. Whig Party
12. Washington Irving
13. Henry Longfellow
14. Nathaniel Hawthorne
15. Martin Van Buren
16. Ralph Waldo Emerson
17. Oliver Wendell Holmes
18. James Fenimore Cooper
19. John Greenleaf Whittier
20. William Gilmore Simms
21. John Quincy Adams
22. William Lloyd Garrison

What Do You Think?

1. Although John Quincy Adams was an able public official who did what he thought was best for the country, he was not popular with the people. Do you think he was a good President? What makes a good President?

2. Do you agree with Calhoun that a state should have the right to nullify an act of Congress? Why?

3. (a) How are public schools supported today? (b) How far may a student continue his education in public schools? (c) Name some colleges or universities in your state or section that are supported by taxes.

4. Name several ways in which the life of the average American has improved since Jackson's time.

5. (a) Why is the spoils system a poor way of choosing public officials? (b) Can you think of a better way? Explain.

The analysis of why Chicago became a great city suggests things to look for in explaining why other cities grew.

LINKING PAST AND PRESENT

Andrew Jackson's home. Many visitors to Nashville, Tennessee, go to see the old mansion called the Hermitage. This beautiful house was built by Andrew Jackson for his wife soon after he returned from the Indian wars in Florida. Before the Hermitage was built, the Jacksons had lived in log cabins. Today the Hermitage looks much as it did during their lifetime. The white two-storied house has the wide verandas and tall columns of the fine southern homes of that period. Many pieces of Jackson's own furniture are to be found in the spacious rooms. Both Jackson and his wife are buried in the beautiful garden of the Hermitage, where visitors may see their graves today.

Chicago, Illinois. The story of Chicago, our nation's second largest city, goes back to the 1600's, when the French explorers Joliet, Mar-

quette, and La Salle visited the place where the city now stands. Here was an easy portage between Lake Michigan and the Illinois River, which emptied into the Mississippi. The area soon became an important trading post, and in 1803 the United States built Fort Dearborn on the site. By 1831, about 350 people lived around the fort. Then, suddenly, the settlement began to grow rapidly. By 1837, there were 5000 people in Chicago.

The secret of Chicago's growth was her location as a crossroads for trade. After the Erie Canal was built, for instance, manufactured goods from the East could be shipped by water from New York to Lake Erie and by way of the Great Lakes to Chicago. Farmers of the Midwest began to think of Chicago as their chief trading center, a place where they could sell their goods for shipment to the East, and where they could buy the things they needed. Another boom came in 1848, when the Illinois Canal was completed. It was now possible to ship goods from New York City to Chicago and from there, by way of the Illinois Canal and the Mississippi River, all the way to New Orleans!

The first railroad from the East reached Chicago in 1852. Soon every important east-west railroad made Chicago one of its terminal points, until today Chicago is one of the greatest rail centers in the world. Since the building of the St. Lawrence Seaway, the city has also become the chief midwestern port for ocean-going merchant ships.

TO CLINCH YOUR

UNDERSTANDING OF

Unit 5

Check ideas contained in the Summary against the questions in the Review.

Summary of Important Ideas

In Unit Five you have read about important changes which·had taken place in the United States by 1850.

1. Different ways of living developed in various sections of the country during the first half of the 1800's.
   a. Although New England sea captains were barred from British ports after the Revolutionary War, they found new markets and ways of making money. American commerce again suffered before and during the War of 1812, but it increased greatly after 1815. A profitable trade was developed with China and the Far East. Meanwhile, the use of machinery and the factory system spread from England to America. When the War of 1812 cut off manufactured goods from foreign countries, there was an industrial boom in New England and the Middle Atlantic states. After the war, tariffs were adopted to keep out cheaper British goods.
   b. By present-day standards, wages, hours, and working conditions were unsatisfactory in the early factories. The growth of

industry increased the number and size of cities. Many new conveniences (especially for city dwellers) and improved transportation and communication (turnpikes, canals, steamboats, railroads, and telegraph) were developed.
   c. The invention of the cotton gin by Eli Whitney in 1793 led to a great increase in the planting of cotton. When the land in the Old South "wore out," the planters sought new and more fertile land to the southwest. Though a small part of the population, the plantation owners were the leaders in the South.
   d. Differences in ways of living in the North and the South led to disagreements. The manufacturing North came to favor protective tariffs, the agricultural South to oppose them. Because of its spreading factory system and its·small farms, the North favored free labor; the plantation South depended on slave labor.
   e. Opportunities offered by the West (the frontier region between settled areas and the wilderness) attracted thousands of pioneer families. The Ordinance of 1787 provided for a territorial government in the Northwest Territory and also for the

Are there important points developed in this unit which should be added to the Summary? Do the Review questions cover the most important points?

admission, in time, of new states in that region. The pattern set by this law was followed in the case of later territories.

2. The United States became more democratic in the first half of the 1800's.

a. Different ways of living which had developed in the North, the South, and the West led to rivalry between the three sections. Andrew Jackson's election as President was hailed as a victory for the West.

b. During his administration, Jackson refused to recognize the right claimed by South Carolina to nullify a protective tariff law. He also vetoed a bill to renew the charter of the Bank of the United States. When unsound trading in western land caused the government to require that payments be made in gold and silver, a severe panic swept the country (1837).

c. During Andrew Jackson's administration, the right to vote was extended to practically all free white men. National conventions began to nominate candidates for the presidency. In the 1830's, reformers worked for the abolition of slavery, for women's rights and temperance, and for the better treatment of criminals and the insane. Free public schools were established, a new interest in reading and literature developed, and inexpensive newspapers were published.

Unit Review

1. (a) Why did commerce and manufacturing develop in New England and the Middle Atlantic states? (b) Why did manufacturing become increasingly important during the War of 1812? (c) What step was taken to protect American manufactures after the war? (d) How did the increase in industry affect the growth of cities? (e) How did it affect communication and transportation? Why?

2. (a) Why did the South need more land after 1793? (b) Why were the plantation owners the most influential group in the South?

3. (a) What stand did the North and the South take on the tariff question? Why? (b) On the question of slavery? Why?

4. (a) What were the chief needs of the West? (b) Why did Westerners tend to be more democratic than the people of other sections? (c) What issues did Andrew Jackson fight for? (d) What new political parties were formed during Jackson's presidency?

5. (a) Why did a panic develop in 1837? (b) What were the results?

6. (a) What advances were made in education in the first half of the 1800's? (b) Why were Americans able to keep better informed about what was going on in the world? (c) What movements were started to improve conditions in the United States? (d) How were these movements linked with the growth of democracy?

Gaining Skill

How to Make Reports

In a history class you will often make reports. You may be asked to review a book you have read or to look up information on a subject in several books and report to the class.

For each of the units we have listed books which you may wish to read for pleasure (beginning on page A33). Doubtless your teacher, librarian, classmates, and you yourself can suggest other books. In reading a book for pleasure, read it rapidly for the story. Do the setting and action of the story agree with what you already know about the period or the events under discussion? Be able to tell the class why you like or do not like a book you have read.

If you are going to report on a particular subject, you will want to read books for information. To locate books on your subject, use the suggestions in "How to Use the Library" on page 260. In reading the maps and pictures in such books, keep in mind the suggestions in "How to Read Maps" and "How to Read Pictures" (pages 132 and 420).

While reading for your report, you will

Students need help in learning how to organize information for an oral or written report.

want to take notes on what you read. To take useful notes, you must have clearly in mind the purpose for which you want to use the notes. Think what the members of the class will want to know about the subject you have chosen. If you were preparing either a written or an oral report on Henry Clay, as suggested in project number 5 in *Interesting Things to Do* on this page, you might decide that the class would want information on three main topics:

    I. General information about Clay's life
    II. Clay and the War of 1812
    III. Clay's work as a "compromise maker" in the tariff and slavery disputes

Keep in mind these main divisions or topics as you take notes on the material you read. Write each note on a separate card, or put the notes for each main division on a separate sheet of paper. Copy exactly any information which you intend to quote; otherwise, express ideas in your own words. Before you actually prepare the biography, you will want to look through your notes and arrange them in order under each main topic. You may find it helpful to make an outline, particularly if you are to give your report orally. You will find that your notes for each main topic will fall into groups. Each group will be represented in your outline by a subtopic, as shown in this suggested outline for the first main topic in Clay's biography:

    I. General information
      A. When and where Clay was born
      B. His early life
      C. The offices Clay held
      D. The men Clay was associated with in public life

If you give an oral report, make the report in your own words and look at your outline and notes as little as possible. If you write the report, follow the outline you have developed, and write what you have to say clearly and in your own words.

Interesting Things to Do

The items marked with an asterisk (*) are for the whole class.

*1. Start a new set of cards for Unit Five. Include the items in "Can you Identify?" for Chapters 14, 15, 16, and 17.

2. Make a map showing one of the following: (a) the Erie Canal and the Hudson River route; (b) the Cumberland Road; (c) the Cotton Kingdom, including the chief cities and rivers used for transportation; (d) the Ohio River Valley, showing the tributaries of the Ohio and the chief settlements north and south of the river; (e) the Northeast with its chief ports and factory towns.

3. Draw a cartoon to show (a) how clipper ship captains felt about the steamship; (b) how farmers felt about the early railroads; (c) the special interests of the North, South, and West; (d) South Carolina and nullification; (e) Jackson and the Bank; (f) the rise of the Democratic and Whig Parties.

4. Write an article as it might have appeared in a newspaper of the times on (a) the completion of the Erie Canal; (b) the factory built by Samuel Slater; (c) the voyage of the *Flying Cloud;* (d) the election of John Quincy Adams; (e) the invention of the cotton gin; (f) sending the first message by telegraph; (g) the first ocean-going steamboat.

5. Prepare an oral or written report on (a) Henry Clay or John C. Calhoun; (b) any one of the famous inventors or writers mentioned in this unit.

6. Write a letter to a friend describing (a) your visit to Washington at the time of Jackson's inauguration; (b) the race between *Tom Thumb* and the horse; (c) your trip to a southern plantation.

7. Prepare and take part in an imaginary conversation between (a) an abolitionist and a southern plantation owner; (b) a northern manufacturer and a southern plantation owner on the tariff; (c) a Westerner and a wealthy Easterner in the year 1800 on who should be allowed to vote; (d) a New England farmer and a factory worker on living conditions in the North; (e) an Easterner and a Westerner on the election of Andrew Jackson.

Item #7 calls for the ability to understand various points of view.

The United States Expand

When our country won its independence, some people thought the nation was too big to live under a single central government. These men said that the people of one section would be so far from the people of another, and their ways of living would be so different, that each section would want a government of its own. When the Constitution of the United States was written, James Madison in "The Federalist" answered this objection. He wrote to his fellow countrymen:

"Hearken not to the . . . voice which tells you that the people of America, knit together . . . by so many cords of affection, can no longer live together as members of the same family; . . . can no longer be fellow-citizens of one great, respectable, and flourishing empire. . . . No, my countrymen. . . . The kindred blood which flows in the veins of American citizens . . . consecrates this Union, and excites horror at the idea of their becoming . . . enemies."

Yet there came a time when Americans in the North and South were rivals and enemies. They carried different flags and fought a bloody conflict that abolished slavery and determined that no state could

and Is Torn by War

withdraw from the Union. The tragic story of how American fought American will be told in this unit.

As background for understanding this conflict, Chapter 18 tells how the United States expanded until it stretched across the whole continent. In Chapter 19, we shall learn how the question of whether or not slavery should exist in the new territories brought differences between the two sections to a head. Following Lincoln's election as President, the southern states seceded and war began. In Chapter 20 we shall trace the course of the war and learn about some of the great battles that took place. Gettysburg, the turning point of the war, is illustrated above by the courageous but ill-fated charge by General Pickett's forces against the northern lines. We shall also learn the outcome of this bitter war and read how the country set about trying to solve the problems that it created.

Doubtless some of your students have visited battlefields of the Civil War. Encourage them to report what they learned.

"A house divided against itself cannot stand."
I believe this government cannot endure perma-
nently half slave and half free.

— ABRAHAM LINCOLN

The United States Gains More
Land and Reaches from Sea to Sea

What this chapter is about —

Our forefathers wanted their country to grow stronger and larger. As they marched steadily westward, they looked eagerly at the unsettled land still farther away. They wanted to own that land. One enthusiastic American, speaking about the need for land, compared the United States with the buffalo, which roamed widely over the western plains:

✳ Make way, I say, for the young American Buffalo — he has not yet got land enough; he wants more land as his cool shelter in summer — he wants more land for his beautiful pasture grounds. I tell you, we will give him Oregon for his summer shade, and the region of Texas as his winter pasture. Like all of his race, he wants salt, too. Well,

People in our story — frontier scout, explorer, American soldier, Mexican officer, prospector.

he shall have the use of two oceans — the mighty Pacific and the turbulent Atlantic shall be his. . . .

In 1783, our country stretched from Canada to Florida and from the Atlantic Ocean to the Mississippi River. Twenty years later, as you have learned in Chapter 13, President Jefferson purchased the Louisiana Territory. Although the Louisiana Purchase doubled the size of the United States, Americans were not satisfied. The speaker whose words are quoted here was correct in thinking that the "American Buffalo" would not be content with the territory it possessed in 1803.

This chapter explains how the United States gained more and more territory, until it reached the shores of the Pacific. You will find answers to these questions:

▶ 1. How was the Louisiana Territory explored and settled?

▶ 2. How did the United States acquire Florida?

▶ 3. How did our country gain Texas, the Southwest, and California?

▶ 4. How did the discovery of gold bring California into the Union?

▶ 5. How did the United States gain part of the Oregon Country?

↘ Recall that control of the fur trade was the chief French goal, and that large-scale settlement was not.

1 How Was the Louisiana Territory Explored and Settled?

What was the Louisiana Territory like in 1803?   When Jefferson surprised the entire country by buying Louisiana from France, neither he nor anyone else knew much about this vast territory. Louisiana lay between the Mississippi River and the Rocky Mountains; it stretched northward to Canada and southward to the Gulf of Mexico. (See map on page 349.) Here indeed was land for the "American Buffalo"! Great plains extended westward from the Mississippi, rising gradually to the Rockies. In the upper Mississippi Valley were forests abounding in deer and other game. Farther south and west, enormous herds of shaggy buffaloes roamed the plains, feeding on the prairie grass which stretched for hundreds of miles. The broad Missouri River, with its headwaters in the snowy summits of the northern Rockies, made its way across these plains to join the Mississippi. And the Mississippi, swollen by the waters of the Missouri, wound in and out through endless acres of fertile land on its way to the Gulf of Mexico.

Except for New Orleans, the Louisiana Territory contained few settlers.   A few thousand Frenchmen and Americans lived along the Mississippi in 1803, most of them in villages founded long before by the French. (You remember that the entire river valley had once been a part of New France.) The chief settlements in the Louisiana Purchase were St. Louis and New Orleans. St. Louis was only a small

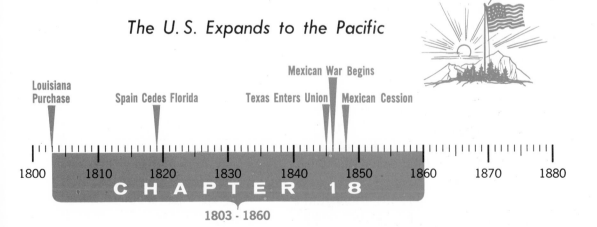

The U. S. Expands to the Pacific

Louisiana Purchase

Spain Cedes Florida

Texas Enters Union

Mexican War Begins

Mexican Cession

1800   1810   1820   1830   1840   1850   1860   1870   1880

CHAPTER 18

1803 - 1860

CAPTAIN WILLIAM CLARK (in the foreground) and his companions ride alongside the Yellowstone River on their return from the west coast. (Lewis and Clark returned by different routes.) Note Sacajawea holding her child on the horse.

fur-trading town of about 160 log cabins. New Orleans, however, was a thriving city of 10,000 people located a hundred miles from the mouth of the Mississippi.

New Orleans had had a colorful history. Founded by the French in 1718, it had been given to Spain with the rest of Louisiana at the end of the French and Indian War (page 130). During the late 1700's, wealthy Spaniards moved to New Orleans and lived there in grand style. Then Louisiana again fell into the hands of the French. Finally it changed owners for the last time when it was bought by the United States in 1803. At that time New Orleans was a city of French and Spanish people and many Negroes, both slave and free. It was the chief port for the products of the Mississippi Valley. Near the city were large plantations of indigo, sugar cane, and cotton.

Lewis and Clark explore the Louisiana Territory. President Jefferson was eager to learn more about this vast land the United States had purchased. So he sent a small expedition of soldiers to explore the Louisiana Territory. The leaders were Captain Meriwether Lewis and Captain William Clark, a younger brother of George Rogers Clark of Revolutionary War fame. Setting out from St. Louis in 1804, they journeyed up the Missouri through the lands of the Sioux (*soo*) Indians. Follow the route of Lewis and Clark on the map on the next page.

Lewis and Clark spent the winter in what is now North Dakota. They continued their journey in the spring, following the Missouri River into the Rockies until it became so narrow that a man could straddle it! Instead of turning back when they reached the Rockies, they crossed the mountains with the help of an Indian woman guide named Sacajawea (*sak' uh-juh-wee' uh*). They kept careful notes of such things as the birds, animals, trees, and flowers they saw, and the locations of rivers and mountains. Their records show that they suffered most, not from the Indians, but from mosquitoes and flies during the summer! Lewis and Clark finally reached the Columbia River and floated down its waters to the Pacific. They made the return trip safely and reached St. Louis in 1806 after a journey of 8000 miles.

The expedition of Lewis and Clark not only gave the people of the United States information about the new lands; it also paved the way for hunters, traders, and pioneer farmers. The record of Lewis and Clark's journey has been published and may be found in many libraries. It still makes interesting reading.

Zebulon Pike explores more of the Louisiana Territory. At about this time

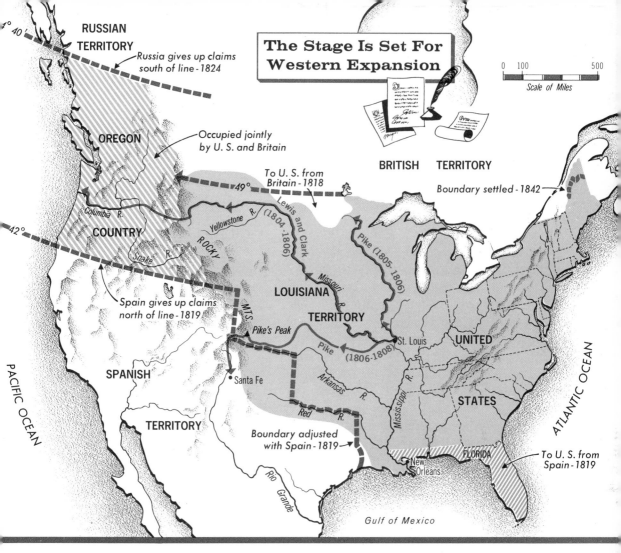

The Stage Is Set For Western Expansion

RUSSIAN TERRITORY

Russia gives up claims south of line - 1824

OREGON

Occupied jointly by U. S. and Britain

BRITISH TERRITORY

Boundary settled - 1842

To U. S. from Britain - 1818

49°

Columbia R.

Lewis and Clark (1804-1806)

Yellowstone R.

COUNTRY

ROCKY

Snake R.

Missouri R.

Pike (1805-1806)

42°

LOUISIANA

Spain gives up claims north of line - 1819

MTS.

TERRITORY

Pike's Peak

Pike (1806-1808)

St. Louis

UNITED

SPANISH

Santa Fe

Arkansas R.

Mississippi R.

STATES

TERRITORY

Red R.

Boundary adjusted with Spain - 1819

FLORIDA

To U. S. from Spain - 1819

New Orleans

Rio Grande

PACIFIC OCEAN

ATLANTIC OCEAN

Gulf of Mexico

Scale of Miles
0   100   500

MAP STUDY United States territory right after the Louisiana Purchase is shown here in solid color. The colored broken lines show later boundary changes. (1) What two areas were gained in 1818 and 1819? (2) What countries occupied Oregon after 1818?

another explorer named Zebulon Pike led an expedition northward to search for the source of the Mississippi. Although he did not find it, he learned a great deal about the region of the upper Mississippi. After returning from this exploration, Pike set out again from St. Louis in 1806. This time he headed westward. His purpose was to explore the Louisiana Territory south of the route taken by Lewis and Clark. After following the Arkansas River for many weeks, Pike came to the Rockies. Pike's Peak in Colorado, which he discovered, is named for this brave explorer.

It was winter when Pike and his men reached the Rockies. Cold and tired, they turned south in search of the Red River. Actually they entered territory along the river called the Rio Grande — land that was not a part of Louisiana but belonged to Spain. There Pike and his men built a fort and raised the American flag above it. They were taken prisoners by the Spaniards, and Pike was brought before the Spanish governor of the region. He was later released and returned through Spanish territory to American soil with valuable maps and a rich store of information.

The boundary of Louisiana Territory was not well **349** defined. Pike, however, was clearly on Spanish soil.

Pioneers flock to Louisiana Territory. When Americans read about the explorations of Lewis and Clark and Zebulon Pike, they became eager to push westward once again. Pioneers in flatboats floated down rivers flowing westward and southward. Others crossed the country in covered wagons. Within a few years pioneers could travel down the Ohio to the Mississippi by steamboat. At several points along the Mississippi there were ferries to take the pioneers to the west side of the river. Thousands of eager settlers crossed the Mississippi into the new territory.

The life of the pioneers who settled in the forests of the upper Mississippi Valley was much like that of the pioneers east of the Mississippi. The settlers who chose the prairies, on the other hand, met with different problems. The rolling prairies might stretch for miles without a tree. Settlers often relied on logs floated down the Mississippi and its branches for lumber to build houses. It was a tough job to plow the wiry grass and sod of the prairies, and farmers had to use huge plows pulled by teams of oxen. But once the land was plowed, fine crops of corn and wheat could be raised. Farther south, in southern Missouri and Arkansas, settlers from the southern states brought their slaves and started cotton plantations.

States are organized west of the Mississippi. Before long, new towns began to appear west of the Mississippi. Some of them grew around forts built to protect the settlers. Des Moines, Iowa, and Leavenworth, Kansas, began as forts. Minneapolis, Minnesota, grew up near Fort Snelling. Other towns, such as Davenport, Iowa, began as fur-trading centers built by fur companies. St. Louis grew rapidly as a fur center and river port. Soon steamboats were traveling the Mississippi, carrying furs and farm produce to New Orleans.

In a few years several new states bordered the west bank of the Mississippi. Louisiana, which had a large population when the territory was bought, entered the Union in 1812. In 1821, the state of Missouri was added, and fifteen years later Arkansas joined the Union. In 1846, Iowa became a state. In 1858, Minnesota completed the row of states on the west bank of the Mississippi. How the western part of Louisiana Territory was settled will be told in a later chapter.

CHECK UP

1. (a) What parts of the Louisiana Territory were explored by Lewis and Clark? (b) By Pike? (c) What were the results of these explorations?

2. How did the life of pioneers on the western prairies compare with pioneer life east of the Mississippi?

3. What states were created in the territory just west of the Mississippi River?

Be sure that students understand the advantages and limitations of the flatboat as a means of transportation.

 ## How Did the United States Acquire Florida?

When our country purchased Louisiana, neither the French nor the Americans were sure just what its boundaries were. You remember that Jefferson wanted particularly to get control of the mouth of the Mississippi so that Westerners could send their products to market through the port of New Orleans. Spain, however, owned

The United States Gains the Gulf Coast

///// Occupied by U. S. by 1813

SOUTH CAROLINA

GEORGIA

ALABAMA

MISSISSIPPI

Mississippi R.

Mobile
FLORIDA
WEST
Pensacola
New Orleans
EAST
St. Augustine
FLORIDA
ATLANTIC OCEAN

Ceded by Spain, 1819

Gulf of Mexico

0   100   200   300
Scale of Miles

MAP STUDY

The striped area was claimed by Americans as part of the Louisiana Purchase, but Spain disputed this claim until 1819. Which states gained an outlet to the Gulf of Mexico through West Florida?

a narrow strip of land along the Gulf of Mexico (called *West Florida*), as well as the peninsula we now call Florida, which was then known as *East Florida*. (See map on this page.) Spain claimed that West Florida extended as far west as New Orleans and the Mississippi River. Jefferson, on the other hand, claimed that the Louisiana Purchase included a considerable amount of land east of the Mississippi River.

The United States expands into West Florida. The dispute went on for years. Finally, when Louisiana became a state in 1812, our government simply added to it all the territory east of the Mississippi which is now included in the present state of Louisiana. Spain was too weak even to try to defend her claim.

The United States, however, was anxious to own all of West Florida. Americans were rapidly settling the land to the north, and the settlers in Alabama and Mississippi wanted to use the rivers which flowed through Spanish territory. The United States offered to buy West Florida, but Spain refused to sell. During the War of 1812, our government occupied more of West Florida. After the war, therefore, the United States was holding a large part of West Florida, although Spain did not admit our right to do so.

Andrew Jackson marches into Florida. In the meantime East Florida had become a trouble spot. Runaway slaves from Georgia had been going into East Florida and hiding there, safe from American authorities. Furthermore, the warlike Indians of Florida often raided frontier settlements just north of the Spanish border. Although Spain had agreed to hold the Indians in check, her troops in Florida were not strong enough to do so. Finally, President Monroe ordered General Andrew Jackson to halt the Indian raids.

Jackson obeyed his orders too well. He marched his men into Florida in pursuit of the Indians, although he had no right to invade Spanish territory. He also captured two Spanish forts. In fact, what he actually did was to invade and conquer Florida. Although the American people applauded Jackson, he had created an embarrassing situation for President Monroe, who had no desire to make an enemy of Spain. So the two forts were returned to Spain, and the American forces were withdrawn.

The United States buys Florida. Jackson's invasion of Florida made it clear to Spain that she was unable to defend this territory. Also, Spain had her hands full at this time with the revolutions going on in Mexico and South America (Chapter 10). So, in a treaty with the United States in 1819, Spain gave up her claims to both East and West Florida. In return, the United States agreed to pay $5,000,000 to Americans who claimed Spain owed them money. This treaty also defined the boundary between the United States and Spanish territory west of the Mississippi. Two years later, the treaty went into effect. For the second time since 1783, the United States had acquired new territory.

C H E C K
U P

1. (a) How did the United States expand into West Florida? (b) Why did General Andrew Jackson invade East Florida?

2. How did the United States obtain Florida?

3 How Did Our Country Gain Texas, the Southwest, and California?

Not long after the purchase of Florida, the eyes of the United States turned to a vast Mexican territory to the southwest. In 1821, as you have learned in Chapter 10, Mexico declared her independence from Spain. The new Republic of Mexico claimed all of the land colonized by Spaniards in what is now the southwestern part of the United States. (The map on page 349 shows the location of this land.) But American pioneers were beginning to move into this region, and there were many people who thought that it should belong to the United States. They believed that it was the destiny of the United States to extend from the Atlantic Ocean to the Pacific. These land-hungry Americans were called *expansionists,* because they wanted to expand or enlarge the territory of the United States. In 1845, James K. Polk, a strong believer in expansion, entered the White House. During his presi-

This price, less than one cent per acre, was much lower than that charged in the United States.

dency a huge amount of territory was added to the United States. The story of how this came about will be told in the following pages.

TEXAS BECOMES A NATION, THEN A STATE

Americans settle in Texas. The story begins about 1820 in Texas. This land was thinly settled. A few wealthy Spaniards owned huge estates worked by mestizos and Indians. There were also several missions, founded by missionary priests, and a few military posts. But most of the inhabitants were Indians.

In 1822, a young man named Stephen F. Austin led a few American families into Texas to make their homes. Two years before, his father had persuaded the Spanish government (which then ruled Texas) to give him a huge tract of land there for American settlers. After his father died, Stephen Austin went ahead with this plan. He arranged with the government of Mexico, which by that time had won its independence from Spain, to bring settlers to Texas. He promised that the colonists would belong to the Catholic faith, would become Mexican citizens, and would obey Mexican laws. Austin was able to offer land to settlers for very little money, and his colony grew rapidly. The land was cultivated, and homes and schools were built.

The Mexican government liked the idea of building up Texas, and opened other parts of Texas for settlement by Americans. A rush for land followed. At one time, a settler could buy 4000 acres for as little as 30 dollars! Many small farmers from the United States bought land. Plantation owners from the South also began to move into the fertile lands of Texas with their families and slaves. By 1835, there

Students may wish to read The Birth of Texas.

were 30,000 colonists from the United States in Texas. This was a much greater number of settlers than Spain had sent during three hundred years.

Mexico becomes alarmed. Mexico realized too late that it had been a mistake to allow Americans to settle in her territory. They did not get along well with the government or with the Spanish people in Texas. The Americans were different in language, religion, and ways of living. Furthermore, they were independent in spirit and disliked living under Mexican law. Nevertheless, the Mexican government naturally expected them to obey its

EARLY AMERICANS in Texas are symbolized by these figures in a mural painting by Tom Lea. From left to right are an army officer, a soldier, and a plainsman.

THE ALAMO (right) still stands in San Antonio as a shrine of the Texan fight for independence. An old print (below) shows how the mission looked in 1836 when Mexican troops attacked the Texan garrison.

laws. It is easy to see that there would be quarrels between the American colonists and the Mexican government. One quarrel was about slavery. Laws had been passed forbidding slavery in Mexican territory, but the Americans brought slaves into Texas anyway.

Texans declare their independence. To prevent these disputes from growing more serious, the Mexican government tried to stop American colonists from entering Texas. This only made the Americans already there angrier, because they did not want to be left alone among people they disliked. When an ambitious general named Santa Anna seized control in Mexico, matters went from bad to worse. The Americans in Texas resented Santa Anna's harsh rule and finally revolted against Mexico. On March 2, 1836, they declared Texas an independent nation.

Mexico tried to crush the revolt. General Santa Anna led troops into Texas to

punish the Americans. The Texans suffered two severe defeats but won a final and glorious victory. The first defeat was at the Alamo (al'uh-moh) in the city of San Antonio. The Alamo was an old Spanish mission surrounded by high walls. A force of 187 Texans, under the command of Colonel William Barrett Travis, barricaded themselves in the mission and were besieged by 3000 Mexican soldiers under Santa Anna. In spite of the unequal odds, the Texans refused to surrender and held out for thirteen days. When the battle was over, all of them were dead. "Remember the Alamo" became the battle cry of all Texans. Soon after the Battle of the Alamo, Mexican troops surrounded and attacked a Texan force at Goliad. Here again the Texans were greatly outnumbered and were forced to surrender. Santa Anna ordered them all massacred, claiming that they were traitors to Mexico. His cruelty aroused all Texas.

Santa Anna referred to himself as the "Napoleon of the West."

Texas wins independence from Mexico.
In the battle of San Jacinto (san juh-*sin'*-toh) on April 21, 1836, the Texans thoroughly avenged these defeats. A Texan force of 800 men under General Sam Houston surprised a larger Mexican army. Shouting their battle cry, "Remember the Alamo! Remember Goliad!" they killed, wounded, or captured almost all of the enemy force. Santa Anna himself was made prisoner. This great victory practically ended the war. The Mexicans were forced to withdraw across the Rio Grande; Texas had won her independence. In 1836, a flag with a single star proclaimed the *Lone Star Republic* of Texas. Sam Houston, once governor of Tennessee, became its first president. The first Congress of the Republic met at Columbia. Later the capital was established at a site on the Colorado River and called Austin, in honor of Stephen F. Austin, the "Father of Texas."

Texas joins the Union. The Texans had no intention of remaining an independent republic for long. They considered themselves Americans, and they wanted to be a part of the United States. Furthermore, they did not feel safe, since Mexico had refused to recognize their independence. So in 1836, Texas petitioned Congress to be annexed, or added, to the United States. But many Americans violently objected to admitting Texas into the Union. Texas, they said, would become a slave state. Her entrance into the Union would mean that there would be more slave states than free states. Other Americans objected because Mexico still claimed Texas and threatened to go to war if the United States accepted Texas. As a result, the Senate refused to approve the request of Texas for admission into the Union.

For nearly ten years the Lone Star Republic remained independent. By 1845,
however, after the election of President Polk, the feeling against admitting Texas had lessened. In December, 1845, Texas was admitted to the Union. Today Texans call their state the *Lone Star State* and fly the Lone Star Flag below Old Glory. They are proud of their heroic fight for independence and of their former republic.

THE UNITED STATES AND MEXICO GO TO WAR

Mexico resents the annexation of Texas.
The government of Mexico, as you have read, had never recognized the independence of Texas. Also, Santa Anna had informed the United States government that if Texas were annexed, it would mean war with Mexico. As a result, when Texas joined the United States, Mexico became very angry. She now believed that Stephen F. Austin had intended from the beginning to win Texas for the United States. To make matters worse, Texas boldly claimed for her western boundary the Rio Grande. Mexico insisted that the Texas Republic had included only the land as far south and west as the Nueces (noo-*ay'*-sehs) River. (See map, page 356.)

Americans eye New Mexico. The annexation of Texas had another result, too. Americans who wanted the United States to expand began to look beyond Texas to other lands belonging to Mexico. For years American traders had been making their way to the region of New Mexico over the Santa Fe (*fay*) Trail. Each year a caravan of wagons creaked out of Independence, Missouri, and crawled across the plains of what is now Kansas to Santa Fe in New Mexico. (Look at the map on page 362.) This town was so far from the sources of Mexican goods that the settlers there would buy almost anything that the American traders brought. Al-

David Lavender's book, The Trail to Santa Fe, describes the long trip through desert and Indian country.

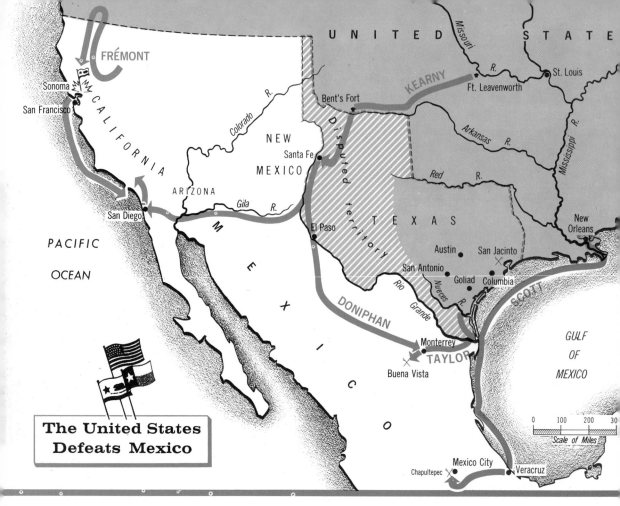

The United States Defeats Mexico

MAP STUDY Trace the routes of Kearny, Taylor, and Scott as you read about them in the text. (When Kearny left Santa Fe, he sent part of his army under Colonel Doniphan south to join Taylor.) Where were important battles fought in Mexico?

though most of the traders took their profits and returned home, a few stayed in Santa Fe. Americans began to want this whole region as a part of the United States.

Americans take an interest in California. The region of California, which also belonged to Mexico, was more thickly settled than the other Mexican possessions. The first settlements in California had been made by missionaries in the days when Spain ruled Mexico. Twenty-one missions, founded to teach Christianity to the Indians, stretched from San Diego in the south to beyond San Francisco in the north. Spanish soldiers occupied forts near the missions, and Indians went to live and Many of these missions can still be visited.

work under the direction of the mission priests. Spanish towns soon grew up around the missions. Wealthy Spaniards had also settled in California on large grants of land, where they raised horses and cattle, fruits and grain. These Spaniards lived well, with Indian servants to do their work. They rode fine horses and dressed like Spanish ladies and gentlemen. But they had little contact with the outside world. Spain, you remember, had allowed only Spaniards to settle in her colonies and did not permit them to trade with other countries.

When Mexico took over the Spanish territories, trade with other countries was

356

SAM HOUSTON

Three years as a runaway among the Indians hardened him for a rugged life on the frontier.

A SOLDIER under General Jackson, young Houston made a one-man charge against the Creek Indians at Horseshoe Bend and was severely wounded. Indians were Houston's friends as well as enemies, however, and he tried to defend their rights.

IN INDIAN DRESS, Houston went to Washington with some Cherokee chiefs to ask for better treatment for the Indians. The Secretary of War's anger caused Houston to resign from the army. He entered politics in Tennessee but moved on farther west to Texas.

TEXAN INDEPENDENCE was the goal as Houston, commander of the Texan forces, led his rain-soaked rebels in the successful battle against the Mexicans at San Jacinto. A hero with the pioneers, Houston helped set up a government for Texas and became its first President.

STATEHOOD for Texas achieved, Houston proudly receives the Lone Star Flag of the state he helped create. Serving as its senator for thirteen years, he tried to preserve the Union of all the states.

Tension increased because Mexico sought to expel United States settlers and to close California to immigration.

358   THE UNITED STATES EXPANDS AND IS TORN BY WAR

encouraged. Americans found that the California trade brought large profits. Many ships made the long trip around Cape Horn to California ports. Other traders made their way overland. Many of these men remained to make their homes in California. Still other Americans joined them and settled on ranches. By 1846, several hundred Americans lived in California. Like all Americans, they preferred to live under their own government. There was much talk about adding California to the United States; in fact, many Americans were willing to go to war to gain California as well as New Mexico.

War begins with Mexico. With so much ill feeling between Mexico and the United States, the stage was set for war. In late 1845, Polk had sent a representative to Mexico City to offer to buy California and New Mexico. But the Mexican government had refused even to see the American representative. When Polk heard about this early in 1846, he decided to take action against Mexico. For several months General Zachary Taylor had been guarding the Nueces River with a small army. Now President Polk ordered Taylor to take his position on the Rio Grande. A Mexican force crossed the river and attacked the American troops. When this news reached the United States, Congress on the recommendation of President Polk declared war early in May, 1846.

IN 1781 the Spanish governor of California founded a village which, after many years, grew into the great city of Los Angeles. Below you see some of the early settlers — twelve families from Mexico and a few soldiers and priests.

AMERICAN CAVALRYMEN slash through the enemy lines in one of the first battles of the Mexican War. News of this victory made General Zachary Taylor a popular hero.

The United States invades Mexico. The two-year war with Mexico was a one-sided conflict. General Taylor marched across the Rio Grande into northern Mexico, and early in 1847 he defeated Santa Anna's troops at Buena Vista (*bway' nah vees'tah*). Meanwhile, General Winfield Scott had sailed with an army from New Orleans and landed at Veracruz on the coast of Mexico. From there he fought his way up the mountains toward Mexico City. When Scott reached Chapultepec (*chuh-pool' tuh-peck*), an ancient palace and fortress near Mexico City, he demanded its surrender. Among the defenders of this fortress were a hundred young cadets from the national military school. When the commander refused to surrender, the Americans stormed and captured Chapultepec. The Mexican cadets who died bravely fighting have become heroes of Mexico just as the men who defended the Alamo are heroes of our country. On September 14, 1847, the American troops entered Mexico City itself. The war was practically over.

California and the New Mexico region are conquered. While fighting was going on in Mexico, the United States had seized control of California and New Mexico. This did not prove difficult because

(1) these regions were far from Mexico City, and (2) they were defended only by small groups of Mexican soldiers. This is how it happened.

Soon after the war began, an American force under Colonel Stephen W. Kearny had set out for Santa Fe. After capturing that city without a struggle, part of his small army moved on westward across the desert to California. Meanwhile, the Americans who lived in California had already overthrown the Mexican government. Their revolt was called the *Bear Flag Revolution* because the Americans carried a flag which showed the figure of a grizzly bear. John C. Frémont, a United States Army officer who was in California at that time, became a leader of the new Bear Flag Republic proclaimed by the Americans. Colonel Kearny arrived soon after the revolt began. After some skirmishes with the Mexican settlers, he took over all of California. The new Bear Flag gave way to the Stars and Stripes.[1] Thus, early in the Mexican War, the United States gained control over the regions of California and New Mexico.

---

[1] In memory of the short-lived Bear Flag Republic, flagstaffs in California today carry the Bear Flag beneath the flag of the United States.

The total Mexican army numbered less than **359** 35,000 men, many of them poorly trained and equipped. They fought bravely, however.

American casulties were about 1,700 killed or died of wounds, and 4,100 wounded. More than 11,000 soldiers, however, died of disease.

360 THE UNITED STATES EXPANDS AND IS TORN BY WAR

THE UNITED STATES ACQUIRES ALL OF THE SOUTHWEST

The war brings a vast territory to the United States. In February, 1848, the Mexican government was forced to make peace. Mexico had to accept the Rio Grande as her border. Thus, she recognized Texas as belonging to the United States. (Texas at this time included not only the present state of Texas but also parts of New Mexico, Colorado, Oklahoma, Wyoming, and Kansas.) As part of the peace treaty, Mexico also had to turn over a huge area called the *Mexican Cession*. It contained the present states of California, Nevada, Utah, most of Arizona, and parts of New Mexico, Wyoming, and Colorado. The Mexican Cession amounted to almost half of Mexico's territory. In return, the United States agreed to pay Mexico $15,000,000 in cash and also to pay American citizens $3,250,000 which the Mexican government owed them.

It is not difficult to understand why the Mexicans felt bitter toward the United States. They had lost a vast area of land. Although today Mexico and our country are good friends, Mexicans continued for many years after the Mexican War to dislike the United States.

The United States buys more land from Mexico. In 1853, the United States paid Mexico $10,000,000 for a stretch of land in the southern part of what are now New Mexico and Arizona. This area was needed to provide a route for a railroad which the United States wanted to build to the west coast. Since the arrangements were made by an American named James Gadsden, this territory was called the *Gadsden Purchase*. (See the map on page 362.) In a few short years, therefore, the United States had acquired a huge amount of land and reached its present boundary in the Southwest.

CHECK UP

1. (a) Why did Americans begin to settle in Texas after 1822? (b) Why did the Texans revolt against Mexico?

2. (a) How did Texas become an independent republic? (b) Why did many Americans oppose the admission of Texas into the Union?

3. (a) How did the annexation of Texas lead to war with Mexico? (b) Where did fighting take place in Mexico? (c) How did the United States win control of California and the New Mexico region?

4. (a) What were the results of the Mexican War? (b) What was the Gadsden Purchase?

4 How Did the Discovery of Gold Bring California into the Union?

The Mexican Cession opened up vast stretches of new land for restless pioneers. But not many American settlers were interested in the dry and mountainous regions which made up most of the Southwest. They did not yet realize the value of these lands for cattle raising. Nor did they know that rich deposits of copper, gold, and silver were located here. So this region was left to the Indians for many

years. In fact, it was not until 1912 that there were enough people in New Mexico and Arizona to form states! The story of California, on the other hand, is quite different. An exciting discovery brought people stampeding into California soon after it became part of the United States.

Gold is discovered in California. In the 1840's, a man named John Sutter lived in California, not far from where the

GOLD, being a heavy metal, can be sifted clear of earth and gravel by the method shown here. As shovelfuls of material from the river bed are washed down the trough, the heavy gold settles out and is caught on ridges inside the trough.

city of Sacramento stands today. Sutter had spent his youth in Switzerland. Strong and restless, longing to see the world and to make his fortune, he had set out for America. In 1839, he had settled in California, where he soon acquired an immense tract of land. As master of this private kingdom in the wilderness, John Sutter ruled over thousands of acres and hundreds of Indians. He raised wheat and corn and owned great herds of cattle, horses, and sheep.

On a rainy afternoon early in 1848, he was visited by James Marshall, a man who was building a sawmill for Sutter some miles away. Marshall was breathless with excitement and demanded to see him alone. This is how John Sutter later described Marshall's visit:

✳ I was surprised to see him. Only the day before I had sent him all the supplies he could possibly need. . . . I could not [understand] the purpose in this unexpected visit. Yet I conducted him from my office to my private rooms — parlor and bedroom — where we shut the door.

"Is the door locked?" said Marshall.

"No," I answered, "but I will lock it if you wish." He was a queer fellow and I only supposed he took this way of telling me some secret.

Then he said distinctly: "Are we alone?"

"Surely," I answered.

[Marshall then asked for some scales.]

Shrugging, and thinking to humor him, I went myself and fetched the scales. On my return I failed to lock the door. Then Marshall dug feverishly into his pantaloon pockets and pulled forth a white cotton rag which had something rolled up in it. Just as he was unfolding it to show me the contents, the door was opened by a clerk who was merely passing through on some business and was not aware we were in the room at all.

"There!" screamed Marshall, "did I not tell you we had listeners!" Quickly he thrust the rag back into his pocket. I [quieted] him, my curiosity aroused. Ordering the surprised clerk to retire, I locked the door.

Then he drew out the rag again. Opening the cloth carefully, he held it before me in his hand. It held what might have been an ounce and a half of gold dust — dust, flakes and grains. The biggest piece was not as large as a pea and varied from that down to less than a pinhead in size.

"I believe it is gold!" whispered Marshall, his eyes wild and restless. "But the people at the mill laughed at me — said I was crazy!" I examined his find closely.

"Yes, it looks like gold," I admitted slowly. "Come let us test it. . . ."

The test showed that Marshall had indeed discovered gold!

During 1849 the population of California increased by 100,000.

362   THE UNITED STATES EXPANDS AND IS TORN BY WAR

Gold seekers rush to California. Not for long was the news of the discovery of gold kept behind locked doors. Quickly it spread through the neighborhood, then through all of California. By 1849 it had leaped across the United States and around the world. Adventurous men by the thousands deserted shops, farms, offices, and headed for California. Why should a man spend all his life earning a bare living when a few weeks of work in the California gold fields might bring him a fortune in gold? Hordes of uninvited visitors rushed to John Sutter's land. They camped in his fields, trampled down his crops, stole his horses and cattle. The present city of Sacramento was founded on part of Sutter's land. From a settlement of four houses in April, 1848, it grew within a short time to a booming city of almost 10,000.

The *forty-niners,* as the people who rushed to California for gold were called, were not like the ordinary American pioneers. They were for the most part men without families, adventurers seeking to make a fortune in gold. Among them were gamblers and desperate criminals as well as decent men.

The forty-niners come by land and sea. The forty-niners had a choice of several routes to California. Look at the map on this page and trace the routes as you read. Independence, Missouri, was the starting point for the overland travelers. From here they could take the old trail to

MAP STUDY   (1) What states lined the western bank of the Mississippi by the mid-1800's? (2) By what routes could people reach the west coast? Tell where each began and ended.

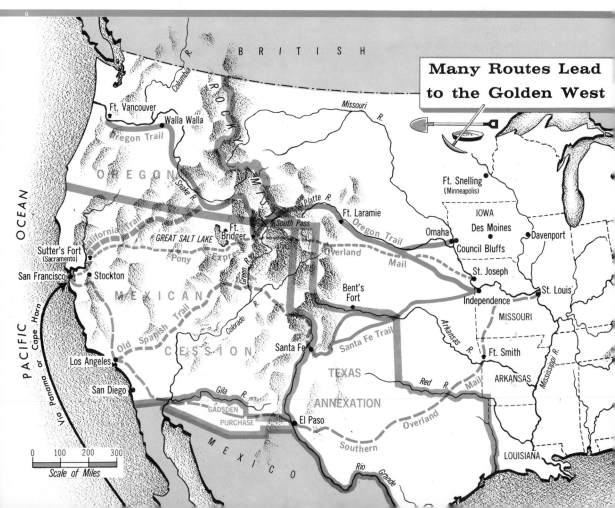

Many Routes Lead to the Golden West

Santa Fe and continue on across the deserts of New Mexico, Arizona, and California. This route took over two months, and those who followed it suffered from heat and thirst. More of the forty-niners followed the Oregon Trail (of which we shall read later) as far as the Great Salt Lake. Then on they struggled across deserts and mountains to northern California. These men ran the dreadful risk of being caught in the mountains by the winter snows. Both of these main overland routes were difficult.

There were also routes by sea which the gold seekers might take. The safest but longest trip was around Cape Horn and north to San Francisco. Because this journey took from six to nine months, many of the forty-niners chose a faster route by way of Panama. Ships of every kind, jammed with men, sailed from the Atlantic coast to the east coast of Panama. From there the men crossed the Isthmus through jungle and swamp to the Pacific coast. Many fell ill from insect bites or died of fever. Those who survived boarded ships for San Francisco.

Life was rough in California in 1849. Once in California, the gold seekers rushed inland from San Francisco to the rivers and mountain sides where gold had been found. There they staked out their *claims* (small plots of land) and started digging gravel and washing it for gold. Life at the mines or *diggings* was rough. A man who tried to take another's claim was tried by a court of miners and punished. Men who stole gold were hanged. Fighting, robbery, and murder were common in the mining camps. The camps often had odd names, such as Hangtown, You-Bet, Red Dog, and Ground Hog Glory! Within ten years about $500,000,000 worth of gold was found in California. Some of the miners who came the first

year, when gold was plentiful, became rich. But the latecomers, for all their trouble, were often no better off than they had been back home.

Many men soon realized that they could make more money by selling food and supplies to the miners than by seeking gold. The miners carried bags of gold dust and paid for goods in ounces of gold instead of with dollars. Prices were unbelievably high. Eggs were 50 cents apiece, onions were a dollar a pound, and bread was 50 cents a loaf. Boots cost as much as 100 dollars!

Among the miners the chief amusements were gambling, racing, and drinking. You can imagine how hard it was to keep law and order when thousands of men were bent on making fortunes by fair means or foul. Crime was especially serious in San Francisco. Men from all over the world passed through that city on their way to the diggings. San Francisco grew rapidly, as boarding houses, hotels, and saloons were hastily put up to serve the hordes of gold seekers. Gamblers, criminals, and desperadoes flocked there to prey on the miners. Murder became an everyday happening. In self-defense, some of the law-abiding citizens formed committees to keep order. They called themselves the *vigilantes* or *vigilance committees*. (To be *vigilant* is to be alert to danger.) Many of the most desperate criminals were arrested, tried, and hanged. Others got out of town before they were caught.

California becomes a state. By the end of 1849, California had grown so tremendously that its people drew up a state constitution. In September, 1850, California was admitted to the Union as a free state. Because travel was so slow, it was over a month before Californians heard the news.

After World War II, the search for uranium produced somewhat similar boom-town conditions in this country and Canada.

THE OVERLAND STAGE dashes through a desolate part of the West. Few passengers made the trip for pleasure, since it meant traveling day and night for three weeks in a lurching, crowded stagecoach.

By 1860, there were 380,000 people in California, most of them in the northern part of the state. This was four times the population ten years earlier. San Francisco had become an important city with more than 50,000 inhabitants. When gold was no longer plentiful, many mining camps became deserted ghost towns; others, however, developed into flourishing communities. Stockton and Sacramento, located at the entrance to the gold regions, grew rapidly. Hangtown changed its name to Placerville and became a settled community. Los Angeles and San Diego in the south were not affected by the gold rush. They remained small, sleepy towns for many years.

The Overland stage connects California with the East. California was 2000 miles away from the settled part of the United States. Naturally travelers to or from the coast did not want to spend several months on the way. So stagecoach lines were established which ran from the Missouri River to points in California. The most important of these was the Overland Mail, which carried mail and passengers from Missouri to San Francisco.

The stagecoaches, called Concord coaches, were pulled by four or six horses and carried as many as nine passengers and three sacks of mail. They traveled day and night, stopping every ten or fifteen miles at wayside stations to change horses. Passengers paid about $200 for the trip, which took from 20 to 25 days. The journey was dangerous. Indians sometimes attacked the coaches, stealing the horses and robbing and killing the passengers. Another danger came from highwaymen, who waylaid the coaches, especially those carrying gold from the mines. Many a traveler was robbed and many a bag of gold stolen by these desperadoes. Not content with stealing, they often killed their victims in cold blood.

The Pony Express furnishes fast mail service. The stagecoach, however, was too slow for important mail. In 1860, the famous Pony Express was established. It took from eight to twelve days to cover the distance from St. Joseph, Missouri, to Sacramento, California. The riders for the Pony Express were carefully picked. They needed to be hardy and brave, for they had to ride over mountain and desert in all kinds of weather and they often had to fight off Indians and robbers. The riders wore buckskin suits, and carried rifles, knives, or six-shooters for protection. The

364 *See also Riders of the Pony Express by Moody.*

men rode for stretches of about one hundred miles apiece. Each man rode at top speed, dashing into a station every ten or fifteen miles to change horses. He would throw his saddlebags containing the mail on a fresh horse, mount, and speed on his way in less than two minutes. One of the best Pony Express riders once covered 120 miles in eight hours, despite being wounded by Indians along the way.

Mark Twain, traveling west on the Overland stagecoach, describes the thrill of seeing a Pony Express rider:

We had had a consuming desire, from the beginning, to see a pony-rider, but somehow or other all that passed us and all that met us managed to streak by in the night, and so we heard only a whiz and a hail, and the swift phantom of the desert was gone before we could get our heads out of the windows. But now we were expecting one along every moment, and would see him in broad daylight. Presently the driver exclaims:

"HERE HE COMES!"

Every neck is stretched further, and every eye strained wider. Away across the endless dead level of the prairie a black speck appears against the sky, and it is plain that it moves. Well, I should think so! In a second or two it becomes a horse and rider, rising and falling, rising and falling — sweeping toward us nearer and nearer — growing more and more distinct, more and more sharply defined — nearer and still nearer — and the flutter of the hoofs comes faintly to the ear — another instant a whoop and a hurrah from our upper deck, a wave of the rider's hand, but no reply, and man and horse burst past our excited faces, and go winging away like a belated fragment of a storm!

The Pony Express operated for only a little more than one year. In that short

WANTED

YOUNG, SKINNY

Wiry fellows not over 18.

Must be expert riders, willing to risk death daily. Orphans preferred.

Wages $25.00 per week

THE PONY EXPRESS, using posters such as this one, advertised for daring young riders. Why do you suppose "wiry," young fellows were wanted?

time, however, its riders became glamorous figures in American life. Their heroic deeds have been told in many stories and motion pictures. The company which operated the Pony Express went out of business in 1861, about the same time that a telegraph line to San Francisco was completed. Mail continued to go by stagecoach until the first transcontinental railroad was completed in 1869. (Locate the routes of the Overland Mail and the Pony Express on the map on page 362.)

CHECK UP

1. (a) Where was gold discovered in California? (b) By what routes did the gold seekers travel to California? (c) What was life like in the gold mining towns?

2. How did the gold rush help California become a state?

3. What means of communication and transportation linked California and the East?

This extract and the one about the discovery of gold (page 361) suggest the type of material that can be read to students.

5 How Did the United States Gain Part of the Oregon Country?

Suppose the map on page 362 were a jigsaw puzzle. It would contain four pieces representing the steps by which the United States extended its territory west of the Louisiana Purchase until it reached the Pacific Ocean. So far in this chapter you have read about the addition of three of these pieces — the Texas Annexation, the Mexican Cession, and the Gadsden Purchase. The remaining piece is labeled Oregon. How was this piece fitted into the puzzle?

Four nations claim Oregon. All the region between Alaska and California was once called Oregon. This beautiful land of mountains, fertile valleys, and rivers abounded in fur-bearing animals. In the early 1800's Oregon was claimed by four nations.

(1) Spain said Oregon was hers chiefly because, when Balboa discovered the Pacific Ocean in 1513, he had claimed all the lands it touched for Spain. Also, later Spanish explorers had cruised along the Oregon coast.

(2) England claimed Oregon because Sir Francis Drake, in his voyage around the world, had sailed along the coast of Oregon in 1579. Still more important were the British explorations by Captain James Cook and Captain George Vancouver. Captain Cook had explored the coast as far as northern Alaska. Captain Vancouver had discovered Puget Sound and had sailed around Vancouver Island, which was named in his honor.

(3) In the 1700's, Russia laid claim to Oregon. A navigator named Vitus Bering had discovered the strait now named for him and crossed it to claim Alaska for Russia. The Russians established colonies in North America and hunted furs along the coast of Alaska and southward to California.

(4) The fourth country to make a bid for Oregon was the United States. Captain Robert Gray, who carried furs from Oregon to China (page 268), had sailed up the mouth of the Columbia River. The explorations of Lewis and Clark, who also reached the mouth of the Columbia, strengthened the claim of the United States.

Rival fur companies compete for furs in Oregon. Early in the 1800's, both British and American fur traders began to see possibilities for a rich fur trade in Oregon. The British already had built up a large and profitable fur trade in the region around the Great Lakes and Hudson Bay. This trade was under the control of the Hudson's Bay Company. John Jacob Astor was a leader in the American fur trade. He had come to America from Germany soon after the Revolutionary War. Astor dreamed of establishing a line of trading posts from the Mississippi to the Pacific. Furs could be sent from these posts to a port in Oregon and from there be shipped to China.

Astor organized the American Fur Company and hired French-Canadian fur traders to work for him. In 1811, Astor's men made the difficult journey to the Pacific coast. They built a fur-trading post, called Astoria, near the mouth of the Columbia River. No sooner had the American company established its post than it discovered that the British had built a post where Spokane, Washington, is today. For a short time these two companies were rivals for the Oregon fur business. But the War of 1812 ruined Astor's plans. At that time, the Americans sold their holdings to the British.

Alexander Mackenzie discovered the first canoe route across the continent to the Pacific. See The First Northwest Passage.

366

(*Continued on page 369*)

THE
Golden West

Before the gold rush, California was a remote land of spacious ranches whose Spanish and Mexican owners spent much of their time on horseback. To them, a good saddle was more important than a fine piece of furniture. Above, note the design of flowers and fruit which was hand-tooled into the leather of a lady's sidesaddle. Many of the first Spanish settlements in California and the Southwest were missions, established to convert the local Indians to Christianity. The early Spanish churchmen built these outposts to last. Shown at left is San Xavier del Bac, a mission still standing near Tucson, Arizona.

A mission included not only a church but other buildings where the priests lived and worked. At right is the library of a mission near Carmel, California, with its store of precious religious books and pictures. Note the ceiling timbers which rest on thick masonry walls.

In the Wild West of gold-rush days, the Colt revolver (right) was valued for its fast-action design. This one, handsomely engraved, was used in warfare against the Apache Indians.

Before a telegraph line had crossed the plains, the Pony Express (above) provided the fastest communication between Missouri and the west coast. This old print shows one of the daring relay riders escaping from Indians. At right can be seen an Indian grave, raised on poles above the hard sod. The painting below shows the busy new navy yard at Mare Island near San Francisco. Built in 1853, it gave the navy a base on the Pacific coast from which it could protect the gold-rich Sacramento valley.

HARDSHIP AND DANGER faced the pioneers on the way to Oregon. Here Indians attack a wagon train. (This is a painting by Frederic Remington, who painted many pictures of the West.)

England and the United States share Oregon. After the war, both the United States and Great Britain still had strong claims to Oregon which neither of them would give up. In 1818, the two countries agreed, therefore, to the *joint occupation* of Oregon; that is, they decided to own Oregon together. Shortly afterward, both Spain and Russia gave up their claims to Oregon. Spain agreed to claim no land north of the forty-second parallel, while Russia gave up any claims south of the latitude of 54° 40′. (See map on page 349.) Thus, the United States and Great Britain were free to try to work out their plan of joint occupation in the Oregon Country.

The British settle Oregon first. For about 20 years after 1818, not many Americans went to Oregon. Only a few fur traders and other daring persons from the East were willing to risk the long and dangerous journey across the western plains and mountains. The British, on the other hand, were making good profits from the Oregon fur trade, which was very largely controlled by the Hudson's Bay Company. There was no regular government in Oregon at this time. In Fort Vancouver Dr. John McLoughlin, a Canadian, was employed by the Hudson's Bay Com-

pany to act as governor. McLoughlin, a fair and kindly man, treated the Indians well and welcomed the few Americans who found their way to Oregon. He believed that the people in Oregon should not rely on fur trading for their living but should also raise their own food. Soon there were crops growing in fertile fields around Fort Vancouver, and farms were being started throughout Oregon.

Americans learn about Oregon. News of this fertile region in the Pacific Northwest did not attract many Americans until the late 1830's. Then the news was spread by missionaries who had gone there to teach Christianity to the Indians. Among these missionaries were Henry Spalding and Dr. Marcus Whitman. In 1836, accompanied by their young wives, they had made the dangerous journey to Fort Vancouver, where they were welcomed by John McLoughlin. Their wives, Narcissa Whitman and Eliza Spalding, were the first white women to cross the western mountains into the Northwest.

The Whitmans started a mission at Walla Walla near the Columbia River. For about eleven years they worked among the Indians, trying to help them and educate them. The Whitmans were finally killed by some Indians who misunderstood

For information about the fur Trade, **369** *see Trappers and Mountain Men.*

An interesting example of how the lay of the land determines a route. This is true of present-day highways and railroads crossing the Rockies.

370 THE UNITED STATES EXPANDS AND IS TORN BY WAR

what they were trying to do. Before this tragedy, however, they had written enthusiastic letters back East describing the rich farm lands, the climate, the forests, and the salmon fishing in Oregon.

Americans follow the Oregon Trail. Reports from the Whitmans and others reached the East soon after the Panic of 1837 broke out, when many people were out of work and discouraged. Soon covered wagons began rolling westward. The route these pioneers followed was the famous Oregon Trail. (See map, page 362.) The pioneers gathered at some town along the Missouri River, such as Independence or St. Joseph or Omaha. Here they banded together in great caravans for protection against the Indians. When the spring grass was high enough to feed the horses and cattle, they set out. Try to

imagine what one of these caravans was like. Scouts on horseback went far ahead of the wagons to be sure the way was safe. The long line of prairie schooners, horses, cattle, and oxen crawled westward from dawn to dusk on the two-thousand-mile journey. Each night the wagons were drawn up in a circle for defense against Indian attacks. If all went well, there was time to reach Oregon before snow fell in the Rockies and made them impassable. Bleached bones along the trail, however, told the story of suffering and death, the fate of many a pioneer.

The trail left the Missouri River and followed the Platte River along its north branch into the Rockies. From here the pioneers climbed a steep grade to the South Pass. Between towering walls of rock they made their way through the Rockies. To the west they found the Green River and from there they crossed to the Snake River. The Snake took them north and west to the great Columbia. Oregon at last!

Oregon is divided. By the early 1840's several thousand Americans had made their way to Oregon, where they had become farmers and had started little villages. But these settlers were not satisfied to have Oregon shared by the United States and Great Britain. Like American settlers in Texas and California, they wanted a government of their own and they wanted to be a part of the United States. Soon the governments of Great Britain and the United States began to realize that the plan of joint occupation would no longer work.

Many Americans insisted that the United States should claim all of Oregon, just as they were clamoring for the annexation of Texas and the whole Southwest. James K. Polk was their champion. When he ran for President in 1844, he warmly supported both causes. Such popular slogans

MAP STUDY The Oregon dispute was settled by extending the border between Canada and the United States to the Pacific. (Compare with the map on page 349.)

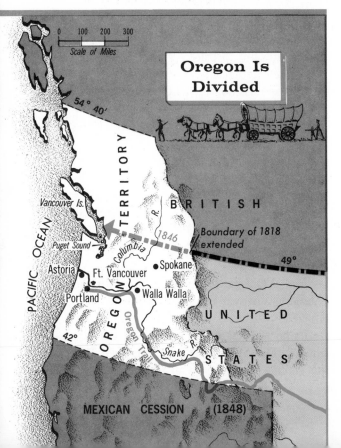

Oregon Is Divided

as "All of Oregon or none" and "Fifty-four forty, or fight" expressed the strong feelings that people had about Oregon. After his election, Polk set out to gain Oregon as well as the Southwest.

So many Americans had been flocking into Oregon that the British fur trade was no longer as profitable as it had been. The British government, realizing this, was willing to compromise but not to give up all of Oregon. The United States also was willing to compromise. Early in 1846, the quarrel between the United States and Mexico threatened to turn into war (page 358). It would have been unwise for President Polk to risk war with the British at the same time. In June of 1846, therefore, an agreement was reached between the governments of Great Britain and the United States. This agreement divided Oregon between the two countries at the forty-ninth parallel of latitude. The border between Canada and the United States had previously been set at that latitude from the Great Lakes to the Rocky Mountains. The agreement of 1846 simply extended this line to the Pacific Ocean. (Look at the map on page 370.)

The land in the Northwest below the forty-ninth parallel was organized by Congress as the Oregon Territory. Its population continued to grow, and in 1859

part of the territory was admitted to the Union as the state of Oregon. The rest of the territory was then called Washington. Out of it, years later, the states of Washington and Idaho were formed.

●

In this chapter you have learned (1) how East and West Florida were secured from Spain, (2) how Texas came to join the Union, (3) how a war with Mexico added California and the Southwest to the United States, and (4) how the great Pacific Northwest became part of our country. The westward march of American pioneers, which began when "the West" was only a few miles inland from the Atlantic seacoast, had reached the Pacific Ocean. The United States now stretched across North America for 2800 miles, "from sea to shining sea."

CHECK UP

1. (a) What four countries claimed the Oregon Country in the early 1800's? (b) What was the basis for the claim of each of these countries? (c) How was Oregon governed after 1818?

2. (a) Why were the British interested in Oregon? (b) Why did Americans begin to settle there? (c) By what route did American settlers reach Oregon?

3. How did Great Britain and the United States settle their rival claims to Oregon?

Call attention to the fact that only 40 years had passed since the Lewis and Clark expedition.

Check Up on Chapter 18

Do You Know the Meaning?

1. annexation	4. diggings
2. expansionist	5. desperado
3. flatboat	6. joint occupation

Can You Identify?

1. Zebulon Pike	4. Lone Star Republic
2. Santa Anna	5. Sam Houston
3. Mexican Cession	6. John Sutter

Can You Identify? (Cont.)

7. Marcus Whitman	15. Overland Mail
8. James K. Polk	16. Gadsden Purchase
9. John J. Astor	17. forty-niners
10. vigilante	18. 1803
11. Lewis and Clark	19. 1819
12. Bear Flag Republic	20. 1845
13. Alamo	21. 1846–48
14. Pony Express	22. 1848

Can You Identify? (Cont.)

23. Stephen Austin   25. Stephen W. Kearny
24. Zachary Taylor   26. John C. Frémont

Can You Locate?

1. St. Louis   9. San Francisco
2. Texas   10. Sacramento
3. St. Joseph   11. San Antonio
4. Independence   12. Platte River
5. Missouri River   13. California
6. Santa Fe   14. Oregon
7. Rio Grande   15. Spokane
8. Nueces River   16. Astoria
          17. Columbia River

What Do You Think?

1. After the War of 1812 many Americans argued that it was the destiny of the United

What Do You Think? (Cont.)

States to acquire Florida and the land westward to the Pacific. (a) Why did they feel this way? (b) How did Spaniards, Mexicans, British, and Canadians feel about it?

2. Why was it fortunate for the United States that it could expand into a thinly settled and little-developed region?

3. Several generals (among them William Henry Harrison, Andrew Jackson, and Zachary Taylor) have become Presidents of the United States. Why? Is a general likely to have the qualities and experience needed to make a good President?

4. (a) Why did the frontier about 1850 jump from the area just west of the Mississippi to the Pacific coast? (b) How would you draw the line of the frontier after that date?

Questions #1 and 2 help students to look at Manifest Destiny from the point of view of others.

LINKING PAST AND PRESENT

Modern pioneers take the Oregon Trail. A strange sight was seen in Portland, Oregon, in the summer of 1959 — a train of covered wagons pulling into town after a long trek on the Oregon Trail! This adventure was a feature of the celebration of the 100th anniversary of Oregon's statehood. Twenty-eight Oregonians with a seven-wagon train set out in early summer from Independence, Missouri, and reached Portland in a hundred days. It took the early pioneers almost twice as long to make the same trip. Of course, the modern pioneers traveled on paved roads and could cross rivers on bridges. And when they camped at night, they could feel safe from Indian ambush, although curious visitors flocked to see them!

Great western cities. Within a remarkably short time great cities sprang up in the West during the period we have been reading about. In many cases favorable locations were responsible for this rapid growth.

In 1841, for example, a log hut was built on a river where Dallas, Texas, stands today. Soon a village grew up. Located in a fertile agricultural region, Dallas became the market for the huge cotton crops produced on nearby plantations. Railroads were built to move the cotton, and factories were started to make cotton gins. Later, oil was discovered nearby, and Dallas grew big and rich.

Seattle, Washington, founded in the 1850's, has grown from a settlement of 21 people to a great ocean port. At first, trade in lumber from the huge forests nearby caused Seattle to grow. Then, in 1884, the Northern Pacific Railroad connected the city with eastern trade. When gold was discovered in Alaska, Seattle became a teeming city where gold seekers bought supplies and booked passage for Alaska. Later, the opening of the Panama Canal brought to Seattle a rich trade with our eastern ports and with Europe.

CHAPTER

19

The North and the South

Come to Blows

The South held that the Federal Union was one of <u>sovereign</u> states. Since sovereign states had joined this union voluntarily, they retained the right to leave it, i. e., to secede.

What this chapter is about —

Of all wars, wars between people of the same country are the most tragic. Oftentimes they are the most bitter as well. Citizens fight their fellow citizens; townsmen fight their fellow townsmen. Sometimes even members of the same family fight on opposite sides. Between 1861 and 1865, our country was torn apart by such a war. At that time, the North and the South came to blows in the Civil War, called by some the War Between the States. The first action of the war took place at Fort Sumter in South Carolina.

This tragic conflict grew out of conditions which have been described in earlier chapters of this book. As you know, different ways of living had developed in the North and in the South. Many Northerners earned their living by trading, shipping, and manufacturing. People in the South, on the other hand, depended on farming for a living, with cotton as their chief crop. Because of these differences in ways of living, the two sections often did not agree on important questions such as the tariff and foreign trade. When questions like these came before Congress, the North and the South frequently lined up on opposite sides. Disagreements are perfectly natural in a country as large as ours, and usually it is possible to settle them fairly and peacefully.

But in the first half of the 1800's, the disagreement over slavery sharply split the

North and South. You remember that the states in the North had given up slavery because it did not pay in that part of the country. The southern states, on the other hand, had held onto slavery because they felt they needed slaves to raise their huge cotton crops. Even this disagreement over slavery might in time have been worked out peacefully if it had not been for one thing — the rapid expansion of our country westward. Again and again, arguments between the North and the South arose over permitting slavery in the new western lands. For some years these arguments were settled by compromises. But finally the quarrel became so bitter that compromise was no longer possible, and our country moved steadily toward war.

In this chapter we shall see how war between the two sections of our country came about. The following questions will help you to understand the events leading up to the Civil War:

1. How did the North and the South settle their differences for many years?

2. How did the two sections move closer to conflict?

3. What events led directly to war between the North and South?

If slave labor were needed chiefly for large-scale growing of cotton, the territory into which slavery would expand was limited.

1 How Did the North and the South Settle Their Differences for Many Years?

In the previous chapter you learned how the United States gained section after section of land, until it stretched across the great plains and mountains to the shores of the Pacific. People from both the North and the South moved into these new lands. Naturally they took with them the ways of living and thinking to which they were accustomed. As more and more settlements were started, new states were sure to be formed. Both the North and the South realized how important the votes of the Westerners in Congress would be. Would these votes add to the strength of the North or the South? Would they favor slavery or oppose it? Both sections felt they needed the votes of the new western states.

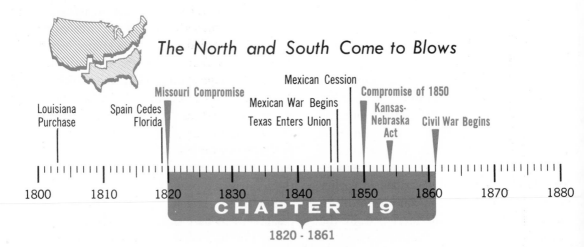

The North and South Come to Blows

Louisiana Purchase

Spain Cedes Florida

Missouri Compromise

Mexican War Begins

Texas Enters Union

Mexican Cession

Compromise of 1850

Kansas-Nebraska Act

Civil War Begins

1800   1810   1820   1830   1840   1850   1860   1870   1880

CHAPTER 19

1820 - 1861

A COMPROMISE SETTLES THE QUESTION OF SLAVERY IN THE LOUISIANA TERRITORY

The admission of Missouri starts a conflict over slavery. The first territory to be added to the United States was the Louisiana Purchase, and the first state to be formed from this territory was Louisiana. There was no question about slavery there. Louisiana was clearly in the lower South, and slavery had existed there since its early days. So Louisiana was admitted to the Union as a slave state. But in 1819, when Missouri asked to be admitted to the Union, an angry dispute broke out between North and South. Missouri, too, was a part of the Louisiana Purchase but lay much farther north than the state of Louisiana.

Many owners of slaves had settled in Missouri. When Missouri asked permission to become a state, its people adopted a rule that would allow slavery in the new state. But when Missouri's request to enter the Union came before Congress, a northern representative demanded that Congress admit Missouri only if Missouri would rid itself of slavery. This angered the South. Southerners feared that if slavery were forbidden in Missouri, it might be forbidden in other states to be carved out of the Louisiana Purchase. Why, asked the South, should northern men without slaves be allowed to go West to settle and form states when southern men with slaves were forbidden to do so?

The Missouri Compromise settles the quarrel. When the dispute was at fever pitch, a fortunate thing occurred. Maine, which was then a part of Massachusetts, asked to be admitted to the Union as a separate state. The people of Maine did not need or want slavery. At once people began to say, "Here is a chance to settle the bitter quarrel over Missouri." In 1820 Congress reached a settlement which is called the *Missouri Compromise* or the *Compromise of 1820.* (See the first map on page 379.)

Under this compromise, (1) Missouri came into the Union as a slave state and (2) Maine as a free state. (3) To settle the question of slavery in the rest of the Louisiana Purchase, a dividing line was agreed upon. This line was a continuation of the southern boundary of Missouri and ran westward across the entire Louisiana Purchase. In the future, all states to be made out of the Louisiana Purchase were to be free states if they lay north of that line. If they lay south of the line, they would be permitted to have slavery.

This compromise seemed fair. The South received what it had asked — slavery in Missouri. The North could count on the votes of Maine in Congress to balance those of Missouri. Both sides were relieved that Congress had passed a law settling the question of slavery within the Louisiana Purchase. The North was especially pleased, for Congress had taken the position that it had a right to decide about slavery in territories still to become states.

The quarrel leaves bitter feelings. Even though the quarrel had ended in the Missouri Compromise, it had aroused bitter feelings. Peering into the future, many men feared that new quarrels would arise over slavery, and that these might be even more dangerous than the one which had just been settled. Thomas Jefferson expressed this fear when he wrote: "This momentous question, like a fire bell in the night, awakened and filled me with terror." He added that in "the gloomiest hour of the Revolutionary War" he had not been so afraid for his country.

THE NORTH AND THE SOUTH ARGUE OVER STATES' RIGHTS

The argument over admitting Missouri to the Union had made Southerners aware of a threat to their way of living. Cotton was wearing out the soil of the South, and Southerners feared that a day might come when they would lack new land on which to grow cotton. They were also troubled (as you read in Chapter 17) by high tariff laws, which raised prices on many articles. Because the South bought quantities of manufactured goods from England, which in turn bought much of the South's cotton, high tariff duties seemed to threaten the prosperity of the South. Southerners were loyal to the Union, but they began to ask: "Is there any way we can live peaceably in the Union and yet be assured of conditions necessary to our way of life?"

The idea of states' rights grows in the South. It seemed to southern leaders that there was a way to stay in the Union and at the same time protect southern interests. Our Constitution, you remember, divides the powers of government between the United States and the states. The United States government has only those powers which are listed in the Constitution. All other powers belong to the states. The Southerners believed that they could protect their way of living by insisting that the United States government keep its hands off all matters over which the Constitution had not given it definite authority. This idea was the basis for what is known as the doctrine of *states' rights.*

Southerners defend states' rights. John C. Calhoun of South Carolina became the South's foremost defender of states' rights. You have already learned that he wrote a strong protest against the high tariff law of 1828. In this protest Calhoun declared that Congress did not have the right to set tariff duties so high that one section of the country would suffer. He spoke for many Southerners when he protested that the tariff law was "unconstitutional, oppressive, and unjust."

One of the most famous debates in the United States Senate took place in 1830 over the question of states' rights. The debate went on for nearly two weeks. Because Calhoun was then Vice-President, he could not take part in the debate. But Senator Robert Y. Hayne, also of South Carolina, spoke eloquently for the South. He argued that in adopting the Constitution the states had surrendered only certain powers to the government of the United States. Any state, he declared, had the right to take steps against a law passed by Congress if the state believed that the law violated the Constitution.

Daniel Webster speaks for a strong Union. Senator Daniel Webster of Massachusetts replied to the speech of Senator Hayne. Webster was a short man, but his large head and his eyes, "that seemed to glow like dull coals," gave him a majestic appearance. On days when he intended to make a long speech, Webster wore a buff-colored vest and an old-fashioned blue coat with brass buttons. This was the dress popular at the time of the Revolution, and made his appearance even more dramatic. Webster did not agree with the South's views on states' rights. He spoke for those Americans who believed that if the Union were to last, the federal government must have more power than the states.

On the day in 1830 when Daniel Webster began his reply to Hayne, the Senate galleries were crowded with visitors who had come to hear him. Webster rose and began to speak in his deep, full voice. What would happen if each state insisted on the right to decide for itself whether a law of Congress was constitutional? His answer was that the United States would soon break apart into separate states or groups of states. In the long and flowery sentences used by speakers of his day,

At the Hartford Convention the New England states had invoked states' rights (see page 254).

CLAY, CALHOUN, AND WEBSTER

First elected to Congress in the early 1800's, these three men spent 40 years in public service during which they became leading spokesmen for the three different sections of the country — West, South, and North.

The Fight for the Union by Margaret Coit makes clear the role of these men during the years when sectionalism grew stronger.

DANIEL WEBSTER of Massachusetts was Representative, Senator, and twice Secretary of State.

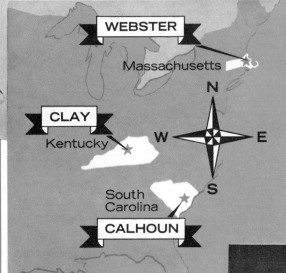

HENRY CLAY of Kentucky served as Representative, Speaker of the House, Senator, and Secretary of State.

THREE OLD STATESMEN met in the Senate for the last time to debate the Compromise of 1850 (below). From left to right, white frames mark Webster, Clay, and Calhoun.

JOHN C. CALHOUN of South Carolina was Secretary of War and State and Vice-President, as well as Representative and Senator.

Webster made a stirring plea for the Union. He ended with these thrilling words:

✷ When my eyes shall be turned to behold for the last time the sun in heaven, may I not see him shining on the broken and dishonored fragments of a once glorious Union; on States dissevered, discordant, belligerent; on a land rent with civil feuds, or drenched, it may be, in fraternal [brothers'] blood. Let their last feeble and lingering glance rather behold the glorious ensign [flag] of the republic, now known and honored throughout the earth, still full high advanced, its arms and trophies streaming in their original luster, not a stripe erased or polluted, not a single star obscured, bearing for its motto no such miserable interrogatory [question] as "What is all this worth?" nor those other words of delusion and folly, "Liberty first and Union afterwards"; but everywhere, spread all over in characters of living light, blazing on all its ample folds, as they float over the sea and over the land, and in every wind under the whole heavens, that other sentiment, dear to every true American heart — Liberty *and* Union, now and forever, one and inseparable.

The famous Webster-Hayne debate was only one in a series of disputes over states' rights. The southern states came to believe so strongly in states' rights that they began to claim the right to withdraw from the Union altogether. And when they finally took this step, as we shall see, the tragic Civil War followed.

NEW QUARRELS LEAD TO THE COMPROMISE OF 1850

By the Missouri Compromise every bit of territory belonging to the United States in 1820 had been marked either "free" or "slave." The addition of new territories, however, was certain to open the debate again. You have already read (Chapter 18) how Americans were divided over the admission of Texas as a slave state.

The Mexican War brings a new quarrel over slavery. When the Mexican War broke out in 1846, it became clear that the United States might win immense new territories. At once there arose the question: "Are the new lands to be slave or free?" Hardly had the war begun when a representative from Pennsylvania named David Wilmot suggested an answer to the question. Wilmot hated slavery. He proposed that Congress agree beforehand that no slavery *"shall ever exist in any part"* of any territory which might be secured from Mexico. This proposal was called the *Wilmot Proviso*. It came up in Congress over and over again but was always defeated. Northerners who disliked slavery voted for it; Southerners voted against it.

The Southerners become alarmed. After the Mexican War ended in 1848, the debate started by Wilmot became more intense. All through the country men argued over the question of slavery in the new territories won from Mexico. Southerners were fearful that the North might try to prevent them from taking slaves into these new territories. To understand their fears, let us listen to a conversation that might have taken place at this time between a well-to-do southern planter and a visiting neighbor. After dinner the two men, whom we shall call Mr. A and Mr. B, might have sat in the parlor, talking.

"I can't help worrying about the future," Mr. A began. "What will happen if the northern states, where there are so many abolitionists, try to keep us from taking our slaves to the western lands or try to interfere with our way of life in the South?"

"I've been thinking about the same thing," said Mr. B. "I'm very much concerned that the North may try to get Congress to take some action against slavery."

"What chance do you think there is that the United States government would do such a thing?" asked Mr. A.

This imaginary conversation (pages 378-380) makes clear why the South felt a balance between free and slave states should be maintained.

The slave and free states are equal in number. "That's what I have been trying to decide," answered Mr. B. "To help me, I have made a list of the original thirteen states and of states that have joined the Union since our country became independent. I have written down the dates when new states entered the Union. My list has two columns, one showing the states where slavery is permitted and one showing the free states. Here it is:

ORIGINAL THIRTEEN STATES	
Slave States	*Free States*
Delaware	New Hampshire
Maryland	Massachusetts
Virginia	Rhode Island
North Carolina	Connecticut
South Carolina	New York
Georgia	New Jersey
	Pennsylvania

NEW STATES			
Slave States		*Free States*	
Kentucky	(1792)		
Tennessee	(1796)	Vermont	(1791)
Louisiana	(1812)	Ohio	(1803)
Mississippi	(1817)	Indiana	(1816)
Alabama	(1819)	Illinois	(1818)
Missouri	(1821)	Maine	(1820)
Arkansas	(1836)	Michigan	(1837)
Florida	(1845)	Iowa	(1846)
Texas	(1845)	Wisconsin	(1848)

What if the free states become stronger? "You see," continued Mr. B, "most of the time the number of slave states and of free states has been equal. New slave states and new free states have been added at about the same time; they

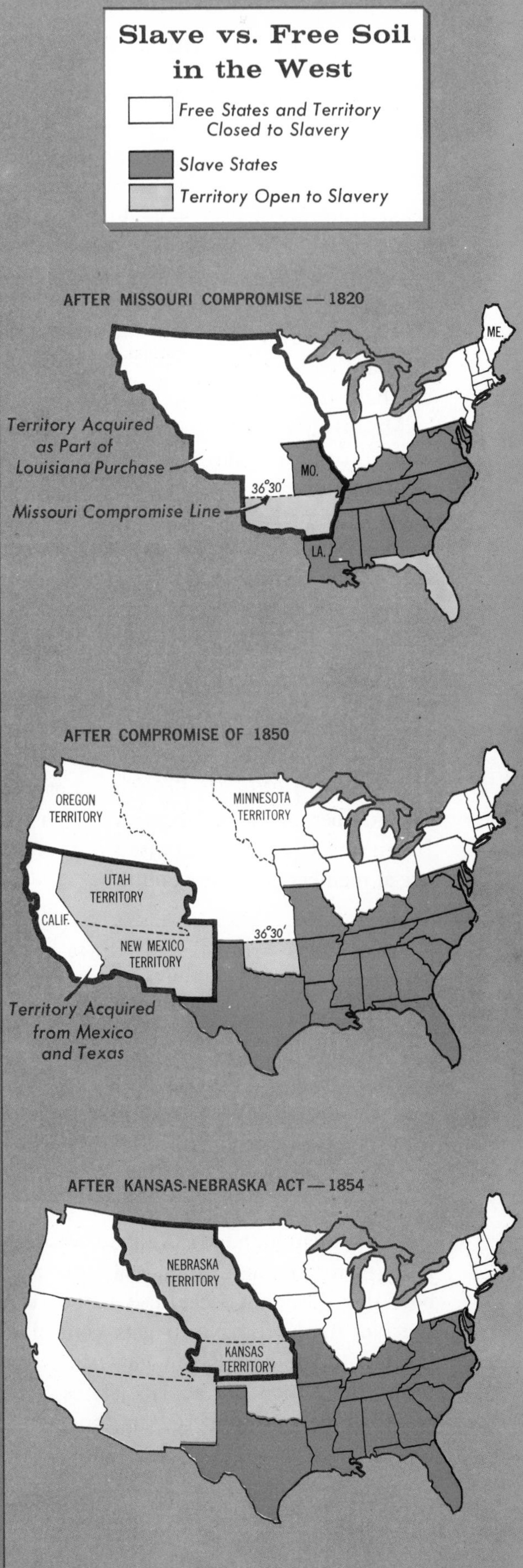

Slave vs. Free Soil in the West

☐ Free States and Territory Closed to Slavery
■ Slave States
▨ Territory Open to Slavery

AFTER MISSOURI COMPROMISE — 1820

ME.

Territory Acquired as Part of Louisiana Purchase

MO.

36°30'

Missouri Compromise Line

LA.

AFTER COMPROMISE OF 1850

OREGON TERRITORY

MINNESOTA TERRITORY

UTAH TERRITORY

CALIF.

36°30'

NEW MEXICO TERRITORY

Territory Acquired from Mexico and Texas

AFTER KANSAS-NEBRASKA ACT — 1854

NEBRASKA TERRITORY

KANSAS TERRITORY

almost come in pairs. There are two senators from each state. So if there is any question on which the South and the North disagree, there will be an even number of senators to vote on each side. Furthermore, most of the Presidents have been southern men, who could be expected to look after the interests of the South."

"So far we are all right," said Mr. A. "We are equal in the Senate and we usually have the President on our side."

Mr. B looked more thoughtful than ever. "Yes," he said, "but the House of Representatives is another story. We both know that in the last 50 years population in the North has been increasing faster than in the South. In the House of Representatives the number of members from each state depends, of course, on population. So the number of representatives from the northern states has been growing rapidly. Here is another list which shows what has been happening in the House since 1800. My list shows not only the number of House members from the North and the South but also the *percentage* of members from the South."

YEAR	1800	1810	1820	1830	1840	1850
Members from free states	76	96	123	141	135	142
Members from slave states	65	79	90	99	88	90
Per cent of southern members	46	45	42	41	39.5	38.8

"Now," concluded Mr. B, "we are rapidly losing voting strength in the House. Suppose the President were also to be from the North. If the North gets control of the territories, and if the new states entering the Union are all free states, then we shall be outnumbered in the Senate too."

"I see," answered Mr. A gravely. "We Southerners must do everything possible to prevent the new territories from entering the Union as free states. We cannot let the North interfere with our way of life."

California wants to become a state. The dispute over what to do about slavery in the lands obtained from Mexico came to a head after the discovery of gold in California. As you learned in Chapter 18, the discovery of gold caused many people to rush to California. These people formed a government of their own and asked to be admitted as a free state. To Southerners this was an outrage. They insisted that California should not be closed to slavery. Northerners insisted that it should be.

If slavery in California was to be discussed in Congress, slavery in the rest of the new territories would need to be discussed too. And if another compromise could not be agreed upon, the country might split in two. The outlook was indeed grave.

Great men represent the states in Congress. The Congress which faced these perplexing problems had many great men in it. There were three men, especially, who had become famous. They had entered Congress about 40 years before and were nearing the close of their careers. There was *Daniel Webster* of Massachusetts, great orator and statesman. Although he disliked slavery, he wanted more than anything else to keep the country united. There was *Henry Clay* of Kentucky, known as the "Great Compromiser." Clay was very skillful at finding ways of keeping peace when men disagreed. In 1820 he had helped make the Missouri Compromise. Now, 30 years later, Clay was to make his last great effort to bring about a compromise between the North and the South. And there was *John C. Calhoun* of South Carolina, champion of

Most of the 100,000 people who came to California in 1849 had no slaves. Mexico had abolished slavery in this territory many years earlier.

JEFFERSON DAVIS (left) and ALEXANDER H. STEPHENS (above) resigned their seats in Congress when their states seceded from the Union in 1861. Davis, a Mississippi cotton planter, had served in the army during the Mexican War. Though Stephens had opposed secession, he remained loyal to Georgia when it left the Union.

states' rights. Although he was now old and sick, he was determined that South Carolina and slavery should have their say. He opposed a compromise.

There were young men, too, whose names would be famous in the years to come. One of them, *Stephen A. Douglas* from Illinois, believed the people in the territories should settle questions like slavery for themselves. Another was *William H. Seward* of New York. Seward declared that God's law made men free and that God's law was "a higher law" than the Constitution of the United States. Brilliant young men also spoke for the South. Among them were *Jefferson Davis* of Mississippi and *Alexander H. Stephens* of Georgia. When the South later formed its own government, these two men became its President and Vice-President.

Congress passes the Compromise of 1850. After lengthy discussions, Congress agreed upon a settlement, known as the *Compromise of 1850*. (See map, page 379.) This compromise dealt with the question of slavery in the new land won from Mexico and with some other things as well. The important parts of the Compromise of 1850 were as follows:

(1) California was admitted to the Union as a free state.

(2) The rest of the territory obtained from Mexico was divided into the New Mexico Territory and Utah Territory. The question of slavery was left to the people who settled there. In other words, the people there were *to decide for themselves* whether slavery should be permitted.

(3) Slaves were not to be bought or sold in the District of Columbia.

(4) To make it harder for slaves to win their freedom by escaping from slave states into free states, a strict *Fugitive Slave Law* was passed. This law required people in the free states to help catch escaped slaves.

This is to say, Congress would not make the decision.

Congress hoped by this compromise to settle the slavery question forever. The members wanted no more angry debates which might prove dangerous to the nation. Americans sighed with relief. Surely, thought many of them, the dispute over slavery could now be forgotten.

CHECK UP

1. (a) What dispute broke out when Missouri requested admission to the Union as a state? (b) How was the dispute settled?

2. (a) What is meant by the term "states' rights"? (b) Why did the South favor this point of view? (c) How did Webster argue against it?

3. (a) Why did the Mexican War lead to a new quarrel over slavery? (b) Why was the South anxious to keep a balance between the number of slave states and free states? (c) How did California's request for statehood add to the dispute?

4. How was the dispute over slavery in the territories settled for the time being by the Compromise of 1850?

How Did the Two Sections Move Closer to Conflict?

Americans who thought the Compromise of 1850 would settle the slavery question and end the quarrels between North and South were too hopeful. Certain events in the next ten years were to make the quarrels more frequent, more angry, and more bitter.

Uncle Tom's Cabin inflames opinion in the North. In 1852, Harriet Beecher Stowe wrote a book called *Uncle Tom's Cabin*. Its description of the suffering of slaves and the cruelties of their masters was hardly a fair picture of conditions throughout the South. But its dramatic story wrung the hearts of the hundreds of thousands of Northerners who read it. In fact, *Uncle Tom's Cabin* influenced Northerners against slavery as nothing else had. Abraham Lincoln in later years is said to have greeted Mrs. Stowe as "the little woman who wrote the book that made this great war." In the South, however, *Uncle Tom's Cabin* aroused a storm of protest and increased the bitter feelings against the abolitionists.

Fugitive slaves are helped by the Underground Railroad. In spite of the Fugitive Slave Law, Northerners continued to help runaway slaves whenever they could. One means they used was the *Underground Railroad.* This was really not a railroad at all but a way of helping runaway slaves to reach places where they would be safe. The slaves who reached the North were sheltered by antislavery men. These men, called *conductors,* took the slaves by night from one house or *station* to another, each farther north than the last. Finally the slaves reached Canada, where they could live as free men. Although not many slaves escaped in this way, the Underground Railroad further inflamed feeling between the North and the South.

Serious quarrels develop as the slavery question is reopened. Differences between the North and the South continued to grow increasingly serious. It was a series of events beginning in 1854, however, which brought the two sections near the breaking point. If it were possible for

When a slave escaped, the owner suffered a substantial financial loss, perhaps $1000 or more, at a time when the dollar had much greater purchasing power than today.

us to sit and watch a telecast of some of these important events, here are the scenes that we might see:

Scene 1: The Kansas-Nebraska Act reopens the slavery quarrel (1854). We see the Senate Chamber of the Capitol in Washington. The senators are discussing the *Kansas-Nebraska Bill,* a proposed law which would set up two new governments, one in Kansas Territory and one in Nebraska Territory. (The map on page 379 shows where these territories were.) If this bill becomes law, the people of these territories are to decide *for themselves* whether slavery shall be permitted there. A northern senator is making a speech, using words like these:

"Gentlemen, look at the map. Kansas is north of the Missouri Compromise line. By the Missouri Compromise slavery was not to be permitted north of that line. Shall we now permit slavery there? No! The people of the North will not stand for it!"

And a southern senator replies:

"The Missouri Compromise did say that slavery was not to be permitted in this territory. But this proposed law, the Kansas-Nebraska Bill, will definitely put an end to the Missouri Compromise.

Wherever the United States flag goes, slavery may go. This is as it should be. Slaves are property. It is our right to take our slave property anywhere into the West, just as you of the North may take your property in horses and cattle there. The people of the South will insist on this right."

The bill passed the Senate and the House and became law. The Missouri Compromise was now dead. The Kansas-Nebraska Act took its place. The people in the territories of Kansas and Nebraska could decide for themselves whether to have slavery or not.

Scene 2: Violence breaks out over slavery in Kansas (1854-1857). We see a tall, gray-bearded man standing against the night sky. He is looking down at five dying men. Someone asks, "Why did you shoot them, John Brown?" He replies: "Men opposed to slavery have been killed, so men who favor slavery must also die."

The place is Kansas, which is now open to freedom or slavery. Settlers from the North and the South have been moving in. The men of the South say, "We will bring our slaves to Kansas. We will even fight to keep them, if we have to." The

Congress has the right to pass a law which does away with legislation passed earlier. But the "repeal" of the Missouri Compromise obviously aroused the ire of people opposed to the extension of slavery.

men of the North say, "We will allow no slaves in Kansas. We will fight to keep them out, if we have to."

John Brown's murder of the proslavery men is only one of many scenes of violence during the settlement of Kansas. Earlier, flames destroyed the village of Lawrence which antislavery men had built. Bands of men on horseback now roam the roads. They carry rifles across their saddles and shoot as they meet other riders. These are proslavery and antislavery men, fighting to win control of Kansas.

Violence in Kansas finally died down, but the struggle for Kansas went on. Because of their greater numbers, the antislavery men finally won, and in 1861 Kansas entered the Union as a free state.

Scene 3: **The Republican Party is born (1854).** We see a group of men holding an outdoor meeting in a Wisconsin town. "We cannot vote for the old parties, the Whigs and the Democrats, any longer," one of them is saying. The other men cheer.

The speaker continues: "The great question today is: Shall there be slavery or freedom in the new territories? The old parties cannot agree on the answer to this question. Congress has just passed the Kansas-Nebraska Act, which says that the people of the territories may decide whether or not to allow slavery. But we men who are meeting here believe that *it is both the right and the duty of Congress to forbid slavery in the territories.* We are strong and we shall become stronger. Let us form a new party and call ourselves Republicans. Let us fight to keep slavery out of the territories!" In other towns throughout the North, scenes like this are taking place. "No slavery in the territories! Join the Republicans!"

The new party gained many members. In the election of 1856, the Republicans won in two thirds of the northern states with John C. Frémont, soldier and explorer, as their candidate. But there were almost no Republicans in the South. So the Democrats in the North and the South were strong enough to elect their candidate, James Buchanan, as President. In spite of their defeat, the Republicans were not downhearted. They knew they had made a good start and hoped to elect a Republican President in 1860.

Scene 4: **The Missouri Compromise is declared unconstitutional in the Dred Scott Case (1857).** We see a small, quiet

Pro-slavery and anti-slavery organizations had encouraged migration to Kansas. The rapid influx of settlers increased the likelihood of conflict.

room where the Supreme Court of the United States is meeting. On the raised platform behind their long carved desk the judges sit solemnly, clad in their black robes. They are the highest court in the land. They explain the meaning of the United States Constitution and decide whether a law of Congress violates the Constitution.

The judges have been considering the case of a Negro, Dred Scott by name. Scott had been a slave in the South, but his master had taken him to a free state and later to territory north of the Missouri Compromise line. The Missouri Compromise had declared that in this territory there could be no slavery and no slaves. Therefore, Dred Scott claimed to be a free man. He had asked the Supreme Court to compel his master to free him.

A judge is slowly reading what the Supreme Court has decided. Dred Scott is not free. Slaves are property, says the judge, and do not have the rights of citizens. The Constitution protects property in the territories as well as in the states. Congress had no right to forbid slavery in any part of the territories. Therefore, the Missouri Compromise is unconstitutional.

In the Kansas-Nebraska Act, Congress had declared the Missouri Compromise dead, but had suggested that the voters in a territory could decide the question of slavery for themselves. Now, in the Dred Scott decision, the United States Supreme Court had declared that *slaves could not be kept out of the territories.*

Southerners were naturally delighted with the Court's decision, but Northerners were astounded. Republicans especially protested that the Supreme Court was favoring the South.

Scene 5: **A great debate takes place in Illinois (1858).** We see an open square in a little Illinois town. On a wooden platform two men stand before a crowd that fills the square. What a contrast the two men make! One is much taller than the other. In fact, if the tall one were to stretch his arm straight out from the shoulder, the short one could walk right under it. The tall one is so carelessly dressed that his coat sleeves do not reach to his wrists nor his trousers to his shoes. The short one is the opposite — carefully dressed in the height of fashion. The tall one is awkward, and his face is lined and sad. The short one is confident, gay, and graceful.

The tall man is Abraham Lincoln — Republican; the short one is Stephen A. Douglas — Democrat. Each hopes to be elected United States senator from Illinois. To let the people know how they will vote in the Senate, they are debating the queston of slavery in the territories. In spite of the Dred Scott decision, Douglas says he believes that the people of a territory should decide for themselves whether to have slavery or not. (This idea is known as *popular sovereignty.*) No wonder Douglas believes this, for he himself had written the Kansas-Nebraska Act.

385

Lincoln says that slavery is wrong. He declares that Congress has the right to get rid of slavery in the land that belongs to all the people of the United States — that is, in the territories, but not in the states. The Republicans, he continues, think slavery is wrong. For this reason they wish to limit slavery to the states where it already exists and prevent its spread to the territories.

But in the back of Lincoln's mind was the fear that a conflict between the North and the South could not be avoided. In an earlier speech he had warned the American people, "A house divided against itself cannot stand. I believe this government cannot endure permanently half slave and half free."

Stephen Douglas won the election. But Abraham Lincoln won fame for making the issues clear.

Scene 6: John Brown attacks the United States Armory at Harpers Ferry, Virginia (1859). In the village of Harpers Ferry on the Potomac River, we see a locomotive roundhouse with thick brick walls. Rifle shots are ringing out. Soldiers rush to the door and capture the building. Inside they find John Brown and a handful of men, most of them dead or wounded. This is the same John Brown we saw in Kansas. What is he doing now?

Brown and a few followers had come to Virginia with the idea of freeing slaves. After seizing the United States Armory at Harpers Ferry in order to get arms, he had cried to nearby slaves: "We are here to set you free! Seize arms and defend your freedom!" But not one slave followed him. John Brown is tried for treason, found guilty, and hanged.

Although the abolitionists looked upon Brown as a "saint," many Northerners considered his act the deed of a madman. But Southerners were filled with dread. They feared that northern abolitionists were working to bring about a Negro uprising and to free the slaves by force. We can't endure much more, the Southerners thought.

There had been slave revolts in the South. The possibility of such an uprising was viewed with terror.

CHECK UP

1. (a) What effect did *Uncle Tom's Cabin* have on the slavery dispute? (b) What was the Underground Railroad?

2. (a) How did the Kansas-Nebraska Act reopen the slavery quarrel? (b) What happened in Kansas in the next few years as a result of the dispute? (c) Why was the Republican Party formed?

3. Why did the Dred Scott decision arouse the North?

4. What were the views of Lincoln and of Douglas on each of the following: (a) the Missouri Compromise? (b) the Kansas-Nebraska Act? (c) the Dred Scott decision? (d) slavery in the states where it already existed?

5. How did John Brown's raid at Harpers Ferry add to the dispute over slavery?

3 What Events Led Directly to War Between the North and South?

Abraham Lincoln is elected President. By 1860, the whole country was alert and tense, as though awaiting the climax of the fateful events of the past years. A presidential election was to be held that year. The chief issue would be the question of slavery. What would be the outcome?

In this election there were four political parties, not two or three as there had been before. The old Democratic Party had split in two. One part, the southern Democratic Party, wished to elect John C. Breckinridge of Kentucky. It believed in states' rights and insisted that slavery should be protected in the territories. The northern Democratic Party believed that the best answer to the slavery question was Stephen A. Douglas's idea of popular sovereignty — let the people in the territories decide for themselves. This party chose Douglas as its candidate. A third party was the Constitutional Union Party. Those who belonged to this party were peaceful men who wished to hold the Union together. They hoped for another compromise over slavery. For President they wanted John Bell of Tennessee.

Finally, there were the Republicans. They demanded what they had demanded in 1854, that slavery be kept out of the territories. But the Republican Party also tried to gain support in the North and West by favoring (1) a tariff, (2) free land for settlers in the West, and (3) the construction of a railroad to the Pacific. For President the Republicans named the backwoods lawyer from Illinois, Abraham Lincoln.

When one party is split, as the Democrats were in 1860, it usually is defeated.

So it was in 1860. The Republicans won the election, even though in most of the southern states their candidates had no place on the ballot. Abraham Lincoln would become President in 1861.

Who was Abraham Lincoln? The man who had won the election of 1860 was one of the most remarkable men in our history. Brought up amid the hardships of the frontier, he lacked the advantages that many of our Presidents have enjoyed. Because he was poor, he had to turn his hand to various ways of making a living. Before he became a lawyer, he cleared and tilled the soil, split rails, worked on a flatboat on the Mississippi, and tended store. Since Lincoln had few chances to attend school, he educated himself in spare moments during the day and by the flickering firelight during the evenings. Even his physical characteristics — unusual height, awkward movements, and high-pitched voice — were against him.

In spite of these handicaps, people liked and respected "Abe" Lincoln. His honesty, clear thinking, friendliness, ability to tell stories, and trust in the common people were qualities which made him popular. Lincoln served several terms in the Illinois legislature. In 1846, he was elected to the House of Representatives, where he served two years.

When his term in Congress was over, Lincoln returned to his work as a lawyer. He felt he was through with politics. But his deep feelings on the matter of slavery forced him back into public life. Although he hated slavery, Lincoln was not an abolitionist. He did not propose to interfere with slavery in the states where it

These three points attracted many voters.

Secession vs. Union

"It was the <u>states</u> which formed the Union and a state can <u>leave</u> the Union. For us, the Union no longer exists!"

"No! The Union was set up for keeps! You're part of one country now, and you can't walk out on us no matter how much you want to!"

existed. But he firmly believed that slavery should not exist in the territories belonging to the United States. His beliefs led him to seek election to the Senate from Illinois, and to take part in the debates with Douglas.

Although Lincoln was well known in the West, he was little more than a name in the East. He was invited to speak at the Cooper Union Hall in New York City early in 1860. Many of the people came out of curiosity to see and hear this man from the West who was becoming an important figure in the Republican Party. How crude and countrified Lincoln must have appeared to the New Yorkers! But when he began to speak, they forgot the queer clothes and awkward appearance of the tall, lanky man. His speech was scholarly; his manner was dignified and convincing. His arguments against slavery in the territories were well thought out and clearly worded. He closed with these words: "Let us have faith that right makes might; and in that faith let us to the end dare to do our duty as we understand it."

At the end, the whole audience rose to its feet in a thunder of applause.

This was the man who in the fall of 1860 was elected the sixteenth President of the United States.

WAR COMES AT LAST

The southern states secede. The southern states had declared that if Lincoln were elected President, they would no longer want to remain part of the United States. It was true that the South still had power in Congress and in the Supreme Court. But a northern man, a Republican, had been elected President. The South no longer felt safe. It feared not only for slavery but also for its way of life, which depended on slavery.

Even before Lincoln became President, southern states had begun to carry out their threat to withdraw, or *secede,* from the Union. First went South Carolina; then in quick succession, Mississippi, Florida, Alabama. Georgia followed, and Louisiana and Texas. These seven states had seceded

These states believed they had the right to   **388**   secede. They called conventions to "un-ratify" the Constitution just as they earlier had called conventions to ratify it.

ABRAHAM LINCOLN

Growing up along the frontier, young Abe cut fuel for his family's crude shelter.

ODD JOBS, such as taking a flatboat down-river from Illinois to New Orleans, won Lincoln a reputation as dependable and honest. At the same time, Lincoln read as much as he could to complete his scanty schooling. Later he studied law.

AS A LAWYER, attending court sessions, Lincoln rode 8000 miles every six months across backwoods Illinois. People looked forward to his arrival. Friendly and entertaining, he had an easy manner and common sense that gradually made him a popular political figure.

"PRESIDENTIAL TIMBER" after the Douglas debates, he spoke at Cooper Union in New York. Despite his awkward appearance and western accent, Lincoln talked eloquently on the slavery issue and won the support of his audience.

A WAR LEADER determined to save the Union at all costs, Lincoln nevertheless found time for the humble soldier and his problems. His understanding and fairness, often expressed in noble words during the war between the North and the South, helped America to survive as one nation.

DELEGATES FROM NORTH AND SOUTH, meeting at Washington in February, 1861, made a last desperate effort to avoid war. But the delegates failed to solve the dispute that split the country.

by February 1, 1861. President Buchanan, who was nearing the end of his term, took no steps to stop the seceding states. He said, "I have no power to interfere."

The Confederate States of America are established. In February, the seven states which had seceded sent representatives to Montgomery, Alabama, to form a new government. These men drew up a constitution for a new nation, the *Confederate States of America* or, as it was often called, the *Confederacy*. The constitution was much like that of the United States. It stated, however, that the Congress of the Confederacy could not interfere with slavery. It also provided that no tariffs could be levied on imports. The President was to serve six years, instead of four, and he could not be re-elected.

Jefferson Davis is elected President of the Confederate States. Jefferson Davis of Mississippi was elected President of the

Confederate States, and Alexander H. Stephens of Georgia was chosen Vice-President. Jefferson Davis was born one year earlier than Abraham Lincoln, and in the same state — Kentucky. But Lincoln's parents took him to Indiana and Illinois, while the Davis family moved to Mississippi. Davis's father was a planter who owned a large plantation and many slaves. Jefferson Davis was well educated and was a graduate of the United States Military Academy at West Point. He made a distinguished record as an officer in the Mexican War. He also had served in the House of Representatives and in the Senate, and as Secretary of War. In the Senate he strongly defended the rights of the South.

Jefferson Davis was a man of commanding appearance, intelligence, and great energy. Upon his shoulders lay the difficult task of helping the seven states of the Confederacy to become an independent nation.

Lincoln hopes for peace. When Abraham Lincoln became President of the United States on March 4, 1861, he faced a very difficult problem. What should he do about the seceded states?

Lincoln did not want war. As he took the oath of office, he said, "Suppose you go to war, you cannot fight always; and when, after much loss on both sides, and no gain on either, you cease fighting, the [same] old questions . . . are again upon you." Slavery in the South was in no danger, for Lincoln promised that he had "no purpose, directly or indirectly, to interfere with . . . slavery in the states where it exists." He went on to say, "In your hands, my dissatisfied fellow countrymen, and not in mine, is the momentous issue of civil war. The government will not assail you." Lincoln, however, made it clear that he had taken a solemn oath to "preserve, protect, and defend" the United States government. Finally he pleaded with the people of the whole country to unite once again. Solemnly he said:

✳ We are not enemies, but friends. We must not be enemies. . . . The mystic chords of memory, stretching from every . . . patriot grave to every living heart and hearthstone all over this broad land, will yet swell the chorus of the Union, when again [they are] touched, as surely they will be, by the better angels of our nature.

Thus Lincoln, with "faith in what he believed was right," took upon his shoulders the responsibility of preserving the Union. Yet, in spite of what he had said, the country remained divided. United States forts in the South had been seized by the Confederacy; the laws of the United States were not being obeyed. Lincoln must act quickly if he hoped to save the Union.

War! The harbor of Charleston, South Carolina, was broad and quiet. Warm in the spring sun, the city lay at the western end of the harbor. In this harbor was a tiny island, and on this island was Fort Sumter. Fort Sumter was occupied by soldiers of the United States Army.

The Confederate leaders demanded that these soldiers leave the fort. But the commander of Fort Sumter refused. Soon the Confederate leaders learned that Lincoln had ordered ships to take food and other supplies to Sumter. Naturally they feared that reinforcements might also be landed. The days and nights seemed to grow longer. People were tense with excitement.

It is now 4:30 in the morning of April 12, 1861, the still hour before the dawn. Suddenly a flash of flame is seen and a deep "Boom!" shatters the silence. From all around the harbor Confederate cannon begin to fire at Fort Sumter. Peace and quiet no longer reign in Charleston Harbor — nor anywhere else in the United States. War has begun!

CHECK UP

1. (a) What political parties had presidential candidates in the election of 1860? (b) What was the stand of each party on the slavery question? (c) Who was the candidate of each party? (d) What party won the election? Why?

2. (a) How did the southern states feel about the results of the election? (b) What action did they take? (c) How was a new government organized in the South?

3. (a) What were President Lincoln's views on slavery and the division of the Union? (b) How did war break out between the North and the South?

The members of the Confederate constitutional convention wished to secede peaceably, and had convinced themselves that this movement would not lead to war.

Check Up on Chapter 19

Do You Know the Meaning?

1. proslavery
2. states' rights
3. treason
4. secede
5. sovereignty
6. popular sovereignty

Can You Identify?

1. Wilmot Proviso
2. 1820
3. Compromise of 1850

Can You Identify? (Cont.)

4. 1854
5. 1857
6. 1861
7. Fort Sumter
8. Harpers Ferry
9. Abraham Lincoln
10. Daniel Webster
11. Kansas-Nebraska Act
12. Republican Party
13. Dred Scott decision
14. Missouri Compromise
15. John C. Calhoun

Can You Identify? (Cont.)

16. Henry Clay
17. John Brown
18. Stephen Douglas
19. Jefferson Davis
20. Confederate States of America

Can You Locate?

1. Kansas Territory
2. Missouri
3. Nebraska Territory
4. Missouri Compromise Line

What Do You Think?

1. Many historians believe that Stephen Douglas's views on slavery helped him win the election for senator in 1858, but cost him the presidency in 1860. Explain why.

What Do You Think? (Cont.)

2. When the slaves were freed in the British West Indies, the government gave their owners money to make up for their losses. Do you think that such a policy could have been followed in this country? Why?

3. At the time, most Americans had high hopes for the success of both the Compromise of 1820 and that of 1850. Why did efforts to work out a permanent settlement of the slavery question fail?

4. Do you think Southerners were justified in feeling that the election of Lincoln made it necessary for them to secede from the Union? Why?

The war cost over $5 billion and 600,000 men lost their lives. The value of slave property in 1860 was over $2 billion.

LINKING PAST AND PRESENT

Lincoln country. Little did the parents of the baby Abraham Lincoln dream that the farm where he was born in 1809 would one day be made a national park in his honor. Today, not only his birthplace (near Hodgenville, Kentucky) but almost every place where Lincoln lived is preserved as a memorial. The farm in Indiana where he grew to manhood is now part of the Lincoln State Park. A stone wall shows the location of the log cabin home; the grave of Lincoln's mother, who died here, is marked by a simple stone. In 1830, the family moved to southeastern Illinois, where their old home and the graves of Lincoln's father and stepmother can be seen. New Salem, Illinois, where Lincoln lived after leaving home in 1831, has been rebuilt. Today it looks like the town he knew, with its log cabins, the tavern, the store he worked in, and the original barrel-maker's shop where he used to study law at night.

In Springfield, Illinois, Lincoln's home after 1837, are many memorials. The house where he lived with his family has been preserved. Furnished with some of the Lincoln family furniture, it looks much as it did a century ago. In Springfield, also, you can see the final resting place of Abraham Lincoln — a beautiful marble tomb at Oak Ridge Cemetery where Lincoln, his wife, and three of his sons are buried.

Pictures of war. Cameramen, using both still and motion picture cameras, have given us a full pictorial record of recent wars. But at the time of the War Between the States, photography was still very new. Cameras were large, difficult to handle, and costly to operate. But some photographs of the war remain, chiefly those taken by Mathew Brady and his assistants. (The photograph on page 406 is a Brady picture.) Most of our pictorial record of the war comes from artists such as A. R. Waud, Winslow Homer, and Thomas Nast. These men would watch a battle, then try to draw an accurate picture of it. Their sketches were cut into wooden blocks and printed in newspapers. Many of these old photographs and sketches are reprinted in books and magazines today. They represent a valuable record of our country's past.

See also, for example, American Heritage Picture History of the Civil War and Mathew Brady: Historian with a Camera by James D. Horan.

The North and the South
Fight a War and Are Reunited

Jonathan Daniels has written an interesting biography : Robert E. Lee.

What this chapter is about —

One day toward the end of the Mexican War, several officers met in the United States Army camp near Mexico City. Two of these men were destined to become famous in American history. One was a colonel; the other was an "untidy young captain." The colonel, described by his commanding officer as "the very best soldier that I ever saw in the field," was Robert E. Lee; the captain was Ulysses S. Grant.

Seventeen years later, these two men met again, this time in a small brick house near Appomattox Court House, Virginia. The years had brought many changes. Once brother officers, they now faced each other as enemies. Grant wore the blue of the United States Army, but Lee was dressed in the gray uniform of the Confederate States of America. Grant had become Lieutenant-General Grant, Commander-in-Chief of the United States Army. Lee was General-in-Chief of all the Confederate armies.

The meeting in the brick house marked the end of a bloody war between the two sections of our country. This war grew out of the clash between the North and the South described in Chapter 19. In this chapter we shall read about the major campaigns and learn how victory was won by the North. We shall learn how the war

*People in our story — Union sailor, general, and
soldier; Confederate soldier and cavalryman; nurse.*

affected both the North and the South and what happened to Lincoln's plans for making the United States once more "one nation, indivisible." In order to understand the war and its outcome, let us keep in mind these questions:

▶ 1. How was the nation divided, and what advantages did each side have?

▶ 2. How did four long years of fighting bring victory to the North?

▶ 3. How did the war affect the lives of people in the North and the South?

▶ 4. How did Abraham Lincoln plan to unite the divided nation?

▶ 5. What happened in the South after the war?

When men said that they felt a greater loyalty to their state than to the nation, they implied that their state had the right to secede.

1 How Was the Nation Divided, and What Advantages Did Each Side Have?

War divides the nation. When the Confederates fired upon Fort Sumter, the nation was too deeply divided to be united again by peaceful means. For several reasons, as you have learned, the North and South had been drifting farther and farther apart. But now that shots had been fired, Americans faced one question above all others: Will the United States remain one nation or become two? Either the Confederate States of America would win the war and become an independent nation, or the United States would win the war and compel the seceding states to rejoin the Union.

The war divided not only the nation but neighborhoods and even families.

Many Northerners went South to fight for the Confederacy; many Southerners fought for the Union. In the "border states" especially — those at the dividing line between North and South — neighbors marched off to fight on opposite sides. What was even sadder, the war often separated members of the same family. Three brothers of Mrs. Abraham Lincoln, wife of the President of the United States, died for the Confederacy. Close relatives of the wife of the President of the Confederacy fought for the Union. The sons of a high-ranking officer of the Union Navy wore Confederate gray. The same story was repeated many times throughout the nation.

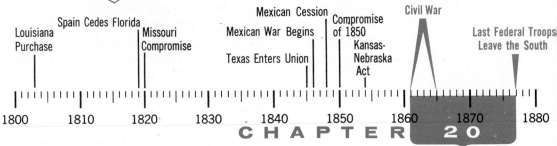

The North and South Fight and Are Reunited

Louisiana Purchase — Spain Cedes Florida — Missouri Compromise — Texas Enters Union — Mexican War Begins — Mexican Cession — Compromise of 1850 — Kansas-Nebraska Act — Civil War — Last Federal Troops Leave the South

1800   1810   1820   1830   1840   1850   1860   1870   1880

C H A P T E R   2 0

1861 - 1877

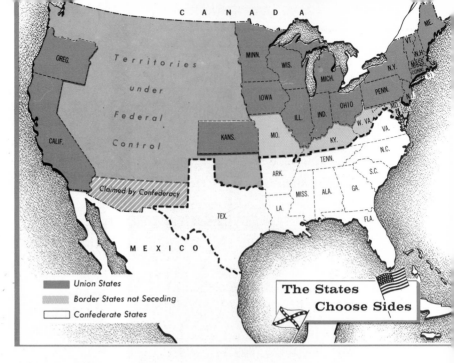

MAP STUDY
This map shows the opposing states in the conflict between the North and South. (1) What states made up the Confederacy? (2) What border states chose to remain in the Union? (West Virginia became a state in 1863.)

Union States
Border States not Seceding
Confederate States

The States Choose Sides

What were the sections fighting for? Men went to war for different reasons. Most men, in both the North and the South, adopted the cause favored by most of their friends and neighbors. Many men in the South believed in slavery and fought to preserve it. Many Southerners also felt sure that their way of life, based upon the growing of cotton, could not survive in the same nation with the trading and manufacturing states of the North. These Southerners fought for the right to secede from the Union and form a new nation.

On the other hand, some Northerners fought because they hated slavery and hoped the war would put an end to it. Many Northerners believed there was no question so difficult that it could not be settled satisfactorily under a democratic government. They felt deeply that the Union should be stronger than any one state or group of states. They fought to preserve the government established by their forefathers.

The remaining slave states choose sides. When fighting broke out, the slave states which had not seceded were forced to decide whether to join the North or the South. Four more states sided with the

Confederacy and seceded soon after the firing on Fort Sumter. These were Virginia, Arkansas, Tennessee, and North Carolina. But the people living in the northwestern part of Virginia refused to join the rest of that state in seceding. They broke away and formed the state of West Virginia, which entered the Union in 1863. The four slave states nearest the North — Missouri, Kentucky, Maryland, and Delaware — remained in the Union. Thus, as the war began, the North had 23 states, the South, 11 states (see map above).

What were the advantages of each side? In the end, a war is usually won by the side having the most men, resources, and supplies. Let us compare the strength of the North and the South.

The North had certain advantages. (1) More than twice as many people lived in the North as in the South — 22 million in the North and 9 million in the South. Of the 9 million people in the South, two out of every five were Negroes, most of whom were slaves. Slaves were not expected to fight. The slaves, however, might do the work at home and thus release white men to join the army. (2) Not only did the North

In comparing the advantages of each side, be sure to refer to the graph on the next page.

395

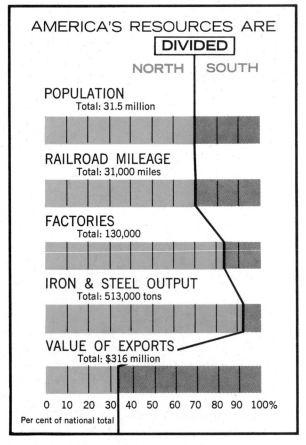

AMERICA'S RESOURCES ARE DIVIDED

NORTH | SOUTH

POPULATION
Total: 31.5 million

RAILROAD MILEAGE
Total: 31,000 miles

FACTORIES
Total: 130,000

IRON & STEEL OUTPUT
Total: 513,000 tons

VALUE OF EXPORTS
Total: $316 million

0 10 20 30 40 50 60 70 80 90 100%
Per cent of national total

THE NORTH outweighed the South in 1861 except in foreign trade, where "cotton was king." The cotton trade, however, depended on keeping sea lanes open to Europe.

have more people, but it had more resources and supplies. Most of the factories which could make guns, ammunition, uniforms, and the thousands of articles needed in war, were in the North. The North had more railroads to move goods and more men to do the fighting. It also had more shipping. (3) Furthermore, the United States government, its army,

and its navy were already established and working. The South had to build these things as it went along.

On the other hand, the South possessed certain advantages over the North. (1) For one thing, the South was fighting for the most part on its own soil. Men fight harder when they are defending their homes than when they are invading enemy territory. Also, they know the territory much better than the invaders possibly could. (2) In addition, the South had many outstanding military leaders who had resigned from the United States Army to fight for the Confederacy. Among these men was Robert E. Lee. Although Lee belonged to an old southern family, he did not believe in slavery and had already freed his slaves. Lee was also against secession and opposed to the war. But he could not bring himself to bear arms against his beloved state, Virginia. When that state seceded, therefore, Lee cast his lot with the Confederacy. Thus the South gained a brilliant general — the ablest in the whole United States Army.

CHECK UP

1. (a) In the conflict between the North and the South, what was the North fighting for? (b) The South? (c) What states were members of the Confederacy? (d) What slave states remained in the Union?

2. (a) What were the advantages of the North in the war? (b) Of the South?

2 How Did Four Long Years of Fighting Bring Victory to the North?

After the attack on Fort Sumter, both the Union and the Confederate States began to raise armies. President Lincoln called for 75,000 volunteers, a call which

was speedily answered. The North felt the need of winning a swift victory. One reason was that Confederate territory began just across the Potomac River from the

This force, enlisted for three months' service, was to supplement the state militia of about 10,000. Neither side had an army ready to fight a war.

AN ARMY ENGINEER after graduation, Lee built levees to save the river port of St. Louis from floods. After seventeen years of peacetime engineering, he was glad to see action at last in the Mexican War. Lee joined General Scott's staff for the invasion of Mexico.

SCOUTING enemy country for a route by which the Americans could attack, Lee barely escaped capture. His ability made him the U.S. Army's outstanding officer, but in 1861 he chose to serve on the southern side.

"GO BACK, GENERAL LEE!" pleaded his men when Lee tried to lead a Confederate charge at the desperate Battle of the Wilderness. To keep their beloved leader out of danger, they then took the Union position on their own. After many battles, plagued by heavy losses, Lee finally was forced to surrender.

A COLLEGE PRESIDENT after the war, Lee helped other ex-Confederates adjust to peace. He took this post as an example to the South that it must "accept the peace and go to work."

Union capital of Washington, D.C. (See the map on the next page.) In fact, the Confederate capital at Richmond, Virginia, was only a little over a hundred miles from Washington.

The defeat at Bull Run awakens the North. In the spring of 1861, the people of the North began to call for action. The cry "On to Richmond!" was heard on all sides. Although the new Union army contained many untrained recruits, Union troops were ordered south to capture Richmond if possible.

The Union forces crossed the Potomac into Virginia early in the summer. The advance into enemy territory was indeed a curious sight. The army was accompanied by many people from Washington who wished to see the Union troops win a victory. There were congressmen, newspapermen, curious citizens, and even society women in elegant carriages! The troops, not used to military discipline, often fell out of line to pick berries and search for water. Meanwhile, Confederate troops had assembled at Manassas Junction, on a small stream called Bull Run. Near this point, about 30 miles from Washington, the two armies met in battle. At first the Confederates seemed to be losing, but they held firm until more Confederate troops arrived. After a few hours of fighting, the Union lines broke, and the army retreated in great confusion to Washington.

The Battle of Bull Run rudely shocked the people of the North and encouraged the people of the South. The leaders of both sides, however, realized that they must raise large armies and prepare for a long war.

The North and South make plans for winning the war. Well-trained troops and plenty of supplies are not enough to win a war. A clear-cut plan for conducting the war is also necessary. This planning is known by the military term, *strategy.*

The strategy of the South was simple. (1) The South planned to hold out until the people of the North grew tired of the war. The Northerners might then say, "If the Confederates want a separate country, let them have it. It's too difficult to force them to return to the Union." (2) Whenever possible, of course, the South would invade the North, hoping to win an important victory. (3) The South counted on help from abroad, especially from England. The South planned to exchange its cotton for badly needed war supplies, such as guns, ammunition, and medical supplies. Because English textile factories needed a steady supply of cotton from the South, the Confederates expected England to take their side in the war.

The North had a different strategy. In order to win the war, it had to invade and conquer the South. This was to be done in three ways: (1) The North planned to follow the strategy of "divide and conquer." A large part of the Confederacy lay west of the Mississippi, as the map on the next page shows. Union plans called for gaining control of the Mississippi. This move would make it impossible for the Confederacy to get supplies from the states west of the river. After cutting the South in two at the Mississippi, the North would try to cut the eastern part of the Confederacy into smaller pieces. (2) The North also planned a blockade of southern ports, to prevent goods from being shipped into or out of the South. This would block the plan of the South to exchange cotton for war supplies. (3) The Confederate capital must be captured and the armies defending it conquered.

The side which was most successful in carrying out its strategy would win the war. Let us see what happened.

Refer to the maps on pages 399 and 400 in helping students understand the war plans of the North.

North and South in Conflict

Union Territory

Confederate States

Atlantic Ocean

ENGLAND
FRANCE

Union arms factories

War supplies from Europe

tobacco

cotton

BLOCKADE

UNION

UNION STRATEGY AT SEA
To blockade the South, cutting off trade with England and France.

UNION STRATEGY ON LAND
To cut the South into three parts and capture its capital, Richmond.

KAN.

MO.

Ohio R.

KY.

W. VA.

Washington

VA.
Richmond ★

"Merrimac"

ARK.

TENN.

N. C.

Supply Lines

Memphis

Chattanooga

Atlanta

Wilmington
S. C.

Mississippi R.

East-West

Charleston

CONFEDERATES TRY TO BREAK THE UNION BLOCKADE
By building ironclad warships. By swift blockade runners.

TEXAS

Vicksburg
MISS.

GA.

ALA.

Savannah

Mobile

LA.

New Orleans

FLA.

R. M. Chapin, Jr.

MAP STUDY   Note that since the South lacked industry, its most important supply line extended all the way to the factories of Europe and could be cut by Union naval power. (1) Where did the Union plan to attack along a water route? (2) Where did the Union plan of attack follow railroad lines?

THE WAR IN THE WEST

For months after the Battle of Bull Run, the important fighting took place, not in the East, but in the West. The army and navy of the Union worked together to win control of the Mississippi River. To follow the story of the fighting in the West, refer to the map below.

Farragut captures New Orleans. In order to gain control of the Mississippi, the North needed to capture the Confederate cities and forts along the river. The most important of these was the city of New Orleans near the mouth of the Mississippi. The man who was ordered to capture New Orleans was David Farragut.

MAP STUDY By winning control of the Mississippi, Union forces split the Confederacy. How did the navy aid Union plans?

Union Forces Split the Confederacy in the West

Farragut had begun his naval career in the War of 1812 when only a boy. He was now a man 60 years old.

In the spring of 1862, Farragut started up the Mississippi with a fleet of wooden ships. In a bold dash, he ran past the fire of Confederate forts on each side of the river. Then he defeated a Confederate fleet guarding New Orleans and captured the city. The lower Mississippi was now in control of Union forces. Farragut was later made the first Admiral of the United States Navy.

General Grant gains some early victories for the North. Meanwhile, other Union forces were moving against Confederate forts farther north on the Mississippi and on the Tennessee and Cumberland Rivers. The leader of these forces was Ulysses S. Grant. Grant was a West Point man and had fought in the Mexican War, but he had not made a name for himself as had Robert E. Lee and others. After the war, he had resigned from the army. The War Between the States gave Grant a chance to re-enter the army and to prove his ability to wage war. A modest man, he was willing to accept good advice, yet he also was able to make wise and quick decisions. Above all, Grant had a will of iron. He refused to turn back after he had once decided on a course of action.

Early in 1862, Grant attacked Fort Henry and Fort Donelson in western Tennessee. With the help of the navy's gunboats, both forts were captured. When the commander of Fort Donelson asked the terms of surrender, Grant replied, "Immediate and unconditional surrender." From then on, U. S. Grant was nicknamed "Unconditional Surrender" Grant. After the capture of the two forts, his armies moved southward. The Confederate forces made a surprise attack on Grant at Shiloh in southern Tennessee. In the furious battle which followed, the Con-

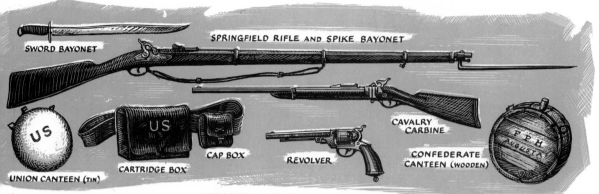

WEAPONS OF THE CIVIL WAR

federates at first seemed to be winning. But when fresh Union soldiers arrived, Grant forced the Confederate troops to retreat.

The capture of Vicksburg gives the North control of the Mississippi. By 1863, the Union forces controlled all the Mississippi except the 250-mile strip between Vicksburg and Port Hudson. (See map, page 400.) General Grant's chief problem now was to capture Vicksburg. This city was situated on high bluffs on the east bank of the river, with swampy ground surrounding it. Its forts were in an excellent position to shell attacking forces. When Grant found he could not take Vicksburg by direct attack, he prepared for a long siege. With Union gunboats guarding the river side and Grant's forces on the land side, no supplies could reach the town. On July 4, 1863, the Confederate commander surrendered Vicksburg on Grant's terms. A short time later Port Hudson also surrendered.

The Union forces now had control of the Mississippi. One part of the North's strategy had succeeded — the Confederacy had been cut in two. Lincoln joyfully announced, "The Father of Waters again goes unvexed to the sea."

THE WAR ON THE SEA

The northern navy cuts off southern shipping. The second part of the Union strategy, you remember, was to strangle the South by blockading its ports. When the war opened, there were only 90 ships in the Union navy. Vessels of every kind, however, were hastily prepared for blockade duty. Soon Union ships were guarding every important Confederate port from Virginia to Texas.

Of course, the blockade was not complete. Because the southern coastline was over 3000 miles long, it proved difficult to seal off every port. In an attempt to break the strangle hold on its shipping, the South used *blockade-runners* built in England. Under cover of the night these swift ships could slip into southern ports with badly needed ammunition, guns, and other supplies. But in spite of all attempts to break the blockade, the South's shipping was slowly strangled. Tea, coffee, soap, and matches became almost impossible to get. Cotton could not be exported, and countless bales of it piled up on the wharves.

To make the blockade even tighter, the

Note how the Northern navy interfered with one of the South's major goals.

FIELD GUN FIRING

THE "MERRIMAC" rammed and sank the Union ship "Cumberland," but met her match in a duel with the "Monitor." The arrow points to dents made in the armor of the "Monitor" (upper right) by gunfire from the "Merrimac."

Union army and navy took steps to capture southern ports. By the end of the war, all important Confederate ports except two were in Union hands. Admiral Farragut added to his fame by taking the great port of Mobile, Alabama. More than any other one plan used by the North, the Union blockade helped bring about the defeat of the South.

Ironclad ships appear in the war on the sea. The first battle ever fought between armored ships took place during this war. Before the war, the navy's ships had all been built of wood. Early in the war, however, the Confederates remodeled the wooden ship *Merrimac,*[1] and covered its sides with iron plates. Five guns were mounted on each side. In

March, 1862, the *Merrimac* attacked Union ships blockading the harbor at Hampton Roads, Virginia. Shells from the Union vessels had no effect on the queer-looking *Merrimac.* She destroyed two ships, ran another one aground, and then withdrew. Her crew planned to return to destroy the remaining ships. On the next day, however, the *Merrimac* was challenged by an ironclad ship which the Union navy had secretly been building. The Union vessel, the *Monitor,* had been designed by a Swedish-American inventor, John Ericsson. This ship was smaller than the *Merrimac.* She had a low, flat iron deck. In a large revolving turret two powerful guns were mounted. The *Monitor* looked like a "tin can on a shingle."

In the battle which followed between the two ironclads, neither ship was able to injure the other greatly. Finally, they

[1] The *Merrimac* was renamed the *Virginia* by the Confederates.

By moving up the James Peninsula McClellan escaped the necessity of having to fight his way through the Wilderness (see maps on pages 404 and 407).

NORTH AND SOUTH FIGHT A WAR AND ARE REUNITED   **403**

both gave up the battle. The North was able to build a large number of additional ironclads, but the South could not. Although the battle between the *Monitor* and the *Merrimac* ended in a draw, it is important in naval history. These strange ironclads proved that wooden warships were a thing of the past and paved the way for the construction of giant steel battleships.

THE WAR IN THE EAST

So far you have read how Union forces gained control of the Mississippi and blockaded the southern coast. Meanwhile, other Union forces in the East had been trying to capture the Confederate capital at Richmond.

McClellan's attack on Richmond fails. After the Union defeat at Bull Run (page 398), General George B. McClellan took charge of reorganizing and drilling the new troops. In a few months the army was a well-disciplined and well-equipped body of 100,000 men. But McClellan was too cautious in attacking the enemy. He did not move against the Confederate army at Richmond until Lincoln ordered him to do so in the spring of 1862. McClellan's army traveled by water and landed on the James Peninsula in order to attack Richmond from the east (map, page 404). The advance up the peninsula against Richmond was so slow, however, that the Confederates decided to attack instead. General Lee sent for General "Stonewall" Jackson to join in the campaign. Jackson had gained his nickname while holding "like a stone wall" against the Union troops in the first Battle of Bull Run. Together Lee and Jackson forced the Union army to retreat in the famous Seven Days' Battles. So the second Union attempt to capture Richmond failed.

Further defeats discourage the North. During the months that followed, the Con-

federates won battle after battle in the East. Another advance by Union forces against Richmond ended in defeat at the second Battle of Bull Run. Lee then led his gray-clad soldiers across the Potomac into Maryland. He was met at Antietam (an-*tee*'tum) Creek by Union troops. After a bloody battle, Lee turned back into Virginia. But he was able to stop the Union advances which followed by winning brilliant victories at Fredericksburg and Chancellorsville. In the latter battle, General Jackson was accidentally shot by his own men and died soon afterward.

BALLOONS launched from this carrier on the Potomac River enabled Union observers to watch Confederate troop movements in Virginia. The balloon carrier was originally a coal barge.

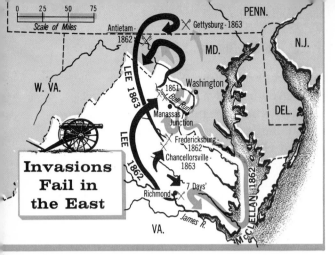

Invasions Fail in the East

MAP STUDY Until Gettysburg the Confederate armies won most of the battles in the East. With what part of the Union strategy were these battles concerned?

When he heard this news, Lee sadly remarked, "I have lost my right arm."

These were discouraging days for the North. Robert E. Lee had outfought Union forces much larger than his own. Lincoln had tried several generals after McClellan's failures, but had not yet been able to find one who could match Lee's military skill. The President himself was bitterly criticized. The people blamed him for the failures of the army. Only Lincoln's stubborn determination to save the Union kept him going in those dark days.

Confederate forces invade Pennsylvania. After his victory at Chancellorsville, General Lee decided to invade the North a second time. He hoped to strike a blow which would end the war. As he swung northward through Maryland and into Pennsylvania, watchful Union armies also marched north, keeping between Lee and the city of Washington.

On June 27, 1863, General Lee and his officers stood looking at a map. As he pointed to the village of Gettysburg in Pennsylvania, the Confederate leader declared, "Hereabouts we shall probably meet the enemy and fight a great battle, and if God gives us the victory, the war will be over, and we shall achieve the recognition of our independence."

Had the Confederates won at Gettysburg, what threatened?

The Battle of Gettysburg stops the Confederate advance. On July 1, the two armies met and the great Battle of Gettysburg began. The Union forces took their position on a series of hills and ridges near Gettysburg. The Confederates occupied a ridge opposite them. Through two and a half days the bitter fighting continued. At noon on July 3, there was a sudden silence on the battlefield. General Lee was preparing to make a bold and desperate attack on the northern position. Then about 15,000 brave Confederates, led by General George Pickett, advanced across a field against the Union forces on Cemetery Ridge. In perfect order they charged through the murderous Union fire and flung themselves at the Union lines. A handful of them succeeded in planting the Confederate flag high on the hill. But then they were forced back. The cannon and musket fire had been so deadly that three fourths of the attackers were killed or wounded. The brave charge had failed. The battle was lost. The next day Lee turned back toward the south.

The President speaks at Gettysburg. Soon after the Battle of Gettysburg, seventeen acres of the battlefield were set aside as a cemetery for the soldiers who had died there. President Lincoln was asked to dedicate the cemetery by making "a few appropriate remarks." Lincoln's "remarks" at Gettysburg on November 19, 1863, have always been remembered because they say so much in so few words and say it so well. His Gettysburg Address, which appears on the next page, is one of the great documents in the history of American democracy. It expresses the ideals which we Americans must keep always before us if our nation is to endure.

Gettysburg marks the turning point of the war. The news of the victory at Gettysburg caused great rejoicing in the North. On its heels came word of Grant's

large northern cities would have been

Four score and seven years ago our fathers brought forth, upon this continent, a new nation, conceived in liberty, and dedicated to the proposition that all men...

The Gettysburg Address

Fourscore and seven years ago our fathers brought forth on this continent a new nation, conceived in liberty, and dedicated to the proposition that all men are created equal.

Now we are engaged in a great civil war, testing whether that nation, or any nation so conceived and so dedicated, can long endure. We are met on a great battlefield of that war. We have come to dedicate a portion of that field as a final resting place for those who here gave their lives that that nation might live. It is altogether fitting and proper that we should do this.

But, in a larger sense, we cannot dedicate — we cannot consecrate — we cannot hallow — this ground. The brave men, living and dead, who struggled here, have consecrated it far above our poor power to add or detract. The world will little note nor long remember what we say here, but it can never forget what they did here. It is for us, the living, rather, to be dedicated here to the unfinished work which they who fought here have thus far so nobly advanced. It is rather for us to be here dedicated to the great task remaining before us — that from these honored dead we take increased devotion to that cause for which they gave the last full measure of devotion; that we here highly resolve that these dead shall not have died in vain; that this nation, under God, shall have a new birth of freedom; and that government of the people, by the people, for the people, shall not perish from the earth.

Be sure to explain words that your students do not understand. Reading the speech aloud will help, too.

success in the West on July 4 — the surrender of Vicksburg (page 401). Grant's victory had cut the Confederacy in two, and the Union success at Gettysburg had hurled back the Confederate invasion of the North. These Union triumphs marked the turning point in the war. In America and abroad, clear-thinking men understood the importance of these victories. Although the South might fight on, it was not likely to win.

General Grant takes command of all the Union armies. Let us now turn again to the fighting in the West. During 1862

The blockade and the campaigns which gave the North control of the Mississippi and cut off the lower South made effective resistance impossible for the Confederacy.

406 THE UNITED STATES EXPANDS AND IS TORN BY WAR

and 1863, Union forces had carried on bitter and bloody campaigns in Tennessee. Their goal was to capture the important city of Chattanooga in the southeastern part of the state. After the surrender of Vicksburg, General Grant took command of these forces. He defeated the Confederate forces at Chattanooga in the late fall of 1863. The Confederate troops had to retreat toward Atlanta, Georgia. (See map, next page.) President Lincoln, impressed by Grant's ability in the West, gave him command of all the Union armies. At last, Lincoln had found a general who might be able to lead the North to final victory.

Grant began to make plans which he hoped would soon end the war: (1) The lower South was to be cut off from the rest of the Confederacy. To accomplish this, Grant ordered General William T. Sherman, who had aided in the capture of Chattanooga, to slash through the Confederacy to Atlanta. (2) As for Grant himself, he was to take the hardest job of all. He would attack Lee in Virginia. No matter what the cost, he would capture Richmond.

Sherman divides the South by marching to the sea. In May, 1864, General Sherman set out from Chattanooga with an army of 100,000 men. Although Confederate troops fought them every step of the way, Sherman's army slowly but surely advanced. In September, Sherman captured Atlanta. (Trace Sherman's advance on the map.)

Shortly afterward, Sherman took a bold step to divide the South still further. With 60,000 men, he struck out for Savannah, Georgia, over 200 miles away on the Atlantic coast. Many southern people have not forgiven General Sherman for the frightful destruction carried out on this march "from Atlanta to the sea." Between Atlanta and Savannah he and his men left behind them a black and desolate strip of country 60 miles wide. They burned houses and barns, towns and crops. They tore up railroads and killed farm animals as they went along. Late in December, 1864, Sherman telegraphed President Lincoln, "I beg to present you, as a Christmas gift, the city of Savannah." The Confederacy had been divided again.

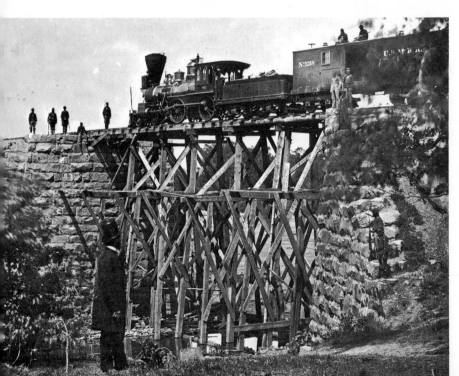

For other Brady photographs see Mathew Brady: Historian with a Camera

UNION SOLDIERS built the wooden railroad bridge in this picture taken by the early photographer Mathew Brady or one of his assistants (page 392). The top-hatted man was a detective assigned to watch the bridge.

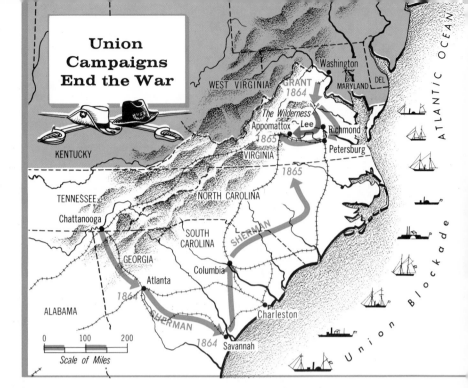

Union Campaigns End the War

MAP STUDY

Two Union thrusts brought the Civil War to an end. What did each of these thrusts accomplish?

Recall the Union strategy outlined on page 398.

The end comes. Meanwhile, General Grant was furiously attacking General Lee's armies in Virginia. The fighting began in a heavily wooded section northwest of Richmond, called the Wilderness. Grant was unable to break through Lee's lines, but he kept hammering at them in spite of frightful losses among his own troops. Step by step the armies moved east and south in a half circle around Richmond. At last, hard-pressed by the enemy, Lee abandoned Richmond to march southwest toward the mountains. But Union armies blocked his way. Lee said sadly, "There is nothing for me to do but go and see General Grant, and I would rather die a thousand deaths." At the village of Appomattox Court House on April 9, 1865, this brave and gallant general surrendered his armies to General Grant.

Grant treated Lee with the respect due a valiant soldier. The two generals began to talk over army experiences during the Mexican War. Then Lee reminded Grant of the purpose of their meeting and asked for the terms of surrender. Grant allowed the Confederate officers to keep their side arms (swords and pistols). He also let the soldiers keep their horses, which, he said, would be needed for spring plowing. Learning that Lee's men were hungry, Grant sent food to them. He forbade his men to fire their guns in celebration of the victory, saying, "The war is over."

About two weeks later in North Carolina, the last important Confederate army surrendered to General Sherman, who had marched north from Savannah to join Grant. The South had fought gallantly. Now the tragic war between countrymen was over. Once more the Stars and Stripes flew over "one nation, indivisible."

CHECK UP

1. (a) What effect did the Battle of Bull Run have on the North? (b) On the South?

2. (a) What was the Confederate plan for winning the war? (b) What was the plan of the North? (c) How did the North carry out each part of its plan?

3. Why did the battles of Gettysburg and Vicksburg mark the turning point in the war?

4. (a) What were Grant's plans for ending the war? (b) How did the war end?

General Grant's policy was approved by President Lincoln but not by many members of Congress.

LEE AND GRANT met again on the morning after the surrender. General Grant, recalling the meeting, later wrote: "We had there, between the lines, sitting on horseback, a very pleasant conversation of over half an hour. . . ."

3 How Did the War Affect the Lives of People in the North and the South?

In time of war, many men are called upon to fight, but those who remain at home also have a job to do. People at home must produce food and supplies for the fighting forces. Every kind of transportation is needed to move supplies. Money must be raised to pay the costs of war. Hours of work are long and every person who can work is called on to help.

The South carries on during the war. The people of the South felt the hardships of the war more keenly than the people of the North. Every man who could fight went into the army. This meant that the work of the South was done for the most part by the slaves and the women. But as the war went on, the slaves began to desert the plantations. Then, too, because of the blockade, the South could not get articles that it usually bought from the North or from foreign countries — clothes, machinery, medicines, and many household goods. The women of the South faced these difficult conditions

bravely. They cut up draperies to make clothes. They tore their linen sheets and towels into bandages for the wounded. Although most of them were not used to hard physical labor, southern women worked on plantations and in hospitals.

As time went on, farms, plantations, and buildings became run-down. Roads were not repaired. Railroad tracks, locomotives, and cars wore out and could not be replaced. It became difficult to transport food and supplies to the armies. Many regions were ruined by invading armies and battles. Homes were burned, cities were shelled, the countryside was stripped of crops and farm animals. War's destruction spread through the South. Thousands of families mourned loved ones lost in battle.

The North prospers during the war. Northern families also felt the grief brought by losses in the war. For several reasons, however, the hardships caused by the war were much less severe in the

Before the age of air power, destruction of invaded country.

property was confined largely to the

Industry always booms during a war, more so in the 20th century than earlier.

NORTH AND SOUTH FIGHT A WAR AND ARE REUNITED **409**

North than in the South. Very little fighting took place on northern soil. Because of its greater population, the North had more men left to carry on at home. The North also had more railroads, factories, and industry of every kind than did the South. Old industries worked at top speed, and new industries sprang up to make the clothes, food, blankets, tents, guns, and ammunition required by the army. Factories also made railroad cars and locomotives, and wagons to transport army supplies.

The boom in northern industry opened up more jobs than there were men to fill them. And when employers need men, wages go up. With wages high, businessmen are forced to ask high prices. High prices in turn help bring greater profits to shopkeepers and others who have something to sell. In spite of great losses and grief, therefore, many people in the North were prosperous during the war.

North and South issue paper money. Both North and South needed money to meet the costs of the war. And in the North as well as the South, the government

issued paper money to pay its bills. But many people feared that these paper dollars might never bring their full worth in gold and silver. In the dark days of 1864, when it seemed the war would never end, the paper dollar in the North was worth only about 40 cents. Since it took more paper dollars to pay for goods, prices went higher and higher. The South, however, was far worse off. To carry on the war, it was forced to issue even greater quantities of paper money. The value of southern money went down much more rapidly than that of northern money. Toward the end of the war, southern money was worth only about three cents on the dollar. These conditions created great hardships for most Southerners.

CHECK UP

1. (a) How did the war affect life in the South? (b) In the North?

2. (a) Why did both sections issue paper money? (b) What was the effect on prices and the value of money?

Northern greenbacks were repaid at full value; Confederate paper money was never redeemed.

 How Did Abraham Lincoln Plan to Unite the Divided Nation?

Even while the war was being fought, Abraham Lincoln struggled with the task of restoring peace after a long and bitter war. He knew, as we do today, that winning the peace is harder than winning a war. Late at night, when the White House stood silent in the darkened city, Lincoln brooded over what would happen when the guns at last ceased firing.

Lincoln proclaims the freedom of the slaves in the Confederate states. From the outset, Lincoln believed that preservation of the Union was the basic war aim of

the North. By focusing on this aim rather than on any other, he could enlist broad support for waging the war. But many people in the North, especially the abolitionists, thought that the chief purpose of the war was to free the slaves. Despite their urging, Lincoln continued to make clear the purpose of the war as he saw it:

* *My paramount object in this struggle is to save the Union. . . . If I could save the Union without freeing any slave, I would do it; if I could save it by freeing all the slaves,*

I would do it; and if I could save it by freeing some and leaving others alone, I would also do that. What I do about slavery and the colored race, I do because I believe it helps to save this Union.

Nevertheless, when Lincoln wrote these words, he had already decided to free the slaves. He realized that freeing the slaves in the Confederacy would be a serious blow to the South. So in the autumn of 1862, he announced that on January 1, 1863, in all parts of the country still fighting the United States, "all persons held as slaves . . . shall be then, thenceforward, and forever free." This statement is known as the *Emancipation Proclamation*.[1] (To *emancipate* means to free.) Now the people of this country and of Europe understood that the war was being fought not only to save the Union but to free the slaves. Since Englishmen did not believe in slavery, their sympathy for the South began to cool. The Proclamation also welcomed Negroes into the Union army. By the end of the war, some 180,000 Negro combat and non-combat troops had joined the Union forces.

Lincoln plans for peace. As Lincoln looked ahead to the end of the war, he saw other problems to be settled. When the Union won the war, as he was sure it would, confusion and disorder would spread through the South. The day the war ended, the Confederate government would collapse. There would be no President, no Congress, no state governments, no police force, no money. Lincoln decided to take steps to meet this situation. He wanted to make it possible for the seceded states to rebuild the South and to enter the

[1] The Emancipation Proclamation was issued under President Lincoln's war power. It did not apply to slaves in the slave states that had remained in the Union. In 1865 the Thirteenth Amendment was added to the Constitution, abolishing slavery forever in the United States.

Union once more. Lincoln proposed this plan: In any southern state, as soon as ten per cent of the persons who had voted in 1860 wished to establish a government loyal to the Union, they could do so.

Lincoln hoped that all Americans would forget the war as soon as possible. He wanted the country to devote all its strength to the building of a new and better nation. When Lincoln took the oath of office as President for the second time, in March of 1865, he expressed this thought in never-to-be-forgotten words:

＊ Fondly do we hope — fervently do we pray — that this mighty scourge of war may speedily pass away. . . .

With malice toward none; with charity for all; with firmness in the right, as God gives us to see the right, let us strive on to finish the work we are in; to bind up the nation's wounds; to care for him who shall have borne the battle and for his widow, and his orphan — to do all which may achieve and cherish a just and lasting peace among ourselves, and with all nations.

Lincoln is assassinated. President Lincoln did not live to put his plans into effect. In the middle of April, 1865, the long struggle was drawing to a close and Lincoln felt the need of relaxation. On the evening of April 14, he arranged to go to Ford's Theater in Washington with Mrs. Lincoln and two guests. Arriving at the theater, he and his guests were shown to the box reserved for them.

In an alley outside the theater a man was restlessly pacing back and forth. His name was John Wilkes Booth. Booth was a Virginian, brooding and desperate over the defeat of the South. He believed that if only Lincoln had not been elected President, if only he were not then President, the South would be better off. Booth had decided to kill Lincoln, and had urged friends to kill other important government

The percentage of casualties among Negro troops was higher than for the Union army as a whole.

PRESIDENT LINCOLN reads the Emancipation Proclamation to his Cabinet officers in this diorama.

officials. Booth himself was an actor. Having often played in Ford's Theater, he was familiar with the building.

As the audience watched the play, John Wilkes Booth stole through the theater to the door of Lincoln's box. Suddenly he threw open the door, stepped into the box, and shot Lincoln in the back of the head. Then he leaped over the railing and half jumped, half fell, to the stage. As he fell, he shouted a Latin phrase which means, "Thus be it ever to tyrants!" He got to his feet, limped across the stage to the back door of the theater, mounted his horse, and rode away. Booth was killed a few days later by soldiers who were sent to capture him.

The wounded President was carried to a house across the street from the theater. There, shortly after seven o'clock the next morning, he died. Thus ended the life of

a great American. Abraham Lincoln had done his work well; the Union had been preserved. It remained for others to "bind up the nation's wounds."

Throughout the North, Lincoln was deeply mourned. Even the people of the South began to realize that this great and kindhearted man had been their friend. Jefferson Davis himself said, "Next to the defeat of the Confederacy, the heaviest blow that fell upon the South was the assassination of Lincoln." In the next few pages we shall learn how true this was.

C H E C K
U P

1. (a) Why did Lincoln issue the Emancipation Proclamation? (b) What slaves were affected by this Proclamation? (c) What effect did the Proclamation have in Europe?

2. What was Lincoln's plan for helping the Confederate states return to the Union?

Help students understand why Jefferson Davis made this statement.

5 What Happened in the South After the War?

THE SOUTH FACES A DIFFICULT PERIOD

War and destruction leave their mark on the South. It is nightfall on a Virginia plantation late in 1865. In the

years before the war, the scene would have been one of gaiety and gracious living. There would have been twinkling lights, charming ladies, courtly gentlemen, Negro servants, and a table spread with good things to eat. On this night, however, an air of gloom hangs over the home. Instead of silver candlesticks, expensive china, and the fine food of prewar days, there are a few dishes of plain food on the table. A single servant, his bowed shoulders and grizzled hair betraying his age, moves slowly about the room. At the table several empty chairs are grim reminders of sons fallen in battle. The master and mistress of the plantation are sharing their scanty meal with a neighbor. Their faces are lined with care, and their clothes are threadbare. They speak with despair of their ruined fields, the loss of their slaves, the destruction of their livestock and farm equipment. "What is to become of us?" they ask. "How are we to rebuild our beloved South?"

Problems must be solved. All over the South men and women were asking the same question, for there were many problems to be solved.

(1) Southerners knew that somehow they must rebuild the South, repair the destruction brought by war, and return to peacetime living.

(2) One of the most important problems had to do with the relation of the seceded states to the national government. How were they to be returned to the Union again? Would they be treated generously or would they be punished as defeated enemies?

(3) There was also the question of setting up state governments. Would the men who fought against the Union be allowed to vote and hold office? If not, who would run the state governments?

(4) Another serious problem was that of the freed slaves. Accustomed to receiving food and clothing from their masters, now they were "on their own." Late in the war Congress had established a *Freedmen's Bureau* which supplied food, cloth-

ing, fuel, and hospital care to a large number of both whites and Negroes. The Bureau also sought to protect freedmen from violence and to defend their right to own property. Its most notable work was in the field of education. Would the Freedmen's Bureau continue this work, or would it be turned over to the reconstructed southern states?

CONGRESS OPPOSES PRESIDENT JOHNSON AND TAKES CHARGE OF RECONSTRUCTION IN THE SOUTH

President Johnson's plans are defeated. After Lincoln's death, the heavy duties of President fell upon Andrew Johnson. The former Vice-President undertook to carry out Lincoln's generous plans for restoring the seceded states to the Union. But the Republican Congress was not willing to leave the *reconstruction* (rebuilding) of the South in the hands of a Democrat and a Southerner.

When Congress convened in December, 1865, newly elected members from the southern states were waiting to take their seats in the two houses. Among them were many men who had held high positions in the Confederacy. Northern senators and congressmen refused to seat the southern delegations.

Congress takes control of reconstruction policy. There were many reasons why Congress demanded its part in working out plans for reconstruction. For one thing, by the end of 1865 it was clear that the former slave states were determined to deny freedmen the rights of free citizens. They adopted *Black Codes* which made it difficult for Negroes to own property, to earn a living, and to acquire an education. None of the states had given freedmen the vote.

The *Thirteenth Amendment* had provided that in determining representation,

Negroes would now be counted the same as whites. Thus the South would soon acquire more seats in the House. Republicans feared that the party which had won the war would lose control of Congress unless a Republican Party open to freedmen could be built in the South. Northerners also felt bitter because of heavy Union losses and the harsh treatment of Union prisoners during the war. As differences with the President over reconstruction policy grew sharper, Republican leaders usually had their way.

Congress passes the Fourteenth Amendment. In 1866 Congress approved the *Fourteenth Amendment,* which would become part of the Constitution when enough states ratified it. This amendment made Negroes citizens by declaring that "all persons born or naturalized in the United States . . . are citizens. . . ." Another section provided that when a state refused to let adult male Negroes vote, its representation in Congress would be reduced. The amendment also forbade former government officials who had taken sides against the Union to hold office again until pardoned by Congress.

Congress passes the Reconstruction Act. When only one of the Confederate states — Tennessee — approved the Fourteenth Amendment, Congress decided to use harsher methods. Congress, therefore, passed the *Reconstruction Act of 1867.* Under this act the governments of the ten unwilling states were swept away, and these states were divided into five military districts. Each district was placed under army rule. The soldiers were to keep order while new state governments more to Congress's liking were formed. In forming these new governments, Congress ruled that the southern whites who had fought against the Union would not be allowed to vote. Negroes, however, would be guaranteed

the right to vote and to hold office. The southern states were not to be admitted to the Union until (1) new state constitutions had been approved by Congress and (2) the new state governments had accepted the Fourteenth Amendment.

The Fifteenth Amendment is added to the Constitution. Congress also passed the *Fifteenth Amendment,* for the purpose of protecting the Negro still further. It stated that no citizen should be kept from voting because of his race or color or the fact that he had once been a slave.

Selfish adventurers gain control of state governments. By the Reconstruction Act, men who only a few years earlier had been slaves were enabled to vote and hold office. Many of them could neither read nor write and did not understand the workings of government. They became easy victims of selfish white men who wanted to gain control of the new southern governments. These white men were known in the South as *carpetbaggers* and *scalawags.* The carpetbaggers were Northerners who tried to carry out Congress's plan of reconstruction. Many also saw a chance to get rich quickly at the expense of the South. They earned their name from the fact that they rushed to the South with all their belongings hastily packed in old-fashioned traveling bags called "carpetbags." The scalawags, on the other hand, were southern white men who had opposed secession or who thought the best plan now was to co-operate with the North. Many carpetbaggers and scalawags were more interested in wealth and power for themselves than in rebuilding the South.

Reconstruction is carried out under carpetbag governments. How did the carpetbaggers and scalawags gain control of the state governments? They joined with the Negroes to form a Republican

Compare the Congressional policy with Lincoln's (page 410).

Party in the South. The three groups controlled the new state legislatures. It was these "carpetbag" governments which carried out the provisions of the Reconstruction Act. By 1870, all the southern states had been admitted once more to the Union.

The new state constitutions and laws contained many admirable provisions. Public schools were established for both whites and Negroes. Voting laws were liberalized and the rights of women enlarged. The courts and the county governments were improved. Many of these reforms have been retained to the present day.

The new legislatures voted huge sums of money for buildings, schools, roads, and railroads. Many of these things were badly needed in the war-torn South, although much money was also spent foolishly. The carpetbag legislatures voted heavy taxes to raise the money they wanted to spend. The heavy taxes fell chiefly on the southern whites who owned property. Many had to sell their lands because they could not pay the taxes.

The southern whites strike back. At first, there seemed no way for the southern whites to get relief from the reconstruction governments. Most of their leaders were not allowed to hold office. Gradually, however, they began to form secret societies. The Ku Klux Klan was the most active of these societies. Its purpose was to frighten the freedmen so that they would not vote for or support the carpetbag governments. Clad in ghostly white hoods and robes, Klan members rode silently around the countryside in the dead of night, terrifying Negroes by their threats. All too often, when their warnings were not heeded, the Klan members returned and used violence. The Ku Klux Klan succeeded so well in frightening the Negroes that Congress ordered federal soldiers to break up the organization.

Note the advances made during reconstruction.

SOUTHERN WHITES REGAIN CONTROL OF THEIR GOVERNMENTS

Reconstruction ends in the South. In time, white people in the South regained much of their power. Those who had been mere boys during the war reached the age of 21. Since they had not fought against the United States, they were permitted to vote and hold office. Also, in 1872, Congress passed a law restoring the right to vote to all but a few ex-Confederates. Carpetbag rule gradually ended, and southern whites regained control of their state governments. Soldiers were withdrawn from the last of the southern states in 1877.

Southerners felt that Negroes should be prevented from voting. So they found ways to get around the Fifteenth Amendment. They passed laws requiring that all voters must have lived for many years in one place, or must pay a tax in order to be eligible to vote. Some states required voters to be able to read and to explain the federal Constitution. These laws were all used to deprive the Negro of the right to vote.

The South becomes solidly Democratic. People in the South found it hard to forgive Congress for the suffering they had endured under the carpetbag governments. Most of the congressmen who had favored harsh treatment of the South belonged to the Republican Party. The Southerners therefore blamed the Republicans for their troubles and became strong supporters of the Democratic Party. In election after election the southern states voted overwhelmingly for Democratic candidates. When people spoke of the "Solid South," they meant that the South could usually be counted on to vote solidly for the Democratic Party. (In recent elections, however, this has been less true.)

A NEW SOUTH DEVELOPS AFTER THE WAR

In time the South, aided by northern capital, repaired the damages caused by war. Cities were rebuilt, railroads repaired, business and trade expanded. Still other changes took place in the South following the Civil War.

Large plantations begin to disappear. One change was the breakdown of the old plantation system. Owners of vast estates had neither the money nor the slave labor to work their land as they had before the war. Also, most of the freed Negroes did not wish to remain on large plantations and toil for wages. Instead, they wanted to start a new life. Because plantation owners lacked workers and because taxes were so high, many of them were forced to sell much of their land. Most of this land was sold in lots of a few acres. As a result, the number of large plantations grew smaller, while the number of separate farms increased.

Sharecropping becomes common. Instead of selling land, many plantation owners rented their land to *tenant farmers.* Some of the tenants paid rent in cash or in crops worth the amount of their rent. But many tenants were poor white men or Negroes who could furnish nothing but their labor. They became *sharecroppers.* The landlord would provide them with food, seed, tools, and a cabin. In return, the sharecropper gave the landowner a share of the crops raised on his plot of land. The share varied from one third to two thirds. Many sharecroppers barely made a living from their share of the crops. They were often in debt to the landowner who charged high prices and might deceive sharecroppers as to the amount due.

New crops are raised in the South. Changes also took place in the crops grown in the South. Cotton remained the chief crop. Large quantities of tobacco, rice,

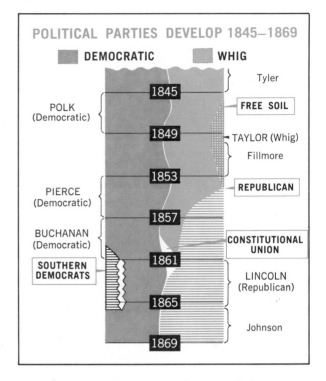

POLITICAL PARTIES DEVELOP 1845–1869

NORTHERNERS who strongly opposed slavery left the Whig Party to form the Free Soil and Republican Parties. Other Whigs joined new middle-of-the-road groups, while the slavery issue split the Democrats into northern and southern parties.

and sugar also continued to be raised. But as transportation improved, farmers found that they could make good profits from fruits and vegetables that were suited to the southern soil and climate. Many southern farmers are now using their land to produce peanuts, pecans, vegetables, and a variety of fruit — peaches, oranges, grapefruit, lemons, and watermelons. Others are raising beef cattle.

Industry begins to flourish in the South. Before the war, most Southerners made their living from farming. After the war, farming was still the chief occupation, but people became more interested in business, trade, and industry. The South was rich in natural resources which had never been developed because cotton-growing with slave labor had seemed more profitable. For example, there were great stretches of forest which would yield quantities of lumber. Beneath southern soil there were large deposits of coal, iron, and oil which were needed in industry. Plentiful cotton and a large supply of workers encouraged the building of mills to manufacture cloth.

The South that has developed since the war, therefore, is very different from the old "land of cotton." Today a network of roads, railroad lines, and airplane routes cover the South. At least a third of the lumber cut in the United States now comes from the South. Quantities of coal and iron are mined in that region. Birmingham, Alabama, has become a thriving steel and industrial center, earning the name of the "Pittsburgh of the South." Oil wells and refineries dot such states as Texas, Louisiana, and Arkansas. Factory towns have grown up in many regions, drawing large numbers of workers into the manufacture of cotton cloth, tobacco, and cottonseed products. New industries continue to spring up in the South. Ports such as New Orleans, Louisiana; Houston and Galveston, Texas; Mobile, Alabama; and Norfolk, Virginia, are busy centers of commerce.

With the passing of years, much of the bitterness caused by the war and recon-struction faded from men's memories. The people of the South had fought for what they believed was right; their cause had been defeated. In spite of the problems of the reconstruction period, the people of the South gradually returned to loyal support of the Union. Differences may arise from time to time, but today Southerners and Northerners — Americans all — are united in their allegiance to our country.

CHECK UP

1. What problems faced the South after the war?

2. (a) How did President Johnson hope to bring the southern states back into the Union? (b) What position did Congress take on reconstruction?

3. (a) What was the purpose of the Fourteenth Amendment? (b) Of the Reconstruction Act of 1867? (c) Of the Fifteenth Amendment? (d) How were new state governments organized and the southern states restored to the Union?

4. (a) How did southern whites regain control of the state governments? (b) What is meant by the term "Solid South"?

5. (a) What effect did the war have on the plantation system? (b) On the development of industry in the South?

Our national welfare has dictated the decentralization of defense-related industries. A favorable climate and good labor supply have attracted light industry to the South.

Check Up on Chapter 20

Do You Know the Meaning?

1. siege
2. strategy
3. emancipation
4. blockade
5. document
6. sharecroppers

7. scalawags
8. unconditional
9. reconstruction
10. assassination
11. carpetbaggers
12. border states

13. tenant farmers

Can You Identify?

1. Robert E. Lee
2. Jefferson Davis
3. Seven Days' Battles
4. 1861
5. 1863
6. 1865

7. Bull Run (Manassas)
8. *Monitor* and *Merrimac*
9. Chancellorsville
10. Freedmen's Bureau
11. Appomattox Court House

Can You Identify? (Cont.)

12. David Farragut
13. Andrew Johnson
14. Ku Klux Klan
15. Antietam
16. Solid South
17. William Sherman
18. U. S. Grant
19. Stonewall Jackson
20. George McClellan
21. John Wilkes Booth
22. 13th, 14th, and 15th Amendments
23. Reconstruction Act
24. Emancipation Proclamation

Can You Locate?

1. Chattanooga
2. Richmond
3. Atlanta
4. New Orleans
5. Savannah
6. Washington, D.C.
7. Vicksburg
8. Gettysburg
9. Mississippi River

What Do You Think?

1. Some historians believe that the South lost the war when Great Britain failed to recognize the Confederacy as an independent

What Do You Think? (Cont.)

country. Why do they think this?
2. (a) Why did Lincoln say that war solves no problems? (b) What problems were not solved by the war between the North and the South? (c) What would have been the result if President Lincoln had made no effort to stop the seceding states?
3. In Georgia and South Carolina, General Sherman carried out widespread destruction to make it impossible for the Confederates to feed and supply their armies. He believed that this policy was justified because it would end the war sooner. How do you feel about this argument? Why?
4. A period of reconstruction for the defeated side follows every war, as it followed the American Civil War. What should be the goal of reconstruction? Should it be based on a policy of revenge and punishment? Explain.

The point raised in question #4 was an issue during and after World Wars I and II.

LINKING PAST AND PRESENT

Modern war. The American Civil War is regarded as the first modern war. It made the first effective use of wire entanglements, booby traps, repeating rifles, and air (balloon) observation. For the first time, masses of men and equipment could be moved by railroad. It was learned that a well-entrenched force equipped with rifles and supported by artillery could beat off many times their number. Most of these developments were a result of the growing use of machines, and the world was shocked to learn how ferocious war could be. Now, atomic and nuclear weapons have made war the terror of civilization.

Wartime Virginia. Virginia was the scene of much heavy fighting during the war between the North and South. This is not surprising when we remember that Richmond,

Virginia, the Confederate capital, was not far across the Potomac from Washington, D.C. Today, many battlefields, monuments, and other reminders of the war can be seen in this state. At Manassas, visitors can see the old stone tavern and a log cabin which survived the battles of Bull Run, and a statue of Stonewall Jackson, who turned back the Union troops. In the wooded Wilderness region, trenches dug by the opposing armies still remain, grim reminders of the battles once fought there. A national military park now preserves the battlefields of Fredericksburg, Chancellorsville, Spotsylvania Court House, and the Wilderness. The old earthworks, trenches, and cannon sites there remind us of events long past. At Appomattox Court House, the brick house where General Lee surrendered to General Grant is still standing. A stone slab commemorates the historic meeting.

Toward the end of the war the North had greatly superior fire power (artillery and units armed with repeating rifles).

The Presidents  of Our Country

JAMES K. POLK 1845–1849

Democrat from Tennessee. Nominated as a compromise candidate, and not a favorite in the race, the short, slightly built Polk became the first "dark horse" to be elected President. Polk favored expansion. During his administration the Mexican War was fought and the boundary dispute with England over the Oregon Territory was settled. Polk's nomination and his inauguration were the first to be reported by telegraph.

ZACHARY TAYLOR 1849–1850

Whig from Louisiana. "Old Rough and Ready" had served in the army for over 40 years when the Whigs nominated him for the presidency. A popular hero in the Mexican War, Taylor had never held public office before his election. Though inexperienced in politics, Taylor was a conscientious President. He took a firm stand in the slavery dispute, threatening to lead an army himself against any attempted secession.

MILLARD FILLMORE 1850–1853

Whig from New York. Distinguished in appearance, Fillmore was a New York legislator and a congressman before he was elected Vice-President. Becoming President at Taylor's death, Fillmore's most important action was to support the Compromise of 1850 — a measure which he mistakenly believed would end the differences between the North and South. Fillmore was the last Whig to serve as President.

FRANKLIN PIERCE 1853–1857

Democrat from New Hampshire. A compromise candidate who didn't want the presidency and made no campaign speeches, Pierce nevertheless won the election by a sweeping majority. The death of their young son just before the family moved to Washington cast a shadow over the Pierces, and there was little entertaining in the White House. Because he favored the South on the slavery issue, Pierce lost northern support during his single term.

JAMES BUCHANAN 1857–1861

Democrat from Pennsylvania. "Old Buck" was our only bachelor President. Buchanan had served as a representative, senator, Secretary of State under Polk, and minister to Russia and England before becoming President. Cautious in nature, he took no action when southern states seceded from the Union. Buchanan believed that although the states had no constitutional right to secede, the federal government had no constitutional right to stop them.

ABRAHAM LINCOLN 1861–1865

Republican from Illinois. Our tallest President, Lincoln had served in the Illinois legislature and for one term in the House of Representatives before becoming President. A grave-looking man with a keen sense of humor, Lincoln was widely admired for his expressive words and writings. The first President to be assassinated, his death deprived the war-torn country of the firm leadership that had held the Union together through the war years.

ANDREW JOHNSON 1865–1869

From Tennessee. A self-educated man of intelligence, honesty, and courage, Johnson had risen from humble beginnings to high public office. Though a southern Democrat, he had opposed secession in the Senate and became Lincoln's second-term Vice-President. When Lincoln died, Johnson inherited the task of restoring the South to the Union. Disagreements with Congress led to Johnson's impeachment, but he was acquitted and completed his term of office.

Ask your students whether they can suggest a summary organized around more (or fewer) than three major points.

TO CLINCH YOUR UNDERSTANDING OF
Unit 6

◾ Summary of Important Ideas

Unit Six has told how the United States expanded and how the North and South fought a bitter war.

1. From 1803 to 1853 the United States, through purchase, annexation, treaty, and conquest, expanded beyond the boundaries of 1783 until it reached the Pacific.

a. Among the reasons for this expansion were (1) a desire to control the inland waterways and to acquire cheap and fertile land, and (2) fear that European countries might become powerful in North America.

b. The areas obtained by the United States included (1) the Louisiana Purchase, (2) Florida, (3) Texas, (4) the Mexican Cession, (5) the Oregon region, and (6) the Gadsden Purchase.

c. The new lands were explored and settled. Just west of the Mississippi River, a number of new states were carved out of the Louisiana Purchase and admitted to the Union. Traveling by wagon train, pioneers followed the Santa Fe Trail to the Southwest or the Oregon Trail to the

419

interior of the country and on to the west coast. With the discovery of gold in California, the population on the Pacific coast increased greatly.

2. A bitter quarrel developed between the North and the South over slavery in the new territories.

   a. For a time, compromises like the Missouri Compromise and the Compromise of 1850 checked the quarrel over slavery.

   b. Finally, further compromise was rejected. Leaders in the South opposed any limitations on slavery in the territories (1) because the soil in the Old South was wearing out and new land was needed for growing cotton, and (2) because Southerners believed that their way of life would be destroyed by the North unless a balance between free and slave states was maintained in the Union. In the North the great majority of the people were opposed to the extension of slavery into the territories.

   c. The victory in 1860 of the Republican Party (which believed that Congress had the power to pass laws prohibiting slavery in the territories) led to the secession of the southern states and to war.

3. The Civil War (1861–1865) caused great destruction in the South and led to great changes in both the North and South.

   a. The North had the advantages of a larger population and greater industrial resources; the South had the advantages of fighting in defense of its own soil and of brilliant military leadership.

   b. After bitter fighting, the northern plan of blockade and of dividing the South resulted in victory. Thus, the Union was saved. In the North, the war greatly increased the national debt, but industry also grew stronger. In the South, property damage was great, Confederate money became worthless, and the slaves were freed.

   c. Following the assassination of Lincoln, Congress insisted on a severe plan for reconstructing the South. This policy was deeply resented by Southerners.

   d. Important changes took place in the

South after the war. Small farms multiplied, new crops were introduced, and industry became increasingly important.

Unit Review

1. How and why did the United States acquire each of the following territories: (a) Louisiana Purchase, (b) Florida, (c) Texas, (d) Oregon Territory, (e) Mexican Cession, (f) Gadsden Purchase?

2. In what way did each of the following contribute to the settlement of the West: (a) the Lewis and Clark expedition, (b) travel by steamboat, (c) the Oregon Trail, (d) Stephen F. Austin, (e) the Santa Fe Trail, (f) the discovery of gold in California, (g) the quarrel over slavery, (h) the fur trade?

3. (a) Why did southern leaders feel that slavery must expand into the new territories? (b) Why did they reject "popular sovereignty"? (c) Why did they favor "states' rights"? (d) Why did the victory of the Republican Party in 1860 lead to the secession of the southern states?

4. (a) What were some of the advantages of each section in the Civil War? (b) Why did the North win the war? (c) How was each of the sections affected by the war?

5. (a) What was Lincoln's plan for reconstruction of the South? (b) Why did Congress develop another plan after his assassination? (c) What were the results?

6. What changes in ways of living took place in the South after the war? Why?

Gaining Skill

How to Read Pictures

The pictures in this book can tell you much about America's story if you look at them carefully and think about them.

Sometimes pictures are better than words because they can *show* you how people dressed in past times, what their homes looked like, and the kinds of tools they used.

It would take many words to describe the appearance of Americans who lived in the Northeast and the South and on the frontier during the early 1800's. But the drawings on the first pages of Chapters 14, 15, and 16 show you at a glance how typical Americans in the different sections looked at that time (pages 264, 289, 304).

Pictures are especially useful in describing how something works. To see what Eli Whitney's first model of the cotton gin looked like, turn to the picture biography on page 291 and look at the second scene. To understand how the gin actually cleaned cotton, look at the diagram on page 292.

＊Pictures can also help you understand a story told in words. On page 167 you read how American Patriots at the Battle of Bunker Hill twice drove back the advancing British troops. Now look at the picture on page 168. It shows you how the height of the hill gave the Patriots an advantage over the British who landed at the foot of it and faced a long climb under enemy fire.

＊In studying pictures you can learn a great deal from details. The illustration on page 105 shows the inside of a colonial ironworks. At the left are the big gear wheels which transmitted power from the outside water wheel. In a modern steel mill such big machinery would be made of steel. Yet in this colonial ironworks the wheels were made of wood. This shows you that in colonial times American industry had barely started to develop. The colonists' use of iron was limited to relatively small parts, like the heads of tools.

Some pictures in this book are printed in pairs to link past and present. Like the links at the ends of chapters, these "picture links" show you the relation between history and our present-day life. On page 297, for example, is a dramatic example of our progress in transportation. The first steamship *Savannah* was little more than a sailing vessel with steam-powered paddle wheels added. Compare this pioneer ship with the present-day *Savannah,* sleek and nuclear-powered, and you can understand at once how transportation has improved in the past 140 years.

Interesting Things to Do

The items marked with an asterisk (＊) are for the whole class.

＊**1.** Make new cards for your game "Can You Identify?" using items in Chapters 18, 19, and 20.

＊**2.** On an outline map show the original territory of the United States in 1783 and each new piece of territory added to the United States up through 1853. Mark the dates on each new territory.

＊**3.** Memorize the Gettysburg Address (page 405). Look up the meaning of the words you do not know so that you will understand it better.

＊**4.** The 13th, 14th, and 15th Amendments were passed as a result of the Civil War. With the help of your teacher make a simple outline showing the main ideas of each of these amendments.

5. Make a pictorial map showing one of the following: (a) the four routes used by the forty-niners; (b) the Oregon Trail; (c) the explorations of Lewis and Clark, and Pike; (d) five flags which have flown over Texas since 1763; (e) four flags which have flown over California.

6. Prepare a "Who's Who" of the leading men of the North and South during the war. Write a paragraph about each man.

7. Write an imaginary letter by (a) an American boy living in Texas when Texas was annexed; (b) a southern boy or girl telling of the changes in the South during the war or reconstruction; (c) a northern soldier at the Battle of Bull Run.

8. Look up some of the songs, such as *Dixie* and the *Battle Hymn of the Republic,* sung during the American Civil War. Others are *Tenting Tonight* and *Tramp! Tramp! Tramp!* Tell the story of these songs and have a group sing them.

9. Study and prepare to read to the class one of these poems: (a) *O Captain! My Captain!* by Walt Whitman; (b) *Lincoln, the Man of the People* by Edwin Markham; (c) *Abraham Lincoln Walks at Midnight* by Vachel Lindsay.

Similar use should be made of other pictures included in the text.

Modern America Takes Shape

In 1876, one hundred years after the Thirteen Colonies had declared their independence, a great fair or exposition was held in Philadelphia. Called the Centennial Exposition, it attracted nearly ten million visitors (see illustration above). During its first hundred years, America had come a long way. Its territory stretched from one ocean to another; its population had multiplied many times. Yet the changes in the first century of our history were dwarfed by the changes that were to take place in the years to come.

One reason was that the United States had proved it was "one nation, indivisible." It had taken a terrible war to decide that the Union should be preserved. Even after the thunder of cannon died, the problems of reconstruction, especially serious in the South, had to be solved. But the country as a whole was now free to make plans for the future.

Moreover, the United States had entered a period of industrial growth. The rich resources of our country had barely been touched. Recent inventions speeded up travel and communication between distant parts of the country. New machines, such as those exhibited at the Centennial

Exposition, made it possible to produce an ever-growing quantity of goods. Vast stretches of land beyond the Mississippi beckoned to pioneers. Endless opportunities awaited people who had the courage and skill to grasp them. A new America was in the making.

Unit Seven tells the story of our country's progress from 1865 to the present. In Chapter 21 you will learn how pioneers moved into the last open spaces in the West. Chapter 22 tells how inventions caused the United States to become the world's leading industrial nation. Our industrial growth brought many benefits but also created new problems. Chapter 23 describes some of these problems and some steps that were taken to meet them. And in Chapter 24 you will learn what happened when new machines and new methods were applied to farming.

Help students understand what the poet refers to in using the word "giant;" what is the source of his strength, and what is his future.

Here the free spirit of mankind, at length
Throws its last fetters off; and who shall place
A limit to the giant's unchained strength,
Or curb his swiftness in the forward race?

— WILLIAM CULLEN BRYANT

The Last Frontier in the West
Is Settled

The material in this paragraph and reference to the map story following page 432 will suggest a way of teaching important real understandings.

What this chapter is about —

"The West" has been a magic term throughout American history. To countless Americans it spelled hardship and danger on the one hand, and adventure, freedom, and a satisfying life on the other. The advice of one famous American to young men just starting out in life was: "Go West, young man, go West, and grow up with the country." For many years the vast stretches of the West seemed endless. But by the end of the 1800's there no longer were large areas of open land fit for settlement by pioneers.

From the very start of American history, as you have learned in earlier chapters, adventurous pioneers had moved westward. For the most part, this westwa advance came in waves, each wave pu: ing the frontier farther westward. Fir the territory between the Atlantic co and the Appalachians was filled in. Th in the early 1800's, settlers poured throu the mountains and into the rich valley the Ohio. Next, the frontier reached Mississippi and beyond. In the mid 1800's, lured by the promise of gold a rich farm lands, pioneers made their w by land or sea to the Pacific coast a settled California and Oregon. There s remained in the West, however, a v unsettled territory. It stretched roug from the present state of Minnesota so

People in our story — plains Indians, cavalryman, cowboy, homesteading family.

The West Is Settled

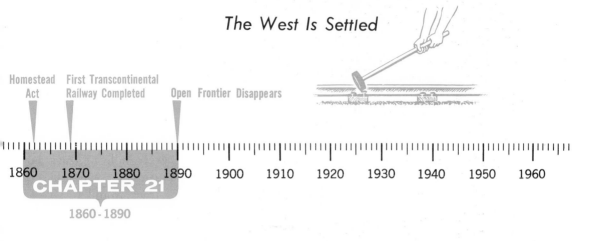

Homestead Act — First Transcontinental Railway Completed — Open Frontier Disappears

1860   1870   1880   1890   1900   1910   1920   1930   1940   1950   1960

CHAPTER 21

1860-1890

to Texas and westward beyond the Rocky Mountains. This territory was the last American frontier. (Turn to the special map story following page 432 to follow the filling in of the West.)

For a long time most Americans doubted that this part of the West would ever be settled. Blocking the paths of the white settlers were thousands of Indians for whom this land was a last hunting ground.

[1] When our government announced in 1890 that the last frontier had disappeared, it referred to the territory of our first 48 states. We should remember, however, that parts of Alaska (which became a state in 1959) still offer frontier conditions and opportunities for adventuresome settlers.

But in the years following the war between the North and South, pioneers streamed into the open spaces west of the Mississippi. So great was this advance that by 1890 the frontier had disappeared.[1]

In this chapter we shall read how miners, cattlemen, and farmers moved into the West and we shall learn what happened to the Indians. The following questions will help you understand what happened:

▶ 1. Why did people move into the last unsettled territory in the West?

▶ 2. What happened to the Indians who resisted western settlement?

▶ 3. How did miners, cowboys, and farmers help to settle the last frontier?

Why Did People Move into the Last Unsettled Territory in the West?

The Homestead Act aids western settlement. In the 1860's, two events encouraged Americans to settle west of the Mississippi. The first was the *Homestead Act,* passed by Congress in 1862. It had to do with public lands, that is, the lands that belonged to the national government. Before this time, the United States had sold public lands to pioneers for as little as $1.25 an acre (page 316). But even this low price kept many poor families from settling in the West. The Homestead Act made public lands easier to obtain. By this Act any head of a family could become the owner of a farm or homestead of 160 acres. The only requirement was that he live on it and work the land for five years.

THIS GOLDEN SPIKE marked the joining of the two sections of the transcontinental railroad. The inscription reads: "May God continue the unity of our country, as this railroad unites the two great oceans of the world." The spike also bears the names of the directors of the Central Pacific Railroad.

See also Wellman, Race to the Golden Spike.

Coming at the time it did, the Homestead Act had very important results. Before the end of the war between the North and the South, many families had moved into the states of Wisconsin, Illinois, Minnesota, and Iowa. At the close of the war, large numbers of soldiers were discharged from military service. These soldiers had given up jobs to go to war; they had led exciting and dangerous lives in battle. Many of them wished to strike out on some bold new venture rather than return to their homes and their former way of living. The Homestead Act made it easy for war veterans to make a new start. Large numbers of them took up homesteads in the western lands.

A transcontinental railroad is built. The second important event followed close on the heels of the Homestead Act. This was the building of the first railroad line across the continent. For many years a few men had dreamed of linking the East and West by railroad. In 1862, these dreams developed into plans. Two companies, the Union Pacific and the Central Pacific, were organized to build a railroad between the Middle West and the Pacific coast. The Union Pacific was to push westward from Omaha, Nebraska, while the Central Pacific would build eastward from Sacramento, California. Somewhere in the huge unsettled region the two roads would meet. The United States government took steps to encourage this plan. It offered to lend generous amounts of money to the railroad builders and to give them large tracts of land on each side of

the railroad for every mile of track laid. Thus, the railroad company which laid the longest stretch of track would receive the most land and money.

A race started between the two railroads. Across broad prairies and through narrow mountain passes the workers pushed their way. At the height of the race nearly 20,000 men toiled and sweated. They suffered from scorching heat, blinding snowstorms, and Indian attacks, but mile by mile the two roads crept closer together. On May 10, 1869, two locomotives — *Number 119* of the Union Pacific and *Jupiter* of the Central Pacific — "touched noses" at Promontory Point near Ogden, Utah. The race had been won by the Union Pacific. Because it crossed level country for much of the way, the Union Pacific had succeeded in laying 1086 miles of track. The Central Pacific, which had to cross the western mountains, had laid only 689 miles of track. There was great rejoicing as Governor Leland Stanford of California drove a gold spike into the final railroad tie. Telegraph wires flashed the news all over the country. The dream of spanning the continent had come true.

The transcontinental railroad helps the settlement of the West. Traveling by railroad, an increasing number of people crossed the open spaces of the West. They sent back news of what they had seen to friends and relatives in the East, many of whom joined the westward stream of pioneers. People who wished to set up homes in the West found the task of moving their families and belongings much

Union veterans in time also received pensions.

easier, safer, and more comfortable after the transcontinental railroad was built. The railroad also made it easier for western farmers to send their crops to market, and cattle could be shipped directly to meat-packing centers. By 1884, three more railroads — the Northern Pacific, the Southern Pacific, and the Santa Fe — had lines stretching to the Pacific coast. The railroads sold land given them by the government to settlers at low prices. Towns grew up along all the railroad lines.

Because of the transcontinental railroads as well as the Homestead Act, a mighty wave of settlers moved westward during the 1870's and '80's. Not only Americans but people from far-distant Europe joined the throng of pioneers in search of land and new homes. This wave of eager settlers pushed the frontier farther and farther westward.

The pioneers endure many hardships. The pushing back of the frontier, however, was still far from easy. The early pioneer had to face and overcome many dangers and hardships. Bitter blizzards in winter might destroy his livestock, and many pioneers themselves were frozen to death. In summer, a pioneer might have to stand by helplessly while his cattle died or his crops withered for lack of water. At other times, floods might sweep away all of his work. But his greatest danger in the early years was from Indian raids.

CHECK UP   *See Long Winter by Wilder, for example.*

1. (a) What was the Homestead Act? (b) Why did it encourage settlement of the West?

2. (a) Why was a transcontinental railroad built? (b) How did the government encourage its construction? (c) How did the railroad help to settle the West?

LOCOMOTIVES were never far behind as workers laid track for the western railroads. This scene, showing how an early railroad was built, is from a modern motion picture.

2 What Happened to the Indians Who Resisted Western Settlement?

This is a moving statement explaining how the Indians felt about the white man's "westward movement."

The Indians fight the advance of the white men. When explorers and settlers first landed on America's shores, they found the Indians here before them. The Indians had been lords of the forests and prairies long before the white men appeared. Naturally they looked upon the land as theirs and theirs alone. But, as the white settlers moved westward, the Indians were pushed out of their homes and hunting grounds. The Indians did not yield easily, however. They bitterly opposed each advance by the pioneers and were often at war with the white men.

One Indian chief, speaking to white men in 1805, explained his people's side of the story in this way:

Brother: Listen to what we say. There was a time when our forefathers owned this great island [by which he meant the whole continent]. Their [lands] extended from the rising to the setting sun. The Great Spirit had made it for the use of Indians. He had created the buffalo, the deer, and other animals for food. He had made the bear and the beaver. Their skins served us for clothing. He had scattered them over the country, and taught us how to take them. He had caused the earth to produce corn for bread. All this He had done for his red children, because He loved them. If we had some disputes about our hunting ground, they were generally settled without the shedding of much blood. But an evil day came upon us. Your forefathers crossed the great water and landed on this island. Their numbers were small. They found friends and not enemies. They told us they had fled from their own country for fear of wicked men, and had come here to enjoy their religion. They asked for a small [area of land]. We took pity on them, granted their request; and they sat down amongst us. We gave them corn and meat; they gave us poison [rum and whiskey] in return.

The white people, Brother, had now found our country. Tidings were carried back, and more came amongst us. Yet we did not fear them. We took them to be friends. They called us brothers. We believed them and gave them a larger [area of land]. At length their numbers had greatly increased. They wanted more land; they wanted our country. Our eyes were opened, and our minds became uneasy. Wars took place. Indians were hired to fight against Indians, and many of our people were destroyed. They also brought strong liquor amongst us. It was strong and powerful, and has slain thousands.

Brother: Our [lands] were once large and yours were small. You have now become a great people, and we have scarcely a

A CHEROKEE BOY on a reservation in North Carolina shows how his ancestors set traps for fish. In 1838 many Cherokees were moved from their eastern homes to lands west of the Mississippi in what is now Oklahoma.

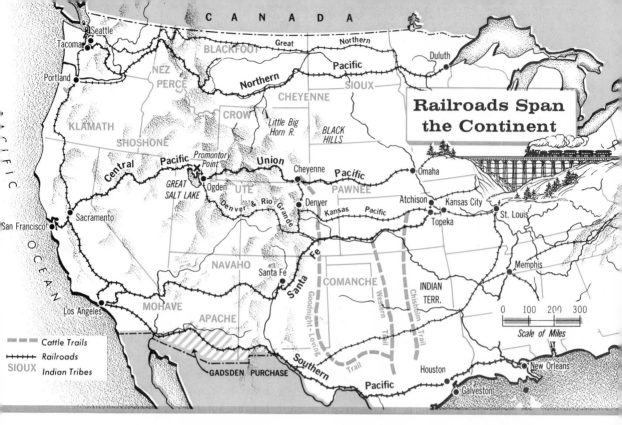

Railroads Span
the Continent

Cattle Trails
Railroads
SIOUX **Indian Tribes**

MAP STUDY   Note that western railroads crossed Indian lands.   (1) What were the chief railroads
that linked the Middle West with the Pacific coast?   (2) Why did the principal cattle
trails run in a north-south direction?

place left to spread our blankets. You have
got our country, but are not satisfied. . . .

In the many battles between the white
men and the Indians, the latter sometimes
won. Usually, however, the white men
were victorious because of their greater
numbers and better weapons. Slowly but
surely the Indians were pushed farther
inland. In fact, by the early 1800's the
Indians had been forced out of most of the
lands east of the Appalachian Mountains.
Even after many white settlers had pushed
their way into the territory beyond the
mountains, however, certain Indian tribes
still claimed large areas of land east of the
Mississippi. Sometimes they occupied fertile lands that the white men wanted.

**The government sets aside an Indian
territory.** In the years following the War
of 1812, the United States government

followed the so-called *removal policy*. This
was a plan to remove the Indians to the
area beyond the Mississippi River. To
carry out the removal policy, the government made treaties with the Indian tribes.
The Indians *east* of the Mississippi agreed
to give up their lands in return for money
and the promise of new tribal lands *west*
of that river. The treaties stated that these
new lands were to belong to the Indians
forever. Our government acted in good
faith, for at that time no one believed
Americans would want to settle on the
western plains which made up the Indian
territory. The eastern Indians were mostly
resettled west and south of the point where
the Missouri River bends northward. Since
there were already many Indian tribes west
of the Missouri, the government had to
make treaties with these tribes also to get
them to move still farther west.

Bring out that Indian tribes were regarded as   **429**   "nations" by the national government.
These treaties were soon broken or "renegotiated."

See also Indians of the Plains *by Rachlis and Ewers.*

White men invade the Indian hunting grounds beyond the Mississippi. If the Indians had been left alone in the unsettled West beyond the Mississippi, there might have been little further warfare with the whites. But there were definite signs in the mid-1800's that this was not to be. (1) The pioneers who followed the Oregon Trail passed through the heart of the Indian country. Many forty-niners also crossed the great plains on their way to California. But small groups of white people sometimes gave up their plans to go all the way to the west coast. Instead, they settled along the Santa Fe and Oregon Trails in the present states of Kansas and Nebraska. (2) In 1847, a band of religious people called Mormons set out to find a "promised land." The Mormons braved many dangers to cross Indian country and settle in the valley of the Great Salt Lake (in what is now Utah). (3) Trappers roamed the northern forests in search of furs. Hunters entered the Indian lands and killed buffaloes by the thousands to obtain the skins, which were highly valued in the East. (4) Then, following the Homestead Act and the building of the transcontinental railroad, came large groups of settlers.

The Indians resolve to defend their homes and hunting grounds. As more and more white men moved westward, the Indians became desperate. In many cases, settlers took lands which had been granted to the Indians by solemn treaty. The United States government did not approve the breaking of treaties, but was unable to control the westward surge of pioneers. Even worse, the Indians faced the loss of their homes and their means of making a living. Fast-growing white settlements cut down the areas in which the Indians could roam freely, and the buffaloes were being killed off at a tremendous rate. William F. Cody, better known as "Buffalo Bill,"

MAN OR BIRD? An Indian wears an eagle mask and feathers to perform the traditional Eagle Dance at the Indian festival held each year at Gallup, New Mexico.

The great plains beyond the Mississippi furnished good homes for the Indians. As yet, there were few white settlements. Instead, there were stretches of open country over which great herds of buffaloes thundered. The huge, shaggy creatures were important to the Indians. They furnished an abundant supply of food, and from their hides the Indians made skins for clothing and coverings for tepees or wigwams. From the buffalo bones the Indians made tools of various kinds.

430

WHEN WHITE SETTLERS and herds of cattle moved into a region, the Indians and the buffalo moved out. This story, which was repeated throughout the West, is well illustrated by the symbolic painting above.

killed more than 4000 animals in less than two years to provide food for the workers building railroads across the West. Many white hunters slaughtered the shaggy animals merely for sport, leaving them where they fell. The buffalo herds grew smaller and smaller, and that meant starvation for the Indians. Faced by hunger and encircled by their white enemies, the Indians took up arms in a desperate attempt to save their lands.

Indian attacks grow into wars. At first, bands of Indian warriors struck at wagon trains and stagecoaches. Then they became bolder and attacked trains. They also swooped down on lonely farms, small settlements, and trading posts. Naturally the white men fought back. To keep the Indians in check, the federal government built army posts in the Indian country. But the attacks continued and finally grew into a series of wars.

The Indian wars were an unhappy chapter in American history. Large numbers of white soldiers and Indian braves were killed. Families were broken up, homes destroyed, and women and children slaughtered. Cruelty was shown on both sides. Unfortunately, there seemed to be no way to prevent these Indian wars, since each side felt that it was in the right. The

Indians were fighting for their lives and their way of living. The white people, on the other hand, felt there would be no peace until the power of the Indian tribes was broken. In the centuries that Indians had inhabited North America they had done little to improve the country or advance their way of life. Should the Indian be allowed to stop settlement and progress? the white men asked. The more they suffered from Indian attacks, the stronger the frontiersmen felt that "the only good Indian is a dead Indian."

The white men break the resistance of the Indians. Because each side believed so strongly in its cause, the Indian wars went on for many years. White settlers lived in fear of the dreaded war whoops that signaled an attack. Sometimes Indian braves wiped out whole settlements in surprise attacks. But the Indians were not the only ones guilty of wholesale massacre. For example, one band of Colorado Indians who thought they had made peace were attacked by cavalry and slaughtered — men, women, and children alike.

One of the most famous Indian victories was in the valley of the Little Big Horn River in Montana. White men had entered the territory given the Sioux (*soo*) Indians by treaty. The Sioux decided they must fight. In June, 1876, more than 200 cavalrymen under George A. Custer were ambushed by a large band of Sioux braves. In the bloody battle that followed, General Custer himself was killed and his force wiped out. There were not many such Indian victories, however. The white soldiers proved too strong for their Indian enemies. One chieftain after another died in battle or made peace. By 1877, most of the fighting was over, although clashes between Indians and whites occurred here and there for another ten years.

The United States government settles the Indians on reservations. In the 1870's, the government began to place the Indians on *reservations*. The reservations were areas set aside for the different Indian tribes. At about the same time the government stopped treating the Indian tribes as separate nations and making treaties with them. A *Bureau of Indian Affairs* was established within the Department of the Interior. The Commissioner of Indian Affairs in Washington was now responsible for all the government officials and agents who looked after the Indians. Today there are about 300 Indian reservations scattered over the country, most of them west of the Mississippi.

The government promised to protect the Indians who lived on reservations and to furnish them with food and other supplies. But the reservation system did not work very well. The defeated Indians longed for the freedom of the plains; they felt hemmed in. In addition, many of the white agents cheated the Indians on the reservations and treated them with contempt and even cruelty.

The attitude of white men toward the Indians changes. Meanwhile, more and more Americans began to take a different view of Indian affairs. Investigations made by the government showed that the whites had been to blame as often as the Indians for trouble between the races. The old frontier attitude began to change. More and more Americans were ashamed when they read stories of how the white men had tricked the Indians and treated them cruelly. Americans began to study the problems of the Indians and to consider new ways of dealing with them.

The government changes its Indian policy. For its part, the United States government accepted the responsibility for protecting Indian lands and of helping the Indians to learn the white man's way of life. Doctors and nurses showed them how to lead healthy lives. Schools were built, and teachers were sent out to the reservations. Thousands of Indian boys and girls now attend such schools. The

(*Continued on page 433*)

See also A Pictorial History of the American Indian by La Farge.

INDIANS drive a burro along a dusty road in New Mexico. Many Indians, valuing traditional ways of life, continue to live much as their ancestors did.

LAND OF CONTINUING GROWTH
A Special Map Story

The hard-riding horsemen pictured above by the artist Frederic Remington remind us of an exciting episode in the story of America's growth. As restless Americans and newcomers from other lands pushed ever westward, the old West with its buffalo, Indians, cowboys, and wide-open spaces (see pictures on page H) gradually disappeared. The maps and charts on the following pages illustrate not only the westward expansion of our nation but other kinds and stages of growth as well.

The maps on pages B, C, and D show the continuing growth of the *territory* of the United States. The map on page B shows the growth of our nation in its early history, from 1790 to 1820. The map on page C shows the stages by which the United States attained its present size. To see our country and its territories overseas, turn to page D.

Size alone is not the only way in which our country has grown. The graphs on pages B and C show how the number of Americans has grown from about 4 million in 1790 to approximately 200 million today. The map on page E shows how people moved ever westward to settle the land during the hundred years from 1790 to 1890. The graph on that page indicates another kind of growth during the same years — the increase in the percentage of people living in towns and cities.

How did Americans travel westward in the first century of our nation's history? The chart on page F gives the answer in terms of roads, canals, and railroads.

Finally, page G brings up to the present the story of increasing density of population, changes in transportation, and growth of cities and towns.

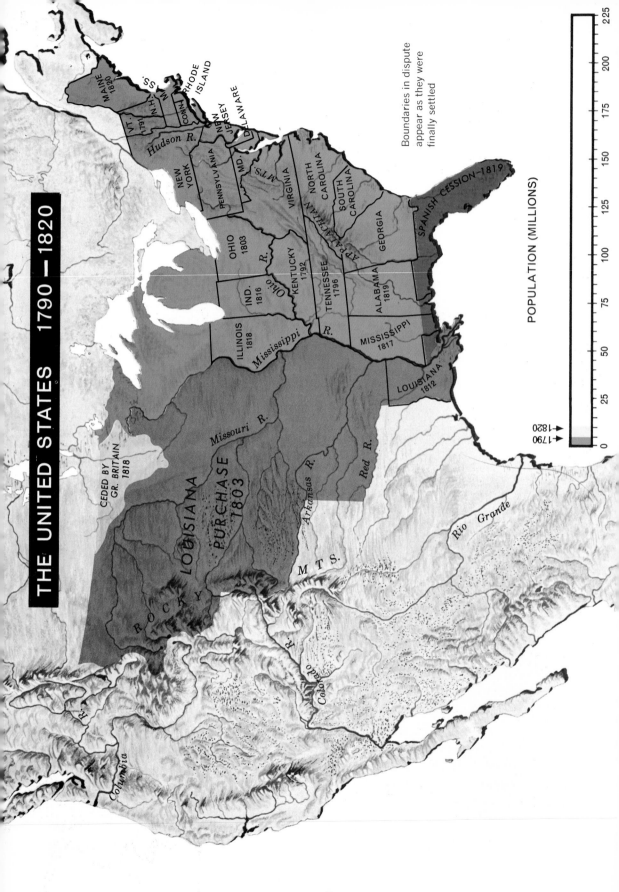

THE UNITED STATES 1790—1820

MAINE 1820

MASS.

N.H.

VT. 1791

RHODE ISLAND

CONN.

NEW JERSEY

DELAWARE

Hudson R.

NEW YORK

PENNSYLVANIA

MD.

S. MTS.

VIRGINIA

NORTH CAROLINA

SOUTH CAROLINA

GEORGIA

SPANISH CESSION—1819

OHIO 1803

Ohio R.

KENTUCKY 1792

APPALACHIAN

TENNESSEE 1796

ALABAMA 1819

IND. 1816

ILLINOIS 1818

MISSISSIPPI 1817

Mississippi R.

LOUISIANA 1812

CEDED BY GR. BRITAIN 1818

Missouri R.

LOUISIANA PURCHASE 1803

Arkansas R.

Red R.

ROCKY

MTS.

R.

Colorado R.

Rio Grande

Columbia

R.

Boundaries in dispute appear as they were finally settled

POPULATION (MILLIONS)

←1790
←1820

0   25   50   75   100   125   150   175   200   225

B

THE UNITED STATES — TODAY

MAINE 1820

VT. 1791

N.H.

MASS.

CONN.

RHODE ISLAND

NEW JERSEY

DELAWARE

Hudson R.

NEW YORK

PENNSYLVANIA

MD.

W.VA. 1863

VIRGINIA

MTS.

NORTH CAROLINA

SOUTH CAROLINA

GEORGIA

SPANISH CESSION—1819

FLORIDA 1845

OHIO 1803

KENTUCKY 1792

TENNESSEE 1796

ALABAMA 1819

MICHIGAN 1837

IND. 1816

Ohio R.

Miami R.

ILLINOIS 1818

Mississippi

MISSISSIPPI 1817

R.

WISCONSIN 1848

MINNESOTA 1858

IOWA 1846

MISSOURI 1821

ARKANSAS 1836

LOUISIANA 1812

Missouri R.

CEDED BY GR. BRITAIN 1818

NORTH DAKOTA 1889

SOUTH DAKOTA 1889

NEBRASKA 1867

KANSAS 1861

OKLAHOMA 1907

Arkansas R.

Red R.

LOUISIANA PURCHASE 1803

TEXAS ANNEXATION 1845

TEXAS 1845

Rio Grande

MONTANA 1889

WYOMING 1890

COLORADO 1876

NEW MEXICO 1912

ROCKY

MTS.

IDAHO 1890

UTAH 1896

Colorado R.

ARIZONA 1912

GADSDEN PURCHASE 1853

WASH. 1889

Columbia R.

OREGON COUNTRY 1846

OREGON 1859

NEVADA 1864

MEXICAN CESSION 1848

CALIFORNIA 1850

HAWAII 1959

HAWAII ANNEXATION 1898

ALASKA 1959

ALASKA PURCHASE 1867

POPULATION (MILLIONS)

225
200 — 1970
175
150
125
100
75 — 1890
50
25 — 1860
0 — 1820
1790

C

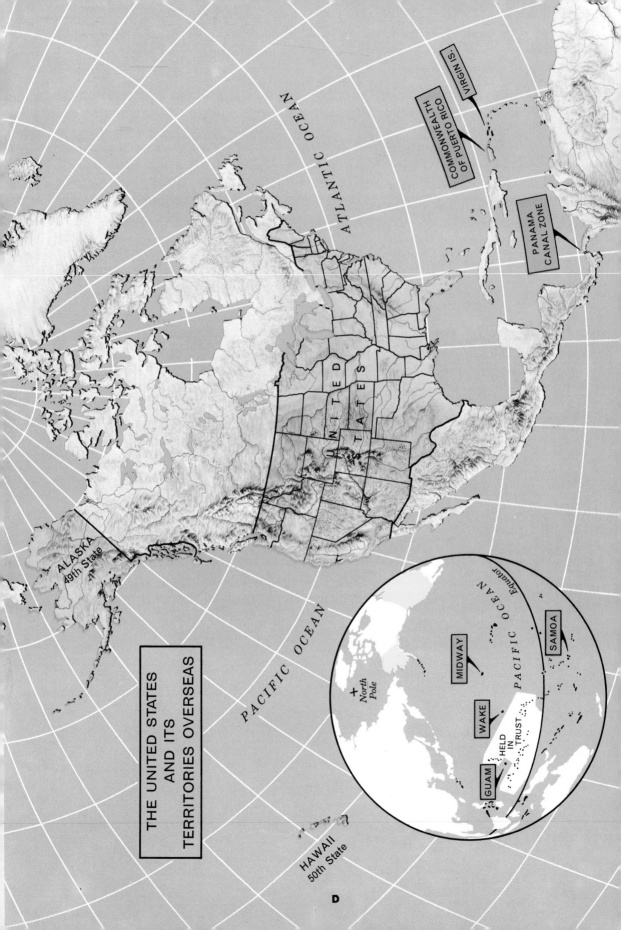

THE UNITED STATES
AND ITS
TERRITORIES OVERSEAS

ATLANTIC OCEAN

COMMONWEALTH
OF PUERTO RICO

VIRGIN IS.

PANAMA
CANAL ZONE

UNITED
STATES

ALASKA
49th State

PACIFIC OCEAN

HAWAII
50th State

PACIFIC OCEAN

North
Pole

MIDWAY

WAKE

GUAM

HELD
IN
TRUST

Equator

SAMOA

PACIFIC OCEAN

D

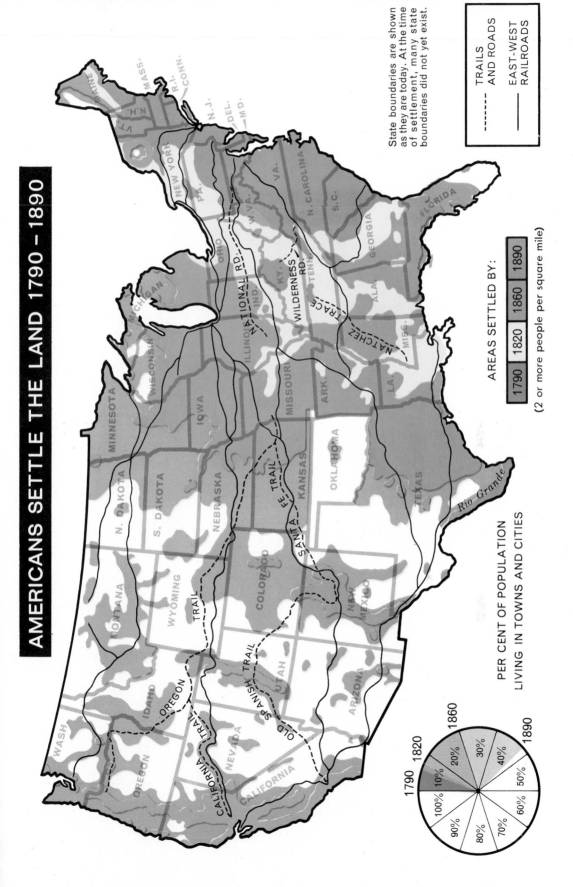

AMERICANS SETTLE THE LAND 1790 – 1890

TRAILS AND ROADS

EAST-WEST RAILROADS

State boundaries are shown as they are today. At the time of settlement, many state boundaries did not yet exist.

AREAS SETTLED BY:

| 1790 | 1820 | 1860 | 1890 |

(2 or more people per square mile)

PER CENT OF POPULATION LIVING IN TOWNS AND CITIES

1790
1820
1860
1890

10%
20%
30%
40%
50%
60%
70%
80%
90%
100%

MAINE

MASS.

R.I.

CONN.

N.H.

VT.

NEW YORK

PA.

N.J.

DEL.

MD.

W.VA.

VA.

N. CAROLINA

S.C.

FLORIDA

GEORGIA

ALA.

TENN.

KY.

OHIO

IND.

ILLINOIS

MICHIGAN

WISCONSIN

IOWA

MINNESOTA

N. DAKOTA

S. DAKOTA

NEBRASKA

KANSAS

OKLAHOMA

MISSOURI

ARK.

MISS.

LA.

TEXAS

Rio Grande

NEW MEXICO

ARIZONA

UTAH

COLORADO

WYOMING

MONTANA

IDAHO

NEVADA

CALIFORNIA

OREGON

WASH.

NATIONAL RD.

WILDERNESS RD.

NATCHEZ TRACE

SANTA FE TRAIL

OREGON TRAIL

CALIFORNIA TRAIL

OLD SPANISH TRAIL

E

GROWTH OF TRANSPORTATION
1790 – 1890

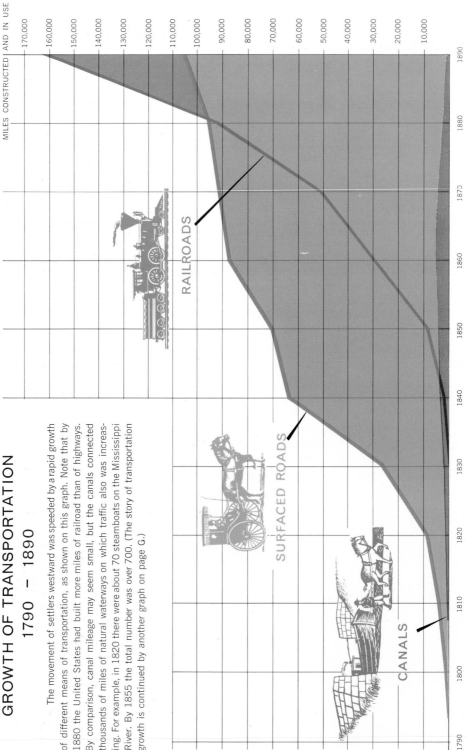

The movement of settlers westward was speeded by a rapid growth of different means of transportation, as shown on this graph. Note that by 1880 the United States had built more miles of railroad than of highways. By comparison, canal mileage may seem small, but the canals connected thousands of miles of natural waterways on which traffic also was increasing. For example, in 1820 there were about 70 steamboats on the Mississippi River. By 1855 the total number was over 700. (The story of transportation growth is continued by another graph on page G.)

MILES CONSTRUCTED AND IN USE

170,000
160,000
150,000
140,000
130,000
120,000
110,000
100,000
90,000
80,000
70,000
60,000
50,000
40,000
30,000
20,000
10,000

1790   1800   1810   1820   1830   1840   1850   1860   1870   1880   1890

RAILROADS

SURFACED ROADS

CANALS

GROWTH OF TRANSPORTATION
1890 – 1960

PER CENT OF POPULATION LIVING IN TOWNS AND CITIES

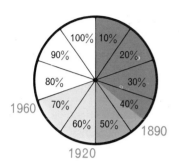

Since 1890 the percentage of people living in towns and cities has kept on rising. By 1920 half of all Americans were town-dwellers. Today the figure is 70 per cent.

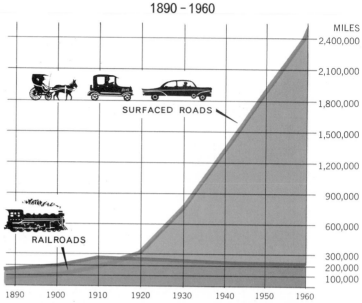

New roads were built more and more rapidly after the automobile was invented in the 1890's. By 1920 America had more miles of highways than of railroads.

DENSITY OF POPULATION IN THE UNITED STATES
1960

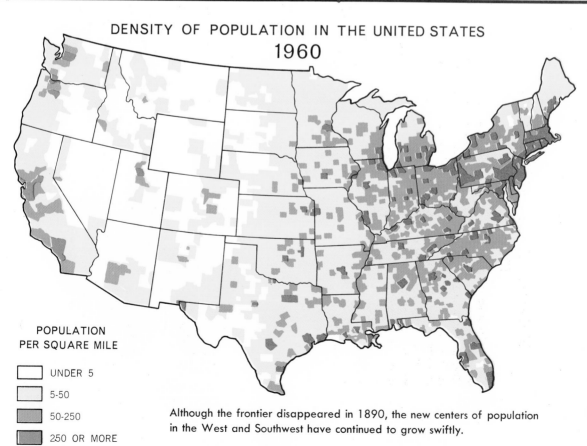

POPULATION PER SQUARE MILE

- UNDER 5
- 5-50
- 50-250
- 250 OR MORE

Although the frontier disappeared in 1890, the new centers of population in the West and Southwest have continued to grow swiftly.

In the 1830's a traveling artist named George Catlin painted the picture below of a buffalo hunt on the great plains. Today, Catlin's paintings are valued as eyewitness accounts of the free life of the plains Indians "before barbed wire."

Statue of a bronco-buster by Charles M. Russell, a former cowboy, is in the Amon Carter Museum at Fort Worth, Texas, along with other sculptures and paintings which capture the spirit of the Old West.

The wide-open spaces of the West which lured the early pioneers still bring a thrill to the hearts of millions of Americans who vacation there, inspiring such beautiful photographs as the one below of Picket Post Mountain in Arizona.

MORE AND MORE INDIANS are taking jobs in industry. This natural gas plant on the Navaho reservation is staffed almost entirely by Indians.

This illustration suggests better than words that Indians are getting away from a subsistence farming economy.

schools for younger children are much like other elementary schools. For older children there are boarding schools where pupils live. The girls learn cooking, sewing, and other household jobs; the boys learn farming, carpentering, and other trades. Also, many Indian students are enrolled in public schools and in colleges and universities as well.

The government also tried to make it possible for Indians to own land. In 1887, the Dawes Act was passed. It permitted the head of an Indian family to obtain 160 acres for farming. The only condition was that he give up his loyalty to his tribe; if he did so, he could become a citizen of the United States. At the end of 25 years he would become full owner of the property. Under a law passed in 1924 all Indians are citizens.

How do the Indians live today? Today over 500,000 Indians are living in the United States, about half of them on reservations. Many do farming and also work at arts and crafts. Indians on reservations may also work in nearby factories. During World War II, for example, many Indians did war work in factories while others served in the armed forces.

Conditions on reservations vary a great deal. Some Indian lands are quite valuable because of their timber, oil, or minerals.

Thus, for the past twenty years, an Apache tribe in New Mexico has received a yearly income of a million dollars from mineral and timber lands. But some Indian tribes are not so fortunate and have suffered real hardship.

The government helps Indians help themselves. The United States government continues to help the Indians. It provides free medical care and special schools for those who need them and helps Indians to find jobs. It has also begun long-range plans to improve ways of living among the Indians. Thus Congress in 1950 authorized a ten-year program for the Navaho and Hopi tribes to provide more schools and better roads and to introduce new methods of farming in order to improve crops and conserve the soil. On the other hand, Indian tribes have become more active in bringing to an end the long period of government control over their affairs. Tribal councils have taken steps to put natural resources on their land to the best use. Where reservation lands have been taken for flood control or other projects, the tribe has used money received in payment for the lost lands to relocate or assist Indian families that had been compelled to move. In brief, Indians wish to be full-fledged American citizens but also to retain their tribal organization.

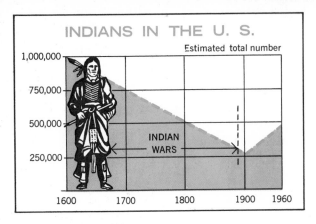

INDIANS IN THE U. S.

Estimated total number

1,000,000					
750,000					
500,000		INDIAN WARS			
250,000					

1600　1700　1800　1900　1960

NUMBERS shown here for early times are estimates. (1) Why did the Indian population decline until 1900? (2) Why has it since increased?

CHECK UP

1. Why did the Indians resist the western advance of the white men?

2. (a) How did the United States government try to solve the Indian problem in the first half of the 1800's? (b) Why was this policy not successful? (c) What was the result of the Indian wars?

3. (a) What was the reservation system? (b) Why did this system not work well? (c) How did the government change its policy toward the Indians?

3 How Did Miners, Cowboys, and Farmers Help to Settle the Last Frontier?

In 1890, a United States government report announced that the frontier had disappeared. This statement did not mean that the area between the Mississippi and the west coast was thickly settled with prosperous farms and busy cities and towns. What it did mean was that there was no longer a clear line where the settlements of white people stopped. Pioneers had pushed into most parts of the West, but much hard work remained before the West was to become what it is today. In this task, three groups of people — the miners, the cattlemen, and the farmers — played an important part. They led lives of hardship and danger, of heartbreaking failure, and of high adventure.

PROSPECTORS OPEN UP THE ROCKY MOUNTAIN COUNTRY

The story of the miners comes first. It goes back to the time when gold was discovered in California (Chapter 18). When the first gold seekers rushed westward to make fortunes in California, there seemed to be plenty of gold. Men needed only to sift it out of the soil in creek and river bottoms or dig it close to the earth's surface. As these fortune seekers swelled into the thousands, however, the "easy" gold was soon exhausted. Only those with money to install expensive machinery could afford to mine gold deep down in the earth. But if easy gold had been found in the hilly country of California, might it not also be discovered in the Rocky Mountain region? Many men turned back from California to the rugged mountain country. Still others stopped in these mountains on their way to the west coast. They wandered here and there, drawn by rumors of rich veins of precious metals. Such men were called *prospectors*.

Gold and silver are found in the Rockies. The hopes of many prospectors were rewarded during the 1850's and '60's. Rich deposits of silver were found in what is now Nevada. About the same time gold was discovered in Colorado, especially in the neighborhood of Pike's Peak. Fortune seekers toiled toward Colorado in wagons bearing the sign "Pike's Peak or Bust." The luckier ones struck gold. Others who

WESTERN MINERS, always in search of gold, inch their wagon train along a dangerous mountain path as they look for new diggings in the Rockies.

were disappointed changed their signs to "Busted, by Gosh!" and moved to other spots. Still later, gold and silver were found in what are now the states of Idaho, Montana, and Wyoming. Gold was also discovered in Arizona, New Mexico, and in the Black Hills of South Dakota.

Life is rough in the mining towns. Wherever adventurers swarmed in search of gold, towns sprang up almost overnight. These early mining towns were far different from most American towns of to-day. Visitors found the streets filled with choking dust, deep ruts, or oozing mud. The few buildings were crudely built and ugly. A wild and noisy throng swarmed through the streets, intent on just one thing — finding a fortune quickly. In the early mining towns there was little government, and wrongdoers often escaped being brought to justice.

Here is the description one visitor gave of a mining town:

✳ This human hive, numbering at least ten thousand people, was the product of ninety days. Into it were crowded all the elements of a rough and active civilization. Thousands of cabins and tents . . . were seen on every hand. Every foot of the gulch [a narrow rocky valley] . . . was already disfigured by huge heaps of gravel. . . . Gold was abundant, and every possible device was employed by the gamblers, the traders, the vile men and women that had come in with the miners into the locality, to obtain it. Nearly every third cabin was a saloon where vile whiskey was peddled out for fifty cents a drink in gold dust. Many of these places were filled with gambling tables and gamblers. . . . Hurdy-gurdy dance-houses were numerous. . . . Not a day or night passed which did not yield its full [amount] of

Mark Twain and Bret Harte have **435** *described life in the mining towns.*

vice, quarrels, wounds, or murder. The crack of the revolver was often heard above the merry notes of the violin. Street fights were frequent, and as no one knew when or where they would occur, every one was on his guard against a random shot.

The mining rush causes the mountain states to grow rapidly. Today, except for a few ghost towns, there is little left in the mountain regions of the West to remind us of those early reckless days. How did this change take place? As the rich "strikes" of gold and silver were exhausted, prospectors moved on to other places. Decent, law-abiding men formed groups to bring the outlaws and bandits of the Wild West to justice. Mining became a business, run by big companies. With expensive machinery, miners tunneled deeper and deeper into the mountain sides to bring forth not only gold and silver but copper, coal, lead, and zinc. Many pioneers who had failed to "strike it rich" settled down, following some trade or farming the soil. The mountain regions would have been settled anyway sooner or later. But the mining rush of the 1850's and '60's speeded up the organization of such states as Nevada (1864), Colorado (1876), Montana (1889), Idaho (1890), and Wyoming (1890).

CATTLE RAISING SPREADS ACROSS THE WESTERN PLAINS

Just as mining helped to settle the mountain regions of the Far West, so cattle raising helped to develop the western plains. When the Spaniards had settled Mexico and, later, parts of what is now our Southwest, they brought with them cattle and horses. Allowed to roam the open spaces freely, the cattle developed in time into half-wild animals with a huge spread of horns. The horses used to herd the cattle were wiry broncos, small but swift. When American settlers spread into Texas, New Mexico, and California, many of them became interested in cattle raising. The Spanish cattle were bred with good strains from the East. Because transportation to the East was difficult, however, cattle raising did not promise big profits.

Cattle raising begins to boom. Then two things happened. (1) The killing of the buffalo herds made available great stretches of grass-covered prairie extending north from Texas to Canada. Cattlemen discovered that the prairie grass was good food for their cattle. Before long, cattle were grazing on the *open range* (the wide, open spaces of unfenced land belonging to the government). (2) When the railroad crossed the prairies, cattlemen found

HELENA, MONTANA, a typical mining town, had a small but busy main street in the 1860's. Gold dust could be deposited or exchanged for cash at the bank.

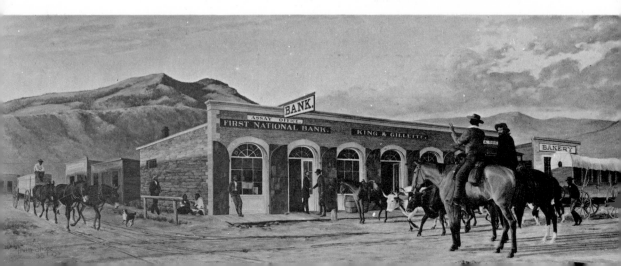

THESE COWBOYS have just completed the fall round-up of a herd of cattle amid the Idaho mountains.

that they could drive their steers northward over the plains to railroad points in Kansas and Nebraska.

Each year Texas cattlemen would collect huge herds of cattle and start them northward on what was called the *long drive*. Often a herd numbered 2000 or 3000 cattle. Grazing leisurely across the prairies, the steers finally reached the "cow towns" along the railroad. Imagine the excitement and noise when the herds thundered into town and were loaded on railroad cars bound for Kansas City or Chicago! Sometimes cattle were driven north to Wyoming or Montana for grazing. The success of the long drive caused cattle raising to boom throughout the open West.

The American cowboy becomes part of the western scene. The long drive would have been impossible without the cowboy. It was his job to protect the cattle from Indians and wild animals and to keep them from straying away. At roundups the young cattle were branded with the mark of their owner, and the steers belonging to various ranches were sorted out. All these activities meant hard work but a free and happy life for the cowboy. The well-known costume of the cowboy was not worn for show. Each part had a use. Here is a description of what the cowboy wore and why he wore it:

✳ The heavy woolen shirt, loose and open at the neck, was the common wear at all seasons of the year excepting winter, and one has often seen cowboys in the wintertime engaged in work about the yard or corral of the ranch wearing no other cover for the upper part of the body but one or more of these heavy shirts. . . . The cowboy's boots were of fine leather and fitted tightly, with light narrow soles, extremely small and high heels. . . . If we rode beside him and watched his seat in the big cow saddle we found that his high and narrow heels prevented the slipping forward of the foot in the stirrup, into which he jammed his feet nearly full length. If there was a fall, the cowboy's foot never hung in the stirrup. . . .

The cowboy was very careful in the selection of his gloves. They were made of the finest buckskin, which could not be injured by wetting. Generally they were tanned white and cut with a deep cuff or gauntlet from which hung a little fringe to flutter in the wind when he rode at full speed on horseback.

The cowboy's hat was one of the typical and striking features of his costumes. It was a heavy, wide, white felt hat with a heavy leather band buckled about it. . . . The boardlike felt was practically indestructible. The brim flapped a little and, in time, was turned up and perhaps held fast to the crown by a thong. . . . He could depend upon his hat in all weathers. In the rain it was an umbrella; in the sun, a shield; in

The best True story about cowboys **437** *is* Lone Cowboy *by William James.*

the winter he could tie it down about his ears with a handkerchief.

Loosely thrown about the cowboy's shirt collar was a silk kerchief. It was tied in a hard knot in front, and though it could scarcely be said to be devoted to the uses of a neck scarf, yet it was a great comfort to the back of the neck when one was riding in a hot wind. It was sure to be of some bright color, usually red. . . .

A peculiar and distinctive feature of the cowboy's costume was his "chaps." The chaps were two very wide and full-length trouser-legs made of heavy calfskin and connected by a narrow belt or strap. They were cut away entirely at front and back so that they covered only the thigh and lower legs and did not heat the body as a complete leather garment would. They were intended solely as a protection against the branches, thorns, briers, and the like, but they were prized in cold or wet weather. Sometimes there was seen, more often on the southern range, a cowboy wearing chaps made of skins tanned with the hair on; for the cowboy of the Southwest early learned that goatskin left with the hair on would turn the cactus thorns better than any other material. . . .

Dressed in this costume and equipped with revolver, lasso, whip, and spurs, the cowboy made a striking figure as he herded cattle or rode into town. Equally colorful were his songs. Cowboys sang a great deal, both to pass the lonely hours and to prevent panic among the steers. The songs of the American cowboy told the story of his life and surroundings in a way that set them apart from other kinds of American music. The following verses furnish a sample of the cowboy songs:

At midnight when cattle are sleeping
On my saddle I pillow my head,
And up at the heavens lie peeping
From out of my cold, grassy bed.
Often and often I wondered

At night when lying alone
If every bright star up yonder
Is a big peopled world like our own.

Are they worlds with ranges and ranches?
Do they ring with rough rider refrains?
Do the cowboys scrap there with Comanches
And other red men of the plains?
Are the hills covered over with cattle
In those mystic worlds far, far away,
Do the ranch houses ring with the prattle
Of sweet little children at play?

In the east the great daylight is breaking
And into my saddle I spring;
The cattle from sleep are awaking,
The heaven-thoughts from me take wing.
The eyes of my bronco are flashing,
Impatient he pulls at the reins,
And off round the herd I go dashing,
A reckless cowboy of the plains.[1]

The days of the open range were limited. Cattle raising on the open range, however, did not continue for many years. There were several reasons.

(1) The open country became so overstocked with cattle that good grazing lands became scarce. In the foothills of the Rockies, sheep raisers took over many feeding grounds formerly used by the cattlemen. Sheep chew the grass so close to the ground that they leave little for cattle. Many bitter fights took place between cattlemen and sheepherders for possession of the range.

(2) Farmers came in great numbers from the East to stake out homesteads on the range. To protect their crops from roving cattle, the farmers fenced in their property with barbed wire. The cattle-

[1] "The Cowboy's Meditation." Collected, adapted & arranged by John A. & Alan Lomax. Copyright 1938 by John A. & Alan Lomax in the book "Cowboy Songs & Other Frontier Ballads." Copyright assigned 1958 to Ludlow Music, Inc., New York, N.Y. Used by permission.

The numbered summary (pages 438 and 439) is an important aid to learning.

A NEBRASKA FAMILY of the 1880's poses for a picture in front of their house built of prairie sod. The horses on the roof are pulling a wagonload of new sod for patching the house.

men fought the homesteaders in every way they could, but the amount of grazing land open to cattle grew smaller and smaller.

(3) The introduction of the windmill made it possible to pump water which was deep in the ground. The cattle ranchers had built their ranch houses and other buildings near springs and streams. But with windmills, farmers no longer had to settle only along rivers and creeks.

(4) When more railroads had been built through the West, it no longer was necessary to drive cattle long distances to market.

As a result of these changes, cattle raising by 1885 was largely confined to fenced-in ranches. There are still many cowboys working on the cattle ranches, but the colorful cowboy of the '70's vanished with the open range.

HOMESTEADERS CHANGE THE GREAT PLAINS INTO A FOOD-GROWING REGION

Both the miner and the cowboy, who helped to open the unsettled West, were restless figures, often on the move. But wherever the farmer took up land, he came to stay. Pioneer life on the great plains was not easy. Since trees were scarce, settlers lived in dugouts or in houses built of the prairie sod. But more and more families staked out homesteads, and the amount of good farm land which was free grew less.

The last frontier is settled. In 1889, the government opened up to settlers much of the old Indian Territory in what is now Oklahoma. A great land rush then took place. Some 100,000 eager settlers lined up. When a signal was given at noon one spring day, they rushed across the boundary in a wild scramble to stake out desirable homesteads. In the next few years more Indian lands were added to the Oklahoma Territory, and in 1907, it became a state. Other western states which entered the Union as a result of the settling of the last frontier were Nebraska (1867), North and South Dakota (1889), Utah (1896), New Mexico and Arizona (1912).

Grain becomes the chief crop of the great plains. Many farmers discovered to their sorrow that much of the West was not fertile or was too dry for regular farming. We shall learn later how the lack of rainfall was overcome. But on the fertile land of the Dakotas and Nebraska, large farms soon developed. Grain was the chief crop; wheat was grown in some places and corn in others. What vast fields of waving grain meant to many a farmer boy is told in Hamlin Garland's words on the following page:

Sheep Wagon by Richardson describes **439** *the efforts of cattlemen to keep sheepherders out of Wyoming Territory.*

✳As I look back over my life . . . the song of the reaper fills a large place in my mind. We were all worshipers of wheat in those days. The men thought and talked of little else between seeding and harvest. . . .

Deep as the breast of a man, wide as the sea . . . our fields ran to the world's end.

We trembled when the storm lay hard upon the wheat, we exulted as the lilac shadows of noonday drifted over it! We went out into it at noon when all was still — so still we could hear the pulse of the transforming sap as it crept from cool root to swaying plume. We stood before it at evening when the setting sun flooded it with crimson, the bearded heads lazily swirling under the wings of the wind . . . and our hearts expanded with the beauty and the mystery of it — and back of all this was the knowledge that its abundance meant a new carriage, an addition to the house, or a new suit of clothes.

Haying was over, and day by day we boys watched with deepening interest while the hot sun transformed the juices of the soil into those stately stalks. I loved to go out into the fairy forest of it. . . . Day by day I studied the barley as it turned yellow, first at the root and then at the neck . . . until at last the lower leaves began to wither and the stems to stiffen in order to uphold the daily increasing weight of the milky berries, and then almost in an hour — lo! the edge of the field became a banded ribbon of green and yellow, languidly waving in and out with every rush of the breeze.

Now we got out the reaper, put the sickles in order, and Father laid in a store of provisions. Extra hands were hired, and at last, early on a hot July morning, the boss mounted to his seat on the self-rake Mc-Cormick and drove into the field. Frank rode the lead horse, four stalwart hands and myself took stations behind the reaper, and the battle was on!

The old West disappears. The miners, the cowboys, and the farmers not only filled in the West but brought to a close an important chapter in our country's history. As the frontier vanished, the reckless and independent way of living which had so great an influence on American life began to disappear also. As travel became speedier and communication improved, differences between the East and the West became less marked. Although some of its old customs still linger, the "West" no longer means a completely different way of life.

CHECK UP

1. (a) How did the discovery of gold and silver help to settle the Rocky Mountain area? (b) What was life like in a mining town?

2. (a) What two events made cattle raising boom on the western plains? (b) What was the life of the cowboy like? (c) Why did cattle raising on the open range come to an end?

3. (a) What was the last territory opened for settlement? (b) What way of life developed on the great plains?

Frederic Remington, Artist of the Old West by McCracken contains over 80 reproductions of paintings and sketches.

Check Up on Chapter 21

Do You Know the Meaning?

1. long drive
2. prairie
3. bronco
4. open range
5. roundup
6. cow town
7. reservation
8. prospector
9. transcontinental
10. brand

Can You Identify?

1. Homestead Act
2. Mormons
3. 1862
4. 1869
5. Dawes Act
6. William F. Cody
7. George A. Custer
8. removal policy
9. Bureau of Indian Affairs

Can You Locate?

1. Omaha
2. Ogden, Utah
3. Sacramento
4. Black Hills
5. Little Big Horn River
6. Great Salt Lake
7. route of Union Pacific
8. route of Central Pacific
9. route of Sante Fe

What Do You Think?

1. Many people believe that the time has come to treat Indians exactly like other American citizens. Do you agree? Give reasons for your answer.

2. It has been said that the settlement of the great plains was made possible by (a) the killing of the buffalo, (b) the transcon-

What Do You Think? (Cont.)

tinental railroads, and (c) the windmill. Why was each important? (d) Would you add any items to this list? Why?

3. With the disappearance of the western frontier, many Americans believed that they no longer had an opportunity to live adventurous lives. Do you agree? Why? Are there any other "frontiers" to be conquered? What about science and invention?

4. (a) What differences were there between the miners, cattlemen, and farmers? (b) How did each contribute to the settlement of the West?

5. Why has western life been so popular as a subject for American songs, stories, television plays, and motion pictures?

Question #2 should intrigue able students.

LINKING PAST AND PRESENT

Indians of the West. At the end of Chapter 5 you learned something about the Indian people who live in the eastern United States. About four fifths of all the Indians in our country, however, are found west of the Mississippi. The roving Indians of the great plains once depended on the buffalo for meat, for skins to make tepees and clothing, and for bones to make tools. Today the great buffalo hunts are only a memory. The plains tribes make their homes for the most part in Montana, Oklahoma, the Dakotas, and other states between the Rockies and the Mississippi.

The Indians of the northwestern states used to hunt whale and sea otter in giant dugout canoes. For their main source of food they depended on the salmon that filled the rivers each spring. To this day the Indians along the Columbia River are given free rights to fish for salmon. But their life has changed. Men put out to sea in gasoline-powered fishing boats instead of cedar dugouts. Their hunters kill wild game with guns

instead of bows and arrows. Many Indians now work in salmon canneries or in some other part of the huge salmon industry of the Pacific Northwest.

By far the largest number of western Indians live in the Southwest. The Hopis live in eleven villages in Arizona and New Mexico. They live in adobe (clay) "apartment houses," built high on cliffs and entered by long ladders. Some of these *pueblos*, as the homes are called, were built before the time of Columbus. The Hopis are noted for their beautiful pottery, basket work, and fine silver and turquoise jewelry. A famous ceremony of their tribe is the Snake Dance, in which live rattlesnakes are coiled round the bodies of the dancers. Sprawling across the four corners where the states of Utah, Colorado, New Mexico, and Arizona meet, is the huge Navaho reservation, largest in the United States. The Navahos are traditionally sheepherders. They are also known for their silver jewelry and fine woven rugs.

The United States Becomes a Great Industrial Nation

What this chapter is about —

Have you any idea how greatly ways of living in America have changed in the last hundred years? In 1865, at the close of the war between the North and the South, people lived in much the same manner that their grandparents had. They had, of course, a few more conveniences in their homes, and could travel faster and a little more comfortably. But in those days the great majority of Americans still made their living by farming. Cities were fewer in number and much smaller than they are today. There were none of the home conveniences — such as electric lights and refrigerators, vacuum cleaners, air conditioners, radios and TV sets, tele-

phones, and washing machines — that people now take for granted. There were no automobiles, high-speed trains, or jet-powered airplanes to whisk travelers swiftly from one place to another. And if anyone had suggested that within a hundred years men would orbit around the earth in space vehicles, he would have been thought completely mad.

The striking changes in American homes, food and clothing, work, and amusements resulted from the rapid growth of industry in the United States. In the years following the end of the Civil War, new sources of power were discovered. Inventors perfected new ma-

People in our story — manufacturer and wife, coal miner, steelworker, early motorist, telephone lineman.

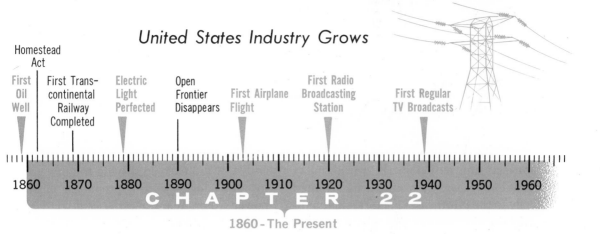

United States Industry Grows

Homestead Act

First Oil Well | First Transcontinental Railway Completed | Electric Light Perfected | Open Frontier Disappears | First Airplane Flight | First Radio Broadcasting Station | First Regular TV Broadcasts

1860   1870   1880   1890   1900   1910   1920   1930   1940   1950   1960

CHAPTER 22

1860 – The Present

chines and scientists worked out new ideas. Bold business leaders backed new ventures. Since 1900, science and industry have taken giant steps forward. At the present rate of progress, who knows what undreamed-of wonders may become a part of daily living within the next few years!

This chapter will explain how the United States became the greatest industrial nation in the world. It will tell you about the inventions which speeded the growth of industry, about conditions which aided that growth, and about the men who

had a hand in our progress. As you read, be on the lookout for answers to the following questions:

▷ 1. What basic conditions made the United States a leading industrial nation?

▷ 2. How did mass production and the growth of corporations aid industry?

▷ 3. How did improved communication and transportation affect American life?

▷ 4. How have business methods changed with the growth of industry?

See *Miracle in Motion: The Story of America's Industry* by Shippen. Causes and far-reaching results are made clear.

1   What Basic Conditions Made the United States a Leading Industrial Nation?

The growth of industry in the United States began, you will recall, when the Industrial Revolution reached this country from England in the late 1700's (Chapter 14). You remember that machines, run by water power, were invented to produce many of the articles which in colonial days had been made by hand. Factories were built, particularly in the Northeast, and workers from nearby farms, as well as newcomers from Europe, flocked to take jobs in the mill towns.

By the middle of the 1800's, steam power had begun to take the place of water power for driving machines. New inventions, more factories, and the spreading network of railroads — all these helped manufacturing to continue to grow. And, as we have seen in Chapter 20, the demand for war materials of all kinds during the war between the North and the South further stepped up the rate of production.

The Industrial Revolution gathers speed. When the war between the North

443

and the South ended, the United States was still far behind England as an industrial nation. Only 35 years later, however, this country had caught up with and passed England in the value of its manufactured goods. And by the 1920's, the United States had become the greatest manufacturing nation in the world.

No longer was manufacturing limited chiefly to the Northeast. Factories had multiplied in the South, and wherever railroads were built in the fast-growing West, industry quickly developed. Because the use of machines increased so rapidly after 1900, this period is often called the Machine Age. You have only to look around you to realize the enormous quantity of goods now produced by machines in America. Machines make our homes comfortable, provide swift means of travel, and save us from much backbreaking labor. The steam shovels whose iron jaws bite into the earth; the great cranes that load and unload vast quantities of material; the tractors, plows, and harvesters used by farmers — these are made largely from American raw materials in American factories by American workmen.

How did it happen that our country became a great industrial power? There are several answers to this question. Let us see what they are.

The United States is blessed with rich natural resources. When our forefathers came to North America, they found a vast undeveloped continent. Its chief value to them lay in the great stretches of rich soil suitable for farming. When manufacturing became important, however, our country turned out to be a rich treasure house of the materials needed in industry. In mineral wealth, for example, the United States was far more fortunate than most countries. Below the ground were the world's most plentiful known supplies of coal. It was estimated that there were 500,000 square miles of coal fields in the United States, or almost half of the world's coal. Most of these deposits were in Pennsylvania, the Appalachian regions, and the Mississippi Valley states. Coal has been tremendously important in the iron and steel industry, in driving the machines in our factories, and in producing electric power. For many years, coal has also been widely used for heating homes and other buildings.

Our country also possessed great quantities of iron ore from which steel is made. Though ore was found in many places, the chief iron ore fields were located around the western end of Lake Superior. The United States was also blessed with generous quantities of copper, lead, and bauxite (from which aluminum is made). In fact, the United States lacked only a few necessary minerals, such as manganese (for hardening steel), tin, nickel, and platinum. When petroleum (oil) became important in industry, our country was found to have the greatest reserves of this precious fluid then known in the world. Because we have drawn heavily upon our own supply of natural resources, however, the United States now imports from other countries large quantities of the raw materials it needs.

Not all of America's natural riches lie below the soil. Our vast forests have supplied the timber needed in industry. Unfortunately, wasteful cutting has destroyed a great part of America's timber resources. Large reserves of timber still remain, however, and lumbering companies now plant new trees to replace those that are cut down. America's rich soil, as we have seen, has made it possible to produce the food crops needed to feed our people. And now that science is discovering ways of using plant materials to make

Students may wish to read Pandora's Box: The Story of Conservation by Baer.

cloth and other products, America's soil is even more valuable.

Today America's natural resources, and products made directly from them, are increasingly supplemented by *synthetics* and *plastics* produced in our chemical laboratories. Synthetic fibers such as nylon, Orlon, and Dacron, because they have certain advantages, are being widely used. Dyes, precious stones, sponges, and furs are among the products made synthetically. Plastics come "originally" from coal, limestone, petroleum, water, and air. But first they are made into "intermediates" in the laboratory. From the intermediate products come a variety of things that are used in everyday life. These include camera film, the glue used in plywood, insulators against heat and electricity, raincoats, garden hose, dishes, squeeze bottles and other containers, and upholstery materials.

There are many hands to do America's work. The United States has also been fortunate in having a large supply of skilled workers for our industries. Since 1860, the number of people in the United States has grown from about 31 million to about 200 million. Much of this growth resulted from the large numbers of immigrants who left their homes in Europe to come to America.

Most of these Americans-to-be were not wealthy. They came to this country to make a new start in life. Large numbers of them sought the fertile farm lands of America, but many others settled in the cities and towns of the East and Midwest. These immigrants were used to hard work. Their hands supplied the labor in factories and mines to turn raw materials into manufactured articles.

Foreign money helps the United States to develop its industries. Large amounts of raw materials and many willing hands, however, were not enough to develop the

CHANGING SOURCES of America's iron ore are shown by this map and series of pictures. (1) In colonial times, iron ore was dug by hand from local bogs. (2) Later, our growing steel industry was fed by huge mines discovered inland, especially in Minnesota. (3) Today, increasing amounts of ore come from foreign sources, such as Venezuela, where barges bring the ore down-river to be reshipped.

This map and the **445** *pictures throw light on how Technological change and the depletion of natural resources may affect the location and nature of an industry.*

giant industries of our country. Factories and machines cost money. In 1865 there were few Americans who had enough money to make large investments in industry. Fortunately, however, there were wealthy Europeans who were eager to put their money into American industry in the hope of making profits. By 1910, over six billion dollars of foreign money, most of it English, was invested in mines, factories, and business concerns in the United States. These large investments had much to do with the rapid growth of our industries. Since the early 1900's, foreign investments have become less and less important in American industry. In fact, after World War I, American business firms began to invest heavily in foreign countries.

The inventive spirit aids the growth of industry. Americans have always shown a talent for invention. In an earlier chapter you learned that Eli Whitney's invention of the cotton gin caused cotton grow-ing to boom. In a similar way, Elias Howe's sewing machine paved the way for the making of clothes in factories (page 274). After 1865, American inventions played an even more important part in helping the United States to become an industrial giant. They made it possible to enlarge existing industries and create new ones. Not all inventions were practical, but any man who had inventive skill, ambition, and persistence had a chance to win success.

Thomas A. Edison — inventor. No one man illustrates the American inventive spirit better than Thomas Alva Edison. In 1847 Edison was born in an average American home in Ohio. Even as a young boy, he had a keen and restless mind and showed an interest in science. Tom became a newsboy on a train and did so well that he soon had other boys working for him. Much of his spare time was spent eagerly reading in the public library and

The Patent System

Inventions have played an important part in encouraging the growth of industry and raising the standard of living in the United States. Inventions in turn owe a great deal to the wisdom of the writers of the Constitution. Among the powers granted to Congress in Article 1, Section 8, of the Constitution is the power "to promote the progress of science and useful arts by securing for limited times to authors and inventors the exclusive right to their respective writings and discoveries" (page A8).

Under this power Congress set up a Patent Office and has passed numerous laws regulating the filing of patents. A patent gives an inventor the sole right to make, use, or sell his product for a period of seventeen years. On the other hand, the inventor must describe his invention fully, so that someone else can make use of the idea after his patent has expired.

The patent system serves two important purposes. (1) It encourages an inventor to put time and money into developing a new invention because he knows that no one can copy or use his invention for the period of his patent. Thomas Jefferson said of the first patent law in 1790 that it "has given a spring to invention beyond my conception."

(2) By providing that descriptions of patented inventions be open to the public, our patent system stimulates someone else to invent an even better product or process. Thus industry works more efficiently and the American standard of living is continually improved. Since 1790 the United States Patent Office has issued a total of more than three million patents.

THOMAS EDISON

At 14, he sold newspapers on a train, using his profits to buy books and laboratory equipment.

Students may wish to read Great Inventors and Their Inventions by Bachman. See also Young Thomas Edison by North.

A "ROLLING LABORATORY" on the train from Port Huron to Detroit occupied Edison's spare time. In a corner of the baggage car he conducted experiments between his trips through the cars to sell papers. He later became a telegrapher and began tinkering with the telegraph instruments, trying to improve them.

INVENTION took up more and more of Edison's time. He designed a new stock ticker and, with the money he received for it, opened in Menlo Park, New Jersey, his own laboratory, where he could work full-time.

THE "WIZARD OF MENLO PARK" had invented a machine that talked! Edison's phonograph worked on the first test, though it often took years to perfect a new device. At times, Edison and his associates worked on over a hundred projects at once.

THE ELECTRIC LIGHT drew hundreds of visitors to the lab in 1879. It marked the end of a year of toil — averaging 100 hours a week for Edison and his assistants. Edison worked for half a century more on inventions which have shaped our modern world.

working in a small laboratory which he set up at home.

As a young man, Edison held a variety of jobs but kept up his interest in science and especially in electricity. In 1868 he patented his first invention. From then until his death in 1931, his active mind and great energy produced a steady stream of inventions. His genius lay in his knack of putting scientific ideas to practical use rather than in the discovery of new scientific truths. He held more than 1200 patents on inventions, and his laboratory at Menlo Park, New Jersey, was truly a storehouse of magic.

Probably Edison's greatest gift to the world was inventing the electric light. The first bulb, which he invented in 1879, gave only a feeble glow, but repeated improvements resulted in the marvels of lighting which we now enjoy. Whether by invention or improvement, Edison's name is also connected with the phonograph, the automatic telegraph, the stock ticker, generators and power stations, electric street railways, motion pictures, and the microphone.

•

Rich natural resources, our American system of private ownership, and the skill, hard work, and inventiveness of the American people — all played a part in making the United States a great industrial nation. Just as important, however, to America's industrial growth were new manufacturing methods and new kinds of business organizations.

CHECK UP

1. What are some important natural resources found in the United States?

2. How did a growing population contribute to the growth of American industry?

3. Why was the investment of foreign money important to American industry?

4. What part has the American inventive spirit played in industry?

Make sure that students understand the importance of "division of labor," "standard parts," and "the assembly line" in large-scale production.

2 How Did Mass Production and the Growth of Corporations Aid Industry?

New manufacturing methods lead to mass production of goods. The United States could never have become the industrial giant it is today unless a method had been discovered to produce vast quantities of goods to sell at low prices. To accomplish this, a new system, called *mass production,* was developed. What steps made mass production possible?

1. *Division of labor.* Before the Industrial Revolution, a single skilled worker usually did every task in changing raw material into a finished product. One shoemaker, for example, would do all the work required to make a pair of shoes. When machines came into use, a change took place. The labor of making an article was divided among several workers. Each worker was limited to doing just one or two things. For example, a punch-press operator, punching holes in a metal part, may repeat the same operation over and over hundreds of times a day. A welder may fasten two pieces of metal together, nothing more. This *division of labor* speeded up production and lowered costs because each

AN EARLY ASSEMBLY LINE is shown in this scene from a Ford plant about 1914. A chain lowers the engine onto the framework of the automobile.

This assembly line is a far cry from those used in present-day automobile plants.

worker soon became very skilled in his particular task.

2. *Standard parts.* Production was also greatly aided by the use of *standard parts.* Eli Whitney did much to develop this idea. After he invented the cotton gin, he became interested in manufacturing guns. He decided to use standard or interchangeable parts in his guns. In other words, all triggers or gun barrels manufactured for a certain model of gun were to be made exactly the same in shape and measurements. If the parts were identical, reasoned Whitney, guns could be put together faster and more efficiently. Or, if a certain part were damaged, another one, exactly like it, could be substituted. Thus the gun could be repaired easily. In the 1900's, Henry Ford developed the idea of standard parts for cars. All industrial plants now make standard parts which can be interchanged easily.

3. *The assembly line.* The most important step in the development of mass production came with the *assembly line* in the 1900's. It was first used in an important way by Henry Ford in the production of automobiles. The assembly line combines on a large scale the use of standard parts and the limiting of each worker to a single task. An automobile factory, for instance, has a long conveyor belt (a slowly moving track) with many workers stationed at different points beside it. The motor is assembled part by part, the frame of the automobile is added, and other parts and fixtures are attached. When the end of the line is reached, the car is complete — motor, body, wheels, and all. Each worker does a single task as the automobile-to-be passes him. In this way the time needed to make a car is greatly reduced.

Mass production methods spread. Division of labor, standard parts, and the assembly line all play a part in mass production. Through mass production methods, Ford employees were able to turn out thousands of cars each day and thereby greatly reduce the price of automobiles. Ford's methods spread not only through-

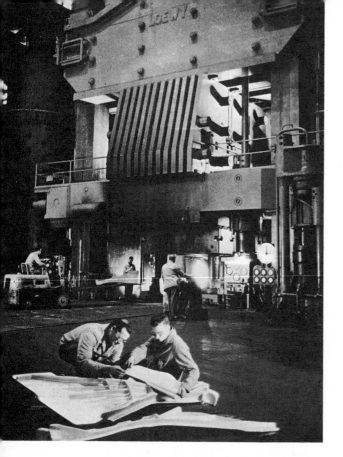

THIS HUGE MACHINE, one of the largest ever built, is used for making airplane parts. Not completely visible because part of it is underground, the machine is eleven stories high.

out the automobile industry but into many other kinds of manufacturing.

During recent years another advance in industrial methods, called *automation*, has been making rapid progress. In automation, the machines which make products are operated or controlled by other machines rather than by workers. Automation also makes possible the use of systems which carry a product from one machine to another until the finished product emerges. Other high-speed automatic machines, called *computers,* are revolutionizing business procedures and research. These machines, handling information much faster than could a large team of people, keep

records and handle payrolls; they can even translate Russian newspapers into English. Although automation tends to cut down the number of jobs for semi-skilled workers, it creates a demand for highly trained workers to maintain and repair the new machines.

AMERICAN INDUSTRY CREATES A GROWING MARKET FOR ITS PRODUCTS

We have been learning how new methods of production swelled the output of American factories. At the same time, businessmen began to find new markets for their products and new ways of selling them.

New markets are found. As the population of the United States grew by leaps and bounds, there were more people eager to buy goods. And because mass production made it possible to produce greater quantities of goods at lower prices, people could buy more and more. Newer forms of transportation also opened up new markets. The growth of the nation's railroads helped businessmen to sell their products throughout the country, rather than only in a small area near their factories. Steamships hauled American-made products to other parts of the world, particularly to Europe.

New ways of selling develop. Before the growth of big businesses, there were small general stores throughout the country where people could buy the few things they needed. But after the war ended in 1865, merchants discovered new and more effective ways to sell their goods. They began to discover the power of advertising to make customers want more of their products. They also developed several new kinds of stores:

(1) One was the *specialty store.* The old general store sold cloth, groceries,

hardware, meat, and about everything else. Now stores began to specialize in selling clothes, or hardware, or groceries. These stores could carry a larger stock of their particular line of goods.

(2) In large cities, glorified general stores, called *department stores,* sprang up. Here, in different departments, the customer could find almost anything he might need. Through careful management and buying in large quantities, a department store could reduce the cost of its goods and thus attract a larger number of customers. Pioneers in this kind of selling included John Wanamaker, who established a store in Philadelphia in 1875, and Marshall Field, who founded his famous store in Chicago in 1881.

(3) *Chain stores* also began to develop in the late 1800's. A number of stores under the same management were scattered in various cities and towns. The chain stores, like the department stores, were able to sell goods at low prices because of large-scale buying and skillful management. Pioneers in chain-store selling included the Great Atlantic and Pacific Tea Company (1859) and F. W. Woolworth Company (1879).

(4) Still another form of mass selling brought low-priced goods to the people of small villages and farms. This was the *mail-order* house. Companies like Montgomery Ward (1872) and Sears Roebuck (1884) sent out catalogs showing pictures of products and directions telling how the products could be purchased by mail. On farms throughout America, the arrival of the rural mail carrier with the mail-order catalogs was one of the most exciting events of the year. Many thousands of American families still order goods from catalogs. (See page 465 for new methods of selling that have developed in more recent years.)

Whereas Sears and Ward's have introduced retail stores, the number of concerns engaged in mail-order selling has increased greatly.

A NEW FORM OF BUSINESS ORGANIZATION AIDS THE GROWTH OF INDUSTRY

In early times, most businesses in the United States were easy to run. Not much money or equipment was needed to start them, and they employed only a handful of workers. They were owned and managed by a single person or a small group known as a *partnership*. As more and more goods were manufactured and sold, these simpler forms of business ownership became less satisfactory. Railroads and factories with expensive machinery cost huge sums. A single owner could neither afford to start such a business nor carry on all the duties of managing it. Gradually a new kind of organization, known as the *corporation,* came into use.

A corporation has many owners. These owners provide the money needed to start and carry on the business. When a corporation is formed, *shares of stock* are offered for sale. The persons who buy these shares of stock are called *stockholders*. The stockholders are the actual owners of a corporation. They usually choose a board of directors to manage the corporation's affairs. The stockholders also have the right to vote on all important matters. If the corporation fails, they lose only the money they have invested in it. If it succeeds, the stockholders receive a share of the profits, or *dividends*.

COUNTRY STORE — ABOUT 1840

There are many advantages to organizing a large business as a corporation. By selling many shares of stock, huge sums can be collected to carry on giant industries. Also, stockholders are free at any time to sell their stock to someone else. Thus a corporation continues along year after year, whereas a business owned by a single person may stop or be seriously upset by his death.

After 1865, the number of corporations in the United States multiplied rapidly. Their growth was speeded up by the fact that they could buy large quantities of raw materials more cheaply and could operate more efficiently. You will read more about the huge business organizations of recent years later in this chapter.

CHECK UP

1. (a) What is mass production? (b) How did each of the following help in the development of mass production: division of labor? standard parts? the assembly line? (c) What is automation?

2. What new ways of selling were developed in the late 1800's?

3. (a) What is a corporation? (b) What are the advantages of organizing a large business as a corporation?

Point out that shares in large corporations are owned by large numbers of stockholders (see page 464).

3   How Did Improved Communication and Transportation Affect American Life?

Americans living a hundred years ago would perhaps be most startled by present-day methods of travel and communication. They would stare in wonder at our multilane highways crowded with speeding cars and trucks, and at sleek jet planes taking off across broad oceans for Europe, Asia, and Africa. In fact, many of the marvels we take for granted today have been developed just within the past fifty years or so. Talking movies and colored movies, for example, date from the 1920's and 1930's, while television has come into common use only since 1945. With the rapid growth of industry, these advances have come within the reach of most people.

INSTANT COMMUNICATION LINKS AMERICA AND THE WORLD

The world is made smaller by telegraph and cable. The telegraph, as we learned in Chapter 14, had been in use since the 1840's. Telegraph lines increased rapidly, and new inventions made it possible to send several messages over the same wire at the same time. Then men began to think that they might use telegraph lines to link the United States with other parts of the world.

An American named Cyrus Field developed a plan to lay a line across the bed of the Atlantic Ocean. This *cable,* as it was called, was reeled out from two ships starting in mid-ocean, one sailing toward the British Isles and the other toward the United States. Field had many disappointments, for the heavy cable broke again and again. Once he succeeded in laying a cable only to have the wires burn out after a month's use. Finally, in 1866, after several attempts, the cable was successfully laid, connecting America and Europe. Important messages no longer had to go by ship but could be flashed in a few moments across thousands of miles of ocean.

LAYING A CABLE across the ocean involved many difficulties. In this scene the problem seems to be: Will the whale attack the cable?

In time, additional cables were laid across the Atlantic, and the United States was also linked by cable with other parts of the world. Cables are used by newspapers, by businessmen, by government officials, and to send personal messages.

The human voice is transmitted by wire. Soon after the war ended in 1865, a young Scotsman named Alexander Graham Bell came to America to teach people who were deaf and dumb. Bell became interested in sending the actual sound of the human voice over a wire charged with electricity. He worked for many years on this problem. One day Bell's assistant heard him speak these words over a wire from an upstairs room: "Come here. I want you." This was the first time the human voice had been sent over a wire.

At a great exhibition in Philadelphia in 1876, Bell showed his telephone, a strange cone-like instrument. Most visitors at the exhibition looked upon the invention as an interesting toy, but Bell was determined to develop it into a useful machine. Shortly afterward, Bell and his assistant were able to talk over a wire strung a distance of two miles between Boston and Cambridge, Massachusetts. Two years later, in 1878, the first telephone exchange

in the United States was set up at New Haven, Connecticut.

Alexander Bell had succeeded in his dream of making a practical machine to transmit the human voice. But the first telephones were poor instruments compared with those of today! This is what one writer has to say about the difficulties of telephoning in the early days:

In the first place . . . you would talk into a funnel-shaped contrivance and then place it against your ear to get the returning message. In order to make yourself heard, you would have to shout like a Gloucester sea-captain at the height of a storm. More than the speakers' voices would come over the wire. It seemed to have become the playground of a million devils; moanings, shriekings, mutterings, and noises of all kinds would interrupt the flow of speech.

To call up your "party," you would not merely lift the receiver as today; you would tap with a lead pencil, or some other appliance, upon the diaphragm of your transmitter. There were no separate telephone wires. The talking at first was done over the telegraph wires. The earliest "centrals" reminded most persons of madhouses, for the day of the polite, soft-spoken telephone girl had not arrived. Instead, boys were rushing around with the ends of wires which they were frantically attempting to peg into the holes

This source extract points out progress after all.

453 *that dial telephones may represent*

These paragraphs bring out the variety of applications made of Marconi's original discovery.

454   MODERN AMERICA TAKES SHAPE

of the primitive switchboard and so establish "connections."

The telephone becomes important in American life. Queer as the early instruments were, they were forerunners of the modern telephone. Constant improvements were worked out and service was expanded. Each year saw an increase in the number of telephone lines and in the number of instruments placed in homes and in business offices. Early in the 1900's, the telephone became an important part of American life. It was no longer a luxury but a necessity to large numbers of people. Long-distance calls were made possible, and in 1915 New York and San Francisco were linked by telephone. When dial telephones came into use, calls could be made without the help of the

THIS "PYRAMID" SWITCHBOARD handled telephone calls in Richmond, Virginia, in 1881, three years after the first telephone exchange in the country had been set up.

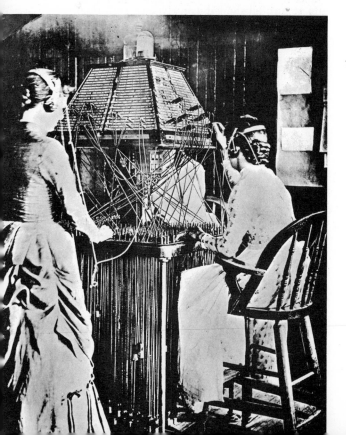

operator. By the early 1960's, people in many areas could even dial calls to distant cities. Today we can talk by telephone to almost any place in the world with greater ease and clearness than people a century ago could shout to their neighbors only a hundred yards away.

Radio serves America and the world. It is difficult for us today to imagine a world without radio. Actually, the first American broadcasting station, KDKA in Pittsburgh, was not built until 1920, and receiving sets did not become common in American homes until several years later. The story of radio, however, dates back to the 1890's. Marconi (mahr-*koh′nih*), an Italian, discovered a way to send "wireless" messages through the air by means of electric waves. Before long, he was able to communicate by wireless between Newfoundland and Great Britain. For some time wireless messages were in code, like telegraph messages. The invention was highly useful, especially to ships in distress at sea. Soon, however, scientists turned their efforts toward sending music and the human voice through the air. The result is the radio of today.

Radio not only brings pleasure but has many useful purposes as well. Radio brings music, sports events, plays, newscasts, and other features into millions of homes. Weather and market reports, health and safety information, charity appeals, and political campaign speeches, as well as the advertising which pays for programs, are broadcast by radio. Some factories have public-address systems which use radio broadcasting. Two-way "telephones" in cabs, private cars, boats, and planes and the "walkie-talkies" used by troops are other important forms of radio communication. Special uses are the radio beams, *radar* and *sonar,* used by ships and airplanes and by submarines to detect approaching objects before they can be seen. Air travel has been made safer because radio beams keep commercial airliners on course and also help them to land safely when airports are "fogged in." Radio waves "send" pictures for newspapers as well as the moving pictures which we know as television.

Television develops rapidly. Television had been invented before World War II, but sets for private use did not become available until after 1945. By the early 1960's, however, over 55 million television sets were in use in the United States. Television brings into our homes news reports and a variety of programs for our entertainment. TV has also become important in the nation's classrooms. Television has added to America's industrial progress because the making, selling, and repairing of sets, as well as the preparing and producing of programs, have created giant new industries, employing many workers.

THIRSTY PASSENGERS on an early train would be offered a drink of water from a kettle like this one equipped with two glasses.

RAILROADS TIE THE NATION TOGETHER WITH BANDS OF STEEL

Railroad building increases. While communication was being speeded up, travel also was being made easier. You have read in Chapter 14 about the early railroads. After peace was restored between the North and the South in 1865, there was a great burst of railroad construction. The southern railroads, damaged during the war, were rebuilt and extended. The North and Midwest were crisscrossed with an ever-increasing number of railroad lines.

Because the United States was growing rapidly, the need for railroads was greater than ever. New villages and towns were clamoring for railroad service. American farms were producing more food and American factories were manufacturing more goods. But to start a railroad is ex-

pensive. The roadbed must be prepared, tracks must be laid, stations must be built, and locomotives and cars must be bought. Nevertheless, some men saw a chance to become rich by operating railroads. To provide the money, companies were formed and people were persuaded to invest money in the railroads. Many of the new railroads paid large profits to the builders and to the people who had invested in them.

Eastern railroads are joined into a few great systems. The early railroad lines were short, linking two or three important cities. There were few connecting lines. This meant delay and inconvenience in moving goods and passengers over long distances. Freight had to be unloaded from cars on one line and hauled to cars on another line. On a long trip goods might have to be loaded and unloaded several times. For example, in the early days of railroads, freight between New York and

In 1884 loaded produce wagons from farms far out on Long Island were carried on railroad flatcars (above) to a New York City terminal. From there horses pulled the wagons to market. Today, loaded truck trailers are backed onto flatcars (right) and carried "piggy-back" by train to destinations hundreds of miles away.

Living proof that the "piggy-back" is not new.

Chicago had to be moved from one line to another nineteen times!

The man who first joined several short lines into one main *trunk line* was Cornelius Vanderbilt, a former ship captain. By buying and uniting many of the short lines in New York State, Vanderbilt developed the great New York Central System. In much the same way, railroads in Pennsylvania were united to form the Pennsylvania Railroad. The Baltimore and Ohio was another important early railroad system. (See map, page 284.)

Railroad travel becomes safer and more comfortable. As time went on, Americans were able not only to ride greater distances but to travel with more safety and comfort. Wrecks and breakdowns were reduced when air brakes and automatic couplers were added to trains. Block signals, requiring trains to halt unless the track ahead was clear, also cut down accidents. Steel instead of iron was used for locomotives, cars, and rails. Smoother roadbeds and better springs, as well as new methods of lighting and heating, increased riding comfort. In time the Pullman Company built comfortable day coaches, sleeping cars, and dining cars. More powerful locomotives, capable of drawing heavy trains at greater speed, replaced the older engines. In large cities huge stations were erected to provide services for travelers.

Railroads face competition from new forms of transportation. During the late 1800's and early 1900's the railroads were America's most important means of transportation. Since then, railroads have continued to make improvements. The huge, puffing steam locomotives have been replaced by electric or oil-burning engines. These trains carry the bulk of the nation's freight. In the last 50 years railroads have greatly increased their carrying capacity. They made a great contribution to the nation's war effort in both World Wars. But good roads and the automobile and increasingly rapid airplane transportation have cut into railroad passenger business. By dropping little-used branch lines and by merging into larger organizations, the railroads have been trying to operate more economically.

THE AUTOMOBILE PUTS AMERICA ON WHEELS

The "horseless carriage" replaces the horse and buggy. It is not possible to fix a single date for the invention of the automobile. A number of men in America and Europe had been tinkering with a "horseless carriage" — a vehicle that could be driven under its own power. Some of these carriages were driven by steam; others, which proved more successful, were powered by a new invention — the gasoline engine. Among the American experimenters in the 1890's were George Selden, Charles Duryea, Elwood Haynes, Alexander Winton, and Henry Ford.

Soon after 1900, automobiles began to appear on the roads. At first they were regarded with amazement and caused a good deal of trouble. Every breakdown, and there were many of them, was greeted with shouts of "Get a horse!" from curious and amused bystanders. The driver of one of these queer-looking vehicles had to be a sort of mechanical wizard, for no service stations lined the highways to furnish gasoline, repair tires, or take care of breakdowns. Roads were poor and so dusty in dry weather that passengers wore coats called "dusters" as well as goggles to protect their eyes. A rapid and steady stream of inventions, however, soon made possible the production of better cars at a lower cost. No longer was the automobile the plaything of the wealthy but a necessary part of American living. In our day there are more cars in the United States than there are families.

Goodyear's experiments in rubber make automobile tires possible. There have been countless inventions and developments without which the present-day automobile would not have been possible. Special steel, chromium, and other metals had to be developed for parts and fixtures. Electrical systems had to be perfected to light and heat cars and to keep motors running smoothly. High-powered gasoline was developed. One of the greatest needs was for an elastic tire, without which high-speed travel would be impossible.

We can thank a New Englander named Charles Goodyear for the discovery that

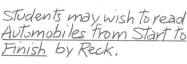

Students may wish to read _Automobiles from Start to Finish_ by Reck.

CHARLES DURYEA'S automobile, like other early models, looked much like a converted buggy. This was one of the first to have inflated rubber tires.

AIRPLANE VS. AUTOMOBILE. In 1919 the two means of transportation, though still young, were developing rapidly. This race between the two took place on the hard-packed sand at Daytona Beach, Florida.

led to the easy-riding tires on our automobiles today. Although Goodyear died in 1860, long before automobiles were invented, he developed a remarkable process for hardening rubber. Raw rubber had been known to the white man since the days of Columbus, but it was not useful because it was affected by changes in temperature. It became brittle in cold weather and sticky in summer.

Charles Goodyear spent his life experimenting with raw rubber to overcome these faults. His experiments kept him poor, and he borrowed money from all his friends in order to carry on his work. Once he even sold his furniture to get money; another time he sold his children's schoolbooks. He made rubber shoes and wore them; he made and wore a rubber coat which caused people in the streets to laugh at him. In spite of every difficulty, Goodyear kept on. He learned that sulfur added to the rubber would prevent stickiness. One day when he dropped some rubber on his wife's stove, he accidentally discovered that heat would harden and improve rubber. Goodyear tried various degrees of heat until he finally produced a rubber that was not affected by changes in temperature. This process, known as *vulcanizing*, became especially valuable for

tires when automobiles came into use. It led to the growth of the great rubber industry in the United States.

During World War II, when America's usual supply of raw rubber was cut off by the enemy, American scientists and industrialists developed synthetic (artificial) rubber. After the war, natural rubber was again imported, but many peacetime uses have also been found for synthetic rubber.

THE AIRPLANE SPEEDS TRAVEL

Man learns to fly. The railroad and the automobile did not end man's search for swifter transportation. For centuries he had dreamed of flying through the air. By the late 1800's balloons had been used for years, and men in England, Germany, and America began to experiment in building airplanes. But not until the invention of the gasoline engine were modern airplanes possible.

Samuel Langley, an American scientist, watched the birds sweep and turn gracefully in the air. He asked himself: Why can't man fly as well as birds? Langley made several types of flying machines, but none of them was practical. After several attempts to launch his machines failed, Langley gave up his efforts. Other in-

Note the kind of landing wheels **458** *used on the airplane. What can be concluded about the weight of the craft and its landing speed?*

ventors also experimented with heavier-than-air machines. But the honor of building the first airplane actually to fly went to two young mechanics named Wilbur and Orville Wright of Dayton, Ohio. They had been interested in flying since childhood. In December, 1903, an airplane they had built made a successful flight at Kittyhawk, North Carolina. On the fourth trial Wilbur Wright flew it for 59 seconds over a distance of 852 feet. Man's dream of flying had been realized!

Pioneers of aviation prove flying is practical. Many years were to pass before people took seriously the efforts to perfect a flying machine. After all, they thought, there were plenty of ways for men to be killed or injured on the ground without risking their lives in the air. Now that speedy travel was possible by train and automobile, what was the use of trying to fly? Attempts to improve the airplane, however, continued. In the First World War airplanes were used for scouting and fighting. During the 1920's many airfields were built, and regular schedules for flying the mail were established.

A number of dramatic flights did much to draw people's attention to the possibilities of air transportation. In May, 1927, a young air-mail pilot named Charles Lindbergh flew alone from Long Island to Paris in a non-stop flight which took little more than 30 hours. Four years later, Wiley Post and Harold Gatty astonished everyone by flying around the world in eight days. The first woman to fly the Atlantic alone was Amelia Earhart, and three years later, in 1935, she flew alone from Honolulu to California. Her career ended tragically in 1937 when her plane disappeared on a flight across the Pacific. The flights of these pioneers of aviation do not seem unusual to us today, but they blazed the trail for our modern airplanes.

The airplane brings great changes in travel. Air travel became more common in the 1930's. But it was during World War II that aviation made amazing progress. Huge factories turned out thousands of fighters and bombers. New types of planes were developed, each bigger and faster than the one before. Rockets were used to speed a plane's take-off, and jet planes came into use.

After 1945 the new developments were applied to peacetime flying. Regular airline flights now carry passengers all over the United States and the world. The speed with which flying has become popular is made clear when we look at the figures. It was some 20 years before American passenger airlines carried their 100 millionth passenger in 1950. In only four years more they reached the 200 million mark. Now America's airlines carry some 60 million passengers every year. The time of long-distance flights has been greatly shortened by the use of jet airplanes that can fly at 600 miles an hour. So many airplanes are flying nowadays that there is danger of overcrowding the airways. To reduce the possibility of collision, the Federal Aviation Agency co-operates with military authorities in finding ways to guide planes more safely and efficiently.

IMPROVEMENTS IN TRAVEL AND COMMUNICATION AID THE GROWTH OF INDUSTRY IN THE UNITED STATES

It is easy to see how new forms of transportation and communication have affected the daily life of the average American. But why were the changes in travel and communication so important to the growth of American industry? As an example, consider a businessman in Detroit. He is an officer of one of the big automobile companies there. To manufacture

Airplanes are discussed in Great Inventors and Their Inventions.

the cars, he orders steel from Pittsburgh or Chicago, rubber from Akron, electrical items from Toledo. "Assembly plants" — factories where cars are finally assembled, or put together — are scattered all over the country. They may be located in Los Angeles, Newark (N.J.), Minneapolis, St. Louis, Dallas, and so on.

The businessman needs quick delivery of materials. The fast freight trains, the giant trucks provide it. Typewriters (which appeared in the 1870's) enable the businessman to keep records and communicate with his fellow businessmen. If he is in a hurry, he can talk with customers or other businessmen by long-distance telephone. Often he has to visit his plants or those of the companies which supply him with materials. On swift trains and planes he can reach other cities quickly and easily. Without this great web of transportation and communication, our industries would be unable to operate as they do.

Improvements in transportation and communication also created vast new industries. Think for a moment of all the raw materials needed to build railroads, automobiles, airplanes, telephones, and radios. Think of the huge factories and the machinery required to make finished parts out of the raw materials. Think of the army of trained workers needed to assemble the parts; to operate trains, trucks, and airplanes; and to repair and service cars, telephones, and radios. When you add up all the people who take part in the building and operating of these newer means of travel and communication, you have included a large portion of all American workers.

CHECK UP

1. (a) How did the telegraph, the cable, and the telephone improve communication? (b) What useful purposes are served by radio and television?

2. (a) Why was there an increased need for railroads in the late 1800's? (b) Why were the railroads joined into a few great systems? (c) How was train travel improved?

3. (a) How has the automobile become an important part of American life? (b) Why is rubber important in modern transportation? (c) How was the safety and usefulness of airplane travel proved?

4. How have better transportation and communication aided the growth of industry?

The Master Builders by Wade includes biographical sketches of Hill, Bell, Carnegie, and Ford.

4 How Have Business Methods Changed with the Growth of Industry?

BUSINESS LEADERS BUILD GIANT INDUSTRIES

We have seen that certain things encouraged the growth of American industry after 1865 — rich natural resources, mass production of goods, swifter transportation and communication, and the growth of corporations. During the closing years of the 1800's, the forward march of industry was also aided by the activities of a small number of business leaders. Often a single one of these men, by his boldness and vision, founded and managed a giant company and built up a huge fortune. Let us glance at the careers of three of the most successful "captains of industry."

James J. Hill — railroad builder. One of the most interesting figures in the building of the American railroad industry was James J. Hill. He was born in 1838, in a log cabin on a little frontier farm in Canada. On such a farm there was much hard work to be done, and young James had his full share of daily chores. After the death of his father, he decided to strike out for himself. Shipping on a lake freighter, he came to the United States. A variety of jobs led him to St. Paul, Minnesota. There he became an agent for a steamboat company and a small railroad.

Until he was about 40 years old, Hill had done nothing out of the ordinary. He had great ideas, but no one took them seriously. One of these ideas was to develop the northwestern part of the country. Hill had traveled through this sparsely settled area on foot and by wagon and dog sledge. He finally persuaded a small group of men to take over the railroad for which he worked, and Hill was appointed general manager. The road was in poor condition and the outlook not too promising. Yet from this modest beginning, Hill built a railroad empire.

The secret of Hill's success lay in his understanding that the Northwest must be dotted with prosperous farms if his railroads were to succeed. He arranged for would-be settlers to be taken on trips to view the country. He imported fine cattle and horses from Europe to encourage cattle raising, and aided farmers to get seed and farm machinery on reasonable terms. He arranged for hundreds of boys to be sent to schools where they learned scientific farming.

By 1893, the Great Northern railway system, under Hill's direction, spanned the country between St. Paul, Minnesota, and Seattle, Washington. In later years, James J. Hill controlled most of the railroad lines in the Northwest, totaling about 20,000 miles of track.

This paragraph calls attention to the great problem of building a long railroad across a sparsely settled area.

Andrew Carnegie — maker of steel.
America owes its progress as an industrial nation in large part to its ability to produce tremendous quantities of steel. Railway rails and cars, automobiles, all sorts of machinery, and huge buildings are only a few of the things which are made from steel. For centuries, steel was known to have qualities of strength and toughness not found in iron. But steel was too expensive to be widely used. Certain impurities had to be removed from iron to make steel, and no cheap method of removing these impurities had been discovered. Then, in the 1850's, an Englishman, Henry Bessemer, and an American, William Kelly, each discovered a startling fact. Working on the same problem separately, they found that a blast of air directed at melted iron would remove its impurities. This new process of making steel was so cheap and easy that steel could be produced in large quantities and at low cost.

The rapid growth of the steel industry in the United States, however, was largely brought about by a man who was not a steelmaker by trade. Andrew Carnegie was a poor Scottish boy brought to America by his parents in 1848, when he was thirteen years old. Young Andrew started work in a Pennsylvania cotton mill where his pay was only a dollar and twenty cents a week. Later he worked in the telegraph office of a railroad company. Then he became secretary to a railroad official. By hard work and shrewd common sense, Carnegie advanced rapidly in the business world. From railroading he went into bridge building. Since steel played an important part in both these industries, he became interested in it.

Carnegie was daring as well as shrewd. He finally decided to risk his entire future in producing steel by the new air-blast method discovered by Kelly and Bessemer.

Carnegie was tremendously successful. By 1900, the Carnegie Steel Company, with headquarters in Pittsburgh, Pennsylvania, was the leading producer of steel in this country. To keep his huge blast furnaces and steel mills working at full speed, Carnegie bought vast deposits of iron ore in the region of the upper Great Lakes. He also controlled a fleet of vessels on the Great Lakes and a railroad which carried the ore from Lake Erie to the blast furnaces in Pittsburgh.

In 1901, Andrew Carnegie decided to retire. He sold out his steel business, which kept on growing as the United States Steel Corporation, the country's largest producer of steel. Carnegie is remembered today not only for his business success but for the generous gifts he made from his tremendous fortune. Many a town and city in the United States has a public library built with funds left by Carnegie. When asked why he gave away so much of his money, he said, "I started life as a poor man, and I wish to end it that way." Carnegie was by no means a poor man when he died, yet he gave away 350 million dollars!

John D. Rockefeller — founder of Standard Oil. While steelmaking was being revolutionized by Andrew Carnegie, another great modern American industry was getting its start. Petroleum, or oil as we commonly call it, lay in great quantities below the earth in Pennsylvania. In some places it seeped through the rock and formed a scum on the surface of creeks. Farmers sometimes skimmed off the oil to grease their wagons, and a few shrewd men even bottled it and sold it as medicine. But no one understood the real value of petroleum until a scientist, Benjamin Silliman, tested it. He found that it could be refined and used for lighting homes and buildings.

In 1859, the first oil well was drilled at Titusville, Pennsylvania. The news that oil wells could be successfully drilled had much the same effect as the discovery of gold in California. Here was a chance to make huge fortunes! All over the country people were certain to use coal oil (kerosene) for lighting in place of candles and whale-oil lamps. Prospectors, therefore, flocked by the thousands to Pennsylvania. Almost overnight, wells were drilled and oil derricks dotted the landscape. Western Pennsylvania became the center of a new industry. Towns and cities sprang up like magic, and refineries for producing kerosene began to appear.

About this time, John D. Rockefeller, a 23-year-old merchant in Cleveland, became interested in oil and determined to get control of the entire oil-refining business. Starting with a single oil refinery, Rockefeller and his partners branched out until in the 1880's they controlled 90 per cent of all the oil-refining plants in the country. But Rockefeller did not stop there. He bought factories to make barrels; he got control of most of the pipe lines which carried oil from the wells; he built warehouses to store the kerosene. Rockefeller also organized a vast selling force to market his product throughout the country. By the 1900's, Rockefeller and his Standard Oil Company controlled practically all the oil business in the United States.

Rockefeller was able to gain a monopoly in oil because of his company's financial power. In the early years, instead of spending all the profits, he put back as much money into the business as he could spare. He advised his partners to do the same. "Take out what you've got to have to live on," he said, "but leave the rest in. Don't buy new clothes and fast horses; let your wife wear her last year's bonnet." As a

This paragraph illustrates how a corporation expands.

ANDREW CARNEGIE

was a Scottish immigrant boy who delivered telegrams to get a start in industrial Pittsburgh.

FROM A TELEGRAPHER for the Pennsylvania Railroad, Carnegie soon rose to division manager. Later, by promoting a railroad sleeping car he started the Carnegie fortune and went into business for himself.

BRIDGE BUILDING was next for Carnegie, since his railroad experience had shown him the need for iron bridges to replace old wooden trestles. A good salesman, he made his bridge company a success. Then he learned of a new, inexpensive method to manufacture steel.

LOW-COST STEEL, Carnegie realized, would find a ready market in industrial America. He set about expanding and organizing the steel industry to meet the demand — and made a fortune. In 1901, however, Carnegie retired, believing that rich men should spend their later years distributing their wealth.

A LIBRARY which Carnegie built for his hometown was visited by President Benjamin Harrison on opening day. It was only the first of Carnegie's huge gifts in support of education, research, and world peace.

However, these many small companies employed a minority of all industrial workers.

464   MODERN AMERICA TAKES SHAPE

result of this thrift, Rockefeller had the money with which to buy out rival refineries. In fact, many a man who tried to get ahead in the oil industry was forced to sell out to Rockefeller. If he refused, Rockefeller would set the price of his kerosene so low that he drove his rival out of business. The money which Rockefeller had put aside carried him along even though he was selling at a loss. This "cutthroat competition" was common in the days when American industry grew big.

Although the use of the electric light cut down the demand for kerosene in the United States, the oil industry continued to grow. The invention of the gasoline engine created a tremendous demand for petroleum products. Also, in recent years oil has been increasingly used for heating homes and other buildings. By 1960 the value of the petroleum produced by American oil companies was about seven and a half billion dollars a year.

•

What Hill, Carnegie, and Rockefeller did to promote American industry is only a part of the story. Other business leaders who had worked their way up from humble beginnings helped to advance industry and achieved fame and fortune as well. Sometimes they used selfish and ruthless methods which our laws today do not permit. Nevertheless, present-day American industry owes much to their boldness, energy, and ability.

OUR CENTURY BRINGS CHANGES IN BUSINESS METHODS

During the 1900's America's industrial power has continued to grow. Much of this growth is due to still further changes in methods of doing business. We shall describe a few of these briefly.

The number of giant corporations has increased. Not only in the production of steel and oil but in most branches of American industry huge business organizations have grown up. This is to be expected since large corporations with ample funds can produce goods efficiently, sell them at low prices, and give attention to developing new products. Sometimes these giant business organizations buy up smaller companies; sometimes two or more companies combine to form larger companies. Today, also, a growing number of giant corporations produce not one but a great variety of products. In spite of this trend toward larger business organizations, it is interesting to note that in the late 1950's, 90 per cent of all the companies in major fields of industry employed fewer than a hundred people.

Business management has changed. Nowadays it is unusual for one man to establish and manage a big business organization. As you know, corporations are owned by stockholders. By the early 1960's, about seventeen million Americans owned stock (and so were owners) in corporations. The American Telephone and Telegraph Company, for example, has two million stockholders. The men who actually *run* large businesses are highly trained managers who are paid salaries. They devote their careers to improving the business and increasing its profits.

Business sponsors scientific research. Leaders in business and industry realize the importance of science in our times. Many corporations give large sums of

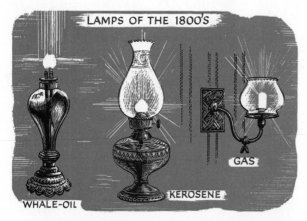

LAMPS OF THE 1800'S

WHALE-OIL   KEROSENE   GAS

THE FIRST OIL WELL (left) was drilled in 1859 in the Pennsylvania town of Titusville by Edwin Drake (the bearded man in the foreground). From this crude wooden structure has grown our modern oil industry with its huge refineries, like the one shown above. Here crude oil is refined in tall towers, and the resulting gasoline and other products are pumped into acres of storage tanks.

money to universities and scientific foundations to advance the study of science. Many large industries also maintain their own laboratories where scientists seek to improve existing products and develop new ones. Research scientists working for a large corporation, for example, developed nylon, the synthetic material (page 445) used in clothing, parachutes, brushes, rope and thread, and many other products. Since the invention of nylon, many other useful synthetic textiles have been developed in industrial laboratories.

In the branch of electricity known as electronics, research has opened up a whole new industry. Radio and television are only the most familiar developments in this new field. Among other electronic devices are radar, X-ray, and computers with "electronic brains" that solve complicated mathematical problems in a few seconds (page 450). New weapons of war and man-made satellites depend heavily upon electronic devices. Scientists and engineers are constantly studying new ways of applying knowledge of electronics and inventing the equipment to use this knowledge. This in turn has caused a tremendous increase in the number of business organizations in the field of electronics.

New methods of selling are developed. In recent years new selling establishments have offered more convenient services to customers. *Supermarkets* set up groceries and other products in long open aisles, where the customer can pick out for himself whatever appeals to his eye. The 1940's and 1950's saw the rise of spacious new *shopping centers* which bring together stores of several kinds — a supermarket, a drug store, a dress shop, and so on. The centers often are located at the edges of cities and provide plenty of parking space. Thus the family can drive up and do all kinds of shopping at one time. *Discount houses,* and many other kinds of stores, sell some products at lower than list prices — usually requiring cash payment, discouraging special services, and eliminating return privileges on merchandise.

Small corporations find it impossible to compete **465** with large corporations in the fields of research and product development.

Advertising has grown enormously. Along with new methods of selling goods has come an increase in advertising. In order to sell large quantities of goods, a manufacturer must advertise his products to the public. In 1900, only a small number of companies advertised their products on a national scale. There were probably no more than a dozen or fifteen agencies to handle advertising campaigns, and most advertising was limited to newspapers and magazines. Today advertising itself is a huge industry. Newspaper and magazine advertising as well as radio and television commercials now reach millions of people. Colorful "ads" inform the public about new products or urge people to buy one particular brand. Advertising experts search for the most effective ways to appeal to buyers. Although some advertisements make questionable claims for their products, advertising as a whole has done much to create a market for the flood of articles turned out by American industry.

CHECK UP

1. (a) How did James J. Hill develop a great railroad system in the Northwest? (b) How did Andrew Carnegie develop the steel industry? (c) How did John D. Rockefeller develop the oil industry?

2. (a) Why has the trend toward large business organizations continued? (b) How has business management changed? (c) How do business and industry encourage scientific research?

3. (a) What new ideas of selling have developed? (b) How has advertising become an important business?

Check Up on Chapter 22

Do You Know the Meaning?

1. mineral
2. dividend
3. radar
4. synthetics
5. electronics
6. corporation
7. investment
8. trunk line
9. standard parts
10. assembly line
11. automation
12. stockholder
13. natural resources
14. vulcanizing
15. mass production

Can You Identify?

1. Machine Age
2. Thomas Edison
3. Henry Ford
4. Cyrus Field
5. 1859
6. 1876
7. James J. Hill
8. Marconi
9. 1903
10. Wright brothers
11. Andrew Carnegie
12. John D. Rockefeller
13. Charles Goodyear
14. Cornelius Vanderbilt
15. Alexander Graham Bell
16. Charles Lindbergh

What Do You Think?

1. (a) Could the United States have become a great industrial nation without her rich natural resources? Why? (b) Why is it important for Americans not to waste these natural resources?

2. Why do invention and industrial progress go hand in hand? In discussing this question use the development of the automobile as an example.

3. (a) What are the advantages of mass production? (b) Are there any disadvantages? Explain.

4. Which American inventor or industrial leader do you think made the greatest contribution to American life? Why?

5. (a) How have the airplane and automobile changed our ways of living? (b) What recent inventions or discoveries are likely to affect our way of life?

6. Was John D. Rockefeller a Public Benefactor or a cheat and a scoundrel why?

The horseless carriage. A forerunner of our speedy, modern auto was simply a buggy moved by a one-cylinder engine. The "horseless carriage" of 1896 could make about twelve miles an hour if it didn't break down! President Theodore Roosevelt was always a daring fellow, but when he rode in an auto in 1902, he had a horse and buggy follow along in case of accident. The early automobiles were considered so dangerous that the state of Tennessee passed a law about their use. The law required a person to publish a warning in the newspaper a week ahead of time if he intended to drive an automobile anywhere!

Movies of yesterday. Perhaps you have seen and laughed at some of the old-time movies. Funny as they are, it was from these early films that our modern motion pictures developed. One of the first pictures to tell a complete story was "The Great Train Robbery," released by the Edison studio in 1903. Soon one- and two-reel pictures took the country by storm. The action in these early movies was fast and jerky, but nobody minded. Such pictures as "Trapped by the Bloodhounds" or "Raffles, the Amateur Cracksman" were shown as fillers between acts in the vaudeville theaters. Then came the separate movie-houses, often called Nickelodeons because the price of admission was a nickel.

The silent films used a piano player, and later an orchestra, to play music suited to the action of the film. "Cue sheets" were supplied to the theaters along with the films. These cue sheets suggested the right kind of music to be played — fast and lively, sad and slow, or soft and sentimental. The music was also needed to keep people quiet while the reels were being changed every fifteen minutes, or when the film broke, as happened quite often. As time went on, pictures were improved, and movie-making became an important industry. Today's movies, shown on a wide screen with sound and color, are a far cry from the silent films of the past.

Bicycle beginnings. The "ancestor" of our modern bicycle was introduced in America in 1876. It was a strange-looking contraption. The front wheel was about five feet in diameter, with pedals on its axle. The rear wheel was only about 18 inches high. The rider, perched high on a seat above the front wheel, needed a good sense of balance! Soon, new inventions, such as equal-sized wheels, inflatable tires, and a sprocket chain connecting the pedals and the rear wheel, made riding easier; and the bicycle quickly became popular. In the days before the automobile, nearly everyone used a bicycle for business and pleasure. A young man could take his girl riding on a *tandem* or two-seated bicycle. Perhaps you have heard the old song which goes:

"It won't be a stylish marriage,
I can't afford a carriage,
But you'll look sweet upon the seat
Of a bicycle built for two."

Greenfield Village. To preserve a part of our country's past, Henry Ford created a typical village of the 1800's outside his home town of Dearborn, Michigan. To make his town true to life, he moved many entire buildings to Greenfield Village — an old schoolhouse, a shoemaker's shop, a silk mill, the house in which Noah Webster wrote his famous dictionary, and many others. Ford also built a museum and filled it with original models of inventions and machines which had helped America to become a great industrial nation. Among these were several of Thomas Edison's original inventions, which Ford had collected and put into working order. Ford, who was a friend and great admirer of the inventor, also had Edison's old laboratory rebuilt in Greenfield Village.

The early cars were accident prone and the roads **467** of those days made fast driving hazardous and at times impossible.

Growing Business and Industry
Face and Solve New Problems

Note how terms such as "business" and "industry" are explained.

What this chapter is about —

Everyone in a modern industrial nation like the United States depends upon business and industry to satisfy many of his needs. These needs include shelter and clothing; bus, train, and airplane service; books, newspapers, and amusements; and a thousand other things. The companies which *produce* the goods to satisfy our needs are usually lumped under the term *industry,* On the other hand, the companies which *help to bring* products or services to the people who need them are commonly called *business* concerns. These include wholesale and retail stores; banks; water, gas, and electric companies; and so on. As you can see, business and industry work hand in hand to supply the needs of modern communities.

Without the rapid growth of industry and business since 1865, it would be impossible to satisfy the needs of your town and all the other communities throughout the country. Americans owe their high standard of living in large part to new inventions, new machines, and new means of manufacturing and transportation.

But the growth of industry and business has also brought to the American people many problems that their ancestors did not have to face. Among these are unemployment and business depressions. To understand such problems and the efforts that

People in our story — working woman and child, picket, union organizer, government official, stockbroker.

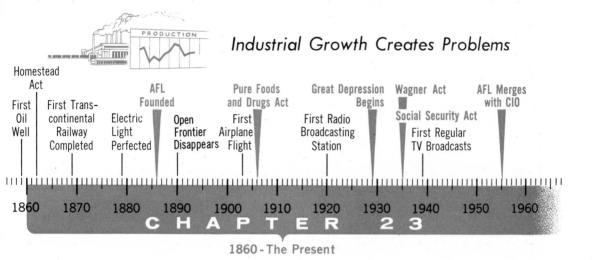

Homestead Act

First Oil Well

First Transcontinental Railway Completed

Electric Light Perfected

AFL Founded

Open Frontier Disappears

First Airplane Flight

Pure Foods and Drugs Act

First Radio Broadcasting Station

Great Depression Begins

Wagner Act

Social Security Act

First Regular TV Broadcasts

AFL Merges with CIO

1860   1870   1880   1890   1900   1910   1920   1930   1940   1950   1960

C H A P T E R   2 3

1860 - The Present

have been made to solve them, look for the answers to the following questions:

▶ 1. What were some important problems that arose in the Machine Age?

▶ 2. What have labor and business done to solve the problems of the Machine Age?

▶ 3. How has government tried to solve some problems of business and industry?

What Were Some Important Problems That Arose in the Machine Age?

In Chapter 22 we learned how the growth of American business and industry brought about the many conveniences which make our lives comfortable today. This chapter will point out some of the less happy results of changes in business and industry. In the following pages we shall read about Mr. Charles Jackson, an American businessman of the 1890's. Mr. Jackson is not a real person, but his story will help us to understand how the growth of industry brought problems as well as benefits.

New machinery tempts Mr. Jackson to increase his production. Mr. Jackson is president of the Jackson Manufacturing Company, which makes furniture of steel and wood. Mr. Jackson is sitting in his office looking at the production figures for

his company. He has just ordered some new machinery. At present his factory can produce 25 chairs each day. With the new machinery, however, Mr. Jackson's company will be able to make 100 chairs a day. Mr. Jackson is pleased for two reasons: (1) The amount of human labor needed to make each chair will be reduced by the use of machinery. Since he will have to pay less money for labor per chair, he hopes to be able to make a larger profit than before. (2) Mr. Jackson's profits will also be greatly increased because his company will be making four times as many chairs each day.

Mr. Jackson now writes letters to the companies from which he buys his steel and wood. "I shall need," he writes, "much more steel and wood than I have

469

A GANG OF STRONG MEN (below) was needed to lay this oil pipe line in New Jersey during the 1890's. Today, as shown at left, pipe-line workers have powerful machines to help them. These two men are using an automatic wrapping machine to waterproof a length of new pipe while it is held up by the tractor crane seen in the background.

been buying." He explains the exact quantities. When these letters reach the steel and wood companies, they too are pleased at the chance to sell more of their products and to make larger profits. The steel company orders more iron ore and more coal. It is just as though the steel company said to the miners, "Get more men! Dig more coal and iron!" The lumber company sends orders to the loggers in the woods, and to the sawmills, to provide more wood.

Increased production uses up natural resources. Other factory owners, like Mr. Jackson, are using new machinery and turning out more and more products. The miners and loggers, therefore, can sell all the ore and wood they can produce. They dig and cut more than ever before with bigger crews and better tools. They dig where the deposits of ore are richest and the digging is easiest, and they cut where they can get the most wood with the least work. They must provide huge quantities of ore and wood so that Mr. Jackson's fac-

tory and thousands of other factories may have the raw materials which they need.

This is what happened to America's natural resources after the war between the North and the South. Everywhere orders were pouring in. Everywhere men acted on this idea: "Hurry up! Provide the materials quickly!" So men dug frantically into the stores of iron that could never be replaced. They dug into the richest veins of coal with no concern for future needs. They cut down trees without considering the needs of their children and grandchildren. In this way, America's natural resources were recklessly used. In recent years more thought has been given to *conserving* our natural resources, that is, using them more wisely. Even so, the United States imports from other parts of the world increasing quantities of raw materials, such as iron ore (page 445).

Mr. Jackson expands his business too far. We return again to the story of Mr. Jackson. Finding, as he expected, that his

An interesting discussion of **470** *America's resources is found in Great Heritage by Shippen.*

new machinery turns out more chairs each day and increases his profits, he decides to buy even more machines. So he orders the machines. He orders more steel and more wood. He hires more workmen to operate the new machines and to increase his output of chairs. To be sure, he does not have the money to pay cash for all he buys. "But," he thinks, "what does it matter? With prices so high and profits so large, I can borrow the money and pay it back out of my profits later on."

Other manufacturers have the same idea. They enlarge their factories. They buy more materials, hire more workers, make more goods. Like Mr. Jackson, they also borrow money. But after a while the creditors (the men who lend money) become alarmed because so much money has been borrowed and so many goods have been manufactured. Mr. Smith, the banker, for example, begins to worry about Mr. Jackson, who has borrowed more money than his business can repay in many years. Mr. Smith has lunch with another banker, Mr. Jones, and finds that he, too, is worrying about the same thing. "What shall I do," wonders Mr. Smith, "if Mr. Jackson, who owes me so much money, doesn't find enough buyers for his products? How will he be able to repay me?"

Thoroughly frightened, Mr. Smith decides to cut down on the amount of money owed to his bank. He gets in touch with the firms to whom the bank has lent money and asks that the loans be paid back. So Mr. Jackson, who owes the bank money, pays his debt. But this takes so much of Mr. Jackson's money that he can buy no more machinery and must spend less for steel and wood and wages paid to workmen. He therefore tells the steel company and the lumber company not to send the materials he has ordered. With fewer materials to work with, he has to go

through his factory saying to a workman here and to another one there something like this: "I'm sorry, Joe, but after this Saturday we won't have any work for you. I'll call you back to the factory the minute there's work for you to do."

Fear sweeps the country. All around the country sweeps a feeling of fear. Just as Mr. Jackson cuts down his orders for steel and wood, the steel and lumber companies, in turn, are forced to reduce their orders for raw materials. Out goes the word to the loggers and the miners: "Less ore. Less coal. Fewer logs." "I'm sorry, Tom." "I'm sorry, Jim." And the workers go home to their wives and tell them, "I'm sorry, Mary, but the boss says no work after Saturday. Better not buy that pair of shoes for the youngster. Better buy less at the grocery store." And so it goes in countless communities throughout the nation. The shoemaker, the grocer, and other merchants have less business. They begin to cut down, to order less, to discharge their helpers. Many businesses fail because they cannot sell their products. Many families · are hungry because men have lost their jobs.

America enjoys booms and suffers depressions. This chain of events has been repeated many times in American history. First there has been a time of confidence and growth of business, then a period of fear and falling-off in business. This first kind of period is called a *boom,* and the time of fear is called a *panic.* The period of falling business and rising unemployment which follows a panic is usually called a *depression.* You read in Chapter 17 about the panic and depression at the time when Van Buren was President.

When most Americans were farmers, panics and depressions did not bring hardship to as many people as they did in later years. Living ·on farms, people could take care of most of their needs even if

This is a graphic description of the business cycle. Economists are not in agreement on the relative importance of factors that make for either a boom or a depression.

BUSINESS PROSPERS AS MONEY MOVES FREELY

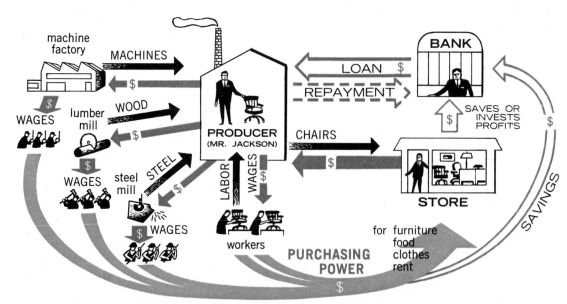

the nation's business was poor. As business and industry have grown, however, an ever-increasing number of Americans make their living in business and manufacturing. A factory worker or a businessman depends on the money he receives to buy what he needs. He does not actually make or grow what his family needs to eat, wear, and use. Thus, in the Machine Age, more people suffer during periods of panic and depression.

There have been a number of depressions since 1865. Three of these have been especially severe. They followed the panics of 1873, 1893, and 1929. In each case the story was much the same. Business expanded rapidly, wages were high, prices rose. People invested their money recklessly in the hope of making big profits. In the years before 1873 and 1893, they lent money for the building of new railroads; before 1929, they invested heavily in stocks and bonds. In each case, when the bubble of good times broke, panic and suffering followed. The Panic of 1929 and the depression that came afterward were the worst the United States has ever known.

Business did not get back to normal for about ten years. Then, during World War II, business increased greatly in order to supply the needs of our military forces. During the 1950's a new term, *recession,* came into use to describe a business decline that was not too long or too serious.

Mr. Jackson plans a monopoly. Let us turn once more to the story of Mr. Jackson to understand another problem that arose in industry and business. One day, as Mr. Jackson is thinking about his business, he jumps suddenly to his feet. "I've got a great idea!" he says excitedly. "This will make me rich. Why didn't I think of it before? I'll try to get control of all the manufacturing of chairs in the United States. Of course, I shall need a great deal of money because I shall have to buy out many other furniture factories. I may even have to sell chairs so cheaply that some other manufacturers cannot afford to stay in business. But when I control all chair manufacturing, every person who wants to buy chairs will be forced to buy from Jackson. Then, when there are no other chairs for people to buy, I can ask almost any price I like. People will have no choice but to pay it."

The number of monopolies increases after 1865. As a matter of fact, neither our imaginary Mr. Jackson nor anyone else ever controlled all the manufacture of chairs in the United States. But some forms of business or industry have been controlled, or practically controlled, by one company or a small group of companies. You have learned already how John D. Rockefeller obtained control of most of the oil refining in the country (Chapter 22). To control a product, as you know, is to have a monopoly of it. When a group of corporations with common interests has a monopoly of a product, the group is called a *trust*. Since 1865, powerful trusts have at some time held monopolies of steel, tobacco, sugar, beef, and other products.

What are the benefits and evils of monopolies? In general, trusts or monopolies are huge organizations. Large business organizations have certain advantages: (1) They can buy raw materials in large quantities. (2) They can hire scientists to discover new products, and experts to make their factories more efficient. (3) They can afford to purchase expensive machinery. (4) They can develop ways to use waste materials that might

otherwise be thrown away. These advantages can mean more products at lower prices for the public.

Monopolies, on the other hand, may bring serious problems: (1) There is a temptation for monopolies to keep their prices high in order to make larger profits. When this happens, the public does not receive the benefit of lower costs. (2) Monopolies also work a hardship on small businesses, which cannot compete successfully with them. (3) New ideas may be discouraged if a monopoly controls all the business in a particular field. Thus new processes and improved products may be kept off the market. Later in this chapter you will learn how the government has taken steps to prevent harmful monopolies.

**C H E C K
✓ U P**

1. (a) Why does new machinery tempt manufacturers to increase production? (b) How does increased production affect companies which sell raw materials? (c) What are some unfortunate results of overproduction?

2. What is meant by the statement "business has followed a pattern of boom, panic, and depression"?

3. (a) What is a monopoly? (b) What are the advantages of monopolies? (c) What problems may they create?

A large corporation is not necessarily a monopoly. Consider Chrysler, Ford, General Motors.

② What Have Labor and Business Done to Solve the Problems of the Machine Age?

So far, we have considered three problems brought about by the growth of industry and business: (1) Natural resources have been wasted. (2) The country has experienced periods of boom and depression. (3) Some of the giant

business concerns that have grown up have tried to establish monopolies. These three problems affect all American citizens. There have been other problems, however, which have more directly affected industrial workers themselves.

COAL MINERS often meet danger in their work. This diorama shows rescue operations following a coal mine explosion.

WORKERS UNITE TO IMPROVE CONDITIONS

You have already learned how the use of machinery and the growth of factories changed conditions for many workers. Operating a machine usually means doing the same thing over and over again. The work is likely to be less interesting than handwork, where the workman has a variety of tasks to do. In addition, carrying out only one or two steps at a machine requires less skill than many kinds of handwork. As a result, workers can more easily be replaced and their jobs are less secure. The use of machines also has an effect on wages. To illustrate these points, let us turn once more to Mr. Jackson's factory in the 1890's.

Mr. Jackson keeps his labor costs down. Mr. Jackson likes the men who work in his factory. At the same time, the wages he pays them are an important part of the cost of making chairs. Mr. Jackson, therefore, offers them the lowest wages they will accept and still continue to work for him. He also wants the workers to do as much work as possible in return for their wages. For this reason they must work

steadily and hard for long hours each day. The workers, on their part, respect Mr. Jackson. Now that the factory is larger and employs more workmen, however, they see less of Mr. Jackson than in the old days. The workers have a feeling that Mr. Jackson is not as interested in their welfare as he was when the factory was smaller. They also believe that they have to work too many hours and that their wages are too low.

Dissatisfied workers join together to win better conditions. Like Mr. Jackson, most factory owners at this time paid workers as low wages as possible. In many factories, also, little attention was paid to the health and safety of the employees. Accidents often crippled workers, making it difficult for them to earn a living. Such conditions made workers discontented. And in times of depression when they lost their jobs, they grumbled still more. "It's unfair," they said, "after we have worked hard and faithfully for our employer in good times, that he should fire us as soon as business falls off."

What could a single workman in the mines, the mills, or the factories do to obtain higher wages or better working conditions? Unhappily there was very little he could do. His boss might simply fire him and hire someone else in his place. But if a great number of workmen were to join together and demand changes, they might succeed in improving their wages and working conditions. An employer could not replace large numbers of workers as easily as he could fill one man's job. As the old saying goes, "In union there is strength." This idea of union led to the formation of *labor unions.*

Some labor unions were formed as early as the 1830's (Chapter 14), but these early attempts were not lasting. Most people at that time were farmers, so that the number of workers in industry who were affected by low pay or poor conditions was limited. Also, most early unions were local; they did not bring together large numbers of workers throughout the country.

The Knights of Labor is organized. When business and industry began to expand after the Civil War, more and more workers felt the need to band together for better conditions. In 1869, a Philadelphia tailor, named Uriah S.

Stephens, founded a union known as the *Knights of Labor.* The Knights of Labor was a single big union open to all workers, both those doing tasks that required long training and those engaged in simple tasks. Nor did it matter whether they were men or women, Negro or white.

At first the Knights of Labor grew slowly. After the union had succeeded in getting a number of employers to treat their workers better, however, hundreds of thousands joined. But the Knights of Labor was not always wisely led. And it was difficult for so many different kinds of people, in so many different kinds of jobs, to work together well in a single union. The Knights of Labor, therefore, lost power rapidly. By the 1890's it had practically disappeared.

The American Federation of Labor is founded. In a shop in New York City worked a young cigarmaker named Samuel Gompers. When he was a boy, he and his parents had come from England to seek a new life in America. As his nimble fingers flew at his task, Gompers thought and talked about the problems of workingmen. Instead of a big general union like the

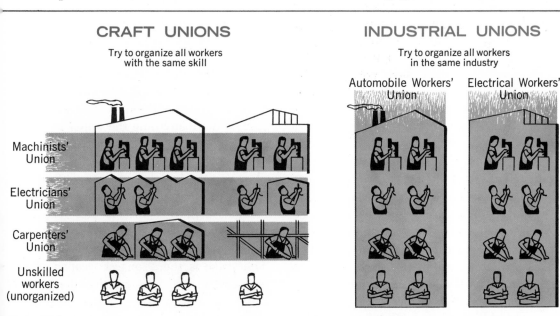

CRAFT UNIONS
Try to organize all workers with the same skill

Machinists' Union

Electricians' Union

Carpenters' Union

Unskilled workers (unorganized)

INDUSTRIAL UNIONS
Try to organize all workers in the same industry

Automobile Workers' Union   Electrical Workers' Union

Knights of Labor, Gompers believed that there should be a separate union for skilled workers in each trade or craft — a cigarmakers' union, a carpenters' union, a hatmakers' union, or a steamfitters' union. Skilled workers are those who have special training and experience. Therefore, they are harder to replace than unskilled workers. Gompers believed that employers would have to listen to the requests of large groups of skilled workers.

In 1886, the American Federation of Labor was organized. It was based on many of Gompers' ideas. Local unions of skilled workers were formed in many trades. The local unions of each trade or craft were then joined in state and national groups. Gompers was the first president of the American Federation of Labor, and held the office for almost 40 years.

The CIO is founded on a new idea. For a long time the American Federation of Labor (commonly called the AFL) was the chief labor organization in the country. Its membership numbered in the millions. Then, in the 1930's, another strong labor organization developed. This was the Congress of Industrial Organizations, or CIO.

Why did the CIO grow up as a rival of the AFL? As you know, the AFL was made up of unions of skilled workers. This meant that there were large numbers of unskilled workers who did not belong to the AFL. The CIO was based on the idea of *industrial* rather than *craft* unions. An industrial union takes into its membership all the workers in a particular industry. The CIO recruited most of its members from mass-production industries which employ large numbers of workers, such as the steel, rubber, and automobile industries. The leader in starting the CIO was John L. Lewis, forceful and powerful head of the United Mine Workers' Union.

The AFL and the CIO became keen rivals. For years each tried to add new

unions and to increase its membership. Some workers were members of smaller independent unions, like the four Railroad Brotherhoods, but many workers belonged to no union. Then, in 1955, the two large union organizations united in the AFL–CIO. This powerful union had 15 million members when it was formed.

HOW HAVE LABOR UNIONS TRIED TO WIN BETTER WORKING CONDITIONS?

Unions use arbitration and strikes to gain their ends. When union leaders representing a group of workingmen ask an employer for higher wages, shorter hours of work, or better conditions, the employer may refuse to grant the request. The union can then try to persuade him that its request is fair and should be granted. Often when representatives of the union and the employer sit down together to discuss terms, they are able to reach an agreement. This is called *collective bargaining*.

If the union and the employer cannot agree, the union may take its demand before a board of fair-minded men. When the members of the board have studied all sides of the question, they try to reach a decision which both the employer and the union will accept. This method of settling labor disputes is called *arbitration*.

If no agreement can be reached, however, is there anything the union workingmen can do to force their employer to grant their request? Naturally the employer needs the labor of his workers if he is to carry on his business. So if other methods fail, the workers can refuse to work. When many men at the same time refuse to work, this action is called a *strike*. The strike is the strongest weapon workingmen can use. Some strikes have been small and unimportant; others have been widespread and costly. Let us follow the story of one early strike.

John L. Lewis later took the United Mine Workers' Union out of the CIO.

SAMUEL GOMPERS

arrived from England when he was thirteen, and had to go to work instead of attending school.

EVENING CLASSES at Cooper Union in New York helped satisfy young Gompers' zeal for learning. For 20 years he attended lectures there, and formed a club with his young friends to debate important issues of the time.

A CIGARMAKER like his father, Gompers was often chosen to read aloud to his fellow workers. In the discussions that followed, he became familiar with their opinions and problems. Using this knowledge, he took the lead in organizing a labor union among the cigarmakers.

NATIONWIDE UNIONS were Gompers' goal as first president of the new American Federation of Labor. At the humble one-room AFL headquarters, and traveling across the country, he tried to organize the skilled workers of every craft into unions of their own.

LEADER of the growing AFL, Gompers was hailed by American labor unions as their chief spokes-man. For 40 years he fought for the right of working men to organize and bargain with employers for better working conditions.

A railroad strike occurs in 1877. After the Panic of 1873 (page 472), jobs were hard to get, and workers' families were suffering. The railroad companies believed that men would take work at any wages, no matter how low, rather than be idle and hungry. In the summer of 1877, therefore, the railroads east of the Mississippi announced that the wages of all railroad workers would be cut ten per cent. The men went out on strike.

This was the first big strike ever held in the United States. It was also one of the most bitter. When the strike began, trains could not run for lack of men to operate them. But the railroad companies were as determined to break the strike as the strikers were to stop the trains. In city after city — Baltimore, Pittsburgh, Reading, Buffalo, Columbus, Chicago, and St. Louis — fierce riots took place. In Pittsburgh, for example, 25 people were killed and many more wounded. The Union Station was burned, and 125 locomotives and 2000 freight cars were destroyed.

In the end this strike failed. The men had to have wages to live, so they could not stay out on strike indefinitely. When federal troops were finally called in to restore order, the railroad workers sullenly accepted the lowered wages and went back to work. But such a failure only made workingmen feel more convinced than ever that they must have powerful unions to improve working conditions.

Unions continue their battle for better conditions. Since the railroad strike of 1877, there have been many long and bitter and costly strikes. In 1886 a struggle for an eight-hour work day was marked by the "Haymarket riot." A bomb exploded in Haymarket Square, Chicago, killing and wounding many people. Another strike in the steel mills at Homestead, Pennsylvania, in 1892 caused the loss of a number of lives. Twenty-six men were

killed in a coal mine strike at Herrin, Illinois, in 1922. Strikes in the steel and automobile industries in the depression days of the 1930's caused much bitterness.

Often unions tried to make strikes more effective by organizing *picket lines;* that is, the strikers would form lines around the shop or factory against which they were striking. The pickets would urge other workers or customers not to cross the picket line to enter the shop or factory. When employers hired strikebreakers to cross the picket lines, fighting would often break out. Sometimes, too, employers would call in police to break strikes. Strikes in our own day still arouse bitter feelings, but they are not likely to be so violent.

Since the early 1930's, unions have become more powerful. They have built up large welfare funds to help their members. They continue to work for higher wages, shorter hours, and better working conditions. Unions have also sought to force employers to hire union workers. They have worked against the *open shop,* which employs both union and non-union workers. (A factory which hires only union members is called a *closed shop.* In a *union shop,* workers must join the union within a certain period of time after they are hired.)

In our fast-changing world both employers and workers face new problems. Workers, especially those who have no special skill, fear that automation (page 450) may affect their jobs. And in recent years, manufacturing in countries where costs and wages are lower threatens America's position of industrial leadership.

EMPLOYERS INTRODUCE IMPROVEMENTS IN WORKING CONDITIONS

Although labor unions have done much to improve the lot of their members, better conditions have also been brought about by

SAFETY DEVICES are essential equipment in modern industry. A safety mask protects this workman's eyes and face from flying sparks.

employers. More and more employers have come to realize that contented workers do more and better work than those who are worried or dissatisfied. Such employers listen carefully to requests for better wages and shorter working hours and to suggestions for improvements. They provide lunchrooms and opportunities for sports and recreation on the factory grounds. They safeguard the health of their workers by employing nurses and doctors and by providing plenty of fresh air and good lighting. Safety fixtures attached to the machinery help to prevent accidents. Some companies enable their workers to buy shares of stock and thus become part owners of the company and share in its profits. In addition, a large number of companies now provide paid vacations, health insurance, and pension plans for their retired employees.

CHECK UP

1. (a) How did machines make the jobs of factory workers less secure? (b) What working conditions made workers dissatisfied?

2. (a) Why did workers form unions? (b) What groups were included in the Knights of Labor? (c) How did the AFL and CIO differ in organization?

3. (a) What methods have unions used to win their demands? (b) How have unions become more powerful? (c) How have employers improved working conditions?

There are advantages in permitting a monopoly, e.g. in such local services as water, telephone, electricity, gas, bus transportation.

3 How Has Government Tried to Solve Some Problems of Business and Industry?

In a democracy, the people request the government to do things which they want done but cannot do themselves. When the rapid growth of business and industry brought about certain problems, both our national and state governments did something about them.

Harmful monopolies are outlawed. One of the problems, as we have seen (pages 472–473), was the forming of monopolies. To prevent groups of corporations or trusts from setting up harmful monopolies, Congress in 1890 passed the *Sherman Anti-Trust Law*. The Sherman Act prohibited businesses that shipped products between states or to other nations from setting up monopolies. This meant that no trust could control the sale of oil or sugar or beef or other products in more than one state.

For a number of years, however, the government did not strictly enforce the Sherman Law. Even when the government did try to break up monopolies, the attempts were not always successful. Oftentimes the companies which the government accused of being monopolies took their cases to court and won. Congress in later years, therefore, passed other laws to break up monopolies. The *Clayton Act* (1914) clearly stated what kinds of business combinations were unlawful.

The government regulates some monopolies. It should be remembered that monopolies are not harmful just because they are big. Rather they are harmful when they try to get unfair advantages as a result of their bigness. In some kinds of business the government recognizes that it would be unwise to forbid monopolies. Electric or telephone service, for example, is more efficient if it is provided by a single business organization rather than by a number of small, separate companies. Instead of forbidding monopolies in such cases, Congress decided to control them. In 1887, Congress passed the *Interstate Commerce Act* to regulate the rates which railroads could charge when hauling freight between states. Later, it also approved laws regulating telephone, telegraph, and radio companies. In such cases, monopolies are not broken up but are required to furnish good service at fair rates to the public, as well as profits to the owners.

Laws regulate the use of harmful products. The government has also found it necessary to pass laws to prevent the manufacture and sale of harmful products. For example, in the early 1900's, Congress passed a law which allowed government officials to inspect meat sold in interstate trade and the conditions under which it

was packed. Meat which has passed inspection carries a government stamp. Another law, the *Pure Food and Drugs Act,* forbade the manufacture and sale of impure or dishonestly labeled foods and drugs. President Theodore Roosevelt, during whose term this law was adopted, said, "No man may poison the people for his private profit." Later laws have further tightened regulations against impure foods, drugs, and cosmetics. Today, when you buy any packaged food or drugs, the label must tell you exactly what it contains.

The states pass labor laws. The government has also passed laws to protect workers. Most of the early labor laws were passed not by the national government but by various states. State laws provided the following kinds of regulations:

(1) *Work by women and children.* To run machines requires less strength and skill than to do work by hand. Women and children, with machines to help them, could do the work as well as men. But for women and children to work twelve or fourteen hours a day, as men did in some industries, seemed harmful and dangerous. So laws were passed by many states limiting the number of hours a woman or child could work in a day.

(2) *Working conditions.* Workers often had to do their jobs under dangerous or unhealthy conditions — in bad air, in unsafe mines, or with materials that might injure their health. They might be employed in factories which were poorly lighted, badly heated, or unsanitary. Laws were passed to protect working men and women from such harmful conditions.

(3) *Accidents.* Even though working conditions were improved, accidents could not be prevented entirely. Therefore, many states passed *employers' liability* or *workmen's compensation laws.* Such laws required the employer to pay the worker for injuries suffered on the job. At first

State and local governments also protect the public health, e.g. the state licenses physicians. A city may inspect restaurants to make sure they meet health standards.

the laws applied only to especially dangerous occupations. Later, they were extended to other types of work as well.

(4) *Minimum wages.* When wages were so low that a person could not earn a decent living, the states passed laws fixing the lowest wages that could be paid.

The national government passes laws to assist workers. During the great depression of the 1930's, the national government passed several laws to aid workers. Among them were the following:

(1) *The National Labor Relations Act.* Many strikes were brought about not only by poor wages and working conditions but because employers refused to do business with labor unions. The National Labor Relations Act, more commonly called the *Wagner Act,* upheld the right of workers to form unions and to bargain collectively with their employers. It also gave the National Labor Relations Board the power to keep employers "from engaging in any unfair labor practices."

(2) *The Social Security Act.* This law, which was passed in 1935, has had far-reaching effects. It provides payments to workers who are sick or unemployed and to older men and women when they retire. The funds to cover these payments are contributed both by workers themselves and by employers. Social Security benefits relieve people of some of their worry about losing jobs, falling sick, or being unable to support themselves in their later years. Social Security has had another effect. Because people receive payments even when they cannot work, they can still make purchases. This prevents business from falling off and makes depressions less likely.

(3) *Wages and Hours Act.* This law regulated the hours of work and minimum wages to be paid to workers who made goods sold in interstate trade. Since the 1930's both the Wages and Hours Act and the Social Security Act have been

changed several times to provide greater benefits for more workers.

The national government passes laws to regulate labor unions. By the mid-1900's, labor unions in the United States had grown strong. They had more members and their leaders had a great deal of power. Just as in earlier years our national government passed laws to regulate huge business concerns, it now passed laws to regulate unions. In 1947 the Taft-Hartley Act placed limits on certain union activities. Among other things, it (1) outlawed the closed shop, (2) required a 60-day "cooling off" period before a union could strike, and (3) provided that both employers and unions might sue each other for breaking contracts. Twelve years later Congress passed the Landrum-Griffin Act to safeguard the rights of union members in such matters as union elections and dues. It also forbade Communists, racketeers, and convicts to hold union offices.

When the Wagner Act was passed, business leaders protested that it gave unfair advantages to labor unions. On the other hand, labor leaders bitterly criticized the Taft-Hartley and Landrum-Griffin Acts. In a democracy, we should remember, the rights of all — employers, workers, and the general public — must be protected. In solving the problems brought by the Machine Age, labor, industry, and government have all had a share.

CHECK UP

1. (a) How has the national government regulated monopolies? (b) How has it regulated the manufacture and sale of food and drugs?

2. (a) What kinds of laws have state governments passed to protect workers? (b) What laws has the national government passed to protect workers? (c) How has the government regulated labor unions?

Check Up on Chapter 23

Do You Know the Meaning?

1. profit
2. conserve
3. boom
4. panic
5. depression
6. recession
7. monopoly
8. picket line
9. labor union
10. strike
11. trust
12. closed shop
13. union shop
14. arbitration
15. prosperity
16. collective bargaining

Can You Identify?

1. Clayton Act
2. Wagner Act
3. 1887
4. 1890
5. 1929
6. 1947
7. John L. Lewis
8. AFL
9. CIO
10. Sherman Act
11. Knights of Labor
12. Interstate Commerce Act
13. Pure Food and Drugs Act
14. Samuel Gompers
15. Social Security Act
16. Wages and Hours Act
17. Taft-Hartley Act
18. Landrum-Griffin Act

What Do You Think?

1. (a) How have machines helped workers? (b) Why have workers sometimes opposed the use of new machines?
2. (a) Have big corporations helped the industrial growth of the United States? (b) Could this growth have taken place if there had been only small companies? Explain.
3. (a) Why has the government passed legislation to regulate business? (b) Why has government also passed laws to regulate labor unions?
4. Can disputes between workers and employers affect the welfare of the general public? Explain.
5. Do booms and depressions affect agriculture as well as industry? Why?
6. Do you think that labor laws are needed or should workers and employers be able to settle their own problems? Why?

The fact that the national government has passed laws both to help and to regulate industry and labor suggests that its role is that of an umpire. The government always has responsibility for furthering the general welfare. See questions #3 and 4.

LINKING PAST AND PRESENT

Labor Day. An important American holiday is Labor Day, the first Monday in September. In 1882, the Knights of Labor established the first Labor Day to honor the American workingman. The idea of a workers' holiday soon became popular. In 1894, Congress made Labor Day a national holiday, and Americans have enjoyed this holiday ever since.

Wall Street once had a wall. The story of Wall Street — the famous street in New York City — goes back to the days when the Dutch came to the New World. In the 1620's, you remember, the Dutch founded the town of New Amsterdam on Manhattan Island. Later, the hot-tempered governor, Peter Stuyvesant, built a wall at the lower end of Manhattan to keep out the Indians and also the

English. The narrow street along the wall was known as Wall Street. But the wall did little good against the English, for in 1664 New Amsterdam surrendered to them and became the city of New York. As New York City grew, Wall Street became important. By 1870, it was a busy trading center for stocks and bonds.

Today Wall Street is the heart of one of the world's great financial districts. Here are located not only the New York Stock Exchange but also the main offices of huge industrial corporations, banking concerns, and other businesses. The term "Wall Street" is often used to refer to big bankers and powerful financial interests in the United States, whether they have offices on Wall Street or not.

New Methods of Farming Create
New Problems

Industrial workers clearly depend on farmers for food. But can one say that farms are primarily responsible for the nation's industrial growth?

What this chapter is about —

Farming is important to every nation, large or small. A country that cannot produce enough food for its people has to depend on other nations for its food supply. An American statesman, William Jennings Bryan, once expressed the importance of farming in these words:

✳ . . . The great cities rest upon our broad and fertile prairies. Burn down your cities and leave our farms, and your cities will spring up again as if by magic; but destroy our farms, and the grass will grow in the streets of every city in the country.

From its early days, our country has been more fortunate than many nations.

Because there were tremendous areas of fertile soil in this country, farmers were able to provide enough food for our rapidly growing population. Even before the time of the Civil War, changes had taken place in the size of farms, in the crops raised on them, and in the tools and methods used by farmers. In the years since 1865, however, new machinery and improved methods have affected farming to a far greater extent.

In this chapter we shall learn how the life of the American farmer has changed in the last hundred years and what new problems he has faced. In order to understand recent changes and problems, we shall answer the following questions:

People in our story — granger of the 1880's, agricultural scientist, county agent, modern farmer and wife.

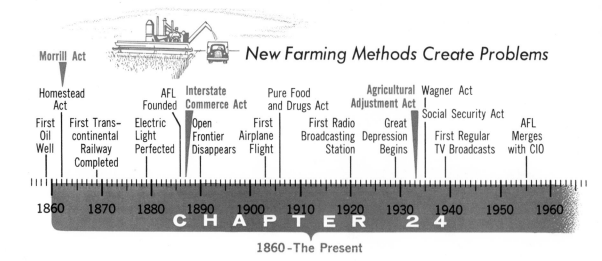

Morrill Act

New Farming Methods Create Problems

Homestead Act

AFL Founded · Interstate Commerce Act

Pure Food and Drugs Act

Agricultural Adjustment Act · Wagner Act

Social Security Act

First Oil Well

First Trans-continental Railway Completed

Electric Light Perfected

Open Frontier Disappears

First Airplane Flight

First Radio Broadcasting Station

Great Depression Begins

First Regular TV Broadcasts

AFL Merges with CIO

1860   1870   1880   1890   1900   1910   1920   1930   1940   1950   1960

CHAPTER 24

1860 - The Present

▷ 1. How did new machines and new methods change farm production?

▷ 2. How did changes in farming bring new problems?

▷ 3. How did farmers try to overcome their problems?

▷ 4. How has the government tried to help the farmers?

There still are examples of subsistence farming in this country in the sense that the farm "provides a living" for the farm family.

1 How Did New Machines and New Methods Change Farm Production?

To understand better the great changes which have taken place on America's farms since 1865, let us first get a picture of farming in the 1840's.

Small farms provide a living. In the South, as you know, there were large plantations where cotton and other crops were raised to be sold abroad (Chapter 15). Most American farms in the 1840's, however, were small. Except on special occasions, when his neighbors lent a helping hand, the farmer and his family did all their own work. Frequently the farmer had only a few simple tools with which to till the soil. These included a plow, a scythe, a wooden "cradle" for harvesting the grain, and a few others. In addition to human strength, the farmer relied on the help of horses, mules, or oxen.

His farm was not a means of *earning a*

living in the sense in which we use these words today. Nowadays most men work, are paid wages, and buy what they need with the money they receive. But the small farms of the 1840's brought little money to the farmer. Instead, the farm *provided a living* for him and his family. The farmer raised most of his family's food, as well as most of the materials from which they made their clothes. He sold a few hogs and cattle and some wheat or corn or oats. With the small amount of cash he received, the farmer bought the few things he could not raise or make at home.

Some improvement in farm tools takes place. It would be wrong, however, to think that the farmer in the 1840's produced his crops in exactly the same manner as had his father and grandfather.

484

Certain improvements in farm tools had already taken place. To the wooden plow of colonial days, a clumsy and inefficient tool at best, had been added an iron tip and iron sheathing on the sides. A few plows with blades entirely of iron had been made. Some new plows also appeared with slight changes in shape. With them the plowman could easily cut a straight furrow in the soil, clean and deep. In addition, plows were manufactured with parts which could be easily replaced if they were broken or damaged.

There were other improved farm implements as well as some new ones. A horse-drawn hayrake, which could do the work of eight or ten men, came into use in the 1820's. Some machines for planting seeds had also been developed. One very important invention speeded up the harvesting of grain. Farmers in earlier times had not planted large fields of grain because cutting the grain by hand was so slow. In the 1830's, a Virginian named Cyrus McCormick patented a successful *reaper.* Drawn by horses, it swept the grain stalks against a cutter and dropped them in large bundles. Workers followed the reaper and tied up these bundles, making what are called *sheaves.* Still another step was the development of a *thresher.* This machine could separate the grain from the husks, or chaff, much more rapidly than it could be done by hand.

Many advances in farm machinery take place after 1865. In spite of these improvements and new machines, most farmers in the 1840's still had to work very hard to make a living from their small farms. During the next fifty years, however, far-reaching improvements in farm tools and machinery completely changed farming. In 1869, James Oliver perfected a plow of steel, a much stronger and tougher material than iron. *Planters* were

FARMERS of the early 1800's sowed their seed by hand and used few machines.

developed that would cut the furrows, break up the clods of earth, and plant the grain in several rows at a time. New *seeders* could sow the seed, cover it with earth, and spread fertilizer on the soil all at the same time.

Even more striking changes took place in reapers. By about 1860, there were reapers in use which not only cut the wheat but even tied it into sheaves automatically. Finally, there was a giant machine, almost human in its skill, that crossed a field of wheat and cut, threshed, and cleaned the wheat, and put it into bags. When this *combine* began its work, there was only a field of waving grain; when the combine had finished, the grain was ready for the market.

New sources of power aid farmers. After 1865 farmers' tasks were lightened not only by new machines but also by

THEY REAPED the ripe grain with cradle scythes and loaded the sheaves on wagons.

KANSAS FARMERS use gasoline-powered harvesting machines to cut and thresh wheat. Notice the farm in the background with the windmill to pump water for cattle.

new kinds of power to run them. At first, farm machines were drawn by horses; later, some machines were driven by steam power. Soon after 1920, tractors, powered first by a gasoline and later by a diesel engine, pulled the plow or the seeder or the combine. Farmers also found many different uses for electrical power, although power lines did not reach farm areas as early as they came to cities and towns. (By 1955, however, almost all farms were served by electricity.) In addition, the rapid growth of industry made it possible to manufacture new and better farm machines at a lower cost. Although the purchase of farm machines still required a large investment of money, more farmers were able to buy them. Not only did the farmer have less to do by hand, but machines did the work faster and better.

THE IMPROVEMENT IN FARM MACHINERY BRINGS CHANGES

Greater production is possible. Besides making his work easier, the new farm machinery permitted the farmer to do many times the work he had formerly done. A hard worker, using an old-fashioned cradle scythe, could cut perhaps an acre and a half of grain in a day. Using a reaper, he could cut ten or twelve acres.

To produce a bushel of wheat in 1840 took a little more than three hours of human labor; in 1894, it took only ten minutes. Much the same thing was true with corn. In 1840, about four hours and a half of human labor were required to produce a bushel of corn; by 1894, only about forty minutes were needed.

Larger farms are possible. With the new machinery, a farmer could take care of a small farm and have time to spare. Because the new machinery was expensive, however, few farmers could afford to buy machines and let them stand idle much of the time. If a farmer could plant larger crops, he could make greater use of his equipment. He could also earn larger profits and thus more easily pay for his new tools and machines. Farmers who could afford to do so, therefore, decided to buy more land, and the size of farms grew steadily. Although there are two million fewer farms today than in 1900, the average farm is now about two hundred acres larger than the average farm of 1900.

The farmer becomes a businessman. As farmers increased the size of their farms and purchased expensive machinery, many of them found that it paid to devote all their land and time to raising a single crop, such as wheat or cotton. This single crop, which they sold for cash, was called a

The increased use of machines and of power average, to produce food for more than 20 other persons.

enables a present-day farm worker, on the

A COTTON-PICKING MACHINE can harvest a field of cotton in a fraction of the time it would take a crew of hand-workers.

This cotton picker is a much more modern machine than the harvester on the opposite page.

money crop. With the cash they received from the money crop they bought whatever they needed. Sometimes they even bought food that formerly they would have grown on their own farms. So farming became more and more a means of *earning* a living rather than of *providing* a living. In fact, farming has become a business, and the farmer a businessman who depends on his profits for his living.

FARMERS DEVELOP WESTERN LANDS

In the years following the war between the North and South, farmers were buying new machinery and wondering how they might get enough land to use the machinery profitably. It was only natural for them to turn their thoughts to the unsettled lands west of the Mississippi. To those lands, as you learned in Chapter 21, they rushed in such numbers that by 1890 the open frontier had disappeared.

Some western lands lack sufficient rainfall. Where there was ample rainfall, the corn and wheat lands of the great plains produced fine crops. But many farmers were disappointed as they went farther west. In much of the western part of our country, there are years when

IRRIGATION is the key to successful farming in many parts of the West. In this New Mexico scene, water for the irrigation canals comes from the mountains seen in the background.

KERR DAM on the Flathead River supplies water for irrigating farm lands in Montana.

there is too little rainfall to grow farm crops. Sometimes the pioneers arrived in years when the rainfall was heavier than usual, and were deceived by the greenness of the land. But when normal dry years followed, crops wilted and died and the families fled from the dry land.

Dry lands become fertile farms. There was rich soil in many of these regions; all that was needed was water. Just as skillful men had invented new farm machinery, so others conquered the problem of growing crops in dry ground. This was largely done by *irrigation*, which means bringing water from a natural source through canals or pipes. Ditches then carry the water into the fields where it runs between the rows of plants or trees. The Mormons in Utah (page 430) had been especially successful in irrigating dry lands, and their example was followed by

Irrigation has also led to disputes between may divert from a given river.

later settlers. Farmers, of course, must pay the cost of irrigation, but many are willing to pay these costs rather than depend on uncertain rainfall.

In order to provide the water to irrigate large areas, the national government has built dams and reservoirs to collect and store water. Some of these dams are marvels of construction. Hoover Dam between Nevada and Arizona stores waters of the Colorado River to irrigate vast regions of the Southwest. Grand Coulee Dam on the Columbia River furnishes water for large sections of the Northwest. Fort Peck Dam and other dams on the Missouri River store up water for lands in Nebraska, the Dakotas, and Montana. In many western states, former desert lands now bloom with fruit trees and other crops.

Farmers have also developed a process known as *dry farming*. This method makes the best use of a small amount of rainfall. The soil is plowed deep before planting. After each rain it is cultivated in order to keep the soil loose. Loose soil not only holds the rain but prevents the moisture below from evaporating. Usually the farmer lets half his land lie idle each year, so that each crop he plants will have two years' supply of moisture.

CHECK UP

1. (a) Why is farming in the 1840's described as a way of "providing" a living? (b) What improvements had been made in farm tools by about 1860?

2. What new farm machines and methods have come into use in the last hundred years?

3. (a) How did new machinery make greater production possible? (b) Why have farms grown larger? (c) Why is farming now considered a business?

4. What methods of farming have been developed in areas of little rainfall?

states over the share of water which each

2 How Did Changes in Farming Bring New Problems?

Even under the best of conditions farming can be discouraging. Nature, upon which the farmer depends for a successful harvest, can often prove cruel. You have just read of the trouble farmers had when they settled on western lands where there was not enough rain. But sometimes there is too much rain and a crop is washed out. Whole crops can also be destroyed by frost, hail, tornadoes, dust storms, or insects. In short, the farmer must carry on a continual battle, often against forces that he cannot control.

Price changes seriously affect the farmer. Other difficulties began to plague the American farmer in the late 1800's. Many of them had to do with the problem of prices. The farmer of the 1840's had not been greatly troubled by prices because his small farm provided for most of his needs. For his son and grandson, however, the story was quite different. As modern farmers, they grew a money crop. If the price of this crop was high, they received a good income. If the price was low, they felt the pinch of hard times.

How are prices determined? Prices go up or down for several reasons. But probably nothing is more important in setting prices than what is known as the rule of *supply and demand.* You have no doubt seen how this rule works. Suppose a boy in your school has something everyone else wants — a sweater, an autographed baseball, a new record. If he has the only one of its kind, some of his schoolmates will offer him a high price for it. But if plenty of the articles are available, nobody will pay a high price for the one the boy possesses. In other words, when the *supply* is small and the *demand* is great, the price is high. But when the supply is equal to the demand or greater than the demand, the price is low. This rule of supply and demand also works with other goods. When fresh strawberries first appear in the summer, for example, the price is high because they are still scarce, and people are hungry for them. When the berries become plentiful, the price drops.

Farmers face low prices and high costs. Now let us see how this rule of supply and demand affected American farmers in the late 1800's. Because they were producing huge crops of wheat, oats, barley, corn, and cotton, the price of each product went down. Since more and more farmers were depending on money crops, lower prices caused hardship. At the same time, as you have learned, there had been a great rush to buy farm land. In other words, the supply of good farm land diminished as the demand for it increased. The price of land, therefore, rose steadily. To make matters worse, most farmers had not been able to pay cash for their farms; they had been forced to borrow money and pay high interest rates on it. Nor had most farmers paid cash for their expensive farm machinery. So, on the one hand, farmers

489

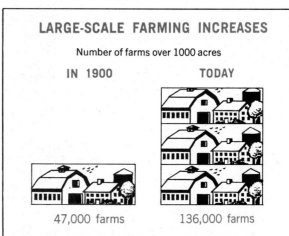

LARGE-SCALE FARMING INCREASES

Number of farms over 1000 acres

IN 1900   TODAY

47,000 farms   136,000 farms

Increased use of machinery has also led to an increase in the size of the average family-operated farm.

"We have enough grain already. We'll buy yours only at a lower price."

"It'll cost you more to ship your grain to market this year. The railroad has raised the rates again."

owed large amounts of money, while, on the other hand, they received less and less cash from their crops as prices fell. Farmers who could not meet the payments on their debts were in danger of losing their machinery and their farms.

Transportation costs rise. You might think that low prices, added to heavy debts for land and machinery, would make enough problems for farmers in the late 1800's. But they had other troubles, too. Trucks had not yet come into use, so farmers depended almost entirely on the railroads to carry their crops to market. A field of grain is a beautiful sight as it stands, but the grain is worth nothing until it reaches the buyers who want it. No matter how much money the railroads asked for shipping his crops, therefore, a farmer had to pay their price. Farmers, particularly in the West, believed that the railroads charged higher freight rates than were necessary. Many a farmer who sold his crop at low prices and had to pay high shipping costs found he had little or nothing to show for his year's labor.

The farmer tries producing larger crops. Facing all these troubles, the farmer at first said to himself: "It's easy to see what I should do about falling prices. If the selling price of a bushel of wheat or corn is $1.50, I get $150 for 100 bushels. If the price falls to $1, I'll get only $100 for my 100 bushels. To make up for the lowered price, I'll plan to raise 150 bushels." American farmers everywhere had the same thought. The result was that they produced larger crops than ever. But the more they produced, the bigger became the supply; and the bigger the supply became, the lower the price fell. This happened not only in the United States but all over the world. Thus the idea of producing more and more not only failed to increase farm incomes but made prices of farm products drop even lower.

Intense production ruins the soil. The idea of producing larger crops had another unfortunate result. It wore out the soil. The soil is somewhat like a man. A man can work hard and steadily for a long period of time, but then he needs

When the farmer becomes a businessman, his described for business.

problems become similar to those already

"You should have bought new equipment last year. Prices are on the way up."

"If we get together, we can elect Joe to Congress where maybe he can do something about our problems!"

change and refreshment. If he tries to work too long without resting, he wears himself out and becomes ill. It is the same with the soil. If a farmer uses the soil over and over again for the same crop, and if he fails to add fertilizer or to care for the soil in other ways, the earth simply wears out. Finally there comes a time when the soil cannot produce anything worthwhile.

American farmers had been in the habit of treating the land carelessly. When the first settlers landed in America, a wide continent stretched before them. Why worry if a little land should be worn out? There always was more to the west! Even after nearly all the land was occupied, farmers still acted as though they could wear out a piece of land and then move on to another.

The results of such careless use of the soil have been tragic. We have already seen how the soil in some parts of the South was worn out because cotton was grown on it year after year (page 292). Although we think of our country as rich, there are many areas where the soil has

been ill-treated. A traveler sees desolate stretches of worn-out land. Trees have been cut down; the land is bare. The forlorn remains of a house may still stand to remind the traveler of the men who thoughtlessly ruined the land. There are ugly gashes where the earth has been *eroded,* or washed away. Now, when heavy rains come, there is nothing to prevent them from turning into destructive floods. Experts say that at least a hundred million acres of American soil have been worn out and destroyed in this fashion. This is an area equal to the size of Maryland, North Carolina, Ohio, and Illinois!

CHECK UP

1. (a) What is the rule of supply and demand? (b) How did this rule affect American farmers in the late 1800's?

2. (a) How did high transportation costs affect the farmers? (b) Why did the production of larger crops only make the farmers' problem worse?

3. What practices have ruined large areas of farm land?

See Pandora's Box: The Story of Conservation.

491

3 How Did Farmers Try to Overcome Their Problems?

Debt, high interest on loans, high railroad rates, ever-larger crops and ever-falling prices, worn-out land — what a collection of difficult problems! Thousands of farmers, each worried by his own troubles, felt that such problems were too big for farmers to solve by themselves. But if they joined together, might they not overcome some of their troubles?

The farmers organize. One man who firmly believed that farmers should get together to work out their problems was Oliver H. Kelley. In 1867, he and a few friends organized a society known as the *National Grange of the Patrons of Husbandry,* commonly called the *Grange.* At first, few farmers showed interest in the Grange, but Kelley was not discouraged. He traveled about the country, talking to farmers and urging them to form local Grange chapters. During the 1870's the Grange took root in many states. It was especially strong in the Midwest — in Indiana, Illinois, Wisconsin, Minnesota, and Iowa.

What could the Grange do to help its farmer-members? It could teach them to plan their work better. It could teach them that better prices could be obtained by marketing their crops in groups rather than as individuals. It could point out that farmers were not wise to depend too much on a single money crop. The Grange could show them how, as a united group, they could better fight the high freight rates charged by the railroads. Also, as a group, they could demand lower interest rates from the banks on loans for farms and farm machinery. All these things the Grange did, and more. At the Grange meetings, men, women, and children from lonely farms were brought together for friendly visits and good times.

The farmer turns to politics for help. The Grange, and other organizations like it, convinced farmers that united in groups they could gain greater power. "But," thought many farmers, "the best way to protect ourselves is to get laws passed that will get us what we want." Soon after 1870, therefore, farmers in several states formed political groups. They voted for governors and members of state legislatures who were interested in farm problems and succeeded in electing a number of these candidates. As a result, the legislatures of several states passed laws compelling railroads to charge lower freight rates for shipping farm products to market. In the late 1870's, the railroads fought these state laws in the courts but were unsuccessful.

Most railroads, however, ran through more than one state. In 1886 the United States Supreme Court decided that interstate railroad rates were a matter for the national government rather than the states to control. Farmers then brought pressure on members of Congress to take action on railroad rates. In 1887, as you have learned, Congress passed the *Interstate Commerce Act* (page 480). This law forbade railroads to charge unreasonable railroad rates or to engage in other unfair acts, many of which had been harmful to the farmers. It provided for a committee of five members called the *Interstate Commerce Commission.* People who had complaints against the railroads could bring them to this commission. In 1920, the commission was given power to set the rates to be charged by railroads.

EROSION did this. Over a period of years uncontrolled floods have cut deep gorges into a once fertile plain.

The western farmer joins political parties. Many farmers also joined national political parties which promised to help their cause. One of these parties was called the *National Greenback Party.* Its members wanted to keep in use large amounts of the paper money issued by the government during the war between the North and the South (page 409). These bills were called *greenbacks* because they were printed with green ink. The western farmers supported the Greenback Party because they believed that the more money there was, the higher farm prices would be and the more easily they could pay their debts. The Greenback Party, however, did not win enough supporters to carry out its program.

Many farmers also supported the *Populist* ("people's") *Party,* which appeared about 1890. The Populists promised to coin large quantities of silver dollars and to carry out reforms favorable to the farmers. The Populists succeeded in electing several members to Congress. In 1896 some Populist ideas were taken over by the Democratic Party. In the election that year, therefore, many of the farmers, especially in the West and the South, enthusiastically supported William Jennings Bryan,

the Democratic candidate for President. Bryan sympathized with the western farmers and spoke eloquently of their problems. His stirring speeches won him the title of "the silver-tongued orator of the West." The presidential campaign of 1896 was one of the most exciting in American history. In the end, Bryan was defeated by the Republican candidate, William McKinley.

Trouble hits the farmer in the 1920's. In the early 1900's, the future looked a little brighter to the farmer. European nations were beginning to buy more farm products from the United States, such as beef and wheat. So Americans received higher prices for their products. When World War I broke out in 1914, European farmers had to leave their farms to fight in defense of their countries. The demand for American farm products, therefore, increased enormously. To grow larger crops, American farmers borrowed money and bought more land and machinery. But at the close of the war the demand for farm products dropped off. European farmers returned to their farms, and the European countries began to buy more wheat from Argentina and Canada. They also turned to other markets for cotton and beef.

The Populists also favored a graduated income **493** tax, the direct election of senators, postal savings banks, the secret ballot, and an eight-hour day for government workers.

Once more the American farmer found himself in trouble. His huge crops were more than the United States needed. Farm prices dropped to less than one third of what they had been during the war. Farmers could not pay their taxes or their debts. During the 1920's, many a farmer lost his farm because he was unable to pay even the interest on his debts.

The farmer again seeks a remedy in politics. In addition to the Grange, several new farm organizations had grown up in the early 1900's. The *Farmer's Union,* which started in Texas, became a national organization. The *American Farm Bureau Federation* grew rapidly and had over two million members by 1920. These groups favored laws helpful to the farmer. Still another, the *Non-Partisan League,* worked actively for state laws to benefit the farmer.

Members of Congress from the farm states organized themselves into a group called a *farm bloc.* They had enough votes in Congress to pass laws to help the farmer. One law enabled farmers who borrowed money on their land to have a longer time to pay it back. Another law made it legal for farmers to organize in large groups called *co-operative associations,* which could get better prices for crops than an individual farmer could. Farmers' co-operatives today have about seven million members. People were beginning to realize that the farmers' problems are important to the whole nation and that the farmers' welfare is of concern to the government.

CHECK UP

1. What did the Granges do to help the farmers?

2. (a) Why did the farmers turn to politics to improve their lot? (b) What political parties did they join? (c) What did each party promise to do for the farmers?

3. (a) What problems did farmers face in the 1920's? (b) How did they try to solve these problems?

Farmers' co-operatives have been successful, for example, in the marketing of fruit -- safeguarding quality, introducing freezing and canning, maintaining an orderly flow of production to market, and using advertising to increase sales.

 How Has the Government Tried to Help the Farmers?

You have just read about a few laws that were passed to help farmers. Actually the government has been aware of the farmer's problems for many years and has taken a number of steps to help solve them.

The government helps the farmer to raise larger and better crops. Here are a few of the many things the national government has done to assist American farmers:

(1) *Agricultural colleges.* In 1862, Congress passed the *Morrill Act.* Under this act the government set aside lands for the use of colleges which would teach agriculture and engineering. As a result, agricultural colleges have been established in every state in the Union. These colleges have done much to make farming scientific. They offer courses to young farmers. In these courses, for example, farmers learn what kind of crops to plant, how to increase the yield, what to feed cows to produce more milk, and how to prevent disease among farm animals. In the college laboratories, scientists carry on experiments. They study soil improvement, diseases that affect plants and animals, and countless other things. The colleges also

IN 1862 Representative Justin Morrill of Vermont (left) sponsored an act granting government lands to establish colleges. Among the 68 land-grant colleges is Colorado State University, founded in 1870 with 19 students. From the small campus shown below it has grown into a modern university with over 6000 students. Its agricultural research includes the use of Geiger counters (right).

have experimental farms where new methods of planting, fertilizing, stock-feeding, and other farm activities are tried out. At first, a good many farmers were suspicious of "new-fangled" ideas, but most farmers today realize that they need to know something about scientific farming to be successful.

(2) *The Department of Agriculture.* Another aid to the farmer is the United States Department of Agriculture, whose Secretary is a member of the President's Cabinet. The work of this department, which was first organized in 1862, is of great value to farmers. Its many bureaus carry on research dealing with farm problems of all kinds. The Department and its agents keep up a continual fight against animal and plant diseases. Soil conservation is one of its important interests. Its scientists study how to develop better plants and animals and how to find more uses for crops. The Department of Agriculture publishes bulletins giving the latest

information on an endless number of topics of interest to the farmer. It also publishes a *Yearbook* which summarizes the latest research on farm problems. These are only a few of the services the Department of Agriculture offers to farmers. The Weather Bureau, whose stations all over the country give warnings of storms, frosts, or heavy floods, was formerly a part of the Department of Agriculture. Now it is under the Department of Commerce.

(3) *Aid to states.* In addition to helping the farmer through the services of the Department of Agriculture, the national government has given money to the states to encourage agricultural education among farmers. In most states this work is carried on in connection with the state colleges of agriculture. Also, the government makes funds available to send a farming expert called a *county agent* to work directly with the farmers in a particular county and to give advice on all kinds of farm problems.

Research related to the development of improved **495** seed, better fertilizers, and the elimination of pests and blight has helped to increase yield.

MOUNTAINS of sugar beets piled outside a western processing plant suggest the huge crops that American farmers now raise every year.

(4) *Farm loans.* The national government has made it easier for the farmer to borrow money to pay for his land or to buy seed and machinery. Government agencies have been set up to help farmers obtain loans at fair rates of interest.

The ups and downs of prices continue to plague the farmer. The several kinds of government services just described helped American farmers to increase and improve their crops. But the problem of getting a fair price for their money crops continued to trouble farmers. Farm prices rose and fell because of conditions over which farmers had no control. As you remember, farmers had a hard time in the years following World War I. During the great depression of the 1930's, conditions went from bad to worse (page 472). Farm prices dropped still further, and more and more farmers lost their farms because they could not pay their debts. Then, during World War II, the demand for American farm products skyrocketed, and farmers again became prosperous. But a decline in farm prices during the 1950's once more caused farmers' incomes to drop.

Congress tackles the problem of farm prices. Beginning with the *Agricultural Adjustment Act* of 1933[1], Congress has passed a series of laws to give American farmers more direct aid. These laws have had different names but they have had several features or ideas in common:

(1) *Price supports.* To protect the farmer, the government sets minimum support prices for basic crops, such as wheat, corn, and cotton. These prices are usually based on the prices the farmer has to pay for the things he buys. If the prices of the things he buys go up, then the minimum support prices for his crops can be raised accordingly.

(2) *Control of production.* The government attempts to discourage farmers from raising too much corn, too much wheat, and so on. If, for example, the farmers raise less wheat than they have been growing, then the law of supply and demand will tend to keep the price of wheat up.

[1] This first Agricultural Adjustment Act was declared unconstitutional by the Supreme Court in 1936. Two years later, a second Agricultural Adjustment Act became law. This act was similar to the earlier law, but was written to avoid the objections of the Supreme Court.

(*Continued on page 499*)

Despite production controls, huge surpluses have **496** accumulated. Price supports have made it difficult to sell staple crops in the world market and have increased costs to manufacturers.

The Industrial Age

The toy above is a faithful copy in cast iron of one of the many new machines of the mid-1800's — a fire engine with steam-powered pumps. Note the boiler mounted on the rear. The Christmas scene at left is an old magic-lantern slide. It could be projected on the curtain of a stage while an entertainer sang an appropriate song. Hand-colored photographs (below) were also used as slides.

Engineers of the late 1800's built on a grand scale. Brooklyn Bridge (right) has 275-foot towers to support its steel cables.

Carriage-makers often designed the bodies of the first automobiles (below) and gave them the same lines as horse-drawn vehicles.

Wooden figures (above) were set up outside stores as a form of advertising to attract customers. This baseball player reflects the growing nationwide interest in sports.

The "new look" of growing American cities was captured in this painting by John Sloan of the corner of Sixth Avenue and 3rd Street in New York City. Pedestrians dodge an automobile (left) while elevated trains roar overhead.

SCIENTIFIC FARMING applies to the growing of fruit trees too. At left a tree is being planted. The mature trees (background) are sprayed to keep them free of diseases and destructive insects.

(3) *Soil conservation.* The government encourages farmers to build up worn-out land by fertilizing it properly and by planting certain soil-building crops. In so doing, farmers are helping to make less productive land more fertile and to conserve our nation's natural resources. At the same time the government's soil conservation program helps to reduce the number of acres planted with basic crops.

How well has government aid to farmers worked? The Agricultural Adjustment Act and other farm laws led to sharp differences of opinion among Americans. Some thought it was wrong to encourage farmers to raise less than they could produce. There were also objections to carrying on a costly government program for just a small part of the population. Others argued that the government had aided industry for many years by passing protective tariffs. Those who favored a government farm program also pointed out that farm income grew from a little over four billion dollars in 1932 to nearly twelve billion dollars in 1941.

During the 1950's, arguments over government aid to farmers continued. It appeared that the aid program was helping the big farm producers more than the small farmer. The government was burdened with huge surpluses of basic crops which it had bought to keep prices from going down. And sharp differences of opinion developed among farmers and members of Congress over the best method of tackling farm problems — whether to increase or reduce the government aid program. In spite of all the thought given to the farmers' problems, then, no final solution of them has yet been found.

CHECK UP

1. How has each of the following helped American farmers: (a) state agricultural colleges? (b) the Department of Agriculture? (c) county agents? (d) government farm loans?

2. How does each of the following types of government aid seek to help the farmer: (a) price supports? (b) production control? (c) encouragement of soil conservation?

Some critics of our farm program argue that efficient producers.

support prices are not needed by the more

Check Up on Chapter 24

Do You Know the Meaning?

1. scythe	7. surplus
2. thresher	8. diesel engine
3. combine	9. dry farming
4. money crop	10. farm bloc
5. irrigation	11. co-operatives
6. erode	12. county agent

13. rule of supply and demand

Can You Identify?

1. Grange	7. Oliver H. Kelley
2. 1862	8. Populist Party
3. 1933	9. National Green-
4. James Oliver	back Party
5. Morrill Act	10. William Jennings
6. Cyrus McCormick	Bryan

11. Department of Agriculture

What Do You Think?

1. (a) Explain how the rule of supply and demand affects prices. (b) What are some examples?

2. Farmers think of farming as a "way of life" as well as a way of earning a living. What does this mean?

3. Is it possible for American farmers to have hard times when Americans who work in business and industry are prosperous? Explain.

4. Many people in other countries, and even some Americans, do not get enough to eat. If that is the case, can the farmers produce too much food? Why have surplus crops been a problem for American farmers?

In answering #4, consider the fact that gifts of United States farm surpluses create a problem for countries which need to sell the same commodities to foreign lands.

LINKING PAST AND PRESENT

"Don't fence me in." A simple invention helped farming to become established on the western plains. This was the wire fence, so common today that we hardly notice it. East of the Mississippi there had been plenty of timber to make split rail fences around a farmer's fields. But farmers who settled on the prairies of the West found little timber there for fences. Then, in 1873, J. F. Glidden of Illinois patented an inexpensive wire fence. With their lands enclosed by wire fences, farmers could grow crops without danger of having them trampled by wandering cattle or sheep. At first, western cattle and sheep ranchers resented the fencing in of the land, and they had many battles with the farmers. The western cowboys, used to riding the open range with nothing in their way, were especially annoyed. In time, however, the stockmen learned that they could raise better animals if they knew where their herds were and could control them. The roaming cowboy was "fenced in,"

but western farming and cattle raising profited from the invention of the wire fence.

Young farmers in America. Many young people who live on farms belong to a 4–H Club ("head, heart, hands, and health"). These clubs began just before the First World War. They are directed by the United States Department of Agriculture and by the land-grant colleges, and their aim is to train better farmers and better citizens. In 4–H Clubs, farm boys or girls compete with each other to see who can grow the finest cows or pigs or the best corn or wheat. The girls try to outdo each other at cooking and sewing. Club members also study good citizenship, help hungry children in foreign lands, and get together just to have fun, too.

The United States Office of Education also plays an important part in helping to train good farmers. It directs an organization called Future Farmers of America. The FFA co-operates with high schools in setting up courses in agriculture. These courses teach young farmers how to raise better animals and crops, repair farm machinery, and so on. The members of Future Farmers of America often meet for good times, too. But the chief goal of the 4-H Clubs and the FFA is to help young Americans become well-informed, efficient farmers.

Buffalo still roam.   Fertile farms and great ranches now cover much of the land where herds of buffalo once grazed. But if you know where to look, you can still see buffalo roaming over the western grasslands. These herds are carefully fenced in and protected by the United States government. At one time fifty million or more of the shaggy beasts grazed on the grasslands of the West.

Then, as Americans pushed westward, vast numbers of buffalo were killed for their meat and hides and often merely for sport. This slaughter went on until the late 1800's, when Americans finally woke up to the fact that the buffalo had almost disappeared. In 1894 the national government passed a law prohibiting the killing of these animals. By that time there were only a few hundred wild buffalo left in the United States. In the early 1900's, the government set aside land where the buffalo would be protected. Today Montana, Oklahoma, North Dakota, and Nebraska have national buffalo refuges. In the last fifty years the herds have increased to several thousand head, and fortunately the American buffalo is no longer in danger of dying out.

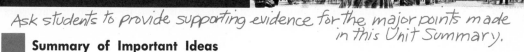

TO CLINCH YOUR

UNDERSTANDING OF

Unit 7

Ask students to provide supporting evidence for the major points made in this Unit Summary.

Summary of Important Ideas

In Unit Seven you have read how farming and industry developed after the Civil War.

1. After 1865, farming and industry expanded rapidly.
   a. The Homestead Act and the transcontinental railroad encouraged settlers to come to the great plains and Rocky Mountain region. Although the Indians fought bitterly against the advancing white man, the region was opened to mining, ranching, and farming.
   b. The growth of industry was made possible by our great natural resources, a large labor supply, foreign investments, inventions, and improved methods for the mass production of goods. Improved transportation and communication knit the country together and also promoted industrial expansion by speeding up production and selling.
   c. The invention and increased use of farm machinery, as well as improved transportation, revolutionized agriculture.

2. The growth of industry and increased agricultural production have been accompanied by a number of problems.
   a. Business has tended to follow a "boom, panic, and depression" pattern. The "ups and downs" of business have caused suffering to employers and employees and also to the general public.
   b. To further their interests, manufacturers have tended to create monopolies.

To improve their condition, workers have organized unions. The government has sought to regulate business, industry, and labor in the public interest.

c. Farming, like manufacturing, has tended to follow a boom and depression pattern. Among the problems of the farmer are debt, high interest rates, "overproduction" and falling prices, and worn-out land.

d. To meet these problems the farmer has formed such organizations as the Grange, and has turned to politics. He has received much help from the government and from agricultural colleges.

3. Increasingly, people have come to understand that the welfare of one group depends on the welfare of other groups. Farmers depend on city dwellers, and the other way around. Likewise, employers and employees depend on each other, and so also do consumers and producers.

Unit Review

1. (a) Why did settlers in large numbers move to the great plains and Rocky Mountain region after the Civil War? (b) What were the results?

2. (a) How have improved communication and transportation led to increased production in agriculture and industry? (b) What other factors help to explain the great expansion of American industry after 1865?

3. (a) How has farming changed in the last hundred years? (b) Why have these changes taken place?

4. (a) Why have agriculture and industry tended to follow a "boom, panic, and depression" pattern? (b) What problems have arisen as a result?

5. (a) How has each of the following groups tried to protect its special interests: manufacturers, workers, farmers? (b) How has the government tried to help these groups and also the general public?

Gaining Skill

How to Explore Local History

Some American communities were first settled in the early 1600's; others have been started much more recently. But any community, old or young, contains interesting records and remains which you may use to get a better understanding of the past.

Just as this book has presented the story of the nation's early beginnings, so you can prepare an account of your own community's beginnings and growth. Your class could write a play, an article for the local newspaper, or even a book of stories about your community's "yesterdays." One class, in North Salem, New York, wrote a history of their town that was published as a book under the title *When Our Town Was Young*. But whether you write a book or a newspaper article, or put on an assembly program, you will need to (1) determine the topics you wish to learn about, and (2) explore your community to locate information concerning its past.

The topics of local history you may wish to learn about are the same as those we have followed in this book in describing early life in the various sections of the country:

1. When and where settlements were made; early settlers

2. How people lived long ago
   a. Their food, clothing, tools, shelter, furniture
   b. Their churches, schools, libraries, amusements
   c. Their means of communication and transportation
   d. Their ways of earning a living
   e. Interesting and exciting adventures of earlier times

Here are some of the sources you may investigate to gather this information:

1. Written sources
   a. State, county, and local histories; biographies of leaders
   b. Old newspapers, anniversary editions of newspapers, records, programs, maps

Writing in the field of local history can be an enjoyable hobby and a springboard to writing for publication.

c. Letters, diaries, account books

d. Markers, tombstones

2. Oral sources

   a. Interviews with "old-timers" in the community

   b. Songs

3. Remains

   a. Town Hall, meeting houses, churches, schools

   b. Old houses in the community

   c. Old grist mills, factories

   d. Old furniture, clothing, tools, jewelry, machinery

   e. Museums

4. Pictorial sources

   a. Pictures

   b. Slides

   c. Movies

Of course, this list is quite complete. Not all these materials may be available in your community. Even if they were, you could not be expected to use them all. But by setting up committees, a great many sources can be investigated and a surprising amount of information collected.

Interesting Things to Do

The "things to do" which are marked with an asterisk (*) are for the whole class. The others are to be used as your teacher directs.

*1. Start a new set of drill cards using the items under "Can You Identify?" at the end of each chapter. A quick drill at the beginning of the class period is a good way to learn the important men and events which you should know.

*2. Make a map of the last frontier in the United States showing the following: the great plains region; Rocky Mountain region; Pacific Northwest and Pacific Southwest; the route of the transcontinental railroad; the cattle country and the long drive; the wheat lands; the mining territory.

*3. Make a time line showing the important inventions which have made the United States a great manufacturing nation.

4. Make a pictorial map of the United States showing the important manufacturing cities and the articles manufactured. You may draw illustrations or paste in small pictures you have found in magazines.

5. Write a newspaper article on one of these events: (a) the completion of the transcontinental railroad; (b) the completion of the transatlantic cable; (c) the Wright brothers' flight; (d) the invention of the telephone or the wireless; (e) Lindbergh's flight to Paris.

6. Write and present to the class an imaginary dialogue (conversation) between: (a) an Indian chief and a white settler on the great plains; (b) a man born in 1850 and his grandson born in 1900; (c) James J. Hill and John D. Rockefeller; (d) a sheepherder and a cattleman.

7. Write a page or two in a diary that might have been written by: (a) the wife of Charles Goodyear; (b) a girl whose father owned one of the first automobiles; (c) a worker in a factory in the late 1800's; (d) a cowboy in the days of the open range.

8. Select a committee to prepare a report to the class on the Indians of North America. Let each member of the committee select one of the following topics: (a) where the Indians came from and what they looked like; (b) the most important tribes and the regions in which they lived; (c) food, homes, and handicrafts of the Indians; (d) religion, music, and amusements of the Indians; (f) Indian schools of today. See the book lists on pages A33-A38 for some books on Indians.

9. Interview someone who belongs to a labor union. Find out what advantages and what disadvantages he finds in being a member.

10. Write or give orally a short report on one of the following men: Samuel Gompers, John L. Lewis, William Green, Philip Murray.

New Conditions Brin

Stress the point that the greatness of a nation depends on the vision and will of the people.

In the earlier units of this book you have followed the march of America's progress. You have learned of the discovery and settlement of the New World and its separation from the Old. You have seen a young nation grow in strength and win the respect of other countries. You have watched this nation become reunited after a shattering war and spread across a continent. You have noted changes in farming and industry, in transportation and communication, which have made the United States the wealthiest and most powerful nation in the world.

But what is a nation? A nation is made up of individuals — of men and women and boys and girls just like ourselves. What makes a nation great? Not only wise leaders but a people who have the vision and the will to make a dream come true. The story of a nation is no more nor less than the story of the accomplishments of its people.

This unit is about the American people. Chapter 25 describes some of the effects which the Machine Age has had on our population. You will find that the number of Americans has increased tremendously since

Changes in American Life

1865. During the late 1800's and early 1900's the need for more workers in factories and mines drew large numbers of immigrants to our shores. The scene above, for example, shows a group of immigrants arriving in New York City. These new Americans are awed by the size and bustle of our largest city. Skyscrapers, automobiles, the elevated railway — all are signs of the Machine Age which caused American cities to grow in size and number. The growth of industry also brought changes in ways of living in cities and towns and on farms.

Not all the changes in living were for the best. Chapter 26 tells about efforts to overcome certain problems in American life. But it also describes changes that have taken place in education, in literature, in science and the arts, and in the use of leisure time.

Mary Antin effectively made the point that each of us is heir to the priceless heritage of the past.

It is not I that belong to the past but the past that belongs to me. . . . I am the youngest of America's children, and into my hands is given all her priceless heritage. . . . Mine is the whole majestic past and mine is the shining future. — MARY ANTIN

The Machine Age Changes Life
in Cities and on Farms

Can your students list any great changes that have taken place during their lifetime? Bring out that change is continuous even if not always dramatic.

What this chapter is about —

It was not until August, 1956, that death came to the last veteran of the Union army in the American Civil War. The aged veteran, Albert Woolson, had been born in 1847 and lived to be 109 years old. Astonishing as it may seem, Mr. Woolson's life spanned more than half the history of the United States!

Think of the changes which this man saw in our ways of living! When he was born, there were only 29 states in the Union. The population of the United States was about 23 million, and the largest city in the country had only 500,000 inhabitants. At the time of Mr. Woolson's birth there were no electric lights, no tele-

phones, and, of course, no radio or television. The invention of the automobile was about 45 years in the future. The first college football game would not be played for 22 years. Basketball would not even be invented until Mr. Woolson was about 50 years old. The list of changes could be continued indefinitely. Most of them took place after the war between the North and the South and resulted from the rapid growth of business and industry.

In this chapter we shall learn how the growth of industry brought large numbers of immigrants to our shores. We shall also see how the Machine Age caused striking changes in the ways Americans lived in

People in our story — immigrant couple, construction worker, policeman, fireman, suburban commuter.

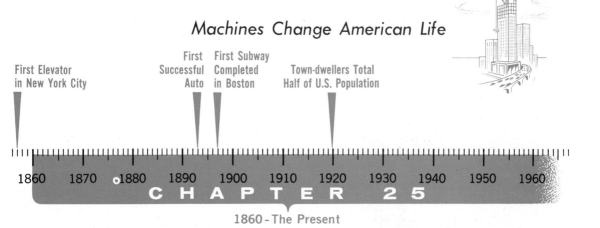

Machines Change American Life

First Elevator in New York City

First Successful Auto

First Subway Completed in Boston

Town-dwellers Total Half of U.S. Population

1860   1870   1880   1890   1900   1910   1920   1930   1940   1950   1960

C H A P T E R   2 5

1860 - The Present

cities, on farms, and in towns. Look for answers to these questions:

▶ 1. How did the growth of industry encourage immigration?

▶ 2. Why have cities grown so rapidly

since the Civil War?

▶ 3. How have ways of living changed in American cities?

▶ 4. How have ways of living changed on American farms and in small towns?

1 How Did the Growth of Industry Encourage Immigration?

Explain the expression, "land of the second chance."

The United States is a nation of immigrants. All of us are immigrants or come from immigrant parents or ancestors. In fact, the dream of America as a "land of the second chance" has played an important part in the growth of the United States. From the earliest times down to the most recent immigrant, people of other countries have felt, in the words of William Cullen Bryant,

There's freedom at thy gates, and rest
For Earth's downtrodden and opprest,
A shelter for the hunted head,
For the starved laborer toil and bread.

Drawn by this dream, immigrants from many lands have come in search of freedom, homes, and jobs.

At first the stream of immigrants to America was small. During the 1600's and 1700's, it took great courage to cross the Atlantic and establish a new home in the wilderness. As conditions became more settled along the Atlantic coast, more people set out for the English colonies from their homes in Europe. Still, the number of newcomers to America's shores remained small for two hundred years after the first English settlements. Most of these early immigrants were farmers. But as towns grew, more people became merchants, craftsmen, ministers, lawyers, and so on.

Because the Thirteen Colonies were under British control, most of the immigrants who came in the 1600's were of British stock, that is, from England, Scotland, or Wales. Then in the 1700's sizable

507

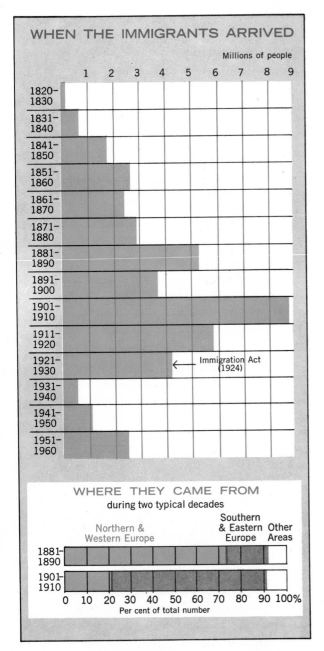

WHEN THE IMMIGRANTS ARRIVED

Millions of people

	1	2	3	4	5	6	7	8	9
1820–1830									
1831–1840									
1841–1850									
1851–1860									
1861–1870									
1871–1880									
1881–1890									
1891–1900									
1901–1910									
1911–1920									
1921–1930									
1931–1940									
1941–1950									
1951–1960									

← Immigration Act (1924)

WHERE THEY CAME FROM
during two typical decades

Northern & Western Europe Southern & Eastern Europe Other Areas

	0	10	20	30	40	50	60	70	80	90	100%
1881–1890											
1901–1910											

Per cent of total number

THE NUMBER of immigrants during ten-year periods is compared in this graph. (1) In what years did immigration reach a peak? (2) Why did it decline later?

numbers of Scotch-Irish (page 113) and Germans came to the English colonies as well. As we read earlier, the Scotch-Irish became famous frontiersmen. They pushed their way inland in Pennsylvania, Virginia, the Carolinas, and even beyond

The German word for Germany is "Deutschland." the mountains into Kentucky and Tennessee. Many Germans settled in southern Pennsylvania. Known as "Pennsylvania Dutch," they built stout stone houses and great barns on their fertile and prosperous farms (page 97). There was also a scattering of immigrants from other countries.

We should remember, however, that there were some people who did not come to America as willing immigrants. For a long time Negroes were brought to America against their will. Instead of coming in search of freedom and better living conditions, they were seized by slave traders in Africa and sold into slavery in America.

A growing America attracts more immigrants. No one knows exactly how many people have come to what is now the United States. In fact, no attempt was made to count immigrants until 1820. Since that time, however, some 40 million men, women, and children have come to our shores. (See the chart on this page.)

Why did the small stream of immigrants in the early 1800's broaden into a mighty flood during the late 1800's and early 1900's? The answer is that a growing America offered more and more opportunities. During these years, for one thing, many immigrants came to America because it was easy to obtain land for farming. As the frontier moved ever westward, new groups of families, many of them immigrants, established farms on lands which had formerly been forest or endless prairie.

Even more important in bringing immigrants to our shores was the growth of industry. You remember how factories and mills spread throughout the Northeast during the first half of the 1800's (Chapter 14). Many workers were needed to operate the factory machines. Others were needed to ship and sell manufactured goods. The building and running of rail-

To understand the implications of this migration for Ireland, one must remember that Ireland's population was much smaller than Germany's.

THE MACHINE AGE CHANGES CITY AND FARM LIFE   509

roads also opened up more jobs. After 1865, the number of workers needed in industry increased sharply. Workers by the millions were needed to dig in the mines, construct buildings and bridges, build and operate machines, and transport goods from factories to the people who would use them.

During most of the 1800's, immigrants come from northern and western Europe. People from many lands swelled the growing tide of immigration. Until the 1890's, these waves of newcomers came chiefly from the countries of northern and western Europe. From time to time, however, more immigrants arrived from one particular country than from any other.

The great Irish immigration. Large numbers of Irish people had come to America from early colonial times on. John Barry, for example, served as an outstanding naval officer in the Revolutionary War. Many Irish left their homeland to escape harsh British rule. Also, many people left Ireland in the 1840's when a great famine swept over the country. From 1820 until 1850, more men and women came to the United States from Ireland than from any other country.

For the most part, Irish immigrants preferred to live in America's cities. Many of them took jobs in industry and as policemen and firemen. Because of their interest in government, others rose to positions of influence and leadership in local, state, and national government. Thousands of Irishmen worked on the building of canals and railroads and thus played a valuable part in building modern America.

German immigration. The next great wave of immigrants came from Germany. Political unrest and the failure of a revolution in the late 1840's sent many Germans to seek freedom in America. Carl Schurz (*shoortz*), who became a noted American journalist and statesman, was one of these. Thousands of other Germans came to earn a better living. From 1850 to 1890, Germany led all countries in the number of immigrants that came to America. For the most part, the newcomers from Germany settled in the Middle West. They became prosperous farmers and helped to develop new states in that region. They also gave to

---

The French, Dutch, and Spanish in America

People from France, Holland, and Spain have added much to American life, not so much because they came as immigrants in large numbers but because the United States includes lands formerly owned by these countries.

French influence is especially important in Louisiana, which was once a French colony. Louisiana law is based on French law, and many French customs are still followed. French influence is also found in New England. Many Canadians of French descent have come from Canada to take up farms or find jobs in New England factories.

The Dutch left a lasting mark on the Hudson River Valley. As you remember, the valley was settled by the Dutch and belonged to Holland in the early 1600's. Later Dutch immigrants settled in Michigan, Iowa, and other states. The city of Holland, Michigan, has a colorful tulip festival every spring which keeps alive the Dutch traditions of that community.

In our southwestern states, especially California, New Mexico, Arizona, and Texas, there are many reminders of the time when Spaniards lived there. In such a city as Santa Fe, New Mexico, many descendants of the old Spanish frontier still proudly bear Spanish names and speak Spanish as well as English.

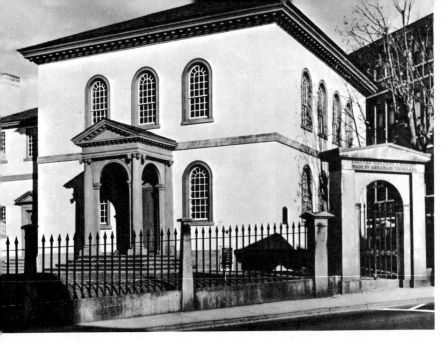

such cities as Milwaukee, St. Louis, and Cincinnati a background of German customs and ways of living.

Scandinavian immigration. While the German immigration was still at its height, large numbers of immigrants came from the Scandinavian countries — Sweden, Norway, and Denmark. The Scandinavian immigration reached its peak in the 1880's. Like many of the Germans, the Scandinavians were interested in farming. Most of them found homes in the prairie lands of the north central states. In Minnesota and the Dakotas, especially, these hardworking new Americans peopled the land and established prosperous farms.

The tide of immigration shifts to eastern and southern Europe. From about 1890 to the 1920's, most immigrants to the United States came, not from northern and western Europe, but from southern and eastern Europe. Newcomers flocked from Italy, Russia, Poland, the many countries which were part of Austria-Hungary, and the Balkan Peninsula. It was during these same years that the total number of immigrants reached an all-time high.

Most of the immigrants from southern and eastern Europe found jobs in the mines and factories. Thus they settled in industrial cities and communities. These were the years when the United States was becoming a great manufacturing and industrial nation. Workers were needed to do the thousand and one back-breaking jobs that industry requires. Just as Irish workers had helped build the canals and early railroads, so these newer immigrants supplied the muscle and sweat that made the United States an industrial giant.

Not all of the newer immigrants took jobs in industry. Many of them entered business in the large cities and so aided in the commercial growth of our country.

The Jews in America. Many of the immigrants who came from eastern Europe after 1890 were Jews who had fled from Russia. For hundreds of years, Jews had no homeland but were scattered about in small groups in many countries. Because they were persecuted from time to time in one country or another, Jews have come to America since its earliest days.

The first Jews, in fact, came before the American Revolution. Some sought religious freedom in colonial times in Rhode Island. During the Revolutionary War, Haym Salomon, a Jewish banker of Phila-

Jews came to America from Portugal, Spain, and still other countries. **510** Russia, Poland, Germany, Austria-Hungary,

delphia, raised large sums of money (much of which came from his own fortune) to aid the fight for independence. Jewish immigrants came in larger numbers in the late 1800's and early 1900's. Most of them settled in cities. They became doctors, lawyers, or businessmen, or enriched America's art, literature, music, and theater.

The Jews who have come to America do not represent a separate race or a particular nation. Throughout centuries of persecution they were held together by their steadfast loyalty to the ancient Hebrew religion. Of the Jews in America it has been said:

The Jews as a group by no means form a . . . unique segment of the American population. . . . Their callings are as diverse as those of their fellow Americans. There are rich Jews, just as there are rich non-Jews. And there are just as many poor Jews, relatively, as there are poor non-Jews. Far from being a homogeneous [uniform] group, the

American Jews are . . . individuals among whom one can find conservatives as well as progressives, Republicans as well as Democrats, employers as well as employees, shopkeepers as well as factory workers. In their opinions, attitudes, and political leanings they differ as much among themselves as do Americans in general.

CHECK
UP

1. During the 1600's and 1700's from what European countries did most of the immigrants to America come?

2. Why did the number of immigrants to America increase greatly in the late 1800's and early 1900's?

3. (a) When did each of the following groups come to America in the greatest numbers: Irish, Germans, Scandinavians, people from eastern and southern Europe? (b) Where did they tend to settle? (c) How did they earn a living? (d) How did they influence American life?

2 Why Have Cities Grown So Rapidly Since the Civil War?

A very important result of the rise of industry was the growth of American cities. There were cities, of course, long before 1865, and the beginnings of many of them stretch far back in our history. Both in size and number, however, cities grew at a rapid rate as the United States became a leading industrial nation.

Each community has its own special history, but in some ways the growth of all cities and towns has been much the same. The following description will show you how a typical city grew.

A village is founded on a river. In the latter part of the 1700's a pioneer strode out of the deep woods and stood upon the

banks of a stream. He was looking for a place to build his home. After exploring the surrounding country for a few days, he decided to build his cabin near the river.

Soon other pioneer families came, and a village grew up. In addition to the homes of the settlers, it contained a blacksmith shop, a tavern, a general store, and other shops. There was a mill to grind flour, its huge water wheel turned by the flow of water from the river. A sawmill also was set up. The small village prospered.

Steamboats and a canal help the village grow. About 1825 a canal was dug to connect the settlement with another, larger river which ran into the Atlantic

Are there similarities in the development of your community and the one described below?

AMERICAN CITIES INCREASE IN SIZE

Our 12 largest cities and their populations

IN 1890

New York	2,507,000
Chicago	1,100,000
Philadelphia	1,047,000
St. Louis	452,000
Boston	448,000
Baltimore	434,000
San Francisco	299,000
Cincinnati	297,000
Cleveland	261,000
Buffalo	256,000
New Orleans	242,000
Pittsburgh	239,000

IN 1960

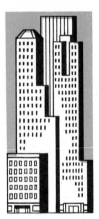

New York	7,782,000
Chicago	3,550,000
*Los Angeles	2,479,000
Philadelphia	2,002,000
*Detroit	1,670,000
Baltimore	939,000
*Houston	938,000
Cleveland	876,000
*Washington	764,000
St. Louis	750,000
*Milwaukee	741,000
San Francisco	740,000

*Not on 1890 list

Ocean. On this larger river were ports where big ships could load and unload their cargoes. Smaller boats floated down the stream which flowed by the village, or were poled upstream. Men in the village spoke of the steamboats which moved easily up and down many rivers. "Why not on our river?" they asked. Before long, steamboats were busily puffing along between the tree-shaded banks of this river. As commerce moved up and down the river, much of it was unloaded at the wharves of the village for shipment on the canal. Warehouses were built. More and more men took part in trade.

The village becomes a city, a railroad center, and a center of industry. Fifteen years after the canal was opened, large gangs of husky, boisterous laborers appeared. They started laying the railroad tracks which were to run through the town. Soon their work was finished, and then they moved on to extend the track farther and farther west. Every man, woman, and child in town gathered at the railroad station to watch the first train come puffing out of the east and rumble to a stop at the new station. Before long,

however, railroads had reached the town from other directions, and trains were a common sight.

More families flocked to the town. By now it might well be called a city. Factories and mills had been established because the city had so many means of transportation. Hundreds of men worked in the factories and mills. Because the city was a junction where several railroad lines crossed, large yards were developed for handling freight, assembling trains, and making repairs. Many men were employed in these railroad yards. Each new industry attracted others because for each new one there were advantages in having the others close by. As the number of workers increased, the city continued to grow.

American cities increase in size and number. The growth of the city we have described above is just an example of what has taken place all over the United States. This has been especially true during the past hundred years. We shall point out some important reasons why cities have grown more rapidly during this period than ever before. These reasons are related to the coming of the Machine Age.

Population increase contributes to the growth of cities. For one thing cities have been affected by our rapidly mounting population. Only about 38½ million people lived in the United States in 1870. By 1950 we had 150½ million. Today we have about 200 million. What caused this mighty increase? In part it came from the birth of new American citizens. In part, also, it resulted from the huge numbers of new Americans who came from abroad. (See the chart on page 508.)

The growth of industry takes place chiefly in cities. Spurred by the needs of the Union army during the Civil War, many northern businessmen had built new factories and new warehouses. As industry in the United States grew, railroads reached more cities and the number of factories and business offices multiplied. Cities grew noisier and busier. Heavy smoke rose from the tall chimneys of factories and mills. Early each morning the city streets were filled with crowds of people hurrying to the day's work. In the evening, city traffic flowed just as strongly from factories to homes. It was natural that the men who worked in factories and shops should live in the cities where industries were located. Business and industry were no longer centered largely in the Northeast but had expanded all across the face of America.

Immigrants and farm people settle in cities. New job opportunities in industry drew more and more of our nation's growing population to cities. Immigrants from Ireland, as we read earlier, made their homes in cities. Likewise, most immigrants from southern and eastern Europe settled in industrial cities like Chicago, Cleveland, and Buffalo. In addition, people from farm areas flocked to the cities. New inventions and new methods of farming enabled the farmers to raise larger crops

1833

1860'S

1928

CHICAGO grew within a century from a small lakeside settlement into the country's second largest city. These three views of Chicago show roughly the same area in 1833, in the 1860's, and in 1928.

Test the ability of students to use charts and tables.

Rising land values in the cities caused more skyscrapers to be built.

with less labor (Chapter 24). As a result, fewer farm workers were needed to raise enough wheat, corn, cattle, and other food to supply the nation.

New inventions make possible the growth of cities. Great cities could not exist without the use of many new ideas developed since 1865. One of the most familiar features of our cities, for example, is their tall buildings — their "skyscrapers." Such buildings could not have been erected before iron and steel came into widespread use as building materials. Again, people are unwilling to climb up and down many flights of stairs. Tall buildings, therefore, require elevators. In 1857 an elevator with safety features was installed in a building in New York City. Fifteen years later an improved elevator was invented, and taller buildings became more practical.

As cities grew ever larger, improved transportation was also needed. American inventiveness supplied the answer to this need. Cities had "elevated railroads," with small steam locomotives pulling cars on tracks raised above the streets. Soon electricity replaced steam. No longer did the elevated railroads shower sparks on the walkers below and pour smoke into the windows of nearby buildings. Another important development was the telephone, invented in the 1870's. City dwellers could now communicate directly with each other; they no longer had to depend on messenger boys.

The United States becomes a nation of city dwellers. For many years, our country had been a nation of farmers and of dwellers in small towns. As late as 1880, only about two people out of every ten lived in cities or in towns of over 2500 people. But during the late 1800's, an increasing number of people began to live in cities. By 1920, five out of every ten Americans lived in communities of more than 2500 people. At the present time about seven out of ten people live in such communities.

CHECK
UP

1. (a) How might a typical town come to be founded? (b) What developments might help it grow?

2. How has each of the following stimulated the growth of cities: (a) immigration? (b) the growth of industry? (c) new inventions?

3 How Have Ways of Living Changed in American Cities?

To the visitor, cities always seem the same: busy, noisy, and crowded. Yet cities have changed in many respects since the 1880's. To give us an idea of the changes, let us visit a city of 1880 and a present-day city. Our visit to the city of the 1880's will be made with an imaginary visitor named Mr. John Countryman.

A CITY IN THE 1880'S

The visitor goes to the city by train. Mr. Countryman, who had never been to the city, finally decided to pay it a visit. One day he boarded the train for his journey. He had several hundred miles to go, so he had reserved space on the sleep-

In recent years the population of many large cities has declined because people have moved to adjacent suburbs.

CEDAR RAPIDS, IOWA, in the early 1900's had electric trolleys (notice the overhead wires), but horse-drawn vehicles still accounted for most of the traffic.

ing car. Pullman sleeping cars, with seats which were transformed into private beds at night, had been made popular some years before (page 456). They were large, comfortable, and brightly lighted.

As Mr. Countryman continued on his long journey, he had a choice of ways to get his meals. The train stopped at stations for 20 minutes at breakfast, lunch, and dinner time. At these stops he could rush into the station restaurant and eat a hurried meal. Or, if he chose, he could have his meals in a more leisurely manner in a dining car on the train.

At last Mr. Countryman reached the city. He alighted from the train in a large station. It was one of the showplaces of the city, with high ceilings and decorated stone walls. To Mr. Countryman the crowds of passengers seemed almost frightening. He made his way out of the railroad station and rode in a horse-drawn cab to a hotel.

A country visitor sees strange sights in a city of 1880. To Mr. Countryman this city of 100,000 looked immense. Today a city of this size does not seem large. But in 1880 there were only nineteen cities in the country having as many as 100,000 people. Only three of these cities had populations of more than half a million — New York, Philadelphia, and Chicago.

The country visitor of 1880 was sure to exclaim about the high buildings. The tallest of them might reach a dozen stories! He would notice, also, the crowded streets filled with horse-drawn vehicles of every sort. There were streetcars drawn by horses (the electric streetcar had not yet been invented) and horse-drawn wagons and carts for transporting goods. Carriages and buggies for private use were everywhere. On the sidewalks throngs of citizens hurried to offices and shops.

Above the vehicles and the people was a maze of wires. In 1880 they were mostly telegraph wires. If Mr. Countryman had delayed his visit for a few years, he would have seen electric and telephone wires too. The poles then sprouted new crossbars, and the many wires threatened to blot out the sun. Indeed, in a few years some cities began to require that wires be placed underground. If New York had been the city visited by Mr. Countryman, he would have seen something else overhead. The elevated railroad, or the "El" as it commonly was called, had first been constructed in 1869. By the time of Mr. Countryman's visit it was spreading over many parts of the city.

Many people live in slum areas. As he walked about the city, Mr. Countryman enjoyed the gas lamps which lighted his

Perhaps the grandfather of one of early memories of a large city. **515** *the students can describe his*

PITTSBURGH, as it looked in 1947, is shown in this photograph of the "Golden Triangle," formed by the junction of two great rivers.

Try to find photographs to illustrate growth and change in your community.

way after dark. In the daytime he noticed that in the better parts of the city there were single-family houses. In other sections, however, he was shocked at the conditions he saw. In these districts there were dingy tenement houses — large buildings, often in run-down condition, which housed many families. The crowded tenement sections of many cities developed into *slums,* where poorer people huddled together in misery and wretchedness.

To know just what Mr. Countryman saw in the slums, we can turn to the writings of a man who did much to alert Americans of the 1800's to this problem. Jacob Riis had come to America from Denmark when he was 21 years old. While getting his start in this new land, Riis lived in the slums of New York City. He not only became a newspaper reporter but wrote several books about the problems existing in large cities. Here is a sample of what he reported about conditions in the slums:

✳ When, in the midnight hour, . . . I have gone the rounds of Ludlow and Hester and Essex Streets . . . [I have] counted often four, five, and even six of the little ones in a single bed. . . . In one I visited very lately, the only bed was occupied by the entire family lying lengthwise and crosswise, literally in layers, three children at the feet, all except a boy of ten or twelve, for whom there was no room. He slept, with his clothes on

to keep him warm, in a pile of rags just inside the door. It seemed to me impossible that families of children could be raised at all in such dens as I had my daily and nightly walks in.

Jacob Riis also noticed things like this:

✳ There were 360 tenants in [one tenement in 1888], and 40 of them were babies. How many were romping children I do not know. The "yard" they had to play in was just 5 feet 10 inches wide, and a dozen steps below the street level. The closets of all the buildings are in the cellar of the rear houses and open upon this "yard," where it is always dark and damp as in a dungeon.

THE AMERICAN CITY OF TODAY

Today we have many large cities. How different is the city of our day from the one visited by Mr. Countryman in 1880! The most obvious difference, of course, is that today's cities are much larger. By 1960 there were five cities in the United States of more than one million population. Another sixteen cities had between half a million and a million inhabitants. All together, 130 cities had populations of more than 100,000.

Suburbs develop near cities. Another difference is that our cities have spread into the regions around them. The fast-growing cities of the late 1800's were noisy,

PITTSBURGH will look like this in the future, when a far-reaching rebuilding program is completed. Compare the photograph on the opposite page with this artist's sketch of the same area.

crowded, smoky, dirty. Would it be possible, wondered some city dwellers, to work in an office in the city, yet live in the green and quiet country nearby? In the mid-1800's a dozen men, at the end of the business day, boarded the train from New York City to Greenwich, Connecticut. When the train slowed before crossing a bridge near their homes, they jumped to the ground. In the mornings they rode back to the city on the train.

From this small beginning has grown the *suburb,* so familiar in the United States today. Smaller communities have grown up around our large cities. From the suburbs the workers go to the city each morning and return each night. At first they went by train. Later they went by electric railways. In still more recent years they have traveled by automobile. Morning and evening, newly constructed highways are crowded with cars, often bumper to bumper on their way to and from the city.

In other words, modern American cities have grown into what are called "metropolitan areas." The center of the area lies within the actual city boundaries — the

"city limits." Beyond are the suburbs, reaching out in every direction from the city itself. At the present time the people living in a city may be outnumbered by those living in its suburbs. In the largest metropolitan area, around New York City, there are 2.6 city dwellers for every one whose home is in a suburb. But in Seattle and Cleveland the suburb dwellers and city dwellers are about equal in number. In Boston and Pittsburgh there are almost three dwellers in the suburbs to every inhabitant of the city itself.

Cities provide necessary services. The smaller cities of earlier days did not require many of the services which we take for granted nowadays. As cities grew larger, however, they needed ample supplies of pure water, good sewage systems, and well-paved streets. They needed means of disposing of garbage; they needed police and fire-fighting forces. Some of these services were slow in coming. But come they did. Water, for example, often is piped from lakes and streams at a distance from the city. This service provides not only drinking water but water for bathing, cleaning, fire-fighting, and industry.

The larger the city, the higher the cost of providing essential services.

NEW YORK CITY'S KENNEDY INTERNATIONAL AIRPORT is almost a city in itself, with its own police force, newspaper, hospital and hotel, churches, shops, and restaurants. This artist's drawing shows how the airport will look when improvements and new buildings are completed.

Buildings grow taller. Many of our modern cities have tall, soaring skylines, quite different from earlier cities. When Mr. Countryman paid his visit to the city in 1880, large buildings were constructed of stone and brick. The use of these materials placed a limit on the height of buildings. Thus, the Monadnock Building in Chicago, erected in the early 1890's, had walls fifteen feet thick at the base to support the weight of its sixteen stories.

As more businesses crowded into big cities, land became scarce and expensive. The only way to house more businesses was to erect taller buildings. When new building materials — first iron and then steel — came into use, the buildings could go up and up without the need for thick walls. Now we are accustomed to skyscrapers 30, 40, or 60 stories high.

Means of transportation and lighting change. A visitor to the city nowadays might make his journey, like Mr. Countryman, by train. But he can also travel by airplane. Or he can drive to the city in his own car. Once he arrives, he is caught up in the swarming automobile traffic. An elevated railroad — electric now, of course — may still exist. He may find, in addition, subways in the larger cities. In many cities, buses have replaced streetcars. If the out-of-town visitor comes by airplane, he might even take advantage of helicopter service to get from the airport to the center of the city.

The streets of our cities are brightly lighted by electric lights. Shops keep their display windows lighted until late in the evening. Advertising signs stare or blink at the beholder. Until the middle 1920's, when a Frenchman named Georges Claude invented the neon tube, all the lights were white. Now you see electric signs in red, green, blue, and other colors.

Cities are remaking themselves. Recently many of our cities have been studying their problems and rebuilding in an effort to solve them. Much progress has been made, for example, in tearing down slums. In their places have risen new, clean apartment houses. Often the new dwellings are set in the midst of green areas of trees and lawns. The people living in these new buildings have comfortable homes with airy, open surroundings. The United States government, and often state and city governments as well, have paid much of the cost of the new developments.

518

Slum clearance and urban renewal projects are improving housing for low-income families.

An example of the traffic problem is the time required to go from the center of a city to its airport.

THE MACHINE AGE CHANGES CITY AND FARM LIFE   519

In some cities whole blocks of run-down buildings have been torn down so that modern office or apartment buildings can be erected. Streets are being widened and made more attractive with stretches of grass and beds of flowers. Historic old homes are being restored so that visitors can see them as they used to be. Steps have been taken to rid cities of chimney smoke and industrial fumes. Private contractors are erecting huge modern apartment buildings. With all these changes, cities will become pleasanter places in which to live. It is even likely that people living in suburbs will return to the cities and save themselves the need to travel long distances to their jobs.

Cities wrestle with the problem of traffic. The automobile has caused much rebuilding in cities. In its early years, the automobile was no problem except when its noisy engine frightened the horses as it passed. Now, however, the automobile is everywhere. Our millions of automobiles need countless miles of broad, smooth streets; otherwise they become hopelessly tied up in traffic jams. Cities are now constructing great express highways to let the cars enter and leave cities quickly. Often buildings, and whole blocks of buildings, are torn down to make way for the new roads and parking areas. Nevertheless, the number of cars grows each year, and the cities still are crowded with traffic.

CHECK UP

1. (a) Describe a typical American city of 1880. (b) What are slums?

2. (a) Why have suburbs developed around modern cities? (b) What services do cities now provide?

3. (a) How have transportation and lighting been improved in American cities? (b) How have cities dealt with the problems of slums and traffic?

4 How Have Ways of Living Changed on American Farms and in Small Towns?

Just as new inventions have altered life in the cities, so have they changed ways of living on the farms. We learned in Chapter 24 how new machines and methods affected working conditions on the farms. But how has the Machine Age changed the daily living of the farmer and his family? How has it affected their lives during

MUDDY ROADS gave drivers as many headaches when cars were first used as traffic tie-ups do today. A team of mules tries to drag this car through the thick mud.

their leisure time? We can get an idea of the differences by comparing farm life in the 1880's with farm life today.

An Iowa farm in the 1880's. It is night over the wide lands of Iowa. In the limitless darkness each farmhouse, set far from its neighbors, seems as lonely as a ship at sea. Inside the farmhouse of John Jones, the family sits a few minutes by the kerosene lamps before going to bed. John Jones himself is reading a farmers' newspaper. He is tired from a long day of hard work, aided only by horses and the few machines they draw. His wife sits near him, bending over a pile of clothes she is mending. She, too, is tired from long hours of cooking in a kitchen which has only a wood-burning stove. She is tired, as well, from pumping water which she had to heat so that she could do the washing in her wooden tubs. The children are studying the lessons they must have ready for school the next day.

John Jones and his family do not often see their friends. To visit them means hitching the horses to the wagon and driving slowly over rough roads. They do meet their neighbors at church on Sunday. Now and again they drive to the small town nearby. Here at the general store they trade farm produce for the articles they need. Occasionally John Jones attends a meeting of the Grange. The family goes to hear speeches at great "rallies" when an election is being held. A few years ago they went to Chicago to visit Mrs. Jones's mother. This meant driving in their wagon to the railroad and then taking a tiring and dirty trip on the train. But they thought the railroad a marvelous thing. Its rails, stretching into the distance, were practically the only connection they had with the rest of the world.

An Iowa farm in the 1960's. Now it is another evening in Iowa some 80 years later. Albert Jones, grandson of John Jones, sits with his family in their comfortable living room. Electric lamps light the room, and two teenagers are viewing their favorite program on television. Earlier Mr. Jones and his wife had listened to the President's speech on foreign affairs; later they will hear the late news. At the moment Mr. Jones is reading a bulletin for farmers which describes a new formula for feeding steers. On the telephone Mrs. Jones is calling members of the committee which is planning the program for the next PTA meeting at the regional high school. She has time for such activities because central heating, hot and cold running water, and electric appliances have taken most of the drudgery out of housework.

Farm life is no longer as lonely as it was 80 years ago. The telephone brings the Jones family into close contact with their neighbors. Shopping in Des Moines or Chicago is no problem because of the family car. Next Saturday the whole family will drive to Iowa City for the homecoming football game. Albert Jones, Jr., entered the State University of Iowa two years ago.

As for Mr. Jones, the radio brings him the daily weather forecast and market report. Truck, tractor, cornpicker, and other machinery make it easier for him to manage a farm of 480 acres than it was for Grandfather Jones to farm 160 acres. It is true that Albert Jones has problems which never troubled his grandfather. He must keep careful records in order to make his federal and state income tax reports. But better seed and fertilizing have improved his crops, while power and machines have made farm work much easier.

The small town see many changes. Like the city and the farm, the small town has changed a great deal in this century. To understand what kinds of changes these were, let us make an imaginary visit to such a town. We shall go with young Lisbeth Brown as she visits her grandmother, who has lived in the town all her life. As they sit talking, Lisbeth asks Grandmother Brown to tell how life in the town has changed since she was young.

"When I was a girl," says Grandmother Brown, "Waterville was smaller than it is now. The town hasn't grown as much as the big cities have, but it has grown some. The greatest changes are in our comforts and conveniences.

"When I was young, we had harder work to do. Each house stood by itself, in the midst of its own lawn. We had to draw water by pumping it from the well, with a hand pump. Only a few of us had central heating in our homes; in many houses there were only stoves and fireplaces. Even if we had central heat, we had to shovel coal into our furnaces by hand. Our light came from kerosene lamps."

Streets and services were crude. "And," went on Grandmother Brown, "our streets were not paved. They were dusty in summer and muddy in spring and fall. The sidewalks were built of wood. We had only a few gas lamps to light our way if we walked. In the country outside of town it was dark as dark could be. As for amusements, we made them ourselves. We got together for parties and sang or played games. When a circus or other show came to town, we had great times indeed."

"Grandma," asked Lisbeth, "weren't you lonely and bored in those days?"

"I don't think so," replied Grandmother Brown. "It is true, though, that life in our town today is more like life in the rest of the country than it was when I was a girl. Now we have television and radio, and we see and hear the same things the people in big cities do. We see the same movies everybody else sees. In my girlhood we could not travel far except by train.

"Or take clothes. When I was a girl, we had several dressmakers in town. They came to the house and made clothes for us. Now our local stores have for sale the same kinds of clothes that people everywhere else are buying. Or we can go on a shopping trip to the city and buy our clothes."

Grandmother Brown sat silently for a few moments. Then she said: "Life has changed greatly in Waterville. We are far more comfortable than we used to be. We have just about every convenience that city people have. Yet our young people are inclined to move away. They go to the cities. They think that they will find more opportunities there, or that life will be more exciting. I am worried. What will become of towns like ours if we cannot hold our young people?"

•

Americans, always restless and energetic, have brought about far-reaching changes in their ways of living. Life on

If your students live in a smaller community, do they feel as Grandmother Brown did about Waterville's future?

farms and in towns is very different from what it was a century ago. Moreover, in the last 100 years Americans have created great cities. By developing industry, they have caused their cities to grow larger and faster. Remarkable inventions have made city life more comfortable but also noisy and crowded. The great cities, shimmering piles of steel and stone, have become the very mark and sign of America.

CHECK UP

1. What are some ways in which inventions have changed life on American farms?
2. How has life in small towns changed?

Check Up on Chapter 25

Do You Know the Meaning?

1. immigrant
2. suburb
3. skyscraper
4. helicopter
5. slums
6. elevated railroad
7. metropolitan area

What Do You Think?

1. The 1960 census showed that suburbs had been growing at a much faster rate than cities or towns. (a) Why do people move to the suburbs? (b) Are there any disadvantages to living in suburbs?

What Do You Think? (Cont.)

2. What advantages did British immigrants have over other newcomers to America?
3. What services that we think of as "necessary" in a modern city did not exist in earlier cities?
4. Why did so many immigrants who came after the Civil War settle in the cities?
5. Are there slums in present-day American cities? What efforts are being made to eliminate them?

Do your students feel that services not now regarded as necessary should be provided at public expense (tax-supported)?

LINKING PAST   AND PRESENT

Where do cities grow? Why did our cities grow up where they did? One reason is that certain locations were ideal for the growth of industry. *Pittsburgh, Pennsylvania,* became the first great steel center because it was near all the needed raw materials. Before the discovery of high-grade iron ore around Lake Superior, iron ore was mined near Pittsburgh. Coke, which is necessary for smelting iron ore, could be made from coal mined near Pittsburgh. Water and rail transportation were good, and immigrants from Europe furnished plenty of labor.

Minneapolis, Minnesota, is a large producer of flour. Wheat is grown nearby in the great wheat belt of Minnesota and the Dakotas. Waterfalls furnished power to run the early flour mills. The city has good railroad connections, and lies near the head of navigation on the Mississippi River.

In the West, *San Francisco, California,* grew by leaps and bounds during the Gold Rush because it was a seaport where would-be miners landed and moved on to the nearby gold fields. After the railroads linking San Francisco with the East were completed, the city continued to grow rapidly. Settlers from other parts of the country came in a steady stream to San Francisco and to nearby farming regions. The city became an important shipping center for mining and agricultural products.

Involvement in more varied activities, including community service, may well mean that mothers and fathers today have less free time than those of a generation or two ago.

America Provides More
Opportunities for More People

What this chapter is about —

Much of America's story, as we have seen, has been a story of growth and change. Our nation has expanded in size and population, and new ways of living have developed. To be sure, change sometimes creates new problems. Thus, the settlers in colonial times did not have to worry about unemployment or the market prices of crops, as people do today. But change has also brought more leisure time and new opportunities. Few of us, for example, would like to work as hard or as long as people had to in colonial times. Nor would we want to do without the modern conveniences and labor-saving machinery which have shortened our workday.

Moreover, greater leisure and increased opportunities have made it possible to improve and enrich American life. During the mid-1800's, as we learned in Chapter 17, some Americans gladly gave their time and energy to help unfortunate people, to abolish slavery, and to increase women's rights. At the same time, there was greater interest in schooling and in the reading and writing of books.

In the last century, and especially since 1900, changes in American life have affected more and more people. The increased use of machines has reduced working hours for most Americans. There have been greater opportunities for education

People in our story — college students (1920's), visiting nurse, scientist, baseball player, movie cameraman, architect.

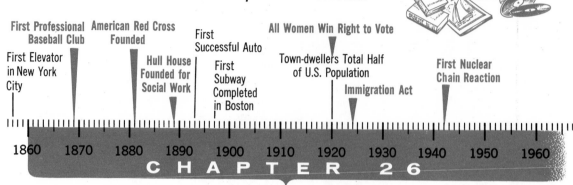

New Possibilities Develop for Americans

First Elevator in New York City

First Professional Baseball Club

American Red Cross Founded

Hull House Founded for Social Work

First Successful Auto

First Subway Completed in Boston

All Women Win Right to Vote

Town-dwellers Total Half of U.S. Population

Immigration Act

First Nuclear Chain Reaction

1860 1870 1880 1890 1900 1910 1920 1930 1940 1950 1960

C H A P T E R   2 6

1860–The Present

and recreation. More Americans have taken an interest in literature, music, and art. To learn what has been accomplished in these fields and what social changes have taken place, we shall answer the following questions:

▶ 1. What important social changes have come about in recent years?

▶ 2. How have opportunities for education and recreation increased?

▶ 3. What advances have been made in science, literature, and art?

1 What Important Social Changes Have Come About in Recent Years?

IMPORTANT POPULATION CHANGES

During the last hundred years, as we saw in Chapter 25, the population of the United States has grown tremendously. It has multiplied more than fivefold, from 36 million at the close of the Civil War to nearly 200 million today. Related to the rapid growth of our nation are certain other important population changes.

A boom in the birth rate begins in the 1940's. Our nation has not grown at a steady rate. During the 1930's, the population of our country increased at a far slower pace than it had in earlier years. This change was partly due to laws limiting immigration (page 527) and partly to a falling *birth rate*. The 1930's, you re-

member, were depression years when jobs were scarce and wages low. Under these conditions fewer people got married, and fewer babies were born. Men who studied population figures in these years believed that by 1985 the population of the United States would total about 160 million. During the 1940's and 1950's, however, the birth rate jumped sharply, increasing the size of the average American family. By 1960, as the number of Americans passed 180 million, population estimates for the next 25 years had to be sharply revised.

The number of senior citizens increases. In recent years there have not only been more babies but an increasing number of older people. Important discoveries in

This mobility can be illustrated by having members of the class list how long they have lived in the community and the state, and tabulating the results.

medical science have reduced the number of deaths due to many diseases. Americans have learned to eat more healthful foods. They have more time to relax on week ends and vacations. More attention has been paid to *preventing* disease. As a result of all these things, more and more Americans are living longer and the number of older people is growing larger.

Large numbers of Americans are on the move. Americans have always been a restless and energetic people. If this were not so, they would not have settled a whole continent, or developed our natural resources, or built up American industry. But a hundred years ago a much larger percentage of people grew up, married, and lived out their lives in the same place. Often their parents and grandparents had done so before them.

Today American families move about and change their homes more frequently than ever before. Perhaps you were born in one town or city, started your schooling in another, and are now living in a third. Of the many reasons for this frequent movement, or *mobility,* of Americans, we shall mention only a few.

(1) So long as a large part of the American people were farming land that they owned, more families tended to remain in one place. But today, because of modern farm machinery, it takes less manpower to supply food for the nation's needs. More farm people, therefore, have left the "old homestead" for jobs in cities and towns.

(2) It is easy for a family to move long distances these days. To the railroads of 1865 have been added the airplane and the family car. Our vast highway system makes the transfer of a family to another state or part of the country swift and comfortable.

(3) Many heads of families work for large companies with factories and offices in many different locations. Often these persons are transferred from a plant in one part of the United States to another plant.

(4) As the number of people who live longer has increased, more retired persons move to parts of the country where the climate and mode of living is more comfortable.

Many Negroes move to northern states. One particular movement of population — that of Negroes to the North — deserves mention. Before the war between the North and the South, most Negroes lived in the South. After the war they began to move northward in search of better opportunities. Not until World War I, however, did Negroes move to the North in large numbers. The nation at that time was bending all its energies toward winning the war. With factories turning out huge amounts of goods and with millions of men in the armed services, jobs became plentiful. So hundreds of thousands of Negroes went north to find employment. The same thing happened again on an even larger scale during World War II. After each of these wars, most Negroes who went north for jobs stayed and made their homes in the large cities of the North. Since World War II, Negroes have continued to move north. By 1960 almost half of the nineteen million Negroes in this country were living in northern states.

The movement of Negroes to northern cities was part of an effort to improve themselves. We must remember that the road of the Negro in this country has not been easy. Even though their freedom and citizenship were guaranteed after the war between the North and South, most Negroes were very poor. They had little or no education and found it difficult to get good jobs and adequate housing. But American Negroes have achieved wonders against great odds. Today there are many Negro

TWO FAMOUS NEGRO LEADERS have been honored on U.S. postage stamps. Booker T. Washington (left) founded Tuskegee Institute. George W. Carver did outstanding work in agricultural chemistry (page 541).

doctors, lawyers, teachers, artists, actors, and business leaders. They have founded banks, insurance companies, and other businesses. Since 1900 the number of Negro college graduates has increased rapidly. Negroes have become famous in many different fields: *education* — Mary McLeod Bethune; *science* — George Washington Carver; *international affairs* — Ralph J. Bunche; *music* — Marian Anderson; and *sports* — Joe Louis, Jackie Robinson, and a number of Olympic stars, including Rafer Johnson and Wilma Rudolph.

IMMIGRATION IS LIMITED

Immigrants face many problems. From 1880 to 1930, millions of immigrants came to our shores in search of a better life (page 510). Many of the new arrivals during these years did not have an easy time. Most of them had little or no knowledge of English. Yet in order to secure jobs, to buy food and clothing, and to find their way from one place to another, they needed to know at least a few words of English. Newcomers also had to get used to customs that were new and strange to them. It was only natural that many of them chose to live near earlier immigrants from their own country. Then they were able not only to speak the same language

but to share customs and memories of the old country. Whole sections of cities and towns, therefore, were settled by people of one nationality. Often these families formed a community within a city.

Most immigrants had little or no money when they arrived in our country. And getting a job was difficult unless the newcomers had special skills which were needed by employers. Often they had to accept the jobs with the hardest work, the longest hours, and the lowest pay. Because it took time for immigrants to learn American ways, greedy and selfish men were able to take advantage of them.

Immigrants become less welcome. Not all people were friendly to immigrants. (Some people dislike anybody or anything which seems strange to them.) Nevertheless, in its earlier years, the United States welcomed immigrants. It was as though our country said: "Come one, come all. We are a big country. We have much work to do. We want to conquer the wilderness, to build new cities, to create more farms, to produce even more goods in our factories. We need willing workers for all our tasks. Come to our shores and help to make America great and prosperous."

By the closing years of the 1800's, however, many Americans began to doubt whether this attitude toward immigration was wise. This doubt grew stronger as the number of immigrants arriving grew larger and larger. Could such great numbers of immigrants be taught American ways? Were they endangering our democracy? In raising these questions, some Americans pointed to the foreign settlements in our cities. Here, they stated, was proof that we were not showing immigrants how to adopt our ways of living and thinking. Those who opposed the flood of newcomers also argued that, by their willingness to

During these years an important function of the **526** schools was "Americanization."

work for low pay, immigrants were lowering wages for American workers.

Limits are placed upon the number of immigrants. As a result of these fears a cry arose that immigration should be restricted. Even as early as 1882 a law had been passed which forbade the immigration of Chinese laborers. Californians, in particular, objected to letting in Chinese, as well as Japanese, because they were willing to work for low wages. From time to time other laws were made restricting immigration. In 1917, for example, a law was passed barring immigrants who could not read. Then in 1924 a law limiting immigration in general was passed. This law forbade most immigration from Asian countries and limited the number of other newcomers to about 150,000 a year.

The number of immigrants to come from each country was known as a *quota*. Quotas were based upon the number of persons of each nationality in the United States. The quota system did not cut down the number of immigrants from the countries of western Europe as sharply as it did immigration from other parts of Europe. (This was because immigrants from eastern and southern Europe did not start arriving in large numbers until 1890.) Because of this law the total number of newcomers to our shores each year was greatly reduced. The McCarran Act, passed in 1952, continued the quota system but lifted the ban against immigration from Asian countries. In recent years, Congress has assigned immigration quotas to a number of new nations in Asia and Africa.

‍*️**There are exceptions to the quota system.** The McCarran Act limits quota immigration to about 155,000 persons per year. Even so, in a typical year only about two thirds of this number actually enter the country as "quota" immigrants.

Over half the number of people who come into this country each year to live are not counted in any quotas. For instance, there are no limits on the number of persons who come into the United States from Canada or the independent countries of Latin America. Also, foreign-born husbands, wives, and children of American citizens are not counted in quotas.

*️**Displaced persons enter this country.** After World War II, millions of people, uprooted by the war, sought new homes. More than 400,000 displaced Europeans were admitted to this country between 1948 and 1952. In general, these refugees were considered part of future quotas for their country of origin. In this way the annual quotas for some European nations have been partly filled for hundreds of years to come. Under the Refugee Relief Act of 1953, however, about 190,000 quota-free immigrants from Europe and Asia were allowed to enter the United States. (Look at the chart on page 508 to see the amount of immigration in recent years.)

THE PROBLEM OF SLUMS

In Chapter 25 you learned that the rapid growth of cities in the late 1800's and early 1900's created slum areas. Large numbers of poor people, many of them immigrants, were herded together in wretched tenement houses in crowded streets. Fortunately there were men and women in the United States who were determined to do something to wipe out slum conditions. One of these persons, Jacob Riis, helped make Americans aware of living conditions in slums through his vivid newspaper reporting and his books (page 516).

Jane Addams fights slum conditions. Another person who devoted her life to helping unfortunate people in the cities

(*Continued on page 530*)

America has drawn its strength from people of varied backgrounds. Throughout this book, and particularly in this unit, such persons are mentioned in story or picture. Shown on these two pages are some Americans who have contributed in one field or another to American life. Whatever their field of activity or how well known they may be, they are Americans all.

Negro lawyer THURGOOD MARSHALL argued the school segregation case that led to the Supreme Court's historic decision in 1954 (page 688). In 1965 he became the first Negro to hold the office of U.S. Solicitor General.

Born in Russia, aircraft manufacturer IGOR SIKORSKY came to the United States to escape the Bolshevik Revolution. Among his many accomplishments was the development of America's first successful helicopter.

JACOB RIIS, Danish immigrant, worked as a New York newspaper reporter for many years. His vivid articles exposing slum conditions awakened public interest in reform (page 516).

MRS. PATRICIA HARRIS was appointed as Ambassador to Luxemburg in 1965. Formerly a teacher of law at Howard University, she became the first Negro woman to serve as an ambassador.

Of Italian background, FIORELLO LA GUARDIA was one of New York City's most colorful mayors (1933–1945). His interest in civic problems led to many effective reforms.

LUIS MUÑOZ MARÍN served as governor of Puerto Rico for sixteen years. Under his leadership Puerto Rico made remarkable progress toward solving its economic problems in Operation Bootstrap (page 585).

HIRAM FONG, lawyer, businessman, and former member of the Hawaiian legislature, became one of Hawaii's first United States senators after that territory won statehood in 1959.

A Jewish merchant and banker, HAYM SALOMON was forced to flee from Poland for his part in a struggle for Polish freedom. During the American Revolution, he devoted much of his fortune to the Patriot cause (page 510).

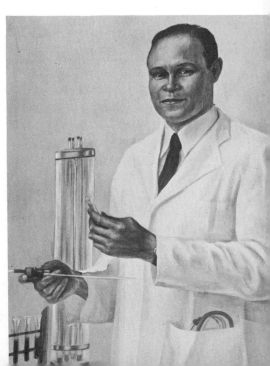

Negro surgeon CHARLES R. DREW, through research in blood preservation and organization of blood banks, helped save millions of lives during and since World War II.

HULL HOUSE, CHICAGO
ABOUT 1890

was Jane Addams. Brought up in a comfortable midwestern home, Miss Addams was deeply troubled when she first saw conditions in the slums of Chicago. Although she was not physically strong, she made up her mind to do what she could to improve conditions among the poor.

After study in Europe, Miss Addams returned to Chicago. In an old mansion in the heart of Chicago's tenement district she established Hull House in 1889. Here she labored to help the families of the neighborhood. Mothers who had jobs or were sick could leave their children in day nurseries where they would be sure of good care. Nourishing food was provided for the underfed children of the neighborhood. Inexpensive rooms in good surroundings were offered to working girls. Clubs and classes provided instruction and happy times for boys and girls. Immigrants were helped to get a better start in the new country to which they had come.

The example of Jane Addams inspired other people to action. They banded together to improve conditions in other cities. They organized settlement houses like Hull House. They formed boys' clubs to furnish wholesome activities — bowling, swimming, hiking, games of all sorts, and study groups. Given a chance to put their time to good use in good surroundings, the members of boys' clubs were far less likely to turn to crime.

Slum conditions are improved. These reformers also turned to the government for help to clean up the slums. As we have seen, whenever enough people are deeply aroused, they force the government to act. City, state, and federal governments took steps to improve undesirable conditions in the crowded cities. Laws were passed controlling the ways in which buildings could be constructed. The laws stated that a certain amount of light and air should reach every room and that fire escapes should be provided. The public water supply was checked carefully to see that the water was pure and that there was enough of it for every purpose. Sewage systems were improved. Street-cleaning departments did much to clear the filth and litter from the streets. Parks and playgrounds were built. Old buildings were torn down and replaced by modern, low-rent public housing developments. In many ways the government has tried to improve conditions in our great cities.

THE PROBLEM OF INTOXICATING LIQUOR

Groups of reformers fight against the use of liquor. Another problem which caught the attention of reformers in the late 1800's was the liquor problem. You have already learned (Chapter 17) about the beginnings of the temperance movement. After the Civil War was over, people once more took up the fight against the use of liquor. They felt something should be done to prevent the crime, misery, and poverty which the use of strong drink often brings. The reformers' aim was to forbid or *prohibit* the manufacture and sale of intoxicating drinks.

Beginning in 1872, a new political party, called the *Prohibition Party,* was

Unsatisfactory living conditions are found in rural as well as urban areas.

(*Continued on page 533*)

The New
PACIFIC
WORLD

Long ago, the original inhabitants of America's Pacific frontier had a colorful and abundant way of life. The sculptured coat of arms above dates from the time when Hawaii was an independent island kingdom and its chiefs wore red cloaks made out of thousands of wild bird feathers. Along the northwest coast of America, the fishing grounds provided the Indians with more food than they needed. Using the plentiful timber of the region, the Indians fashioned such striking buildings as the meeting house (left) near Ketchikan, Alaska, with its painted totem poles.

Grand Coulee Dam (right) in the state of Washington shows how the modern inhabitants of the Pacific region are using its resources to enrich American life. Harnessed by the dam, the Columbia River yields electric power for new industry, and water to irrigate new cropland.

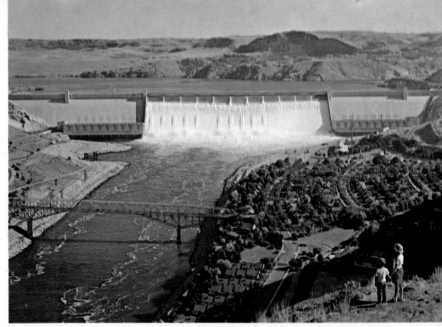

Soaring arches (left) called attention to the Science Pavilion of the World's Fair held at Seattle, Washington. The fair was a showcase for American advances in scientific discovery, many of which have been made in the universities and laboratories of the Pacific coast.

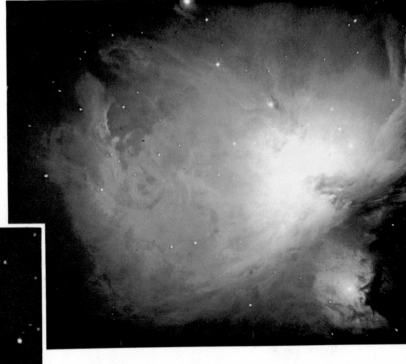

One of the Pacific world's greatest scientific resources is the astronomical observatory at Mount Palomar in California. Through its 200-inch telescope the first photographs were taken which recorded the colors of the Great Nebula of Orion (above) and the Ring Nebula of Lyra (left).

MANY CITIES are beginning to replace areas like this one with new low-rent housing developments, which are less crowded, less of a fire hazard, and more attractive.

formed. The Prohibition Party, however, was not as successful in arousing public interest as the efforts of earnest private citizens. Through churches, clubs, and organizations like the Women's Christian Temperance Union (the W.C.T.U.) and the Anti-Saloon League, they held meetings and published articles urging prohibition. Women even went into saloons and held prayer meetings. One of the greatest workers for prohibition was Frances E. Willard, who for many years was the energetic leader of the W.C.T.U.

National prohibition is tried. As a result of all these efforts, many states passed laws forbidding the sale of intoxicating liquors. Such states were called "dry" states. There was a serious drawback, however, to state prohibition; liquor could easily be smuggled into dry states from nearby states where the liquor business was permitted. So an active campaign was carried on to bring about nation-wide prohibition. In 1919, the Eighteenth Amendment to our Constitution went into effect. It forbade the manufacture, transportation, and sale of intoxicating liquor within the United States (page A28).

National prohibition led to a bitter dispute. Those who favored prohibition pointed to a decrease in the liquor consumed, fewer arrests for drunkenness, and higher amounts in savings banks as proof of its success. But national prohibition was difficult to enforce because many people did not want it. Liquor was smuggled in from other countries by lawless gangs and distributed by men known as "bootleggers." After fourteen years (in 1933), national prohibition was brought to an end by the Twenty-First Amendment to the Constitution. By this amendment the control of the liquor problem was returned to the states.

Note that a state still has the right to vote itself "dry."

A BRIDE of a century ago might have chosen a gown like this one, actually worn by a Connecticut girl in 1866. Notice the full skirt and delicate bonnet and fan.

WOMEN FIGHT TO GAIN EQUALITY

Women take part in activities outside the home. The struggle to win the same rights and opportunities for women as for men began in the 1830's and '40's (Chapter 17). After the Civil War was over, women took an increasing interest in improving living conditions and in public affairs. For example, women like Jane Addams worked to get rid of slums. Clara Barton, who had helped nurse sick and wounded soldiers during the war, founded the American Red Cross in 1881. She was its able and energetic leader for many years.

The growth of industry also helped to change the earlier ideas about women's rights. As factories and businesses multiplied, more and more opportunities outside the home were opened to women. The wages women received in these jobs gave them more freedom. New industries also turned out labor-saving aids to help women in their homes — such as gas and electric stoves, vacuum cleaners, electric refrigerators, and washing machines. Housework thus became easier, and women had more time for interests outside their homes.

Many colleges, formerly limited to men, now accepted women students. Also, by 1901, over 120 women's colleges had been founded. Because the opportunities for college education were greater, women were able to enter the professions, such as law and medicine.

Women win the right to vote. As women became more active outside the home, there seemed less and less reason to deny them the right to vote. Susan B. Anthony and Elizabeth Cady Stanton were leaders of the National Woman's Suffrage Association. They carried on their efforts to win equal rights for women in the face of scorn and strong opposition. By 1900, four states west of the Mississippi River had approved *woman suffrage;* that is, they had granted women the right to vote. But leaders in the battle for women's rights had to fight long and hard to win suffrage for all American women. Women wrote newspaper articles and gave lectures. They even paraded before the White House to awaken the public to the need for this reform. In 1920, the Nineteenth Amendment (page A29) was added to the Constitution, extending to women the right to vote. Women in all parts of the country voted in the election of 1920. Since that time they have taken more and more interest in government. Women today not only vote but hold many offices in our national, state, and local governments.

In countries where there is a shortage of labor **534** (USSR and Red China, for example) even a higher per cent of women work outside the home than in this country.

CLARA BARTON

A youth spent outdoors with her brother helped ready her for the hard life of army camps.

NURSING her brother for two years, after he'd been injured in a house-raising, made thirteen-year-old Clara deeply aware of the needs of others. A self-reliant person, she later taught school in Massachusetts, then went to Washington as a clerk just before the Civil War.

IN WASHINGTON, Clara brought news from home and food to lonely troops who had lost their baggage. Collecting and distributing food and clothing soon became a full-time occupation, and she determined to carry her work to the front.

"ANGEL OF THE BATTLEFIELD" was the name given to Clara because of her work in nursing the wounded and carrying supplies. In 1864, the government appointed her a superintendent of nurses. After the war, she served as a nurse in Europe where she first witnessed and admired the work of the International Red Cross.

THE RED CROSS in America was established in 1881 with Clara as president. Bringing help to flood victims, she established the idea of Red Cross relief for peacetime disasters.

CHECK UP

1. (a) Why has the nation's population in recent years included greater numbers of both children and old people? (b) Why do Americans today tend to move more frequently from one community to another? (c) When did Negroes begin to move to northern cities? Why? (d) How have American Negroes made progress?

2. (a) What problems have immigrants faced on first arriving in this country? (b) Why did some Americans want to restrict immigration? (c) In what ways has immigration been limited?

3. (a) How did reformers try to improve slum conditions? (b) How has government sought to improve conditions in the cities?

4. (a) How did reformers fight against the use of liquor? (b) What was national prohibition? (c) How was it ended?

5. (a) How did the growth of industry lead to greater freedom for women? (b) How did women gain the right to vote?

Questions #1 and 2 effectively probe the students' understanding of population and immigration.

How Have Opportunities for Education and Recreation Increased?

During our early history, there were few schools and fewer colleges. Nor did most Americans have much time for education or for amusements either. People worked from sunup to sundown to obtain the food, clothing, and shelter they needed. By the 1900's, however, the greater use of machines and new kinds of power had shortened the workday. With more free hours, Americans have been able to increase their schooling and to enjoy many kinds of recreation.

EDUCATION

The American public school system develops. By the mid–1800's, interest in education was much greater than in colonial days (Chapter 17). Public elementary schools paid for by taxes had started, and a few public high schools had been opened. Still, school terms were short and boys and girls were not required to attend school. Many of those who did go to school dropped out after completing a few grades, in order to go to work.

Nowadays the picture is quite different. As the population of the country has increased, the number of schools has multiplied and the number of pupils in school has soared. About nine out of ten young people of school age attend school. The aim of most Americans is to complete at least a high school education. The "little red school house," where a single teacher taught children of different grades in one room, has almost disappeared. New, modern school buildings are to be found in most communities. In many cases, too, a regional high school has taken the place of several very small high schools in towns or farm areas. The high schools of today offer a wide variety of subjects and many extracurricular programs.

College enrollments increase. Just as more children go to school these days, so more young people go to college. In fact, all indications are that in coming years more young people will seek admission to college than the colleges have room for. Most of our earlier American colleges were private; that is, they were built and supported by gifts of money from generous citizens. In later years, however, colleges and universities were established by states

POUNDING CORKS into medicine bottles (left) was one way for a girl to earn a living in the 1800's, when women were just beginning to work in factories and offices. Nowadays jobs in the drug industry — as a research technician, for instance (right) — require a background of skill and education.

Most of the land-grant colleges have become large universities offering a variety of programs in addition to agriculture and engineering.

and even by cities. The Morrill Act (page 494) made it possible to set up state colleges which specialized in agriculture and engineering. Today over half of all the college students in the country are enrolled in publicly supported colleges and universities.

Education is important for Americans. The United States has gone farther than any other nation in making it possible for citizens to obtain an education. Perhaps you have thought of going to school only in terms of getting a better job and enjoying a richer, fuller life. But education is also important for the future of our nation. A free democracy cannot exist unless its citizens are well informed, can think clearly, and are able to choose their leaders wisely. Nor can the United States successfully meet the challenge of Communist Russia and China unless it has talented scientists and engineers, skilled technicians, able diplomats, and wise statesmen.

Amusements and sports play a larger part in American life. In early times, as we have seen, Americans had few opportunities for amusement and play. During the early 1800's, people began to find more time for recreation. But most amusements were simple and were still centered about the home. People continued to frown upon those who spent much time on sports or other amusements.

BASEBALL — ABOUT 1875

FOOTBALL — ABOUT 1880

Since the time of the Civil War, however, sports and amusements have come to hold an important place in the lives of the American people. The growth of cities and towns, where large numbers of people live close together and have more leisure hours, has encouraged new forms of amusement. Schools and colleges support athletic programs. As a result, millions of present-day Americans enjoy football, baseball, hockey, golf, swimming, tennis, boating, basketball, wrestling, boxing, bowling, and other sports.

Baseball becomes the national sport. Most Americans consider baseball the national sport. It began in the early 1800's with such games as "old-cat" and "rounders." The following description of "rounders" shows how different this early game was from baseball today:

✳ We used to dig a hole in the ground for the home position, and place four stones in a circle, or nearly so, for the bases and, choosing up sides, we went in for a lively time at what was the parent game of baseball. When the ball tosser, or "feeder," sent a ball to the bat, and it was hit into the field, the player running round the bases at once became the target of the fielders. Their efforts, if the ball was not caught, were directed at hitting him with the ball, in which case he was out. Failing to do this, they would try and toss the ball into the hole at "home."

Your students may wish to supplement this list of baseball's immortals.

About 1840, rules were proposed which led to baseball as we know it today. The diamond-shaped playing field came into use and players were limited to nine on each side. The Knickerbocker Baseball Club of New York City was perhaps the first group to play under the new rules. The Knickerbockers also adopted uniforms of blue trousers, white shirts, and straw hats.

In the late 1800's, baseball grew rapidly. Baseball clubs were formed in many cities. The first paid professional team, known as the Cincinnati Red Stockings, appeared in 1869. By 1900, two major leagues, the National and the American Leagues, had been formed. Three years later, the first post-season or World Series games between the champions of the two leagues took place. Today baseball is played on sandlots by American boys throughout the country as well as in schools and colleges. Millions follow the progress not only of the major league teams but also of teams in the many minor leagues. Although the fans of each team have their favorites, baseball's immortals include such players as Honus Wagner, Christy Mathewson, Ty Cobb, Tris Speaker, Cy Young, Lou Gehrig, Babe Ruth, Joe DiMaggio, Ted Williams, Stan Musial, and Willie Mays.

Football wins great popularity. Another favorite American sport is football. The American game had its beginnings in

BASKETBALL — ABOUT 1905

the English game of rugby. In the early days, as played by American schoolboys and college students, it was largely a game of kicking the ball. The first real college game of football was played between Princeton and Rutgers in 1869. Football spread rapidly to other colleges.

Today the golden autumn days find football games taking place all over the country as throngs of onlookers cheer their favorite teams. New rules and the use of the forward pass and the T-formation make the modern game of football far different from that of former days. Famous coaches, such as Knute Rockne of Notre Dame, have produced great teams. Professional football teams now share the spotlight with schools and colleges.

Basketball catches up with baseball and football in popularity. Basketball is an American sport which did not appear until the 1890's. Dr. James Naismith of Springfield Y.M.C.A. College wanted a winter sport to keep his football and baseball players in trim. He worked out the rules for a new game to be played indoors, called basketball. He set up peach baskets at each end of a hall. The referee had to climb a stepladder to remove the ball from the basket after a shot had been placed. Because basketball required little equipment, it spread rapidly in popularity. Today professional, college, and high school basketball games attract much interest.

Spectator amusements grow tremendously. Sports are recreation not only for those who take part in them but for those who watch athletic contests. Each year millions of spectators watch baseball, football, basketball, and hockey games, boxing and wrestling matches, and the like. Other forms of spectator amusements have become popular in recent years.

The movies. Motion pictures created a whole new field of amusement for the

A MULE-DRAWN BARGE glides along the historic Chesapeake and Ohio Canal, near Washington, D.C., on a hot summer afternoon. Boating in any form is a favorite American pastime.

American people. Pioneered by Thomas Edison, early motion pictures were very different from those we see today. The film flickered and was dim. The motions of the actors were quick and jerky; and their facial expressions as they registered fear, joy, or sadness would seem to us rather silly. But the movies improved rapidly. In 1915, the success of *Birth of a Nation* encouraged the building of silent-movie theaters in cities and towns throughout the country. A second landmark in the history of motion pictures as entertainment occurred in 1927 when Al Jolson's *The Jazz Singer* successfully introduced the talking picture. During the 1930's, pictures in color added to the enjoyment of movie-goers. Each week millions of people attend some motion picture theater or "drive-in," though television has reduced the number of movie-goers in recent years.

Today greater stress is being placed on physical **539** fitness for all; i.e. greater participation in body-building sports.

Radio and television. Since the 1920's, radio has been bringing musical programs, newscasts, sports events, and a variety of other programs to an increasing audience. The addition of sight to sound accounts for the widespread popularity of television since World War II, although television has not displaced the radio in American homes. Taken together, radio and television present an amazing variety of free entertainment to the American people.

Vacations become an American habit. Vacations are another example of how Americans have found new uses for their leisure time. In the late 1800's only the well-to-do left home for a vacation. They went to "resorts" — expensive hotels in the mountains or at the seashore. Some families went to board at a farm house or had their own summer camps or cottages.

In the last 75 years the situation has changed completely. More families have leisure and can afford vacations. More families, also, have automobiles to take them where they want to go. Today millions of families go away for vacations. They may go to a lake, to the mountains, or to the seashore. Perhaps they merely drive a short distance to visit relatives. Or they may visit one of the scores of national parks which are scattered all across the nation. The Grand Canyon in Arizona is such a park; so are Yellowstone, Yosemite, and many others. In 1960, 72 million Americans visited these and the other national parks.

CHECK UP

1. (a) How has education changed since the 1800's at the high school level? (b) At the college level?

2. How have baseball, football, and basketball become America's national sports?

3. What other forms of recreation have become popular?

The fact that science is international (results are published and scientists build on the work of other scientists) needs to be stressed. Defense-related research is an exception.

3 What Advances Have Been Made in Science, Literature, and Art?

SCIENCE

The United States becomes a leader in science and learning. For hundreds of years the universities of Europe were the world's great centers of learning. During the 1800's, however, a few professors in American colleges gained fame in certain fields of knowledge. Benjamin Silliman and Louis Agassiz (*ag'uh-sih*) did much to advance the science of geology, or the study of the earth. Agassiz also won fame through his study of animals (zoology), while Asa Gray became a noted authority on plants and flowers (botany). Following the Civil War, the number of famous scholars in American universities greatly increased. Later, in the years before World War II, when Germany and Italy were ruled by dictators, many European scholars sought refuge in our country. One of these was Albert Einstein, whose scientific theories paved the way for splitting the atom. Today American universities include on their faculties world leaders in all fields of learning.

Americans live in a wonder world created by science. We have already learned how science and invention have

Progress in public health and medical science have greatly increased life expectancy even in underdeveloped countries.

changed travel, communication, industry, and farming since the days of the Civil War. But scientific research has had an even wider influence upon our ways of living in recent years. For example, home life has been entirely changed by the use of electrical appliances. Chemical research has shown the way to new products and to the making of old products from new sources. Synthetics, plastics, and other materials have sprung from the chemist's test tube (page 445). Chemistry has found how to make dyes, perfumes, and explosives from coal tar. The Negro scientist George Washington Carver discovered that over three hundred articles could be made from peanuts, and that over a hundred products could be made from the sweet potato. These are but a few examples of the influence of science on what we eat, what we wear, and what we use.

Medical science points the way to better health and longer life. Just as startling have been the advances in medical science in recent years. For centuries man has been the helpless victim of dread diseases, many of which have now been conquered. Tuberculosis, if discovered in its early stages, can be controlled. The spread of smallpox, yellow fever, typhoid, and diphtheria can be prevented by inoculation. Although no cure for diabetes has been discovered, people who suffer from this disease can live normal lives by using insulin. Wonder drugs like penicillin have greatly reduced the dangers of pneumonia and other infections. During World War II, thousands of lives were saved through blood transfusions and the use of blood plasma. The percentage of babies who die each year has been greatly reduced. Operations which were formerly considered rare and unusual are now performed almost every day. The use of new vaccines has cut down the number of polio cases and may soon wipe out this crippling disease. Meanwhile, doctors and scientists continue their research to conquer cancer and heart disease. As a result of improvements in medicine and surgery, people can look forward to increasingly longer lives.

We enter the atomic age. In the summer of 1945, atomic bombs were dropped on two Japanese cities, Hiroshima and Nagasaki. These events hastened the end of World War II and gave man a new and fearful source of power.

The tiny particles which make up all substances in the world are called *atoms*. When an atom is split or smashed, tremendous energy is released. By splitting the atoms in a pound of uranium, for example, scientists can produce as much energy as can be obtained from millions of pounds of gasoline or thousands of tons of coal. Used in warfare, atomic power becomes a fearful weapon capable of destroying mankind. But used as a source of power in a peaceful world, atomic energy promises fuller and richer ways of living.

ALBERT EINSTEIN'S theories laid the basis for man's use of atomic energy. He also personally urged in 1939 that the United States begin work on the atomic bomb. Born in Germany, Einstein became an American citizen in 1940.

READING AND LITERATURE

American literature depicts American life. Great changes have taken place in American reading and literature in the last hundred years. Not only has the number of published books increased enormously, but American writers have turned more and more to writing about America itself. In their books they have portrayed America — its people, its customs, and its problems.

"Local color" writers. In the last half of the 1800's, there grew up a group of authors known as the "local color" writers. Each of these writers wrote about the section of the country in which he lived or with which he was familiar. Some authors wrote about the Middle West, others about the South, still others about New England. Perhaps the best known of the "local color" writers was Bret Harte, who wrote vivid tales, such as *The Luck of Roaring Camp,* about the mining camps of California.

Great American storytellers. The greatest American writer of stories and novels in the last half of the 1800's — and one of the greatest authors in all American literature — was Mark Twain. Twain, whose real name was Samuel Langhorne Clemens, painted an unforgettable picture of life along the Mississippi. *The Adventures of Tom Sawyer, Adventures of Huckleberry Finn,* and *Life on the Mississippi* are favorites of Americans of all ages. Another storyteller, Jack London, wrote gripping stories of the sea and the frozen northland in Alaska and Canada. O. Henry (his real name was William Sydney Porter) added to America's fame in the field of the short story by giving his stories an unexpected or surprise ending.

The West in literature. Important in the new American literature were the writers who told about the West and the frontier. Among the many authors who wrote realistically about pioneers was Willa Cather. In her novels *My Antonia* and *O Pioneers!* she described the life and the people of the western prairies.

The South in literature. Another section of the country which inspired many books was the South. Some authors wrote historical novels dealing with the founding and early history of the South. Ellen Glasgow of Virginia wrote many stories about the changes that took place in southern society after the war between the North and the South. Margaret Mitchell wrote the novel *Gone with the Wind,* which was a best-seller in the 1930's. It tells the story of the Civil War from the point of view of a family in Georgia and describes efforts to build a new South after the war. Perhaps you have read Marjorie Kinnan Rawlings' *The Yearling,* about a boy growing up in rural Florida.

American authors write about modern life and its problems. Many recent authors have been concerned with present-day life in our country. Some have pointed out problems in the American scene that they felt needed attention. Others, such as John P. Marquand and Sinclair Lewis, described how Americans in different walks of life reacted to the changes and confusions of our age. For example, Sinclair Lewis, winner of a Nobel Prize in literature, vividly described in his novels the people of a small midwestern town, the life of a typical American businessman, a physician, and so on. Another Nobel Prize winner of recent years was Ernest Hemingway, whose novels and stories reflected his world-wide interests.

Americans are proud of famous playwrights and poets. America has had poets and playwrights as well as writers of fiction. Eugene O'Neill, America's best-known dramatist, wrote one-act plays of

In the section, "For Further Reading," are listed books by and about Mark Twain.

MARK TWAIN

A boyhood spent along the Mississippi was the background for many of his best-loved writings.

"MARK TWAIN!" was the cry river men used when their soundings showed safe water. To Sam Clemens it recalled the exciting years he spent as a steamboat pilot, and he adopted the river cry for his pen name. First, however, he went west as a prospector.

PROSPECTING in Nevada brought Twain little wealth but many experiences which he turned into amusing stories. One was written, for example, after a mule fell through the canvas roof of Twain's dugout. He began writing for a local newspaper and soon became a full-time reporter.

"INNOCENTS ABROAD" was a humorous book about Twain's experiences with a party of Americans on a European tour including a caravan trip through the Holy Land. Within a year, 100,000 copies were sold, making Twain a successful author, well-known in England as well as America.

DRAMATIZING his new stories with his children was one of Twain's favorite pastimes as he continued to write the famous books which have brought pleasure to millions of American readers.

COMMEMORATIVE POSTAGE STAMPS remind us how foreign-born Americans have contributed to life in this country. From left to right, stamps honor John Audubon (born in French West Indies), known for lifelike paintings of birds; John Ericsson (born in Sweden), designer of the "Monitor"; Joseph Pulitzer (born in Hungary), famous newspaperman; Victor Herbert (born in Ireland), composer of operettas.

"For Further Reading" lists an interesting biographical sketch of Whitman.

the sea as well as full-length dramas. One of his plays, *Ah Wilderness!*, describes with sympathy the problems of a young boy growing up.

Walt Whitman is one of the world's great poets. You have probably read *O Captain! My Captain!*, which expresses Whitman's grief over the death of Lincoln. Whitman was stirred by America's past and exulted in the promise of its future. Through all his poems shines a strong faith in democracy and in people. Much of Whitman's poetry is in the form of free verse, which does not rhyme. A good example is *Pioneers! O Pioneers!*, part of which is quoted on page 304.

Two of America's most important recent poets have been Carl Sandburg and Robert Frost. Like Whitman's poems, Carl Sandburg's writings reveal his understanding and love of America. Though Robert Frost's poems often concern New England people and scenes, they actually tell us much about people anywhere. The poem called *Stopping by Woods on a Snowy Evening* is one of his best-known:

Whose woods these are I think I know.
His house is in the village though;
He will not see me stopping here
To watch his woods fill up with snow.

My little horse must think it queer
To stop without a farmhouse near
Between the woods and frozen lake
The darkest evening of the year.

He gives his harness bells a shake
To ask if there is some mistake.
The only other sound's the sweep
Of easy wind and downy flake.

The woods are lovely, dark and deep.
But I have promises to keep,
And miles to go before I sleep,
And miles to go before I sleep.[1]

Newspapers and magazines change to meet modern conditions. In the years since 1865, newspapers have undergone many changes and have reached larger and larger numbers of people. With the aid of the telephone, cable, and radio, they now print up-to-the-minute information from all over the world. This news is gathered by such news services as the Associated Press and the United Press. Popular features (including sports pages, comic strips, and women's pages) and the

[1] From NEW HAMPSHIRE by Robert Frost, published by Holt, Rinehart and Winston, Inc. Copyright 1923, Holt, Rinehart and Winston, Inc. Copyright 1951, Robert Frost. Published in Great Britain by Jonathan Cape, Ltd.

wide use of pictures have increased the number of readers. Columnists, who interpret or comment on the news, write articles which appear in papers from coast to coast. Another change that has taken place is the growth of the newspaper chain — that is, a group of newspapers owned and controlled by the same company. Since newspapers reach great numbers of readers, the power of the modern newspaper to influence public opinion is enormous.

In the United States today hundreds of magazines of all kinds are published, some weekly and some monthly. One of the pioneers who helped to develop a magazine read by millions across the nation was Edward Bok. Bok, who came from Holland as a small boy in 1870, in time became the editor of the *Ladies' Home Journal*. The new ideas he introduced made the *Journal* for many years one of the most widely read magazines in America.

Whatever his taste may be, the American can find on almost any newsstand magazines which will interest him. Some are news magazines. Others are magazines of opinion which express the views of their editors and contributors on questions facing the country and the world. Still others offer articles and short stories. Some magazines publish the best writing of present-day American authors. Two of the chief changes that have taken place in American magazines in recent years are (1) the growth of "picture" magazines and (2) the introduction of "digests" which condense articles from other magazines and papers.

Public libraries increase. The education and reading of the American people have been influenced by the spread of public libraries. Some libraries were established even in colonial times, but there were not many until after the period of the Civil War. The generous gifts of Andrew Carnegie (page 462) did much to bring good books and magazines within the reach of many people. The number of public libraries increased rapidly in the 1900's, until today there are few towns of any size which do not have library service. A recent development has been the use of traveling libraries or "bookmobiles" to bring books to areas where there is no public library close at hand.

Students may wish to read Dutch Boy Fifty Years After, written by Edward Bok.

"TORNADO," a painting by John Steuart Curry, depicts a midwestern farm family seeking shelter in their storm cellar as a threatening tornado approaches.

ART AND ARCHITECTURE

American art portrays American life Interest in all forms of art has grown in the United States in recent years. A steadily growing number of art schools offer instruction to those interested in the fine arts. Art museums and wealthy men and women have brought large numbers of the world's finest paintings and art objects to our country, where they can be viewed with pleasure by millions of Americans. In a recent year almost four million people visited the Metropolitan Museum of Art in New York City.

Among America's famous sculptors have been Daniel Chester French and Augustus Saint-Gaudens. French's statue of Lincoln in the Lincoln Memorial, Washington, D.C., and the one of the Minuteman at Concord, Massachusetts, have stirred the hearts of millions of people. Saint-Gaudens' statues and memorials are found in Boston, New York, Philadelphia, and many other cities.

There have been many fine American painters. Two well-known artists of the late 1800's were Frederic Remington and James McNeill Whistler. Remington painted exciting scenes of life in the Far West (see pictures on page 369 and facing page 432). You have probably seen Whistler's portrait of his mother.

Three more recent artists are especially noted for their paintings of the American scene. They are Thomas Benton, John Steuart Curry, and Grant Wood, all from the Middle West. Benton lived as a boy in Missouri, in the same surroundings as Mark Twain's famous characters Huck Finn and Tom Sawyer. The color and vigor of American life are dramatized in his paintings. Two of his murals used in this book (pages 44 and 122) also show his interest in American history. Curry was a farm boy who grew up to paint the people and the plains of his native Kansas (page 545). Grant Wood, sometimes called America's "Painter of the Soil," pictured in exact and clear details the homely scenes of Iowa farms and farm people.

American architecture is distinctly American. America has made its greatest contribution to modern art in the field of architecture — in the building of bridges

"ARBOR DAY," by Grant Wood, shows the teacher and pupils of a one-room school in Iowa planting a tree. Notice the fields stretching into the distance.

Art in the New Land contains stories of American artists and their works.

THE WORLD'S FAIR at Chicago in 1893 (below) helped set an elaborate style for buildings which was slow to change. Now, many modern architects prefer glass walls and a simpler shape which corresponds to the building's own steel framework, like that of the Union Carbide skyscraper in New York City (right).

"For Further Reading" lists a fictional biography of Stephen Foster.

and towering skyscrapers. The Golden Gate Bridge at San Francisco is a good example of the grace and skill of modern architecture. To gain space in the crowded cities, architects and engineers created the modern steel skyscraper — a breathtaking example of engineering skill. In the late 1800's, Louis Henri Sullivan fought for the idea that buildings should not be cluttered up from top to bottom with useless decoration but should express simply the use for which they were intended. He is known as "the father of the modern skyscraper."

Of all American architects, Frank Lloyd Wright probably contributed the most to modern American architecture. He boldly thrust aside the old styles of buildings, which were often poorly planned, and developed new designs. The many homes which he designed are well suited to the needs of modern living. Wright's influence can be seen in the work of many present-day American architects.

MUSIC

America develops music of its own. Music has always been a part of American life. As men and women struggled to build America, they sang at their work. Negro spirituals, sailors' chanteys, cowboy songs, canal and river songs, songs of pioneers, ballads — all these became the folk music of America. In the 1800's, a favorite way of spending the evenings was for a group to gather around an organ or a piano and sing. Old and young went to community "sings." The tender songs of Stephen Foster, such as *My Old Kentucky Home* and *Old Folks at Home,* were favorites.

After the war between the North and the South, American music became more varied. John Philip Sousa, who won fame as a bandmaster, composed a number of popular march tunes. Edward MacDowell became known as one of America's leading composers of serious music. He wrote hauntingly lovely music on American subjects. In the field of light opera the name

Radio, television, and phonographs, however, have reduced employment opportunities for musicians.

548 NEW CONDITIONS BRING CHANGES IN AMERICAN LIFE

of Victor Herbert stands out. An immigrant from Ireland, Herbert composed nearly 40 light operas, some of whose catchy tunes are still sung and played.

Opportunities to enjoy good music increase. More and more opportunities to enjoy music have developed in the 1900's. Music instruction has become a regular subject in our schools. High schools and junior high schools have their bands, orchestras, and glee clubs. Opera companies, such as the Metropolitan Opera Company of New York City, bring the world's best operas to large audiences. Symphony orchestras, led by famous conductors, present programs for music lovers. This is true not only in the older eastern cities like Philadelphia, Boston, and New York but also in other major cities throughout the country. In fact, there are well over a thousand symphony orchestras in the United States today. Orchestras in many of our cities have provided greater opportunities to hear good music by giving outdoor concerts "under the stars."

With the coming of the phonograph and the radio, Americans began to spend much more time listening to music. Today, as we play records on the phonograph in our living rooms, we may hear Rubinstein at the piano, Heifetz on the violin, and the voices of Marian Anderson and other famed singers, both past and present. A mere turning of the radio or television dial will bring us almost any kind of music, from the latest popular "hits" to the swelling tones of a great symphony orchestra.

Newer forms of music become popular in America. In the early 1900's, a new kind of music called *ragtime* appeared. It was distinctly American and expressed the vigor and fast movement of modern life. Ragtime, first played by American Negroes, soon became popular all over the country. One song that swept the nation was *Alexander's Ragtime Band*. Irving Berlin, who wrote this song, became one of the leading composers of what we now call popular music. Probably Berlin's best-known song is *White Christmas*.

After World War I a new form of ragtime was given the name *jazz*. One of the first great jazz orchestras was led by Duke Ellington. Paul Whiteman, "King of Jazz,"

MARIAN ANDERSON, American contralto, has won fame throughout the world. "A voice like hers," said the conductor Arturo Toscanini, "comes once in a century."

At 74 Irving Berlin wrote the songs for a new musical, "Mr. President."

IRVING BERLIN, born in Russia, came to America as a small boy. Though he never had musical training, he became one of America's best-loved songwriters.

was another famous orchestra leader. An offshoot of jazz is *swing* music, which features solo instruments. The swing band plays an accompaniment while the soloist improvises a melody. Benny Goodman's swing band of the 1930's was outstanding. George Gershwin borrowed the rhythms of jazz in composing music for symphony orchestras. His *Rhapsody in Blue* and the opera *Porgy and Bess* have been performed both in this country and abroad. Jazz, once frowned upon, is now a recognized form of music.

Many of our most popular songs have been written for musical comedies, which combine music and dancing with a story. Among musical comedies whose songs are still sung must be included: *Showboat* by Jerome Kern, *Kiss Me, Kate* by Cole Porter, *Of Thee I Sing* by George Gershwin. A famous team, Richard Rodgers and Oscar Hammerstein II, produced a number of great hits: *Oklahoma!, South Pacific,* and *The King and I.* A play written by George Bernard Shaw, *Pygmalion,* provided the story for *My Fair Lady.* This musical comedy, created by Frederick Loewe and Alan Jay Lerner, has been one of the most successful of recent years.

In reading about America's achievements in science, literature, art, and music, we have come across the names of many famous Americans. Famous names also stand out in other fields of activity — government service, business and industry, engineering, sports, and so on. We honor these people for their part in making life in America richer and fuller.

Proud as we are, however, of the famous "names" in our country's story, we must not forget that ordinary Americans have been key figures in building America. Thousands of men and women from our Atlantic seaboard states went west, conquered the wilderness, and established

new communities. Wherever they went, they carried with them American ideals. They were joined by groups of "unknown" men from all over the world. All these nameless Americans — from many lands, of all races, of different religions — by their work and their faith in American liberty and democracy have made America what it is today.

CHECK UP

1. (a) What are some scientific discoveries that have made possible a more comfortable life and better health? (b) What are the dangers and the opportunities of living in the atomic age?

2. (a) What is a "local color" writer? (b) Who have been some of the great American storytellers? (c) What authors have written about the West? (d) About the South? (e) Name some outstanding American poets.

3. (a) How have American newspapers and magazines changed in the last hundred years? (b) How have libraries served Americans' reading needs?

4. (a) What contributions have Americans made in art? (b) Architecture? (c) Music?

549

Check Up on Chapter 26

Do You Know the Meaning?

1. birth rate
2. mobility
3. nationality
4. quota
5. suffrage
6. penicillin
7. vaccine
8. local color
9. atomic energy
10. columnist
11. digest
12. bookmobile
13. symphony
14. jazz
15. extracurricular
16. spectator amusements

Can You Identify?

1. Robert Frost
2. Jane Addams
3. 1919
4. 1920
5. 1924
6. 1933
7. McCarran Act
8. W.C.T.U.
9. Clara Barton
10. Mark Twain
11. Willa Cather
12. Louis Agassiz
13. Albert Einstein
14. Susan B. Anthony
15. Prohibition Party
16. Sinclair Lewis
17. Walt Whitman
18. Frederic Remington
19. Frank Lloyd Wright
20. Stephen Foster
21. Irving Berlin
22. George Gershwin
23. George Washington Carver

What Do You Think?

1. Should the United States remove its restrictions on immigration? Give reasons.
2. Name some immigrants who have been outstanding, for example, in music, sports, or science. Explain what they have contributed to American life.
3. (a) Should every student be required to complete a high school education? Why? (b) Should every student go on to college? Why? (c) What type of education would you like to have? Why?
4. (a) Some people think that Americans get too much of their recreation from "spectator" amusements. Do you agree? Why? (b) Is there value in taking part in sports or in playing a musical instrument, for example, that cannot be achieved by watching others?
5. Would you rather live in one town for most of your life or move every few years to see different parts of the country? Explain why you feel as you do.

Questions #3-5 deal with problems about which your students will have views.

LINKING PAST AND PRESENT

What is an American? Almost no American (except the Indians) can trace his ancestors in this country back beyond the 1600's. Most of us would find that our ancestors came to North America much later — probably in the 1800's or perhaps in the 1900's. For America is a nation of immigrants or descendants of immigrants, whether our forefathers came to the New World in colonial days or in the years of the great immigrations or later. Americans today, therefore, are a mixture of nationalities. We believe that America has blended the best features of many peoples to produce a vigorous new national stock. Dorothy Thompson, a well-known writer, gave us a humorous description of the American nationality: "What is an American? — An American is a fellow whose grandfather was a German forty-eighter who settled in Wisconsin and married a Swede, whose mother's father married an Englishwoman, whose son met a girl at college, whose mother was an Austrian and whose father was a Hungarian Jew and their son in the twentieth century right now is six feet tall and goes to a state college, plays football, and can't speak a word of any language except American."

Women in politics. Today we are used to having women take an active part in politics as party workers, voters, and office-holders.

But when the woman suffrage amendment was passed almost 50 years ago, neither men nor women were used to the idea of females in politics. It took courage for women of the 1920's to go to the polls to vote, to say nothing of running for office! Nevertheless, they made a start. Before long, the governors of two states were women, and each house of Congress had a woman member.

As time passed, the number of women voters and office-holders increased. In the national government, Presidents Franklin Roosevelt and Dwight Eisenhower each appointed a woman Cabinet member, and each named a woman as the minister or ambassador to a foreign country. Seventeen women held seats in the 87th Congress — fifteen in the House of Representatives and two in the Senate. Many more women, of course, also hold offices in local and state governments. Moreover, women often serve their communities by arousing public interest in political issues and elections. In the 1960's, women are taking an even greater part in politics than they have done in the past. Since there are a few million more women of voting age in the United States than there are men, they could decide an election!

TO CLINCH YOUR

UNDERSTANDING OF

Unit 8

Summary of Important Ideas

In Unit Eight you have read how American life has been affected by the Machine Age, by social changes, and by greater opportunities for education and recreation.

1. Since 1820 more than 40 million people have immigrated to the United States.

   a. Among the reasons why immigrants have come to America are the desire for greater freedom and the hope of earning a better living. Millions of immigrants, settling on farms and in the city, have made great contributions to American life.

   b. When the good free land was gone and the demand for labor had begun to decline, the United States began a policy of restricting immigration.

2. With the growth of industry following the Civil War, American cities expanded rapidly in both number and size. Job opportunities in industry attracted immigrants and reduced the percentage of Americans living in farm areas. With the growth of cities came increased conveniences of living but also more serious social problems.

   a. Cities began to provide special services (such as pure water supplies) and to build tall buildings and new systems of transportation and lighting.

   b. City slums and intemperance were two evils which engaged the attention of Americans.

   c. In this period women achieved greater rights and became increasingly active outside the home.

Call attention to work done by the League of Women Voters.

d. Important population changes included increasing numbers of both babies and older people, the tendency of Americans to be on the move, and the migration of Negroes northward.

3. Industrialization has also affected American farms and small towns, where life is very different from a century ago.

4. With increased leisure, Americans have more time to become informed and to be entertained.

a. Education on all levels has become generally available.

b. Both newspapers and magazines have changed to meet new conditions. Books are readily available through purchase or library loan. The radio and television bring news of the world and entertainment into the home. Movies and sports events attract millions daily.

c. Distinctly American types of literature, art, music, and architecture have developed.

Unit Review

1. (a) For what reasons have immigrants come to this country? (b) From what countries have the largest numbers of immigrants come? (c) Where have they tended to settle? (d) Why was immigration restricted after World War I?

2. (a) Why did the percentage of the population living in cities increase rapidly after about 1880? (b) What were some problems resulting from the crowding of large numbers of people into American cities?

3. (a) How has life on farms and in small towns changed in the last hundred years? (b) Why have these changes come about?

4. (a) How have women gained increased rights? (b) Why have they become increasingly active in work outside the home?

5. (a) How is education changing in this country? (b) How has science made better living possible?

6. (a) What new games or sports have been developed in the United States? (b) What contributions have Americans made to music? art? architecture? literature?

Gaining Skill

How to Use Charts and Graphs

Many graphs and charts are included in this book to help you in the study of history. Once you learn how to get the most out of them, you will find that they are very helpful study tools.

It would take many words to present all of the information which charts can clearly illustrate. For example, the chart on page 232 pulls together many ideas explained in the text and shows in a "graphic" way the organization of our government. The top chart on page 141 diagrams local government in the Southern and New England Colonies and helps you compare them and note any differences. Throughout the book, you will find charts on political parties which will help you keep all of the parties' names straight (pages 240, 338, 415, 568, 686). If you were to put these charts together, you'd see the different steps and changes in the growth of political parties throughout our country's history. A chart, then, is a means of summing up information in a form which will make it easier to understand.

When you are preparing a report to give to the class or reviewing material you have studied, you will find it helpful not only to be able to use available charts but to make one for your own use. The first thing to do in making a chart is to select a topic. Let's say you decide to make a chart dealing with immigration to America. Because "Immigration" includes so many things, it will be necessary to limit this topic. Do you see why the topic "Contributions of Immigrants to America, 1850–1920" would be better? The next step is to determine what are the things you should remember about this topic. Ask yourself — which items of information are important? In this way, you will work out the major "categories" of information. Categories might include the names of immigrants, their native countries, and the fields in which they made contributions. Place each "category" in a separate column: one column for the person's name, another for his accomplishments, and so on. Before you read further, see if you can make such a chart.

Graphs are another kind of useful illustration. They present facts expressed in figures which are sometimes difficult to keep in mind. Graphs, such as the one on page 175, may present a comparison in time and amount. Or they may use measurement to show trends, as does the graph on page 296. The means of measurement may be a rising or falling line, a series of bars, or a symbol which represents a certain quantity.

To see what a particular graph does and how it should be used, look at the "bar" graph on page 219. Try to answer the following questions about this graph:

1. What kinds of information are presented?
2. Why is it called a bar graph? What is the means of measurement?
3. How many people does each division on the scale represent?
4. Are the divisions on the scale of equal size? Why is this important?
5. Does the scale begin with zero? Why is this important?
6. How would one find out the population of a particular state?
7. Which state had the largest population?
8. Which *two* states were the smallest?
9. Approximately how many people lived in Georgia at that time?
10. What states had populations of less than 300,000 people?
11. How many people were living in the two Carolinas at this time?
12. What period in our history does this graph illustrate?
13. How does this graph compare with the information in the text?
14. What is the purpose of this graph?
15. Does it do what it intends to do?
16. What did you learn from it?

There is a great deal of information shown in this graph. All of the charts and graphs in this book can help you if you study them as carefully as you have studied the graph discussed above.

Interesting Things to Do

The "things to do" which are marked with an asterisk (*) are for the whole class. The others are to be used as your teacher directs.

*1. Add to the drill cards the items marked "Can You Identify?" at the end of each chapter in Unit Eight.
*2. America was made by immigrants. What nationality are you descended from? Draw your "family tree" showing in what country your parents and grandparents were born. If necessary, go farther back to find an immigrant ancestor.
*3. On a map, locate the ten largest American cities and indicate the population of each.
4. Prepare a report to the class on one of these outstanding Negroes: Marian Anderson, Ralph Bunche, Booker T. Washington, George Washington Carver, Jackie Robinson.
5. If you read poetry well, select and read to the class some of the poems of Walt Whitman, Carl Sandburg, or Robert Frost.
6. Find out about the federal government's program to improve housing in cities and report to the class.
7. Find some pictures of paintings by one of the American artists mentioned in the text and show them to the class.
8. Tell the class about the life and work of one of the following: Mark Twain, Augustus Saint-Gaudens, George Gershwin, Irving Berlin, John Barry, Jacob Riis, John Philip Sousa, Albert Einstein, Jane Addams.
9. Consult *The American Songbag* by Carl Sandburg for typical American songs of the late 1800's. Read some of the verses to the class or, better yet, sing the songs.

"For Further Reading" lists books about Burbank, Muir, Carver, Clemens, and Whitman.

The United State

In Units Seven and Eight we read about many changes in the American way of life since 1865. As a result of these developments, Americans enjoy a higher standard of living than the people of any other nation. We also learned that difficult problems have arisen from time to time and that the government has taken steps to solve some of them. So far, however, we have said little of our Presidents since 1865 or of the growing importance of our country among the nations of the world.

For a hundred years after our government was set up in 1789, Americans were chiefly occupied with the big job which faced them at home — pushing their boundaries westward, conquering the wilderness, and peopling a continent. But at last the mighty march across the continent neared its end. Empty spaces became fewer; towns and cities multiplied. America's farms and factories were producing a flood of goods, more than enough for her own people. Speedier methods of transportation and communication brought all nations of the world closer together. As a result, since the late 1800's, the United States has become increasingly active in world affairs. Now events in distant lands, once of little con-

This statement calls attention to the fact that Presidents **554** since Grover Cleveland increasingly have had to concern themselves with foreign affairs and international problems.

Widens Its Horizons

cern to us, may affect our country and each one of us. America's new interest and influence in world affairs were dramatized in 1907 when President Theodore Roosevelt sent the fleet round the world on a goodwill trip, which included the visit to a Japanese port shown above.

We shall read about America's growing part in world affairs in the last two units of this book. Unit Nine will cover the period from 1865 to about 1920. Chapter 27 will tell how some of our Presidents during these years took steps to meet important problems. Chapter 28 will point out how the United States became interested in affairs beyond our borders and gained new possessions. By the early 1900's the United States had embarked on new foreign policies, particularly toward countries in Latin America and the Far East. In Chapter 29 you will read about these events and about World War I and the peace treaty that followed.

This quotation supports the idea that the Declaration of Independence was for all peoples for all time.

We seek to maintain the dignity and authority of the United States only because we wish always to keep our great influence unimpaired for the uses of liberty, both in the United States and wherever else it may be employed for the benefit of mankind. — WOODROW WILSON

American Leaders Branch Out

Along New Paths

Our Presidents by Morgan contains biographical sketches of the Presidents.

What this chapter is about —

Whenever you have a new teacher, a new president of your club, a new captain of your team — even when you make New Year's resolutions on December 31 — a feeling of change is in the air. You resolve to begin again, to do old things in a different way, and to do them better. You say to yourself, "This is a chance for a new start. This time I'll avoid old mistakes; this time I'll do the job right!"

The same thing happens in history. Every now and then there comes a time when large groups of people feel there is a chance to make a new start. In the United States such a time may come when a new President is elected. People say,

"What does the President intend to do? How well will he succeed?"

This chapter is concerned with the Presidents and the national government from the 1860's to the 1920's. We shall not attempt to cover fully the activities of all the Presidents during these years. (You will find brief sketches of the Presidents of this period on pages 559–560.) We shall find that some Presidents were unable or unwilling to make any important changes. But we shall tell about a few of the more important occasions when the country had a new President who felt we should make a "fresh start." These Presidents believed that it was time for the country to study

People in our story — political bosses, civil service applicant and inspector, forest ranger, government drug inspector.

556

itself more closely and to clear up certain problems which were troubling the American people. To pick out the important parts of the story, look for answers to the following questions:

1. How did the Presidents of the late 1800's deal with America's changing needs?

2. What evils did President Theodore Roosevelt fight to overcome?

3. What did President Wilson's plans for a "New Freedom" accomplish?

1 How Did the Presidents of the Late 1800's Deal with America's Changing Needs?

PRESIDENTS JOHNSON AND GRANT DO LITTLE TO MEET NEW PROBLEMS

It is easy for us today to look back and realize that after 1865 the United States was entering a new era. Growing use of machines and new methods of manufacturing goods enabled the United States to become a leading industrial nation. New machines and improved methods of farming made it possible for fewer farmers to raise larger crops than ever before. Trade with other nations increased. As the population of the United States soared, our cities increased in size and number. These and other developments not only changed the face of America but created new problems. You have already read about such problems as business booms and depres-

sions, monopolies, farm prices, and city housing. It took time for people to become fully aware of these new problems and for bold leaders to tackle them.

The Civil War saddled the country with many difficult problems. For a number of years after 1865, Americans had to deal with problems arising out of the past instead of looking to the future. Four years of bitter warfare had left deep wounds. The South, as you know, was especially hard hit. Thousands of its soldiers had given their lives for the southern cause. Because most of the fighting had taken place on southern soil, the destruction of property had been frightful. Returning soldiers found homes burnt to the ground, railroads torn up, cities badly

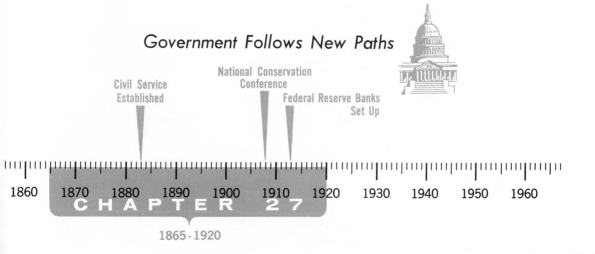

Government Follows New Paths

Civil Service Established

National Conservation Conference

Federal Reserve Banks Set Up

1860   1870   1880   1890   1900   1910   1920   1930   1940   1950   1960

C H A P T E R   2 7

1865-1920

damaged, and many necessities of life lacking. Confederate money was worthless.

The war created some pressing problems in the North as well. The number of northern soldiers killed or wounded exceeded the losses of the southern armies. To be sure, the North had suffered little property damage, and the need for wartime materials — guns, ammunition, uniforms, and so on — had caused northern industry to boom. But after the war, factories had to shift over to making articles for normal living. Many of the returning soldiers had trouble fitting back into a peacetime world quite different from the world they had known before.

Perhaps the most difficult problem resulting from the war was restoring the Confederate states to the Union (Chapter 20). The harsh measures Congress forced upon the South aroused resentment. Even after the last southern state was readmitted to the Union, the bitter memory of the years of reconstruction government lingered on in the South.

Political parties fail to deal with new problems. In the years following the end of the Civil War, political parties looked backward instead of forward. The Republicans, for example, were in control of the government in Washington from 1861 to 1885. In election after election they reminded the American people that the Republican Party had saved the Union. In other words, Republican candidates asked the voters to elect them because of their party's past record rather than for what they might do about new problems. Both Republicans and Democrats seemed more interested in building up their political power than in carrying out the wishes of the people. (See the chart of political parties on page 568.)

Because both the Republican and Democratic Parties were slow to respond to public needs, those who strongly favored re-

forms sometimes organized a new party. Several of these third parties were formed in the late 1800's, though none gained enough supporters to elect a President. But one third party was able to get a major party to adopt its reform programs. This happened in the 1890's when discontented farmers of the West and South organized the Populist Party (page 493). In the election of 1896 the Democratic Party adopted the chief reforms of the Populist program.

Presidents Johnson and Grant have troubled terms of office. Neither of the first two Presidents who followed Lincoln undertook any important reforms. In the election of 1864, Andrew Johnson had been named by the Republicans as their candidate for Vice-President. Johnson was a Democrat from Tennessee who was fiercely loyal to the Union. The Republicans had nominated him in hopes that he would bring southern votes to their side. When Lincoln was killed, Johnson became President. During most of his term of office, Johnson and leading Republicans in Congress carried on a furious quarrel that grew out of their conflicting plans for readmitting the southern states (page 413). In fact, Johnson was the only one of our Presidents to be impeached (accused of misconduct) by the House of Representatives, though he was found not guilty by a close vote in the Senate.

U. S. Grant, our next President, had been the leading northern general during the War Between the States. He was elected for two terms. As President, Grant was honest and upright but was inexperienced in politics and unable to tell good advice from bad. Although he attempted some reforms, Grant's eight years in the White House were clouded by public scandals and problems left by the war. Little was done to deal with the new problems facing the American people.

This is the longest time one political party has been in power in this country.

The Presidents *of Our Country*

ULYSSES S. GRANT 1869–1877

Republican from Illinois. Grant had retired from the army after serving in the Mexican War but returned to serve as an officer in the Civil War. He eventually became general of all the Union forces. Though well-meaning himself, Grant's administration was marred by scandals involving dishonest government officials. Later, he failed in business but spent his last months writing his life story to pay his debts and provide for his family.

RUTHERFORD B. HAYES 1877–1881

Republican from Ohio. Hayes was an officer in the Union Army when elected to Congress. In Congress, and later as governor of Ohio, he earned a reputation for complete honesty. As President, Hayes encouraged civil service reform and tried to reconcile the North and the South by withdrawing the last federal troops from southern states. Hayes installed the first telephone in the White House.

JAMES A. GARFIELD 1881

Republican from Ohio. In his youth, this tall, genial man had worked as a canal boy to support his widowed mother and put himself through college. Garfield served as president of Hiram College in Ohio, as the youngest brigadier general in the Union Army, and in Congress. In 1880 he was nominated as a compromise candidate for President. Four months after his inauguration he was shot by a disappointed office-seeker.

CHESTER A. ARTHUR 1881–1885

Republican from New York. A tall, courtly gentleman, he dressed so stylishly that he was called "Elegant Arthur." His association with political bosses won him the nomination for Vice-President. After Garfield's death, however, Arthur proved to be an upright, efficient President who put duty to his country first. His endorsement of the civil service law cost him the support of the bosses and chances of renomination.

GROVER CLEVELAND 1885–1889   1893–1897

Democrat from New York. A stout, stubbornly honest man, Cleveland had taught school, studied law, and been a sheriff, a mayor, and governor of New York. As President, he helped improve the civil service and tried to lower the tariff. Though Cleveland won the popular vote in the election of 1888, he lost the electoral vote. In 1892, however, he won easily and returned to the presidency. His second term was plagued by a severe depression.

The Presidents  of Our Country

BENJAMIN HARRISON 1889–1893

Republican from Indiana. This President was the only one whose grandfather — William Henry Harrison — had also been President. A cautious man, Harrison let Congress initiate measures, while he tried to maintain a "middle-of-the-road" policy to please various groups. A program to build a two-ocean navy was begun during his term. The Harrisons were the first family to have electric lights in the White House.

WILLIAM McKINLEY 1897–1901

Republican from Ohio. McKinley had been a soldier, lawyer, congressman, and governor of Ohio. His presidency was marked by booming business and by the growing activity of the United States in world affairs, including the short war with Spain, which brought overseas territories under American control. He was assassinated six months after his second term began.

THEODORE ROOSEVELT 1901–1909

Republican from New York. Big-game hunter and author of over 30 books, "Teddy" (or "T.R.") became President at McKinley's death. He started the air force in 1909 by purchasing a $25,000 plane from the Wright brothers. For helping to end the Japanese-Russian War, he became the first President to receive the Nobel Peace Prize. He was also the first President to ride in an automobile.

WILLIAM HOWARD TAFT 1909–1913

Republican from Ohio. Our largest President, Taft was over six feet tall and weighed at one time more than 300 pounds. A judge for nearly 20 years and governor of the Philippines, this genial man was Secretary of War under Roosevelt but later became his rival for the presidency. Taft was named Chief Justice of the Supreme Court in 1921, the only President who has held this position.

WOODROW WILSON 1913–1921

Democrat from New Jersey. President of Princeton University, he had been a college professor and noted historian but had never held political office until elected governor of New Jersey. Within two years he was elected President. A strong executive, he led Congress in lowering tariffs and passing the Federal Reserve Act. At the close of World War I, Wilson's peace proposals made him the second President to win the Nobel Peace Prize.

Hayes is named President by an Electoral Commission. On March 4, 1877, a new President took office under unusual conditions. Many Americans, perhaps half the nation, did not believe that he had a right to his high position. Cartoons appeared in the newspapers hinting that he had gained his election through fraud. How could this be?

Rutherford B. Hayes, the new President, was a Republican from Ohio. He had served ably as governor of that state. During the presidential election of 1876, an exciting race had developed between Hayes and the Democratic candidate, Samuel J. Tilden. A dispute arose over the election returns from four states. Three of these were southern states still under carpetbag rule (page 413). The Democrats insisted that the majority of the people in these states favored Tilden but had been prevented from registering their votes. To settle the dispute, Congress appointed a special Electoral Commission. This Commission decided by a single vote in favor of Hayes. Many Americans did not agree with the Commission's decision, but Hayes was declared elected.

Hayes removes federal troops from the South. In spite of this unfortunate beginning, President Hayes undertook several important changes. Before the Electoral Commission had given its decision on the election, carpetbag rule had ended in Florida, one of the three southern states whose election returns had been disputed. President Hayes now ordered the removal of troops from the other two states (South Carolina and Louisiana) that had been under carpetbag rule.

Hayes begins the fight for civil service reform. President Hayes also undertook an important change in the method of

"ANOTHER SUCH VICTORY and I am undone," says the wounded Republican elephant in this political cartoon published after the bitter election of 1876 left the Republican Party victorious but battered.

appointing people to government jobs. Ever since the days of President Andrew Jackson (Chapter 17), the spoils system had been widely used. Victorious Presidents had removed large numbers of government officials to make room for their own friends and supporters. They often gave government positions to their relatives. As a result, many government offices had been held by men who had neither the ability nor the training to carry out their duties efficiently. Most of these men were anxious to keep their political party in power so as to hold their jobs.

President Hayes thought this system of using public office as a reward to the victors was wrong. Hayes believed that "he serves his party best who serves his country best." In other words, only well-qualified men should be appointed to public office. One

A **BAND** of unemployed men, called Coxey's Army, marched on Washington in 1894 (during Cleveland's second administration) to protest the lack of jobs. The army broke up after its leader, Jacob Coxey, was arrested for walking on the Capitol lawn.

way to obtain good officials is to have people take examinations, with government jobs going to those who make the highest scores. Government employees who secure their positions in this way are said to be under the *merit system*. The movement to establish the merit system is often spoken of as *civil service reform*.

Although many members of his own party opposed him, President Hayes was determined to fight for civil service reform. When he entered the White House, Hayes did not replace large numbers of office-holders with his own friends or supporters. He chose Carl Schurz, who had come from Germany as a young man (page 509), to be a member of his Cabinet. A tireless worker for good government, Schurz is remembered as one of the most enthusiastic supporters of the merit system. President Hayes also tried, without success, to get Congress to set up a commission to select government officials who were well trained for their jobs. Finally, he caused the removal from the New York Custom House of several leading Republicans who were firm supporters of the spoils system.

Civil service reforms are adopted. Small though these beginnings were, they aroused interest throughout the country. Then a dramatic event occurred. President Garfield, who followed Hayes, was shot by a disappointed office-seeker. People now saw clearly the need for the merit system in selecting persons for government jobs. In 1883, Congress established a *Civil Service Commission*. This group of men was to set up a system of examinations for various government departments. For example, some employees of the postal service, customs officers, and so on, were required to take examinations to qualify for their jobs. Positions were filled from the three highest candidates on the list. Since 1883, the merit system has been extended so that now it covers a great variety of government jobs. Many states and cities also use the merit system in selecting their employees.

Cleveland becomes President. March 4, 1885, marked still another unusual inauguration day. For the first time in 25 years, there was a Democratic President in the White House. The new President, Grover Cleveland, had risen from poverty to fame through his hard work, honesty, and courage. He had been a sheriff, mayor of Buffalo, and finally governor of New York State. Even when it might

A band of unemployed men (ex-soldiers) also descended on Washington in 1932. Force
finally was used to disperse this group.

cost him popularity, he did not hesitate to say "no." In Cleveland's mind a public office was a public trust, or responsibility.

Cleveland works for many reforms. Grover Cleveland greatly increased the number of positions to be filled by civil service examinations. During his first term of office, several important laws were passed, including the Interstate Commerce Act to regulate railroad rates (page 480). Cleveland also worked hard but unsuccessfully to lower the tariff.

Since the war between the North and the South, tariffs on goods imported from foreign countries had been high. Tariff duties had been kept at high levels to protect American-made goods from cheaper foreign-made goods. President Cleveland found that these high taxes were bringing in so much money to the government that there was a large surplus in the Treasury. Cleveland felt that American industries were now so strong that high tariff duties were no longer needed to protect them from foreign competition. He also argued that heavy tariff duties raised the prices of many goods and increased the cost of living for the average American. Under pressure from President Cleveland, a bill to reduce the tariff was introduced into Congress. Although the bill failed to pass, President Cleveland kept up his fight to lower the tariff.

Cleveland returns to the White House. President Cleveland was defeated in his attempt at re-election. But four years later (in 1892), he was again elected President. Thus he has the distinction of being the only President who has served a second term in office after having once left the presidency. Cleveland's second term was clouded by a severe depression. Many of his actions at the time were not popular. But in later years it became clear that Cleveland had done his duty as he saw it, and had worked for what he thought were the best interests of the American people.

CHECK UP

1. (a) What new problems arose in American life in the second half of the 1800's? (b) Why were the political parties slow to deal with these problems? (c) Why was little accomplished during the administrations of Presidents Johnson and Grant?

2. (a) What is civil service reform? (b) Why was it needed? (c) How did President Hayes try to improve the civil service? (d) What improvements were introduced by the Civil Service Commission?

3. (a) What reforms did President Cleveland favor? (b) Why did he want to lower the tariff?

What Evils Did President Theodore Roosevelt Fight to Overcome?

A sick boy becomes a vigorous man. In a comfortable house in a fashionable district of New York City, a worried man paced the floor with a baby in his arms. Although it was night, the baby could not sleep. Fighting for breath, the baby struggled with terrible coughing spells. Sometimes the father would call for a carriage and drive swiftly through the streets. It didn't matter where they went, so long as a breeze made it easier for the boy to breathe.

Father and son were both named Theodore Roosevelt. Theodore, Jr., continued to be sickly until he was well into his teens. But he was studious and read everything he could lay his hands on. Nature study was one of his chief hobbies. As his health began to improve, young Theodore grew more active physically and became interested in sports. While at Harvard College, he took up boxing. Still later he lived on a ranch in the Dakota Bad Lands, where he fished and hunted and came to love outdoor life.

Over the years, the sickly boy developed into a vigorous man. Roosevelt became, in fact, a bundle of energy. He moved quickly, talked rapidly, laughed loudly, and cut the air with sharp, wide movements of his arms as he talked. He seemed to burst into rooms, not enter them. He seemed to shout, not talk. He seemed to run, not walk. Wherever Theodore Roosevelt was, there was plenty of action.

Roosevelt chooses a career of public service. Very soon after his graduation from college, Roosevelt turned his great energy to the field of government. He became a member of the New York state legislature. Later he served as one of the United States Civil Service Commissioners, who arranged for the selection of qualified government workers. As president of the Police Board of New York City, Roosevelt spurred on the police in their fight against crime. In the spring of 1897, he was appointed Assistant Secretary of the Navy.

Then, in April, 1898, the United States declared war on Spain (Chapter 28). Roosevelt resigned at once to form the regiment of cavalry which became known as the "Rough Riders." This was a group of dashing, hard-riding, quick-shooting volunteers that included western cowboys as well as fashionable "gentlemen riders." Roosevelt's war record made him so popular that he was elected governor of New York. Soon afterward he was nominated for the vice-presidency by the Republican Party and was elected. Many people believed that Theodore Roosevelt had made a mistake in taking this office, for a Vice-President in those days did not have great responsibilities. Roosevelt himself once said that he would rather be almost anything than Vice-President. But in 1901, President McKinley was shot and killed by an anarchist (a man who does not believe in any government). Roosevelt became President of the United States when he was not quite 43, the youngest man ever to hold that high office.[1]

President Roosevelt follows a vigorous foreign policy. As President, Theodore Roosevelt was quick-witted, well-informed, and had the will to get things done. In Chapters 28 and 29 we shall find out about the active part he took in foreign affairs: in settling the Russian-Japanese War, in building the Panama Canal, and in using force to keep order in Latin America. Roosevelt believed that the United States should be strong. He built up a powerful navy and sent it around the world to impress other countries with our strength. Long before he became President, he had said in a speech, "Speak softly and carry a big stick, and you will go far." His attitude toward foreign affairs has often been called the "Big Stick" Policy.

Roosevelt fights evils in American life. Theodore Roosevelt was equally vigorous in affairs at home. He believed that the American people should have a "square deal." Where he found conditions in American life that needed correcting, he set out to change them.

(1) *Trusts and monopolies.* One problem, in Roosevelt's opinion, was the wealth and power held in those days by the big

---

[1] The youngest man ever to be *elected* to the presidency, however, was John F. Kennedy, elected President in 1960 at the age of 43.

Theodore Roosevelt: Strenuous American tells about this President's life as rancher, soldier, statesman, and reformer.

business monopolies or trusts. These trusts not only controlled a large share of American business but also had a strong influence in politics. They spent money to elect government officials who would do their bidding. Roosevelt believed that in a democratic country it was wrong for a few men to have such power. He set out to break up the huge business monopolies. The Sherman Anti-Trust Law (page 479) had already been passed, but a law is of no use unless it is enforced. Former Presidents had done very little to stop monopolies. Under Roosevelt, however, the government went to court against several great trusts to compel them to obey the Sherman Law. Because of his fight against these trusts, Roosevelt was given the nickname of "trust-buster."

(2) *Conservation.* Theodore Roosevelt was also greatly troubled by the reckless way in which people of the United States had been wasting their natural wealth — their forests, soil, water power, and coal and other minerals (page 444). Experts who had studied this problem predicted that in a few years most of our rich resources might be entirely used up. Roosevelt decided to take measures to save or conserve these resources. He saw that laws were passed to keep forest lands under government control. Millions of acres were set aside as national forests and parks. Other laws made it possible to build dams to make use of our water power and to provide irrigation for dry western lands. Roosevelt also encouraged laws to conserve mineral resources. At a conference in 1908 he called together important national leaders to study conservation problems. His efforts made people aware of the need to use natural resources wisely.

(3) *Better government.* Theodore Roosevelt was interested in still another problem. Our government had become so large that it was carried on mainly by representatives of the people rather than by the people themselves. This system works well if the representatives sincerely seek to carry out the people's wishes. Many Americans in the early 1900's, including Roosevelt, did not believe that this was being done. They felt that many representatives and officials listened only to the leaders of their political party or to special groups who put pressure on them to favor or oppose certain matters.

WISE USE of our natural resources means that scenes like this (a mountain valley in the state of Washington) will not disappear from our country.

Several reforms were suggested, especially in western states. One was called the *direct primary.* It permitted members of a political party to nominate their candidates by secret ballot instead of having the candidates selected by party leaders at a convention. Another, called the *referendum,* provided that a bill passed by members of a legislature be submitted, or referred, to the voters for their approval before it went into effect. A third reform, the *initiative,* enabled citizens to take steps to introduce

One of the great conservation problems of today **565** is preventing the pollution of water and making an adequate supply of water available to metropolitan areas.

THEODORE ROOSEVELT

As President, "T.R." launched a national program of conservation to preserve for all Americans the great outdoors which he himself enjoyed so much. (The picture at right shows him riding in the mountains of Colorado.) Active in international affairs, he won the Nobel Peace Prize for bringing Russians and Japanese together (below) to end the Russian-Japanese War.

legislation which they wanted considered. Still another, the *recall,* would allow the voters to remove from office an official whose services were unsatisfactory, even before his term was completed.

President Theodore Roosevelt was much interested in these efforts to give the people a more direct voice in their government. He did what he could to help these reforms. Neither in his day nor since have any of these measures been put into practice by the national government in Washington. But many states have adopted the direct primary, the referendum, and the initiative, and several hundred cities permit the use of the recall.

How successful was Theodore Roosevelt? There is no doubt that Theodore Roosevelt succeeded in many things. He made America's influence felt in world affairs. Later Presidents carried on and expanded his plans to preserve our natural

resources. But in some ways Theodore Roosevelt may remind us of a man racing against an automobile. Although the man runs hard and fast, the automobile leaves him farther and farther behind. For example, Roosevelt sought to break up powerful business groups, yet there were more monopolies when he ceased to be President than when he began. Nevertheless, by his vigorous actions and stirring speeches, Roosevelt awakened the American people and helped them to understand better the problems they faced.

CHECK UP

1. Describe Theodore Roosevelt's career before he became President.

2. (a) What were Theodore Roosevelt's views on (1) monopolies? (2) conservation? (3) reforms in government? (b) How successful was he in carrying out these ideas?

At least three presidents have campaigned on a program which included NEW in its title (Freedom, Deal, Frontier).

3 What Did President Wilson's Plans for a "New Freedom" Accomplish?

When the election of 1908 drew near, Theodore Roosevelt had completed nearly two terms in the White House. Although he had declared he would not run for re-election, he was powerful enough to force the Republican Party to nominate the man he wanted. His choice was William Howard Taft, a stout, good-natured Ohioan who had held several government offices and who had been Roosevelt's Secretary of War. With Roosevelt's support, Taft was elected.

The Democrats win the 1912 election. In many ways President Taft continued the work begun by Roosevelt. Under Taft, for example, the government carried forward the fight against trusts and monopolies. But Taft did not go fast enough or far enough in his reforms to please the vigorous Roosevelt. Before long, in fact, Theodore Roosevelt became convinced that Taft was not carrying on the policies that he, Roosevelt, favored. The split between the two former friends became so deep that Roosevelt decided to seek the Republican nomination for President in 1912. Failing to win it, he ran for President as the candidate of a new third party called the *Progressive Party*. Although the Republican Party renominated Taft, many Republicans voted for Roosevelt. The Democrats, who were united, won the election.

Woodrow Wilson becomes President. The man whom the Democrats had elected was Woodrow Wilson. Like Theodore Roosevelt, he wanted to solve the important problems facing the country. But in many ways he was different from Roosevelt. Roosevelt was born in New York; Wilson was born in Virginia. Roosevelt was short, stocky, and energetic. Wilson was tall, slender, and more dignified.

Roosevelt, the soldier and outdoor man, believed in action; Wilson, on the other hand, was a thinker whose most effective weapons were words. Roosevelt was almost boyish in his hot enthusiasms and sudden changes of mood. Wilson's manner was calm and composed.

Woodrow Wilson had been a scholar and teacher almost all his life. He had been president of Princeton University and had served one term as governor of New Jersey. Except for Grover Cleveland, he was the only Democrat who had been elected President since before the Civil War. Wilson had campaigned on a program which he called a "New Freedom" for the American people.

Wilson puts through several important reforms. Woodrow Wilson went to Congress in person to read his important messages, a thing no President had done since John Adams. When he took the oath of office as President, and in his messages to Congress, Wilson spoke in favor of a number of reforms.

(1) *The tariff.* President Wilson asked Congress to lower the tariff duties on many articles so that trade could flow freely between the United States and other nations. He believed that foreign countries could not buy our goods unless they could sell their own goods. Cleveland, you remember, had fought for a lower tariff but had not been successful. In fact, tariff laws passed in the 1890's and early 1900's had set higher tariff duties. But Congress now followed Wilson's wishes and passed the *Underwood Tariff Law,* lowering tariff rates.

(2) *Banking reforms.* President Wilson also asked for changes in the banking system. During panics many banks had been

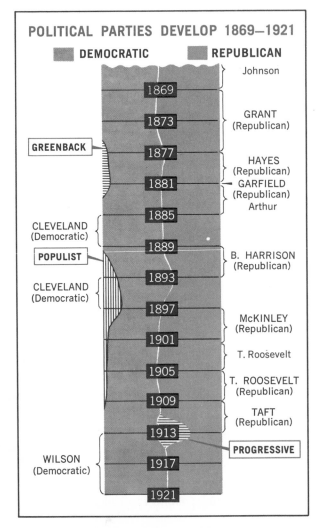

POLITICAL PARTIES DEVELOP 1869–1921

DEMOCRATIC **REPUBLICAN**

Johnson
1869
1873 — GRANT (Republican)
GREENBACK
1877 — HAYES (Republican)
1881 — GARFIELD (Republican) / Arthur
1885
CLEVELAND (Democratic)
1889 — B. HARRISON (Republican)
POPULIST
1893
CLEVELAND (Democratic)
1897 — McKINLEY (Republican)
1901 — T. Roosevelt
1905 — T. ROOSEVELT (Republican)
1909 — TAFT (Republican)
1913 — PROGRESSIVE
WILSON (Democratic)
1917
1921

THIRD PARTIES appeared, urging reforms, but their members drifted back into the two big parties, which adopted some ideas from the reformers.

forced to close their doors when large numbers of depositors tried to draw out their funds. Wilson wished to set up a banking system which would make it possible for banks to obtain the money needed to meet the demands upon them. Congress therefore passed the *Federal Reserve Act.* This act set up a central bank in each of twelve major regions of the country, all under the control of the Federal Reserve Board. The Federal Reserve Banks had broad powers to regulate business conditions and help local banks which were in difficulty.

Today the income tax produces far more revenue than any other tax.

(3) *The income tax.* For a number of years many people had favored a new form of taxation — a tax on a person's wages or income. Their argument for an income tax was that people with large incomes are able to pay a higher tax than people with small incomes. Congress had tried to levy an income tax before, but the Supreme Court had declared it unconstitutional. In 1913, however, just before Wilson took office, the Sixteenth Amendment was added to the Constitution, permitting Congress to levy such a tax (page A28). At President Wilson's request, an income tax law was passed, and we have had income taxes ever since.

(4) *Business and monopolies.* Wherever Wilson turned, he saw some problem which he wanted to set right. Like Theodore Roosevelt, he believed that powerful monopolies were dangerous. He urged Congress to pass laws to control such monopolies. One of these was the *Clayton Act,* which listed things that big corporations should not do (page 480). Another law set up a government bureau, the *Federal Trade Commission,* with power to find out facts about business and to prevent companies from building monopolies.

(5) *Farmers and workers.* Under Wilson's guidance, arrangements were made so that farmers could borrow money more easily when they needed it and for longer periods of time. The United States government also began to spend millions of dollars every year to teach farmers how to do their work more efficiently. Nor were workers in industry forgotten. A law was passed to reduce the regular working day on interstate railroads to eight hours. Meanwhile, a number of individual states passed laws to prevent children from going to work and, so far as possible, to require safe and healthful working conditions (page 480).

War halts reform at home. We shall never know how far-reaching President

Wilson's New Freedom program might have been, because it was interrupted by the First World War (Chapter 29). This conflict, which broke out just a little over a year after Wilson took office, grew into the greatest war fought up to that time. The attention of the President and Congress and indeed of all Americans centered more and more on this conflict. At last in 1917 the United States entered the war Woodrow Wilson had to turn from his program of reforms at home to the problems created by a great war abroad.

When World War I ended, world problems continued to demand President Wilson's attention. He went to Europe to help write a peace treaty and to push plans for a world peace organization. On his return to the United States, Wilson wore himself out trying to interest Congress and the nation in his plans for the League of Nations. In 1921, he ended his second term in office a sick and disappointed man. He died three years later. Although he failed to achieve his dream of a peaceful world, Wilson is recognized today as one of our great Americans.

•

Between 1865 and 1920, Woodrow Wilson was the only President who had to face the crushing burden of a world war and of trying to make a world-wide peace. But you will learn in the remaining chapters of this book that foreign affairs brought increasing responsibilities to all our Presidents after the late 1890's.

CHECK UP

1. Why was Woodrow Wilson elected President in 1912?

2. What were Wilson's ideas on each of the following, and what action was taken in each case: (a) the tariff? (b) banking reforms? (c) the income tax? (d) monopolies? (e) farm aid and labor laws?

3. Why did reforms receive little attention during Wilson's second term?

Check Up on Chapter 27

Make sure that students can answer question #2.

Do You Know the Meaning?

1. impeach
2. income tax
3. recall
4. initiative
5. secret ballot
6. referendum
7. anarchist
8. civil service
9. merit system
10. direct primary

Can You Identify?

1. Carl Schurz
2. Grover Cleveland
3. 1876
4. 1883
5. 1912
6. 1913
7. Woodrow Wilson
8. New Freedom
9. Federal Reserve Act
10. Theodore Roosevelt
11. Big Stick Policy
12. Progressive Party
13. Rutherford B. Hayes
14. Electoral Commission
15. William Howard Taft
16. Underwood Tariff Law

What Do You Think?

1. Why is conservation of our natural resources one of the serious problems of this country today?

2. Explain why a high tariff on foreign goods may prevent other countries from buying goods in this country.

3. (a) Why have third political parties sometimes been organized in this country? (b) How successful have these third parties been in achieving their goals?

4. (a) Why have most people favored civil service reform? (b) Why have some opposed it?

5. (a) Why does "trust-busting" have a popular appeal? (b) Are monopolies necessarily bad?

How old have our Presidents been? According to the Constitution, a man must have reached the age of 35 to be eligible for the office of President. The ages of our Presidents, at the time each *first* took office, have ranged from 42 to 68 years. Twenty-one, including Lyndon B. Johnson, were in their fifties when they became President; seven were in their sixties; and seven were in their forties. The oldest man to take office was William Henry Harrison, who was 68 years old when inaugurated. Theodore Roosevelt was only 42 when he succeeded to the presidency after the death of President McKinley. But since Roosevelt had not been elected to the office, the honor of being the youngest man to be *elected* President goes to John F. Kennedy.

Our national parks. Over 13 million acres in various parts of our country have been set aside by the national government as permanent parks for Americans to visit and enjoy. These areas have been left in their natural state as much as possible. They include some of the most beautiful and unusual sights to be found anywhere — snow-capped mountains, rock formations, deep river gorges, geysers, and glaciers, as well as all kinds of wild life. Yellowstone National Park was the first to be established, in the year 1872. Here you can see steaming geysers, volcanoes that spout mud, and other wonders of nature. Sequoia National Park, with its ancient redwoods, and Yosemite, with its magnificent cliffs and waterfalls, were established in 1890. One of the newest parks is the Virgin Islands National Park, founded in 1956 on the American island of St. John. Its chief attractions are white sandy beaches and beautiful Caribbean scenery.

It was Theodore Roosevelt who did most to preserve our natural heritage. Working with Gifford Pinchot of the Forestry Service, he reserved great stretches of western land for national parks. Since 1916, our parks have been in the care of the National Park Service of the Department of the Interior. Most parks have cabins you can rent for a small sum and campsites where you can pitch a tent. It is good to know that our country is preserving these regions, so that Americans may enjoy the natural beauty of the land.

Numbering the Presidents. Although 35 individuals have served as President of the United States, we have had a total of 36 Presidents. To find out why, we must turn back to the 1890's. It is easy to count the Presidents from Washington, our first President, to Benjamin Harrison, our 23rd. The trouble starts when we come to Grover Cleveland. A glance at the list of Presidents on pages A44–A45 shows that Cleveland served a term *after* Harrison as well as *before* him. Should Cleveland be counted once or twice? If you count him once, Lyndon Johnson would be our 35th President. If you count Cleveland twice, as the 22nd *and* the 24th President, then President Johnson is the 36th. The second method of counting now seems to be accepted as official, because the United States Department of State has ruled that Cleveland is to be counted twice.

Can your students explain why each of these "people in our story" is pictured in the introduction to Chapter 28?

The United States Gains
Possessions Overseas

What this chapter is about —

Throughout his life a man's activities and interests change. As a boy his time is occupied by school work, sports, and perhaps a part-time job. As a young man he finds a job and gets married. He then becomes interested in seeking a better job and larger salary and in providing for his family. He may begin to take part in politics or community affairs. He joins a neighborhood club, is active in the local government, or gives time to help his church. By the time he is fifty years old, his interests and activities are different from those he had at the age of fifteen.

Nations, like people, grow and change. A small, weak nation acts one way, but a big, powerful country acts another way. Thus when the United States was young, it was interested in conquering the wilderness, in expanding westward across the continent, in creating and enlarging industries. But the time came when the United States began to take a greater interest in world affairs. This interest, which was only natural for a country grown large and powerful, led the United States to accept control of territory outside its existing borders.

In this chapter we shall learn how the United States began to look beyond its own boundaries. We shall seek answers to these questions:

People in our story — American missionary, businessman, soldier and sailor; Pacific islanders; American engineer and doctor.

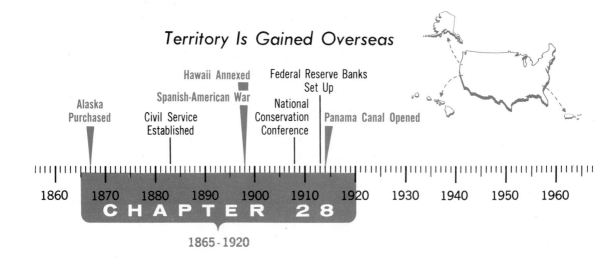

Territory Is Gained Overseas

Alaska Purchased

Civil Service Established

Spanish-American War

Hawaii Annexed

National Conservation Conference

Federal Reserve Banks Set Up

Panama Canal Opened

1860 1870 1880 1890 1900 1910 1920 1930 1940 1950 1960

CHAPTER 28

1865-1920

▶ 1. Why did Americans begin to take a greater interest in world affairs?

▶ 2. How did our country acquire Alaska and uphold the Monroe Doctrine?

▶ 3. How did the United States gain islands in the Pacific and Caribbean?

▶ 4. How did the United States handle problems in lands freed from Spain?

▶ 5. How was the United States able to build the Panama Canal?

▶ 6. How did we gain more island possessions?

Today this country is involved not only in the affairs of Europe but of Africa and Asia as well.

1 Why Did Americans Begin to Take a Greater Interest in World Affairs?

What is foreign policy? When a nation follows a certain plan of action toward other nations over a period of time, such a plan of action is called the nation's *foreign policy*. Early in the 1800's, for example, the United States decided that it did not want to be drawn into the affairs of European nations and did not want them to interfere in the Western Hemisphere. The United States, therefore, announced and supported the *Monroe Doctrine*. A century later, the United States government decided to act together with other countries in North and South America for the common good. It therefore launched the *Good Neighbor Policy*. These are examples of foreign policy.

The United States had little interest in foreign affairs before the late 1800's. For a while after 1865, the United States was not much concerned with foreign policy. Americans were too busy with things close at home. The War Between the States was over. Great open spaces waited to be settled. Railroads had to be built, mines had to be dug, farms had to be established. How well Americans succeeded in these tasks between 1860 and 1890 is shown by a few significant facts. In 1860, for example, only 31 million people lived in the United States, most of them east of the Mississippi. In 1890, thirty years later, the number of people living in the United States had

572

doubled to 63 million. The homes of these 63 million Americans were scattered from the Atlantic to the Pacific and from Canada to Mexico. In 1860, there were about 30,000 miles of railroad track in the United States, but no railroad yet spanned the continent. In 1890, there were over 160,000 miles of track, and several railroads had reached the Pacific. In 1890, American farmers produced twice as much corn, and more than twice as much wheat and cotton, as in 1860. The value of goods manufactured in the United States in 1890 was five times as great as in 1860.

Growth like this calls for much hard work. Most men fixed their eyes on their own share of the work — on the busy factories, the lengthening railroads, the plows turning long, deep furrows in the rich soil. The job at hand was big enough for most Americans. What need had they to think of other, distant lands?

Americans look abroad for new markets. After a time, however, the very success of their work at home led Americans to look beyond their country. The American farmer, for example, grew more cotton and wheat and tobacco and produced more ham and bacon and lard than his fellow Americans could buy and use. The American miner, also, dug more copper

and more coal than could be sold in the United States. The American logger and sawmill owner produced more lumber than was required in this country. And the American manufacturer of machinery made more than his countrymen needed or could buy. This extra supply of goods is called a *surplus.*

Because these producers could not sell their surplus goods in this country, they had to look abroad for new markets. The American businessman also found that at times he had more money than he could invest at home. He, too, began to look to other countries for chances to put his money to good use. In foreign countries that lacked money to develop their own resources, businessmen and bankers could invest in mining, industry, or business and often make large profits. One American, thinking of all these things, remarked, "Whether they will or no, Americans must now begin to look outward."

Trade increases the interest of this country in world affairs. As Americans increased their foreign trade or invested their money abroad, they became more interested in the affairs of other countries. Businessmen are always keenly interested in countries where they do business. If a businessman makes money, he naturally

Overseas countries provide raw materials, markets for surplus products, and investment opportunities.

THE GROWTH of American industry affected our trade with foreign nations. (1) What per cent of our imports consisted of manufactured goods in 1865? Today? (2) What per cent of our exports consisted of manufactured goods in 1865? In 1929?

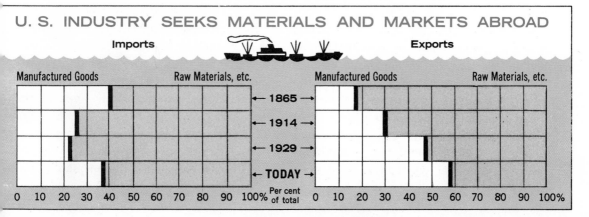

U. S. INDUSTRY SEEKS MATERIALS AND MARKETS ABROAD

Imports   Exports

Manufactured Goods   Raw Materials, etc.   Manufactured Goods   Raw Materials, etc.

← 1865 →
← 1914 →
← 1929 →
← TODAY →

Per cent of total

0 10 20 30 40 50 60 70 80 90 100%   0 10 20 30 40 50 60 70 80 90 100%

wants to increase his profits by widening his market or by finding ways to invest more money. On the other hand, if he loses money, he wants to know why. Perhaps conditions in a foreign country are upset or its government is unfriendly or weak. A businessman cannot do much by himself to change such conditions. So he may ask the aid of his own government. The United States on several occasions took a hand in the affairs of foreign countries in order to protect the interests of American businessmen.

Thus, with the growth of American trade came a growth of interest in other

This country no longer intervenes in Latin American countries to protect American investments.

parts of the globe. Beginning slowly at first, this interest increased as the years went by.

CHECK UP

1. (a) What is a nation's "foreign policy"? (b) Why were Americans little concerned with foreign affairs before the late 1800's?

2. Why did the growth of American industry and agriculture lead Americans to seek new markets?

3. How did overseas trade cause Americans to become interested in the affairs of other countries?

2   How Did Our Country Acquire Alaska and Uphold the Monroe Doctrine?

THE UNITED STATES PURCHASES ALASKA

There is an old saying, "Don't bite off more than you can chew." As you have just read, most Americans after 1865 felt that they had enough to do just to build a strong America at home. They thought that to do anything more would be to "bite off more than they could chew." But a few Americans had other ideas. One of these was William H. Seward.

Secretary of State Seward believes in expansion. Seward had been Secretary of State since 1861, when Abraham Lincoln became President. In 1867 Seward was a slender, white-haired man with stooped shoulders and a habit of slouching. As Secretary of State, he had charge of all the dealings of our government with the other countries of the world. Seward knew how the United States, with giant strides, had marched westward across the continent. "But," he thought, "why stop at the water's

edge? Having advanced to the shoreline of the Pacific, why not go even farther?"

Alaska is purchased. One day in March, 1867, the Russian representative to the United States called at Seward's office and began to talk of Alaska. (Alaska, as you read on page 366, had been claimed for Russia by Vitus Bering in the 1700's.) This vast region, complained the Russian minister, was much too far from European Russia. Furthermore, Alaska was expensive to protect and to develop. Did that mean, asked Seward, that Russia would consider selling Alaska to the United States? The minister said he believed Russia would sell. Seward felt that such an opportunity might never come again. Acting quickly, he persuaded the Senate to approve the necessary treaty and sealed the bargain. The price for Alaska was set at $7,200,-000. This was less than two cents an acre for a region of half a million square miles.

To understand the importance of Alaskan air bases see the map on page 579. It shows how close Alaska is to Russian territory.

THE UNITED STATES GAINS POSSESSIONS OVERSEAS 575

Many Americans joked about Seward's purchase of Alaska. They called Alaska "Seward's Folly" and "Seward's Icebox." But Seward was a wiser man than they realized. The fur seals which were caught in the waters near Alaska were very valuable. Later, gold was discovered in Alaska and plentiful supplies of other minerals also were found. The United States established naval bases in Alaska. And now, in the age of airplanes, Alaska has very important air bases as well. No longer does anyone speak of Alaska as "Seward's Folly." Alaska has paid for itself many times over, especially in natural resources and military importance. For many years a territory of the United States, Alaska was admitted to the Union as the forty-ninth state in 1959. (Locate Alaska on the map on page 579.)

Americans lose interest in further expansion. Seward's dreams of expansion did not end with Alaska. In the autumn of 1867, the same year that Alaska was purchased, the United States took possession of the Midway Islands, far out in the Pacific Ocean northwest of Hawaii. But here William H. Seward had to stop. Although he dreamed of obtaining more and more land, the Senate would not approve his plans for further expansion. Americans were still too much wrapped up in affairs at home to look very far beyond their shores. Thirty years were to pass before the United States again acquired any important amount of territory.

THE UNITED STATES ENFORCES THE MONROE DOCTRINE

Every nation tries to protect certain vital interests such as its independence, its security, and its foreign trade. The United States believed that the Monroe Doctrine helped to protect its vital interests. The Doctrine had declared that European nations should not interfere with the governments of American countries (page 257). On two important occasions between 1860 and 1900 the United States used the Monroe Doctrine to protect its interests and those of other American states.

France feels the force of the Monroe Doctrine. Although Napoleon had sold Louisiana to the United States (page 250), France had never quite given up the hope

HARBOR of Juneau, Alaska's capital, shelters amphibian planes used along the rugged coast. The Juneau museum has this wooden figure (left) of Lincoln, the "Great Emancipator," carved by Indian slaves who were freed when Alaska became American.

of regaining an empire in the Western Hemisphere. During the American Civil War, Napoleon III of France (the nephew of the great Napoleon) planned to set up a government in Mexico under French control. He believed that the United States would be too busy with the war to object. Using debts owed to France by Mexico as an excuse, Napoleon III sent an army to invade Mexico. The invasion was successful, and Napoleon made an Austrian archduke, Maximilian, Emperor of Mexico. Aided by French soldiers and Mexicans who approved the scheme, Maximilian ruled Mexico for a few years. As soon as the War Between the States came to a close, however, the United States government showed that it meant to enforce the Monroe Doctrine. Since Napoleon III did not want war with the United States, he began to withdraw his troops from Mexico. The Mexicans then rose in revolt against the helpless Maximilian. They put him to death and regained control of their country.

The United States uses the Monroe Doctrine against Great Britain. In 1895 the Monroe Doctrine met another serious challenge. The cause was a quarrel between Venezuela and Great Britain. Great Britain owned the colony of British Guiana on the coast of South America just east of Venezuela (map, page 586). Exactly where British Guiana ended and Venezuela began had never been settled. When Great Britain suggested a boundary cutting deeper into Venezuela than had ever been thought of before, the United States became concerned. The Monroe Doctrine forbade the establishment of new colonies in the Americas, but did it also apply to making a colony larger? Believing that it did, President Cleveland demanded that Great Britain agree to arbitrate the dispute. Great Britain, however, felt that the United States had no right to interfere in the boundary dispute with Venezuela. For a time it seemed that there might be war between England and the United States. But the British government finally agreed to arbitration. As it turned out, Britain received a large part of the disputed land. Nevertheless, the United States had made it clear to the world that the Monroe Doctrine could not be ignored.

CHECK UP

1. How did the United States acquire Alaska?

2. How did the United States enforce the Monroe Doctrine in each of the following situations: (a) the French attempt to set up an emperor in Mexico? (b) the dispute between Great Britain and Venezuela?

For centuries English policy has been to keep a strong power from taking possession of the Low Countries (modern Holland and Belgium). That policy is similar in a way to our Monroe Doctrine.

3 How Did the United States Gain Islands in the Pacific and Caribbean?

Americans settle in Hawaii. In the sun-drenched Pacific Ocean, more than 2000 miles southwest of San Francisco, lies a group of islands topped by jagged mountains. These islands, called Hawaii, have an area about the size of New Jersey. At one time the islands were occupied by happy people who led a simple and leisurely life. They were governed by native rulers. (Locate Hawaii on the map on page 579.)

In the late 1700's, Yankee sailors from whaling ships and trading vessels stopped

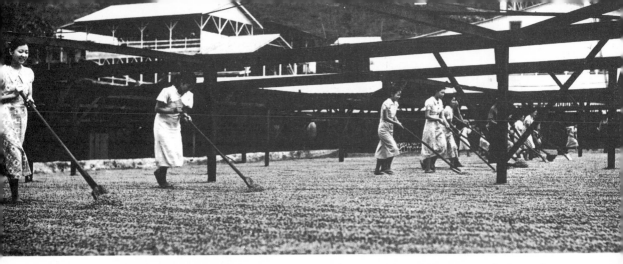

HAWAII'S IDEAL CLIMATE and rich soil produce many crops. Sugar cane and pineapple are most important but other fruits, vegetables, flowers, and even coffee are grown. These girls use long paddles to rake coffee beans drying in the sun.

at these islands for water and supplies. Then American missionaries, traders, and storekeepers began to settle in Hawaii. Peoples of other countries also went there to live — Chinese, Japanese, British, and Germans. But the Americans gained control of most of the land and business.

The American government becomes interested in Hawaii. Because Americans had settled in Hawaii, the American government began to take a keen interest in these small Pacific islands. The United States made an agreement with the ruler of Hawaii (1) that no part of the islands should be given to any foreign country and (2) that only Americans might use Pearl Harbor, the best harbor in the islands.

The Americans who lived in Hawaii, however, wanted even closer ties with the United States. Most of them made their living by growing sugar cane, and most of the huge sugar crop was sold in the United States. The prosperity of Americans in Hawaii, therefore, depended on good trade relations between the United States and Hawaii.

Hawaii is annexed to the United States. So long as Hawaii was an independent country, there was always the danger that

something might happen to disturb relations between Hawaii and the United States. This thought worried the American sugar growers in Hawaii. "Why," they asked each other, "shouldn't Hawaii become a part of the United States? Then there would no longer be a threat to our trade and prosperity." This idea gained more and more support. Finally, a revolution, led by American sugar planters, broke out in 1893. The native ruler of Hawaii, Queen Liliuokalani (lee-*lee'*oo-oh-kah-*lah'*-nee), was forced to give up her throne. But when those taking part in the revolution asked that Hawaii be made a part of the United States, their request was refused. President Grover Cleveland objected because he did not believe that the uprising was supported by the Hawaiian people themselves. He disapproved of the part played by Americans in the revolution. He was especially disturbed because the uprising had been aided by marines from an American warship.

Disappointed by the failure of their plan, the leaders of the revolution declared Hawaii to be a republic. Matters were allowed to drift until McKinley became President. In 1898, Congress finally voted the annexation of Hawaii to the United

Once Hawaii became part of the United States, there would be no tariff on Hawaiian sugar.

States. It was organized as an American territory, and American citizenship was given to all citizens of the islands. Under American rule, Hawaii prospered, exporting sugar and pineapples to the mainland and in turn buying large amounts of manufactured goods.

More than once, the Hawaiians voted to become a state in the Union. In 1959 Congress accepted their petition, and Hawaii became our fiftieth state.

WAR WITH SPAIN BRINGS NEW TERRITORIES TO THE UNITED STATES

The annexation of Hawaii did not seem as important to most Americans as events taking place about the same time on the island of Cuba. This lizard-shaped island lies some 90 miles south of Key West, Florida. It had been discovered by Christopher Columbus in 1492 and had been ruled ever since by Spain. When the rest of Spanish America revolted and won independence, Cuba and tiny Puerto Rico, another Caribbean island, remained loyal to Spain.

Cuba revolts against Spain. In the late 1800's, however, the Cubans became restless under Spanish rule. Several times they rebelled and tried to win their independence. Each time the soldiers of Spain overpowered them. In 1895, however, they tried once again. In a village of eastern Cuba, a small group of men unfurled a flag with five bars and a single star. Standing beneath this flag, they declared Cuba an independent country.

When Spain refused to give Cuba its freedom, rebellion flamed from one end of Cuba to the other. Spanish troops marched against the Cubans, seeking to stamp out the uprising. But the Cubans avoided open battle. They fell upon the Spanish

soldiers in surprise attacks, did what damage they could, and dashed away again. They burned supplies and acres of sugar cane, the island's chief crop. The Spanish soldiers fought back, hoping to trap enough Cubans in one place to put an end to the revolt.

The United States is interested in the Cuban revolt. The United States watched with deep interest the struggle between Cuba and Spain. American businessmen and planters had gone to Cuba as they had to Hawaii. They had invested money in sugar plantations, mines, and other businesses. Also, a good deal of trade was carried on between Cuba and the United States. The American ambassador to Spain pointed out that because of the revolt, the United States was deprived of the large amount of sugar normally imported from Cuba. And the United States in turn was unable to export meat, flour, and manufactured goods to Cuba.

There was still another reason why Americans were interested in Cuba. They remembered how the Thirteen Colonies had revolted from England and won their independence. The people of the United States, therefore, had sympathy for other peoples who struggled for freedom. The Republican Party announced in 1896: "We watch with deep and abiding interest the heroic battles of the Cuban patriots against cruelty and oppression. . . . We believe that the government of the United States should [try] to restore peace and give independence to the island."

American newspapers were full of news about the revolt, and large headlines played up the events in Cuba.

The battleship "Maine" blows up. As the Cuban revolt continued, the United States government felt that the lives and property of American citizens in Cuba

After Castro came to power in Cuba, American-owned business and industry were taken over.

America Advances Across the Pacific

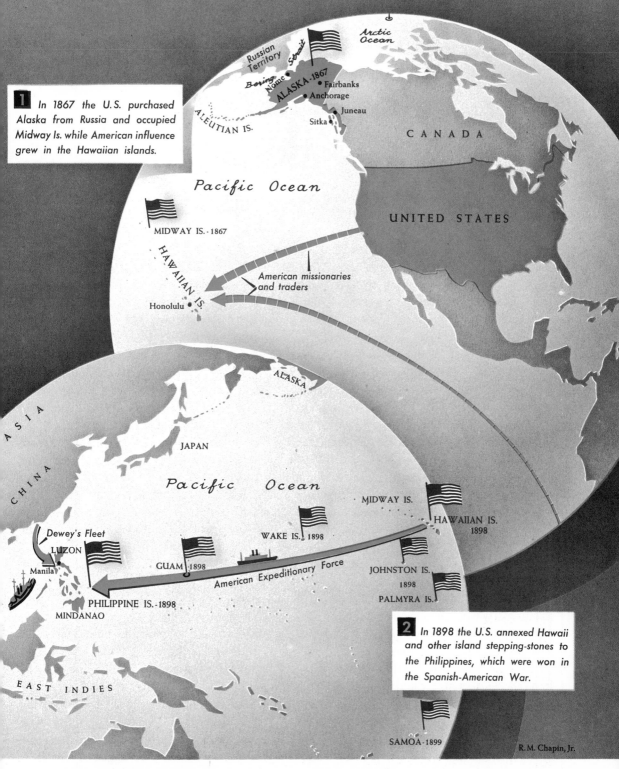

1 In 1867 the U.S. purchased Alaska from Russia and occupied Midway Is. while American influence grew in the Hawaiian islands.

Arctic Ocean

Russian Territory

Bering Strait

Nome

ALASKA - 1867

Fairbanks

Anchorage

Juneau

Sitka

ALEUTIAN IS.

CANADA

Pacific Ocean

MIDWAY IS. - 1867

UNITED STATES

HAWAIIAN IS.

American missionaries and traders

Honolulu

ALASKA

ASIA

JAPAN

CHINA

Pacific Ocean

MIDWAY IS.

HAWAIIAN IS. 1898

Dewey's Fleet

LUZON

Manila

WAKE IS. 1898

GUAM 1898

American Expeditionary Force

JOHNSTON IS. 1898

PHILIPPINE IS. - 1898

MINDANAO

PALMYRA IS.

2 In 1898 the U.S. annexed Hawaii and other island stepping-stones to the Philippines, which were won in the Spanish-American War.

EAST INDIES

SAMOA - 1899

R. M. Chapin, Jr.

MAP STUDY Locate Hawaii on each of these two views of the globe, which show how American influence moved westward across the Pacific in two main stages. (1) When was Alaska purchased? (2) How did the United States become interested in Hawaii? (3) What other American possessions are shown, and when was each acquired?

were in danger. To protect these citizens, an American battleship, the *Maine,* steamed into the harbor of Havana, Cuba, late in January, 1898.

Three weeks passed. On a hot, still night the *Maine* rode gently at her moorings. Her captain sat in his cabin writing a letter to his wife. Suddenly there was a dull roar and a terrific explosion shook the city. The *Maine* had blown up! She sank immediately, and soon only the tangled wreckage of her masts showed above the surface. Of the 350 officers and men on board, 260 were killed by the explosion or drowned in the sinking ship. Eight others were so badly wounded that they later died.

War comes between the United States and Spain. To this day, nobody knows for certain who or what caused the explosion on the *Maine.* It would certainly have been foolish of the Spaniards to blow up the ship, for the last thing Spain wanted was war with the United States. Nevertheless, in 1898, excited Americans blamed the Spaniards for the destruction of the ship and the loss of life. Everywhere the cry was "Remember the *Maine!*" Americans said, "Spain must be taught a lesson! The people of Cuba, and of other Spanish colonies as well, must be freed from the control of the Spanish government!"

Spain tried to avoid war. Her government did much to meet the wishes of the United States with regard to Cuba. But Congress was in a fighting mood. It voted that Cuba should be independent and that the armed forces of the United States should be used to help Cuba win her freedom. Congress also voted that after Cuba became free, the United States would "leave the government and control of the island to its people." This announcement was meant to show that the United States had no intention of selfishly grabbing

Cuba for itself. On April 25, 1898, war with Spain was declared.

America prepares for the war. The Spanish navy was both weak and ill-prepared; the United States Navy was more powerful and ready for war. On the other hand, the entire American army contained fewer than 30,000 officers and men, while Spain had about 80,000 soldiers in Cuba alone. So immediate steps were taken to enlarge the American army and to prepare the men for battle. The plan was for the American army to invade and occupy the islands owned by Spain in the Caribbean Sea. As for the United States Navy, it would blockade the Cuban coast so that more men and supplies from Spain could not reach Cuba. It would also seek to destroy the enemy's ships, wherever they might be.

Dewey destroys the Spanish fleet at Manila. The first important battle of the war took place thousands of miles from Cuba or the United States. Hardly had war been declared when Commodore George Dewey with several American warships set sail from a port in China. His goal was the Philippine Islands, then owned by Spain. On the morning of May 1, Dewey boldly attacked a Spanish squadron of several ships in Manila Bay in the Philippines. Back and forth steamed the American warships, firing upon the Spanish vessels until they were utterly destroyed.

In spite of Dewey's victory, the Philippine Islands could not be conquered until American soldiers arrived to defeat the Spanish land forces. Dewey blockaded the capital city of Manila, but it took many months to send an army all the way from the United States. In August, 1898, after an attack by American soldiers and Filipino patriots who were eager to win freedom from Spain, Manila surrendered.

The Splendid Little War is told largely in the words of men who took part in the Spanish American War. It contains 300 illustrations.

THE AMERICAN NAVY trapped a Spanish fleet in the harbor of Santiago, Cuba. This painting shows how the Americans sank one of their own ships (right background) in an effort to block the channel and prevent the Spanish ships from escaping.

Swift victories are won in Cuba. Meanwhile, American forces had been winning victories in the Spanish islands in the Caribbean Sea. Late in June a force of American soldiers landed in Cuba. In the campaign that followed, these soldiers fought under serious handicaps. When they left the United States, they wore heavy woolen uniforms which were unsuited to the stifling Cuban heat. The soldiers did not receive proper food. Furthermore, there was little protection from malaria and yellow fever, diseases which flourished in the tropical climate. More American soldiers in Cuba actually died from disease than were killed on the battlefields. Nevertheless, the American army prepared to attack the city of Santiago in southern Cuba. (map, page 586).

One of the famous battles of the war occurred just outside Santiago. An American army unit, known as the Rough Riders, stormed and captured San Juan (sahn *hwahn'*) Hill. The Rough Riders, as we have seen, were a group of volunteers commanded by Colonel Leonard Wood and Lieutenant Colonel Theodore Roosevelt (page 564). After the Americans had

seized San Juan Hill as well as other hills surrounding the city, Santiago could not be defended and it later surrendered.

Meanwhile, an American naval squadron in Cuban waters won nearly as complete a victory as Dewey had at Manila. A few Spanish ships had crossed the Atlantic early in the war but had been bottled up in the harbor of Santiago by American vessels. One July morning the Spanish ships made a dash for freedom. The American fleet attacked and destroyed every enemy ship.

After the surrender of Santiago, American forces landed on the island of Puerto Rico. Within a short time they had occupied most of that island.

Peace brings new territories to the United States. With the war going against it everywhere, the Spanish government sought to end the conflict. On August 12, 1898, less than four months after Congress had declared war, the United States and Spain agreed to end the fighting. But to stop fighting does not make a peace. What was to be done with Cuba? With Puerto Rico? With the Philippines? Because the United States had defeated the Spanish

Naval battles in the War with Battles and Heroes.

Spain are described in Naval

army and fleet, the fate of these islands rested chiefly in the hands of our country.

The American people were not agreed about what to do with the islands. Some believed that the United States should not take any responsibility for lands outside our mainland boundaries. These persons also felt that a democracy should not force its rule on foreign peoples. Others believed that Americans had a duty toward the people they had freed from Spain. In the end, Puerto Rico in the Caribbean Sea, and Guam and the Philippines in the far-distant Pacific, were transferred to the United States. (Find these islands on the maps, pages 579, 586.) In return for the Philippines, however, the United States

paid Spain $20,000,000. In addition, Spain agreed to give up its control of Cuba.

CHECK UP

1. (a) Why did Americans become interested in Hawaii? (b) How did the United States acquire Hawaii?

2. (a) Why did Americans become interested in the Cuban revolt against Spain? (b) What event led to war between Spain and the United States?

3. (a) What was the American plan for action against Spain? (b) What were the results of the fighting?

4. What territories did the United States acquire in the peace settlement?

How Did the United States Handle Problems in Lands Freed from Spain?

The United States gives a helping hand to Cuba. Although the Spanish-American War freed Cuba, she was hardly ready to manage her own affairs as an independent country. There was no organized government in Cuba. Many Cubans were homeless, poorly clothed, and starving. Disease, especially yellow fever, was widespread. To leave the Cubans to struggle with these problems alone would have increased their misery. American troops, therefore, remained in Cuba to lend a helping hand. The sick and hungry were cared for, and schools were established.

Yellow fever is conquered in Cuba. One of the most important things that Americans did for Cuba was to stamp out yellow fever. For many centuries yellow fever had been a dreaded disease in tropical countries, but no one knew what caused it. A Cuban doctor, Carlos Finlay, had long

believed that yellow fever was carried by mosquitoes which bred in swamps and in standing pools of water. But so far he had not been able to prove his theory. One sure test was to allow healthy humans to be bitten by mosquitoes that had previously bitten yellow fever victims. A number of soldiers volunteered to risk their lives in this experiment. As a result, Major Walter Reed and other army doctors proved beyond a doubt that yellow fever was carried by a certain kind of mosquito.

The remedy for yellow fever, then, was to wipe out all mosquitoes wherever they were found. Swamps were drained, and oil was spread over pools of standing water so that the young mosquitoes would be destroyed. In three months Major William C. Gorgas, in charge of health conditions in Cuba, was able to rid Havana of yellow fever. Thus brave men, with the aid of

Walter Reed: Doctor in Uniform tells how he discovered the cause of yellow fever.

FORTRESS EL MORRO, built by the Spanish in the 1500's, guarded the city of San Juan, Puerto Rico, from the ships of Spain's enemies. Today the rugged fortress overlooking San Juan harbor attracts many visitors.

science, conquered this age-old scourge of the tropics.

Cubans resent America's protection. The United States also helped Cuba establish a government. Cubans adopted a constitution and elected a president and a legislature. In 1902, American soldiers were withdrawn from the island, but the United States kept some control over Cuba. A special treaty was made which allowed the United States to maintain naval bases there. It also gave our country the right to intervene in Cuban affairs if the lives and property of American citizens or the freedom of Cuba were threatened. Under this treaty American forces returned to Cuba more than once when revolutions broke out and helped to restore order. Cubans, however, resented American interference because it reminded them that Cuba was not completely independent. In Chapter 31 you will learn how the United States later changed its policy toward Cuba.

The Philippines, Guam, and Puerto Rico present problems. The United States faced much more difficult problems in the Philippine Islands, Guam, and Puerto Rico. Because these islands were owned by the United States, we felt greater responsibility for· them than for Cuba. Unlike earlier additions to American territory (such as Florida, Louisiana, California, and Oregon), these islands were separated from our mainland by oceans. They were inhabited by peoples unfamiliar with our language, customs, and form of government. Even if the United States succeeded in improving conditions in these former possessions of Spain, what was their future to be? Were they to remain American colonies? Were they to become independent? Few Americans felt certain about these matters. The "march of the flag" outside our borders had brought heavy responsibilities to the United States. Many people believed that we had undertaken too much.

The United States improves conditions in the Philippines. The Philippines had special problems of its own. On its many islands lived people of many different tribes and languages. The largest island, Luzon, with its capital at Manila, was inhabited by Spanish-speaking natives. On other islands lived tribes of savage people. Most of the Filipinos were poor and lacked education. Moreover, they did not welcome American control. They had expected that the United States would give them freedom, just as we had promised freedom to the people of Cuba. After the surrender of the Spanish, Filipino troops had fought for their independence against American forces. Jungle fighting took many lives on both sides before the revolt finally ended.

Capitán: the Story of a Mule Tells **583** _about an army mule that saw service in Cuba, the Philippines, China, Mexico, and France._

This century has produced ample evidence that no people wishes to be ruled by another country.

584   THE UNITED STATES WIDENS ITS HORIZONS

After order had been restored, the United States was able to improve conditions in the Philippines. A bureau of health did much to stamp out disease and to teach the Filipinos the simple rules of healthful living. To provide education, teachers were sent from America and Filipino teachers were trained. By the 1930's, more than 7000 schools had been established. Local government was organized in towns and villages. Good roads were built. To provide farms for poor people, the government bought great stretches of land which were divided into small plots. Modern ways of farming and better tools were introduced. All these activities cost large sums of money, most of which was furnished by the United States.

Growing trade also helped the Filipino people. Americans bought great quantities of Philippine sugar, hemp, and tobacco. After 1909, these products entered the United States free of tariff duties.

The Filipinos desire independence. As conditions in the islands improved, the United States gave the Filipinos a greater share in their government. Beginning in 1907, they elected members to their own Philippine Assembly. In 1916, Congress approved a constitution for the Philippine Islands. This constitution provided for a senate and a house of representatives to be elected by the Filipinos. Laws made by the Philippine legislature, however, could be vetoed by the American governor-general if he did not consider them wise. Except for the governor-general and a few other officials, government positions were to be held by Filipinos. The United States also promised to withdraw its control from the islands as soon as the Filipino people had proved fully capable of governing themselves. Because of this plan for Philippine independence, the Filipinos were not given United States citizenship as the Hawaiians were.

Many Filipinos, however, were not satisfied with greater self-government under American control. They felt they were already capable of governing themselves and continued to ask for immediate independence. You will read in Chapter 30 how the Philippines finally won full independence at the close of World War II.

American rule brings some benefits to Puerto Rico. After the United States took over Puerto Rico, conditions were improved on that island. The way was made

FILIPINO GIRLS enjoy a lesson in child care in this photograph taken about 1928. Home nursing demonstrations were part of the American program to help improve life in the Philippine Islands.

SMALL BUSINESSES have been given a boost by Puerto Rico's Operation Bootstrap. These women are spraying dishes in a chinaware factory.

clear for Puerto Rican products to enter the United States without tariff duties. As a result, sugar, tobacco, and banana production boomed. The United States built roads, improved health conditions, and increased the number of schools.

In spite of these improvements, Puerto Rico still had serious problems. For several reasons the islanders did not progress as rapidly as the Filipinos did. The population was large for the size of the island and there was much overcrowding. Although trade with the United States brought more wealth to Puerto Rico, very little of it reached the ordinary person. There was much unemployment and poverty; thousands of Puerto Ricans were hungry and sick.

Then, the Puerto Ricans decided to do something about their problems. They started a program called *Operation Bootstrap*,[1] which encouraged the establishment of manufacturing and attracted investments from the United States. The many new factories started since then have created thousands of jobs and added greatly to the island's income. Agricultural production has also increased and farmers are en-

[1] This name comes from the old saying "to pull yourself up by the bootstraps."

couraged to grow other crops as well as sugar cane. In addition, Puerto Rico's tropical scenery has attracted many vacationers, and so the tourist trade has become an important source of income. All of these developments have meant a better life for the islanders. Many problems remain to be solved, and large numbers of Puerto Ricans have migrated to large cities of the United States in hopes of finding a better life. But those who stay in Puerto Rico now have a standard of living twice as high as it was twenty years ago. In Chapter 32 you will read how Puerto Rico governs itself as a commonwealth under the protection of the United States.

CHECK UP

1. (a) How did Americans help Cuba after 1898? (b) What sort of control did the United States keep in Cuba? (c) How did the Cubans feel about this control?

2. (a) How did the United States try to improve conditions in the Philippines? (b) By what steps did the Filipinos make progress toward self-government?

3. (a) How did conditions improve in Puerto Rico after 1898? (b) What problems remained? (c) How have the Puerto Ricans tried to deal with these problems?

5 How Was the United States Able to Build the Panama Canal?

The canal was also needed for commercial purposes.

At the beginning of the 1900's, the United States found herself in a new position. Her territory stretched not only from the Atlantic to the Pacific but halfway across the world. Yet there was no short cut by which our navy and merchant ships could reach the Pacific coast from the Atlantic coast. They had to travel south the full length of South America, around Cape Horn, and north again, a trip of about 12,000 miles. To protect our possessions in the Pacific and to help American commerce, it became important to shorten this long trip. A glance at the map on this page will show you that the narrowest place between North and South America is the neck of land which Balboa crossed in 1513 — the Isthmus of Panama. Why not cut the continents apart by building a canal through the Isthmus?

The United States decides to dig a canal. The idea of building a canal across Panama was not a new one. During the 1800's, France and England as well as the United States had considered such a canal. But in 1898 the United States government became fully aware of how necessary a canal was for the defense of its coasts. When the Spanish-American War broke out in that year, the *Oregon,* a battleship of the United States Navy, was in the Pacific. Ordered to Cuba, the *Oregon* made the long trip around South America and did not arrive until the short war was almost over! The government was convinced that a canal must be built and that the United States must build it.

For many years the United States had had an agreement with Great Britain that neither country should control by itself a

MAP STUDY Colored arrows show American campaigns against Spain's Caribbean possessions during the Spanish-American War. Dates tell when territories came under American control. (1) When was the Panama Canal Zone acquired? (2) The Virgin Islands?

The U. S. Expands into the Caribbean

THOUSANDS OF MEN, using huge machinery, moved earth and mountains to dig the Panama Canal.

canal route across Central America. In 1901, our government made a new treaty with Great Britain. This agreement stated that the United States alone might build and control a canal if ships of all nations were allowed to use it. Great Britain realized that she would profit from the new and much shorter trade route that such a canal would make possible.

The next step was to decide where to build the canal. Two routes were considered — one across Nicaragua, which was longer but easier to build; the other across Panama, which was shorter. The shorter route was finally recommended, although it meant cutting through mountains in the interior of Panama. A French company had already tried unsuccessfully to build a canal through the Isthmus of Panama. But the company had not been prepared to battle the dread diseases of malaria and yellow fever. The French company finally failed after losing 40,000 workmen and spending millions of dollars. The United States bought the property rights of this French company.

The United States secures land for the canal. The next step was to make arrangements for the right to build the canal across Panama. At that time Panama was a part of the Republic of Colombia in South America. Colombia refused to give

the United States permission to dig a canal in Panama. But the people of Panama were eager to have the canal built and feared that the United States might turn to the Nicaraguan route. In 1903, with the encouragement of the American President, Theodore Roosevelt, Panama revolted from Colombia and set up an independent republic. It is well known that American warships off the coast of Panama prevented Colombian troops from landing to put down the revolt. Also, the United States hastily made an agreement with the new Republic of Panama. For a down payment of $10,000,000 and rent of $250,000 a year,[1] its government leased to the United States a strip of land ten miles wide "in perpetuity," or to the end of time.

Disease is conquered in Panama. Our government had not forgotten the reason for the French failure in Panama. Colonel William Gorgas, the man who had stamped out yellow fever in Cuba, was sent to Panama. In the ten-mile-wide strip called the Canal Zone, Colonel Gorgas drained swamps and ponds so that the deadly mosquitoes could not breed. Not only the Zone, but much of Panama sur-

---

[1] The amount of rent has been increased until it now totals $1,930,000 a year.

See _Soldier Doctor: The Story of_ **587** _William Gorgas._

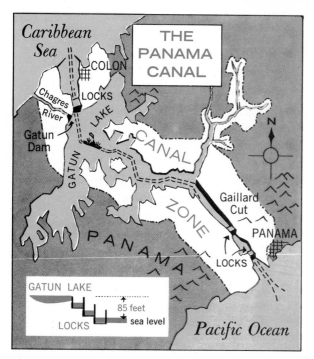

THE PANAMA CANAL

Caribbean Sea

COLON

Chagres River

LOCKS

Gatun Dam

GATUN

CANAL LAKE

ZONE

N

Gaillard Cut

PANAMA

LOCKS

PANAMA

GATUN LAKE

85 feet
sea level

LOCKS

Pacific Ocean

GATUN DAM (top, left) backed up the waters of the Chagres River to form an artificial lake above sea level. Ships are raised to it by means of locks. Where was the canal cut through mountains?

rounding it, was freed of mosquitoes. Deaths from malaria and yellow fever became rare. After two years it was safe for men to work on the canal.

The "Big Ditch" is dug. Colonel George Goethals (*goh'*thalz), of the United States Army Engineers, was given the tremendous task of building the canal. Because of the mountains in the interior, it was decided to build a canal which would be 85 feet above sea level in the middle of the Isthmus. Locks were to be built to raise and lower ships, and rivers were to be dammed to furnish a waterway in the interior. For seven years, using huge steam shovels and other powerful machinery, men blasted and dug and dredged. The most difficult task was cutting a channel, eight or nine miles long, through mountains of solid rock. This channel is called the Gaillard Cut, in honor of David Gaillard (*gil-yard'*), the engineer in charge.

In August, 1914, the great engineering feat was at last completed. In faraway Washington, President Wilson pushed a switch which released the dammed-up waters and filled the "Big Ditch." Soon ships were passing from one ocean to the other. These ships could now travel from the east coast of our country to the west coast at a saving of 7000 miles! Many ports in other parts of the world were also brought closer together. And the United States had acquired some more territory outside its borders.

The Canal Zone is governed by the United States. The Canal Zone, a slice of land ten miles wide and about forty miles long, is controlled by the American government. Most people in the Zone have some connection with the canal — workmen, engineers, members of the army and navy, and so on. There are attractive, modern government-owned houses for rent, schools, stores, clubs, and movies.

As you can imagine, the canal is vital to the defense of the Western Hemisphere. If it should be damaged by enemy bombs, our navy would be seriously handicapped, for ships could not move speedily from one ocean to the other. During World War II both army and navy kept watch, not only over the canal itself, but far out to sea. Because of a great increase in canal traffic, in 1964 the United States announced plans to build a new sea-level canal in Central America.

CHECK UP

1. (a) Why was the United States interested in building a canal across Central America? (b) How did the United States acquire the right to build the canal in Panama?

2. (a) What problems were overcome in building the canal? (b) How is the Canal Zone governed today?

The story of how the canal came **588** to be built is told in _Bridge of Water: the story of Panama and the Canal._

How Did We Gain More Island Possessions?

See also <u>Ocean Outposts</u> *by Helen Follett.*

The story of American possessions would not be complete without mentioning the other islands in the Pacific and Caribbean which are owned by the United States. As you read about these islands, refer to the maps on pages 579 and 586.

Wake Island and Guam become American possessions. We learned earlier in this chapter that our government owns the Midway Islands, so named because they lie halfway between America and Asia. When the first cable was laid across the Pacific, it went by way of the main island, Midway. About 2000 miles straight west of Honolulu lies Wake Island, three square miles in area. In 1898, the United States Navy took possession of it. Midway and Wake, both of which are barren coral islands and have no native inhabitants, are used as stopping points for planes winging their way across the Pacific.

Guam, ceded to us by Spain, is the largest of the Pacific island group called the Marianas. It was first important as a naval station. Later, a government wireless station was set up there. Guam also became a stop on the air route to the Far East. For many years Guam was governed by an American naval officer. But in 1950 the people of Guam became United States citizens. Their governor is appointed by the President of the United States but they elect the members of the law-making body.

The United States also controls American Samoa, the Virgin Islands, and others. On the ocean route between San Francisco and Australia lie the Samoan Islands. Because of its excellent harbor, Pago Pago (*pong'oh pong'oh*), the United States became interested in Tutuila (*too-too-ee'lah*), one of the islands in the Samoan group. In 1899, our country took possession of Tutuila and four other tiny islands nearby. A powerful wireless station was erected on Tutuila. Thanks to schools started by the United States, most Samoans can read and write. The governor of American Samoa is appointed by the United States government, but the Samoans have their own legislature. They are not yet citizens of the United States, although they would like to be.

Our government has also claimed small groups of uninhabited Pacific islands or atolls. They were valuable at first for guano, which was greatly in demand for fertilizer in the 1800's. Someday they may be important as stops on plane routes.

The last territory acquired by the United States was in the Caribbean. In 1917, we paid $25,000,000 to Denmark for three small islands in the Virgin Islands group. World War I was going on, and we wanted them as bases for the defense of the Panama Canal. For several years they were governed by a naval officer. Today a governor is appointed by the President of the United States, and the people are citizens of the United States.

•

By the early 1900's, then, the island possessions of the United States stretched from the nearby Caribbean Sea to the remote Pacific. In accepting responsibility for these islands and their peoples, the United States took a long step toward the role of world leader.

CHECK UP

1. (a) What islands has the United States acquired in the Pacific? (b) In the Caribbean?

2. How are the more important of these islands governed?

589

Check Up on Chapter 28

Do You Know the Meaning?

1. isthmus
2. canal lock
3. yellow fever
4. foreign policy
5. vital interests

Can You Identify?

1. Maximilian
2. 1867
3. 1895
4. 1898
5. 1917
6. *Maine*
7. Napoleon III
8. George Dewey
9. Rough Riders
10. Walter Reed
11. William Gorgas
12. William H. Seward
13. Operation Bootstrap

Can You Locate?

1. Alaska
2. Hawaii
3. Havana
4. Cuba
5. Guam
6. Midway Islands
7. Puerto Rico
8. Philippine Islands
9. Wake Island
10. American Samoa

Can You Locate? (Cont.)

11. Manila
12. Santiago
13. Virgin Islands
14. Panama Canal Zone

What Do You Think?

1. Is the Panama Canal as important today as when it was opened? Why?
2. Could the Spanish-American War have been avoided? Give reasons for your answer.
3. American rule helped improve conditions in both Cuba and the Philippines after the Spanish-American War. Yet the people of both areas strongly wanted independence. Why?
4. Is the United States less interested in East Asia now that the Philippines are independent? Explain.
5. Are nations today interested in acquiring colonies? Why?

Questions #3 and 5 are fundamental.

LINKING PAST AND PRESENT

How cold is Alaska? Probably no one in 1867 ever dreamed that the Alaskan "icebox" would become a state of the Union. Oddly enough, many people today still think of Alaska as an icebox. There are of course vast frozen areas in the arctic region to the north. But in central and southern Alaska, people live comfortably. One reason is that the coastal region is warmed by an ocean stream called the Japan Current. The interior of Alaska is warm and often hot during the short summer; and in the winter it is no colder than some of the states just south of Canada. It is true that the winters are long and the summer season is short, lasting only about two months. But during these summer months the sun shines up to nineteen hours a day! The long hours of sunshine produce fine crops of vegetables, fruits, and flowers.

Who are the Hawaiians? The first inhabitants of Hawaii were brown-skinned Polynesians from other Pacific islands. Paddling giant canoes, they made their way to Hawaii over 1000 years ago. In the 1800's, American trading ships began to stop at the islands, and missionaries soon arrived, bringing a new religion and way of life. Other Americans started sugar plantations and brought in thousands of Chinese and, later, Japanese to work in the fields. People from other countries also came to the islands. All these immigrants had a part in building Hawaii. Of the 630,000 people there today, only a few are of pure Polynesian stock. Diseases brought by foreigners killed thousands of the original Hawaiians. But their culture survives in musical words, graceful dances, and Hawaiian food and water sports.

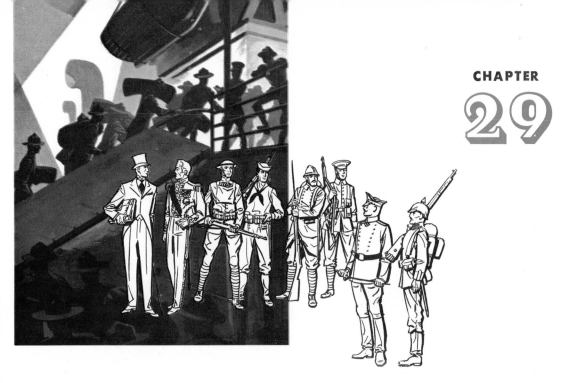

The United States Plays a Larger

Part in World Affairs

America Grows Up by Johnson deals with the Monroe Doctrine, the Spanish-American War, and the Open Door.

What this chapter is about —

The course of history does not always move in a straight line. Nations, like people, change their plans and policies. A plan or policy that seems wise and desirable at one time may seem less attractive, or even dangerous, at another time. The affairs of a nation, it should be remembered, are more complicated than those of a man or a family. A man can make his personal decisions — to accept a new job, for example, or to buy a new house — largely by himself. In a democracy like the United States, however, millions of voters have opinions on a subject that affects the whole nation. These opinions naturally differ. Voters and political parties debate the subject, and it takes time and thought before the country finally decides what course to follow.

In this chapter we shall learn about a period when the United States had some difficulty in making up its mind. In the early 1900's, our nation, growing ever larger and stronger, still could not quite decide what part to play in world affairs. At times Americans took a vigorous and important part in world events. At other times they favored a less active part. For example, after a period of neutrality from 1914 to 1917, the United States entered World War I.

As you read how the foreign policy of

People in our story — American and European diplomats; U.S. infantryman and sailor; French soldier; British soldier; German officer and soldier.

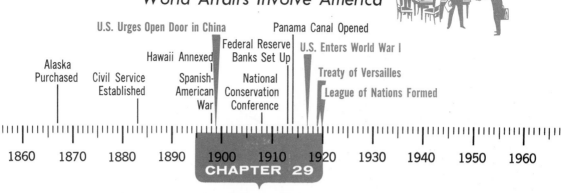

World Affairs Involve America

U.S. Urges Open Door in China · Panama Canal Opened

Alaska Purchased · Hawaii Annexed · Federal Reserve Banks Set Up · U.S. Enters World War I

Civil Service Established · Spanish-American War · National Conservation Conference · Treaty of Versailles · League of Nations Formed

1860 1870 1880 1890 1900 1910 1920 1930 1940 1950 1960

CHAPTER 29

1895 - 1920

the United States developed and changed, look for the answers to these questions:

▶ 1. How did American foreign policy develop in the early 1900's?

▶ 2. What part did the United States play in World War I?

▶ 3. How did the victorious nations fail to lay the basis of a lasting peace?

How Did American Foreign Policy Develop in the Early 1900's?

You read in the last chapter how the Spanish-American War marked a turning point in America's relations with the rest of the world. As a result of the war, the United States had possessions and important interests in the far Pacific area as well as in the Western Hemisphere. As Theodore Roosevelt said, it was no longer a question whether we would take part in world affairs, but "whether we should play that part well or ill." Even so, Americans still differed on the question of how active a part the United States should play in world affairs. Many Americans felt that overseas responsibilities were troublesome and expensive. When government leaders urged that the United States adopt an active foreign policy, they could expect a good deal of opposition. Nevertheless, our country continued to develop new policies in its foreign relations.

THE UNITED STATES DEVELOPS THE OPEN DOOR POLICY FOR CHINA

Trade brings the United States in contact with far-off China. Suppose a piece of string is tied tightly around a world globe so that it runs through Washington, D.C., and through the North and South Poles. On the side of the globe opposite Washington, this string will pass through Chungking, an important city in China.

Half a world away! We might suppose that people on opposite sides of the globe would have no interest in each other. This is far from true. Very early in American history, Yankee ships made their way to China and began a brisk trade between the two countries (Chapter 14). At one time the finest and speediest sailing vessels were the China clippers running between American and Chinese ports. In recent years, one of the earliest airplanes to fly

You may still need to call **592** *attention to cross-references.*

AMERICAN TROOPS storm a wall in Peking during the Boxer Rebellion. These Americans were part of an international army of about 20,000 men that rescued besieged foreigners in China.

regularly across the Pacific Ocean was named the *China Clipper* after the earlier sailing ships. For 150 years, until after World War II, the United States and China were for the most part on friendly terms. Americans helped build hospitals and schools in China. American missionaries brought education and better health, as well as the Christian religion, to the people of China. Many Chinese students studied in American colleges.

European powers and Japan help themselves to parts of China. China was a united country long before the European nations were formed. Over many hundreds of years, the Chinese had developed their own art and literature and their own way of living. The Chinese people, however, had not kept up with the progress which European countries had made — especially in such things as modern machinery and weapons and means of transportation. Thus it happened that, although China had many millions of people, she was unable to resist the armed strength of the newer nations. In the 1800's, therefore, when Western countries wanted to gain more trade and colonies, they were able to seize parts of China.

Great Britain, for example, forced China to give up Hong Kong and to permit Englishmen to live and trade in five other Chinese cities. Later on, France seized part of China and ruled it under the name of French Indo-China. Russia forced China to give her special privileges in Manchuria and Port Arthur. (Locate these places on the map on page 594.) In the 1890's, Japan (the only Asian nation to copy Western ways) made war on China and forced her to give up territory. As each power obtained more land and rights in China, the others, becoming jealous, made further demands. It seemed likely that China would be nibbled away until nothing remained.

The "Fists" of China strike back. Patriotic Chinese became angry. Why, they asked, should our country be handed out bit by bit to foreigners? Why should so many foreigners come to live and make money in China? Let us get rid of them! So patriotic Chinese formed secret societies known by strange names — "Great Sword Society," the "Plum-Blossom Fists," the "Fists of Public Harmony." By mistake, foreigners thought the secret societies engaged in boxing, so they called them "boxers." In their secret meetings the "boxers" talked of the great day when foreigners would be driven out of China.

Sooner or later, such angry feelings were bound to result in trouble. In 1900, the Chinese people rose in revolt. They killed

Today British-held Hong Kong and Portuguese Macao are the last of these holdings on the Chinese mainland.

some foreigners and destroyed property held by foreigners. Embassies and foreign business houses in Peking, the capital, were surrounded. Because the societies of "boxers" had been leaders in teaching the Chinese to hate the "foreign devils," this uprising was known as the *Boxer Rebellion.*

Foreign soldiers crush the Boxer Rebellion. The foreign powers — Russia, France, Great Britain, Germany, Japan, and the United States — took steps to aid their fellow countrymen in China. They sent soldiers who put down the Boxer Rebellion and restored order. The Chinese government was forced to pay large sums of money for the damages suffered by foreigners and the trouble which the rebellion had caused. The European powers and Japan kept their shares of this money, but the United States later returned more than half of its share. The money returned was used to send Chinese students to

schools and colleges in this country. The Chinese people were grateful to the United States for this generous act.

Our Open Door Policy urges fair play for China. In 1899, just the year before the Boxer Rebellion, the United States showed its friendliness for China in another way. John Hay, the American Secretary of State, asked the other leading powers to declare that the people of all nations should be treated alike when they lived and traded in China. None were to seek special favors. Since Hay's idea meant that the door of China should be open to all, it was called the *Open Door Policy.* This policy would not only benefit all who peacefully sought trade in China but would protect China's independence.

In time, other powers halfheartedly agreed to Hay's idea. The Open Door Policy became the basis of American foreign policy in China and the Far East. More than once in the early 1900's the

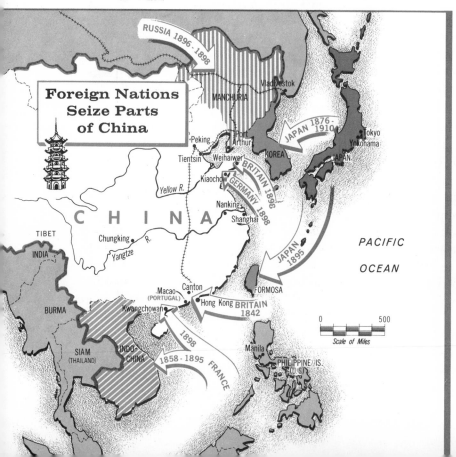

MAP STUDY
(1) What countries had acquired important rights by about 1900 in Hong Kong? (2) In Port Arthur? (3) Why do you think Japan would be interested in Korea and Manchuria on mainland Asia?

THE GIFT OF A MINIATURE RAILROAD TRAIN and 370 feet of track won many friends for Commodore Perry on his visit to Japan. This Japanese drawing exaggerates the size of the train; actually people could not fit inside it. But the delighted Japanese would perch on the roof as the train puffed along at 20 miles an hour.

United States lent support to the notion of fair play in China.

THE UNITED STATES HELPS JAPAN, BUT OPPOSES JAPANESE EFFORTS TO CONTROL CHINA

Perry opens Japan to the world. The year 1854 is an important date in the history of Japan. For hundreds of years Japan had little to do with foreigners. She would not allow any foreign ships (except a few Dutch vessels) to enter her ports to carry on trade. Japan was almost completely shut off from the rest of the world.

Then, in 1854, Commodore Matthew C. Perry (a brother of Oliver H. Perry, the naval hero of the War of 1812) visited Japan with part of the United States fleet. The Japanese government was greatly awed by the strength of the American navy. It therefore agreed to Perry's demand that Japan make a treaty with the United States, allowing Americans to trade in her ports. As a result of this treaty, Japan was opened to the world.

Japan becomes a strong, modern country. Before Perry's visit, the Japanese people lived in much the same way that Europeans had lived in the Middle Ages (pages 17–18). But the Japanese were quick to learn. Once they came into contact with the rest of the world, they determined to make Japan a modern industrial country. Unlike China, Japan made rapid progress in adopting some European and American ways. In less than fifty years she became one of the world's great powers and a strong commercial and industrial nation.

President Theodore Roosevelt helps settle Japan's war with Russia. For many years after Perry's visit, the United States and Japan were on friendly terms. Japan, to be sure, had been one of the countries that had "helped themselves" to parts of China. But Japan seemed to accept our Open Door Policy and joined the United States and the other foreign powers in putting down the Boxer Rebellion.

During the early 1900's, the country which seemed the most eager to expand into Chinese territory was Russia. Russia

How Perry opened Japan to Trade **595** *is Told in Square Sails and the Spice Islands.*

appeared to be trying to get a stronger grip on Manchuria, China's large northern territory. But Japan did not want any other country to obtain special rights in Manchuria. Manchuria was rich in iron and other minerals which Japan lacked and which she felt she needed to become a strong industrial country. So, in 1904, Japan went to war against Russia. Americans generally sympathized with Japan, much the smaller of the two nations.

To the surprise of many, Japan won victory after victory over Russia, both on land and at sea. When President Theodore Roosevelt offered his help in bringing the war to a close, Russia was glad to accept. As a result of Roosevelt's efforts, delegates from Russia and Japan met at Portsmouth, New Hampshire, and agreed on a treaty of peace ending the war. By the terms of the treaty Japan was awarded the special rights which Russia had previously held in Manchuria. The treaty also recognized that Japan had special interests in Korea (map, page 594). But the Japanese were disappointed. They had hoped their victories would bring them even greater gains.

The friendly relations of the United States and Japan come to an end. With the end of the Russian-Japanese War, a change took place in the relations between Japan and the United States. The Japanese, on the one hand, felt that President Roosevelt had favored Russia in the peace settlement. The Japanese also resented the restrictions placed on Japanese immigration into this country (page 527). Many Americans, on the other hand, feared that a strong Japan would try to take the Philippines away from us. They watched with alarm as Japan's growing commerce began to cut into America's trade.

Japan fails to support the Open Door Policy in China. The most important reason for less friendly relations between Japan and the United States, however, grew out of Japan's attitude toward China. Japan seemed intent on controlling China and "shutting the door" on the rest of the world. Japan openly annexed Korea in 1910. Many Japanese spoke of a "Monroe Doctrine" for Asia, which would exclude Americans and Europeans. Then, during World War I, Japan made harsh demands on China. These were withdrawn only when the United States and other countries strongly objected. Though Japan declared war on Germany in World War I, she did little except take over German rights and territories in China and the Pacific.

THE UNITED STATES USES THE MONROE DOCTRINE TO INTERVENE IN LATIN AMERICA

Let us turn now from the Far East to the Americas. What foreign policy did the United States follow during the early 1900's toward the countries south of the Rio Grande?

You will recall (Chapter 10) the long struggle of Latin Americans to win their independence. Independence, however, brought new problems. Latin Americans had had little chance to practice self-government while under the strict control of Spain. The people of the separate Latin American republics set up after independence, therefore, were ill-prepared to manage their affairs. Instead, in country after country, ambitious leaders seized control for their own selfish purposes. Revolutions frequently toppled such leaders from power, but their places were taken by others who were no more interested in the welfare of the people.

Latin Americans grow suspicious of the Monroe Doctrine. In 1823, just about the time Latin Americans gained freedom from Spain, President Monroe announced

The Japanese policy for Asia obviously was not approved by the Chinese.

the Monroe Doctrine (page 257). At first, the countries of Latin America welcomed the Doctrine. They were glad to accept its protection. They knew they could not hold their own against European nations which might want to gain territory in the Americas. As time went on, however, the countries of Latin America came to look at their powerful neighbor to the north with suspicion. They saw the United States annex Mexican territory as a result of the Mexican War (page 360). They saw it make Puerto Rico and the Philippines American possessions, interfere in Cuban affairs, and obtain the Panama Canal Zone. What if the United States should look to the south for more territory? Then in the early 1900's certain events made it seem that their fears were coming true.

Theodore Roosevelt expands the Monroe Doctrine. The republics of Central America and those in the Caribbean Sea suffered from bad government. They had piled up big debts and had borrowed large sums from European countries. Soon after 1900, conditions became desperate in several of these countries. There were frequent revolts. Furthermore, European governments were demanding the repayment of their loans and threatening to send warships to collect them.

Theodore Roosevelt was President of the United States at this time. He reminded Congress that the Monroe Doctrine forbade European nations to interfere in this hemisphere. He declared that the United States should step in and manage the affairs of any Latin American country that could not keep order or pay its debts.

The United States becomes a policeman in Latin America. In 1905, the United States did step in to straighten out the tangled affairs of the Dominican Republic. American officials took charge of its money affairs and arranged for the payment of its debts. Under United States control, conditions in the little country improved greatly, but the people of the Dominican Republic did not like our interference. The United States also took over control of finances in the neighboring republic of Haiti. To maintain order, United States marines were sent to Haiti in 1915 and stayed for nineteen years. The Haitians naturally resented the presence of foreign soldiers. Even earlier, in 1912, the United States had begun to "police" Nicaragua in Central America.

The actions of the United States arouse fear and suspicion. To many people, especially Latin Americans, the United States seemed to be depriving these small republics of their independence. They began to ask, "Does the United States intend to use its Monroe Doctrine as an excuse to gain control of all Latin America?" Latin American newspapers wrote bitterly about the actions of the United States. Authors of books and magazine articles compared the United States to a huge octopus reaching out to seize the republics of Latin America in its tentacles.

A revolution takes place in Mexico. Meanwhile, trouble broke out in Mexico. For almost 35 years (1877–1911) Mexico had been under the rule of a heavy-handed dictator named Diaz (*dee'*ahs). Diaz had allowed foreign businessmen to obtain large tracts of land, to build railroads, and to develop Mexico's rich oil wells. In return, the Mexican government received a share of the large profits made by the foreign companies. While foreign businessmen and a few Mexican politicians grew rich, conditions among the common people of Mexico grew no better. Most of them lived in miserable houses, working the land for rich landlords.

At last the Mexican people rose in revolt. From 1910 to 1920, all Mexico was a

Latin American countries resented the Roosevelt Corollary. The Good Neighbor Policy (page 669) was intended to allay this resentment.

GENERAL PERSHING led the American expedition in pursuit of Pancho Villa. Within a few months Pershing was to go to France as commander of the American forces in World War I (page 604).

bloody battlefield. First, the people fought to get rid of Diaz, and then they took part in the struggles between rival leaders fighting each other for power. In the end the people triumphed. A new constitution provided for a president who could serve one term only and a congress to be elected by the people. Rights to oil and minerals were to belong to the nation. The government was also given power to buy land from large landowners and divide it among the peons, or peasants. These changes did not come about at once, but over the years the Mexicans have gained many of the things for which they fought.

The United States interferes in Mexico. What did the United States have to do with the Mexican Revolution? During the revolution, as you can imagine, Mexico was in a state of great confusion. Its government was not strong enough to protect the property and the lives of Americans and other foreigners who lived there. Through our representative in Mexico, the United States tried to bring about the establishment of an orderly government. This action was resented by the Mexicans as interference with their government. Then an unfortunate incident occurred.

One of the revolutionary leaders was a man named Pancho Villa (*vee'*yuh). In 1916, he seized eighteen Americans from a train and killed them. Two months later, Villa's men crossed the border and killed seventeen more Americans in a town in New Mexico. An American force under General John J. Pershing was sent into Mexico to catch and punish Villa and his men. American troops had several skirmishes with Villa, but he escaped into the mountains. In 1917, our soldiers returned home. The United States at that time was about to enter World War I and the American troops in Mexico might soon be needed in Europe. The withdrawal of American forces prevented further trouble in Mexico, but it did not end the bitterness felt by Mexicans toward the United States.

THE UNITED STATES LENDS SUPPORT TO PLANS FOR WORLD PEACE

You have already read about several important changes in our country's foreign

A sovereign state unquestionably has the right to determine that oil and minerals belong to the nation.

policy that occurred in 1898 and the years that followed: (1) The United States acquired possessions outside the North American continent. (2) It supported the Open Door Policy in the Far East. (3) And it broadened the Monroe Doctrine in its relations with the countries of Latin America.

Still another policy that the United States followed after 1898 was to support plans for keeping peace between nations. For centuries, wise and kindly men have wondered whether war could not be stamped out. They thought of the men killed or crippled in battle and of their sorrowing widows and orphaned children. They considered the crops, buildings, and cities laid waste, and the vast sums of money spent for wars. And these men asked, "Why can't we put an end to war? Why can't we use our strength for peaceful progress instead of for destruction? We have policemen to keep peace in cities; we have governments to keep peace within nations. Can't we find ways to keep peace *between* nations? At least we can try."

The Hague Court is formed. Down through the years different plans have been suggested for keeping peace among the nations of the world. In 1899, many governments sent representatives to a meeting at The Hague, a city in Holland. Another meeting was held at The Hague in 1907. At these meetings plans were drawn up for a court which would settle disputes between nations. The quarreling nations could select judges, from a list made beforehand, to act as umpires. These judges would listen to both sides of the quarrel and then give a decision.

The United States took a leading part in the meetings at The Hague. It sent representatives to assist in making plans. Andrew Carnegie gave the money to erect a building at The Hague where the judges in such disputes would meet. The United States also was the first country to use this method of avoiding war. It referred an old dispute with Mexico to the Hague Court for settlement.

World peace is difficult to enforce. Unhappily the hopes for peace aroused by the meetings at The Hague were soon dashed. In a world of many nations each nation considered itself the equal of every other. Each country insisted upon the right to act as it saw fit, without outside interference. Nations might agree to observe a set of rules or customs (called *international law*). They might agree to submit disputes to an umpire like the Hague Court. But when a dispute arose or a quarrel developed, there was no way of *compelling* nations to keep their promises or to settle their differences peacefully. The outbreak of World War I in 1914 made this fact all too clear.

CHECK UP

1. (a) Why did the European powers and Japan seize parts of China in the late 1800's? (b) How did China strike back? (c) What were the results? (d) What was the Open Door Policy?

2. (a) How was Japan opened to trade with the rest of the world? (b) Why did Japan and Russia go to war? (c) How was the war ended?

3. (a) Why did Japan and the United States become less friendly? (b) What was Japan's attitude toward the Open Door Policy? Why?

4. (a) Why were Latin Americans suspicious of the Monroe Doctrine? (b) What new meaning did Theodore Roosevelt give to the Monroe Doctrine? (c) Where was the Doctrine applied in Latin America?

5. (a) Why did a revolution break out in Mexico in 1910? (b) What action was taken by the United States in Mexico?

6. (a) What was the Hague Court? (b) Why was it formed? (c) Why is it difficult to maintain world peace?

There still is no way of compelling great powers to submit a dispute to arbitration. Smaller ones usually yield to pressure.

World War I begins. On a night early in August, 1914, the citizens of a little Belgian village on the border of Germany awoke with a feeling of fear. Into the village rode the advance guard of the German army. Soon, long columns of gray-clad infantry followed, and there could be heard the rumble and thunder of guns. The citizens knew what all this meant — Germany was at war with France. Belgium was a neutral country, but that fact meant nothing to the German army, which wanted to make a lightning thrust at France. The Belgian villagers had reason to be fearful and sad. As the battle surged around them, their homes went up in flames and many of the people were killed.

At other towns and villages along the border, the news was the same. The million and a half German soldiers invading Belgium and France expected to crush the French army in a few weeks. Gone were the high hopes of leading peaceful lives in a peaceful world. Once more war had come to Europe — the worst war the world had known up to that time.

What were the causes of World War I? The real causes of the conflict lay in the jealousies and desires for power among the leading European countries. For a number of years, there had been two rival groups of nations in Europe. All that was needed was a spark to set off the explosion of war. That spark came from a quarrel between Austria-Hungary and Serbia.[1] When a Serbian sympathizer murdered the Archduke who was heir to the Austro-Hungarian throne, Austria declared war on Serbia.

Immediately the different nations in

[1] Serbia today is part of Yugoslavia. Austria and Hungary are now separate nations.

the two groups sprang to action. Russia, which considered itself the protector of several small countries in the Balkan Peninsula, went to Serbia's aid. France and Great Britain had a friendly understanding with Russia and so could be expected to take her side. But Germany, having promised support to Austria-Hungary, declared war on Russia and France. One by one the countries of Europe took sides. Soon the war was in full swing. On one side were the *Central Powers,* including Germany, Austria-Hungary, Bulgaria, and Turkey. On the other side were the *Allies,* including France, Great Britain, Russia, Belgium, and later Italy.

Before the war ended, 27 nations took part in it, and their combined armies made up a total of 65 million men. It was indeed a "World War."

THE UNITED STATES TRIES UNSUCCESSFULLY TO REMAIN AT PEACE

President Wilson urges neutrality. Americans were shocked at the way European nations rushed into war. They were horrified at the cruel invasion of little Belgium, which had no quarrel with Germany. To the United States, however, Europe and its quarrels seemed far away. Americans remembered how George Washington had warned them to keep out of the quarrels of Europe. Now they listened to President Woodrow Wilson. As soon as World War I began, he advised them to be "neutral in fact as well as in name . . . impartial in thought as well as in action." "Good," they thought; "the United States will not have to fight in this war. We will remain neutral."

The United States finds it hard not to take sides. Through 1914, through 1915

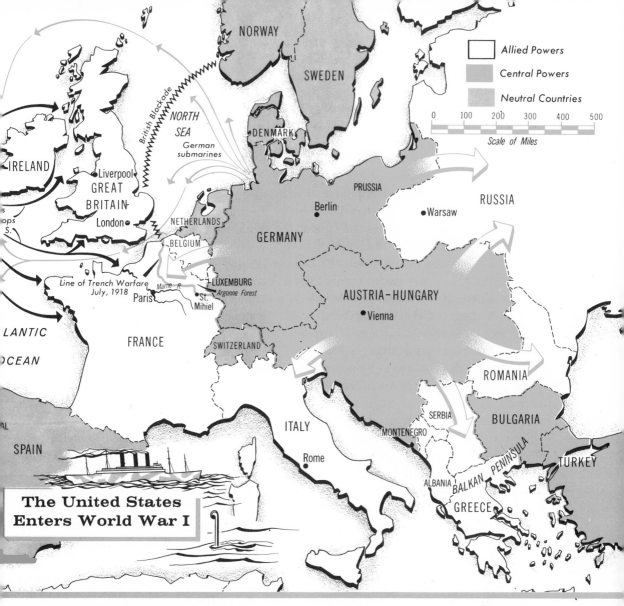

The United States
Enters World War I

and 1916, war continued to rage. Slowly, first in one way and then in another, America was drawn closer to the conflict in Europe. (1) It appeared to most Americans that Austria and Germany were chiefly responsible for the war. (2) Also, most of the war news which reached the United States came through the Allies and was favorable to the Allied cause. This fact helped to strengthen the belief that the Allies were right and the Central Powers wrong. (3) Then, too, there was an enormous demand for American goods of all kinds. Because the British navy was blockading Germany, Americans found it easier to trade with the Allies. American shipping was a tremendous help to the Allies. The United States was naturally more sympathetic toward the side it was helping. (4) Probably Americans were influenced most

There was a growing conviction also that the defeat of France and Britain by Germany would threaten the security of this country.

Britain as well as Germany disregarded the rights of neutrals, but Germany's policy cost hundreds of lives.

602 — THE UNITED STATES WIDENS ITS HORIZONS

of all by the submarine warfare carried on by Germany.

The Germans start submarine warfare. Germany was determined to cut Great Britain off from the rest of the world. Because Great Britain is a small island kingdom, it has to get most of its supplies from other places. These supplies had to reach her by sea. Germany, therefore, sent large numbers of submarines, or U-boats, to roam the seas and sink the ships of any nation that engaged in trade with Britain.

Sometimes Germany issued orders limiting the actions of her U-boat commanders. At other times Germany ordered *unrestricted* submarine warfare. This allowed U-boats to send ships, passengers, and crews to the bottom without warning. The neutral rights of American vessels, and of United States citizens on other vessels, were often disregarded. American ships were sunk; American lives were lost. Our government protested strongly to Germany, but the protests were ignored. If Germany could cut the supply lines of Great Britain and starve that country out of the war, she did not care what neutral countries might think.

The Germans sink the "Lusitania." May 7, 1915, was a clear day, and off the coast of southern Ireland the sea was calm. In the early afternoon, a large steamship was making its way past a landmark on the coast known as the "Old Head of Kinsale." The ship was one of the largest and fastest in the world at that time — the British *Lusitania,* bound for Liverpool from New York. Steaming proudly through familiar waters near the end of her voyage, she headed toward St. George's Channel, between Ireland and Britain. The *Lusitania's* moves, however, were being watched by the German submarine *U-20.* The *U-20* submerged, and without warning discharged a single torpedo at the huge liner. There was one explosion, then another, and fire broke out in the *Lusitania.* She slowed down and tilted sharply to starboard. In eighteen minutes she sank. Of nearly two thousand passengers and crew members, 1198 died. Among those lost were 128 Americans.

After this sinking, the United States issued strong warnings to the German government that the lives of American citizens must not be put in danger. For a time,

FRENCH BIPLANE

BRITISH TANK

RAILWAY GUN

GERMAN SUBMARINE

AIR, SEA, AND LAND WEAPONS — WORLD WAR I

AN AMERICAN DESTROYER rescues the crew of an English airplane forced down in the ocean. World War I saw the first use of airplanes as weapons, not so much for bombing as for aerial observation and fighting with enemy aircraft.

Germany gave up her unrestricted submarine warfare. But early in 1917 she announced that she would begin it again. Altogether, submarine warfare cost 209 American lives on the high seas between 1914 and April, 1917.

Must the United States enter the war? President Wilson realized how horrible war was. He knew full well the grave responsibility he carried as President. For two and a half years he had kept the United States out of war. Yet there were times when President Wilson wondered whether it was not this country's duty to help defeat Germany. He realized that this country could not afford to let Germany crush Great Britain and take Britain's place as mistress of the seas.

In April, 1917, soon after German U-boats had sunk several American ships, Wilson prepared a message to Congress saying that the United States must go to war. But on the night before he delivered this fateful message to Congress he walked restlessly in the White House. Thinking of the awful results of war, he said to a friend, "What else can I do? Is there anything else I can do?" "No," replied his friend, "Germany has forced the war upon the United States." Sadly the President

spoke of things destroyed in war: not only lives and money, but the spirit of good will and perhaps even freedom itself.

When, on the next day, he asked Congress to declare war on Germany, his words showed how carefully he had weighed his decision:

It is a fearful thing to lead this great peaceful people into war, into the most terrible and disastrous of all wars, civilization itself seeming to be in the balance. But the right is more precious than peace, and we shall fight for the things which we have always carried nearest our hearts — for democracy, for the right of those who submit to authority to have a voice in their own government, for the rights and liberties of small nations, for a universal dominion of right by such a concert of free peoples as shall bring peace and safety to all nations and make the world itself at last free. To such a task we can dedicate our lives and our fortunes, everything that we are and everything that we have, with the pride of those who know that the day has come when America is privileged to spend her blood and her might for the principles that gave her birth and happiness and the peace which she has treasured. God helping her, she can do no other.

On April 6, 1917, Congress declared war.

EVEN SCHOOL CHILDREN did their part in the war effort during World War I. This girl and boy display a prize cabbage grown in their school's "victory garden" near New York City.

THE UNITED STATES PLAYS A VALIANT PART IN THE FIRST WORLD WAR

America prepares for war. Once war had been declared, the United States bent all its efforts to the tasks that lay ahead. Congress at once passed a Selective Service Act. This act required all men between the ages of 21 and 31 to register for possible call to military duty. Later the age limits were extended to 18 through 44. Before the war ended, nearly 4,500,000 men wore the uniform of the armed forces of the United States.

These men could not be trained and sent into battle overnight. They needed food and clothing and shelter. They had to have weapons and ammunition. Far greater supplies were needed than in any earlier war. Locomotives, freight cars, railroad tracks, and trucks, together with weapons and supplies, had to be shipped to France for the army's use.

To provide all these things, America's factories and shipyards increased their production. Farmers worked into the night. The railroads strained to move supplies and men to the points where they were needed. The people saved light and heat, observed meatless days, and bought Liberty bonds. Everywhere the nation put every ounce of strength into winning the war for ourselves and our allies. As President Wilson said, "It is not an army that we must shape and train for war, it is a nation."

While the country was working at top speed to supply the needs of its armed forces, the army itself was preparing for its grim task in France. General John J. Pershing was placed in command. Pershing said he would need three million soldiers, of whom at least one million must be ready to fight in France by the spring of 1918. The American navy had already swung into action. Its ships swept the seas for mines and tracked down German U-boats. The navy also escorted the ships carrying soldiers and supplies across the Atlantic.

Both sides adopt trench warfare in France. At the opening of the war in 1914, the Germans had high hopes for a quick victory. They planned to defeat the French army, capture Paris, and force France out of the war. But these plans fell through. The French massed their strength along the Marne River near Paris and halted the onrushing enemy (map, page 601).

Since neither side had been able to win a clear-cut victory, both the Allies and the Germans dug deep trenches into which the soldiers burrowed for protection. Each side put up miles of tangled barbed wire to

America Moves Forward by Johnson **604** *begins with This country's participation in World War I.*

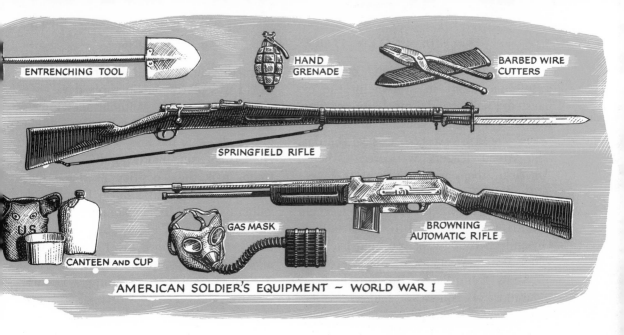

ENTRENCHING TOOL

HAND GRENADE

BARBED WIRE CUTTERS

SPRINGFIELD RIFLE

U.S.

CANTEEN AND CUP

GAS MASK

BROWNING AUTOMATIC RIFLE

AMERICAN SOLDIER'S EQUIPMENT ~ WORLD WAR I

guard against surprise attacks. In a few months the trenches extended for miles, like an irregular gash in the earth. They ran from a point on the North Sea coast of Belgium across northern France and southward to the boundary of Switzerland. From these trenches the opposing armies thundered and smashed at each other from 1914 to 1917. Sometimes one side made gains, sometimes the other. But neither could break through the other's lines to victory. Always the armies dug in again and stood firm.

The Allies suffer discouraging setbacks. Toward the end of 1917, however, the fortunes of war so favored the Central Powers that it seemed they might soon win. Crushing defeats at the hands of the German army and a great revolution within its own borders forced Russia to quit the war. German troops which had been stationed on the Russian front could now be moved to France to prepare for the winning blow. On the Italian front, German and Austrian forces had smashed the Italian army and sent it reeling back. In

AMERICAN SOLDIERS fire a small cannon at the front in war-torn France.

Compared to the trench warfare of World War I, World War II was a war of movement--tank breakthroughs, island-hopping, and paratroop attacks.

the spring, the Germans surely would make a supreme effort to overwhelm the exhausted English and French forces. Only the United States, pouring in its fresh troops, could be expected to save the day. The Allied leaders wondered, "Would American troops appear in time . . . ?"

The tide of war finally turns against the Germans. In March, 1918, the German infantry moved forward in a great attack. On and on they swept, pushing back the Allied lines. At one point they were only 50 miles from Paris. But hundreds of thousands of American soldiers (affectionately called "doughboys") had arrived to back up the battle-weary French and English troops. The fiercely fighting Allies slowed down the German advance and finally, in mid-July, brought the German attack to a standstill. The American troops, fresh and confident of victory, had helped turn the tide of war against the Germans. The chancellor (prime minister) of Germany said: "On the 18th [of July] even the most optimistic among us

knew that all was lost. The history of the world was played out in three days."

The war is won. Without allowing the Germans to rest, the Allies began a counterattack all along the line, pushing back the enemy more and more rapidly. American troops took their position at the eastern end of the long battle line. They fought valiantly at St. Mihiel (san'mee-yell') and in the Argonne Forest. (See map, page 601.) On November 11, 1918, the Germans finally gave up and signed an *armistice* (agreement to stop fighting). The war was over.

CHECK
UP

1. (a) What conditions in Europe led to the outbreak of World War I? (b) What groups of powers opposed each other in the war?

2. (a) Why did the United States find it hard to remain neutral? (b) Why did this country finally enter the war?

3. (a) What part did the United States play in winning the war? (b) How did the Allies finally turn back the German advance?

The role of aviation in World War I is told in Falcons of France by Nordhoff and Hall, members of the Lafayette Flying Corps.

3 How Did the Victorious Nations Fail to Lay the Basis of a Lasting Peace?

The Allies had won World War I but at a frightful cost. Thirty-seven million men were killed, wounded, or missing. Three hundred *billion* dollars' worth of property had been used up. Much land had been laid waste. An enormous amount of energy had been spent in destruction which in peacetime might have been put to useful purposes. Little wonder, then, that people everywhere looked forward with hope to plans for peace. They said, "Can't we build a peace that will last?

Can't we save our children and our children's children from other terrible wars?"

The victorious Allies disagree over terms of peace. The peace was made at a meeting of representatives from the victorious Allied countries at Versailles (vehr-sigh'), just outside Paris, in 1919. It was the men at this conference who could begin to plan for a better world. President Woodrow Wilson himself represented the United States at the conference. Great Britain sent her Prime Minister, David Lloyd

In 1915 when President Wilson attended the World Series (left) with his bride-to-be, he was working on reforms at home to give Americans "a new freedom." Later, while leading the nation through World War I, he set up the goal of a lasting peace for the whole world. Below, he is welcomed by the Belgians and their king (in uniform) while on his way to the peace conference at Versailles.

George; France, her Premier, Georges Clemenceau (kleh-mahn-*soh'*); and Italy, her Prime Minister, Vittorio Orlando. The last three came from countries worn out by the war and full of hatred for their enemies. When it came to deciding how much Germany should pay for war damages, where boundary lines should be drawn, or how other questions should be settled, these three statesmen insisted upon severe terms for Germany.

President Wilson, on the other hand, came from a country 3000 miles away from the fighting. The United States had entered the war late and finished still fresh and strong. It wanted no territorial gains. In Wilson's words, its chief aims were to "make the world safe for democracy" and to make the war "a war to end wars."

Wilson proposes a peace based on his Fourteen Points. Even while the fighting still raged, President Wilson had stated plainly the kind of world the United States was fighting for. He listed *Fourteen Points* as a basis for a better world. The chief items in the Fourteen Points were these: (1) Agreements among nations should be open and public. (2) There should be freedom of the seas "alike in peace and war." (3) Trade barriers between nations should be broken down. (4) Nations should reduce their armies and navies. (5) Colonial claims should be settled as fairly as possible. (6) Nations should have the right to self-determination (the right to govern themselves). (7) "A general association of nations" should be set up to promise independence and safety "to great and small nations alike."

The Treaty of Versailles is written. President Wilson's peace plans did not win the support of the other members of the "Big Four" at the peace table. Lloyd George, Clemenceau, and Orlando were more eager to get advantages for their own countries than to help make a better world.

It is not surprising that countries which had **607** suffered more from war than had the United States found Wilson's terms idealistic. These countries also had reached agreements among themselves prior to our entry into the war.

TREATY
of
Versailles

NORWAY
SWEDEN
FINLAND
NORTH
SEA
DENMARK
U.S.S.R.
ESTONIA
LATVIA
LITHUANIA
GREAT
BRITAIN
NETHERLANDS
Danzig
EAST
PRUSSIA
BELGIUM
GERMANY
POLAND
LUX.
Versailles
CZECHOSLOVAKIA
FRANCE
SWITZ.
AUSTRIA HUNGARY
Trieste
YUGOSLAVIA
ROMANIA
SPAIN
ITALY
MONTE-
NEGRO
SERBIA
BULGARIA
BLACK
SEA
ALBANIA
GREECE
TURKEY
MEDITERRANEAN
SEA

Postwar boundaries
Prewar extent of:
  German Empire
  Austria-Hungary
  Russian Empire

0   200   400
Scale of Miles

MAP STUDY In 1919 new nations were formed in eastern Europe from lands formerly part of Austria-Hungary, Russia, and Germany. Which countries surrendered territory to form Poland?

Very reluctantly, Wilson was forced to give up most of his Fourteen Points. On one point, however, President Wilson refused to give in. He insisted that the peace treaty should set up an association of nations to help keep peace. This association would be called a *League of Nations.*

The Versailles Treaty and other peace treaties signed with the defeated countries included the following points: (1) Germany was held responsible for starting the war; hence, she should pay for the losses and damage. (2) Not only was Germany stripped of a huge quantity of supplies, but she also had to pay a large sum of money, called *reparations.* (3) Germany was disarmed and deprived of her colonies and some territory in Europe. (4) Several new nations were formed in Europe out of land

taken from the defeated countries and Russia. The boundaries of these new nations were so planned as to include national groups within one country. Among these countries were Poland and Czechoslovakia. (See map on this page.) (5) Woodrow Wilson's dream, a League of Nations, was made a reality.

The League of Nations is formed. The League of Nations, which was provided for in the Treaty of Versailles, included an assembly. All member nations were to have a voice in this body. There was also a council in which the leading powers had seats and to which the smaller nations elected representatives. In addition, there was a *World Court,* which was organized by the League in 1921. This body could decide certain disputes between nations.

The countries which joined the League of Nations agreed that its purpose was to promote co-operation among nations and bring about international peace. If a country attacked another country and continued fighting in spite of the League's orders, the members could take action against it. They could stop lending money to such a nation or cut off trade with it. The League might even call upon its members to use force against a warring country.

The United States rejects the League of Nations. President Wilson returned to the United States sure that the League of Nations provided a way to preserve peace. But our Constitution requires that treaties such as the one drawn up at Versailles must be approved by the United States Senate. Some senators were frankly angry because President Wilson had ignored them in working out the peace treaty. Others were tired of Europe and its troubles. They thought Wilson had made a mistake in insisting on the League of Nations. Might not the League draw the United States into

Actually it was impossible to achieve this ideal. **608** Each new country contained minority groups which were disaffected.

new European quarrels? Many senators also did not believe that the United States should become a leader in the effort to keep peace in the world. They wanted the government to stay out of the League and out of foreign difficulties. This attitude came to be known as *isolationism,* and the people who supported it as *isolationists.* Many Americans were isolationists after World War I.

When some senators proposed to attach "reservations" or restrictions on American membership in the League, Wilson decided he must appeal to the people of the United States for their support of the peace treaty and the League. He began a speaking tour. In glowing words he explained to his hearers what the League meant to him and what benefits it might bring to the world. But one night as Wilson's train sped through the countryside from Colorado to Kansas, he became seriously ill. Although he remained in office until the end of his term, President Wilson never recovered.

The failure of Wilson to involve Republican senators in the peace mission and his unwillingness to accept reservations made certain the defeat of the Versailles Treaty in the Senate.

In spite of his efforts, many Americans were not ready to accept responsibility in affairs outside of the Americas. The United States, therefore, did not join the League of Nations or approve the Treaty of Versailles. Instead, it made a separate peace with Germany in 1921. The League was set up without the United States, but, as we shall learn, this new association of nations was not strong enough to carry out Wilson's dream of a peaceful world.

CHECK UP

1. (a) What countries had most to say about the peace treaty? (b) How did their spokesmen at Versailles disagree? (c) What were the Fourteen Points? (d) What did they provide?

2. What were the chief points of the final peace treaties?

3. (a) What was the League of Nations? (b) How was it designed to lessen the chance of war? (c) Why did the United States fail to join the League?

Check Up on Chapter 29

Do You Know the Meaning?

1. embassy	7. chancellor
2. archduke	8. armistice
3. sympathizer	9. reparations
4. submarine	10. isolationism
5. torpedo	11. trench warfare
6. doughboy	12. international law

Can You Identify?

1. Boxer Rebellion	7. 1918
2. John Hay	8. 1919
3. 1854	9. Big Four
4. 1904–05	10. Allies
5. 1914	11. *Lusitania*
6. 1917	12. Open Door Policy

Can You Identify? (Cont.)

13. Matthew C. Perry	18. Fourteen Points
14. Pancho Villa	19. League of Nations
15. John J. Pershing	20. World Court
16. Hague Court	21. Treaty of
17. Central Powers	Versailles
22. Woodrow Wilson	

Can You Locate?

1. China	7. Austria-Hungary
2. Manchuria	8. Belgium
3. Japan	9. Great Britain
4. Russia	10. Marne River
5. Serbia	11. Paris
6. Germany	12. St. Mihiel

Can You Locate? (Cont.)

13. France
14. Bulgaria
15. Turkey
16. Italy

17. Argonne Forest
18. Versailles
19. Poland
20. Czechoslovakia

What Do You Think?

1. China has the largest population of any country in the world. Yet it has been the victim of invasion many times throughout history. Why?
2. (a) Why did the United States favor the

What Do You Think? (Cont.)

Open Door Policy in China? (b) Why did Japan oppose it?
3. Is it wise for the winning side in a war to favor a harsh treaty for the defeated country? Why?
4. Do you think the United States should have joined the League of Nations? Why?
5. If you were helping to make a plan by which all nations would agree to disarm, how could you make sure that all members would live up to the agreement?

Questions #3 and 5 get at important issues.

LINKING PAST AND PRESENT

more

The Unknown Soldiers. On a marble terrace in Arlington National Cemetery in Washington, D. C., stands the Tomb of the Unknown Soldier. Inside the simple and dignified tomb lies the body of an American soldier killed in World War I. This Unknown Soldier was buried in Arlington on November 11, 1921 — the third anniversary of the armistice ending World War I. The inscription on the tomb reads: "Here rests in honored glory an American soldier known but to God."

On Memorial Day, 1958, two unidentified soldiers — one killed in World War II and the other in the Korean War — were buried beside the original tomb. By honoring the Unknown Soldiers, our nation honors all the men who have fought and died for their country.

The Nobel Peace Prize. Every year the Nobel Peace Prize is awarded to the person who has contributed most toward world peace. Several Americans have received this prize; among them are two of our Presidents. Theodore Roosevelt received it in 1906 for helping to end the Russian-Japanese War and for supporting the Hague

Court. In 1919, the peace prize was given to Woodrow Wilson for his part in establishing the League of Nations. The money for the prize comes from a fund left by Alfred Nobel, a Swedish chemist and inventor who died in 1896. Although Nobel invented explosives used in war, he was a man of high ideals. His will provided for a fund of $9,000,000, the interest to be distributed each year among those who have benefited mankind most. In addition to the peace prize, four other awards are given — in physics, chemistry, medicine and physiology, and literature.

Khaki uniforms. The "doughboys" of World War I, like American soldiers of more recent years, wore uniforms of khaki — a dull yellow-brown color. American soldiers first wore uniforms of this color in the Spanish-American War. The first troops that had been sent to the Philippines and Cuba had sweltered in the regulation dark blue uniforms. So the United States Army began to issue uniforms of khaki cloth, which was lighter and cooler. But the change was made chiefly because of a lesson learned by the British army in India many years before.

The British soldiers in bright red or white uniforms were easy targets in battle. On one occasion British troops under heavy fire rolled in muddy pools to make their uniforms less conspicuous! So British troops were soon issued khaki uniforms. The word "khaki" comes from a Persian word "khak" meaning "earth."

TO CLINCH YOUR

UNDERSTANDING OF

Unit 9

◼ Summary of Important Ideas

In this unit you have read about the American Presidents from 1865 to 1920 and how the United States became more active in foreign affairs during this period.

1. Demands for change after the Civil War led, in time, to reforms.
a. Federal legislation established the merit system in civil service, curbed trusts and monopolies, and halted the waste of natural resources. Later, the tariff was cut and the Federal Reserve banking system adopted. Laws also cut the working day to eight hours for interstate railroad workers and made it easier for farmers to borrow money.
b. An amendment to the Constitution provided for a federal income tax.
c. Some states adopted the initiative, referendum, and recall.
2. The growth of American farming and industry after 1865 caused the United States to seek new markets. Commercial expansion in turn led to a more active interest in world affairs.
a. The United States obtained territories outside this country by purchase (Alaska), annexation (Hawaii), and war with

Spain (the Philippines, Puerto Rico, and Guam). The United States helped the islands freed from Spain, and maintained for a time the right to intervene in Cuba.
b. To aid commerce and to protect our possessions, the United States wished a shorter water route between the east and the west coasts. This desire was fulfilled when the United States leased land from Panama and built the Panama Canal.
3. The basis of American foreign policy was the Monroe Doctrine for the Western Hemisphere and the Open Door for eastern Asia.
a. The Monroe Doctrine was used in forcing the French to leave Mexico and in the Venezuelan boundary dispute with Great Britain.
b. In the early 1900's the Latin American republics came to fear that the United States meant to use the Monroe Doctrine, and especially Theodore Roosevelt's broad interpretation of the Doctrine, to extend its influence over the Western Hemisphere.
c. The Boxer Rebellion broke out in China as a protest against the European powers and Japan, who had forced China to give up land and rights. After the rebellion was put down, the United States proposed

Make sure that your students can elaborate the points about our foreign policy briefly stated in item #3.

the Open Door Policy — that trade with China should be open to all.

d. In the mid-1850's the United States opened Japan to Western influence, but later opposed Japan's efforts to expand at the expense of China.

4. In the early 1900's the United States supported plans for maintaining peace among nations. When World War I broke out in Europe, this country at first sought to remain neutral.

a. German submarine policy, and the threat to this country implied in a German victory, finally caused the United States to enter the war.

b. President Wilson was able to make the League of Nations a part of the peace settlement. The United States, however, failed to join the League and returned to a policy of isolation after the war.

Unit Review

1. What reforms were favored by these Presidents: (a) Hayes, (b) Cleveland, (c) Theodore Roosevelt, and (d) Wilson?

2. (a) Why did the United States become interested in overseas territories in the late 1800's? (b) What possessions did the United States acquire? Explain how and why in each case.

3. (a) Why did the United States become interested in a canal connecting the Atlantic and the Pacific? (b) Why was the Panama route favored? (c) How was it obtained?

4. (a) Why did the United States go to war with Spain? (b) What efforts were made to help the people in the islands freed from Spain? (c) What were the results?

5. (a) What is the Monroe Doctrine? (b) Give examples of how and when it was applied. (c) How did Latin American countries feel about intervention by the United States in Cuba, Haiti, Nicaragua, and Mexico? Why?

6. (a) What is the Open Door Policy? (b) Why did we favor this policy in east-

ern Asia? (c) What countries were out of sympathy with this policy? Why?

7. (a) Why did the United States try to remain neutral in World War I? (b) Why did it finally go to war in 1917? (c) Why did Wilson urge the establishment of the League of Nations? (d) Why did this country fail to join it?

Gaining Skill

How to Evaluate Information

For several months now, you have been studying the history of the United States. Meanwhile, even as you have been studying American history, more history has been made. Many of the problems you have been reading about in this book are not yet settled. They are going to be worked out in the future, and you are going to have a part in dealing with them. For that reason you will need to keep informed about public affairs through reading, listening to radio and television reports, and taking part in discussions. On many issues you will read conflicting reports and discover differences of opinion. To help you reach sound conclusions, apply these rules to what you read and hear:

(1) *Did the reporter himself observe what he describes?* If not, his story is second-hand. It may be incorrect because the person who first told it might have included errors. Stories have a way of "growing" as they are told and retold. When possible, you should use original sources.

(2) *Is the reporter qualified to make an accurate report?* A person may be fitted to report on one situation and not on another. A doctor can best judge the seriousness of injuries suffered in a traffic accident; an engineer whether a bridge is safe for traffic. In a foreign country, a person who does not understand the language and customs of the people has great difficulty reporting accurately on what is happening. In judging the truth of a report, always consider whether or not the reporter is qualified to give an accurate account.

(3) *Is the reporter trustworthy?* Some persons and some sources of information develop over the years a reputation for being trustworthy; others do not. An account may be untrustworthy because the reporter is careless or because he sets out to misrepresent things. Try to locate and use trustworthy sources of information.

(4) *Is there a special reason why a reporter who usually is trustworthy may not be in a particular case?* There are many reasons why a trustworthy reporter may give an inaccurate account in a certain instance. He may not have been in a position to see or hear exactly what happened. His sight and hearing may not be as good as they should be. It is possible also that some emotion — fear, anger, excitement — influenced him.

(5) *Is the report a statement of fact or of opinion?* Opinion is how the reporter feels about what he sees, hears, reads, or experiences. Almost all reports include both fact and opinion. Be sure you know whether a particular statement is fact or opinion.

Sometimes a reporter selects the facts which square with his opinion and disregards other facts. In that case his report is untrustworthy. To judge the worth of a report, therefore, you need to know something about the reporter's tastes (what he likes and does not like) and standards (what he feels is poor, average, and superior).

Incidentally, you should listen to both sides of a question. It is important for you to know what people whose opinions differ from yours think about various issues.

■ Interesting Things to Do

The "things to do" marked with an asterisk (*) are for the whole class. Select from the others as your teacher directs.

*1. Start a new set of cards for Unit Nine, using the items under "Can You Identify?" at the end of each chapter. A class quiz two or three times a week with these cards will help you remember the important dates, events, and people.

*2. Make a chart giving the following information about the important possessions of the United States: size, population, imports, exports, how acquired, how governed. Use a geography book or an encyclopedia for the information not given in the text.

3. Draw a cartoon to show one of the following: (a) sinking of the *Maine;* (b) Open Door Policy; (c) Good Neighbor Policy; (d) Boxer Rebellion; (e) Senate vote against the League of Nations.

4. Present to the class some statistics on the Panama Canal, such as the cost of passage through the canal, the number of ships a day, etc. Consult the *World Almanac* for information. Also show on a globe or world map how the canal shortens the distance between some of the world's important ports, such as New York to San Francisco, New York to Yokohama, Japan, etc.

5. Read and report to the class on one of the following topics: (a) the Alaskan gold rush; (b) the conquest of yellow fever; (c) building and opening of the Panama Canal; (d) the industries of Alaska; (e) Operation Bootstrap.

6. Write an account of one of these events as it might have appeared in a newspaper of the time: (a) purchase of Alaska; (b) Battle of Manila Bay or Santiago; (c) Villa's raid in New Mexico; (d) sinking of the *Lusitania;* (e) declaration of war against Germany, April 6, 1917.

7. Write a newspaper editorial taking a stand for or against one of these questions of the day: (a) the annexation of Hawaii; (b) war with Spain; (c) United States interference in Haiti and the Dominican Republic; (d) the Open Door Policy; (e) the United States and the League of Nations.

8. Make a list of popular songs of World War I or World War II. Tell the class a little about each song and organize a group to sing them.

#7 provides a way of testing understanding.

The United State

Unit Nine carried our story through World War I. In this final unit we bring it up to the present. In this century Americans have seen many remarkable advances in new products and sources of power, in the invention and use of intricate machines, in the field of health. They have witnessed man's first efforts to pierce the unknown universe that lies beyond our earth. But the story of recent years is also the story of war, of human misery, and a <u>continuing struggle</u> between those who believe in freedom and democracy and others who would crush these ideals.

Although we can see no end to this "continuing struggle," we must not despair of the outcome.

After World War I most Americans hoped to live again in the kind of world they had lived in before. But this was not to be. In the late 1920's the worst depression in our history began. Then, in Germany and Italy new governments arose, which were determined to expand their territory at the expense of weaker nations. In 1939 World War II broke out. The United States entered the war both to help other nations whose freedom was endangered and to defend our own safety.

World War II has been followed by the "cold war," in which the United States and the nations that believe in freedom have been opposed

Becomes a World Leader

by Communist countries led by Russia and China. Always there hangs over the world the threat of a war with nuclear weapons in which no one would win. But Americans have a heritage of freedom which was won and preserved by great sacrifice in the face of danger. In this same spirit they look forward to the promise of a better world. Many Americans, like the doctors and nurses shown above on their way to a foreign country, are helping to bring this better world into being.

In Chapter 30 you will read the story of World War II and America's part in world events since then. All of us are caught up in the world struggle between freedom and communism. Chapter 31 describes the progress of our neighbors to the north and south and our relations with them. In Chapter 32 you will learn about our recent Presidents and the steps they have taken to deal with the crises they have faced.

The idea of "liberty as the heritage of all men" was in the thinking of Jefferson, Wilson, and F.D. Roosevelt, as well as Lincoln.

Our reliance is in the love of liberty which God has planted in us. Our defense is in the spirit which prized liberty as the heritage of all men, in all lands everywhere. — ABRAHAM LINCOLN

Our Country Meets Threats to Freedom and Works for World Peace

What this chapter is about —

People of every period in history have probably believed their own times to be unusual. Our fathers, our grandfathers, our great-grandfathers all have believed that there was something special about the age they lived in. Our own age is no exception. We think it is unusual. But perhaps in the 1900's we have better reasons for thinking so than earlier generations had. Twice within 25 years our world has been engulfed in terrible wars. The family of nations has grown tremendously as many peoples in Asia and Africa have gained independence. Striking advances have come about in science, in medicine, in satisfying man's everyday needs. Science, for ex-

ample, has made possible the development of atomic energy and the exploration of outer space. In all the great changes of recent times, the United States has taken a leading part.

Out of these great changes there could grow a new and better world, but only if the nations of the world can maintain law and order and keep the peace. In this chapter we shall learn why the peace which people hoped for at the close of World War I did not last. We shall see how the leaders of certain countries, anxious to gain power, brought about the outbreak of World War II. And we shall learn what steps the United States has taken to maintain peace

People in our story — Nazi storm trooper; Japanese soldier; American marine, aircraft carrier crewman, pilot, and soldier; Russian soldier.

and freedom since World War II. We shall seek answers to these questions:

1. What events after World War I destroyed hopes for world peace?
2. How did the United States and its allies gain victory in World War II?
3. How did a "cold war" develop between the United States and the Soviet Union?
4. What steps has America taken to defend the free world against the Communist threat?

Bring out the fact that the United States, though not a member of the League, took part in the programs of many international organizations.

What Events After World War I Destroyed Hopes for World Peace?

PEACE EFFORTS FALTER AFTER WORLD WAR I

The United States was the only great power to come out of World War I stronger than ever before. President Wilson's ringing words and his efforts to create the League of Nations gave promise of a better, peaceful world. It was only natural, therefore, that the people of the world looked to the United States for leadership. After World War I, however, most Americans were not ready to undertake the responsibilities of world leadership. They were anxious to return to their own interests and activities and let other countries solve their own problems.

The United States takes part in peace efforts. It would be a mistake, however, to think that our country showed no interest in peace movements during the 1920's and 1930's. Individual Americans and the United States government continued to work for a peaceful world. Americans served as judges on the World Court. The United States, although not a member of the League of Nations, took part in its efforts to control the international drug traffic and to improve world labor conditions. No country was more interested than the United States in keeping world peace.

The United States takes the lead in reducing the size of navies. One peace

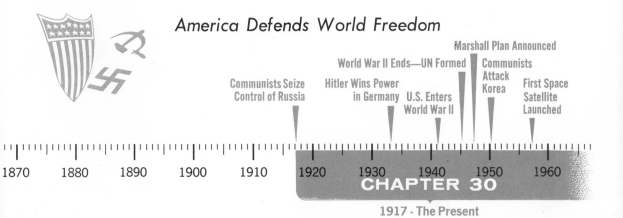

America Defends World Freedom

Marshall Plan Announced

World War II Ends—UN Formed — Communists Attack Korea

Communists Seize Control of Russia

Hitler Wins Power in Germany — U.S. Enters World War II

First Space Satellite Launched

1870   1880   1890   1900   1910   1920   1930   1940   1950   1960

CHAPTER 30

1917 - The Present

movement in which the United States took a leading part was the effort to cut down the size of armed forces. In 1921 several world powers were invited to meet in Washington, D.C., to discuss what could be done to reduce the size of navies. At the Washington Conference, Secretary of State Charles Evans Hughes declared that our government would reduce its navy if other countries would do the same. As a result of the conference, the United States, Great Britain, Japan, France, and Italy agreed to limit the number of their largest warships.

At a conference in London in 1930 another agreement was made to limit the size of navies. Within a few years, however, all the plans to reduce armaments were abandoned. As we shall learn, Germany disregarded the Versailles Treaty and began rebuilding her army and navy. Japan withdrew from the disarmament agreements. Other nations felt they must have large armed forces in case war broke out. Nations once more began to rearm.

Efforts to outlaw war prove disappointing. In 1928 the American Secretary of State, Frank B. Kellogg, and the French Minister of Foreign Affairs, Aristide Briand (bree-*ahn'*), joined in another effort to secure peace. They urged the nations of the world to condemn war and agree to use peaceful means to settle disputes. Most of the world's governments promised to outlaw war by signing this agreement, which became known as the *Kellogg-Briand Pact.*

But agreements to reduce armed forces or to settle disputes by peaceful means are of little value unless (1) the nations involved *want* to live up to these agreements or (2) there is some means of *compelling* nations to live up to them. And the League of Nations never was strong enough to keep the peace.

These two points are extremely important.

NEW GOVERNMENTS ARE FORMED

A great war upsets the whole world, much as a violent explosion damages a building. After a war, nations often need rebuilding, just as damaged buildings need to be repaired. But should they be restored just as they were before, or rebuilt along different lines? After World War I, the people of some countries wanted to return to the conditions which had existed before the fighting. These people wished only to live out their lives in peace and quiet. But in other nations people were bitterly discontented. When the people of a nation are dissatisfied, they are likely to follow leaders who promise them better conditions. They may even be persuaded to change the form of government of their country. In three important countries — Russia, Germany, and Italy — World War I brought such changes.

Russia establishes a new government and way of life. The change in Russia came first and was the greatest change of all. In 1917, while World War I was still going on (page 605), the Russian people revolted. They overthrew the government and imprisoned their ruler, the czar (*zahr*). Later in 1917, a small party called the *Bolshevists* used armed force to overthrow the government that had replaced the czar's. The Bolshevists established a Communist dictatorship and forced their way of life on all the Russian people. The official name of the country was changed to the Union of Soviet Socialist Republics. It is often referred to as the USSR or the Soviet Union.

The Communists did not stop with taking over the government. They also made great changes in the ways the Russian people earned their living. In the United States, as you know, the land, the mines, and other natural resources are

VETERANS of the Russian Revolution march across Red Square in Moscow in the 1930's. Photographs of the Communist leaders Lenin and Stalin appear in the background.

privately owned. Individual persons or groups of people own and operate the railroads and other means of transportation; they also own the factories and the stores and the businesses. This system of private ownership is called *capitalism* or the *free enterprise* system.

The Communists did away with the system of private ownership. In the Soviet Union, the government now owns and operates the factories and the farms, the railroads and the mines, the stores and the newspapers and the hospitals. The people work for the government. This system is called *communism,* because supposedly all the factories and businesses and property are owned *in common* by all the people. But as it has worked out, everything in Soviet Russia is controlled by a small group, the leaders of the government, who are also the leaders of the Communist Party. The people of Soviet Russia are not free to engage in business as they wish or to select their own jobs.

Furthermore, the Russian people do not have the freedoms — such as freedom of speech and the press — which have meant so much to Americans and other democratic peoples. The Russians call their system a "people's republic" and "demo-cratic," but it is not what we think of as democracy. There are elections but the people can vote only for candidates of the Communist Party.

A new government is formed in Italy. The Communist leaders boldly proclaimed that their seizure of power in Russia was only the first step in a revolution which would sweep the world. Because of the fear that this might actually happen, people in other countries listened to leaders who promised to save them from communism. In Italy, a man named Benito Mussolini (moos-oh-*lee'*nih) used this fear to make himself all-powerful in Italy. He convinced the Italian people that communism might spread to Italy and that he was the man who could save them from it.

In 1922 Mussolini seized control of the government for himself and his followers, who were called *Fascists* (*fash'*ists). Italy kept her king, but he was only a figurehead with no power. The Fascists controlled Italy, and Mussolini, chief of the Fascists, controlled them. Mussolini thus became dictator of Italy. Those who opposed Mussolini and the Fascists were driven out of the country, thrown into prison, or killed. The Italian people were repeatedly told that under the Fascists their country would

For a discussion of communism, 619 see *The World of Communism* by Swearingen.

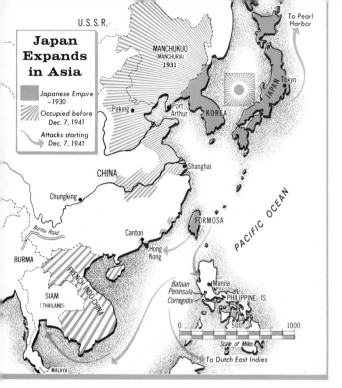

MAP STUDY Japan had already built an empire by 1930. What areas did Japan occupy between 1930 and 1941?

gain power and become great. Mussolini spent great sums of money on an army, navy, and air force, because a dictator depends on force to keep his power.

Germany's new republic is taken over by the Nazis. Germany was another country where discontent brought changes. At the close of World War I, the Germans set up a republic with a constitution, a president, and a congress. But the German people had never been given much responsibility in their own government. No people can learn democratic ways in a few years, and so the republic did not work well. Unfortunately, many Germans linked the new republic with their defeat in the war and the hated Treaty of Versailles. As you learned in Chapter 29, the Treaty of Versailles held Germany guilty of starting World War I and had reduced her power, wealth, and territory. In spite of these difficulties, the republic might have succeeded if hard times had not hit Germany. In the

The fact that the German Republic had accepted the government.

years following the war many Germans could not find jobs. During the world-wide depression in the early 1930's, conditions went from bad to worse. The German people felt bitter and helpless.

Taking advantage of widespread discontent, a dictator seized power in Germany in 1933, much as Mussolini had done in Italy. The German dictator was Adolf Hitler, and his followers were called *Nazis* (*nah'*tsihz). Hitler promised to make Germany a great nation again and to recover the land it had lost. To carry out his ambitions, Hitler began to rearm Germany and set its factories to making war materials.

Under Hitler the Germans once more became a proud people with high hopes for the future. But this gain was achieved at heavy cost. People were no longer free in Germany; those who disagreed with Hitler dared not say so. Many lived in dread of the Nazi secret police. The Nazis imprisoned, tortured, killed, or drove from the country anyone who dared speak out against them. They were especially cruel to Jews, whom they blamed for all of Germany's troubles. Jews were stripped of their property, and thousands of them were sent to concentration camps, where they suffered starvation, torture, and death. Some six million European Jews had been destroyed by the Nazis by the close of World War II.

THE WORLD IS DISTURBED BY AMBITIOUS NATIONS

To be rich and powerful, a nation must have many men and women to do its work. It also needs mines and factories and farms and forests. If all these are not found within its borders, an ambitious nation may be tempted to seize the land of neighboring countries. It may even try to conquer distant regions which will serve as

the Treaty of Versailles was used to discredit

_71_ Recall that Japan had displayed an interest in dominating East Asia even before World War I.

OUR COUNTRY WORKS FOR WORLD PEACE **621**

colonies. If a nation wishes to grow in this way, it can always find excuses for seizing what it wants. If necessary, a quarrel can be started just as an excuse to seize territory belonging to another nation.

Japan sets out to control China. There were a number of "land-hungry" countries after World War I. The first of these to cause trouble was Japan. As explained in Chapter 29, Japan was eager to gain power over China. A group of military and naval leaders obtained control of the Japanese government and got rid of leaders who favored peaceful relations with other countries. Already Japan had acquired the island of Formosa, a number of small Pacific islands, and Korea on the mainland of Asia.

Japan, however, was not satisfied. Late in 1931, the Japanese army marched without warning into Manchuria, the northern area of China. In a short time Japan made Manchuria into a Japanese-controlled state known as Manchukuo (man-choo-*kwoh'*). Even that was not enough. In 1937, on the excuse that they had been fired on by the Chinese, Japanese troops advanced into China. Japan's attacks on China may well be considered the beginning of World War II.

Italy and Germany also want more land. Germany and Italy also wanted more territory. Germany had lost her colonies and some land in Europe because she was defeated in World War I. Italy, though one of the victorious Allies, had received less in the treaty of peace than she had demanded. So the ambitious dictators of these dissatisfied countries, tempted by Japan's success in China, set out to grab what they wanted.

The strong attack the weak. Mussolini, for example, wished to increase Italy's empire in Africa. In 1935, he sent Italian troops into the African kingdom of Ethiopia. After a few months, Emperor Haile Selassie (*high'*leh seh-*las'*ih) was driven from his throne. Ethiopia became part of the Italian empire.

Germany, for her part, made conquests nearer home. By the terms of the Versailles Treaty, Germany was supposed to have only a small army. Moreover, no troops were to be permitted in the land along the Rhine River, between Germany and France. But Hitler ignored these rules. In 1936, he sent German troops into the land along the Rhine. Because France could not count on the support of her former allies, she had to permit Germany to reoccupy and fortify the Rhineland. When this move succeeded, Hitler became bolder. Perhaps now he could ignore other treaty agreements.

What next? To the south and east of Germany lay Austria, a small nation one

MAP STUDY By 1939 Nazi Germany had seized the lands shown here. (1) Why was the Polish Corridor important to Germany? (2) What country did Italy conquer?

The Axis Expands in Europe

HITLER AND MUSSOLINI met a number of times to discuss their plans for conquest. Here the two dictators review Nazi troops in Germany.

tenth the size of Germany. Austria had been a weak nation since World War I. Many Austrians felt they would be better off if they joined with Germany. Seeing his chance, Hitler sent German troops to the Austrian border. The chancellor of Austria then submitted to Hitler's demands, and the German army entered Austria to "preserve order." Thus, Austria became part of "Greater Germany." (See the map on page 621.)

What next? Czechoslovakia, another neighbor, was surrounded by German territory on three sides. Many Germans lived in Czechoslovakia. Before long, Adolf Hitler began to complain that these Germans were being mistreated. Soon he was demanding control of western Czechoslovakia, where most of these Germans lived. None of the great powers seemed willing to risk war to help Czechoslovakia. Once more Hitler had his way. Late in 1938, he obtained portions of Czechoslovakia. The next year Hitler took over the remainder of this helpless nation.

Why did other nations permit these conquests? Small countries like Ethiopia and Austria and Czechoslovakia could not resist powerful nations like Italy and Germany. But what were the other European powers doing while Italy and Germany swallowed up one small country after another?

Perhaps Great Britain, France, and Russia could have prevented Italy and Germany from conquering other countries. But the people of these three nations had had enough of war from 1914 to 1918. They did not wish to fight again. Furthermore, Great Britain and France were not prepared for war. So rather than risk another war, they stood aside. This policy of giving in to the demands of the dictators became known as *appeasement*.

The League of Nations lacks power to prevent attacks. What about the League of Nations, which had been formed to prevent all future wars? Some countries, like the United States, did not belong to the League. Germany and Japan had both withdrawn from the League in the early 1930's and so were not bound by its decisions. Even the nations which were League members seemed unwilling to act together to carry out a League decision.

A good many disputes were brought before the League, some of which were settled. When Italy attacked Ethiopia, the League members voted to stop trade with Italy. But some nations failed to live up to this agreement. So this method of punishing warring nations proved useless.

Another world war looms. With Germany and Italy determined to take what they wanted, and with the League too weak to stop them, there seemed only one thing for the other nations to do. Slowly, unwillingly, they began to get ready for the day when they might have to fight. Gone were the bright hopes of lasting peace; forgotten were the agreements to cut down armed forces. Countries began to increase their armies and to build more warships and guns and airplanes and tanks. But Germany and Italy were hopeful about the future. They had started to rearm long before the other nations, and they continued to prepare for the possibility of war.

CHECK UP

1. (a) How did the United States show its interest in world peace after World War I? (b) Why did peace efforts prove useless?

2. (a) What kind of government was established in Russia after the war? (b) How was the Russian way of life affected by this change? (c) How did Mussolini come to power in Italy? (d) What kind of rule did Hitler set up in Germany?

3. (a) What areas had Japan conquered before World War II? (b) What territorial gains were made by Italy? (c) By Germany?

4. (a) What attitude did other nations take toward these conquests? Why? (b) Why did the League of Nations fail to prevent the conquests?

There is a useful discussion of causes of the war in First Book of World War II by Snyder.

2 How Did the United States and Its Allies Gain Victory in World War II?

World War II begins. It was in September, 1939, that the world once more heard the heavy tramp of marching feet in Europe. To the crack of rifles and the roar of artillery were added the whine of diving airplanes and the "crump" of bombs striking their targets. In Europe it was the citizens of Poland who first heard these terrifying sounds in World War II.

In the late summer of 1939, Hitler demanded a strip of Polish territory which separated East Prussia from the rest of Germany. Meanwhile, Germany and the Soviet Union signed a neutrality pact, which left Hitler free to act without danger of Russian interference. When his demand for Polish territory was refused, he angrily ordered an invasion of Poland. This time, however, Hitler did not go unchallenged. There was no appeasement as there had been in the case of Czechoslo-

vakia. Although neither Great Britain nor France was prepared for war, they came to Poland's assistance and declared war on Germany on September 3, 1939. But the German forces attacked Poland swiftly and fiercely in what they called a *blitzkrieg* (lightning war). Poland was overcome before the British and French could furnish any real aid.

The war spreads over western Europe. For a few months after the conquest of Poland there was little real fighting. The German forces and the British and French armies settled down behind strongly fortified lines. Some people felt that this was a "phony war," and believed that a peaceful agreement might still be reached. But in the spring of 1940, the Nazis unleashed a terrific attack. Norway and Denmark were easily overrun. Then the German blitzkrieg hit Belgium, Holland, and France.

Swiftly the motorized columns of German soldiers swept forward. So deadly were the attacks of their airplanes and tanks that in a few weeks Holland, Belgium, and finally France surrendered to Hitler's forces. German troops rushed to cut off the retreating British army before it could escape across the English Channel. But by a frantic effort, 338,000 British and French soldiers were ferried across the Channel in naval vessels, tugs, yachts, and other craft sent from England.

It looked as if England would be the next to fall. Hitler's plans for invasion, however, did not work out. Wave after wave of German airplanes bombed England, but the valiant fliers of the British Royal Air Force outfought Hitler's bombers in the air. When Hitler collected a huge fleet of barges to invade England, R.A.F. bombers smashed them to pieces. The Germans then took to night bombing. During most of the war the British people endured terrific air attacks, but England was not invaded.

Hitler attacks on other fronts. Elsewhere in Europe, however, the German armies met with great successes. Most of the little states of eastern Europe and the Balkan Peninsula were forced to join the Nazis or were conquered and enslaved. In 1941, in spite of the peace pact that the German and Soviet governments had signed just before the war, Hitler launched a tremendous attack against Russia. Though the Russians fought fiercely, German forces occupied western Russia. The battle line extended from near Leningrad in the north to near Stalingrad on the Volga River before the German advances could be checked. German forces even pushed into North Africa. Meanwhile, on the seas German submarine attacks caused heavy damage to English shipping. (Look at the map on page 625 to see how much

territory had been conquered by the Axis in Europe.)

Italy and Japan join Germany. In some of these victories Germany had aid from Italy. Even before the war began, Mussolini and Hitler had formed an alliance. Then, when the defeat of France seemed certain, Mussolini brought his country into the war on Germany's side. Italy and Germany became known as the *Axis Powers.* The Axis had also gained a partner in the Far East. Japan, which had been busy gobbling up China (page 621), became allied with Germany and Italy as the third member of the Axis.

The Japanese gain most of China and look for further conquests. On the other side of the world, the Chinese continued to fight doggedly but unsuccessfully to halt the Japanese invasion, which had begun in 1937. Japan rapidly took over many of the cities and the best farm land in China. But the Chinese leader, Chiang Kai-shek (chee-*ahng' kye'shek'*), refused to give in. Under his leadership, thousands of Chinese made their way into the mountainous interior region of China. There they established a new capital at Chungking. The Chinese people carried on their shoulders as much machinery and tools as they could, and built new factories for producing supplies to continue the war. From their mountain strongholds the Chinese launched raids behind the Japanese lines, destroying railroads and supply depots controlled by the Japanese.

Instead of completing their conquest of China, the Japanese turned their eyes to other parts of the Far East. Why not take over French Indo-China, Siam, the Malay Peninsula, the Dutch East Indies, the Philippines, and, who knows, perhaps Australia? (Locate these countries on the map on page 631.) And why not go west to Burma — and even beyond, to seize the

Hitler possibly hoped that Britain might accept peace if Germany directed its attack eastward. He also needed Russian resources.

The Allies Win in the West

Farthest extent of Axis occupation

Neutral Countries

U. S. supply line to U.S.S.R.

ICELAND

ATLANTIC OCEAN

Murmansk

SWEDEN

FINLAND

NORWAY

Leningrad

1943

Moscow

ESTONIA

LATVIA

LITHUANIA

U. S. S. R.

NORTH SEA

DENMARK

GREAT BRITAIN

EIRE

London

Dunkirk

English Channel

NORMANDY 1944

Paris

FRANCE

Elbe

Berlin

Rhine R.

1945

GERMANY

BELG.

1945

Vistula R.

Warsaw POLAND 1944

Stalingrad

Volga R.

Don R.

1942 – 1943

SWITZ.

1945 Budapest

CZECHOSLOVAKIA

AUSTRIA

HUNGARY

ROMANIA

1944

BLACK SEA

ITALY

Rome

Anzio

Salerno

1944

YUGOSLAVIA

Danube R.

BULGARIA

ALBANIA

GREECE

TURKEY

ORTUGAL

SPAIN

1942

MEDITERRANEAN SEA

1943

Sicily

NORTH AFRICA

0 200 400

Scale of Miles

MAP STUDY This map shows how much territory in Europe the German and Italian armies held at one time. (1) In what part of Europe did the western Allies make their first invasion? (2) Where did later invasions take place?

wealth of India? Great Britain was besieged in Europe. France was defeated. Only the United States stood in the way.

The United States hopes to keep peace. What had the United States been doing while war raged in other parts of the world? When Japan seized Manchuria, our Secretary of State, Henry L. Stimson, strongly objected. The United States, he declared, would not recognize any "situation, treaty, or agreement which may be brought about" by war. Again and again our President appealed to Hitler and Mussolini not to disturb the peace of Europe.

Meanwhile, Congress passed *neutrality laws* stating that we would not take sides in foreign wars. These laws forbade Americans to lend money or to ship military

When the danger of a German victory became apparent, Congress and the President found ways of helping nations fighting the Axis.

626 THE UNITED STATES BECOMES A WORLD LEADER

supplies to nations at war. Americans were not to travel on any ships belonging to warring countries. The idea behind these neutrality laws was, of course, to keep our country from being drawn into another world war. Americans at this time believed strongly that the United States should keep out of World War II.

American sympathy for nations fighting the Axis grows. Just as in the early years of World War I, Americans found it more and more difficult to keep neutral. As German victories continued, the threat of war approached our own shores. What if Hitler succeeded in conquering all of Europe? Would he be content to stop there or would he seek to extend his power to the Americas?

Moreover, as German conquests spread, freedom and liberty disappeared. Wherever the Nazi armies triumphed, the people were enslaved. Because the Germans considered themselves a "master race," defeated peoples everywhere were forced to labor in the fields and factories for their conquerors. It seemed that unless the Nazis were checked, human freedom

and democratic government would be destroyed throughout the world. Great Britain appeared to be fighting not only to defend itself but to defend the rights of free men everywhere. Americans, therefore, felt increasing friendship for the people fighting against Germany and Italy.

The United States takes a stronger stand against the Axis Powers. During 1940 and 1941, then, Americans became less strictly neutral. For one thing, our government took steps to enlarge and strengthen its army and navy. In exchange for 50 over-age American destroyers, the United States received naval and air bases in the British-owned islands of the Caribbean and the Atlantic. These bases would help to defend our shores and the Panama Canal from attack. Congress also passed a law permitting countries at war to purchase munitions in America and later passed the *Lend-Lease Act.* This act allowed the President to sell or lend war materials to any nation whose defense was considered essential to America's safety. The production of war materials was speeded up.

A CLOSE-UP of part of the chapter time line shows important events which led to World War II, such as Japan's invasion of Manchuria in 1931. The Japanese invasion of China in 1937 is sometimes regarded as the start of the war in Asia.

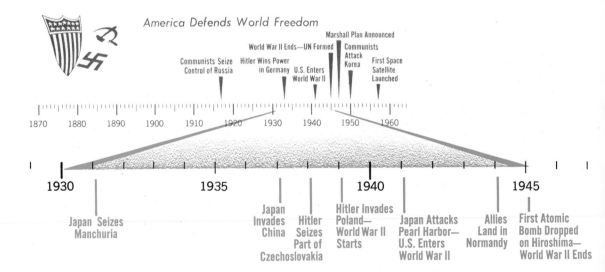

America Defends World Freedom

| Communists Seize Control of Russia | Hitler Wins Power in Germany | World War II Ends—UN Formed | Marshall Plan Announced Communists Attack Korea | First Space Satellite Launched |

U.S. Enters World War II

1870 1880 1890 1900 1910 1920 1930 1940 1950 1960

1930 1935 1940 1945

Japan Seizes Manchuria

Japan Invades China

Hitler Seizes Part of Czechoslovakia

Hitler Invades Poland— World War II Starts

Japan Attacks Pearl Harbor— U.S. Enters World War II

Allies Land in Normandy

First Atomic Bomb Dropped on Hiroshima— World War II Ends

USO recreation centers are leisure-time headquarters for American servicemen at home and overseas (at right, in Tokyo). Though founded in 1941, the idea of the USO (United Service Organizations) goes back to the war between the North and the South, when a Soldiers' Free Library established in Washington, D.C. (above), provided recreation for Union soldiers.

Meanwhile, our relations with Japan became steadily worse. Japan insisted that her goal was to help Asian peoples. Our government, however, believed that Japan's main purpose was to enlarge her empire at the expense of weaker nations. The United States insisted upon protecting American rights in the Far East. Our government also gave aid to war-torn China and broke off a long-standing trade agreement with Japan. To achieve her ambitions, Japan decided that the United States must be crushed. So, while outwardly seeking to iron out differences with the United States, Japan prepared for a surprise attack.

War! The blow fell on December 7, 1941. Without warning, waves of Japanese bombers attacked the great American base at Pearl Harbor in Hawaii. Caught by surprise, the Americans fought bravely, but the Japanese caused heavy damage. Most of our airplanes were destroyed on the ground. Five battleships were sunk or disabled, and fourteen other vessels were badly damaged. Nearly 2500 soldiers, sailors, and civilians were killed. Our entire nation was shocked and angered.

On December 8, President Franklin D. Roosevelt asked Congress for an immediate declaration of war against Japan. Congress followed the President's request and declared war that same day. Britain also declared war against Japan. A few days later, Germany and Italy declared war against the United States. The United States thus joined Britain, Russia, and China, who were known as the Allies, against the Axis Powers.

The American nation goes "all out" for victory. Now that war had been declared, the American people bent all their efforts toward victory. Men between 18 and 45 were called into military service. At top strength, the armed forces included over twelve million men and women. Among them were over one million Negroes, half of whom served overseas.

Japan hoped that this attack would make it **627** impossible for the United States to block Japanese expansion in Asia.

BENJAMIN O. DAVIS, JR., earned a distinguished record as a fighter pilot in both World War II and the Korean War. Now a lieutenant general in the Air Force, he serves as chief of staff of United States forces in Korea.

To provide needed war materials, mines and factories worked day and night. Managers of industry and workers pulled together to meet the tremendous demands of war, and American production became the marvel of the world. Meanwhile, American farmers were outdoing themselves to produce the food needed by this country and our allies. To help pay the terrific costs of war, high taxes were levied. Boys and girls, as well as men and women, bought billions of dollars' worth of war bonds.

The war brings great changes in the American way of living. Americans quickly adjusted to war conditions. Civilians learned what to do in case of air raids. Because enormous quantities of food were needed for our forces overseas, as well as for our allies, many peacetime goods disappeared entirely from the stores. Other articles — such as meat, fats, coffee, sugar, gasoline, and fuel oil — were so scarce they were rationed; that is, people were permitted to buy them only in small quantities. To prevent *inflation* (higher prices), the government set limits or "ceilings" on the prices of food, clothing, and other things, and also on rents.

People did all sorts of extra or unusual jobs during the war. They helped as airplane spotters and air-raid wardens. They assisted in hospitals and in entertaining servicemen. Millions of Americans gave blood, which could be used to save the lives of the wounded. Women took jobs usually done by men in shipyards, airplane factories, and in other industries. Boys and girls harvested crops; helped collect rubber, scrap metal, and paper; or took jobs in stores and factories. To release more men for actual fighting, women enlisted in the WAC (army), the WAVES (navy), the SPARS (Coast Guard), and the Marine Corps.

Italy is defeated. The United States found itself fighting two wars, one in Europe and one in the Pacific. Under General George C. Marshall, Chief of Staff of the United States Army, the defeat of Germany and Italy became our first goal.

Late in 1942, a combined American and British force, commanded by General Dwight D. Eisenhower, made a surprise landing in North Africa. After several months of fighting, the Nazi troops in

Battle Stations tells about airplane pilots, and infantry men. **628** *paratroopers, submariners,*

Had the war in Europe ended earlier, Russian forces would not have been able to push so far westward.

OUR COUNTRY WORKS FOR WORLD PEACE   **629**

Africa were completely defeated. The next step was a landing on the Italian island of Sicily, where the Germans were forced out in a few weeks. Then, combined American and British forces succeeded in getting a foothold on the Italian mainland. The conquest of Italy was a long and bitter struggle which lasted until nearly the end of the war in Europe. Although Italy surrendered to the Allies in 1943, a few weeks after Mussolini had been forced out of power, the German troops in Italy kept on fighting. (See map, page 625.)

Nazi Germany is forced to surrender. Meanwhile, hard-fighting Russian forces, aided by American lend-lease supplies, not only turned back the savage German thrusts but regained much of their lost territory. British and American bombers were pounding the Germans continuously from the air. With the Germans suffering from air attacks and hard-pressed in Italy and on the Russian front, the time seemed ripe for the invasion of western Europe. Eisenhower and his staff spent long months planning the details of the invasion, collecting supplies, and training their forces.

On June 6, 1944, a great force of Americans, Canadians, and British struck at the Normandy beaches of France. Naval guns bombarded the coast, and hordes of bombers gave protection in the air as the soldiers scrambled ashore. The landings were successful, and by August, France had been freed from Nazi control. The Americans and British then pushed on against Germany. After bitter fighting, they succeeded in crossing the Rhine River. With Nazi armies being cut to pieces by Allied drives from the east and the west, and with round-the-clock bombing of its cities and factories, Germany's cause was hopeless. She was forced to surrender unconditionally. On May 8, 1945, the war in Europe was declared officially over.[1]

[1] Mussolini was captured and killed in April, 1945, by some of his own countrymen. Hitler's suicide was reported just before the Russians captured Berlin.

A VAST FLEET OF SHIPS lines the Normandy coast as supplies pour onto the beach in support of the Allied landing in June, 1944. Notice the barrage balloons floating overhead to protect the ships from strafing by enemy airplanes.

Hull-Down for Action is an exciting story of adventure in the southwest Pacific.

BAZOOKA

"WALKIE-TALKIE"

The United States fights a bitter war with Japan. In the Pacific the task of defeating Japan fell mainly upon the United States. At first the war went badly. Soon after Pearl Harbor, the Japanese launched an invasion of the Philippine Islands. Although greatly outnumbered, American forces and loyal Filipinos fought stubbornly to hold the Bataan Peninsula. In June, 1942, the exhausted remnants of the American forces finally surrendered. Though the Japanese overran the islands, the Filipinos showed great courage as they continued to fight in outlying districts.

The Japanese were equally successful in other parts of Asia. They had already occupied French Indo-China and now took the British colony of Hong Kong. Advancing through the jungles, Japanese soldiers overran the Malay Peninsula and captured the great British stronghold at Singapore. The Dutch Empire in the East Indies fell before their attacks. Japanese forces then pushed on through Burma and broke the supply line to China over the Burma Road. The Chinese, worn out by war, fell back still farther before enemy attacks. The Japanese also seized Pacific islands as far north as the Aleutians, off the coast of Alaska. Japanese dreams of becoming mas-

ter of the Far East seemed about to be realized. (See map, page 631.)

American forces push back the Japanese. Slowly but surely, however, the tide turned. Our navy won two smashing victories. One, in the Coral Sea, blocked an invasion of Australia; the other, at Midway, saved Hawaii. General Douglas MacArthur, chief of the Allied forces in the Far East, mapped plans to recapture lost ground. Beginning with Guadalcanal, American marines and soldiers, supported by the navy, began to capture important bases. Combined American forces, working together, seized important islands and leapfrogged others, pushing ever closer to Japan. When Saipan, Guam, and Tinian were taken, American planes used these islands as bases for the bombing of the Japanese homeland. Some of the island attacks — Guadalcanal, Iwo Jima, and

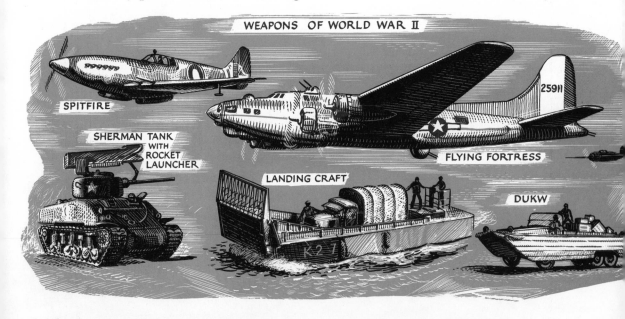

WEAPONS OF WORLD WAR II

SPITFIRE

SHERMAN TANK WITH ROCKET LAUNCHER

LANDING CRAFT

FLYING FORTRESS

25911

DUKW

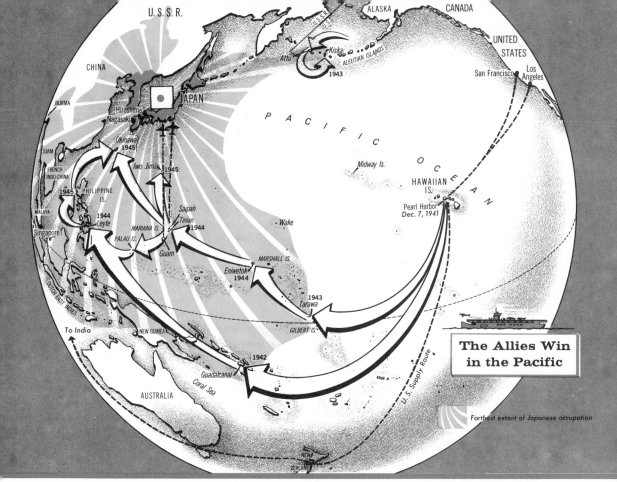

The Allies Win in the Pacific

Farthest extent of Japanese occupation

MAP STUDY American forces closed in on Japan by "island hopping" across the vast distances of the Pacific Ocean. They followed one main route across the south Pacific and another across the central Pacific. (1) Which route finally brought U.S. forces to the Philippines? (2) Which route brought them to Iwo Jima?

Semper Fidelis is a story of the Marines in action.

Okinawa — were among the most costly battles of the Pacific war.

By October, 1944, it was possible to launch a successful attack on the Philippines. American forces landed at Leyte and in a few months regained control of the Philippine Islands. One of the greatest naval battles of history, in which the Japanese lost a large part of their fleet, took place near Leyte.

World War II ends. These successes, as well as others on the mainland of Asia, dashed Japan's hopes of empire. But Japan itself still had to be conquered. American bombers, based on huge carriers and Pacific islands, began hammering Japanese cities. Allied plans for invading Japan, however, never had to be used.

For years scientists in America had been working at top speed to develop a bomb which would make use of atomic energy. Men from many countries — Allied scientists as well as refugees from Nazi and Fascist tyranny — assembled in the United States. They combined their knowledge and skill with that of American scientists and leaders of industry. Almost overnight whole new towns with laboratories, factories, and living quarters were built. Cut off from the world, these engineers and scientists carried on their research. At last their efforts were successful.

During the Mexican War, U.S. marines waged amphibious warfare (above) hundreds of miles away from American bases. Arriving in a paddle-wheel steamer (left), they used small wooden boats to land and fight their way inland.

In World War II, landing ships specially designed for amphibious attacks were used, for example, at the Japanese island of Iwo Jima (above). Their bows opened, allowing tanks and trucks to roll quickly onto the enemy beach.

On August 6, 1945, the first atomic bomb used against an enemy was dropped on the unfortunate Japanese city of Hiroshima, causing frightful loss of life and property. Two days later, a second atomic bomb practically wiped out the city of Nagasaki. Faced with utter destruction, the Japanese government opened peace talks. On August 14, Japan agreed to surrender, and on September 2 the peace terms were signed. Emperor Hirohito was permitted to remain at the head of the Japanese government, but he was required to take orders from General MacArthur.

As throngs of people either celebrated wildly or quietly offered prayers of thanksgiving, World War II came to an end — the most destructive war in history. It is estimated that 22 million people were killed and over 34 million wounded. The cost in money is even more difficult to imagine — over 1,000,000,000,000 (one trillion) dollars.

CHECK UP

1. (a) Why did war break out in Europe in 1939? (b) What nations were conquered by Nazi Germany? (c) How was Great Britain able to hold out? (d) Against what other countries did Nazi Germany launch attacks?

2. (a) How successful had Japan been in the war with China? (b) What other areas did Japan seek to conquer?

3. (a) What did the United States do to keep out of the war? (b) Why did this country's attitude change? (c) How did the United States become involved in the war? (d) In what ways did Americans take part in the war effort?

4. (a) Describe the Allied campaigns in North Africa and Italy. (b) Tell how the Allies landed in France and pressed on into Germany.

5. (a) What was the extent of the Japanese conquests? (b) How did American forces in the Pacific push back the Japanese? (c) What event finally brought about Japan's surrender?

These bombs were used because the military believed that the Japanese otherwise would not surrender unless the home islands were invaded and conquered.

3   How Did a "Cold War" Develop Between the United States and the Soviet Union?

During World War II there were encouraging signs that the nations might work together, after the conflict, for a free and peaceful world. One example was the meeting of President Roosevelt and Prime Minister Churchill of Great Britain on a ship off the coast of Newfoundland in August, 1941. In a statement known as the *Atlantic Charter,* the two statesmen summarized the aims of their countries for a better world. The Atlantic Charter pledged that all peoples should have the right to choose their own form of government. It stated that the United States and Britain desired no changes of territory without the approval of the people living in that territory. Roosevelt and Churchill also promised to work for a fairer division of world trade and natural resources.

The President and the Prime Minister held several other important conferences during the war. On two occasions — at Teheran (teh-uh-*rahn'*) in Iran and at Yalta in the Russian Crimea — they were joined by Premier Stalin (*stah'*lin) of Russia. At these meetings, the leaders naturally devoted much of their time to mapping plans to win the war. But they also gave thought to the problems of peace after victory. In the case of the Yalta Conference, many Americans have come to believe that the Western leaders acted unwisely when they promised certain territories to Soviet Russia in return for her aid against Japan.

The United Nations gets under way. World leaders agreed on one thing. A new start should be made toward a world organization of nations, in which all countries might co-operate for peaceful purposes. In April, 1945, representatives of 46 nations gathered at San Francisco to complete the first plans for a world organization. In two months they wrote the Charter of the *United Nations.*

Fifty-one nations joined the new organization at the start. In the early sentences of the Charter the member nations stated the purpose of the United Nations. They said they were "determined to save" later generations from war and reaffirmed their "faith in fundamental human rights, in the dignity and worth of the human person, in the equal rights of men and women and of nations large and small." They promised to "live together in peace with one another as good neighbors," to "unite [their] strength to maintain international peace and security," and to insure that "armed force shall not be used, [except] in the common interest."

What is the organization of the United Nations? To carry out the purposes of the United Nations, the UN Charter set up several groups or bodies. These are:

(1) *The General Assembly,* in which every member nation has a seat and each of these countries, large or small, has one vote. The Assembly may discuss any subject which comes under the Charter.

(2) The *Security Council,* which is directly responsible for keeping peace. Five countries — the United States, Great Britain, Russia, Nationalist China (page 636), and France — have permanent seats on the Council. Six other members are elected by the Assembly for two-year terms. Before any action can be taken, all five permanent members must agree to it. Thus, any one of the great powers has a *veto* over the decisions of the Council. The Security Council has the power to study disputes

The history of the UN is told in by Gait.

How the United Nations Works

between nations and recommend settlements. If this fails, the Council may call on members to stop all trade and communication with the offending nation. As a last resort, the Council can call upon the member nations to provide military forces for the UN to use against offenders.

(3) The *International Court of Justice,* which decides questions of international law submitted to it.

(4) The *Economic and Social Council,* which was set up to work toward higher standards of living, fuller employment, and improved education throughout the world. To carry out these goals, the Economic and Social Council has the help of a number of specialized groups or *agencies.*

(5) The *Trusteeship Council,* which entrusts colonies to the care of member nations. After World War II, for example, the UN granted the United States "trusteeships" for a number of islands in the Pacific which our forces had captured from the Japanese. The United States is responsible for these islands but does not own them. It must make regular reports about them to the United Nations.

(6) The *Secretariat,* which is the permanent staff of officials for the UN. It is headed by a Secretary-General elected by the General Assembly.

The headquarters of the United Nations is a group of modern buildings near the East River in New York City. By 1962 membership in the United Nations had passed the one-hundred mark.

What has the United Nations accomplished? During the postwar years the United Nations gave much valuable aid to people and to nations. For example, UNRRA (United Nations Relief and Rehabilitation Administration) provided food and supplies to war-torn countries at the close of World War II. The International Refugee Organization helped find new homes for more than a million people who fled or were driven from their homes during World War II. UNESCO (United Nations Educational, Scientific, and Cultural Organization) has taught people in underdeveloped countries to read and write. The World Health Organization and the Food and Agricultural Organization have tried to create better health conditions and to increase and improve the food supply in underprivileged nations. The General Assembly has adopted a Declaration of Human Rights, which sets up certain basic goals for peoples all over the world.

The UN also worked out peaceful solutions in some disputes. It helped to bring about the creation of the republics of Israel and Indonesia and the kingdom of Libya. Though a permanent UN military force was not established, UN member nations several times contributed soldiers and military equipment when crises threatened to upset world peace. As we shall see later in this chapter, recent world events have cast a shadow over the UN's future. Nevertheless, on the tenth anniversary of the United Nations, President Eisenhower remarked that "with all the defects, with all the failures that we can chalk up against it, the UN still represents man's best-organized hope to substitute the conference table for the battlefield."

WORLD PEACE IS THREATENED BY THE COLD WAR

In spite of the United Nations, the true and lasting peace that the world longed for has not been achieved. Instead, since World War II ended in 1945, there has been a sort of uneasy peace. Again and again, trouble in one part of the globe or another has threatened to provoke another major war. This period of uneasy peace has been called the "cold war."

The willingness of member states to contribute men and supplies when a crisis threatens world peace represents an advance over what was possible in the days of the League of Nations.

The world splits into two opposing
groups of nations. The great barrier to
real peace grew out of a split of nations
into two opposing groups after 1945. These
two groups, one led by the United States
and one by Communist Russia, faced
each other in anger. Gone was the friendship which had existed between the Russians and their allies during the Second
World War. Russia refused to withdraw
her armies from eastern Germany or to co-
operate in working out a final peace treaty
with Germany. In the United Nations,
Soviet Russia refused to work with her
former allies. Russia, for example, stalled
a plan to control the atomic bomb because
the plan called for inspection within her
territory by an international committee.
Again and again in the Security Council,
Russia used her veto power to kill proposals
by the United States and other nations. By
1962 the Soviet Union had cast its hun-
dredth veto in the Security Council.

**The Communists build up Russia's
power.** To understand the Soviet Union's
unfriendly actions, we need to look back
to events during World War I. In 1917,
you remember, the Communist Party seized
control of Russia (page 618). At that
time, Soviet Russia was far behind the
United States and the western European
nations in the production of goods. But
Stalin, who became the dictator of Russia
in the 1920's, was determined to make
Russia into a modern industrial nation.
Under the Communist system, business
and industry came under the direct control of the government, and the Communist Party controlled the government. The
Russian people worked for the state, not
for themselves.

**The Communists take over eastern
Europe.** When Hitler's forces swept eastward during World War II, Russia suffered
enormous losses. Soviet troops, however,

Russia Seizes Eastern Europe

Prewar Russia
Annexed by Russia since 1939
Communist-ruled

MAP STUDY Soviet armies turned the nations of
eastern Europe into satellites of the
USSR. Yugoslavia later followed an independent course, and Albania now
looks to Communist China for leadership.

not only turned back the invaders but
helped to conquer Germany. At the close
of the war, Russia took control of the European countries through which its armies
had advanced. (See map, page 625.) Between these countries and western Europe,
Soviet Russia dropped an "iron curtain" of
secrecy. The people behind the iron curtain lost their freedom and the right to
govern themselves. The countries of eastern Europe which became dominated by
Russia are known as the *satellite* nations.

Communism becomes a world threat.
An important goal of Soviet Russia has
been to spread communism throughout the
world. To carry out this purpose, Communist agents have been sent into many
countries. Working from within, these
agents seek to spread Communist influence

by embarrassing or destroying the governments of these countries.

Perhaps the greatest Communist victory was in China. Just before the Japanese surrendered in the summer of 1945, Soviet Russia declared war on Japan and began an invasion of Manchuria. Meanwhile, a bitter struggle was taking place between our war ally, Chiang Kai-shek's Nationalist government, and the Chinese Communists, whose leaders had been trained in Russia. Finally, in 1949, Chiang Kai-shek and his supporters were forced to take refuge on the island of Formosa. The millions of people on the Chinese mainland had to live under a Communist government and adopt Communist ways of living. The Chinese Communists also took steps to dominate all Asia.

The desire for freedom grows. Conditions in Asia and in Africa offered Soviet Russia and Communist China an unusual opportunity. Millions of Asians and Africans who had lived under the rule of colonial powers (such as Britain, France, Holland, and Belgium) longed for freedom to govern themselves. To understand better how colonial peoples in these parts of the world felt about independence, let us turn for a moment to the story of the Philippines.

You remember that the United States took over control of the Philippine Islands after the Spanish-American War (page 582). Our government improved living conditions in the Philippine Islands, provided teachers and schools, and gave the Filipinos an ever-increasing share in their government. But many Filipinos were not satisfied with anything less than independence. Freedom, as we Americans know, is one of the most valuable things an individual or a group of people can possess. So in 1935, Congress created the self-governing Philippine Commonwealth. It

was to remain under American protection for ten years, after which the Philippine Islands would become completely independent. World War II caused some delay in these plans, but on July 4, 1946, the Philippine Commonwealth became the independent Philippine Republic. The wisdom of America's policy was shown in World War II when the Filipinos remained loyal to the United States during the Japanese occupation (page 630). Without the promise of independence, the Filipinos might have sided with the Japanese.

Peoples in Asia and Africa demand an end to colonialism. World War II upset conditions in large areas of Asia and Africa which still belonged to European powers. France, Holland, and Belgium were occupied by Hitler's forces early in the war, while Great Britain fought desperately to ward off German invasion. Many colonies of these European countries, especially in Asia (see map, page 631), were occupied by Axis forces until the tide of battle turned in favor of the Allies. By the war's close the demand for independence among colonial peoples in Asia and Africa had spread like wildfire. They were unwilling to wait until their European masters had recovered from the war and might take steps to set them free. They demanded independence immediately. Between 1945 and 1960, 23 new independent nations were created in Africa alone.

The Communist powers seek to expand their influence in Asia and Africa. The break-up of colonial empires in Asia and Africa into independent nations made it easier for the Communists to carry out their plans for world power. Many of these new nations faced serious problems. After years under the rule of outsiders, they were ill-prepared to govern themselves. Nor were they able to defend themselves against more powerful countries. Above

The foreign policy of Red China, if anything, has been more militant than that of the Soviet Union.

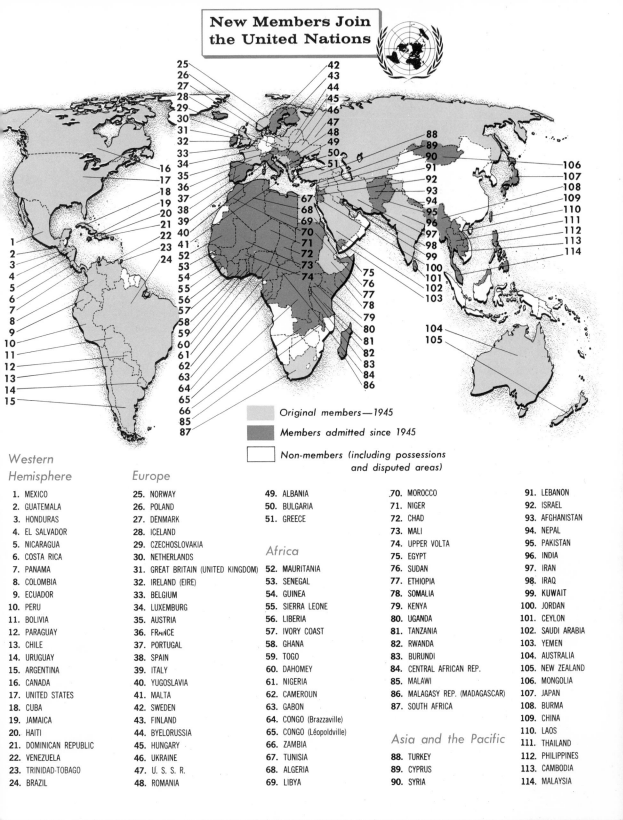

New Members Join the United Nations

Original members—1945

Members admitted since 1945

Non-members (including possessions and disputed areas)

Western Hemisphere

1. MEXICO
2. GUATEMALA
3. HONDURAS
4. EL SALVADOR
5. NICARAGUA
6. COSTA RICA
7. PANAMA
8. COLOMBIA
9. ECUADOR
10. PERU
11. BOLIVIA
12. PARAGUAY
13. CHILE
14. URUGUAY
15. ARGENTINA
16. CANADA
17. UNITED STATES
18. CUBA
19. JAMAICA
20. HAITI
21. DOMINICAN REPUBLIC
22. VENEZUELA
23. TRINIDAD-TOBAGO
24. BRAZIL

Europe

25. NORWAY
26. POLAND
27. DENMARK
28. ICELAND
29. CZECHOSLOVAKIA
30. NETHERLANDS
31. GREAT BRITAIN (UNITED KINGDOM)
32. IRELAND (EIRE)
33. BELGIUM
34. LUXEMBURG
35. AUSTRIA
36. FRANCE
37. PORTUGAL
38. SPAIN
39. ITALY
40. YUGOSLAVIA
41. MALTA
42. SWEDEN
43. FINLAND
44. BYELORUSSIA
45. HUNGARY
46. UKRAINE
47. U. S. S. R.
48. ROMANIA
49. ALBANIA
50. BULGARIA
51. GREECE

Africa

52. MAURITANIA
53. SENEGAL
54. GUINEA
55. SIERRA LEONE
56. LIBERIA
57. IVORY COAST
58. GHANA
59. TOGO
60. DAHOMEY
61. NIGERIA
62. CAMEROUN
63. GABON
64. CONGO (Brazzaville)
65. CONGO (Léopoldville)
66. ZAMBIA
67. TUNISIA
68. ALGERIA
69. LIBYA
70. MOROCCO
71. NIGER
72. CHAD
73. MALI
74. UPPER VOLTA
75. EGYPT
76. SUDAN
77. ETHIOPIA
78. SOMALIA
79. KENYA
80. UGANDA
81. TANZANIA
82. RWANDA
83. BURUNDI
84. CENTRAL AFRICAN REP.
85. MALAWI
86. MALAGASY REP. (MADAGASCAR)
87. SOUTH AFRICA

Asia and the Pacific

88. TURKEY
89. CYPRUS
90. SYRIA
91. LEBANON
92. ISRAEL
93. AFGHANISTAN
94. NEPAL
95. PAKISTAN
96. INDIA
97. IRAN
98. IRAQ
99. KUWAIT
100. JORDAN
101. CEYLON
102. SAUDI ARABIA
103. YEMEN
104. AUSTRALIA
105. NEW ZEALAND
106. MONGOLIA
107. JAPAN
108. BURMA
109. CHINA
110. LAOS
111. THAILAND
112. PHILIPPINES
113. CAMBODIA
114. MALAYSIA

MAP STUDY United Nations members are listed above with numbers which identify them on the world map. Many of the new members are former colonies which have become independent since 1945. Which has contributed more new members — Asia or Africa?

AERIAL TORPEDOES dropped by U.S. Navy airplanes smashed the floodgates of this Korean dam. The waters thus released slowed down a Communist spring offensive.

all, the peoples of Asia and Africa desired improved living conditions. They believed this goal could be reached only by industrializing their countries. Since the new nations lacked money and trained workers to build factories and develop their resources, they needed outside help.

Most of the new nations were suspicious of Western powers that had formerly held colonies. Soviet Russia and Communist China made good use of this anti-Western feeling. They pointed to the rapid growth in industry that Russia had made under communism. They tried to win over new nations to the Communist side — in some cases by tempting offers of loans and trade and in others by threats and armed force.

At times the cold war turns hot. The efforts of the Communist nations to expand their power have been resisted by the free nations. Although both sides have tried to make gains without actually fighting, outbreaks which might have led to a third world war have sometimes taken place. One of the most important outbreaks was in Korea. After World War II, Korea was divided at the 38th parallel of latitude. The northern half was placed under Russian control and the southern

half under the supervision of the United States. The United States helped the Republic of Korea get started, and then the American soldiers were withdrawn. The Russian soldiers also withdrew from their portion of Korea. But North Korea remained under a Communist government.

Fighting breaks out in Korea. Suddenly, on June 25, 1950, the North Koreans invaded the Republic of Korea. At once the Security Council of the United Nations asked the North Koreans to stop fighting and withdraw north of the 38th parallel. The Security Council also asked members of the UN to help the Republic of Korea repel the attack and restore peace. President Truman announced immediately that the United States would support the UN. He ordered General Douglas MacArthur, commander of American troops in Japan, to send forces to Korea. President Truman also directed an American fleet to prevent any attack upon the island of Formosa held by the Chinese Nationalist government.

Following the invasion by the North Koreans in 1950, fighting raged up and down Korea. While not officially called a war, it was a savagely fought conflict.

Most of the soldiers in the UN force were contributed by the Republic of Korea and the United States.

Although the United States furnished most of the supplies and the United States and South Korea provided most of the troops, other members of the United Nations sent men or ships or planes.

In November, 1950, as the UN army approached the Chinese border, large numbers of soldiers from Communist China joined the North Korean forces. The greatly outnumbered UN troops retreated into South Korea. Yet, even after China's entry into the conflict, the UN troops drove the enemy back to the 38th parallel. Though both sides suffered many losses, those of the Communists were far greater.

Truce efforts drag on. After a year of fighting, officers from each army met to discuss a truce. (To make a truce is to stop the fighting for a time so that plans can be made to end it for good.) For more than two years the officers held meetings off and on. They could not agree on many things. Sometimes no meetings took place for months. At last, however, on July 27, 1953, a truce was signed. But troops still guard both sides of the boundary between North and South Korea.

CHECK UP

1. (a) What was the Atlantic Charter? (b) How was the United Nations created? (c) What was its purpose?

2. (a) What are the chief bodies of the United Nations? (b) What is the purpose of each? (c) What have been some of the achievements of the UN?

3. (a) How has the cold war divided the world? (b) How did Russia extend communism in eastern Europe? (c) Where else in the world did communism become a threat? (d) What methods have the Communists used to extend their influence?

4. (a) Why did colonial peoples in Asia and Africa demand independence after World War II? (b) How did the Philippines become an independent nation? (c) What problems did the new nations of Asia and Africa face?

5. (a) What led to the outbreak of war in Korea? (b) How did the UN and the United States meet this threat? (c) What part did Communist China play in this conflict?

4 What Steps Has America Taken to Defend the Free World Against the Communist Threat?

When World War II came to a close, the American people had high hopes for a lasting peace. They believed that the United Nations would become a powerful force in maintaining such a peace. As you already know, however, Soviet Russia used its veto power in the Security Council to block many UN plans. And although the UN Charter permitted the formation of a permanent military force to stop threats of war, no such force was set up. Yet the constant attempts of Soviet Russia and its allies to expand their power after 1945 showed the free world that it must be prepared to meet the Communist threat. Because of its strength, the United States realized that it had to take the lead in working for peace and halting Communist expansion. One way to do this was to help countries that had suffered in the war.

The United States aids other countries. Early in 1947 President Truman asked Congress to vote large sums of money to help Greece and Turkey resist the spread of communism. This idea of aiding nations which would oppose communism is

AMERICAN AID to foreign countries includes not only money and material but also technical assistance. Here trainees in Pakistan are learning to operate a grain thresher.

The United States takes part in reaching peace settlements. Because of Russia's unfriendly attitude, the business of peacemaking after World War II was slowed up. Treaties were worked out with Italy and some smaller nations. But Russia blocked a general peace treaty for Europe, such as the Treaty of Versailles at the end of World War I. The free nations grew impatient, and in May, 1952, agreements were signed by the United States, Britain, France, and West Germany. (West Germany was the part of Germany not occupied by Russian forces.) The agreements ended the state of war, and West Germany became an independent republic in 1955. The rest of Germany, known as East Germany, remained under Russian control. Also in 1955 a peace treaty, to which Soviet Russia agreed, was finally worked out with Austria.

THE FREE WORLD FORMS ALLIANCES

The United States begins to build a series of alliances. As ill feeling between the Communists and the Western powers grew stronger, the United States began to form agreements for defense, or alliances, with other nations. The first alliance made after World War II was in the region nearest the United States. In 1947, the United States signed an agreement with nineteen Central and South American countries. The treaty provided that all these nations should act together against an armed attack on any of them. The signers of the treaty agreed, also, to refer such an attack to the Security Council of the United Nations. A few years later several of the same nations made still another agreement for the defense of the Americas.

The North Atlantic nations make an alliance. Many of the nations of the free world lie on one side or the other of the

called the *Truman Doctrine*. Later in that same year, Secretary of State George C. Marshall announced that the United States would give "friendly aid" to European nations to help them recover from the damage of war. Russia and the satellite countries refused this offer of assistance. But the western European countries accepted. Under this *Marshall Plan* the United States provided huge sums of money so that the farms and factories of Europe might produce effectively once more. The Marshall Plan was responsible for helping western Europe to become prosperous again in a remarkably short time.

In 1950 our government also announced the *Point Four* program. This program was intended to help underdeveloped countries improve health conditions, increase food supplies, and develop their trade, natural resources, and industry. If living conditions were improved, these nations, it was believed, would be better able to resist Communist pressures or attacks.

Shirt Sleeve Diplomacy describes Point Four programs.

640

FOREIGN STUDENTS come from around the globe to attend American universities. These students represent countries of Europe, Asia, and Africa.

North Atlantic Ocean. In 1949 these countries formed the North Atlantic Treaty Organization, commonly called NATO. This organization was made up originally of Great Britain, France, Belgium, the Netherlands, Luxemburg, the United States, Canada, Norway, Denmark, Iceland, Italy, and Portugal. Greece, Turkey, and West Germany joined later. The members of NATO declared that they supported the United Nations and wished to settle all disputes by peaceful means. But they also said that an attack upon one of them should be considered an attack upon them all. They would unite, they declared, to resist such an attack. Each nation contributes to the armed forces of NATO, and each has representatives on the Council of NATO.

Alliances stretch around the globe. Across the Pacific spreads a whole network of alliances. When a peace treaty was made with Japan in 1951, the Japanese agreed that the United States might keep armed forces there. Later the two nations agreed to co-operate in defense. In 1952 the United States and the Philippines agreed upon joint defense. In the same year Australia, New Zealand, and the United States made a similar agreement (called, from the initials of the signers, ANZUS). In 1954 a Southeast Asia de-

fense treaty was signed. SEATO, as this alliance is called, included Australia, France, New Zealand, Pakistan, the Philippines, Thailand, Great Britain, and the United States. Although the treaty did not set up a common defense force such as NATO has, each member nation of SEATO declared it would respond to an attack on another member.

Alliances do not fully guarantee peace. These alliances assure aid to member nations in case of sudden attack. But they provide no guarantee of a lasting peace. In recent years, NATO nations have sometimes disagreed on general defense policies. Thus, ties within the organization have been loosened. A number of nations, furthermore, are not members of any alliance. Many of them, especially those created since 1945, have been unwilling to take sides in the cold war. These "uncommitted" nations have accepted help from both Communist and free-world countries but have avoided entering any alliance.

Secondly, because of their ambitions for power, the Communist leaders have continued to threaten the peace of the world. By their false charges they seek to turn the new and uncommitted nations against the free world. By threats or use of force they have caused crises to break out in different parts of the world.

"Uncommitted" India, for example, has **641** maintained that the evolution of the Communist and Free World alliance systems is a major threat to peace. India, however, has also been compelled to resist Communist Chinese aggression.

TROUBLE SPOTS DEVELOP THROUGHOUT THE WORLD

A crisis arises in the Middle East. Many of the new nations created in recent years lie in the Middle East. Except for the Jewish state of Israel, all these new states are Arab. Of the new Arab states, Egypt was one of the most important, and its President, Gamal Abdel Nasser, hoped to become the most powerful leader in the Middle East.

In 1956 President Nasser declared that Egypt would take over the Suez Canal, which had been operated by a private company for many years. The countries using the canal became alarmed. What if Egypt, for some reason, should close the canal to the ships of any country? Such a step would be a serious blow to a country's trade. For weeks the Suez problem was discussed in the United Nations.

Meanwhile, relations between Egypt and Israel grew more tense. The Arab nations of the Middle East had opposed the creation of this modern Jewish state. For years border raids had taken place between Israel and Egypt. In the middle of the Suez crisis, Israel suddenly launched an invasion of Egypt. Israeli troops fought their way deep into Egypt and almost to the canal itself. The situation became more critical when French and British troops entered Egypt and occupied the canal zone.

The United Nations and the United States take action in the Middle East. The United Nations General Assembly held an emergency session. It called for a cease-fire and created a UN security force to supervise the cease-fire. Great Britain, France, and Israel reluctantly withdrew their troops from Egypt.

As leader of the free world, the United States feared that Soviet Russia might use troubled conditions in the Middle East as

MAP STUDY

On the world map on the opposite page, colored circles locate some of the places which today are sources of international tension or conflict. The smaller maps at top and bottom provide close-up views of certain of these areas. Note that most of the trouble spots include Communist-controlled lands. What is the situation today in each of the areas shown here?

an excuse to extend its power. Early in 1957, therefore, Congress gave President Eisenhower authority to use American armed forces to protect Middle Eastern nations which requested help against "any nation controlled by international communism." Under this Doctrine, United States marines were sent to Lebanon for a few weeks in 1958 to protect that country's independence. A crisis every so often in one of the nations of the Middle East reminds us that this area continues to be a world trouble spot.

Red China threatens to overrun Asia. Over much of the rest of Asia looms the shadow of Communist China. You have learned that hordes of soldiers from Communist China took part in the conflict in Korea (page 639). The activities of Red China, however, did not end with the Korean truce. Since the early 1950's, Chinese Communists have given aid and support to native Communists in their efforts to take control of the newly independent states in Southeast Asia. (See map on page 643.) North Vietnam was lost to the Communists, while Communist forces seized much of Laos and invaded South Vietnam. Though Laos was proclaimed neutral in 1962, Communist forces attacked again in 1963. The United States has poured financial and military aid into South Vietnam in an effort to save

Note that in the case of Egypt this country **642** supported the UN and opposed the policy of two NATO allies--Britain and France.

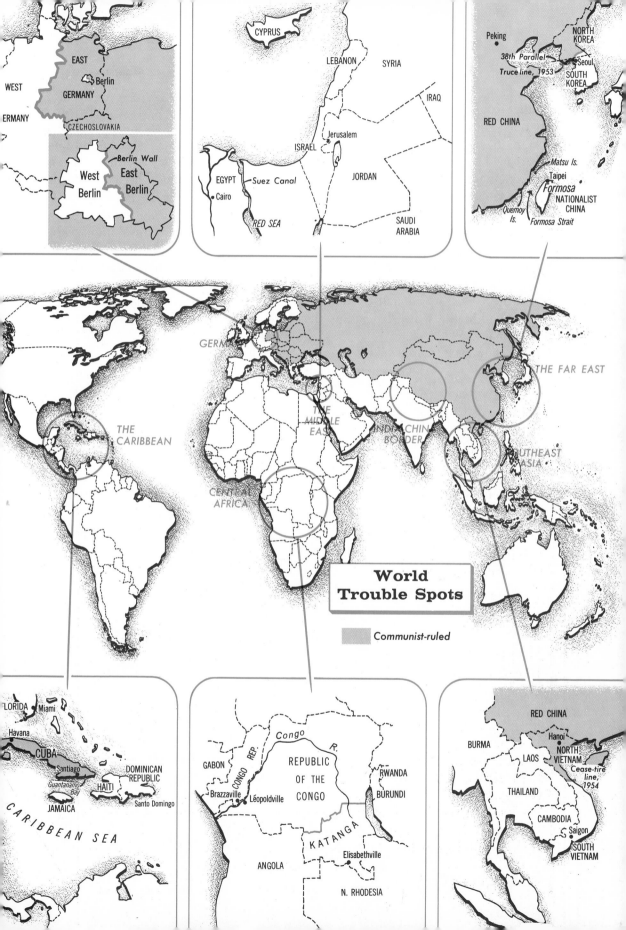

Inset: Germany / Berlin

WEST GERMANY

EAST GERMANY

Berlin

CZECHOSLOVAKIA

Berlin Wall

West Berlin

East Berlin

Inset: The Middle East

CYPRUS

LEBANON

SYRIA

IRAQ

ISRAEL

Jerusalem

JORDAN

EGYPT

Suez Canal

Cairo

RED SEA

SAUDI ARABIA

Inset: The Far East

Peking

38th Parallel

Truce line, 1953

NORTH KOREA

Seoul

SOUTH KOREA

RED CHINA

Matsu Is.

Taipei

Formosa

NATIONALIST CHINA

Quemoy Is.

Formosa Strait

Main Map

GERMANY

THE MIDDLE EAST

INDOCHINA BORDER

THE FAR EAST

THE CARIBBEAN

CENTRAL AFRICA

SOUTHEAST ASIA

World Trouble Spots

Communist-ruled

Inset: The Caribbean

FLORIDA

Miami

Havana

CUBA

Santiago

Guantanamo Bay

JAMAICA

DOMINICAN REPUBLIC

HAITI

Santo Domingo

CARIBBEAN SEA

Inset: Central Africa

Congo R.

GABON

CONGO REP.

REPUBLIC OF THE CONGO

RWANDA

BURUNDI

Brazzaville

Léopoldville

KATANGA

Elisabethville

ANGOLA

N. RHODESIA

Inset: Southeast Asia

RED CHINA

BURMA

Hanoi

NORTH VIETNAM

LAOS

Cease-fire line, 1954

THAILAND

CAMBODIA

Saigon

SOUTH VIETNAM

that country from falling under Communist control (page 699).

Other countries in Asia have felt the heavy hand of Red China. The Chinese overran the mountain kingdom of Tibet and crushed with great savagery the efforts of Tibetans to defend their country. Red Chinese soldiers crossed the northern border of India, claiming that land south of the long-established boundary belonged to China. For years also the Chinese Communists have threatened to seize the island of Formosa. Off and on they have bombarded the Chinese Nationalist islands of Quemoy and Matsu, which lie close to the Chinese mainland.

Berlin remains a trouble spot in Europe. In Europe the cold war has centered about the divided city of Berlin. Soviet Russia and the Western powers were unable to reach an agreement concerning the future of Germany after World War II ended. While West Germany became a prosperous, democratic state having close ties with western Europe, East Germany remained a satellite of Communist Russia. Within East Germany lies the city of Berlin. Since 1945, Great Britain, France, and the United States have occupied the western part of Berlin; East Berlin, under Soviet control, is the capital of Communist East Germany. The Russians have repeatedly threatened to force the Western powers out of West Berlin. But the United States, Britain, and France have refused to withdraw because their wartime agreements with Russia give them the right to be there.

In 1961, conditions in Berlin seemed likely to touch off a war. For years East Germans had sought freedom by escaping into West Berlin. Finally, to stop the loss of skilled workers, Soviet troops and tanks moved into East Berlin, and the Communists built a wall separating East and West Berlin. The American, British, and French governments responded by increasing their military forces in West Berlin. They insisted they would protect the people of West Berlin. But tension in Berlin continues and new crises could lead to war.

The Communists stir up trouble in Latin America and Africa. Two other trouble areas mentioned frequently in the news during the early 1960's were Cuba and the Congo. In Cuba the government was controlled by a revolutionary leader named Castro. Soviet Russia saw in the confused situation in Cuba an opportunity to use that country as a base from which to stir up trouble in other Latin American republics. (You will read more about Cuba in Chapters 31 and 32.)

Meanwhile, trouble was boiling up in Africa. One of the many new African nations was the Republic of Congo. The Congolese had been poorly prepared by their former Belgian masters to govern themselves. While rival leaders and tribes battled one another, some Congolese turned violently on white people who remained in the Congo. To help restore order, the UN sent a military force made up of soldiers of various member nations. As in the case of Cuba, however, Soviet Russia took steps to turn the confusion in the Congo to its own advantage. It sent airplanes, trucks, and "technicians" in an attempt to win influence in the struggle between rival Congolese leaders. Russia even refused to support the UN's efforts to restore law and order in the Congo. The efforts of Soviet and Chinese Communists to influence the newly independent countries in Africa pose a constant threat of trouble between the Communist and free-world nations.

THE COLD WAR CONTINUES

The struggle between Communist and free nations continues to keep the world in turmoil. It has led to a build-up of atomic,

The dispute over Berlin would never have arisen if the Soviet Union had lived up to the agreement to let the Germans in a plebiscite decide for themselves the kind of government they wanted.

ROBERT GODDARD
believed from boyhood that man could use rockets to reach the unknown world of high altitudes.

EARLY EXPERIMENTS nearly caused Goddard to be expelled from college when a rocket-fuel test filled the lab with thick smoke. He became a physics professor, however, and later proved that rockets could work in a vacuum — a discovery vital to space travel.

IN THE SIGNAL CORPS during World War I, Goddard demonstrated his new antitank rocket, forerunner of the bazooka. Peace came before it was taken seriously. Meanwhile, experimenting on his own, he designed the first multi-stage rocket.

THE HISTORIC FIRST FLIGHT of his liquid-fueled rocket from a Massachusetts farm only got Goddard in trouble with the alarmed neighbors. Ridiculed as "Moony" Goddard because of his theory that rockets could reach the moon, the quiet, determined scientist moved to New Mexico to work full-time on rocket development.

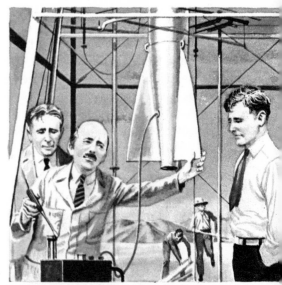

BIGGER and more powerful rockets were Goddard's goal in the 1930's, as, aided by scientific foundations and Charles Lindbergh, he continued the research on which all modern rocketry is based.

or nuclear, weapons and touched off a race to explore (and perhaps control) outer space. New crises have arisen and the UN has been affected.

New weapons make war more destructive. World War II ended amid the terrible thunder of the atomic bomb (page 632). During the cold war both Communist Russia and the Western powers have developed new and even more terrifying weapons. These are marvels of science and engineering but are also destructive beyond imagination. Some of them can be dropped from airplanes; another kind, the intercontinental ballistic missile (commonly nicknamed ICBM), can be launched from one continent to another. One of the most important American missiles is the Polaris, which can be fired from an atomic submarine under water. Because of the immense power of the new weapons, it has often been said that in an all-out nuclear war, "there will be no winners, only losers."

East and West compete in space. The same science which develops weapons of war has also led toward the exploration of outer space. In October, 1957, Russia launched its first "Sputnik," a small sphere which circled the earth for three months. Other Sputniks followed. In 1959 Russia announced that it had hit the moon with one space rocket, and with another had photographed the side of the moon always turned away from the earth. On April 12, 1961, Russia launched the world's first spaceman. Major Yuri Gagarin, the Soviet "Cosmonaut," circled the earth and returned safely. Since then, a number of Cosmonauts have carried out much longer and more spectacular flights.

The United States was also busy exploring outer space. Early in 1958 the United States launched its first small earth satellite, Explorer I, and since then has sent up more satellites than the Russians. While the Russian satellites have been heavier, the American satellites have yielded more information of value to scientists. The Tiros and Nimbus satellites, for example, have sent back to earth much valuable information concerning weather. Also, such satellites as Telstar and "Early Bird" have relayed live television programs from continent to continent.

In 1959 the government selected seven experienced jet pilots as our first Astronauts, and on May 5, 1961, an Astronaut rocketed into space for the first time. Navy Commander Alan B. Shepard reached an altitude of 115 miles in a Mercury capsule. The first Astronaut to go into orbit was John Glenn, in February, 1962. Other Astronauts made successful orbital flights. The last, and longest, Mercury flight came in May, 1963, when Gordon Cooper orbited the earth 22 times. While the Soviet space missions have been carried out under conditions of secrecy, America's man-in-space efforts have been openly broadcast to the world. (See page 699 for more recent achievements in space.)

Relations between the East and West grow better, then worse. For a time during the late 1950's the cold war seemed to ease. Following Stalin's death, Nikita Khrushchev (kroosh-*choff'*) became the new "strong man" of Russia. Khrushchev appeared willing to improve relations with the nations of the free world. The iron curtain was lifted enough to allow groups of Russians and Americans to visit each other's countries. Khrushchev himself visited the United States in 1959. Plans were made for President Eisenhower to make a return visit to Russia and for a "summit meeting" of top world leaders to be held in Paris in 1960.

Suddenly in the spring of 1960, however, hopes for a more peaceful world out-

Students may wish to read Rockets, Satellites, and Space Travel.

NIKITA KHRUSHCHEV, accompanied by two other members of the Soviet government, is shown making an emphatic point during his visit to New York City in 1960. Four years later Khrushchev was replaced by younger leaders in a shake-up of the Soviet government.

look were rudely dashed. Using as an excuse the flight of an American U–2 airplane over Russia, Khrushchev refused to sit down with the Western leaders who had gathered in Paris for the summit talks. He hurled insults at President Eisenhower and the United States. The world outlook during the months that followed were grim as the Soviet Union and Red China carried on a campaign to downgrade the United States in the eyes of other nations.

The cold war affects the UN. When the General Assembly of the UN met in the fall of 1960, the meetings were attended by the heads of several Communist governments as well as by the regular delegates. Khrushchev kept the Assembly in an uproar. He noisily thumped his desk when he disagreed with other speakers. He condemned the UN's policy in the Congo and tried to abolish the position of Secretary-General. And he repeatedly hurled the charge of "colonialism" against the leading nations of the free world. But the Russian accusation sounded silly in view of the number of new nations given independence

in recent years by western European powers. Such charges actually apply more accurately to the Soviet Union and Red China, in view of the number of small countries they have brought under their control.

Nevertheless, the position and future of the UN had been thrown into doubt. Other nations besides those of the Soviet bloc refused to contribute funds for the UN force in the Congo. As a result, a financial crisis developed, which threatened to halt the work of the United Nations. Furthermore, the balance of power in the UN has significantly shifted in recent years. Of over a hundred members, a large number represent the newly independent nations of Africa and Asia. Many of these nations regard themselves as uncommitted in the cold war. They prefer not to ally themselves with either the Western nations or the Communist bloc. With this large group of uncertain votes in the UN General Assembly, neither the United States nor the Soviet Union can be certain of winning support on any stand they might take.

At the very time that Free World nations are abandoning "colonialism" as a policy, the Soviet Union and Red China are extending imperial control over neighboring states.

CHECK UP

1. (a) How has our country fought communism through (1) the Truman Doctrine? (2) the Marshall Plan? (3) Point Four? (b) How did West Germany become an independent nation?

2. What alliances has the United States formed with other countries for the defense of the free world?

3. (a) How has peace been threatened in the Middle East? (b) In Asia? (c) In Berlin? (d) In Cuba? (e) In the Congo?

4. (a) What new weapons have made the possibility of war more fearful than ever before? (b) What progress has been made in the exploration of space?

5. (a) Why did relations between East and West improve for a time in the late 1950's? (b) Why did they worsen again? (c) What have recent developments been?

In discussing Question #2, take into account that Hitler would have backed down in the Rhineland if France and Great Britain had brought up troops. Italy was vulnerable to economic pressure. Whether Japanese aggression in Manchuria could have been stopped short of war is less certain.

Check Up on Chapter 30

Do You Know the Meaning?

1. outer space	10. summit meeting
2. disarmament	11. cease-fire
3. czar	12. atomic bomb
4. communism	13. veto
5. missile	14. trusteeship
6. appeasement	15. cold war
7. blitzkrieg	16. satellite
8. air base	17. truce
9. inflation	18. free enterprise

Can You Identify?

1. Mussolini	18. Chiang Kai-shek
2. NATO	19. Lend-Lease Act
3. Hitler	20. Franklin D. Roosevelt
4. Nazis	21. Dwight D. Eisenhower
5. 1933	22. George C. Marshall
6. 1939	23. Douglas MacArthur
7. 1941	24. Harry S. Truman
8. 1945	25. Truman Doctrine
9. 1957	26. Joseph Stalin
10. 1961	27. Communist Party
11. ICBM	28. Winston Churchill
12. Axis Powers	29. Atlantic Charter
13. Suez Canal	30. United Nations
14. Sputnik	31. Nikita Khrushchev
15. Explorer I	32. Henry L. Stimson
16. Point Four	33. Gamal Nasser
17. Marshall Plan	34. Yuri Gagarin
	35. John Glenn

Can You Locate?

1. Germany	11. North Africa
2. Italy	12. East Indies
3. Sicily	13. USSR
4. Japan	14. Stalingrad
5. Formosa	15. Coral Sea
6. Korea	16. Guadalcanal
7. Ethiopia	17. Okinawa
8. Burma	18. Hiroshima
9. Normandy	19. Yalta
10. Congo	20. Israel
	21. French Indo-China

What Do You Think?

1. Why were nations that had suffered staggering losses in World War I ready to spend huge sums for armaments in the 1930's?

2. Could World War II have been prevented if the League of Nations had been able to stop Japan, Italy, and Germany when they first seized territory illegally? Why?

3. Do you think the United States should have used the atomic bomb against Japan?

4. What problems has the UN so far been unable to solve?

5. How does life in Soviet Russia differ from life in the United States?

6. How have the alliances built up by the free nations contributed to world peace?

Remember Pearl Harbor! Beneath the waters of Pearl Harbor in Hawaii lies the rusting hulk of the U. S. battleship *Arizona,* a sad reminder of a black day in American history. During the Japanese attack on December 7, 1941, the *Arizona* was hit by bombs. The ship blew up and sank, carrying with her a crew of a thousand men. Over twenty years have passed, but the *Arizona* is not forgotten. The ship has become a Navy memorial to all the men who lost their lives in the Japanese attack. Each day and night a Navy honor guard raises and lowers a flag from a platform built over the sunken ship.

"Sighted sub — sank same." At crucial times in our history, many a man has made a short, dramatic report on some important victory or event, such as Commodore Perry's "We have met the enemy and they are ours" in the War of 1812 (page 255). The story goes, too, that when American troops arrived in France in World War I, General Pershing, their commander, said "Lafayette, we are here." In this way he expressed our country's gratitude to the young Frenchman who had fought in our Revolutionary War.

Out of World War II came another short and dramatic report. After the United States entered the war, the Germans sent packs of submarines to prey on our Atlantic coast shipping. Many a ship was torpedoed and many a crew left to drown. The Army and Navy sent out planes and drafted small boats of all kinds to spot the deadly submarines. On a January day in 1942, an aviation machinist's mate named Donald Mason was flying a Navy bomber over the Atlantic. Suddenly the periscope of a German sub was sighted below. After dropping two depth bombs on the target, the crew of the plane watched eagerly. They saw a submarine rise to the surface, turn on its side, and plunge into the ocean. Only an oil slick was left to tell the tale. Mason radioed back the news in four short words: "Sighted sub — sank same."

Integration on the battlefield. Although often denied their rights, Negroes have fought for the cause of freedom in all of this country's wars. In the early conflicts they fought shoulder to shoulder with white soldiers and sailors. During the Civil War and the Spanish-American War, Negro troops usually had white officers. But in World War I, Negro regiments were commanded by colored officers, and in World War II, a much larger number of Negro officers commanded both white and Negro troops. Although many Negro officers and enlisted men were decorated for gallantry in action, the practice of racially separate regiments was continued until 1948. At that time, President Truman ordered the integration of troops in all branches of the service. This has been the practice ever since — among troops stationed in this country and in Korea, Berlin, and South Vietnam.

"The rockets' red glare." The American troops who defended Baltimore during the War of 1812 were startled when the British fired volleys of rockets at them. As you know from "The Star-Spangled Banner," Fort McHenry stood up under attack by the British "wonder weapon," and rockets did not become important in warfare until modern times. In World War II, rockets were fired from ships, tanks, airplanes, and long tubes called "bazookas." Using the same principle, powerful rockets today launch satellites and manned spacecraft, and before long may carry men to the moon.

The United States Looks to Its
Neighbors in the Americas

Students may need to review Chapter 10.

What this chapter is about —

Neighbors are important to nations as well as to people. You know that it makes a good deal of difference whether the families living near you are pleasant and helpful, or unfriendly and quarrelsome. In much the same way, it is important to a nation whether its neighbors are peace-loving or warlike. Fortunately our neighbor Canada is a friendly, democratic nation, and the 4000-mile border between the two countries is unarmed. But in recent years the United States has learned what it is like to have an unfriendly near neighbor. Our relations with that neighbor, Cuba, have helped us realize this fact all too clearly.

Chapter 30 described our country's foreign policy as a world leader in recent years. It pointed out that events in far-distant places like Korea or the Congo can have important effects on our lives. If this is true, how much more would we be affected by trouble in nearby nations. In this chapter, therefore, we shall find out how the United States has gotten along with our neighbors in the Western Hemisphere. First, however, we need to pick up the stories of Canada and Latin America where we left off in Chapter 10. We shall learn how Canada became an independent member of the British family of nations and how the republics of Latin

---

People in our story — Canadian Mounted Policeman, prospector, and logger; Latin American Indian couple, army officer, and student and professor.

America have developed. This chapter will answer the following questions:

▶ 1. How did Canada become an independent nation?

▶ 2. What progress have Latin American

nations made since winning independence?

▶ 3. What relations have developed between the United States and its neighbors?

Building the Canadian Nation is a history used in Canadian schools.

How Did Canada Become an Independent Nation?

In 1850 Canada was a small group of provinces governed by Great Britain. Today, a little over a hundred years later, Canada is a strong, independent nation with many new industries and a growing foreign trade. It holds an important place not only in the Western Hemisphere but among the nations of the world. How did Canada progress from a British colony to an important independent nation?

CANADA GAINS CONTROL OF ITS OWN AFFAIRS

In Chapter 10 you read about the large numbers of English-speaking people who moved to French Canada after it became a possession of Great Britain. Many were Loyalists from the newly independent

United States; others were immigrants from the British Isles. It was these English-speaking people who demanded a government for Canada which would represent the people. By 1850, the separate provinces had won control of their own provincial governments. Two more important steps, however, had to be taken before Canada won complete independence. To find out about these steps, let us imagine that we are talking to James King, a Canadian boy who lives in Ottawa, the capital city of Canada.

"Did Canada, like the United States, fight a war to win its freedom from Great Britain?" we ask. "No indeed," James answers with a smile. "The people of Canada were able to gain the independence they wanted without war, and yet remain a

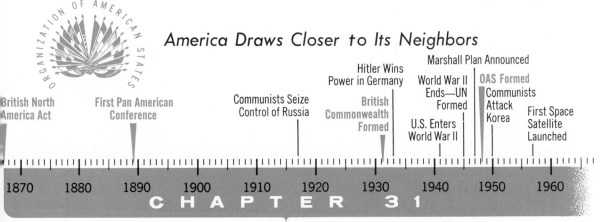

America Draws Closer to Its Neighbors

British North America Act

First Pan American Conference

Communists Seize Control of Russia

British Commonwealth Formed

Hitler Wins Power in Germany

World War II Ends—UN Formed

U.S. Enters World War II

Marshall Plan Announced

OAS Formed

Communists Attack Korea

First Space Satellite Launched

1870   1880   1890   1900   1910   1920   1930   1940   1950   1960

C H A P T E R   3 1

1867 - The Present

part of the British family of nations. Very briefly this is how my country became a self-governing and independent nation."

Canada in 1850 was much smaller than it is today. To begin with, James explains what Canada was like in 1850 when it was still a colony of Great Britain. At that time there were only half as many provinces as there are today. In the eastern part of Canada three small provinces bordered the Atlantic Ocean — Nova Scotia, Prince Edward Island, and New Brunswick. The people of these provinces earned a living by fishing and shipbuilding. Most Canadians lived in the United Provinces of Upper and Lower Canada. Their farms and cities clustered about the Great Lakes and the St. Lawrence River. Only a few white people lived west of the Great Lakes. Indians and a few half-breeds (part Indian and part white) hunted buffalo in this vast region and carried on trapping and fur trading. Most of the western territory of present-day Canada was controlled by the Hudson's Bay Company, which had many fur-trading posts in that region. As for the government, it was a good deal like that of the American colonies in 1750. Each province had its own government, but Great Britain controlled trade with foreign nations and was responsible for the defense of Canada in case of war.

Canadians work for a union of the provinces. Canadians were not satisfied for long with merely gaining control of their provincial governments. Many people began to talk about forming a Canadian nation. As James King says, "They wanted to unite the provinces under a central government in much the same way as your American states are united." He goes on to explain that the most important reason for union was fear of the United States, which was then sweeping westward across the continent. Canadians had not forgotten that the United States had twice invaded their soil — at the beginning of the American Revolution and again during the War of 1812. They still remembered the rivalry over control of the Oregon Territory (page 366). What is more, American pioneers in large numbers were beginning to cross over into the western regions of Canada. Canadians began to ask each other, "Will the United States try to swallow up our lands as they did other western lands?"

Many people believed that a United Canada would be better able to protect itself against the United States. Of course, there were other good reasons for union. As a nation, Canada expected to control her own affairs and would be in a better position to develop her natural resources and trade.

Canada becomes a Dominion. "The year 1867," says James King, "is as important to us Canadians as 1776 is to you Americans. It marks the birth of our nation. In 1867 the Parliament of Great Britain passed the *British North America Act,* which united the provinces under a single government. At the head of the new nation, called the Dominion of Canada, was John A. Macdonald, a wise and able leader from Upper Canada. Macdonald became one of Canada's greatest statesmen."

The Dominion grows. James King goes on to describe the new Dominion. At first, he tells us, Canada was small. It had only four provinces — Nova Scotia, New Brunswick, and the two new provinces of Quebec and Ontario which were formed from Lower and Upper Canada. Except for Newfoundland and Prince Edward Island, the rest of what is now Canada still belonged to Great Britain and was controlled by the Hudson's Bay Company. The Cana-

It is important for students to understand that the same events (Quebec Act, American Revolution, War of 1812, dispute over Oregon) were viewed differently by Canadians and Americans in the 1860's.

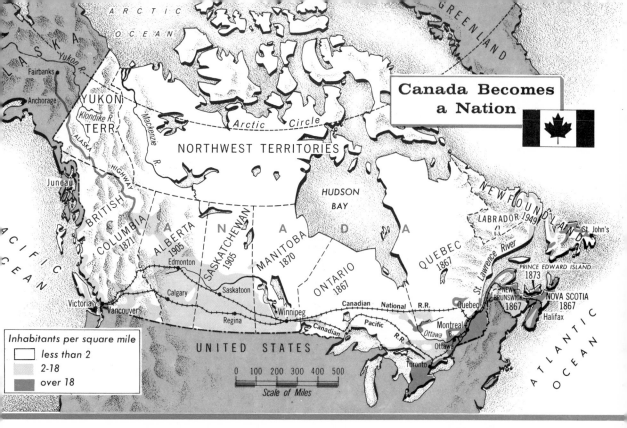

Canada Becomes
a Nation

Inhabitants per square mile
☐ less than 2
▨ 2-18
■ over 18

0 100 200 300 400 500
Scale of Miles

MAP STUDY (1) What are the provinces of present-day Canada? (2) When did each become a province? (3) What provinces did Canada include when it became a Dominion in 1867?

Have students compare density of population in Canada, Latin America

dian government soon bought up the company's rights to the land, and Great Britain turned over to Canada all the territory as far west as the Canadian Rockies. But the company kept its trading posts and its right to trade for furs.

Like the United States, Canada grew until its territory stretched from sea to sea. In the 1870's three new provinces were added to the Dominion. These were Manitoba, in the region north of the Dakota prairies; British Columbia, formed from Britain's share of the Oregon Territory; and Prince Edward Island, in the east. When the Canadian Pacific Railroad was completed across the continent, people began to throng into the western prairie region. In the early 1900's, the provinces of Alberta and Saskatchewan joined the Dominion. Finally, in 1949,

the people of Newfoundland voted to become part of Canada. Labrador, which belongs to Newfoundland, also became a part of Canada, but not as a separate province. Today Canada includes ten provinces and the Yukon and Northwest Territories. (See the map on this page.)

Canada becomes an independent and self-governing member of the British Commonwealth of Nations. "You must not think that Canada was completely independent after she became a Dominion," James King continues. "Even though we had our own government, Canada could not deal directly with foreign countries. Our foreign affairs were still controlled by Great Britain."

When World War I broke out in 1914, and Great Britain went to war with Germany, Canada also found herself at war.

(p. 659) and the United States   **653**   *(p. 432-3). Can the students explain why the areas of greatest density are where they are?*

THE BUILDINGS OF PARLIAMENT in Ottawa, the capital of Canada, stand in a beautiful park area along the Ottawa River.

own right. "We Canadians," says James King, "have close ties with Great Britain, but we are citizens of Canada. We are proud of our Canadian nationality, just as you Americans are proud of yours."

Canada's system of government differs somewhat from ours. We ask James if Canada has a form of government like that of the United States. "My country, like the United States, has a democratic government," he answers, "and our federal government is a union of provinces similar to your union of states. But our government works more like that of Great Britain."

The Canadian *Parliament*, which makes the laws, is made up of two houses — the *Senate* and the *House of Commons*. The members of the Senate represent the provinces rather than the people. They are not elected but are appointed for life. The members of the House of Commons, however, are elected by the people, and each member represents a certain portion of the population.

You may be surprised to learn that Canada, as a member of the Commonwealth

She was willing to fight on the side of the mother country, but wanted to be recognized as a nation. The Canadian government won the right to work as an equal with Great Britain and the other Allies in planning and directing the war. And when World War I ended, Canada signed the peace treaties as a separate country, not as a colony.

After the war Canadians wanted complete control of their foreign affairs. They were no longer willing to have the government in London deal with the United States and other countries on Canadian affairs. In 1931, the British government passed the *Statute of Westminster* which recognized Canada as an independent, self-governing member of the British Commonwealth of Nations. This was Canada's final step on her long road to independence. When World War II broke out, the Canadian government of its own choice declared war on Germany and Japan. Today Canada is an important nation in her

The fact that members **654** of the Canadian Senate are appointed for life may cause that body not to be representative of current political views in the provinces.

The Commonwealth of Nations

A number of former British possessions are now self-governing, equal partners with Great Britain in the Commonwealth of Nations. Canada, Australia, and New Zealand have been members for some time. India, Pakistan, and Ceylon became self-governing members in the 1940's and Ghana and Malaysia in the 1950's. Recent members of the Commonwealth include Nigeria, Sierra Leone, Cyprus, Tanzania, Jamaica, Trinidad-Tobago, Uganda, Kenya, Malawi, Malta, and Zambia. Ireland and South Africa are no longer members of the Commonwealth.

of Nations, has a governor-general who represents the king or queen of England. But the governor-general has no real authority over Canada. The actual head of the Canadian government, and the man who holds the real power, is the *Prime Minister*. Like the President of the United States, he is responsible for carrying out the laws. But he is also responsible for getting laws passed. The Prime Minister is not elected to that office but is chosen because he is the leader of the party which has a majority of members in the House of Commons.

In order to remain in office, the Prime Minister must have the support of the House of Commons. If a majority of the members votes against an important bill proposed by his party, he either resigns or calls for a new election. If in this election the opposition wins a majority of the members in the House, he must resign. The leader of the new majority party then becomes Prime Minister. "As you see," says James, "our system of government is somewhat different from yours, but it works well for Canada."

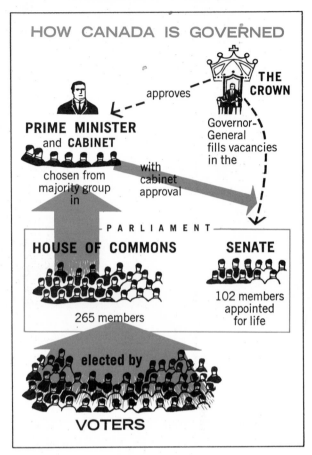

HOW CANADA IS GOVERNED

THE CROWN

PRIME MINISTER and CABINET — approves

Governor-General fills vacancies in the

chosen from majority group in

with cabinet approval

PARLIAMENT

HOUSE OF COMMONS

SENATE

265 members

102 members appointed for life

elected by

VOTERS

THE PRIME MINISTER, chosen with his cabinet from the legislative branch, is Canada's chief executive. The governor-general, representing the Queen, has little power.

CANADA DEVELOPS HER RESOURCES, INDUSTRIES, AND TRADE

Our neighbor to the north has been called a "great small nation." Canada is great in territory (ranking as second largest nation in the world) and great in natural wealth and in her rapidly growing industry and trade. But Canada's population is only one tenth that of our country, or about nineteen million people. In spite of her small population, Canada has become an important and prosperous nation.

Most Canadians are of French or British descent. As you look at the map on page 653, imagine a line running across Canada about two hundred miles north of the United States border. In the belt between this line and the border are located most of Canada's farms and towns and cities. About half of her people live in the eastern part of the belt between Lake Huron and Canada's largest city, Montreal.

Canadians, like Americans, are immigrants or descendants of immigrants. But while Americans represent many nationalities, most Canadians are of French or British descent. The French Canadians, who live for the most part in the province of Quebec, make up one third of Canada's population. Almost one half are of English, Irish, or Scottish stock. People with various other national backgrounds have also settled in Canada. In recent years

ALUMINUM is refined at this huge plant in British Columbia, 70 miles inland from the Pacific coast. A mountain river flowing down steep coastal mountains provides electric power.

Europeans uprooted from their homes by war or discouraged by conditions in their homeland have entered Canada in large numbers. They are drawn by the dream of living in a free country which offers them opportunities for a better life.

Canada develops its natural wealth. Few nations are as rich in natural resources as our northern neighbor. Canada's fertile soil has made it possible for her to become a great agricultural nation. Although she raises vegetables, fruits, and many kinds of grain, her most important crop is wheat. Like the United States, Canada has developed large-scale farming by using modern agricultural machinery. Enormous crops of wheat are grown on the fertile prairies west of the Great Lakes.

Canada has a large supply of most of the minerals needed in the world today. Canada, for example, leads the world in the production of nickel and asbestos. Petroleum, gold, copper, zinc, platinum, and lead are also produced in large quantities. In recent years vast new deposits of iron ore have been found in eastern Canada. This discovery is important not only to Canada but also to the United States, whose supplies of high-grade iron ore are shrinking each year. Of great importance in this atomic age are Canada's large supplies of uranium ore, which is used to produce atomic power. She has already become a leading country in the mining and refining of this valuable ore, much of which goes to the United States. No one knows the full extent of Canada's mineral resources, for new deposits of petroleum, iron ore, and uranium are still being discovered.

Canada's vast forests are another source of wealth. Canada produces large amounts of both lumber and wood pulp, used to make paper for newspapers and magazines. Plentiful supplies of fish and furs add to her wealth. The great inland waterway of the Great Lakes-St. Lawrence system furnishes water power as well as transportation. Along the river, power plants produce electric power in abundance for factories and mills. Inexpensive power has led to the development of many new industries in Canada.

Canada becomes an important trading and manufacturing nation. Since World War II, Canada's industries have increased at a tremendous rate. The largest industrial areas are in the provinces of Ontario,

A great deal of American capital is invested in Canada and has speeded the development of Canadian resources (see page 667).

A CANAL runs alongside the St. Lawrence River in this aerial view of Canadian locks in the St. Lawrence Seaway.

Quebec, and British Columbia. Among Canada's important manufactures are food products, iron and steel goods, chemicals, paper pulp and paper, wood products, and electrical equipment. Although Canada does not mine aluminum ore (bauxite), she ranks as one of the three leading countries in the production of aluminum. Industrial companies have found that it pays to import bauxite from other countries and refine it in Canada where electric power is cheap. Two of the largest aluminum refineries in the world are located in thinly settled parts of Quebec and British Columbia. Entire towns for the workers and their families have been built near these refineries.

Since Canada produces more food and manufactured products than her own people can use, she sells the surplus to other nations. In recent years Canada has become one of the most important trading nations in the world. A large part of Canada's exports go to the United States, the rest to Britain and other countries. In exchange for wheat, wood pulp, metals, and other products, Canada imports such things as heavy machinery, coal, textiles, coffee, tropical fruits, and so on. For

transportation of its products across the country, Canada has two transcontinental railroads as well as the St. Lawrence Seaway. Transportation by airplane has also increased rapidly in recent years.

Canada and the United States build the St. Lawrence Seaway. Before 1959, deep-sea ships were able to travel up the St. Lawrence only as far as Montreal. For many years the United States and Canada talked about extending this water route to allow ocean-going ships to reach the ports on the Great Lakes. Working together, the two countries began the construction of the St. Lawrence Seaway in 1954. Channels in the river were deepened; new locks and canals were built. Today ocean vessels can travel inland from the Atlantic to the important port of Chicago and even to the westernmost ports on Lake Superior. The St. Lawrence Seaway has benefited trade and industry in both Canada and the United States. As part of the Seaway project, huge electric-power plants were installed at International Rapids upstream from Montreal. These plants furnish electric power to industrial areas in Canada and to northern New York State and other regions on the American side.

**CHECK
UP**

1. (a) What areas did Canada include in 1850? (b) Why did Canadians begin to favor a union of the provinces? (c) How was such a union achieved?

2. (a) What provinces joined Canada after 1867? (b) How did the Statute of West-minster affect Canada? (c) How is Canada governed today?

3. (a) What is the national background of the Canadian people? (b) What natural resources does Canada possess? (c) How has Canada developed her trade and industry? (d) What is the importance of the St. Lawrence Seaway?

What Progress Have Latin American Nations Made Since Winning Independence?

We now turn to our neighbors in Latin America, the 20 republics south of the Rio Grande. As you learned in Chapter 10, most of the Spanish colonies and the Portuguese colony of Brazil had won their independence by 1825. To tell the story of each republic since then would require an entire book. But we need to know something about the countries south of us and the progress they have made since becoming independent. It is true that all the countries formed from the Spanish colonies inherited the language, the religion (Roman Catholic), and the customs of Spain. There are distinct differences, however, among the people and their ways of living in the Latin American countries. As you read about each of these countries, locate it on the map on the next page.

A GLANCE AT OUR LATIN AMERICAN NEIGHBORS

Mexico is our nearest neighbor to the south. Every year, thousands of Americans visit Mexico, the only Latin American country which shares a boundary with the United States. These visitors find Mexico a fascinating land of contrasts. They see many reminders of the Aztec and Spanish past, but they also find much in present-day Mexico that resembles our own way of living. Along with villages where people live much as they did in 1500, there are modern bustling cities. In Mexico City, up-to-date shops rub elbows with Spanish buildings that are centuries old. Many Mexicans still farm the land or turn out handmade articles as their ancestors did, but others work in factories, in oil fields, and in stores and businesses.

Mexico is rapidly becoming a modern nation. In recent years the government has done a great deal to educate its people, to provide irrigation systems for dry farm lands, and to help the farmer improve his crops. In addition to raising food crops and cattle for their own use, Mexicans grow large amounts of coffee and other tropical products for export. Mexico also grows half the world's supply of *sisal*, a cactus fiber used for making rope. Mining is important too. Mexico leads the world in silver production, and produces more petroleum than any other Latin American country except Venezuela. Mexican factories supply a variety of goods for the use of its people.

Six small republics occupy Central America. South of Mexico lies Central

Mexico has achieved greater economic and political stability than most republics in South America.

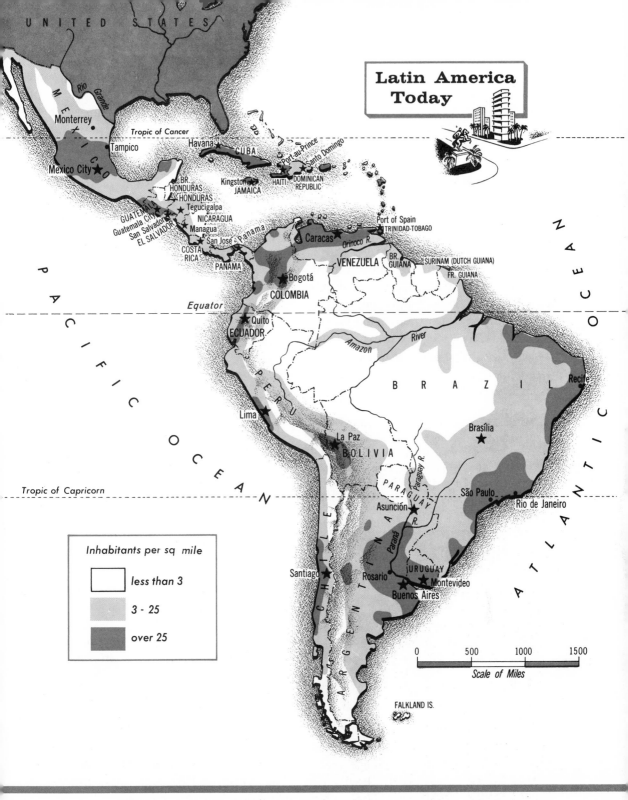

Latin America Today

UNITED STATES

Monterrey

Rio Grande

MEXICO

Tropic of Cancer

Tampico

Mexico City

Havana

CUBA

Port-au-Prince
Santo Domingo

BR.
HONDURAS

Kingston
JAMAICA

HAITI
DOMINICAN
REPUBLIC

GUATEMALA

Tegucigalpa
HONDURAS

NICARAGUA

Guatemala City
San Salvador
EL SALVADOR

Managua

San José

Costa
RICA

Panama

Port of Spain
TRINIDAD-TOBAGO

Caracas

Orinoco R.

VENEZUELA

BR.
GUIANA

SURINAM (DUTCH GUIANA)

FR. GUIANA

PANAMA

Bogotá

COLOMBIA

Equator

Quito

ECUADOR

Amazon

River

BRAZIL

Recife

PERU

Lima

La Paz

BOLIVIA

Brasília

Tropic of Capricorn

Paraguay R.

São Paulo

Rio de Janeiro

PARAGUAY

Asunción

Paraná R.

ARGENTINA

CHILE

Santiago

Rosario

URUGUAY

Montevideo

Buenos Aires

PACIFIC OCEAN

ATLANTIC OCEAN

Inhabitants per sq mile

	less than 3
	3 - 25
	over 25

0   500   1000   1500

Scale of Miles

FALKLAND IS.

MAP STUDY Name the nations of Latin America and their capital cities. Notice the three Guianas in northeastern South America and British Honduras in Central America. These territories retain ties with their mother countries. Jamaica and Trinidad-Tobago, in the West Indies, are self-governing members of the Commonwealth of Nations.

The Castro regime has worked to increase Communist influence in Central America and republics farther south.

660   THE UNITED STATES BECOMES A WORLD LEADER

America, the narrow strip of land that connects North and South America. Today it contains six Latin American republics — Guatemala, El Salvador, Honduras, Nicaragua, Costa Rica, and Panama. Panama was formerly a part of the South American republic of Colombia. But at the time we wanted to build the Panama Canal, Panama broke away and set up its own independent government (page 587).

These six republics, which stretch southward from Mexico, are alike in many ways. Their people .(except in Costa Rica) are of Indian or Indian and Spanish descent, and they earn their living mainly by farming. The fertile soil of these countries produces valuable tropical crops, of which bananas and coffee are the most important in world trade. They are alike in

MEXICO'S "LIBERTY BELL" is rung by the Mexican president in celebration of his country's independence day (page 206). The stamp shown here pictures the famous bell and was issued jointly by the United States and Mexico in 1960.

MEXICAN INDEPENDENCE 1810 1960

4¢ JOINT ISSUE MEXICO-UNITED STATES U.S. POSTAGE

another respect — most have not had orderly or democratic governments. In revolution after revolution strong men have seized office and ruled as dictators.

There are also some interesting differences among the six countries. For example, in Guatemala, half of the people are full-blooded Indians descended from the Mayan tribes. Their villages and their ways of life have changed very little since the time of Columbus. On the other hand, the people of El Salvador, the smallest republic, are a mixture of Spanish and Indian. Honduras is an undeveloped country often called the "banana republic," because bananas are its chief crop. Nicaragua, the largest country of Central America, has a history of frequent revolutions, while little Costa Rica is noted for its democratic government. All its citizens are required to vote, and all its children are required to go to school. Because there were few Indians in this region when the Spaniards conquered it, Costa Rica's people are largely of Spanish descent. And although Panama is independent, the Canal Zone, which is governed by the United States (page 588), runs across it.

The Caribbean Sea contains three island republics. To the northeast of Central America lie three more Latin American republics. You have already read about one of these, Cuba, in Chapter 28. The other two, Haiti and the Dominican Republic, are located on the island of Hispaniola. Centuries ago, Columbus founded a settlement in the eastern part of Hispaniola. After a time, Frenchmen settled in the western end of the island, and it became a French colony. The French started large coffee and sugar plantations there, and brought in Negro slaves to do the heavy labor. The slaves, who made up a vast majority of the population, were cruelly treated, and in the late

This was the first Latin American country to achieve independence.

1700's they rose in revolt against their French masters. Under the leadership of a remarkable Negro named Toussaint L'Ouverture (see page 198), they defeated the French and set up a Negro republic. Although French troops were sent to reconquer the island, savage fighting and deadly yellow fever forced them to leave. In 1804, years before the Spanish colonies on the mainland won their freedom, the Republic of Haiti became the first Latin American nation to gain independence. It is the only one of the Latin American republics whose people speak French. In time, the eastern part of Hispaniola became the Spanish-speaking Dominican Republic.

The mountains influence life in the Andean countries. The next group of Latin American republics lies in northern South America. These countries — Colombia, Venezuela, Ecuador, Peru, and Bolivia — all lie in the tropics. And through them all, from north to south, stretch the Andes Mountains, towering in lofty splendor. The mountains affect ways of living in these Andean republics, for they are both a help and a hindrance.

The Andes separate the narrow coastal plains from the steaming jungles of the interior and provide the cool highlands where most of the people live. However, the high mountains make travel and transportation in the Andean countries very difficult. There are few railroads, and even the building of roads across the mountains is a tremendous task. In the mountain regions of Ecuador, Peru, and Bolivia, the Indians depend upon the *llama* for carrying goods. This sure-footed beast can travel long distances over steep mountain trails with very little food and water. In the last few years, new roads have been built to connect the coast with the highlands and the jungle region beyond. And airplanes make up for the lack of trains,

A GIRL IN EL SALVADOR lays out sisal fiber to dry in the sun. The fibers come from the spikes of a cactus plant that grows in several Latin American countries.

carrying passengers and freight of all kinds back and forth from the seacoasts.

Farming is important in the Andean countries. Tropical farm products such as coffee, bananas, cotton, sugar, and cacao (kuh-*kah'*oh) are grown in the coastal regions and on the lower slopes of the Andes. Colombia is the second largest exporter of coffee in the world. Mining is also important in most of these countries. Bolivia is noted for its tin, Peru for copper, and Venezuela is one of the world's largest oil producers. From Ecuador come lightweight balsa wood and the fine straw hats mistakenly called "Panama hats."

In all the Andean countries there is a small Spanish upper class. Many Negroes live in the seaport towns of Venezuela and Colombia. In the mountains of Ecuador, Peru, and Bolivia the people are largely pure-blooded Indians, descendants of the Incas and other tribes. They speak their native languages and live in much the same way that their ancestors did hundreds of years ago.

The most distant Latin American countries lie in a temperate region. In the southern part of South America is still another group of republics — Chile, Argentina, Uruguay, and Paraguay. Paraguay, a hot, inland country, does not have much in common with the other three republics. Two long and bitter wars with other South American states killed off large numbers of her men. Since then, Paraguay has been a backward country and has not made much progress in developing her resources. Chile, Argentina, and Uruguay, on the other hand, are forward-looking Latin American nations. All lie in the temperate zone and their climate is cool and stimulating. Because their seasons are opposite to ours, their people enjoy June weather in December. Although people of Spanish descent still make up the bulk of their population, thousands of other Europeans have settled in these three countries within the last hundred years.

Chile. Glancing at the map, you will see that Chile occupies a long, narrow strip between the Andes and the Pacific Ocean. Four fifths of its people, however, live in a sunny valley between the Andes and another range of mountains near the coast. Here grains, vegetables, and fruits of all kinds are grown. Much of Chile's wealth comes from its valuable mineral deposits. Nitrate, used for fertilizer, is found in the northern desert. Most of the world's supply of iodine is produced in Chile as a by-product of the nitrate industry. Chile is also a leading producer of copper. In recent years manufacturing has grown rapidly in this Latin American country.

Argentina. Argentina shares the southern part of South America with Chile. In size it is greater than the part of the United States east of the Mississippi. Its capital, Buenos Aires, is the largest city in South America and one of the largest in the entire Western Hemisphere. Argentina is noted for its vast *pampas* (prairies), where cattle and sheep are raised. In earlier days the gauchos (*gow'chose*), or Argentine cowboys, roamed the pampas with huge herds of cattle in much the same way as

POWER for new industries is supplied by this hydroelectric plant recently built in a mountain canyon in Peru.

TWIN TOWERS rise over the new Congressional buildings in Brasília. Brazil's senators meet under the dome at left; the other house of the Congress under the inverted dome at right.

American cowboys rode our western plains. The people of Argentina are mostly of Spanish and Italian descent. They export large quantities of beef and lamb, and they raise great crops of wheat, corn, and other grains. Meat packing, the manufacture of meat by-products, and the processing of leather are important industries. Efforts to expand other kinds of industries in recent years have brought about financial troubles in Argentina.

Uruguay. Uruguay is the smallest South American republic. In many ways it is an Argentina on a small scale, because it, too, raises sheep and cattle, wheat and corn. Uruguay's standard of living is high, and education is free through college. Its people enjoy advantages such as old-age pensions and medical care for the poor, which are not common in Latin America. Uruguayans are proud of their modern country and their up-to-date and democratic government.

Brazil is the giant of South America. Finally we come to Brazil, the largest Latin American country in size and population. After winning its independence from Portugal (Chapter 10), Brazil was ruled by emperors for many years. It was not until the late 1880's that the last emperor was forced out and a republic called the United States of Brazil was established. As the map shows, Brazil borders on every South American country except Chile and Ecuador. It stretches from the vast hot basin of the mighty Amazon River in the north to the cool grasslands of the south.

Brazil has a wealth of natural resources, with its fertile soil, plentiful rainfall, rushing rivers, dense tropical forests, and enormous mineral deposits. Manganese ore, used in hardening steel, is mined in large quantities for export to the United States. Brazil has vast stores of iron ore which it has only recently begun to develop. It also has the largest steel mill in South America. The coastal rivers have been harnessed to produce electric power, and manufacturing has become increasingly important. It has been said that Brazil can grow almost every crop known to man. Brazil is the world's biggest coffee producer, and its sugar crop is one of the largest in the world. Cotton and cacao are also important crops. In recent years, soaring prices, a dependence on foreign loans, and other financial problems have plagued Brazil.

Brazil has several important cities. São Paulo (sown *pow'*loh) is the leading industrial center. Everyone has heard of Rio de Janeiro, the most important port

Uneven economic development (industrial São Paulo to subsistence farming in the northeast) poses a problem for Brazil.

LATIN AMERICAN NATIONS DEPEND ON TRADE WITH U. S.

TOTAL EXPORTS
← Sold to the U.S. →

Panama
Colombia
Haiti
Mexico
Costa Rica
Brazil
Chile
Peru
Argentina

0 10 20 30 40 50 60 70 80 90 100%

Per cent of total

PERCENTAGES show how representative Latin American nations depend on the United States to buy their products.

and for many years the capital of Brazil. Recently, a wholly new capital city, called Brasília, has been built hundreds of miles inland. Brazil hopes to open up its vast inland regions so that people from overcrowded areas can make new homes and develop rich natural resources never before touched.

PROGRESS HAS BEEN DIFFICULT IN LATIN AMERICA

After reading about our neighbors to the south, you may wonder why they have not moved forward more rapidly since winning their independence over a century ago. We have already seen that Latin Americans had no chance to govern themselves as long as they were ruled as colonies of European governments. When they became inde-

pendent, therefore, they were not prepared to manage their own affairs. Nor were the majority of Latin Americans given much chance to improve their way of life. During these years, for the most part, there were only two classes of people in Latin American countries. A small upper class owned most of the land and ran the government for their own benefit. A large lower class of peons worked on the great estates. The peons were miserably poor and unable to read or write. They lived and died on the land with no hope of owning any of it for themselves. There was little effort to develop natural resources or to build up industries. Few people belonged to what we would call the middle class — farmers who owned their own land, shopkeepers, and so on.

One-man governments have been bad for Latin America. Perhaps the greatest drawback to Latin American progress was bad government. When the people became independent, they wanted a democratic form of government like that of the United States. The constitutions of the new republics called for the election of presidents and legislatures. But true democracy depends on more than just a plan of government. Unfortunately, there were men who cared more about gaining power than safeguarding such liberties as free elections, free speech, and freedom of the press. So at one time or another in almost every country of Latin America selfish and ambitious men have seized control of the government by force. Although they have had the title of president, most of them have been all-powerful dictators. Few of them have had much interest in the welfare of the people.

Revolutions are still not uncommon. Under such leaders it is no wonder that some nations of Latin America have made little progress. There have been frequent revolutions in these countries. Usually these have come about when a strong leader overthrows a dictator in power and then sets up his own dictatorship. Such revolutions usually have had little effect upon the lives of the people. But sometimes the people themselves have risen against a hated dictator and overthrown his government. You read in Chapter 29 how the Mexican people revolted against a powerful dictator in 1910, and how they finally gained a more democratic government. In Argentina the people had for many years enjoyed a democratic government and certain rights as citizens. Then, after World War II, a dictator-president named Perón gained control of the government. In 1955, however, Perón was forced out by a revolution. Since 1950, there have also been popular uprisings in Colombia, Venezuela, Cuba, and the Dominican Republic. As long as dictators are able to gain control of governments in Latin America, revolutions against them will probably continue.

Latin American countries are making progress. In spite of the difficulties we have mentioned, some countries of Latin America have managed to move forward. One reason is that the middle class in these countries is growing larger. Mexico, Costa Rica, Colombia, Chile, Argentina, Brazil, and Uruguay have become modern nations. Although a few Latin American presidents today are still the "strong man" type, most countries have learned to choose their presidents in orderly elections, that is, by "ballots, not bullets."

Today Latin American countries realize the importance of education and a better standard of living for their people. The governments are building roads, schools, and hospitals; they are training doctors, nurses, and teachers. They are also working to improve farming methods and are developing industries and trade. Although much of the land is still held by wealthy landowners, more and more ordinary people are being given the opportunity to own their own land. Mexico has been a leader in breaking up the large estates and dividing the land among the people who work it. Yet progress is spotty. Most of the Latin American republics lack the wealth or capital to make needed reforms and to develop modern industry. Progress is particularly difficult in those countries where large numbers of Indians live in remote areas and follow the centuries-old ways of their forefathers.

New problems arise. In recent years the Latin American countries have faced the problem of a rapid rise in population. Even where progress has been made in industry and agriculture, these countries are finding that their production cannot keep up with the huge increase in population. As a result, their cities are becoming overcrowded, and more and more people are not getting adequate food, clothing, and shelter. One answer to this problem would be to develop the vast unsettled areas of South America and to make more use of the continent's rich natural resources. But few of the Latin American countries have the money to do this.

CHECK UP

1. (a) In what ways is Mexico becoming a modern country? (b) What are the six republics of Central America? (c) How are they alike? (d) How are they different?

2. (a) What are the three republics in the Caribbean? (b) Name the five Andean republics. (c) How does geography affect life in the Andean countries?

3. (a) Which South American republics lie in the temperate zone? (b) What are the important resources of each? (c) Why is Brazil important?

4. (a) Why have many Latin American countries found it difficult to achieve stable, democratic governments? (b) What other difficulties have these countries faced? (c) In what ways have they made progress?

The fact that population is increasing more rapidly than productivity creates a problem in many Latin American countries.

So far in this chapter we have learned about the growth of Canada and Latin America. Now we want to know something of their relations with our own country Let us first consider our northern neighbor, Canada.

AMERICANS AND CANADIANS LEARN TO SETTLE DISPUTES PEACEFULLY

Arguments between two countries often lead to war. At various times disputes have arisen between the United States and Canada which might have led to trouble. Because the two countries wanted peace, however, they have been willing to talk over their differences and settle them without war. The friendly relations between these two neighboring countries over the last 150 years can hardly be matched elsewhere in the world.

An unfortified boundary aids peace. Many nations of the world guard their borders with soldiers and guns, but Canada and the United States are proud that the border they share is unarmed. The idea of a peaceful border began back in the early 1800's when Canada was still a colony of Great Britain. In 1817, both the United States and Britain had armed ships on the Great Lakes. Believing it was not necessary to guard the boundary between two nations that truly wanted peace, they signed an agreement forbidding armed ships on the lakes (except for a few gunboats to keep order when necessary). This was the first step toward establishing an unarmed border between the two countries.

Later the idea of a peaceful border was extended to the land boundaries as well. This was made possible by the peaceful settlement of several disputes affecting Canada and our own country. (1) One dispute was over the northern boundary of the Louisiana Purchase. In 1818 Great Britain and the United States signed a treaty establishing the 49th parallel of latitude as the boundary line from northern Minnesota to the Rockies. (2) In the late 1840's, you recall, rivalry over the Oregon Country almost led to war. Again, the United States and Great Britain agreed to a peaceful settlement which divided Oregon at the 49th parallel. This extended the boundary between the United States and Canada from the Rocky Mountains to the Pacific Ocean. (3) Meanwhile, another dispute had broken out over the boundary between Canada and the northeastern part of the state of Maine. In 1842, this quarrel also was settled by a treaty dividing the disputed land between the United States and Canada. Today the long 4000-mile border between the two countries is a friendly border without forts, guns, or warships.

Later disputes are ironed out. As might be expected, Canada and the United States had other disputes. One disagreement was over fishing rights. American fishermen had been following the schools of mackerel as they moved north into Canadian waters off the coast of Newfoundland. Canadian fishermen claimed that Americans had no right to fish in Canadian waters, and violent arguments had taken place. This was one of several problems which were dealt with in a treaty in 1871. The United States agreed to pay for the use of Canadian fishing grounds. A commission was appointed to decide how much should be paid.

Still later, an argument developed over the boundaries of the Alaskan panhandle,

Canadians have sometimes wondered whether the **666** great "flow" of United States publications and radio and television programs into their country tends to impose our standards and tastes on them.

GOLD SEEKERS had to pack their supplies over treacherous snow-covered mountains to get to the Klondike. This is an actual photograph of Klondike prospectors taken in the 1890's.

that narrow strip of land which extends southward along the Pacific. (Look at the map on page 653.) Gold had been discovered in the Klondike, a region of Canada next door to Alaska. Canadians wishing to reach the gold fields from the Pacific coast first had to cross the Alaskan panhandle, which was American territory. Canadians claimed parts of the panhandle which would have permitted the miners to land directly on Canadian soil. This question, too, was submitted to a commission, and the decision was in favor of the United States. Although Canadians were not pleased by this decision, they accepted it.

TRADE AND DEFENSE HAVE BOUND THE UNITED STATES AND CANADA CLOSELY TOGETHER

Canada and the United States are friendly neighbors who in recent years have realized that they are important to each other in many ways.

Trade and business ties grow. For one thing, both countries profit from trading with each other. Canada has many raw materials which Americans need. Among these are nickel, high-grade iron ore, and uranium. Canada, on the other hand, depends on the United States for many of the manufactured goods she needs. In recent years, almost three fourths of all the

goods Canada has bought have come from our country, while the United States has bought over a half of Canada's exports.

Canada is important to American business in other ways. Many large American industries, such as the Ford Motor Company, have branches in Canada. These branches manufacture in Canada products for use in that country. American capital invested in Canada is helping to develop its new industries, such as the iron and steel, petroleum, and fast-growing aluminum industries.

Canada and the United States cooperate in the defense of the Western Hemisphere. Canada and the United States are important to each other in another way — in the defense of the Western Hemisphere. When World War II started, Canada became a vital part of this defense. Located between Alaska and the United States, she was in the path of any invasion from the north. Both countries worked together on plans for defending North America. The Alaska Highway was rushed through Canada to Alaska for military use. Preparations were also made to defend the Canadian as well as the American Pacific coast. Fortunately, the enemy did not attempt to invade the mainland of North America.

Since World War II, the defense ties of these two North American countries have

Canada, however, has been reluctant to have Canadian soil.

American atomic weapons made available on

U.S. COAST GUARD ICEBREAKERS, like the one above, keep navigation open through the frozen waters of the Arctic Ocean so that supplies may reach DEW Line radar stations (right).

grown even closer. Both Canada and the United States are important members of the North Atlantic Treaty Organization. Together they maintain a radar warning system stretching across arctic Canada from Alaska to Greenland. The air forces of the two countries co-operate in guarding the skies along this DEW (Distant Early Warning) Line. Such joint efforts are extremely important in these days of rocket missiles and bitter rivalry between Communist and free-world nations.

The basic ties between Canada and the United States remain firm. From time to time, even the best of friends have differences of opinion. In recent years, as Canada has "grown up" as a nation, her people have had an increasing desire to control their own affairs. Canadians, for example, realize how much the investment of huge sums from our country has helped Canada to become a leading industrial nation. But they wish the actual management of Canadian industry to be in their own hands. Canadians have felt that America's plans for giving surplus food to some countries has hurt the sale of Canadian

farm products abroad. Canadians have also been troubled because of the flood of books and magazines from the United States and the American radio and television programs which the air waves carry into Canadian homes.

In short, some Canadians feel that these developments tie their country too closely to our policies and influence the Canadian way of life. But the fact remains that Canadians and Americans are much alike in their outlook and way of life. As President Kennedy said during a visit to Canada in 1961, "Geography has made us neighbors. History has made us friends. Economics has made us partners; and necessity has made us allies."

THE UNITED STATES ADOPTS THE GOOD NEIGHBOR POLICY

Why were relations with Latin America unfriendly in the early 1900's? Relations with Latin America have been more difficult than with Canada. One reason, of course, is that the United States has had to deal not with one government but with

This quotation states the picture perfectly.

twenty. More important, however, is the fact that our actions have not always seemed friendly to Latin America. Starting with President Theodore Roosevelt, our government interfered in Latin American nations which were having trouble managing their affairs (page 597). Marines were sent to Nicaragua and the Caribbean countries to keep order. The United States acted as a policeman in Latin America for about twenty-five years. However good the reasons for this policy may have seemed at the time, it caused the Latin American nations to fear and dislike our country. Our government began to realize the importance of gaining the good will of our neighbors to the south. But the United States could not expect good will while our marines were still stationed in some of these neighbor republics.

The United States adopts the Good Neighbor Policy. In the 1920's and '30's, three American Presidents took steps to improve relations with Latin America. Calvin Coolidge withdrew marines from the Dominican Republic. He also sent an ambassador to Mexico whose friendly attitude did much to improve relations between the two countries. Later, Herbert Hoover made a good-will visit to eleven of the southern republics and spoke for better understanding between Latin America and the United States. To prove his good faith, Hoover recalled the marines from Nicaragua.

When Franklin D. Roosevelt became President in 1933, he announced in his inaugural address that the United States would not interfere in Latin American affairs. Instead it would follow the "policy of the good neighbor — the neighbor who resolutely respects himself and, because he does so, respects the rights of others."

Actions speak louder than words. Franklin Roosevelt soon proved that he

meant what he said. When the Cubans revolted to overthrow a dictator in the 1930's, the United States for the first time did not send American troops to keep order. What is more, the United States gave up the right to interfere in Cuban affairs which it had secured when Cuba became independent (page 583). As another proof of our Good Neighbor Policy, the last marines on Latin American soil were withdrawn from Haiti.

Still another test of our new policy had to do with Mexico. In 1938, the Mexican government, acting under its constitution, took over the oil wells and other oil property belonging to American and British oil companies. This was an almost unheard-of thing for any Latin American government to do and could easily have led to serious trouble. It is true that the Mexican government offered to pay the oil companies for their property. But the price offered was only about one sixth of what these oil properties were thought to be worth. Rather than go to war, however, the United States government asked the oil companies to accept the lower price. This was another proof that our country was sincere in its wishes to become a good neighbor of the Latin American republics.

THE AMERICAN REPUBLICS SEEK TO WORK TOGETHER

As long ago as 1889, the republics of the Western Hemisphere made a small beginning toward working out in a peaceful manner problems that arose among them. In that year delegates from the various American republics met at Washington, D.C., to discuss questions of trade and the settlement of disputes between nations. Since that time, a number of Pan American[1] (or inter-American) Conferences have

[1] *Pan* means "all."

This explains why the United States in the early 1960's found it difficult to oppose the Communist take-over in Castro's Cuba.

How Our Approach to Latin America Has Changed

Monroe Doctrine

"Hey, leave them alone! We don't want any trouble in this neighborhood from you Europeans!"

Early 1900's

"You'd better let me run your business for a while so you won't get into any more trouble."

been held in different national capitals. Matters of importance to the member-nations are discussed and acted upon.

The Pan American Conferences promote understanding. At first these conferences were not very friendly affairs. They were controlled almost entirely by the United States, and the United States was not popular in Latin America. But when the Seventh Pan American Conference met in the capital of Uruguay in 1933, there was a change for the better. For the first time a real feeling of friendliness and co-operation developed among the delegates. Our Secretary of State declared that the United States, as a good neighbor, was willing to discuss any questions the delegates of other countries wished to bring up.

At this conference all the nations, including the United States, signed an important declaration. It stated that no nation had the right to meddle in the affairs of any other nation. By signing this declaration, our government showed clearly that

the United States had given up its policy of interfering in the affairs of Latin America. With this change in the attitude of our government, the conferences became meetings where all the delegates shared equally in the discussions.

The Pan American Union encourages friendship among the American republics. One significant result of the first inter-American conference was the establishing of the Pan American Union. The Union has its headquarters in a beautiful marble building in Washington, D.C., and is supported by funds contributed by the member-nations. It carries on many activities to encourage co-operation among its members and performs many services for them. For instance, the Pan American Union gives information on almost any subject connected with the American nations — their trade, crops, new methods of farming, education, tropical diseases, wages in the various countries, and music, art, and literature of the Americas. Countries wishing to improve their trade, their

Good Neighbor Policy

"I'm going to swear you all in as deputies, all right? Then we'll all keep order together in this hemisphere."

Cold War

"Well, what are we going to do about him? I'll bet that Communist was the one who put him up to making trouble for us!"

schools, or the health of their people can learn from the Union what other member-nations have accomplished.

Knowledge of other countries and peoples leads to better understanding. For this reason the Union has done a great deal to increase friendship and understanding among the countries of the Americas. Among other things, it encourages the exchange of students and teachers between the United States and Latin America. The Union also publishes an interesting magazine called *Américas*. It is printed in three languages — English, Spanish, and Portuguese — and gives news of what is going on throughout the Americas.

The American republics work together in the face of common danger. In recent years inter-American conferences have reached a series of agreements for keeping peace in the Western Hemisphere:

(1) All the nations have signed treaties agreeing that disputes between American republics are to be settled by arbitration and not by force. There have been several

times when this agreement has prevented war between two countries or stopped a war already started.

(2) When World War II broke out in Europe, it became clear that if a warlike nation should attack anywhere in the Americas, the entire Western Hemisphere would be in danger. The American republics pledged themselves to stand together against attack on any of them. After the Japanese attacked Pearl Harbor and the United States went to war with the Axis Powers, the Latin American republics stood by their promise. Eighteen of them broke off friendly relations with Germany, Japan, and Italy, and fourteen of them declared war on the Axis countries.

(3) After the war, as you read on page 640, the American nations made further agreements to aid each other in case of attack and to resist Communist activities within their borders.

The Organization of American States is formed. In 1948, an inter-American conference held at Bogotá, Colombia, took

The larger Latin American republics, however, **671** have been reluctant to take firm action against Communist Cuba.

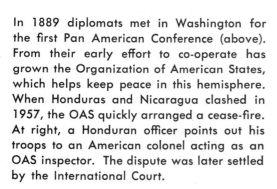

In 1889 diplomats met in Washington for the first Pan American Conference (above). From their early effort to co-operate has grown the Organization of American States, which helps keep peace in this hemisphere. When Honduras and Nicaragua clashed in 1957, the OAS quickly arranged a cease-fire. At right, a Honduran officer points out his troops to an American colonel acting as an OAS inspector. The dispute was later settled by the International Court.

a very important step. It formed the Organization of American States, which included the United States and the 20 Latin American republics. (Canada does not belong to the Organization of American States, though she has been invited to join.) The Organization of American States (OAS) holds regular inter-American conferences every five years. To deal with important matters which may come up in the meantime, there is a Council which is composed of a representative from each nation. Also, the foreign ministers of the member nations may hold meetings to deal with emergency situations. The day-to-day work of the OAS is carried on by the Pan American Union.

The OAS seeks to deal with various problems affecting the American republics. Trade is one of these problems. The Latin American nations want to increase the amount of goods they export. By selling more of their products, they can buy more

The Latin American countries have discussed has been done in Western Europe.

of the manufactured goods they need. But their export trade is handicapped in several ways.

Many Latin American countries, for example, rely on one product — such as coffee or bananas — as their chief export. If world prices drop, or if there is less demand for these products, trade falls off and these countries suffer. Trade *between* Latin American countries is limited because many of them produce the same crops or goods for export. Not only do they have little to offer to one another, but several countries may try to sell the same products to the same customers outside Latin America. About fifteen Latin American countries, for instance, compete in selling coffee to Europe and the United States.

Another serious problem facing Latin American governments is the need to improve living conditions for their people. They want to build better roads, better houses, and more schools. To do this, how-

the creation of a "Common Market," much as

ever, requires money they do not have. The OAS has been working out plans for borrowing the funds they would need, the loans to be paid back later. If the American republics can co-operate in solving their trade and other problems, the result will be a stronger and more prosperous Western Hemisphere. The first and foremost purpose of the OAS, however, is to settle disputes and help maintain the peace of the Western Hemisphere.

The cold war affects Latin America. The creation of the Organization of American States marked a high point in improving relations between the United States and its southern neighbors. But these friendly ties have been severely tested during the cold war years. Since World War II, there has been increasing unrest among the Latin American people. For one thing, after the war Latin America lost some of its foreign markets. Furthermore, the demand of Latin American people for a higher standard of living meant that their governments had to do more to develop their resources, industries, and trade. Looking at their prosperous northern neighbor, Latin Americans were inclined to blame the United States for not purchasing more of their products. And while the United States gave foreign aid to Latin American governments, until recently our government paid less attention to Latin American needs than it did to the new nations in Asia and Africa. Under these conditions, anti-American feeling spread among Latin Americans.

During the 1950's, too, the Communists sought to take advantage of discontent and the desire for a higher standard of living among Latin Americans. Whenever possible, Communist groups tried to stir up feelings against the "Yanquis." By blaming the United States for Latin American problems, the Communists hoped to convince

HUGE PICTURES of Fidel Castro and Lenin, a Russian Communist hero, are displayed at a parade of Soviet-built military vehicles in Havana, Cuba.

Latin Americans that they should form closer ties with Soviet Russia and Red China. This purpose was shown most clearly in Cuba.

A serious crisis arises in Cuba. Early in 1959, a revolutionary leader named Fidel Castro succeeded in overthrowing a dictator in Cuba. At first Americans were inclined to sympathize with Castro because he promised the Cubans a democratic government. As time went on, however, sympathy for the hero of the Cuban revolution dwindled. Castro postponed elections and drew steadily closer to Soviet Russia. He hurled a continuous stream of threats and insults at the United States. Americans in Cuba were imprisoned, and American property was seized. At first, the United States government tried to ignore this situation, but matters only became

It is unfortunate that countries which need foreign capital to develop resources often impose conditions that tend to keep out private capital.

worse. Our government finally faced the fact that the Communists might gain a stronghold less than a hundred miles from our shores. From Cuba the Communists could step up their campaigns against the United States in other Latin American countries.

The United States breaks with Cuba. The foreign ministers of the countries belonging to the Organization of American States met in 1960 at San José, Costa Rica. They issued a warning to the Communists not to meddle in the affairs of Latin America. But the Cuban crisis grew worse rather than better as Soviet Russia proclaimed its support of Castro. In January, 1961, the United States broke off diplomatic relations with Cuba.

Meanwhile, many Cubans had fled from Castro's dictatorial rule to seek refuge in the United States. Then, in April, a force of Cuban exiles landed in their native country, hoping the people would join them in an uprising. But within a few days Castro's troops defeated the rebel landing force. The failure of the rebellion against Castro was more than a bitter disappointment to Cubans who wanted their country to be free. It was also a setback to the efforts of the United States to keep communism out of the Western Hemisphere. Our government was criticized by some because it had encouraged the invasion plans of the Cuban exiles; by others it was criticized for not having provided adequate support to make the invasion successful.

The OAS takes action against Cuba. The Cuban government continued its war of words against the United States. Castro finally publicly declared that he was a Communist and that he intended to make Cuba a Communist state. Now it became clearer than ever that the Communists were strengthening their grip on Cuba. The number of Russian and Chinese technical experts in Cuba increased. Moreover, the Communists even seemed to be taking over dictatorial powers formerly held only by Castro. Those who criticized the government were silenced, and the flow of Cuban refugees to the United States continued.

In early 1962, Cuba was the major topic of a meeting of the OAS in Uruguay. Many of the Latin American republics, especially the small countries of Central America, had become fully aware of the dangers of having a Communist neighbor. To show the world that communism was unacceptable in the Americas, a majority of the OAS members voted to exclude Cuba from participation in that organization. Later, when Communist Russia stepped up its military aid to Cuba, the United States warned that it would use force to defend countries threatened by Cuba.

The Alliance for Progress is launched. Meanwhile, the OAS had approved a program proposed by President Kennedy to speed up economic growth and to improve social conditions in Latin America. Under this program, called the *Alliance for Progress,* the United States pledged to Latin America a greatly enlarged amount of financial aid over a ten-year period. One important condition was that funds would go to those republics that showed they were willing to help themselves. Cuba, however, would not receive aid while it remained under Communist control.

The Alliance for Progress got off to a slow start, despite the urgent need for long-range development programs. Few of the Latin American countries worked out detailed plans for self-improvement. And reforms were opposed in many countries by the small groups who controlled most of the land and business.

CHECK
UP

1. (a) What is unusual about the border between the United States and Canada? (b) What were some of the disputes concerning

the American-Canadian border? (c) How was each settled? (d) What other disputes involving the United States and Canada were peacefully settled?

2. (a) How are Canada and the United States important to each other in trade and industry? (b) How have they co-operated in defense of this hemisphere?

3. (a) How did the Latin American countries regard the American policy of intervention in the early 1900's? (b) What was the Good Neighbor Policy? (c) How was this policy put into effect in the 1930's?

4. (a) How have the Pan American Conferences affected relations between the United States and the Latin American republics? (b) How have the American republics agreed to co-operate for defense? (c) What is the purpose of the OAS?

5. (a) What problems have at times hurt friendly relations between the United States and the Latin American countries since World War II? (b) Why has Cuba presented a special problem?

Check Up on Chapter 31

Do You Know the Meaning?

1. dominion
2. majority
3. uranium
4. tropics
5. temperate
6. llama
7. cacao
8. nitrate
9. pampas
10. gauchos
11. governor-general

Can You Identify?

1. 1818
2. 1867
3. 1889
4. 1931
5. Toussaint L'Ouverture
6. Perón
7. St. Lawrence Seaway
8. Good Neighbor Policy
9. DEW Line
10. OAS
11. Fidel Castro
12. Alaska Highway
13. Statute of Westminster
14. Pan American Union
15. British North America Act
16. Commonwealth of Nations
17. John A. Macdonald
18. Alliance for Progress

Can You Locate?

1. Ecuador
2. Ottawa
3. Ontario
4. Manitoba
5. Panama
6. Haiti
7. Alberta
8. Honduras
9. Nicaragua
10. Costa Rica
11. Quebec (province)
12. British Columbia
13. El Salvador
14. Uruguay

Can You Locate? (Cont.)

15. Saskatchewan
16. Newfoundland
17. Guatemala
18. Bolivia
19. Paraguay
20. Buenos Aires
21. Amazon River
22. Brasília
23. Dominican Republic

What Do You Think?

1. If Canada's government is independent of Great Britain, why does a governor-general still represent the British king or queen?

2. In several congressional elections in the 1950's, the majority of men sent to Congress belonged to a different political party from that of the President. This could not happen in Canada. (a) Why? (b) Do you favor the American or Canadian system? Why?

3. Why has industrialization in Canada been more rapid and successful than in the Latin American countries?

4. (a) Why do neighboring countries wish to attract United States investments? (b) Why are these countries nevertheless sometimes uneasy about such investments?

5. How have advances in science and medicine created problems for Latin American countries?

6. What would be the advantages of having Canada as a member of the Organization of American States?

Questions #2–5 should receive careful consideration.

Our Canadian neighbors. Citizens of Canada pride themselves on some customs and manners which are different from those of the United States. But actually the differences, except perhaps in Quebec Province, are few. It is easier to tell an Arizona cowboy from a native New Englander than it is to tell a Canadian wheat farmer from an American wheat farmer. Probably the finest portrayals of Abraham Lincoln in the movies and on the stage were made by Raymond Massey, who was born in Canada!

Opening the St. Lawrence Seaway. On April 25, 1959, the St. Lawrence Seaway was officially opened to traffic. A Canadian icebreaker was the first ship to enter the Seaway at Montreal. It was followed by a procession of ocean-going ships from many nations. Crowds waved from shore, and ships blew their whistles as the icebreaker moved slowly westward into the first of the Seaway's seven locks. At the same time another group of ships entered the western end of the Seaway to travel eastward. On June 26, President Eisenhower and Queen Elizabeth formally dedicated the St. Lawrence Seaway in a ceremony near Montreal. Later, the President and his wife were guests of Queen Elizabeth on a cruise in the royal yacht. At one point on the Seaway, the yacht passed ships of the Canadian and United States navies. A 21-gun salute was fired to honor the heads of the two nations. These were the first armed ships (except for a few gunboats) allowed on the waterway since 1817. At that time, you remember, the United States and Canada forbade warships on the waters between the two countries.

Brasília, city of the future. As you may know, our national capital is a *planned city.* That is, instead of "just growing" like most cities, Washington, D.C., was laid out and built according to a carefully prepared plan. A more recent planned city is Brazil's gleaming new capital, Brasília. This city rose from a wilderness in only three years. Before 1957, it was just a dream; in the spring of 1960, the government of Brazil started moving to the new capital. Brasília is located on a plateau 600 miles northwest of Rio de Janeiro, the old capital. The new city was carefully laid out, and designs drawn for every building. Roads had to be built; men, machines, materials, and equipment had to be transported. The thousands of workers had to be fed and housed. But Brazil's president was confident that these obstacles could be overcome.

Once the job started, all the workers, from the architects and engineers to the humblest laborer, caught the president's enthusiasm and the city began to take shape. Noted architects and designers made the capital a model of the finest modern design. The people live in superblocks (groups of apartment houses) which accommodate hundreds of families. Each superblock has its own elementary school and shopping center. A great deal of work still remains to be done, however. Building will go on in Brasília and people will continue to move in for years to come.

The location of Brasília was an effort to speed economic development of the interior. The great expense of building this city contributed to the inflation which plagues Brazil.

Americans Face the Challenge of
a Modern World

What this chapter is about —

In 1789, George Washington became the first President of a small country which had little influence in world affairs. Yet as leader of this new republic, Washington realized that he would have to face grave problems. As he left his Mount Vernon home to take up his new duties, he was filled with dread at quitting "a peaceful abode for an ocean of difficulties."

All our Presidents since Washington have carried heavy burdens, and many have had to make agonizing decisions. This has been especially true since the close of World War I. During the 1920's most Americans hoped to return to the kind of life they had known before the war broke

out. But during the 1930's, the United States was plunged into the worst depression in its history. Then in the early 1940's our country entered World War II.

When the fighting ceased, most Americans realized that the United States, as a leading power, could not withdraw from world affairs. They did, however, hope for a lasting peace. But this was not to be. The ambitions of the Communists to take over the world brought not only fighting in Korea but also years of cold war tension. In this chapter we shall learn how the Presidents since 1920 have dealt with difficult problems at home and abroad. We shall seek answers to these questions:

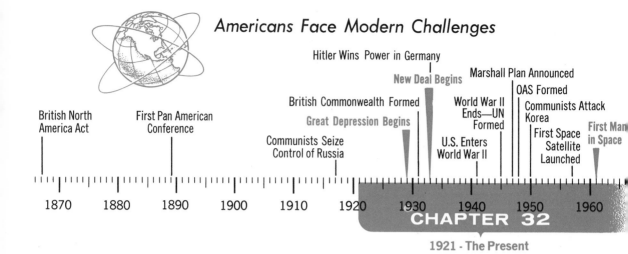

Americans Face Modern Challenges

British North America Act

First Pan American Conference

Communists Seize Control of Russia

British Commonwealth Formed

Great Depression Begins

Hitler Wins Power in Germany

New Deal Begins

U.S. Enters World War II

World War II Ends—UN Formed

Marshall Plan Announced

OAS Formed

Communists Attack Korea

First Space Satellite Launched

First Man in Space

1870   1880   1890   1900   1910   1920   1930   1940   1950   1960

CHAPTER 32

1921 - The Present

1. What goals did Presidents Harding, Coolidge, and Hoover seek?

2. What changes took place under President Franklin Roosevelt's "New Deal"?

3. How did Presidents Truman and Eisenhower deal with postwar conditions?

4. What challenges did Presidents Kennedy and Johnson face?

1   What Goals Did Presidents Harding, Coolidge, and Hoover Seek?

We have already learned that two American Presidents in the early 1900's took steps to solve some of the problems facing the American people (Chapter 27). Theodore Roosevelt and Woodrow Wilson were not alike in personality and they were leaders of different political parties. But both believed that the great problems of their day called for reforms. Then came World War I. Reforms were forgotten as the American people, led by President Wilson, devoted all their energies to winning the war.

President Harding seeks a return to "normalcy." By the time of the election of 1920, the nation's mood had changed. People wanted to forget everything connected with war — the death and destruction, the heavy taxes, the strain and the worry. Americans, in brief, wanted a chance to enjoy life. Warren G. Harding, a Senator from Ohio, was elected President on the Republican ticket in 1920. Harding was a genial, folksy person, who fully agreed with the views of most Americans. So the United States under Harding turned its back on reform at home and membership in the League of Nations abroad. The country, so it was said, wished to "get back to normal."

Calvin Coolidge favors less expense in government and non-interference in business. Before his term was completed, President Harding died. He was succeeded by the Vice-President, Calvin Coolidge of Massachusetts. Then, in 1924, Coolidge was elected President in his own right. A shrewd man who never wasted words, he was quite a different kind of person from Harding. Yet Coolidge, like Harding, was not a reformer. He believed that Americans should be left alone to live their lives without interference from the government. Coolidge lowered taxes and cut down government expenses. Under President Coolidge, several laws were passed to help business. A higher tariff, which had been put into effect under Harding, was continued.

During President Coolidge's administration, the country, except for the farmers, enjoyed great prosperity. Business activity and profits increased, and the incomes of many people rose. The Coolidge years were often referred to as "the Golden Twenties."

Herbert Hoover becomes President. In 1928, Herbert Hoover was elected President, the third Republican to be chosen since World War I. Hoover had been an engineer and possessed great organizing ability. During World War I, he had won fame as food administrator in the United States and as director of war relief in Belgium. Later, he had served as Secretary of Commerce under Presidents Harding and Coolidge.

Hoover won the election on a pledge to continue the prosperity which the country had enjoyed under the preceding Republican Presidents. Popular with businessmen, he believed firmly in leaving people and business free from government controls. But Hoover was no mere follower of Coolidge and Harding; he had ideas of his own. During his administration the great Hoover Dam was begun on the Colorado River, to provide electric power and water for irrigation. Hoover also made an important good-will visit to Latin America (page 669). His Committee on Social Trends made a thorough study of the social problems which Americans faced. If prosperity had continued,

For over thirty years President Hoover was a respected elder statesman.

HERBERT HOOVER

As food administrator during World War I, Hoover (shown below with beet-sugar producers) coped with wartime shortages, developing the skill he later used to organize postwar relief in Europe. The picture at left shows the former President dedicating a dam in California. Out of office, Hoover continued to be a spokesman for conservative Americans and served effectively on special government committees.

Hoover's term in office might have been remembered for its great achievements.

The Hoover years are overshadowed by a depression. Hoover had hardly settled down in the White House, however, when he was faced with the worst depression the country had ever known (page 472). Factories stood idle, their empty windows staring blankly at passers-by. Farmers became desperate when they could find no one to buy their crops even at the lowest prices. When farmers could no longer pay their debts, their farms were taken over by those to whom they owed money. Many farms were abandoned.

In the cities, millions of Americans wanted work but could not find it. Men and women stood in long lines to apply for the few jobs that were offered. The unlucky ones formed other lines to receive food and clothing from organizations which care for unfortunate people. Month after month, for one year, a second year, a third year, the distress grew worse.

The depression was not President Hoov-

er's fault, of course. It was the result of world-wide conditions beyond the power of any one man or country to prevent. Yet the President in office usually receives the credit when things go well with the country and the blame when things go wrong. President Hoover was the first President to use the power of the national government to try to stop a depression. But many people believed that he was not doing enough. When the election of 1932 came along, the voters in large numbers turned against President Hoover. They chose in his place Franklin D. Roosevelt, a Democrat who was a distant cousin of Theodore Roosevelt.

CHECK UP

1. (a) What did President Harding think the country needed after World War I? (b) What role did President Coolidge favor for the national government?

2. (a) What were some accomplishments of President Hoover's administration? (b) What great problem arose during his term?

For farmers depressed conditions began in the early 1920's.

What Changes Took Place Under President Franklin Roosevelt's "New Deal"?

Franklin D. Roosevelt had wide experience in public affairs. In many ways the early career of President Franklin D. Roosevelt was similar to the careers of other Presidents. Born in New York State, he went to college and studied law. He became interested in politics and served for two years in the New York legislature. In World War I he was Assistant Secretary of the Navy. Although he failed to be elected Vice-President in 1920, he later served two terms as Governor of New York.

In his career in public office, however, there was one unusual thing. When Franklin D. Roosevelt was 39 years old, he was stricken with polio. The doctors said his legs were so badly paralyzed that he might never walk again. But Roosevelt refused to give up. He triumphed over the disease, although it left him badly crippled. His uphill fight against polio not only strengthened Roosevelt's determination but also made him well-acquainted with sorrow and suffering.

HUNGRY PEOPLE stood in line for food when the depression of the 1930's threw millions out of work. Here a federal relief agency distributes potatoes.

Roosevelt tries to end the depression.
When Franklin D. Roosevelt became President, people were suffering and fearful of the future. Millions of men had lost their jobs, their homes, and their farms. Banks all over the country had closed their doors as panicky depositors tried to withdraw their savings. Roosevelt was determined to put all the power and wealth of the United States to work to end the depression. He said that he would try to protect Americans against the effects of depressions then and in the future. As he expressed it, the country needed a change — a *New Deal.*

In the early days of the New Deal, Congress passed a long list of laws at the request of President Roosevelt.

Agriculture. Government organizations were created to lend money to farmers. Laws were passed to encourage farmers to grow smaller crops so that prices would be higher and farmers would have larger profits (page 496).

Unemployment. For the unemployed the government tried to find work. Much of this work was on projects such as roads, dams, parks, and public buildings. A Civilian Conservation Corps (CCC) was organized to give work to the thousands of young men who could not get jobs. They lived in camps and worked at such tasks as clearing forests and planting trees. But in the public works projects, less useful work was sometimes arranged quickly, just to give the unemployed something to do. The government spent huge amounts of money to provide jobs. Other large sums supplied food and clothing and shelter to the families of those who could not find work.

Business and banking. Money was lent to businessmen, so that mines, mills, and stores could provide jobs. At the same time, laws were passed to regulate and control industry and business. The New Deal did not stop there. Because many Americans had lost their savings when banks failed, banking laws were passed to insure people's savings.

The New Deal adopts labor laws.
Many laws of the 1930's were passed just to lift the American people out of the depression. But there were several laws (like the law to insure people's savings) which are still important today. Two of these laws have to do with workingmen (page 481). President Roosevelt believed that workers should be protected in the right to join labor unions and to bargain collectively (in groups) with employers. In 1935, Congress passed the *National*

In discussing the New Deal it is important to stop-gap measures to relieve unemployment.

681

distinguish between permanent reforms and

Labor Relations Act (often called the Wagner Act), which stated that the government would protect these rights.

Roosevelt also believed that the country would be more prosperous if wages were increased and working hours reduced so that more men could be given employment. The *Wages and Hours Act* of 1938 said that the regular work week of all persons making goods to be sold in interstate commerce (outside the state where they were made) should be limited to 40 hours. It also said that the least a worker could be paid was 40 cents an hour. (This *minimum wage* has been increased several times since then.) If a man worked more than 40 hours, he was to be paid a higher rate for the extra work. The law also provided that as a general rule young people under sixteen should not be employed.

The Social Security Act is passed. One of the most important laws passed under President Roosevelt was the *Social Security Act* (1935). For years many people had been asking, "What would happen to me and my family if I should lose my job and could not get another one right away? Even if I am lucky enough to keep my job, what will I do when I am too old to work? I have not been able to save enough to support myself and my wife in our old age." These are serious problems which may affect any one of us.

Congress passed the Social Security Act in the belief that people should be protected against unemployment as well as poverty in old age. This act provides for the payment of certain amounts of money for as long as three or four months to workers out of a job. When workers retire, they are paid a monthly sum as long as they live. In order to get the money for these benefits, a certain percentage is taken out of the wages of each worker, and his employer contributes an equal amount. The states work with the federal government in the handling of unemployment payments. Old-age insurance, however, is the responsibility of the federal government. In recent years the Social Security system has included more people and provided more generous payments.

The New Deal helps to conserve natural resources. Like Theodore Roosevelt, Franklin D. Roosevelt was interested in the conservation of natural resources. Many of the laws passed to help the farmer included plans for conserving the soil. The CCC, which furnished work for many young men, also helped to protect our forests. The building of dams like Grand Coulee not only created more jobs but made possible flood control and the irrigation of large sections of land.

An important project started under the New Deal was the Tennessee Valley Au-

CCC WORKERS in doing useful conservation work also improved recreation areas. Here a young man builds a picnic fireplace at a campground.

FRANKLIN D. ROOSEVELT

A masterful speaker, "F.D.R." used the radio (left) for frequent "fireside chats" in which he urged Americans to support his New Deal program for ending the depression. As commander-in-chief of America's global operations in World War II, he visited the North African front (below), lunching with Generals Mark Clark (left) and George Patton (right).

thority (TVA). The TVA was a long-range plan to improve a whole region covering parts of seven southern states. The TVA provided for flood control, irrigation, soil conservation, and electric power. Also, the TVA was given authority to do other things which would improve living conditions in the Tennessee Valley.

The New Deal increases the cost and the power of the federal government. To carry out the many New Deal reforms, new government agencies were created. These agencies or boards hired thousands of additional workers and spent large sums of money. The government departments in Washington greatly expanded in size. Many Americans criticized the New Deal for spending too much money and piling up a huge debt. These people believed that the government was interfering too much with business. The TVA, for example, was criticized as providing unfair competition for private power companies. Critics

of the New Deal objected that the country was being governed by boards and bureaus in Washington. Furthermore, President Roosevelt was accused of building up a powerful government to keep the Democrats in power. In fact, most of the criticism of the New Deal was directed against Roosevelt himself. But the President also had strong admirers and supporters, especially among working people. Roosevelt was re-elected President in 1936, carrying every state except Maine and Vermont. Four years later, he was elected a third time, the only President in our history to be elected for more than two terms.[1]

Roosevelt becomes a world leader. World events brought President Roosevelt's New Deal to a close, just as World War I had ended Woodrow Wilson's New Freedom reforms. World War II, as you

[1] The Twenty-Second Amendment, added to the Constitution in 1951, prevents any future President from serving more than two terms.

There has been some sentiment in favor of repealing this Amendment because it reduces the control a President has over his party during his second term in office.

know, began in Europe in September, 1939. The United States remained neutral at first. But, as the fighting spread, Americans became increasingly aware that they might be forced to take part in the struggle. Our country's role in a world at war seemed more important than New Deal reforms at home.

The attack on Pearl Harbor brought the United States into World War II (page 627). Americans once again turned all their efforts toward winning a war. Under the President's leadership, the Allied leaders worked together for victory. Franklin D. Roosevelt was elected for a fourth term in 1944. But on April 12, 1945, less than a month before the surrender of Germany, the President died suddenly. Worn out by the responsibilities he had shouldered for many years, Roosevelt did not live to see the final victory for which he had worked so hard.

People felt strongly about Franklin D. Roosevelt, just as people in the 1830's did about Andrew Jackson. Roosevelt probably was the most loved and at the same time the most hated of recent American Presidents. Whatever the final verdict of history may be, the American people will remember him as their leader through a critical time of depression and war.

CHECK UP

1. (a) How did President Franklin Roosevelt try to help the farmers? (b) To find work for the unemployed? (c) To stimulate business and regulate banks?

2. (a) What laws were passed to protect workers? (b) How did the New Deal plan to conserve natural resources?

3. (a) How did the New Deal affect the cost and the power of federal government? Why? (b) How did President Roosevelt become a world leader?

---

3 How Did Presidents Truman and Eisenhower Deal with Postwar Conditions?

TRUMAN FACES POSTWAR CONDITIONS

With the death of Franklin D. Roosevelt, Harry S. Truman entered the White House. The new President was the seventh Vice-President to succeed to the highest office in the land because of the death of a President. Harry Truman had seen action as an artillery captain in World War I. After serving as a judge in Missouri, he was elected to the Senate in 1934 and re-elected six years later. Nominated for the vice-presidency in 1944, Truman had actually held that office only three months when he was summoned to lead the nation.

The end of World War II brings perplexing problems. The new President's first and most pressing task was to end World War II quickly and on satisfactory terms. The complete defeat of Germany came within a month, while the Japanese surrendered soon after atomic bombs fell on the cities of Hiroshima and Nagasaki in August, 1945.

Next, the Truman administration had to struggle with problems that arose when Americans changed back to peacetime living. In 1945 and 1946, millions of veterans came home and were discharged from the armed forces. Wartime rationing and price controls were abandoned. Industries shifted from producing war materials to making goods for peacetime use. But the public demanded more goods than industries could produce. Americans who had been denied many things during the war wanted them at once. With so much demand for too few goods, prices shot up. Labor unions demanded higher wages to meet the increased cost of living and frequently went on strike to obtain them. Inflation became an increasingly serious problem.

Truman wins the 1948 election. In the midst of these conditions, the presidential election of 1948 took place. The Democrats nominated President Truman. The Republicans named Thomas E. Dewey, Governor of New York, as their candidate. Almost every newspaper writer and public opinion poll predicted that Governor Dewey would win. But President Truman fought a vigorous campaign, speaking in almost every part of the country. He promised higher wages, more liberal labor laws, and equal rights for all Americans. His program also included help to elderly people, price controls, the building of inexpensive houses, and a government-supported health program. To the great surprise of the political experts, Truman won the election.

The President believed his victory proved that the people wanted the measures he had favored. Greatly encouraged, he asked Congress to approve such a program. He called it the *Fair Deal*. Some measures were adopted, providing for better housing, raising the minimum wage level, and expanding Social Security benefits. But Congress did not pass an equal rights law, repeal the Taft-Hartley labor law (page 481), or adopt a plan of health insurance, as President Truman had suggested. The Congresses elected in 1948 and in 1950 included more Demo-

PRESIDENT TRUMAN toured the country in 1948 to tell Americans what he thought were the issues of the election. Here he speaks from the platform of his campaign train.

crats than Republicans.[1] But on many issues some Democrats sided with the Republicans. For this and other reasons, President Truman could not get Congress to approve much of his Fair Deal program.

Truman seeks world peace through co-operation among nations. Meanwhile, President Truman had been wrestling with the problem of establishing world peace. Americans felt differently at the end of World War II than they had after World War I. They realized that trouble anywhere in the world might again plunge their country into a destructive war. They

[1] While our Presidents are elected every four years, all members of the House of Representatives and one third of the senators are elected every two years. (See Article I of the Constitution, pages A2–A4.)

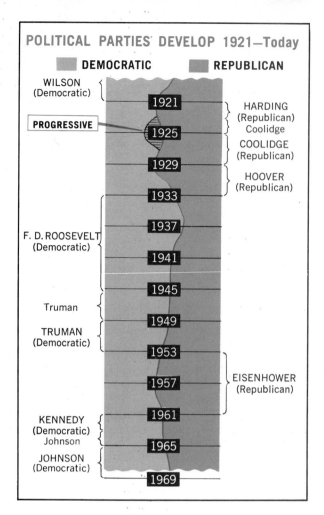

POLITICAL PARTIES DEVELOP 1921–Today

◼ DEMOCRATIC ◼ REPUBLICAN

WILSON
(Democratic)

1921 — HARDING
(Republican)
Coolidge

PROGRESSIVE

1925 — COOLIDGE
(Republican)

1929 — HOOVER
(Republican)

1933

1937

F. D. ROOSEVELT
(Democratic)

1941

1945

Truman

1949

TRUMAN
(Democratic)

1953

1957 — EISENHOWER
(Republican)

KENNEDY
(Democratic)
Johnson

1961

1965

JOHNSON
(Democratic)

1969

TWO PARTIES continue to win the support of most voters. This chart does not show such smaller groups as the Socialist Party, Prohibition Party, and States' Rights Democrats.

knew that Americans must be alert to what was happening outside their borders.

America's hopes of working with other nations for world peace met with disappointing setbacks. Always a strong supporter of the United Nations, President Truman tried to arrange through that organization for control of the dread power of the atomic bomb. But Communist Russia, as we have seen, would not agree to any plan which allowed outsiders to inspect her atomic plants. Russia also slowed up the making of peace treaties (pages 635, 640).

World conditions worsen. The development of the cold war interrupted President Truman's Fair Deal program. This was especially true after North Korean forces invaded South Korea (page 638). Once again, America faced the possibility of all-out war. Once more Selective Service Boards began sending young men into the armed forces and factories turned to making war materials. Once more the public faced shortages of goods, and the government began to control prices and wages. The American people were obliged to think seriously about the threat to peace and freedom from Communist Russia and China. The activities of Communist spies and sympathizers in our country led to stricter measures against those aiding the Communist cause.

Even before fighting broke out in Korea, President Truman had taken steps to create alliances which would strengthen the free world against possible attack (page 640). While making such preparations in case war could not be avoided, the United States also proposed plans for disarmament. But the United States and Soviet Russia could not agree on disarmament plans, so the two powers strove to develop more deadly atomic weapons. The President had announced in September, 1949, that Soviet Russia apparently had developed an atomic bomb. Soon after the United States had tested a hydrogen bomb in 1952, Russia also had successfully exploded a hydrogen bomb of its own. The development of such terrible weapons of destruction cast a long shadow over the world's outlook for peace.

PRESIDENT DWIGHT D. EISENHOWER HEADS THE NATION

New presidential candidates appear. In the spring of 1952, President Truman let it be known that he would not seek re-election. To lead their party the Democrats selected Adlai E. Stevenson, Governor of Illinois. Trained as a lawyer, Stevenson had held several positions in the United States government. Then, returning to his native state, he had been elected governor in 1948 by a large vote. Stevenson's running mate for Vice-President was Senator John Sparkman of Alabama.

For their presidential candidate the Republicans chose General Dwight D. Eisenhower. Born in Texas and reared in Kansas, he had attended the United States Military Academy and had been an officer in the army almost all of his life. In 1942 he became commander-in-chief of the Allied forces in North Africa during World War II. He commanded the Allied armies which invaded Europe on D-Day and received the surrender of the German generals when the war in Europe ended. After serving as Army Chief of Staff for three years, General Eisenhower became president of Columbia University. He returned to Europe in 1951 to organize the defense forces under the North Atlantic Treaty Organization. Eisenhower's warm and friendly manner attracted people quite as much as his military fame. Senator Richard M. Nixon was the Republican choice for Vice-President.

The 1952 election arouses keen interest.
General Eisenhower and Governor Stevenson carried on vigorous election campaigns. General Eisenhower, of course, was far better known to Americans than his opponent. Both presidential candidates used radio and television to place their viewpoints before the voters. Eisenhower urged that it was "time for a change," since the Democratic Party had been in control for 20 years. Toward the end of the campaign, General Eisenhower announced that, if elected, he would fly to Korea to study the situation personally.

General Eisenhower wins a sweeping victory. Eisenhower won the presidency by a landslide. He received the electoral votes of 39 states, including several southern states which normally vote Democratic. Soon after the election, President-elect Eisenhower fulfilled his campaign promise. He flew to Korea and made an inspection tour of the battle area.

Aided by the popularity of General Eisenhower, many Republican senators and representatives were elected. Though its majorities were slight, especially in the Senate, the Republican Party gained control of both houses of Congress.

Congress passes important laws. One of the first acts of Congress under the new administration was to carry out Eisenhower's campaign promise concerning "tidelands oil." Oil is found not only deep in the earth of many states but also under the ocean off the shores, or *tidelands,* of California and several Gulf states, particularly Texas and Louisiana. President Eisenhower believed that the states, not the United States government, should control tidelands oil. Congress soon passed a law transferring the tidelands to the states.

Another early act of Congress was to increase the number of executive departments from nine to ten. The name of the new department — Health, Education and Welfare — indicates the nature of its work. Still another law created an Air Force Academy. Located in magnificent new buildings in the mountains of Colorado, it trains officers for the Air Force just as the Military Academy at West Point and the Naval Academy at Annapolis prepare them for the Army and Navy.

The Democrats win control of Congress.
In the Congressional elections of 1954, the Democrats won a majority in both houses. Their margin in the Senate, however, was

Each of our major wars has produced presidential candidates.

exceedingly narrow. The Democrats also elected many governors and won control of more state legislatures than they had in the 1952 election.

In the next two years Congress passed laws which were to have far-reaching effects on the lives of Americans. The minimum wage rate, for example, was raised to one dollar per hour, and plans for an enlarged military reserve were also adopted. In 1956 Congress approved a vast road-building program, providing for over 40,000 miles of four-lane roads.

The Supreme Court rules on the schools. An important event of President Eisenhower's first administration was neither an action of his nor of the Congress but a decision of the Supreme Court. On May 17, 1954, the Court declared unanimously that state laws requiring Negro children to attend separate public schools were unconstitutional. In a later decision the Supreme Court directed that "a prompt and reasonable start" should be made toward allowing both white and Negro pupils to attend the same schools. In some states much was done to carry out the Court's decision. Other states proceeded slowly, while in a few no action was taken. But each year has seen more school systems making a start toward carrying out the Court's decision.

President Eisenhower is re-elected. In spite of two serious illnesses during his first term, President Eisenhower regained his health and decided to run for re-election in 1956. The Republicans chose not only President Eisenhower but also Vice-President Nixon to be candidates for re-election. The Democrats turned again to Adlai Stevenson as their nominee for President. As his running mate they chose Senator Estes Kefauver of Tennessee.

The election showed that President Eisenhower still was overwhelmingly popular with the voters. He and Vice-President Nixon received 457 electoral votes to only 74 for Stevenson and Kefauver. The Democrats, however, once again gained control of Congress. Two years later, in the Congressional elections of 1958, the Democrats won control of the House and Senate by even wider margins. Thus, for six of President Eisenhower's eight years in office Congress was controlled by Democrats. Even so, Congress followed President Eisenhower's recommendations more closely than might be expected when both houses were controlled by the opposing party.

Congress acts on civil rights. During the 1957 session of Congress, the bill which received most attention was the "civil rights" bill. In some southern states Negroes had been prevented, by one means or another, from voting in elections. Under the proposed law they could turn to the courts, which would order that all qualified persons be permitted to vote. The civil rights bill, with some changes, was finally passed. In 1960, another civil rights bill was passed. The 1960 law gave the national government more powers to protect the Negro's right to vote.

The St. Lawrence Seaway is opened. An important accomplishment of the Eisenhower administration was the St. Lawrence Seaway (page 657). The Seaway project deepened the St. Lawrence River above Montreal so that sea-going ships can sail to ports on the Great Lakes. A related project develops electric power along the river. On April 30, 1959, a Dutch freighter docked at Chicago, the first ocean-going vessel to reach that port.

Alaska and Hawaii become states. The year 1959 also saw the admission of two new states. It was the first time new states had been admitted since Arizona and New Mexico had joined the Union in

This decision affects tax-supported institutions of higher education as well as public elementary and secondary schools.

TWO NEW STATES in 1959 meant a new look for the American flag. Workers in this flag factory are inspecting new 50-star flags.

1912. Alaska had adopted a constitution in 1956 and requested admission as a state. Two years later Congress voted to admit Alaska. Alaska immediately set up its state government and elected two senators and one representative to Congress. Then on January 3, 1959, President Eisenhower signed a proclamation announcing the admission of Alaska.

Congress approved the admission of Hawaii in March, 1959. In signing the statehood bill, President Eisenhower said that Hawaii's admission would "demonstrate anew to the world the vitality of the principles of freedom and self-determination — the principles upon which this nation was founded 172 years ago." The 50-star flag was officially raised on July 4, 1960.

Puerto Rico remains a free Commonwealth. After the admission of Hawaii and Alaska, Puerto Rico remained the one heavily populated territory belonging to the United States (page 585). Puerto Ricans have been American citizens since 1917, and for many years they have elected representatives to make their own laws. In 1952 Puerto Rico became a self-governing Commonwealth under the protection of the United States. As a Commonwealth, Puerto Rico has had cer-

tain advantages, such as free trade with the United States and unrestricted migration to this country. In recent years industry has expanded and Puerto Rico has made a good start toward working out many of its problems. Many Puerto Ricans now want their homeland to become a state, like Hawaii and Alaska. Some hope to become fully independent. But other Puerto Ricans realize the advantages of remaining a Commonwealth.

Inflation and labor reforms become important issues. As his presidency neared its end, President Eisenhower became deeply concerned over inflation. Inflation, you remember, is the steady rise of costs and prices. As inflation continues, the value of every man's dollar goes down. This is because, with higher and higher prices, each dollar buys less. One way to fight inflation, the President stated, was to reduce government spending. Eisenhower vetoed many bills passed by Congress which, in his judgment, would have spent government funds unwisely.

Labor reform also became an important issue. People were deeply disturbed by evidence presented before a Senate committee showing that in a few labor unions certain leaders had misused their power. After long debate, Congress passed the

Inflation poses a problem for people living on **689** fixed income, and especially those who have retired.

Communist trade and aid programs often involve barter - for example, cotton for armaments.

690   THE UNITED STATES BECOMES A WORLD LEADER

Landrum-Griffin Act, the first important labor law since the Taft-Hartley Act (page 481).

World affairs require much attention. Throughout his eight years in the White House, President Eisenhower had to deal with many critical world events. It is true that soon after he became President, the fighting in Korea was ended by a truce (page 639). But the truce fell far short of a real peace, and both sides continued to keep armed forces in Korea.

Furthermore, as you learned in Chapter 30, the Communist nations sought to bring more and more of the world under their control. Red China, which was trying by giant strides to become a modern industrial country, constantly threatened the weaker countries of Asia. Soviet Russia, with tempting offers of aid, tried to extend Communist influence into the newly independent countries. At times Khrushchev seemed anxious to improve relations between the East and the West. At other times, however, his threats of force and his anti-Western talk increased world tension. During his administration, President Eisenhower had to deal with crises over the Suez Canal, Formosa, Berlin, Cuba, and the Congo (Chapter 30).

Eisenhower works for peace with freedom. Although he had been a military leader most of his life, President Eisenhower wanted to bring an end to war and the creation of deadlier weapons. Late in 1953, in a speech before the United Nations, he proposed a plan to use atomic power for peaceful uses. Time and again he pledged America's willingness to control or reduce nuclear weapons under any plan which included proper supervision and inspection. And in an address before the UN General Assembly in September, 1960, he pledged (1) full support to the United Nations, (2) aid to underdeveloped nations, particularly the many new African states, and (3) co-operation in halting the arms race. But the President did not want "peace at any price." To have peace with freedom, the United States needed to keep its defenses strong. American scientists and military leaders continued to develop new weapons and methods of detecting enemy attacks.

PRESIDENT EISENHOWER traveled many miles to speak directly to the people and leaders of other countries. Here he greets a welcoming crowd in the Middle East.

CHECK UP

1. What problems did President Truman face after the end of World War II?

2. (a) What were the results of the election of 1948? (b) What was the Fair Deal?

3. What steps did President Truman take to maintain world peace and security?

4. (a) What were the results of the election of 1952? (b) What were the important events of President Eisenhower's first term?

5. (a) What happened in the election of 1956? (b) What were the highlights of the second Eisenhower administration?

6. In what ways did President Eisenhower work for world peace?

 ## What Challenges Did Presidents Kennedy and Johnson Face?

Kennedy wins the election of 1960. President Eisenhower was not eligible to seek a third term. Early in 1960 it appeared that Vice-President Richard Nixon was most likely to be nominated as the Republican candidate for the presidency. Within the Democratic Party, however, a race developed among several prominent leaders. When the Democrats held their convention in July, they nominated Senator John F. Kennedy of Massachusetts for President and Senator Lyndon Johnson of Texas for Vice-President. At their convention two weeks later, the Republicans chose Vice-President Nixon as their presidential candidate and Henry Cabot Lodge, then ambassador to the United Nations, as his running mate.

In the hard-fought campaign which followed, both Kennedy and Nixon crisscrossed the United States by airplane, making numerous speeches. For the first time in a presidential campaign the two candidates appeared together on television to debate important issues. Because of his two terms as Vice-President, Nixon was perhaps better known than Senator Kennedy. But Kennedy's appearances in the four debates made him as familiar to the voters as his opponent. Senator Kennedy told the American people that if elected he would call for a New Frontier program of action to tackle the country's problems.

The election itself was one of the closest in our history. Kennedy received only about 118,000 more popular votes than Nixon. His margin in the electoral college, however, was 303 to 219 (another candidate receiving the remaining 15 votes). Senator Kennedy, 43 years old, was the youngest man ever to be elected President of the United States. He was also the first member of the Roman Catholic Church to be elected President.

The Kennedy administration gets under way. In January, 1961, President Kennedy plunged into the business of his new office with enthusiasm. During the preceding months business activity had slackened throughout the country and the number of unemployed workers had increased. President Kennedy requested Congress to give additional aid to jobless workers, especially in areas where unemployment had been widespread for some time. To get the New Frontier under way, he also submitted a number of other messages to the new Congress. The President called for federal aid to schools, a higher minimum wage law, more housing, and new programs to aid farmers and to provide medical care for aged people. President Kennedy also called for more funds to build up America's defenses.

Another early development in the Kennedy administration was the ratification of

Television debates viewed by some 60 million Americans are a far cry from the Lincoln-Douglas debates

The Peace Corps idea has been adopted by a number of other countries.

692   THE UNITED STATES BECOMES A WORLD LEADER

a new amendment to the Constitution. The Twenty-Third Amendment permits the residents of the District of Columbia to vote in presidential elections.

The Peace Corps is established. Soon after his inauguration, President Kennedy announced the formation of the Peace Corps. Its purpose was to send people with useful skills abroad to help foreign peoples develop their countries. Most of the Peace Corps volunteers were to teach school, train workers, or introduce better methods of farming and sanitation. They were to live in the same way as the people of the countries to which they were sent: doing the same work, eating the same food, and, as far as possible, speaking the language of the country. After four years, 14,000 volunteers were serving in scores of countries around the world.

Congress reacts to the President's program. When President Kennedy began his administration, it seemed probable that the various programs he proposed would win approval. The fact that the Democrats had a clear majority in both the House and Senate pointed in this direction. But by October, 1962, when Congress adjourned, some parts of the New Frontier program had been defeated, while action on other parts fell short of the President's wishes. For example, Congress turned down his proposals to provide medical insurance for aged persons, furnish federal aid to schools, and create a Department of Urban Affairs. And while Congress finally approved a tax bill, a foreign aid program, and a farm bill, these measures fell short of the President's original requests.

Congress, however, did approve two especially important parts of the President's program. (1) One bill provided for the purchase of up to 100 million dollars worth of bonds issued by the United Nations. The UN had run into financial trouble because of the failure of some of its members to pay their share of its expenses (page 647). (2) The Trade Expansion Act empowered the President to make sweeping changes in tariff rates to encourage foreign trade, especially trade with the Common Market. This group of countries in western Europe has been moving toward the elimination of tariffs in trade among themselves, and they have adopted a common tariff in their trade with outside countries.

The President stresses tax legislation. In the congressional elections of November, 1962, the Democrats retained their majorities in both the House and Senate. President Kennedy asked the new Congress which met in January, 1963, to reconsider some of his New Frontier proposals which had been turned down by the previous Congress. But he particularly urged favorable action on certain tax cuts and tax reforms. Although the President's tax program would reduce the government's income by eleven billion dollars, he believed it would stimulate business and reduce unemployment.

The civil rights movement gets under way. Much of President Kennedy's time and thought were claimed by a new movement which had been gaining strength since the 1950's. American Negroes had not won the equality in citizenship to which they were entitled. Spurred by the Supreme Court school decision of 1954 (page 688) and by the frustrations experienced since emancipation, Negroes began a drive to attain true equality in America.

On a December day in 1955, Mrs. Rosa Parks, a Negro woman who worked in a department store in Montgomery, Alabama, boarded a bus on her way home from work. She sat in the back half of the bus, as a local law required Negroes to do. As the bus filled up, there were more white passengers than there were seats in

CIVIL RIGHTS LEADERS, including Martin Luther King, hold up their hands to greet the crowds during the march in Washington, D.C., in the summer of 1963.

the white section toward the front of the bus. The bus driver ordered Mrs. Parks to move back so that a white passenger could have her seat. She refused to move, and was arrested.

The arrest of Mrs. Parks caused Negroes to boycott the buses in Montgomery. They refused to ride on the buses until Negroes should receive equal treatment as passengers. A leader in the Montgomery bus boycott was Dr. Martin Luther King, a young Baptist minister. He and others, both white and Negro, led many other protests against the unfair treatment of Negroes. Dr. King became the leader of the Southern Christian Leadership Conference. This organization sought equal treatment for Negroes but insisted that Negroes should secure such treatment without using force or violence. Dr. King and his methods became so successful and well-known that he was awarded the Nobel Peace Prize in 1964.

Injustices to Negroes are widespread. The Montgomery bus boycott dealt with only one situation in one city. In many parts of the South, particularly in the Deep

South, there were customs and laws which denied equal treatment to Negroes. They were barred from using "white" hotels, lunch counters, waiting rooms, beaches, and other public places. Progress in carrying out the Supreme Court decision against separate schools for Negroes and whites had been painfully slow. Moreover, despite the civil rights laws passed under President Eisenhower (page 688), Negroes in many states were still prevented from voting.

Not only in the South but in other sections of the country Negroes were limited in the jobs they could get and the places where they could live. Because many Negroes had an inadequate education, they could not obtain better-paying jobs. Low income in turn kept them in poor housing.

Negro demands for equal treatment sweep across the nation. By the early 1960's, the nation's attention was focused on the growing number of demonstrations for civil rights. There were protest marches, including a massive but orderly march in Washington, D.C. Other forms

The question of de facto segregation has been **693** raised in northern cities. Because of residential patterns, a neighborhood school may enroll chiefly Negro children.

of demonstrations were boycotts, "freedom rides," "sit-ins," and picketing. Negroes were joined in many of their protests by white people who believed in the justice of their cause. Demonstrations took place not only in the South but in northern and western cities as well. Sometimes violence and riots broke out in connection with these efforts. To meet the civil rights challenge, President Kennedy called on Congress to pass laws which would end discrimination.

Congress acts on civil rights. In 1962 Congress approved the Twenty-Fourth Amendment to the Constitution. This Amendment said that in elections for President, Vice-President, senators, and representatives, no voter should be required to pay "any poll tax or other tax." (A poll tax is a tax of a certain amount per person.) The Amendment was ratified by the necessary number of states in 1964, and became part of the Constitution.

In 1964 Congress adopted a wide-ranging civil rights law. This law protected the right of all qualified citizens to vote and forbade employers to use unfair practices in hiring. It also required that all persons be allowed to use such public places as hotels and motels, restaurants, lunch counters, stores, theaters, parks, and sports arenas. In 1965 still another law sought to protect the right of Negroes to vote.

President Kennedy and Khrushchev meet in Vienna. From the very start of his administration, President Kennedy faced serious problems brought on by the cold war. In Southeast Asia, Communist forces threatened to take over Laos (page 642). In Cuba, as you read earlier (page 674), an invading force of Cuban exiles failed to overthrow Castro's dictatorial rule. Moreover, Khrushchev was threatening to stir up a new crisis over Berlin.

For most people, the baffling thing about the Cold War is that it promises to continue indefinitely.

These and other cold war problems led President Kennedy and his advisers to feel that he and Khrushchev should meet. In June, 1961, President Kennedy flew to Vienna, where he conferred with the Russian leader on questions of urgent importance. No agreements or decisions of significance were reached. But the two leaders took advantage of the meeting to exchange views on such vital issues as nuclear testing and the future of Laos.

Following their meetings, each of the leaders made his own statement concerning the state of the cold war. In Moscow, Premier Khrushchev declared that the tide of history was running in favor of communism. President Kennedy, in his report to the American people, stated: ". . . I believe just as strongly that time will prove . . . that liberty and independence and self-determination, not communism, is the future of man, and that free men have the will and the resources to win the struggle for freedom."

The United States builds up its military strength. The unyielding attitude adopted by Khrushchev at the Vienna meeting convinced the President that the United States must build up its military strength. Our government would continue to discuss plans for disarmament. But neither Soviet Russia nor Red China would be allowed to conclude that willingness to work for peace meant military weakness. Thus, in the fall of 1961, when conditions became tense in Berlin (page 644), additional American forces were sent to that divided city.

The United States also saw the need of training troops in the type of guerrilla warfare waged by the Communists in Southeast Asia. There Communist jungle fighters had won control of much of Laos and threatened the independent state of South Vietnam (page 642).

(Continued on page 696)

The Presidents  of Our Country

WARREN G. HARDING 1921–1923

Republican from Ohio. A handsome, successful businessman, newspaper owner, and senator, Harding's platform called for a "return to normalcy" — that is, a return to peaceful times and the enjoyment of life. His election as President was the first to be broadcast over the radio. The Washington Disarmament Conference was held during his administration. Harding died two years after taking office.

CALVIN COOLIDGE 1923–1929

Republican from Massachusetts. As Governor of Massachusetts, Coolidge became famous for his handling of a Boston police strike in 1919. Elected Vice-President in 1920, he became President at Harding's death. He was a quiet man of few words who believed in working hard, spending little, and limiting the powers of the federal government. During his administration, the country enjoyed a period of prosperity.

HERBERT HOOVER 1929–1933

Republican from California. A successful mining engineer, Hoover was also known as a great humanitarian for his organization of food relief projects in Europe after World War I. He later served as Secretary of Commerce. Because he was President at the time, Hoover was blamed for the depression that followed the panic of 1929. In later years, he gave valuable service as chairman of the committees on reorganization of the executive branch of the government.

FRANKLIN D. ROOSEVELT 1933–1945

Democrat from New York. Roosevelt had served as a New York state senator, Assistant Secretary of the Navy, and Governor of New York. The only President to serve more than two terms, "F.D.R." led the country through its worst depression and greatest war. In office he introduced the "New Deal" program and made wide use of radio and news conferences. He was the first President to fly while in office. Roosevelt died in 1945 at the beginning of his fourth term.

HARRY S. TRUMAN 1945–1953

Democrat from Missouri. Captain of artillery in World War I, Truman rose through local politics to become a United States senator. As Vice-President he became President at Roosevelt's death and continued the "New Deal" approach in his "Fair Deal" program. During his administration, World War II ended, the United States adopted plans for aiding the recovery of Europe, and American troops fought in the Korean War.

The Presidents *of Our Country*

DWIGHT D. EISENHOWER 1953–1961

Republican. Born in Texas and raised in Kansas, Eisenhower was a soldier for most of his life. During World War II he commanded the Allied forces in the invasion of Europe. Later, he served as Chief of Staff of the Army, president of Columbia University, and NATO commander in Europe. As President he had to deal with the growing threat of world communism. In 1961, the Eisenhowers retired to their farm in historic Gettysburg, Pennsylvania.

JOHN F. KENNEDY 1961–1963

Democrat from Massachusetts. A Navy PT boat commander during World War II, Kennedy began his political career as a representative and became a senator in 1953. As President, he proposed "New Frontier" legislation to solve national problems. In foreign affairs, Kennedy called for the removal of nuclear missiles from Cuba and secured a test-ban treaty with Russia and Britain. President Kennedy was assassinated in November, 1963.

LYNDON B. JOHNSON 1963–

Democrat from Texas. Johnson's 24 years in Congress, first as representative and later as senator, covered the administrations of three Presidents. As Vice-President, he also served as Chairman of the National Aeronautics and Space Council. Sworn in as President after the assassination of John Kennedy in 1963, Johnson pledged himself to carry on Kennedy's policies. In 1964 he won election as President in his own right.

President Kennedy quarantines Cuba. The turn of events in Cuba in the fall of 1962 furnished proof of our country's need to stand ready for instant action. President Kennedy reported to the nation that Soviet Russia was arming Cuba with intermediate-range nuclear missiles, despite earlier Soviet assurances that Cuba was receiving only defensive weapons. The President announced a "strict quarantine on all offensive military equipment under shipment to Cuba" and ordered American ships to use force if necessary to keep such cargo from reaching Cuba.

After a few tense days, Khrushchev agreed to dismantle and remove offensive weapons from Cuba. In return, he requested that the United States end the quarantine and agree not to invade Cuba. President Kennedy was unwilling, however, to pledge no invasion of the island without an on-the-spot inspection to check

696
The President s firm action was approved throughout the free world.

the removal of all offensive weapons. This Castro flatly refused to permit. But Castro's position among the Latin American countries had suffered, and in the crisis the Organization of American States had supported the United States' position.

The world seeks controls on nuclear tests. President Kennedy faced the same problems as former Presidents in seeking agreements on the control of nuclear weapons. In disarmament talks at Geneva, the United States tried to secure a treaty by which the nuclear powers would agree not to test nuclear weapons and would permit international inspection to enforce such an agreement. But Soviet Russia refused to permit foreigners to make inspections on her territory.

In 1958, the United States, Great Britain, and Russia had voluntarily given up nuclear testing when disarmament talks began at Geneva. But three years later the world was shocked to hear that Russia had begun a series of nuclear explosions in the atmosphere over Siberia and the Arctic. Despite protests from many countries, Russia continued the series of tests.

The United States government realized that it must upgrade its own arsenal of nuclear weapons in order to protect the free world. In the spring of 1962 it began a series of nuclear tests over the Pacific. Soviet Russia in turn began still another series of tests.

In 1963, however, the United States, Britain, and the Soviet Union agreed to hold a test-ban conference. At this meeting, held in Moscow in July, the three powers agreed not to carry out nuclear tests in the atmosphere, in outer space, or under water. It was recognized by all that the treaty did not end the threat of nuclear warfare. But the three powers had taken, in the words of Secretary of State Dean Rusk, "what all mankind must hope will

PRESIDENT KENNEDY inspected a sentry post at the Berlin Wall during his visit to Germany in 1963.

be a first step on the road to a secure and peaceful world."

President Kennedy is assassinated. On November 22, 1963, President Kennedy made a visit to Dallas, Texas. As his automobile passed along the street, a young man named Lee Harvey Oswald fired three shots at the President. Kennedy slumped into the arms of his wife, who was riding beside him, and died almost at once.

Vice-President Lyndon B. Johnson had been riding in another car behind President Kennedy. Two hours after the assassination, he took the oath of office as President, and then flew immediately to Washington. Even as the nation mourned for its young former leader, Johnson vigorously took up the duties of the presidency. A native of Texas, Lyndon Johnson was 55 years old when he became President. After serving several terms in

The treaty, however, permits underground testing, which does not pollute the atmosphere.

Many of these were measures originally proposed to Congress by President Kennedy.

698 THE UNITED STATES BECOMES A WORLD LEADER

the House of Representatives, he had been elected to the Senate in 1948. He became Democratic floor leader of the Senate in 1953 and showed much skill in that position.

Johnson wins the election of 1964. During his first year in office, President Johnson pursued policies that the late President Kennedy had started. Then, in the summer of 1964, Johnson was nominated for the presidency in his own right. The Democrats chose Hubert Humphrey, Senator from Minnesota, as their candidate for the vice-presidency. The Republicans selected Barry Goldwater, Senator from Arizona, and Representative William E. Miller of New York as their nominees. President Johnson and Senator Humphrey won the election by a huge margin. They received over fifteen million more votes than the Republican candidates, and car-

ried 44 states and the District of Columbia (with 486 electoral votes) to six states (with 52 electoral votes) for Goldwater and Miller.

President Johnson proposes new measures. President Johnson displayed much vigor and worked long hours. He was fond of talking to newspaper reporters as he walked rapidly in the White House grounds. His habit of personally telephoning people whose advice or support he wanted became well-known. As a former Senate leader, he used his influence to obtain the passage of laws he recommended to Congress.

The result was the enactment of much important legislation. Among the measures passed were a reduction in income taxes and the removal of excise taxes from many articles. Johnson proposed and secured passage of the Economic Oppor-

ASTRONAUT EDWARD WHITE left his Gemini capsule and floated in space more than a hundred miles above the earth. Only the coiling lifeline connected the Astronaut with his spaceship during the historic flight in June, 1965.

tunity Act of 1964. Its purpose was to help young people who were out of school and out of work by training them for jobs. He also suggested, and secured, laws to give financial aid to schools and colleges. Congress acted favorably on still another bill proposed by the President. It was the Voting Rights Act of 1965, intended to enable all qualified citizens, including Negroes, to vote without restriction. In addition, Congress passed the Medicare bill to provide medical insurance for people over 65.

Congress also approved a Twenty-Fifth Amendment to the Constitution. When ratified by the states, the Amendment would authorize the President to fill a vacancy in the office of Vice-President. It would also make clear how the duties of the presidency could be turned over to the Vice-President whenever a President was seriously disabled.

Gemini flights continue the American space program. The country's manned spaceflight program entered a new phase in 1965. After the completion of the Mercury project (page 646), a series of two-man "Gemini" flights began. During one of these flights, an American Astronaut duplicated the feat of a Soviet Cosmonaut a few months before by leaving an orbiting space ship and floating freely in space. In other spectacular achievements, American space probes succeeded in sending back to earth close-up photographs of both the moon and the planet Mars.

Foreign policy presents difficulties. President Johnson wanted to create what he called "the Great Society" in the United States. But events in other countries also demanded a great deal of his time and attention. Half-way around the world, the situation in Vietnam grew steadily more serious. President Johnson sent more and

PRESIDENT JOHNSON announced the appointment of Supreme Court Justice Arthur J. Goldberg as Ambassador to the United Nations during this ceremony in the White House Rose Garden. Goldberg replaced Adlai Stevenson, who had served in this post from 1961 until his death in 1965.

more American forces to South Vietnam to prevent that country from falling under Communist control. "Our objective," he said in a speech in early 1965, "is the independence of South Vietnam, and its freedom from attack. We want nothing for ourselves — only that the people of South Vietnam be allowed to guide their own country in their own way." As America's military support of South Vietnam mounted, President Johnson time and again stated his willingness to support peace efforts.

A trouble spot closer to home erupted in April, 1965, when revolution broke out in the Dominican Republic, an island nation in the West Indies. Responding quickly, President Johnson sent American marines and other forces to protect American lives and to try to preserve peace in the Dominican Republic.

The United Nations and the Organization of American States also took action. In late May an Inter-American Peace Force, consisting of troops from several Latin American countries as well as the United States, was formed under the command of a Brazilian general. It was the first time that such a force had been organized in the Western Hemisphere. The Peace Force established an uneasy truce among the opposing parties. Meanwhile, a three-man committee of the Organization of American States tried to work out a more permanent solution in the Dominican conflict.

Some Americans argued that this action, taken without consultation with the OAS, violated our promise not to use intervention (page 669).

CHECK UP

1. (a) What were the results of the 1960 election? (b) What legislation was passed during President Kennedy's administration?

2. (a) What conditions caused Negro leaders to start the civil rights movement? (b) What success has this movement had?

3. What cold war developments occurred during President Kennedy's years in office?

4. (a) What were the highlights and results of the 1964 election? (b) What legislation did President Johnson ask Congress to enact? (c) With what success?

5. What international problems developed during the Johnson administration?

Check Up on Chapter 32

Do you Know the Meaning?

1. administrator
2. minimum wage
3. price controls
4. health insurance
5. hydrogen bomb
6. tidelands
7. civil rights
8. public opinion poll

Can You Identify?

1. Warren Harding
2. Calvin Coolidge
3. Herbert Hoover
4. 1932
5. 1945
6. 1952
7. 1960
8. 1961
9. CCC
10. TVA
11. Franklin D. Roosevelt
12. New Deal
13. Harry S. Truman
14. Fair Deal
15. Dwight D. Eisenhower
16. Adlai Stevenson
17. John F. Kennedy
18. Peace Corps
19. Lyndon Johnson

What Do You Think?

1. Should a President be given credit for prosperous times and blamed for hard times? Why?

2. Franklin D. Roosevelt was elected President four times. The Twenty-Second Amendment now prevents anyone from being elected President more than twice. Do you believe such a limitation is wise?

3. What are the chief problems that the President and Congress face today?

4. (a) How are the Democratic Party and Republican Party different? In general, what does each party support? (b) Do all members of each party hold the same political views?

5. What do you think is the most important decision made by this country since 1945?

Ideals of government, then and now. When our government was being established, many men wrote about what they believed would make the most successful kind of government. Some of their thoughts seem as vital to us today as when they were written. John Adams, for example, said:

"As the happiness of the people is the sole end of government, so the consent of the people is the only foundation for it."

And Thomas Jefferson wrote:

"When the people are well-informed, they can be trusted with their own government; whenever things get so far wrong as to attract their attention, they can be relied on to set them to rights."

Our national capital. It is not often that a nation builds a brand-new city for its capital as did the United States. The fine capital city we have today is the result of the wise planning of its founders. President George Washington was asked by Congress to select a site for the new capital somewhere in the southern states. He traveled on horseback up and down the Potomac River, and finally selected the location where the city of Washington is today. The land was donated by the states of Maryland and Virginia, and was named the District of Columbia.

To design the capital, Washington chose Pierre Charles L'Enfant (lahn-*fahn*'), a French artist and engineer who had come to America with Lafayette during the Revolution. L'Enfant set about to plan a capital "magnificent enough to grace a great nation." He wanted a city of grandeur, with plenty of open spaces. On a hill overlooking the Potomac, he placed the Capitol, where Congress meets today. A mile away would

be the President's house, the beautiful White House we all know so well. To the west of the Capitol Building, he planned a monument to honor George Washington. Between the two was to be a broad park. That is the beautiful Mall which you can see today, with the Capitol at one end and the Washington Monument at the other.

L'Enfant laid out, between the Capitol and the White House, the broad avenue we know as Pennsylvania Avenue. He planned other wide boulevards to run through the city, radiating like spokes of a wheel from the various circles and plazas. Many of these were built and may be seen today, usually with fine statues and other memorials. They slow up present-day traffic since they were planned before the time of automobiles, but they give the city a feeling of space and openness not usually found in our large cities.

L'Enfant's plans were followed as far as possible, but they were too expensive for a new nation to work out quickly or completely. When the government moved to Washington in 1800, for example, President Adams and his wife found the plaster still damp in the White House and many of the rooms unfinished! The boulevard which was planned to connect the President's house with the Capitol was only a muddy road, and the Capitol itself had only one completed room. But these buildings and the monuments planned by L'Enfant were finally finished, and as time went on, many more were added. Today Washington is a busy city of about a million people. Thanks to the vision of Pierre L'Enfant, it is one of the beautiful cities of the world, truly a capital "magnificent enough to grace a great nation."

Students may wish to be on the lookout for other succinct statements about "ideals of government."

PIER 5

Summary of Important Ideas

In Unit Ten you have read about our country's part in international affairs from about 1920 to the present and about the Presidents who have guided the country during that period.

1. The peaceful world which the League of Nations was intended to insure did not come about.

   a. After World War I, dictatorships gained power in Russia, Italy, and Germany. Because other nations did not want war, the Axis powers — Italy, Germany, and Japan — were tempted to expand their territories.

   b. World War II broke out in Europe when Germany invaded Poland in 1939. The United States at first followed a policy of strict neutrality but later gave aid to the victims of aggression. The Japanese attack on Pearl Harbor brought the United States into World War II.

   c. The heroic resistance of the British, the unwise German attack on Russia, and the all-out efforts of American industry and manpower contributed to the defeat of the Axis countries in World War II.

2. World War II was followed by a "cold war" which divided the world into two hostile sides.

   a. The nations allied against the Axis powers formed the United Nations to keep peace in the postwar world. The UN has had to deal with a world split by differences between communism and the free world.

   b. In recent years the United States has continued its efforts for world peace. It has met Communist aggression by arranging regional defense pacts, working through the UN, helping underdeveloped countries, and building up the defense of the free world.

   c. The cold war at times has become a shooting war, as in Korea. Freedom-loving nations must be prepared to resist Communist aggression all over the world.

   d. The desire of former colonial peoples for freedom, and of underdeveloped peoples in general to improve their lot quickly, has led some of them to look with favor on the rapid gains achieved by Russia and Red China under Communist dictatorships.

   e. Rapid scientific advances, such as nuclear energy and the exploration of space, may lead to the use of great sources of power for the good of man rather than his destruction.

3. The relations of the United States with its neighbors to the north and to the south have become increasingly friendly.

   a. Impressed by the growth of the United States, Canada worked toward a union of its provinces. Canada's steady growth and the aid she gave in World War I led England to grant Canada independence within the Commonwealth of Nations.

   b. The friendship between the United States and Canada is shown by their long record of settling disputes by peaceful means and the unfortified boundary between the two countries. Canada and the United States depend on each other for commerce and protection.

   c. The lack of experience in self-government under Spanish rule and widespread poverty have held back progress in Latin

Do your students feel that any Summary need to be qualified?

702

statements included in this

America. Nevertheless, many of these republics are moving ahead rapidly.

d. In the early 1900's the Latin American republics mistrusted the United States. The Good Neighbor Policy and the increasing readiness of this country to help underdeveloped peoples led to improved relations.

e. The Organization of American States provides a means for this country to work together with the Latin American lands.

4. Since 1920 our country's domestic policies have passed through a series of stages.

a. From 1920 to 1929 the emphasis was on a return to "normalcy," with little government interference in business.

b. During the period of 1930 to 1940 various efforts were made to end the depression and to provide social security.

c. The wartime period from 1941 to 1945 was one of full employment and peak production.

d. Since 1946 the country has generally been prosperous. Rising prices and the failure to achieve full employment, however, have been causes of concern. So also are tensions growing out of efforts to provide equal civil rights for all.

Unit Review

1. (a) By what steps did Canada obtain independence? (b) How do the governments of the United States and Canada differ? (c) Why are the two countries important to each other?

2. (a) Why has progress been slow in some Latin American countries? (b) Why did the Latin American republics mistrust the United States early in the 1900's? (c) Why have our relations with these countries improved?

3. (a) Why did Japan, Italy, and Germany seek to expand their territories after World War I? (b) What were the results? (c) What was the attitude of the United States? (d) Why did this country take part in World War II?

4. (a) What is the UN? (b) Why was it formed? (c) What differences do you see between the UN and the League of Nations? (d) What has the UN accomplished? (e) What are some of the great problems of the world today?

5. (a) Why have colonial peoples become increasingly interested in freedom since World War II? (b) What has been our country's policy in this matter? Why?

6. (a) Why has communism sought to gain power in newly independent and underdeveloped countries? (b) How? (c) With what success?

Gaining Skill

Developing Opinions and Attitudes

All of us have opinions on many subjects. We may prefer vanilla ice cream to strawberry, or a musical program on TV to a quiz show, or playing tennis to softball, or history class to mathematics, or practically any food to oysters. When used in this sense, the word *opinion* means *what one tends to like or not to like.* The source of such an opinion may be the likes and dislikes of parents and friends; or an interest, as in the case of music; or what one does better, as in the case of sports; or what is easier, as in the case of school subjects; or the appearance of something, as in the case of the raw oyster. Some people may express such an opinion without trying the thing first and then reaching a decision.

Such opinions are matters of personal preference or *taste.* There is no way of proving a person's taste wrong. If a boy prefers sneakers to moccasins, he will wear them more often. But when he dresses for a party, the boy doubtless will wear more formal shoes. Why does he do that? Perhaps because he knows that it is expected of him, or possibly because his mother insisted. In either case, he is following a *standard* rather than his personal taste; that is, he is following a rule of conduct expected and approved by other people.

There are standards for judging many things: the quality of an automobile tire or the greatest American League slugger. Sometimes standards are based on expert opinion: the most valuable player in the National League, or the best motion picture, or the athlete of the year. Do you know who are the experts that reach decisions of this kind? Do you think they are right? Always? Most of the time?

Sometimes opinion or attitude involves the question of whether a person has the right to do something. Suppose he wants to drive his car on the left side of the road. That is the *custom* in Great Britain but not in this country. Does he drive 60 miles an hour in a 35-mile zone? That is against the *law*. Is he critical of the policies of the Secretary of State? That is permitted because the Constitution guarantees *freedom of speech.* Some countries have no such guarantees, and citizens in those countries tend to keep their views to themselves. Are there no limitations to freedom of speech? There are indeed. No one has the right to utter *libel.* Look up the meaning of this word. Nor would one have the right to start a panic by shouting "fire" in a crowded theater. Such action would be a threat to the welfare of others.

What are some ways of forming sound opinions and attitudes on controversial issues? One way is to read in order to be *informed* and to discuss the issue with others who are informed. Another is to seek the views of *experts* on the issue in question. A third is to check each position on the issue to see if it is in conflict with the *basic social beliefs* of Americans. Some of these basic beliefs are:

All persons should be judged on their merits.

All persons should possess equal rights and liberties.

The rights of no person should be exercised so as to interfere with the rights of others.

The actions of no person should threaten the welfare of the people or the security of the nation.

Interesting Things to Do

The "things to do" marked with an asterisk (*) are for the whole class.

*1. Start a new set of cards for Unit Ten, using the items under "Can You Identify?" at the ends of Chapters 30, 31, and 32. A class quiz two or three times a week with these cards will help you remember the important dates, events, and people.

*2. Make a map showing the twenty Latin American republics and their capital cities. Show by arrows what products are exchanged in trade between Latin America and the United States. Consult a geography book for information.

*3. Trace an outline map of Canada, showing the ten provinces with their capitals. Show the Canada-United States border, and use arrows to show important items in Canadian trade with the United States.

4. Draw a cartoon to show one of the following: (a) Good Neighbor Policy; (b) Hitler and Mussolini threaten the peace; (c) Atlantic Charter; (d) the problems of the cold war; (e) the United Nations as the hope for peace.

5. Imagine that you were a delegate to the House of Representatives from Alaska or Hawaii before 1958. What arguments would you have used in supporting a bill to make your territory a state?

6. Write a report on one of the following: John Macdonald; Winston Churchill; Franklin D. Roosevelt; Dwight Eisenhower; Douglas MacArthur; rockets and missiles; atomic-powered submarines; the cold war.

7. Write an account of one of these events as it might have appeared in a newspaper of the time: (a) the attack on Pearl Harbor; (b) the Pan American Conference at Rio; (c) VE day; (d) VJ day; (e) the completion of the UN Charter; (f) around the world in an atomic submarine; (g) the first space flight by an American Astronaut; (h) Chinese intervention in Korea; (i) the most recent presidential election.

America Faces the Future

The purpose of *This Is America's Story* has been to give you a better understanding of our nation's history and its remarkable record of achievement. At times serious dangers have threatened the nation. Some of these dangers have arisen within our own country; others have resulted from relations with other nations. But the United States has emerged from each crisis to reach its present position of power and leadership.

Has the remarkable growth of the United States been merely a matter of good luck? The answer to this question is decidedly "No!" Of course, America's open spaces and rich natural resources have played an important part in our country's progress. Then, too, until new inventions made swift transportation and communication possible, the Atlantic and Pacific Oceans kept us separated from troubles elsewhere in the world and helped to protect us from attack. This was an important advantage when the United States was a young nation. To understand our country's growth, however, we must look beyond favorable geographic conditions.

The founders of this nation believed the principles of *liberty and self-government* to be all-important. They fought to obtain these rights and, on many occasions, to preserve them. As a result of their efforts and those of succeeding generations of Americans, we today enjoy freedom of speech and of worship; the right to assemble in groups and to petition the government; and the right to a fair trial. Also, because of their efforts, we live today under a government based upon the will of the majority of citizens, expressed through elected representatives. To be sure, life in the United States has changed greatly since our republic was founded. Most of America's open spaces have been filled in. A country inhabited largely by farmers who supplied their own needs has given way to an America of giant industries and teeming cities. In spite of these changes, however, we today enjoy the same basic freedoms that our forefathers had.

Though life has changed greatly since 1787, the principles of government which seemed basic then are basic today.

Our nation has also grown great because of its *leaders*. Some have served our country in battle or in government affairs. Others have made possible our progress in industry, in science and invention, in education, and in human welfare. In times of national crisis, a Washington or a Lincoln has come forward to provide much-needed leadership.

Moreover, the United States has benefited from the hard work of countless men and women who have made use of the opportunity to get ahead offered by our free way of life. Equally important has been the ability of the American people to work together toward a common purpose, as did the early settlers and pioneers who pushed back the frontier. Finally our country has won the loyal devotion of its citizens. These qualities have continued throughout our history.

Principles of liberty and self-government, great leaders, a loyal devotion — these form our American heritage. A nation without a sound heritage rarely reaches greatness. But it is equally true that a nation which does not *guard* its heritage rarely remains great.

This sentence presents a challenge to all Americans.

THE PRESENT CHALLENGE

Today the United States, great and powerful as it is, faces important tests both at home and abroad. At home there are many perplexing problems to solve if the American way of life is to be carried forward and if all Americans are to have a chance to live satisfying lives. Solutions must be found for such problems as declining natural resources, crime and corruption, pollution of air and water, lack of full employment, and the heavy death rate resulting from traffic accidents. But the severest test of our times is the dangerous conflict between the world of communism and the free world.

In the final chapters of this book you learned how communism has grown since Communist leaders seized control of Russia during World War I. Since World War II, communism has spread at an alarming rate. It has taken over eastern Europe and China and other parts of Asia and has even penetrated into Africa. It has brought within its grip the island of Cuba in the Western Hemisphere. Today the Communist world includes nations covering one third of the world's land surface.

Why is communism a deadly threat? One answer lies in the difference between Communist ideas and the heritage upon which the United States has grown. (1) In the United States the individual is important. Under communism the individual is the servant of the

Sackets Harbor (left), an American naval base on Lake Ontario, was attacked from Canada in the War of 1812.

After the war, the United States and Britain agreed to disarm along the Canadian border. In 1962 a shipload of Canadian Sea Cadets (right) visited Sackets Harbor to celebrate more than 140 years of Canadian-American peace.

President Buchanan greeted the first Japanese envoys who came to Washington after Perry's visit to Japan.

Today, an American teacher (right) shares her knowledge of home economics with a class in the West Indies. Below, a visiting Japanese architect introduces American college students to some new ideas.

Americans Seek Friendly Relations

with Other Countries

Can your students add to this list of differences?

state. (2) Americans cherish personal rights and freedom. Under communism the people have few rights. (3) Our American way of life includes the private ownership of property and the right of the individual to choose his job and to own a business. In Communist countries the government owns the means of production and determines what jobs people will hold. (4) Finally, control of a free government rests in its citizens; the policies of our government are determined by representatives and officials elected by the voters in free elections. In a Communist country, a small group of Communist Party leaders, not the people themselves, determines policies. When elections are held in Communist countries, the people have no opportunity to choose one of several candidates. They are merely allowed to vote "yes" for the candidates selected by the Communist Party.

Of course, conditions vary at different times and in different Communist countries. But the differences between Communist government and free government are obvious.

Another answer to the question — "Why is communism a dangerous threat?" — grows out of the determination of the Communists to spread their ideas throughout the world. Americans believe in the right of each nation to be independent and to govern itself as it wishes. Not so the Communists. Again and again Communist leaders of Russia and China have made it plain that they intend to dominate the world. Khrushchev, former premier of Soviet Russia, promised Americans that he would "bury" us and proclaimed communism to be the wave of the future. To reach their goals, Communist countries have used different means. We will mention these only briefly.

(1) They have put their greatest efforts into those industries which will build up their military strength and trade. This task is made easier by the fact that in Communist countries the government decides what goods are to be produced and tells workers what work they shall do.

(2) They have used their military strength both to take over and to keep control of other countries. Thus, Soviet Russia used her armies at the end of World War II to seize control of the nations of eastern Europe (page 635) and savagely crushed a revolt in Hungary in 1956. Chinese Communists used force to make mainland China into a Communist country (page 636). Red Chinese forces also fought in the Korean War (page 639) and later took over Tibet (page 644).

(3) Many times the Communists have used the threat of war to gain their ends. This threat has been held repeatedly over Berlin by the Russians (page 644) and over the new nations of Southeast Asia by the Chinese Communists (page 642). The threat of war is espe-

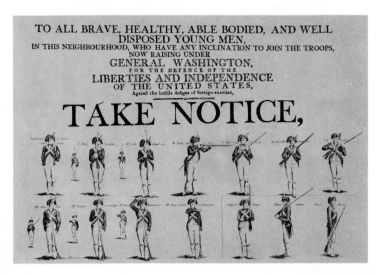

An old recruiting poster (left) reminds us that Americans have had to be prepared to fight for their rights ever since our nation was born.

During World War I, college students trained for military service on campus. At right they are shown throwing dummy grenades, supervised by an ROTC instructor.

Americans Stand Ready
to Defend Their Rights

Above, left, American naval vessels patrol Asian waters to prevent Communist aggression. In 1804 American ships had to bombard a pirate stronghold in North Africa (above) to protect our merchant seamen.

cially effective in these days because a full-scale war would involve the use of nuclear weapons. Nowhere in the world would there be a safe place to hide from the devastating effects of such a war.

(4) The Communists have also spread lies and discontent by sending agents into other countries, particularly those which have become independent since World War II. In this way, for example, they hope to make nations in Asia and Africa part of the Communist world. The Communist take-over of Cuba has given them a new base from which to carry on such activities in Latin America.

(5) Often the Communists try to win over weak governments by offering aid and favorable trade treaties. They know that one of the best ways to gain influence in another country is to make that country dependent on them.

MEETING THE CHALLENGE

How can the United States and its free-world allies meet the Communist threat? There are several things our nation can do:

(1) We do not have to accept as true the Soviet claim that "communism is the wave of the future." There was a time not too long ago when people in most European countries were the subjects of kings who had unlimited power. Yet today there are few kings, and the powers of those who remain are strictly limited. Dictators have come and gone. Hitler proclaimed that his Nazi state would last for 1000 years. But at the close of World War II, Nazi Germany was defeated, its military might destroyed, its leader dead. In the long run, the trend of history has been toward more freedom for more people, provided they count their freedom worth keeping.

(2) We must keep the military forces of our country strong enough to defend ourselves and to help protect other free nations. America must also boost the production of its factories and farms to meet the rapidly growing industrial power of the Communist world, especially of Russia. These goals are not just the responsibility of our leaders. They require the support of all American citizens — both to build up the level of our nation's production and to pay the taxes which are needed for national defense.

(3) Even though the United States must keep its defenses strong in order to protect itself and its allies, our government must at the same time continue to seek a sound plan of disarmament and be willing to settle disputes by peaceful means.

No one can object if Communists believe that "communism is the wave of the future." Our objection is to having communism imposed on people against their wishes.

When a newspaper arrived in the 1840's (left), Americans were eager to read the latest news of the Mexican War.

After World War I began in 1914, Americans studied the situation in Europe on a big map outside a newspaper office (above). Although the war was 3000 miles away, it soon involved our country. At left, Americans in a railroad station watch a television broadcast of a space-launching in 1962.

Americans Need To Be Well-Informed About the World

To learn about Asia's problems, students hold a forum in which they present the viewpoints of historical figures and modern Asian leaders. Note maps of China and India on the blackboard.

(4) At the same time that we maintain military might and industrial output, we must preserve those values of liberty and democracy that have made the United States a model for other nations. The world and particularly the new nations of Asia and Africa are watching to see if our free government and way of life can meet the present challenge. The Communists are quick to point out any conditions in the United States which do not square with the principles we proclaim. Our success in making the American way of life work may well sway the world balance in favor of freedom and democracy.

So far we have mentioned the steps which Americans as a nation can take to create a better America and to turn back the menace of communism. But what can we as *individuals* do? Often you hear someone say: "I am only one among 200 million people. I'm not a leader or a government official. What can I do?"

Our democratic form of government suggests several answers. The first is that all of us, students in school as well as adults, can take full advantage of our opportunities to become well informed. Such opportunities do not exist in a dictatorship. In a dictatorship — whether it be a Nazi government under Hitler or a Communist government under the Kremlin bosses — newspapers can print only the news approved by the government. Radio stations broadcast only the government's side of the news. Citizens are not allowed to criticize their rulers or their policies. In the United States, however, information is easily available. Newspapers, magazines, and radio and television broadcasts not only tell all the news but also express opinions about it. In these disturbed times, all Americans need to keep informed about the problems which face our country.

In the second place, adult citizens have the right to vote. They can choose local officials; they can select leading state officers and members of their state legislatures. They can vote for members of Congress and for presidential electors from their state. The electors from all the states elect the President and Vice-President. In America, then, citizens control their government through representatives chosen in free elections.

Freedom to vote, to form one's own opinions on public questions, and to express these opinions without fear make it possible for individual citizens to help their country. Mr. Average Citizen can vote for men who, he believes, will serve our country wisely and well. He can refuse to vote for those in whom he has no faith. He can study the party platforms or statements of the political parties and vote for those candidates who support the things he thinks America needs. If government officials and political parties fail to keep their promises, the voter can refuse to support them in the next election.

The obligations implied in these sentences are as vitally important as the freedoms.

When the Pilgrims signed the Mayflower Compact in 1620 (left), they agreed to govern themselves through laws enacted by common consent.

Americans still meet to set up rules for self-government. At right, elected delegates work out a new state constitution.

As voters, Americans have the important responsibility of choosing the nation's leaders. The young people shown at left are reminding their fellow citizens of this duty. Below, students are checking the addresses of voters who will be sent election information.

VOTE AUG 5TH

All Americans Must Help to Carry On Their Free Government

Mr. Average Citizen can do even more if he has read widely and listened carefully. If he is convinced that the government should take some action, he can talk about it with his friends. He can join organizations which will voice his opinion in Washington. He can also write to his representative and senator. All too often people neglect the power of public opinion. They merely grumble and do nothing. Finally, if he has the necessary qualifications, Mr. Average Citizen can seek election to office in his community or state or in the national government. We recognize that our government is not perfect; our way of life falls short of what we would like it to be. But they can be improved if each individual does his full share.

•

Years ago, when the Constitutional Convention had finished its work, Benjamin Franklin was asked, "What have you given us?" This wise old gentleman replied, "A republic, if you can keep it." Franklin knew that if liberty and self-government were to endure, citizens must accept responsibilities. This truth applies just as much in the world in which we live today as it did when the United States was created.

Franklin's words echo the same challenge that was made on page 706

THE
CONSTITUTION
OF THE
UNITED STATES

On the following pages you will find the Constitution, a document drawn up 175 years ago, which continues to serve our nation well.

The actual text of the Constitution appears in the wide left-hand column on each page. Headings and subheadings have been added to help you read the text with greater understanding. Those parts of the Constitution no longer in effect are enclosed in brackets and printed in italic type like this [*which shall be determined*].

Throughout the text of the Constitution, you will also find explanatory notes under the title **WHAT TO LOOK FOR.** Each of these notes will alert you to important topics in the portion of the Constitution that follows.

Finally, in the narrow right-hand column of each page there are definitions or explanations to help you understand unfamiliar words or terms that occur in the neighboring portion of the text of the Constitution.

PREAMBLE

WE THE PEOPLE of the United States, in order to form a more perfect union, establish justice, insure domestic tranquillity, provide for the common defense, promote the general welfare, and secure the blessings of liberty to ourselves and our posterity, do ordain and establish this Constitution for the United States of America.

▶ *Preamble* · An introduction.

▶ *Insure domestic tranquillity* · To guarantee peace within the country.

▶ *Posterity* · Descendants; later generations.

▶ *Ordain and establish* · To announce officially; to declare as law.

ARTICLE I

Legislative Department

WHAT TO LOOK FOR IN ARTICLE I, SECTIONS 1, 2, AND 3

Our federal government has three branches — one (Congress) that makes laws, one (the executive branch) that carries them out, and one (the courts) that explains them and says how they apply in certain cases. You may want to look back at pages 231–232 in this book where the reasons for setting up the three branches are given.

Article I of the Constitution tells how the law-making body — Congress — shall be organized and shall carry on its business.

Congress has two houses. Section 1 explains that Congress is made up of two houses, the Senate and the House of Representatives. Section 2 tells how long the members of the House of Representatives shall serve, who chooses them, what qualifications they must have, on what basis they shall be chosen, and how vacancies shall be filled. Section 3 gives the same information for the Senate. The qualifications for representatives differ from those for senators, as you will see if you compare Sections 2b and 3c. Today members of the Senate, as well as members of the House, are elected directly by the voters. The reasons for this change in the original Constitution are explained in the note for Amendment XVII on page A27.

Number of members. There are 435 members of the House of Representatives. Our states are divided into districts on the basis of population, and one representative is elected from each district. Thus a state with a large population has more districts and sends more representatives to Washington than a state with fewer people. No matter how small a state may be, however, it still sends one representative. To see how many representatives your state has, look at the chart of states on pages A42–A43. The Senate, on the other hand, contains two senators from each state. Because there are 50 states, there are 100 senators in all.

Section 1. **Congress in General**

All legislative powers herein granted shall be vested in a Congress of the United States, which shall consist of a Senate and House of Representatives.

▶ *Legislative* · Law-making.

▶ *Vested in a Congress* · Granted, or assigned, to Congress.

Section 2. **The House of Representatives**

a. Election and term of members. The House of Representatives shall be composed of members chosen every second year by the people of the several States,

Difficult terms are explained in This column.

and the electors in each State shall have the qualifications requisite for electors of the most numerous branch of the State Legislature.

▶ *Qualifications requisite* · Required qualifications.
▶ *Most numerous branch* · In a state legislature, the house which has the most members.
▶ *Attained to* · Reached.

b. Qualifications of members. No person shall be a Representative who shall not have attained to the age of twenty-five years, and been seven years a citizen of the United States, and who shall not, when elected, be an inhabitant of that State in which he shall be chosen.

c. Apportionment of representatives and of direct taxes. Representatives and direct taxes shall be apportioned among the several States which may be included within this Union, according to their respective numbers, [*which shall be determined by adding to the whole number of free persons, including those bound to service for a term of years, and excluding Indians not taxed, three fifths of all other persons.*] The actual enumeration shall be made within three years after the first meeting of the Congress of the United States, and within every subsequent term of ten years, in such manner as they shall by law direct. The number of Representatives shall not exceed one for every thirty thousand, but each state shall have at least one representative; [*and until such enumeration shall be made, the state of New Hampshire shall be entitled to choose three; Massachusetts, eight; Rhode Island and Providence Plantations, one; Connecticut, five; New York, six; New Jersey, four; Pennsylvania, eight; Delaware, one; Maryland, six; Virginia, ten; North Carolina, five; South Carolina, five; and Georgia, three.*]

▶ *Direct taxes* · Taxes paid per person or on property or income.
▶ *Apportioned . . . according to their respective numbers* · Distributed among the states according to their populations.

▶ *Enumeration* · Counting; census.

▶ *Every subsequent term of ten years* · The first census was taken in 1790, and one has been taken every ten years since.

d. Filling vacancies. When vacancies happen in the representation from any State, the Executive authority thereof shall issue writs of election to fill such vacancies.

▶ *Executive authority* · Chief officer; in this case, the state governor.
▶ *Writs of election* · Official orders calling for elections.

e. Officers; impeachment. The House of Representatives shall choose their Speaker and other officers; and shall have the sole power of impeachment.

▶ *Sole power of impeachment* · The power, granted only to the House of Representatives, to make official accusations against federal officials, charging that they have not properly carried out their duties.

Section 3. **The Senate**

a. Number and election of members. The Senate of the United States shall be composed of two Senators from each state, chosen [*by the legislature thereof,*] for six years, and each Senator shall have one vote.

b. Classification. Immediately after they shall be assembled in consequence of the first election, they shall be divided as equally as may be into three classes. [*The seats of the Senators of the first class*

Parts of the Constitution no longer in effect are bracketed and printed in italics.

shall be vacated at the expiration of the second year, of the second class at the expiration of the fourth year, and of the third class at the expiration of the sixth year,] so that one third may be chosen every second year; [*and if vacancies happen by resignation, or otherwise, during the recess of the legislature of any State, the Executive thereof may make temporary appointments until the next meeting of the legislature, which shall then fill such vacancies.*]

c. Qualifications of members.   No person shall be a Senator who shall not have attained to the age of thirty years, and been nine years a citizen of the United States, and who shall not, when elected, be an inhabitant of that State for which he shall be chosen.

d. President of Senate.   The Vice President of the United States shall be President of the Senate, but shall have no vote, unless they be equally divided.

e. Other officers.   The Senate shall choose their own officers, and also a President pro tempore, in the absence of the Vice President, or when he shall exercise the office of President of the United States.

f. Trial of impeachment.   The Senate shall have the sole power to try all impeachments. When sitting for that purpose, they shall be on oath or affirmation. When the President of the United States is tried, the Chief Justice shall preside; and no person shall be convicted without the concurrence of two thirds of the members present.

g. Judgment in case of conviction.   Judgment in cases of impeachment shall not extend further than to removal from office, and disqualification to hold and enjoy any office of honor, trust or profit under the United States; but the party convicted shall nevertheless be liable and subject to indictment, trial, judgment and punishment, according to law.

Note the precise definition of terms.

▶ **Equally divided** · The Vice-President votes on a bill only if the vote in the Senate is equally divided for and against the bill.

▶ **President pro tempore** · The senator chosen to preside over the Senate when the Vice-President is absent.

▶ **Exercise the office of President** · Carry out the duties of the presidency.

▶ **Sole power to try all impeachments** · The power, granted only to the Senate, to conduct the trials of impeached officials.

▶ **On oath or affirmation** · Bound by a solemn declaration or promise to be honest and just.

▶ **Chief Justice** · The chief justice of the Supreme Court.

▶ **Convicted** · Declared guilty.

▶ **Concurrence** · Agreement.

▶ **Indictment** · Being charged with a crime.

▶ **Punishment, according to law** · An impeached official found guilty by the Senate is removed from office. After that he can be tried for his crime in a regular court and punished if convicted.

Students probably should read the headnote before reading the part of the Constitution to which it refers.

WHAT TO LOOK FOR IN ARTICLE I, SECTIONS 4, 5, AND 6

Sections 4, 5, and 6 describe how members of Congress shall be elected, when Congress shall meet, the way it shall conduct business, the pay the members shall receive, and the privileges they shall have. Notice that each house is given wide powers to conduct its business and control its members.

Elections, time of meeting, and privileges. Three items in these sections deserve special attention.

(1) **The governments of the different states have control over elections of representatives and senators.** Your own state, for example, decides how candidates for office shall be named, prints the ballots, and conducts the elections.

(2) The time when Congress meets has been changed by the 20th Amendment. To find an explanation of this change, look at the note explaining Amendments XX, XXII, and XXIII on page A29.

(3) Members of Congress are not to be "questioned in any other place" about what they say in the House or the Senate (Section 6a). Senators and representatives, therefore, may feel free to say what they think without fear that they may be taken to court and forced to stand trial for their remarks. Although this privilege may be abused sometimes, it is a necessary one. Under its protection congressmen may without fear criticize the executive branch of the government or discuss any subject of concern to the nation.

Section 4. Election of Senators and Representatives and Meeting of Congress

a. Method of holding elections. The times, places and manner of holding elections for Senators and Representatives shall be prescribed in each State by the Legislature thereof; but the Congress may at any time by law make or alter such regulations, except as to the places of choosing Senators.

▶ *Prescribed* · Decided or designated.

b. Meeting of Congress. The Congress shall assemble at least once in every year, [*and such meeting shall be on the first Monday in December,*] unless they shall by law appoint a different day.

Section 5. Rules of Procedure

a. Organization. Each house shall be the judge of the elections, returns and qualifications of its own members, and a majority of each shall constitute a quorum to do business; but a smaller number may adjourn from day to day, and may be authorized to compel the attendance of absent members, in such manner, and under such penalties, as each house may provide.

▶ *Quorum* · The number of members which must be present for official business to be carried on. In each house a majority (over half) of the members is a quorum.
▶ *Adjourn* · To put off meeting until a later time.

b. Rules of proceedings. Each house may determine the rules of its proceedings, punish its members for disorderly behavior, and, with the concurrence of two thirds, expel a member.

▶ *Concurrence of two thirds* · By a two-thirds vote either house may expel one of its members.

c. Journal. Each house shall keep a journal of its proceedings, and from time to time publish the same, excepting such parts as may in their judgment require secrecy; and the yeas and nays of the members of either house on any question shall, at the desire of one fifth of those present, be entered on the journal.

▶ *Yeas and nays* · The votes for (yeas) and against (nays) a measure.

d. Adjournment. Neither house, during the session of Congress, shall, without the consent of the other, adjourn for more than three days, nor to any other place than that in which the two houses shall be sitting.

Section 6. Compensation, Privileges, and Restrictions

a. Pay and privileges of members. The Senators and Representatives shall receive a compensation for their services, to be ascertained by law, and paid out of the Treasury of the United States. They shall in all cases except treason, felony and breach of the peace, be privileged from arrest during their attendance at the session of their respective houses, and in going to and returning from the same; and for any speech or debate in either house, they shall not be questioned in any other place.

b. Holding other offices prohibited. No Senator or Representative shall, during the time for which he was elected, be appointed to any civil office under the authority of the United States which shall have been created, or the emoluments whereof shall have been increased during such time; and no person holding any office under the United States shall be a member of either house during his continuance in office.

In Canada, for example, all members of the cabinet also are members of Parliament, the lawmaking body.

▶ *Compensation · Salary.* Congressmen also receive travel and office expenses.
▶ *Ascertained by law ·* Provided for by law.
▶ *Treason ·* See Article III, Section 3, for definition of treason.
▶ *Felony and breach of the peace ·* A serious crime and illegal violence.

▶ *Civil office ·* A non-military government office.
▶ *Emoluments ·* Salary.

▶ *Continuance in office ·* No person holding a position in the federal government can also be a member of Congress. For example, a senator elected to the presidency would resign his seat in the Senate.

WHAT TO LOOK FOR IN ARTICLE I, SECTION 7

This section tells how laws shall be passed. In order for a bill to become a law, it must be passed in exactly the same form by both House and Senate. With one exception, any bill can be started in either house. The exception is that bills to raise revenue, that is, tax bills, must start in the House of Representatives.

Passage of bills. Actually, the business of lawmaking today is not as simple as it sounds, for of the thousands of bills introduced into each house each year only a small number become law. A bill is usually studied and reported on by one of several committees in each house before it is debated and put to a vote. Committees have great power in that they can kill a bill in two ways: (1) by reporting unfavorably on it and (2) by not reporting on it at all and thus preventing the bill from being voted on in the House or Senate.

The President signs or vetoes. Ordinarily, the President must approve a bill before it can become a law. If the President disapproves, he is said to "veto" a bill. It still can become a law, however, if both the House and the Senate pass it again by a two-thirds vote.

The President must act on a bill within ten days; if he neither signs nor vetoes the bill within this period, it becomes law. The exception is what is called a "pocket veto." If a bill is presented to him within ten days of the adjournment of Congress, and if he does not sign it, the bill does not become law. It is as though he had killed the bill by putting it in his pocket and leaving it there.

Section 7. **Method of Passing Laws**

a. Revenue bills. All bills for raising revenue shall originate in the House of Representatives; but the Senate may propose or concur with amendments as on other bills.

▷ *Bills* · Written statements of proposed laws.

▷ *Raising revenue* · Raising income for government expenses.

▷ *Propose or concur with amendments* · Add or approve of changes.

b. How bills become laws. Every bill which shall have passed the House of Representatives and the Senate shall, before it become a law, be presented to the President of the United States; if he approve he shall sign it, but if not he shall return it, with his objections to that house in which it shall have originated, who shall enter the objections at large on their journal, and proceed to reconsider it. If after such reconsideration two thirds of that house shall agree to pass the bill, it shall be sent, together with the objections, to the other house, by which it shall likewise be reconsidered, and if approved by two thirds of that house, it shall become a law. But in all such cases the votes of both houses shall be determined by yeas and nays, and the names of the persons voting for and against the bill shall be entered on the journal of each house respectively. If any bill shall not be returned by the President within ten days (Sundays excepted) after it shall have been presented to him, the same shall be a law, in like manner as if he had signed it, unless the Congress by their adjournment prevent its return, in which case it shall not be a law.

▷ *Objections at large* · The basic reasons given by the President for his refusing to sign the bill.

c. Approval or disapproval by the President. Every order, resolution, or vote to which the concurrence of the Senate and House of Representatives may be necessary (except on a question of adjournment) shall be presented to the President of the United States; and before the same shall take effect, shall be approved by him, or being disapproved by him, shall be repassed by two thirds of the Senate and House of Representatives, according to the rules and limitations prescribed in the case of a bill.

▷ *Resolution* · A declaration which states a rule or expresses an opinion. If a resolution is adopted by both houses, it is called a "joint resolution" and must be presented, like a bill, to the President for his approval or veto.

WHAT TO LOOK FOR IN ARTICLE I, SECTIONS 8, 9, AND 10

At the very heart of our form of government is the question of what powers the United States government shall have, what powers the states shall have, and what powers are denied to both state and national governments. The men who framed the Constitution showed great wisdom in solving this problem, as you will find by turning back to pages 228–229 of this book.

Powers granted to Congress.   Section 8 lists definite powers granted to Congress. It also empowers Congress to pass laws "necessary and proper" to carry out these listed powers. This "necessary and proper" clause has enabled Congress to widen its powers considerably.

Powers denied to the federal and state governments.   The powers purposely denied to the United States and to the states are named in Sections 9 and 10. To refresh your memory of why Section 9a forbade Congress to prohibit the importing of slaves, look back at page 221. By its own wording, this paragraph was in effect only until 1808.

The powers denied to the states in Section 10 make clear the relations between the states and the national government. If the states had the power to make treaties, coin money, tax imports and exports, and keep their own armies, they would really be independent countries. The central government would then be weak and meaningless.

Powers belonging to both federal and state governments.   Though the Constitution does not say so, some powers belong to both the state and federal governments. Both, for instance, have the power of taxation.

Section 8. Powers Granted to Congress

The Congress shall have power

a. To lay and collect taxes, duties, imposts, and excises, to pay the debts and provide for the common defence and general welfare of the United States; but all duties, imposts and excises shall be uniform throughout the United States;

▶ *Duties, imposts, and excises* · A duty is a tax. An impost is a tax on imported goods. An excise is a tax on products manufactured within the country.
▶ *Uniform* · Standard; the same.

b. To borrow money on the credit of the United States;

▶ *Credit* · Trustworthiness in paying debts.

c. To regulate commerce with foreign nations, and among the several States, and with the Indian tribes;

▶ *Naturalization* · The steps by which a foreign-born person becomes a citizen.
▶ *Bankruptcies* · Businesses which are unable to pay their debts and whose property is therefore sold to meet these debts.

d. To establish an uniform rule of naturalization, and uniform laws on the subject of bankruptcies throughout the United States;

e. To coin money, regulate the value thereof, and of foreign coin, and fix the standard of weights and measures;

▶ *Standard of weights and measures* · The units of weight and measurement (for example, pounds and inches) that are used throughout the country.
▶ *Securities* · Includes money and government bonds.

f. To provide for the punishment of counterfeiting the securities and current coin of the United States;

g. To establish post offices and post roads;

▶ *Post roads* · Improved roads on which mail was carried.

h. To promote the progress of science and useful arts by securing for limited times to authors and inventors the exclusive right to their respective writings and discoveries;

▶ *Useful arts* · Writing books, composing music, and inventing are examples.
▶ *Securing for limited times . . . the exclusive right* · Patent and copyright laws protect the rights of authors and inventors. (See the box on page 446.)

i. To constitute tribunals inferior to the Supreme Court;

▶ *To constitute tribunals inferior. . . . ·* To establish courts lower in rank than the Supreme Court.

j. To define and punish piracies and felonies committed on the high seas and offences against the law of nations;

▶ *High seas* · The open sea, not within the jurisdiction of any nation.

k. To declare war, grant letters of marque and reprisal, and make rules concerning captures on land and water;

Letters of marque and reprisal · Government licenses authorizing the holders to fit out armed ships for use in capturing enemy merchant ships.

l. To raise and support armies, but no appropriation of money to that use shall be for a longer term than two years;

Appropriation · An amount set aside for a certain purpose.

m. To provide and maintain a navy;

n. To make rules for the government and regulation of the land and naval forces;

o. To provide for calling forth the militia to execute the laws of the Union, suppress insurrections, and repel invasions;

Militia · Citizen soldiers who are not in the regular army; for instance, the state militia.

Execute the laws · Carry out the laws.

Insurrections · Uprisings; rebellions.

Disciplining · Training.

p. To provide for organizing, arming and disciplining the militia, and for governing such part of them as may be employed in the service of the United States, reserving to the States respectively the appointment of the officers, and the authority of training the militia according to the discipline prescribed by Congress;

q. To exercise exclusive legislation in all cases whatsoever, over such district (not exceeding ten miles square) as may, by cession of particular States, and the acceptance of Congress, become the seat of the government of the United States, and to exercise like authority over all places purchased by the consent of the legislature of the State, in which the same shall be, for the erection of forts, magazines, arsenals, dockyards, and other needful buildings; — and

Exercise exclusive legislation · Have the sole right to pass laws.

Cession · Yielding of property.

Exercise like authority · To have the same power. Congress enacts laws for other federal areas, such as army bases, as well as the District of Columbia.

Magazines, arsenals · Buildings for the storage of weapons, munitions, and other military supplies.

r. To make all laws which shall be necessary and proper for carrying into execution the foregoing powers, and all other powers vested by this Constitution in the government of the United States, or in any department or officer thereof.

Section 9. Powers Denied to the Federal Government

a. [*The migration or importation of such persons as any of the States now existing shall think proper to admit, shall not be prohibited by the Congress prior to the year one thousand eight hundred and eight, but a tax or duty may be imposed on such importation, not exceeding ten dollars for each person.*]

b. The privilege of the writ of habeas corpus shall not be suspended, unless when in cases of rebellion or invasion the public safety may require it.

Writ of habeas corpus · A court order directing that a prisoner be given a hearing so that the court may decide whether he should be held and charged with a crime or released.

Why was Congress denied the right to pass ex post facto laws?

A10 THE CONSTITUTION OF THE UNITED STATES

c. No bill of attainder or ex post facto law shall be passed.

d. No capitation, or other direct, tax shall be laid, unless in proportion to the census or enumeration herein before directed to be taken.

e. No tax or duty shall be laid on articles exported from any State.

f. No preference shall be given by any regulation of commerce or revenue to the ports of one State over those of another: nor shall vessels bound to, or from, one State be obliged to enter, clear, or pay duties in another.

g. No money shall be drawn from the Treasury, but in consequence of appropriations made by law; and a regular statement and account of the receipts and expenditures of all public money shall be published from time to time.

h. No title of nobility shall be granted by the United States: and no person holding any office of profit or trust under them shall, without the consent of the Congress, accept of any present, emolument, office, or title, of any kind whatever, from any king, prince, or foreign state.

Section 10. Powers Denied to the States

a. No State shall enter into any treaty, alliance, or confederation; grant letters of marque and reprisal; coin money; emit bills of credit; make any thing but gold and silver coin a tender in payment of debts; pass any bill of attainder; ex post facto law, or law impairing the obligation of contracts, or grant any title of nobility.

b. No State shall, without the consent of the Congress, lay any imposts or duties on imports or exports, except what may be absolutely necessary for executing its inspection laws; and the net produce of all duties and imposts, laid by any State on imports or exports, shall be for the use of the treasury of the United States; and all such laws shall be subject to the revision and control of the Congress.

c. No State shall, without the consent of Congress, lay any duty of tonnage, keep troops, or ships of war in time of peace, enter into any agreement or compact with another State, or with a foreign power, or engage in war, unless actually invaded, or in such imminent danger as will not admit of delay.

▶ *Bill of attainder* · A legislative act that imposes a punishment without a trial or a specific charge.

▶ *Ex post facto law* · A law which declares that a certain action is illegal and which permits persons who have already committed such an action to be prosecuted for it.

▶ *Capitation* · A head tax; a tax paid for each person.

▶ *Unless in proportion to the census* · The amount of a capitation or direct tax paid by a state would depend on its population. Note, however, that the Sixteenth Amendment (page A28) provides for the income tax, which is levied "without regard to any census or enumeration."

▶ *Be obliged to . . . clear* · Be required to pay harbor dues or customs duties.

▶ *Expenditures* · Spending.

▶ *Title of nobility* · A title such as count, baron, duke, etc.

▶ *Accept of any present* · Actually, high officials like the President may exchange personal presents with leaders of foreign states.

▶ *Emit bills of credit* · Issue letters or bonds to be used by the holder as money.

▶ *A tender* · Money offered in payment of a debt.

▶ *Impairing the obligation of contracts* · Making a contract (a legal agreement between two persons) of less value; for example, permitting a person to pay off a contract for less than its face value.

▶ *Net produce* · Income from duties and imposts after expenses have been paid.

▶ *Duty of tonnage* · Duty collected at a given amount per ton of cargo.

▶ *Imminent* · Immediate, or threatening to happen soon.

ARTICLE II

Executive Department

WHAT TO LOOK FOR IN ARTICLE II, SECTION I

Article II establishes the executive branch of the government. Section I describes the term of office of the President and the Vice-President, the original method of electing these officials, the qualifications that they must possess, and their salaries.

Election of the President and his salary. The President and the Vice-President serve for four years. They are elected in the autumn of the years which can be exactly divided by four (1960, 1964, 1968, etc.). Their term of office, however, begins in the year following their election (1961, 1965, 1969, etc.). Using the power given in Section 1c of Article II, Congress provides that voters shall cast their ballots in presidential elections on the Tuesday after the first Monday in November. The salary of the President is now $100,000 a year, and he receives additional amounts for his expenses. He also receives the use of the White House, automobiles and airplanes, and other conveniences necessary for a man holding this important position.

Electors. To this day, Americans do not vote directly for President and Vice-President. The voters of each state choose *electors,* who have the right under the Constitution to choose both President and Vice-President. The reasons for this arrangement are given in the paragraph numbered (3) on page 221 of this book. But for years the electors have generally cast their votes in the same way as do the majority of the voters of their states. For this reason we know soon after a national election is over who will be the next President and Vice-President.

You will notice that the way of choosing the President and Vice-President (Section 1b) has been changed. To understand the reasons for this change, look at the explanation preceding the 11th and 12th Amendments on page A23.

Section 1. **President and Vice-President**

a. Term of office. The executive power shall be vested in a President of the United States of America. He shall hold his office during the term of four years, and together with the Vice President, chosen for the same term, be elected as follows:

b. Electors. Each State shall appoint, in such manner as the legislature thereof may direct, a number of electors, equal to the whole number of Senators and Representatives to which the State may be entitled in the Congress; but no Senator or Representative, or person holding an office of trust or profit under the United States, shall be appointed an elector.

Former method of electing President and Vice-President. [*The electors shall meet in their respective States, and vote by ballot for two persons, of whom one at least shall not be an inhabitant of the same State with themselves. And they shall make a list of all the persons voted for, and of the number of votes for each; which list they shall sign and certify, and transmit sealed to the seat of government of the*

▸ *Each state shall appoint . . . a number of electors* · Electors are usually nominated by conventions or committees of the parties in each state. In the presidential election the people then elect the group of electors who, with the electors of other states, will choose the President.

▸ *Equal to the whole number of Senators and Representatives* · A state's electoral vote equals the number of representatives it has in the House plus two (the number of senators).

United States, directed to the President of the Senate. The President of the Senate shall, in the presence of the Senate and House of Representatives, open all the certificates, and the votes shall then be counted. The person having the greatest number of votes shall be the President, if such number be a majority of the whole number of electors appointed; and if there be more than one who have such majority, and have an equal number of votes, then the House of Representatives shall immediately choose by ballot one of them for President; and if no person have a majority, then from the five highest on the list the said house shall in like manner choose the President. But in choosing the President the votes shall be taken by States, the representation from each State having one vote; a quorum for this purpose shall consist of a member or members from two thirds of the States, and a majority of all the States shall be necessary to a choice. In every case, after the choice of the President, the person having the greatest number of votes of the electors shall be the Vice President. But if there should remain two or more who have equal votes, the Senate shall choose from them by ballot the Vice President.]

c. Time of elections. The Congress may determine the time of choosing the electors, and the day on which they shall give their votes; which day shall be the same throughout the United States.

d. Qualifications of the President. No person except a natural born citizen, [*or a citizen of the United States, at the time of the adoption of this Constitution,*] shall be eligible to the office of President; neither shall any person be eligible to that office who shall not have attained to the age of thirty-five years, and been fourteen years a resident within the United States.

▶ *Natural born citizen* • A natural born citizen is one born in this country or born to American citizens who are living outside the country.

e. Vacancy. In case of the removal of the President from office or of his death, resignation, or inability to discharge the powers and duties of the said office, the same shall devolve on the Vice President, and the Congress may by law provide for the case of removal, death, resignation, or inability, both of the President and Vice President, declaring what officer shall then act as President, and such officer shall act accordingly, until the disability be removed, or a President shall be elected.

▶ *Discharge the powers and duties* • To carry out powers and responsibilities.
▶ *Devolve on* • Become the responsibility of.

f. The President's salary. The President shall, at stated times, receive for his services, a compensation, which shall neither be increased nor diminished dur-

▶ *Diminished* • Reduced.

ing the period for which he shall have been elected, and he shall not receive within that period any other emolument from the United States, or any of them.

▶ *Period for which he shall have been elected* · His term of office: four years.

g. Oath of office. Before he enter on the execution of his office, he shall take the following oath or affirmation: — "I do solemnly swear (or affirm) that I will faithfully execute the office of President of the United States, and will to the best of my ability, preserve, protect and defend the Constitution of the United States."

WHAT TO LOOK FOR IN ARTICLE II, SECTIONS 2, 3, AND 4

Powers and duties of the President. It may seem strange that the powers and duties of the President of the United States can be described in two short sections (2 and 3) of this Article. That they can be stated so briefly illustrates an important strength of our Constitution. This great document did not spell out every detail of the government. As a result, our government has been able to grow as conditions in our country have changed, without having to add a great many amendments to the Constitution.

Power to appoint. For instance, the Constitution merely says that Congress may give power to appoint officers of the government to "the President alone," or to "the heads of departments." The President is now head of a branch of the government which has hundreds of thousands of employees. These people carry on the work of the departments and agencies of the executive branch of the government. A few words in the Constitution, therefore, provide the foundation for all their jobs.

Impeachment. Section 4 of this Article states for what reasons a President may be removed from office. Only one President — Andrew Johnson — has ever been impeached (accused), and he was not convicted and removed.

Section 2. **Powers of the President**

a. Military powers; reprieves and pardons. The President shall be commander in chief of the army and navy of the United States, and of the militia of the several States, when called into the actual service of the United States; he may require the opinion, in writing, of the principal officer in each of the executive departments, upon any subject relating to the duties of their respective offices, and he shall have power to grant reprieves and pardons for offences against the United States, except in cases of impeachment.

▶ *Commander in chief of the army and navy* · The President is commander in chief of all the armed forces, which today also includes the Air Force.

▶ *Executive departments* · The departments represented in the President's Cabinet, such as State, Treasury, etc.

▶ *To grant reprieves and pardons* · To postpone punishments (reprieves) and to release persons from punishment (pardons).

b. Treaties; appointments. He shall have power, by and with the advice and consent of the Senate, to make treaties, provided two thirds of the Senators present concur; and he shall nominate, and by and with the advice and consent of the Senate, shall appoint ambassadors, other public ministers and consuls, judges of the Supreme Court, and all other officers of the United States, whose appointments are not herein otherwise provided for, and which shall be established by law; but the Congress may by law vest the appointment of such inferior officers as they think proper, in the President alone, in the courts of law, or in the heads of departments.

c. **Filling vacancies.** The President shall have power to fill up all vacancies that may happen during the recess of the Senate, by granting commissions which shall expire at the end of their next session.

Section 3. Duties of the President

He shall from time to time give to the Congress information of the state of the Union, and recommend to their consideration such measures as he shall judge necessary and expedient; he may, on extraordinary occasions, convene both houses, or either of them, and in case of disagreement between them with respect to the time of adjournment, he may adjourn them to such time as he shall think proper; he shall receive ambassadors and other public ministers; he shall take care that the laws be faithfully executed, and shall commission all the officers of the United States.

Section 4. Impeachment

The President, Vice President and all civil officers of the United States shall be removed from office on impeachment for, and conviction of, treason, bribery, or other high crimes and misdemeanors.

▸ *Ambassadors, other public ministers and consuls* • Official representatives of the United States to other countries.

▸ *Congress may by law vest the appointment* • Congress may pass laws giving the power of appointing officers to the President only, to the law courts, or to department heads.

▸ *Fill up all vacancies* • When the Senate is not in session, the President may appoint persons on a temporary basis to positions for which the Senate's approval is needed.

▸ *Recess* • A period when a legislative body is not in session.

▸ *Commissions* • Appointments.

▸ *Expire* • To end; run out.

▸ *Expedient* • Desirable and suitable.

▸ *Extraordinary* • Special, or emergency.

▸ *Convene* • Call together.

▸ *High crimes and misdemeanors* • Serious crimes and offenses.

ARTICLE III
Judicial Department ← *The subject of the article is stated.*

WHAT TO LOOK FOR IN ARTICLE III

Congress establishes courts. This Article establishes the third great branch of our government — the judicial branch. Section 1 states that there shall be a Supreme Court and such other courts as Congress may see fit to establish. Thus Congress has set up district and appeals courts throughout the country as well as some special courts.

Judges of the Supreme Court. Congress also determines the number of judges in the Supreme Court. (For a good many years there have been nine.) The Constitution goes on to say that the judges of all the United States courts shall hold their offices "during good behavior," and that their salaries may not be reduced. As a result, judges are able to make decisions under the laws without fear of being dismissed from their positions or of having their salaries lowered.

On what cases may the courts act? The different parts of Section 2 tell what kinds of cases may be tried in federal courts. Every United States court, when it is requested to consider a subject, asks first of all: "Have we the right to act in this matter?" The answer depends on Section 2 of Article III.

The right of trial by jury. Part c of Section 2 guarantees trial by jury. Such a trial is important in making sure that Americans are not unjustly convicted. Moreover, a trial must be held in the state where the crime was committed. If you will look back to pages 138 and 230, you will find why this right to a trial by jury is important.

Treason and its punishment. Section 3 defines treason. Treason is such a serious crime that the members of the Constitutional Convention thought it should be clearly defined in the Constitution itself. In dictatorships treason is not defined clearly, so that people may be convicted of treason merely because they oppose the government or fail to abide by its laws. This section also restricts the kind of punishment that may be imposed for treason.

Note that only the Supreme Court is mentioned specifically.

Section 1. The Federal Courts

The judicial power of the United States shall be vested in one Supreme Court, and in such inferior courts as the Congress may from time to time ordain and establish. The judges, both of the Supreme and inferior courts, shall hold their offices during good behavior, and shall, at stated times, receive for their services, a compensation, which shall not be diminished during their continuance in office.

Inferior courts · Courts lower in rank than the Supreme Court.

A compensation, which shall not be diminished · The salary of a federal judge cannot be reduced during his period of service (but it can be increased).

Section 2. Jurisdiction of the Federal Courts

a. **Federal courts in general.** The judicial power shall extend to all cases, in law and equity, arising under this Constitution, the laws of the United States, and treaties made or which shall be made, under their authority; — to all cases affecting ambassadors, other public ministers and consuls; — to all cases of admiralty jurisdiction; — to controversies to which the United States shall be a party; — to controversies between two or more States; — [*between a State and citizens of another State;*] — between citizens of different States; — between citizens of the same State claiming lands under grants of different States, and between a State, or the citizens thereof, and foreign states, citizens or subjects.

b. **Supreme Court.** In all cases affecting ambassadors, other public ministers and consuls, and those in which a State shall be a party, the Supreme Court shall have original jurisdiction. In all the other cases before mentioned, the Supreme Court shall have

Cases, in . . . equity · Cases based on general principles of justice rather than on particular laws.

Cases of admiralty jurisdiction · Cases based on situations that develop on the high seas. (*Jurisdiction* means the right or power to hear a case and administer justice.)

Controversies · Disputes.

Party · One of the two sides in a lawsuit.

Original jurisdiction; appellate jurisdiction · In original jurisdiction a case is

appellate jurisdiction, both as to law and fact, with such exceptions, and under such regulations as the Congress shall make.

    c. Rules respecting trials. The trial of all crimes, except in cases of impeachment, shall be by jury; and such trial shall be held in the State where the said crimes shall have been committed; but when not committed within any State, the trial shall be at such place or places as the Congress may by law have directed.

Section 3. Treason

    a. Definition of treason. Treason against the United States shall consist only in levying war against them, or in adhering to their enemies, giving them aid and comfort. No person shall be convicted of treason unless on the testimony of two witnesses to the same overt act, or on confession in open court.

    b. Punishment of treason. The Congress shall have power to declare the punishment of treason, but no attainder of treason shall work corruption of blood, or forfeiture except during the life of the person attainted.

Why was treason defined so carefully?

brought directly to a court for its first hearing. In appellate jurisdiction the case comes to a higher court because of an appeal (claim) that a lower court was in error.

▸*Both as to law and fact* • Whether the law applies and whether the facts were correctly determined.

▸*Levying war* • Making war.
▸*Adhering to* • Supporting.

▸*Overt act* • An act seen by others.

▸No *attainder of treason . . . .* • The children of a citizen *attainted* (convicted of treason) shall not be denied the right to inherit their father's property nor be deprived of the rights of citizenship because of the father's wrongdoing.

ARTICLE IV

The States and the Federal Government

WHAT TO LOOK FOR IN ARTICLE IV

    Article IV describes the relationships between the United States and the states, and between one state and other states. For example, Section 1 provides that one state must accept the official acts of other states. Section 2a says that citizens of one state shall have the privileges of citizens of the other states. Section 2b states that if a person accused of crime flees to another state, the second state shall return him to the first state for trial. Without this provision, crime could flourish.

    Admission of new states. Section 3a permits Congress to admit new states. This section guarantees, however, that no states may be reduced in size to make new ones, unless these states themselves and Congress agree. In Section 3b Congress is given power to govern territory belonging to the United States.

Protection of the states by the federal government. Section 4 guarantees to the states help from the United States government when they need it. The United States will protect the states from invasion, for example. In the same way, the United States is to protect the states if serious riots or other violence should occur. The various provisions of this Article help to make the United States a strong and united nation.

Section 1. State Records

Full faith and credit shall be given in each State to the public acts, records, and judicial proceedings of every other State. And the Congress may by general laws prescribe the manner in which such acts, records, and proceedings shall be proved, and the effect thereof.

▶ *Full faith and credit . . . .* • Each state must accept the official acts of other states.

▶ *Public acts, records, and judicial proceedings* • Laws, official files (such as birth records), and court actions.

Section 2. Privileges and Immunities of Citizens

a. Privileges. The citizens of each State shall be entitled to all privileges and immunities of citizens in the several States.

▶ *Immunities* • Freedoms or exemptions.

b. Surrender of fugitives. A person charged in any State with treason, felony, or other crime, who shall flee from justice, and be found in another State, shall, on demand of the executive authority of the State from which he fled, be delivered up, to be removed to the State having jurisdiction of the crime.

c. Fugitive workers. [*No person held to service or labor in one State, under the laws thereof, escaping into another shall in consequence of any law or regulation therein, be discharged from such service or labor, but shall be delivered upon claim of the party to whom such service or labor may be due.*]

Section 3. New States and Territories

a. Admission of new states. New States may be admitted by the Congress into this Union; but no new State shall be formed or erected within the jurisdiction of any other State; nor any State be formed by the junction of two or more States, or parts of States, without the consent of the legislatures of the States concerned, as well as of the Congress.

▶ *Junction* • Combination.

b. Power of Congress over territory and property. The Congress shall have power to dispose of and make all needful rules and regulations respecting the territory or other property belonging to the United States; and nothing in this Constitution shall be so construed as to prejudice any claims of the United States, or of any particular State.

▶ *Dispose of* • Sell or transfer ownership.

▶ *Construed as to prejudice any claims* • Interpreted so as to raise questions about claims (of property).

Recall the privilege granted Texas at the time of its annexation.

Guarantees to the States

The United States shall guarantee to every State in this Union a republican form of government, and shall protect each of them against invasion; and on application of the legislature, or of the executive (when the legislature cannot be convened) against domestic violence.

> *Republican form of government* • The representative form of government characteristic of a republic. (See box on page 327 for definitions of "republic" and "democracy.")
> *Convened* • Assembled; called into session.
> *Domestic violence* • Riots or uprisings within a state.

ARTICLE V
Method of Amendment

WHAT TO LOOK FOR IN ARTICLE V

In this short Article the ways of changing, or amending, the Constitution are set forth. "Amendment" is the legal word for a change in the Constitution.

Ways of amending.   According to this Article, amendments may be suggested in two ways and approved in two ways. They may be proposed either by a two-thirds vote of both houses of Congress or by a convention (special body) called at the request of two thirds of the states. Amendments may be approved either by the legislatures of three fourths of the states or by conventions in three fourths of the states. Up to this time every amendment but one has been suggested by a two-thirds vote in both the House and the Senate, and approved by the legislatures in three fourths of the states. For the one exception read Section 3 of the Twenty-First Amendment.

Number of amendments.   Since the Constitution was written in 1787, 24 amendments have been adopted. (See pages A20–A32.)

The Congress, whenever two thirds of both houses shall deem it necessary, shall propose amendments to this Constitution, or, on the application of the legislatures of two thirds of the several States, shall call a convention for proposing amendments, which, in either case shall be valid to all intents and purposes, as part of this Constitution, when ratified by the legislatures of three fourths of the several States, or by conventions in three fourths thereof, as the one or the other mode of ratification may be proposed by the Congress; provided that [*no amendments which may be made prior to the year one thousand eight hundred and eight shall in any manner affect the first and fourth clauses in the ninth section of the first article,*

> *Deem* • Believe.

> *Valid to all intents and purposes* • Fully legal.

> *Mode* • Method.

and that] no State, without its consent, shall be deprived of its equal suffrage in the Senate.

> *Equal suffrage in the Senate* • Since each state has two senators, each state has two votes in the Senate.

ARTICLE VI

General Provisions

WHAT TO LOOK FOR IN ARTICLE VI

Federal law is supreme. Article VI contains, in Section b, a most important provision. It states that the Constitution, the laws of the United States, and the agreements (treaties) made by the United States with other nations shall be the supreme law. If such a provision did not exist, the states might have as much power as the United States. We would then have a loose federation of states rather than a single united nation. To strengthen this idea still further, Section c requires that all officials, both of the United States government and of the state governments, as well as members of Congress and of the state legislatures, take an oath to support the Constitution.

The nation's earlier debts are binding. The first part of this Article was important when the Constitution was written, although it is not important now. It states that the debts of the old government, the Confederation (pages 214–216), would become the debts also of the new government. It was a promise that the new government was not being formed to escape the payment of debts incurred during and after the Revolutionary War.

a. Public debt. All debts contracted and engagements entered into, before the adoption of this Constitution, shall be as valid against the United States under this Constitution, as under the Confederation.

> *Engagements* • Agreements and contracts.

b. Supremacy of the Constitution. This Constitution, and the laws of the United States which shall be made in pursuance thereof; and all treaties made, or which shall be made, under the authority of the United States, shall be the supreme law of the land; and the judges in every State shall be bound thereby, anything in the Constitution or laws of any State to the contrary notwithstanding.

> *Laws . . . made in pursuance thereof* • Laws passed for the purpose of putting the Constitution into effect.

> *Anything . . . to the contrary notwithstanding* • Regardless of whether any state law or constitution contradicts the federal Constitution and laws.

c. Oath of office; no religious test. The Senators and Representatives before mentioned, and the members of the several State legislatures, and all executive and judicial officers, both of the United States and of the several States, shall be bound by oath or affirmation, to support this Constitution; but no religious test shall ever be required as a qualification to any office or public trust under the United States.

> *No religious test* • Membership in no particular church is needed to qualify for public office, nor does membership in any particular church disqualify a person for public office.

Note that state executive and judicial officers and members of the state legislatures are bound by oath to support the Constitution.

ARTICLE VII

Ratification of the Constitution

WHAT TO LOOK FOR IN ARTICLE VII
    This Article made it fairly easy to put the Constitution into effect. The Article states that the new Constitution would go into effect when nine of the thirteen states had approved it. Nowadays it is difficult to believe that there ever was any doubt whether the Constitution would be approved. But there was. The contest between those for and against the Constitution is described on pages 222–224 of this book.

    The ratification of the conventions of nine States shall be sufficient for the establishment of this Constitution between the States so ratifying the same.

AMENDMENTS
TO THE CONSTITUTION
Amendments I–X are called the Bill of Rights.

WHAT TO LOOK FOR IN AMENDMENTS I–X
    The Bill of Rights. Americans are proud that they are a free people. The basis of their freedom, in law, is found in the first ten amendments to the Constitution. These amendments are generally called the American Bill of Rights. If you will look back to pages 229–230, you may read again why Americans decided to write down, clearly and definitely, their basic rights.

    General rights. The rights guaranteed in these amendments fall into several classes. In Amendments I, IV, VI, and VII, you will find certain broad general rights. These include freedom to speak as one sees fit, write and print what one believes, hold meetings and petition the government, and worship as one thinks most fitting; freedom from unjust searches of one's house and other property; and the right to a trial by jury.

    Rights of people accused of crimes. The second group of rights provides protection for people accused of crimes (Amendments V, VI, VIII). Here we find listed not only the right to a trial by jury but also certain other safeguards. There are, for example, guarantees against cruel and unusual punishments.

    Less important rights. The rights in the third group (Amendments II and III) are perhaps not as important now as when these amendments were written. Nowadays in the United States, for example, soldiers are not likely to be assigned to live in people's houses.

    Protection of other rights. Amendments IX and X strengthen the first eight. Failure to list a right in the first eight amendments, says the Ninth Amendment, does not mean that Americans do not possess the right. It may mean only that the writers of the Constitution did not mention the right. Amendment X emphasizes that ours is a limited form of government. If a power is not given to the United States by the Constitution, or denied by the Constitution to the states, then the power belongs to the states (see page 229). Or perhaps it still belongs to the people, because the people have not given it to either the United States or the state governments.

AMENDMENT I · *Adopted 1791*

Freedom of Religion, Speech, and the Press; Right of Assembly

Congress shall make no law respecting an establishment of religion, or prohibiting the free exercise thereof; or abridging the freedom of speech, or of the press; or the right of the people peaceably to assemble, and to petition the government for a redress of grievances.

▸ *An establishment of religion* · **A government-supported church.**

▸ *Free exercise thereof* · **Freedom of worship.**

▸ *Abridging* · **Restricting.**

▸ *Redress of grievances* · **Correction of injustices.**

AMENDMENT II · *Adopted 1791*

Right to Keep and Bear Arms

A well-regulated militia, being necessary to the security of a free State, the right of the people to keep and bear arms, shall not be infringed.

▸ *Infringed* · **Violated or restricted.**

AMENDMENT III · *Adopted 1791*

Quartering Troops

No soldier shall, in time of peace be quartered in any house, without the consent of the owner, nor in time of war, but in a manner to be prescribed by law.

▸ *Quartered* · **Lodged or assigned to live in.**

▸ *Prescribed* · **Provided for or regulated.**

AMENDMENT IV · *Adopted 1791*

Limiting the Right of Search

The right of the people to be secure in their persons, houses, papers, and effects, against unreasonable searches and seizures, shall not be violated, and no warrants shall issue but upon probable cause, supported by oath or affirmation, and particularly describing the place to be searched, and the persons or things to be seized.

▸ *Effects* · **Possessions.**

▸ *Warrants* · **Documents issued by a cout giving authority, in this case, for a search.**

▸ *Probable cause* · **A reasonable cause for suspicion that a crime has been committed.**

AMENDMENT V · *Adopted 1791*

Safeguards for Accused Persons; Property Rights to Be Respected

▸ *Held to answer* · **Brought to trial.**

▸ *Capital, or otherwise infamous crime* · **A capital crime is punishable by death.**

No person shall be held to answer for a capital, or otherwise infamous crime, unless on a presentment or indictment of a grand jury, except in cases arising in the land or naval forces, or in the militia, when in actual service in time of war and public danger; nor shall any person be subject for the same offense to be twice put in jeopardy of life or limb; nor shall be compelled in any criminal case to be a witness against himself, nor be deprived of life, liberty, or property, without due process of law; nor shall private property be taken for public use without just compensation.

An infamous crime, while not requiring the death penalty, is so serious as to require severe punishment.

▸ *Presentment or indictment of a grand jury* • Recommendation by a grand jury that a person be charged with a crime and brought to trial. (A *grand jury* investigates accusations made against persons and decides whether or not they should be charged and brought to trial.)

▸ *Twice put in jeopardy of life or limb* • Put on trial a second time for an offense for which the person has already once been tried.

▸ *Without due process of law* • Without fair and legal proceedings, for example, trial by jury.

AMENDMENT VI · *Adopted 1791*

Rights of Accused Persons

In all criminal prosecutions, the accused shall enjoy the right to a speedy and public trial, by an impartial jury of the State and district wherein the crime shall have been committed, which districts shall have been previously ascertained by law, and to be informed of the nature and cause of the accusation; to be confronted with the witnesses against him; to have compulsory process for obtaining witnesses in his favor, and to have the assistance of counsel for his defense.

▸ *Criminal prosecutions* • Trials of persons accused of crimes.

▸ *Impartial* • Fair; not favoring one or the other.

▸ *Compulsory process for obtaining witnesses* • Court order commanding a witness to appear in court.

▸ *Counsel for his defense* • A lawyer who defends an accused person in court.

AMENDMENT VII · *Adopted 1791*

Rules of the Common Law

In suits at common law, where the value in controversy shall exceed twenty dollars, the right of trial by jury shall be preserved, and no fact tried by a jury, shall be otherwise re-examined in any court of the United States than according to the rules of common law.

▸ *Common law* • The basic legal system developed in England through custom and interpretation and brought to the lands colonized by the British.

▸ *Value in controversy* • The value of the thing over which a dispute has arisen.

AMENDMENT VIII · *Adopted 1791*

Excessive Bail, Fines, and Punishment Prohibited

Excessive bail shall not be required, nor excessive fines imposed, nor cruel and unusual punishments inflicted.

▶ *Bail* · Money or property pledged as a guarantee that an accused person will appear at his trial. If the accused fails to appear, the state keeps the bail.

Make sure that students understand the purpose of Amendments IX and X.

AMENDMENT IX · *Adopted 1791*

Rights Retained by the People

The enumeration in the Constitution of certain rights, shall not be construed to deny or disparage others retained by the people.

▶ *Construed to deny or disparage* · Interpreted so as to deny or reduce.

AMENDMENT X · *Adopted 1791*

Powers Reserved to States and People

The powers not delegated to the United States by the Constitution, nor prohibited by it to the States, are reserved to the States respectively, or to the people.

WHAT TO LOOK FOR IN AMENDMENTS XI AND XII

In the early years of the government under the Constitution, two parts of the document did not work as had been intended. These two parts were changed by Amendments XI and XII. These two amendments are therefore called the "corrective" amendments.

Lawsuits against states. The Eleventh Amendment prevents certain kinds of cases from coming to trial in the federal law courts. It prevents a citizen of one state from bringing suit against the government of another state unless the state agrees to be sued. It also forbids a foreigner to do the same thing.

Separate ballots for President and Vice-President. The Twelfth Amendment grew out of the election of 1800. Under the system originally set up in the Constitution in Article II, Section 1b, the presidential electors voted for President and for Vice-President on the same ballot. The man having the highest number of votes was to be President, and the man having the second highest number was to be Vice-President. In the case of a tie the Constitution said that the House of Representatives was to choose the President.

By 1800 political parties were firmly established in this country. In the election held that year all the electors chosen by the Democratic-Republican Party (page 238) voted for Thomas Jefferson to be President and for Aaron Burr to be Vice-President. Thus Jefferson and Burr received the same number of electoral votes. But the House of Representatives almost chose Burr to be President instead of Jefferson. It would never do for the House to select for President a man whom the electors had not had in mind. So the Twelfth Amendment was passed. It provided that the electors use *separate* ballots in voting for the President and the Vice-President. Henceforth, only a tie on the same ballot would be important.

AMENDMENT XI · *Adopted 1798*

Limiting the Powers of Federal Courts

The judicial power of the United States shall not be construed to extend to any suit in law or equity, commenced or prosecuted against one of the United States by citizens of another State, or by citizens or subjects of any foreign state.

▶ Construed · Interpreted.

AMENDMENT XII · *Adopted 1804*

Election of President and Vice President

The electors shall meet in their respective States, and vote by ballot for President and Vice President, one of whom, at least, shall not be an inhabitant of the same State with themselves; they shall name in their ballots the person voted for as President, and in distinct ballots the person voted for as Vice President, and they shall make distinct lists of all persons voted for as President, and of all persons voted for as Vice President, and of the number of votes for each, which lists they shall sign and certify, and transmit sealed to the seat of government of the United States, directed to the President of the Senate; — the President of the Senate shall, in the presence of the Senate and House of Representatives, open all the certificates and the votes shall then be counted; — the person having the greatest number of votes for President shall be the President, if such number be a majority of the whole number of electors appointed; and if no person have such majority, then from the persons having the highest numbers not exceeding three on the list of those voted for as President, the House of Representatives shall choose immediately, by ballot, the President. But in choosing the President, the votes shall be taken by States, the representation from each State having one vote; a quorum for this purpose shall consist of a member or members from two thirds of the States, and a majority of all the States shall be necessary to a choice. And if the House of Representatives shall not choose a President whenever the right of choice shall devolve upon them, [*before the fourth day of March next following*], then the Vice President shall act as President, as in the case of the death or other constitutional disability of the President. — The person having the greatest number of votes as Vice President, shall be the Vice President, if such number be a majority of the whole number of electors ap-

▶ *Shall not be an inhabitant of the same State with themselves* · Thus, electors in Iowa, for example, could not vote for candidates for President and Vice-President, both of whom were from Iowa.

▶ *Distinct ballots* · Separate ballots.

▶ *Certify* · Declare to be correct.

▶ *Transmit* · Send.

▶ *Certificates* · The lists certified by the electors of the various states.

▶ *The representation from each State having one vote* · In this case, all the representatives of each state shall be considered as a unit with a single vote.

▶ *Quorum* · To have a legal vote for this purpose, two thirds of the states must have a member or members present.

▶ *A majority of all the States shall be necessary to a choice* · Over half of the states must vote for one person if he is to qualify for President.

▶ *Constitutional disability* · Illness or physical injury.

pointed, and if no person have a majority, then from the two highest numbers on the list, the Senate shall choose the Vice President; a quorum for the purpose shall consist of two thirds of the whole number of Senators, and a majority of the whole number shall be necessary to a choice. But no person constitutionally ineligible to the office of President shall be eligible to that of Vice President of the United States.

▶ *Constitutionally ineligible* · Lacking the qualifications set forth in the Constitution.

Bring out the importance of Section 1 of Amendment XIV.

WHAT TO LOOK FOR IN AMENDMENTS XIII, XIV, AND XV

These three amendments were adopted as a result of the war between the North and the South. The Thirteenth Amendment freed the former slaves. It said that slavery should not exist in the United States. The Fifteenth Amendment gave Negroes the right to vote.

The Fourteenth Amendment dealt with a number of questions arising out of the Civil War. The Fourteenth Amendment said, for example, that the Confederate debt should not be paid. It also said that any state that refused the right to vote to eligible citizens should have fewer representatives in the House. This provision was aimed at any former Confederate state which might prevent Negroes from voting.

Look at Section 1 of the Fourteenth Amendment to find out who are citizens of the United States. When this amendment was first adopted, its purpose was to make clear that Negroes were citizens. But because the Constitution itself did not define citizenship, this provision of Amendment XIV continues to be important. It tells us clearly who are American citizens.

Section 1 is important for another reason. The original Constitution had protected Americans against unjust actions by the United States government. This section of the Fourteenth Amendment also protects citizens against unjust actions on the part of state governments.

Look back to pages 410 and 413 for the background of these three amendments.

AMENDMENT XIII · *Adopted 1865*

Slavery Abolished

Section 1. Abolition of Slavery

Neither slavery nor involuntary servitude, except as a punishment for crime whereof the party shall have been duly convicted, shall exist within the United States, or any place subject to their jurisdiction.

▶ *Involuntary servitude* · A condition in which one is forced to work, for example, as a slave or prisoner.

Section 2. Enforcement

Congress shall have power to enforce this article by appropriate legislation.

▶ *Appropriate* · Suitable and proper.

AMENDMENT XIV · *Adopted 1868*

Citizenship Defined

Section 1. Definition of Citizenship

All persons born or naturalized in the United States, and subject to the jurisdiction thereof, are citizens

▶ *Naturalized* · Having secured the rights and privileges of a native-born citizen.

of the United States and of the State wherein they reside. No State shall make or enforce any law which shall abridge the privileges or immunities of citizens of the United States; nor shall any State deprive any person of life, liberty, or property, without due process of law; nor deny to any person within its jurisdiction the equal protection of the laws.

▸ *No State . . . shall abridge the privileges or immunities. . . . •* No state may take away from a United States citizen the rights and freedoms to which he is entitled.

▸ *Without due process of law •* Without fair and legal proceedings.

Section 2. Apportionment of Representatives

Representatives shall be apportioned among the several States according to their respective numbers, counting the whole number of persons in each State, excluding Indians not taxed. But when the right to vote at any election for the choice of electors for President and Vice President of the United States, Representatives in Congress, the executive and judicial officers of a State, or the members of the legislature thereof, is denied to any of the male inhabitants of such State, being twenty-one years of age, and citizens of the United States, or in any way abridged, except for participation in rebellion, or other crime, the basis of representation therein shall be reduced in the proportion which the number of such male citizens shall bear to the whole number of male citizens twenty-one years of age in such State.

▸ *Apportioned •* Divided or allotted.

Section 3. Disability Resulting from Insurrection

No person shall be a Senator or Representative in Congress, or Elector of President and Vice President, or hold any office, civil or military, under the United States, or under any State, who, having previously taken an oath, as a member of Congress, or as an officer of the United States, or as a member of any State legislature, or as an executive or judicial officer of any State to support the Constitution of the United States, shall have engaged in insurrection or rebellion against the same, or given aid or comfort to the enemies thereof. But Congress may by vote of two thirds of each house, remove such disability.

▸ *Such disability •* This disqualification (that is, the denial of the right to hold office in the national or state governments).

Section 4. Public Debt of the United States Valid; Confederate Debt Void

The validity of the public debt of the United States, authorized by law, including debts incurred for payment of pensions and bounties for services in suppressing insurrection or rebellion, shall not be questioned. But neither the United States nor any State shall assume or pay any debt or obligation incurred in aid of insurrection or rebellion against the United

▸ *Validity •* Legality.
▸ *Incurred for •* Made necessary by.
▸ *Bounties •* Payments made to men willing to serve in the armed forces.

▸ *Debt or obligation •* The debts and financial obligations incurred by the states

States, or any claim for the loss or emancipation of any slave; but all such debts, obligations, and claims shall be held illegal and void.

Section 5. Enforcement

The Congress shall have power to enforce by appropriate legislation the provisions of this article.

▶ which had seceded were not to be paid by them or by the United States.

▶ *Loss or emancipation of any slave* · No slaveholder received payment for freed slaves.

AMENDMENT XV · *Adopted 1870*

Right of Suffrage

Section 1. The Suffrage

The right of citizens of the United States to vote shall not be denied or abridged by the United States or any State on account of race, color, or previous condition of servitude.

▶ *Abridged* · Restricted or limited.

▶ *Condition of servitude* · Slavery.

Section 2. Enforcement

The Congress shall have power to enforce this article by appropriate legislation.

Call attention to the statement, "Income tax permitted," and to Amendment XVI on the next page.

WHAT TO LOOK FOR IN AMENDMENTS XVI, XVII, XVIII, XIX, AND XXI

After the passage of the Thirteenth, Fourteenth, and Fifteenth Amendments, over 40 years went by before another was added to the Constitution. Then, in quick succession, four amendments were added to the Constitution.

Income tax permitted. Amendment XVI is called the income tax amendment. The Supreme Court had ruled that such a tax was not constitutional. So the Sixteenth Amendment was adopted, permitting a federal income tax (page 568). Today the income tax raises more money for the United States government than any other tax.

Popular election of senators. During the 1800's, as we have learned (page 327), more people obtained the right to vote. By 1913 it seemed to most Americans that it was not democratic for the state legislatures to choose United States senators. Amendment XVII provided that the voters themselves should elect their senators.

Women's right to vote. Like the Seventeenth Amendment, Amendment XIX was another example of the growth of democracy. Because increasing numbers of women were holding jobs in business and industry, were entering professions, and were taking part in many activities outside the home, more and more people asked: "Is it right to deny the vote to women?" (Look back to page 534 for a fuller account of women's activities.) Soon after World War I, this amendment gave women the right to vote.

Prohibition and repeal. Amendment XVIII prohibited the making or sale of intoxicating liquors. For fourteen years the amendment was in effect. But prohibition did not work well. People made and sold liquor in spite of the amendment, and there was much lawlessness. In 1933, therefore, Amendment XXI "repealed" — or did away with — Amendment XVIII. Amendment XVIII is the only amendment ever to have been repealed.

AMENDMENT XVI · *Adopted 1913*

Income Tax

The Congress shall have power to lay and collect taxes on incomes, from whatever source derived, without apportionment among the several States, and without regard to any census or enumeration.

▶ *Derived · Obtained.*

AMENDMENT XVII · *Adopted 1913*

Direct Election of Senators

a. Election by the people. The Senate of the United States shall be composed of two Senators from each State, elected by the people thereof, for six years; and each Senator shall have one vote. The electors in each State shall have the qualifications requisite for electors of the most numerous branch of the State legislatures.

b. Vacancies. When vacancies happen in the representation of any State in the Senate, the executive authority of such State shall issue writs of election to fill such vacancies: Provided that the legislature of any State may empower the executive thereof to make temporary appointments until the people fill the vacancies by election as the legislature may direct.

▶ *Provided that · With the understanding that.*
▶ *Empower · Give authority to.*

c. Not retroactive. This amendment shall not be so construed as to affect the election or term of any Senator chosen before it becomes valid as part of the Constitution.

AMENDMENT XVIII · *Adopted 1919*

National Prohibition

Section 1. **Prohibition of Intoxicating Liquors**

[*After one year from the ratification of this article the manufacture, sale, or transportation of intoxicating liquors within, the importation thereof into, or the exportation thereof from the United States and all territory subject to the jurisdiction thereof for beverage purposes is hereby prohibited.*]

Section 2. **Enforcement**

[*The Congress and the several States shall have concurrent power to enforce this article by appropriate legislation.*]

Section 3. Limited Time for Ratification

[*This article shall be inoperative unless it shall have been ratified as an amendment to the Constitution by the legislatures of the several States, as provided by the Constitution, within seven years from the date of the submission hereof to the States by the Congress.*]

AMENDMENT XIX · *Adopted 1920*

Extending the Vote to Women

Section 1. Woman Suffrage

The right of citizens of the United States to vote shall not be denied or abridged by the United States or by any State on account of sex.

Amendment XIX illustrates how an amendment to the Constitution can limit a power given the states. Note that Congress is given the right to enact laws to insure enforcement.

Section 2. Enforcement

The Congress shall have power to enforce this article by appropriate legislation.

WHAT TO LOOK FOR IN AMENDMENTS XX, XXII, XXIII, AND XXIV

Inaugurations and the opening of Congress. Until Amendment XX was adopted, sessions of Congress began early in December and new Presidents were inaugurated the following March 4. Congress now meets each year on January 3. New Presidents are inaugurated on January 20. Amendment XX also tells what is to happen if a President-elect dies before his inauguration or if no President has been chosen by January 20.

The presidential term limited. Although the Constitution did not prevent a President from serving longer, up to 1940 no President had served more than two terms. Then Franklin D. Roosevelt was elected for a third term in 1940 and for a fourth term in 1944. Because many people believed that the old custom was a good one, Amendment XXII was added to the Constitution. It states that nobody shall be elected President more than twice.

Voting for President in the District of Columbia. Amendment XXIII permits residents of Washington, D.C., to vote in presidential elections. Previously only states could choose presidential electors. Washington residents still have no voice in their local government and are not represented in Congress.

Prohibition of the poll tax. Since the 1870's, some states had used the poll tax to prevent Negroes from voting. Amendment XXIV prohibits the states from requiring a tax as a condition for voting in federal elections, but it does not apply to state or local elections.

AMENDMENT XX · *Adopted 1933*

Beginning of Presidential and Congressional Terms

Section 1. Terms of President, Vice-President, and Congress

The terms of the President and Vice President shall end at noon on the 20th day of January, and the terms of Senators and Representatives at noon on the 3d day of January, of the years in which such terms would have ended if this article had not been ratified; and the terms of their successors shall then begin.

Section 2. Sessions of Congress

The Congress shall assemble at least once in every year, and such meeting shall begin at noon on the 3d day of January, unless they shall by law appoint a different day.

Section 3. Presidential Succession

If, at the time fixed for the beginning of the term of the President, the President elect shall have died, the Vice President elect shall become President. If a President shall not have been chosen before the time fixed for the beginning of his term, or if the President elect shall have failed to qualify, then the Vice President elect shall act as President until a President shall have qualified; and the Congress may by law provide for the case wherein neither a President elect nor a Vice President elect shall have qualified, declaring who shall then act as President, or the manner in which one who is to act shall be selected, and such person shall act accordingly until a President or a Vice President shall have qualified.

Section 4. Choice of President by the House

The Congress may by law provide for the case of the death of any of the persons from whom the House of Representatives may choose a President, whenever the right of choice shall have devolved upon them, and for the case of the death of any of the persons from whom the Senate may choose a Vice President whenever the right of choice shall have devolved upon them.

Section 5. Date Effective

Sections 1 and 2 shall take effect on the fifteenth day of October following the ratification of this article.

Section 6. Limited Time for Ratification

This article shall be inoperative unless it shall have been ratified as an amendment to the Constitution by the legislatures of three fourths of the several States within seven years from the date of its submission.

▶ *Article* · Amendment.
▶ *Ratified* · Approved.
▶ *Successors* · Those who follow in office.

▶ *President elect* · A person who has been elected President but who has not yet taken office.

▶ *Inoperative* · Invalid; not law.

▶ *Submission* · Being presented (in this case, to the states for their approval).

AMENDMENT XXI · *Adopted 1933*

Repeal of Prohibition

Section 1. Repeal of Amendment XVIII

The eighteenth article of amendment to the Constitution of the United States is hereby repealed.

▶ *Repealed* · Abolished or withdrawn.

Section 2. States Protected

The transportation or importation into any State, territory or possession of the United States for delivery or use therein of intoxicating liquors in violation of the laws thereof, is hereby prohibited.

▶ *In violation of the laws thereof* · Although this amendment repealed national prohibition, it recognized the right of the states to pass laws prohibiting the use of liquor.

Section 3. Limited Time for Ratification

This article shall be inoperative unless it shall have been ratified as an amendment to the Constitution by conventions in the several States, as provided in the Constitution, within seven years from the date of the submission hereof to the States by the Congress.

By having Amendment XXI ratified by state conventions speedy action was insured.

AMENDMENT XXII · *Adopted 1951*

Presidential Term Limited

Section 1. Definition of Limitation

No person shall be elected to the office of the President more than twice, and no person who has held the office of President, or acted as President, for more than two years of a term to which some other person was elected President shall be elected to the office of the President more than once. But this article shall not apply to any person holding the office of President when this article was proposed by the Congress, and shall not prevent any person who may be holding the office of President, or acting as President, during the term within which this article becomes operative from holding the office of President, or acting as President during the remainder of such term.

Section 2. Limited Time for Ratification

This article shall be inoperative unless it shall have been ratified as an amendment to the Constitution by the legislatures of three-fourths of the several States within seven years from the date of its submission to the States by the Congress.

AMENDMENT XXIII · *Adopted 1961*

Presidential Voting in the District of Columbia

Section 1. Appointment of Electors

The District constituting the seat of Government of the United States shall appoint in such manner as the Congress may direct:

A number of electors of President and Vice President equal to the whole number of Senators and Representatives in Congress to which the District would be entitled if it were a State, but in no event more than the least populous State; they shall be in addition to those appointed by the States, but they shall be considered, for the purposes of the election of President and Vice President, to be electors appointed by a State; and they shall meet in the District and perform such duties as provided by the twelfth article of amendment.

Section 2. Enforcement

The Congress shall have power to enforce this article by appropriate legislation.

Note that Amendment XXIII does not give residents of the District of Columbia the same rights to vote as are enjoyed by the residents of a state.

▶ *But in no event more than the least populous State* · At present the least populous state (the one with the fewest people) has three electors (because it has two senators and one representative), so the District of Columbia may have no more than three electors. Thus, there are a total of 538 presidential electors (based upon 100 senators, 435 representatives, and the three District of Columbia electors), with 270 electoral votes needed for a majority.

AMENDMENT XXIV · *Adopted 1964*

Prohibition of the Poll Tax

Section 1. Prohibition in National Elections

The right of citizens of the United States to vote in any primary or other election for President or Vice President, for electors for President or Vice President, or for senator or representative in Congress, shall not be denied or abridged by the United States or any state by reason of failure to pay any poll tax or other tax.

Section 2. Enforcement

The Congress shall have the power to enforce this article by appropriate legislation.

▶ *Poll tax* · The poll tax, or head tax, was introduced in colonial times, and was originally levied on men who owned no property and paid no other local taxes.

For Further Reading

BOOKS FOR GENERAL USE

These books will prove useful throughout the course.

American Heritage: The Magazine of History. Published every two months since 1954. Each issue contains interesting historical material — articles, picture-stories, and original documents.

American Heritage Book of Great Historic Places. Simon & Schuster. This land is rich in history, legends, and great stories.

American Heritage Book of Indians. Simon & Schuster. The story of the native Americans, beautifully illustrated in full color.

American Heritage Book of the Pioneer Spirit. Simon & Schuster. The pioneer spirit spread to everything Americans did, their inventions, their arts and politics, the confident way that they talked and thought.

Blow, Michael, and Multhaus, Robert, *Men of Science and Invention.* American Heritage Publishing Co. The story of science and invention from colonial days to the present-day exploration of the universe.

Boni, Margaret M. (Editor), *The Fireside Book of Favorite American Songs.* Simon & Schuster. The songs which have settled into the general treasury of American music.

Brown, Harriett M., and Guadagnolo, Joseph F., *America Is My Country.* Houghton. Tells about the symbols of our democracy, our national documents, our monuments and shrines, our patriotic songs, poems, and holidays.

Cross, Wilbur, III, and Heffernan, John B., *Naval Battles and Heroes.* American Heritage Publishing Co. Pictures and narrative tell the story of battles from the Revolutionary War to World War II.

Eliot, Alexander, and Editors of *Time, Three*

Hundred Years of American Painting. Random House. Interesting text and beautiful illustrations.

Johnson, Gerald W., *The Presidency.* Morrow. A description of our country's highest office and how it has developed.

La Farge, Oliver, *A Pictorial History of the American Indian.* Crown. An authority on American Indians reconstructs their life in every section of North America. Over 350 illustrations.

Morgan, James, *Our Presidents.* Macmillan. Interesting biographical sketches plus a brief history of the presidency.

Morris, Richard B. (Editor), *Encyclopedia of American History.* Harper. A readable reference book which presents the essential historical facts from pre-Columbian times to the present.

Peck, Anne M., *Pageant of Canadian History.* Longmans. From discovery and exploration to independence within the Commonwealth of Nations.

Peck, Anne M., *Pageant of South American History.* Longmans. South America, past and present.

Stevenson, Augusta, *Scenes from American History.* Houghton. Students will enjoy reading these plays. One or more might be included in an assembly program.

Stevenson, Burton E., *American History in Verse for Boys and Girls.* Houghton. Poems about historical events.

World Almanac and Book of Facts (annual edition). *New York World-Telegram and The Sun.* A valuable collection of statistics and general information.

BOOKS FOR EACH UNIT

Unit One

Averill, Esther H., *Cartier Sails the St. Lawrence.* Harper. Based on Cartier's logbooks for three voyages to the New World.

Berger, Josef, and Wroth, Lawrence C., *Discoverers of the New World.* American Heritage Publishing Co. Explorations of perilous seas and unknown lands.

Fox, Frances Margaret, *They Sailed and Sailed.*

Dutton. Short stories about 21 famous explorers and their discoveries.

Gaither, Frances O., *The Scarlet Coat.* Macmillan. La Salle's search for the mouth of the Mississippi.

Hartman, Gertrude, *Medieval Days and Ways.* Macmillan. Life in western Europe before the great explorations.

Both fiction and books on history are included.

Hewes, Agnes D., *Spice Ho! A Story of Discovery*. Knopf. This book explains how the desire for spices led explorers to seek new routes.

Hodges, C. Walter, *Columbus Sails*. Coward. How Columbus seemed to the men who knew him.

Johnson, Gerald W., *America Is Born*. Morrow. The story of America from its discovery to 1787. Written by the author for his own grandson.

Lucas, Mary, *Vast Horizons*. Viking. Great explorers and what they discovered.

Means, Philip A., *Tupak of the Incas*. Scribner. How the Indians of Peru lived before the coming of the Spaniards.

Pond, Seymour, *Ferdinand Magellan: Master Mariner*. Random House. His ship was the first to sail around the world.

Tharp, Louise, *Champlain: Northwest Voyager*. Little, Brown. The great explorer who also founded Quebec.

Walsh, Richard J., *Adventures and Discoveries of Marco Polo*. Random House. Marco Polo's tales of wondrous things seen in Cathay aroused interest in exploration.

West, Anthony, *The Crusades*. Random House. An exciting story brings out reasons for and results of the wars to free the Holy Land.

Unit Two

Cochran, Hamilton, *Pirates of the Spanish Main*. American Heritage Publishing Co. Stories and pictures about pirates.

Eaton, Jeanette, *Lone Journey*. Harcourt. The story of Roger Williams, an American who fought for freedom of speech and religion.

Foster, Genevieve, *The World of Captain John Smith*. Scribner. World events in the late 1500's and early 1600's are linked with periods in John Smith's life.

Gray, Elizabeth J., *Penn*. Viking. A biography of the Quaker who founded Pennsylvania.

Johnson, Gerald W., *America Is Born*. Morrow. From the discovery of America to 1787.

Jones, Evan, *Trappers and Mountain Men*. American Heritage Publishing Co. Competition for beaver fur led to rivalries among nations and to the destruction of Indian peoples.

Lancaster, Bruce, *Ticonderoga, the Story of a Fort*. Houghton. The hero is the star-shaped fort between Lake Champlain and Lake George, which played an important part in early American history.

Langdon, William C., *Everyday Things in American Life, 1607–1776*. Scribner. Early American food and dress, houses and furniture.

Lobdell, Helen, *Golden Conquest*. Houghton. The exciting story of the conquest of Mexico by Cortés.

Morison, Samuel E., *Story of the Old Colony of New Plymouth*. Knopf. From its beginnings until it was joined with Massachusetts Bay Colony.

North, Sterling, *Captured by the Mohawks*. Houghton. The exciting story of Radison, famous French Canadian fur trader, who became one of the founders of the Hudson's Bay Company.

Riesenberg, Felix, Jr., *Balboa: Swordsman and Conquistador*. Random House. He crossed Panama and discovered the Pacific.

Shippen, Katherine B., *New Found World*. Viking. Tells about Cortés and Pizarro and Latin American lands.

Sickels, Eleanor M., *In Calico and Crinoline: True Stories of American Women, 1608–1865*. Viking. Read about the part women played in colonial days.

Speare, Elizabeth George, *The Witch of Blackbird Pond*. Houghton. A story about Puritan Connecticut. A witch is hunted and tried in court.

Wellman, Paul I., *Indian Wars and Warriors (East)*. Houghton. Struggles between white men and Indians, from Champlain's attack on the Iroquois to the defeat of the Seminoles in Florida 200 years later.

Ziner, Feenie, and Willison, George F., *The Pilgrims and Plymouth Colony*. American Heritage Publishing Co. They stood ready to sacrifice their lives to achieve their ideals.

Unit Three

American Heritage Book of the Revolution. Simon & Schuster. Makes Washington and the men he led come alive for us.

Brown, George, *Building the Canadian Nation*. Dent (Canada). You may enjoy reading a text used by students in Canada.

Daugherty, James H., *The Magna Charta*. Random House. The story of the Great Charter of England and its relation to later documents of freedom.

Fisher, Dorothy Canfield, *Our Independence and the Constitution*. Random House. The writing of our great patriotic documents as seen through the eyes of a Philadelphia family.

Forbes, Esther, *Johnny Tremain*. Houghton. An apprentice boy takes part in the Boston Tea Party and other exciting events.

Foster, Genevieve, *George Washington's World*. Scribner. What was taking place all over the world during Washington's lifetime.

Johnson, Gerald W., *America Is Born*. Morrow. The history of this country to 1787.

Judson, Clara I., *Benjamin Franklin*. Follett. Stresses the political activities of the foremost American of his day.

Langdon, William C., *Everyday Things in American Life, 1607–1776*. Scribner. Interesting drawings and descriptions.

Maurois, André, *Lafayette in America*. Houghton. A major general at nineteen, he was a youth who did a man's job.

Montross, Lynn, *Washington and the Revolution*. Houghton. Boys as young as fourteen fought in an army that wouldn't stay beaten.

Moscow, Henry, and Malone, Dumas, *Thomas Jefferson and His World*. American Heritage Publishing Co. A man of many talents — legislator, diplomat, farmer, scientist, architect, inventor, patron of education and the arts.

Shippen, Katherine B., *New Found World*. Viking. The independence movements in Argentina, Peru, Brazil, Mexico, and Haiti.

Sickels, Eleanor M., *In Calico and Crinoline: True Stories of American Women, 1608–1865*. Viking. Read about the part women played in the Revolutionary War.

Wellman, Paul I., *Indian Wars and Warriors (East)*. Houghton. Pontiac's conspiracy; Indians and Tories in the Revolutionary War.

Unit Four

Allen, Florence E., *This Constitution of Ours*. Putnam. A federal court judge explains the Constitution.

Brown, George, *Building the Canadian Nation*. Dent (Canada). You may wish to compare the discussion of the period from 1783 to 1815 in this Canadian book with that in your text.

Elting, Mary, and Gossett, Margaret, *We Are the Government*. Doubleday. An interesting explanation of our form of government.

Finger, Charles J., *Cape Horn Snorter*. Houghton. The exploits of the U.S. Frigate *Essex* in the War of 1812.

Fisher, Dorothy Canfield, *Our Independence and the Constitution*. Random House. How the Constitution was written.

Foster, Genevieve, *Abraham Lincoln's World*. Scribner. What was taking place all over the world, 1809–1865.

Foster, Genevieve, *George Washington's World*. Scribner. What was taking place all over the world during Washington's lifetime.

Holland, Rupert S., *Freedom's Flag: the Story of Francis Scott Key*. Macrae Smith. How Key wrote our national anthem.

Johnson, Gerald W., *America Grows Up*. Morrow. The second volume of this history tells about our country's story from 1787 to 1917.

Judson, Clara I., *Andrew Jackson*. Follett. Before he became President, Jackson was an Indian fighter and a hero of the War of 1812.

Mason, F. van Wyck, *The Battles for New Orleans*. Houghton. A dramatic account of General Jackson's campaign.

Moscow, Henry, and Malone, Dumas, *Thomas Jefferson and His World*. American Heritage Publishing Co. Jefferson in Paris and in the White House.

Schachner, Nathan, *Alexander Hamilton, Nation Builder*. McGraw-Hill. An interesting biography of one of the nation's ablest men.

Wellman, Paul I., *Indian Wars and Warriors (East)*. Houghton. The Indians make war in the Northwest Territory.

Wilson, W. E., *Shooting Star*. Rinehart. The story of the great Indian chief Tecumseh.

Unit Five

Chase, Mary Ellen, *Donald McKay and the Clipper Ships*. Houghton. He built the fastest ships of his day.

Chase, Mary Ellen, *The Fishing Fleets of New England*. Houghton. These fishermen braved the storms of the North Atlantic.

Chase, Mary Ellen, *Sailing the Seven Seas*. Houghton. A true story of sea-going New England families and the ships they sailed.

Daugherty, James H., *Daniel Boone*. Viking. He blazed a trail into the wilderness.

Foster, Genevieve, *Abraham Lincoln's World.* Scribner. Happenings in other lands and in this country during Lincoln's lifetime.

Hough, Henry Beetle, *Great Days of Whaling.* Houghton. The adventures told in this book really happened.

Johnson, Gerald W., *America Grows Up.* Morrow. Deals with the period 1787–1917.

Judson, Clara I., *Andrew Jackson: Frontier Statesman.* Follett. Old Hickory as President.

Latham, Jean Lee, *Carry On, Mr. Bowditch.* Houghton. Young seamen still study Nat Bowditch's book on navigation.

North, Sterling, *Thoreau of Walden Pond.* Houghton. He loved nature and the simple life.

Reck, Franklin M., *Romance of American Transportation.* Crowell. Early canals and railroads; the first steamboats.

Sandburg, Carl, *Abe Lincoln Grows Up.* Harcourt. Reprinted from the early chapters of the two-volume biography.

Seton, Anya, *Washington Irving.* Houghton. Irving was not only an author but also an able diplomat.

✳Shapiro, Irwin, and Stackpole, Edwin, *The Story of Yankee Whaling.* American Heritage Publishing Co. Colorful pictures and an interesting account.

Shippen, Katherine B., *Great Heritage.* Viking. A vivid discussion of America's resources.

Shippen, Katherine B., *Miracle in Motion: the Story of America's Industry.* Harper. Important changes in America's industry and why they happened.

Sickels, Eleanor M., *In Calico and Crinoline: True Stories of American Women, 1608–1865.* Viking. This book contains interesting material on the South.

Unit Six

✳*American Heritage Picture History of the Civil War.* Doubleday. The story of the war told in vivid words and pictures.

Andrist, Ralph K., and Hanna, Archibald, *The California Gold Rush.* American Heritage Publishing Co. Nearly 100,000 people poured into California in two years.

Bakeless, John, *The Adventures of Lewis and Clark.* Houghton. Based on the actual journals of these daring explorers.

These picture books are interesting.

Coit, Margaret, *The Fight for Union.* Houghton. Tells about the dramatic years before the Civil War and statesmen like Webster, Clay, and Calhoun.

Daniels, Jonathan, *Robert E. Lee.* Houghton. The great general of the Confederacy.

Daugherty, James H., *Of Courage Undaunted: Across the Continent with Lewis and Clark.* Viking. They explored the wilderness of western America.

Foster, Genevieve, *Abraham Lincoln's World.* Scribner. Most of the events described in this unit happened during his lifetime.

✳Horan, James D., *Mathew Brady: Historian with a Camera.* Crown. The story of the famous photographer's life and work. More than 500 pictures are included.

Johnson, Gerald W., *America Grows Up.* Morrow. Important developments, 1787–1917.

Johnson, William W., *The Birth of Texas.* Houghton. Stephen Austin, the Lone Star Republic, the Alamo.

Jones, Evan, *Trappers and Mountain Men.* American Heritage Publishing Co. Fur trade in the Louisiana Purchase and Oregon Country.

Lavender, David, *The Trail to Santa Fe.* Houghton. Across deserts, over mountains, and through Indian country, the wagon trains brought goods to Santa Fe.

Lomask, Milton, *Andy Johnson: The Tailor Who Became President.* Farrar. Johnson's rise to the presidency makes a dramatic story.

Moody, Ralph, *Riders of the Pony Express.* Houghton. Every trip was a race against time.

O'Meara, Walter, *The First Northwest Passage.* Houghton. Alexander Mackenzie discovers the first canoe route to the Western Sea.

Rourke, Constance M., *Davy Crockett.* Harcourt. Hunter, frontier statesman, and soldier.

Sickels, Eleanor M., *In Calico and Crinoline: True Stories of American Women, 1608–1865.* Viking. Tells about the role of women in the Civil War.

Wellman, Paul I., *Gold in California.* Houghton. Some struck it rich; more failed.

Unit Seven

Bachman, Frank P., *Great Inventors and Their Inventions.* American Book. Bell, Edison, automobiles, airplanes, television, movies.

Baer, Marian E., *Pandora's Box: the Story of Conservation*. Rinehart. Conservation is everyone's concern.

James, Will, *Lone Cowboy*. Scribner. A true story about cowboys.

Johnson, Gerald W., *America Grows Up*. Morrow. Our nation's history, 1787–1917.

McCracken, Harold, *Frederic Remington, Artist of the Old West*. Lippincott. The story of his life. More than 80 reproductions of sketches and pictures.

McCready, Albert L., and Sagle, Lawrence W., *Railroads in the Days of Steam*. American Heritage Publishing Co. The story of America's railroads is the story of the growth and development of the nation itself.

Moody, Ralph, *Wells Fargo*. Houghton. The story of the famous stagecoach company.

North, Sterling, *Young Thomas Edison*. Houghton. At fourteen he was learning telegraphy, making experiments, and trying to read every book in the Detroit library!

Rachlis, Eugene, and Ewers, John C., *Indians of the Plains*. American Heritage Publishing Co. Their customs and ways of living; their relations with white men.

Reck, Franklin M., *Automobiles from Start to Finish*. Crowell. How this country became a nation on wheels.

Richardson, Myra R., *Sheep Wagon*. McBride. In Wyoming Territory in 1882 cattlemen were determined to keep out sheepherders.

Shippen, Katherine B., *Great Heritage*, Viking. A vivid discussion of America's resources.

Shippen, Katherine B., *Miracle in Motion: the Story of America's Industry*. Harper. Highlights major changes; brings out causes and far-reaching results.

Ullman, James R., *Down the Colorado with Major Powell*. Houghton. Brave men in four little boats explored the canyons of the Green and Colorado Rivers.

Wade, Mary H., *The Master Builders*. Little, Brown. Hill, Bell, Carnegie, Ford.

Ward, Don, and Dykes, J. C., *Cowboys and Cattle Country*. American Heritage Publishing Co. Cowboys and herding, from the Indian vaquero of Mexico and California to the jeep-riding and helicopter-flying ranchers of today.

Wellman, Paul I., *Indian Wars and Warriors (West)*. Houghton. For nearly a century, trappers, gold seekers, and settlers were in almost constant conflict with the western Indians.

Wellman, Paul I., *Race to the Golden Spike*. Houghton. An exciting account of the race to build the transcontinental railroad.

Wilder, Laura Ingalls, *Long Winter*. Harper. Frontier life in Dakota as experienced by the author.

Unit Eight

Antin, Mary, *The Promised Land*. Houghton. The story of an immigrant girl.

Beaty, John Y., *Luther Burbank: Plant Magician*. Messner. His experiments with flowers, fruit trees, and farm products made him famous.

Bok, Edward, *Dutch Boy Fifty Years After*. Scribner. A famous journalist tells how he became an American.

Clemens, Samuel L. (Mark Twain), *The Adventures of Huckleberry Finn* and *The Adventures of Tom Sawyer*. Harper. The famous stories about life in a small town on the Mississippi.

Deutsch, Babette, *Walt Whitman: Builder for America*. Messner. A great poet who was a champion of democracy.

Douglas, William O., *Muir of the Mountains*. Houghton. The thrilling story of one of the country's first great conservationists.

Graham, Shirley, and Lipscomb, George D., *Dr. George Washington Carver: Scientist*. Messner. A poor but gifted Negro boy who became a distinguished scientist.

Hahn, Emily, *Around the World with Nellie Bly*. Houghton. The story of one of America's earliest and ablest girl reporters. She visited factories and slums and described what she saw.

Johnson, Gerald W., *America Grows Up*. Morrow. Important developments in this country, 1787–1917.

Nolan, Jeannette, *Clara Barton of the Red Cross*. Messner. Tells about Clara Barton's work and the times in which she lived.

North, Sterling, *Mark Twain and the River*. Houghton. A biography of America's great storyteller.

Purdy, Claire Lee, *He Heard America Sing: the Story of Stephen Foster*. Messner. A fictional biography; contains the music of many of Stephen Foster's songs.

Shippen, Katherine B., *Passage to America*. Harper. The dramatic story of the many nationality groups that came to America.

Simon, Charlie, *Art in the New Land*. Dutton. Stories of American artists and their works.

Terres, John K. (Editor), *The Audubon Book of True Nature Stories*. Crowell. Best-loved stories from the *Audubon Magazine*.

Unit Nine

Crockett, Lucy H., *Capitan; the Story of an Army Mule*. Holt. An army mule that saw service in Cuba, China, the Philippines, Mexico, and France.

Follett, Helen, *Ocean Outposts*. Scribner. This country's outlying possessions.

Freidel, Frank, *The Splendid Little War*. Little, Brown. The Spanish-American War told largely in the words of those who were there.

Harlow, Alvin F., *Theodore Roosevelt: Strenuous American*. Messner. Rancher, soldier, President, conservationist.

Hoyt, Edwin P., *Grover Cleveland*. Reilly and Lee. An interesting and accurate account of a President known for his fight against political corruption.

Johnson, Gerald W., *America Grows Up*. Morrow. The Monroe Doctrine, the Spanish-American War, the Open Door.

Johnson, Gerald W., *America Moves Forward*. Morrow. The third volume starts with the United States in World War I.

Judson, Clara I., *Soldier Doctor: the Story of William Gorgas*. Scribner. His fight against mosquitoes made the Panama Canal possible.

London, Jack, *Call of the Wild*. Macmillan. The story of a dog in the Klondike region.

Long, Laura, *Square Sails and Spice Islands*. Longmans. Perry opens Japan to world trade.

Nicolay, Helen, *Bridge of Water: the Story of Panama and the Canal*. Appleton. How the canal came to be built and its construction.

Nordhoff, Charles, and Hall, James Norman, *Falcons of France*. Little, Brown (Atlantic Monthly Press). The Lafayette Flying Corps in World War I.

Shippen, Katherine B., *Miracle in Motion: the Story of America's Industry*. Harper. Industrial growth has led to increased trade.

Wood, Laura N., *Walter Reed: Doctor in Uniform*. Messner. He discovered the cause of yellow fever.

Unit Ten

Ayling, Keith, *Semper Fidelis*. Houghton. U.S. Marines in action!

Bingham, Jonathan B., *Shirt-Sleeve Diplomacy*. Day. The story of Point Four in action.

Brown, George, *Building the Canadian Nation*. Dent (Canada). Read about recent Canadian history in this book written for Canadian schools.

Brown, Harriett M., and Bailey, Helen Miller, *Our Latin American Neighbors*. Houghton. Tells about Latin America in general and each of the countries as well.

Coggins, Jack, and Pratt, Fletcher, *Rockets, Satellites, and Space Travel*. Random House. Use of rockets in war and recent space research.

Colegrove, Kenneth, *Democracy versus Communism*. Van Nostrand. A comparison of two contrasting political and economic systems.

Considine, Bob, and Lawson, Ted, *Thirty Seconds Over Tokyo*. Random House. A pilot tells his part in the Doolittle raid in World War II.

Cooper, Gordon L., Jr., and others, *The Astronauts: Pioneers in Space*. Golden Press. The seven Astronauts of Project Mercury give us their own story of how they prepared for this mission.

Gait, Tom, *How the United Nations Works*. Crowell. A history of the UN.

Johnson, Gerald W., *America Moves Forward*. Morrow. This country's history since 1917.

Lewis, Elizabeth F., *To Beat a Tiger*. Winston. Chinese boys band together to survive during the Japanese occupation.

Peare, Catherine Owens, *The FDR Story*. Crowell. An interesting account of Roosevelt's personal story.

Scoggin, Margaret C., *Battle Stations*. Knopf. Stories about paratroopers, submariners, airplane pilots, infantrymen.

Shippen, Katherine B., *New Found World*. Viking. Read about developments in the last 40 years in our hemisphere.

Snyder, Louis L., *First Book of World War II*. Watts. A helpful discussion of causes and results.

Sperry, Armstrong, *Hull-Down for Action*. Doubleday. Adventures in the southwest Pacific during World War II.

Students may wish to recommend books to be added to the bibliography for Unit Nine.

Important Dates in American History

1095 Pope calls for Crusades.
1215 Magna Carta.
1275 Marco Polo reaches China on Asian travels (1271–1295).
1418 Prince Henry sends expedition to explore African coast.
1450 Printing begins in Europe about this time.
1487 Dias reaches Cape of Good Hope.
1492 Columbus discovers New World.
1493 Line of Demarcation.
1497 Cabot explores North American coast.
1498 Da Gama reaches India.
1500 Cabral discovers Brazil.
1513 Balboa discovers the Pacific. Ponce de Leon explores Florida.
1519 Cortés lands in Mexico; conquers Aztec capital (1521).
1519–1522 Magellan's crew sails around world.
1524 Verrazano explores North American coast.
1532 Pizarro begins conquest of Peru.
1534 Cartier discovers and explores St. Lawrence River.
1540–1542 Coronado explores the Southwest.
1541 De Soto discovers Mississippi.
1551 University of Mexico founded.
1565 Spanish found St. Augustine.
1576 Frobisher explores North American coast.
1577–1580 Drake sails around the world.
1585 "Lost Colony" founded on Roanoke Island.
1588 Spanish Armada defeated.
1607 English found Jamestown.
1608 Champlain founds Quebec.
1609 Hudson explores Hudson River.
1610 Hudson discovers Hudson Bay.
1619 Virginia House of Burgesses established.
1620 Pilgrims found Plymouth; draw up Mayflower Compact.
1623 Dutch found New Amsterdam.
1630 Puritans found Boston.
1636 Roger Williams founds Rhode Island.
Connecticut settlements are founded.
Harvard College started.
1647 Massachusetts school law.
1649 Toleration Act in Maryland.
1660–1663 Navigation Acts passed.
1664 English capture New Netherland.
1670 Charles Town (Charleston), South Carolina, founded.
1673 Marquette and Joliet explore Mississippi River.
1682 Pennsylvania founded by Penn and Quakers.
La Salle reaches mouth of Mississippi River.
1689 English Bill of Rights.

1689–1763 English and French fight for North America.
1691 Plymouth and Massachusetts Bay Colony unite.
1693 College of William and Mary founded.
1704 Deerfield Massacre.
1710 English seize Acadia.
1733 Georgia founded.
1745 English take Louisburg.
1754 Albany Plan of Union.
1754–1763 French and Indian War.
1755 Braddock defeated.
1759 Battle of Quebec.
1763 Peace of Paris. France is driven out of North America.
1763 Proclamation of 1763.
Pontiac's War.
1765 Stamp Act passed.
Virginia Resolutions.
Stamp Act Congress.
Colonial boycott.
1766 Stamp Act repealed.
1767 Townshend Acts passed.
1769 Spanish found first mission in California.
First settlement in Tennessee.
1770 Boston Massacre.
1773 Boston Tea Party.
1774 Intolerable Acts.
First Continental Congress meets.
First settlement in Kentucky.
1775 Boonesborough founded.
1775–1783 Revolutionary War.
1775 Battles of Lexington and Concord.
Second Continental Congress meets.
Ethan Allen captures Crown Point and Ticonderoga.
Battle of Bunker Hill.
1776 Tom Paine's *Common Sense.*
British troops leave Boston.
Declaration of Independence.
Battle of Trenton.
1777 Battle of Princeton.
Battle of Saratoga; Burgoyne surrenders.
1777–1778 Washington at Valley Forge.
1778 Treaty of alliance with France.
1779 George Rogers Clark captures Vincennes.
Bonhomme Richard defeats *Serapis.*
1780 Battles of King's Mountain and Cowpens.
1781 Cornwallis surrenders at Yorktown.
1783 Treaty of Paris; Thirteen States win independence.
1781 Articles of Confederation go into effect.
1784 *Empress of China* opens trade with China.

1785 Land Ordinance in Northwest.
1787 Northwest Ordinance.
Constitution drafted.
1788 Marietta, Ohio, first town in Northwest Territory, founded.
1789 George Washington becomes President.
First Congress meets.
Supreme Court established.
French Revolution begins.
1790 Slater starts U.S. factory system.
1791 Vermont becomes a state.
Bill of Rights added to Constitution.
Quebec divided into Upper and Lower Canada.
1792 Kentucky becomes a state.
1793 Whitney invents cotton gin.
1794 Whiskey Rebellion.
1795 Jay's Treaty approved.
1796 Tennessee becomes a state.
1797 John Adams becomes President.
XYZ Affair.
1798 Sedition Act.
1801 Thomas Jefferson becomes President.
American fleet sent to fight Barbary pirates.
1803 Ohio becomes a state.
Fort Dearborn (Chicago) founded.
Louisiana Purchase.
1804 Lewis and Clark set out to explore Louisiana Territory.
1806 Pike explores more of Louisiana Territory.
1807 Embargo Act.
Fulton's steamboat is successful.
1809 James Madison becomes President.
1810 Father Hidalgo starts Mexican revolt against Spain.
Miranda starts Venezuelan revolt against Spain.
1811 National Road is begun.
1812 Louisiana becomes a state.
1812–1814 War of 1812.
1814 Francis Scott Key writes Star-Spangled Banner.
Hartford Convention.
Treaty of Ghent.
1815 Jackson defeats British at New Orleans.
1816 Congress approves a protective tariff.
Indiana becomes a state.
1817 James Monroe becomes President.
U.S. and Canada agree on unarmed border.
Mississippi becomes a state.
1818 Illinois becomes a state.
1819 Spain cedes Florida to U.S.
Alabama becomes a state.
1820 Missouri Compromise.
Maine becomes a state.
Land law makes public lands cheaper.
1821 First public high school (Boston).

Missouri becomes a state.

Mexico and Peru proclaim independence from Spain.

Bolívar's victory frees Venezuela.

1822 Austin leads group of American colonists into Texas.

Brazil proclaims independence from Portugal.

1823 Monroe Doctrine proclaimed.

1824 Battle of Ayacucho. All Spanish South America liberated.

1825 John Quincy Adams becomes President.

Erie Canal completed.

1829 Andrew Jackson becomes President.

1830 Cooper's locomotive makes successful run.

Webster-Hayne debate.

1831 McCormick reaper invented.

First issue of *The Liberator*.

1832 South Carolina nullifies protective tariffs.

Jackson vetoes the Bank Bill.

1833 Compromise tariff.

New York *Sun* begins first penny daily newspaper.

Oberlin accepts women students.

1836 Texas declares independence from Mexico; Battles at Alamo, San Jacinto.

Arkansas becomes a state.

First women's college opens.

1837 Martin Van Buren becomes President.

Panic of 1837.

Horace Mann fights for free schools.

Michigan becomes a state.

1838 Lord Durham's Report recommends responsible government for Canada.

1839 Goodyear successfully vulcanizes rubber.

1841 William Henry Harrison becomes President.

John Tyler becomes President on Harrison's death (April).

1844 Morse telegraph successful.

1845 James K. Polk becomes President.

Texas and Florida become states.

Howe perfects sewing machine.

1846 Oregon divided between England and U.S.

Iowa becomes a state.

Canada gains responsible government.

1846–1848 Mexican War.

1847 Mormons settle in Utah.

1848 Gold discovered in California.

Mexican Cession.

Women's Rights Convention at Seneca Falls.

Wisconsin becomes a state.

1849 Zachary Taylor becomes President.

California gold rush.

1850 Millard Fillmore becomes President on Taylor's death (July).

Compromise of 1850.

California becomes a state.

Cotton crop amounts to two million bales.

1852 *Uncle Tom's Cabin* published.

First railroad from East reaches Chicago.

1853 Franklin Pierce becomes President.

Gadsden Purchase.

1854 Perry persuades Japan to make trade treaty with U.S.

Kansas-Nebraska Act.

Republican Party founded.

1856 Bessemer process for making steel.

1857 James Buchanan becomes President.

Dred Scott decision.

First elevator in New York City.

1858 Lincoln-Douglas debates.

Minnesota becomes a state.

1859 John Brown attacks U.S. Armory at Harpers Ferry.

First oil well drilled, in Pennsylvania.

Oregon becomes a state.

1860 South Carolina secedes.

Pony Express established.

1861 Abraham Lincoln becomes President.

Kansas becomes a state.

Confederacy is formed in the South.

1861–1865 Civil War.

1861 Fort Sumter fired upon.

First Battle of Bull Run.

1862 *Monitor* fights the *Merrimac*.

Farragut captures New Orleans for North.

Battles of Shiloh, Seven Days, Fredericksburg.

1863 Emancipation Proclamation.

Battle of Chancellorsville.

Battle of Gettysburg.

Surrender of Vicksburg.

Gettysburg Address.

1864 Sherman captures Atlanta and Savannah.

1865 Lee surrenders to Grant at Appomattox Court House.

1862 Homestead Act passed.

Morrill Act paves way for land-grant colleges.

1863 West Virginia becomes a state.

1864 Nevada becomes a state.

1865 Andrew Johnson becomes President on Lincoln's assassination (April).

Thirteenth Amendment abolishes slavery.

1866 Atlantic cable successfully laid.

1867 Nebraska becomes a state.

First Reconstruction Act.

British North America Act.

Alaska bought from Russia.

Midway Islands acquired.

Grange movement starts.

1868 Fourteenth Amendment defines citizenship.

1869 Ulysses S. Grant becomes President.

First transcontinental railroad completed.

Knights of Labor founded.

First professional baseball club.

1870 Fifteenth Amendment states voters' rights.

1873 The Panic.

1876 Bell invents telephone.

Custer's force wiped out by Sioux Indians.

Colorado becomes a state.

1877 Rutherford B. Hayes becomes President.

Last Union troops withdrawn from South.

Railroad strike — first big strike.

1879 Edison invents electric light.

1881 James A. Garfield becomes President.

Chester A. Arthur becomes President on Garfield's death (September).

American Red Cross founded.

1882 Chinese immigration restricted.

1883 Civil Service Commission established.

1885 Grover Cleveland becomes President.

1886 AFL (American Federation of Labor) founded.

1887 Interstate Commerce Act.

Dawes Act provides land and citizenship for Indians.

1889 Benjamin Harrison becomes President.

First Pan American Conference.

Jane Addams founds Hull House.

Montana, North Dakota, South Dakota, Washington become states.

1890 Disappearance of frontier announced.

Sherman Anti-Trust Law.

Idaho and Wyoming become states.

1893 Grover Cleveland becomes President for second time.

First successful automobile.

1896 Utah becomes a state.

1897 William McKinley becomes President.

First subway built (Boston).

1898 Spanish-American War: U.S. acquires Philippines, Puerto Rico, Guam; frees Cuba.

U.S. annexes Hawaii.

1899 "Open Door" Policy proposed.

First Hague Peace Conference.

U.S. acquires Wake Island

and Tutuila.
1900 Boxer Rebellion.
1901 Theodore Roosevelt becomes President on McKinley's assassination (September).
1903 U.S. leases Canal Zone in Panama.
Wright brothers make first successful airplane flight.
1905 U.S. expands Monroe Doctrine.
1906 Pure Food and Drugs Act.
1907 Second Hague Peace Conference.
Oklahoma becomes a state.
1908 National Conservation Conference.
1909 William H. Taft becomes President.
1912 New Mexico and Arizona become states.
1913 Woodrow Wilson becomes President.
Sixteenth Amendment makes income tax legal.
Seventeenth Amendment provides for election of senators by voters.
Underwood Tariff Law.
Federal Reserve Act.
1914 Panama Canal opened.
Federal Trade Commission formed.
Clayton Anti-Trust Act.
1914–1918 World War I.
1915 *Lusitania* sunk by Germans.
1917 U.S. enters the war.
1918 Battles of St. Mihiel, Argonne.
Armistice ends war.
1917 Virgin Islands purchased from Denmark.
Communists seize power in Russia.
1918 First regular air mail service.
1919 Eighteenth Amendment establishes prohibition.
Treaty of Versailles.
1919–1920 U.S. rejects League of Nations.
1920 League of Nations formed.
Nineteenth Amendment gives all women the vote.
First American radio broadcasting station.
Half of U.S. population counted as urban.
1921 Warren G. Harding becomes President.
Washington Arms Conference.
World Court organized.
1922 Mussolini seizes power in Italy.
1923 Calvin Coolidge becomes President on Harding's death (August).
1924 Immigration Act sets up quotas.
All Indians made citizens.

1927 Lindbergh flies non-stop from New York to Paris.
The Jazz Singer — first talking movie.
1928 Kellogg-Briand Pact.
1929 Herbert Hoover becomes President.
Great Depression begins.
1931 Japan invades Manchuria.
Statute of Westminster.
1933 Franklin D. Roosevelt becomes President.
Hitler seizes power in Germany.
Twentieth Amendment. Presidential and congressional terms begin earlier.
Roosevelt pledges Good Neighbor policy.
First Agricultural Adjustment Act.
Tennessee Valley Authority.
Twenty-First Amendment repeals prohibition.
1934 U.S. Marines leave Latin America.
U.S. gives up right of interference in Cuba.
1935 Philippine Commonwealth created.
Wagner Labor Act.
Social Security Act.
Italy attacks Ethiopia.
1937 Japanese invade China.
1938 CIO (Congress of Industrial Organizations) formed.
Wages and Hours Act.
1938–1939 Germany occupies Austria and Czechoslovakia.
1939 First regular television broadcasts.
1939–1945 World War II.
1939 Germany invades Poland.
1940 Nazis conquer Norway, Denmark, Belgium, Holland, France.
U.S. leases bases in Atlantic and Caribbean.
1941 Lend-Lease Act.
Germany attacks Russia.
Atlantic Charter.
Pearl Harbor attacked by Japan — U.S. enters war.
1942 American troops in Philippines forced to surrender.
U.S. victories at Coral Sea, Midway, Guadalcanal.
Allies land in North Africa.
1943 Allies land in Sicily and Italy.
1944 Allied invasion of Normandy.
U.S. victories at Saipan, Guam, Leyte.
1945 Battles of Iwo Jima and Okinawa.

UN formed.
Germany surrenders.
Atomic bombs dropped on Japan — Japan surrenders.
1942 First nuclear chain reaction.
1945 Harry S. Truman becomes President on Roosevelt's death (April).
1946 Philippines become independent.
1947 Truman Doctrine announced.
Marshall Plan.
Taft-Hartley Act.
1948 OAS formed.
1949 NATO created.
Communists take over China.
1950 Point Four program announced.
UN intervention in Korea.
1951 Twenty-Second Amendment puts two-term limit on presidency.
Japanese peace treaty signed.
1952 McCarran Immigration Act.
Puerto Rico becomes self-governing Commonwealth.
Nationwide television used in presidential campaign.
First hydrogen bomb.
1953 Dwight D. Eisenhower becomes President.
Korean truce signed.
Refugee Relief Act.
1954 Supreme Court decision on school segregation.
SEATO formed.
1955 AFL–CIO merger.
1956 Suez Canal crisis.
1957 Russia launches first Sputnik.
1958 U.S. launches its first satellite.
1959 Alaska and Hawaii become states.
Castro leads Cuban revolt.
St. Lawrence Seaway opens.
Landrum-Griffin Labor Act.
1960 Summit meeting cancelled over U-2 incident.
1961 John F. Kennedy becomes President.
Peace Corps formed.
Twenty-Third Amendment allows D.C. residents to vote for President.
First men in space.
1962 First U.S. manned orbital space flight.
Trade Expansion Act.
U.S. quarantines Cuba.
1963 Negro demonstrations for civil rights.
Test-ban treaty.
1963 Lyndon Johnson becomes President on Kennedy's assassination (November).
1964 Twenty-Fourth Amendment abolishes poll tax.
Civil Rights Act.
1965 Increased American involvement in Vietnam.
Medicare and Voting Rights Act adopted.

What effect did reapportionment following the 1960 census have on the representation of your state?

THE STATES OF THE UNITED STATES OF AMERICA

NO.	STATE NAME	DATE OF ADMISSION	POPULATION (1960 CENSUS)	NUMBER OF REPRESENTATIVES (1960 APPORTIONMENT)	AREA IN SQUARE MILES	CAPITAL	LARGEST CITY
1	Delaware	1787	446,292	1	2,057	Dover	Wilmington
2	Pennsylvania	1787	11,319,366	27	45,333	Harrisburg	Philadelphia
3	New Jersey	1787	6,066,782	15	7,836	Trenton	Newark
4	Georgia	1788	3,943,116	10	58,876	Atlanta	Atlanta
5	Connecticut	1788	2,535,234	6	5,009	Hartford	Hartford
6	Massachusetts	1788	5,148,578	12	8,257	Boston	Boston
7	Maryland	1788	3,100,689	8	10,577	Annapolis	Baltimore
8	South Carolina	1788	2,382,594	6	31,055	Columbia	Columbia
9	New Hampshire	1788	606,921	2	9,304	Concord	Manchester
10	Virginia	1788	3,966,949	10	40,815	Richmond	Norfolk
11	New York	1788	16,782,304	41	49,576	Albany	New York
12	North Carolina	1789	4,556,155	11	52,712	Raleigh	Charlotte
13	Rhode Island	1790	859,488	2	1,214	Providence	Providence
14	Vermont	1791	389,881	1	9,609	Montpelier	Burlington
15	Kentucky	1792	3,038,156	7	40,395	Frankfort	Louisville
16	Tennessee	1796	3,567,089	9	42,244	Nashville	Memphis
17	Ohio	1803	9,706,397	24	41,222	Columbus	Cleveland
18	Louisiana	1812	3,257,022	8	48,523	Baton Rouge	New Orleans
19	Indiana	1816	4,662,498	11	36,291	Indianapolis	Indianapolis
20	Mississippi	1817	2,178,141	5	47,716	Jackson	Jackson
21	Illinois	1818	10,081,158	24	56,400	Springfield	Chicago
22	Alabama	1819	3,266,740	8	51,609	Montgomery	Birmingham
23	Maine	1820	969,265	2	33,215	Augusta	Portland
24	Missouri	1821	4,319,813	10	69,686	Jefferson City	St. Louis
25	Arkansas	1836	1,786,272	4	53,104	Little Rock	Little Rock
26	Michigan	1837	7,823,194	19	58,216	Lansing	Detroit
27	Florida	1845	4,951,560	12	58,560	Tallahassee	Miami
28	Texas	1845	9,579,677	23	267,339	Austin	Houston
29	Iowa	1846	2,757,537	7	56,290	Des Moines	Des Moines
30	Wisconsin	1848	3,951,777	10	56,154	Madison	Milwaukee
31	California	1850	15,717,204	38	158,693	Sacramento	Los Angeles

A42

32	Minnesota	1858	8	3,413,864	84,068	St. Paul	Minneapolis
33	Oregon	1859	4	1,786,687	96,981	Salem	Portland
34	Kansas	1861	5	2,178,611	82,264	Topeka	Wichita
35	West Virginia	1863	5	1,860,421	24,181	Charleston	Charleston
36	Nevada	1864	1	285,278	110,540	Carson City	Las Vegas
37	Nebraska	1867	3	1,411,330	77,227	Lincoln	Omaha
38	Colorado	1876	4	1,753,947	104,247	Denver	Denver
39	North Dakota	1889	2	632,446	70,665	Bismarck	Fargo
40	South Dakota	1889	2	680,514	77,047	Pierre	Sioux Falls
41	Montana	1889	2	674,767	147,138	Helena	Great Falls
42	Washington	1889	7	2,853,214	68,192	Olympia	Seattle
43	Idaho	1890	2	667,191	83,557	Boise	Boise
44	Wyoming	1890	1	330,066	97,914	Cheyenne	Cheyenne
45	Utah	1896	2	890,627	84,916	Salt Lake City	Salt Lake City
46	Oklahoma	1907	6	2,328,284	69,919	Oklahoma City	Oklahoma City
47	New Mexico	1912	2	951,023	121,666	Santa Fe	Albuquerque
48	Arizona	1912	3	1,302,161	113,909	Phoenix	Phoenix
49	Alaska	1959	1	226,167	586,400	Juneau	Anchorage
50	Hawaii	1959	2	632,772	6,424	Honolulu	Honolulu
	District of Columbia			763,956	69		
			435	179,323,175	3,615,211		

PRINCIPAL DEPENDENCIES OF THE UNITED STATES

DEPENDENCY	DATE OF ACQUISITION	POPULATION (1960 CENSUS)	AREA IN SQUARE MILES	CAPITAL, OR PRINCIPAL CITY
Puerto Rico	1899	2,349,544	3,435	San Juan
Guam	1899	67,044	212	Agana
American Samoa	1900	20,051	76	Pago Pago
Panama Canal Zone	1904	42,122	553	Balboa
Virgin Islands	1917	32,099	133	Charlotte Amalie
Total		2,510,860	4,409	

PRESIDENTS AND VICE-PRESIDENTS OF THE UNITED STATES

PRESIDENT	BORN	DIED	DATE OF INAUGURATION	PARTY ELECTING PRESIDENT	STATE *	VICE-PRESIDENT	STATE *
George Washington	1732	1799	1789	None	Virginia	John Adams	Massachusetts
George Washington	1732	1799	1793	None	Virginia	John Adams	Massachusetts
John Adams	1735	1826	1797	Federalist	Massachusetts	Thomas Jefferson	Virginia
Thomas Jefferson	1743	1826	1801	Dem.-Republican	Virginia	Aaron Burr	New York
Thomas Jefferson	1743	1826	1805	Dem.-Republican	Virginia	George Clinton	New York
James Madison	1751	1836	1809	Dem.-Republican	Virginia	George Clinton	New York
James Madison	1751	1836	1813	Dem.-Republican	Virginia	Elbridge Gerry	Massachusetts
James Monroe	1758	1831	1817	Dem.-Republican	Virginia	Daniel D. Tompkins	New York
James Monroe	1758	1831	1821	Dem.-Republican	Virginia	Daniel D. Tompkins	New York
John Quincy Adams	1767	1848	1825	Nat.-Republican	Massachusetts	John C. Calhoun	South Carolina
Andrew Jackson	1767	1845	1829	Democratic	Tennessee	John C. Calhoun	South Carolina
Andrew Jackson	1767	1845	1833	Democratic	Tennessee	Martin Van Buren	New York
Martin Van Buren	1782	1862	1837	Democratic	New York	Richard M. Johnson	Kentucky
William H. Harrison	1773	1841	1841	Whig	Ohio	John Tyler	Virginia
John Tyler	1790	1862	(1841, April)	Whig	Virginia		
James K. Polk	1795	1849	1845	Democratic	Tennessee	George M. Dallas	Pennsylvania
Zachary Taylor	1784	1850	1849	Whig	Louisiana	Millard Fillmore	New York
Millard Fillmore	1800	1874	(1850, July)	Whig	New York		
Franklin Pierce	1804	1869	1853	Democratic	New Hampshire	William R. King	Alabama
James Buchanan	1791	1868	1857	Democratic	Pennsylvania	John C. Breckinridge	Kentucky
Abraham Lincoln	1809	1865	1861	Republican	Illinois	Hannibal Hamlin	Maine
Abraham Lincoln	1809	1865	1865	Republican	Illinois	Andrew Johnson	Tennessee
Andrew Johnson	1808	1875	(1865, April)	Republican	Tennessee		
Ulysses S. Grant	1822	1885	1869	Republican	Illinois	Schuyler Colfax	Indiana
Ulysses S. Grant	1822	1885	1873	Republican	Illinois	Henry Wilson	Massachusetts
Rutherford B. Hayes	1822	1893	1877	Republican	Ohio	William A. Wheeler	New York

PRESIDENT	BORN	DIED	DATE OF INAUGURATION	PARTY ELECTING PRESIDENT	STATE *	VICE–PRESIDENT	STATE *
James A. Garfield	1831	1881	1881	Republican	Ohio	Chester A. Arthur	New York
Chester A. Arthur	1830	1886	(1881, Sept.)	Republican	New York		
Grover Cleveland	1837	1908	1885	Democratic	New York	Thomas A. Hendricks	Indiana
Benjamin Harrison	1833	1901	1889	Republican	Indiana	Levi P. Morton	New York
Grover Cleveland	1837	1908	1893	Democratic	New York	Adlai E. Stevenson	Illinois
William McKinley	1843	1901	1897	Republican	Ohio	Garret A. Hobart	New Jersey
William McKinley	1843	1901	1901	Republican	Ohio	Theodore Roosevelt	New York
Theodore Roosevelt	1858	1919	(1901, Sept.)	Republican	New York		
Theodore Roosevelt	1858	1919	1905	Republican	New York	Charles W. Fairbanks	Indiana
William H. Taft	1857	1930	1909	Republican	Ohio	James S. Sherman	New York
Woodrow Wilson	1856	1924	1913	Democratic	New Jersey	Thomas R. Marshall	Indiana
Woodrow Wilson	1856	1924	1917	Democratic	New Jersey	Thomas R. Marshall	Indiana
Warren G. Harding	1865	1923	1921	Republican	Ohio	Calvin Coolidge	Massachusetts
Calvin Coolidge	1872	1933	(1923, August)	Republican	Massachusetts		
Calvin Coolidge	1872	1933	1925	Republican	Massachusetts	Charles G. Dawes	Illinois
Herbert Hoover	1874	1964	1929	Republican	California	Charles Curtis	Kansas
Franklin D. Roosevelt	1882	1945	1933	Democratic	New York	John N. Garner	Texas
Franklin D. Roosevelt	1882	1945	1937	Democratic	New York	John N. Garner	Texas
Franklin D. Roosevelt	1882	1945	1941	Democratic	New York	Henry A. Wallace	Iowa
Franklin D. Roosevelt	1882	1945	1945	Democratic	New York	Harry S. Truman	Missouri
Harry S. Truman	1884		(1945, April)	Democratic	Missouri		
Harry S. Truman	1884		1949	Democratic	Missouri	Alben W. Barkley	Kentucky
Dwight D. Eisenhower	1890		1953	Republican	New York	Richard M. Nixon	California
Dwight D. Eisenhower	1890		1957	Republican	Pennsylvania	Richard M. Nixon	California
John F. Kennedy	1917	1963	1961	Democratic	Massachusetts	Lyndon B. Johnson	Texas
Lyndon B. Johnson	1908		(1963, Nov.)	Democratic	Texas		
Lyndon B. Johnson	1908		1965	Democratic	Texas	Hubert H. Humphrey	Minnesota

* Residence at time of election.

Here are identified sources which have been used.

Sources and Acknowledgments

Grateful acknowledgment is made to authors, publishers, and other copyright holders for permission to reprint (and in some selections to adapt slightly) copyright material listed below. Numbers in parentheses refer to pages where the following selections are to be found in this book.

The Travels of Marco Polo, Everyman's Library Edition. Reprinted by permission of E. P. Dutton & Co., Inc., and J. M. Dent & Sons Ltd. (22–23)

The Journal of Christopher Columbus, translated by Clements R. Markham. Reprinted by permission of the Hakluyt Society (32, 34)

From *The Spanish Conquerors,* by I. B. Richman, Volume 2, The Chronicles of America. Copyright Yale University Press (60)

Landing of the Pilgrim Fathers, by Felicia Hemans (80)

Mayflower Compact, November 11, 1620 (90)

History of Plimouth Plantation, by William Bradford (91)

New England Primer (100)

The Life of George Mason, by Kate Rowland, 1892. Reprinted by permission of G. P. Putnam's Sons (110)

A Retrospect of the Boston Tea Party with a Memoir of George R. T. Hewes, 1834 (157–158)

An Ancient Prophecy, by Philip Freneau (158)

Speech by Patrick Henry in the Virginia House of Burgesses, March 23, 1775 (161)

Paul Revere's Ride, by Henry Wadsworth Longfellow (162)

Concord Hymn, by Ralph Waldo Emerson (163)

Common Sense, by Thomas Paine (169)

Excerpts from Declaration of Independence (169–170)

Military Journal during the American Revolutionary War, from 1775 to 1783, by James Thacher, 1854 (187)

Letter from Thomas Jefferson to James Madison, December 20, 1787 (223)

Preamble to the United States Constitution (228)

Letter from Thomas Jefferson to Robert R. Livingston, April 18, 1802 (250)

Leading American Inventors, by George Iles, Henry Holt and Sons, 1912 (283)

"Oliver Evans and His Inventions" by Coleman Sellers, *Journal of the Franklin Institute* (July, 1886: vol. CXXII) (283–284)

American Notes, by Charles Dickens, 1842 (285)

"Correspondence of Eli Whitney," edited by M. B. Hammond, *The American Historical Review,* Vol. III, 1897–98 (290, 292)

Pioneers! O Pioneers! by Walt Whitman (304)

Recollections of Life in Ohio from 1813 to 1840, by William C. Howells. Copyright 1895 by The Robert Clarke Company. Reprinted by permission of Appleton-Century-Crofts, Inc. (314–316)

Speech by Major Davezac at the New Jersey State Democratic Convention, 1844 (346)

Sutter of California, by Julian Dana. Reprinted by permission of Julian Dana. Published by The Macmillan Company, 1934 (361)

Roughing It, by Mark Twain. Reprinted by permission of Harper & Brothers (365)

Speech by Daniel Webster in the United States Senate, January 26, 1830 (378)

Lincoln's First Inaugural Address, March 4, 1861 (391)

Letter from Lincoln to Horace Greeley, August 22, 1862 (409–410)

Lincoln's Second Inaugural Address, March 4, 1865 (410)

The Life and Times of Red-Jacket, or Sa-Go-Ye-Wat-Ha; Being the Sequel to the History of the Six Nations, by William L. Stone, 1841 (428–429)

Vigilante Days and Ways, by Nathaniel P. Langford. A. C. McClurg & Co., 1912 (435–436)

The Story of the Cowboy, by Emerson Hough. Reprinted by permission of Appleton-Century-Crofts, Inc. (437–438)

A Son of the Middle Border, by Hamlin Garland. Copyright 1917 by Hamlin Garland. Reprinted by permission of The Macmillan Company (440)

From *The Age of Big Business,* by Burton J. Hendrick, Volume 39, The Chronicles of America. Copyright Yale University Press (453–454)

Speech by William Jennings Bryan at the Democratic National Convention, July, 1896 (483)

America, by William Cullen Bryant (507)

One America, by F. J. Brown & J. S. Roucek. Adapted by permission. © 1945, Rev. Prentice-Hall, Inc. (511)

The Making of an American, by Jacob Riis. Copyright 1929 by Mary Riis. Reprinted by permission of The Macmillan Company (516)

The Game of Baseball. George Munro and Son, 1868 (538)

Speech by Woodrow Wilson to the United States Congress, April 2, 1917 (603)

The authors and publisher are indebted to many people and institutions for help in producing this book. Most maps and all time lines were prepared by John V. Morris. Maps on pages 31, 41, 145, 253, 269, 399, and 579 were prepared by Robert M. Chapin, Jr. Lilli Mautner prepared the special maps following page 432. Other artists were Samuel H. Bryant — scratchboard drawings; Cheslie D'Andrea — chapter opening drawings; Ed Emberley — cartoons; Victor Mays — unit opening drawings and picture biographies; and Donald Mackay — charts.

Thanks are extended to the following for their courtesy in making pictures available for reproduction on the pages indicated: (Where several pictures appear on one page, they are referred to from left to right, top to bottom.)

ii Collection of Washington University, St. Louis, photo by Sandak, Inc.
iii Stern from Foto-Find
iv Courtesy, The Mariners' Museum, Newport News, Va.
v Nielson from Shostal
vi Ford from Alpha; Smithsonian Institution
vii Zehrt from Freelance Photographers Guild, Inc.; Somogyi from Freelance Photographers Guild, Inc.
viii Owned by the Henry Ford Museum, photo by Sandak, Inc.; Wilson from Alpha
ix Morton from Shostal; General Electric Co.
x Courtesy, Map Division, New York Public Library and American Heritage Publishing Co., Inc.; courtesy, British Museum
xi Collection of American Heritage Publishing Co., Inc.; Coast and Geodetic Survey
xii, 1 Courtesy, *The Texaco Star*, Texaco, Inc.
2 Brown Brothers; Morton from Shostal
3 State Department of Archives and History, Raleigh, N.C.; Hemmet from F.P.G.
4 Culver Pictures, Inc.; Lowry from Rapho-Guillumette
5 Brown Brothers; E. I. du Pont de Nemours & Co.
6 *Harper's New Monthly* magazine; News Bureau, California Institute of Technology
7 Weston Kemp; Culver Pictures, Inc.
8 Bettmann Archive; U.S. Air Force Academy

18 Austrian National Library, Vienna
21 Information Bureau, American Spice Trade Association; courtesy, Museum of Fine Arts, Boston
27 George Peabody and Associates, Inc.
29 Norwegian Information Service, Washington, D.C., and Antiquity Collections, Oslo University; courtesy, *Holiday Magazine*
34 Bahamas Development Board, photo by Maura
44 Mural by Thomas Benton, courtesy, Power Authority of the State of New York
47 Museum of the City of New York
60 Bettmann Archive
62 Courtesy, The American Museum of Natural History; Pan American Union, Washington, D.C.
65 Photo by Canadian Pacific Railways; Pan American Union, Washington, D.C.
69 Courtesy, Museum of the American Indian; McGibbeny from Shostal; Evens from Shostal
70 Collection of Cranbrook Institute of Science, photo by Sandak, Inc.; Manley from Shostal; courtesy, The American Museum of Natural History; courtesy, Philbrook Art Center, Tulsa, Okla., photo by Sandak, Inc.
72 Pan American World Airways
74 Painting by Tom Lea; Dallas Museum of Fine Arts, gift of *Life Magazine,* 1960
77 Ewing Galloway
84 Wide World Photo
90, 91 One of eight mural paintings by Charles Hoffbauer in the lobby of New England Mutual Life Insurance Co., Boston
92 From *Chesapeake Bay and Tidewater* by A. Aubrey Bodine, Hastings House, 1954; photo courtesy of the author
94 Division of Philately, Post Office Department
96 Historical Society of Pennsylvania; Long Island Historical Society
103 National Gallery of Art, Index of American Design; North Carolina News Bureau, photo by Kelly; Willinger from Shostal
104 (top left, right, and bottom) Courtesy, Museum of Fine Arts, Boston; Heatly from Freelance Photographers Guild, Inc.
105 Saugus Ironworks Restoration,

Saugus, Mass., and Hill & Knowlton, Inc.
106 Lambert Pharmacal Co.
108 Governor Dummer Academy, South Byfield, Mass.
112 Virginia Chamber of Commerce, photo by Flournoy
113 Continental Distilling Corp., Philadelphia, and Colonial Williamsburg
116 Aetna Life Affiliated Companies, Hartford
122, 123 Mural by Thomas Benton, courtesy, Power Authority of the State of New York
124 Maine Department of Economic Development
126 See above, pp. 90, 91
128 Iconographic Collections, State Historical Society of Wisconsin
139 State Capitol mural by Albert Herter, courtesy, State Historical Society of Wisconsin
142 Courtesy of Belt, Lemmon and Lo, Architects-Engineers, Honolulu, in association with John Carl Warnecke and Associates, Architects and Planning Consultants, San Francisco; Colonial National Historical Park, National Park Service Photo
146 New York Public Library
153 Brown Brothers
158 John Hancock Life Insurance Co.
159 Chicago Historical Society
160 New Hampshire State Planning and Development Commission
161 John Hancock Life Insurance Co.
167 Massachusetts Department of Commerce
171 National Archives
174 John Hancock Life Insurance Co.
177 Division of Philately, Post Office Department
180 American Iron and Steel Institute and Hill & Knowlton, Inc.
184 Indiana State Library
186 Colonial National Historical Park, National Park Service Photo
192 From *Book of the American Spirit* by Howard Pyle, Harper & Brothers, 1923
193 Hunting Survey Corp., Ltd., Toronto, Canada
198 Three Lions
199 Hamilton Wright, New York
200 Standard Oil Co. (N.J.)
202 Mural detail from Anfiteatro Bolívar, Mexico City
203, 205 Pan American World Airways
218 Tourist Division, Maryland Department of Economic Development
221 State Capitol mural by Albert Herter, courtesy, State Histori-

This index tells you where to locate on maps the geographical names appearing in the text. ("Fol. 432" refers to the special map section following that page.)

Index to Names on Maps

The purpose of this General Index is to help you locate quickly in this book any information on a certain topic. To be sure you know how to use the index, look at the suggestions on page 260.

This index includes references not only to the text but to the pictures and charts as well. These may be identified as follows: *p* 21 refers to a picture on page 21; *c* 125 refers to a chart on page 125. ("Fol. 432" refers to the special map section following that page.)

There is a separate map index starting on page A50. In that index you will find references to maps in this book where you can find geographical locations.

The fact that five pages are devoted to the Index to Names on Maps and twenty pages to the General Index makes it easy to locate names and topics discussed in this textbook.